The Works of ... Vindicating the Church of England, as Truly Christian, and Duly Reformed

THE
WORKS
OF
Mr. Richard Hooker,

(That *Learned, Godly, Judicious,* and *Eloquent Divine*)

Vindicating the

CHURCH of ENGLAND,

As truly *Christian,* and duly *Reformed:*

In Eight BOOKS of

ECCLESIASTICAL POLITY.

Now compleated,

As with the *Sixth* and *Eighth*, so with the SEVENTH,
(touching *Episcopacy,* as the Primitive, Catholick and Apostolick
Government of the Church) out of his own Manuscripts, never
before Published.

With an account of his *Holy Life,* and *Happy Death,*

Written by Dr. *John Gauden,* now Bishop of *Exeter.*

The entire *Edition* Dedicated to the Kings Most
Excellent Majestie,

CHARLS the II.

By whose ROYAL FATHER (near His Mar-
tyrdom) the former Five Books (then onely extant) were
commended to his dear Children, as an excellent means
to satisfie Private Scruples, and settle the Publique
Peace of this Church and Kingdom.

James 3.17. *The wisdom from above, is first pure, then peaceable, gentle, easie to be intreated, full of mercy and good works, without partiality and hypocrisie.*

Μωρά τ᾿ ἀληθινα ᾿Cιζαια, κ᾿ τ᾿ ἀρι ᾿στα ᾿σωνια· Plat.
Multi tædio investigandæ veritatis ad proximos divertunt errores. Min. Fel.

London, Printed by *J. Best,* for *Andrew Crook,* at the *Green Dragon* in S. *Pauls*
Church-yard. 1662.

TO THE
KINGS

Moſt EXCELLENT MAJESTIE

CHARLS the II.

By the Grace of God,

King of *Great Britany*, *France* and *Ireland*,
Defender of the Faith, *&c.*

Moſt Gracions Soveraign,

 *Lthough I know how little leiſure*
Great Kings have to read Large
Books, *or indeed any, ſave one-*
ly Gods (the ſtudy, belief and
obedience of which, is Preciſely
commanded, even to Kings, Deut.
17.18,19. *And from which, whatever wholly* diverts
them, will bazard to damn *them: there being no af-*
fairs of ſo great importance, as their ſerving God, and
ſaving their own ſouls; *nor any Precepts ſo wiſe, juſt,*
holy and ſafe, as thoſe of the Divine Oracles; *nor*
any Empire *ſo glorious, as that by which Kings being*
ſubject to Gods Law, *have* Dominion *over them-*

A 2   ſelves,

felves, *and so best deserve and exercise it over their*
Subjects.)

Yet having lived to see the wonderful and happy Reftauration *of your* Majefty *to your Rightful* Kingdoms, *and of this* reformed Church *to its* juft rights,
primitive order, and priftine conftitution, *by your Ma-*
jefties prudent care, and unparallel'd *bounty, I know*
not what to prefent more worthy of your Majefties acceptance, *and my duty, then thefe* elaborate *and fea-*
fonable Works *of the Famous and Prudent* Mr.
Richard Hooker *now augmented, and I hope com-*
pleated with the three laft Books, *fo much defired, and*
fo long concealed.

The publifhing of which Volume *fo* intire, *and thus*
prefenting *it to your* Majefty, *feems to be a* bleffing
and honor *referved by Gods Providence, to adde a*
further Lufture *to your Majefties* glorious Name,
and happy Reign, *whofe* tranfcendent *favour, juftice,*
merit and munificence *to the* long afflicted Church
of England, is a fubject no lefs worthy of admiration
then gratitude *to all pofterity : And of all things (next*
Gods *grace)not to be abufed or turned into wantonnefs*
by any of your Majefties Clergy, *who are highly obliged*
beyond all other Subjects *to piety, loyalty and induftry.*

I fhall need nothing more to ingratiate this Incomparable Piece *to your Majefties acceptance, and all the*
English worlds , then thofe high commendations *it*
hath ever had, as from all prudent, peaceable and impar-
tial Readers, fo efpecially from your Majefties Royal
Father, *who a few days before he was* Crowned with
Martyrdom, *commended to his* deareft Children,
the diligent Reading *of Mr.* Hookers Ecclefiaftical
Polity, *even next the* Bible *; as an excellent means to*
fettle

settle them in the truth of Religion, *and in the* peace of this Church, *as much* Christian, *and as well* Reformed *as any under* Heaven: *As if God had reserved this* signal Honor *to be done by the* best of Kings, *and* greatest Sufferers for this Church, *to him who was one of the best* Writers, *and ablest* Defenders *of it.*

To this compleated Edition, *I have added such particular accounts as I could get, of the* Authors *person, education, temper, manners, fortunes, life and death, which no man hath hitherto done to any* exactness or *proportion: That hereby* your Majesty *and all the world may see (if I have been able at this distance of time to take his* Effigies *aright) what sort of men are fittest for* Church-work *(which like the building of* Solomons Temple, *is best carried on with most evenness of* Judgement, *and* least noise of *passion*;) *Also what manner of man he was,* to whom we all owe *this* noble work, *and* durable *defence.*

Which is indeed at once (as the Tongues of Eloquent Princes *are to themselves, and their* Subjects*) both a* Treasury *&* an Armory, *to inrich the friends, and* defend *against the* Enemies of the Church of England: *a rare* composition of *unpassionate* Reason, *and* unpartial Religion: *the mature product of a* judicious *Scholar, a* loyal *Subject, an* humble *Preacher, and a most* eloquent *Writer: the very* abstract *and* quintessence of Laws Humane *and* Divine, *a* summary of the grounds, rules *and* proportions of *true* Polity *in Church and State: upon which* clear, solid, *and* safe *foundations, the* good Order, Peace, *and* Government of this Church was anciently *settled, and on which, while it stands firm, it will be* flourishing: *All other* popular *and* specious *pretensions being found by*
late

late *ſad experiences, to be, as* novel *and* unfit, *ſo* factious *and* fallacious, *yea dangerous and deſtructive to the* peace *and* proſperity *of this Church and Kingdom, whoſe inſeparable* happineſs *and* Intereſts *are bound up in* Monarchy *and* Epiſcopacy.

The Politick and viſible managing of both which, God hath now graciouſly reſtored, and committed to your Majeſties Soveraign VViſdom *and* Authority, *after the many & long* Tragedies *ſuffered from thoſe* Club-maſters *and* Tub-miniſters, *who ſought not fairly to obtain* Reformation *of what might ſeem amiſs, but violently and wholly to overthrow the ancient and* goodly Fabrick *of this* Church and Kingdom : *For finding themſelves not able in many years to* Anſwer *this one* Book, *long ago written in defence of the* Truth, Order, Government, Authority *and* Liberty *(in things* indifferent*) of this Reformed Church, agreeable to right* Reaſon, *and true* Religion *(which makes this well-tempered* Peice *a file capable to break the teeth of any that venture to bite it:) they conſpired at laſt to betake themſelves to* Arms, *to kindle thoſe horrid fires of Civil VVars, which this wiſe* Author *foreſaw and* foretold *in his* admirable Preface, *would follow thoſe* ſparks, *and that ſmoak which he ſaw riſe in his* days: *So that from* impertinent Diſputes *(ſeconded with* ſcurrilous Pamphlets*) they fled to* tumults, ſedition, rebellion, ſacriledge, paracide, *yea* regicide; counſels, weapons *and* practices, *certainly, no way becoming the hearts and hands of* Chriſtian ſubjects, *nor ever ſanctified by* Chriſt, *for his ſervice, or his Churches* good.

VVhat now remains, *but your Majeſties perfecting and preſerving that (in this Church) which you have*

with

with much prudence and tenderness so happily *begun and prosecuted, with more* zeal *then the* establishment *of your* own Throne. *The still* crazy Church of England, *together with this* Book (*its great and impregnable Shield*) *do further need, and humbly implore your Majesties* Royal Protection under God: *Nor can your Majesty by any generous instance and perseverance* (*most worthy of a Christian King*) *more express that pious and grateful sense which God and all good men expect from your Majesty, as some retribution for his many* miraculous mercies *to your self, then in a wise, speedy, and happy settling of our Religious peace, with the least* grievance, *and most* satisfaction *to all your* good Subjects; *Sacred Order and Uniformity being the* centre and circumference *of our* Civil Tranquillity: *Sedition naturally rising out of Schism, and Rebellion out of faction; The onely* cure and Antidote *against* both, *are good* Laws and Canons, *first, wisely made, with all Christian Moderation, and Seasonable Charity; next, duly* executed *with Justice, and impartiality; which sober severity, is indeed the greatest Charity to the Publique. Whose Verity, Unity, Sanctity and Solemnity in Religious Concernments, being once duly* established, *must not be shaken or sacrificed to any private varieties and extravagancies. Where the intervals of Doctrine, Morality, Mysteries, and Evangelical Duties, being (as they are in the* Church of *England) sound and sacred, the externals of decent Forms, Circumstances, Rites and Ceremonies, being subordinate and servient to the main, cannot be either evil or unsafe, neither offensive to God nor good Christians.*

                                        For

For the attaining of which bleſſed ends *of Piety and Peace, that the ſacred* Sun *and* Shield *of the* Divine Grace *and* Power *directing and protecting, may ever ſhine upon Your Maieſties Perſon and Family, Counſels and Power, is the humble prayer of*

Your *Sacred Majeſties*

moſt Loyal *Subject,*

and devoted *Servant,*

January 1. 1661.

Ioh. Exon.

THE

THE
LIFE & DEATH
OF
Mr. Richard Hooker,
(The Learned and juftly Renowned Author of
the *ECCLESIASTICAL POLITIE.*)

Written by
John Gauden D.D. and Bifhop of *Exon.*

Eing not more earneftly defired by others, then Ambitioufly devoted of my felf, to exprefs my fingular refpect and gratitude
to the memory of Mr. *Richard Hooker,* by whofe Labours I
have profited, in giving fome account to the now *reftored Church
of England,* of the Perfon and Manners, the Life and Death
of this its great *Friend,* faithful *Servant,* and valiant *Champion,*
by way of Ornament to this *new Edition* of his *incomparable
Work of Eccleſiaſtical Polity;* to which, by the care of fome
Learned men, efpecially of the Right Reverend Father in
God, *Gilbert* now Lord Bifhop of *London,* thofe genuine additions are now made
of the *three laſt Books,* promifed and performed by him, but long concealed from
publique view, not without great injury to the publique good. I muft confefs,
I was never more encouraged to fuch an undertaking by the real worth and il-
luftrious merit (in general) of any Church-man, being fet beyond all flattery or
falfity on this part, and fubject to do neither *him* nor *myfelf* any injury, but by my
own defects: Nor was I ever lefs enabled to perform fo *publike a fervice,* as to thofe
fupplies of particular *remarks,* and exact *memorials* of his Life and Death, which
are neceffary to make a compleat Hiftory or Pourtrait of him; in whom fome things
were admirable, many things *imitable,* and all things *commendable,* yet hath no account publique or private hitherto been given of him, by any Writing or Infor-

B   mation

mation proportionate to his Dimenfions, who merited a Volume, and is not to be made up in fhort and obfcure Narratives: For nothing is more deformed, then to fee the *Heroick eminencies* of grand Perfons fhrunk to *pittiful Epitomies*, like *Æfops Fables*, wrapping up *Achilles* in an *Enchiridion*, and putting *Hercules* into a *pinte pot*; (*Auguftiffimas virtutes fcripti Anguftiis minuendo*) fetting Vertue as it were in the ftocks, and wire-drawing ample worth, through the ftraits of an envious pen, or penurious ftile: Great Saints do merit great fhrines; eminent wifdom and valour may well expect Iliads.

Why no full account heretofore given of Mr. R. Hooker.

Not that Mr. *Hooker* wanted either *Excellencies* capable to have invited and employed the moft accurate pens of his age; nor yet did he want learned *Friends*, and juft *Admirers*, who were highly devoted to his honor; yea, indeed to Gods glory, which deferved and required fome juft and grateful defcription of thofe *rare gifts* and *graces*, which were liberally beftowed on him, and excellently ufed by him.

But the nobler and better fort of the *Englifh Clergie* (who were conformable to this Church) feemed fo fatisfied with thofe illuftrions (though till now defective) *Monuments*, which he left in his writings, that they thought he wanted nothing more to preferve his memory, or to keep Pofterity in a perpetual admiration of him, then the reading of his works: They judged the *Jewel* of his name was fo well fet in his folid and fplendid Writings, that there needed no other *foil*: And perhaps that was Mr. *Hookers* fortune, which oft befals rare faces, and fingular beauties, to have no picture left of them, becaufe no hand was fo prefumptuous of its skill, as to venture to take their Pourtraicture. So that the defect on this fide may be imputed to a modeft defpair of emulating the *Original*, or hitting the life.

Others (who warped from the Church of *England*) and have ventured to be (*Biogrrphers*) writers of the lives of fome Englifh *Divines* (as fome of late have done during the *Ataxy* or *Anarchy* of *Presbytery* and *Independency*) thefe have either envioufly paffed by this Mr. *Hooker*, becaufe they took him to be no friend to their parties (which were then to be cried up among the vulgar;) or they did him this right, to efteem him (*graviffimum & in tractabilem adverfarium*) as a very learned, fo a very heavy *Adverfary*; not to be commended by them, becaufe never to be anfwered, in his juft, valiant and Victorious oppofitions againft their Defigns, Principles, and Interefts, who were either a little crofs-grained, or more rudely non-conform to the Church of *England*.

Whofe *fcurrilous Petulancy* (as to the meaner and more Plebean fort of thofe Scriblers) Mr. *Hooker* then moft feverely chaftifed, when being intent onely to Reafon and Religion, he difdained to anfwer *them according to their folly* and railing, but left them to be punifhed by their own impotent paffions, and impudent manners: Others of that party, who feemed to be the fobereft and ftrongeft Pillars of it, this grand *Hero* couragioufly encountred, notably routed, and utterly vanquifhed, even to the filencing of them; ferioufly difcovering their machinations and devices, gravely anfwering all their *Sophiftical* and Popular Fallacies, fully *confuting* all their ftrongeft Arguments, *beating* them out of their *Faftneffes* and *Retreats*, demolifhing their very Fortifications, and thofe Towers of *Babel*, which their confufed fancies and tongues had built in their own crowns, and fought to fet up in this Church.

Mr. *Hookers* name fet off with equal wifdom and meeknefs, for the ftrength of truth managed by modeft eloquence, gave fuch a terror to fuch writers, that they kept an aftonifhed diftance from him: And indeed this fort of *partial Hiftorians*, chofe to be wilfully ignorant of Mr. *Hooker*, and fo to keep the world; afraid to read his works, and afhamed (if they did read them) to own that pregnancy of Reafon which doth encounter them in all his writings: Hence they were fo wary, as not to meddle with what they had no minde to perform, and thought it fafer to let him reft in quiet, or to bury him in *Silence*, then either by difparaging of him to expofe themfelves to the laughter and fcorn of all wife men; or by *commending* him, to *difadvantage* their *party* and *caufe*, which for many years after his *Ecclefiaftical Polity* was publifhed, lay gafping and fprawling for breath, as *Antæus* under the ftrict preffures or grafpings of this mighty *Hercules*; out of whofe *arms*

arms they defpaired to get, unlefs fome lucky opportunity, would offer it felf, to
act, not by *Arguments*, but by *Arms* ; not by rational or *Religious, demonftrations*,
but *tumultuous* force, and violent impreffions, cutting thofe cords afunder by, *Sedition* and *Rebellion*, which they could not diffolve by juft *difputation:* As it came
to pafs after many days, when the Goblin *Smectymnuus* firft appeared, and con-
fured up thofe *Presbyterian* and *Independent Spirits*, from the North and South,
which could not be allayed; until they had quite *tired out* themfelves, by *tormenting*
others.

So partial, blinde, and bold doth *Faction* make all men (how able and plaufi- **The blinde-**
ble foever they feem to be for gifts and graces) if they have not humble and **nefs, boldnefs**
honeft hearts, meek and quiet fpirits; if they be not lovers of God, his, truth, **and partiali-**
and the Churches publique peace, more then of their own private interefts, of pro- **ty of faction.**
fit or reputation. The *mifts* which *prejudice* and *popularity* firft; next, *pride* and
paffion, caft on mens judgements, do at length turn their very light into darknefs,
being loath to fee or own worth in any perfon or performance, but what makes
for their party. All their parts for *Learning* and *Oratory*, nay their very *Zeal*,
muft (*τῇ ἀλλὰ ſchebel*) ferve their *caufe* and *credit*, as an over-hot liver, and bilious
temper, turns the fweeteft nourifhment into chollar and bitternefs. At laft they fer-
ment to fuch prefumptuous and precipitant practices of piety, as will adventure
to fhake and overthrow all that is fettled in Church or State, as Sacred or Civil, rather then mifcarry of their *wills :* What the *Heaven* of Reafon and Religion, of Chriftian patience, and Loyal obedience cannot, yea will not do, that the
gate and *powers of Hell*, fury and confufion muft endeavour, though to the *eternal*
reproach of the Authors and Abetters of that caufe and means, which are carried
on by *fuch methods*, as do in the end ruine fuch a Reformed Church, and flourifhing Kingdom as *England* once was, and may again be by Gods bleffing.

Whofe publique honor and happinefs, fome mens heady zeal, and proud *fuperftition*, made no fcruple grievoufly to revile, and terribly to threaten, even in
Mr. *Hookers* days, and in after times to fet all on a light fire; endeavouring to confume, and utterly bury fo goodly *a Fabrick* as the Church of *England* was, in its
own afhes and ruines ; rather then endure fome innocent *carved work* on *its walls*,
or fome *duft and cobwebs* in its windows : All which (as S. *Auftin* in a like cafe
againft the fury of Novatians and Donatifts of his time) were better born with
Chriftian patience, or excufed with *Charity*, or rightly interpreted without any prejudice or offence, then reformed with fuch fury, clamor, and confufion, as ufe
not the *beefome of lawful Authority*, but onely the *firebrands* of popular infolency,
forgetting all bounds of Modefty, Loyalty, and Charity, becoming Men, Subjects,
and Chriftians.

This *great Prophet* Mr. *Hooker* (not fuch by *extraordinary infpiration*, but *pru-* **Mr. Hookers**
dential confideration; (for, *prudentia eft quædam divinatio;* and, *bonus conjectator eft* **Prophetick**
vates optimus; Wife men dwell next door to Prophets) wifely *forefaw*, and notably **Spirit.**
foretold above forty years before they came to pafs, the probability of thofe diftempers and conflagrations, which were likely to befal the Church of *England*, by
the plaufible, but inordinate pretenfions of fome mens opinions and practices; of
whofe pernicious principles and events he gives a large account by *Foreign experience*, alfo excellent counfel and caution againft them, in his *Learned and Eloquent*
Preface before his Ecclefiaftical Polity.

And certainly, if the hand of any one man had been able to have applied an effectual *antidote or defenfative*, againft thofe then prefaged, and now accomplifhed
mifchiefs, Mr. *Hooker* was likely to have done it : Such *fatisfaction* his writings gave
to all ingenious and impartial men, as to the *fcruples* objected againft the Church
of *England*, not about its *inward health, and foundnefs of conftitution for faith and
manners*, for *doctrine and true devotion* (which few but *Papifts* durft, or did then
oppofe) but as to its *cloathing* and *ornaments* ; the outward form and modes of
publique and folemn performing Religious Duties, which properly fall under the
Cognizance, Care, and Appointment of Publique Wifdom, and *Supreme Authority.*

Hence

Mr. *Hookers* atchieve-ments in his writings.

Hence he made, *first*, a very godly and grave *Vindication* of the Church of *England*, as to its *Conformity to the Word of God*, in all things that are the main essen-tial, and immutable parts of Religion. *Next*, he justified its Power and Prudence, even in those minute and mutable *Circumstances* and *Ceremonies*, modes and Rites of outward Administrations of Religion; in which it either followed the *purest* and *primitive Antiquity*, or exercised its *own Christian liberty*, prudence and autho-rity in the choice, use, and appointment of such things, as it esteemed most con-venient for that publique Order and Decency, that uniformity and peace which must be kept in the Church of Christ; not either judging or imposing these things as matters of religious *necessity* or *sanctity*, in their general nature, or particular in-stance; but as objects of *Rational prudence*, *Christian liberty*, and *Supreme Autho-rity* under God, in things not precisely commanded or forbidden by Him, but receiving such stamps of Religion, of Moral or Religious good or evil, as are set upon them by the relation they have to the end whereto they are applied; also to that lawful Authority, by which they are enjoyned, agreeable to Gods Word: Which first commands all things to be *done decently, and in order*. *Next*, it intrusteth not private fancies, but publique Authority, and Soveraign Wisdom, with the particular determining and executing those general injunctions. *Lastly*, it com-mands obedience for the Lords sake to *Superiors*, in all such things as God hath thus put under their *Prudence* and *Regulation*.

Mr. *Hookers* compleat defence of the Church of *England* in-effectual.

Indeed Mr. *Hooker* left no part of the *Church* of England *unfortified*, but so sub-stantially defended, even as to its very out-works, that one would wonder how it came in after ages to be so assaulted, stormed and slighted, as it was by a *ge-neration* of men, whom he left so weak and inconsiderable, as the rigid *non-Con-formists* were for many years in *England*, after his writings came to be read and admired by all wise men. It were a *superfluous curiosity*, to examine how *the Church of England* came to fall under the insolence of its *enemies*, after so strong and ra-tional a defence made by Mr. *Hooker*, and when it had so resolute a Defender as the *late excellent King Charls* the first was.

How the Church of *England* came to be so de-sperately af-faulted, after Mr. *Hookers* just defence of it.

This is certain, that (besides the *Traytors* of our epidemical and immoral sins, which were within us, and which are capable to betray the most assured peace of *Church* or *State*) the strength of the Church of *England* was much decayed and un-dermined, before it was openly battered; partly by some superfluous, illegal and unauthorized innovations in point of Ceremony, which some men affected to use in publique, and impose upon others, which provoked people to jealousie and fury, even against things lawful, every man judging truly, that the measure of all *publique obedience* ought to be *publique Laws*; partly by a supine *neglect* in others of the main matters in which the *Kingdom of God*, the peace of *Conscience*, and of the *Churches* happiness do chiefly consist, while they were immoderately intent upon meer *Formalities*, and more zealous for an *outward conformity* to those sha-dows, then for that inward or outward conformity with Christ, in *holy hearts*, and *unblameable lives*, which most adorn true Religion.

Hence, as the Learned Dr. *Holsworth* observes in his first Lecture, did the vigi-lant Enemies of the Church of *England* take *their rise*; by these *leaks* in our own sides, the waters came in which *sank* us: Not that legal *Conformity* was either the *sin* or *shame* of this Church, or any good man: Decent Ceremonies, or Rites for Solemnity, as *motes in the Sun*, neither adding to the sacred light of Religion, nor detracting from it, where the conscience is pure, and the life unspotted: But to be *super-ceremonial*, or *solely-ceremonial*, is no less folly then to be *anti-ceremonial*; for it doth not onely prejudice the wisdom and authority of the Church, as if it wholly, or too much doted on these *petty matters* (which is the great blemish, and just blame of the Church of *Rome*, where too much of Ceremonies, hath smothered and overlaid much of the true Religion, as ashes do the fire) but it gives an ad-vantage to the novellizing insolency of its *Adversaries*, as great as *Dalilah* did to the *Philistines* against *Sampson*, when by cutting off *his hair*, she bereaved him of his great strength; not that it lay in his hair, which was but a *symbole of his vow*, as a *Naza-rite*; no more then the health, honor and happiness of the Church of *England*, lies in its *legal Ceremonies*: But these are such publique instances and *evidences of its Authority*; such *boundaries*, against all visible *extravagances*, such *demonstrations of*
its

its *unanimity*, such ties and bonds of publique Uniformity, and such Ornaments of Reverend *Solemnity*; or visible sanctity, that whoever openly despiseth; forsaketh, or violateth the *Authority* and wisdom of the Church in these things, either adding to, or taking from its customs or *Constitutions*, takes the course either to betray her, or *destroy* her: For fancying himself to *be wiser* then the Law, he wants nothing but power to make him Master of it, that so he and his party may (as *Julius Cæsar*) become *Dictators* to the Publique: Nothing keeping the peace of any *Polity, Ecclesiastical* or *Civil*, so firm and sure, as the strict keeping of all men to its *Laws*, without going to the right hand, or to the left: No man may diminish from, or adde to publique *Constitutions*; which like currant Coyn, are stamped with the *Image of supreme* Wisdom and Authority, and may not be clipped or defaced by any private hand, nor yet heightned or abased by any private judgement, signifying neither more nor less, then the publique *esteem* and *declared use* hath set upon them.

Although this *admirable* Writer was not so happy to *purge out* the disease and humour *wholly from* this Church, yet (as the *Jesuites powder* doth in quartanes) he very much *damped* and *quenched* it; so that for a long time, the fits and paroxysms of *Non-conformity* were allayed: Nor do I doubt, but that God of his mercy stirred up so great an instrument of his glory in those times (when the *Disciplinarian faction* boiled *very high*; yea, and *bristled too* against the *Queen* and *Parliaments*) as well as against *Bishops*; petitioning, remonstrating, monishing, murmuring, menacing, and mutyning; that he might (*frigidam suffundere*), give them a cool dash, and thereby the tranquility of this Church might be lengthned (as it was, for the space of forty years; after the *blasphemy* and *execution* of *Hacket* and his Complices, had brought an infinite shame and horror upon all that *dissenting party*. ^{margin: *Mr. Hookers* pains strengthned the Churches tranquility.}

Yet at length, the confluence of our *common and personal sins*, brought on the feared and foretold Calamities, prevailing against Gods patience, and long suffering: And when there was no remedy, wrath broke forth upon all estates and degrees in Church and Kingdom: Not for any Legal, *sober and due* conformity to that Reformed Religion, which was established with truth and holiness for the substance, as with order and decency, for the *Ceremony and Solemnity*; without any known error in the former, or any *superstition* in the latter: But the sin, the *Achan*, the cursed thing that troubled *Israel*, chiefly lay in the *emptiness, formality, unthankefulness, hypocrisie*, and *unfaithfulness* of those, who knew not how to prize and use so great *mercies temporal* and *spiritual*, as were to be enjoyed in the Church of *England*, by Loyal and Religious Christians. ^{margin: Conformity to the Laws, no cause of the Church of *England's* miseries.}

Nor did the *Divine Vengeance* chuse or use any other rod of his wrath, wherewith to afflict this Church, but that which Mr. *Hooker* foresaw, and foretold: For all other *Sects* and *Factions* were but the slips and *surculations* of that old *root of bitterness*, which went under the name of *Non-conformity*; the *head* or *tail*, the *sting* and *poyson* of which, were the *Disciplinarians*; or *Presbyterians*, of all late *dissenters*, the most dangerous: For they moved not so much upon their scruples and dissatisfaction in point of some little Ceremonies (as many well-meaning men did but (*pro summæ imperii*) they had an ambition to *govern* in common, as *Presbyters*: The better to promote this, they set up the new *Title* and *Office* of lay-Elders, that the *common people* in every Parish might be *sprinkled* with the *same leaven*, and swell to the height of Mole-hills, as to some part of *Church* Rule or *Government* in them. ^{margin: The rod chosen by divine vengeance to chastise the Church of *England*.}

These Presbyterian *Pompeys*, rather then fail of this so specious and popular design of governing, resolved to hazard all, having much to get, and little to lose of *estate* or *repute*, (such (old and young) Monsters indeed there were of *Non-conformity*; for I do in charity believe, their cruel plots of late practiced, were beyond the intent, and utterly against the minde of many more modest *Non-conformists* of old time; who had onely some fear, lest one or two of our *Ceremonies*, might savour still of *Superstition* or *Popery* (not considering, if abuse of things good and lawful be capable to *desecrate them* for a time, sure the restored *right use of them* is as able to *consecrate them a new*, as it hath done our *Churches* (which some *Fanaticks* would have all *demolished*, because they are elder then the late *Reformation*;) but those *meeker spirits*, *Non-conformists*, never opposed *Liturgy* or *Episcopacy*, much ^{margin: The ambitious presumption of some Presbyters.}

C   less

less the *whole frame* and being of the Church of *England*, to whole Articles and Canons they subscribed: However, many of them were carried down the latter *streams of violence*, which pretended at first onely to *Reformation*, not to *extirpation*: Ambitious projects never wanting specious vizo's and pretentions by which to begin, and ever wanting moderation in their procedures.

The fury of some Non conformists. The intemperate heat of those high-spirited and *hot-spur'd Non-Conformists*, at last so *over-boyled*, that they quenched for a time *the light of our Israel*, deformed the *beauty of Order and Holiness*, Law and Religion, Church and Kingdom, casting themselves and all things into such an Hell of horror, deformity and confusion, as nothing but *multiplied miracles* of Divine Mercy, could recover us out of that *Abyss of despair*; which had no hope left in it, but these *maximes* of Eternal Truth, which in the worst of times were some *stay to pious mindes*: *That God is merciful as well as just*; That when *wicked men* are the rod to punish their betters, the chastisement will not be long, and is less to the sufferers, then to the unjust doers: That sin and hypocrisie can never prosper long, though it may prevail: That all sin is its own severest punishment: That evil opinions, are at last most severely confuted by their own evil practices, and fatal events: That patient obedience to God and man, will give a better account of it self *to Conscience*, though it be suffering, then the most *prosperous* sinning, upon any *presumption* whatsoever: That if man aim at *Gods ends* in *good earnest*, he will enquire, finde out and follow *Gods means*, which must ever be holy and just, according to Gods and mans Laws: That *riotous* and *rebellious* Reformations, are the greatest deformities of *true Religion*, prostituting the Sanctity and Virginity of it to vulgar lusts; like the *Israelites Golden Calf*, which they made without the presence, counsel or consent of *Moses*, which became their sin and snare, though they had cryed it up as the *Gods of Israel*, by popular *acclamations*.

The mercy of restored tranquilry to the Church of England. These principles of Christian *hopes*, no *times*, no *Tyrants*, or *Tragedies*, were able to banish out of good mens mindes: And blessed be God, we have not onely lived to see and feel the predictions of this great Prophet fulfilled; but we have *outlived their dreadful accomplishments*, and after the *earthquake, tempest* and *fire* are past, we have heard the *soft voyce of Gods presence*; we are come to that *serenity* and *safety*, as may dare to own the sin and shame of former times and actions; to weep over our past calamities, and to joy in present mercies. It was of late *capital* to complain, a *crime to mourn* over bad, or to pray for *better times*; it was *Treason*, to speak *truly* of *Treason*; and loss of *liberty*, to deplore the publique *slavery*; to such a *predominancy* had the *overflowing scourge*, and the *abomination of desolation* prevailed, till God from above, rebuked the proud waves, and caused the *dry land* to appear in this Church and Kingdom; in which Religion, Loyalty and Learning, may now outface *Hypocrisie, Rebellion*, and *Ignorance*: We have now *liberty*, not onely to *read*, but *reprint* and practice Mr. *Hookers* Ecclesiastical Polity; to which, as to *Jeremies Prophesie*, many more like words *are now added*, together with some larger *Commentary* upon his life and death: All which may be both pleasant and profitable to the *present age, restored now* (as the *dispossessed Demoniac*) to its *right wits* and *estates*; to its *former laws*, and true liberties in *Church* and *State*.

How hard it is to write Mr. *Hookers* Life exactly I well know, that a *Picture* taken at so great a distance from the life and death of Mr. *Hooker* (now sixty years past) can hardly hit the life exactly, Time with its black and impartial mantle wrapping up all things in darkness and oblivion, burying pearls no less then pebbles, in dust and ashes; especially where no care hath been taken (except in some *superficial* and *general* ways) to preserve any special characters of such a person, in whom no doubt, many particulars were rare, remarkable, both in Nature, Art, and Grace. But my aim is so far, at least, to *retrive* the *footsteps*, not onely of his well-known fame and worth; but, 1. Of his Birth and Education. 2. *His genius and temper* of body and minde, with the most critical *instances* of his *life and actions*; his Person also, and outward Mine, or Aspect, which is no small indication of mens *mindes* and *manners*. 3. *Works*, or κατορθώματα, as to his *Writings*. 4, His (ἀγῶνες or ἀσκήσεις) *Sufferings* and *Tryals*. 5. His *Rewards* and *Preferments*. 6. and *lastly*, His *Death*, and *Burial*, and *Monument*: That so the English World may see by a Retrospection (as glasses which present those *objects before* us, which are indeed behinde us) what kinde of Lamp that was, which

contained

contained such *Golden Oyl* ; which shined with so bright a light of *Reason*, and *Religion* ; which burned with so discreet a Zeal, and holy Fervency of united Gifts and Graces; as cheared the Friends, and *dazled* the Enemies of the Church of *England*.

If I seem to come short in any of these his true proportions, it must not be imputed to my want of *good will*, or *good colours*, but to the want of a full view, and free *Prospect* of him ; whom the long intervail of time, and the negligence of former *Writers*, have left so unobserved, that my best intelligence hitherto, hath not been able to assure me, as to *the first head of his birth*, what *Village*, *Town* or *City* had the *honor* of his *Nativity* ; for which, as for *Homers* birth, many places would ambitiously contend. This onley is certain on all hands, that he was born in the West, either in, or not far from the City of *Exeter*; onely Dr. *Vilvain*, an Ancient and Learned Physician in *Exeter*, informs me, that he was born in *Southgate street* in *Exeter*, *Anno* 1550. His Countrey (as Mr. *Cambden* observes) is indeed *ferax ingeniorum*, pregnant with *good wits*, and *great spirits* ; *necessitated* to industry, by the *native tenuity* of the soil : addicted to Piety and Vertue, as having no great leisure for *luxury* ; much encouraged to all ingenious Arts and Studies, by the health and long life they enjoy : But of what Parents, or with what *presages* of his future Eminency, there is not any notice to be had, although I have made diligent enquiry *upon the place* ; where the name is not yet extinct : One of his Uncles, Mr. *John Hooker*, elder Brother to his Father, was *Chamberlain of Exeter* in Mr. *Hookers* youth, and contributed both care and cost toward his Education in the Free-School at *Exeter* : His *Parents* of no further note, then that they lived *contentedly*, did all things *commendably*, and departed this life *comfortably*, enjoying *competency* with industry and piety, and dying in peace; as they lived without envy ; needing no other renown or Monument of honor and happiness, then this, that they were the blessed Parents of so worthy a Son.

So that, his *Originals*, like that of *Nilus*, are left obscure ; but as the *nobleness* of that River *recompenceth* in its streams and exuberancy, the *obscurity* of its Fountains ; so it is in this *illustrious Person*, what he seems to want in the honor of his Birth and Progeny, is made up in that of his Life and Labors. God oft raiseth as noble *Plants* out of *small beds*, as out of the *stateliest Gardens* : *Literate* and pious *Nobility*, may be as honorable upon the account of the publique good, and grace, as that of *Blood* and *Parentage*, which is then most to be esteemed, when it is the least *excellency* of him *that hath it.*

Nor do I hear of any *Astrological calculations* made from *the stars* at his *Nativity*, the usual *cheats* and flatteries of *vain* men : But yet we have such *Theological demonstrations* in his life, of his *rare worth, and gracious endowments* (whose inclinations come from an higher and better influence then *the stars*) that we may conclude him to have been born, not onely with *happy and propitious stars*, but by the *special Providence* of the *God of Heaven*, who furnished him, by the *ministration* of Elementary principles, or second causes, with such a temper of body and minde, as were rarely fitted to each other, and both to those *great designs* for which the wise God intended him ; to whose Omnipotent goodness, all things are equally easie : And however, he can work effectually by weak means, and *unprobable instruments*, when he is pleased to exert his *mighty arm* in extraordinary operations, or special inspirations, by which he made Prophets of Shepheards, and Apostles of Fishermen (that mankinde might sometimes look up to the *first cause* of causes, who is in, and above all second causes;) yet in the usual methods of his Providence, this (μίγας Δημιεργος) this great *Worker* gives his *tools* that *temper* in nature, for *constitution* of body, and *disposition* of minde, which is most proportionable to the work they are to do, as we see in *Moses*, *Aaron*, *Joshua*, *Sampson*, *Samuel*, *Eliah*, and others.

It is oft seen, that mens souls do (*male habitare*) lodge inconveniently ; bodily *indispositions* or preponderancies of *constitution*, being great *allays* and *impediments* to the operations and improvements of their souls, either by the weakness of *organs*, or by the *redundancy of indigested*, dull, and phlegmatick humors, or by the *Incubus* of a moroser *Melancholy* ; or by the *over-activity* of a sanguinary easiness,

and

1. Mr. *Hookers* birth and education.

2. The temper of his body and mind.

The symbolizing of souls and bodies.

and unfettledness; or by the too great *fharpnefs* and brittlenefs of a *cholerick* edge, which makes men *fharp* and *untractable*. Sometimes the foul is *too keen* for the body, as a *knife* which cuts through its fheath; fometimes the body is too fluggifh and cumberfome for the foul, like *Birds*, whofe feathers load them; as the *Oftrich*, of which it is a queftion, whether its *plumes* do more help, or hinder its flight: fometimes the Light cannot fhine through the thicknefs of the *lanthorn*, otherwhile the Candle is fo great, or *mifplaced*, that it burns the thin and horny fides of it.

Mr. *Hookers* excellent conftitution. This excellent perfon Mr. *Hooker*, had a body and foul every way fo adjufted and fuited to each other, that they were like *meet pairs* happily married together, and living peaceably. His great foul feemed to be well pleafed with the *fize* of his body, which was not grand, but moderate; not *Pygmean*, nor Cyclopick; neither as a *narrow Clofet*, nor a vaft Hall, but an handfome *Parlour*, or Chappel: The habit alfo of his body was neither *grofs* nor *meager*, fparing indeed, but not *withered*; he was neither (πολύσαρχος nor ἰσχός) large nor little. It is in mens *ftatures* obfervable, as in *trees*, if very tall, they are commonly *barren*; if fhrubs and dwarfs, they bear but *little fruit*, though good: His *outward afpect* and carriage was rather *comely* then *courtly*,

His outward garb, deportment and afpect. his looks always grave and referved, not as *fullenly difcontented*, but as *Ammianus Marcellinus* obferves of *primitive Bifhops* and Churchmen, modeftly *dejected*: His foul feemed more retired and looking inward, then *expatiating* at his eyes, or taking the outward profpect of *his fenfes*: His whole *garb* and *prefence* was rather *plain* then *polifhed*, and not very promifing beyond a *ftudious fimplicity*, and fuch a fevere, but *fpeculative gravity*, as becomes a great Scholar, and *folemn Divine*: He went always, as if he meditated fome great and good defign; and was forming it, as it were, behinde the *vail*, or *curtain*, in fome more retired room of his *fpacious foul*, before he would let the world fee it.

His aptitude to ftudy and induftry. The happy conftitution of Mr. *Hooker*, which was neither *airy*, nor *earthy*, nor *watery*, nor *fiery*, but all, made him capable to bear that great *fedulity* and *fedentary* pains, which his *reading*, *meditating*, *digefting*, and *writing* did require for the production of fo profound and grave a Work, as he happily effected, without any *remarkable* injury to either health of body or minde.

The blefling of fober and found Parents. Which blefling (and a great one is *as* to this life) health being *flos vitæ*, the *flower and life of life*) he owed principally to God, but fecondarily to his *Parents*, whofe honefty and induftry kept them in health, and derived this to *their children*, in fuch temperature of body and minde, as were *benign*, *adequate*, and *compleat*, without any notable *flaws*, *defects*, *exceffes*, or *deformities*; which very oft vifit the Parents *fins on the children*, who oft owe their *rheumatique*, ricketly, *dwindling*, *difeafed*, *impotent*, and *indifpofed* tempers of body and minde, to the diftempers and *debaucheries* of their *Progenitors*, who have more care and caution for the *breed of their horfes and hounds*, then of their children (whofe health commonly follows the *honefty and fobriety of their parents*, as plenty *doth peace* and induftry.) Nor are any *injuries* lefs reparable, then thofe that are thus *feminal* and connate with our very Genitures (as bricks ill *tempered*, and worfe *burnt* in the *clay*, are never good in the *building*, but always mouldring and decaying.) Againft other *accidents* which may for a time *deprefs natures* vigour, yet at length a juft and generous *conftitution* raifeth up it *felf*, and makes a valiant *oppofition*; yea, in time *conquers its* oppreffors, expels its *Tyrants*, and eftablifheth the *Empire* of its health to a greater *firmnefs* and *conftancy*, then perhaps it would otherwife have enjoyed; ftrength encreafing by fuch contefts, as valour doth by *difficulties*, and health enriching it felf by the *fpoils* of its fubdued *infirmities*.

Hereditary maladies hardly overcome. But *Hereditary cankers*, like thofe of *Scions*, taken from fretted *trees*, are hardly, if ever *outgrown*, but become *everlafting chains* and *clogs* to *poor mortals*; whofe fouls either always live like *Prifoners and Galley-flaves*, tugging at the *chains* and oars of their depreffing bodies; or if they have a *generous ambition* to get above thofe wearifome dejections and preffures, they commonly make their way fooner out of *their bodies*; as the fire that once breaks out, fooner confumes *the houfe*, then that which is *fmothered within the walls*: Hence that of the Poet is true of pregnant fpirits in puling bodies,

Præmaturis brevis eft ætas & rara fenectus.

which

which *Cardan* foretold of our *Edward* the fixth: Those whose bodies are too weak, or too ftrait, or too heavy for their fouls, are not long *lived*, nor much at eafe while they live, which makes them foon weary of life, and *covetous of death*, as their onely freedom from that captivity, in which their infirm amd decayed bodies detain their *nobler fouls.*

As the *ftrings* of Mr. *Hookers* temper or conftitution were true and well tuned, **His Equable** or fet to an happy *harmony* between his *foul* and *body*, fo did they always carry a **conversation** grave and fober accord, or *unifone* in his converfation (ἀσύν θερμότερον, ἀσύν τρεμώδες, as *Marcus Aurelius* adviseth:) nothing was fudden, rafh, violent, precipitant, extravagant, in his words, geftures, undertaking or actions: What he thought within his duty, reach, and capacity, that he defigned; and what he fo defigned, he induftrioufly and effectually acted, with due deliberation, diligence, *conftancy* and *modefty*: Never *vapouring* or *vexing*, without any affectation or oftentation, always even at home *compofed*, wrapt up *in himfelf*, and intire, feldom *erring*, and therefore feldom *repenting.*

His words, which are the pulfe of the rational foul, were always fober, fteddy, **His words or** apt, well-chofen, and well-ordered, not more in number then weight, if in a *feri-* **Affability.** *ous difcourfe*; nor beyond civility and *Sanctity*, if remifs or *jocofe*, which he rather not hated, then much loved: So far from being prodigal of fpeech (as fome are, whofe mindes are always not onely fet a broach, but running out at the tap of their tongues) that he was rather *parfimonious*, and *fcarce liberal*, unlefs he were well acquainted: He laid but little of his *finer ware* on the *fhopboard*, or *ftall*, as thofe do, whofe ftock of *wit* or *knowledge*, like a *Pedlars* pack, is prefently open, and falls under one view; but as thofe that deal by *whole-fale* in rich *commodities*, he kept his *treafure* fhut up, and under *lock* and key, in a large, but retired *warehoufe*: He was like an *hive full of honey*, of a plain outfide, and a *narrow accefs* or *orifice*; but *heavy*, as having in him all manner of *good Literature*, as that hath the *quinteffence* of all *vegetable* or *florid fweetnefs*, induftrioufly gathered, and aptly digefted, very *fweet*, and very *fluent*, when he lift to give it vent.

His Friends or *Confidents* were few, but choife, as one that had no great *opinion of* **His Friends** *himfelf* nor captated the applaufe of others, nor was much at leifure or vacant, **or confidents** more difpofed to a *reclufe* or *eremetical* life, then to the *Ayr* or *Sun*; and fitter for *chamber practice* at his *ftudy* and *pen*, then for the *bar* or *pulpit*: But however, his natural temper was flow and referved, as fome Rivers, yet he had that in *depth* and *clearnefs*, which he feemed to want in *noife* and *fwiftnefs*.

He began betimes, even in the *Grammar School* of *Exeter*, to difcover a great foul, **His firft ef-** pregnant as to wit and invention, capacious and extenfive as to a largenefs of *un-* **fays and in-** *derftanding*, fixed as to a gravity of *judgement*, bleffed with fidelity of memory, and **dications of** advancing daily by an *indefatigable diligence*, a filent, fedentary, and aftonifhed way **learned in-** of induftry in *ftudy*; which like a *ponderous* and fharp wedge, followed with *con-* **duftry.** *tinual little ftrokes*, did make its way through all things, on which it could fix.

At the fame *rate*, or pace, *flow*, but *fure*, he went on in his *Academical* ftudies **His Acade-** at *Oxford*, in acquiring the *learned and facred Languages*, in attaining thofe intellectu- **mical profi-** al *Arts* and *Sciences*, which are excellent *handmaids* to *Divinity*, in fpoiling the **ciency.** Egyptians of their *Jewels*; the Heathen Philofophers, Hiftorians, Poets, and Philologers, daily paying tribute to his victorious diligence. Thefe (as his *Works* every where *difcover*) he not onely tafted *fuperficially*, but throughly *imbibed*, *fully exhaufted*, and *methodically digefted*, in that ftill and fober way of *his ftudies*, which made not fo much *noife* and *flourifh* in the *Schools* and *Univerfity*, as many other young men; but he daily rooted *deeper*, and *encreafed* more in all wifdom and *underftanding Humane* and *Divine*; able, but not *forward*, to teach others, judging it the beft *method of a good Scholar*, who intends to be a *Preacher*, firft to be well inftructed, before he undertakes to inftruct others, to fill the *ciftern* before he give it vent, not driving the *hive*, till it be well *laden* with *honey*.

This made him *demur* for fome years after he was *Mafter of Arts*, and *Fellow* of **His flownefs** *Corpus Chrifti Colledge*, before he undertook any *Minifterial Office* or *charge*, having **to appear or** obferved many *prefocious Preachers*, and *preproperous Writers*, to be like *prodigal young* **preach.** *Gallants*, newly come to their *eftates*, who fancy they have nothing more to get, or to save, but all the *care is, to finde* ways to *spend fast* enough: hence, like *hot mettall'd horses*, they soon tire, or founder by their too great activity and *confidence* at their first setting out; nothing *spoiling* a good *Scholar*, and making a bad Preacher, so much as *over-hasty preaching*, and *impatient scribbling*. As good husbandry is the foundation of *hospitality*, and *thrift* the fewel of *magnificence*, in domestick and Civil affairs: so in *intellectual*; neither *fields* nor *mindes* will be fruitful, unless they have good *manure*, and due tillage, before the crop be expected.

His retiredness at the Colledge.

While Mr. *Hooker* continued in *Corpus Christi Colledge*, few men of any note in either University, but promised more then he did, as to any great and publique undertaking: Not that he wanted a publique spirit, or excellent abilities in Nature and Education; but he was so locked up and reserved by a natural modesty, and *self-deficiency* or distrust, that he seemed to think it *reward* sufficient to have the conscience of well-doing; and *pleasure* enough, to see himself daily profit in his studies; and *preferment* even to an envy, to enjoy vertue, though never so cloistered and confined to his own breast: And although his face, as to the inward man, and as to *his life*, shined with all splendor of Gifts and Graces, yet he *chose* as *Moses*, to put *a vail* on himself, left he should lose the true glory of it, by seeming in the least kinde to glory in it.

His obscuring of himself a long time.

Neither his great dimensions nor deserts did yet appear in their true lustre; but as the *Sun* in a misty morn, he was clouded, till *almost noon*, before he brake through those *native obscurities*, for which the after brightness and heat of his day *made a great amends*. Nothing is more *injudicious* then to *pass hasty judgement*, or to take up mean prejudices against men of good breeding, ingenuity and industry, before they come to *their proof*: Men of *modest* and *reserved* tempers, like the more lasting fruit, ripen later then others seem to do; but they are more solid, sapid and lasting, as good liquor, which conceives greater spirits, by being long *close bottled* up, and stopped. Men of *excellent Naturals*, may as *Brutus* the younger, seem very dull and *gros Garzons* while they are young, who afterward prove very eminent in all true worth, even beyond what was expectable from them: As did this *worthy*, but *wary Scholar*, who was not so active and forward as many others of his time, but *less idle* in his *reserves*, then most men are in *their more ayry* appearances, and *pragmatick ostentations*: His *retirings* were his *ripenings*, and his being still *wrapped up* in himself, was his thickning or fulling, before he came to be put on the *teinters*, and laid forth to those *great employments*, to which he is judged by all wise men to be one of the most adequate of any man that ever entred the lists of combate with the *Adversaries* of the Order, Unity, Liberty, Authority and Peace of the *Church of England*. Few men were found upon just proof, to have had so much sound learning so well marshalled and disposed; few had so *trusty memories*, so profound and impartial judgements, so unperturbed passions, so copious, clear and current expressions; none more cogent in demonstrations, either for right Reason, or true Religion; none more pathetick in his excitation of serious and sober affections.

Not much nored or famed in the Colledge or University.

Yet while he lived in the *Colledge* and *University*, there seems to have been no great notice of him, further then that of a good *plodding Student*, one that lay heavy on the plow, and was *daily sowing* good seed, but few expected so rich *an harvest* as afterward grew up in his soul, and was reaped by *his pen*: He was like a *rich mine* not yet fully discovered, but daily improving upon the Explorators. At last he made up the *Triumviri* of that little *Colledge*, those three men of Renown, in whose names it justly glories, as of the *first three* and highest form, for learned, great, and *godly Divines*.

B.shop *Iewel* of the same Colledge.

The first was Bishop *Jewel*, who (*vir sui nominis*) verified his name, esteemed at home and abroad by all *reformed Divines* one of the most *splendid Gems* that ever this, or any Church was adorned withal: Nor could the *Romish* envy or malice be so impudent, as either to deny or depreciate his incomparable worth, both for learning and holiness: However, *reason of State* and worldly Policy, would not suffer them to subscribe to those Reformed, but *ancient* Truths, which that *excellent* Prelate most convincingly maintained against them by Scriptures and Antiquity.

So was Dr. Reynolds.

The second was Dr. *Reynolds*, who was very good mettal and full *weight* for Learning and Piety, however he seemed a while something *bowed* and *disfigured* (by his Education and relations) as to the stamp of *exact Conformity* with the *Church of England*,

England, until the Conference at *Hampton-Court* (where he was the onely *Atlas* on that side) But the *learned* wisdom of King *James,* set off with his potent *Eloquence,* and a benignity more imperial then his Kingly Authority, restored that excellent Scholar to the perfect *Character* and *Superscription* of a *good Subject,* and a good *Church-man :* For after that Conference, which concluded with some gracious *con-defcentions* of the King, this Dr. *Reynolds,* though neither tempted nor rewarded with a Bishoprick, fully conformed to the *Church of England,* and advised others so to do.

The third *Colofs* of fair, solid marble, which came out of that *rich Quarry,* was Mr. *Hooker,* though he was some time in hewing and polishing, before the ampleness and goodliness of his figure, as to the soul and minde, did appear by his pen; which yet seemed not to have been to any great *conspicuity* or *expectance,* while he continued in the *Colledge,* if we may take an *estimate* of the opinion had of him by the first *offer of preferment,* or rather imployment, made to him, yea and accepted by him, as to those small obscure livings; one of which was first given him by the Colledge, and *leaving* that, another was conferred on him by some private Patron, each of them being thought *competent entertainments,* even for Mr. *Hookers plainness* and *simplicity of living,* at least they were better then some Fellowships of that Colledge.

Mr. *Hooker* made the third worthy of that Colledge.

Nor did the good man disdain either the one or the other (when he left the first:) And this not out of covetousness or *ambition,* alas there was no such bait or temptation in either ; but chiefly out of a conscientious sense of the duty he owed *to God* and *the Church,* that he might pay them some *grateful tribute* by his pains in the Ministery, for that liberal *Education* he had enjoyed : And being now by years and enclination got above and beyond *those juvenile and florid studies,* which like flowers in the *Spring,* or *first-fruits* in *Summer,* adorn an *Academical* life, he began to confider *what harvest* he was now to bring forth to Gods glory, and the good of mens souls, proportionable to the seed that had been bestowed on him in the *University studies.*

His retiring to small Countrey Livings.

For the worthy person thought nothing less *became the honor of Learning,* and the *dignity of the famous Universities,* or the *pious design* of the munificent Founders, then for *Schollars* to grow too old, ripe and rotten too in their *Chambers,* as *Monks* in their Cells : Not but that as in *Woods* that are *fell'd once in* twelve years, some fair *Standers* may be left, of such as are *proper for* the support, exemplary conduct, and honor of *Academical learning* and Government : But for the *general* growth of *the underwood,* it is *ill husbandry* to let them continue too long in the shade and nursery, which not onely deprives the publique of the benefit they owe to it, but themselves also of that fruitfulness, beauty and sweetness which they might sooner attain, if they came sooner *into the Sunshine,* and freer conversation of the World, where they might more communicate their useful *abilities* ; not burying their many *talents in a Napkin,* which is the way to lose them ; nor confining their ambition to the narrow *Empire* of a *Fellowship,* or the *confines* of a *chamber,* which is to put that Light *under a bushel,* which is fit to be set on the *table,* or on *an hill,* to bless Parishes, Towns, Cities, and whole Countreys.

Why he left the University.

Many wise men have oft deplored the *detriment* that befals *Church* and *State,* by the not timely imploying and improving to the publique good, Scholars of *excellent abilities,* well bred up in the Universities, but not so soon or happily transplanted as were meet. Which defect seems to arise from a *twofold cause :*

1. Many ingenious and learned men suffer themselves (as those *that have the scurvy*) by degrees so to be pleased with a sedentary way of life, that they contract, if not a *laziness,* yet a great indisposition and loathness to come abroad, being so in love with *speculation,* that they *abhor action* ; and being now wedded to their own content and ease, they grow *divorced* from the main *ends of their studies,* Gods glory, and the publique good, thinking it enough to be ever *whetting the sithe,* but never *mowing* ; collecting *materials* and contriving, but never building : As if it were sufficient to commend a *rich peice of scarlet,* that dwells long in the dye-fat in order to imbibe a *noble tincture,* but is never to be put on the *teinture,* or worn in garments : Which *backwardness* and *barrenness* is indeed to defeat, not onely the good intentions of the Founders, and the expectations of their friends, but to *smother* and *stifle*

Scholars when ripe, are best transplanted out of the Universities. Two hindrances of timely transplantation. 1. Too great delight in speculation and ease.

their

their own more capacious fouls ; which like *veffels* fill'd with *generous wine* , are therefore filled, as Chrift commanded the *water pots* to be at the marriage, that thence they may draw forth and fatisfie others more then themfelves, that like the *Vine, Olive* and *Fig-tree* in *Jothans* Parable , they may *chear* and honour both *God* and *men.*

Improve-ment comes by feafonable employment of mens a-bilities,

Doubtlefs from fit *imployment* comes daily *improvement,* and to him that *hath ſhall be given,* if he ufe well that which he hath ; induftry being the *price* and *meafure of pro-ficiency,* as proficiency is the *firft reward* of induftry : From too long *refervednefs* good Scholars grow *reſtive* ; from *reſtive* they become averfe ; from averfion they contract an *enmity* to activity ; and thence an abhorrency of any thing that puts them upon more *publique pains* , or ufeful operations : At length filently and infenfibly *paſſing* the *Meridian of life* , the *ſhadows* of the *evening* grow upon them, they feel or fancy thofe *infirmities* which muft be now their *Apology* for their future filence: At laft (as the *Monks* of old) they are as loth to leave *their Cells* as to put off *their skins,* like *Birds* or *Squirrils* bred in *a Cage,* they know not how to ſhift for themfelves abroad: In fine, they wrapt themfelves up in their *Cynical* way with *Diogenes,* grow morofe, tetrical and cenforious, like old and neglected maids that contemn all marriages, re-folving to lay *their bones* there where they have fo many *years ſlept in quiet*; they dread being tranfpanted when they are old, and burn at laft to the very *ſnuff,* as *candles* that are hidden in a *dark-lanthorn,* without any other *account* of their lives, beyond what is to be found in the *Buttery book ,* and deferve his *Epitaph, Fui non vixi, & habui quod edi : Didici, non docui.*

The fecond caufe of Scholars non-im-provement want of pre-ferment.

2. A fecond *defect* much contributing to the publique *detriment,* by the *non-im-provement* of Scholars when they are well trained in the Univerfity, and fit to be tran-fplanted out of thofe *Nurferies* (that being fet *thinner* they may fpread *wider,* grow *bigger,* and bear much *more fruit*) is the want of *publique care* and Patrociny to prefer and *difpofe* of them, fo as may be moft agreeable to *their abilities*; Many times their *modeſty* much *curbs* their activity (like ears of corn and *boughs* of trees, the more loaden, the more hidden and *dejected*) and being wholly deftitute of fuch friends and relations as might put them forward, they have this to anfwer any *that ask* why they ftand ftill till the *ninth hour* of the day, *becaufe no man hath hired them,* or fet them on work, or preferred them : Befides this, the *ſwarms* or *leſſer fry* of other meaner *Scholars,* who have but a *little tincture* of learning in comparifon, and who like *Bar-nacles* or *Soleme Geefe,* too foon drop off *from the Univerfity,* betaking themfelves to Country Cures, according as their neceffities compel them: Thefe fo *foreſtal the markets of Parochial Livings* and Church Preferments, gaining by their obfequioufnefs and adherencies, the favour and friendfhip of fuch *Patrons* as have any thing worth ac-ceptance in their difpofe, that many other good *Scholars* are left to *fuperannuate* in their *folitudes,* to be confined to their Mufes everlaftingly, as if their ears had been bored through and fixed to the Colledge gates, or Study doors; as *Democritus junior* moft elegantly and pathetically deplores this *dereliction* of rare men in the Univer-fity, which makes the *Mufes melancholy,* and depriving both merit of reward, and the publique of that good which thefe men might do as Mafter Builders *in Gods Temple.*

His humble ftooping to a Countrey Cure.

Mr. *Hooker* did not look upon the eafe and quietnefs of a *Colledge* life, as the *ul-timate defign of his ſtudies* ; nor did he fay with the Apoftles, *It is good to be here,* as in a fettled Tabernacle ; but gently embraced thofe fmall *offers of Miniſterial Em-ployments* in the Countrey which were made to him, by fuch as thought them fome-what *proportionate,* if not to his *worth* and learning, yet to that *humble plainnefs* and *fimplicity* of his *genius and mode of living.*

Hence I finde him (as moft mens *manners* and fortunes generally follows their *conſtitution* and *temper*) very eafily removed, as if he chofe a *Countrey* and *retired life,* even in the greateft *vigor* and *activity,* tamely embracing without any *check* or *fcruple,* the firft offer of a *little Living* called *Bufcomb,* in the *Weft,* to which the *Colledge of Corpus Chriſti* prefented him ; and afterward that other, not much better in *Lincoln-*

His zeal to ferve God and the Church in the Miniftry.

ſhire, called *Drayton Beauchamp.*

Not that he was weary of a *Collegiate* and *ſtudious* life, any more then Bees are of gathering honey ; nor that he haftned to *marriage* as the *Sanctuary of Chaſtity* to fome men (for he ever lived a fingle and *unſpotted life*) but he did not think an *Academi-*

cal

cal life either *solitude* enough, or (poffibly) not *work* *enough*, willingly going about his *Fathers bufinefs*, and undertaking that *husbandry* of fouls which fhould be the main end, and timely employment of thofe *Scholars*, who have by *holy Orders* put their *hand* to that Sacred Plow.

Mr. *Hooker* looked more to his employment and retirement then his *Prefer-*
ment: hence I finde him *aground* as foon as *lanched* out, and as it were buried fo foon as he parted from his *Mother the Univerfity*, ftill fhut up for many years in *Coun-trey obfcurities*, where there could be no great profit nor pleafure, onely he fancied this way of living (*procul a turba*) out of the *crowd, noife* and *tintamar* of the great *World*, chufing a little *Creek*, rather then a great *arm* of the *Sea* to anchor in; where, as there is more water, fo there are greater winds and waves.

Nor is it probable he would of himfelf have ftirred by any ambitious impatience from either of thefe *ruftical retirements*, or *living Sepulchres* of him (no more then a *gentle horfe* will move from *that place* on which his bridle hangs, rather *ftarving then ftirring*) if others who had a truer eftimate of him, then he had of himfelf, had not taken notice of his fo fo fecluded *worth*, both pitying and envying to fee fuch a rich *treafury* of eloquent *Learning* buried, and almoft quite loft in a *ruftical obfcurity*, confined to *Cottages*, when he was capable to ferve whole *Churches* and *King-doms*.

It is not feldom feen, that as fome mens vapouring or crowing fancies are prone to fet too great a value on themfelves, having never well ftudied that *Socratick Leffon*, or *Oracle of* Apollo, *the knowledge of themfelves*; fo others are of that great modefty and native humility, that they are prone to *undervalue* themfelves very much, and thereby much miftake that work to which they are moft prepared by God in nature and education.

Indeed Mr. *Hooker* was not cut out for *the plain*, yet *profitable* work of preaching to
a *Countrey Auditory*; he deferved to be employed with *Bezaliel*, in the curious and fine Embroideries, the rich and coftly Gravings of the Tabernacle and Temple, ra-ther then about the tacking together of boards and Badgers skins, or hewing of courfe ftones: This great and well charged *Cannon* was *planted, mounted* and *directed* to another *level*, to a far *higher pitch*, not onely to fight againft the immoralities and fen-fualities of mean peoples *manners* in the *Countrey* (whom Minifters have much ado, like *Ulyffes* with his Companions, to keep from degenerating to Beafts, by thofe en-chantments of *bruitifh pleafures*:) But he was to keep both the *out-works* of the Church of *England*, its innocent Rites and Ceremonies; and alfo to defend its ancient Liberty, Honor and Authority againft factious and ufurping novelties; he was to batter down thofe (ὀχυρώματα) *ftrong-holds*, and fpiritual *wickednesses* which were fpe-eioufly raifed in the High places, the popular and proud *imaginations* of fome *ambi-tious Presbyters* and people, againft the good Order, Catholick Government, and lawful Conftitution of the Church of *England*; which had no fooner come out of the houfe of *bondage*, the *Romifh* oppreffion; and out of the hot *furnace* of the *Ma-rian Perfecution*, but it met with *fiery Serpents* and *Amalekites*, who fought by pri-vate opinions and prefumption to overthrow publique *Laws* and *Conftitutions*: Cry-ing out againft Pride and Superftition (as *Diogenes* trampled upon *Plato's mantle*) with far greater *pride* and *fuperftition*, denying the publique wifdom and power of Church and State that *liberty*, which themfelves daily and boldly ufurped; yea, and making fuch things fins, which no right Reafon or Scripture any way *condemns* as fuch, but rather *approves* or *allows*.

Thefe were the *Antagonifts*, the *Anakims*, againft whofe proud boafting and defy-
ings of the Church of *England* Mr. *Hooker* was to be fet, thefe he was to undertake, and to encounter: With thefe, though *an hoft of men*, he fought fuch a duel, like *Sampfon*, that he wounded and wafted them; he fo routed and difcomfited them by his potent and perfpicuous *demonftrations*, that they never made any confiderable head again during his life, until long *peace* and *plenty* had betrayed the Nation to thofe un-doubted fins, which called for a *fore fcourge* upon us, and this to be inflicted by that *arrogant* hand, which of all others was fitteft to be an *Executioner* of wrath firft upon *others*, and laft *upon it felf*.

His Countrey retirement was for his improvement to his great work.

And however this retired courſe of Mr. *Hookers* life might ſeem leſs *diſpoſitive* of him *for that great work* (moſt Scholars learned abilities being prone to grow as *ruſty* or retrograde in the Countrey through diſuſe (as the old Armour that hangs up in a Countrey Juſtices damp Hall ;) yet the providence of God, who orders all things in *wiſdom* and *mercy* to thoſe that fear and love him (as he made *Joſephs* pit the *firſt ſtep to his preferment*) of whoſe thread we muſt not judge, till it be all wound on the bottom, no more then we can of *an Arras* hanging while it is on the *loom*, and *unfiniſhed* : God, I ſay, not onely led Mr. *Hooker* to, but kept him in this *ſimple* Countrey privacy for eight years ; in which he had leiſure not onely to proſecute his former ſtudies, but alſo to mature and *digeſt them*, yea and to lay out his great deſign of aſſerting the Church of *England* ; in whoſe honor and peace he was now more *ſenſibly concerned*, then when he lived in a *Collegiate retirement*, out of the *daſh* and *importunity* of thoſe *Pamphlets* and *Petitions* of ſome *Miniſters* and *people*, whoſe *petulancy* gloried as much to *bay unceſſantly* at the Church of *England*, as ſome *Dogs do* at the Moon in the *brighteſt* and *calmeſt* night, as if they had more cauſe to quarrel at her *ſpots*, then to commend her *light*.

Mr. Hookers firſt alarm and ſenſe for the Church of Englands danger and defence.

Thoſe unſeaſonable and tedious noiſes which *ſome Non-conformiſts made*, kept this good Countrey *Parſon awake*, who however he could bear with *patience* and *ſilence* the reproaches that might be caſt upon himſelf as a private man for his *conformity* (which was by ſome made a great ſin) yet he thought it a *ſtupor* next to ſin, or *Lethargy*, for any Son to *bear*, without juſt indignation, his *Father* or *Mother* reviled or *deſpiſed*, by *peeviſh*, *ignorant* and *ingrateful children* : This *rowſed* up Mr. *Hookers* modeſt, but *generous courage* ; this made this *little David reſolved* to have a bout with theſe *uncircumciſed Philiſtins*, who diſdained to *conform* to the *Wiſdom*, Piety and Authority of the *whole Church and Kingdom* : He firſt takes an exact view of the *ground* theſe *Mutineers* had ſo long traverſed ; what *armature* or *artillery* of Reaſon and Religion they pretended to bring, what *counſels* and *correſpondencies* they had from Scripture and Antiquity : what deſign they *managed* under the name of this *holy War*, and new Diſcipline, wherewith they threatned the *Queen*, the *Parliament*, and all *Eſtates* in *England*, that did not ſpeedily ſubmit to their yet wooden *ferula*, which was ſhortly to be turned to an *iron rod*, and after that to *a golden* Scepter, even the Scepter of *Jeſus* Chriſt, in the hands of *Parochial Presbyters* and their *Lay-Elders*.

This *popular vapour*, and *factious fallacy* growing every day louder, by the ſubſcription of a thouſand Miniſters hands to one Supplication, gave the alarm to Mr. *Hooker* : this put him, contrary *to his meek* and *calm genius*, to arm himſelf with the whole *Armour of God*, both in Reaſon and Scripture : This gave (as his *privacy did opportunity*) reſolution to undertake the *cauſe of the Church of England*, which he knew *was the cauſe of God*, and *of this Kingdom* : Hence *ſprang that excellent Work* of the *Eccleſiaſtical Polity*, which ſpeaks ſufficiently for it ſelf to ſuch as are capable to read and *underſtand it*, without *prejudice* or *partiality*.

The matter and manner of his Eccleſiaſtical Polity.

The manner of his writing is at once *liberal* and *elegant*, copious and comely, with a majeſtick kinde of *ampleneſs*, and ſtately luxuriancy, as the ancient Roman Buildings; or as bodies that are *fair* and *full*, *ſinewy* and *beautiful*, handſome, and yet *athletick*, having no flat redundancy *in his ſtile or matter*, nothing *defective* or *impertinent* : ſo *unaffected*, *impartial*, *profound*, *ſolid*, *conſpicuous* and *conſcientious*, that as was ſaid of *Pindars Odes*, he is both *full*, *fluent* and *ſublime*, yet *ſerene* as the firmament : a Torrent indeed, but untroubled, carrying all before him with weighty and convincing *reaſonings* : the *whole* Work, as the *vail of the Temple*, is *enterwoven* and *curiouſly wrought* with *Scripture demonſtrations*, adorned with apt and *true allegations* of antiquity from *Councils*, *Fathers*, *Church Hiſtories*, *Schoolmen*, *Philoſophers* and *Philologiſts*, with all ſorts of excellent Obſervations, for wiſdom and prudence, Theory and Practice ; that bate him a little of the *length* of *ſome* of *his periods* and *parentheſes* (in which his *premiſes being* pregnant *with many* and *complicated* conceptions, ſeek to make the way firm and free *for bringing* up the *concluſion*) we may ſay of him, *Omne tulit punctum* : many *Writers* have *done well*, but in *his vein* he excels them all : Tis true of him what *Photius* in his *Bibliotheke* writes by way of *cenſure* of ſome *Authors*, that they were *weighty* and *grave* for their matter, *ſublime* and *accurate* for their manner of Writing ; ſtrong in their *arguings*, clear *in their deductions*, true in *their Narratives,*

Narratives, and *impartial in their judgements*, pure in their stile, and compleat in all things, beginning their Works wisely, and finishing *them happily*.

So are Mr. *Hookers Workers* to those that can read with *understanding*: The truth is, they require a very *judicious*, *steddy* and *undistracted* Reader; in many things he is too deep for *shallow* capacities, whose cord is short, and their *bucket* but *little*; in many places he is very *profound* and *sublime*, leading the Reader either to the *foundations of all Polity* and Government, or to the very *pinacle of the Temple*; such high and abstracted notions he hath from Reason, Experience and Religion, so fair a way he makes for *a wise* man and good Christian to walk in, with peace with God, himself, and others, according to Laws Natural, Moral, Evangelical, Civil and Ecclesiastical: Weak *brains* are either afraid or loth to *ascend* so high, or *descend* so low, as the upper and nether *springs* of Law from God or man: Though Mr. *Hooker* hath made the steps very fair and easie, some cannot bear the *terror* of so goodly *a prospect*, being wonted to mount no higher then their own *Closets* and *Families*, fancying it as easie for them to prescribe *ways of Government* to such a great *Church* and *Kingdom* as England is, as it is to model their petty Oeconomy of their little Cottages or Families.

The profoundness of his writing.

The *Grandeur* and *Majestie* of his Writings hath occasioned some Scholars and Ministers (especially if toucht with *Non-conformity*) to be wholly *strangers to them*; some men chusing easie and *obvious errors*, rather then *difficult and retired truths*; others were afraid lest they might *grasp* more then they *could hold*, or else be beaten from those *petty opinions* and prejudices of *a non-conformable party*, in whose *clouts* they had been *swadled*, and with whose milk they had been suckled, and from which they were loth to be *weaned*, hoping that the *breast of faction* would afford as liberal *nourishment* to the Patrons and *Chaplains* of it, as others enjoyed who were of a more peaceable temper, and conformable to the Church of *England*: There being nothing more acceptable to common people and their Abettors (as this *excellent Author* observes) then to be told by their Preachers, that they are not so well governed or disciplined as they might be, if these young Masters had the power to dispose of all things in Church and State, so as might most mend their *own Livings*, and gratifie the ambition of their *Patrons*, upon whom they *much depend*, daily encouraging them to *censure* all men and all things severely but *themselves*, as a great point of zeal and piety, capable to go with their party for *current repentance*, to expiate their own fatuities, and hide all their infirmities.

Why many Ministers such strangers to Mr. *Hookers* writings.

I cannot punctually tell what *special stimulation* Mr. *Hooker* had from *persons of eminency* in Church and State, to excite and encourage him to write *these Books*, which required both strength and valour, for he well knew he should *meet with opposition* enough: There is no doubt but the excellent *Archbishop Whitgift* added much quickning edge to his, otherwise slow and *hesitant temper*; and no less did others of his favourers and friends, who knew him better for his sufficiencies, then he did himself.

His motives and encouragements to this work.

But the main and *uncessant motive* (no doubt) to begin, carry on and compleat so useful and *laboursom a work*, was from the *good Spirit* of God working upon Mr. *Hookers* heart, and deeply affecting him with that sense of *duty*, *gratitude* and *compassion* which he owed to the Church of *England*, which he saw conflicting with so much *faction*; tedious, importune, petulant, and never to be *satisfied* with Reason or Religion: He foresaw that it was likely to be evermore so *afflicted* (as *Hannah* with *Peninnahs* reproaches) unless the *Authority* of Gods and mans Laws did timely prevail against those *specious* principles, and *desperate* designs, which he knew some men meditated, yea declared, and hoped to carry on by the popular prejudices which they daily raised against the Church of *England*, the better to accomplish the modest designs of *their party*, which was onely to rule *all things* in *Church and State*, to bring both *Princes* and *Parliaments* to receive *Dictates* and *Oracles* of Government from this *Tripos* of *Presbytery*, which was to be instituted by Jesus Christ, abetted with *Teaching* and *Ruling Elders*, who were all to be better *then Bishops*, even *Kings* and *Priests*, sitting and reigning *with Jesus Christ* on his Throne.

He saw that *the ambition* of some heady men, was to be *skreened* by the *superstition* of others, *well meaning Christians*, whom they kept in a kinde of *twilight Religion*, forbidding them the use of *right Reason* in any *matter of Religion*, but enjoyning them to live in such an *implicite faith* as made them *infinitely fhy* and *boggling* at thofe things as *great fins*, which he proves to be very *lawful* and *fafe* : Left free by Chrift, as in their *nature*, fo in *their ufe* agreeable to their nature, and not *enjoyned* by the Church under any other notion ; not as fixed parts or *effentials* of Religion, but as *circumftantials* and mutable ornaments ; which falling under the *cognizance of publique authority*, were to be *limitted* by publique *wifdom*, in order to *decency*, *peace* and *uniformity* in the publique *worfhip* of God ; the care and regulation of which, as to *things of indifferency*, is by God committed to the Supreme power in every Polity and Kingdom, as he unanfwerably proves.

This learned, fober and wife man could not but be fecretly grieved to fee the Church of *England* (which was fo *happily reformed*, fo flourifhing in all Piety, Learning and Peace, fo *famous* in this Weftern world, fo eftablifhed by excellent *Laws*, fo every way compleat and moft conform, for the main, to the paterns primitive and Gods Word, to fee this (like *Naaman* the *Syrian*, (who was a *valiant man*, but a *Leper*) thus continually infefted with the itch and tetter of *endlefs cavilling*, and eager *contending* about *fmall matters*, which are not, cannot be evil in *themfelves* ; becaufe no where forbidden of God, no *way contrary* to *faith* or good *manners*, no way *ufed* or *impofed* beyond what their *nature bears*, and God allows, as to outward Rites, Decency and Solemnity of publique Religion.

It grieved him to fee fo much *inordinate* heat in fome mens fpirits (otherways commendable for Learning and Piety (breaking out at *their tongues* and *pens*, in their prayers and Sermons, not againft herefies and errors, vice and immorality, fin and profanenefs, but againft fuch forms and fhadows, as their own needlefs jealoufie and uncharitable fufpicion made to them *Superftitions*, and fo to their fequacious Difciples, who rather took their bare word, then the whole Churches authentick teftimony ; nor would they be fo fair mannered as to give the *Church* and *Kingdom* leave to interpret its own *conftitutions*, or to declare its *true intentions*, which it hath oft and fully in thefe things, to be as far from Superftition, Idolatry, or any addition to the Word and Worfhip of God, as any effential and neceffary part of them, as the intention of the three Tribes was from *Apoftatizing* from the true God, when they erected that Altar of *memory*, witnefs hiftorick, and record on this fide *Jordan*, in token of their fraternal Communion with the other Tribes in their Religion.

When this Learned and Prudent perfon had for fome time duly confidered the *state of the controverfie*, the nature of the things difputed, light and fmall of themfelves, yet as ftubble or wifps of ftraw, fit to kindle and fet all on fire ; when he weighed the danger even of fuch petty divifion ; how fuch differences daily ventilated by new paffions, which are (*flabella opinionum*) the *fan* or *bellows* of their opinions, did grow to high animofities, diffentions and factions in Church and State, apt to ferve the *lufts of any ambitious* and difcontented people, who commonly take their fires from the Temple, and their *coals* from the Altar with which they intend to give light and heat to their defigns : He did not like thofe *Twins of Conformity* and *Nonconformity* ftruggling in one womb, to the *torture and terror of the Mother*. Hence he applied himfelf to examine the general and particular nature of things difputed, thence to clear and compofe differences, to fatisfie fcruples, and to juftifie the Churches liberty and authority, if by any means he might extinguifh thofe fires whofe fmoakings he already felt, and whofe *flames* he feared would at laft break out to *dreadful conflagrations*, as they did, after they had by his Writings been much allayed for a time, and rather *fmothered* then fincerely *quenched*.

VVhen once he had fully confidered, with what force he was able to meet thofe that came *againft him*, and *fought againft* the Churches Honor, *Peace, Liberty, Authority* and *Unity*, he muftred up all his ftrength ; he became wholly *captive* to this great and good defign : This poffeffed him intirely, to this all his ftudies and meditations were reduced : This, as a *ftrong byas*, fwayed all his thoughts, counfels and conferences, as the building of the Temple was the grand defign of *Davids* and *Solomons* munificence : Nor did the giver of every good and perfect gift, fail to furnifh this large and liberal foul with all *Sufficiencies* for fo great a work, having vaft abilities for Learning, a full *maturity* for his judgement, a great *integrity* in his defign, an exact magiftery over his paffions, a Dove-like *innocency* in his manners, and

an

an undefatigable *induſtry* in ſo good an undertaking, nothing was *impoſſible*, which this *Wiſeman* would endeavour; being ſo judicious as not to take upon him more then his ſhoulders could bear, and ſo *induſtrious* as not to give over whatever was within the ſphere of a Learned, Grave, Humble, Devout and diligent Divine.

Having thus fully debated the undertaking with himſelf, and wholly devoted himſelf (σὺν Θεῷ) by Gods direction and aſſiſtance to this *heroick deſign*, as another *Hercules* to tame *Schiſmatical Monſters*, to crop off the reviving heads of *factious Hydra's*, to cleanſe the *Augean* filth, which ſome mens tongues and pens by their impotent railings, and ſcurrilous writings had caſt on the beauty and honor of the Church of *England*: It is not to be imagined what *mighty aſſiſtances*, what *generous ſucceſſes* he daily had in this ſo honeſt and honorable an undertaking.

His courage and encouragements to the work,

Such *plenty of matter*, ſuch *variety of reading*, ſuch full and pertinent citations, ſuch clear and copious expreſſions, ſuch methodical *diſtributions*, ſuch powerful *demonſtrations*, ſuch *fundamentals* of reaſon, ſuch *originals* of Law, ſuch *eſſentials* of Religion, ſuch *proportions* of *Polity* and Order, ſuch *boundaries of Government*, ſuch neceſſary principles and *ingredients* to make up the peace and happineſs of mankinde, both Temporal and Eternal, Perſonal and Political, did flow in upon his capacious ſoul, that he had matter more then enough to ſerve his turn; and he did ſo artificially diſpoſe of his plenty and variety, that he hath juſtly obtained this *Encomium* from all intelligent Readers, both Forreign and Domeſtick, that never any man undertook ſince the ancient conflicts of the Fathers, *Iræneus*, *Cyprian*, *Tertullian*, *Auſtin*, *Optatus*, *Hilary*, *Proſper*, and others, againſt the *Valentinians*, *Novatians*, *Maniches*, *Donatiſts*, and others, a better cauſe, or handled it with an honeſter heart, an abler judgement, or an eloquenter ſtile.

His ſupplies and ſufficiencies to the work.

He ſearcheth, as a wiſe *Phyſitian* and *Chyrurgion*, the bottom of real or pretended ſores and diſeaſes; He evinceth the greateſt complainiers, and forwardeſt healers of the Church of *England*, to be the moſt *diſeaſed* and *depraved parts* of it, either blinde in their judgements, or blear-eyed with their paſſions, or partial in their intereſts, or lame in their obedience to God and man, uncharitably ſevere, and arrogantly cenſorious to others; impotent in their popular preſumptions, confident in their vulgar errors, ſuperſtitious in their *ſeverities*, inordinate in their motions, and ſubject to ſuch various diſtempers, that ſometime they are too hot in the *calentures* of their uncomely zeal beyond *underſtanding*; otherwhile they are *too cold* as to the glowings of their partial charity; the novelizing itch of their ambition to dictate and to domineer, being no leſs their own affliction and inquietude, then it threatned to be the leproſie or plague-ſore of this whole Church and Kingdom (and the event hath too truly verified his prudent *conjecture*.)

His fidelity in the work.

Hence, like a skilful undertaker to cure a dangerous and ſpreading diſeaſe, he ſpares no time or labour to furniſh himſelf with all ſorts of apt and ſoveraign Medicines; he ſearcheth at home and abroad, he collects and applies what he thinketh moſt proper to ſtop the Gangreen of Faction, to allay the inflammation, to abate the tumors, to purge out the ill humors, to recover health and beauty to the Body Politick: For this purpoſe he rifles all Antiquity, deflours the Chriſtian and Heathen Writers of thoſe excellent principles, preſcriptions and experiments, which he judged moſt ſuitable and ſeaſonable for his deſign; nothing eſcapes his *Eagle-eye* that was remarkable in Philoſophers, Poets, Orators, Fathers, Councils, Hiſtorians, School-men, Caſuiſts and Civilians; he extracts the ſpirits and quinteſcence of all Law: and Reaſon, of all Order and Government out of the *Greek* and *Roman Lawyers*, the *Imperial* or *Civil*, the *Canon* or *Eccleſiaſtical*, alſo the Common and Engliſh Law: Theſe he very artificially digeſts into ſuch a Confection or Plaiſter as he thought moſt apt to abate the diſeaſe, and to advance ſincere health: He infuſeth all theſe in ſuch *Celeſtial waters*, or *Scriptural diſtillations*, as were dropt from Heaven, from the *Father and Fountain of all light and health*, all true and ſaving wiſdom: So that there wants nothing in his Writings, as in a rare *compoſition*, to make it grateful as well as uſeful, palatable as well as profitable, to mindes that are either curious for ancient Learning, or Admirers of ſtrong reaſon, or adorers of Divine Revelation, or delighted with elegant expreſſions: So that he that will confute *Mr. Hookers Books*, muſt contradict the Scriptures, oppoſe Antiquity, cut the ſinews of Reaſon, maim all true Religion, put all Order out of joynt, and give the ſtrapado to all

The exactneſs of his induſtry, and compleatneſs of his deſign.

F Government

Government in Families, Cities, Churches and Kingdoms, yea he muſt deny himſelf to be a man and a Chriſtian, fitter for brutiſh Solitudes, then for Civil or Eccleſiaſtical Societies, which are the conſervatories of men and Chriſtians, the Sanctuaries in which Reaſon and Religion are to be conſecrated and preſerved inviolable.

This wiſe Maſter-builder Mr. *Hooker*, was not now to lay the foundations of this Church anew, in Doctrine, Devotion, Diſcipline or Government (which work by the ſingular goodneſs of God had been done long before his days, by the learned pains and patience of many worthy Biſhops and others, Martyrs and Confeſſors in the *Church of England*, to whoſe prudence and piety the favour of Princes and Parliaments had given the *ſanction and ſtability of the Laws*.

He was onely to repair and fortifie thoſe parts of its *outworks*, as to Order, Decency, Polity and Government, which either the Romiſh Arts and Policies, or *Schiſmatical diſcontents* and factious deſigns ſought to undermine and overthrow. For this end, he like an excellent Engineer, lays out his work or line of *circumvallation* by that exact method, that every one of *his eight Books*, like ſo many *Sconces* and *Bulwarks* well placed, aptly correſpond and ſerve both to adorn and defend each other: There is ſo rare a *ſymmetry* and proportion in the *whole Fabrick*, both as to the foundation and ſuperſtructure, that neither can want the other, and together they are invincible; nothing can undermine his foundations of Eternal verity, equity and neceſſity; nothing can batter or demoliſh his ſuperſtructures of Humanity, Chriſtanity and Polity: It will not be amiſs to give the Reader a brief model of each Book.

In the *firſt Book* Mr. *Hooker* ſearcheth and diſcovereth *Fontes legis*, the bottom of that *great deep* which we *call Law*; the ſource of which is from the *abyſs* of Divine Wiſdom, that *eternal* and *eſſential reaſon*, the emanations whereof, as the Rivers of Paradiſe, water the whole *Creation* in Nature and Providence; but the moſt eminent *courſe* thereof is contained within the current of rational and free *natures*, *Angeli* and *men*, to whom *Reaſon* and *Divine revelation*, as the waters below and above the *firmament*, are diſpenſed as the dictates or Placita of that one great *Lawgiver*, God *bleſſed for ever*: Here he admirably expreſſeth as the *original*, ſo the neceſſity, *uſe* and *end* of all *Laws* for the *good order*, *well-being*, *peace* and *Government* of all things, ſpecially of *of Men and Angels*, who are not onely paſſive under the Law of Gods power, but may be active in obeying his will, either under the more immediate (θεοπαλία) diſpenſation of Gods preſence and pleaſure; or by thoſe *interventions*, of Princes and Lieutenancies which he hath appointed in Churches and Kingdoms by way of Magiſtrates, or Prieſts and Miniſters: That all Law is but the circle of the Divine wiſdom and goodneſs, drawn by *his holy will and juſt power*, about all things in heaven, earth and hell, keeping them within compaſs, and directing them to *his glory*, in which their own happineſs, if willingly obedient, is included; or others welfare, if they are curbed and conſtrained thereunto: That by having Laws both in Reaſon and Religion, we men are manifeſted to be of higher extraction, nobler capacity, and neerer relation to the Divine Nature then other Creatures, vaſtly differing from beaſts, next degree to *Angels*, and not far from the *glory of the Creator*; the expreſs image or ſtamp of whoſe Beauty and Majeſtie, is moſt manifeſted by our *conformity* to him in *Righteouſneſs* and *Holineſs*; the firſt is wrought by the Laws of right Reaſon or *Morality*, the ſecond by the Laws of true *Religion*, or Chriſtian Sanctity.

In the *ſecond Book* Mr. *Hooker* notably aſſerteth againſt Papiſts and Enthuſiaſts, the Supremacy and ſufficiency of that Law of Sanctity or Religion, which God hath revealed to his Church in the *Holy Scriptures*, thereby ſupplying thoſe defects, and diſpelling the miſts which our luſts and paſſions have brought upon the *Law of Nature* or *right Reaſon*, which teacheth Humanity, Morality, and Natural Divinity, from which the *ignorances*, *prejudices*, *prides* and *rebellions* of mens hearts have now ſo perverted them, that without ſpecial grace *teaching and aſſiſting*, they cannot attain to that *ſupreme good* and *happineſs* which mankinde is capable of, by an holy conformity to Gods will in *grace, and in glory*. Not that Scripture-light doth null or extinguiſh the light of *true reaſon*, ſo far as concerns the lower region of *humane prudence* and

Polity

Polity in this World, but rather *confirms* it : Nor that the *Scripture-revelation*, which is sufficient to make a Christian perfect to *Salvation* and *Sanctification*, is so *precise*, *punctual* and *exact* a *rule*, or *Law* of all our inferior and exterior actions Natural, Civil and Religious, in respect of the particular *circumstantiating* or modifying of them, that nothing circumstantial or ceremonial is to be thought *good* or *lawful*, which hath not a *special command* in *Gods Word* to determine the particular manner, method, time, place, and other general circumstances which as inseparably doth all actions done under the Sun, as our skins do our bodies; without which exact regulations and proportions, the whole duty must be thought *superstitious*, condemned as *will-worship*, cryed down as vain traditions of *men*; all customs and forms must be Antichristian Rites, and sinful *ceremonies*, with the like *territulaments* of expressions severely used as *specious* terrors, and *popular fallacies*, by the opposers of conformity, to take off mens esteem, reverence and observance to the Peace, Order, Decency, Providence and Authority of the Church of *England*, wisely limiting things of this nature so as it seems best for the publique Solemnities of Religion, and enjoyning such a decent conformity thereunto, as may avoid variety, novelty, faction and confusion.

This *excellent Writer* hath beyond all just reply, manifested these great truths, That as nothing can be *necessary* and *essential* to *Religion*, but what God hath *prescribed* in his Word (which is the doctrine of *the Church of England*;) so in *lesser matters*, which concern the *individualing* of general circumstances and things *left indifferent* (that is under *no express command* of God affirmative or negative; as to what time and place, in what method and manner, how long, and how much, in what time or language, to what phrase and fashion, what gesture and vesture are to be used, what is to be first or last, with other like limitations or regulations which concern the visible Order, Decency, Solemnity and Uniformity of publique worship, and holy Ministrations) the *indulgence of God* hath not tied us up under *the Gospel* to *Judaick strictnesses* of this circumstance, and that ceremony, except in some things of the blessed Sacraments, divinely instituted as visible signs of invisible grace, but hath left every private Christian to *his liberty* in his closet: Also every *chief Ruler of the Family*, to his choice in his family duties; and every *Ecclesiastical Polity or Body*, to its freedom and choice what modes either by the *civil use* and *custom of the Countrey*, or any other measures of *decency* it lists to chuse to it self and the members of its community, where the *major part* in *publique suffrages* is to be esteemed the vote and law of all; and the *minor part*, however they do in their judgements prefer other forms; which possibly may be as well, or seem better in some respects, yet are they peaceably to conform to the spirits and result of *the most*, unless they will make Religion to enterfere with *right reason*, and cease to live orderly as men, under a pretence of living piously as Christians; which is also the judgement of the most learned and holy Primate of *Armagh* in his excellent Sermon upon that Text, *God is not the Author of confusion, &c.*

This Law of Christian liberty, managed by due Authority in humane Societies both *Civil* and *Ecclesiastical*, Mr. *Hooker* justly and *fully vindicates*, after S. *Austin*, as a *Law of God* both in reason and in Scripture *commanding obedience* to Superior power, and prudence in all these things, where they are commanded and used under no other *notion* then that which their *nature bears*; and *God allows*; not as essential, internal, necessary and immutable *parts of Religion*, but as external and mutable, onely for Order, Decency, Unity and Edification, no way prejudicial either to true *faith*, or *good manners*.

Nor may Christians under any *fancies of Reformation* and *antendment*, be rude *Novellizers*, or refractory Non-conformists in these things to publique usages, customs and appointments; since *Christian Religion*, which gives the greatest liberty to *Christians* in these things, both as to their *judgement* or *conscience*, and use of them in their private and *proper sphere*, doth also give to chief *Magistrates* and *Governors in Church* and *State*, a full and *paramount Authority* therein, obliging all private and *subjected Christians* to a more exact obedience as such, both to avoid *scandal* or *offence* against Governors, also to give testimonies of their *charity*, *humility* and ready *obedience*, as of all men furthest from peevishness, headiness, refractoriness and rebellions, whose judgements are still free to think of those things no otherwise then they are left by

Side notes:
Of the Churches power in circumstantials of Religion.

Christian Liberty consistent with conformity to mans Laws.

F 2   God

God and the Church indifferent in their natures, and onely circumscribed or limitted in their temporary use; not therefore enjoyned because necessary, but onely so far necessary in point of use, as they are enjoyned for Order, Decency, Peace and Unity.

Mr. *Hooker's* striking the right vein of Non-conformity.

This one great *sinew or vein of Sophistry* being thus cut in sunder, as Mr. *Hooker* doth it most *effectually*, both the *Negative Superstition* of *Non-conformists* is evinced, and justly *perstringed*, as an enemy to the *Liberty and Authority* of Christian Churches in these things; also the *bonds of needless scrupulosity*, by which they hamper many poor souls and well-meaning people, are *utterly dissolved*: Nor will the repeated *Crambes of the pattern in the Mount*; and, Christ being *faithful in the house of God*, and, *not an hoof must be left in Egypt*, and the like *enchantments of vulgar, weak* and *silly souls*; these will not any longer serve as *fig-leaves*, to cover the *infamy or obstinacy* of these eager disputers against the Church of *Englands* Liberty, Prudence and Authority in these things, so far as it judgeth and declareth them expedient for the publique good of Church and State.

The great vertue and operation of this principle.

This principle being thus fully asserted by him: 1. *It justifies the Church of England* in its Constitutions. 2. It leaves *other Churches* to the like *liberty and variety* with charity. 3. It *solves* the great objection and fear of *private scandal*, which *scares* some, but is not to be *considered*, when in *competition* with publique duty and obedience in *lawful things*, to *lawful Authority*, to which we must not give any offence or publique scandal, in order to gratify any private scrupulosity. And indeed Mr. *Hooker* in this *discourse* maintaining the *use of right reason*, subordinate to true *Religion*, and of *prudence* consistent with piety, and of discretion with good conscience, did cast the *Tortoise of Non-conformity on its back*; nor could it ever *recover it self*, better then it represented false *terrors to vulgar mindes*, bringing *silly people* by new clamors into the *bondage of their own* and others needless imaginations, when indeed *they had God's* not onely permission, but warrant and injunction in such things to obey the Ordinances of men in point of outward Order, Polity and Peace for the Lords sake.

Here the long and hotly agitated *controversie of limitted circumstances* and *ceremonies* of outward Rites, and customary Solemnities in the *publique forms of Religion*, where the faith is kept found, and all superstitious fancies are abandoned, as in the declaration of the Church of *England*, had found a full period and *solution*; their death and burial, if *homility, modesty, ingenuity, right reason*, and *peaceable* Religion had been able to prevail against *prejudices, animosities, adherences to parties emulation, ambition, reputation* and *self-interests* of some popular Preachers and their Disciples, who all *pretended* they should do God good service, if they fought against the *few innocent Ceremonies* of the Church, rather then the *insolent passions* and *presumptions* of their own hearts, being unluckily advanced in the *opposition* of these things beyond any *handsome retreat*. This made some of them persist (while others came in and submitted) not in *reasoning*, but in *railing* or *clamouring* most sadly against these poor shadows, that they were *Jewish* and *Popish*, *Impious* and *Antichristian*, Superstitious and Idolatrous; when the superstition was onely in themselves, who feared, where no fear was, and called good evil, and evil good, challenging a liberty to *disuse these* Forms and Rites which the Church had chosen, and to chuse *such others* as they thought most *comely* or *convenient* for the discrimination, credit and support of their party: Nor indeed was any answer ever made to these *Demonstrations*, but such as violence, tumult and Rebellion put at length into some mens hearts and hands, bringing all things by a most horrid Non-conformity to a most abominable Confusion.

The summary of his third book.

In the third Book Mr. *Hooker* applies the former general rules of *Christian Liberty*, and lawful Authority *in things of indifferency*, to the particular state of the Church of *England*, or any other Ecclesiastical Polity, which is made up of one Magistratick Head as Supreme; and of subjects, as members of that body united by the ligatures of Laws, as the results of publique *counsel* and *consent*; no way contrary to the Word of God, but agreeable to that wisdom, freedom and power which he hath given Christian Societies to provide, as they see best for the publique solemnity and decency of his worship, together with their own peace and good order.

Here he manifesteth, That the Church of *England* did (*jure suo & Authoritate uti*) do as God allowed, enabled, yea, and commanded her to do, by his general

commands

commands of, *Let all things be done decently, and in order*; of, *Subjects obedience to Superiors in the Lord*; who is the God of Peace, Polity and Order, as well as of Piety, Zeal and Verity; an Enemy *to Faction* and *Confusion*, as well as to *Heresie* and *Error*; requiring outward Reverence and Solemnity, as well as inward Sanctity in his Worship. Here this great *Master* of the Assembly, not onely *drives* home to the head these (*Clavos Trabales*, strong nails, which by the hammer of Reason he forged on the Anvil of *Religion*) but he *clencheth* them so fast, that they are not to be drawn out: The main head of them, is the *Essential Sanctity* of all religious duties, to be measured onely by Gods Word, and Divine Institution: The return, or fastning of their points, is the necessity of Solemnity, Order and Decency in the outward Form, and publique Performance of such duties; in which the publique Laws and Constitutions are to be obeyed, as having that wisdom and authority which is least to be disputed, as the best chuser, and most authentick determiner of those things; provided they be enjoyned and used under no other notion, and to no other ends then those to which they are fitted in their nature, and so left free by the Divine Indulgence.

In the *fourth Book*, the Learned Author answers the many little cavils, which are importunely and particularly urged by *Non-conformists*, against some Rites and Ceremonies settled in the Church of *England*, according to the liberty and authority it hath from the God of Reason and Religion; in these things to advise for its own Peace and Order, as well as for the Reverence and Solemnity of Publique Worship: Against which neither the *use*, nor the *abuse* of the Church of *Rome* (which is odiously and popularly objected) nor the *disuse of any Reformed Foreign Churches*, can be any bar or prejudice to the Liberty and Authority of the Church of *England*; if the Objectors would seriously weigh the nature and truth of things, or give leave to the Church of *England* to interpret its *own meaning* in them, which they either pervert, or are willingly ignorant of: If they would cease to think themselves wiser then the Laws, then Kings, Prelates, and Convocations: If they would indulge the Church the same publique Liberty which they affect to take in these things, while they fear not to use what others have abused, in lifting up and opening their hands and eyes, or in shutting and closing them fast; in standing, kneeling, or sitting as they list: If they would cease to be children in understanding, and in peevishness: If they would be as wary of the Camel of Sedition, as they are of the Gnats of Ceremonies; this quarrel would soon be at an end, the Laws would be obeyed, the Church composed, Charity revived, dangers dispelled, the Kingdom settled, good Christians edified, and God in all things glorified; by our uniform obedience first to his holy commands, next to the *Ordinances of our Superiors*, for the Lords sake; while they keep within the bounds of his Word, free from *Superstition* and *Prophaneness*.

The sum of his fourth book.

The *fifth and last Book* of Mr. *Hookers Ecclesiastical Polity*, heretofore extant, and owned as Authentick, expatiates into all the windings and turnings, the *labyrinths* and *diverticles*, by which the versatile Adversaries of the Church of *Englands* peace sought to amuse the Vulgar, losing them in a *Wood* or *Wilderness of petty Scruples and Objections*, about Words and Expressions, Modes and Forms, Rites and Ceremonies, rather then any thing *Essential* or *Moral* as to the main of Religion, in *Faith*, *Doctrine*, or *Devotion*.

The sum of the fifth book.

Here that he might not onely skin over the *sore* or *orifice*, but search the very bottom of this running old Ulcer, *this Fistula* or *Canker* of Superstition, Schism and Sedition, which he saw festered in the minds of many well-meaning people, by the scrupulosity and pragmaticalness of some Ministers, either weak or wilful: This excellent *Author* gives a short, but solid account of true Religion and its opposites; *Atheism*, which is below it; *Prophaneness*, which is against it; and *Superstition*, which affects to be above it, by an over-weening, and pragmatical kinde of righteousness.

After this, he opposeth a large *shield of honest and unanswerable defence*, full of Truth and Charity, Reason and Religion; of vast reading, and acute observation, against all those *darts* and *arrows*, greater or less, which the fierce *Non-conformists* cast against the Church of *Englands* Order, Beauty, Peace, Solemnity and Piety. He not onely makes a general *outwork for defence*, but takes notice of every *shot*

F 3   and

and *battery* made againſt the Church of *England*, as to the places of *Publique Worſhip*, our *matereal Churches*, their *Names, Forms, Sumptuouſneſs, Dedication, ends* and *uſes* &c. ſo the *times* ſet apart for publique Worſhip, either the *Lords Day*, or other Eccleſiaſtick Feſtivals: He conſiders what true preaching is, and what are the ſeveral ways of due inſtructing people in Religion; alſo by reading and catechiſing: Of publike *Prayer*, and ſolemn *Devotion*, by way of ſet Forms, or *publique Liturgies* in general, and this of the Church of *England* in particular, inferior to none that is, or ever was extant in any Church: After this, he weighs in the Balance of the Sanctuary, by *Religion* and *right Reaſen*, all the publique Offices and Liturgical appointments in the Church of *England*, for *matter and form*, ſubſtance and ceremony; not juſtifying all things, as beſt in their kinde or degree, or as neceſſary, but as good, apt, expedient, and better in ſome reſpects then the *novelties* obtruded by men that admire nothing ſo much as their own inventions; and inſtead of being humbly thankful to God and Chriſtian Kings, for the rich means of ſalvation freely afforded them in the Church, they are ever quarrelling at the manner of it; deſpiſing, as the Jews in their wanton ſurfeits, that *Manna* which was liberally caſt upon them, becauſe it is not dreſt, or diſhed for them, as they forſooth do moſt fancy in their lunatick or changeable humors.

A Work worthy indeed of ſo able a pen, and fit to exerceiſe ſo *Divine a patience*, which muſt attend ſo *minute objections*, and weigh very *atomes of circumſtances*, and *motes* of *ceremonies*; yet with which he ſaw the Enemies of the Churches peace would vex the *eyes of poor people*, firſt to water or tears, next to *bloodſhottenneſs* and *fury*. Here I know not which moſt to *admire* and *commend*, whether his Learning and Eloquence, which dreſſeth up every mean thing *handſomely*; or his *candor* and meekneſs, which handles all things with evenneſs and integrity, neither perturbed with paſſion, nor conquered with oppoſition, nor tired with importunity.

Indeed his zeal for Gods glory, and this Churches both *honor* and *happineſs*, that it might be free from *rent* and *reproach*, was ſo intenſive, together with his charity and compaſſion even to the *Enemies of the Churches*, and their *own peace*, that he ſeems onely ambitious, as a *Silk-worm*, to bury himſelf in his *own Web*; to exhauſt himſelf, that he might effect ſomething of uſe or ornament to the Church.

No man that hath not tryed what it is to follow the *circulations* of impotent objections, and *Sceptical Criticks*, can imagine what a weariſome buſineſs this fifth Book muſt needs be to this grave Divine, whoſe profound judgement enabled him for *better work*, then thus to purſue every *bubble* of *froth* and *ſpittle*, which ſome mens *wanton breath* lifted to *raiſe*, and blow off *into the ayr*, among the *common people*, with whom not the *weight*, but the number of *objections* is conſiderable: What a clear, calm and compoſed ſpirit he muſt needs have, duly to *weigh*, leiſurely to *examine*, orderly *to digeſt*, and ſoberly to *determine* thoſe things, whoſe very lightneſs and thinneſs makes them ſcarce fall under a wiſe mans *meditation*, or fit to be put into the balance of his judgement! To which purpoſe, he muſt have all *meaſures* and *weights*, even to *ſcruples* and *grains* of right reaſon, as well as *talents of Religion* at hand; not onely the pretended *allegations* of *Scriptures*, but the very circumſtances of things, the ſeveral cuſtoms of Churches, the very *Ceremonies* for decency and reverence, muſt be brought to the *teſt or touchſtone*: Alſo he was to carry a civil reſpect to the judgement of Foreign, as well as *Domeſtick Divines*; yet we finde this *Atlas* no where complaining, or ſtooping; no where tediouſly affected, or abating *his vigour*, but ſtill ſo proſecuting every new particular, aſif he had handled none *before it*; his devotion and zeal every day ſetting a *new edge*, and giving a freſh *quickneſs* to his induſtry: So indefatigable *is the love* of the Churches peace, ſo ſevere a Taskmaſter is true *Charity to its ſelf*; never ſatisfied, while any thing remains to be done that *concerns its duty*, deſpiſing nothing that may advance *its great deſign*, Gods Glory, and the good of Souls; nor thinking any thing ſmall which toucheth upon Religion or Conſcience, or the Churches Peace; the skirt or lap of whoſe *Garments* may not be *cut off by any private* Preſumption: No Pin or Utenſil of the Tabernacle and Temple of God but was holy, and worthy of the Prieſts care, as well as the Levites carrying.

In this fifth Book Mr. *Hooker* being lead on by the importune *molestations* of *T.C.* and others, to *try all things*; and being commanded by the *Apostle*, to *hold fast what is good*, omits nothing that *was objected*, giving full force to the Adversaries *Arguments* (which is (ρωμαιωτερον) to *strive lawfully*) and as full answers, as the nature of the things is *capable of* in Reason or Religion: Not that this *Wiseman Magnifies* every particular *Rite and Ceremony* used in the Church of *England*, as either *necessary*, or *absolutely* the best in it self; but onely *justifying* the use of them, because in *themselves* lawful and good, yea better then any mans private *novelties*, because settled by *Publique Wisdom*, and due *Authority*. Possibly he might in the abstract or general think, that some things in our *Singing* or *Musick*, in our *Liturgy* and *Polity*, or Church Government, might be *altered* and improved, when it should be thought convenient by the publique *Wisdom* and *Piety*; but he did not think that the Church was bound to alter its good *Constitutions* and *Customes*, so oft as every private fancy or *faction* shall pretend to a *better Platform*; as if a man should still be pulling *down his house*, so oft as any one *list* to commend a new *Model* of Building to him: Nay, he did not think (as no wise man doth) that any Church is always bound in these things, to alter *for the better*; its sufficeth, if what is appointed, and in use, be good; for the matter, not contrary to the Word of God; for the *manner*, such as is not thought uncomely by the publique Prudence, which must set bounds to the vanity and variety *of private fancies*; which by daily novelty will destroy Unity and Constancy, introducing Faction, Levity and Confusion, under the pretence of *bettering*, altering, and endless *Reforming*; of which, who shall be Judge, if things be not confined to the publique *determination*?

Many things he justifies to be, as very ancient, so very good; others to be more convenient then better, because apt and wonted; the *old Wine* being to be preferred before the new, because, though this be more spiritful and heady, yet the other is more *pure* and *wholesome*: He vindicates all things to be, if not highly commendable, yet not *justly blameable*, and at worst *tolerable*, because accompanied with so many *blessed Advantages* of true Faith, with all Piety, Grace, and Vertue; all which are fully set forth, and to be enjoyed with peace, by humble and thankful Christians in the *Church of England*; where every one may be as good as they can for *their hearts*, if they be not wanting to themselves: Nor doth any man lightly despise the *Publique Laws*, and settled *Constitutions*, but he that hath a mind to begin *greater troubles* by his *Novelties*, then those *inconveniencies* can amount to, which he seems so offended at; which if not bad, that is, not against Faith and Holiness, are better, with the Churches Peace, then better things, brought in with Perturbation and Reproach to Church and State, as Saint *Austin* long ago observed, judging an old suit, that is easie and comely, to be better, though plain, then a new one that is *finer*, but less fit.

And here, after this, *Phœnix of Learning* and *Grace*, of Prudence and Eloquence, had collected this Fair Pile of his *Ecclesiastical Polity*, and furnished it with all Curiosities of Humane and Divine, Ancient and Modern Wisdom, himself expired amidst his great Undertakings, to the impotent joy of his *Antagonists*; who finding themselves worsted, and sorely wounded, between the joynts of their *Armour*, Popular Inventions, and Ambitious Objections, by this Great *Archer*, in his Five first Books, which he lived to publish; yet received some comfort in this, that they escaped the *shot of his last Three*, which he never published, and which they hoped, he had never finished; or if he did compleat them, they found (as is by some imagined) some *Artifice* so long to smother and conceal them from the Publique, till they had played such an After-game, as they thought was onely able to confute Mr. *Hooker*, and to blot out by the Sword, the impressions of his pen.

Mr. Hooker's moderation in his vindication of Rites and Ceremonies; &c.

Mr. Hooker's death, before he had finished, at least published all his intended Books.

But Providence in time, hath not onely confuted thofe mens projects and confidences, but alfo brought forth thofe efteemed *Abortives*, the three laft Books, with fuch *lineaments* of their Fathers Vertue and Vigor on them, that they may be eafily and juftly owned for *genuine*; although (perhaps) they had not the laft politure of their Parents hands: Their ftrength fhews them to be a *legitimate Progeny*, however they may feem to want *fomething* of that *beauty* and *luftre* which always attended Mr. *Hookers confummations*.

The defign and fum of the fixth book.

In the firft of thefe, which is the *fixth Book*, He makes *Nehuftan* of the *Brazen Serpent*, and grinds to powder the golden Calf or Teraphin of the *Difciplinarian Project*, as to the claim of Power of Ordination and Jurifdiction in *Presbyters* apart from Bifhops, yea againft them; much more that filly Idol which was fet up firft in *Lay-Elders*, and afterwards licked to fome more plaufible fhape of Independency, or Congregational power, as to Church affairs. Thefe Presbyterian prefumptuous and popular *Novelties*, he notably refutes; as did, after him, Mr. *Clumbald*, in an excellent Tract of his, the *lofs* of which I have oft *deplored* in vain, when I faw it vilely *embezzled* by fome of the *Scotifh Affembly*, to whom it was imparted by a perfon, who had greater *confidence of fome mens honefty*, then ever his *experience did make good*.

The defign of Mr *Hookers* feventh book.

His *feventh Book* notably *vindicates Ecclefiaftical Government and Jurifdiction*, as fettled by the *Catholick* cuftom of this, and all ancient *Churches*; alfo by the Laws of this Kingdom, in *Bifhops* or *Prelates*, either *Metropolitan* or *Diocefan*: Evidently proving by the *Canons* of *Councils*, by the known *Laws* of this Realm, by the Scripture *grounds*, right *Reafon*, and true *proportions* of all Polity and good Government; alfo by long and happy *experience*, that the *intereft of Epifcopacy* is the *true intereft*, as of the *Church of Chrift in general*, fo fpecially of this *Church* and *Kingdom*, and all Eftates herein.

The intereft of Epifcopacy, is the true intereft of all Eftates in *england*

1. Of the Populacy.

1. Of the *common People*, who muft be governed in Religion, as well as Civil concerns, being prone, like water, in both refpects, to dangerous *Extravagancies*: Nor can they be governed by Minifters either their *inferiors* or *equals*; but by fuch whofe *Learning*, *Age*, *Prudence*, and legal *Authority* derived *from the Prince*, worthily fets them in a deferved and meet *Superiority*, as Judges over them, both able and Venerable.

2. Of the Clergy.

2. *Epifcopacy* or *Prelacy*, is the *true intereft* of all the learned and fober *Clergy*; who have the moft *fafety, reputation, honor, fatisfaction* and *tranquillity*, when they are in *caufes Ecclefiaftical*, under the *protection* and *cognizance*, or jurifdiction of their *Fathers* and *Brethren*, who have moft *regard* for them, as being of the fame *Calling* and *Profeffion*; whofe very *corrections* of them, are fulleft of *compaffion* for them; and ftudy their good in charity, when they are forced to ufe fome neceffary feverity to them.

3. Of the Gentry.

3. It is the true *intereft of the Englifh Gentry*, or *leffer Nobility*, who are too *knowing*, and too high-*fpirited*, to be curbed by, and concluded under the *difcipline and decrees of every Parochial Minifter*; who may have competent gifts for a *Preacher*, but not *gravity* fufficient for a *Governor*; there being as great a diftance between a *Preacher* and a *Ruler*, as between a *Pleader* and a *Judge*: There is a vaft difference between making a Sermon, and giving a Sentence.

4. Of the Nobility.

4. Epifcopacy beft fuits with the *intereft* of the *grand nobility* in *England*, whofe honor is beft preferved by the *eminency* and *proportion of venerable* and *prudent Bifhops*, paying all due refpects to them; as it would be greatly *diminifhed* and *abafed* by the pertnefs and infolency of every petty Presbyter, and their popular adherents, who think it *honor enough* to make the beft *Nobleman* in the Parifh, one of their layElders, or a member of their pitiful Congregations; thereby rending him off from that duty he ows to, and communion he ought in honor and confcience to keep with the Church of *England*, yea the Catholick Church, rather then any felect and fchifmatical party whatfoever.

5. Of Kings.

5. It is the intereft of Majeftie and *Soveraignity in our Kings and Princes*, as to that *Dominion they* juftly have, and that influence they *muft maintain* and exercife over all degrees of their Subjects; whom they can never *govern* as to Civil fubjection, unlefs they have a religious eye to, and hand over their fouls and confciences, as well as their bodies and eftates; no more then the *wheels of the Watch* will move orderly,

without the spring be right set; or the ship steer well, unlels the rudders be discreetly hung and handled: Not onely the open practices of subjects, but their opinions are to be under such coercion, as may best keep them within the bonds of truth and obedience to God and man. Due inspections and regulations of Religion, are the greatest securings of Loyalty; and no Profession teacheth and urgeth greater subjection to Princes, then the Christian and Reformed doth, specially where Bishops are servants to Christ and Kings; nor are any men so fit to receive and use this Ecclesiastical inspection and authority as Bishops who can best take account, as of people, so of Ministers doctrines and examples, and may best give account of them to Soveraign Magistrates; so much truth and weight was there in King James his Prophetick maxime, No Bishop, no King; both Presbytery and Independency being the cloud and Eclypse of Kingly Majestie, as Episcopacy is a great lustre and radiancy of it.

6. Sad experience tells us, that Episcopacy is beyond all doubt or dispute (now) the true interest of this Churches Honor, Peace and Happiness, which never flourished so much as under Bishops; nor was ever so shaken, abused, deformed and desolated, as when Presbyterian and popular Novelties were brought in by violence, to the subversion of Monarchy, no less then Episcopacy.

7. Episcopacy rightly managed, is manifested to be the great Interest of God's glory, and our Saviours honor, as they have by precepts and examples constituted a visible Church, regular Flock, and orderly Family in this world, distinguished by Institutions and Mysteries of Religion proper to Christians; who yet must not be as rude and disorderly rabbles, occasionally hudled together; but as becometh the Wisdom of the God of Order and Peace, and the Houshold of faith, with such due subordinations under Fathers and Pastors, Stewards and Overseers, or Bishops over them, as sorts with the Majestie of our God, the pristine examples of his wisdom among the Jews, and the Soveraignity also of our Saviour, who is the chief Lord, King, Captain, and Bishop of the Church; nothing being more dissonant from Christianity, in its ends and rules, in its holy Order and Beauty, then levelling spirits, and such popular projects as tend to nothing but Faction and Schism, to Anarchy and Confusion; which events, this Wiseman Mr. Hooker foresaw, and foretold, as we have seen unhappily fulfilled: Nor was ever Episcopacy more advanced, then by being so much depressed, the woful want of it shewing how useful, yea necessary it is for the well-being of this Church and Kingdom, as the late excellent King oft in vain Remonstrated to those deaf Adders, who refused to be charmed, till they had destroyed both his Sacred Person, and all Kingly Majesty, with this Church, and venerable Episcopacy; whose Offices and Revenues (both of Church and Crown) those gentle and modest Deformers, either as Presbyters or People, made no scruple to usurp, enjoy and exercise; fancying themselves at once both Kings and Priests, till they appeared either fools, or knaves, or both, being once unfortunate, and confuted not more by the frowns of Providence, then by their own confusions.

In the eighth Book, Mr. Hooker asserts by Scripture and Reason, Laws of God and man, the Supremacy of Soveraign Princes, such as the Kings of England are by Law, as to all Supreme and executive power Ecclesiastical, or Civil jurisdiction in Church and State, both against all Papal claim and usurpation, which was the old terriculament of Christian Kings and Emperors; also against all popular and Presbyterian invasions; who possessed with the same spirit of ambition (as unbeseeming Christian people and Preachers, as Prelates) have found out new notions, phrases and macainations, at once to cheat the Christian and incautious world; also to ruine flourishing Churches and Kingdoms, with their Kings and Bishops, under pretence of setting up the Throne, Kingdom, Discipline and Government of Jesus Christ; which must be first moulded in these mens odde fancies; and then managed by their rude hands, as great Masters forsooth in our Israel, and sole Dictators of all Laws and Government both in Church and State, if they can but any way get power into their hands, answerable to the pride and ambition of their hearts; who like fishes, onely live by providence, and swim down the stream of success, but presently expire, when once these fail, and they are cast on dry ground.

The

Mr. Hookers
design de-
clared by
himself.

The Venerable *Author of these eight Books*, had formerly given the world an account of *his design in each of them:* Of which, five have many year been *extant in publique;* the last three were thought to have been *never finished,* and to be sure, they
have been for many ages *suppressed;* which are now come to light, after our late
long troubles (as some buried *Statues,* and *hidden Monuments* are oft discovered
by *Earthquakes:*) Such as they are, it is thought meet to present them to the *Reader;*
each of them is by *learned Criticks* judged to be *genuine,* or *Authentick,* though possibly not so compleat and exact as the curious Author intended: The seventh book,
by comparing the writing of it with *other indisputable Papers,* or known *Manuscripts*
of Mr. *Hookers,* is undoubtedly his *own hand* throughout: The eighth is written by
another hand (as a Copy) but interlined in many places with Mr. *Hookers own characters,* as owned by him.

The genui-
ness of the
three last
books

The *best and surest test* of the *genuiness* or *legitimacy* of these three now *added
Books,* will be the *weight,* or *learned solidity* of the matter; also the grave, but *eloquent and potent* manner of handling each subject, there being nothing in Mr. *Hookers
Writings* either *trivial,* or *plebean and vulgar:* Nor is it easie to *emaculate* or *counterfeit* either his *stile, method,* or *notions:* This onely may be suspected (as is said)
that in some places he had not put too *his last* polishing, or consummating hand;
yet as in the *rougher hewn parts of a well figured Statue,* one may see in them the
grandeur of the design, and *majesty* of the *lineaments,* even through the *unpoliter* skin
which yet hangs as a mist or cloud over them.

The grand,
useful
subjects
handled in
the three
added books

To be sure, the *subjects* he undertook in these three last Books are very noble,
and *deserved to be amply handled,* as indeed they are: Nor is it to be doubted, but
they will, by Gods blessing, contribute much to the *restoring and establishing* of that
Ecclesiastical *Order,* ancient *Polity,* meet *Jurisdiction,* and necessary *Peace,* which is
truly Christian, and which was in the way of Episcopacy, most *primitive* and Catholick in this, and all famous Churches, until the affected *novelties,* or *fatal necessities* of latter times, *tempted* some Christians and Churches to vary from all *Antiquity;*
which the piety and prudence of the Church of *England* never yet did, as judging such
innovations neither just, nor safe, nor expedient, for its honor and happiness, nor yet
for *Gods glory,* or the repute of the *Christian and Reformed Religion;* whose aim
ever was, and is, to recover and restore the *grateful forms of venerable* and decayed
Antiquity, but not to *reproach* or utterly *ruine* them, under pretence of *pairing off*
some *accretions* or superfluities, which time possibly had brought upon the *Beauty*
and Order of Christs Church, which is always *adorned with modesty and humility,* no
less then veracity and innocency: Nor may it, without great uncharitableness, be
suspected of the *Spouse of Christ,* the Church Catholick, that either it omitted or falsified
any point of saving Doctrine; or that it degenerated and failed in so great a concern
of *Order, Peace,* and Charity, as this of Church Government, which it had received
(by way of Episcopal Precedency) from *the Apostles;* and so ever retained it
both in judgement and practice, by as *clear a use,* and *examplary a constancy,* as it
did *observe either in the Canon of the Scripture,* or the *Baptism* of Infants, or the observation of the Lords day; whose Precepts are not so precise or punctually evident in Scripture, as their practice is in the Churches use, agreeable to the general
tenor and *analogy* of the Scripture; and not to be decryed by any but sawcy and
Phanatick fancies, who had rather run their heads against this *Pillar and ground of
Truth,* the Churches undoubted veracity and constancy, then fairly read those
evident Characters which are to be seen in the Doctrine it ever maintained, and
in the practice which it had constantly used: Nor doth any thing so baffle the
most impudent and canting novelty, as the universal prejudice of Antiquity, which
certainly was as faithful a *Keeper* of the meaning and *minde* of God in Scripture,
as of the Letter, or Books in which it was written.

Mr. Hookers
trials, or mo-
ral exercises.

Having thus given some account of Mr. *Hookers* Works, as to the studying,
composing and writing part of his life; my second undertaking is to set forth his
Asceticks, or Athleticks, his (ἀσκησία or ἄθλησις) agonies or sufferings; at least the
exercises and foils of his other excellent gifts and graces; for his Moral and Christian Vertues, were answerable to his intellectual endowments; the whole man
was raised to a very great height; not his head lofty, and his heart debased, as
high hills, whose tops are raised up to heaven, but their foundations are in the
valleys;

are in the valleys; or as ricketly bodies with great heads, and weak limbs: But as *Moses* his hands, when they were lifted up, so were his actions and his sufferings too, both exercises and exaltations of his great abilities.

And here I cannot but observe from the *tryals* and *temptations* which adventured to attacque this learned and godly person, that no goodness is so *innocent*, no vertue so *unspotted*, no piety so venerable, but they shall finde some *envy* to malign, and some enmity to molest them, as they did Mr. *Hooker*; after his Life and labours came to be most conspicuous.

It was indeed a matter, not of displeasure and regret so much as of just rejoycing, to see those publique *Antipathies* and *Batteries*, which like waves of the Sea, most importuned the peace and honor of the Church of *England*, that they did fall upon so *firm a Rock*, so solid and *invincible a Defence*; whose Learning was equal, yea exceeding the best of its Opponents; whose unblameable life was inferiour to none of them; his *Intellectuals* as sublime, his *Morals* as pure, his *Spirituals* as Divine, and *Politicals*, as more *prudent*, so more *obedient*; that in attacquing Mr. *Hooker*, they met with *their match* in all, and their Superior in many things; they not onely encountred great Learning, but they dashed themselves against a profound and solid judgement; they affronted Gravity, they opposed Wisdom, and sought to shake or discompose a most orderly and harmonious soul; which they found by their sad experience to *their cost*, and too late repented, that they had provoked such a *Gyant* as he was to undertake the cause of this Church; which if he had lived to finish, and set forth in his own accurate form, certainly no man had led a more ample *Triumph*, or had seen more Conquerors and *Captives* to follow his *Triumphant Pen*; some joyfully partaking in his Victory over their own Prejudices and errors; others unable to resist the strength of his reason, continued *Prisoners to* their own Passions and parties, rather then have their share in that rational and ingenuous freedom which he proposed to them.

In this publique and long contest, which he maintained, like some of *Davids Worthies*, against whole *Armies and Legions of Opposites*, his purpose and happiness was to assert the *Church of England*, both in its Constitution, and Legal Execution, as to Ecclesiastical Laws and Canons, Orders and Offices, together with its *Discipline and Government*; that in the main of matter and form, end and use, they were very Christian and commendable, pious and prudent; nothing in them justly *scandalous* or blameable, much less dangerous or *damnable*; yea, that upon the whole view and design, things were settled with very great charity and discretion, considering the proportions of those men, and times, and things, from which *Reformation* first began, and through which it had been with some vicissitudes carried on, before it came to so fair and full a *consistency*: In all which, some lesser things were not onely tolerable and allowable, but so far useful and desirable, as they contributed much to a publique closing of Fractions, or at least hindred greater Ruptures; Schismes and Dissentions, in matters of greater weight.

It was fit at first to condescend somewhat to the use of such things, in themselves not evil, nor yet morally good; not for the necessity or Sanctity of them, but onely for the long use and custom of them among the people; who would not have had the just Reformation, in the grand *Points and Essentials of it*, so much in esteem and veneration, if they had without any Reason or Religion, been forced to forgo all those decent Rites, and innocent Ceremonies, to which they had been long accustomed; without which, as a good face without hair on its head, the *Reformed Religion* would have appeared bald and uncomely, though it might have Health, and good Symmetry;

After all things had been duly scanned, judiciously approved, and legally settled, by the Wisdom of Soveraign *Princes*, *Parliaments*, and *Convocations*; after they had been highly applauded by Learned and Godly men both at home and abroad; yea, after they had for some years been blessed of God, and prospered with all Temporal and Spiritual Blessings, with Peace, Plenty, and Piety;

He

Marginal notes:

Mr. *Hooker* compared with his Antagonists.

The piety, prudence, & charity of the first Reformers vindicated.

The mischief of alteration where things are once well settled.

he then juftly and fully concludes againft the itch of all *Innovations*; that then no *Moral* or *Political* neceffity could be alledged, for daily unfettling and altering of things fo once well fettled, meerly under the colours and clamours of fome petty *Reformation* in things of *Outward Form, Circumftance*, or *Ceremonies*; or in fome Words, Phrafes, and Expreffions; where the change required, was not from any thing *abfolutely evil*, or precifely forbidden of God; nor yet to any thing *pofitively good*, as punctually commanded or required by his Holy Word; but onely from that which feemed not *fo good*, to that which *feemed better* in fome private mens *apprehenfions*; and thefe not onely the fewer for number, but far inferior in all eminency, either *Civil* or *Ecclefiaftical*: Which imaginary amendment of things that were judged to be good, and fettled as moft convenient, by Publique, Supreme, and Authoritative Wifdom, cannot in Reafon or Religion be a fufficient motive to mutation, nor any way counterpoife the danger of fuch eafie alterations; which do not onely very much diminifh the *Majeftie of any Government*, but weaken the Authority, fhake the Foundation, and expofe the very *Legiflative power* to every *pragmatick fpirit*, *and fanciful noveller*; cutting every moneth, or week, or day thofe banks, which long experience and ufe had raifed and preferved, purpofely to keep out thofe *inundations* which prefs upon all *fettled States* and Churches, from thofe Springs of *novellizing*, which do rife in moft mens inventions; and which by felf love and admiration are encreafed, as Rivulets, in their progrefs to thofe factions; which firft feek to break in by pious *importunities*, weeping over corruption of *Church and State*, as *Ifhmael* did over the captivity, until they get fuch advantages, as may give not onely colour, but *countenance* to their ambitious threats and infolencies, which march under the Banner of Religion and Reformation, undecerned by vulgar eyes, until the mifchiefs in the bottom of thefe Reformations, difcover themfelves to be far worfe then any thing, for the amendment of which they are fo cruelly eager and importune.

Of thefe publique Agonies which exercifed Mr. *Hookers* minde and pen fo long, and fo happily, his Works will give the beft and ampleft account; there the Reader will fee what Weapons Offenfive, and Defenfive, either *Scriptural* or *Rational* he ufed; what ftrength he collected and employed; what Auxiliary Forces from ancient Authorities he made ufe of; what skill and vigilancy he applyed in all parts; with what courage and conftancy he kept his ground, or ftation, againft all oppofition; defending, though it were but a field of *Lentils*, as *Shammah*, one of *Davids* Worthies did, 2 Sam. 23. 11. againft many hundreds of the Philiftines; when not the profit or value of the things (being but a few *mutable Rites*, *outward Forms, and Ceremonies*) were fo confiderable, but the *Authority of the Laws*, the *Majeftie of Government*, alfo the Safety, Sanctity, and Unity of the Church; together with that *Loyal Duty*, Courage and Conftancy which he, as a Chriftian member of the Church, no lefs then a Subject of his Prince did owe to the honour of his Soveraign, alfo to the Churches, and to his Countreys Peace, yea more then thefe; to his Religion, God and Saviour: To all which, thefe men will never be faithful in great things, who are not fo in fmall; for from the prefumption to cut off the skirt, or lap of the Churches Garment, men eafily rife to higher infolencies: Such as were oppofite to Ceremonies, at laft deftroyed Liturgies, Epifcopacy, Kings and Bifhops, Church and Kingdom.

The joynt caufe therefore of all Interefts Civil and Sacred, was refolutely undertaken, and valiantly maintained by this *excellent Perfon*, who had as much *cool and fober valour* as any man living; not giving way to the *Churches Enemies, Perturbers, Calumniators*, no not for an hour; nor enriching them with one *fhooelatchet*: And this he did with as much more juftifiable rigor and pertinacy, then thofe men, on the other fide, who made fuch popular pretenfions of ftrictneffe, that not *one hoof muft be left in Egypt*; that all muft be after the *pattern in the Mount*, that Chrift, as a Son, was more *faithful* then *Mofes*, and fo had preferibed every *pin of the Evangelical Tabernacle*, every punctillio and circumftance in Religion: Hence they drive amain againft all things of *indifferences*, againft any impofed *form, or outward ceremonies* for Order, Uniformity, and Decency, fo *fhaving Religion*
from

from all the excrescencies of superstition (as they called all that was not of Sacred Institution) till they had brought *Reformation* to be not onely *undecent*, and *deformed*, but *rude* and *ridiculous*; expecting that this Tree of Publique and Solemn *Devotion* should bear better fruits, when it was quite *peeled of its bark*, and *stripped of its leaves*; when nothing should be left either for *defence* or *decency*, for *Reverence* or *Solemnity*, which is a kinde of *sensible Sanctity*, in our outward or bodily Worship of God.

In which to be *negligent* or *rude*, *slovenly* or *unmannerly*, *antick* or *fanatick*, is a *sort of prophaness*: Here private affectations are not onely a degree of folly, but madness, since both Reason and Religion command us by common dictates in all mankinde, *versri numen*, outwardly to reverence the Divine Glory in his Sanctuary, and to conform to the publique customs not contrary to Gods Word: Nor is the *simplicity of the Gospel* here to be pleaded in such a sense as some men intend, which is to run all things of *outward Administration*, and *social Profession*, to a kinde of *Bacchinal riot*, and *rustick confusion*: when the *Simplicity of the Gospel* is meant onely of such a *sincere*, *unmixt*, and *uncorrupted* way of *worshipping* God, as neither addes nor detracts ought in point of *necessary* duties, or of the *integral* and *essential* points of *Religion*; which must ever be punctually commanded by the *Word of God*, and founded upon a special *Divine Institution*, without any additional of the same kinde and degree, or that are expresly contrary to *the Word of God*, as that is of *worshipping the true God by any way* of *erroneous imagination*, or *Image-Adoration*, which is prone to debase the *Majestie of the Divine Nature*; and that *Spirituality* which ought to be in all our Devotions, as the very life and soul of them, without which the outward formality, with never so much pomp and ceremony, is but a dead carkase, not onely unacceptable, but an Abominable Sacrifice to the Living God.

Besides all these, which were *publique Contests* (in which he did ἀνδρίζειν ἡ ὑπερνῶν) quit *himself like a man*, and came off more then *Conqueror*, in the judgement of all that were impartial, and able Spectators (that is, *diligent Readers of his Books of Ecclesiastical Polity*) the good man had other *notable tryals*, more *personal* and *private*, which fell between him and one Mr. *Travers* at the *Temple* (one of the *Inns of Court* so called) not onely upon the general distance of their parties, as conform, or not, *to the Church of England*; for which each of them there stood as *Sentinel* or *Standard-bearer*; but from a kinde of *Natural Antipathy* of their *spirits* and *tempers*: Both *magnetical*, but *differing* as much as the *North* and *South* points of the *Loadstone*, or *Terella*: So that when they came to stand in the same *Point*, or *Pulpit*, they easily grew to a kinde of *Justling* or *Duel*, even to an *emulation* and *envy*; if not in their Persons, yet in their opinions and Partisans.

Mr. *Hooker* was there settled by the care of the *Archbishop Whitgift*, and the Authority of the *Queen*, to preach in the forenoon as *Master* or *Guardian of the Temple*; Mr. *Travers* was popularly chosen by the Society, to be *Lecturer* in the afternoon; a man of *esteemed* piety and good *learning*, but *warping* to the *Disciplinarian* party, or *Non-conformity*, wherewith many *lawyers* and other *Gentlemen* were then leavened; not so much out of judgement and conscience, as out of a secret kinde of *envy* and *Rivalry*, which had always been nourished by many of that *long Robe*, or practicers of the *common Law*, against the *Ecclesiastical Jurisdiction* and *Church Government*, hoping that the *stream* of their gain and practice would run stronger to drive their *mills*, if all causes were wholly diverted from the *channel of the Episcopal Courts*, or Ecclesiastical Jurisdictions, to their Bars.

Here Mr. *Hooker* did not so much summon up his courage and valour, as exercise his *candor* and *patience*: Though there was no compare between the *amplitude* of their *Learning*, and *latitude* of their *real abilities*; yet Mr. *Hooker* meekly suffered himself to be *eclipsed* and *undervalued* in comparison of Mr. *Travers*: If the paucity of vulgar *hearers* when Mr. *Hooker* preached, and the frequency or crowd when Mr. *Travers*, were the *competent Judge* and discrimination of their worth, Mr. *Hookers* Sermons were as some rougher coyn, good gold, and full weight, but not of so fair and smooth a stamp to vulgar eyes and hands as Mr. *Travers*.

The one had more of *Geometrical*, the other of *Arithmetical* proportions: They were as *musical Harmonies*, which are made up, some by Unisons, others by deeper *Antiphonies*

Marginal notes:
The contests between Mr. *Hooker* and Mr. *Travers* at the *Temple*.

Mr. *Hookers* meekness.

Their different veins in preaching.

g

Antiphonies or correspondencies of founds, that are Diapafons to the other: Mr. *Travers* was a more plaufible and *profitable Preacher* to vulgar Auditors, as well as more *popular*; having much more of the *Oratorian* decoy, a pleafing *voyce*, a *pathetick* pronunciation, and an infinuating fafhionior *gefture*, to captivate his Auditors, by his agreeable *prefence*, *vigorous fpeech*, and *grateful activity*: Nor were his *Texts* and matter ufually *ill chofen*, or *impertinently* or dully *handled*, upon *practical heads* and *Common-places* of Divinity. Both had honeft hearts, and good heads: Mr. *Hooker* was more profound, and the other more *fluent*: *Different gifts* they had from the *fame Spirit*, for feveral *ufes of the Church*, to the fame end of Gods glory, and fouls good, though in different ways of Miniftrations.

Mr. *Hooker* was a *deeper*, but *filenter ftream*; running, as more flowly and quietly, fo with fome *obfcurity* and *dulnefs* to common Auditors; fo confident of the facred power and efficacy of the matter he delivered, that he thought it needed no great fetting off: This made him fo far from *any life* in his looks, geftures or pronunciations, that he preached like *a living*, but fcarce *moving ftatue*: His eyes *ftedfaftly* fixed on the fame place from the beginning to the end of his *Sermons*; his *body* unmoved, his *tone* much to an *Unifone*, and very *unemphatick*; fo varioufly doth God diftribute *his gifts*, not *lading* all *in one* bottom.

Mr. *Travers* had the *broader fails*, the fairer *wafteloaths*, and *larger ftreams*: Mr. *Hooker* had the *ampler hold*, the truer *Compafs*, the richer *lading*, and the *firmer rudder*. Both were *good fhips*, and *well built*, though of *different moulds*; and both might make *good voyages*, arriving at laft to the fame fair *Haven of Heaven*.

But (as *Paul* and *Silas*, in their earthly pilgrimage) took *feveral voyages*: The face of Mr. *Hooker* was toward *Jerufalem*, the Church of *England*; Mr. *Travers* was as if he came from, or would go to *Samaria*, *Geneva*, *Amfterdam* or *Edinburgh*: At laft the contention grew fo *fharp*, and the *Scholaftick fewds fo hot*, that this fire from the *Temple* brake out to more *publique flames*; fo far, as to engage many perfons both in *City* and *Countrey*, yea in the *Queens Court* and *Council*: Some were for *Paul*, others for *Apollos*. Their perfons were not fo much at odds, nor drew *Difciples after them*, as the caufe which either of them had *efpoufed*, and were now publiquely engaged for as chief *Champions*: This drew *Spectators*, *Abettors* and *Admirers* of each mans perfon, parts, opinions and practices, according as mens mindes being touched or pointed by their affections, prejudices and *interefts* did encline them.

Their different Tenents as to the Church of Rome. In one point they were moft *openly Diametrous*, Mr. *Hooker* affirming and proving the *Church of Rome* to be, though not a *pure*, *found* and *perfect* Church, yet a *true one*, in which the neceffary and fundamental means of falvation are preferved, but much difeafed and obfcured by *fuperftitious Superftructures*, to the great danger of peoples fouls and detriment, as well as difhonor of *Chriftian Religion*, in its holy *Inftitutions*, *Morals* and *Myfteries*. Mr. *Travers* (on the other fide) earneftly contended againft the *Church of Rome*, as no Church of Chrift, but wholly a *Synagogue of Satan*, and the *feat of Antichrift*, denying falvation to all thofe that held *communion with her*: Thus *charity* in the one, and *zeal* in the other (both Chriftian and commendable Graces) carried them further from *each other*: The firft thought that the abufe of humane *Superftition*, did not *null* or *vacate* the *ufe* and *vertue* of *Divine Inftitutions*; that no mens *ufurpations* upon any Churches, can preclude Gods right and property to them, while his Gofpel and Sacraments are in any kinde among them: The policies and corruptions of the *Roman Court*, did much *overlay*, but not quite fmother *to death*, the Truth and Church of Chrift which was among them; as gold may be among much drofs, which the great Refiner at laft would fo diftinguifh and feparate, as not to *deftroy* one with the other, but fave thofe *Roman Chriftians*, whofe *profeffion* brought them to true *faith* in Jefus Chrift, to *repentance* from fin, and holy *obedience* to the Gofpel, notwithftanding that in many things, by reafon of *prejudice* and *education*, they were ignorant of, and fo *enemies* to fome truths profeffed in the *Reformed Churches*.

But Mr. *Travers* was for no *quarter to be given* to the *Romanifts*, condemning one and all, the fimple and the malicious, the fincere and the hypocritical; breaking at once all the bruifed reeds, quenching the *fmoaking flax*, which may be in many of *the plain and fimpler hearted-Papifts*, who wilfully detain *no truth in unrighteoufnefs*, *ness,* but *believe, love* and *obey* those truths of the Gospel which are there set forth, after their *way* and *fashion*; and may not in charity be thought wholly to lose their enlightning, converting, sanctifying and saving efficacy, especially when the power of Gods Spirit may supply Humane defects and infirmities in humble and honest hearts.

This one *Capital Controversie,* drew after it a long tail of all Controversies between *the Reformed* and *Roman parties:* Mr. *Hookers milde temper* (as mens constitutions have great *influence* over their *Religions, Opinions,* and *Consciences*) studied by all safe *condescentions* to *invite* to *union,* and to *heal* those great and *justly deplored breaches* in the Christian and *Western* World; the accommodation or close of which, many learned men have endeavoured. Mr. *Travers* being of a more hot and *cholerick complexion,* was for *fire to come down from Heaven and destroy them all* : The *blessed God,* whose equal and just hand holds the *Balance of the Sanctuary* without any varying, weighing impartially all mens Affections, Actions and Opinions, knows how to *sever* the *charity* of the one, and the *zeal* of the other, from their personal *infirmities* : These his mercy will *pardon,* and the other his bounty will *reward.*

When the *conflagration* grew too flaming and publique (*agitated* by the breath of How these men of quality on either side) both of them were brought *before the Queen* and hears were Council, who sought to take up the *controversie,* and allay that (*ἀμετρία*) transport, allayed. to which either might be carried, if not beyond truth (which commonly lies in the midst between the extreams of mens passions and *disputes*) yet beyond the *peace of the Church,* and that charity which is due to the Publique; to which all disputes and opinions, yea all *gifts* and *graces* must *vale,* and come under the *lee*; except onely those which are *constitutive of a Church,* which are not *very many,* and of which few *Christian Churches* in the world (I believe) are, or ever were wholly *destitute*: Each hath enough of *soveraign Medicines* to cure the *maladies* of *their souls,* if they would on all hands, Bishops, Ministers and People, use *discreet Applications,* and not trouble themselves too much with Superstructures and *Impertinencies* : Nor is it *improbable,* but wherever there is such means of Grace offered, as for neglect of it, men *will be damned*; so there is also so much, by the right use of which, men may be *saved.*

At last prudent *Applications* and time (*magnus rerum Dominus!*) the great tamer of all our *juvenile confidences,* heights and heats of spirit (which makes us always *impatient to be worsted,* and *ambitious* to have the victory and dominion over all men, *rather then our selves*) cooled the *calentures* on *both sides*; chiefly by parting the *Antagonists,* and placing them in *several stations* : Mr. *Hooker* was by his worthy and deserving Patron *Archbishop Whitgifts* means, removed to another place of less *envy,* and more privacy in *Kent,* being loth to have so excellent a light too much *wasted,* by its standing too long in the *blaze* and *wind*: At *distance* they grew nearer to each other in their mutual good esteem and *affections*; each of them, as occasion offered, *professing* an high value of the other.

There was no gift or grace more eminent in Mr. *Hooker,* then that *Mosaick* work of a *meek* and *smooth* temper, free from the roughness of *rancor* and *malice* : Though he were *shaken* by disputes, and much *agitated by peevish controversies,* yet like a *vial of clear water,* he discovered no soil of *uncharitableness* at the *bottom*; which testimony all his *Writings* do verifie, being as a *two-edged sword* very *bright* and *weighty,* good *mettal,* and *sharp-edged,* doing its work without any *bluntness* or *raggedness,* yet without any *ponit* or *pungency,* by way of *personal reflexions,* or *Satyrick bitterness* : He writes as intent to the *cause* and subject matter, not to the quality or infirmity of the *person*; keeping to that *Golden saying* in his Preface, *There will come a time when three words uttered with Charity and Meekness, will receive a far more blessed reward, then Three Thousand Volumes Written with Disdainful Sharpness of Wit.*

And no less *calm,* after the quick *Paroxysms* of some jevenile and popular passions were *breathed* out and allayed by *Grace* and *Experience,* was Mr. *Travers* towards Mr. *Hooker* : Though they misunderstood each other in *lesser matters,* yet they corresponded in the main of sound *Doctrine,* and *Holy life*; like *generous Rivals,* they honored and loved what they saw good in one *another*; what seemed otherways, they either pardoned, excused, or in charity supplied. Hence that very *worthy speech* of Mr. *Travers*, when being asked what *he thought* of some vile *aspersion* cast upon Mr. *Hooker?* he answered, *In truth I take* Mr. *Hooker to be a very holy man.*

A vile and horrible plot against Mr. Hookers honor.
As indeed he was in *word* and *deed*; yet wanted there not a Devil so impudent, as not daring to *tempt him*, yet dared to hamper him, as it were, with that *sin*, from which no man was more severely free, *unspotted*, and *unsuspected*. Some well advised men of *former* years have told me, that it was thought by some to have been a *plot* and *practice* laid by some of Mr. *Hookers* and the Church of *Englands* more cowardly *Enemies*, who were wont to bark against all in their *scurrilous Pamphlets*, thus by thus blasting Mr. *Hookers* reputation, to *discredit* the glory of his *excellent Writings*, with which the wiser and better world was then so greatly and *justly* taken.

Hence (they say) a *design* was laid (as of old against the *great Athanasius*) that he should be assaulted by an *impudent Woman*, as he was diverting in the fields *neer London*: Her presence and speech was presently seconded by a *man as base as* her self, who came in as Mr. *Hooker* was talking with the woman, and challenged her for his wife: Together they threaten the *good man*, to accuse him of what ever *shameless Villany* could invent, to scare his pious and thus *surprized simplicity*, that so he might be wrought upon to redeem *his reputation* and honor, by such moneys as they now demanded of him.

He (*good man*) amazed at this unwonted and most unwelcome encounter, and finding that it amounted no higher then his *purse*, with *much blushing* for their *shameless demands* and *demeanor*, and with a most *innocent simplicity*, gives them *what money* he had about him, that he might be rid of them at any rate: They unsatisfied with that small pittance he gave them, insolently demanded more: They renew and encrease their *threatnings*; he willing by any means to get free of these *Hornets*, promised them the *sum* they demanded, appoints them to come to his *lodging*, and there made good his word, hoping at once to *silence them*, and to be quit of their *further importunity*.

These Wretches finding the *facility* and *fear* of this *Holy man* to render him so *malleable*, rather then he would fall under such vile and *desperate calumnies*, frequent his *lodging* once in ten days continually, *draining*, as Leeches, what money he had, and more then he could well spare; yet he *gently parted* with it, that he might *conceal* and *conquer*, if *possible*, their *Villany*. After these *evil spirits* had for some moneths haunted him, by chance, or rather by good *Providence*, there comes to his Chamber while one or both of these *Imps* were there, a noble Friend of Mr. *Hookers*, Sir *Edwin Sands* (one of the sons of that famous *Archbishop* of *York*, who was so happy in the *learning* and *good fortunes* of all his sons:) This *Knight* seeing so inauspicious Attendants with the good man, like *Satan* standing at the right hand of *Joshua* the High Priest, demanded of him when they were gone, what unsuitable *society* these were whom he met in his *Chamber*, who looked so impudently, and ugly, one as a Bawd, the other as a Pander.

How Mr. Hooker was freed from that injury and indignity in which he was captivated.
Mr. *Hooker* very mildly replied, with some *sadness* and *dejection* beyond his ordinary *serenity*, That they were poor people, who came to him for *some relief*. The committing looks of the *Varlets*, and the manner of Mr. *Hookers* answer, occasioned the more *inquisitive curiosity* in his *Noble Friend*, who was jealous of some cheat or imposturage put upon the *innocent simplicity* of Mr. *Hooker*, who had more of the *Dove* then *Serpent*; replying therefore with some *quickness* upon him, he desired a more *exact account* of that riddle, which seemed to be in his *relieving persons*, who had so little to invite *charity* in their very *meen* and *presence*: At last, after some *faint reserves*, Mr. *Hooker* was won freely to tell him the *concealed*, but costly *Tragedy* of his *first encounter*; what *captivity*, as to his *fame* and *fears*, he had been in; what use, or abuse rather, these *Miscreants* and *Monsters* had made of his *civil* and *enforced Charity*, which had impoverished his *goodness*, to enrich their wickedness.

Sir *Edwin Sands* with *infinite indignation* and disdain, hearing of *this mysterie of Iniquity*, resolves speedily to *disinchant* the good man of such *evil Spirits*; he makes an appointment so, that the next time one or both of the *Harpies came*, he might be sent for: Which *was done*, and two *Constables* (as *Exorcists*) brought with him;

                                                  who

who, without much ado, meeting with those *Comrades*, seize on them both, carry them to the next *Justice*, cause them to be *examined* apart, finde them in so *grossly* and *contradictions*, that they were both sent to the *Purgatory* of *Bridewel*. One of them impatient of so *uneasie a lodging* and penance, confesseth all their execrable *design* and *practice*. At last, these *Vipers* which had so long *seized* on the *good mans* hand, fell off without any further *harm* to him, save the *drawing some* money from him, and some little *whisperings* of his enemies, when they had got that report by *the end*, which the more ingenuous were ashamed to hear of, and abhorred to believe.

3. Others were wholly defeated, as to their hopes of *gaining* some repute to their worsted cause, by the *disrepute* of such a person, whom all the learned and sober World looked now upon with so much *Veneration*, as one that had an unquestioned conquest over both *Papists* and *Catharists*, having battered the pretended *Conformity* of the Church of *Rome*, as to their novel *Errors* and *Traditions*, while he *vindicated* the *Conformity* of the *Church of England*, both with the Word of God, and the *primitive Churches* examples.

This strange *Narrative* I was loth to omit (whereof Mr. *Fuller* gives some *little obscure touch*) but I have long since *in my youth* heard it at large from *persons of credit*: If I fail in some *circumstances* of it, yet for the substance it is that *which all agree to*; The impu- That the Devil had a *prank* to play upon this excellent *Person*, but he laid his scene dence of the so *unfitly*, and had such *unlikely Actors*, that he lost his design; nor did any other Devils temp- evil befal Mr. *Hookers* innocency, then what is prone to light on those whose sim- tations. plicity may invite *Temptation*, but their sanctity *fortifies them* against all evil *impressions*: He was so good, that he knew not how to resist *evil* but by *well-doing*; and chose rather to suffer silently, then rathly to hazard his good name by any more *brisk vindication* of himself, or open contestation with so *odious* and *impudent* a *Devil*: Against the assaults of which, no defence is so sure *in point* of *Conscience*, as that of *Joseph*, the fear of sinning *against God*; and *nothing so great a compurgation for a mans reputation*, as the constancy of his former *unspotted conversation*, no man easily degenerating to so great sins, who hath long kept at *distance* from them: And however such *Flesh-flies* sent by *Belzebub*, may be sometime suffered to appear in the *Temple*, and to light on the *Sacrifices* of God (chaste and unspotted souls) yet they are never *permitted* to fly-blow, taint and infect them so as to pollute their *Consciences*, or much *deface* their credit; God in time pleading their cause by ways of Providence not ordinary, making their *Righteousness to shine forth as the Sun* out of mists and clouds, with the greater lustre: Nor is there any *Defensative* so firm against the assaults of good mens honor, as the integrity of their mindes and manners before God.

> *Vivendum est recte, cum propter plurima, tum hoc*
> *Ut discas linguas contemnere mancipiorum.*

As the fruits of *Vertue* are many, fair and *sweet to the Conscience*, so the very *leaves* of it, as to credit, are both a great shelter and ornament.

Other more private or personal *accounts* of Mr. *Hookers* own observations and ex- The want of periences, I have none to offer to the World; having never gained any such me- Mr. *Hookers* morials of his more *retired life* from any man, and least of all from his *own* pen: His private me- native modesty and humility not permitting him to record any thing of himself, lest morials: he should seem to glory, either in his *abilities* or *infirmities*; not but that I think it would be much to the advance of Gods glory, and the good of posterity, if (as in all other *Arts* and *Sciences*, the notable experiments of learned men give great advantages) in this practical *part* of private *Piety*, eminent *Persons* (such as Mr. *Hooker* was) would leave the World so much of their *Pictures*, as might well consist with the modester gravity, yea severity of Christian *Vertues* and *Graces*, which are not bound wholly to hide and vail their beauties, for fear of *affectation* or vain-glory; but let their *light so shine before men*, that they may have cause *to glorifie their heavenly Father*; which was the design of that excellent *Father* S. *Augustine*, who hath enriched the World with those fair *glasses* of his *Confessions*, *Retractations* and *Soliloquies*, which give us as it were a prospect into the *very inside* of so *Learned*, *Holy*, and *Devout* a man; who after *various agitations* of body and foul, where he almost made shipwrack of both, he was happily reduced by *Gods grace*, from wantonness both *Carnal* and *Spiritual*, from Manichean *opinions*, and sensual *pleasures*, after many Conflicts, to embrace a most holy and strict life, as a good *Christian*, and a most *excellent Bishop*.

Certainly (as *Pancirolla* observes in Art and Nature, many things in the greater world of excellent use, are lost and buried in oblivion, for want of such particular Records as might best *preserve them* : So the works of God in his gracious and particular dispensations to the lesser world, mens persons, as to their souls and bodies, many things might (if registred by wise *Observators* of themselves or *others*) be added to the *Treasury* of Gods glory, and the stock of others improvement : After the rare *pattern* of *Marcus Aurelius*, who opens his breast *to all Spectators*, that they might see by his *Writings*, what his *Principles* were as to Piety, Vertue, Gratitude, and Honor toward God and Man ; also what his conscientious reflections were upon the review of his actions and experiences, in so great a *sphere* of life and liberty, as that was of the *Roman Empire* : In which he exceeded all that went before or after him ; not so much in the latitude and tranquillity of *his Empire*, as in that happy and absolute *Dominion* his Reason and Natural Religion kept above his *Senses, Passions,* and *Affections*.

Nor have there been wanting great *examples* of Learned and Pious men in this kinde ; who (as *Franciscus Junius*) have been the Historians of their own lives, being best able to give a true and impartial account of things, free from vain-glory and envy, being best acquainted with the pulse of their *own hearts*, and *events of their lives*: Doubtless, in so rich a mine as Mr. *Hooker*, was besides the works of a publique *interest and proportion* with which he hath blessed the Church of *England*, there were many other *gems* and *rarieties* wherewith he might have *enriched the World*.

But I must not repine at modest and humble mens *self-concealments* ; nor is it fit to be *curiously inquisitive* after them, where they thought best to be *reserved*, it being a part of incivility unimited, to follow any man to his closet : Onely this I cannot but occasionally *note*, that if *Astrological observations* made of the *Stars* and *Planets* in their several *Aspects* and *Motions*, are worthy of so *Learned mens waking hours*, diligent eyes, and *accurate pens* (such as were *Ptolomy*, *Alphonso*, *Tichobrahe*, *Kepler, Briggs*, and others) doubtless there might be no less *useful* observations made and *communicated* to the World, of the *various Aspects* and *Correspondencies* between Gods Spirit and our own ; provided they be *taken*, not by *fantick Astrologers*, who take every *Blazing-star*, or *Meteore* for a *fixed Light in the Firmament*, or *Heaven of the* foul ; but by godly, wise, and serious persons, who judge of *heavenly motions*, not by *occasional Apparitions*, but by *habitual* or *constant* holy dispositions, consonant to the *clearest lights* of *Precepts* and *Promises* in the Word of God

3 Of Mr. Hookers preferments in the Church of *England*.

But I apply my self to the *third Head* I proposed in *writing* Mr. *Hookers* Life ; which is, To take a short view of his *Preferments* in the Church, where he deserved so well. Here the *shadow of this Pyramide* was not proportionable to his Dimensions and Height ; either for his abilities or eminent Services and Merits.

The steps of *his preferments* were but few and easie, never to any great height : He moved oft indeed, but was not much *promoted* at last : Not that he wanted either desert, or friends both able and willing, who knew to *value* and *reward* his worth ; but they chose (as it seems) rather to make use of his *abilities* in ways more suitable to them, then to put him beyond *that Sphere*, to which they saw his *modester genius* most disposed him ; who was more devoted to a *useful* and laborious *latency*, then to a troublesome and envyed *eminency* : His *Ambition* was rather to do *good things, then enjoy great* : He was so far from affecting Honor, and then *cumulating Plurality of Livings*, and adding to them *Ecclesiastical Dignities*, beyond what any one or two men can with good conscience discharge or enjoy, that I finde he contented himself, as with one living at a time, and one or two Prebendaries at most, so with the *onely degree of Mr. of Arts* ; for so all his subscriptions run, not so much as *Batchelor* in Divinity, that I can find ; I am sure *not Doctor in any faculty*, though well learned in all that became a great Scholar and good Divine.

Nor

Nor can I here *charge the age* in which he lived of *Envy* or *Ingratitude* to him
(though this be frequent, especially in times when pragmatick and partial activity, makes a prey of Ecclesiastical Dignities and Preferments, still crowding out
those that are the most *meritorious, modest,* and *consciencious;*) but I will impute the
mediocrity of his advancements, to the aptitude he had rather for teaching then governing, and for writing then ruling: To be sure, it is a great part of Publique
Wisdom, so to employ and prefer men, as they are *adapted* to *dutie;* not to put
Souls Armour on those shoulders which are less fit to bear or manage them: Every
Bird flies best with its own feathers, and in its own sphere.

His first *Publique rise* was (as I have touched) to be Fellow of *Corpus Christi*
Colledge in *Oxford;* a preferment that seems very desirable to young Masters of
Art, and is much to their advantage, if they remove not too soon, and if they
seriously improve their time and talents; and lastly, if they stay not over-long, till
they have contracted a *morose* and *supercilious habit of manners,* fancying that to be
an Empire, and settled condition, which is indeed but a kinde of Apprentiship, or
preparation for more publique and grand employments, which render Learning
and Scholars both more sociable and useful.

On this *narrow pedestal,* or basis of a Fellowship, stood this *living Statue* for some
seven years, till the uneasiness of his small maintenance, and his willingness to go
out to the wider World, invited him to accept the offer of a small Living called
Buscomb, in the West; thence *Anno* 1584. he was removed to *Drayton Beauchamp*
in *Lincolnshire,* no very great Benefice; *Anno* 1592. he had the Dignities of a *Pre-
bendary* in *Salisbury,* and the *Subdeanry* bestowed on him; and by the Queen he was
preferred to be *Master of the Temple;* that is, the *publique Preacher* in that *great Auditory,* which requires an *excellent Preacher,* and where he may well *deserve an honora-
able maintenance;* hence *Anno* 1594. he was removed to his last station, at *Bishops-
bourn* in *Kent,* and was made also Prebend of *Canterbury,* by the favour of the Archbishop *Whitgift,* whose valiant and able second he was in that *Conflict;* which he
so notably *maintained* against the *Disciplinarian* Faction, or the *unruly Non-conformists.*

This was the period of Mr. *Hookers promotion,* much below indeed his merit, but
adequate, it seems, to the retiredness of his temper, and most suitable to the policies of
those times, where Church Governors were to be rather active then contemplative spirits. And from this something rising, but not very high ground, did this excellent person take his ascent and rise to Heaven, the onely preferment worthy of
him. 4 Mr. *Hookers* death.

After he had finished *his course with joy,* because with all good *Conscience,* fighting a good fight, both for the Faith and Peace of this *Reformed Church,* wasted not
by age, so much as *much study;* dying with great comfort at his Parsonage in
Kent, about fifty year old, in the year of our Lord 1599. says Mr. *Cambden,* in
Anno 1603. says his Monument; so uncertain are the Chronological calculations of
his Birth, Life, and Death, always living in a single life with all sanctity and severity; not onely *unmarried,* but *unspotted;* and more venerable for his *chastity,* then
his *celibacy.*

I cannot finde upon search *any Will* he made; which makes me believe he made
none; but while he lived was his own *Executor,* distributing his charity as occasion offered; and not deferring it, till by death it was turned to *necessity,* as good
wines sometimes soure to Vinegar, for want of timely spending: like ill debtors,
who never pay their debts, till the Baily Arrests, and hales them to prison. I presume he had not much to give; onely his excellent *Library* was his Treasury, Ar-
moury, and best Houshold-stuff, nor can I finde how that was disposed of: Other
Furniture it is like he had, but very plain and little, as S. *Austin,* when he dyed,
having like a good Husband, put his superfluity to usury, as soon as it came in,
trusting God with repayment of what he credited to the poor, whose onely hand
(not writing, but receiving) he had for the receipt, acknowledgement, and security of what he gave: Nor did it ill become Mr. *Hooker* thus to live, and thus to dye,
with less incumbrance and care, having neither wife, nor childe, nor any kindred,
whose eyes had failed for his charity till his death; he rather prevented them, and
as he could spare it, spent it, not in *Epicurism* and Luxury, but in such a frugal
decency,

decency as beſt became him, his relations, his neighbours, and the poor: To theſe laſt, he thought he owed, and ſo paid more then to himſelf. His diet, as his apparel, plain, but decent: His entertainments hoſpitable, but Philoſophical, yea Theological: His recreation, as to expenſiveneſs, none; for he took pleaſure in nothing ſo much as that by which he profited moſt, in *ſtudy* or *diſcourſe*: He lived daily as in the *Confines of Heaven*, and *next door to Death*, which is the *porch of Eternity*: He never had the levity of youth, much leſs the lubricity, being grave and good betimes; nor did he grow moroſe, or tetrical, or covetous, or ambitious, or proud with *years*, though crowned with the *garlands* of Applauſe, and the *laurels* of great Learning, yea with the *fruits* of noble and excellent *Works*: His humble ſoul was as a fruitful field, nothing elevated, when moſt enriched; or as the heavenly lights, ſatisfied with ſhining to others.

His funerals.

His *Funerals* were ſolemnized with a kinde of *Victorious ſorrow*, and *Triumphant grief*, by the frequency of many perſons of Honor and Learning, beſides the common people, who eſteemed Mr. *Hooker* as κοινον αγαθον, a common bleſſing or publique good to all the Vicinity and Countrey; being acceſſible to all, ready to communicate any Counſel, Comfort, or Charity in his power: Perſons of higher quality eſteemed him as a *Tutelary Angel*; Divines, as an *Oracle* among them; all admired his Learning, more his Humility, and moſt of all his *Charity*: Theſe at once to counterpoiſe the grief and bitterneſs of his loſs, *gloried* in the works he had *written*, and the excellent example he had given to all Miniſters, the more gifts and learning they have, to be more humble and peaceable; while they alſo mourned unfeignedly for his immature departure, and deplored the publique privation of ſo uſeful a Perſon: Who was Religious, without affectation; Wiſe, without any notable mixture of folly: Grave, without any ſcorn or brow; Good, without any oſtentation; Learned, without any extravagancy; Judiciouſly Conformable to the Church of *England*, without any either *formality* or reſtiveneſs; and loyal to his Soveraign, without any ambition or reſervation.

He was interred in the *Chancel* of *Biſhopsbourn*, where a fair *Marble* and *Alabaſter Monument*, no way violated or deformed in all our late years of confuſion, ſuch reverence even the Enemies of the Church of *England* had for Mr. *Hookers* name and ſhrine; this I ſay, was long after in *Anno* 1634. erected to his *deſerving memory*, with that *Effigies* and *Epitaph* you ſee in the *Front* of the *Book*, by Sir *William Cowper* of *Ratling-court* in the County of *Kent*, Knight and Baronet; whoſe *pious gratitude* thought nothing more worthy of his own honor, and the others vertue, then to expreſs a thankful *Veneration* toward that *Perſon*, whom God had made his *Spiritual-Father*, a means of his *Regeneration* and *Converſion* to Chriſt, by that Miniſtery of the *Goſpel*, which Mr. *Hooker* diſpenced in ſo ſtill *a voyce* and ſilent *geſture*, but with potent demonſtrations of Scripture and Reaſon, which are the greateſt vertue and efficaciouſneſs of a *Preacher*, whoſe meer *Stentorian* noiſe, and *Theatrick geſticulations* in a Pulpit, ſerve more to *amuſe* and *ſcare*, or to decoy or lowbel the gaping, ſleeping, or frighted people, then much to edifie, inform or amend them; the ſweet and ſecret *incubations*, or *hatchings* of the *bleſſed Spirit* to the life of grace, being made on the ſouls of men, not by *culinary* and paſſionate heats, which ſcorch and dry; but by ſuch heavenly and gentle influences, as carry a ſweet *temperament* of light and warmth together, like the Suns beams in the Spring time: This one great inſtance ſufficiently confutes that *vulgar prejudice* which many have againſt ſome calmer Miniſters, as that they could never profit by their preaching, becauſe they uſe not that *vociferation* and *earneſtneſs* which others do, while they bait themſelves, rather then purſue their Texts; as if mens hearts could never *burn within them*, till their *ears do glow* with a *vehement* noiſe, and a tearing kinde of *Oratory*; which many times like hail more then rain, makes a great ratling, but comes from a *cold Region*, and neither moiſtens nor enters. The ſureſt way of *profiting* by any *Preacher*, is to weigh the Authority by which he preaches, and the matter which he delivers, by the Balance of the Sanctuary, right Reaſon, the Laws of the Land, and the Sacred Scriptures, as the Noble *Bereans* did when S. *Paul* preached to them; and not to be taken with any meer *pomp* or *artifice* of ſpeech and pronuntiation, which no men have more accurate and affected,

then

then those who like *Mountebanks* and *Charlatans*, act a popular part, and are least in good earnest; whose interest it is, like *Hernshaws*, to hide the *meagerness* of their bodies, by the flushness of their feathers, and to compensate the known defect of real abilities by such pretty *pageantries*; whereas the spiritual and moral goodness of the heart, depends wholly upon that sound illumination, which first duly informs the understanding, and so moves the will from a consent to the truth, to a desire, love and delight in that good, which is thus aptly, agreeably conveyed to the rational soul. It is but a *vulgar fallacy* in some Ministers and People, to delight in that drink which runs out more to froth then good liquor; filling their mindes with the *windyness* of empty notions, and airy opinions, rather then with any sanctity and solidity of saving wisdom; which grows but from one holy root, and is seldom either rightly plucked, or duly planted, but by such Preachers as have solid judgements, honest hearts, and humble spirits; which carried on by competent *Ministerial Abilities*, will do more at the years end, then all the *truculency* and *terror* which some Ministers affect; as modest and frequent showers do more advance the fruitfulness and growth of all things, then those violent storms which are not brought forth but with much wind, thunder and lightning: Ministers of Christ, as *Ambassadors*, must not be sheepish and discountenanced, or discomposed in doing their Embassy; nor yet may they appear *Thrasonick* and *impudent*, as if they had forgot not onely themselves, but the Majestie of their Master: the sanctity of their service, and that *reverence* they owe to the Church of Christ, met in his name and presence, whom they are soberly to serve, not rudely to affront.

Long before his Tomb or Inscription were made, there were some *Elegant Epitaphs* made and scattered, *as flowers upon his Fragrant Hearse:* That of *Corpus Christi* Colledge I may not omit, which was sent to Sir *William Cowper*, as the joynt testimony of their just sense of his worth, and their loss.

Honor done to Mr. *Hookers* memory.

*E*cclesiæ labantis Atlas unicus,
*E*t veritatis grande propugnaculum,
Hic Magnus ille, Hookerus, hic magnus jacet:
Integritatem cujus, & vitam piam
Scientiamq; quanta nemini data est,
Alteq; cunctis pectus incoctum bonis;
Non marmor istud referat, non surdus lapis;
Libri loquuntur, & volumen nobile,
Authoris immortale Monumentum sui:
Quo Numinis vexata turpiter sacra,
Ritusq; nullo jure spretos vindicat.
Et, quæ volebat Schisma dirui, suo
Veneranda Divum fana sustentat stylo;
Qui sacra sic defendit, & Templa omnia,
Templis meretur ipse Monumentum omnibus.

The sense of which lines, a little varied, Sir *William Cowper* thus presented with a fair Monument, as an honorary of gratitude to his deceased and justly admired Friend, yea his Spiritual Father.

1 Cor. 4. 15. *In Christ Jesus I have begotten you through the Gospel.*

Though nothing can be spoke worthy his fame,
Or the remembrance of that precious Name
Judicious Hooker: Though this cost be spent
On him, that hath a lasting Monument
In his own Books; yet ought we to express,
If not his worth, yet our respectfulness.
Church Ceremonies he maintain'd; then why
Without all Ceremony should he dye?

W 2

Was it becaufe his Life and Death fhould be
Both equal patterns of Humility ?
Or that perhaps this onely glorious one
Was above all to ask, Why he had none ?
Yet he that lay fo long obfcurely low,
Doth now preferr'd, to greater Honors go.
Ambitious men, learn hence to be more wife,
Humility is the true way to rife :
And God in me this Leffon did infpire,
To bid this humble man, *Friend fit up higher.*

WILLIAM COWPER.

I have met alfo with another Paper, made I fuppofe, foon after his Death, as appears by the *Poetry* ; which I will venture to the Readers candor, becaufe what is wanting in the Elegancy of the Verfe, is made up in the veracity of the matter.

The Character of Mr. *Richard Hooker.*

THe Painted Whore *and* Naked Matron *he*
 Diflik'd , both Rome *and her quite contrary ;*
He ftrove for Tythes, *and* Ceremonies *too,*
That fo Chrifts Spoufe *might* warm *and* decent *go :*
He gave her power, not to do what fhe pleafe,
But took away the Sword, *and left the* Keys.
When brain-fick men reeled to either hand,
He gave his judgement, bade them upright ftand :
Having got out of Romes Pollution,
Croffing the way they now were pofting on
Into a new extreme ; he bade them ftay ,
And fhew'd between each ditch the fafeft way.
He did Democracy and mifrule hate,
And lov'd the Order both of Church and State.
If he attain what's aim'd at by his quill,
Kings *fhall be* Kings, *and* Bifhops, Bifhops *ftill.*
He was nor Prince *nor* Bifhop, *yet did write,*
Not to uphold his Fortunes, but their right :
Go read his Book ; it will thee, if thou art
True Proteftant, *confirm ; if not, convert.*

Thefe few collections I have made ; probably many other private pens highly devoted to Mr. *Hookers* praifes, and affected with his death, were then exercifed in fuch like *Encomiaftical Elegies* ; all which the ftream of Time hath carried out of fight. Publique *Threnodies* from either Univerfity, I never heard of, as to this fubject , who deferved much more then many of thofe whom the fick and flattering *Mufes* fometime fought to Deifie, living and dead ; ftooping fo low (in our latter times) as to bring *fpices* and *fweet odours* to the putid Carkaffes , and worfer Confciences of the moft *impudent Traytors,* and flagitious *Regicides* in the world ; yet thefe mens rotten names muft (forfooth) be *embalmed* by the joynt tears of our degenerated Univerfities, which deferve to be wafht with news ones ; for to praife *men of Blood,* Hypocrifie and Cruelty, when dead, is as much to adopt the guilt of their fins, as to bid them *Godfpeed* when living : Nothing is a more abject and infolent way of *flattery,* then to fet the body of *Vertue,* which is Honor and Commendation, upon the *Devils fleeve* ; or to put the imprefs and matter of *praife* upon the *Banner of* Schifm *and* Sedition.

It were endlefs to enumerate the many other high *commendations* given by men of eminent Learning and Piety to Mr. *Hooker,* when ever they made publique mention of him, or his works ; counting it a kinde of *Sacriledge* to be filent of *his merits,* or to rob his good name of that *fragrancy* which was *in it ,* and reputation
due

The many juft Encomiums of him.

due to it. Therefore I thought it a needless curiosity to muster up that cloud of witnesses, which have all either dropped down some *Epithites* and *Titles of Honor*, or showered larger *Paragraphs*, and whole *Panygericks* upon Mr. *Hooker*. I will content my self with onely two at present, which are at hand, and under my eye.

One is Mr. *Cambden*, a Learned, Eloquent, and grave *Historian* of our own, in his *Annales* 42 of Q. *Eliz. Anno Dom.* 1599. *This year*, saith he, *Mr.* Richard Hooker *rendred his soul to God: A Divine to be imitated for his Modesty, Temperance, Meekness, and other Vertues; famous for his manifold commendations in Learning, as his Books of Ecclesiastical Polity, set forth in English, and worthy to be turned into Latine, do abundantly testifie.*

The next is the late *Learned and Eloquent*, both *Preacher* and *Professor* in *Divinity*, Dr. *Richard Holdsworth*, a *Confessor* and *Martyr* in the late Persecution, who thus writes in his *Lect.* 14. *Hookerus magnus ille mysta, quem pro sanctissimo & modestissimo viro nostreq; doctrinæ conscio habendum esse, & inter nos Pontificii liberrime fateri non aspernantur.* The very Papists owned Mr. *Hooker* that profound Divine, to be one of the most Learned, Holy, and Modest of those that have asserted the Church of *England*, and Reformed Religion.

But it is *superfluous* to cumulate *commendations* upon those whom none can *disparage*, without *discovering* their *Ignorance, Envy*, or *Malice*: As in nature the Sun and other things of known, useful, and publique *excellencies*, are (like *Paragon Jewels*) their own *Heralds* and *Commentaries*, though all tongues should be silent; so is it in *some persons*, the conspicuity of whose Authentick worth is such, that nothing can *Eclipse* it: And of this first three of men, of *Christians*, of *Divines*, of *Writers* and of *Livers*, was this famous Mr. *Hooker*, ὁ μακαρίτης, ὁ πολυθρύλλητος, ὁ θαυμάσιος, ὁ θεῖος, ὁ πάνυ, who thought it very ingrate and impudent, rashly to disparage or desert the *Religion chosen by his King and Countrey*; especially when upon tryal he saw it so *piously intent*, and wholly conform (for the main) in all *Faith, Mysteries, Morals*, and *Evangelicals*, to the *Word of God*, and the Primitive Churches: He thought it became not onely Christian Charity, but *common Modesty* and *humanity*, for sons candidly to interpret the meaning of their Mother the Church, and thankfully to accept with the right hand, what was so wisely offered by her just Authority: not to be too much *morose* or *curious*, or *censorious* or *critical*, or *severe* and *magisterial* in *lesser* matters of Circumstance and Ceremony; the publique use and *Arbitrement* of which depends not on private mens *fancies*, but on the publique Prudence in Church and State: He did not think any morality or bond lay upon Governors or Lawgivers, to have always that which may be, or seems to some men best in its kinde for *language* and *words*, or *Rites* and *modes*, or *forms* and *methods* of Religion; but what is most *expedient* to times and places, to peoples capacities, customs, and other *political proportions*: That as there is no true piety without Christianity, nor Christianity without charity; so no charity without such humble, *tender*, and *equanimous* submissions to that Authority in Church and State (in such *small, outward Regulations*) which doth *liberally furnish* all Christians with those *great things* of God, which pertain to *salvation*: That it is very uningenuous, and rudely *ingrate* for *sons*, or *servants*, or *guests*, that are *liberally* treated with all things wholesome, decent and necessary, to quarrel with the *dress of things*, and *separate* from the *entertaintment*, because every *dish* and *garnish* is not of their own *contrivance* and *minted in their fancies*.

His judgement was as *searching* and *serene*, as any mans, his *conscience* as *pure* and strict in things that had any *tincture of sin*, that is, were opposite to Law or Gospel; but he had a juster *latitude* of Christian *liberty* in general, then others had, and a stricter sense of his obedience to Ecclesiastical and Civil Laws, in their limitations of Christian liberty; not in its general nature, but in its regular exercise and use of particulars; he did with more candor both enjoy this liberty himself in this Church, and allow it to others both Christians and Churches, either in their *private or personal*, or their *politick* and *social communities*; what he judged free and indifferent in its *nature*, as to any *precedent, moral*, or *divine necessity* imposing, that he *thought himself* bound to *use and observe*, when it was once restrained, and enjoyned in some particular and prudential instance by lawful Authority: Not as if the nature of things was changed, but because the use of them *was lawfully limited* for publique Order, Decency and Solemnity.

He

The med um
he kept.

He was happy to keep the *mean* between the *extremes* then *pregnant in England*, and *distinguished* by Recusancy and *Non-conformity*, afterwards by *Papists* and *Puritans* : He avoided *superstition* on either hand; neither calling *that evil* which was *good*, nor that good which was *evil* : He abhorred Prophaneſs, Superſtition and Schiſm, the firſt as poyſoning, the ſecond as infecting, the third as rending a Church ; all killing, if not cured by *seasonable applications*.

He was happy in his *undertaking*, happier in the rare *management* of it, and had been with the whole Church *most happy* in the event, or effect, and deſign rather of his learned labours, if he had met with no men but ſuch as were onely *intent* to conquer, or to be *conquered* with truth ; not *addicted* to endleſs *janglings*, and *pertinacious* either to parties, or prepoſſeſſed opinions : If his *Antagonists* had been all *maſters* of ſo much candor, generoſity and juſtice as *Cecilius* the Heathen owned, after his *ſmart conference* with *Octavius* a Chriſtian ; when being convicted in his judgement, and yielding to *the Empire of Truth*, which is a beam of Gods Omnipotent Wiſdom, he thus with great *Elegancy* and *Ingenuity* concludes (in *Minutius Felix*) *Vicimus, & ita, ut improbe uſurpo victoriam* ; *nam ut ille* (Octavius) *mei victor eſt, ita ego erroris triumphator* ; which is, and ought to be the *Epinicion* of every good Chriſtian, who entring the liſts of *Religious Diſputation*, muſt not look to the intereſt of his *reputation* or party, but to the love of truth, the ſatisfaction of conſcience, the peace of the Church, and the glory of God ; and be more delighted to ſee himſelf *ſubdued* to all theſe, then to *obtain* an impious and fallacious victory : Which holy end I believe was the ſole byas and ſway of Mr. *Hooker* in theſe and *other his writings*, and ſo I *wiſh it may of all his Readers*.

Concluſion.

What now remains, but after the *example* of the late *Judicious, Pious*, and *ever-glorious King* and *Martyr Charls* the firſt, to recommend (as *His Majeſty* now dying did to his *dear and Orphan Children*) theſe excellent *Labours* of Mr. *Richard Hooker*, to the diligent reading of all Learned and Conſcientious men Miniſters eſpecially, when they are come to that *maturity* of judgement, as to be able to bear the weight of his Reaſonings, and the ampleneſs of his ſtile (for mindes that are yet but feeble, or griſly and gelly, will hardly read them with pleaſure, or reap the profit to be had *by them* (as tender ſtomacks muſt not be charged with *ſtronger meats*, till they have firmer digeſtion;) yet when they come to be fit for theſe perplexed, yet profitable ſtudies, they will finde in Mr. *Hookers Works* a *Treaſury* and an *Armory* ; wherewith to *enrich* and defend *themſelves*, and the *Church of England*, according to that ſtation in which they are placed : For want of which ſkilful and faithful Aſſertor, ſhe hath lately been ſo *aſſaulted, ſpoiled* and *deſpiſed* by ignorant and inſolent Enemies. When theſe *excellent Books* ſhall obtain their deſerved place in *mens heads and hearts*, inſtead of factions, frothy, ſeditious and ſenſeleſs Pamphlets, which are the ſhame and poyſon of this Church and Kingdom, I ſhall have no cauſe to repent of the pains, yea *pleaſure* I have taken in giving the World this *renewed view* of Mr. *Richard Hooker*, and his now *compleated Works* : Which while they remain in the *Engliſh World*, and are underſtood, the Church cannot want a ſufficient *Antidote* againſt any Factious Infuſions, until the ſins of a degenerous, idle, ſupercilious and impertinent Clergy, added (as *Pelion* to *Oſſa*) to debaucheries of other people (which will grow like weed in neglected gardens) ſhall give fire again to thoſe *Conflagrations* which our moſt merciful God, our gracious King, and our late wiſe Parliaments have thus far *reſtinguiſhed* : Nothing but the Clergies *Impudence* or *Impiety*, turning Grace into Wantonneſs, and miraculous Reſtaurations to ingrateful Apoſtaſies, can give opportunity and power to factious ſpirits again to turn their *Plowſhares* into ſwords, and their *pruning hooks* into pikes: Theſe Sects cannot be ſtrong, but by our weakneſs ; nor *armed*, but by our *nakedneſs* ; by ſtripping our ſelves of *Gods protection*, the *Laws* defences, and the *love* of good men ; which will all fail us, if we fail to do *our duty* in thoſe ways of Piety, Prudence, Induſtry and Charity, which are expected of us as Biſhops and Presbyters, both by God and man : Neither loſing friends by negligences in the main concerns of holineſs and peace, nor multiplying enemies by cauſeleſs, exaſperations and extravagancies : Both which Rocks are beſt avoided, if on all hands we follow the counſel and example of this Humble, Learned, Induſtrious and Charitable Mr. *Hooker*, one of the Honors of our Engliſh Nation, and Glories of our Reformed Church.

T O

The moſt Reverend Father in God, my very good Lord, the Lord Arch-Biſhop of *Canterbury* His Grace, *Primate* and *Metropolitan* of all ENGLAND.

MOST Reverend in Chriſt, the long continued, and more then ordinary favour, which hitherto your Grace hath been pleaſed to ſhew towards me, may juſtly claim at my hands ſome thankful acknowledgment thereof. In which conſideration, as alſo for that I embrace willingly the ancient received courſe, and conveniency of that Diſcipline, which teacheth inferior degrees, and Order in the Church of God, to ſubmit their writings to the ſame Authority, from which their allowable dealings whatſoever, in ſuch affairs, muſt receive approbation, I nothing fear but that your accuſtomed clemency will take in good worth the offer of theſe my ſimple and mean labours, beſtowed for the neceſſary juſtification of laws heretofore made queſtionable, becauſe, as I take it, they were not perfectly underſtood. For ſurely, I cannot find any great cauſe of juſt complaint, that good Laws have ſo much been wanting unto us, as we to them. To ſeek reformation of civil laws is a commendable endevour, but for us the more neceſſary is a ſpeedy redreſs of our ſelves. We have on all ſides loſt much of our fervency towards God ; and therefore concerning our own degenerated ways, ſhe have reaſon to exhort with S. *Gregory*, ὅπερ ἧμεν πρότερον, *Let us return again unto that which we ſometimes were* ; but touching the exchange of Laws in practice with Laws in device, which, they ſay, are better for the ſtate of the Church, if they might take place, the farther we examine them, the greater cauſe we finde to conclude μένωμεν ὅπερ ἐσμέν, *although we continue the ſame we are, the harm is not great*. Theſe fervent reprehenders of things eſtabliſhed by publique authority, are always confident and bold ſpirited men. But their confidence for the moſt part riſeth from too much credit given to their own wits, for which cauſe they are ſeldom free from errors. The errors which we ſeek to reform in this kind of men, are ſuch as both received at your own hands their firſt wound, and from that time to this preſent, have been proceeded in with that moderation, which uſeth by patience

to

to fupprefs boldnefs, and to make them conquer that fuffer. Wherein confidering the nature and kind of thefe controverfies, the dangerous fequels whereunto they were likely to grow, and how many ways we have been thereby taught wifdom, I may boldly aver concerning the firft, that as the weightieft conflicts the Church hath had, were thofe which touched the head, the Perfon of our Saviour Chrift; andthe next of importance, thofe queftions, which are at this day between us and the Church of *Rome*, about the actions of the body of the Church of God; fo thefe which have laftly fprung up from Complements, rites and ceremonies of Church actions, are in truth for the greateft part fuch filly things, that very eafinefs doth make them hard to be difputed of in ferious manner. Which alfo may feem to be the caufe, why divers of the Reverend Prelacy, and other moft judicious men, have efecially beftowed their pains about the matter of jurifdiction. Notwithftanding led by your Graces example, my felf have thought it convenient to wade through the whole caufe, following that method, which fearcheth the truth by the caufes of truth. Now if any marvaile, how a thing in it felf fo weak, could import any great danger, they muft confider not fo much how fmall the fpark is that flieth up, as how apt things about it are to take fire. Bodies politique, being fubject as much as natural, to diffolution, by divers meanes; there are undoubtedly more eftates overthrown through difeafes, bred within themfelves, then through violence from abroad; becaufe our manner is always to caft a doubtful and a more fufpicious eye towards that over which we know we have leaft power; and therefore, the fear of external dangers, caufeth forces at home to be the more united; it is to all forts a kind of bridle, it maketh vertuous minds watch, it holdeth contrary difpofitions in fufpence, and it fetteth thofe wits on work in better things which would be elfe imployed in worfe; whereas on the other fide, domeftical evils, for that we think we can mafter them at all times, are often permitted to run forward, till it be too late to recal them. In the mean while the Common-wealth is not onely through unfoundnefs fo far impared, as thofe evils chance to prevaile; but farther alfo through oppofition arifing between the unfound parts and the found, where each endeavoreth to draw evermore contrary ways, till deftruction in the end bring the whole to ruine. To reckon up how many caufes there are, by force whereof divifions may grow in Common-wealths, is not here neceffary. Such as rife from variety in matter of Religion, are not onely the fartheft fpread, becaufe in Religion all men prefume themfelves interessed alike, but they are alfo for the moft part hotlier profecuted and perfued then other ftrifes; for as much as coldnefs, which in other contentions may be thought to proceed from moderation, is not in thefe fo favourably conftrued. The part which in this prefent quarrel ftriveth againft the current and ftream of Laws, was a long while nothing feared, the wifeft contented not to call to mind how errors have their effect many times not proportioned to that little appearance of reafon whereupon they would feem built, but rather to the vehement affection or fancy which is caft towards them, and proceedeth from other caufes. For there are divers motives, drawing men to favour mightily thofe opinions, wherein their perfwafion are but weakly fetled, and if the paffions of the mind be ftrong, they eafily fophifticate the underftanding, they make it apt to believe upon every flender warrant, and to imagine infallible truth, where scarce any probable shew appeareth. Thus were those poor seduced creatures *Hacquet* and his other two adherents, whom I can neither speak nor think of but with much commiseration and pity, thus were they trained by fair ways first, accompting their own extraordinary love to his discipline, a token of Gods more then ordinary love towards them; from hence they grew to a strong conceit, that God which had moved them to love his Discipline, more then the common sort of men did, might have a purpose by their means to bring a wonderful work to pass, beyond all mens expectation, for the advancement of the throne of discipline by some tragical execution; with the particularities whereof it was not safe for their friends to be made acquainted, of whom they did therefore but covertly demand what they thought of extraordinary motions of the spirit in these days, and withall request to be commended unto God by their Prayers, whatsoever should be undertaken by men of God, in meer zeal to his glory, and the good of his distressed Church. With this unusual and strange course they went on forward, till God, in whose heaviest worldly judgments, I nothing doubt, but that there may ly hidden mercy, gave them over to their own inventions, and left them made in the end an example for head-strong and inconsiderate zeal, no less fearful then *Achitophel*, for proud and irreligious wisedom. If a spark of error have thus far prevailed, falling even where the wood was green, and farthest off, to all mens thinking, from any inclination unto furious attempts, must not the peril thereof be greater in men whose minds are of themselves as dry fewel, apt before-hand unto tumults, seditions and broyls? But by this we see in a cause of Religion, to how desperate adventures men will strain themselves for relief of their own part, having law and authority against them. Furthermore, let not any man think, that in such divisions, either part can free it self from inconveniencies, sustained not onely through a kind of Truce, which vertue on both sides doth make with vice, during war between truth and error; but also in that there are hereby so fit occasions ministred for men to purchase to themselves wel-willers by the colour, under which they oftentimes prosecute quarrels of envy or inveterate malice, and especially because contentions were as yet never able to prevent two evils, the one a mutual exchange of unseemly and unjust disgraces, offered by men whose tongues and passions are out of rule; the other, a common hazard of both, to be made a prey by such as study how to work upon all occurrents, with most advantage in private. I deny not therefore, but that our Antagonists in these controversies, may peradventure have met with some, not unlike to *Ithacius*, who mightily bending himself by all means against the heresie of *Priscilian*, (the hatred of which one evil was all the vertue he had) became so wise in the end, that every man, careful of vertuous conversations, studious of Scripture, and given unto any abstinence in diet, was set down in his Kalender for suspected Priscillianists, for whom it should be expedient to approve their soundness of faith by a more licencious and loose behaviour. Such Proctors and Patrons the truth might spare. Yet is not their grossness so intolerable, as on the contrary side, the scurrilous and more then Satyrical immodesty of Martinisme, the first published schedules whereof, being brought to the hands of a grave and a very Honorable Knight, with signification given, that the Book would refresh his spirits, he took it, saw what the Title was, read

Sulp. Sever. *sp. hist.* hcel.

over an unſavory ſentence or two, and delivered back the Libel with this anſwer ; *I am ſorry you are of the mind to be ſolaced with theſe ſports, and ſorrier you have herein thought mine affection to be like your own.* But as theſe ſores on all hands lie open, ſo the deepeſt wounds of the Church of God have been more ſoftly and cloſely given. It being perceived that the plot of Diſcipline did not only bend it ſelf to reform ceremonies, but ſeek farther to erect a popular authority of Elders, and to take away Epiſcopal juriſdiction, together with all other Ornaments and means, whereby any difference or inequality is upheld in the Eccleſiaſtical order; towards this diſtructive part, they have found many helping hands, divers although peradventure not willing to be yoaked with Elderſhips, yet contented (for what intent God doth know) to uphold oppoſition againſt Biſhops, not without greater hurt to the courſe of their whole proceedings in the buſineſs of God and her Majeſties ſervice, then otherwiſe much more weighty adverſaries had been able by their own power to have brought to paſs. Men are naturally better contented to have their commendable actions ſuppreſt, then the contrary much divulged. And becauſe the wits of the multitude are ſuch, that many things they cannot lay hold on at once, but being poſſeſt with ſome notable either diſlike or liking of any one thing whatſoever, ſundry other in the mean time may eſcape them unperceived ; therefore if men deſirous to have their vertues noted, do in this reſpect grieve at the fame of others, whoſe glory obſcureth and darkneth theirs, it cannot be choſen, but that when the ears of the people are thus continually beaten with exclamations againſt abuſes in the Church, theſe tunes come alvvays moſt acceptable to them, vvhoſe odious and corrupt dealings in ſecular affairs, both paſs by that mean the more covertly, and vvhatſoever happen do alſo the leaſt feel that ſcourge of vulgar imputation, which notwithſtanding they moſt deſerve. All this conſidered, as behoveth, the ſequel of duty on our part is only that which our Lord and Saviour requireth, harmleſs diſcretion, the wiſdome of Serpents tempered with the innocent meekneſs of Doves. For this world will teach them wiſdome that have capacity to apprehend it. Our wiſdome in this caſe muſt be ſuch, as doth not propoſe to it ſelf π ἴδιον our own particular, the partial and immoderate deſire whereof poiſoneth whereſoever it taketh place : but the ſcope and mark which we are to aim at, is π κοινὸν the publique and common good of all, for the eaſier procurement whereof our diligence muſt ſearch out all helps and furtherances of direction, which Scriptures, Counſels, Fathers, Hiſtories, the laws and practices of all Churches, the mutual conference of all mens collections and obſervations may afford; our induſtry muſt even anatomize every particle of that body, which we are to uphold ſound ; and becauſe, be it never ſo true which we teach the world to believe, yet if once their affections begin to be alienated, a ſmall thing perſwadeth them to change their opinions it behoveth that we vigilantly note and prevent by all means thoſe evils, whereby the hearts of men are loſt, which evils for the moſt part being perſonal, do arm in ſuch ſort the Adverſaries of God and his Church againſt us, that if through our too much neglect and ſecurity the fame ſhould run on, ſoon might we feel our eſtate brought to thoſe lamentable termes, whereof this hard and heavy ſentence was by one of the ancients uttered upon like occaſions,

Leg. Carol, Magd. 411.

Dolens dico, gemens denuncio, ſacerdotium quod apud nos intus cecidit, foris

din

diu stare non poterit. But the gracious providence of Almighty God hath, I trust, put these thornes of contradiction in our sides, lest that should steal upon the Church in a slumber, which now, I doubt not, but through his assistance may be turned away from us, bending thereunto our selves with constancy, constancy in labour to do all men good, constancy in prayer unto God for all men, Her especially, whose sacred power matched with incomparable goodness of nature, hath hitherto been Gods most happy instrument, by him miraculously kept for works of so miraculous preservation and safety unto others ; that as, *By the Sword of God and Gedeon,* was sometime the cry of the people of *Israel*, so it might deservedly be at this day the joyful song of innumerable multitudes, yea the Emblem of some Estates and Dominions in the world, and (which must be eternally confest even with tears of thankfulness) the true inscription, stile or title of all Churches as yet standing within this Realm, *By the goodness of Almighty God and his servant Elizabeth we are.* That God, who is able to make mortality immortal, give her such future continuance as may be no less glorious unto all posterity, then the days of her regiment past have been happy unto our selves; and for his most dear annointeds sake, grant them all prosperity, whose labours, cares and counsels, unfainedly are referred to her endless welfare, through his unspeakable mercy, unto whom we all owe everlasting praise. In which desire I will here rest, humbly beseeching your Grace, to pardon my great boldness, and God to multiply his blessings upon them that fear his name.

Iud. 7. 20.

                    Your Graces in all duty,

                    Richard Hooker.

A
PREFACE.

To them that seek (as they term it) the
Reformation of Laws and Orders *Ecclesiastical*, in
the Church of *England*.

The cause and occasion of handling these things ; and what might be wished in them, 'or whose sakes so much paine is taken

Hough for no other cause, yet for this, that posterity may know, we have not loosely through silence
permitted things to pass away as in a dream, there
shall be for mens information extant thus much concerning the present state of the Church of God established amongst us, and their careful endeavour,
which would have upheld the same. At your hands,
beloved in our Lord and Saviour Jesus Christ (for in
him the love which we bear unto all that would but
seem to be born of him, it is not the Sea of your gall and bitterness that
shall ever drown) I have no great cause to look for other then the self-
same portion and lot, which your manner hath been hitherto to lay on
them that concur not in Opinion and Sentence with you. But our hope is,
that the God of peace shall (notwithstanding mans nature, too impatient
of contumelious malediction) enable us quietly, and even gladly to suffer all
things, for that work sake which we covet to performe. The wonderful
zeal and fervour wherewith ye have withstood the received orders of this
Church, was the first thing which caused me to enter into consideration,
whether (as all your published Books and Writings peremptorily maintain)
every Christian man fearing God, stand bound to joyn with you for the furtherance of that which ye term the *Lords Discipline*. Wherein I must plainly
confess unto you, that before I examined your sundry declarations in that
behalf, it could not settle in my head to think, but that undoubtedly such
numbers of otherwise right well affected and most religiously enclined
minds, had some marvelous reasonable inducements which led them with

so

fo great earneftnefs that way. But when once, as neer as my flender abi
lity would ferve, I had with travel and care performed that part of the A-
poftles advice and counfel in fuch cafes,whereby he willeth to *try all things*;
and was come at the length fo far,that there remained onlythe other claufe
to be fatiffied, wherein he concludeth, that *what good is muft be held*:
there was in my poor underftanding no remedy but to fet down this as my
final refolute perfwafion ; *Surely the prefent form of Church Government
which the Laws of this Land have eftablifhed, is fuch, as no Law of God, nor
reafon of man hath hitherto been alleadged of force fufficient to prove they
do ill, who to the uttermoft of their power withftand the alteration thereof*:
Contrariwife; *The other which inftead of it we are required to accept, is onely
by errour and mifconceipt named the ordinance of Jefus Chrift, no one proof as
yet brought forth, whereby it may clearly appear to be fo in very deed*. The explication of which two things I have here thought good to offer into your
own hands: heartily befeeching you even by the meeknefs of Jefus Chrift,
whom I truft ye love; that, as ye tender the peace and quietnefs of this
Church, if there be in youthat gracious humility which hath ever been the
Crown and glory of a Chriftianly difpofed mind ; if your own fouls,hearts
and confciences, (the found integrity whereof can but hardly ftand with
the refufal of truth in perfonal refpects)be,as I doubt not but the yare,things
moft dear and precious unto you, *Let not the faith which ye have in our Lord
Jefus Chrift, be blemifhed with partialities*, regard not who it is which fpeaketh,but weigh only what is fpoken.Think not that ye read the words of one,
who bendeth himfelf as an adverfaryagainft the truth,which ye have already
imbraced but the words of one who defireth even to imbrace togetherwith
you the felf fame truth,if it be the truth ; and for that caufe(for no other,
God he knoweth)hath undertaken the burthenfome labour of this painful
kind of conference. For the playner accefs whereunto, let it be lawful for
me to rip up the very bottom how and by whom your difcipline was planted, at fuchtime as this age we live in began to make firft trial thereof.

The fi ft (fta
blifhment o
new Difciplir e
by M. *Calvins*
induftry, in
the Church of
Geneva: and
the beginning
of ftrife about
it amongft our
felves. 2. A Founder it had, whom, for mine own part, I think incomparably
the wifeft man that ever the French Church did injoy, fince the hour it injoyed him. His bringing up was in the ftudie of the civil Law. Divine
knowledge he gathered not by hearing or reading fo much, as by teaching
others. For though thoufands were debters to him, as touching knowledg
in that kind ; yet he to none but onely to God, the Author of that moft
bleffed Fountain the book of Life, and of the admirable dexterity of wit,
together with the helps of other learning which were his guides: till being occafioned to leave *France*, he fell at the length upon *Geneva*. Which
City, the Bifhop and Clergy thereof had a little before (as fome affirm)
forfaken, being of likelyhood frighted with the peoples fudden attempt
for abolifhment of Popifh Religion: the event of which enterprize they
thought it not fafe for themfelves to wait for in that place. At the coming
of *Calvine* thither, the forme of their civil Regiment was popular, as it
continueth at this day: neither King nor Duke nor Nobleman of any authority or power over them, but officers chofen by the people out of themfelves, to order all things with publique confent. For fpiritual Government, they had no Laws at all agreed upon, but did what the Paftors of
their fouls by perfwafion could win them unto. *Calvin* being admitted
one of their Preachers and a Divinity-Reader amongft them, confidered
how dangerous it was that the whole eftate of that Church fhould hang
ftill

ſtill on ſo ſlender a thread, as the liking of an ignorant multitude is, if it have power to change whatſoever it ſelf liſteth. Wherefore taking unto him two of the other Miniſters, for more countenance of the action, (albeit the reſt were all againſt it) they moved, and in the end perſwaded with much ado, the people to bind themſelves by ſolemn Oath, firſt, never to admit the Papacy amongſt them again; and ſecondly, to live in obedience unto ſuch orders concerning the exerciſe of their Religion, and the forme of their Eccleſiaſtical Government as thoſe their true and faithful Miniſters of Gods Word had agreeably to Scripture ſet down for that end and purpoſe. When theſe things began to be put in ure, the people alſo (what cauſes moving them thereunto, themſelves beſt know) began to repent them of that they had done, and irefully to champ upon the bit they had taken into their mouthes, the rather for that they grew by means of this innovation, into diſlike with ſome Churches near about them, the benefit of whoſe good friendſhip their ſtate could not well lack. It was the manner of thoſe times; (whether through mens deſire to enjoy alone the glory of their own enterpriſes, or elſe becauſe the quickneſs of their occaſions required preſent diſpatch,) ſo it was, that every particular Church did that within it ſelf, which ſome few of their own thought good, by whom the reſt were all directed. Such number of Churches then being, though free within themſelves, yet ſmall, common conference before-hand might have eaſed them of much after trouble. But a great inconvenience it bred, that every later indeavoured to be certan degrees more removed from conformity with the Church of *Rome* then the reſt before had been, whereupon grew marvelous great diſſimilitudes, and by reaſon thereof, jealouſies, heart-burnings, jars, and diſcords amongſt them. Which notwithſtanding might have eaſily been prevented, if the orders which each Church did think fit and convenient for it ſelf, had not ſo peremptorily been eſtabliſhed under that high commanding form, which rendered them unto the people, as things everlaſtingly required by the law of that Lord of Lords, againſt whoſe ſtatutes there is no exception to be taken. For by this mean it came to paſs, that one Church could not but accuſe and condemn another of diſobedience to the will of Chriſt, in thoſe things vvhere manifeſt difference vvas betvveen them: vvhereas the ſelf-ſame orders allovved, but yet eſtabliſhed in more vvary and ſuſpenſe manner, as being to ſtand in force till God ſhould give the opportunity of ſome general conference vvhat might be beſt for every of them aftervvards to do; this, I ſay, had both prevented all occaſions of juſt diſlike vvhich others might take, and reſerved a greater liberty unto the Authors themſelves of entring into farther conſultation aftervvards. Which though never ſo neceſſary, they could not eaſily novv admit, vvithout ſome fear of derogation from their credit: and therefore that vvhich once they had done, they became for ever after reſolute to maintain. *Calvin* therefore and the other tvvo his Aſſociates, ſtifly refuſing to adminiſter the Holy Communion to ſuch as vvould not quietly vvithout contradiction and murmur ſubmit themſelves unto the orders vvhich their ſolemn Oath had bound them to obey, vvere in that quarrel baniſhed the Town. A few years after (ſuch was the levity of that people) the places of one or two of their Miniſters being fallen voyd, they were not before ſo willing to be rid of their learned Paſtor, as now importunate to obtain him again from them who had given him entertainment, and which were loth to

part

part with him, had not unresistable earnestness been used. One of the Tovvn-Ministers that savv in vvhat manner the people vvere bent for the revocation of *Calvine*, gave him notice of their affection in this sort. *The* *Senate of two hundred being assembled, they all crave* Calvine. *The next day* *a general Convocation ; They cry in like sort again all : We will have* Calvin *that good and learned man Chrifts Minifter. This*, saith he, *when I under-* *stood, I could not choose but praife God, nor was I able to judge otherwife,* *then that this was the Lords doing, and that it was marvelous in our eyes,* And that *the ftone which the builders refufed, was now made the head of the* *Corner.* The other tvvo vvhom they had throvvn out (together vvith *Cal-* *vin*) they vvere content fhould injoy their exile. Many caufes might lead them to be more defirous of him. Firft, his yielding unto them in one thing, might haply put them in hope, that time would breed the like eafinefs of condefcending further unto them. For in his abfence he had perfwaded them, with whom he was able to prevaile, that albeit himfelf did better like of common bread to be ufed in the Eucharift, yet the other they ra- ther fhould accept, then caufe any trouble in the Church about it. Againe, they faw that the name of *Calvin* waxed every day greater abroad, and that together with his fame their infamy was fpread, who had fo rafhly and childifhly ejected him. Befides, it was not unlikely but that his cre- dit in the World, might many ways ftand the poor Town in great ftead: as the truth is, their Minifters forreign eftimation hitherto hath been the beft ftake in their hedge. But whatfoever fecret refpects were likely to move them, for contenting of their minds, *Calvin* returned (as it had been another *Tully*) to his old Home. He ripely confidered how grofs a thing it were for men of his quality, wife and grave men, to live with fuch a multitude, and to be Tenants at will under them, as their Mini- fters, both himfelf and others, had been. For the remedy of which inconvenience, he gave them plainly to underftand, that if he did become their Teacher again, they muft be content to admit a compleat form of Difcipline, which both they and alfo their Paftors fhould now be folemnly fworn to obferve for ever after. Of which difcipline the main and prin- cipal parts were thefe : A ftanding Ecclefiaftical Court to be eftablifhed : perpetual Judges in that Court to be their Minifters, others of the people annually chofen (twice fo many in number as they) to be Judges together with them in the fame Court : thefe tvvo forts to have the care of all mens manners, power of determining of all kind of Ecclefiaftical caufes, and authority to convent ; to control, to punifh, as far as vvith Excommunica- tion, whomfoever they fhould think worthy, none either fmall or great ex- cepted. This device, I fee not, how the wifeft at that time living could have bettered, if we duly confider what the prefent ftate of *Geneva* did then require. For their Bifhop and his Clergy being (as it is faid) departed from them by Moon-light, or however, being departed ; to choofe in his room any other Bifhop, had been a thing altogether impoffible. And for their Minifters to feek, that themfelves alone might have coercive power over the whole Church, would perhaps have been hardly conftrued at that time. But when fo frank an offer was made, that for every one Minifter there fhould be two of the People to fit and give voice in the Ec- clefiaftical Confiftory, what inconvenience could they eafily find vvhich themfelves might not be able alvvays to remedy? Hovvbeit (as ever more the fimpler fort are even vvhen they fee no apparent caufe, jealous not.

with

Epift Cal. 24.

Luc. 33. 1 7.

withstanding over the secret intents and purposes of wiser men) this proposition of his did somewhat trouble them. Of the Ministers themselves which had stayed behind in the City when *Calvin* was gone, some, upon knowledge of the peoples earnest intent to recal him to his place again, had before-hand written their Letters of submission, and assured him of their alleagiance for ever after, if it should like him to harken unto that publique suit. But yet misdoubting what might happen, if this Discipline did go forward, they objected against it the example of other reformed Churches, living quietly and orderly without it. Some of the chiefest place and countenance amonst the Laiety professed with greater stomack their judgments, that such a Discipline was little better then Popish Tyranny, disguised and tendered unto them under a new form. This sort, it may be, had some fear that the filling up of the seats in the Consistory, with so great a number of Lay-men, was but to please the minds of the people, to the end they might think their own sway somewhat, but when things came to tryal of practice, their Pastors learning would be at all times of force to over-perswade simple men, who knowing the time of their own Presidentship to be but short, would always stand in fear of their Ministers perpetual authority. And among the Ministers themselves, one being so far in estimation above the rest, the voices of the rest were likely to be given for the most part respectively with a kind of secret dependency and aw: so that in shew a marvelous indifferently composed Senate Ecclesiastical was to govern, but in effect one onely man should, as the spirit and soul of the residue, do all in all. But what did these vain surmises boot? Brought they were now to so straight an issue, that of two things they must chuse one; Namely, whether they would to their endless disgrace, with ridiculous lightness dismiss him, whose restitution they had in so impotent manner desired, or else condescend unto that demand, wherein he was resolute either to have it, or to leave them. They thought it better to be somewhat hardly yoaked at home, then for ever abroad discredited. Wherefore in the end, those Orders were on all sides assented unto, with no less alacrity of mind, then Cities unable to hold out longer are wont to shew when they take conditions such as liketh him to offer them which hath them in the narrow streights of advantage. Not many years overpassed, before these twice-sworn men adventured to give their last and hottest assault to the Fortress of the same Discipline, childishly granting by common consent of their whole Senate, and that under their Town Seal, a relaxation to one *Bertelier* whom the Eldership had Excommunicated; further also decreeing, with strange absurdity, that to the same Senate it should belong to give final judgment in matter of excommunication, and to absolve whom it pleased them; clean contrary to their own former deeds and Oathes. The report of which decree being forthwith brought unto *Calvin*; *Before* (saith he) *this Decree take place, either my blood or banishment shall sign it.* Again, two days before the Communion should be celebrated, this speech was publiquely to like effect, *Kill me, if ever this hand do reach forth the things that are holy, to them whom the Church hath judged despisers.* Whereupon, for fear of tumult, the forenamed *Bertelier* was by his friends advised for that time not to use the liberty granted him by the Senate, nor to present himself in the Church till they saw somewhat further what would ensue. After the Communion quietly ministred, and some likelyhood of peaceable ending of these troubles without

An. Dom. 1541

out

out any more ado, that very day in the after-noon, besides all mens expecta-tion, concluding his ordinary Sermon, he telleth them, that because he neither had learned nor taught to strive with such as are in authority; there-fore (saith he) *the case so standing as now it doth, let me use these words of the Apostle unto you, I commend you unto God and the Word of his grace,* and so bad them heartily *Adieu.* It sometimes commeth to pass, that the rea-diest way which a wise man hath to conquer, is to fly. This voluntary and unexpected mention of sudden departure, caused presently the Senate (for according to their wonted manner they still continued onely constant in unconstancy) to gather themselves together, and for a time to sus-pend their own Decree, leaving things to proceed as before, till they had heard the judgment of four *Helvetian* Cities concerning the matter which was in strife. This to have done at the first before they gave assent unto any order, had shewed some wit and discretion in them : but now to do it, was as much as to say in effect, that they would play their parts on a Stage ; *Calvin* therefore dispatcheth with all expedition his letters unto some principal Pastor in every of those Cities, craving earnestly at their hands, to respect this cause as a thing whereupon the whole state of Religion and Piety in that Church did so much depend ; that God and all good men were now inevitably certaine to be trampled under foot, unless those four Cities by their good means might be brought to give sen-tence with the Ministers of *Geneva,* when the cause should be brought be-fore them : yea, so to give it, that two things it might effectually con-taine ; the one an absolute approbation of the Discipline of *Geneva,* as con-sonant unto the Word of God, without any cautions, qualifications, ifs, or ands ; the other an earnest admonition not to innovate or change the same. His vehement request herein as touching both points was satisfied. For albeit the said *Helvetian* Churches did never as yet observe that Disci-pline, nevertheless the Senate of *Geneva* having required their judgment concerning these three questions: First, *After what manner, by Gods com-mandement, according to the Scripture and unspotted Religion, Excommuni-cation is to be exercised* : Secondly, *Whether it may not be exercised some other way then by the Consistory* : Thirdly, *What the use of their Churches was to do in this case* : Answer was returned from the said Churches, *That they had heard already of those Consistorial Laws, and did acknowledge them to be godly Ordinances,* drawing towards *the prescript of the Word of God, for which cause they did not think it Good for* the Church of *Geneva, by innovation to change the same, but rather to keep them as they were.* Which answer, although not answering unto the former demands, but respecting what Master *Calvin* had judged requisite for them to answer, was notwith-standing accepted without any further replie : in as much as they plainly saw that when stomack doth strive with wit, the match is not equal. And so the heat of their former contentions began to slake. The present inhabitants of *Geneva,* I hope, will not take it in evil part, that the faultiness of their people heretofore, is by us so far forth laid open, as their own learn-ed Guides and Pastors have thought necessary to discover it unto the world. For out of their Books and Writings it is that I have collected this whole narrative, to the end it might appear in what sort amongst them that dis-cipline was planted, for which so much contention is raised amongst our selves. The reasons which moved *Calvin* herein to be so earnest, was, as *Beza* himself testifieth, *For that he saw how needful these bridles were to be*

Epist. 166.

pu s

pnt in the jaws of that City. That which by wifdome he faw to be requifite
for that people, was by as great wifdome compaffed. But wife men are Quod cam
urbem vide-
ret omnino his
frœnis indi-
gere.
men, and the truth is truth. That which *Calvin* did for eftablifhment of
his Difcipline, feemeth more commendable, then that which he taught
for the countenance of it eftablifhed. Nature worketh in us all a love to
our own Counfels. The contradiction of others is a fan to inflame that love.
Our love fet on fire to maintain that which once we have done, fharpneth
the wit to difpute, to argue, and by all mens to reafon for it. Wherefore
a marvail it were if a man of fo great capacity, having fuch incitements to
make him defirous of all kind of furtherances unto his caufe, could efpy
in the whole Scripture of God nothing which might breed at the leaft a
probable opinion of likelyhood, that divine authority it felf was the fame
way fomewhat inclinable. And all which the wit even of *Calvin* was able
from thence to draw, by fifting the very utmoft fentence and fillable, is
no more then that certain fpeeches there are, which to him did feem to
intimate, that all Chriftian Churches ought to have their Elderfhips indued
with power of Excommunication, and that a part of thofe Elderfhips every
where fhould be chofen out from amongft the Laytie after that form which
himfelf had framed *Geneva* unto. But what argument are ye able to fhew,
whereby it was ever proved by *Calvin*, that any one fentence of Scripture
doth neceffarily inforce thefe things, or the reft wherein your opinion
concurreth with his againft the Orders of your own Church? We fhould
be injurious unto vertue it felf, if we did derogate from them whom
their induftry hath made great. Two things of principal moment there
are which have defervedly procured him honour throughout the World:
the one his exceeding pains in compofing the inftitution of Chriftian Religion; the other, his no lefs induftrious travails for expofition of holy
Scripture according unto the fame Inftitutions. In which two things whofoever they were that after him beftowed their labour, he gained the advantage of prejudice againft them, if they gain-faid; and of glory above
them, if they confented. His Writings, publifhed after the queftion about
that Difcipline was once begun, omit not any the leaft occafion of extolling
the ufe and fingular neceffity thereof. Of vvhat account the Mafter of
fentences was in the Church of *Rome*, the fame and more amongft the
Preachers of reformed Churches *Calvin* had purchafed: fo that the per-
fecteft Divines vvere judged they vvhich vvere skilfulleft in *Calvins* Writings. His books almoft the very Canon to judge both Doctrine and Difcipline by; *French* Churches, both under others abroad, and at home in
their ovvn Countrey, all caft according unto that mold vvhich *Calvin* had
made. The Church of *Scotland* in erecting the fabrick of their reformation, took the felf-fame pattern. Till at length the Difcipline which was
at the firft fo weak, that without the ftaff of their approbation who were
not fubject unto it themfelves it had not brought others under fubjection,
began now to challenge univerfal obedience, and to enter into open conflict with thofe very Churches which in defperate extremity had been
beleivers of it. To one of thofe Churches which lived in moft peaceable
fort, and abounded as well with men for their learning in other profeffi-
ons fingular, as alfo with Divines whofe equals were not elfewhere to be
found, a Church ordered by *Gualters* difciple, and not by that which
Geneva adoreth: unto this Church of *Heidelberge*, there commeth one
who craving leave to difpute publiquely, defendeth with open difdain of
their

their government, that to *a Minister with his Eldership power is given by the Law of God to excommunicate whomsoever, yea even Kings and Princes themselves.* Here were the seeds sown of that controversie which sprang up between *Beza* and *Erastus* about the matter of Excommunication, whether their ought to be in al Churches an Eldership having power to Excommunicate, and a part of that Eldership to be of necessity certain chosen out from amongst the Layty for that purpose. In which disputation they have, as to me it seemeth, divided very equally the truth between them; *Beza* most truly maintaining the necessity of Excommunication; *Erastus* as truely the non-necessity of Lay-elders to be Ministers thereof. Amongst our selves, there was in King *Edwards* days some question moved by reason of a few mens scrupulosity touching certaine things. And beyond Seas, of them which fled in the days of Queen *Mary,* some contenting themselves abroad with the use of their own Service-book, at home authorized before their departure out of the Realm; others liking better the common Prayer Book of the Church of *Geneva* translated, those smaller contentions before begun were by this mean somewhat increased. Under the happy reign of her Majesty which now is, the greatest matter a while contended for, was the wearing of the Cap and Surpless, till there came Admonitions directed unto the High Court of Parliament, by men who concealing their names, thought it glory enough to discover their minds and affections, which now were universally bent even against all the Orders and Laws wherein this Church is found unconformable to the plat-forme of *Geneva.* Concerning the Defender of which Admonitions, all that I mean to say is but this : *There will come a time when three words uttered with charity and meekness, shall receive a far more blessed reward, then three thousand Volumes written with disdainful sharpness of wit.* But the manner of mens writings must not alienate our hearts from the truth, if it appear they have the truth : as the followers of the same defender do think he hath, and in that perswasion they follow him, no otherwise then himself doth *Calvin, Beza,* and others, with the like perswasion that they in this case had the truth· We being as fully perswaded otherwise, it resteth that some kind of trial be used to find out which part is in error.

By what means so many of the people are trained into the liking of or that Discipline.
1 Cor. 10. 11 and 11. 14.
Luc. 12 56, 5.
Acts 17. 11.

3. The first mean whereby Nature teacheth men to judge good from evil, as well in Laws as in other things, is the force of their own discretion. Hereunto therefore S. *Paul* referreth oftimes his own speech to be considered of by them that heard him, *I speak as to them which have understanding, judge ye what I say.* Again afterward, *Judge in your selves, is it comly that a woman pray uncovered ?* The exercise of this kind of judgment our Saviour requireth in the Jews. In them of *Berea* the Scripture commendeth it. Finally, whatsoever we do, if our own secret judgement consent not unto it as fit and good to be done, the doing of it to us is sin, although the thing it self be allowable. S. *Pauls* rule therefore

Rom 14, 5.

general is, *Let every man in his own mind be fully perswaded of that thing which he either alloweth or doth.* Some things are so familiar and plain, that Truth from Falshood, and good from evil is most easily discerned in them, even by men of no deep capacity. And of that nature, for the most part, are things absolutely unto all mens Salvation necessary, either to be held or denied, either to be done or avoided. For which cause S. *Augustine* acknowledgeth that they are not onely set down, but also plainly set down in Scripture : so that he which heareth or readeth, may without any great
difficulty

difficulty underftand. Other things alfo there are belonging) though in a lovver degree of importance (unto the office of Chriftian men: vvhich becaufe they are more obfcure, more intricate and hard to be judged of, therefore God hath appointed fome to fpend their whole time principally in the ftudy of things divine, to the end that in thefe more doubtful cafes, their underftanding might be a light to direct others. *If the underftanding power or faculty of the foul be* (faith the grand Phyfitian) *like unto bodily fight, not of equal fharpnefs in all; what can be more convenient, then that, even as the dark-fighted man is directed by the cleer about things vifible, fo likewife in matters of deeper difcourfe the wife in heart doth fhew the fimple where his way lyeth.* In our doubtful cafes of Law, what man is there who feeth not how requifite it is, that Profeffors of skill in that faculty be our Directors? So it is in all other kinds of knovvledge. And even in this kind likevvife the Lord hath himfelf appointed, *that the Priefts lips fhould preferve knowledge, and that other men fhould feek truth at his mouth, becaufe he is the meffenger of the Lord of Hofts.* Gregory Naziauzen, offended at the peoples too great prefumption in controlling the judgement of them to vvhom in fuch cafes they fhould have rather fubmitted their ovvn, feeketh by earneft intreaty to ftay them vvithin their bounds: Prefume not ye *that are fheep, to make your felves guides of them that fhould guide you, neither feek ye to overflip the fold which they about you have pitched. It fufficeth for your part, if ye can well frame your felves to be ordered. Take not upon you, to judge your felves, nor to make them fubject to your laws who fhould be a law to you, for God is not a God of fedition and confufion, but of order and of peace.* But ye vvill fay, that if the guides of the people be blind, the common fort of men muft not clofe up their ovvn eyes and be led by the conduct of fuch; if the Prieft be partial in the Lavv, the flock muft not therefore depart from the ways of fincere truth, and in fimplicity yield to be followers of him for his place fake and office over them. Which thing though in it felf moft true, is in your defence notwithftanding weak: becaufe the matter, wherein ye think that ye fee and imagine that your ways are fincere, is of far deeper confideration then any one amongft five hundred of you conceiveth. Let the vulgar fort among you know, that there is not the leaft branch of the caufe wherein they are fo refolute, but to the trial of it a great deal more appertaineth then their conceit doth reach unto. I write not this in difgrace of the fimpleft that way given; but I would gladly they knew the nature of that caufe wherein they think themfelves throughly inftructed and are not; by means whereof they dayly run themfelves, without feeling their own hazzard, upon the dint of the Apoftles fentence againft evil fpeakers, as touching things wherein they are ignorant. If it be granted a thing unlawful for private men, not called unto publique confultation, to difpute which is the beft State of civil Policy (with a defire of bringing in fome other kind then that under which they already live, for of fuch difputes I take it his meaning was;) if it be a thing confeft, that of fuch queftions they cannot determine without rafhnefs, in as much as a great part of them confifteth in fpeciall circumftances, and for one kind as many reafons may be brought as for another; is there any reafon in the World, why they fhould better judge what kind of Regiment Ecclefiafticall is the fitteft? For in the civil State more infight, and in thofe affairs more experience a great deal muft needs be granted them, then in this they can poffibly have. When they which write

Galen. de opt. docen. Gen.

Mal. 2. 7.

Greg. Nazian. Orat qua fe ex. ufat.

Matth. 10. 14.

Mal. 2. 9.

Iude ver. 10. 2 Pet. 2. 12.

Calvin. Inftit. liv. 4. cap. 20. fect. 8.

The Author of the Petition directed to her Majesty, p. 3. in defence of your Discipline, and commend it unto the Highest, not in the least cunning manner, are forced notwithstanding to acknowledg, that *with whom the Truth is they know not*, they are not certain, what certaintie or knowledge can the multitude have thereof? Weigh what doth move the common sort so much to favour this innovation, and it shall soon appear unto you, that the force of particular reasons which for your severall opinions are alleaged, is a thing whereof the multitude never did, nor could so consider as to be therewith wholly carried; but certain generall inducements are used to make saleable your Cause in gross: and when once men have cast a fancie towards it, any slight declaration of specialties will serve to lead forward mens inclinable and prepared mindes. The method of winning the peoples affection unto a generall liking of the Cause (for so ye term it) hath been this. First, in the hearing of the multitude, the faults especially of higher callings are ripped up with marvellous exceeding severitie and sharpness of reproof; which being oftentimes done, begetteth a great good opinion of integritie, zeal and holiness, to such constant Reproovers of sin, as by likelyhood would never be so much offended at that which is evil, unless themselves were singularly good. The next thing hereunto is to impute all faults and corruptions wherewith the world aboundeth, unto the kind of Ecclesiastical Government established. Wherein, as before by reproving faults, they purchased unto themselves with the multitude a name to be vertuous; so by finding out this kind of cause, they obtaine to be judged wise above others: whereas in truth unto the form even of Jewish Government, which the Lord himself (they all confess) did establish, with like shew of reason they might impute those faults which the Prophets condemne in the Governors of that common-wealth; as to the English kind of Regiment Ecclesiasticall (whereof also God himself though in another sort is Author) the stains and blemishes found in our State; which springing from the root of humane fralitie and corruption, not only are, but have been always more or less, yea, and (for any thing we know to the contrarie) will be till the worlds end complained of, what forme of Government soever take place. Having gotten thus much sway in the hearts of men, a third step is to propose their own forme of Church-Government, as the only soveraigne remedie of all evils; and to adorn it with all the glorious titles that may be. And the nature, as of men that have sick bodies, so likewise of the people in the crazedness of their minds possest with dislike and discontentment at things present, is to imagine that any thing (the vertue whereof they hear commended) would help them; but that most, which they least have tried. The fourth degree of inducements, is by fashioning the very notions and conceits of mens minds in such sort, that when they read the Scripture, they may think that everie thing soundeth towards the advancement of that Discipline, and to the utter disgrace of the contrarie. *Pythagoras*, by bringing up his Schollars in speculative knowledge of numbers, made their conceits therein so strong, that when they came to the contemplation of things natural, they imagined that in every particular thing they even beheld as it were with their eyes, how the elements of number gave essence and being to the workes of Nature: A thing in reason impossible, which notwithstanding through their misfashioned preconceit, appeared unto them no less certain, then if Nature had written it in the very foreheads of all the creatures of God. When they of the *Family of Love* have

have it once in their heads, that Christ doth not signifie any one person, but a quality whereof many are partakers; that to be raised is nothing else but to be regenerated or indued with the said quality; and that when separation of them which have it from them which have it not, is here made, this is judgment; how plainly do they imagine that the Scripture every where speaketh in the favour of that sect? And assuredly, the very cause which maketh the simple and ignorant to think they even see how the Word of God runneth currantly on your side, is, that their minds are forestalled, and their conceits perverted beforehand, by being taught that that an Elder doth signifie a Lay-man, admitted onely to the office of Rule or Government in the Church; a Doctor, one which may onely teach, and neither Preach nor administer the Sacraments; a Deacon, one which hath charge of the Almes-box, and of nothing else: that the Scepter, the Rod, the Throne and Kingdom of Christ, are a form of Regiment, onely by Pastors, Elders, Doctors and Deacons: that by mystical resemblance Mount *Sion* and *Jerusalem* are the Churches which admit, *Samaria* and *Babylon* the Churches which oppugne the said form of Regiment. And in like sort they are taught to apply all things spoken of repairing the walls and decayed parts of the City and Temple of God by *Esdras*, *Nehemias*, and the rest: as if purposely the Holy Ghost had therein meant to fore-signifie, what the Authors of admonitions to the Parliament, of supplications to the Council, of petitions to her Majesty, and of such other like Writs, should either do or suffer in behalf of this their cause. From hence they proceed to an higher point, which is the perswading of men credulous and over-capable of such pleasing errors, that it is the special illumination of the Holy Ghost, whereby they discern those things in the word, which others reading yet discern them not. *Dearly beloved*, saith S. *John*, *Give not credit unto every spirit.* There are but two ways whereby the spirit leadeth men to all truth: the one extraordinary, the other common: the one belonging but unto some few, the other extending it self unto all that are of God; the one that which we call by a special divine excellency, *Revelation*; the other *Reason*. If the spirit by such revelation have discovered unto them the secrets of that Discipline out of Scripture, they must profess themselves to be all (even men, women, and children) Prophets. Or if reason be the hand which the Spirit hath led them by, for as much as perswasions grounded upon reason, are either weaker or stronger, according to the force of those reasons whereupon the same are grounded, they must every of them from the greatest to the least, be able for every several Article to shew some special reason as strong as their perswasion therein is earnest. Otherwise how can it be, but that some other sinews there are from which that overplus of strength in perswasion doth arise? Most sure it is, that when mens affections do frame their opinions, they are in defence of errour more earnest a great deal, then (for the most part) sound Beleivers in the maintenance of Truth, apprehended according to the nature of that evidence which Scripture yieldeth: which being in some things plain, as in the principles of Christian Doctrine; in some things, as in these matters of discipline, more dark and doubtful, frameth correspondently that inward assent which Gods most gracious Spirit worketh by it as by his effectual instrument. It is not therefore the fervent earnestness of their perswasion, but the soundness of those reasons whereupon the same is built, which must declare their opinions in these things to have been wrought by the

1 John 4. 1.

Holy

2 Thef. 2. 11. Holy Ghoſt, and not by the *fraud* of that evil Spirit which even in his illuſions ſtrong. After that the phancie of the common ſort hath once thorowly apprehended the Spirit to be Author of their perſwaſions concerning Diſcipline, then is inſtilled into their hearts; that the ſame Spirit leading men into this opinion, doth thereby ſeal them to be Gods children; and that as the ſtate of the times now ſtandeth, the moſt ſpecial token to know them that are Gods own from others, is an earneſt affection that way. This hath bred high terms of ſeparation between ſuch and the reſt of the world; whereby the one ſort are named the Brethren, The Godly; and ſo forth; the other, Worldlings, Time-ſervers, Pleaſers of Men, not of God, with ſuch like : From hence they are eaſily drawn on to think it exceeding neceſſary, for fear of quenching that good Spirit, to uſe all means whereby the ſame may be both ſtrengthned in themſelves, and made manifeſt unto others. This maketh them diligent hearers of ſuch as are known that way to incline; this maketh them eager to take and ſeek all occaſions of ſecret conference with ſuch; this maketh them glad to uſe ſuch as Counſellors and Directors in all their dealings which are of weight, as Contracts, Teſtaments, and the like; this maketh them, through an unweariable deſire of receiving inſtruction from the Maſters of that company; to caſt off the care of thoſe very affaires which do moſt concern their eſtate, and to think that then they are like unto *Mary*, commendable for making choyce of the better part. Finally, this is it which maketh them willing to charge, yea often-times even to over-charge themſelves, for ſuch mens ſuſtenance and releif, leſt their zeal to the cauſe ſhould any way be unwitneſſed. For what is it which poor beguiled ſouls will not do through ſo powerful incite-ments? In which reſpect it is alſo noted, that moſt labour hath been be-ſtowed to winne and retain towards this cauſe them whoſe judgements are commonly weakeſt by reaſon of their ſex. And although not women

2 Tim. 3. 6. *loaden with ſins*, as the Apoſtle St. *Paul* ſpeaketh, but (as we verily eſteem of them for the moſt part) women propenſe and inclinable to holineſs, be otherwiſe edified in good things, rather then carried away as Captives, into any kind of ſin and evil, by ſuch as enter into their houſes with pur-poſe to plant there a zeal and a love toward this kind of Diſcipline; yet ſome occaſion is hereby miniſtred for men to think, that if the cauſe which is thus furthered, did gain by the ſoundneſs of proof whereupon it doth build it ſelf, it would not moſt buſily endeavour to prevail, where leaſt abilitie of judgement is : and therefore that this ſo eminent induſtry in making Proſelytes, more of that ſex then of the other, groweth for that they are deemed apter to ſerve as inſtruments and helps in the cauſe. Apter they are through the eagerneſs of their affection, that maketh them which way ſoever they take, diligent in drawing their Husbands, Chil-dren, Servants, Friends and Allies the ſame way : apter through that na-tural inclination unto pitie, which breedeth in them a greater readineſs then in men, to be bountiful towards their Preachers who ſuffer want; apter through ſundry opportunities which they eſpecially have, to procure encouragements for their brethren; finally, apter through a ſingular delight which they take in giving very large and particular intelligence how all neer about them ſtand affected as concerning the ſame cauſe. But be they women or be they men, if once they have taſted of that cup, let any of contrarie opinion open his mouth to perſwade them, they cloſe

up their ears, his reasons they weigh not, all is answered with rehearsal of the words of *John*, *We are of God, he that knoweth God, heareth us ;* as for the rest, ye are of the world, for this worlds pomp and vanity it is that ye speak, and the world whose ye are, heareth you. Which cloke sitteth no less fit on the back of their cause, then of *Anabaptists*, when dignity, authority and honour of Gods Magistrates is upheld against them. Shew these eagerly-affected men their inability to judge of such matters ; their answer is, *God hath chosen the simple.* Convince them of folly, and that so plainly, that very children upbraid them with it ; they have their bucklers of like defence. *Christs own Apostle was accounted mad ; The best men evermore by the sentence of the world have been judged to be out of their right minds.* When instruction doth them no good, let them feel but the least degree of most merciful tempered severity, they fasten on the head of the Lords Vicegerents here on earth, whatsoever they any where find uttered against the cruelty of blood-thirsty men ; and to themselves they draw all the sentences which Scripture hath in the favour of innocency persecuted for the truth : yea they are of their due and deserved sufferings no less proud, then those antient disturbers to whom St. *Augustine* writeth, saying : *Martyrs rightly so named are they, not which suffer for their disorder, and for ungodly breach they have made of Christian unity ; but which for righteousness sake are persecuted. For Agar also suffered persecution at the hands of* Sara *; wherein, she which did impose was holy, and she unrighteous which did bear the burthen. In like sort, with the Theeves was the Lord himself Crucified, but they who were matcht in the pain which they suffered, were in the cause of their sufferings dis-joyned. If that must needs be the true Church which doth endure persecution, and not that which persecuteth, let them ask of the Apostle what Church* Sara *did represent, when she held her Maid in Affliction. For even our Mother which is free, the heavenly* Jerusalem, *that is to say, the true Church of God, was, as he doth affirm, prefigured in that very Woman by whom the Bond-maid was so sharply handled. Although, if all things be throughly skanned, she did in truth more persecute* Sara *by proud resistance, then* Sara *her, by severity of punishment.* These are the pathes wherein ye have walked that are of the ordinary sort of men ; these are the very steps ye have troden, and the manifest degrees whereby ye are of your guides and directors trained up in that School : a custom of injuring your ears with reproof of faults especially in your Governors : and use to attribute those faults to the kind of spiritual Regiment, under which we live ; boldness in warranting the force of their discipline for the cure of all such evils ; a slight of framing your conceits to imagine that Scripture every where favoureth that discipline ; perswasion that the cause, why ye find it in Scripture is the illumination of the Spirit, that the same Spirit is a Seal unto you of your neerness unto God ; that ye are by all means to nourish and witness it in your selves, and to strengthen on every side your minds against whatsoever might be of force to withdraw you from it.

4. Wherefore to come unto you whose judgement is a lantorn of direction for all the rest, you that frame thus the peoples hearts, not altogether (as I willingly perswade my self) of a politique intent or purpose, but your selvs being first over-born with the weight of greater mens judgments : on your shoulders is laid the burthen of upholding the cause by argument. For which purpose sentences out of the word of God alleage the divers: but

1 Ioh. 4. 6.

What hath caused so many of the learneder sort to approve the same discipline

So

so that when the same are discust, thus it always in a manner falleth out; that what things by vertue thereof ye urge, upon us as altogether necessary, are found to be thence collected onely by poor and marvelous slight conjectures. I need not give instance in any one sentence so alleadged, for that I think the instance in any alledged otherwise a thing not easie to be given. A very strange thing sure it were, that such a Discipline as ye speak of should be taught by Christ and his Apostles in the Word of God, and no Church ever have found it out, nor received it till this present time; contrariwise, the government against which ye bend your selves, be observed every where throughout all generations and ages of the Christian World, no Church ever perceiving the Word of God to be against it. We require you to find out but one Church upon the face of the whole Earth, that hath been ordered by your Discipline, or hath not been ordered by ours, that is to say, by Episcopal Regiment, sithence the time that the blessed Apostles were here conversant. Many things out of antiquity ye bring, as if the purest times of the Church had observed the self-same orders which you require; and as though your desire were, that the Churches of old should be patterns for us to follow, and even glasses wherein we might see the practice of that which by you is gathered out of Scripture. But the truth is, ye mean nothing less. All this is done for fashions sake onely; for ye complain of it as of an injury, that men should be willing to seek for examples and patterns of government in any of those times that have been before. Ye plainly hold, that from the very Apostles times till this present age wherein your selves imagine ye have found out a right pattern of sound discipline, there never was any time safe to be followed. Which thing ye thus indeavour to prove. Out of *Egesippus* ye say that *Eusebius* writeth, how although as long as the Apostles lived the Church did remain a pure Virgin, yet after the death of the Apostles, and after they were once gone whom God vouchsafed to make hearers of the Divine Wisdom with their own ears, the placing of wicked errors began to come into the Church. *Clement* also in a certain place; to confirm that there was corruption of Doctrine immediately after the Apostles times, alleadgeth the Proverb, *that there are few sons like their fathers. Socrates* saith of the Church of *Rome* and *Alexandria*, the most famous Churches in the Apostles times, that about the year 430. the *Roman* and *Alexandrian* Bishops leaving the sacred Function, were degenerate to a secular rule or Dominion: Hereupon ye conclude, that it is not safe to fetch our Government from any other then the Apostles times. Wherein by the way it may be noted, that in proposing the Apostles times as a pattern for the Church to follow, though the desire of you all be one, the drift and purpose of you all is not one. The chiefest thing which Lay-reformers yawn for, is, that the Clergy may through conformity in state and condition be Apostolical, poor, as the Apostles of Christ were poor. In which one circumstance if they imagine so great perfection, they must think that Church which hath such store of mendicant Fryers, a Church in that respect most happy. Were it for the glory of God, and the good of his Church indeed, that the Clergy should be left even as bare as the Apostles when they had neither staff nor scrip; that God, which should lay upon them the condition of his Apostles, would I hope, endue them with the self-same affection which was in that holy Apostle, whose words concerning his own right vertuous contentment of heart, *As well how to want, as how to abound*

T. c. l. 1. p. 97.

Euseb. 3. l. 32.

Lib. Strom.
Somewhat after the beginning.
L. 7. C. 11.

Phil. 4. 12.

abound, are a moſt fit Epiſcopal empreſe. The Church of Chriſt is a body myſtical. A body cannot ſtand, unleſs the parts thereof be proportionable. Let it therefore be required on both parts, at the hands of the Clergy, to be in meanneſs of ſtate like the Apoſtles ; at the hands of the Laytie, to be as they were who lived under the Apoſtles : and in this reformation there will be, though little wiſdom, yet ſome indifferency. But your reformation which are of the Clergy (if yet it diſpleaſe you not that I ſhould ſay ye are of the Clergy) ſeemeth to aim at a broader mark. Ye think that he which will perfectly reform, muſt bring the form of Church-Diſcipline unto the ſtate which then it was at. A thing neither poſſible, nor certain, nor abſolutely convenient. Concerning the firſt, what was uſed in the Apoſtles times, the Scripture fully declareth not; ſo that making their times the Rule and Canon of Church-polity, ye make a rule which being not poſſible to be fully known, is as impoſſible to be kept. Again, ſith the later even of the Apoſtles own times, had that which in the former was not thought upon ; in this general propoſing of the Apoſtles times, there is no certainty which ſhould be followed, eſpecially ſeeing that ye give us great cauſe to doubt how far ye allow thoſe times. For albeit the lover of Antichriſtian building were not, ye ſay, as then ſet up, yet the foundations thereof were ſecretly and under the ground laid in the Apoſtles times : ſo that all other times ye plainly reject, and the Apoſtles own times ye approve with marvelous great ſuſpition, leaving it intricate and doubtful wherein we are to keep our ſelves unto the pattern of their times. Thirdly, whereas it is the error of the common multitude, to conſider only what hath been of old, and if the ſame were well, to ſee whether ſtill it continue ; if not, to condemne that preſently which is, and never to ſearch upon what ground or conſideration the change might grow : ſuch rudeneſs cannot be in you ſo well born with, whom learning and judgement hath enabled much more ſoundly to diſcerne how far the times of the Church, and the orders thereof may alter without offence. True it is *(a)* the ancienter, the better ceremonies of Religion are ; howbeit, not abſolutely true, and without exception, but true onely ſo far-forth as thoſe different ages do agree in the ſtate of thoſe things, for which at the firſt thoſe rites, orders, and Ceremonies, were inſtituted. In the Apoſtles times that was harmeleſs, which being now revived would be ſcandalous ; as their *(b)* *obſcula ſancta*. Thoſe *(c)* Feaſts of charity, which being inſtituted by the Apoſtles, were retained in the Church long after, are not now thought any where needful. What man is there of underſtanding, unto whom it is not manifeſt, how the way of providing for the Clergy by Tithes, the device of Almes-houſes for the poor, the ſorting out of the people into their ſeveral Pariſhes, together with ſundry other things which the Apoſtles times could not have, (being now eſtabliſhed) are much more convenient and fit for the Church of Chriſt, then if the ſame ſhould be taken away for conformities ſake with the antienteſt and firſt times ? The orders therefore which were obſerved in the Apoſtles times, are not to be

urged

a Antiquitas ceremoniis atꝗ ſanis tantum ſanctitatis tri- buere conſuevit quantum adſtruxerit vetuſtatis. Am. p. 736. *b* Rom. 16. 16. 1 Cor. 13. 12. 1 Theſ. 5. 25, 1 Pet. 5. 14, In their meetings to ſerve God, their manner was in the end to ſalute one another with a kiſs, uſing theſe words, Peace be with you. For which cauſe, *Tertul.* doth call it *ſignaculum orationis*, the ſeal of Praier, *Lib. de Ora.* *c Epiſt. Iud. verſe* 12. Concerning which feaſts, S. *Chryſ. ſait, taliſ diebus menſas faciebant communes, & peracta ſynaxi poſt ſacramentorum communionem inibant convivium, diviti lis quidem cibos afferentibus, pauperibus autem & qui nihil habebant etiam vocatis,* in 1 Cor. 11. *Hom.* 27. Of the ſame feaſts in like ſort, *Tertul. Cœna noſtra de nomine rat onem ſui oſtendit. Vocatur enim, αγαπη, id quod eſt penes Græcos dilectio. Quantiſcunque ſumtibus conſtet, lucrum eſt pietatis nomine ſumptum* Apolog. c. 39.

urged as a rule universally, either sufficient or necessary. If they be, nevertheless on your part it still remaineth to be better proved, that the form of Discipline which ye intitle Apostolical, was in the Apostles time exercised. For of this very thing ye fail even touching that which ye make most account of, as being matter of substance in Discipline, I mean the power of your Lay-elders, and the difference of your Doctors from the Pastors in all Churches. So that in sum, we may be bold to conclude, that besides these last times, which for insolency, pride, and egregious contempt of all good order are the worst, there are none wherein ye can truely affirme, that the compleat form of your Discipline, or the substance thereof was practized. The evidence therefore of Antiquity failing you, ye fly to the judgments of such Learned men, as seem by their writings, to be of opinion that all Christian Churches should receive your Discipline, and abandon ours. Wherein, as ye heap up the names of a number of men not unworthy to be had in honour; so there are a number whom when ye mention, although it serve ye to purpose with the ignorant and vulgar sort, who measure by tale and not by weight, yet surely they who know what quality and value the men are of, will think ye draw very neer the dregs. But were they all of as great account as the best and chiefest amongst them, with us notwithstanding neither are they, neither ought they to be of such reckoning that their opinion or conjecture should cause the Laws of the Church of *England* to give place. Much less when they neither do all agree in that opinion, and of them which are at agreement, the most part through a courteous inducement, have followed one man as their Guide, finally, that one therein not unlikely to have swerved. If any chance to say it is probable that in the Apostles times there were Lay-elders, or not to mislike the continuance of them in the Church; or to affirme that Bishops at the first were a name, but not a power distinct from Presbyters; or to speak any thing in praise of those Churches which are without Episcopal Regiment; or to reprove the fault of such as abuse that calling; all these ye register for men, perswaded as you are, that every Christian Church standeth bound by the Law of God to put down Bishops, and in their rooms to erect an Eldership so authorized as you would have it for the Government of each Parish. Deceived greatly they are therefore, who think that all they whose names are cited amongst the Favourers of this cause, are on any such verdict agreed. Yet touching some material points of your Discipline, a kind of agreement we grant there is amongst many Divines of Reformed Churches abroad. For first, to do as the Church of *Geneva* did, the Learned in some other Churches must needs be the more willing, who having used in like manner not the slow and tedious help of proceeding by publique authority, but the peoples more quick endeavour for alteration, in such an exigent I see not well how they could have stayed to deliberate about any other Regiment then that which already was devised to their hands, that which in like case had been taken, that which was easiest to be established without delay, that which was likeliest to content the people by reason of some kind of sway which it giveth them. When therefore the example of one Church was thus at the first almost through a kind of constraint or necessity followed by many, their concurrence in perswasion about some material points belonging to the same polity is not strange. For we are not to marvel greatly, if they which have all done the same thing, do easily imbrace the same opinion as concerning their own doings.

Besides

Besides, mark, I beseech you; that which *Galen* in matter of Philosophie noteth; for the like falleth out even in questions of higher knowledge. It fareth many times with mens opinions, as with rumors and reports. That which credible persons telleth, is easily thought probable by such as are well perswaded of him. But if two, or three, or four, agree all in the same tale, they judge it then to be out of Controversie, and so are many times overtaken, for want of due consideration, either some common cause leading them all into errour or one mans oversight deceiving many through their too much credulitie and easiness of beliefe. Though ten persons be brought to to give testimonie in any cause, yet if the knowledge they have of the thing whereunto they come as witnesses, appear to have growne from some one amongst them, and to have spread it self from hand to hand, they all are in force but as one testimonie. Nor is it otherwise here, where the Daughter Churches do speak their Mothers Dialect; here where so many sing one Song, by reason that he is the Guide of the Quire, concerning whose deserved authoritie, amongst even the gravest Divines, we have already spoken at large. Will ye ask what should move those many Learned to be followers of one mans judgement, no necessitie of Argument forcing them thereunto? Your demand is answered by your selves. Loth ye are to think that they whom ye judge to have attained as sound knowledge in all points of Doctrine as any since the Apostles time, should mistake in Discipline. Such is naturally our affection that whom in great things we mightily admire; in them we are not perswaded willingly that any thing should be amiss. The reason wherof is, for that as dead Flyes putrifie the ointment of the Apothecarier, so a little Folly him that is in estimation for wisdome. This in every profession hath too much authorized the judgement of a few. This with *Germans* hath caused *Luther*, and with many other Churches *Calvin*, to prevail in all things. Yet are we not able to define, whether the Wisdom of that God (who setteth before us in Holy Scripture so many admirable patterns of Vertue, and no one of them without somewhat noted wherein they were culpable, to the end that to him alone it might always be acknowledged, *Thou only art Holy, thou only art Iust*) might not permit those worthy Vessels of his Glory to be in some things blemished with the stain of humain frailtie, even for this cause, lest we should esteem of any man above that which behoveth.

5. Notwithstanding, as though ye were able to say a great deale more then hitherto your Books have revealed to the World, earnest Challengers ye are of triall by some publike Disputation. Wherein if the thing ye crave be no more then only leave to dispute openly about those matters that are in question, the Schooles in Universities (for any thing I know) are open unto you: they have their yearly Acts and Commencements, besides other Disputations both ordinarie and upon occasion, wherein the several parts of our own Ecclesiasticall Discipline are often times offered unto that kind of Examination; the Learnedest of you have been of late years noted seldome or never absent from thence at the time of those greater assemblies; and the favour of proposing therein convenient whatsoever ye can object (which thing my self have known them to grant of Scholasticall courtesie unto Strangers) neither hath (as I think) nor never will (I presume) be denied you. If your Suit be to have some great extraordinarie confluence, in expectation whereof the

Laws

Galen. Clas. lib. de cuju[?] adim. pe at. notitia atque medela.

Petit to the Q. M. Pag. 14.

Eccl. 10. 1,

Their calling for triall by Disputation.

Laws that already are should sleep and have no power over you, till in the hearing of thousands ye all did acknowledg your error, and renounce the further prosecution of your cause; haply, they whose authority is required unto the satisfying of your demand, do think it both dangerous to admit such concourse of divided minds, and unmeet that Laws which being once solemnly established are to exact obedience of all men, and to constraine thereunto, should so far stoop, as to hold themselves in suspence from taking any effect upon you, till some disputer can perswade you to be obedient. A Law is the deed of the whole body politique, whereof if ye judge your selves to be any part, then is the Law even your deed also. And were it reason in things of this quality, to give men audience, pleading for the overthrow of that which their own very deed hath ratified? Laws that have been approved, may be (no man doubted) again repealed, and to that end also disputed against, by the Authors thereof themselves. But this is when the whole doth deliberate what laws each part shall observe, and not when a part refuseth the Laws which the whole hath orderly agreed upon. Notwithstanding, for as much as the cause we maintain is (God be thanked) such as needeth not to shun any trial, might it please them on whose approbation the matter dependeth, to condescend so far unto you in this behalf, I wish heartily that proof were made even by solemn conference in orderly and quiet sort, whether you would your selves be satisfied, or else could by satisfying others, draw them to your peace. Provided alway, first, in asmuch as ye go about to destroy a thing which is in force; and to draw in that which hath not as yet been received; to impose on us that which we think not our selves bound unto, and to overthrow those things whereof we are possessed; that therefore ye are not to claim in any conference, other then the Plaintiffes or opponents part which must consist altogether in proof and confirmation of two things: the one, that our Orders by you condemned we ought to abolish; the other, that yours we are bound to accept in the stead thereof. Secondly, because the questions in Controversie between us are many, if once we descend unto particulars; that for the easier and more orderly proceeding therein, the most general be first discussed, nor any question left off, nor in each question the prosecution of any one Argument given over and another taken in hand, till the issue whereunto by replys and answers both parts are come, be collected, read and acknowledged as well on the one side as on the other, to be the plain conclusion which they are grown untos Thirdly, for avoiding of the manifold inconveniences whereunto ordinary and extemporal Disputes are subject, as also because if ye should singly dispute one by one as every mans own wit did best serve, it might be conceived by the rest, that haply some other would have done more, the chiefest of you do all agree in this action, that whom ye shall then chose your speaker, by him that which is publiquely brought into disputation be acknowledged by all your consents not to be his allegation but yours, such as ye all are agreed upon, and have required him to deliver in all your names: the true copie whereof being taken by a Notary, that a reasonable time be allowed for return of answer unto you in the like form. Fourthly, whereas a number of conferences have been had in other causes with the less effectual success by reason of partial and untrue reports, published afterwards unto the World; that to prevent this evil, there be at the first a solemn Declaration made on both parts of their agreement to have that very Book and no other set abroad, wherein their present authorized Notaries do write those things fully and onely, which being Written and there read, are by their own open testimony acknowledged to be their own. Other circumstances hereunto belonging, whether for the choice of time, place, and language, or for prevention of impertinent and needless speech, or to any end and purpose else, they may be thought on when occasion serveth. In this sort to broach my private conceit for the ordering of a publique action, I should be loth, (albeit I do it not otherwise then under correction of them whose gravity and wisdome ought in such cases to over-rule) but that so venturous boldness I see is a thing novv general, and am thereby of good hope that vvhere all men are licenced to offend, no man vvill shevv himself a sharp Accuser.

6. What success God may give unto any such kind of Conference or Disputation, vve cannot tell. But of this vve are right sure, that Nature, Scripture, and experience it self, have all taught the World to seek for the ending of contentions, by submitting it self unto some judicial and definitive sentence, vvhereunto neither part that contendeth may under any pretence or colour refuse to stand, this must needs be effectual and strong. As for other means without this, they seldome prevail. I would therefore know whether for the ending of the irksome strifes, wherein you and your fellows do stand thus formally divided against the authorized guides of this Church, and the rest of the people subject unto their charge, whether, I say, ye be contented to refer your cause to any other higher judgement then your own ; or else intend to persist and proceed as ye have begun, till your selves can be perswaded to condemne your selves. If your determination be this, we can be but sorry that ye should deserve to be reckoned with such, of whom God himself pronounceth, *The way of peace they have not known.* Ways of peaceable conclusion there are but these two certain : the one, a sentence of judicial decision given by authority thereto appointed within our selves ; the other the like kind of sentence given by a more universal authority. The former of which two ways God himself in the law prescribeth, and his spirit it was which directed the very first Christian Churches in the world to use the latter. The ordinance of God in the Law was this. *If there arise a matter too hard for the in judgement between blood and blood, between plea, &c then shalt thou arise, and go up unto the place which the Lord thy God shall choose, and thou shalt come unto the Priests of the Levites, and unto the Judge that shall be in those days, and ask, and they shall shew thee the sentence of judgment, and thou shalt do according to that thing which they of that place which the Lord hath chosen shew thee ; and thou shalt observe to do according to all that they informe thee ; according to the Law which they shall teach thee, and according to the judgment which they shall tell thee shalt thou do, thou shalt not decline from the thing which they shall shew thee, to the right hand, nor to the left. And that man that will do presumptuously, not harkning unto the Priest (that standeth before the Lord thy God to Minister there) or unto the Judge, that man shall dye, and thou shalt take away evil from Israel.* When there grew in the Church of Christ a question, *Whether the Gentiles beleiving might be saved, although they were not Circumcised after the manner of* Moses, *nor did observe the rest of those legal Rites and Ceremonies whereunto the Jews*

No end of contention, without submission of both parts unto some definitive sentence.

Rom. 3. 17.

Deut. 17. 8.

Acts 15.

K 2

were

were bound : After great diffention and difputation about it, their con clufion in the end was to have it determined by fentence at *Jerufa lem* : which was accordingly done in a Council there affembled for the fame purpofe. Are ye able to alleage any juft and fufficient caufe wherefore abfolutely ye fhould not condefcend in this Controverfie, to have your judgments over-ruled by fome fuch definitive fentence, whether it fall out to be given with or againft you, that fo thefe tedious contentions may ceafe ? Ye will perhaps make anfwer, that being perfwaded already as touching the truth of your caufe, ye are not to harken unto any fentence, no not though Angels fhould define otherwife, as the bleffed Apoftles own example teacheth : again, that Men, yea Councels, may erre ; and that unlefs the judgment given do fatisfie your minds, unlefs it be fuch as ye can by no further argument oppugne, in a word, unlefs you perceive and acknowledge it your felves confonant with Gods Word, to ftand unto it not allowing it, were to fin againft your own confciences. But confider, I befeech you, firft, as touching the Apoftle, how that wherein he was fo refolute and peremptory, our Lord Jefus Chrift made manifeft unto him, even by intuitive Revelation, wherein there was no poffibility of errour : That which you are perfwaded of, ye have it no otherwife then by your own onely probable collection ; and therefore fuch bold affeverations as in him were admirable, fhould in your mouths but argue rafhnefs. God was not ignorant that the Priefts and Judges, whofe fentence in matters of Controverfie he ordained fhould ftand, both might and oftentimes would be deceived in their judgement. Howbeit, better it was in the eye of his underftanding, that fometime an erronious fentence definitive fhould prevaile, till the fame authority perceiving fuch over-fight, might afterwards correct or reverfe it, then that ftrifes fhould have refpit to grow, and not come fpeedily unto fome end. Neither wifh we that men fhould do any thing which in their hearts they are perfwaded they ought not to do, but this perfwafion ought (we fay) to be fully fetled in their hearts, that in litigious and controverfed caufes of fuch quality, the will of God is to have them to do whatfoever the fentence of judicial and final decifion fhall determine, yea, though it feem in their private opinion to fwarve utterly from that which is right : as no doubt many times the fentence amongft the Jews did feem unto one part or other contending ; and yet in this cafe God did then allow them to do that which in their private judgement it feemed (yea and perhaps truly feemed) that the Law did difallow. For if God be not the Author of confufion, but of peace ; then can he not be the Author of our refufal, but of our contentment, to ftand unto fome definitive fentence, without which almoft impoffible it is, that either we fhould avoid confufion, or ever hope to attain peace. To fmall purpofe had the Councel of *Jerufalem* been affembled, if once their determination being fet down, men might afterwards have defended their former opinions. When therefore they had given their definitive fentence, all controverfie was at an end. Things were difputed before they came to be determined ; men afterwards were not to difpute any longer, but to obey. The fentence of judgment finifhed their ftrife, which their difputes before judgement could not do. This was ground fufficient for any reafonable mans confcience to build the duty of obedience upon, whatfoever his own opinion were as

touching

touching the matter before in queſtion. So full of wilfulneſs and ſelf-liking is our nature, that without ſome definitive ſentence, which being given may ſtand, and a neceſſity of ſilence on both ſides afterward impoſed; ſmall hope there is that ſtrifes thus far proſecuted, will in ſhort time quickly end. Now it were in vain to ask you whether ye could be content that the ſentence of any Court already erected, ſhould be ſo far authorized as that among the Jews eſtabliſhed by God himſelf, for the determining of all Controverſies: *That man which will do preſumptuouſly, not hearkning unto the Prieſt that ſtandeth before the Lord to miniſter there, nor unto the Judge, let him die;* Ye have given us already to underſtand what your opinion is in part concerning her ſacred Majeſties Court of high Comiſſion, the nature whereof is the ſame with that amongſt the Jews albeit the power be not ſo great. The other way haply may like you better, becauſe Maſter *Beza* in his laſt Book ſave one written about theſe matters, profeſſeth himſelf to be now wearie of ſuch combats and encounters, whether by word or writing, in as much as he findeth that Controverſies thereby are made but Brawls; and therefore wiſheth *that in ſome common lawfull aſſembly of Churches, all theſe ſtrifes may at once be decided.* Shall there be then in the mean while no *doings?* Yes. There are the weightier matters of the Law, *judgement and mercie and fidelitie.* These things we ought to do; and theſe things, while we contend about leſs, we leave undone. Happier are they, whom the Lord, when he commeth, ſhall find doing in theſe things, then diſputing about Doctors, Elders and Deacons. Or if there be no remedy but ſomewhat needs ye muſt do which may tend to the ſetting forward of your Diſcipline; do that which wiſemen, who think ſome Statute of the Realme more fit to be repealed then to ſtand in force, are accuſtomed to do before they come to Parliament where the place of enacting is; that is to ſay, ſpend the time in re-examining more duly your cauſe, and in more throughly conſidering of that which ye labour to overthrow. As for the Orders which are eſtabliſhed, ſith equitie and reaſon, the Law of nature, God and man, do all favour that which is in being, till orderly judgement of deciſion be given againſt it, it is but Iuſtice to exact of you, and perverſneſs in you it ſhould be to denie thereunto your willing obedience. Not that I judge it a thing allowable for men to obſerve thoſe Laws, which in their hearts they are ſtedfaſtly perſwaded to be againſt the Law of God: but your perſwaſion in this caſe ye are all bound for the time to ſuſpend, and in otherwiſe doing, ye offend againſt God, by troubling his Church without any juſt or neceſſary cauſe. Be it that there are ſome reaſons inducing you to think hardly of our laws: Are thoſe reaſons demonſtrative, are they neceſſary, or but meer probabilities only? An argument neceſſary and demonſtrative is ſuch, as being propoſed unto any man and underſtood, the mind cannot chooſe but inwardly aſſent. Any one ſuch reaſon diſchargeth I grant the conſcience, and ſetteth it at full libertie. For the publike approbation given by the body of this whole Church unto thoſe things which are eſtabliſhed, doth make it but probable that they are good: and therefore unto a neceſſary proof that they are not good, it muſt give place. But if the ſkilfulleſt amongſt you can ſhew that all the Books ye have hitherto written be able to afford any one argument of this nature, let the inſtance be given. As for probabilities, what thing was there ever ſet down ſo agreeable with ſound reaſon, but ſome

probable

Praef. c a&. de Excom. & Presbyt.

Mat. 23, 23.

probable fhevv againſt it might be made ? is it meet that vvhen publiquely things are received and have taken place, general obedience thereunto ſhall ceaſe to be exacted, in caſe this or that private perſon led vvith
ſome probable conceit, ſhould make open proteſtation, *Peter* or *John*
diſallow them, and pronounce them naught ? In vvhich caſe your anſvver
vvill be, that concerning the Lavvs of our Church, they are not onely
condemned in the opinion of a *private man, but of thouſands,* yea and
even *of thoſe amongſt which divers are in publique charge and authority.* As
though vvhen publique conſent of the vvhole hath eſtabliſhed any thing,
every mans judgement being thereunto compared vvere not private, hovv-
ſoever his calling be to ſome kind of publique charge. So that of peace
and quietneſs there is not any vvay poſſible unleſs the probable voice of
every intire ſociety or body politique, over-rule all private of like nature
in the ſame body. Which thing effectually proveth, that God being Author of peace and not of confuſion in the Church, muſt needs
be Author of thoſe mens peaceable reſolutions vvho concerning theſe
things have determined vvith themſelves to think and do as the Church
they are of decreeth, till they ſee neceſſary cauſe enforcing them to
the contrary.

T.C l.3.p.171

The matter
contained in
theſe eight
Books.

7. Nor is mine own intent any other in theſe ſeveral books of diſcourſe,
then to make it appear unto you ; that for the Eccleſiaſtical Laws of this
Land, we are led by great reaſon to obſerve them and ye by no neceſſity
bound to impugne them. It is no part of my ſecret meaning to draw you
hereby into hatred, or to ſet upon the face of this cauſe any fairer gloſs
then the naked truth doth afford : but my whole endeavour is to reſolve
the conſcience, and to ſhew as neer as I can what in the controverſie the
heart is to think, if it will follow the light of ſound and ſincere judgement, without either cloud of prejudice or miſt of paſſionate affection.
Wherefore ſeeing that Laws, Ordinances in particular, whether and
ſuch as we obſerve, or ſuch as your ſelves would have eſtabliſhed, when
the mind doth ſift and examine them, it muſt needs have often recourſe
to a number of doubts and queſtions about the nature, kinds, and qualities of Laws in general, whereof unleſs it be throughly informed, there
will appear no certainty to ſtay our perſwaſion upon : I have for that cauſe
ſet down in the firſt place an Introduction on both ſides needful to be conſidered : Declaring therein what Law is, how different kinds of Laws
there are, and what force they are of according unto each kind. This
done, becauſe ye ſuppoſe the Laws for which ye ſtrive are found in Scripture, but thoſe not, againſt which we ſtrive ; and upon this ſurmiſe are
drawn to hold it as the very main pillar of your whole cauſe, that *Scripture*
ought to be the onely rule of all our actions, and conſequently that the
Church-orders which we obſerve being not commanded in Scripture, are
offenſive and diſpleaſant unto God : I have ſpent the ſecond book in ſift-
ing of this point, which ſtandeth with you for the firſt and chiefeſt principle whereon ye build. Whereunto the next in degree is, that as God will
have always a Church upon earth while the World doth continue, and that
Church ſtand in need of Government, of which Government it behoveth
himſelf to be both the Author and Teacher : So it cannot ſtand with duty,
that man ſhould ever preſume in any wiſe to change and alter the ſame; and
therefore, *that in ſcripture there muſt of neceſſity be found ſome particular form*
of Eccleſiaſtical Polity, the Laws whereof admit not any kind of alteration.

The

The firſt three Books being thus ended, the fourth proceedeth from the general grounds and foundations of your cauſe, unto your general accuſations againſt us, as having in the Orders of our Church (for ſo you pretend) *corrupted the right form of Church-polity with manifold Popiſh rites and Ceremonies, which certain reformed Churches have baniſhed from amongſt them, and have thereby given us ſuch example as* (you think) *we ought to follow.* This your aſſertion hath herein drawn us to make ſearch, whether theſe be juſt exceptions againſt the cuſtomes of our Church, when ye plead that they are the ſame which the Church of Rome hath, or that they are not the ſame which ſome other Reformed Churches have deviſed. Of thoſe four Books which remain, and are beſtowed about the ſpecialities of that cauſe which lyeth in Controverſie, the firſt examineth the cauſes by you alledged; wherefore the publique duties of Chriſtian Religion, as our Prayers, our Sacraments and the reſt, ſhould not be ordered in ſuch ſort as with us they are; nor that power whereby the perſons of men are conſecrated unto the Miniſtry, be diſpoſed of in ſuch manner as the Laws of this Church do allow. The ſecond and third are concerning the power of Juriſdiction: the one, whether Lay-men, ſuch as your governing Elders are, ought in all Congregations for ever to be inveſted with that power; the other, whether Biſhops may have that power over other Paſtors, and therewithal that honour which with us they have. And becauſe beſides the power of Order which all conſecrated perſons have, and the power of Juriſdiction which neither they all, nor they onely have, there is a third power, a power of Eccleſiaſticall Dominion, communicable, as we think, unto perſons not Eccleſiaſtical, and moſt fit to be reſtrained unto the Prince our Soveraign Commander over the whole body politique. The eight Book we have allotted unto this queſtion, and have ſifted therein your objections againſt thoſe preeminences Royal which thereunto appertain. Thus have I laid before you the brief of theſe my Travailes; and preſented under your view the limmes of that cauſe litigious between us: the whole intire body whereof being thus compact, it ſhall be no troubleſome thing for any man to find each particular Controverſies reſting place, and the coherence it hath with thoſe things, either on which it dependeth or which depend on it.

8. The caſe ſo ſtanding therefore my brethren, as it doth, the wiſedom of Governours ye muſt not blame, in that they further alſo forecaſting the manifold ſtrange and dangerous innovations, which are more then likely to follow, if your Diſcipline ſhould take place, have for that cauſe thought it hitherto a part of their duty to withſtand your endevours that way: the rather, for that they have ſeen already ſome ſmall beginnings of the fruits thereof, in them, who concurring with you in judgement about the neceſſity of that Diſcipline, have adventured without more ado, to ſeperate themſelves from the reſt of the Church, and to put your ſpeculations in execution. Theſe mens haſtines the warier ſorts of you doth not commend, ye wiſh they had held themſelves longer in, and not ſo dangerouſly flown abroad before the feathers of the cauſe had been grown; their errour with merciful termes ye reprove, naming them in great commiſeration of mind, your *poor brethren.* They on the contrary ſide more bitterly accuſe you as their *falſe Brethren*, and againſt you they plead, ſaying: From your breaſts it is, that we have ſucked thoſe things, which when ye delivered unto us, ye termed that heavenly,

ſincere,

How juſt cauſe there is to fear the manifold dangerous events likely to enſue upon this intended reformation, if it did take place.

1 Pet. 2, 2.

Pſal 5, 13.

sincere, and wholeſome milk of Gods Word, howſoever ye now abhor as poyſon that which the vertue thereof hath wrought and brought forth in us. Ye ſometime our companions, guides, and familiars, with whom we have had moſt ſvveet conſultations, are novv become our profeſſed adverſaries, becauſe vve think the Statute-Congregations in *England* to be no true Chriſtian Churches ; becauſe vve have ſevered our ſelves from them, and becauſe vvithout their leave or licence that are in Civil Authority, vve have ſecretly framed our ovvn Churches according to the platform of the Word of God. For of that point betvveen you and us there is no controverſie. Alas, vvhat vvould ye have us to do ? at ſuch time as ye vvere content to accept us in the number of your ovvn, your teaching we heard, vve read your Writings : and though vve vvould yet able vve are not to forget vvith vvhat zeal ye have ever profeſt, that in the Engliſh Congregations (for ſo many of them as be ordered according unto their own Laws,) the very publique Service of God is fraught, as touching matter, with heaps of intolerable pollutions, and as concerning form, borrowed from the Shop of Antichriſt ; hateful both ways in the eys of the moſt Holy : the kind of their Government by

Pref. againſt D. Biſher.

Biſhops and Archbiſhops, Antichriſtian, that Diſcipline which Chriſt hath eſſentially tied, that is to ſay, ſo united unto his Church, that we cannot account it really to be his Church which hath not in it the ſame Diſcipline, that very Diſcipline no leſs there deſpiſed, then in the higheſt throne of Antichriſt ; all ſuch parts of the Word as do any way concern that Diſcipline, no leſs unſoundly taught and interpreted by all authorized Engliſh Paſtors, then by Antichriſts factors themſelves ; at Baptiſme Croſſing, at the Supper of the Lord kneeling, at both a number of other the moſt notorious badges of Antichriſtian recogniſance uſual. Being moved with theſe and the like your effectual diſcourſes, whereunto we gave moſt attentive ear, till they entred even into our ſouls, and were as fire within our boſomes ; we thought we might hereof be bold to conclude, that ſith no ſuch Antichriſtian Synagogue may be accompted a true Church of Chriſt, ye by accuſing all Congregations ordered according to the Laws of *England* as Antichriſtian, did mean to condemn thoſe Congregations, as not being any of them werthy the name of a true Chriſtian Church. Ye tell us now it is not your meaning. But what meant your often threatnings of them, who profeſſing themſelves the Inhabitants of mount *Sion*, were to loth to depart wholly as they ſhould out of *Babylon* ? Whereat our hearts being fearfully troubled, we durſt not, we durſt not continue longer ſo neer her confines, leſt her plagues might ſuddenly overtake us, before we did ceaſe to be partakers with her ſins : for ſo we could not not chuſe but acknowledge with grief that we were, when they doing evill we by our preſence in their aſſemblies ſeemed to like thereof, or at leaſt wiſe not ſo earneſtly to diſlike, as became men heartily zealous of Gods glory. For adventuring to erect the Diſcipline of Chriſt without the leave of the Chriſtian Magiſtrate, haply ye may condemn us as fools, in that we hazard thereby our eſtates and perſons, further then you which are that way more wiſe think neceſſary : but of any offence or ſin therein committed againſt God, with what conſcience can you accuſe us, when your own poſitions are, that the things we obſerve ſhould every of them be dearer unto us then ten thouſand lives ; that they are the peremptory Commandements of God ; that no mortal man can difpence with them, and that the Magiftrate grie voufly finneth in not conftraining thereunto ? Will ye blame any man for doing that of his own accord , which all men fhould be compelled to do that are not willing of themfelves ? When God commandeth, fhall we anfwer that we will obey, if fo be *Cæfar* will grant us leave ? Is Difcipline an Eccle-fiaftical matter or a civil ? If an Ecclefiaftical , it muft of neceffity belong to the duty of the Minifter. And the Minifter (ye fay) holdeth all his Authority of doing whatfoever belongeth unto the fpiritual charge of the Houfe of God , even immediately from God himfelf, without dependen-cy upon any Magiftrate. Whereupon it followeth, as we fuppofe , that the hearts of the people being willing to be under the Scepter of Chrift, the Minifter of God , into whofe hands the Lord himfelf hath put that Scepter , is without all excufe , if thereby he guide them not. Nor do we find that hitherto greatly ye have difliked thofe Churches abroad where the people vvith direction of their godly Minifters , have even againft the vvill of the Magiftrate brought in either the Doctrine or Difcipline of Jefus Chrift. For vvhich caufe vve muft novv think the very fame thing of you, vvhich our Saviour did fometime utter con-cerning falfehearted Scribes and Pharifes, *They fay and do not.* Thus the foolifh *Barrowift* deriveth his fchifme by vvay of conclufion, as to him it feemeth, directly and plainly out of your principles. Him there-fore vve leave to be fatisfied by you from vvhom he hath fprung. And if fuch by your ovvn acknovvledgement be perfous dangerous, al-though as yet the alterations vvhich they have made are of fmall and tender grovvth ; the changes likely to infue throughout all ftates and vo-cations vvithin this Land , in cafe your defire fhould take place, muft be thought upon. Firft concerning the fupreme povver of the higheft, they are no fmall prerogatives, vvhich novv thereunto belonging the form of your difcipline vvill conftrain it to refigne, as in the laft book of this Trea-tife vve have fhevved at large. Again it may juftly be feared, whether our Englifh Nobility, when the matter came in trial, would content-edly fuffer themfelves to be always at the call, and to ftand to the fentence of a number of mean perfons, affifted with the prefence of their poor Teacher , a man (as fometimes it happeneth) though better able to fpeak , yet little or no whit apter to judge then the reft ; from whom be their dealing never fo abfurd (unlefs it be by way of com-plaint to a Synod) no appeal may be made unto any one of higher power, in afmuch as the order of your Difcipline admitteth no ftanding in equality of Courts, no fpiritual Judge to have any ordinary fuperi-our on earth, but as many Supremacies as there are Parifhes and feveral Congregations. Neither is it altogether without caufe that fo many do fear the overthrow of all learning, as a threatned fequele of this your intended Difcipline. For if the *worlds prefervation* depend upon *the multitude of the wife* ; and of that fort the number hereafter be not like-ly to wax over-great, when that wherewith the fon of *Syrach* profeffeth himfelf *at the heart grieved*) *men of underftanding are* already fo *little fet by* : how fhould their minds, whom the love of fo precious a Jewel fil-leth with fecret jealoufie even in regard of the leaft things which may any way hinder the flourifhing eftate thereof, chufe but mifdoubt left this Difcipline, which always you match with Divine doctrine as her natural and true fifter , be found unto all kinds of knowledge a ftepmother ;

L   feeing

Mat 23, 3.

Sap. 6, 24.

Eccl. 16, 21.

seeing that the greateſt wordly hopes, which are propoſed unto the chiefeſt kind of learning, ye ſeek utterly to extirpate as weeds ; and
have grounded your platform on ſuch propoſitions, as do after a ſort undermine thoſe moſt renowned habitations, where, through the goodneſs of
Almighty God, all commendable Arts and Sciences are with exceeding
great induſtry hitherto (and ſo may they for ever continue) ſtudied, proceeded in, and profeſt? To charge you as purpoſely bent to the overthrow
of that wherein ſo many of you have attained no ſmall perfection, were
injurious. Onely therefore i wiſh that your ſelves did well conſider how
oppoſite certain of your poſitions are unto the ſtate of Collegiate ſocieties,
whereon the two Univerſities conſiſt. Thoſe degrees which their ſtatutes
bind them to take, are by your Laws taken away, your ſelves who have
ſought them ye ſo excuſe, as that ye would have men to think ye judge
them not allowable, but tolerable onely, and to be born with, for ſome
help which ye find in them unto the furtherance of your purpoſes, till the
corrupt eſtate of the Church may be better reformed. Your Laws forbidding Eccleſiaſtical perſons utterly the exerciſe of Civil power, muſt
needs deprive the Heads and Maſters in the ſame Colledges of all ſuch
authority as now they exerciſe, either at home, by puniſhing the faults
of thoſe, who not as children to their parents by the law of Nature, but
altogether by civil authority are ſubject unto them, or abroad, by keeping Courts amongſt their Tenants. Your laws making permanent inequality amongſt Miniſters, a thing repugnant to the Word of God, enforce
thoſe Colledges, the Seniors whereof are all or any part of them Miniſters under the government of a Maſter in the ſame vocation, to chooſe,
as oft as they meet together, a new Preſident. For if ſo ye judge it
neceſſary to do in Synods, for the avoiding of permanent inequality
amongſt Miniſters, the ſame cauſe muſt needs even in theſe Collegiate
aſſemblies enforce the like. Except peradventure ye mean to avoid all
ſuch abſurdities, by diſſolving thoſe corporations, and by bringing the
Univerſities unto the forme of the School of *Geneva*. Which thing men
the rather are inclined to look for, in as much as the Miniſtery, whereinto their founders with ſingular providence have by the ſame Statutes
Humb. Motion
to the L.L. p. 50 appointed them neceſſarily to enter at a certain time, your Laws bind
them much more neceſſarily to forbear, till ſome Pariſh abroad call for
them. Your opinion concerning the Law Civil is, that the knowledge
thereof might be ſpared, as a thing which this Land doth not need. Pro-
feſſors in that kind being few, ye are the bolder to ſpurn at them, and
not to diſſemble your minds as concerning their removal : in whoſe
ſtudies although my ſelf have not much been converſant, nevertheleſs exceeding great cauſe I ſee there is to wiſh that thereunto more encouragement were given, as well for the ſingular treaſures of wiſedome therein
contained, as alſo for the great uſe we have thereof both in deciſion of
certain kinds of cauſes ariſing dayly within our ſelves, and eſpecially for
commerce with Nations abroad, whereunto that knowledge is moſt requiſite. The reaſons wherewith ye would perſwade that Scripture is the
onely rule to frame all our actions by, are in every reſpect as effectual
for proof that the ſame is the onely Law whereby to determine all our
Civil controverſies. And then what doth let, but that as thoſe men
may have their deſire, who franckly broach it already that the work of
Reformation will never be perfect, till the Law of Jeſus Chriſt be received

ved alone; so Pleaders and Councellors may bring their Books of com-   Act. 19.19.
mon-Law, and bestow them as the Students of curious and needless arts
did theirs in the Apostles time ? I leave them to scan how far those words
of yours may reach, wherein ye declare that whereas now many Houses   Act. 19.19.
lye wast through inordinate suits of Law, *This one thing will shew the ex-*   Humb. Met.
cellency of Discipline for the wealth of the Realm, and quiet of Subjects, Pag. 74.
that the Church is to censure such a partie who is apparently troublesome
and contentious, and without Reasonable Cause upon a meer will and stomack
doth vex and molest his Brother, and trouble the Country. For mine own
part I do not see but that it might very well agree with your own principles, if your discipline were fully planted, even to send out your Writs
of Surcease unto all Courts of *England* besides, for the most things handled in them. A great deal further I might proceed and descend lower.
But for as much as against all these and the like difficultys, your answer is,
That we ought to search what things are consonant to Gods will, not
which be most for our own ease; and therefore that your Discipline, be- Counterp.
ing (for such is your errour) the absolute commandement of Almighty Pag. 108.
God it must be received, although the World by receiving it should be
clean turned upside-down; herein lieth the greatest danger of all.
For whereas the name of Divine Authority is used to countenance these
things, which are not the Commandements of God, but your own erroneous collections; on him ye must father whatsoever ye shall afterwards
be led, either to do in withstanding the Adversaries of your cause, or to
think in maintenance of your doings. And what this may be God doth
know. In such kinds of error, the mind once imagining it self to seek
the execution of Gods will, laboureth forth-with to remove both things
and persons, which any way hinder it from taking place; and in such cases
if any strange or new thing seem requisite to be done, a strange and new
opinion concerning the lawfulness thereof, is withal received and broached
under countenance of divine authority. One example herein may serve
for many, to shew that false opinions touching the will of God to have
things done, are wont to bring forth mighty and violent practices against
the hinderances of them; and those practices new opinions more pernici- Mat. 15.13.
ous then the first, yea, most extreamely sometimes opposite to that
which the first did seem to intend. Where the people took upon them the
reformation of the Church by casting out Popish superstition, they having received from their Pastors a general instruction that whatsoever the
heavenly Father hath not planted, must be rooted out, proceeded in some
forrein places so far, that down went oratories and the very Temples of
God themselves. For as they chanced to take the compasse of their Commission stricter or larger, so their dealings were accordingly more or less
moderate. Amongst others there sprang up presently one kind of men,
with whose zeal and forwardness the rest being compared, were thought
to be marvellous cold and dull. These grounding themselves on Rules
more general; that whatsoever the Law of Christ commandeth not,
thereof Antichrist is the author; and that whatsoever Antichrist or his
adherents did in the world; the true professors of Christ are to undo; found
out many things more then others had done, the extirpation whereof was Guy de Bres
in their conceit as necessary as of any thing before removed. Hereupon con relateur
they secretly made their doleful complaints every where as they went, des Anabaptists,
that albeit the world did begin to professe some dislike of that which was Pag. 4.

      evil

evil in the kingdome of Darknefs, yet fruits worthy of a true repentance were not feen ; and that if men did repent as they ought , they muft endevour to purge the truth of all manner of evil , to the end there might follow a new World afterward , wherein righteoufnefs onely fhould dwell. Private repentance they faid muft appear by every mans fafhioning his own life contrary unto the cuftome and order of this prefent World, both in greater things and in lefs. To this purpofe they had always in their mouthes thofe greater things , Charity, Faith , the true fear of God, the Crofs , the mortification of the flefh. All their exhortations were to fet light of the things in this World , to account riches and honours vanity, and in token thereof not onely to feek neither , but if men were poffeffors of both, even to caft away the one and refigne the other, that all men might fee their unfained converfion unto Chrift. They were folliciters of men to fafts , to often meditations of heavenly things, and as it were conferences in fecret with God by prayers , not framed according to the frozen manner of the World , but expreffing fuch fervent defires as might even force God to harken unto them. Where they found men in diet, attire, furniture of Houfe , or any other way obfervers of civility and decent order, fuch they reprove as being carnally and earthly minded. Every word otherwife then feverely and fadly uttered , feemed to pierce like a fword thorow them. If any man were pleafant , their manner was prefently with fighes to repeat thofe words of our Saviour Chrift : *Wo be to you which now laugh, for ye fhall lament.* So great was their delight to be always in trouble , that fuch as did quietly lead their lives, they judged of all other men to be in moft dangerous cafe. They fo much affected to crofs the ordinary cuftome in every thing; that when other mens ufe was to put on better attire , they would be fure to fhew themfelves openly abroad in worfe : the ordinary names of the days in the Week they thought it a kind of prophanefs to ufe , and therefore accuftomed themfelves to make no other diftinctions then by numbers, The Firft, Second , Third day From this they proceed unto publique Reformation , firft Ecclefiaftical, and then Civil. Touching the former , they boldly avouched, that themfelves onely had the Truth, which thing upon peril of their lives they would at all times defend ; and that fince the Apoftles lived , the fame was never before in all points fincerely taught. Wherefore that things might again be brought to that ancient integrity which *Jefus Chrift* by his word requireth , they began to controll the Minifters of the Gofpel for attributing fo much force and Vertue unto the Scriptures of God read , whereas the truth was, that when the Word is faid to engender Faith in the heart, and to convert the foul of man, or to work any fuch fpirituall divine effect; thefe fpeeches are not thereunto appliable as it is read or Preached, but but as it is ingrafted in us by the power of the Holy Ghoft opening the eyes of our underftanding , and fo revealing the myfteries of God, according to that which *Jeremy* promifed before fhould be , faying , *I will put my Law in their inward parts , and I will write it in their hearts.* The Book of God they notwithftanding for the moft part fo admired, that other difputation againft their opinions then onely by allegation of Scripture they would not hear ; befides it, they thought no other Writings in the World fhould be ftudied ; in fo much as one of their great Prophets exhorting them to caft away all refpects unto humane Writiting , fo far

Pag. 5.

Pag. 16,
p. 118, 119

p. 111, 1 0,

P. 114,
Luke 6. 1[.]

F. 117.

P. 5.

Ier. 31. 3[.]

p. 17,
P. 17.

to

to his motion they condescended, that as many as had any Books save the holy Bible in their custody, they brought and set them publiquely on fire. When they and their Bibles were alone together, what strange phantastical opinion soever at any time entred into their heads, their use was to think the spirit taught it them. Their phrensies concerning our Saviours incarnation, the state of souls departed, and such like, are things needless to be rehearsed. And for as much as they were of the same Suit with those of whom the Apostle speaketh, saying, *They are still learning, but never attain to the knowledge of truth*, it was no marvail to see them every day broach some new thing, not heard of before. Which restless levity they did interpret to be their growing to spirituall perfection, and a proceeding from faith to faith. The differences amongst them grew by this mean in a manner infinite, so that scarcely was there found any one of them, the forge of whose brain was not possest with some speciall mystery. Whereupon although their mutuall contentions were most fiercely prosecuted amongst themselves, yet when they came to defend the cause common to them all against the Adversaries of their faction, they had ways to lick one another whole, the sounder in his own perswasion, excusing *The dear Brethren*, which were not so far enlightned, and professing a charitable hope of the mercy of God towards them, notwithstanding their swarving from him in some things. Their own Ministers they highly magnified, as men whose Vocation was from God: the rest their manner was to terme disdainfully *Scribes* and *Pharises*, to account their calling an humane Creature, and to detain the people as much as might be from hearing them. As touching Sacraments, Baptisme administred in the Church of *Rome*, They Judged to be but an execrable Mockery and no Baptisme; both because the Ministers thereof in the Papacy are wicked Idolaters, lewd Persons, Theeves and Murderers, cursed Creatures, ignorant Beasts; and also for that to baptize is a proper action belonging unto none but the Church of Christ, whereas *Rome* is Antichrists Synagogue. The custome of using God-fathers and God-mothers at Christnings they scorned. Baptisme of Infants, although confest by themselves to have been continued even sithence the very Apostles own times, yet they altogether condemned: partly, because sundry errours are of no less antiquity; and partly, for that there is no Commandement in the Gospel of Christ, which saith, *Baptise Infants*; but he contrariwise in saying, *Go Preach and Baptize*, doth appoint that the Minister of Baptisme shall in that action first administer Doctrine, and then Baptisme, as also in saying, *Whosoever doth beleeve and is baptised*, he appointeth that the party to whom Baptisme is administred shall first believe, and then be baptized; to the end that beleeving may go before this Sacrament in the receiver, no otherwise then preaching in the Giver, sith equal in both, the Law of Christ declareth not onely what things are required, but also in what order they are required. The Eucharist they received (pretending our Lord and Saviours example) after Supper: and for avoyding all those impieties which have been grounded upon the mysticall words of Christ, *This is my body*, *This is my blood*, they thought it not safe to mention either body or blood in that Sacrament, but rather to abrogate both, and to use no words but these, *Take, eat, declare the death of our Lord: Drink, shew forth our Lords death.* In Rites and Ceremonies

2. Tim. 3. 7.

p. 65.

p. 6.

p. 135.

p. 25.

p. 71.

p. 124.

p. 764.

p. 748.

p. 512.

p. 513.

N. 722.

p. 725.—

p. 658.

p. 38.

p. 121.

nies their profeffion was hatred of all conformity with the Church of *Rome* : for which caufe they would rather indure any torment then obferve the folemn feftivals which others did, in as much as Antichrift (they faid) was the firft inventer of them. The pretended end of their civil reformation, was that Chrift might have dominion over all ; that all Crowns and Scepters might be thrown down at his feet, that no other might raign over Chriftian men but he ; no Regiment keep them in aw but his Difcipline ; amongft them no Sword at all be carried befides his, the Sword of fpiritual Excommunication. For this caufe they laboured with all their might in over-turning the feats of Magiftracy, becaufe Chrift hath faid, *Kings of Nations* ; in abolifhing the execution of Juftice, becaufe Chrift hath faid, *Refift not evil* ; in forbidding Oaths the neceffary means of judicial tryal, becaufe Chrift hath faid, *Swear not at all* : finally, in bringing in community of goods, becaufe Chrift by his Apoftles hath given the World fuch example to the end that men might excel one another, not in wealth the Pillar of fecular authority, but in vertue. Thefe men at the firft were onely pittied in their errour, and not much withftood by any ; the great Humility, Zeal, and Devotion, which appeared to be in them, was in all mens opinion a pledge of their harmlefs meaning. The hardeft that men of found underftanding conceived of them, was but this, *O quam honefta voluntate miferi errant ? With how good a meaning thefe poor fouls do evil* : *Luther* made requeft unto *Frederick* Duke of *Saxonie*, that within his Dominion they might be favourably dealt with and fpared, for that (their errour exempted) they feemed otherwife right good men. By means of which merciful toleration they gathered ftrength, much more then was fafe for the State of the Common-wealth wherein they lived. They had their fecret corner-meetings and affemblies in the night, the people flocked unto them by thoufands. The means whereby they both allured and retayned fo great multitudes, were moft effectual ; firft, a wonderful fhew of zeal towards God, wherewith they feemed to be even rapt in every thing they fpake : fecondly, an hatred of fin, and a fingular love of integrity, which men did think to be much more then ordinary in them, by reafon of the cuftome which they had to fill the eares of the people with Invectives againft their authorized Guides as well fpiritual as Civil : Thirdly the bountiful relief wherewith they eafed the broken eftate of fuch needy Creatures, as were in that refpect the more apt to be drawn away : Fourthly, a tender compaffion which they were thought to take upon the miferies of the common fort, over whofe heads their manner was even to poure down fhowres of tears in complayning that no refpect was had unto them, that their goods were devoured by wicked Cormorants, their perfons had in contempt, all liberty both Temporal and Spiritual taken from them ; that it was high time for God now to hear their grones, and to fend them deliverance : Laftly, a cunning flight which they had to ftroke and fmooth up the minds of their Followers, as well by appropriating unto them all the favourable Titles, the good words, and the gracious promifes in Scripture; as alfo by cafting the contrary always on the heads of fuch as were fevered from that retinue. Whereupon, the peoples common acclamation unto fuch deceivers was: Thefe are verily the men of God, thefe are his true and fincere

cere

p. 841.
p. 849.

P. 40.

Lactant. de Iuftit. lib. 5. ca. 19

p. 6.

p. 420.

P. 55.

p. 6.
P. 7.

P. 7.

cere Prophets. If any such prophet or man of God did suffer by order of
Law condign and deserved punishment; were it for Fellony, Rebellion,
Murder, or what else: the people (so strangely were their hearts inchanted)
as though blessed St. *Stephen* had been again Martyred, did lament that
God took away his most dear servants from them. In all these things being p. 27.
fully perswaded, that what they did, it was Obedience to the will of God,
and that all men should do the like; there remayned after speculation,
practice, whereby the whole World thereunto (if it were possible)
might be framed. This they saw could not be done, but with mighty op- p. 6.
position and resistance: against which to strengthen themselves, they secretly entred into a League of Association. And peradventure considering, that although they were many, yet long Wars would in time wast
them out; they began to think whether it might not be that God would
have them do for their speedy and mighty increase, the same which sometime Gods own chosen people, the people of *Israel* did. Glad and fain
they were to have it so: which very desire was it self apt to breed both an
opinion of possibility, and a willingness to gather Arguments of likelihood
that so God himself would have it. Nothing more cleer unto their seeming, then that a new *Jerusalem* being often spoken of in Scripture, they
undoubtedly were themselves that new *Jerusalem*, and the old did by way
of a certain figurative resemblance signifie what they should both be and
do. Here they drew in a Sea of matter, by amplifying all things unto their
own Company, which are any where spoken concerning divine favours
and benefits bestowed upon the old Common-wealth of *Israel*; concluding, that as *Israel* was delivered out of *Egypt*, so they spiritually out of the
Egypt of this Worlds servile thraldom unto Sin and Superstition; as *Israel*
was to root out the Idolatrous Nations, and to plant instead of them a
people which feared God; so the same Lords good will and pleasure was
now, that these new *Israelites* should under the conduct of other
Josuaes, *Sampsons* and *Gedeons*, performe a work no less miraculous in
casting out violently the wicked from the Earth, and establishing the
Kingdome of Christ with perfect liberty: and therefore as the cause why
the Children of *Israel* took unto one man many Wives, might be, lest
the casualties of War should any way hinder the promise of God concerning their multitude from taking effect in them; so it was not unlike
that for the necessary propagation of Christs Kingdom under the Gospel,
the Lord was content to allow as much. Now whatsoever they did in
such sort collect out of Scripture, when they came to justifie or perswade
it unto others, all was the heavenly fathers' appointment, his commandement, his will and charge. Which thing is the very point, in regard whereof I have gathered this declaration. For my purpose herein is to shew
that when the minds of men are once erroniously perswaded, that it is
the will of God to have those things done which they Fancy; their opinions are as Thorns in their sides, never suffering them to take rest till
they have brought their speculations into practice: the lets and impediments of which practice their restless desire and study to remove,
leadeth them every day forth by the hand into other more dangerous
opinions, sometimes quite and clean contrary to their first pretended
meanings: so as what will grow out of such errors as go masked under
the cloke of divine authority, impossible it is, that ever the wit of man
should imagine; till time have brought forth the fruits of them: for
which

which cause it behoveth Wisdom to fear the sequels thereof, even beyond all apparent cause of fear. These men, in whose mouths at the first, sounded nothing but onely mortification of the flesh, were come at the length to think they might lawfully have their six or seven Wives a piece: they which at the first thought Judgement and Justice it self to be mercilefs cruelty ; accompted at the length their own hands sanctified with being imbrued in Christian blood : they who at the first were wont to beat down all Dominion, and to urge against poor Constables, *Kings of Nations* ; had at the length both Confels and Kings of their own erection amongst themselves : finally, they which could not brook at the first that any man should feek, no not by law, the recovery of goods injurioufly taken or with-held from him, were grown at the last to think they could not offer unto God more acceptable facrifice, then by turning their Adverfaries clean out of house and home, and by inriching themselves with all kind of fpoile and pillage ; which thing being laid to their charge, they had in a readinefs their anfwer, that now the time was come, when according to our Saviours promife, *The meek ones muft inherit the earth*, and that their title hereunto was the fame which the righteous *Israelites* had unto the goods of the wicked *Egyptians*. Wherefore fith the World hath had in thefe men fo frefh experience, how dangerous fuch active errors are, it muft not offend you though touching the fequel of your prefent mifperfwafions much more be doubted, then your own intents and purpofes do haply aim at. And yet your words already are fomewhat, when ye affirm that your Paftors, Doctors, Elders and Deacons, ought to be in this Church of *England, Whether her Majefty and our State will or no*, when for the animating of your confederates, ye publifh the mufters which ye have made of your own Bands, and proclaim them to amount to I know not how many thoufands ; when ye threaten, that fith neither your fuits to the Parliament, nor fupplications to our convocation-houfe, neither your defences by Writing, nor challenges of Difputation in behalf of that caufe are able to prevaile, we muft blame our felves, if to bring in difcipline fome fuch means hereafter be ufed as fhall caufe all our hearts to ake. *That things doubtful are to be conftrued in the better part*, is a principle not fafe to be followed in matters concerning the publique State of a Common weal. But howfoever thefe and the like fpeeches be accounted as arrows idely fhot at random, without either eye had to any mark, or regard to their lighting place : hath not your longing defire for the practice of your Difcipline, brought the matter already unto this demurre amongft you, whether the people and their godly Paftors that way affected, ought not to make feparation from the reft, and to begin the exercife of Difcipline without Licence of Civil Powers, which Licence they have fought for, and are not heard ? Upon which queftion, as ye have now devided your felves; the warier fort of you taking the one part, and the forwarder in zeal the other ; fo in cafe thefe earneft Ones fhould prevail, what other fequel can any wife man imagine but this, that having firft refolved that attempts for Difcipline without Superiors are lawful, it will follow in the next place to be difputed what may be attempted againft Superiors, which will not have the Scepter of that Difcipline to rule over them ? Yea even by you which have ftayed your felves from running head-long with the other fort, fomewhat notwithftanding there hath been done without the

P. 4:.

Mat. 5.5.

Exod. 11. 2.

Mart. in his 3. Libel, p. 28.

Demonftr. in the Pre.

the leave or liking of your lawful Superiors, for the exercise of a part of your Discipline amongst the Clergy thereunto addicted. And lest examination of principal parties therein should bring those things to light, which might hinder and let your proceedings; behold for a bar against that impediment, one Opinion ye have newly added unto the rest even upon this occasion, an Opinion to exempt you from taking Oaths, which may turn to the molestation of your Brethren in that cause. The next Neighbour Opinion whereunto, when occasion requireth, may follow for Dispensation with Oaths already taken, if they afterwards be found to import a necessity of detecting ought which may bring such good men into trouble or damage, whatsoever the cause be. O merciful God, what mans wit is there able to sound the depth of those dangerous fearful evils, whereinto our weak and impotent nature is inclinable to sink it self, rather then to shew an acknowledgement of errour in that which once we have unadvisedly taken upon us to defend, against the stream as it were of a contrary publique resolution: Wherefore if we any thing respect their errour, who being perswaded even as ye are have gone further upon that perswasion then ye allow, if vve regard the present Stage of the highest Governour placed over us, if the quality and disposition of our Nobles, if the orders and Lavvs of our famous Universities, if the profession of the Civil, or the practice of the Common Lavv amongst us, if the mischiefes vvhereinto even before our eys so many others have faln head-long from no less plausible and fair beginnings then yours are: there is in every of these considerations most just cause to fear, lest our hastiness to embrace a thing of so perilous consequence, should cause Posterity to feel those evils, vvhich as yet are more easie for us to prevent, then they vvould be for them to remedy.

9. The best and safest way for you therefore my dear Breathren is, to call your deeds past to a new reckoning, to re-examine the cause ye have taken in hand, and to try it even point by point, argument by argument, with all the diligent exactness ye can; to lay aside the gall of that bitterness wherein your minds have hitherto over-abounded, and with meekness to search the truth. Think ye are men, deem it not impossible for you to erre: sift unpartially your own hearts, whether it be force of reason, or vehemency of affection, which hath bred, and still doth feed these opinions in you. If Truth do any where manifest it self, seek not to smother it with glozing Delusion, acknowledge the greatness thereof, and think it your best Victory when the same doth prevaile over you. *The conclusi-on of all.*

That ye have been earnest in speaking or writing, again and again the contrary way, should be no blemish or discredit at all unto you. Amongst so many so huge Volumes, as the infinite paines of St. *Augustine* have brought forth, what one hath gotten him greater love, commendation and honour, then the book wherein he carefully collected his own oversights, and sincerely condemneth them? Many speeches there are of *Jobs*, whereby his Wisdom and other Vertues may appear: but the glory of an Ingenuous mind he hath purchased by these words onely, *Behold, I will lay mine hand on my mouth; I have spoken once, yet will I not therefore maintain Argument; yea twice, howbeit for that cause further I will not proceed.* Far more comfort it were for us (so small is the joy we take in these strifes) to labour under the same yoke, as men that look for the *Job 49.37.*

same

same eternal reward of their Labours, to be injoyned with you in bands of indissolvable love and amity; to live as if our persons being many, our souls were but one, rather in such dismembred sort to spend our few and wretched days in a tedious prosecution of wearisome contentions: the end whereof, if they have not some speedy end, will be heavy even on both sides. Brought already we are even to that estate which *Gregory Nazianzen* mournfully describeth, saying,

Greg. Naz. in Apol.

My mind leadeth me (sith there is no remedy) *to flie and to convey my self into some corner out of sight, where I may scape from this cloudie tempest of maliciousness, whereby all parts are entred into a deadly war amongst themselves, and that little remnant of love which was, is now consumed to nothing. The onely godliness we glory in, is to find out somewhat, whereby we may judge others to be ungodly. Each others faults we observe, as matter of exprobration, and not of grief. By these mean we are grown hateful in the eyes of the Heathens themselves; and (which woundeth us the more deeply) able we are not to deny but that we have deserved their hatred. With the better sort of our own, our fame and credit is clean lost. The less we are to marvel if they judge vilely of us, who although we did well, would hardly allow thereof. On our backs they also build that are lewd, and what we object one against another, the same they use to the utter scorn and disgrace of us all. This we have gained by our mutuall home-dissentions. This we are worthily rewarded with, which are more forward to strive, then becommeth men of vertuous and mild disposition.* But our trust in the Almighty is, that with us contentions are at now at the highest flote, and that the day will come (for what cause of despaire is there?) when the passions of former enmity being allayed, we shall with ten times redoubled tokens of our unfained reconciled love, shew our selves each towards other the same, which *Joseph* and the brethren of *Joseph* were at the time of their enter-view in *Egypt*. Our comfortable expectation and most thirsty desire whereof what man soever amongst you shall any way help to satisfie, (as we truely hope there is no one amongst you but some way or other will) the blessings of the God of Peace both in this World and in the World to come, be upon him more then the stars of the Firmament in number.

What things are handled in the Books Following.

THe first *Book*, *concerning Laws in General.*

The second, *Of the use of Divine Law contained in Scripture, whether that be the onely Law which ought to serve for our direction in all things without exception.*

The third, *Of Laws concerning Ecclesiastical Polity: whether the forme thereof be in Scripture so set down, that no addition or change is lawful.*

The fourth, *Of general exceptions taken against the Laws of our Polity, as being Popish and banished out of certain Reformed Churches.*

The fifth, *Of our Laws that concern the publique religious duties of the Church: and the manner of bestowing that power of order, which inableth men in sundry degrees and callings to execute the same.*

The

THE CONTENTS.

OF

OF THE
LAWS
OF
Ecclesiastical Politie.

The First Book.

Concerning Laws, and their several kinds in general.

The Matter contained in this First Book.

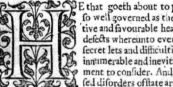

HE that goeth about to perswade a multitude, that they are not so well governed as they ought to be, shall never want attentive and favourable hearers; because they know the manifold defects whereunto every kind of regiment is subject; but the secret lets and difficulties, which in publique proceeding are innumerable and inevitable, they have not ordinarily the judgment to consider. And because such as openly reprove supposed disorders of state are taken for principal friends to the common benifit of all, and for men that carry singular freedome of mind; under this fair and plausible colour whatsoever they utter, passeth for good and currant. That which wanteth in the waight of their speech, is supplyed by the aptnes of mens minds

The cause of writing this general discourse.

M to

to accept and believe it. Whereas on the other fide, if we maintaine things that are eftablifhed, we have not onely to ftrive with a number of heavy prejudices deeply rooted in the hearts of men, who think that herein we ferve the time, and fpeak in favor of the prefent ftate, becaufe thereby we either hold or feek preferment; but, alfo to bear fuch exceptions as minds fo averted before-hand, ufually take againft that which they are loth fhould be poured into them. Albeit therefore much of that we are to fpeak in this prefent caufe, may feem to a number perhaps tedious, perhaps obfcure, dark, and intricate, (for many talk of the truth, which never founded the depth from whence it fpringeth; and therefore when they are led thereunto, they are foon weary, as men drawn from thofe beaten pat is wherewith they have been inured:) yet this may not fo far prevail, as to cut-off that which the matter it felf requireth, howfoever the nice humor of fome be therewith pleafed or no. They unto whom we fhall feem tedious, are in no wife injured by us, becaufe it is in their own hands to fpare that labour which they are not willing to indure. And if any complain of obfcurity, they muft confider, that in thefe matters it commeth not otherwife to pafs, then in fundry the works both of art and alfo of nature; where that which hath greateft force in the very things we fee, is notwithftanding it felf often times not feen. The ftatelinefs of houfes, the goodlinefs of trees, when we behold them delighteth the eye; but that foundation which beareth up the one, that root which Miniftreth unto the other nourifhment and life, is in the bofome of the earth concealed; and if there be occafion at an time to fearch into it, fuch labour is then more neceffary then pleafant, both to them wich undertake it, and for the lookers on. In like manner, the ufe & benefit of good laws, all that live under them may enjoy with delight and comfort, al eit the grounds and firft original caufes from whence they have fprung be unknown, as to the greateft part of men they are. But when they who withdraw their obedience, pretend that the laws which they fhould obey, are corrupt and vicious; for better examination of their quality, it behoveth the very foundation and root, the higheft wel fpring and fountain of them to be difcovered. Which becaufe we are not oftentimes accuftomed to do, when we do it, the paynes we take are more needful a great deal then acceptable, and the matters which we handle feem by reafon of newnefs, (till the mind grow better acquainted with them) dark, intricate, and unfamiliar. For as much help whereof as may be in this cafe, I have endeavoured thorowout the body of this whole difcourfe, that every former part might give ftrength unto all that follow, and every latter bring fome light unto all before. So that if the judgments of men do but hold themfelves in fufpence as touching thefe firft more general meditations, till in order they have perufed the reft that enfue : what may feem dark at the firft, will afterwards be found more plain, even as the latter particular deciſions will appear I doubt not more ftrong, when the other have been read before. The Laws of the Church, whereby for fo many Ages together we have been guided in the exercife of Chriftian Religion, and the fervice of the true God, our Rites, Cuftomes, and Orders of Eclefiaftical Government, are called in queftion; we are accufed as men that will not have Chrift Jefus to rule over them : but have wilfully caft his ftatutes behind their backs, hating to be reformed and made fubject unto the Scepter of his Difcipline. Behold therefore we offer the laws whereby we live, unto the general trial and judgment of the whole world; heartily befeeching Almighty God, whom we defire to ferve according to his own will, that both we and others (all kind of partial affection being clean laid afide) may have eyes to fee, and hearts to imbrace the things that in his fight are moft acceptable. And becaufe the point about which we ftrive is the quality of our laws, our firft entrance hereinto cannot better be made, then with confideration of the nature of law in general; and of that law which giveth life unto all the reft which are commendable, juft, and good; namely the law whereby the Eternal himfelf doth work. Proceeding from hence to the law, firft of Nature, then of Scripture, we fhall have the eafier accefs unto thofe things which come after to be debated, concerning the particular caufe and queftion which we have in hand.

Of that Law which God from before the begining hath fet for himself to do allthings by.

2. All things that are, have fome operations not violent or cafual. Neither doth any thing ever begin to exercife the fame, without fome fore-conceived end for which it worketh. And the end which it worketh for, is not obtained, unlefs the work be alfo fit to obtain it by; for unto every end, every operation will not ferve.

That

That which doth assign unto each thing the kind, that which doth moderate the force and power, that which do th appoint the form and measure of working, the same we term a *Law*. So that no certain end could ever be attained, unless the actions whereby it is attained were regular, that is to say, made sutable, fit, and correspondent unto their end, by some Canon, Rule or Law : Which thing doth first take place in the works even of God himself. All things therefore do work after a sort according to Law : all other things according to a Law, whereof some Superiour unto whom they are subject is Author; onely the works and operations of God, have him both their worker, and for the Law whereby they are wrought. The being of God, is a kind of Law to his working : for that perfection which God is, giveth perfection to that he doth. Those natural, necessary, and internal operations of God, the *generation* of the Son, the *proceeding* of the Spirit, are without the compass of my present intent : which is to touch only such operations as have their beginning and being by a voluntary purpose, wherewith God hath eternally decreed when and how they should be ; Which eternal decree is that we term an eternal Law. Dangerous it were for the feeble brain of man to wade far into the doings of the most High; whom although to know be life, and joy to make mention of his Name ; yet our soundest knowledg is, to know that we know him not as indeed he is, neither can know him ; and our safest eloquence concerning him is our silence, when we confess without confession, that his glory is inexplicable, his greatness above our capacity and reach. He is above, and we upon earth; therefore it behoveth our words to be wary and few. Our God is one, or rather very *Onenefs*, and meer unity, having nothing but it self in it self, and not consisting (as all things do besides God) of many things. In which essential unity of God, a Trinity personal nevertheless subsisteth, after a manner far exceeding the possibility of mans conceit. The works which outwardly are of God, they are in such sort of him being one, that each person hath in them somewhat peculiar and proper. For being three, and they all subsisting in the essence of one deity, from the Father, by the Son, through the spirit, all things are. That which the Son doth hear of the Father, and which the Spirit doth receive of the Father and the Son, the same we have at the hands of the spirit, as being the last, and therefore the nearest unto us in order, although in power the same with the second and the first. The wise and learned amongst the very Heathens themselves have all acknowledged some first cause, whereupon originally the being of all things dependeth. Neither have they otherwise spoken of that cause than as an Agent, which knowing *what* and *why* it worketh, observeth in working a most exact *Order* or *Law*. Thus much is signified by that which *Homer* mentioneth, (a) Διὸς δ᾽ ἐτελείετο βουλή. Thus much acknowledged by *Mercurius Trismegist.* (b) Τὸν πάντα κόσμον ἐποίησεν ὁ δημιουργὸς ὁ χρείων. ἀλλὰ λόγω. Thus much confest by *Anaxagoras* and *Plato*, terming the maker of the world an *Intellectual* worker. Finally the Stoiks, although imagining the first cause of all things to be fire, held nevertheless that the same fire having art, did (c) ὁ δὴ βαδίζειν ὅθι γενέσει κόσμω. They all confess therefore in the working of that first cause, that *Counsel* is used, *Reason* followed, a *Way* observed, that is to say, constant *Order* and *Law* is kept, whereof it self must needs be author unto it self. Otherwise it should have some worthier and higher to direct it, and so could not it self be the first, being the first it can have no other then it self to be the author of that Law which it willingly worketh by. God therefore is a Law both to himself, and to all other things besides. To himself he is a Law in all those things whereof our Saviour speaks, saying, *My Father worketh as yet, so I*. God worketh nothing without cause. All those things which are done by him, have some end for which they are done: and the end for which they are done, is a reason of his will to do them. His will had not inclined to create woman, but that he saw it could not be well if she were not treated; *Non est bonum, It is not good man should be alone*; therefore let us make an helper for him. That and nothing else is done by God, which to leave undone were not so good. If therfore it be demanded, why God having power and ability infinite, the effects notwithstanding of that power are all so limited as we see they are : the reason here of is, the end which he hath proposed, and the Law whereby his wisdome hath stinted the effects of his power in such sort, that it doth not work infinitely, but correspondently unto that end for which it worketh, even all things, γένεσις, in most decent and comely sort, all things in *measure*, *number*, and *weight*. The general end of Gods externall working, is the exercise of his most

Iohn 16. 13. 14. 15.

(a) Iupiters counsel was accomplished:

(b) The creator made the whole world not with hands but by reason. *Stob. in eclog. phyf.*

(c) Proceed by a certain and a set way in the making of the world.

Iohn 5. 17.

Gen. 2. 18.

Sapi 8. 1.
Sapi. 11. 17.

Ephef. 1. 7.
Phil. 4. 19.
Col. 1. 3.
Pvov. 16. 4.

most glorious and most abundant vertue. Which abundance doth shew it self in variety, and for that cause this variety is oftentimes in Scripture exprest by the name of riches. *The Lord hath made all things for his own sake*. Not that any thing is made to be beneficial to him, but all things for him to shew benificence and grace in them. The particular drift of every act proceeding externally from God, we are not able to discern, and therefore cannot alwayes give the proper and certain reason of his works. Howbeit undoubtedly, a proper and certain reason there is of every finite work of God, in as much as there is a law imposed upon it, which if there were not, it should be infinite even as the Worker himself is. They erre therefore who think that of the will of God to do this or that, there is no reason besides his will. Many times no reason known to us; that there is no reason thereof, I judge it most unreasonable to imagine, in as much as he worketh all things, χ⳽ τ Cʋκλω τϛ ϑελήμαι⳽Θ αυτϛ, not onely

Ephef. 1. 11.

Rom. 11. 33.

according to his own will, but *the counsell of his own will*. And whatsoever is done with counsel or wise resolution, hath of necessity some reason why it should be done, albeit that reason be to us in some things so secret, that it forceth the wit of man to stand, as the blessed Apostle himself doth, amazed thereat, *O the depth of the riches, both of the wisdom and knowledg of God! How unsearchable are his judgments, &c.* That Law eternal which God himself hath made to himself, and thereby worketh all things whereof he is the cause and Author, that law in the admirable frame whereof shineth with most perfect beauty the countenance of that wisdom which hath testified concerning her self, *The*

Pro. 8. 13.

Lord possessed me in the beginning of his way, even before his works of old I was set up; that Law which hath been the Pattern to make, and is the Card to guide the World by; that Law which hath been of God, & with God everlastingly; that Law the Author and Observer whereof is one onely God, to be blessed for ever; how should either Men or Angels be able perfectly to behold? The Book of this Law we are neither able nor worthy to open and look into. That little thereof which we darkly apprehend, we admire; the rest, with religious ignorance, we humbly and meekly adore. Seeing therefore that according to this Law he worketh, *of whom, through whom, and for*

Rom. 11. 36.
Boet. lib. 4. de
consol. Phil. 6.

whom are all things; although there seem unto us confusion and disorder in the affairs of this present world; *Tamen quoniam bonus mundum rector temperat, recte fieri cuncta ne dubites*, Let no man doubt but that every thing is well done, because the World is ruled by so good a Guide as transgresseth not his own Law, then which, nothing can be more absolute, perfect, and just. The Law whereby he worketh, is eternal, and therefore can have no shew or colour of mutability: for which cause, a part of that Law being opened in the promises which God hath made (because his promises are nothing else but declarations what God will do for the good of men) touching those promises the Apostle hath witnessed, that God may as possibly deny himself, and not be God, as fail to perform them. And concerning the counsel of

2 Tim. 2. 13.
Heb. 6. 17.

God, he termeth it likewise a thing *unchangeable*; the counsel of God, and that Law of God whereof now we speak being one. Nor is the freedom of the will of God any whit abated, let or hindred by means of this; because the imposition of this Law upon himself, is his own free and voluntary act. This Law therefore we may name eternal, being that *order which God before all Ages hath set down with himself, for himself to do all things by*.

The law which
natural agents
have given
them to ob-
serve, and
their necessity
manner of
keeping it.

3. I am not ignorant, that by *Law Eternal*, the Learned for the most part do understand the order, not which God hath eternally purposed himself in all his works to observe, but rather that which with himself he hath set down as expedient to be kept by all his creatures, according to the several conditions wherewith he hath endued them. They who thus are accustomed to speak, apply the name of *Law* unto that onely rule of working which Superiour Authority imposeth; whereas we somewhat more enlarging the sense thereof, term any kinde of Rule or Canon whereby actions are framed, a Law. Now that Law, which as it is laid up in the bosom of God, they call *Eternal*, receiveth according unto the different kinde of things which are subject unto it, different and sundry kindes of names. That part of it which ordereth natural Agents, we call usually *Natures* Law: that which Angels do clearly behold, and without any swerving observe, is a Law *Celestial* and heavenly: the Law of *Reason*, that which bindeth creatures reasonable in this World, and with which by reason they may most plainly perceive themselves bound; that which bindeth them, and is not known but by special revelation from God, *Divine* Law: *Humane* Law,

that

that which out of the Law either of Reason or of God, men probably gathering to be expedient, they make it a law. All things therefore, which are as they ought to be, are conformed unto *this second Law Eternal* ; and even those things which to this *Eternal* Law are not conformable, are notwithstanding in some sort ordered by *the first Eternal Law.* For what good or evil is there under the Sun, what action correspondent or repugnant unto the Law which God hath imposed upon his creatures, but in or upon it God doth work according to the Law which himself hath eternally purposed to keep ; that is to say, the *first Law Eternal ?* So that a twofold Law Eternal being thus made, it is not hard to conceive how they both take place in ª all things. Wherefore to come to the Law of Nature, albeit thereby we sometimes mean that manner of working which God hath set for each created thing to keep : yet for as much as those things are termed most properly natural Agents, which keep the Law of their kinde unwittingly, as the Heavens and Elements of the World, which can do no otherwise then they do ; and for as much as we give unto intellectual natures the name of *voluntary* Agents, that so we may distinguish them from the other, expedient it will be, that we sever the Law of Nature observed by the one, from that which the other is tied unto.

ª Id omne quod in rebus creatis fit, est materia legis æternæ. *Th.l.1.2.q.23.art.4,5,6.* Nullo modo aliquid legibus summi creatoris ordinationique subtrahitur, à quo pax universitatis administratur. *Aug. de Civit. Dei, lib. 19.c. 21. Imo & peccatum, quatenus à Deo justè permittitur, cadit in legem æternam. Etiam legi æternæ subjicitur peccatum; quatenus voluntaria legis transgressio pœna'e quoddam incommodum animæ inserit, juxta illud Augustini.* Jussisti Domine, & sic est, ut pœna sua sibi sit omnis animus inordinatus. *Confes. lib. 1.cap. 12. Nec male scholastici, Quemadmodum inquiunt videmus res naturales contingentes, hoc ipso quod à fine particulari suo, atq; adeo à lege æterna exorbitant, in eandem legem æternam incidere, quatenus consequuntur alium finem à lege etiam æternâ ipsis in casu particulari constituum ; sic verisimile est homines etiam cùm peccant & desciscunt à lege æternâ ut præcipiente, reincidere in ordinem æternæ legis ut punientis.*

Touching the former, their strict keeping of one Tenure, Statute, and Law is spoken of by all, but hath in it more then men have at yet attained to know, or perhaps ever shall attain, seeing the travel of wading herein is given of God to the sons of men, that perceiving how much the least thing in the world hath in it, more then the wisest are able to reach unto, they may by this means learn humility. *Moses,* in describing the work of Creation, attributeth speech unto God; *God said, Let there be light: let there be a firmament: let the waters under the heavens be gathered together into one place : let the earth bring forth : let there be lights in the firmament of heaven.* Was this onely the intent of *Moses,* to signifie the infinite greatness of Gods Power, by the easiness of his accomplishing such effects, without travel, pain, or labour ? Surely it seemeth that *Moses* had herein, besides this, a further purpose, namely, first, to teach that God did not work as a necessary, but a voluntary Agent, intending before-hand, and decreeing with himself, that which did outwardly proceed from him. Secondly, to shew that God did then institute a Law natural to be observed by creatures; and therefore according to the manner of Laws, the Institution thereof is described, as being established by solemn injunction. His commanding those things to be which are, and to be in such sort as they are, to keep that tenure and course which they do, importeth the establishment of Natures Law. This worlds first Creation, and the preservation since of things created, what is it, but onely so far forth a manifestation by execution, what the eternal Law of God is concerning things natural ? And as it cometh to pass in a Kingdom rightly ordered, that after a Law is once published, it presently takes effect far and wide, all States framing themselves thereunto; even so let us think it fareth in the natural course of the world : Since the time that God did first proclaim the Edicts of his law unto it, Heaven and earth have hearkned unto his voice, and their labour hath been to do his will : *He made a law for the Rain; He gave his decree unto the Sea, that the Waters should not pass his commandment.* Now, if nature should intermit her course, and leave altogether, though it were but for a while, the observation of her own Laws ; those principal and Mother Elements of the World, whereof all things in this lower world are made, should lose the qualities which now they have ; if the frame of that Heavenly Arch erected over our heads should loosen and dissolve it self; if Celestial Spheres should forget their wonted motions, and by irregular volubility turn themselves any way as it might happen ; if the Prince of the Lights of Heaven, which now as a Gyant doth run his unwearied course, should, as it were, through a languishing faintness, begin to stand, and to rest himself; if the Moon should wander from her beaten way, the times and seasons of the yeer blende themselves, by disordered and

Psal. 19. 5.

    con-

confused mixture, the winds breathe out their last gasp, the clouds yield no rain, the earth be defeated of heavenly influence, the fruits of the earth pine away, as children at the withered breasts of their mother, no longer able to yield them relief; what would become of man himself, whom these things now do all serve? See we not plainly, that obedience of creatures unto the Law of Nature, is the stay of the whole world? Notwithstanding, with Nature it cometh sometimes to pass, as with art. Let *Phidias* have rude and obstinate stuff to carve, though his art do that it should, his work will lack that beauty which otherwise in fitter matter it might have had. He that striketh an Instrument with skill, may cause notwithstanding a very unpleasant sound, if the string whereon he striketh chance to be uncapable of harmony.

Theophrast. in Metaph.

In the matter whereof things natural consist, that of *Theophrastus* takes place, Πολυ τι εὐπακυον δε ἀχθμυον τι ἐυ, *Much of it is oftentimes such, as will by no means yield to receive that impression which were best and most perfect.* Which defect in the matter of things natural, they who gave themselves unto the contemplation of nature amongst the Heathen, observed often: but the true original cause thereof, divine malediction, laid for the sin of man upon these creatures, which God had made for the use of man, this being an article of that saving truth which God hath revealed unto his Church, was above the reach of their meerly natural capacity and understanding. But howsoever, these swervings are now and then incident into the course of nature; nevertheless, so constantly the Laws of nature, are by natural Agents observed, that no man denieth but those things which nature worketh, are wrought either always, or for the most part, after one and the same manner.

Arist. Rhet. 1. cap. 39.

If here it be demanded, What that is which keepeth nature in obedience to her own law, we must have recourse to that higher Law whereof we have already spoken; and because all other laws do thereon depend, from thence we must borrow so much as shall need for brief resolution in this point. Although we are not of opinion therefore, as some are, that nature in working hath before her certain exemplary draughts or patterns, which subsisting in the bosom of the Highest, and being thence discovered, she fixeth her eye upon them, as Travellers by Sea upon the Pole-star of the World, and that according thereunto she guideth her hand to work by imitation: Although we rather imbrace the Oracle of *Hippocrates*, that *each thing both in small and in great fulfilleth the task which destiny hath set down*: and concerning the manner of executing and fulfilling the same, *What they do they know not, yet is it in shew and apppearance, as though they did know what they do; and the truth is, they do not discern the things which they look on*:

Τλω παερφω μενλω μοιρλω ἐκαςον ἐκπανεςι κ ὅτι τι μειζον κ ἐπι τι μησον. ὁ πρησ ουσιν, κκ εἰ δαςιν, δε ἐφιανεσι δοκεοντες δι κινεςιν εἰδεναι, κ δ΄ ὀυ ἐρεσι εσιναςι· κετι. Acts 17.23. a

Nevertheless, for as much as the works of nature are no less exact, then if she did both behold and study how to express some absolute shape or mirror always present before her; yea, such her dexterity and skill appeareth, that no intellectual creature in the world were able by capacity, to do that which nature doth without capacity and knowledge; it cannot be but nature hath some Directer of infinite knowledge to guide her in all her ways. Who the guide of nature, but onely the God of nature? *In him we live, move, and are.* Those things which nature is said to do, are by Divine Art performed, using nature as an instrument; nor is there any such Art or Knowledge Divine in Nature her self working, but in the guide of Natures work. Whereas therefore things natural, which are not in the number of voluntary Agents (for of such onely we now speak, and of no other) do so necessarily observe their certain laws, that as long as they keep those *a* forms which give them their being, they cannot possibly be apt or inclinable to do otherwise then they do; seeing the kindes of their operations are both constantly and exactly framed, according to the several ends for which they serve, they themselves in the mean while, though doing that which is fit, yet knowing neither what they do, nor why: it followeth, that all which they do in this sort, proceedeth originally from some such Agent, as knoweth, appointeth, holdeth up, and even actually frameth the same. The manner of this Divine efficiency being far above us, we are no more able to conceive by our reason, then creatures unreasonable by their sense, are able to apprehend after what manner we dispose and order the course of our affairs. Onely thus much is discerned, that the natural generation and process of all things, receiveth order of proceeding from the setled stability of Divine Understanding. This appointeth unto them their kindes of working, the disposition whereof, in the purity of Gods own knowledge and will, is rightly termed by the name of *Providence*. The same being

a Form in other creatures is at ing proportionable unto the soul in living creatures. Sensible it is not, nor otherwise discernable, then only by effect; according to the diversity of inward forms, things of the world are distinguished into their kindes.

re-

referred unto the things themselves here disposed by it, was wont by the Ancient to be called *Natural Destiny*. That Law, the performance whereof we behold in things natural, as it were an authentical, or an original draught written in the bosom of God himself; whose spirit being to execute the same, useth every particular nature, every meer natural agent, onely as an instrument created at the beginning, and ever since the beginning used to work his own will and pleasure withal. Nature therefore is nothing else but Gods instrument: In the course whereof, *Dionysius* perceiving some sudden disturbance, is said to have have cried out, *Aut Deus naturæ patitur, aut mundi machina dissolvetur,* Either God doth suffer impediment, and is by a greater then himself hindred; or if that be impossible, then hath he determined to make a present dissolution of the World, the execution of that law beginning now to stand still, without which the world cannot stand. This workman, whose servitor nature is, being in truth but onely one, the Heathens imagining to be moe, gave him in the skie the name of *Jupiter*, in the ayre the name of *Juno*, in the water the name of *Neptune*, in the earth the name of *Vesta*, and sometimes of *Ceres*; the name of *Apollo* in the Sun, in the Moon the name of *Diana*, the name *Æolus*, and divers other in the winds; and to conclude, even so many guides of Nature they dream'd of, as they saw there were kindes of things natural in the world. These they honoured, as having power to work or cease according as men deserved of them. But unto us there is one onely guide of all agents natural, and he both the Creator and the Worker of all in all, alone to be blessed, adored and honoured by all for ever. That which hitherto hath been spoken, concerneth natural agents considered in themselves. But we must further remember also (which thing to touch in a word shall suffice) that as in this respect they have their law, which law directeth them in the means whereby they tend to their own perfection: So likewise another law there is, which toucheth them as they are sociable parts united into one body; a law which bindeth them each to serve unto others good, and all to prefer the good of the whole before whatsoever their own particular, as we plainly see they do, when things natural in that regard, forget their ordinary natural wont; that which is heavy, mounting sometime upwards of its own accord, and forsaking the center of the earth, which to it self is most natural, even as if it did hear it self commanded to let go the good it privately wisheth, and to relieve the present distress of Nature in common.

4. But now that we may lift up our eyes (as it were) from the footstool, to the Throne of God, and leaving these natural, consider a little the state of heavenly and divine creatures; touching Angels which are Spirits immaterial and intellectual, the glorious Inhabitants of those sacred Pallaces, where nothing but light and blessed immortality, no shadow of matter for tears, discontentments, griefs, and uncomfortable passions to work upon, but all joy, tranquillity, and peace, even for ever & ever do dwell; as in number and order they are huge, mighty, and royal armies, so likewise in perfection of obedience unto that law, which the Highest, whom they adore, love, and imitate, hath imposed upon them; such observants they are thereof, that our Saviour himself being to set down the perfect *Idea* of that which we are to pray and wish for on earth, did not teach to pray or wish for more, then onely that here it might be with us, as with them it is in Heaven. God which moveth meer natural agents as an efficient onely, doth otherwise move intellectual creatures, and especially his holy Angels. For beholding the face of God, in admiration of so great excellency they all adore him; and being rapt with the love of his beauty, they cleave inseparably for ever unto him. Desire to resemble him in goodness, maketh them unweariable, and even unsatiable in their longing, to do by all means all manner of good unto all the creatures of God, but especially unto the children of men; in the countenance of whose nature looking downward, they behold themselves beneath themselves, even as upward in God, beneath whom themselves are, they see that character which is nowhere but in themselves and us resembled. Thus far even the Painims have approached; thus far they have seen into the doings of the Angels of God; *Orpheus* confessing, that the fiery Throne of God is attended on by those most industrious Angels, careful how all things are performed amongst men; and the mirror of humane wisdom plainly teaching, that God moveth Angels, even as that thing doth stir mans heart, which is thereunto presented amiable. Angelical actions may therefore be reduced unto these three general kindes: first, most delectable, &c. 3.

Vide Thom. in compend. Theol. cap. 3.
Omne quod non venit ab aliquo, est quasi instrumentum quoddam primi moventis.
Ridiculum est autem etiam apud indoctos puere instrumentum moventium ab aliquo principali agente.

The law which Angels do work by.
Psal. 104.4.
Heb. 1.7.
Ephes. 3.10.
Dan. 7.10.
Mat. 16.53.
Heb. 12.12.
Luke 1.19.
Matth. 6.10.
& 18.10.
Psa. 91.11,12.
Luke 15.10.
Heb. 1.14.
Acts 10.3.
Dan. 9.23.
Mat. 18.10.
Dan. 4.10.
Τῷ ᾗ θρόνῳ πυρώδει αει εφεστηκασι παρασιν πολυμηχανοι Αγγελοι, οιοι μιμηλοι, οσοι Ζηλους αριστα τελειθ.
Arist. Metaph.
11. cap. 7.
Iohn. 38.7.
Mar. 18.10.
Psal. 148.2.
Hab. 1.6.

This is intimated wheresoever we finde them termed the sons of G. d, as Iob 1. 6. and 38. 7. 2 Pet. 2. 4. Ep. Iud. v. 6. Psal. 148. 2. Luk. 1. 13. Mat. 26, 53. Psal. 148. 2. Heb 1. 11. Apoc. 22. 5.

ble love, arising from the visible apprehension of the purity, glory, and beauty of God, invisible, saving onely unto Spirits that are pure: secondly, adoration, grounded upon the evidence of the greatness of God, on whom they see how all things depend: thirdly, imitation, bred by the presence of his exemplary goodness, who ceaseth not before them daily to fill Heaven and Earth with the rich treasures of most free and undeserved grace. Of Angels, we are not to consider onely what they are, and do, in regard of their own being, but that also which concerneth them as they are linked into a kinde of corporation amongst themselves, and of society or fellowship with men. Consider Angels each of them severally in himself, and their Law is that which the Prophet *David* mentioneth, *All ye his Angels praise him.* Consider the Angels of God associated, and their Law is that which disposeth them as an *Army*, one in order and degree above another. Consider finally the Angels, as having with us that communion which the Apostle to the *Hebrews* noteth, and in regard whereof Angels have not disdained to profess themselves our *fellow-servants*: From hence there springeth up a third Law, which bindeth them to works of ministerial imployment. Every of which their several functions, are by them performed with joy. A part of the Angels of God notwithstanding (we know) have fallen, and that their fall hath been through the voluntary breach of that Law, which did require at their hands continuance in the exercise of their high and admirable vertue. Impossible it was, that ever their will should change or encline to remit any part of their duty, without some object having force to avert their conceit from God, and to draw it another way; and that before they attained that high perfection of bliss, wherein now the elect Angels are without possibility of falling. Of any thing more then of God, they could not by any means like, as long as whatsoever they knew besides God, they apprehended it not in it self, without dependency upon God; because so long God must needs seem infinitely better then any thing which they so could apprehend. Things beneath them, could not in such sort be presented unto their eyes, but that therein they must needs see always how those things did depend on God. It seemeth therefore that there was no other way for Angels to sin, but by reflex of their understanding upon themselves; when being held with admiration of their own sublimity and honour, the memory of their subordination unto God, and their dependency on him was drowned in this conceit, whereupon their adoration, love, and imitation of God, could not choose but be also interrupted. The fall of Angels therefore was pride. Since their fall, their practices have been the clean contrary unto those before mentioned: For being dispersed, some in the ayre, some on the earth, some in the water, some amongst the minerals, dens and caves, that are under the earth; they have by all means laboured to effect an universal rebellion against the laws, and as far as in them lieth, utter destruction of the works of God. These wicked spirits the Heathens honoured instead of Gods, both generally under the name of *Dii inferi*, Gods infernal; and particularly, some in Oracles, some in Idols, some as houshold Gods, some as Nymphs; in a word, no foul and wicked spirit, which was not one way or other honoured of men as God, till such time as light appeared in the World, and dissolved the works of the Devil. Thus much therefore may suffice for Angels, the next unto whom in degree are men.

Iohn 8. 44. 1 Pet. 5. 8. Apoc. 9. 11. Gen. 3. 15. 1 Chro. 21. 1. Iob. 1. 7. & 2. 5. Iohn 13. 2. Acts 5. 3. Apoc. 20. 8.

The law whereby man is in his actions directed to the imitation of God.

5. God alone excepted, who actually and everlastingly is whatsoever he may be, and which cannot hereafter be that which now he is not; all other things besides are somewhat in possibility, which as yet they are not in act. And for this cause, there is in all things an appetite or desire, whereby they incline to something which they may be; and when they are it, they shall be perfecter then now they are. All which perfections are contained under the general name of *Goodness*. And because there is not in the world any thing whereby another may not some way be made the perfecter, therefore all things that are, are good. Again, sith there can be no goodness desired, which proceedeth not from God himself, as from the Supreme cause of all things; and every effect doth after a sort contain, at leastwise resemble the cause from which it proceedeth; all things in the world are said, in some sort, to seek the highest, and to covet more or less the participation of God himself. Yet this doth nowhere so much appear, as it doth in man, because there are so many kindes of perfections which man seeketh. The first degree of goodness, is that general perfection which all things do seek, in desiring the continuance of their being.

Πάντα γὰρ ἐκείνου ὀρέγεται. Arist. de an. lib. 2. cap. 4.

ing.

ing. All things therefore coveting, as much as may be, to be like unto God in being ever, that vvhich cannot hereunto attain personally, doth seek to continue it self another way; that is, by off-spring and propagation. The next degree of goodness, is that which each thing coveteth, by affecting resemblance with God; in the constancy and excellency of those operations which belong unto their kinde. The immutability of God they strive unto, by working either always, or for the most part, after one and the same manner; his absolute exactness they imitate, by tending unto that which is most exquisite in every particular. Hence have risen a number of axiomes in Philosophy, shewing, how *The works of nature do always aim at that which cannot be bettered.* These two kindes of goodness rehearsed, are so neerly united to the things themselves which desire them, that we scarcely perceive the appetite to stir in reaching forth her hand towards them. But the desire of those perfections which grow externally is more apparent; especially of such as are not expresly desired, unless they be first known, or such as are not for any other cause then for knowledge it self desired. Concerning perfections in this kinde, that by proceeding in the knowledge of truth, and by growing in the exercise of vertue, man, amongst the creatures of this inferiour world, aspireth to the greatest conformity with God; this is not onely known unto us, whom he himself hath so instructed, but even they do acknowledge, who amongst men are not judged the neerest unto him. With *Plato*, what one thing more usual, then to excite men unto the love of wisdom, by shewing how much wise men are thereby exalted above men; how knowledge doth raise them up into Heaven, how it maketh them, though not Gods, yet as Gods, high, admirable, and divine? And *Mercurius Trismegistus* speaking of the vertues of a righteous soul: *Such spirits* (saith he) *are never cloyed with praising and speaking well of all men, with doing good unto every one by word and deed, because they study to frame themselves according to* THE PATTERN *of the Father of spirits.*

6. In the matter of knowledge, there is between the Angels of God and the children of men this difference; Angels already have full and compleat knowledge in the highest degree that can be imparted unto them; men, if we view them in their spring, are at the first without understanding or knowledge at all. Nevertheless, from this utter vacuity they grow by degrees, till they come at length to be even as the Angels themselves are. That which agreeth to the one now, the other shall attain unto in the end; they are not so far disjoyned and severed, but that they come at length to meet. The soul of man being therefore at the first as a book, wherein nothing is, and yet all things may be imprinted; we are to search by what steps and degrees it riseth unto perfection of knowledge. Unto that which hath been already set down concerning natural agents, this we must adde, that albeit therein we have comprised as well creatures living, as void of life, if they be in degree of nature beneath men; nevertheless, a difference we must observe between those natural agents that work altogether unwittingly, and those which have, though weak, yet some understanding what they do, as fishes, fowls, and beasts have. Beasts are in sensible capacity as ripe even as men themselves, perpaps more ripe. For as stones, though in dignity of nature inferiour unto plants, yet exceed them in firmness of strength, or durability of being; and plants, though beneath the excellency of creatures indued with sense; yet exceed them in the faculty of vegetation, and of fertility: so beasts, though otherwise behinde men, may notwithstanding in actions of sense and fancy go beyond them; because the endeavours of nature, when it hath an higher perfection to seek, are in lower the more remiss, not esteeming thereof so much as those things do, which have no better proposed unto them. The soul of man therefore, being capable of a more divine perfection, hath (besides the faculties of growing unto sensible knowledge, which is common unto us with beasts) a further ability, whereof in them there is no shew at all, the ability of reaching * higher then unto sensible things. Till we grow to some ripeness of years, the soul of man doth onely store it self with conceits of things of inferiour and more open quality, which afterwards do serve as instruments unto that which is greater: in the mean while, above the reach of meaner creatures it ascendeth not. When once it comprehendeth any thing above this, as the difference of time, affirmations, negations, and contradiction in speech, we then count it to have some use of natural reason. Whereunto, if afterwards there might be added the right helps of true Art and Learning (which helps I must plainly confess, this age of the world, carrying the name of a Learned age, doth neither much

know.

[marginal notes]
'Εν τοῖς φύσει
διὰ τὸ ἴσκνον
ἐὰν ἐνδέχηται
ὑπερχεῖν μᾶλλον, ἡ φύσις
ἀεὶ μετὰ ἔςιν
ἐνδεχομένων
τὸ βέλτιςον.
Ari. de cæl. cap 4.
Matth. 5. 48.
Sap. 7. 27.
Ἡ δὲ τελεία
ψυχὴ κᾶρου
εἰδότι ἔχει,
ὑμνῦσα εὐφη-
μοῦσά τε πᾶσι
τοῖς ἀνθρώποις,
καὶ λέγουσα καὶ ἐρ-
γοῖς πάντας
εὖ ποιοῦσα, μι-
μεῖ ται αὐτῆς
τ πατέρα.

Mens sisi beginning to grow to the knowledge of that law which they are to observe. *Vide Isa. 7. 16.*

* Ὁ δὲ ἄνθρω-
πῶ εἰς τ᾽ ἑρα-
νὸν ἀ γαζαίρει,
ἡ μετεῶ αὐτῶ
καὶ οἶδε πιαμὲν
ἔςιν ἐντὸς ψυχὴ
λα, τοῖαδε τὰ
πεῖα, καὶ τὰ
ἄλλα πάντα
ἀκριῶς μετὰ·
δίσει. Καὶ τὸ
πᾶν τοῦ μέζον,
ἡ δή δὲ ω̃ τα·
πλιμπὺ ἄρα
ὄτε τα·
Mercur. Trism.
Aristotelical
demonstrati-
on.

know, not greatly regard) there would undoubtedly be almoſt as great difference in maturity of judgement between men therewith inured, and that which now men are, as between men that are now and Innocents. Which ſpeech, if any condemn, as being over Hyperbolical, let them conſider but this one thing. No Art is at the firſt finding out ſo perfect, as induſtry may after make it: Yet the very firſt man, that to any purpoſe knew the way we ſpeak of, and followed it, hath alone thereby performed more very neer in all parts of natural knowledge, then ſithence in any one part thereof, the whole World beſides hath done. In the poverty of that other new-deviſed aid, two things there are notwithſtanding ſingular. Of marvellous quick diſpatch it is, and doth ſhew them that have it, as much almoſt in three days, as if it had dwelt threeſcore years with them. Again, becauſe the curioſity of mans wit doth many times with peril wade farther in the ſearch of things, then were convenient: the ſame is thereby reſtrained unto ſuch generalities, as every where offering themſelves, are apparant unto men of the weakeſt conceit that need be. So as following the Rules and Precepts thereof, we may finde it to be an Art, which teacheth the way of ſpeedy Diſcourſe, and reſtraineth the minde of man, that it may not vvax over-vviſe. Education and Inſtruction are the means, the one by uſe, the other by Precept, to make our natural faculty of reaſon, both the better and the ſooner able to judge rightly betvveen Truth and Errour, good and evil. But at vvhat time a man may be ſaid to have attained ſo far forth the uſe of reaſon, as ſufficeth to make him capable of thoſe Laws, whereby he is then bound to guide his actions; this is a great deal more eaſie for common ſenſe to diſcern, then for any man by Skill and Learning to determine; even as it is not in Philoſophers, vvho beſt knovv the nature both of Fire and Gold, to teach vvhat degree of the one vvill ſerve to puriſie the other, ſo vvell as the Artizan (vvho doth this by fire) diſcerneth by ſenſe, vvhen the fire hath that degree of heat vvhich ſufficeth for his purpoſe.

7. By reaſon man attaineth unto the knovvledge of things that are, and are not ſenſible; it reſteth therefore, that vve ſearch hovv man attaineth unto the knovvledge of ſuch things unſenſible, as are to be knovvn that they may be done. Seeing then that nothing can move, unleſs there be ſome end, the deſire vvhereof provoketh unto motion; hovv ſhould that divine povver of the Soul, that *Spirit of our minde*, as the Apoſtle termeth it, ever ſtir it ſelf unto action, unleſs it have alſo the like ſpur? The end for vvhich vve are moved to vvork, is ſometimes the goodneſs vvhich vve conceive of the very vvorking it ſelf, vvithout any further reſpect at all; and the cauſe that procureth action, is the meer deſire of action, no other good beſides being thereby intended. Of certain turbulent vvits it is ſaid, *Illis quieta movere magna merces videbatur.* They thought the very diſturbance of things eſtabliſhed, an hire ſufficient to ſet them on vvork. Sometimes that vvhich vve do is referred to a further end, vvithout the deſire vvhereof, vve vvould leave the ſame undone, as in their actions that gave Alms, to purchaſe thereby the praiſe of men. Man in perfection of nature, being made according to the likeneſs of his Maker, reſembleth him alſo in the manner of vvorking; ſo that vvhatſoever vve vvork as men, the ſame vve do vvittingly vvork, and freely; neither are vve according to the manner of natural agents any way ſo tied, but that it is in our povver to leave the things we do undone. The good which either is gotten by doing, or which conſiſteth in the very doing it ſelf, cauſeth not action, unleſs apprehending it as good, we ſo like and deſire it. That we do unto any ſuch end, the ſame we chooſe and prefer before the leaving of it undone. Choice there is not, unleſs the thing vvhich vve take, be ſo in our povver, that vve might have refuſed and left it. If fire conſume the ſtubble, it chooſeth not ſo to do, becauſe the nature thereof is ſuch, that it can do no other. To chooſe, is to vvill one thing before another; and to vvill, is to bend our ſouls to the having or doing of that vvhich they ſee to be good: Goodneſs is ſeen vvith the eye of the underſtanding; and the light of that eye, is Reaſon: So that tvvo principal fountains there are of humane action, *Knowledge* and *Will*; vvhich vvill in things tending tovvards any end, is termed *Choice.* Concerning Knovvledge; *Behold*, ſaith, *Moſes, I have ſet before you this day good and evil, life and death.* Concerning Will, he addeth immediately *Chooſe life*; that is to ſay, the things that tend unto life, them chooſe. But of one thing vve muſt have ſpecial care, as being a matter of no ſmall moment; and that is, hovv the vvill properly and ſtrictly taken, as it

is

[margin notes:]
Ramiſtry.

Of mans will, which is the thing that laws of action are made to guide. Epheſ. 4. 23.

Saluſt.

Mat. 6. 2.

Deut. 30. 19.

is of things vvhich are referred unto the end that man defireth, differeth greatly from that inferiour natural defire vvhich we call appetite. The object of appetite is, vvhatfoever fenfible good may be vyilhed for; the object of vvill is, that good vvhich reafon doth lead us to feek. Affections, as joy, and grief, and fear, and anger, vvith fuch like, being as it vvere the fundry fafhions and forms of appetite, can neither rife at the conceit of a thing indifferent, nor yet choofe but rife at the fight of fome things. Wherefore it is not altogether in our povver, vvhether vve vvill be ftirred vvita affections or no : vvhereas actions vvhich iffue from the difpofition of the vvill, are in the povver thereof to be performed or ftayed. Finally, appetite is the vvills Sollicitor, and the vvill is appetites Controuler ; vvhat vve covet according to the one, by the other we often reject : neither is any other defire termed properly will, but that where reafon and underftanding, or the fhew of reafon, prefcribeth the thing defired. It may be therefore a queftion, Whether thofe operations of men are to be counted voluntary, wherein that good which is fenfible provoketh appetite, and appetite caufeth action, reafon being never called to counfel ; as when we eat or drink, or betake our felves unto reft, and fuch like. The truth is, that fuch actions in men having attained to the ufe of reafon, are voluntary. For as the authority of higher powers, hath force even in thofe things which are done without their privity, and are of fo mean reckoning, that to acquaint them therewith it needeth not : in like fort, voluntarily we are faid to do that alfo, which the will if it lifted, might hinder from being done, although about the doing thereof, we do not exprefly ufe our reafon or underftanding, and fo immediately apply our wills thereunto. In cafes therefore of fuch facility, the Will doth yield her affent, as it were with a kinde of filence, by not diffenting; in which refpect, her force is not fo apparent as in exprefs Mandates or Prohibitions; efpecially upon advice and confultation going before. Where underftanding therefore needeth in thofe things, Reafon is the Director of mans Will, by difcovering in action what is good. For the Laws of Well-doing, are the Dictates of right Reafon. Children which are not as yet come unto thofe years whereat they may have ; again, Innocents, which are excluded by natural defect from ever having: Thirdly, mad men, which for the prefent cannot poffibly have the ufe of right reafon to guide themfelves, have for their guide the Reafon that guideth other men, which are Tutors over them, to feek and to procure their good for them. In the reft, there is that light of Reafon, whereby good may be known from evil, and which difcovering the fame rightly, is termed right. The Will notwithftanding doth not incline to have or do that which Reafon teacheth to be good, unlefs the fame do alfo teach it to be poffible. For albeit the appetite, being more general, may wifh any thing which feemeth good, be it never fo impoffible : yet for fuch things, the reafonable Will of man doth never feek. Let Reafon teach impoffibility in any thing, and the Will of man doth let it go ; a thing impoffible it doth not affect, the impoffibility thereof being manifeft. There is in the Will of man naturally that freedom, whereby it is apt to take or refufe any particular object whatfoever, being prefented unto it. Whereupon it followeth, that there is no particular object fo good, but it may have the fhew of fome difficult or unpleafant quality annexed to it ; in refpect whereof, the will may fhrink and decline it : contrariwife (for fo things are blended) there is no particular evil which hath not fome appearance of goodnefs whereby to infinuate it felf. For evil, as evil, cannot be defired : if that be defired which is evil, the caufe is the goodnefs which is, or feemeth to be joyned with it. Goodnefs doth not move by being, but by being apparent ; and therefore many things are neglected, which are moft precious, onely becaufe the value of them lieth hid. Senfible goodnefs is moft apparent, neer, and prefent ; which caufeth the appetite to be therewith ftrongly provoked. Now purfuit and refufal in the Will do follow, the one the affirmation, the other the negation of goodnefs; which the underftanding apprehendeth, grounding it felf upon fenfe, unlefs fome higher reafon do chance to teach the contrary. And if reafon have taught it rightly to be good, yet not fo apparently that the minde receiveth it with utter impoffibility of being otherwife : ftill there is place left for the Will to take or leave. Whereas therefore, amongft fo many things as are to be done, there are fo few, the goodnefs whereof reafon in fuch fort doth or eafily can difcover, we are not to marvel at the choice of evil, even then when the contrary is probably known. Hereby it cometh to pafs, that cuftom inuring the minde by long practice,

and

[marginal notes:]
O m'bi præteri. toi referat fi lu- piter aunos !

'Ει ỹ τις ὃλι ησκίας ὁρμᾳ, πρῶτον μ'ιτὸχ– αἰς ὃλι ησκίας αὐλω ὁρμῶσιν, ἀλλ' ωῖςω α fαθῦ. Paulò poſt. Ἀδύναλον γα'ρ ὁρμᾶι ὃλι ησκὰ Cωλόφωι ἔχειν αὐ]ά,ὃτι ἐλπὶ– διὰγαθῦ, ὃτε φόζω μείζονος ησκῦ. Alcin. dedog. mat. Plat.

and so leaving there a sensible impression, prevaileth more then reasonable perswasi-on what way soever. Reason therefore may rightly discern the thing which is good, and yet the Will of man not incline it self thereunto, as oft as the prejudice of sensi-ble experience doth oversway. Nor let any man think that this doth make any thing for the just excuse of iniquity; For there was never sin committed, wherein a less good was not preferred before a greater, and that wilfully; which cannot be done without the singular disgrace of nature, and the utter disturbance of that Divine Or-der, whereby the preheminence of chiefest acceptation, is by the best things wor-thily challenged. There is not that good which concerneth us, but it hath evidence enough for it self, if reason were diligent to search it out. Through neglect thereof, abused we are with the shew of that which is not; sometimes the subtilty of Satan enveigling us, as it did (a) Eve; sometimes the hastiness of our wills preventing the more considerate advice of sound reason, as in the (b) Apostles, when they no sooner saw what they liked not, but they forthwith were desirous of fire from Heaven; some-times the very custom of evil making the heart obdurate against whatsoever instru-ctions to the contrary, as in them over whom our Savior spake weeping, (c) *O Jerusa-lem, how often, and thou wouldst not?* still therefore that wherewith we stand blameable, and can no way excuse it, is, in doing evil, we prefer a less good before a greater, the greatness whereof is by reason investigable, and may be known. The search of know-ledge is a thing painful; and the painfulness of knowledge, is that which maketh the will so hardly inclinable thereunto. The root hereof, divine malediction; whereby the (d) instruments being weakned, wherewithal the soul (especially in reasoning) doth work, it preferreth rest in ignorance, before wearisome labour to know. For a spur of diligence therefore, we have a natural thirst after knowledge ingrafted in us. But by reason of that original weakness in the instruments, without which the understand-ing part is not able in this world by discourse to work, the very conceit of painful-ness is as a bridle to stay us. For which cause the Apostle, who knew right well, that the weariness of the flesh is an heavy clog to the will, striketh mightily upon this Key, *Awake thou that sleepest, cast off all which presseth down; watch, labour, strive to go forward, and to grow in knowledge.*

8. Wherefore to return to our former intent, of discovering the natural way, whereby Rules have been found out concerning that goodness wherewith the will of man ought to be moved in humane actions; as every thing naturally and necessari-ly doth desire the utmost good and greatest perfection whereof nature hath made it capable, even so man. Our felicity therefore being the object and accomplishment of our desire, we cannot chuse but wish and covet it. All particular things which are subject unto action, the will doth so far forth incline unto, as reason judgeth them the better for us, and consequently the more available to our bliss. If reason err, we fall into evil, and are so far forth deprived of the general perfection we seek. Seeing there-fore that for the framing of mens actions, the knowledge of good from evil is neces-sary, it only resteth that we search how this may be had. Nether must we suppose that there needeth one rule to know the good, and another the evil by. For he that knoweth what is straight, doth even thereby discern what is crooked, because the absence of straightness in bodies capable thereof is crookedness. Goodness in actions is like unto straitness; wherefore that which is done well, we term right. For as the strait way is most acceptable to him that travelleth, because by it he cometh soonest to his jour-neys end: so in action, that which doth lie the evenest between us and the end we de-sire, must needs be the fittest for our use. Besides which fitness for use, there is al-so in rectitude, beauty; as contrariwise in obliquity, deformity. And that which is good in the actions of men, doth not onely delight as profitable; but as amiable also. In which consideration, the Grecians most divinely have given to the active perfecti-on of men, a name expressing both beauty and goodness, because goodness in ordina-ry speech is for the most part applied onely to that which is beneficial. But we in the name of Goodness do here imply both. And of discerning goodness, there are but these two ways; the one the knowledge of the causes whereby it is made such; the other the observation of those signs and tokens, which being an-nexed always unto goodness, argue that where they are found, there also good-ness is, although we know not the cause by force whereof it is there. The former of these, is the most sure and infallible way, but so hard, that all shun it, and had

                                                                      rather

rather walk as men do in the dark by hap hazard, then tread so long and intricate Mazes for knowledg sake. As therefore Phylitians are many times forced to leave such Methods of curing as themselves know to be the fittest, and being over-ruled by their Patients impatiency, are fain to try the best they can, in taking that way of cure, which the cured will yield unto : in like sort, considering how the case doth stand with this present age full of tongue, and weak of brain, behold we yield to the stream thereof; into the causes of goodnes we will not make any curious or deep inquiry ; to touch them now and then it shall be sufficient, when they are so neer at hand that easily they may be conceived without any far removed discourse : that way we are contented to prove, which being the worse in it self, is notwithstanding now by reason of common imbecillity the fitter and likelier to be brookt. Signes and tokens to know good by, are of sundry kinds : some more certaine, and some less. The most certain token of evident goodnes is, if the general perswasion of all men do so account it. And therefore a common received error is never utterly overthrown, till such times as we go from signes unto causes, and shew some manifest root or fountain thereof common unto all, whereby it may clearly appear how it hath come to pass that so many have been over-seen. In which case surmises and slight probabilities will not serve; because the universal consent of men is the perfectest and strongest in this kind, which comprehendeth onely the signes and tokens of goodnes. Things casual do varie; and that which a man doth but chance to think well of, cannot still have the like hap. Wherefore although we know not the cause, yet thus much we may know, that some necessary cause there is, whensoever the judgements of all men generally or for the most part run one and the same way, especially in matters of natural discourse. For of things necessarily and naturally done, there is no more affirmed but this, (a) *They keep either always or for the most part one Tenure.* The general and perpetual voyce of men is as the sentence of God himself. (b) For that which all men have at all times learned, Nature her self must needs have taught; and God being the Author of nature, her voice is but his instrument. By her from him we receive whatsoever in such sort we learn. Infinite duties there are, the goodnes whereof is by this rule sufficiently manifested, although we had no other warrant besides to approve them. The Apostle St. *Paul* having speech concerning the Heathen, saith of them, (c) *They are a Law unto themselves.* His meaning is, that by force of the light of reason, wherewith God illuminateth every one which cometh into the world, men being enabled to know Truth from falshood, and good from evil, do thereby learn in many things what the will of God is, which will himself not revealing by any extraordinary means unto them, but they by natural discourse attaining the knowledge thereof, seem the makers of those Laws which indeed are his, and they but onely the finders of them out. A Law therefore generally taken, is a directive rule unto goodnes of operation. The rule of divine operations outward, is the definitive appointment of Gods own wisdome set down within himself. The rule of natural agents that work by simple necessity, is the determination of the Wisdome of God, known to God himself the principal director of them, but not unto them that are directed to execute the same. The rule of natural agents which work after a sort of their own accord, as the beasts do, is the judgment of common sence or fancie concerning the sensible goodnes of those objects wherewith they are moved. The rule of ghostly or immaterial natures, as spirits and Angels, is their intuitive intellectual judgment concerning the amiable beauty and high goodnes of that object which with unspeakable joy and delight doth set them on work. The rule of voluntary agents on earth, is the sentence that reason giveth concerning the goodnes of those things which they are to do. And the sentences which reason giveth, are some more, some less general, before it come to define in particular actions what is good. The main principles of reason are in themselves apparent. For to make nothing evident of it self unto mans understanding, were to take away all possibility of knowing any thing. And herein that of *Theophrastus* is true, *They that seek a reason of all things, do utterly overthrow reason.* In every kind of knowled some such grounds there are, as that being proposed, the mind doth presently embrace them as free from all possibility of error, cleer and manifest without proof. In which kind, axiomes or principles more general are such as this, *That the greater good is to be chosen before the less.* If therefore it should be demanded, what reason there is why the will of man which doth necessarily shun harm, and covet whatsoever

N

is (c Rom. 1. 14.

[marginal notes:]
a δεῖ ὢς ἄϵι τὸ πολὺ ὡσαύ- τως ἀπαντᾶται.

b ἅ τι πολλ̉ error contingere ubi omnes idem opina tur.

in 1 Polit.

Quicquid in omnibus inuivi. dis unius speci- ei cumq̉ uniter iacsi, id caufam communem ha beat oportet, que est earum inuivi. daoium specics & natura. Idem Quodata uà ah- qua specie fit, u. niue falis parti- cular sque natu- ra sit instindu, Fici n. de chrift. Relig.

Si profecerie cu- tis primo farme id uerum puta quod sana mens omnium homi- num aricfiaxur.

Cum in com- pend, cap. 1.

Non licet naiu- ra'e un uersale que hominum md'cium falsum vain m q̉e ex- istima e. Tel. t.

Ὅ γὰ πᾶσι δο- κει, τὸ εἶναι φα- μὲν. τῶ̇ εἶναι γαρ ἠ δὲ ἵ- πίσιν, τα'την Τιν μϵν ὶ πᾶς τυ ἀιστ πραϵρι Arist. l to. 1c. cap. 2.

Ἀντιπῦ ῷ-
πιμῦπς λόγοι,
ἀγατήσει λόγοι
Theoph. in Met. is why the will of man, which doth necessarily shun harm, and covet whatsoever is pleasant and sweet, should be commanded to count the pleasures of sin, gall, and notwithstanding the bitter accidents wherewith vertuous actions are compast, yet still to rejoyce and delight in them; surely this could never stand with reason: but that wisdome thus prescribing, groundeth her Laws upon an infallible rule of comparison, which is, that small difficulties, when exceeding great good is sure to insue; and on the other side momentany benefits, when the hurt which they draw after them is unspeakable, are not at all to be respected. This rule is the ground whereupon the Wisdome of the Apostle buildeth a Law, injoyning patience unto himself, *The present lightness of our affliction worketh unto us even with abundance upon abundance an eternal waight of glory, while we look not on the things which are seen, but on the things which are not seen. For the things which are seen are temporal, but the things which are not seen are eternal.* Therefore Christianity to be embraced, whatsoever calamities in those times, it was accompanied withal. Upon the same ground our Saviour proveth the Law most reasonable, that doth forbid those crimes which men for gains sake fall into. For a man to win the world, if it be with the loss of his soul, what benefit or good is it? Axiomes less general, yet so manifest that they need no farther proof, are such as these, *God to be worshiped, Parents to be honored; Others to be used by us as we our selves would by them.* Such things, as soon as they are alleaged, all men acknowledg to be good; they require no proof or farther discourse to be assured of their goodness. Notwithstanding, whatsoever such principle there is, it was at the first found out by discourse, and drawn from out of the very bowels of heaven and earth. For we are to note, that things in the World are to us discernable, not only so far forth as serveth for our vital preservation, but further also in a two-fold higher respect. For first if all other uses were utterly taken away; yet the mind of man being by nature speculative and delighted with contemplation in it self, they were to be known even for meer knowledg and understandings sake. Yea further besides this, the knowledg of every the least thing in the world, hath in it a second peculiar benefit unto us, in as much as it serveth to minister Rules, Canons, and Laws for men to direct those actions by, which we properly terme humane. This did the very Heathens themselves obscurely insinuate, by making *Themis* which we call *Jus* or Right, to be the Daughter of heaven and earth. We know things either as they are in themselves, or as they are in mutual relation to one another. The knowledg of that which man is in reference unto himself, and other things in relation unto man, I may justly term the Mother of all those principles, which are as it were edicts, statutes, and decrees in that law of nature, whereby humane actions are framed. First therefore having observed that the best things where they are not hindred, do still produce the best operations; (for which cause where many things are to concur unto one effect, the best is in all congruity of reason to guide the residue, that it prevailing most the work principally done by it may have greatest perfection:) when hereupon we come to observe in our selves, of what excellency our souls are in comparison of our bodies, and the diviner part in relation unto the baser of our souls; seeing that all these concur in producing humane actions, it cannot be well unless the chiefest do command and direct the rest. The soul then ought to conduct the body, and the spirit of our minds the soul. This is therefore the first Law, whereby the highest power of the mind requireth general obedience at the hands of all the rest concurring with it unto action. Touching the several grand Mandates, which being imposed by the understanding faculty of the mind, must be obeyed by the will of man, they are by the same method found out, whether they import our duty towards God or towards man. Touching the one, I may not here stand to open, by what degrees of discourse the minds even of meer natural men, have attained to know, not only that there is a God, but also what power, force, wisdome and other properties that God hath, and how all things depend on him. This being therefore presupposed, from that known relation which God hath unto us (a) as unto children, and unto all good things as unto effects, whereof himself is the (b) principal cause, these axiomes and Laws natural concerning our duty have arisen; (c) *That in all things we go about, his aid is by Prayer to be craved*, (d) *That he cannot have sufficient honor done unto him, but the uttermost of that we can do to honor him we must*; which is in effect the same that we read, (e) *Thou shalt love the Lord thy God with all thy heart, with all thy soul, and with all thy mind.* Which Law our Saviour doth terme the (f) *First and the great*

2 Cor. 4. 17.

Matth. 16. 26.

* Arist. Polit. 1.
cap. 5.
αΟὐ δὲς Θεὸς
δύσαυς ἀνθρώ-
πσις. Plat. in
Theæt.
b Ὅτι γὰρ
Θεὸς δοκεῖ τὸ
αἴτιον πᾶσιν
εἶ) ἢ ἀρχή τις.
Arist. διειαρ.
lib. 1. cap 2.
c Ἀλλ᾽ ὦ Σώ-
κρατες τῶν γε
δὴ ἀντίτης ἔσω
ἢ χρὴ ἐραῶ
σωρεγούντε
μετέχουσιν,
ἐπὶ πᾶσιν ὁρμῶ
ἢ μικρῶ ἢ με-
γάλω πράγ-
ματος. Σὺν
ἀπί σε κριλίσι.
Plat. in Tim.
d Arist. Ethic.
lib. 4. cap ult.
e Deut. 6. 4.
f M. 22. 38.

great *Commandment.* Touching the next, which as our Saviour addeth, is like unto this (he meaneth an amplitude and largeness, in as much as it is the root out of which all laws of duty to men-ward have grown, as out of the former all offices of Religion towards God) the like natural inducement hath brought men to know, that it is their duty no less to love others then themselves. For seeing those things which are equal, must needs all have one measure: if I cannot but wish to receive all good, even as much at every mans hand, as any man can wish unto his own soul, how should I look to have any part of my desire herein satisfied, unless my self be careful to satisfie the like defire, which is undoubtedly in other men, we all being of one and the same nature? To have any thing offered them repugnant to this desire, must needs in all respects grieve them as much as me: So that if I do harm, I must look to suffer; there being no reason that others should shew greater measure of love to me, then they have by me shewed unto them. My desire therefore to be loved of my equals in nature as much as possible may be, imposeth upon me a natural duty of bearing to them-ward fully the like affection. From which relation of equality between our selves, and them that are as our selves, what several rules and canons natural reason hath drawn for direction of life, no man is ignorant; as namely, *That because we would take no harm, we must therefore do none; that fith we would not be in any thing extremely dealt with, we must our selves avoid all extremity in our dealings; that from all violence and wrong we are utterly to abstain,* with such like; which further to wade in would be tedious, and to our present purpose not altogether so necessary, seeing that on these two general heads already mentioned, all other specialties are dependent. Wherefore the natural measure whereby to judge our doings, is the sentence of reason, determining and setting down what is good to be done. Which sentence is either mandatory, shewing what must be done; or else permissive, declaring onely what may be done; or thirdly admonitory, opening what is the most convenient for us to do. The first taketh place, where the comparison doth stand altogether between doing and not doing of one thing, which in it self is absolutely good or evil; as it had been for *Joseph* to yield, or not to yield, to the impotent desire of his leud Mistris; the one evil, the other good simply. The second is, when of divers things evil, all being not evitable, we are permitted to take one; which one, saving onely in case of so great urgency, were not otherwise to be taken; as in the matter of divorce amongst the Jews. The last, when of divers things good, one is principal and most eminent; as in their act who sold their possessions and laid the price at the Apostles feet, which possessions they might have retained unto themselves without sin; again, in the Apostle St. *Pauls* own choice, to maintain himself by his own labour, whereas in living by the Churches maintenance, as others did, there had been no offence committed. In goodness therefore there is a latitude of extent, whereby it cometh to pass, that even of good actions, some are better then other some; whereas otherwise one man could not excel another, but all should be either absolutely good, as hiting jump that indivisible point or center wherein goodness consisteth; or else missing it, they should be excluded out of the number of well-doers. Degrees of well-doing there could be none, except perhaps in the seldomness and oftenness of doing well. But the nature of goodness being thus ample, a Law is properly that which reason in such sort defineth to be good, that it must be done. And the Law of Reason or Humane Nature is that, which men by discourse of natural reason have rightly found out themselves to be all for ever bound unto in their actions. Laws of Reason have these marks to be known by. Such as keep them, resemble most lively in their voluntary actions, that very manner of working which Nature her self doth necessarily observe in the course of the whole World. The works of Nature are all behoveful, beautiful, without superfluity or defect; even so theirs, if they be so framed according to that which the Law of Reason teacheth. Secondly, those laws are investigable by reason, without the help of revelation supernatural and divine. Finally, in such sort they are investigable, that the knowledge of them is general, the world hath alwayes been acquainted with them; according to that which one in *Sophocles* observeth concerning a branch of this Law. *It is no childe of two dayes, or yesterdays birth, but hath been no man kneweth how long sithence.* It is not agreed upon by one, or two, or few, but by all; which we may not so understand, as if every particular man in the whole world did know and confess whatsoever the Law of Reason doth contain; but this Law

Marginal notes:
Quod quis in se approbat, in alio reprobare non posse. l. in arenam C. de inos. test. Quod quisque juris in alium statuet t ipsum quoque eodem uti debere.l.quod quis'q; Ab omni peni-tus injuria az qui abstinens dum,l.t.sect.f. quod vi, aut clam.

Mat. 22. 40.
On these two Commandments hang the whole *Law* Gen. 30. 9.
Mark 10. 4.
Acts 4. 37. and 5. 4.
2 Thess. 3. 8.

Greek marginal notes:
Ου γδι νν [...] τωι πηχαχθει; [...] αλλ αει ποιε [...] Σ η ουδον ε-χ η [...] τις ειδεν ο[...]- ποτε φμν. Soph. Anti.

is such, that being proposed, no man can reject it as unreasonable and unjust. Again, there is nothing in it, but any man (having natural perfection of wit, and ripeness of judgement) may by labour and travel finde out. And to conclude, the general principles thereof are such, as it is not easie to finde men ignorant of them. Law rational therefore, which men commonly use to call the Law of Nature, meaning thereby the Law which humane Nature knoweth it self, in reason universally bound unto; which also for that cause may be termed most firly, the Law of Reason: This Law, I say, comprehendeth all those things, which men, by the light of their natural understanding evidently know, or at leastwise may know, to be beseeming or unbeseeming, vertuous or vitious, good or evil for them to do. Now, although it be true, which some have said, that whatsoever is done amiss, the Law of Nature and Reason thereby is transgrest, because even those offences which are by their special qualities breaches of supernatural Laws, do also, for that they are generally evil, violate in general that principle of Reason, which willeth universally to flye from evil: yet do we not therefore so far extend the Law of Reason, as to contain in it all manner of Laws whereunto resonable creatures are bound, but (as hath been shewed) we restrain it to those onely duties, which all men by force of natural wit either do, or might understand

Th.1.2.q94.
art.3. Omnis
peccata sunt
in quiversum
contravationem
& natura legem. Aug. de
Civ. Dei l. 12.
cap. 1.
Omne vitium
natura nocet, ac
pa hoc contra
naturam est.
De Doct: Chr.
l. 3. c. 14.

to be such duties as concern all men. *Certain half-waking men there are* (as St. *Augustine noteth*) *who neither altogether asleep in folly, nor yet throughly awake in the light of true understanding, have thought that there is not at all any thing just and righteous in it self; but look wherewith Nations are injured, the same they take to be right, and just. Whereupon their Conclusion is, That seeing each sort of people hath a different kinde of right from other; and that which is right of its own nature, must be every where one and the same; therefore in it self there is nothing right.* These good folks (saith he, *that I may not trouble their wits with the rehearsal of too many things*) *have not looked so far into the world as to perceive, that,* Do as thou wouldst be done unto, *is a sentence which all Nations under heaven are agreed upon. Refer this sentence to the love of God, and it extinguisheth all heinous crimes: Refer it to the love of thy Neighbour, and all grievous wrongs is banished out of the world.* Wherefore, as touching the Law of Reason, this was (it seemeth) St. *Augustines* judgement; namely, that there are in it some things which stand as Priciples universally agreed upon; and that out of those Principles, which are in themselves evident, the greatest moral duties we owe towards God or Man, may without any great difficulty be concluded. If then it be here demanded, by what means it should come to pass: (the greatest part of the Law moral being so easie for all men to know) that so many thousands of men notwithstanding have been ignorant, even of principal moral duties, not imagining the breach of them to be sin: I deny not, but leud and wicked custom, beginning perhaps at the first amongst few, afterward spreading into greater multitudes, and so continuing from time to time, may be of force even in plain things, to smother the light of natural understanding, because men will not bend their wits to examine, whether things wherewith they have been accustomed be good or evil. For examples sake, that grosser kinde of Heathenish Idolatry, whereby they worshipped the very works of their own hands, was an absurdity to reason so palpable, that the Prophet *David* comparing Idols and Idolaters together, maketh almost no odds between them, but the one in a manner, as much without wit and sense as the other, *They that make them are like unto them, and so are*

Psal. 115. 18.

all that trust in them. That wherein an Idolater doth seem so absurd and foolish, is by the Wiseman thus exprest, *He is not ashamed to speak unto that which hath no life; He calleth on*

Wisd. 13. 17.

him that is weak, for health; He prayeth for life unto him, which is dead; Of him, which hath no experience he requireth help; For his journey he sueth to him, which is not able to go; For gain, and work, and success in his affairs, he seeketh for furtherance of him that hath no manner of power: the cause of which senless stupidity is afterwards imputed to custom.

Wisd. 14. 12.

When a father mourned grievously for his son that was taken away suddenly, he made an image for him that was once dead, whom now he worshipped as a god, ordaining to his servants ceremonies and sacrifices. Thus by process of time this wicked custom prevailed, and was kept as a Law; the authority of Rulers, the ambition of Crafts-men, and such like means, thrusting forward the ignorant, and encreasing their superstition. Unto this which the Wiseman hath spoken, somewhat besides may be added. For whatsoever we have hitherto taught, or shall hereafter, concerning the force of mans natural understanding, this we always desire withal to be understood, that there is no kinde

of

of faculty or power in man, or any other creature, which can rightly perform the functions allotted to it, without perpetual aid and concurrence of that supreme cause of all
things. The benefit whereof as oft as we cause God in his justice to withdraw, there can
no other thing follow then that which the Apostle noteth, even men indued with the
light of Reason to walk notwithstanding *in the vanitie of their mind, having their co-* Ephes. 4. 17.
gitations darkened, and being strangers from the life of God through the ignorance which is
in them, because of the hardness of their hearts. And this cause is mentioned by the Prophet *Isaiah*, speaking of the ignorance of Idolaters, who see not how the manifest Law
of reason condemneth their gross iniquity and sin; they have not in them, saith he, so
much wit as to think, *Shall I bow to the Stock of a tree? All Knowledg and understanding* Isa. 44. 18, 19.
is taken from them. For God hath shut their eyes that they cannot see. That which we say
in this cause of Idolatry, serveth for all other things, wherein the like kind of general
blindness hath prevailed against the manifest Laws of Reason. Within the compass of
which Laws we do not only comprehend whatsoever may be easily known to belong
to the duty of all men; but even whatsoever may possibly be known to be of that qua-
litie, so that the same be by *necessarie* consequence deduced out of cleer and manifest
principles. For if once we descend unto probable collections what is convenient for
men; we are then in the Territorie where free and arbitrary determinations, the
Territorie where humane Laws take place, which Laws are after to be considered.

9. Now the due observation of this Law which Reason teacheth us, cannot but be   The benefit of
effectual unto their great good that observe the same. For we see the whole World   keeping that
and each part thereof so compacted, that as long as each thing performeth onely that   law which rea-
work which is natural unto it, it thereby preserveth both other things, and also it self.   son teacheth.
Contrariwise, let any principal thing, as the Sun, the Moon, any one of the Heavens or
Elements, but once cease or fail, or swerve; and who doth not easily conceive that the
sequel thereof would be ruine both to it self, and whatsoever dependeth on it? And is
it possible that man, being not only the noblest creature in the world, but even a very
World in himself; his transgressing the Law of his Nature should draw no manner of
harme after it? Yes, *tribulation and anguish unto every soul that doth evil.* Good doth
follow unto all things by observing the course of their nature, and on the contrarie
side evil by not observing it: but not unto natural Agents that good wich we call
Reward, nor that evil which we properly terme *Punishment.* The reason whereof
is, because amongst creatures in this world, onely mans observation of the Law of
his nature is *Righteousness*, onely mans transgression *Sin.* And the reason of this is,
the difference in his manner of observing or transgressing the Law of his nature. He
doth not otherwise then voluntarily the one or the other. What we do against our
wills, or constrainedly, we are not properly said to do it; because the motive cause
of doing it is not in our selves, but carrieth us; as if the wind should drive a Feather
in the Aire, we no whit furthering that whereby we are driven. In such cases therefore the evil which is done, moveth compassion; men are pittied for it, as being rather miserable in such respect then culpable. Some things are likewise done by man,
though not through outward force and impulsion, though not against, yet without
their will; as in alienation of mind, or any the like inevitable utter absence of wit
and judgment. For which cause, no man did ever think the hurtful actions of furious Men and Innocents to be punishable. Againe, some things we do neither against
nor without, and yet not simply and meerly with our wills; but with our wills in
such sort moved, that albeit there be no impossibility but that we might, nevertheless we are not so easily able to do otherwise. In this consideration one evil deed is
made more pardonable then another. Finally, that which we do being evil, is not withstanding by so much more pardonable, by how much the exigence of so doing, or the
difficultie of doing otherwise is greater; unless this necessity or difficulty have
originally risen from our selves. It is no excuse therefore unto him, who being
drunk committeth incest, and alleageth that his wits were not his own; in as much
as himself might have chosen whether his wits should to that mean have been taken
from him. Now rewards and punishments do always presuppose some thing willingly done well or ill; without which respect though we may sometimes receive good or
harme; yet then the one is onely a benefit, and not a reward; the other simply an hurt, not a punishment. From the sundrie dispositions of mans will;
which is the root of all his actions, there groweth varietie in the sequele of rewards
and

Voluntate sub-
lata, or nera a-
tium partem esse
l. fædissimam, &
de adult. Ho-
nam voluntatem
plerunq; profa.io
repu.ari l. si quis
in Testamenti.

Divos caste ad-
eunto, pietatem
adhibento Qui
secus faxit, Deus
ipse vindex erit.

How Reason
doth lead men
unto the mak-
ing of humane
laws, whereby
politique soci-
eties are go-
verned, and to
agreement a-
bout Laws,
whereby the
fellowship or
communion of
independent
society stand-
eth.

Εςι γαρ ὁ μας-
τιυον η
παντες ειστι
κοινον δικαιον κ)
αδικον κ)
μεσ εμια κονω-
νια προς αλλη-
λους η μηδεν
συνδικον.
Arist. Rhets 1.

and punishments, which are by these and the like rules measured : *Take away the will,*
and all acts are equal : That which we do not and would do, is commonly accepted as done.
By these and the like rules mens actions are determined of and judged, whether they
be in their own nature rewardable or punishable. Rewards and punishments are not received, but at the hands of such as being above us, have power to examine and judge
our deeds. How men come to have this authority one over another in external actions, we shall more diligently examine in that which followeth. But for this present, so much all do acknowledge, that sith every mans heart and conscience doth
in good or evil, even secretly committed and known to none but it self, either
like or disallow it self, and accordingly either rejoyce, very nature exulting as
it were in certaine hope of reward, or else grieve as it were in a sence of future punishment; neither of which can in this case be looked for from any other, saving
onely from him who discerneth and judgeth the very secrets of all hearts : Therefore he is the onely Rewarder and Revenger of all such actions; although not of such
actions onely, but of all whereby the Law of nature is broken, whereof himself is
Author. For which cause, the Roman Laws, called the Laws of the twelve Tables,
requiring offices of inward affection, which the eye of man cannot reach unto, threaten
the neglecters of them with none but divine punishment.

10. That which hitherto we have set down, is (I hope) sufficient to shew their
brutishness, which imagine that Religion and Vertue are onely as men will account of
them ; that we might make as much account, if we would, of the contrarie, without any harme unto our selves, and that in nature they are as indifferent one as the
other. We see then how nature it self teacheth Laws and Statutes to live by. The
Laws which have been hitherto mentioned, do bind men absolutely, even as they are
men, although they have never any setled fellowship, never any solemn agreement
amongst themselves what to do or not to do. But forasmuch as we are not by our
selves sufficient to furnish our selves with competent store of things needful for such
a life as our nature doth desire, a life fit for the dignity of man; Therefore to supply
those defects and imperfections which are in us living single and solely by our selves,
we are naturally induced to seek communion and fellowship with others. This was the
cause of mens uniting themselves at the first in Politique societies, which societies could
not be without government, nor government without a distinct kind of Law from that
which hath been already declared. Two foundations there are which bear up publique
societies ; the one, a natural inclination, whereby all men desire sociable life and fellowship; the other, an order expresly or secretly agreed upon, touching the manner of their union in living together. The latter is that which we call the law of a
Common-weal, the very soul of a Politique body, the parts whereof are by law
animated, held together, and set on work in such actions as the common good
requireth. Laws politique, ordained for external order and regiment a-
mongst men, are never framed as they should be, unless presuming the will of man to
be inwardly obstinate, rebellious, and averse from all obedience unto the sacred Laws
of his nature in a word, unless presuming man to be inregard of his depraved mind,
little better then a wild beast, they do accordingly provid enotwithstanding so to frame
his outward actions, that they be no hindrance unto the common good for which societies are instituted : unless they do this, they are not perfect. It resteth therefore that we consider how nature findeth out such laws of government, as serve to direct even nature depraved to a right end. All men desire in this world to lead an happy life. The life is led most happily, wherein all vertue is exercised without impedi-

1 Tim 6. 6.

ment or let. The Apostle in exhorting men to contentment, although they have in this
world no more then very bare food and raiment, giveth us thereby to understand,
that those are even the lowest of things necessary , that if we should be stripped of all
those things without which we might possibly be, yet these must be left; that destitution in these is such an impediment, as till it be removed, suffereth not the mind of man

Gen. 1. 29.
Gen. 2. 17.
Ge. 4. 2.
G.n. 4. 26.

to admit any other care. For this cause first God assigned *Adam* maintenance of
Life, and then appointed him a Law to observe. For this cause after men began to
grow to a number, the first thing we read they gave themselves unto, was the tilling of
the earth, and the feeding of cattle. Having by this mean whereon to live, the prin-

Mat. 6. 33.

cipal actions of their life afterward are noted by the exercise of their Religion. True
it is, that the Kingdome of God must be the first thing in our purposes and desires.
But

But in as much as a righteous life presupposeth life, in as much as to live vertuously it is impossible except we live; therefore the first impediment, which naturally we endeavour to remove, is penury and want of things without which we cannot live. Unto life many implements are necessary; most, if we seek (as all men naturally do) such a life as hath in it joy, comfort, delight, and pleasure. To this end we see how quickly sundry Arts Mechanical were found out in the very prime of the World. As things of greatest necessity are alwayes first provided for, so things of greatest dignity are most accounted of by all such as judge rightly. Although therefore Riches be a thing which every man wisheth; yet no man of judgement can esteem it better to be rich, then wise, vertuous, and religious. If we be both or either of these, it is not because we are so born. For into the world we came as empty of the one as of the other, as naked in mind as we are in body. Both which necessities of man had at the first no other help and supplies, then onely domestical; such as that which the Prophet implieth, saying, _Can a mother forget her child ?_ Such as that which the Apostle mentioneth, saying, _He that careth not for his own is worse then an Infidel;_ such as that concerning _Abraham, Abraham will command his sons and his houshold after him, that they keep the way of the Lord._ But neither that which we learned of our selves, nor that which others teach us can prevail, where wickedness and malice have taken deep root. If therefore when there was but as yet one onely family in the world, no meanes of instruction humane or divine, could prevent effusion of blood: how could it be chosen but that when families were multiplied and increased upon earth, after separation, each providing for it self, envy, strife, contention, and violence, must grow amongst them ? For hath not nature furnisht man with wit and valour, and as it were with armour, which may be used as well unto extream evil as good ? yea, were they not used by the rest of the world unto evil ? unto the contrary onely by _Seth, Enoch,_ and those few the rest in that line ? We all make complaint of the iniquity of our times: not unjustly; for the dayes are evil. But compare them with those times wherein there were no civil societies, with those times wherein there was as yet no manner of Publiqe regiment established, with those times wherein there were not above eight righteous persons living upon the face of the earth: and we have surely good cause to think that God hath blessed us exceedingly, and hath made us behold most happy dayes. To take away all such mutual grievances, injuries and wrongs, there was no way but onely by growing upon composition and agreement amongst themselves, by ordaining some kind of government publique, & by yielding themselves subject thereunto; that unto whom they granted authority to rule & govern, by them the peace, tranquillity, & happy estate of the rest might be procured. Men always knew that when force and injury was offered, they might be defenders of themselves; they knew that howsoever men may seek their own commoditie, yet if this were done with injury unto others, it was not to be suffered, but by all men and by all good meanes to be withstood; finally, they knew that no man might in reason take upon him to determine his own right, and according to his own determination proceed in maintenance thereof, in as much as every man is towards himself, & them whom he greatly affecteth, partial; and therefore that strifes & troubles would be endless, except they gave their common consent, all to be ordered by some whom they should agree upon: without which consent, there were no reason that one man should take upon him to be Lord or Judge over another; because although there be according to the opinion of some very great and judicious men, a kind of natural right in the Noble, wise, and vertuous, to govern them which are of servile disposition; nevertheless for manifestation of this their right, and mens more peaceable contentment on both sides, the assent of them who are to be governed, seemeth necessary. To Fathers within their private Families, Nature hath given a supreame power; for which cause we see throughout the world, even from the first foundation thereof, all men have ever been taken as Lords and lawful Kings in their own houses. Howbeit over a whole grand multitude, having no such dependency upon any one, and consisting of so many Families as every politique society in the world doth, impossible it is that any should have complete lawful power, but by consent of men, or immediate appointment of God, because not having the natural superiority of Fathers, their power must needs be either usurped, and then unlawful; or if lawful, then either granted or consented unto by them over whom they exercise the same, or else given extraordinarily

ordinarily

Gen. 4. 20, 21, 22.

Isai 43. 15.

1 Tim. 5. 8.
Gen. 18. 19.

Gen 4. 8.

Gen. 6. 5.
Gen. 5.

2 Pet. 2. 5.

Arist. Pol. lib. 3.
& 4.

Arist. Polit. l. 1
cap. . Vide &
Platonem in 3.
de legibus.

ordinaily from God, unto whom all the World is subject. It is no improbable opinion therefore which the Arch-Philosopher was of, that as the chiefest person in every houshold was always as it were a King ; so when numbers of housholds joyned themselves in Civil Societies together, Kings were the first kind of Governors amongst them. Which is also (as it seemeth) the reason, why the name of *Father* continued still in them, who of Fathers were made Rulers : as also the antient custome of Governors to do as *Melchisedec*, and being Kings to exercise the office of Priests, which Fathers did at the first, grew perhaps by the same occasion. Howbeit not this the only kind of Regiment that hath been received in the World. The inconveniences of one kind, have caused sundry other to be devised. So that in a word, all publiqe Regiment, of what kind so ever, seemeth evidently to have risen from deliberate advice, consultation & composition between men, judging it convenient and behoveful; there being no impossibility in nature considered by it self, but that men might have lived without any publiqe Regiment. Howbeit the corruption of our nature being presupposed, we may not denie but that the Law of nature doth now require of necessity some kind of Regiment ; so that to bring things unto the first course they were in, and utterly to take away all kind of publiqe government in the world, were apparantly to overturn the whole world. The case of mans nature standing therefore as it doth, some kind of Regiment the Law of nature doth require ; yet the kinds thereof being many, nature tyeth not to any one, but leaveth the choice as a thing arbi-

(a) Cum preme
returinitio mul-
t tudo ab iis qui
maieres opes ba-
bebant,ad unum
ali quem confu
giebant v rtute
praestantem; qui
cû profiteб ctin-
iuriâ tenaires,
aequitate consti-
t. endâ summos
cum infimis pari
iure retinebat.
Cum id m nus
contingeret, le-
gesfunt invente
Cic. Offic. lib.2.

trary. At the first when some certain kind of Regiment was once approved, it may be that nothing was then further thought upon for the manner of governing, but all permitted unto their wisdome and discretion which were to rule; (a) till by experience they found this for all parts very inconvenient, so as the thing which they had devised for a remedy, did indeed but increase the sore which it should have cured. They saw that to live by one mans will, became the cause of all mens misery. This constrained them to come unto Laws, wherein all men might see their duties beforehand, and know the penalties of transgressing them. (b) If things be simply good or evil, and withal universally so acknowledged, there needs no new law to be made for such things. The first kind therefore of things appointed by Laws humane, containeth whatsoever being in it self naturally good or evil; is notwithstanding more secret then that it can be discerned by every mans present conceit, without some deeper discourse

Τὸ κριὰς πρῶι
κỳ εἶλκε ἐυ-
μενÌ κỳ τῆς
ἐυεργεσίας χά-
ειν ἀποδιδυαι,
πῦτα κỳ τέτις
ὁμοια ἐ ωργ-
χάσοω τῆς
ἀνθρώπυς ἐι
γεγαμμίνοι
ἡφατι ποιεῖν,
ἀλλ᾽ ἐυδὺς α-
χρεω κỳ κοινῶ
τρόπυ νομ᾽ζε.
Arist. Rhet. ad
Alex.

& judgment. In which discourse, because there is difficulty and possibility many ways to erre, unless such things were set down by laws, many would be ignorant of their dutys, which now are not; & many that know what they should do, would nevertheless dissemble it, & to excuse themselves pretend ignorance and simplicity, which now they cannot. And because the greatest part of men are such as prefer their own private good before all things ; even that good which is sensual, before whatsoever is most Divine; and for that the labour of doing good, together with the pleasures arising from the contrary, doth make men for the most part slower to the one, and proner to the other, then that duty prescribed them by Law can prevaile sufficiently with them : therefore unto Laws that men do make for the benefit of men, it hath seemed always needful to add rewards, which may more allure unto good then any hardness deterreth from it; and punishments, which may more deterre from evil then any sweetness thereto allureth. Wherein as the generality is natural, *Vertue rewardable, and Vice punishable* : So the particular determination of the reward or punishment, belongeth unto them by whom

(b) Tanta est
enim vis to up
tatum, ut & ig-
n rant am crote-
let in occasio-
ne.a.& consci-
entiam terr- m
pat in dissimula-
tioнeм. Tertul.
lib. de Specia-
cul.

Laws are made. Theft is naturally punishable, but the kind of punishment is Positive; and such lawful, as men shall think with discretion convenient by Law to appoint. In Laws that which is natural, bindeth universally; that which is positive not so. To let go those kind of Positive laws, which men impose upon themselves, as by vow unto God, contract with men, or such like ; somewhat it will make unto our purpose, a little more fully to consider, what things are incident unto the making of the Positive Laws for the Government of them that live united in publiqe Societie. Laws do not onely teach what is good, but they injoyn it, they have in them a certain constraining force. And to constrain men unto any thing inconvenient, doth seem unreasonable. Most requisite therefore it is, that to devise Laws which all men shall be forced to obey, none but Wisemen be admitted. Laws are matters of principal consequence ; men of common capacity, and but ordinary judgment, are not able (for how should they?) to discerne what things are fittest for each kind and state of

Regi-

Regiment. We cannot be ignorant how much our obedience unto Laws dependeth upon this point. Let a man, though never so justly, oppose himself unto them that are disordered in their ways, and what one among them commonly doth not, stomack at such contradiction, storm at reproof, and hate such as would reform them? Notwithstanding even they, which brook it worst that men should tell them of their duties, when they are told the same by a Law, think very well and reasonably of it. For why? They presume that the Law doth speak with all indifferency, that the Law hath no side respect to their persons, that the Law is as it were an Oracle proceeding from Wisdom and Understanding. Howbeit, Laws do not take their constraining force from the quality of such as devise them, but from that power which doth give them the strength of Laws. That which we spake before concerning the power of Government, must here be applied unto the power of making Laws whereby to govern, which power God hath over all; and by the natural law whereunto he hath made all subject, the lawful power of making laws, to command whole Politique Societies of men, belongeth so properly unto the same intire Societies, that for any Prince or Potentate, of what kind soever upon earth, to exercise the same of himself, and not either by express commission immediately and personally received from God, or else by authority derived at the first from their consent upon whose persons they impose Laws, it is no better then meer tyranny. Laws they are not therefore which publique approbation hath not made so. But Approbation not onely they give who personally declare their assent by voyce, sign, or act, but also when others do it in their names, by right originally at the least derived from them. As in Parliaments, Councils, and the like Assemblies, although we be not personally our selves present, notwithstanding our assent is by reason of other agents there in our behalf. And what we do by others, no reason but that it should stand as our deed, no less effectually to bind us then if our selves had done it in person. In many things assent is given, they that give it, not imagining they do so, because the manner of their assenting is not apparent. As for example, when an absolute Monarch commandeth his Subjects that which seemeth good in his own discretion, hath not his edict the force of a Law, whether they approve or dislike it? Again, that which hath been received long sithence, and is by custom now established, we keep as a Law which we may not transgress; yet what consent was ever thereunto sought and required at our hands? Of this point therefore we are to note, that sith men naturally have no full and perfect power to command whole politique multitudes of men; therefore utterly without our consent, we could in such sort be at no mans commandment living. And to be commanded we do consent, when that Society whereof we are part, hath at any time before consented, without revoking the same after by the like universal agreement. Wherefore as any mans deed past is good as long as himself continueth: So the act of a publique Society of men done five hundred years sithence, standeth as theirs; who presently are of the same Societies, because Corporations are immortal; we are then alive in our Predecessors, and they in their Successors do live still. Laws therefore humane of what kind soever, are available by consent. If here it be demanded how it cometh to pass, that this being common unto all Laws which are made, there should be found even in good Laws so great variety as there is: we must note the reason hereof to be, the sundry particular ends, whereunto the different disposition of that subject or matter for which laws are provided, causeth them to have a special respect in making Laws. A Law there is mentioned amongst the *Grecians*, whereof *Pittacus* is reported to have been *Arist. polit.l.2.* Author; and by that Law it was agreed, that he which being overcome with drink *cap. ult.* did then strike any man, should suffer punishment double as much as if he had done the same being sober. No man could ever have thought this reasonable, that had intended thereby onely to punish the injury committed, according to the gravity of the fact. For who knoweth not, that harm advisedly done is naturally less pardonable, and therefore worthy of sharper punishment? But for as much as none did so usually this way offend as men in that case, which they wittingly fell into, even because they would be so much the more freely outragious: it was for their publique good where such disorder were grown, to frame a positive Law for remedy thereof accordingly. To this appertain those known laws of making laws; as that Law-makers may have an eye to that place where, and to the men amongst whom; that one kind of laws cannot serve for all kind of Regiment; that where the multitude beareth sway,

Laws

laws that shall tend unto the prefervation of that ftate, muft make common fmaller officers to go by lot, for fear of ftrife and divifion likely to arife, by reafon that ordinary qualities fufficing for difcharge of fuch offices, they could not but by many be defired, and fo with danger contended for, and not miffed without grudge and difcontentment, whereas at an uncertain lot, none can finde themfelves grieved on whomfoever it lighteth; contrariwife the greateft, whereof but few are capable, to pafs by popular election, that neither the people may envy fuch as have thofe honours, in as much as themfelves beftow them, and that the chiefeft may be kindled with defire to exercife all parts of rare and beneficial vertue; knowing they fhall not lofe their labour by growing in fame and eftimation amongft the people: If the helm of chief Government be in the hands of a few of the wealthieft, that then laws providing for continuance thereof, muft make the punifhment of contumely and wrong offered unto any of the common fort, fharp and grievous, that fo the evil may be prevented, whereby the rich are moft likely to bring themfelves into hatred with the people, who are not wont to take fo great offence when they are excluded from honours and offices, as when their perfons are contumelioufly troden upon. In other kinds of regiment the like is obferved concerning the difference of pofitive Laws, which to be every where the fame is impoffible, and againft their nature. Now as the learned in the Laws of this Land obferve, that our Statutes fometimes are onely the affirmation or ratification of that which by common Law was held before: So here it is not to be omitted, that generally all Laws humane, which are made for the ordering of politick Societies, be either fuch as eftablifh fome duty, whereunto all men by the Law of Reafon did before ftand bound; or elfe fuch as make that a duty now, which before was none. The one fort we may for diftinction fake call *mixedly*, and the other *meerly* humane. That which plain or neceffary reafon bindeth men unto, may be in fundry confiderations expedient to be ratified by Humane Law. For example, if confufion of blood in marriage, the liberty of having many wives at once, or any other the like corrupt and unreafonable cuftom doth happen to have prevailed far, and to have gotten the upper hand of right reafon with the greateft part; fo that no way is left to rectifie fuch foul diforder, without prefcribing by law the fame things which reafon neceffarily doth enforce, but it is not perceived that fo it doth; or if many be grown unto that which the Apoftle did lament in fome, concerning whom he writeth, faying, that *Even what things they naturally know, in thofe very things, as Beafts void of reafon, they corrupt themfelves*; or if there be no fuch fpecial accident, yet for as much as the common fort are led by the fway of their fenfual defires, and therefore do more than fin for the fenfible evils which follow it amongft men, then for any kind of fentence which reafon doth pronounce againft it: This very thing is caufe fufficient why duties belonging unto each kind of vertue, albeit the Law of Reafon teach them, fhould notwithftanding be prefcribed even by Humane Law. Which Law in this cafe we term *mixt*, becaufe the matter whereunto it bindeth, is the fame which reafon neceffarily doth require at our hands, and from the Law of Reafon it differeth in the manner of binding only. For whereas men before ftood bound in confcience to do as the Law of Reafon teacheth; they are now by vertue of Humane Law become conftrainable, and if they outwardly tranfgrefs, punifhable. As for Laws which are *meerly* humane, the matter of them is any thing which reafon doth but probably teach to be fit and convenient; fo that till fuch time as Law hath paffed amongft men about it, of it felf it bindeth no man. One example whereof may be this; Lands are by Humane Law in fome places, after the owners deceafe, divided unto all his children; in fome, all defcendeth to the eldeft fon. If the Law of Reafon did neceffarily require but the one of thefe two to be done, they which by law have received the other, fhould be fubject to that heavy fentence, which denounceth againft all that decree wicked, unjuft, and unreafonable things, *woe*. Whereas now, which foever be received, there is no law of reafon tranfgreft; becaufe there is probable reafon why either of them may be expedient, and for either of them more then probable reafon there is not to be found. Laws, whether mixtly, or meerly humane, are made by politick Societies: fome, onely as thofe Societies are civilly united; fome, as they are fpiritually joyned, and make fuch a body as we call the Church. Of Laws humane in this latter kind, we are to fpeak in the third Book following. Let it therefore fuffice; thus far to

have

Staundf. pref. to the Pleas of the Crown.

Ep. f. Iud. v. 10. *Οι πολλοι ακϛιϛαι μανϑανŏϛι ἄλŏγα ταυτα εϊα φϑαρŏϛι ᾗ ζημιŏϛι εϊϛ το κακω* *Arift. Eth. lib. 10 cap. 10.*

Ifi. 10. 1.

have touched the force wherewith Almighty God hath graciously endued our nature, and thereby enabled the same to finde out both those Laws which all men generally are for ever bound to observe, and also such as are most fit for their behoof
who lead their lives in any ordered state of Government. Now besides that Law
which simply concerneth men, as men, and that which belongeth unto them as they
are men linked with others in some form of Politique Society, there is a third kinde
of Law which toucheth all such several bodies Politique, so far forth as one of them
hath publique commerce with another. And this third is the *Law of Nations*. Between men and beasts there is no possibility of sociable communion; because the well-
spring of that communion is a natural delight which man hath to transfuse from himself into others, and to receive from others into himself, especially those things
wherein the excellency of this kinde doth most consist. The chiefest instrument of
humane communion therefore is speech, because thereby we impart mutually one to
another the conceits of our reasonable understanding. And for that cause, seeing beasts
are not hereof capable, forasmuch as with them we can use no such conference, they
being in degree, although above other creatures on earth to whom Nature hath denied sense, yet lower then to be sociable companions of man, to whom Nature hath
given reason; it is of *Adam* said, that amongst the beasts, *He found not for himself any*
meet companion. Civil society doth more content the nature of man, then any private
kinde of solitary living; because in society, this good of mutual participation is so
much larger then otherwise. Herewith notwithstanding we are not satisfied, but we covet (if it might be) to have a kinde of society and fellowship even with all mankinde.
Which thing *Socrates* intending to signifie, professed himself a Citizen, not of this or
that Commonwealth, but of the world. And an effect of that very natural desire in us,
(a manifest token that we wish after a sort an universal fellowship with all men)
appeareth by the wonderful delight men have, some to visit forreign Countreys,
some to discover Nations not heard of in former Ages; we all to know the affairs
and dealings of other people, yea, to be in league of amity with them: and this not
onely for trafficks sake, or to the end that when many are confederated, each may
make other the more strong; but for such cause also, as moved the Queen of *Sheba*
to visit *Solomon*; and in a word, because Nature doth presume, that how many men
there are in the world, so many Gods, as it were, there are, or at leastwise such
they should be towards men. Touching Laws which are to serve men in this behalf;
even as those Laws of reason, which (man retaining his original integrity) had been
sufficient to direct each particular person in all his affairs and duties, are not sufficient,
but require the access of other laws, now that man and his off-spring are grown thus
corrupt and sinful; again, as those laws of Polity and Regiment, which would have served
men living in publike society together with that harmless disposition which then they
should have had, are not able now to serve, when mens iniquity is so hardly restrained
within any tolerable bounds: in like manner, the national laws of natural commerce between societies of that former and better quality might have been other then now,
when Nations are so prone to offer violence, injury and wrong. Hereupon hath grown
in every of these three kindes, that distinction between *Primary* and *Secundary* Laws;
the one grounded upon sincere, the other built upon depraved nature. Primary laws of
Nations are such as concern embassage, such as belong to the courteous entertainment
of Forreigners and Strangers, such as serve for commodious traffick, and the like. Secon-
dary laws in the same kinde, are such as this present unquiet world is most familiarly
acquainted with; I mean laws of Arms; which yet are much better known then kept.
But what matter the law of Nations doth contain, I omit to search. The strength and
vertue of that law is such, that no particular nation can lawfully prejudice the same by
any their several laws and ordinances, more then a man by his private resolutions the
law of the whole Commonwealth or State wherein he liveth. For as civil law being the
act of a whole body Politique, doth therefore over-rule each several part of the same
body: so there is no reason that any one Commonwealth of it self, should to the prejudice of another, annihilate that whereupon the whole world hath agreed. For which
cause, the Lacedemonians forbidding all access of strangers into their coasts, are in that
respect both by *Josephus* and *Theodoret* deservedly blamed, as being enemies to that hospitality, which for common humanities sake all the nations on earth should embrace.
Now as there is great cause of communion, and consequently of laws for the mainte-

Arist. pol. 1. c. 2.

Gen. 1. 20.

Cic. Tusc. 5. & 1 de Legib.

1 King. 10. 1. 2 Chron. 9. 1. Mat. 12. 42. Luke 11. 31.

Iose. lib. 1 contra Apion. Theod. lib. 9. de sanand. Graeca affect.

nance

nance of communion amongſt Nations : So among Nations Chriſtian, the like in re-gard even of Chriſtianity hath been always judged needful And in this kinde of cor-reſpondence among Nations, the force of general Councils doth ſtand For as one and the ſame Law Divine, whereof in the next place we are to ſpeak, is unto all Chri-ſtian Churches a rule for the chiefeſt things, by means whereof they all in that reſpect make one Church, as having all but *one Lord, one Faith, and one Baptiſm* : ſo the ur-gent neceſſity of mutual communion for preſervation of our unity in theſe things, as alſo for order in ſome other things convenient to be everywhere uniformly kept, maketh it requiſite that the Church of God here on earth have her laws of ſpiritual commerce between Chriſtian Nations ; laws, by vertue whereof all Churches may en-joy freely the uſe of thoſe reverend religious and ſacred conſultations, which are term-ed Councils general A thing whereof Gods own bleſſed Spirit was the Author; a thing practiſed by the holy Apoſtles themſelves, a thing always afterwards kept and obſerved throughout the world, a thing never otherwiſe then moſt highly eſteemed of, till pride, ambition and tyranny began by factious and vile endeavours, to abuſe that divine invention, unto the furtherance of wicked purpoſes But as the juſt authority of Civil Courts and Parliaments is not therefore to be aboliſhed, becauſe ſometimes there is cunning uſed to frame them according to the private intents of men over-potent in the Commonwealth . So the grievous abuſe which hath been of Councils, ſhould rather cauſe men to ſtudy how ſo gracious a thing may again be reduced to that firſt perfection, then in regard of ſtains and blemiſhes ſithence growing, be held for ever in extreme diſgrace To ſpeak of this matter as the cauſe requireth, would require very long diſcourſe All I will preſently ſay, is this, Whether it be for the finding out of any thing whereunto divine law bindeth us, but yet in ſuch ſort, that men are not thereof on all ſides reſolved, or for the ſetting down of ſome uniform judge-ment to ſtand touching ſuch things, as being neither way matters of neceſſity, are notwithſtanding offenſive and ſcandalous, when there is open oppoſition about them; be it for the ending of ſtrifes touching matters of Chriſtian belief, wherein the one part may ſeem to have probable cauſe of diſſenting from the other, or be it concern-ing matters of Politie, order and regiment in the Church ; I nothing doubt but that Chriſtian men ſhould much better frame themſelves to thoſe heavenly precepts, which our Lord and Saviour with ſo great inſtancy gave as concerning peace and uni-ty, if we did all concur in deſire to have the uſe of ancient Councils again renewed, rather then theſe proceedings continued, which either make all contentions endleſs, or bring them to one onely determination, and that of all other the worſt, which is by ſword. It followeth therefore, that a new foundation being laid, we now adjoyn hereunto that which cometh in the next place to be ſpoken of, namely, wherefore God hath himſelf by Scripture, made known ſuch laws as ſerve for direction of men.

11. All things (God onely excepted) beſides the nature which they have in them-ſelves, receive externally ſome perfection from other things, as hath been ſhewed. In ſo much, as there is in the whole world no one thing great or ſmall, but either in re-ſpect of knowledge or of uſe, it may unto our perfection add ſomewhat. And whatſo-ever ſuch perfection there is, which our nature may acquire, the ſame we properly term our good, our ſoveraign *good* or *bleſſedneſs*, that wherein the higheſt degree of all our perfection conſiſteth, that which being once attained unto, there can reſt nothing fur-ther to be deſired, and therefore with it our ſouls are fully content and ſatisfied, in that they have they rejoyce, and thirſt for no more. wherefore of good things deſired, ſome are ſuch that for themſelves we covet them not, but onely becauſe they ſerve as inſtru-ments unto that for which we are to ſeek, of this ſort are riches, another kinde there is, which although we deſire for it ſelf, as health, and vertue, and knowledge, ne-vertheleſs, they are not the laſt mark whereat we aim, but have therein further end where-unto they are referred, ſo as in them we are not ſatisfied, as having attained the utmoſt we may, but our deſires do ſtill proceed Theſe things are linked, and as it were chained one to another . we labour to eat, and we eat to live ; and we live to do good, and the good which we do, is as ſeed ſown (*a*) with reference unto a future harveſt. But we muſt come at length to ſome pauſe For if every thing were to be deſired for ſome other without any ſtint, there could be no certain end propoſed unto our actions, we ſhould go on we know not whither, yea, whatſoever we do, were in vain, or rather

nothing

Epheſ. 4.5.

Acts 15 2°.

Iªh, 14. 27.

Whereſore
God hath by
Scripture tur-
ther made
known ſuch
ſupernatural
laws, and do
ſerve for mens
direction.

a Col 4 8. He
that would to
the, &c it ſhall
of the Spirit
repliſh ever
laſting

nothing at all were possible to be done. For as to take away the first efficient of our being, were to annihilate utterly our persons; so we cannot remove the last final cause of our working, but we shall cause whatsoever we work to cease. Therefore something there must be desired for it self simply and for no other. That is simply for it self desirable, unto the nature whereof it is opposite and repugnant to be desired with relation unto any other. The Oxe and the Asse desire their food, neither propose they unto themselves any end wherefore; so that of them this is desired for it self; but why? By reason of their imperfection, which cannot otherwise desire it: whereas that which is desired simply for it self, the excellency thereof is such as permitteth it not in any sort to be referred unto a farther end. Now that which man doth desire with reference to a farther end, the same he desireth in such measure as is unto that end convenient: but what he coveteth as good in it self, towards that his desire is ever infinite. So that unless the last good of all which is desired altogether for it self, be also infinite, we do evil in making it our end, even as they who placed their felicity in wealth, or honour, or pleasure, or any thing here attained, because in desiring any thing as our final perfection, which is not so, we do amisse. Nothing may be infinitely desired, but that good which indeed is infinite. For the better, the more desireable; that therefore most desireable, wherein there is infinity of goodness; so that if any thing desirable may be infinite, that must needs be the highest of all things that are desired. No good is infinite but only God: therefore he our felicity and bliss. Moreover desire tendeth unto union with that it desireth. If then in him we be blessed, it is by force of participation and conjunction with him. Again, it is not the possession of any good thing can make them happy which have it, unless they enjoy the things wherewith they are possessed. Then are we happy therefore, when fully we injoy God, as an object wherein the powers of our souls are satisfied even with everlasting delight: so that although we be men, yet by being unto God united, we live as it were the life of God. Happiness therefore is that estate whereby we attain, so far as possibly may be attained, the full possession of that which simply for it self is to be desired, and containeth in it after an eminent sort the contentation of our desires, the highest degree of all our perfection. Of such perfection capable we are not in this life. For while we are in the world, we are subject unto sundry (*a*) imperfections, grief of body, defects of mind; yea, the best things we do are painful, and the exercise of them grievous, being continued without intermission: so as in those very actions whereby we are especially perfected in this life, we are not able to persist; forced we are with very weariness, and that often, to interrupt them; which tediousness, cannot fall into those operations that are in the state of bliss, when our union with God is compleat. Compleat union with him must be according unto every power and faculty of our minds, apt to receive so glorious an object. Capable we are of God both by understanding and will; by understanding, as he is that Soveraign truth, which comprehends the rich treasures of all wisedome: by will, as he is that Sea of goodness, whereof who so tasteth shall thirst no more. As the will doth now work upon that object by desire, which is as it were a motion towards the end as yet unobtained, so likewise upon the same hereafter received it shall work also by love. *Appetitus inhiantis fit amor fruentis*, saith St. *Augustine: The longing disposition of them that thirst, is changed into the sweet affection of them that tast and are replenished.* Whereas we now love the thing that is good, but good especially in respect of benefit unto us; we shall then love the thing that is good, onely or principally for the goodness of beauty in it self. The soul being in this sort as it is active, perfected by love of that infinite good, shall as it is receptive be also perfected with those supernatural passions of joy, peace and delight: All this endless and everlasting. Which perpetuity, in regard whereof our blessedness is termed *a crown which withereth not*, doth neither depend upon the nature of the thing it self, nor proceed from any natural necessity that our souls should so exercise themselves for ever in beholding and loving God, but from the will of God, which doth both freely perfect our nature in so high a degree, and continue it so perfected. Under man no creature in the world is capable of felicity and bliss; first, because their chiefest perfection consisteth in that which is best for them, but not in that which is simply best, as ours doth; secondly, because whatsoever external perfection they tend unto, it is not better then themselves, as ours is. How just ocasion have we therefore even in this respect with the Prophet to admire the goodness of God; Lord, what is man that thou

Vide Arist. Eth.
lib. cap. 10. &
Metaph. 1. cap.
6. & cap. 4. &
cap. 10.

a Μόνον ὃ Ἀσκλῆπε τὸ ὀνόμα τ᾽ ἀγαθῦ ἐνδίδρυσις τὸ ἔργον ἐδημῶς, τὸ μὴ ἦλαι καὶ κὸν, ἐν δ᾽ δὴ τὸ ἀγαθὸν ἔχι. Τὸ δὲ ἐσθλὸ ἀγαθὸν, μόει ὃ τὸ καλῦ τὸ ἐλάχιστν. Ἀδύνατν ἓν τὸ ἀγαθὸν ἔχ Σαῖς καθαρεύειν τῆ κακίας· καθὸ δὲ χάριι ἔχω τὸ θεῦ τῷ εἰς τὺν μοι μῷ πλήρωμα Cαλὲπ ἥ τι γιώσεως τὰ ἀγαθῦ, ὅτι ἀδύναταὶ ἰσιν αὐτί ἐν τῷ κόσμῳ. D᾽ ἢ γὰρ κόσμῷ πλήρωμα ὅτι τ κακίας, ὁ δὲ θεὸς ἀγαθὸς δὴ, ἥ τὸ ἀγαθῦ Σὲ, Μευ. ιν. Trism.

Mat. 25. The just shall go into life everlasting.

t life everlasting.

Mir. 22. They shall be as the Angels of God

a Tim. 1. 8

1 Pet. 1. 4.

Pfu. 8.

thou ſhouldeſt exalt him above the works of thy hands, ſo far as to make thy ſelf the inheritance of his reſt, and the ſubſtance of his felicity! Now, if men had not naturally this deſire to be happy, how were it poſſible that all men ſhould have it? All men have. Therefore this deſire in man is natural. It is not in our power not to do the ſame: how ſhould it then be in our power to do it coldly or remiſſly? So that our deſire being natural, is alſo in that degree of earneſtneſs whereunto nothing can be added. And is it probable that God ſhould frame the hearts of all men ſo

Comment in proœm.2.Me-taph.

deſirous of that which no man may obtain? It is an axiome of nature, that natural deſire cannot utterly be fruſtrate.This deſire of ours being natural ſhould be fruſtrate, if that which may ſatisfie the ſame were any thing impoſſible for man to aſpire unto. Man doth ſeek a tripple perfection; firſt, a ſenſual conſiſting in thoſe things which very life it ſelf requireth, either as neceſſary ſupplements, or as beauties and orna-ments thereof; then an intellectual, conſiſting in thoſe things which none underneath man is either capable of, or acquainted with; Laſtly, a ſpiritual and divine, conſiſt-ing in thoſe things whereunto we tend by ſupernatural means here, but cannot here attain unto them. They that make the firſt of theſe three the ſcope of their whole life,

Phil. 3.15.

are ſaid by the Apoſtle. to have no God, but onely their belly, to be earthly-minded men. Unto the ſecond they bend themſelves eſpecially,who ſeek eſpecially to excel in all ſuch knowledg and vertue as doth moſt commend men. To this branch belongeth the law of moral and civil perfection. That there is ſomewhat higher then either of theſe two, no other proof doth need then the very proceſs of mans deſire, which being natural ſhould be fruſtrate, if there were not ſome farther thing wherein it might reſt at the length contented, which in the former it cannot do. For man doth not ſeem to reſt ſatisfied either with fruition of that wherewith his life is preſerved, or with performance of ſuch actions as advance him moſt deſervedly in eſtimation; but doth further covet,yea oftentimes manifeſtly purſue with great ſedulity and earneſtneſs,that

Mat. 5.12.Re-joce and be glad;for great is your reward in heaven.

which cannot ſtand him in any ſtead for vital uſe; that which exceedeth the reach of ſenſe, yea ſomewhat above capacity of reaſon, ſomewhat divine and heavenly, which with hidden exultation it rather ſurmiſeth then conceiveth; ſomewhat it ſeeketh; and what that is directly it knoweth not;yet very intentive deſire thereof doth ſo incite it,

Aug. de doct. Chriſt.c.6 Sum-ma merces eſt ut iſſo perfruamur. Ambroſ. con-tra Sym.

that all other known delights and pleaſures are laid aſide, they give place to the ſearch of this but only ſuſpected deſire. If the ſoul of man did ſerve only to give him being in this life,then things appertaining unto this life would content him, as we ſee they do other creatures: which creatures enjoying what they live by, ſeek no further, but in this contentation do ſhew a kinde of acknowledgement, that there is no higher good

Magno & ex-cellenti ingenio viri, cum ſe do-ctrinæ penitus dedißent,quic-quid laboris po-terat impendi (contemptis om-nibus & privatis & publicis acti-onibus)ad inqui-renda veritatis ſtudium contule-runt,exiſt man-tes multo eße præclarius hu-manarum divi-narumꝰ rerum inveſtigare ac ſcire rationem, quàm ſtruendis opibus aut cu-mulandis hono-ribus inhærere.

which doth any way belong unto them.With us it is otherwiſe.For although the Beau-ties, Riches, Honors, Sciences, Vertues and perfections of all men living, were in the preſent poſſeſſion of one: yet ſomewhat beyond and above all this there would ſtill be ſought and earneſtly thirſted for. So that Nature even in this life doth plainly claim and call for a more divine perfection,then either of theſe two that have been mention-ed. This laſt and higheſt eſtate of perfection, whereof we ſpeak, is received of men in the nature of a(a) reward. Rewards do always preſuppoſe ſuch duties performed as are rewardable. Our natural means therefore unto bleſſedneſs are our works: nor is it poſ-ſible that nature ſhould ever find any other way to ſalvation then only this. But exa-mine the works which we do, and ſince the foundation of the world what one can ſay, My ways are pure? Seeing then all fleſh is guilty of that for which God hath threatned eternally to puniſh, what poſſibility is there this way to be ſaved? There reſteth therefore either no way unto ſalvation,or if any,then ſurely a way which is ſu-pernatural,a way which could never have entred into the heart of man as much as once to conceive or imagine,if God himſelf had not revealed it extraordinarily. For which

Sed neꝙ adep i ſunt id quod volebant,& oper am ſimul atꝙ induſtriam perdiderunt: quia veritas, ideſt, arcanum ſummi Dei qui fe-cit omnia, ingenio ac propriis ſenſibus non poteſt c mprehendi. Alioqui nihil inter Deum hominemꝙ diſtaret, ſi conſilia & diſpoſitiones illius majeſtatis æternæ cogitatio aſſequeretur humana. Quod quia fieri non potuit ut homini per ſe ipſum ratio divina noteſceret, non eſt paſſus hominem Deus lumen ſapientiæ quærentem diutius aberrare,ac ſine ullo laboris eſſectu vagari per tenebras inextricabiles: a-peruit oculos ejus aliquando, & notionem veritatis munus ſuum fecit,ut ad humanam ſapientiam nullam eſſe monſtraret, & erranti ac vago viam conſequendæ immortalitatis oſtenderet, Lact.l.1. c.1.

cauſe we term it the myſtery or ſecret way of ſalvation. And therefore St. Ambroſe in this matter appealeth juſtly from man to God, (b) Cæli myſterium doceat me Deus qui condidit,non homo qui ſeipſum ignoravit; Let God himſelf that made me,let not man that knows not himſelf, be my inſtructor concerning the myſtical way to Heaven. (c) When men of excellent wit (ſaith Lactantius) had wholly betaken themſelves unto ſtudy

after

after farewel bidden unto all kinde as well of private as publique actions, they spared no labour that might be spent in the search of truth ; holding it a thing of much more price to seek and to finde out the reason of all affairs, as well Divine as Humane, then to stick fast in the toil of piling up Riches, and gathering together heaps of Honours. Howbeit, they both did fail of their purpose, and got not so much as to quit their charges ; because truth, which is the secret of the Lord, whose proper handywork all things are, cannot be compassed with that wit & those senses which are our own. For God and man should be very neer neighbours, if mans cogitations were able to take a survey of the counsels and appointments of that Majestie everlasting. Which being utterly impossible, that the eye of man by it self should look into the bosom of Divine Reason; God did not suffer him, being desirous of the light of Wisdom, to stray any longer up and down, and with bootless expence of travel, to wander in darkness that had no passage to get out by. His eyes at length God did open, & bestow upon him the knowledge of the truth by way of donative, to the end that man might both be clearly convicted of folly, and being through errour out of the way, have the path that leadeth unto immortality laid plain before him; thus far Lact. Firmian. to shew that God himself is the teacher of the truth, whereby is made known the supernatural way of salvation, and law for them to live in that shall be saved. In the natural path of everlasting life, the first beginning is that ability of doing good, which God in the day of mans creation endued him with; from hence obedience unto the will of his Creator, absolute righteousness and integrity in all his actions ; and last of all, the justice of God rewarding the worthiness of his deserts with the crown of eternal glory. Had *Adam* continued in his first estate, this had been the way of life unto him and all his posterity. Wherein I confess notwithstanding, with the wittiest of the 'School-Divines, that if we speak of strict justice, God could no way have bin bound to requite mans labours in so large & ample maner as humane felicity doth import: inasmuch as the dignity of this exceedeth so far the others value. But be it that God of his great liberality had determined in lieu of mans endeavours to bestow the same, by the rule of that justice which best beseemeth him, namely, the justice of one that requireth nothing mincingly, but all with pressed, and heaped, & even over-inlarged measure: yet could it never hereupon necessarily be gathered, that such justice should add to the nature of that reward the property of everlasting continuance ; sith possession of bliss, though it should be but for a moment, were an abundant retribution. But we are not now to enter into this consideration, how gracious and bountiful our good God might still appear in so rewarding the sons of men, albeit they should exactly perform whatsoever duty their Nature bindeth them unto. Howsoever God did propose this reward, we that were to be rewarded, must have done that which is required at our hands ; we failing in the one, it were in nature an impossibility that the other should be looked for. The light of nature is never able to find out any way of obtaining the reward of bliss, but by performing exactly the duties and works of righteousness. From salvation therefore and life all flesh being excluded this way, behold how the wisdom of God hath revealed a way mystical & supernatural, a way directing unto the same end of life, by a course which groundeth it self upon the guiltiness of sin, and through sin desert of condemnation and death. For in this way the first thing is the tender compassion of *God*, respecting us drown'd & swallow'd up in misery; the next is redemption out of the same by the precious death and merit of a mighty Saviour; which hath witnessed of himself, saying,* *I am the way,* the way that leadeth us from misery into bliss. This supernatural way had God in himself prepared before all worlds. The way of supernatural duty which to us he hath prescribed, our Saviour in the Gospel of S. *John* doth note, terming it by an excellency, The work of God; b *This is the work of God, that ye believe in him whom he hath sent.* Not that God doth require nothing unto happiness at the hands of men, saving onely a naked belief (for hope and charity we may not exclude:)but that without belief all other things are as nothing, and it the ground of those other divine vertues. Concerning faith, the principal object whereof is that eternal verity which hath discovered the treasures of hidden wisdom in *Christ*; concerning hope, the highest object whereof is that everlasting goodness which in *Christ* doth quicken the dead; concerning charity, the final object whereof is that incomprehensible beauty which shineth in the countenance of Christ the Son of the living God: concerning these vertues, the first of which beginning here with a weak apprehension of things not seen, endeth with the intuitive vision of God in the world to come ; the second beginning here with a trembling expectation of things far removed, and as yet but only heard of, endeth with real and actual fruition of that which no tongue can express;

the

Scot. lib. 4.
sent. d 8. qu. 6.
Loquendo de
stricta justitia,
Deus nulli no-
stri importer
quacunque me-
rita est debitor
perfectionis red-
dendae tam in-
tensae, propter
immoderatum
excessum illius
perfectionis ul-
tra illa merita.
Sed esto quod ex
liberalitate sua
determinasset
meritis conferre
actum tam per-
fectum tanquam
praemium tali
quidem justitia
qualis decet
eum, scilicet su-
pererogantis in
praemiis: tamen
non sequitur ex
hoc necessario,
quod per illam
justitiam sit red-
denda perfectio
pereunti tan-
quam praemium,
imo abundans
fieret retributio
in beata indivi-
sibili momenti.
a Joan 1. 6.
b Iohn 6. 29.

[a] The cause
why fo many
na-ural, cr ra-
tional Laws
are fet down in
holy Scripture.
[b] *Jus naturale eſt
quod in lege &
Evangelio conti-
netur, pag. 1.d.1.*
c *Ioſeph. lib.
ſecunda contra
Appio, Lacede-
monii quomodo
non ſunt ob inhe-
ſpitalitatem re-
prehendendi, fæ-
dumq̀ neglectum
nuptiarum ?
Elenſes verò &
Thebani ob coi-
tum cum maſcu-
lis plunè impu-
denem & con-
tra naturam ;
quem reċtè &
utiliter exercere
putabant? cumq̀
hæc omnino per-
petrarent, etiam
ſuis legibus miſ-
cuere, v. de Th.
12.quæſt. 19-4.
5,6. Lex naturæ
ſic corrupta fuit
apud Germanes,
ut latrocinium
non reputarent
peccatum. Aug.
aut quiſquis au-
thor eſt, l b. de
quæſt nov. &
vet.teſt. quis
neſciat quid bo-
næ vitæ conve-
niat, aut ignoret
quiæ quod ſibi fi-
eri non vult,alii
minimè deveat
facere ? At verò
ubi naturalis lex
evanuit oppreſſa
conſuetudine de-
linquenti, tunc
opo tuit manife-
ſtari ſcriptis , ut
Dei judicium
omnes audirent:
non quod peni-
tus oblilerata
eſt, ſed quia
maximæ ejus
authoritate ca-
rebat,idu'e'a-
trie ſtndebatur,
timor Dei inter-
ris non erat, ſun-
nica'io opera'a-
tur, circa rem
proximi avida
erat contupiſcentia. Data ergo lex eſt, ut quæ ſciebantur authoritatem haberent, & quæ latere cæperant,maniſeſtarentur.

the third beginning here with a weak inclination of heart towards him unto whom we are not able to approach,endeth with endleſs union,the myſterie whereof is higher then the reach of the thoughts of men; concerning that faith, hope and charity, without which there can be no ſalvation,was there ever any mention made ſavingonly in that law which God himſelf hath from heaven revealed? There is not in the World a ſyllable muttered with certain truth concerning any of theſe three, more then hath been ſuper-naturally received from the mouth of the eternal God. Laws therefore concerning theſe things are ſupernatural, both in reſpect of the manner of delivering them,which is divine ; and alſo in regard of the things delivered, which are ſuch as have not in na-ture any cauſe from which they flow, but were by the voluntary appointment of God ordained beſides the courſe of Nature, to rectiſie Natures obliquity, withal.

12.[a]When ſupernatural duties are neceſſarily exacted,natural are not rejected as need-leſs:the law of God therefore is,though principally delivered for inſtruction in the one, yet fraught with precepts of the other alſo.The Scripture is fraught even with laws of nature,inſomuch that [b]*Gratian* defining natural right(whereby is meant the right which exacteth thoſe general duties, that concern men naturally , even as they are men) termeth natural right that which the Books of Law and the Goſpel do contain. Neither is it vain,that the Scripture aboundeth with ſo great ſtore of laws in this kind. For they are either ſuch as we of our ſelves could not eaſily have found out,& then the benefit is not ſmall,to have them readily ſet down to our hands;or if they be ſo clear & manifeſt,that no man indued with reaſon can lightly be ignorant of them;yet the Spirit, as it were, borrowing them from the School of Nature, as ſerving to prove things leſs manifeſt, and to induce a perſwaſion of ſomewhat which were in it ſelf more hard and dark,unleſs it ſhould in ſuch ſort be cleared,the very applying of them unto caſes parti-cular,is not without moſt ſingular uſe and profit many ways for mens inſtruction. Be-ſides,be they plain of themſelves or obſcure,the evidence of Gods own teſtimony added unto the natural aſſent of Reaſon, concerning the certainty of them, doth not a little comfort and confirm the ſame.Wherefore,inaſmuch as our actions are converſant about things beſet with many circumſtances,which cauſe men of ſundry wits,to be alſo of ſun-dry judgements concerning that which ought to be done: requiſite it cannot but ſeem the rule of divine law,ſhould herein help our imbecility,that we might the more infalli-bly underſtand what is good & what evil. The firſt principles of the law of nature are ea-ſie;hard it were to find men ignorant of them;but concerning the duty which natures law doth require at the hands of men in a number of things particular, ſo (c) far hath the natural underſtanding even of ſundry whole nations been darkned, that they have not diſcerned,no,not groſs iniquity to be ſin. Again, being ſo prone as we are to fawn upon our ſelves,and to be ignorant as much as may be of our own deformities,without the feeling ſenſe whereof we are moſt wretched ; even ſo much the more becauſe not knowing them,we cannot as much as deſire to have them taken away : how ſhould our feſtered ſores be cured, but that God hath delivered a law as ſharp as the two-edged ſword, piercing the very cloſeſt and moſt unſearchable corners of the heart,which the law of nature can hardly,humane laws by no means poſſibly reach unto?Hereby we know even ſecret concupiſcence to be ſin,and are made fearful to offend,though it be but in a wandring cogitation.Finally, of thoſe things which are for direction of all the parts of our life needful,and not impoſſible to be diſcerned by the light of nature it ſelf,are there not many which few mens natural capacity,and ſome which no mans hath been able to find out ? They are,ſaith S.*Auguſtine*,but a few,and they indued with great ripeneſs of wit and judgment,free from all ſuch affairs as might trouble their meditations,inſtruct-ed in the ſharpeſt and the ſubtileſt points of learning,who have,& that very hardly,been able to find out but only the immortality of the ſoul.The reſurrection of the fleſh,what man did ever at any time dream of,having not heard it otherwiſe then from the ſchool of nature? whereby it appeareth, how much we are bound to yield unto our Creator, the Father of all mercy,eternal thanks;for that he hath delivered his law unto the world, a law wherein ſo many things are laid open , clear, and manifeſt;as a light which other-wiſe would have bin buried in darkneſs,not without the hazard,or rather not with the hazard,but with the certain loſs of infinite thouſands of ſouls moſt undoubtedly how ſa-ved.We ſee therefore that our ſoveraign good is deſir'd naturally,that God the author of that natural deſire, had appointed natural means whereby to fulſil it ; that man having

utterly

itterly disabled his nature unto those means, hath had other revealed from God, and hath received from Heaven a Law to teach him, how that which is desired naturally, must now supernaturally be attained; finally, we see, that because those latter exclude not the former, quite and clean as unnecessary, therefore together with such supernatural duties as could not possibly have been otherwise known to the World, the same Law that teacheth them, teacheth also with them such natural duties as could not by Light of Nature easily have been known.

13. In the first Age of the World God gave Laws unto our Fathers; and by reason of the number of their days, their memories served in stead of Books; whereof the manifold imperfections and defects being known to God, he mercifully relieved the same, by often putting them in minde of that whereof it behoved them to be specially mindeful. In which respect we see how many times one thing hath been iterated unto sundry even of the best and wisest amongst them. After that the lives of men were shortned, means more durable to preserve the Laws of God from oblivion and corruption grew in use, not without precise direction from God himself. First therefore of *Moses* it is said, that he *wrote all the words of God*; not by his own private motion and device: for God taketh this act to himself, *I have written*. Furthermore, were not the Prophets following commanded also to do the like? Unto the holy Evangelist St. *John* how often express charge is given, *Scribe, write these things?* Concerning the rest of our Lords Disciples, the words of S. *Augustine* are, *Quidquid ille de suis factis & dictis nos legere voluit, hoc scribendum illis tanquam suis manibus imperavit.* Now although we do not deny it to be a matter meerly accidental unto the Law of God to be written; although Writing be not that which addeth authority and strength thereunto: finally, though his Laws do require at our hands the same obedience, howsoever they be delivered; his providence notwithstanding, which hath made principal choice of this way to deliver them, who seeth not what cause we have to admire and magnifie? The singular benefit that hath grown unto the World by receiving the Laws of God, even by his own appointment committed unto writing, we are not able to esteem as the value thereof deserveth. When the question therefore is, whether we be now to seek for any revealed Law of God, otherwhere then onely in the sacred Scripture, whether we do now stand bound in the sight of God to yield to Traditions urged by the Church of *Rome*, the same obedience and reverence we do to his written Law, honouring equally, and adoring both as Divine? Our answer is, No. They that so earnestly plead for the authority of Tradition, as if nothing were more safely conveyed, then that which spreadeth it self by report, and descendeth by relation of former generations, unto the ages that succeed, are not all of them (surely a miracle it were if they should be)so simple, as thus to perswade themselves; howsoever, if the simple were so perswaded, they could be content perhaps very well to enjoy the benefit, as they account it, of that common errour. What hazard the truth is in when it passeth through the hands of report, how maimed and deformed it becometh; they are not, they cannot possibly be ignorant. Let them that are indeed of this minde, consider but onely that little of things Divine, which the b Heathen have in such sort received. How miserable had the state of the Church of God been long ere this, if wanting the sacred Scripture, we had no Record of his Laws but onely the memory of man, receiving the same by report and relation from his Predecessors? By Scripture it hath in the wisdom of God seemed meet to deliver unto the world much but personally expedient to be practised of certain men; many deep and profound points of Doctrine, as being the main original ground whereupon the Precepts of duty depend; many Prophesies, the clear performance whereof might confirm the world in belief of things unseen; many Histories to serve as looking-glasses to behold the mercy, the truth, the righteousness of God towards all that faithfully serve, obey and honour him; yea, many intire Meditations of Piety, to be as Paterns and Presidents in cases of like nature; many things needful for explication, many for application unto particular occasions, such as the providence of God from time to time hath taken to have the several Books of his holy Ordinance written. Be it then, that together with the principal necessary Laws of God, there are sundry other things written, whereof we might haply be ignorant, and yet be saved: What? shall we hereupon think them needless? shall we esteem them as riotous branches wherewith we sometimes behold most pleasant Vines over-grown? Surely no more then

Margin notes:
a *The benefit of having Divine Laws written.*
Exod. 14.4.
Hof. 8.12.
Apoc 1.11. & 1.13.
Aug.lib.1.de conf. Evang. cap.ult.
b *I mean those historical matters concerning the antient state of the first world, the Deluge, the sons of Noah, the children of Israel deliverance out of Egypt, the life and doings of Moses, the life and doings of that Captain, with such like: the certain truth whereof delivered in holy scripture, is of the Heathen then which had them one by b. report, so intermingled with fabulous vanities, that the most which remaineth in them to be seen, is the shew of dark and obscure steps, where some part of the truth hath gone.*

then we judge our hands or our eyes superfluous, or what part soever, which if our bodies did want, we might notwithstanding any such defect, receive still the compleat being of men. As therefore a compleat man is neither destitute of any part necessary, and hath some parts, whereof though the want could not deprive him of his essence, yet to have them, standeth him in singular stead in respect of the special uses for which they serve : in like sort, all those writings which contain in them the Law of God, all those venerable books of Scripture, all those sacred tomes and volumes of holy Writ, they are with such absolute perfection framed, that in them there neither wanteth any thing, the lack whereof might deprive us of life ; nor any thing in such wise aboundeth, that as being superfluous, unfruitful, and altogether needless, we should think it no loss or danger at all, if we did want it.

The sufficiency of Scripture unto the end for which it was instituted. Verum cognitio supernaturalis necessaria viatori, sit sufficienter tradita in sacrâ scripturâ? This quæst on proposed by Scotus, is affirmatively concluded.

14. Although the Scripture of God therefore be stored with infinite variety of matter in all kindes, although it abound with all sorts of laws, yet the principal intent of Scripture is to deliver the laws of duties supernatural. Oftentimes it hath been in very solemn manner disputed, whether all things necessary unto salvation, be necessarily set down in the holy Scriptures or no. If we define that necessary unto salvation, whereby the way to salvation is in any sort made more plain, apparent and easie to be known ; then is there no part of true Philosophy, no art of account, no kinde of science, rightly so called, but the Scripture must contain it. If onely those things be necessary, as surely none else are, without the knowledge and practise whereof it is not the will and pleasure of God to make any ordinary grant of salvation ; it may be notwithstanding, and oftentimes hath been demanded, how the books of holy Scripture contain in them all necessary things, when of things necessary the very chief is to know what books we are bound to esteem holy ; which point is confest impossible for the Scripture it self to teach. Whereunto we may answer with truth, that there is not in the world any art or science, which proposing unto it self an end (as every one doth some end or other) hath been therefore thought defective, if it have not delivered simply whatsoever is needful to the same end ; but all kindes of knowledge have their certain bounds and limits ; each of them presupposeth many necessary things learned in other sciences, and known beforehand. He that should take upon him to teach men how to be eloquent in pleading causes, must needs deliver unto them whatsoever precepts are requisite unto that end ; otherwise he doth not the thing which he taketh upon him. Seeing then no man can plead eloquently, unless he be able first to speak, it followeth, that ability of speech is in this case a thing most necessary. Notwithstanding every man would think it ridiculous, that he which undertaketh by writing to instruct an Orator, should therefore deliver all the precepts of Grammar : because his profession is to deliver precepts necessary unto eloquent speech ; yet so, that they which are to receive them be taught beforehand, so much of that which is thereunto necessary, as comprehendeth the skill of speaking. In like sort, albeit Scripture do profess to contain in it all things which are necessary unto salvation ; yet the meaning cannot be simply of all things which are necessary, but all things which are necessary in some certainkinde or form ; as all things that are necessary, and either could not at all, or could not easily be known by the light of natural discourse ; all things which are necessary to be known that we may be saved, but known with presupposal of knowledge concerning certain principles, whereof it receiveth us already perswaded, and then instructeth us in all the residue that are necessary:In the number of these principles, one is the sacred Authority of Scripture. Being therefore perswaded by other means, that these Scriptures are the Oracles of God, themselves do then teach us the rest, and lay before us all the duties which God requireth at our hands, as necessary unto salvation. Further, there hath been some doubt likewise, whether *containing in Scripture*, do import express setting down in plain terms, or else *comprehending* in such sort, that by reason we may from thence conclude all things which are necessary. Against the former of these two constructions, instance hath sundry ways been given. For our belief in the Trinity, the Co-eternity of the Son of God with his Father, the proceeding of the Spirit from the Father and the Son, the duty of baptizing infants ; these, with such other principal points, the necessity whereof is by none denied, are notwithstanding in Scripture nowhere to be found by express literal mention, onely deduced they are out of Scripture by collection. This kinde of comprehension in
Scripture

Scripture being therefore received, still there is no doubt how far we are to proceed by collection, before the full and compleat measure of things necessary be made up. For let us not think, that as long as the world doth endure, the wit of man shall be able to found the bottom of that which may be conclued out of the Scripture; especially if things contained by collection do so far extend, as to draw in whatsoever may be at any time out of Scripture, but probably and conjecturally surmized. But let necessary collection be made requisite, and we may boldly deny, that of all those things which at this day are with so great necessity urged upon this Church, under the name of Reformed Church Discipline, there is any one which their books hitherto have made manifest to be contained in the Scripture. Let them, if they can, alledge but one properly belonging to their cause, and not common to them and us, and shew the deduction thereof out of Scripture to be necessary. It hath been already shewed, how all things necessary unto salvation, in such sort as before we have maintained, must needs be possible for men to know; and that many things are in such sort necessary, the knowledge whereof is by the light of nature impossible to be attained. Whereupon it followeth, that either all flesh is excluded from possibility of salvation, which to think were most barbarous; or else that God hath by supernatural means revealed the way of life so far forth as doth suffice. For this cause God hath so many times and ways spoken to the sons of men. Neither hath he by speech onely, but by writing also instructed and taught his Church. The cause of writing hath been, to the end that things by him revealed unto the world, might have the longer continuance, and the greater certainty of assurance; by how much that which standeth on record, hath in both those respects preheminence above that which passeth from hand to hand, and hath no pens, but the tongues; no book, but the ears of men to record it. The several Books of Scripture having had each some several occasion and particular purpose which caused them to be written, the contents thereof are according to the exigence of that special end whereunto they are intended. Hereupon it groweth, that every Book of holy Scripture doth take out of all kindes of truth, (a) natural, (b) historical, (c) forreign, (d) supernatural, so much as the matter handled requireth. Now forasmuch as there have been reasons alledged sufficient to conclude, that all things necessary unto salvation must be made known, and that God himself hath therefore revealed his will, because otherwise men could not have known so much as is necessary; his surceasing to speak to the world, since the publishing of the Gospel of Jesus Christ, and the delivery of the same in writing, is unto us a manifest token that the way of salvation is now sufficiently opened, and that we need no other means for our full instruction, then God hath already furnished us withall. The main drift of the whole New-Testament, is that which Saint *John* setteth down as the purpose of his own History, *These things are written, that ye might believe that Jesus is Christ the Son of God, and that in believing, ye might have life through his name.* The drift of the Old, that which the Apostle mentioneth to *Timothy, The holy Scriptures are able to make thee wise unto salvation.* So that the general end both of Old and New is one; the difference between them consisting in this, that the Old did make wise by teaching salvation through Christ that should come; the New, by teaching that Christ the Saviour is come; and that Jesus whom the Jews did crucifie, and whom God did raise again from the dead, is he. When the Apostle therefore affirmeth unto *Timothy*, that the Old was able to make him wise to salvation, it was not his meaning that the Old alone can do this unto us, which live sithence the publication of the New. For he speaketh with presupposal of the Doctrine of Christ known also to *Timothy*; and therefore first it is said, *Continue thou in those things which thou hast learned, and art perswaded, knowing of whom thou hast been taught them.* Again, those Scriptures he granteth, were able to make him wise to salvation; but he addeth, *through the faith which is in Christ.* Wherefore without the Doctrine of the New-Testament, teaching that Christ hath wrought the Redemption of the World, which Redemption the Old did foreshew he should work; it is not the former alone which can on our behalf perform so much as the Apostle doth avouch, who presupposeth this, when he magnifieth that so highly. And as his words concerning the Books of ancient Scripture, do not take place, but with presupposal of the Gospel of Christ embraced; so our own words also, when we extoll the compleat sufficiency of

the

(a) Eph. 5. 29.
(b) 2 Tim. 3. 8.
(c) Tit. 1. 12.
(d) 2 Pet. 1. 4.

John 20. 31.

2 Tim. 3. 15.

2 Tim. 3. 14.

Vers. 15.

the whole intire body of the Scripture, must in like sort be understood with this caution, that the benefit of natures light be not thought excluded as unnecessary, because the necessity of a Diviner light is magnified. There is in Scripture therefore no defect, but that any man, what place or calling soever he hold in the Church of God, may have thereby the light of his natural understanding so perfected, that the one being relieved by the other, there can want no part of needful instruction unto any good work which God himself requireth, be it natural, or supernatural, belonging simply unto men, as men ; or unto men, as they are united in whatsoever kinde of Society. It sufficeth therefore, that Nature and Scripture do serve in such full sort, that they both joyntly, and not severally either of them, be so compleat, that unto everlasting felicity we need not the knowledge of any thing more then these two may easily furnish our mindes with on all sides : and therefore they which adde traditions as a part of supernatural necessary truth, have not the truth, but are in errour : For they onely plead, that whatsoever God revealeth as necessary for all Christian men to do or believe, the same we ought to embrace, whether we have received it by writing or otherwise ; which no man denieth ; when that which they should confirm, who claim so great reverence unto traditions, is, that the same traditions are necessarily to be acknowledged divine and holy. For we do not reject them onely, because they are not in Scripture, but because they are neither in Scripture, nor can otherwise sufficently by any reason be proved to be of God. That which is of God, and may be evidently proved to be so, we deny not but it hath in his kinde, although unwritten, yet the self same force and authority with the written Laws of God. It is by ours acknowledged, *that the Apostles did in every*

Whitakerus adversus Bellarmin. quæst 6. cap. 6.

Church institute and ordain some rites and customs serving for the seemlines of Church regiment, which rites and customs they have not committed unto writing. Those rites and customs being known to be Apostolical, and having the nature of things changeable, were no less to be accounted of in the Church, then other things of the like degree ; that is to say, capable in like sort of alteration, although set down in the Apostles writings. For both being known to be Apostolical, it is not the manner of delivering them unto the Church, but the Authour from whom they proceed ; which doth give them their force and credit.

Of Laws positive contained in Scripture : the mutability of certain of them, and the general use of Scripture.

15. Laws being imposed either by each man upon himself, or by a Publique Society upon the particulars thereof ; or by all the Nations of men, upon every several Society ; or by the Lord himself, upon any or every of these : there is not amongst these four kindes any one, but containeth sundry both natural and positive laws. Impossible it is, but that they should fall into a number of gross errours, who onely take such Laws for positive, as have been made or invented of men ; and holding this position, hold also, that all positive, and none but positive laws are mutable. Laws natural do always binde ; Laws positive not so, but onely after they have been expresly and wittingly imposed. Laws positive there are in every of those kindes before mentioned. As in the first kinde, the promises which we have past unto men, and the vows we have made unto God ; for these are Laws which we tie our selves unto, and till we have so tied our selves, they binde us not. Laws positive in the second kinde, are such as the civil constitutions peculiar unto each particular common weal. In the third kinde, the Law of Heraldry in War, is positive : And in the last, all the Judicials which God gave unto the people of *Israel* to observe. And although no laws but positive be mutable, yet all are not mutable which be positive. Positive laws are either permanent, or else changeable, according as the matter it self is concerning which they were first made. Whether God or man be the maker of them, alteration they so far forth admit, as positive ; and either concern men supernaturally, as men, or else as parts of a supernatural Society, which Society we call the Church. To concern men as men supernaturally, is to concern them as duties which belong of necessity to all, and yet could not have been known by any to belong unto them, unless God had opened them himself, in as much as they do not depend upon any natural ground at all out of which they may be deduced, but are appointed of God to supply the defect of those natural ways of salvation, by which we are not now able to attain thereunto. The Church being a supernatural society, doth differ from natural societies in this, that the persons unto whom we associate our selves, in the one, are men, simply considered as men ; but

they

they to whom we be joyned in the other, are God, Angels, and holy Men. Again, the Church being both a Society, and a Society Supernatural; although as it is a Society, it have the self-same original grounds which other Politique Societies have, namely, the natural inclination which all men have unto sociable life, and consent to some certain bond of association; which bond is the Law that appointeth what kinde of order they shall be associated in : yet unto the Church, as it is a Society Supernatural, this is peculiar, that part of the bond of their association which belongs to the Church of God, must be a Law Supernatural, which God himself hath revealed concerning that kinde of worship which his people shall do unto him. The substance of the service of God therefore, so far forth as it hath in it any thing more then the Law of Reason doth teach, may not be invented of men, as it is amongst the Heathens; but must be received from God himself, as always it hath been in the Church, saving onely when the Church hath been forgetful of her duty. Wherefore to end with a general Rule concerning all the Laws which God hath tied men unto : Those Laws Divine that belong whether naturally or supernaturally, either to men as men, or to men as they live in Politique Societie, or to men as they are of that Politique Society which is the Church, without any further respect had unto any such variable accident, as the estate of men, and of Societies of men, and of the Church it self in this world is subject unto; all Laws that so belong unto men, they belong for ever, yea, although they be positive Laws, unless being positive, God himself which made them alter them. The reason is, because the subject or matter of Laws in general is thus far forth constant : Which matter is that for the ordering whereof Laws were instituted, and being instituted, are not changeable without cause; neither can they have cause of change, when that which gave them their first institution, remaineth for ever one and the same. On the other side, Laws that were made for men, or Societies, or Churches, in regard of their being such, as they do not always continue, but may perhaps be clean otherwise awhile after, and so may require to be otherwise ordered then before; the Laws of God himself which are of this nature, no man indued with common sense, will ever deny to be of a different constitution from the former, in respect of the ones constancy, and the mutability of the other. And this doth seem to have been the very cause why St. *John* doth so peculiarly term the doctrine that teacheth salvation by Jesus Christ, *Evangelium eternum*, *An eternal Gospel*; because there can be no reason wherefore the publishing thereof should be taken away, and any other instead of it proclaimed, as long as the World doth continue : whereas the whole Law of Rites and Ceremonies, although delivered with so great solemnity, is notwithstanding clean abrogated, inasmuch as it had but temporary cause of Gods ordaining it. But that we may at the length conclude this first general introduction unto the nature and original birth, as of all other Laws, so likewise of those which the sacred Scripture containeth ; concerning the Author whereof, even Infidels have confessed, that he can neither erre nor deceive; albeit, about things easie and manifest unto all men by common sense, there needeth no higher consultation; because as a man whose wisdom is in weighty affairs admired, would take it in some disdain to have his counsel solemnly asked about a toy;so the meanness of some things is such,that to search the Scripture of God for the ordering of them, were to derogate from the reverend authority and dignity of the Scripture, no less then they do by whom Scriptures are in ordinary talk very idly applied unto vain and childish trifles : yet better it were to be superstitious, then prophane ; to take from thence our direction even in all things great or small, then to wade through matters of principal weight and moment, without ever caring what the Law of God hath, either for or against our designs. Concerning the customs of the very Paynims , thus much *Strabo* witnesseth, * *Men that are civil, do lead their lives after one common Law appointing them what to do. For that otherwise a multitude should without harmony amongst themselves , concur in the doing of one thing, (for this is civilly to live) or that they should in any sort manage community of life, it is not possible. Now Laws or Statutes are of two sorts : For they are either received from Gods, or else from men. And our ancient Predecessors did surely most honour and revence that which was from the Gods.; for which cause consultation with Oracles was a thing very usual and frequent in their times.Did they make so much account of the voyce of their gods,which in truth were no Gods :*
and

Isa.29.13. Their fear towards me was taught by the precept of men.

Apud 1 Co. Κοινῇ ἄρα ὁ νοῦς ἀπνῶν καὶ ἀληθὴς ἐν τῷ ἰσῷ, καὶ ἐν λόγῳ καὶ ὅτε αὐτὸς μεθίσταται, ὅτε ἄλλος ἐκλεαται, ὅτε χι φαντασίας, ὅτε κατὰ λόγας ὅτε καθ᾽ ὁρμίαν ποιητάς, καθ᾽ ὑπερβολὴν. ὀναρ. Plato in fine 2. Polit.

* Πολιτικοὶ ὄντες ἀπὸ προςτάγματος κοινῇ ζῶσιν. Ἄλλως γὰρ ἐχ οἷόντε τὰς πολλοὺς ἕν τι κατὰ ταυτὸ ποιεῖν ἡμέως ὠψίως ἀ νλήλοις, ὅπερ ἐν τὸ πολιτεύεσθαι, καὶ ἄλλως πως τέμειν βίον κοινὸν. Τὸ δ᾽ προτασμα διττὸν τῶν γὰρ παρὰ θεῶν ἢ παρὰ ἀνθρώπων. Καὶ οἱ γὰρ χαιοὶ τὸ παρὰ τῶν θεῶν ἐτρεπον Ϛδιον μᾶλλον ἢ διὰ τοῦτο κ χρησιμεύεο ὁ λὼ τότε πολύτε Stra.Geogr. lib. 16.

and ſhall we neglect the precious benefit of conference with thoſe Oracles of the true and living God, whereof ſo great ſtore is left to the Church, and whereunto there is ſo free, ſo plain, and ſo eaſie acceſſ for all men ? [a] *By thy commandments* (this was *Davids* confeſſion unto God) *thou haſt made me wiſer then mine Enemies ;* again, *I have had more underſtanding then all my Teachers, becauſe thy teſtimonies are my meditations.* What pains would not they have beſtowed in the ſtudy of theſe Books, who travelled Sea and Land to gain the treaſure of ſome fews days talk with men, whoſe wiſdom the world did make any reckoning of ? [b] That little which ſome of the Heathens did chance to hear, concerning ſuch matter as the Sacred Scripture plentifully containeth, they did in wonderful ſort affect, their ſpeeches, as oft as they make mention thereof, are ſtrange, and ſuch as themſelves could not utter as they did other things ; but ſtill acknowledged that their wits, which did everywhere elſe conquer hardneſſ, were with profoundneſſ here over-matched. Wherefore ſeeing that God hath indued us with ſenſe, to the end that we might perceive ſuch things as this preſent life doth need, and with reaſon, left that which ſenſe cannot reach unto, being both now, and alſo in regard of a future eſtate hereafter neceſſary to be known, ſhould he obſcure. Finally, with the heavenly ſupport of * Prophetical Revelation, which doth open thoſe hidden Myſteries which Reaſon could never have been able to finde out, or to have known the neceſſity of them unto our everlaſting good: Uſe we the precious gifts of God, unto his glory and honour that gave them, ſeeking by all means to know what the will of our God is, what righteous before him, in his ſight what holy, perfect, and good, that we may truly and faithfully do it.

16 Thus far therefore we have endeavoured in part to open, of what nature and force Laws are, according unto their ſeveral kindes ; the Law, which God with himſelf hath eternally ſet down to follow in his own works, the Law, which he hath made for his creatures to keep ; the Law of natural and neceſſary Agents ; the Law, which Angels in Heaven obey ; the Law, whereunto by the light of Reaſon, men finde themſelves bound, in that they are men ; the Law, which they make by compoſition for multitudes and politique Societies of men to be guided by; the Law, which belongeth unto each Nation ; the Law, that concerneth the fellowſhip of all ; and laſtly, the Law which God himſelf hath ſupernaturally revealed. It might peradventure have been more popular and more plauſible to vulgar ears, if this firſt diſcourſe had been ſpent in extolling the force of Laws, in ſhewing the great neceſſity of them when they are good, and aggravating their offence, by whom publique Laws are injuriouſly traduced. But foraſmuch as with ſuch kinde of matter the paſſions of men are rather ſtirred one way or other, then their knowledge any way ſet forward unto the trial of that whereof there is doubt made, I have therefore turned aſide from that beaten path, and choſen, though a leſſ eaſie, yet a more profitable way, in regard of the end we propoſe. Leſt therefore any man ſhould marvel whereunto all theſe things tend, the drift and purpoſe of all is this, even to ſhew in what manner, a ſuch very good and perfect gift, ſo this very gift of good and perfect Laws is derived from the Father of lights; to teach men a reaſon why juſt and reaſonable Laws are of ſo great force, of ſo great uſe in the world ; and to inform their mindes with ſome method of reducing the Laws, whereof there is preſent controverſie, unto their firſt original cauſes, that ſo it may be in every particular Ordinance thereby the better diſcerned, whether the ſame be reaſonable, juſt and righteous, or no. Is there any thing which can either be thorowly underſtood, or ſoundly judged of, till the very firſt cauſes and principles from which originally it ſpringeth be made manifeſt ? If all parts of knowledge have been thought by wiſe men to be then moſt orderly delivered and proceeded in, when they are drawn to their firſt original ; ſeeing that our whole queſtion concerneth the quality of Eccleſiaſtical Laws, let it not ſeem a labour ſuperfluous, that in the entrance thereunto all theſe ſeveral kindes of Laws have been conſidered, inaſmuch as they all concur as principles, they all have forcible operations therein, although not all in like apparent and manifeſt manner: By means whereof it cometh to paſſ, that the force which they have, is not obſerved of many. Eaſier a great deal it is for men by law to be taught what they ought to do, then inſtructed how to judge as they ſhould do of law; the one being a thing which belongeth generally unto all, the other ſuch as none but the wiſer and more judicious ſort

can

[a] Pſal. 119.98.

[b] Vide Orphei Carmina.

+ *Ὃν γὰρ ὁ θεὸς ἀποκείπται, ὄψις τότε ἱεροφανεία φθάνει*
b lo de Moſ.

A concluſion, ſhewing how all this belongeth to the cauſe in queſtion.

Iam.1.17.

Ariſt Phyſ. l. 1. cap.1.

can perform. Yea the wisest are always touching this point the readiest to acknowledge, that soundly to judge of a Law, is the weightiest thing that any man can take
upon him. But if we will give judgement of the Laws under which we live, first, let
that Law eternal be always before our eyes, as being of principal force and moment
to breed in religious minds a dutiful estimation of all Laws, the use and benefit whereof we see; because there can be no doubt but that Laws apparently good, are (as it
were) things copied out of the very Tables of that high everlasting Law, even as the
Book of that Law hath said concerning it self, *By me Kings reign, and by me Princes de-*
cree justice. Not as if men did behold that Book, and accordingly frame their Laws;
but because it worketh in them, because it discovereth, and (as it were) readeth it self
to the world by them, when the Laws which they make are righteous. Furthermore,
although we perceive not the goodness of Laws made; nevertheless, sith things in
themselves may have that which we peradventure discern not; should not this breed
a fear in our hearts, how we speak or judge in the worse part concerning that, the
unadvised disgrace whereof may be no mean dishonour to him, towards whom we
profess all submission and awe? Surely there must be very manifest iniquity in Laws,
against which we shall be able to justifie our contumelious Invectives. The chiefest
root whereof, when we use them without cause, is ignorance, how Laws inferiour are
derived from that supream or highest Law. The first that receive impression from
thence, are natural agents. The Law of whose operations might be haply thought
the less pertinent, when the question is about Laws for humane actions, but that in
those very actions which most spiritually and supernaturally concern men, the Rules
and Axiomes of natural operations have their force. What can be more immediate to
our salvation, then our perswasion concerning the Law of Christ toward his Church?
What greater assurance of love towards his Church, then the knowledge of that mystical Union, whereby the Church is become as near unto Christ, as any one part of
his flesh is unto other? That the Church being in such sort his, he must needs protect
it; what proof more strong, then if a manifest Law so require, which Law it is not
possible for Christ to violate? and what other Law doth the Apostle for this alleage,
but such as is both common unto Christ with us, and unto us with other things natural; *No man hateth his own flesh, but doth love and cherish it?* The Axiomes of
that Law therefore, whereby natural agents are guided, have their use in the moral, yea, even in the spiritual actions of men, and consequently in all Laws belonging unto men howsoever. Neither are the Angels themselves so far severed from
us in their kinde and manner of working, but that between the Law of their
heavenly operations, and the actions of men in this our state of mortality, such
correspondence there is, as maketh it expedient to know in some sort the one, for
the others more perfect direction. Would Angels acknowledge themselves Fellow-servants with the Sons of men, but that both having One Lord, there must
be some kinde of Law which is one and the same to both, whereunto their obedience being perfecter, is to our weaker both a pattern and a spur? Or would
the Apostles, speaking of that which belongeth unto Saints, as they are linked together in the bond of spiritual society, so often make mention how Angels are
therewith delighted, if in things publiquely done by the Church we are not somewhat to respect what the Angels of Heaven do? Yea, so far hath the Apostle Saint
Paul proceeded, as to signifie that even about the outward orders of the Church,
which serve but for comeliness, some regard is to be had of Angels; who best like us
when we are like unto them in all parts of decent demeanor. So that the Law of Angels
we cannot judge altogether impertinent unto the affairs of the Church of God.
Our largeness of speech, how men do finde out what things reason bindeth them of
necessity to observe, and what it giveth them to chuse in things that are left as arbitrary, the care we have had to declare the different nature of Laws which severally
concern all men, from such as belong unto men either civilly or spiritually associated,
such as pertain to the fellowship which Nations, or which Christian Nations have a-
mong themselves, and in the last place, such as concerning every or any of these God
himself hath revealed by his holy word; all serveth but to make manifest, that as
the actions of men are of sundry distinct kindes, so the Laws thereof must accordingly be distinguished. There are in men operations, some natural, some rational, some
supernatural, some politique, some finally Ecclesiastical. Which if we measure
not

not each by his own proper Law, whereas the things themſelves are ſo different, there will be in our underſtanding and judgment of them confuſion. As that firſt errour ſheweth whereon our oppoſites in this cauſe have grounded themſelves: For as they rightly maintain, that God muſt be glorified in all things, and that the actions of men cannot tend unto his glory, unleſs they be framed after his Law: So it is their error, to think that the onely Law which God hath appointed unto men in that behalf is the ſacred Scripture. By that which we work naturally, as when we breath, ſleep, move, we ſet forth the glory of God as natural agents do; albeit we have no expreſs purpoſe to make that our end, nor any adviſed determination therein to follow a Law, but do that we do (for the moſt part) not as much as thinking thereon. In reaſonable and moral actions another Law taketh place, a law by the obſervation whereof we glorifie God in ſuch ſort as no creature elſe under man is able to do; becauſe other creatures have not judgement to examine the quality of that which is done by them, and therefore in that they do, they neither can accuſe nor approve themſelves. Men do both, as the Apoſtle teacheth; yea, thoſe men which have no written law of God to ſhew what is good or evil, carry written in their hearts the univerſal Law of mankind, the Law of reaſon, whereby they judge as by a rule which God hath given unto men for that purpoſe. The Law of reaſon doth ſomewhat direct men how to honour God as their Creatour; but how to glorifie God in ſuch ſort as is required to the end he may be an everlaſting Saviour, this we are taught by divine Law, which Law both aſcertaineth the truth, and ſupplieth unto us the want of that other Law. So that in moral actions, divine Law helpeth exceedingly the Law of reaſon to guide mans life; but in ſupernatural it alone guideth. Proceed we further, let us place man in ſome publique ſocietie with others, whether Civil or Spiritual: and in this caſe there is no remedie but we muſt add yet a further Law. For although even here likewiſe the Laws of Nature and Reaſon be of neceſſary uſe; yet ſomewhat over and beſides them is neceſſary, namely humane and poſitive Law, together with that Law which is of commerce between grand Societies, the Law of Nations, and of Nations Chriſtian. For which cauſe the Law of God hath likewiſe ſaid, *Let every ſoul be ſubject to the higher powers.* The publike power of all Societies is above every ſoul contained in the ſame Societies. And the principal uſe of that power is to give Laws to all that are under it; which Laws in ſuch caſe we muſt obey, unleſs there be reaſon ſhewed which may neceſſarily inforce, that the Law of Reaſon or of God doth enjoyn the contrary. Becauſe except our own private, and but probable reſolutions, be by the Law of publike determinations over-ruled, we take away all poſſibility of ſociable life in the world. A plainer example whereof then our ſelves we cannot have. How cometh it to paſs that we are at this preſent day ſo rent with mutual contentions, and that the Church is ſo much troubled about the Polity of the Church? No doubt, if men had been willing to learn how many Laws their actions in this life are ſubject unto, and what the true force of each law is, all theſe controverſies might have died the very day they were firſt brought forth. It is both commonly ſaid, and truly, that the beſt men are not always the beſt in regard of ſociety. The reaſon whereof is, for that the Law of mens actions is one, if they be reſpected only as men; and another, when they are conſidered as parts of a Politike body. Many men there are, then whom nothing is more commendable when they are ſingled. And yet in ſociety with others, none leſs fit to anſwer the duties which are looked for at their hands. Yea, I am perſwaded, that of them with whom in this cauſe we ſtrive, there are whoſe betters among men would be hardly found, if they did not live amongſt men, but in ſome Wilderneſs by themſelves. The cauſe of which their diſpoſition ſo unframable unto ſocieties wherein they live, is for that they diſcern not aright what place and force theſe ſeveral kinds of Laws ought to have in all their actions. Is there queſtion either concerning the Regiment of the Church in general, or about conformity between one Church and another, or of Ceremonies, Offices, Powers, Juriſdiction in our own Church? Of all theſe things they judge by that rule which they frame to themſelves with ſome ſhew of probability; and what ſeemeth in that ſort convenient, the ſame they think themſelves bound to practiſe, the ſame by all means they labour mightily to uphold; whatſoever any Law of man to the contrary hath determined, they weigh it not. Thus by following the Law of private reaſon, where the Law of publike ſhould take place, they breed diſturbance. For the better inuring therefore

of

Mat. 18: 7, 8, 9

Rom. 1. 21.

Rom. 1. 15.

Rom. 13. 1.

Πολλοὶ γὰρ ἐν
μὲν τ̓ῖς ἰδιώτοις
τῇ ἀρετῇ δια-
φέρω τὰ γινώσκω,
ἐν δὲ τοῖς πρὸς
ἕτερον ἀδυνα-
τοῦσιν. Ariſt.
Eth. l. 5. c. 3.

of mens mindes with the true distinction of Laws and of their several force, according to the different kind and quality of our actions, it shall not peradventure be amiss to shew in some one example how they all take place. To seek no further; let but that be considered, then which there is not any thing more familiar unto us, our food. What things are food, and what are not, we judge naturally by sense, neither need we any other Law to be our directer in that behalf then the self same which is common unto us with beasts. But when we come to consider of food, as of a benefit which God of his bounteous goodness hath provided for all things living; the Law of reason doth here require the duty of thankfulness at our hands, towards him at whose hands we have it. And lest appetite in the use of food, should lead us beyond that which is meet, we owe in this case obedience to that Law of Reason, which teacheth mediocrity in meats and drinks. The same things Divine Law teacheth also, as at large we have shewed it doth all parts of moral duty, whereunto we all of necessity stand bound, in regard of the life to come. But of certain kindes of food the Jews somtime had, and we our selves likewise have a mystical, religious, and supernatural use; they of their Paschal Lamb and Oblations; we of our Bread and Wine in the Eucharist; which use none but Divine Law could institute. Now as we live in Civil society, the state of the Commonwealth wherein we live, both may and doth require certain Laws concerning food; which Laws, saving onely that we are members of the Commonwealth where they are of force, we should not need to respect as rules of action, whereas now in their place and kinde they must be respected and obeyed. Yea, the self-same matter is also a subject wherein sometime Ecclesiastical Laws have place; so that unless we will be Authors of confusion in the Church, our private discretion, which otherwise might guide us a contrary way, must here submit it self to be that way guided, which the publique judgement of the Church hath thought better. In which case that of *Zonaras* concerning fasts may be remembred. *Fastings are good, but let good things be done in good and convenient manner. He that transgresseth in his fasting the orders of the holy Fathers,* the positive Laws of the Church of Christ, must be plainly told, *that good things do lose the grace of their goodness, when in good sort they are not performed.* And as here mens private fancies must give place to the higher judgement of that Church which is in authority a Mother over them: so the very actions of whole Churches have, in regard of commerce and fellowship with other Churches, been subject to Laws concerning food, the contrary unto which Laws had else been thought more convenient for them to observe; as by that order of abstinence from strangled and blood may appear; an order grounded upon that fellowship which the Churches of the Gentiles had with the Jews. Thus we see how even one and the self same thing is under divers considerations conveyed through many Laws, and that to measure by any one kinde of Law all the actions of men, were to confound the admirable order wherein God hath disposed all Laws, each as in nature, so in degree, distinct from other. Wherefore that here we may briefly end, of Law there can be no less acknowledged, then that her seat is the bosom of God, her voyce the harmony of the World; all things in Heaven and Earth do her homage, the very least as feeling her care, and the greatest as not exempted from her power; both Angels, and men, and creatures of what condition soever, though each in different sort and manner, yet all with uniform consent, admiring her as the Mother of their peace and joy.

Io. 24.3
Psal. 145.15,16.

Ὅτι ἐ καλὸν τὸ καλὸν, ὅταν μὴ καλῶς γένη[τ].
Zonar. in Can. Apost. 66.

Acts 15.20.

OF THE
LAWS
OF
Ecclefiaftical Politie.

The Second BOOK.

Concerning their Firſt Poſition who urge Reformation in the Church of *England.*

Namely, That Scripture is the onely rule of all things which in this life may be done by men.

The matter contained in this ſecond Book.

1. **A**N Anſwer to their firſt proof brought out of Scripture, Prov.2.9.
2. To their ſecond, 1 Cor. 10.31.
3. To their third, 1 Tim.4.5.
4. To their fourth. Rom.14.23.
5. To their proofs out of Fathers, who diſpute negatively from the Authority of Holy Scripture.
6. To their proof by the Scriptures cuſtom of diſputing from Divine Authority negatively.
7. An examination of their opinion concerning the force of Arguments taken from humane Authority, for the ordering of mens-actions and perſwaſions.
8. A Declaration what the truth is in this matter.

AS that which in the title hath been propoſed for the matter whereof we treat, is onely the Eccleſiaſtical Law whereby we are governed ; So neither is it my purpoſe to maintain any other thing, then that which therein truth and reaſon ſhall approve. For concerning the dealings of men who adminiſter Government, and unto whom the execution of that law belongeth , they have their Judge who ſitteth in Heaven, and before whoſe Tribunal Seat they are accountable for whatſoever abuſe or corruption, which (being worthily miſliked in this Church) the want either of care or of conſcience in them hath bred. We are no Patrons of thoſe things therefore; the beſt defence whereof is ſpeedy redreſs and amendment. That which is of God we defend, to the uttermoſt of that ability which he hath given : that which is otherwiſe, let it wither even in the root from whence it hath ſprung. Wherefore all theſe abuſes being ſevered and ſet apart, which riſe from the corruption of men, and not

from

from the Laws themselves. Come we to those things which in the very whole intire form of our Church-Polity have been (as we perswade our selves) injuriously blamed by them who indeavour to overthrow the same, and instead thereof to establish a much worse; onely through a strong misconceit they have, that the same is grounded on Divine Authority. Now, whether it be that through an earnest longing desire to see things brought to a peaceable end, I do but imagine the matters whereof we contend, to be fewer then indeed they are; or else for that in truth they are fewer when they come to be discust by reason, then otherwise they seem, when by heat of contention they are divided into many slips, and of every branch an heap is made: surely, as now we have drawn them together, choosing out those things which are requisite to be severally all discust, and omitting such mean specialities as are likely (without any great labour) to fall afterwards of themselves; I know no cause why either the number or the length of these Controversies should diminish our hope of seeing them end with concord and love on all sides; which of his infinite love and goodness the Father of all peace and unity grant. Unto which scope that our endeavour may the more directly tend, it seemeth fittest that first those things be examined, which are as seeds from whence the rest that ensue have grown. And of such the most general is that, wherewith we are here to make our entrance: a question not moved (I think) anywhere in other Churches, and therefore in ours the more likely to be soon (I trust) determined: the rather for that it hath grown from no other root, then onely a desire to enlarge the necessary use of the Word of God; which desire hath begotten an errour enlarging it further then (as we are perswaded) soundness of truth will bear. For whereas God hath left sundry kindes of Laws unto men, and by all those Laws the actions of men are in some sort directed: they hold that one onely Law, the Scripture, must be the rule to direct in all things, even so far as to the *taking up of a Rush or straw.* About which point there should not need any question to grow, and that which is grown might presently end, if they did yield but to these two restraints: the first is, Not to extend the actions whereof they speak, so low as that instance doth import, of taking up a straw, but rather keep themselves at the least within the compass of moral actions, actions which have in them Vice or Vertue: the second, Not to exact at our hands for every action the knowledge of some place of Scripture out of which we stand bound to deduce it, as by divers testimonies they seek to enforce; but rather as the truth is, so to acknowledge, that it sufficeth if such actions be framed according to the Law of Reason; the general Axiomes, Rules and Principles of which Law being so frequent in holy Scripture, there is no let but in that regard, even out of Scripture such duties may be deduced by some kinde of consequence (as by long circuit of deduction it may be that even all truth out of any truth may be concluded) howbeit no man bound in such sort to deduce all his actions out of Scripture, as if either the place be to him unknown whereon they may be concluded, or the reference unto that place not presently considered of, the action shall in that respect be condemned as unlawful. In this we dissent, and this we are presently to examine.

T.C. l. 1. p. 59, 60.

1. In all parts of knowledge rightly so termed, things most general are most strong; Thus it must be, inasmuch as the certainty of our perswasion touching particulars, dependeth altogether upon the credit of those generalities out of which they grow. Albeit therefore every cause admit not such infallible evidence of proof, as leaveth no possibility of doubt or scruple behinde it; yet they who claim the general assent of the whole world unto that which they teach, and do not fear to give very hard and heavy sentence upon as many as refuse to embrace the same, must have special regard that their first foundations and grounds be more then slender probabilities. This whole question which hath been moved about the kinde of Church-Regiment, we could not but for our own resolution sake, endeavour to unrip and sift; following therein as near as we might, the conduct of that judicial method which serveth best for invention of truth. By means whereof having found this the head Theorem of all their Discourses, who plead for the change of Ecclesiastical Government in *England,* namely, *That the Scripture of God is in such sort the rule of humane actions, that simply whatsoever we do, and are not by it directed thereunto, the same is sin;* we hold it for Solomon saith in the second Chapter of the *Proverbs, My son, if thou receive my words, &c. then thou shalt understand justice, and judgement, and equity, and every good way.*

The first pretended proof of the first Position out of Scripture. *Prov. 2. 9.*
T.C. lib. 1. p. 20.
I say, that the Word of God containeth whatsoever things can fall into any part of mans life.
For so Solomon

necessary

necessary that the proofs hereof be weighed: Be they of weight sufficient or otherwise, it is not ours to judge and determine; onely what difficulties there are, which as yet withhold our assent, till we be further and better satisfied, I hope, no indifferent amongst them will scorn or refuse to hear. First, therefore, whereas they alledge, *That Wisdom doth teach men every good way*; and have thereupon inferred, that no way is good in any kinde of action, unless wisdom do by Scripture lead unto it: See they not plainly how they restrain the manifold ways which Wisdom hath to teach men by, unto one onely way of teaching, which is by Scripture? The bounds of Wisdom are large, and within them much is contained. Wisdom was *Adams* Instructer in Paradise: Wisdom endued the Fathers who lived before the Law, with the knowledge of holy things;

Psal. 119. 95.

by the wisdom of the Law of God, *David* attained to, excell others in understanding; and *Solomon* likewise to excel *David*, by the self-same wisdom of God, teaching him many things besides the Law. The ways of well-doing are in number even as many, as are the kindes of voluntary actions: so that whatsoever we

a 2 Tim. 3. 16.
The whole Scripture is given by inspiration of God, and is profitable to teach, to improve, to correct, and to instruct in righteousness, that the man of God may be absolute, being made perfect unto all good works. He meaneth all and only those good works which belong unto us as we are men of God, & which

do in this World, and may do it ill, we shew our selves therein by well-doing to be wise. Now if wisdom did teach men by Scripture not onely all the ways that are right and good in some certain kinde, according to that of S. *Paul*, concerning the use of Scripture; but did simply without any manner of exception, restraint, or distinction, teach every way of doing well: There is no Art but Scripture should teach it, because every Art doth teach the way how to do some thing or other well. To teach men therefore Wisdom professeth, and to teach them every good way: but not every good way by one way of teaching. Whatsoever either men on Earth, or the Angels of Heaven do know, it is as a drop of that uneuptiable Fountain of wisdom; which Wisdom hath diversly imparted her treasures unto the World. As her ways are of sundry kindes, so her manner of teaching is not meerly one and the same. Some things she openeth by the sacred Books of Scripture; some things by the glorious works of Nature: with some things she inspireth them from above by spiritual influence; with some things she leadeth and traineth them onely by worldly experience and practice. We may not so in any one special kinde admire her, that we disgrace her in any other; but let all her ways be according unto their place and degree adored.

unto salvation are necessary. Or if we understand by men of God, Gods Ministers, there is not required in them an universal skill of every good work or way, but an ability to teach whatsoever men are bound to do that they may be saved. And with this kinde of knowledge the Scripture sufficeth to furnish them as touching matter.

The second proof out of scripture, 1 Cor 10.31. T. C. l. p. 26. S. Paul saith, that whether we eat or drink, or what soever we do, we must do it to the glory of God: but no man can glorifie God in any thing but by obedience; and there is no obedience but in respect of the commandment & word of God; therefore it followeth that the word of God directeth a man in all his actions.

2. That *all things be done to the glory of God*, the blessed Apostle (it is true) exhorteth. The glory of God is the admirable excellency of that Vertue Divine, which being made manifest, causeth Men and Angels to extoll his greatness, and in regard thereof to fear him. By being glorified, it is not meant, that he doth receive any augmentation of glory at our hands; but his Name we glorifie, when we testifie our acknowledgement of his glory. Which albeit we most effectually do by the vertue of obedience; nevertheless it may be perhaps a question, Whether St. *Paul* did mean that we sin as oft as ever we go about any thing, without an express intent and purpose to obey God therein. He saith of himself, *I do in all things please all men, seeking not mine own commodity, but rather the good of many, that they may be saved.* Shall it hereupon be thought, that St. *Paul* did not move either hand or foot, but with express intent even thereby to further the common salvation of men? We move, we sleep, we take the cup at the hand of our friend, a number of things we oftentimes do, onely to satisfie some natural desire, without present express and actual reference unto any Commandment of God. Unto his glory even these things are done which we naturally perform, and not onely that which morally and spiritually we do. For by every effect proceeding from the most concealed instincts of Nature, his power is made manifest. But it doth not therefore follow, that of necessity we shall sin, unless we expresly intend this in every such particular: But be it a thing which requireth no more then onely our general presupposed willingness to please God in all things, or be it a matter wherein we cannot so glorifie the Name of God as we should, without an actual intent to do him in that particular some special obedience; yet for any thing there is in this sentence alledged to

the

the contrary, God may be glorified by obedience, and obeyed by performance of his will, and his will be performed with an actual intelligent desire to fulfil that Law which maketh known what his will is, although no special clause or sentence of Scripture be in every such action set before mens eyes to warrant it. For Scripture is not the onely Law whereby God hath opened his will touching all things that may be done; but there are other kinde of Laws which notifie the will of God, as in the former Book hath been proved at large: nor is there any Law of God, whereunto he doth not account our obedience his glory. *Do therefore all things unto the glory of God,* (saith the Apostle) *be inoffensive both to the Jews and Grecians, and the Church of God; even as I please all men in all things, not seeking mine own commodity, but manies, that they may be saved.* In the least thing done disobediently towards God, or offensively against the good of men whose benefit we ought to seek for as for our own, we plainly shew that we do not acknowledge God to be such as indeed he is, and consequently that we glorifie him not. This the blessed Apostle teacheth: but doth any Apostle teach, that we cannot glorifie God otherwise then onely in doing what we finde that God in Scripture commandeth us to do? The Churches dispersed amongst the Heathen in the East part of the World, are by the Apostle S. *Peter* exhorted, to have their *conversation honest amongst the Gentiles, that they which spake evil of them as of evil doers, might by the good works which they should see, glorifie God in the day of visitation.* As long as that which Christians did was good, and no way subject to just reproof, their vertuous conversation was a mean to work the Heathens conversion unto Christ. Seeing therefore this had been a thing altogether impossible, but that Infidels themselves did discern, in matters of life and conversation, when Believers did well, and when otherwise; when they glorified their Heavenly Father, and when not: it followeth, that some things wherein God is glorified, may be some other way known then onely by the sacred Scriptures; of which Scripture the Gentiles being utterly ignorant, did notwithstanding judge rightly of the quality of Christian mens actions. Most certain it is, that nothing but onely sin doth dishonour God. So that to glorifie him in all things, is to do nothing whereby the Name of God may be blasphemed; nothing whereby the salvation of Jew or Grecian, or any in the Church of Christ may be let or hindred, nothing whereby his Law is transgrest. But the question is, whether onely Scripture do shew whatsoever God is glorified in.

1 Pet. 2.12.

Rom. 2.24.

1 Cor. 10.31.
Rom. 2.13.

3. And though meats and drinks be said to be sanctified by the Word of God, and by Prayer: yet neither is this a reason sufficient to prove, that by Scripture we must of necessity be directed, in every light and common thing which is incident unto any part of mans life. Onely it sheweth that unto us the Word, that is to say, the Gospel of Christ, having not delivered any such difference of things clean and unclean, as the Law of *Moses* did unto the Jews; there is no cause but that we may use indifferently all things, as long as we do not (like Swine) take the benefit of them without a thankful acknowledgement of his liberality and goodness, by whose providence they are enjoyed: and therefore the Apostle gave warning beforehand to take heed of such as should enjoyn to *abstain from meats, which God hath created to be received with thanksgiving, by them which believe and know the Truth. For every creature of God is good, and nothing to be refused, if it be received with thanksgiving, because it is sanctified by the Word of God and Prayer.* The Gospel, by not making many things unclean, as the Law did, hath sanctified those things generally to all, which particularly each man unto himself must sanctifie by a reverend and holy use: which will hardly be drawn so far as to serve their purpose, who have imagined the Word in such sort to sanctifie all things, that neither food can be tasted, nor rayment put on, nor in the World any thing done, but this deed must needs be sin in them which do not first know it appointed unto them by Scripture before they do it.

The third scripture proof, 1 Tim. 4. 5. and that which St. *Paul* said of meats and drinks, that they are sanctified unto us by the word of God, the same is to be understood of all things else whatsoever we have the use of, T.C. l. 1. p. 10.
1 Tim. 4.

4. But to come unto that which of all other things in Scripture is most stood upon, that place of S. *Paul* they say, is of *all other most clear, where speaking of those things which are called indifferent, in the end he concludeth, that whatsoever is not of faith, is sin. But faith is not but in respect of the Word of God. Therefore whatsoever is not done by* the Word of God, *is sin.* Whereunto we answer, that albeit the name of faith being properly and strictly taken, it must needs have reference unto some uttered word,

The fourth scripture proof, Rom. 14.
T. C. l. 1. p. 171

as the object of belief: nevertheless, sith the ground of credit is the credibility of things credited; and things are made credible, either by the known condition and quality of the utterer, or by the manifest likelihood of Truth which they have in themselves; hereupon it riseth, that whatsoever we are perswaded of, the same we are generally said to believe. In which generality the object of faith may not so narrowly be restrained, as if the same did extend no further then to the onely Scriptures of God. *Though* (saith our Saviour) *ye believe not me, belive my works, that ye may know and believe that the Father is in me, and I in him.* The other Disciples said unto Thomas, *We have seen the Lord;* but his answer unto them was, *Except I see in his hands the print of the nails, and put my finger into them, I will not believe.* Can there be any thing more plain, then that which by these two sentences appeareth? namely, that there may be a certain belief grounded upon other assurance then Scripture; any thing more clear then that we are said not only to believe the things which we know by anothers relation, but even whatsoever we are certainly perswaded of, whether it be by reason, or by sense?

Pfal. 19.8.
Apoc 3.14.
2 Cor.1.18.

Iohn 10.38.

Iohn 20.25.

Forasmuch therefore as it is granted that S. *Paul* doth mean nothing else by *Faith,* but only *a full perswasion that that which we do is well done;* against which kinde of faith or perswasion as S. *Paul* doth count it sin to enterprize any thing; [b] so likewise some of the very Heathen have taught, as *Tully, That nothing ought to be done whereof thou doubtest whether it be right or wrong; whereby it appeareth that even those which had no knowledge of the Word of God, did see much of the equity of this which the Apostle requireth of a Christian man:* I hope we shall not seem altogether unnecessarily to doubt of the soundness

[a] And if any will say, that S. *Paul* meaneth there a full *perswasion* and perswasion that that which he doth is well done, *I* grant it. But from whence can that spring but from faith? how can we perswade and assure our selves that we do well, but whereas we have the word of God for our warrant? *T.C. l. 1. c. 27.* [b] What also that some even of those Heathen men have taught, that nothing ought to be done, whereof thou doubtest whether it be right or wrong? Whereby it appeareth, that even those which had no knowledge of the Word of God, did see much of the equity of this which the Apostle requireth of a Christian man: and that the chiefest difference is, that where they sent men for the difference of good and evil to the light of reason, in such things the Apostle sendeth them to the School of Christ in his Word, which onely is able through faith to give them assurance and resolution in their doings. *T.C. l. 1. p. 60.*

of their opinion, who think simply that nothing but onely the Word of God, can give us assurance in any thing we are to do, and resolve us that we do well. For might not the Jews have been fully perswaded that they did well to think (if they had so thought) that in Christ God the Father was, although the onely ground of this their faith had been the wonderful works they saw him do? Might not, yea, did not *Thomas* fully in the end perswade himself, that he did well to think that body which now was raised, to be the same which had been crucified? That which gave *Thomas* this assurance was his sence; *Thomas, because thou hast seen, thou believest,* saith our Saviour. What Scripture had *Tully* for his assurance? Yet I nothing doubt, but that they who alledge him, think he did well to set down in writing a thing so consonant unto truth. Finally, we all believe that the Scriptures of God are Sacred, and that they have proceeded from God; our selves we assure that we do right well in so believing. We have for this point a demonstration sound & infallible. But it is not the word of God which doth or can possibly assure us, that we do well to think it his word. For if any one Book of Scripture did give testimony to all; yet still that Scripture which giveth credit to the rest, would require another Scripture to give credit unto it: neither could we ever come unto any pause whereon to rest our assurance this way; so that unless besides Scripture there were something which might assure us that we do well, we could not think we do well, no not in being assured that Scripture is a sacred and holy Rule of well doing. On which determination we might be contented to stay our selves without further proceeding herein, but that we are drawn on into a larger speech by reason of their so great earnestness, who beat more and more upon these last alledged words, as being of all other most pregnant. Whereas therefore they still argue, that *wheresoever faith is wanting, there is sin;* and, *in every action not commanded, faith is wanting;* Ergo, *in every action not commanded, there is sin:* I would demand of them; first, forasmuch as the nature of things indifferent is neither to be commanded nor forbidden, but left free and arbitrary; how there can be any thing indifferent, if for want of faith sin be committed, when any thing not commanded is done? So that of necessity they must adde somewhat, and at leastwise thus set it down: In every action not commanded of God or permitted with approbation, Faith

Iohn 10. 21.

T.C. l. 2. p. 55.

is wanting, and for want of Faith there is sin. The next thing we are to enquire is, What those things be which God permitteth with approbation, and how we may know them to be so permitted? When there are unto one end sundry means; as for example, for the sustenance of our bodies many kindes of food; many sorts of rayment to cloath our nakedness, and so in other things of like condition: here the end it self being necessary, but not so any one mean thereunto; necessary that our bodies should be both fed and cloathed, howbeit no one kinde of food or raiment necessary; therefore we hold these things free in their own nature and indifferent. The choice is left to our own discretion, except a principal bond of some higher duty remove the indifferency that such things have in themselves. Their indifferency is removed, if either we take away our own liberty, as *Ananias* did, for whom to have sold or held his possessions it was indifferent, till his solemn Vow and Promise unto God had strictly bound him one onely way: or if God himself have precisely abridged the same, by restraining us unto, or by barring us from some one or more things of many, which otherwise were in themselves altogether indifferent. Many fashions of Priestly attire there were, whereof *Aaron* and his sons might have had their free choice without sin, but that God expresly tied them unto one. All meats indifferent unto the Jew, were it not that God by name excepted some, as Swines flesh. Impossible therefore it is we should otherwise think, then that what things God doth neither command nor forbid, the same he permitteth with approbation either to be done or left undone. *All things are lawful unto me,* saith the Apostle, speaking as it seemeth, in the person of the Christian Gentile, for maintenance of liberty in things indifferent: whereunto his answer is, that nevertheless, *All things are not expedient;* in things indifferent there is a choice, they are not always equally expedient. Now in things although not commanded of God, yet lawful, because they are permitted, the question is, What light shall shew us the conveniency which one hath above another? For answer, their final determination is, that *whereas the Heathen did send men for the difference of good and evil to the light of reason, in such things the Apostle sendeth us to the School of Christ in his word, which onely is able through faith to give us assurance and resolution in our doings.* Which word *Onely,* is utterly without possibility of ever being proved. For what if it were true concerning things indifferent, that unless the Word of the Lord had determined of the free use of them, there could have been no lawful use of them at all; which notwithstanding is untrue; because it is not the Scriptures setting down such things as indifferent, but their not setting down as necessary, that doth make them to be indifferent: yet this to our present purpose serveth nothing at all. We enquire not now, Whether any thing be free to be used, which Scripture hath not set down as free? but concerning things known and acknowledged to be indifferent, whether particularly in chusing any one of them before another we sin, if any thing but Scripture direct us into this our choice. When many meats are set before me, all are indifferent, none unlawful; I take one as most convenient. If Scripture require me so to do, then is not the thing indifferent, because I must do what Scripture requireth. They are all indifferent; I might take any, Scripture doth not require me to make any special choice of one: I do notwithstanding make choice of one, my discretion teaching me so to do. A hard case, that hereupon I should be justly condemned of sin. Nor let any man think, that following the judgement of natural discretion in such cases, we can have no assurance that we please God. For to the author and God of our nature, how shall any operation proceeding in natural sort, be in that respect unacceptable? The nature which himself hath given to work by, he cannot but be delighted with, when we exercise the same any way without Commandment of his to the contrary. My desire is to make this cause so manifest, that if it were possible, no doubt or scruple concerning the same, might remain in any mans cogitation. Some truths there are, the verity whereof time doth alter: as it is now true that Christ is risen from the dead; which thing was not true at such time as Christ was living on earth, and had not suffered. It would be known therefore, whether this which they teach concerning the sinful stain of all actions not commanded of God, be a truth that doth now appertain unto us onely, or a perpetual truth, in such sort that from the first beginning of the world, unto the last consummation thereof, it neither hath been, nor can be otherwise. I see not how they can restrain this unto any particular time, how they can think it true now, and not always true, that in every action not commanded

there

there is for want of faith fin. Then let them caft back their eyes unto former generations of men, and mark what was done in the prime of the World: *Seth, Enoch, Noah, Sem, Abraham, Job,* and the reft that lived before any fyllable of the Law of God was written, did they not fin as much as we do in every action not commanded? That which God is unto us by his Sacred Word, the fame he was unto them by fuch like means as *Eliphas* in *Job* defcribeth. If therefore we fin in every action which the Scripture commandeth us not, it followeth that they did the like in all fuch actions as were not by revelation from Heaven exacted at their hands. Unlefs God from Heaven did by vifion ftill fhew them what to do, they might do nothing; not eat, not drink, not fleep, not move. Yea, but even as in darknefs, candle-light may ferve to guide mens fteps, which to ufe in the day were madnefs; fo when God had once delivered his Law in writing, it may be, they are of opinion, that it muft needs be fin for men to do any thing, which was not there commanded them to do, whatfoever they might do before. Let this be granted, and it fhall hereupon plainly enfue, either that the light of Scripture once fhining in the world, all other light of nature is therewith in fuch fort drowned, that now we need it not, neither

Iob 4.19.

may we longer ufe it; or if it ftand us in any ftead, yet as *Ariftotle* fpeaketh of men whom nature hath framed for the ftate of fervitude, faying, *They have reafon fo far forth as to conceive when others direct them,* but little or none in directing themfelves by themfelves; fo likewife our natural capacity and judgement muft ferve us onely for the right underftanding of that which the facred Scripture teacheth. Had the Prophets who fucceeded *Mofes,* or the bleffed Apoftles which followed them, been fettled in this perfwafion, never would they have taken fo great pains in gathering together natural Arguments, thereby to teach the faithful their duties. To ufe unto them any other motive then *Scriptum eft, Thus it is written,* had been to teach them other grounds of their actions then Scripture; which I grant, they alledge commonly, but not onely. Onely Scripture they fhould have alledged, had they been thus perfwaded, that fo far forth we do fin, as we do any thing otherwife directed then by Scripture. S. *Auguftine* was refolute in points of Chriftianity to credit none, how godly and learned foever he were, unlefs he confirmed his fentence by the Scripture,

Arift. Pol. 1.

Auguft. Ep. 18.

or by fome reafon not contrary to them. Let them therefore with S. *Auguftine,* reject and condemn that which is not grounded either on the Scripture, or on fome reafon not contrary to Scripture, and we are ready to give them our hands in token of friendly confent with them.

The fixt affertion endeavoured to be proved by the ufe of taking arguments negatively from the authority of Scripture: which kinde of difputing is ufual in the Fathers.

5. But againft this it may be objected, and is, That the Fathers do nothing more ufually in their Books, then draw arguments from the Scripture negatively in reproof that which is evil; *Scriptures teach it not, avoid it therefore;* thefe difputes with the Fathers are ordinary, neither is it hard to fhew that the Prophets themfelves have fo reafoned: Which Arguments being found and good, it fhould feem that it cannot be unfound or evil to hold ftill the fame affertion, againft which hitherto we have difputed. For if it ftand with reafon thus to argue, Such a thing is not taught us in Scripture, therefore we may not receive or allow it: how fhould it feem unreafonable to think, that whatfoever we may lawfully do, the Scripture by commanding it muft make it lawful? But how far fuch arguments do reach, it fhall the better appear by confidering the matter wherein they have been urged. Firft therefore this we conftantly deny, that of fo many teftimonies as they are able to produce for the ftrength of negative arguments, any one doth generally (which is the point in queftion) condemn either all opinions as falfe, or all actions as unlawful, which the Scripture teacheth us not. The moft that can be collected out of them is onely, that in fome cafes a negative argument taken from Scripture is ftrong, whereof no man endued with judgement can doubt. But doth the ftrength of fome negative Argument prove this kinde of negative Argument ftrong, by force whereof all things are denied whith Scripture affirmeth not, or all things which Scripture prefcribeth not condemned? The queftion between us is concerning matter of action, what things are lawful or unlawful for men to do. The fentences alledged out of the Fathers, are as peremptory and as large in every refpect for matter of opinion, as of action; which argueth that in truth they never meant any otherwife to tie the one then the other unto Scripture, both being thereunto equally tied, as far as each is required in the fame kinde of neceffity unto Salvation. If therefore it be not unlawful to know, and with full

perfwafion

perswasion to believe much more then Scripture alone doth teach ; if it be against all sense and reason to condemn the knowledge of so many Arts and Sciences as are otherwise learned then in holy Scripture, notwithstanding the manifest speeches of ancient Catholick Fathers which seem to close up within the bosom thereof all manner of good and lawful knowledge : wherefore should these words be thought more effectual, to shew that we may not in deeds and practice, then they are to prove that in speculation and knowledge we ought not to go any further then the Scripture? Which Scripture being given to teach matters of belief no less then of action ; the Fathers must need be, and are even as plain against credit, besides the relation, as against practice, without the Injunction of the Scripture. S. *Augustine* hath said, *Whether it be question of Christ, or whether it be question of his Church, or of what thing soever the question be : I say not , if we, but if an Angel from Heaven shall tell us any thing beside that you have received in the Scripture under the Law and Gospel, let him be accursed.* In like sort *Tertullian, We may not give our selves this liberty to bring in any thing of our will, nor choose any thing that other men bring in of their will ; we have the Apostles themselves for Authors, which themselves brought nothing of their own will ; but the discipline which they received of Christ, they delivered faithfully unto the people ;* in which place the name of Discipline importeth not as they who alledge it would fain have it construed ; but as any man who noteth the circumstance of the place, and the occasion of uttering the words, will easily acknowledge ; even the self-same thing it signifieth , which the name of Doctrine doth ; as well might the one as the other there have been used. To help them farther, doth not S. *Jerome* after the self-same manner dispute, *We believe it not, because we read it not ? yea, we ought not so much as to know the things which the Book of the Law containeth not,* saith S. *Hilarie.* Shall we hereupon then conclude, that we may not take knowledge of, or give credit unto any thing which sense, or experience, or report, or art doth propose, unless, we finde the same in Scripture ? No, it is too plain that so far to extend their speeches, is to wrest them against their true intent and meaning. To urge any thing upon the Church, requiring thereunto that religious assent of Christian belief, wherewith the words of the holy Prophets are received ; to urge any thing as part of that supernatural and celestially revealed truth which God hath taught, and not to shew it in Scripture, this did the ancient Fathers evermore think unlawful, impious, execrable. And thus as their speeches were meant, so by us they must be restrained. As for those alledged words of *Cyprian, The Christian Religion shall finde, that out of this Scripture Rules of all Doctrines have sprung, and that from hence doth spring, and hither doth return whatsoever the Ecclesiastical Discipline doth contain.* Surely this place would never have been brought forth in this cause, if it had been but once read over in the Author himself, out of whom it is cited. For the words are uttered concerning that one principal commandment of Love ; in the honour whereof he speaketh after this sort, *Surely this commandment containeth the Law and the Prophets, and in this one word is the abridgement of all the Volumes of Scripture : This Nature, and Reason, and the authority of thy Word, O Lord, doth proclaim ; this we have heard out of thy mouth : herein the perfection of all Religion doth consist. This is the first commandment and the last : this being written in the Book of Life, is (as it were) an everlasting lesson both to men and Angels. Let Christian Religion read this one word, and meditate upon this commandment, and out of this Scripture it shall finde the Rules of all Learning to have sprung, and from hence to have risen, and hither to return, whatsoever the Ecclesiastical Discipline containeth ; and that in all things it is vain and bootless which Charity confirmeth not.* Was this a sentence (trow you) of so great force to prove that Scripture is the onely rule of all the actions of men ? Might they not hereby even as well prove, that

one

Aug. contr. litter. Petil. l. 3. c. 6.

Tertul. de præscrip. adversus.

T. C. l. 1. p. 51. Augustine saith, Whether it be question of Christ, or whether it be question of his Church, &c. And lest the answer should restrain the general saying of *Augustine* unto the Doctrine of the Gospel, so that he would thereby shut out the Discipline ; even *Tertullian* himself, before he was embrued with the Heresie of *Montanus,* giveth testimony unto the Discipline in these words, *We may not give our selves, &c.*

Hierom. contra Heluid. Hilar. in Psal. 131.

T. C. lib. 2. p. 8. Let him hear what *Cyprian* saith, The Christian Religion (saith he) shall finde, that, &c. *Vere hoc mandatum legem complectitur et Prophetias, & in hoc verbo omnium Scripturarum volumina coarctantur. Hoc natura, hoc ratio, hoc Domine, verbi tui clamat authoritas, hoc ex ore tuo audivimus, hic invenit consummationem omnis Religio. Primum est hoc mandatum & ultimum, hoc in libro vitæ conscriptum inde sufficientem & hominibus & Angelis exhibet lectionem. Legat hoc unum verbum & in hoc mandato meditetur Christiana Religio, & inveniet ex Hac Scriptura omnium doctrinarum regulas emanasse, & hinc nasci & huc reverti quicquid Ecclesiastica continet disciplina, & in omnibus irritum esse & frivolum quicquid dilectio non confirmat.*

one Commandment of Scripture is the onely rule of all things, and so exclude the rest of the Scripture, as now they do all means besides Scripture? But thus it fareth, when too much desire of contradiction causeth our speeches rather to pass by number, then to stay for weight. Well, but *Tertullian* doth in this case speak yet more plainly: *The Scripture* (saith he) *denieth what it noteth not*: which are indeed the words of *Tertullian*. But what? the Scripture reckoneth up the Kings of Israel, and amongst those Kings, *David*; the Scripture reckoneth up the sons of *David*,

and amongst those sons, *Solomon*. To prove that amongst the Kings of Israel, there was no *David* but onely one; no *Solomon* but one in the sons of *David*, *Tertullians* Argument will fitly prove. For inasmuch as the Scripture did propose to reckon up all; if there were more, it would have named them. In this case *the Scripture doth deny the thing it noteth not*. Howbeit, I could not but think that man to do me some piece of manifest injury, which would hereby fasten upon me a general opinion, as if I did think the Scripture to deny the very Reign of King *Henry* the Eighth, because it nowhere noteth that any such King did reign. *Tertullians* speech is probable concerning such matter as he there speaketh of. There was, saith *Tertullian*, no second *Lamech*, like to him that had two wives, the Scripture denieth what it noteth not. As therefore it noteth one such to have been in that age of the World; so had there been moe, it would by likelihood as well have noted many as one. What infer we now hereupon? *There was no second Lamech; the Scripture denieth what it noteth not*. Were it consonant unto reason to divorce these two sentences, the former of which doth shew how the latter is restrained, and not marking the former, to conclude by the latter of them, that simply whatsoever any man at this day doth think true; is by the Scripture denied, unless it be there affirmed to be true? I wonder that a case so weak and feeble hath been so much persisted in. But to come unto those their sentences, wherein matters of action are more apparently touched, the name of *Tertullian* is as before, so here again pretended; who writing unto his wife two Books, and exhorting her in the one to live a widow, in case God before her should take him unto his mercy; and in the other, if she did marry, yet not to joyn her self to an Infidel, as in those times some Widows, Christian had done for the advancement of their estate in this present world, he urgeth very earnestly S. *Pauls* words, *Only in the Lord*. Whereupon he demandeth of them that think they may do the contrary, what Scripture they can shew where God hath dispenced and granted licenfe to do against that which the blessed Apostle so strictly doth enjoyn? And because in defence it might perhaps be replied, Seeing God doth will that couples which are married when both are Infidels, if either party chance to be after converted unto Christianity, this should not make separation between them, as long as the unconverted was willing to retain the other on whom the grace of Christ had shined, wherefore then should that let the making of marriage, which doth not dissolve marriage being made? After great reasons shewed why God doth in Converts being married, allow continuance with Infidels, and yet disallow that the faithful when they are free should enter into bonds of Wedlock with such, concludeth in the end concerning those women that so marry, *They that please not the Lord, do even thereby offend the Lord, they do even thereby throw themselves into evil*; that is to say, while they please him not by marrying in him, they do that whereby they concur his displeasure; they make an offer of themselves into the service of that enemy with whose servants they link themselves in so near a bond. What one syllable is there in all this, prejudicial any way to that we hold? For the words of *Tertullian* as they are by them alledged, are two ways misunderstood; both in the former part, where that is extended generally to *all things* in the neuter gender, which he speaketh in the feminine gender of womens persons; and in the latter, where, *received with hurt*, is put instead of *wilful incurring that which is evil*. And so in sum, *Tertullian* doth neither mean nor say as is pretended, *Whatsoever pleaseth not the Lord, displeaseth him, and with hurt is received*; but, *Those women that please not the Lord by their kinde of marrying, do even thereby offend the Lord,*

Tertul lib de Monog.
T. C. l. p. 81.
And in another place *Tertull. on both*, that the Scripture denieth that which it noteth not.

Lord, they do even thereby throw themselves into evil. Somewhat more shew there is in a second place of *Tertullian*, which notwithstanding when we have examined, it will be found as the rest are. The Roman Emperours custom was at certain solemn times to bestow on his Souldiers a donative; which donative they received, wearing garlands upon their heads. There were in the time of the Emperors *Severus* and *Antonius*, many who being Souldiers had been converted unto Christ, and notwithstanding continued still in that Military course of life. In which number, one man there was amongst all the rest, who at such a time coming to the Tribune of the Army to receive his Donative, came but with a Garland in his hand, and not in such sort as others did. The Tribune offended hereat, demandeth what this great singularity would mean. To whom the Souldier, *Christianus sum, I am a Christian.* Many there were so besides him, which yet did otherwise at that time; whereup-

T. C. l. 2. p. 81. And to come yet neerer, where he disputeth against the wearing of crown or garland(which is indifferent in it self)to those which objecting asked, Where the Scripture saith, that a man might not wear a Crown? He answereth by asking where the Scripture saith that they may wear? And unto them replying that it is permitted, which is not forbidden, he answereth that it is forbidden which is not permitted. Whereby appeareth, that the argument of the Scriptures negatively, holdeth not onely in the Doctrine and Ecclesiastical Discipline, but even in matters arbitrary and variable by the advice of the Church. Where it is not enough that they be not forbidden, unless there be some word which doth permit the use of them: It is not enough that the Scripture speaketh not against them, unless it speak for them; and finally, where it displeaseth the Lord which pleaseth him not, we must of necessity have the Word of his mouth to declare his pleasure.

on grew a question, whether a Christian Souldier might herein do as the unchristian did, and wear as they wore. Many of them, which were very found in Christian belief, did rather commend the zeal of this man, then approve his action. *Tertullian* was at the same time a *Montanist*, and an enemy unto the Church for condemning that Prophetical Spirit, which *Montanus* and his followers did boast they had received; as if in them Christ had performed his last promise; as if to them he had sent the Spirit that should be their perfecter and final instructer in the mysteries of Christian truth. Which exulceration of mind made him apt to take all occasions of contradiction. Wherefore in honour of that action, and to gall their mindes who did not so much commend it, he wrote his book *de Corona Militis*, not dissembling the stomach wherewith he wrote it. For first the man he commended as one more constant then the rest of his Brethren, *Who presumed*, saith he, *that they might well enough serve two Lords.* Afterwards choler somewhat rising within him, he addeth, *It doth even remain that they should also devise how to rid themselves of his Martyrdom, towards the Prophesies of whose Holy Spirit they have already shewed their disdain. They mutter that their good and long peace is now in hazard. I doubt not but some of them send the Scriptures before, truss up bag and baggage, make themselves in a readiness, that they may fly from City to City. For that is the onely point of the Gospel which they are careful not to forget. I know even their Pastors very well what they are, in peace Lyons, Harts in time of trouble and fear.* Now these men, saith *Tertullian, They must be answered, Where do we finde it written in Scripture,* that a Christian man may not wear a Garland? And as mens speeches uttered in heat of distempered affection, have oftentimes much more eagerness then weight; so he that shall mark the proofs alledged, and the answers to things objected in that Book, will now and then perhaps espy the like imbecillity. Such is that argument whereby they that wore on their heads Garlands, are charged as transgressors of Natures Law, and guilty of Sacriledge against God the Lord of Nature, inasmuch as Flowers in such sort worn, can neither be smelt nor seen well by those that wear them: and God made Flowers sweet and beautiful, that being seen and smelt unto, they might so delight. Neither doth *Tertullian* bewray this weakness in striking onely, but also in repelling their strokes with whom he contendeth. They ask, saith he, *What Scripture is there which doth teach that we should not be crowned? And what Scripture is there which doth teach that we should?* For in requiring on the contrary part the ayd of Scripture, they do give sentence beforehand that their part ought also by Scripture to be aided. Which answer is of no great force. There is no necessity, that if I confess I ought not to do that which the Scripture forbiddeth me, I should thereby acknowledge my self bound to do nothing which the Scripture commandeth me not. For many inducements besides Scripture may lead me to that, which if Scripture be against, they all give place, and are of no value; yet otherwise are strong and effectual to perswade. Which thing himself well enough understanding, and being not ignorant that Scripture in many things doth neither

command

Tert. de Coron. Milit.

command nor forbid, but use silence; his resolution in fine, is, that in the Church a number of things are strictly observed, whereof no Law of Scripture maketh mention one way or other; that of things once received and confirmed by use, long usage is a Law sufficient; that in civil affairs when there is no other Law, custom it self doth stand for Law; that inasmuch as Law doth stand upon reason, to alledge reason serveth as well as to cite Scripture; that whatsoever is reasonable, the same is lawful, whosoever is Authour of it; that the authority of custom is great; finally, that the custom of Christians was then, and had been a long time, not to wear Garlands; and therefore that undoubtedly they did offend, who presumed to violate such a custom by not observing that thing: the very inveterate observation whereof was a Law sufficient to binde all men to observe it, unless they could shew some higher Law, some Law of Scripture to the contrary. This presupposed, it may stand then very well with strength and soundness of reason, even thus to answer, *Whereas they ask what Scripture forbiddeth them to wear a Garland? we are in this case rather to demand, What Scripture commandeth them? they cannot here alledge, that that is permitted with is not forbidden them: no, that is forbidden them which is not permitted.* For long received custom forbidding them to do as they did (if so be it did forbid them) there was no excuse in the world to justifie their act, unless in the Scripture they could shew some Law that did licence them thus to break a received custom. Now whereas in all the Books of *Tertullian* besides, there is not so much found as in that one, to prove not onely that we may do, but that we ought to do sundry things which the Scripture commandeth not; out of that very Book these sentences are brought to make us believe that *Tertullian* was of a clean contrary minde: We cannot therefore hereupon yield, we cannot grant, that hereby is made manifest the argument of Scripture negative to be of force, not onely in doctrine and Ecclesiastical discipline, but even in matters arbitrary. For *Tertullian* doth plainly hold even in that Book, that neither the matter which he entreateth of was arbitrary, but necessary, inasmuch as the received custom of the Church did tie and binde them not to wear Garlands as the Heathens did; yea, and further also he reckoneth up particularly a number of things, whereof he expresly concludeth, *Harum & aliarum ejusmodi disciplinarum si legem expostules Scripturarum, nullam invenies*; which is as much as if he had said in express words, Many things there are which concern the discipline of the Church and the duties of men, which to abrogate and take away, the Scriptures negatively urged may not in any case perswade us, but they must be observed, yea although no Scripture be found which requireth any such thing. *Tertullian* therefore undoubtedly doth not in this Book shew himself to be of the same minde with them by whom his name is pretended.

The first assertion endeavoured to be confirmed by the Scriptures custom of disputing from Divine authority negatively, *1 Iohn* 1. 5.

6. But sith the sacred Scriptures themselves afford oftentimes such Arguments as are taken from divine authority both one way and other; *The Lord hath commanded, therefore it must be*: and again, in like sort, *He hath not, therefore it must not be*: some certainty concerning this point seemeth requisite to be set down: God himself can neither possibly err, nor lead into errour. For this cause his testimonies, whatsoever he affirmeth, are always truth and most infallible certainty. Yea further, because the things that proceed from him are perfect without any manner of defect or maims; it cannot be but that the words of his mouth are absolute, and lack nothing which they should

God is light, and there is in him no darkness at all. *Hebr.* 6. 18. It is impossible that God should lie. *Numb.* 23. 19. God is not as man, that he should lye. *T. C. l. 2. p. 48.* It is not hard to shew that the Prophets have reasoned negatively. As when in the person of the Lord the Prophet saith, Whereof I have not spoken, *Ier.* 19. 5. And which never entred into my heart, *Iere* 7. 31, 32. And where he condemneth them, because they have not asked counsel at the mouth of the Lord, *Isa.* 30. 2. And it may be shewed, that the same kinde of Argument hath been used in things which are not of the substance of salvation or damnation, and whereof there was no commandment to the contrary (as in the former there was, *Levit.* 18. 21, and 20. 3. *Deut.* 1. 16.) In *Ioshua* the Children of *Israel* are charged by the Prophet, that they asked not counsel of the mouth of the Lord, when they entred into Covenant with the *Gibeonites*, *Ioshua* 9. 14. And yet that Covenant was not made contrary unto any Commandment of God. Moreover, we read that when *David* had taken this counsel, to build a Temple unto the Lord, albeit the Lord had revealed before in his Word, that there should be such a standing place, where the Ark of the Covenant and the service should have a certain abiding: and albeit there was no Word of God which forbad *David* to build the Temple; yet the Lord (with commendation of his good affection and zeale he had to the advancement of his glory) concludeth against *Davids* resolution to build the Temple, with this Reason, namely, That he had given no Commandment of this who should build it, *1 Chron.* 17. 6.

have

have, for performance of that thing whereunto they tend. Whereupon it followeth, that the end being known whereunto he directeth his speech, the argument negatively is evermore strong and forcible, concerning those things that are apparently requisite unto the same end. As for example, God intending to set down sundry times that which in Angels is most excellent, hath not anywhere spoken so highly of them as he hath of our Lord and Saviour Jesus Christ; therefore they are not in dignity equal unto him. It is the Apostle S. *Pauls* argument. The purpose of God was to teach his people, both unto whom they should offer sacrifice, and what sacrifice was to be offered. To burn their sons in fire unto *Baal* he did not command them, he spake no such thing, neither came it into his minde: therefore this they ought not to have done. Which argument the Prophet *Jeremy* useth more then once, as being so effectual and strong, that although the thing he reproveth were not onely not commanded, but forbidden them, and that expresly; yet the Prophet chooseth rather to charge them with the fault of making a Law unto themselves, than the crime of transgressing a Law which God had made. For when the Lord had once himself precisely set down a form of executing that wherein we are to serve him, the fault appeareth greater to do that which we are not, then not to do that which we are commanded. In this we seem to charge the Law of God with hardness onely, in that with foolishness; in this we shew our selves weak and unapt to be doers of his will, in that we take upon us to be Controllers of his wisdom: in this we fail to perform the thing which God seeth meet, convenient, and good; in that we presume to see what is meet and convenient better then God himself. In those actions therefore, the whole form whereof God hath of purpose set down to be observed, we may not otherwise do then exactly, as he hath prescribed: In such things negative Arguments are strong. Again, with a negative argument *David* is pressed concerning the purpose he had to build a Temple unto the Lord: *Thus saith the Lord, Thou shalt not build me an House to dwell in. Wheresoever I have walked with all Israel, spake I one word to any of the Judges of Israel, whom I commanded to feed my people, saying, Why have ye not built me an house?* The Jews urged with a negative argument touching the aid which they sought at the hands of the King of *Egypt*; *Wo to those rebellious children* (saith the Lord) *which walk forth to go down into Egypt, and have not asked counsel at my mouth, to strengthen themselves with the strength of Pharaoh.* Finally, the league of *Joshua* with the Gibeonites is likewise with a negative Argument touched. It was not as it should be: And why? the Lord gave them not that advice: *They sought not counsel at the mouth of the Lord.* By the vertue of which examples, if any man should suppose the force of negative arguments approved, when they are taken from Scripture, in such sort as we in this question are pressed therewith, they greatly deceive themselves. For unto which of all these was it said, that they had done amiss in purposing to do, or in doing any thing at all which the Scripture commanded them not? Our question is, Whether all be un which is done without direction by Scripture, and not whether the Israelites did at any time amiss by following their own mindes, without asking counsel of God. No, it was that peoples singular priviledge, a favour which God vouchsafed them above the rest of the world, that in the affairs of their estate, which were not determinable one way or other by the Scripture, himself gave them extraordinarily direction and counsel, as oft as they sought it at his hands. Thus God did first by speech unto *Moses*; after by *Urim* and *Thummim* unto Priests; lastly, by dreams and visions unto Prophets, from whom in such cases they were to receive the answer of God. Concerning *Joshua* therefore, thus spake the Lord unto *Moses*, saying, *He shall stand before Eleazer the Priest, who shall ask counsel for him by the judgement of* Urim *before the Lord:* whereof had *Joshua* been mindeful, the fraud of the Gibeonites could not so smoothly have past unespied till there was no help. The Jews had Prophets to have resolved them from the mouth of God himself whether Egyptian aids should profit them, yea, or no: but they thought themselves wise enough, and him unworthy to be of their counsel. In this respect therefore was their reproof, though sharp, yet just, albeit there had been no charge precisely given them that they should always take heed of *Egypt*. But as for *David*, to think that he did evil in determining to build God a Temple, because there was in Scripture no Commandment that he should build it, were very injurious: the purpose of his heart was religious and godly, the act most worthy of honour and renown;

Levit 11. 21.
Num. 3.
Deut. 8. 10.

1 Chron. 17. 6.

Isa. 3. 1.

Josh. 1. 14.

Num 27. 21.

Q.

nown; neither could *Nathan* choose but admire his vertuous intent, exhort him to go forward, and befeech God to profper him, therein. But God faw the endlefs troubles which *David* fhould be fubject unto, during the whole time of his Regiment, and therefore gave charge to defer fo good a work till the days of tranquillity and peace, wherein it might without interruption be performed. *David* fuppofed that it could not ftand with the duty which he owed unto God, to fet himfelf in an houfe of Cedartrees, and to behold the Ark of the Lords Covenant unfettled. This opinion the Lord abateth, by caufing *Nathan* to fhew him plainly, that it fhould be no more imputed unto him for a fault, then it had been unto the Judges of Ifrael before him, his cafe being the fame which theirs was, their times not more unquiet then his, nor more unfit for fuch an action. Wherefore concerning the force of negative Arguments fo taken from the authority of Scripture, as by us they are denied, there is in all this lefs then nothing. And touching that which unto this purpofe is borrowed from the Controverfies fometimes handled between Mr. *Harding*, and the

1 Chron. 17. T.C. l.2.p. 50. M. Harding reproacheth the Bifhop of *Salisbury* with this kinde of reafoning: unto whom the Bifhop anfwereth, The argument of authority negatively, is taken to be good, whenfoever proof is taken of Gods Word; and is ufed not onely by us, but alfo by many of the Catholick Fathers. A little after he fheweth the reafon why the argument of authority of the Scripture negatively is good; namely, for that the Word of God is perfect. In another place unto M. *Harding*, cafting him in the teeth with negative arguments, he alledgeth places out of *Irenæus, Chrysoftome, Leo*, which reafoned negatively of the authority of the Scripture. The places which he alledgeth be very full and plain in generality, without any fuch reftraints as the Anfwerer imagined, as they are there to be feen.

worthieft Divine that Chriftendom hath bred for the fpace of fome hundreds of years, who being brought up together in one Univerfity, it fell out in them which was fpoken of two others, *a* *They learned in the fame, that which in contrary Camps they did practife.* Of thefe two the one objecting that with us Arguments taken from authority negatively are over-common; the Bifhops anfwer hereunto is, that *this kinde of Argument is thought to be good, whenfoever proof is taken of Gods Word; and is ufed not onely by us, but alfo by St. Paul, and by many of the Catholick Fathers.* St. *Paul* faith, *God faid not unto Abraham, In thy feeds all the Nations of the earth fhall be bleffed ; but, In thy feeed, which is Chrift ; and thereof he thought he made a good argument.* Likewife, faith Origen, *The Bread which the Lord gave unto his Difciples, faying unto them, Take and eat, he deferred not, nor commanded to be referved till the next day. Such arguments* Origen *and other learned Fathers thought to ftand for good, whatfoever mifliking Mr.* Harding *hath found in them. This kinde of proof is thought to hold in Gods Commandments, for that they be full and perfect : and God hath fpecially charged us, that we fhould neither put to them, nor take from them : and therefore it feemeth good unto them that have learned of Chrift,* Unus eft magifter vefter Chriftus, *and have heard the voyce of God the Father from Heaven,* Ipfum audite. *But unto them that adde to the Word of God what them lifteth, and make Gods will fubject unto their will, and break Gods Commandments for their own traditions fake, unto them it feemeth not good.* Again, the Englifh Apologie alledging the example of the Greeks, how they have neither private Maffes, nor mangled Sacraments, nor Purgatories, nor Pardons ; it pleafeth Mr. *Harding* to jeft out the matter, to ufe the help of his wits where ftrength of truth failed him, and to anfwer with fcoffing at negatives. The Bifhops defence in this cafe, *The ancient learned Fathers having to deal with politique Hereticks, that in defence of their errours avouched the judgement of all the old Bifhops and Doctors that had been before them, and the general confent of the primitive and whole univerfal Church, and that with as good regard of truth, and as faithfully as you do now ; the better to difcover the fhamelefs boldnefs, and nakednefs of their doctrine, were oftentimes likewife forced to ufe the negative, and fo to drive the fame Hereticks, as we do you, to prove their affirmatives ; which thing to do was never poffible. The ancient Father* Irenæus *thus ftayed himfelf, as we do, by the negative,* Hoc neq; Prophetæ prædicaverunt, neq; Dominus docuit, neq; Apoftoli tradiderunt ; *This thing neither did the Prophets publifh, nor our Lord teach, nor the Apoftles deliver. By a like negative* Chryfoftome *faith, This tree neither Paul planted, nor Apollos watered, nor God increafed. In like fort* Leo *faith, What needeth it to believe that thing that neither the Law hath taught, nor the Prophets have fpoken, nor the Gofpel hath preached, nor the Apoftles have delivered ? And again, How are the new devices brought in that our Fathers never knew ?* S. *Auguftine having reckoned up a great number of the Bifhops of* Rome *, by a general negative faith thus, In all this order of fucceffion of Bifhops, there is not one Bifhop found that was a Donatift.* S. *Gregory being himfelf*

a Vell. Paterc. Iugurtha ad Marius fub eodem Africano militantes, in iifdem caftris d dicere quæ poftea in contrariis facerent. Art.1.Divif.14. Gal.3. Orig. in Levit. Hom. 5.

Matth. 23. Matth. 17.

Defens. par. 5. ed. 15. divif. ..

Lib. 1 cap.

De incomp. nat. Dei, ho. 3 Epifl.93.c 12

1 pift.9 .cap.3. 1 pift.165.

Lib 3. ep. 32.

*himself a Bishop of Rome, and writing against the Title of Universal Bishop, faith thus,
None of all my Predecessors ever consented to use this ungodly Title; No Bishop of Rome ever
took upon him this name of singularity.* By such negatives, Mr. Harding, we reprove the
vanity and novelty of your Religion; we tell you, none of the Catholique antient, learned
Fathers, either Greek or Latine, ever used either your private Mass or half Communion,
or your barbarous unknown prayers. Paul never planted them, Apollos never watered them,
God never encreased them; they are of your selves, they are not of God. In all this there
is not a syllable which any way crosseth us. For concerning arguments negative
taken from humane authority, they are here proved to be in some cases very
strong and forcible. They are not in our estimation idle reproofs, when the
Authours of needless innovations are opposed with such negatives, as that of
Leo; *How are these new devices brought in which our Fathers never knew?* when their
grave and reverend Superiors do reckon up unto them, as *Austin* did unto the *Donatists*,
large Catalogues of Fathers, wondred at for their wisdom, piety, and learning, amongst
whom for so many ages before us, no one did ever so think of the Churches affairs,
as, now the world doth begin to be perswaded; surely by us they are not taught to
take exception hereat, because such arguments are negative. Much less when
the like are taken from the sacred authority of Scripture, if the matter it self do
bear them. For in truth the question is not, whether an argument from Scripture
negatively, may be good, but whether it be so generally good, that in all actions men may urge it? The Fathers, I grant, do use very general and large terms,
even as *Hiero* the King did in speaking of *Archimedes*, *From henceforward whatsoever
Archimedes speaketh, it must be beleeved.* His meaning was not that *Archimedes* could
simply in nothing be deceived; but that he had in such sort approved his skill, that
he seemed worthy of credit for ever after in matters appertaining unto the science, he
was skilful in. In speaking thus largely it is presumed, that mens speeches will be
taken according to the matter whereof they speak. Let any man therefore that
carrieth indifferency of judgement, peruse the Bishops speeches, and consider well
of those negatives concerning Scripture, which he produceth out of *Ireneus*, *Chrysostom*, and *Leo*, which three are chosen from among the residue, because the senten- Their opinion
ces of the others (even as one of theirs also) do make for defence of negative argu- concerning
ments taken from humane authority, and not from divine onely. They mention no the force of
more restraint in one then in the other: yet I think themselves will not hereby judge, Arguments,
that the Fathers took both to be strong without restraint unto any special kind of mat- taken from
ter, wherein they held such arguments forcible. Nor doth the Bishop either say or humane au-
prove any more, then that an argument in some kind of matter may be good, although thority for
taken negatively from Scripture. the ordering
of mens acti-
ons or per-

7. An earnest desire to draw all things to the determination of bare and naked swasions.
Scripture, hath caused here much pains to be taken in abating
the estimation and credit of man. Which if we labour to *T. C. l. 1. p. 95.* When the question is
maintain as far as truth and reason will bear, let not any think of the authority of a man, it holdeth
we travail about a matter not greatly needful. For the scope neither affirmatively nor negatively. The
of all their pleading against mans authority, is, to over- reason is, because the infirmity of man
throw such orders, laws and constitutions in the Church, can never attain to the perfection of any
as depending thereupon; if they should therefore be taken thing whereby he might speak all things
away, would peradventure leave neither face nor memory that are to be spoken of it; neither yet be
of Church to continue long in the world, the world especi- free from error in those things which he
ally being such as now it is. That which they have in this speaketh or giveth out. And therefore
case spoken, I would for brevity sake let pass, but that the this argument neither affirmatively nor
drift of their speech being so dangerous, their words are not negatively compelleth the hearer, but
to be neglected. Wherefore to say that simply an Argu- onely induceth him to some liking or
ment taken from mans authority doth hold no way, nei- disliking of that for which it is brought,
ther affirmatively nor negatively, is hard. By a mans au- and is rather for an Orator to perswade
thority we here understand, the force which his word hath for the assurance of
anothers mind that buildeth upon it; as the Apostle somewhat did upon their report
of the house of *Cloe*; and the *Samaritans* in a matter of far greater moment upon the
report of a simple woman. For so it is said in S. *Johns* Gospel, *Many of the Samaritans
of that City beleeved in him for the saying of the woman, which testified, He hath told me
all things that ever I did.* The strength of mans authority is affirmatively such,

that

that the wightieft affairs in the world depend thereon. In judgement and juftice are not hereupon proceedings grounded? Saith not the Law, that *in the mouth of two or three witneffes every word fhall be confirmed ?* This the law of God would not fay, if there were in a mans teftimony no force at all to prove any thing. And if it be admitted that in matter of fact there is fome credit to be given to the teftimony of man, but not in matter of opinion and judgement, we fee the contrary, both acknowledged and univerfally practifed alfo throughout the World. The fentences of wife and expert men were never but highly efteemed. Let the title of a mans right be called in queftion, are we not bold to relie and build upon the judgement of fuch as are famous for their skil in the laws of this land? In matter of State, the weight many times of fome one mans authority is thought reafon fufficient even to fway over whole Nations. And this is not onely with the fimple fort, but the learneder and wifer we are, the more fuch arguments in fome cafes prevail with us. The reafon why the fimpler fort are moved with authority, is the confcience of their own ignorance; whereby it cometh to pafs, that having learned men in admiration, they rather fear to diflike them, then know wherefore they fhould allow and follow their judgements. Contrariwife with them that are skilfull, authority is much more ftrong and forcible; becaufe they onely are able to difcern how juft caufe there is, why to fome mens authority fo much fhould be attributed. For which caufe the name of *Hippocrates* (no doubt) were more effectual to perfwade even fuch men as *Galen* himfelf, then to move a filly Emprick. So that the very felf-fame argument in this kind, which doth but induce the vulgar fort to like, may conftrain the wifer to yeild. And therefore not Orators onely with the people, but even the very profoundeft of Difputers in all faculties have hereby often with the beft learned prevailed moft. As for arguments taken from humane authority, and that negatively, for example fake, if we fhould think the affembling of the people of God together by the found of a Bell, the prefenting of Infants at the holy Font, by fuch as we commonly call their Godfathers, or any other the like received cuftom to be impious, becaufe fome men of whom we think very reverently, have in their books and writings no where mentioned or taught that fuch things fhould be in the Church; this reafoning were fubject unto juft reproof; it were but feable, weak, and unfound. Notwithftand even negatively an argument from humane authority may be ftrong; as namely thus : The Chronicles of *England* mention no more then onely fix Kings bearing the name of *Edward*, fince the time of the laft Conqueft; therefore it cannot be there fhould be more. So that if the queftion be of the authority of a mans teftimony, we cannot fimply avouch, either that affirmatively it doth not any way hold, or that it hath onely force to induce the fimpler fort, and not to conftrain men of underftanding and ripe judgement to yield affent, or that negatively it hath in it no ftrength at all. For unto every of thefe the contrary is moft plain. Neither doth that which is alledged concerning the infirmity of men, overthrow or difprove this. Men are blinded with ignorance and error ; many things may efcape them, and in many things they may be deceived ; yea, thofe things which they do know, they may either forget, or upon fundry indirect confiderations let pafs, and although themfelves do not erre, yet may they through malice or vanity, even of purpofe deceive others. Howbeit, infinite cafes there are wherein all thefe impediments and lets are fo manifeftly excluded, that there is no fhew or colour whereby any fuch exception may be taken, but that the teftimony of man will ftand as a ground of infallible affurance. That there is a City of *Rome*, that *Pius Quintus* and *Gregory* the thirteenth, and others, have been Popes of *Rome*, I fuppofe we are certainly enough perfwaded. The ground of our perfwafion, who never faw the place nor perfons beforenamed, can be nothing but mans teftimony. Will any man here notwithftanding alledge thofe mentioned humane infirmities as reafons, why thefe things fhould be miftrufted or doubted of ? yea, that which is more, utterly to infringe the force and ftrength of mans teftimony, were to fhake the very Fortrefs of Gods truth. For whatfoever we beleive concerning falvation by Chrift, although the Scripture be therein the ground of our beleif ; yet the authority of man is, if we mark it, the key which openeth the door of entrance into the knowledge of the Scripture. The Scripture doth not teach us the things that are of God, unlefs we did credit men who have taught us that the words of Scripture do fignifie thofe things. Some way therefore, notwithftanding mans infirmity, yet his authority may inforce affent. So much is perceived, and at the length confeft, that Arguments taken from the authority of men, may not onely fo far forth as hath been declared, but further alfo be of fome force in *Humane Sciences*; which force be it never fo fmall, doth fhew that they are not utterly naught. But in *Matters Divine* it is ftill maintained ftifly, that they have no manner force at all. Howbeit, the very felf fame reafon, which caufeth to yield that they are of fome force in the one, will at the length conftrain alfo to acknowledge that they are not in the other altogether unforcible. For if the natural ftrength of mans wit may by experience and ftudy attain unto fuch ripenefs in the knowledge of things humane, that men in this refpect may prefume to build fomewhat upon their judgement; what reafon have we to think but that even in mat-

Upon better advice and deliberation

T.C. l. 1. p. 10. Akhough that kinde of argument of authority of men is good neither in humane nor divine fciences; yet it hath fome fmall force in humane fciences, foraimuch as naturally, and in that he is a man, he may come to fon é ripenefs of judgement in thofe fciences, which in divine matters hath no force at all: as of him which naturally, and as he is a man, can no more judge of them then a blinde man of colours; yea, fo far is it from drawing credit, if it be barely fpoken without reafon and teftimony of Scripture, that it carrieth alfo a fufpicion of untruth whatfoever proceedeth from him; which the Apoftle did well note, when to fignifie a thing corruptly fpoken, and againft the truth, he faith, that it is fpoken according to man, *Rom* 3. He faith not as a wicked and lying man, but fimply as a man: And although this corruption be reformed in many, yet for fo much as in whom the knowledge of the truth is moft advanced, there remaineth both ignorance and difordered affections (whereof either of them turneth him from fpeaking of the truth) no mans authority, with the Church efpecially, and thofe that are called and perfwaded of the authority of the Word of God, can bring any affurance unto the confcience.

ters Divine, the like wits furnifht with neceffary helps, exercifed in Scripture with like diligence, and affifted with the grace of Almighty God, may grow unto fo much perfection of knowledge, that men fhall have juft caufe, when any thing pertinent unto Faith and Religion is doubted of, the more willingly to encline their mindes towards that which the fentence of fo grave, wife, and learned in that faculty fhall judge moft found? For the controverfie is of the weight of fuch mens judgements. Let it therefore be fufpected, let it be taken as grofs, corrupt, repugnant unto the truth, whatfoever concerning things divine above nature fhall at any time be fpoken as out of the mouthes of meer natural men, which have not the eyes wherewith heavenly things are difcerned. For this we contend not. But whom God hath endued with principal gifts to afpire unto knowledge by; whofe exercifes, labours, and divine ftudies he hath fo bleft, that the World for their great and rare skill that way, hath them in fingular admiration; may we reject even their judgement likewife, as being utterly of no moment? For mine own part, I dare not fo lightly efteem of the Church, and of the principal pillars therein. The truth is, that the minde of man defireth evermore to know the truth according to the moft infallible certainty which the nature of things can yield. The greateft affurance generally with all men, is that which we have by plain afpect and intuitive beholding. Where we cannot attain unto this, there what appeareth to be true by ftrong and invincible demonftration, fuch as wherein it is not by any way poffible to be deceived, thereunto the minde doth neceffarily affent, neither is it in the choice thereof to do otherwife. And in cafe thefe both do fail; then which way greateft probability leadeth, thither the minde doth evermore encline. Scripture with Chriftian men being received as the Word of God; that for which we have probable, yea, that which we have neceffary reafon for, yea, that which we fee with our eyes, is not thought fo fure as that which the Scripture of God teacheth; becaufe we hold that his fpeech revealeth there what himfelf feeth, and therefore the ftrongeft proof of all, and the moft neceffarily affented unto by us (which do thus receive the Scripture) is the Scripture. Now it is not required, nor can be exacted at our hands, that we fhould yield unto any thing other affent, then fuch as doth anfwer the evidence which is to be had of that we affent unto. For which caufe even in matters divine, concerning fome things we may lawfully doubt and fufpend our judgement, enclining neither to one fide or other, as namely touching the time of the fall both of man and Angels; of fome things we may very well retain an opinion that they are probable and not unlikely to be true, as when we hold that men have their fouls rather by creation then propagation, or that the Mother of our Lord lived always in the ftate of Virginity as well after his birth as before (for of thefe two, the one, her virginity before, is a thing which of neceffity we muft believe; the other, her continuance in the fame ftate always, hath more likelihood of truth then the contrary;) finally in all things then are our confciences beft refolved, and in moft agreeable fort unto God and Nature settled, when they are so far perswaded as those grounds of perswasion which are to be had will bear. Which thing I do so much the rather set down, for that I see how a number of souls are, for want of right information in this point, oftentimes grievously vexed. When bare and unbuilded conclusions are put into their mindes, they finding not themselves to have thereof any great certainty, imagine that this proceedeth onely from lack of faith, and that the Spirit of God doth not work in them, as it doth in true believers; by this means their hearts are much troubled, they fall into anguish and perplexity: whereas the truth is, that how bold and confident soever we may be in words, when it cometh to the point of trial, such as the evidence is which the truth hath either in it self or through proof, such is the hearts assent thereunto; neither can it be stronger, being grounded as it should be. I grant that proof derived from the authority of mans judgement, is not able to work that assurance which doth grow by a stronger proof; and therefore although ten thousand General Councils would set down one and the same definitive sentence concerning any point of Religion whatsoever, yet one demonstrative reason alledged, or one manifest testimony cited from the mouth of God himself to the contrary, could not choose but over-weigh them all; inasmuch as for them to have been deceived, it is not impossible; it is, that demonstrative reason or testimony Divine should deceive. Howbeit, in defect of proof infallible, because the minde doth rather follow probable perswasions, then approve the things that have in them no likelihood of truth at all; surely if a question concerning matter of doctrine were propoled, and on the one side no kinde of proof appearing, there should on the other be alledged and shewed that so a number of the learnedest Divines in the World have ever thought; although it did not appear what reason or what Scripture led them to be of that judgement, yet to their very bare judgement somewhat a reasonable man would attribute, notwithstanding the common imbecillities which are incident unto our nature. And whereas it is thought, that especially with the Church, and those that are called and perswaded of the authority of the Word of God, mans authority with them especially should not prevail; it must and doth prevail even with them, yea with them especially as far as equity requireth, and farther we maintain it not. For men to be tied and led by authority, as it were with a kinde of captivity of judgement, and though there be reason to the contrary, not to listen unto it, but to follow like beasts the first in the herd, they know not nor care not whither, this were brutish. Again, that authority of men should prevail with men either against or above reason, is no part of our be-

T. C. l. 2, p. 21. Of divers sentences of the Fathers themselves (where by some have likened them to brute beasts without reason, which suffer themselves to be led by the judgement and authority of others, some have prefered the judgement of one simple rude man alledging reason, unto companies of learned men) I will content my self at this time with two or three sentences. *Ireneus* saith, Whatsoever is to be shewed in the Scripture, cannot be shewed but out of the Scriptures themselves, *lib. 3. cap. 12. Ierome* saith, No man, be he never so holy or eloquent, hath any authority after the Apostle, in *Psal. 16. Augustine* saith, That he will believe none, how godly and learned soever he be, unless he confirm his sentence by the Scriptures, or by some reason not contrary to them, *Ep. 18.* And in another place, Hear this, the Lord saith; hear not this, *Donatus* saith, *Rogatus* saith, *Vincentius* saith, *Hilarius* saith, *Ambrose* saith, *Augustine* saith, but hearken unto this, the Lord saith, *Ep. 48.* And again, having to do with an Arrian, he affirmeth, that neither he ought to bring forth the Council of *Nice*, nor the other the Council of *Arimine*, thereby to bring prejudice each to other; neither ought the Arrian to be holden by the authority of the one, nor himself by the authority of the other, but by the Scriptures which are witnesses proper to neither, but common to both; matter with matter, cause with cause, reason with reason ought to be debated, *Cont. Max. Arrian. 3. 14. cap.* And in another place against *Iesil*, the Donatist, he saith, Let not these words be heard between us, I say, You say, let us hear this, Thus saith the Lord. And by and by speaking of the Scriptures he saith, There let us seek the Church, there let us try the cause, *De unita. Ecclef cap. 3.* Hereby it is manifest, that the argument of the authority of man affirmatively is nothing worth.

lief. Companies of learned men, be they never so great and reverend, are to yield unto reason; the weight whereof is no whit prejudiced by the simplicity of his person which doth alledge it, but being found to be sound and good, the bare opinion of men to the contrary, must of necessity stoop and give place. *Ireneus* writing against *Marcion*, which held one God Authour of the Old-Testament, and another of the New; to prove that the Apostles preached the same God which was known before to the Jews, he copiously alledgeth sundry their Sermons and speeches uttered concerning that matter, and recorded in Scripture. And lest any should be wearied with such store of allegations, in the end he concludeth, *While we labour for these demonstrations out of Scripture, and do summarily declare the things which many ways have been spoken, be contented quietly to hear, and do not think my speech tedious:* Quoniam

niam oftenfiones quæ funt in Scripturis, non poffunt oftendi nifi ex ipfis Scripturis, *Becaufe demonftrations that are in Scripture, may not otherwife be fhewed, then by citing them out of the Scriptures themfelves where they are.* Which words make fo little unto the purpofe, that they feem, as it were, offended at him which hath called them thus folemnly forth to fay nothing. And concerning the verdict of *Jerome,* If no man, be he never fo well learned, have after the Apoftles any authority to publifh new Doctrine as from Heaven, and to require the Worlds affent as unto truth received by Prophetical revelation ; doth this prejudice the credit of learned mens judgements in opening that truth, which by being converfant in the Apoftles writings, they have themfelves from thence learned ? S. *Auguftine* exhorteth not to hear men, but to hearken what God fpeaketh. His purpofe is not (I think) that we fhould ftop our ears againft his own exhortation, and therefore he cannot mean fimply that audience fhould altogether be denied unto men ; but either that if men fpeak one thing, and God himfelf teach another, then he, not they to be obeyed ; or if they both fpeak the fame thing, yet then alfo mans fpeech unworthy of hearing, not fimply, but in comparifon of that which proceedeth from the mouth of God. Yea, but we doubt what the will of God is. Are we in this cafe forbidden to hear what men of judgement think it to be ? If not, then this allegation alfo might very well have been fpared. In that ancient ftrife which was between the Catholick Fathers and Arrians, Donatifts, and others of like perverfe and froward difpofition, as long as to Fathers or Councils alledged on the one fide, the like by the contrary fide were impofed, impoffible it was that ever the queftion fhould by this mean grow unto any iffue or end. The Scripture they both believed ; the Scripture they knew could not give fentence on both fides ; by Scripture the controverfie between them was fuch as might be determined. In this cafe what madnefs was it with fuch kindes of proofs to nourifh their contention, when there were fuch effectual means to end all controverfie that was between them ? Hereby therefore it doth not as yet appear, that an argument of Authority of man affirmatively is in matters Divine nothing worth. Which opinion being once inferted into the mindes of the vulgar fort, what it may grow unto God knoweth. Thus much we fee, it hath already made thoufands fo headftrong, even in grofs and palpable errours, that a man whofe capacity will fcarce ferve him to utter five words in fenfible manner, blufheth not in any doubt concerning matter of Scripture to think his own bare *Tea,* as good as the *Nay* of all the wife, grave and learned judgements that are in the whole world. Which infolency muft be repreft, or it will be the very bane of Chriftian Religion. Our Lords Difciples marking what fpeech he uttered unto them, and at the fame time calling to minde a common opinion held by the Scribes, between which opinion and the words of their Mafter, it feemed unto them that there was fome contradiction ; which they could not themfelves anfwer with full fatisfaction of their own mindes ; the doubt they propofe to our Saviour, faying, *Why then fay the Scribes that Elias muft firft come ?* They knew that the Scribes did erre greatly, and that many ways even in matters of their own profeffion. They notwithftanding thought the judgement of the very Scribes in matters Divine to be of fome value ; fome probability they thought there was that *Elias* fhould come, in as much as the Scribes faid it. Now no truth can contradict any truth ; defirous therefore they were to be taught, how both might ftand together ; that which they knew could not be falfe, becaufe Chrift fpake it ; and this which to them did feem true, onely becaufe the Scribes had faid it. For the Scripture from whence the Scribes did gather it, was not then in their heads. We do not finde that our Saviour reproved them of errour, for thinking the judgement of the Scribes to be worth the objecting, for efteeming it to be of any moment or value in matters concerning God. We cannot therefore be perfwaded that the will of God is, we fhould fo far reject the authority of men, as to reckon it nothing. No, it may be a queftion, whether they that urge us unto this be themfelves fo perfwaded indeed. Men do fometimes bewray that by deeds, which to confefs they are hardly drawn. Mark then if this be not general with all men for the moft part. When the judgements of learned men are alledged againft them ; what do they but either elevate their credit, or oppofe unto them the judgements of others as learned ? Which thing doth argue that all men acknowledge in them fome force and weight, for which they are loth the caufe they maintain fhould be fo much

weakned

weakned as their teſtimony is available. Again, what reaſon is there why alledging teſtimonies as proofs, men give them ſome title of credit, honour and eſtimation whom they alledge, unleſs beforehand it be ſufficiently known who they are? what reaſon hereof but onely a common engraffed perſwaſion, that in ſome men there may be found ſuch qualities as are able to countervail thoſe exceptions which might be taken againſt them, and that ſuch mens authority is not lightly to be ſhaken off? Shall I adde further, that the force of arguments drawn from the Authority of Scripture it ſelf, as Scriptures commonly are alledged, ſhall (being ſifted) be found to depend upon the ſtrength of this ſo much deſpiſed and debaſed authority of man? Surely it doth, and that oftner then we are aware of. For although Scripture be of God, and therefore the proof which is taken from thence muſt needs be of all other moſt invincible; yet this ſtrength it hath not, unleſs it avouch the ſelf ſame thing for which it is brought. If there be either undeniable apparence that ſo it doth, or reaſon ſuch as cannot deceive, then Scripture-proof (no doubt) in ſtrength and value exceedeth all. But for the moſt part, even ſuch as are readieſt to cite for one thing five hundred ſentences of holy Scripture; what warrant have they, that any one of them doth mean the thing for which it is alledged? Is it not their ſureſt ground moſt commonly, either ſome probable conjecture of their own, or the judgement of others taking thoſe Scriptures as they do? Which notwithſtanding

T.C. l.2. 21. If at any time it hapned unto Auguſtine (as it did againſt the Donatiſts and others) to alledge the authority of the ancient Fathers, which had been before him; yet this was not done before he had laid a ſure foundation of his cauſe in the Scriptures, and that alſo being provoked by the adverſaries of the truth who bare themſelves high of ſome Council, or of ſome man of name that had favoured that part.

to mean otherwiſe then they take them, it is not ſtill altogether impoſſible. So that now and then they ground themſelves on humane authority, even when they moſt pretend Divine. Thus it fareth even clean throughout the whole controveſie about that diſcipline which is ſo earneſtly urged and laboured for. Scriptures are plentifully alledged to prove that the whole Chriſtian World for ever ought to embrace it. Hereupon men term it, *The Diſcipline of God.* Howbeit, examine, ſift, and reſolve their alledged proofs, till you come to the very root from whence they ſpring, the heart wherein their ſtrength lieth; and it ſhall clearly appear unto any man of judgement, that the moſt which can be inferred upon ſuch plenty of Divine Teſtimonies is onely this, That *ſome things* which they maintain as far as *ſome men can probably conjecture,* do *ſeem* to have been out of Scripture *not abſurdly* gathered. Is this a warrant ſufficient for any mans conſcience to build ſuch proceedings upon, as have been, and are put in ure for the eſtabliſhment of that cauſe? But to conclude, I would gladly underſtand how it cometh to paſs, that they which ſo peremptorily do maintain that Humane Authority is nothing worth, are in the cauſe which they favour ſo careful to have the common ſort of men perſwaded, that the wiſeſt, the godlieſt, and the beſt learned in all Chriſtendom are that way given, ſeeing they judge this to make nothing in the World for them? Again, how cometh it to paſs, they cannot abide that Authority ſhould be alledged on the other ſide, if there be no force at all in Authorities on one ſide or other? Wherefore labour they to ſtrip their Adverſaries of ſuch furniture as doth not help? Why take they ſuch needleſs pains to furniſh alſo their own cauſe with the like? If it be void and to no purpoſe that the names of men are ſo frequent in their Books, what did move them to bring them in, or doth to ſuffer them there remaining? Ignorant I am not how this is ſalved, *They do it but after the truth made manifeſt, firſt, by reaſon or by Scripture; they do it not but to controul the enemies of truth, who bear themſelves bold upon Humane Authority, making not for them, but againſt them rather.* Which anſwers are nothing. For in what place, or upon what conſideration ſoever it be they do it, were it in their own opinion of no force being done, they would undoubtedly refrain to do it.

A Declaration what the truth is in this matter.

8. But to the end it may more plainly appear, what we are to judge of their ſentences, and the cauſe it ſelf wherein they are alledged; firſt, it may not well be denied, that all actions of men endued with the uſe of reaſon, are generally either good or evil. For although it be granted that no action is properly termed good or evil, unleſs it be voluntary; yet this can be no let to our former aſſertion, That all actions of men endued with the uſe of reaſon, are generally either good or evil; becauſe even thoſe things are done voluntary by us, which other creatures do naturally, inaſmuch as we might ſtay our doing of them if we would. Beaſts naturally do take their food and reſt, when it offereth it ſelf unto them. If men did ſo too, and could not do otherwiſe of themſelves, there were no place for any ſuch reproof as that

Mat 26.40.

of our Saviour Chriſt unto his Diſciples, *Could ye not watch with me one hour?*

That

That which is voluntarily performed in things tending to the end, if it be well done, must needs be done with deliberate confideration of some reasonable cause, wherefore we rather should do it then not. Whereupon it seemeth, that in such actions onely those are said to be good or evil, which are capable of deliberation: So that many things being hourly done by men, wherein they need not use with themselves any manner of consultation at all, it may perhaps hereby seem that well or ill doing belongeth onely to our weightier affairs, and to those deeds which are of so great importance that they require advice. But thus to determine were perillous, and peradventure unsound also. I do rather incline to think, that seeing all the unforced actions of men are voluntary; and all voluntary actions tending to the end have choice; and all choice presupposeth the knowledge of some cause wherefore we make it; where the reasonable cause of such actions so readily offereth it self, that it needeth not be sought for, in those things though we do not deliberate, yet they are of their nature apt to be deliberated on, in regard of the will which may encline either way; and would not any one way bend it self, if there were not some apparent motive to lead it. Deliberation actual we use, when there is no doubt what we should encline our wills unto. Where no doubt is, deliberation is not excluded as impertinent unto the thing, but as needless in regard of the agent, which seeth already what to resolve upon. It hath no apparent absurdity therefore in it to think, that all actions of men endued with the use of reason, are generally either good or evil. Whatsoever is good, the same is also approved of God; and according unto the sundry degrees of goodness, the kinds of Divine approbation are in like sort multiplied. Some things are good, yet in so mean a degree of goodness, that men are onely not disproved nor disallowed of God for them. *No man eateth his own flesh.* If ye do good unto them that do so to you, the very *Publicans* themselves do as much. They are worse then Infidels that have no care to provide for their own. In actions of this sort, the very light of nature alone may discover that which is so far forth in the sight of God allowable. Some things in such sort are allowed, that they be also required as necessary unto salvation, by way of direct immediate and proper necessity final; so that without performance of them we cannot by ordinary course be saved, nor by any means be excluded from life observing them. In actions of this kind our chiefest directions is from Scripture; for Nature is no sufficient Teacher what we should do that may attain unto life everlasting. The unsufficiency of the light of nature, is by the light of Scripture so fully and so perfectly herein supplied, that further light then this hath added, there doth not need unto that end. Finally, some things, although not so required of necessity, that to leave them undone excludeth from salvation, are notwithstanding of so great dignity and acceptation with God, that most ample reward in Heaven is laid up for them. Hereof we have no commandment either in Nature or Scripture which doth exact them at our hands; yet those motives there are in both, which draw most effectually our minds unto them: In this kind there is not the least action, but it doth somewhat make to the accessory augmentation of our bliss. For which cause our Saviour doth plainly witness, that there should not be as much as a cup of cold water bestowed for his sake without reward. Hereupon dependeth whatsoever difference there is between the states of Saints in glory: hither we refer whatsoever belongeth unto the highest perfection of man by way of service towards God: Hereunto that fervour and first love of Christians did bend it self, causing them to sell their possessions; and lay down the price at the blessed Apostles feet. Hereat S. *Paul* undoubtedly did aim, in so far abridging his own liberty, and exceeding that which the bond of necessary and enjoyned duty tied him unto. Wherefore seeing that in all these several kinds of actions, there can be nothing possibly evil which God approveth; and that he approveth much more then he doth command; and that his very Commandments in some kind, as namely his precepts comprehended in the Law of Nature, may be otherwise known then onely by Scipture; and that do to them, howsoever we know them, must needs be acceptable in his sight: let them, with whom we have hitherto disputed, consider well, how it can stand with reason to make this bare mandate of sacred Scripture the onely Rule of all good and evil in the actions of mortal men. The testimonies of God are true, the Testimonies of God are perfect, the Testimonies of God are all-sufficient unto that end for which they were given. Therefore accordingly we do

Ephes. 5. 29.
Mat. 5. 46.
1 Tim. 5. 8.

Mat. 10. 42.

Act. 20. ult.
1 Thes. 2. 7,9.

do receive them, we do not think that in them God hath omitted any thing needfull unto his purpose, and left his intent to be accomplished by our devisings. What the Scripture purposeth, the same in all points it doth perform. Howbeit, that here we swerve not in judgment, one thing especially we must observe, namely, that the absolute perfection of Scripture is seen by relation unto that end whereto it tendeth. And even hereby it commeth to pass, that first such as imagine the general and main drift of the body of sacred Scripture not to be so large as it is, nor that God did thereby intend to deliver, as in truth he doth, a full instruction in all things unto salvation necessary, the knowledge whereof man by nature could not otherwise in this life attain unto : they are by this very means induced, either still to look for new revelations from Heaven, or else dangerously to adde to the Word of God uncertain Tradition, that so the Doctrine of mans salvation may be compleat; which Doctrine we constantly hold in all respects without any such things added to be so compleat, that we utterly refuse as much as once to acquaint our selves with any thing further. Whatsoever, to make up the doctrine of mans salvation, is added as in supply of the Scriptures unsufficiency, we reject it : Scripture purposing this, hath perfectly and fully done it. Again, the scope and purpose of God in delivering the holy Scripture, such as do take more largely then behoveth, they on the contrary side racking and stretching it further then by him was meant, are drawn into sundry as great inconveniences. They pretending the Scriptures perfection, infer thereupon, that in Scripture all things lawfull to be done must needs be contained. We count

T. c. lib. 1 p. 9.
Where this doctrine is accused of bringing men to despair, it hath wrong. For when doubting is the way to despair, against which this Doctrine objecteth the remedy; it must needs be that it bringeth comfort and joy to the conscience of man.

those things perfect which want nothing requisite for the end whereto they were instituted : as therefore God created every part and particle of man exactly perfect, that is to say, in all points sufficient unto that use for which he appointed it; so the Scripture, yea, every sentence thereof is perfect, and wanteth nothing requisite unto that purpose for which God delivered the same. So that if hereupon we conclude, that because the Scripture is perfect, therefore all things lawfull to be done are comprehended in the Scripture; we may even as well conclude so of every sentence, as of the whole sum and body thereof, unless we first of all prove that it was the drift, scope and purpose of Almighty God in holy Scripture, to comprize all things which man may practise. But admit this, and mark, I beseech you, what would follow. God in delivering Scripture to his Church, should clean have abrogated amongst them the Law of Nature; which is an infallible knowledge imprinted in the minds of all the children of men, whereby both general principles for directing of humane actions are comprehended, and conclusions derived from them; upon which conclusions groweth in particularity the choise of good and evil in the daily affairs of this life. Admit this, and what shall the Scripture be but a snare and a torment to weak consciences, filling them with infinite perplexities, scrupolosities, doubts insoluble, and extreme despairs? Not that the Scripture it self doth cause any such thing (for it tendeth to the clean contrary, and the fruit thereof is resolute assurance and certainty in that it teacheth :) but the necessities of this life urging men to do that which the light of Nature, common discretion, and judgement of it self directeth them unto; on the other side, this doctrine teaching them that so to do were to sin against their own souls, and that they put forth their hands to iniquity, whatsoever they go about, and have not first the sacred Scripture of God for direction; how can it chuse but bring the simple a thousand times to their wits end, how can it chuse but vex and amaze them? For in every action of common life to finde out some sentence clearly and infallibly setting before our eyes what we ought to do (seem we in Scripture never so expert) would trouble us more then we are aware. In weak and tender minds we little know what misery this strict opinion would breed, besides the stops it would make in the whole course of all mens lives and actions; make all things sin which we do by direction of Natures light, and by the rule of common discretion without thinking at all upon Scripture. Admit this Position, and Parents shall cause their children to sin, as oft as they cause them to do any thing before they come to years of capacity and be ripe for Knowledge in the Scripture. Admit this, and it shall not be with Masters as it was with him in the Gospel; but servants being commanded to go, shall stand still, till they have their errand warranted unto them by Scripture. Which as it standeth with Christian duty in some cases, so in common affairs to require it, were most unfit. Two opinions therefore there are concerning sufficiency

of

of holy Scripture, each extreamly oppofite unto the other, and both repugnant unto truth. The Schools of *Rome* teach Scripture to be unfufficient, as if, except Traditions were added, it did not contain all revealed and fupernatural Truth, which abfolutely is neceffary for the children of Men in this life to know, that they may in the next be faved. Others juftly condemning this opinion, grow likewife unto a dangerous extremity, as if Scripture did not onely contain all things in that kinde neceffary, but all things fimply, and in fuch fort, that to do any thing according to any other Law, were not onely unneceffary, but even oppofite unto falvation, unlawful and finful. Whatfoever is fpoken of God, or of things appertaining to God, otherwife then as the truth is, though it feem an honour, it is an injury. And as incredible praifes given unto men, do oftentimes abate and impair the credit of their deferved commendation ; fo we muft likewife take great heed, left in attributing unto Scripture more then it can have, the incredibility of that, do caufe even thofe things which indeed it hath moft abundantly, to be lefs reverendly efteemed. I therefore leave it to themfelves to confider, whether they have in this firft point or not over-fhot themfelves; which, God doth know, is quickly done, even when our meaning is moft fincere, as I am verily perfwaded theirs in this cafe was.

OF

OF THE
L A W S
O F
Ecclefiaftical Politie.

The third B o o κ.

Concerning their fecond Affertion, *That in Scripture
there muſt be of neceſsity contained a form of Church-
Polity, the Laws whereof may in no wiſe
be altered.*

The matter contained in this third Book.

1. VV Hat the Church is, and in what reſpeᶜᵗ Laws of Polity are thereunto neceſſarily required.
2. Whether it be neceſſary that ſome particular form of Church-Polity be ſet down
in Scripture, ſith the things that belong particularly to any ſuch form are not of
neceſſity to ſalvation.
3. That matters of Church-Polity are different from matters of faith and ſalvation, and
that they themſelves ſo teach which are our reprovers for ſo teaching.
4. That hereby we take not from Scripture any thing, which thereunto with the ſoundneſs of truth may be given.
5. Their meaning who fiᵣſt urged againſt the Polity of the Church of England, that
nothing ought to be eſtabliſhed in the Church more then is commanded by the
Word of God.
6. How great injury men by ſo thinking ſhould offer unto all the Churches of God.
7. A ſhift notwithſtanding to maintain it, by interpreting Commanded as though it were
meant that greater things onely ought to be found ſet down in Scripture particularly,
and leſſer framed by the general rules of Scripture.
8. Another device to defend the ſame, by expounding Commanded as if it did ſigniſie
grounded in Scripture, and were oppoſed to things found out by light of natural
reaſon onely.
9. How Laws for the Polity of the Church may be made by the advice of men, and how
thoſe Laws being not repugnant to the Word of God, are approved in his ſight.
10. That neither Gods being the Author of Laws, nor yet his committing of them to
Scripture, is any reaſon ſufficient to prove that they admit no addition or change.
11. Whether Chriſt muſt needs intend Laws unchangeable altogether, or have forbidden
any where to make any other Law then himſelf did deliver.

Albeit

Lbeit the substance of those controversies whereinto we have begun to wade, be rather of outward things appertaining to the Church of Christ, then of any thing wherein the nature and being of the Church consisteth: yet because the subject or matter which this position concerneth, is *A form of Church-government or Church Polity*, It therefore behoveth us so far forth to consider the nature or the Church, as is requisite for mens more clear and plain understanding, in what respect Laws of Polity or Government are necessary thereunto. That Church of Christ, which we properly term his body mystical, can be but one; neither can that one be sensibly discerned by any man, in as much as the parts thereof are some in Heaven already with Christ, and the rest that are on earth (albeit their natural persons be visible) we do not discern under this property whereby they are truly and infallibly of that body. Only our minds by intellectual conceit are able to apprehend, that such a real body there is, a body collective, because it containeth an huge multitude; a body mystical, because the mystery of their conjunction is removed altogether from sense. Whatsoever we read in Scripture, concerning the endless love and the saving mercy, which God sheweth towards his Church, the only proper subject thereof is this Church. Concerning this flock, it is that our Lord and Saviour hath promised, *I give them eternal life, and they shall never perish, neither shall any pluck them out of my hands.* They who are of this society have such marks and notes of distinction from all others, as are not object unto our sense; only unto God, who seeth their hearts, and understandeth all their secret cogitations, unto him they are clear and manifest. All men knew *Nathaniel* to be an *Israelite.* But our Saviour piercing deeper, giveth further testimony of him then men could have done with such certainty as he did, *Behold indeed an Israelite in whom there is no guile.* If we profess as *Peter* did, that we love the Lord, and profess it in the hearing of men; charity is prone to believe all things, and therefore charitable men are likely to think we do so, as long as they see no proof to the contrary. But that our love is sound and sincere, that it cometh from *a pure heart, a good conscience, and faith unfeigned,* who can pronounce, saving only the searcher of all mens hearts, who alone intuitively doth know in this kind who are his? And as those everlasting promises of Love, Mercy, and Blessedness, belong to the mystical Church; even so on the other side, when we read of any duty which the Church of God is bound unto, the Church whom this doth concern is a sensible known company. And this visible Church in like sort is but one, continued from the first beginning of the World to the last end. Which company being divided into two moyeties; the one before the other since the coming of Christ, that part which since the coming of Christ, partly hath embraced, and partly shall hereafter embrace the Christian Religion, we term as by a more proper name the Church of Christ. And therefore the Apostle affirmeth plainly of all men Christians, that be they Jew or Gentiles, bond or free, they are all incorporated into one company, they all make but (a) one body. The unity of which visible body and Church of Christ, consisteth in that uniformity which all several persons thereunto belonging have, by reason of that *one Lord,* whose Servants they all profess themselves; that *one Faith,* which they all acknowledge, that *one Baptism,* wherewith they are all initiated. The visible Church of Jesus Christ therefore one, in outward profession of those things which supernaturally appertain to the very essence of Christianity, and are necessarily required in every particular Christian man. *Let all the house of Israel know for certainty, saith Peter, that God hath made him both Lord and Christ, even this Jesus whom ye have crucified.* Christians therefore they are not, which call not him their Master and Lord. And from hence it came, that first at *Antioch,* and afterward throughout the whole world, all that were of the Church visible were called Christians, even amongst the Heathen: which name unto them was precious and glorious; but in the estimation of the rest of the world, even Christ Jesus himself was (b) execrable, for whose sake all men were so likewise which

What the Church is, and in what respect Laws of Polities are therefore unto necessarily required.

Ioh. 10. 28.

and 1. 47.

and 21. 15.

1 Tim. 1. 5.

a Ephes 2. 16. that he might reconcile both unto God in one body. Eph. 3. 6. that the Gentiles should be inheritors also of the same body. Vide T. p. 3. q. 7. art. 3. 1 Cor. 12. 13. Eph. 4. 5. Act 1. 2. et 11. 1. Col. 3. 24. Col. 1. b 1 Cor. 1. 23. Vide & Tacitum l 6. Annal. 15.

Nero quaesitissimis poenis afficit quos per flagitia invisos vulgus christianos appellabat. Auctor nominis ejus Christus, qui Tiberio imperitante per procuratorem Pontium Pilatum supplicio affectus erat. Repressaq; in praesens exitiabilis superstitio rursus erumpebat, non modo per Judaeam originem ejus mali, sed per urbem etiam, quo cuncta undiq; atrocia aut pudenda confluunt celebranturq;.

did

did acknowledge him to be their Lord. This himself did foresee, and therefore armed his Church, to the end they might sustain it without discomfort : *All these things they will do us to you for my names sake ; yea the time shall come, that whosoever killeth you will think that he doth God good service. These things I tell you, that when the hour shall come ye may then call to minde how I told you beforehand of them.* But our naming of Jesus Christ the Lord is not enough to prove us Christians, unless we also embrace that faith which Christ hath published unto the world. To shew that the Angel of *Pergamus* continued in Christianity, behold how the spirit of Christ speaketh, *Thou keepest my name, and hast not denied my faith.* Concerning which Faith, *The rule thereof*, saith Tertullian, *is one alone, immoveable, and no way possible to be better framed anew.* What rule that is he sheweth by rehearsing those few Articles of Christian-belief. And before *Tertullian*, Ireney ; *The Church though scattered through the whole world unto the uttermost borders of the earth, hath from the Apostles and their Disciples received belief.* The parts of which Belief he also reciteth in substance the very same with *Tertullian*, and thereupon inferreth, *This faith the Church being spread far and wide preserveth, as if one house did contain them ; these things it equally embraceth, as though it had even one soul, one heart, and no more ; it publisheth, teacheth, and delivereth these things with uniform consent, as if God had given it but one onely tongue wherewith to speak. He which amongst the guides of the Church is best able to speak, uttereth no more then this ; and less then this the most simple do not utter,* when they make profession of their Faith. Now although we know the Christian Faith, and allow of it, yet in this respect we are but entring ; entred we are not into the visible Church, before our admittance by the door of Baptism. Wherefore immediately upon the acknowledgement of Christian faith, the Eunuch (we see) was baptized by *Philip*, Paul by *Ananias*, by Peter a huge multitude containing three thousand souls ; which being once baptized, were reckoned in the number of souls added to the visible Church. As for those vertues that belong unto moral righteousness and honesty of life, we do not mention them, because they are not proper unto Christian men as they are Christian, but do concern them as they are men. True it is, the want of these vertues excludeth from salvation. So doth much more the absence of inward belief of heart ; so doth despair and lack of hope ; so emptiness of Christian love and charity. But we speak now of the visible Church, whose children are signed with this mark, *One Lord, one Faith, one Baptism.* In whomsoever these things are, the Church doth acknowledge them for her children ; them only she holdeth for Aliens and Strangers, in whom these things are not found. For want of these it is, that Saracens, Jews, and Infidels, are excluded out of the bounds of the Church. Others we may not deny to be of the visible Church, as long as these things are not wanting in them. For apparent it is, that all men are of necessity either Christians or not Christians. If by external profession they be Christians, then are they of the visible Church of Christ : and Christians by external profession they are all, whose mark of recognizance hath in it those things which we have mentioned, yea, although they be impious Idolaters, wicked Hereticks, persons excommunicable, yea, and cast out for notorious improbity. Such withal we deny not to be the Imps and limbs of Satan, even as long as they continue such. It is then possible that the self-same men should belong both to the Synagogue of Satan, and to the Church of Jesus Christ? Unto that Church which is his Mystical Body, not possible ; because that body consisteth of none but only true Israelites, true sons of *Abraham*, true servants and Saints of God. Howbeit of the visible body and Church of Jesus Christ, those may be and oftentimes are, in respect of the main parts of their outward profession ; who in regard of their inward disposition of mind, yea of external conversation, yea even of some parts of their very profession, are most worthily both hateful in the sight of God himself, and in the eyes of the sounder part of the visible Church most execrable. Our Saviour therefore compareth the Kingdom of heaven to a Net, whereunto all which cometh, neither is nor seemeth fish ; his Church he compareth unto a field, where Tares manifestly known and seen by all men, do grow intermingled with good corn, and even so shall continue till the final consummation of the world. God hath had ever, and ever shall have some Church visible upon the earth. When the people of God worshipped the Calf in the wilderness ; when they adored the brazen Serpent ; when they served

the

Ioh. 15. 2.
Ioh. 16. 2, 4.

Apoc. 2. 13.
Tertul. de Virgin. veland.

Iren. adverf.
Lar. lib. 1.
cap. 2, & .

Act. 8. 38.
and 12. 16.
and 2. 41.

Matt. 13. 45.
and 3. 24.

Exod. 32.
Psa. 106. 19, 20.
2 King. 18, 4.
Ier. 11. 14.

the Gods of Nations; when they bowed their knees to *Baal*; when they burnt Incense
and offered Sacrifice unto Idols; true it is, the wrath of God was most fiercely inflamed ^{1 *Kings* 22. 17.}
against them, their Prophets justly condemned them, as an adulterous seed and a wick- ^{*Isai.* 57. 3.}
ed generation of Miscreants, which had forsaken the living God; and of him were ^{*Isai.* 1. 4.}
likewise forsaken, in respect of that singular mercy wherewith he kindly and lovingly ^{*Isai.* 60. 15.}
imbraceth his faithful Children. Howbeit retaining the Law of God, and the Holy
Seal of his Covenant, the Sheep of his visible Flock they continued even in the depth
of their Disobedience and Rebellion. Wherefore not only amongst them God always ^{*Ier.* 13. 11.}
had his Church, because he had thousands which never bowed their knees to *Baal*; ^{1 *Kings*, 19 8.}
but whose knees were bowed unto *Baal*, even they were also of the visible Church
of God. Nor did the Prophet so complain, as if that Church had been quite and
clean extinguished; but he took it as though there had not been remaining in the ^{*Ier.* 1. 11.}
World any besides himself, that carried a true and an upright heart towards God, ^{1 *Kings* 19. 8.}
with care to serve him according to his holy will. For lack of diligent observing the
difference, first, between the Church of God mystical and visible, then between the
visible sound and corrupted, sometimes more, sometimes less; the oversights are neither
few nor light that have been committed. This deceiveth them, and nothing else,
who think that in the time of the first World, the Family of *Noah* did contain all
that were of the visible Church of God. From hence it grew and from no other
cause in the World, that the *African* Bishops in the Council of Carthage, knowing how the administration of Baptism belongeth only to the Church of Christ, and
supposing that Hereticks which were apparently severed from the sound beleiving
Church, could not possibly be of the Church of Jesus Christ; thought it utterly against
reason, that Baptisme administred by men of corrupt belief, should be accounted as
a Sacrament. And therefore in maintenance of Rebaptization, their arguments are
built upon the fore-alleadged ground, *That Hereticks are not at all any part of the* ^{*Fortunat. in*}
Church of Christ. Our Saviour founded his Church on a Rock, and not upon Heresie; ^{*Concil. Car.*}
power of Baptizing he gave to his Apostles, unto Hereticks he gave it not: Wherefore ^{*Mat. 7. 24.*}
they that are without the Church, and oppose themselves against Christ, do but scat- ^{*Mat. 16. 8.*}
ter his Sheep and Flock. Without the Church Baptize they cannot. Again, are He- ^{*Mat. 2. 8. 29.*}
reticks Christians, or are they not? If they be Christians, wherefore remain they not
in Gods Church? If they be no Christians, how make they Christians? Or to what
purpose shall those words of the Lord serve, He which is not with me, is against me: and,
He which gathereth not with me, scattereth? Wherefore evident it is, that upon misbegotten ^{*Secundinus in*}
children and the brood of Antichrist, without rebaptization the Holy Ghost cannot de- ^{*eodem Concil.*}
scend. But none in this case so earnest as *Cyprian*; *I know no Baptisme but one, and* ^{*Mat. 12. 30.*}
that in the Church only; none without the Church, where he that doth cast out the Devil, hath
the Devil: He doth examine about belief, whose lips and words do breath forth as a Canker:
The faithless doth offer the Articles of Faith, a wicked creature forgiveth wickedness; in
the name of Christ, Antichrist signeth; he which is cursed of God, blesseth; a dead carri-
on promiseth life, a man unpeaceable giveth peace, a Blasphemer calleth upon the name of
God, a prophane person doth exercise Priesthood, a Sacrilegious wretch doth prepare the Altar,
and in the neck of all these that evil also commeth, the Eucharist a very Bishop of the
Devil doth presume to consecrate. All this was true, but not sufficient to prove that
Hereticks were in no sort any part of the visible Church of Christ, and consequently their Baptism, no Baptisme. This opinion therefore was afterwards both condemned by a better advised Councel, and also revoked by the chiefest of the Authours thereof themselves. What is it but only the self-same errour and miscon-
ceit, wherewith others being at this day likewise possest, they ask us where our ^{*In concilio Ni-*}
Church did lurk, in what Cave of the Earth it slept for so many hundreds of years ^{*ceno, vide Hie-*}
together before the birth of *Martin Luther*? As if we were of opinion that *Luther* ^{*ron. dial. adversus*}
did erect a new Church of Christ. No, the Church of Christ which was from the ^{*Luciferia.*}
beginning, is, and continueth unto the end. Of which Church all parts have not
been always equally sincere and sound. In the days of *Abia* it plainly appeareth, that
Juda was by many degrees more free from pollution then *Israel*, as that solemn Ora-
tion sheweth, wherein he pleadeth for the one against the other in this wise: O
Jeroboam, *and all Israel, hear you me; Have ye not driven away the Priests of the*
Lord, the Sons of Aaron, and the Levites, and have made you Priests like the people
of nations? Whosoever commeth to consecrate with a young Bullock and seven Rams, the same ^{1 *Chron.* 13.}
may.

may be a Prieſt of them that are no Gods. But we belong unto the Lord our God, and have not forſaken him ; and the Prieſts the ſons of Aaron miniſter unto the Lord every morning and every evening burnt Offerings, and ſweet Incenſe, and the Bread is ſet in order upon the pure Table, and the Candleſtick of gold with be Lamps thereof to burn every evening ; for we keep the watch of the Lord our God, but ye have forſaken him. In S. Pauls time the integrity of *Rome* was famous ; *Corinth* many ways reproved ; they of *Galatia* much more out of ſquare. In S. *Johns* time, *Epheſus* and *Smyrna* in far better ſtate then *Thyatira* and *Pergamus* were. We hope therefore, that to reform our ſelves, if at any time we have done amiſs, is not to ſever our ſelves from the Church we were of before. In the Church we were, and we are ſo ſtill. Other difference between our eſtate before and now, we know none, but only ſuch as we ſee in *Judah*, which having ſometime been Idolatrous, became afterward more ſoundly religious, by renouncing Idolatry and Superſtition. If *Ephraim* be joyned to Idols, the counſel of the Pro

Hoſ. 14. 1 , & 17. 1 Chron. 24. 5.

phet is, *Let him alone.* If *Iſrael* play the Harlot, let not *Judah* ſin. If it ſeem evil unto you, ſaith *Joſhua*, to ſerve the Lord, chuſe you this day whom you will ſerve; whether the gods whom your Fathers ſerved beyond the flood, or the gods of the Amorites in whoſe land ye dwell: But I and mine houſe will ſerve the Lord. The indiſpoſition therefore of the Church of *Rome* to reform her ſelf, muſt be no ſtay unto us from performing our duty to God ; even as deſire of retaining conformity with them, could be no excuſe if we did not perform that duty. Notwithſtanding ſo far as lawfully we may, we have held and do hold fellowſhip with them. For even as the

Rom. 11. 28.

Apoſtle doth ſay of *Iſrael*, that they are in one reſpect enemies, but in another beloved of God : In like ſort with *Rome*, we dare not communicate concerning ſundry her groſs and grievous abominations ; yet touching thoſe main parts of Chriſtian truth wherein they conſtantly ſtill perſiſt, we gladly acknowledge them to be of the Family of Jeſus Chriſt ; and our hearty prayer unto God Almighty is, that being conjoyned ſo far forth with them, they may at the length (if it be his will) ſo yield to frame and reform themſelves, that no diſtraction remain in any thing, but that we all may with one heart and one mouth, glorifie God the Father of our Lord and Saviour, whoſe Church we are. As there are that make the Church of *Rome* utterly no Church at all, by reaſon of ſo many, ſo grievous errors in their Doctrines : So we have them amongſt us, who under pretence of imagined corruptions in our Diſcipline, do give even as hard a judgement of the Church of *England* it ſelf. But whatſoever the one ſort or the other teach, we muſt acknowledge even Hereticks themſelves to be though a maimed part, yet a part of the viſible Church. If an Infidel ſhould purſue to death an Heretick profeſſing Chriſtianity, onely for Chriſtian profeſſion ſake, could we deny unto him the honour of Martyrdom ? Yet this honour all men know to be proper unto the Church. Hereticks therefore are not utterly cut off from the viſible Church of Chriſt. If the Fathers do anywhere, as oftentimes they do, make the true viſible Church of Chriſt, and Heretical companies oppoſite, they are to be conſtrued as ſeparating Hereticks not altogether from the company of Believers, but from the fellowſhip of ſound Believers. For where profeſt unbelief is, there can be no viſible Church of Chriſt ; there may be, where ſound belief wanteth. Infidels being clean without the Church, deny directly, and utterly reject the very Principles of Chriſtianity ; which Hereticks embrace, and err onely by miſconſtruction ; whereupon their opinions, although repugnant indeed to the Principles of Chriſtian Faith, are notwithſtanding by them held otherwiſe, and maintained as moſt conſonant thereunto. Wherefore being Chriſtians in regard of the general Truth of Chriſt which they openly profeſs ; yet they are by the Fathers everywhere ſpoken of, as men clean excluded out of the right believing Church, by reaſon of their particular Errours, for which all that are of a ſound belief

Calvin. Epiſt. 1.

muſt needs condemn them. In this conſideration the anſwer of *Calvin* unto *Farell*, concerning the children of Popiſh Parents doth ſeem crazed. *Whereas*, ſaith he, *you ask our judgement about a matter, whereof there is doubt amongſt you, whether Miniſters of our order profeſſing the pure Doctrine of the Goſpel, may lawfully admit unto Baptiſm an Infant whoſe Father is a ſtranger unto our Churches, and whoſe Mother hath fallen from us unto the Papacy, ſo that both the Parents are Popiſh; thus we have thought good to anſwer; namely, that it is an abſurd thing for us to baptize them which cannot be*

reckoned

reckoned members of our body. And sith Papists children are such, we see not how it should be lawfull to minister Baptism unto them. Sounder a great deal is the answer of the Ecclesiastical Colledge of *Geneva* unto *Knox,* who having signified unto them, that himself did not think it lawful to baptize Bastards, or the children of Idolaters (he meaneth Papists) or of persons Excommunicate, till either the Parents had by repentance submitted themselves unto the Church, or else the children being grown unto the years of understanding, should come and sue for their own Baptism: *For thus thinking,* saith he, *I am thought to be over severe, and that not only by them which are Popish; but even in their judgements also who think themselves Maintainers of Truth.* Master *Knoxes* over-sight herein they controuled. Their Sentence was, *Wheresoever the profession of Christianity hath not utterly perished and been extinct, Infants are beguiled of their right, if the common Seal be denied them.* Which conclusion in it self is found, although it seemeth the ground is but weak whereupon they build it. For the reason which they yield of their sentence is this; *The promise which God doth make to the faithfull concerning their Seed, reacheth unto a thousand Generations; it resteth not only in the first Degree of Descent. Infants therefore whose great-Grandfathers have been holy and godly, do in that respect belong to the body of the Church, although the Fathers and Grandfathers of whom they descend, have been Apostates: Because the tenure of the Grace of God which did adopt them three hundred years ago and more in their Ancient Predecessors, cannot with justice be defeated and broken off by their Parents impiety coming between.* By which reason of theirs, although it seem that all the world may be baptized, inasmuch as no man living is a thousand Descents removed from *Adam* himself; yet we mean not at this time either to uphold or to overthrow it : oney their alleagded conclusion we embrace, so it be construed in this sort; *That forasmuch as men remain in the visible Church, till they utterly renounce the profession of Christianity, we may not deny unto Infants their right, by with-holding from them the publick sign of holy Baptism, if they be born where the outward acknowledgement of Christianity is not clean gone and extinguished.* For being in such sort born, their Parents are within the Church, and therefore their birth doth give them interest and right in Baptism. Albeit not every error and fault, yet Heresies and Crimes which are not actually repented of and forsaken, exclude quite and clean from that salvation, which belongeth unto the Mystical Body of Christ; yea, they also make a separation from the sound visible Church of Christ; altogether from the visible Church neither the one nor the other doth sever. As for the act of Excommunication, it neither shutteth out from the Mystical, nor clean from the visible; but onely from fellowship with the visible in holy Duties. With what congruity then doth the Church of *Rome* deny, that her Enemies, whom she holdeth always for Hereticks, do at all appertain to the Church of Christ; when her own do freely grant, that albeit the *Pope* (as they say) cannot teach Heresie, nor propound Error, he may notwithstanding himself worship Idols, think amiss concerning matters of Faith, yea, give himself unto acts Diabolical, even being Pope ? How exclude they us from being any part of the Church of Christ under the colour and pretence of Heresie, when they cannot but grant it possible even for him to be as touching his own personal perswasion Heretical, who in their opinion not onely is of the Church, but holdeth the chiefest place of authority over the same ? But of these things we are not now to dispute. That which already we have set down, is for our present purpose sufficient. By the Church therefore in this question we understand no other than onely the visible Church. For preservation of Christianity there is not any thing more needful, then that such as are of the visible Church, have mutual fellowship and society one with another. In which consideration, as the main body of the Sea being one, yet within divers Precincts hath divers names; so the Catholick Church is in like sort divided into a number of distinct Societies, every of which is termed a Church within it self. In this sense the Church is always a visible Society of men; not an assembly; but a Society. For although the name of the Church be given to Christian Assemblies, although any number of Christian men congregated may be termed by the name of a Church, yet Assemblies properly are rather things that belong to a Church. Men are assembled for performance of publick actions; which actions being ended, the Assembly dissolveth it self, and is no longer in being; whereas the Church which was

R 3   assembled,

Epist. 283.

Epist. 85.

assembled, doth no less continue afterwards then before. *Where but three are, and they of the Laity also,* saith *Tertullian, yet there is a Church,* that is to say, a Christian assembly. But a Church, as now we are to understand it, is a Society, that is, a number of men belonging unto some Christian fellowship, the place and limits whereof are certain. That wherein they have communion, is the publick exercise of such duties as those mentioned in the Apostles Acts, *Instruction, Breaking of bread and Prayer.* As therefore they that are of the Mystical body of Christ, have those inward Graces and Vertues, whereby they differ from all other which are not of the same body; again, whosoever appertain to the visible Body of the Church, they have also the notes of external Profession, whereby the world knoweth what they are: After the same manner, even the several Societies of Christian men, unto every of which the name of a Church is given, with addition betokening severally, as the Church of *Rome, Corinth, Ephesus, England,* and so the rest, must be indued with correspondent general properties belonging unto them, as they are publick Christian Societies. And of such properties common unto all Societies Christian, it may not be denied, that one of the very cheifest is Ecclesiastical Polity. Which word I therefore the rather use, because the name of Government, as commonly men understand it in ordinary speech, doth not comprize the largeness of that whereunto in this question it is applied. For when we speak of Government, what doth the greatest part conceive thereby, but only the exercise of superiority peculiar unto Rulers and Guides of others ? To our purpose therefore the name of Church-Polity will better serve, because it containeth both Government, and also whatsoever besides belongeth to the ordering of the Church in publick. Neither is any thing in this degree more necessary then Church-Polity, which is a form of ordering publick spiritual affairs of the Church of God.

A&s 1.47.

2. But we must note, that he which affirmeth speech to be necessary amongst all men throughout the World, doth not thereby import that all men must necessarily speak one kind of Language; Even so the necessity of Polity, and Regiment in all Churches may be held, without holding any one certain form to be necessary in them all, nor is it possible that any form of Polity, much less of Polity Ecclesiastical, should be good, unless God himself be author of it. *Those things that are not of God* (saith *Tertullian*) *they can have no other then Gods Adversary for their Author.* Be it whatsoever in the Church of God, if it be not of God, we hate it. Of God it must be; either as those things sometimes were, which God supernaturally revealed, and so delivered them unto *Moses* for Government of the Commonwealth of *Israel*; or else as those things which men finde out by help of that light, which God hath given them unto that end. The very Law of Nature it self, which no man can deny but God hath instituted, is not of God, unless that be of God, whereof God is the Author as well this latter way as the former. But forasmuch as no form of Church-Polity is thought by them to be lawful, or to be of God, unless God be so the Author of it, that it be also set down in Scripture; they should tell us plainly, whether their meaning be that it must be there set down in whole, or in part. For if wholly, let them shew what one form of Polity ever was so. Their own to be so taken out of Scripture they will not affirm; neither deny they that in part, even this which they so much oppugn is also from thence taken. Again, they should tell us, whether only that be taken out of Scripture, which is actually and particularly there set down; or else that also, which the general Principles and Rules of Scripture potentially contain. The one way they cannot so much as pretend, that all the parties of their own Discipline are in Scripture; and the other way their mouthes are stopped, when they would plead against all other forms besides their own; seeing the general Principles are such, as do not particularly prescribe any one, but sundry may equally be consonant unto the general Axiomes of the Scripture. But to give them some larger scope, and not to close them up in these streights: let their allegations be considered, wherewith they earnestly bend themselves against all, which deny it necessary that any one compleat form of Church-Polity should be in Scripture. First therefore, whereas it hath been told them, that matters of Faith, and in general, matters necessary unto salvation, are of a different nature from Ceremonies, Order, and the kind of Church-government; and that the one is necessary to be expresly contained

Whether it be necessary that some particular form of Church-polity he set down in Scripture, sith the things that belong particularly unto any such form, are not of necessity to salvation.

Tertul de habitu mul. Æmulisint necesse est, quæ Dei non sunt. Rom.1.15.
Lect.lib.6.c.8. Ille legis hujus inventor disceptator,lator.Cic. 3. de Reput.

in

i.

in the Word of God, or else manifestly collected out of the same, the other not so; that it is necessary not to receive the one, unless there be something in Scripture for them; the other free, if nothing against them may thence be alledged: although there do not appear any just or reasonable cause to reject or dislike of this: nevertheless, as it is not easie to speak to the contentation of mindes exulcerated in themselves, but that somewhat there will be always which displeaseth; so herein for two things we are reproved; the first *misdistinguishing*, because matters of Discipline and Church-Government are (as they say) matters necessary to salvation, and of Faith, whereas we put a difference betwixt the one and the other; our second fault is *injurious dealing* with the Scripture of God, as if it contained onely the principal points of Religion, some rude and unfashioned matter of building the Church, but had left out that which belongeth unto the form and fashion of it; as if there were in the Scripture no more then onely to cover the Churches nakedness, and not Chains, Bracelets, Rings, Jewels to adorn her; sufficient to quench her thirst, to kill her hunger, but not to minister a more liberal, and (as it were) a more delicious and dainty diet. In which case our Apology shall not need to be very long.

Two things misliked; the one, that we distinguish matters of discipline or Church-Government from matters of faith and necessary unto salvation; the other, that we are injurious to the Scripture of God, in abridging the large and rich contents thereof; Their

words are these, You which distinguish between these, and say that matters of faith and necessary unto Salvation, may not be tolerated in the Church, unless they be expressly contained in the Word of God, or manifestly gathered; but that Ceremonies, Order, Discipline, Government in the Church, may not be received against them: You (I say) distinguishing or dividing after this sort, do prove your self an evil divider. As though matters of Discipline and kinde of Government were not matters necessary to salvation, and of Faith. It is no small injury which you do unto the Word of God to pin it in to narrow room, as that it should be able to direct us but in the principal points of our Religion; or as though the substance of Religion, or some rude and unfashioned matter of building of the Church were uttered in them, and those things were left out that should pertain to the form and fashion of it; or as if there were in the Scriptures onely to cover the Churches nakedness, and not also Chains, and Bracelets, and Rings, and other Jewels to adorn her and set her out; or that to conclude, there were sufficient to quench her thirst and kill her hunger, but not to minister unto her a more liberal, and (as it were) a more delicious and dainty diet. These things you seem to say when you say that matters necessary to salvation, and of faith, are contained in Scripture, especially, when you oppose these things to Ceremonies, Order, Discipline and Government. *T.C. lib. 1. pag. 26.*

3. [a] The mixture of those things by speech, which by nature are divided, is the Mother of all Errour. To take away therefore that errour which Confusion breedeth, distinction is requisite. Rightly to distinguish, is by conceit of minde to sever things different in Nature, and to discern wherein they differ. So that if we imagine a difference where there is none, because we distinguish where we should not, it may not be denied that we misdistinguish. The one trial whether we do so, yea or no, dependeth upon comparison between our conceit and the nature of things conceived. Touching matters belonging to the Church of Christ this we conceive, that they are not of one sute. Some things are *meerly* of faith, which things it doth suffice that that we know and believe: some things not onely to be known, but done because they concern the actions of men. Articles about the Trinity are matters of meer faith, and must be believed. Precepts concerning the works of Charity, are matters of action; which to know, unless they be practised, is not enough. This being so clear to all mens understanding, I somewhat marvel that they especially should think it absurd to oppose *Church-Government*, a plain matter of action, unto matter of faith, who know that themselves divide the Gospel into Doctrine and Discipline. For if matters of Discipline be rightly by them distinguished from matters of Doctrine, why not matters of Government by us as reasonably set against matters of Faith? Do not they under Doctrine comprehend the same which we intend by matters of faith? Do not they under Discipline comprize the Regiment of the Church? When they blame that

[a] That matters of Discipline are different from matters of faith and salvation; and that they themselves so teach which are our Reprovers.

T.C. lib. 1. pa. 1. We offer to shew the Discipline to be a part of the Gospel. And again, *pag 5.* I speak of the Discipline as of a part of the Gospel. If the Discipline be one part of the Gospel, what other part can they assign but Doctrine, to answer in division to the Discipline?

in us, which themselves follow, they give men great cause to doubt that some other thing then judgement doth guide their speech. What the Church of God standeth bound to know or do, the same in part Nature teacheth. And because Nature can teach them but onely in part, neither so fully as is requisite for mans salvation; nor so easily, as to make the way plain and expedite enough, that many may come to the knowledge of it, and so be saved; therefore in Scripture hath God both collected the most necessary things, that the School of Nature teacheth unto that end; and revealeth

vealeth also whatſoever we neither could with ſafety be ignorant of, nor at all be
inſtructed in but by ſupernatural Revelation from him. So that Scripture containing all things that are in this kinde any way needful for the Church, and the
principal of the other ſort; this is the next thing wherewith we are charged as
with an errour : we teach that whatſoever is unto ſalvation termed *neceſſary* by way
of excellency, whatſoever it ſtandeth all men upon to know or do that they may
be ſaved, whatſoever there is whereof it may truly be ſaid, *This not to believe is*
eternal death and damnation ; or , *This every ſoul that will live muſt duly obſerve*, of
which ſort the Articles of Chriſtian Faith, and the Sacraments of the Church of
Chriſt are ; all ſuch things if Scripture did not comprehend, the Church of God
ſhould not be able to meaſure out the length and breadth of that way wherein for
ever ſhe is to walk ; Hereticks and Schiſmaticks never ceaſing, ſome to abridge,
ſome to enlarge, all to pervert and obſcure the ſame. But as for thoſe things that
are acceſſary hereunto, thoſe things that ſo belong to the way of ſalvation, as to alter them is no otherwiſe to change that way, then a path is changed by altering onely
the uppermoſt face thereof, which be it laid with gravel, or ſet with graſs, or paved
with ſtones, remaineth ſtill the ſame path ; in ſuch things becauſe diſcretion may
teach the Church what is convenient, we hold not the Church further tied herein unto Scripture, then that againſt Scripture nothing be admitted in the Church, leſt that
path which ought alwayes to be kept even, do thereby come to be over-grown with

Mat. 23. 23.
Brambles and Thorns. If this be unſound, wherein doth the point of unſoundneſs
lie ? Is it not that we make ſome things *neceſſary*, ſome things *acceſſory* and appen-
dant onely? For our Lord and Saviour himſelf doth make that difference, by terming Judgement, and Mercy, and Fidelity, with other things of like nature, *The*
greater and weightier matters of the Law. Is it then in that we account *Ceremonies*,
(wherein we do not compriſe Sacraments, or any other the like ſubſtantial duties in
the exerciſe of Religion, but onely ſuch external Rites as are uſually annexed unto Church actions) is it an overſight, that we

[a] The Government of the Church of Chriſt granted
by *Fenner* himſelf to be thought a matter of great
moment, yet not of the ſubſtance of Religion. Againſt
Doctor Bridges, pag. 124, if it be *Fenner* which was the
Author of that Book.
reckon theſe things and [a] matters of Government
in the number of things acceſſory, not things neceſſary in ſuch ſort as hath been declared? Let them
which therefore think us blameable, conſider well
their own words. Do they not plainly compare
the one unto Garments, which cover the body of the Church; the other unto Rings,
Bracelets and Jewels that onely adorn it ? the one to that Food which the Church
doth live by, the other to that which maketh her Diet liberal, dainty, and more delicious ? Is dainty fare a thing neceſſary to the ſuſtenance, or to the cloathing of the
body rich Attire ? If not, how can they urge the neceſſity of that which themſelves
reſemble by things not neceſſary ? Or by what conſtruction ſhall any man living be
able to make thoſe compariſons true, holding that diſtinction untrue, which putteth
a difference between things of external Regiment in the Church, and things neceſſary unto ſalvation ?

That we do
not take from
Scripture any
thing which
may be there-
unto given
with ſound-
neſs of truth.
Ariſt. Pol. lib. 1.
cap. 8. & Plato
in Menex.
Ariſt. lib. 3. de
Anima, cap. 5.
4. Now as it can be to Nature no injury, that of her we ſay the ſame which diligent
beholders of her works have obſerved ; namely, that ſhe provideth for all living
creatures nouriſhment which may ſuffice ; that ſhe bringeth forth no kinde of creature
whereto ſhe is wanting in that which is needful ; although we do not ſo far magnifie
her exceeding bounty, as to affirm that ſhe bringeth into the World the ſons of men
adorned with gorgeous attire, or maketh coſtly buildings to ſpring up out of the
Earth for them : So I truſt that to mention what the Scripture of God leaveth unto
the Churches diſcretion in ſome things, is not in any thing to impair the honour
which the Church of God yieldeth to the ſacred Scriptures perfection. Wherein
ſeeing that no more is by us maintained, than onely that Scripture muſt needs teach
the Church whatſoever is in ſuch ſort neceſſary, as hath been ſet down ; and that it is
no more diſgrace for Scripture to have left a number of other things free to be ordered at the diſcretion of the Church, then for Nature to have left it unto the wit of
man to deviſe his own attire, and not to look for it as the beaſts of the field have
theirs. If neither this can import, nor any other proof ſufficient be brought forth,
that we either will at any time, or ever did affirm the Sacred Scripture to comprehend no more then onely thoſe bare neceſſaries ; if we acknowledge that as well for
particular

particular application to special occasions, as also in other manifold respects infinite Treasures of Wisdom are over and besides abundantly to be found in the Holy Scripture; yea, that scarcely there is any noble part of knowledge, worthy the minde of man, but from thence it may have some direction and light; yea, that although there be no necessity it should of purpose prescribe any one particular form of Church-Government; yet touching the manner of governing in general, the Precepts that Scripture setteth down are not few, and the Examples many, which it proposeth for all Church-Governours, even in particularities to follow; yea, that those things, finally, which are of principal weight in the very particular form of Church-Politie (although not that form which they imagine; but that which we against them uphold) are in the self same Scriptures contained: if all this be willingly granted by us, which are accused to pin the Word of God in so narrow room, as that it should be able to direct us but in principal points of our Religion, or as though the substance of Religion, or some rude or unfashioned matter of building the Church were uttered in them, and those things left out that should pertain to the form and fashion of it; let the cause of the Accused be referred to the Accusers own conscience, and let that judge whether this accusation be deserved where it hath been laid.

5. But so easie it is for every man living to erre, and so hard to wrest from any mans mouth the plain acknowledgement of errour, that what hath been once inconsiderately defended, the same is commonly persisted in, as long as wit by whetting it self is able to finde out any shift, be it never so sleight, whereby to escape out of the hands of present contradiction. So that it cometh herein to pass with men unadvisedly faln into errour, as with them whose state hath no ground to uphold it, but onely the help which by subtil conveyance they draw out of casual events arising from day to day, till at length they be clean spent. They which first gave out, that *Nothing ought to be established in the Church which is not commanded by the Word of God*, thought this principle plainly warranted by the manifest words of the Law, *Ye shall put nothing unto the Word which I command you, neither shall ye take ought therefrom, that ye may keep the Commandments of the Lord our God, which I command you.* Wherefore having an eye to a number of Rites and Orders in the Church of *England*, as marrying with a Ring, Crossing in the one Sacrament, Kneeling at the other, observing of Festival days more then onely that which is called the *Lords Day*, enjoyning Abstinence at certain times from some kindes of Meat, Churching of Women after Childe-birth, Degrees taken by Divines in Universities, sundry Church-offices, Dignities, and Callings, for which they found no Commandment in the holy Scripture, they thought by the one onely stroke of that Axiome to have cut them off. But that which they took for an Oracle, being sifted, was repeld. True it is concerning the Word of God, whether it be by misconstruction of the sense, or by falsification of the words, wittingly to endeavour that any thing may seem Divine which is not, or any thing not seem which is, were plainly to abuse and even to falsifie Divine Evidence, which injury offered but unto men, is most worthily counted hainous. Which point I wish they did well observe, with whom nothing is more familiar, then to plead in these Causes, *The Law of God, the Word of the Lord*: who notwithstanding when they come to alledge what Word and what Law they mean, their common ordinary practice is; to quote by-speeches in some historical Narration or other, and to urge them as if they were written in most exact form of Law. What is to adde to the Law of God, if this be not? When that which the Word of God doth but deliver historically, we consture without any warrant, as if it were legally meant, and so urge it further then we can prove that it was intended, do we not adde to the Laws of God, and make them in number seem more then they are? It standeth us upon to be careful in this case. For the sentence of God is heavy against them, that wittingly shall presume thus to use the Scripture.

6. But let that which they do hereby intend be granted them; let it once stand as consonant to reason, that because we are forbidden to adde to the Law of God any thing, or to take ought from it; therefore we may not for matters of the Church make any Law more then is already set down in Scriptures: who seeth not what sentence it shall enforce us to give against all Churches in the World, inasmuch as there is not one, but hath had many things established in it, which though the Scripture did

The irmeaning who first did plead against the Polity of the Church of *England*, urging that, *Nothing ought to be established in the Church, which is not commanded by the Word of God*; and what Scripture they thought they might ground this Assertion upon.
Deut. 4. 2. and 12. 32.
Whatsoever I command you take heed you do it; thou shalt put nothing thereto, nor take ought therefrom.

The same assertion we cannot hold, without doing wrong unto all Churches.

did never command, yet for us to condemn were rashnefs. Let the Church of God even in the time of our Saviour Christ serve for example unto all the rest. In their Domestical celebration of the Pasfoever, which Supper they divided (as it were) into two courses; what Scripture did give commandment that between the first and the fecond, he that was chief should put off the residue of his garments, and keeping on his Feast-robe onely, wash the feet of them that were with him? What Scripture did command them never to lift up their hands unwasht in Prayer unto God, which custom *Aristæus* (be the credit of the Author more or lefs) sheweth wherefore they did fo religioufly obferve? What Scripture did command the Jews every Festival day to fast till the fixt hour? The custom both mentioned by *Josephus* in the History of his own life, and by the words of *Peter* signified. Tedious it were to rip up all such things, as were in that Church established, yea, by Christ himfelf, and by his Apostles obferved, though not commanded anywhere in Scripture.

margin: Iohn 13. *Cænævium: de quo Mat. 22, 12. Ibi de Cænætorio nuptia'i.*

margin: Acts 1.

margin: ª A shift to maintain that, Nothing ought to be established in the Church, which is not commanded in the Word of God: namely, that Commandments are of two forts; and that al things lawful in the church are commanded, if not by special Precepts, yet by general Rules in the Word. 1 Cor. 10. 31. and 14. 40. and 14. 26. Rom 14. 6, 7. T. C. l. p. 35.

7. ª Well, yet a glofs there is to colour that paradox, and notwithstanding all this, still to make it appear in shew not to be altogether unreasonable. And therefore till further reply come, the cause is held by a feeble distinction; that the commandments of God being either general or special, although there be no exprefs word for every thing in fpecialty; yet there are general commandments for all things, to the end that even fuch cafes as are not in Scripture particularly mentioned, might not be left to any to order at their pleafure, onely with caution that nothing be done against the Word of God: And that for this caufe the Apostle hath fet down in Scripture four general Rules, requiring fuch things alone to be received in the Church, as do best and neareft agree with the fame Rules, that fo all things in the Church may be appointed, not onely *not against*, but *by* and *according* to the Word of God. The Rules are thefe, *Nothing fcandalous* or offensive unto any, especially unto the Church of God; *All things* in order and with feemlinefs; *All unto edification*; finally, *All to the glory of God*. Of which kinde how many might be gathered out of the Scripture, if it were neceffary to take fo much pains? Which Rules they that urge, minding thereby to prove that nothing may be done in the Church but what Scripture commandeth, must needs hold that they tie the Church of Christ no otherwife, then onely becaufe we finde them there fet down by the finger of the Holy Ghoft. So that unlefs the Apostle by writing had delivered thofe Rules to the Church, we fhould by obferving them have finned, as now by not obferving them. In the Church of the Jews is it not granted, that, *the appointment of the hour for daily Sacrifices*; the building of *Synagogues* throughout the Land to hear the Word of God and to pray in, when they came not up to *Jerusalem*; the erecting of *Pulpits and Chairs* to teach in; the order of *Burial*, the *Rites of marriage*, with fuch like, being matters appertaining to the Church, yet are not anywhere prefcribed in the Law, but were by the Churches difcretion instituted? What then shall we think? Did they hereby adde to the Law, and fo displeafe God by that which they did? None fo hardly perfwaded of them. Doth their Law deliver unto them the felf fame general rules of the Apostles, that framing thereby their Orders, they might in that refpect cleer themfelves from doing amifs? S. *Paul* would then of likelihood have cited them out of the Law, which we fee he doth not. The truth is, they are Rules and Canons of that Law which is written in all mens hearts; the Church had for ever no lefs then now ftood bound to obferve them, whether the Apostle had mentioned them or no. Seeing therefore thofe Canons do binde as they are edicts of Nature, which the Jews obferving as yet unwritten, and thereby framing fuch Church-Orders as in their Law were not prefcribed, are notwithstanding in that refpect unculpable; it followeth, that fundry things may be lawfully done in the Church, fo as they be not done against the Scripture, although no Scripture do command them, but the Church onely following the Light of Reafon, judge them to be in difcretion meet. Secondly, unto our purpofe, and for the question in hand, whether the commandments of God in Scripture be general or special, it skilleth not. For if being particularly applied, they have in regard of fuch particulars a force conftraining us to take fome one certain thing of many, and to leave the reft; whereby it would come to pafs, that any other particular but that one being established, the general Rules themfelves in that cafe would be broken; then is it utterly impoffible that God fhould

leave

leave any thing great or small free for the Church to establish or not. Thirdly, if so be they shall grant, as they cannot otherwise do, that these Rules are no such Laws as require any one particular thing to be done, but serve rather to direct the Church in all things which she doth; so that free and lawful it is to devise any Ceremony, to receive any Order, and to authorize any kinde of Regiment, no special commandment being thereby violated; and the same being thought such by them to whom the judgement thereof appertaineth, as that it is not scandalous, but decent, tending unto edification, and setting forth the glory of God; that is to say, agreeable unto the general Rules of the Scripture; this doth them no good in the World for the furtherance of their purpose. That which should make for them, must prove that men ought not to make Laws for Church-Regiment, but onely keep those Laws which in Scripture they finde made. The plain intent of the Book of Ecclesiastial Discipline is to shew, that men may not devise Laws of Church-Government; but are bound for ever to use and execute onely those, which God himself hath already devised and delivered in the Scripture. The self same drift the Admotioners also had, in urging that nothing ought to be done in the Church according unto any Law of mans devising, but all according to that which God in his Word hath commanded. Which not remembring, they gather out of Scripture general Rules to be followed in making Laws; and so in effect they plainly grant, that we our selves may lawfully make Laws for the Church, and are not bound out of Scripture onely to take Laws already made, as they meant who first alledged that principle whereof we speak. One particular plat-form it is which they respected, and which they laboured thereby to force upon all Churches; whereas these general rules do not let, but that there may well enough be sundry. It is the particular order established in the Church of *England*, which thereby they did intend to alter, as being not commanded of God; whereas unto those general Rules they know, we do not defend that we may hold any thing unconformable. Obscure it is not what meaning they had, who first gave out that grand Axiome; and according unto that meaning, it doth prevail far and wide with the Favourers of that part. Demand of them, wherefore they conform not themselves unto the Order of our Church? and in every particular their answer for the most part is, *We finde no such thing commanded in the Word.* Whereby they plainly require some special commandment for that which is exacted at their hands; neither are they content to have matters of the Church examined by general Rules and Canons. As therefore in controversies between us and the Church of *Rome*, that which they practise, is many times even according to the very grossness of that which the vulgar sort conceiveth; when that which they teach to maintain it, is so nice and subtil, that hold can very hardly be taken thereupon; in which cases we should do the Church of God small benefit, by disputing with them according unto the finest points of their dark conveyance, and suffering that sense of their Doctrine to go uncontrolled, wherein by the common sort it is ordinarily received and practised. So considering what disturbance hath grown in the Church among our selves, and how the Authors thereof do commonly build altogether on this as a sure foundation, *Nothing ought to be established in the Church, which in the Word of God is not commanded*; were it reason that we should suffer the same to pass without controlement, in that current meaning whereby every where it prevaileth, and stay till some strange construction were made thereof, which no man would lightly have thought on, but being driven thereunto for a shift?

8. The last refuge in maintaining this Position, is thus to construe it, *Nothing ought to be established in the Church, but that which is commanded in the Word of God*; that is to say, All Church-Orders must be *grounded upon the Word of God*, in such sort grounded upon the Word, not that being found out by some *Star, or Light of Reason, or Learning, or other help*, they may be received, so they be not against the Word of God; but according at leastwise unto the general Rules of Scripture they must be made. Which is in effect as much as to say, *We know not what to say well in defence of this Position: and therefore lest we should say it is false, there is no remedy but to say that in some sense or other it may be true, if we could tell how*. For that *Scholie* had need of a very favourable Reader, and a tractable, that should think it plain construction, when to be *commanded in the Word*, and grounded

Another answer in defence of the former assertion, whereby the meaning thereof is opened in this sort. All Church-Orders must be commanded in the Word, that is, to say, grounded upon the Word, and made according, at the leastwise unto the general Rules of holy Scripture. As for such things as are found out by any star or light of reason, and are in that respect received, so they be not against the Word of God, all such things it hold th unlawfully received, drift dit, to

grounded upon the Word are made all one. If when a man may live in the ſtate of Matrimony, ſeeking that good thereby which Nature principally deſireth, he make rather
choice of a contrary life in regard of S. *Pauls* judgement ; that which he doth is
manifeſtly *grounded* upon the Word of God, yet *not commanded* in his Word, becauſe

1 Cor. 7.

without breach of any commandment he might do otherwiſe. Secondly, whereas no
man in juſtice and reaſon can be reproved, for thoſe actions which are framed according unto that known will of God, whereby they are to be judged ; and the
will of God which we are to judge our actions by, no found Divine in the World
ever denied to be in part made manifeſt even by light of Nature, and not by Scripture alone ; if the Church being directed by the former of theſe two (which
God hath given who gave the other, that man might in different ſort be guided by
them both) it the Church, I ſay, do approve and eſtabliſh that which thereby it
judgeth meet, and findeth not repugnant to any word or ſyllable of Holy Scripture, who ſhall warrant our preſumptuous boldneſs, controlling herein the Church
of Chriſt ? But ſo it is, the name of the Light of Nature is made hateful with men ;
the *Star of Reaſon and Learning*, and all other ſuch like helps, beginneth no otherwiſe
to be thought of, then if it were an unlucky Comet, or as if God had ſo accurſed it,
that it ſhould never ſhine or give light in things concerning our duty any way to-

Apoc 8 10.

wards him, but be eſteemed as that *Star* in the *Revelation* called *Wormwood*; which
being fallen from Heaven, maketh Rivers and Waters in which it falleth, ſo bitter,
that men taſting them dye thereof. A number there are, who think they cannot admire as they ought the power and authority of the Word of God, if in things divine
they ſhould attribute any force to mans reaſon. For which cauſe they never uſe
reaſon ſo willingly as to diſgrace reaſon. Their uſual and common diſcourſes

1 Cor. 14.

are unto this effect : Firſt, *The natural man perceiveth not the things of the Spirit of
God : for they are fooliſhneſs unto him, neither can he know them, becauſe they are ſpiri-

Col. 1. 8.

tually diſcerned.* Secondly, it is not for nothing that S. *Paul* giveth charge to *beware
of Philoſophy*, that is to ſay, ſuch knowledge as men by Natural Reaſon attain unto.
Thirdly, Conſider them that have from time to time oppoſed themſelves againſt the
Goſpel of Chriſt, and moſt troubled the Church with Hereſie. Have they not alwayes been great admirers of Humane Reaſon ? Hath their deep and profound ſkill
in Secular Learning, made them more obedient to the Truth, and not armed them
rather againſt it ? Fourthly, They that fear God will remember how heavy his
ſentences are in this caſe ; *I will deſtroy the wiſdom of the wiſe, and will caſt away the

1 Cor 19.

underſtanding of the prudent. Where is the wiſe ? Where is the Scribe ? Where is the
Diſputer of this World ? Hath not God made the wiſdom of this World fooliſhneſs ?
Seeing the World by wiſdom knew not God; in the wiſdom of God, it pleaſed God by the
fooliſhneſs of preaching to ſave Believers.* Fifthly, the Word of God in it ſelf is abſolute, exact, and perfect. The Word of God is a two-edged ſword : as for the weapons of Natural Reaſon, they are as the Armour of *Saul*, rather cumberſome about
the Souldier of Chriſt, then needful. They are not of force to do that, which the
Apoſtles of Chriſt did by the power of the Holy Ghoſt, *My preaching,* therefore ſaith

1 Cor. 2. 5.

*Paul, hath not been in the inticing ſpeech of mans wiſdom, but in plain evidence of the
Spirit of power ; that your faith might not be in the wiſdom of men, but in the power of
God.* Sixthly, if I believe the Goſpel, there needeth no reaſoning about it to perſwade me : if I do not believe, it muſt be the Spirit of God, and not the reaſon of
man that ſhall convert my heart unto him. By theſe and the like diſputes an opinion
hath ſpread it ſelf very far in the world, as if the way to be ripe in faith, were to be raw
in wit and judgement ; as if Reaſon were an enemy unto Religion, childiſh ſimplicity the mother of Ghoſtly and Divine Wiſdom. The cauſe why ſuch declamations prevail ſo greatly, is, for that men ſuffer themſelves in two reſpects to be deluded ; one is, that the wiſdom of men being debaſed, either in compariſon with that
of God, or in regard of ſome ſpecial thing, exceeding the reach and compaſs thereof, it ſeemeth to them (not marking ſo much) as if ſimply it were condemned ; another, that learning, knowledge, or wiſdom falſly ſo termed, uſurping a name
whereof they are not worthy, and being under that name controlled, their reproof is
by ſo much the more eaſily miſapplied, and through equivocation wreſted againſt thoſe
things whereunto ſo precious names do properly and of right belong. This duly obſerved, doth to the former allegations it ſelf make ſufficient anſwer. Howbeit, for all

mens

mens plainer and fuller fatisfaction. Firft, Concerning the inability of reafon to
fearch out and to judge of things Divine, if they be fuch as thofe properties of God,
and thofe duties of men towards him, which may be conceived by attentive confideration of Heaven and Earth : we know that of meer natural men, the Apoftle teftifieth, how they *knew both God, and the Law of God.* Other things of God there be, Rom. 1. 21. 31
which are neither fo found, nor though they be fhewed, can ever be approved without the *fpecial* operation of Gods good grace and Spirit. Of fuch things fometime
fpake the Apoftle S. *Paul,* declaring how Chrift had called him to be a witnefs of his
death and refurrection from the dead, according to that which the Prophets and
Mofes had forefhewed. *Feftus* a meer natural man, an Infidel, a Roman, one whofe Acts. 25. 19.
ears were unacquainted with fuch matter, heard him, but could not reach unto that
whereof he fpake; the fuffering and the rifing of Chrift from the dead, he rejected Acts. 19. 24.
as idle fuperftitious fancies, not worth the hearing. The Apoftle that knew them by
the Spirit, and fpake of them with power of the Holy Ghoft, feemed in his eyes but 1 Cor 2. 14.
learnedly mad. Which example maketh manifeft what elfewhere the fame Apoftle
teacheth, namely, that nature hath need of grace, whereunto I hope we are not
oppofite, by holding that grace hath ufe of nature. Secondly, Philofophy we are
warned to take heed of; not that Philofophy which is true and found knowledge
attained by natural difcourfe of reafon; but that Philofophy which to bolfter Herefie
or Error, cafteth a fraudulent fhew of reafon upon things which are indeed unreafonable, and by that mean as by a ftratageme fpoileth the fimple which are not able to
withftand fuch cunning. *Take heed leaft any fpoile you through Philofophy and vain* Col. 1. 8.
deceit. He that exhorteth to beware of an enemies policy, doth not give counfel to
be impolitick; but rather to ufe all prudent forefight and circumfpection, left our
fimplicity be over-reacht by cunning fleights. The way not to be enveigled by them
that are fo guileful through skill, is throughly to be inftructed in that which maketh
skilful against guile, and to be armed with that true and fincere Philofophy, which
doth teach against that deceitful and vain, which fpoileth. Thirdly, But many great
Philofophers have been very unfound in belief. And many found in belief have been alfo
great Philofophers. Could fecular knowledge bring the one fort unto the love of
Chriftian Faith? Nor Chriftian faith the other fort out of love with fecular knowledge.
The harm that Hereticks did, they did it unto fuch as were unable to difcern between
found and deceitful reafoning; and the remedy against it, was ever the skill which the
ancient Fathers had to difcry and difcover fuch deceit. Infomuch that *Crefconius* the
Heretick complained greatly of St. *Auguftine,* as being too full of Logical fubtilties.
Herefie prevaileth onely by a counterfeit fhew of reafon; whereby notwithftanding it
becommeth invincible, unlefs it be convicted of fraud by manifeft remonftrance,
cleerly true, and unable to be withftood. When therefore the Apoftle requireth ha- Tit. 1. 9. 11.
bility to convict Hereticks, can we think he judgeth it a thing unlawful, and not rather needful to ufe the principal inftrument of their conviction, the light of reafon?
It may not be denied but that in the Fathers writings, there are fundry fharp invectives against Hereticks, even for their very Philofophical reafonings. The caufe whereof *Tertullian* confeffeth, not to have been any diflike conceived against the kind of Tert. de Refur.
fuch reafonings, but the end. *We may* (faith he) *even in matters of God, be made* carnis.
wifer by reafons drawn from the publick perfwafions which are grafted in mens minds,
fo they be ufed to further the truth, not to bolfter errour : fo they make with, not against
that which God hath determined. For there are fome things even known by nature, as
the immortality of the foul to many, one God unto all. I will therefore my felf alfo
ufe the fentence of fome fuch as Plato, pronouncing every foul immortal. I my felf too
will ufe the fecret acknowledgment of the communalty bearing record of the God of gods.
But when I hear men alledg, That which is dead is dead : and, While thou art alive, be
alive : and, After death an end of all, even of death it felf : then will I call to mind
both that the heart of the people with God is accounted duft, and that the very wifdome of
the World is pronounced folly. If then an Heretick flie alfo unto fuch vicious, popular,
and fecular conceits, my anfwer unto him fhall be; Thou Heretick, avoid the Heathen; al-
though in this ye be one, that ye both belye God; yet thou that doft this under the name of Chrift,
differeft from the Heathen, in that thou feemeft to thy felf a Chriftian. Leave him there-
fore his conceits, feeing that neither will he learn thine. Why doft thou, having fight, truft
to a blind guide ? thou which haft put on Chrift, take raiment of him that is naked ?

S If

If the Apostle have armed thee, why doft thou borrow a strangers shield ? Let him rather learn of thee to acknowledge, then thou of him to renounce the refurrection of the flesh. In a word, the Catholick Fathers did good unto all by that knowledge, whereby Hereticks hindering the truth in many, might have furthered therewith themselves, but that obftinately following their own ambitious or otherwise corrupted affections, inftead of framing their wills to maintain that which reafon taught, they bent their wits to find how reafon might feem to teach that which their wils were fet to maintain. For which caufe the Apoftle faith of them juftly, that they are

Tit. 3. 11.

for the moft part αυτοσατάχριτοι men condemned even in and of themfelves. For though they be not all perfwaded that it is truth which they withftand; yet that to be errour which they uphold, they might undoubtedly the fooner a great deal attain to know ; but that their ftudy is more to defend what once they have ftood in, than to find out fincerely and fimply what truth they ought to per-fift in for ever. Fourthly, there is in the world no kind of knowledge, whereby

4.

any part of truth is feen, but we juftly account it precious ; yea, that principal truth, in comparifon whereof all other knowledg is vile, may receive from it fome kind of light, whether it be that Egyptian and Caldean wifdome Mathemati-cal, wherewith *Mofes* and *Daniel* were furnifht ; or that natural, moral, and civil

Acts 7. 22.
Dan. 1. 17.
1 Kin. 4. 29, 30.
Acts 22. 13.

wifdom wherewith *Salomon* excelled all men ; or that rational and oratorial wif-dom of the Grecians, which the Apoftle St. *Paul* brought from *Tarfus* ; or that Judaical, which he learned in *Jerufalem*, fitting at the feet. of *Gamaliel* : to de-tract from the dignity thereof, were to injure even God himfelf, who being that light which none can approach unto, hath fent out thefe lights whereof we are ca-pable, even as fo many fparkles refembling the bright Fountain from which they rife. But there are that bear the title of wife men, and Scribes, and great Dif-puters of the World, and are nothing indeed lefs then what in fhew they moft ap-pear. Thefe being wholly addicted unto their own wils, ufe their wit, their learning, and all the wifdome they have, to maintain that which their obftinate hearts are delighted with, efteeming in the frantick errour of their minds, the greateft madnefs in the world to be wifdom, and the higheft wifdom foolifhnefs. Such were both Jews and Grecians which profefled, the one fort legal, and the other fecular skil, neither indureing to be taught the myftery of Chrift : unto the glory of whofe moft blefled Name, who fo ftudy to ufe both their reafon and all other gifts, as well which nature as which grace hath indued them with, let them never doubt but that the fame God, who is to deftroy and confound utterly

Mat. 13. 52.

that wifdom falfely fo named in others, doth make reckoning of them as of true Scribes, Scribes by wifdom inftructed to the Kingdom of Heaven, Scribes againft that Kingdom hardned in a vain opinion of wifdome, which in the end being proved folly, muft needs perifh; true underftanding, knowledge, judgment, and reafon, continuing for evermore. Fifthly, unto the Word of God, being in refpect of that end for which God

5

ordained it, perfect, exact, and abfolute in it felf, we do not add reafon as a fup-plement of any maim or defect therein, but as a necefſary inftrument, without which we could not reap by the Scriptures perfection, that fruit and benefit which

Heb. 4. 12.

it yieldeth. The Word of God is a two-edged fword, put in the hands of reafonable men ; and reafon as the weapon that flew *Goliah*, if they be as *David* was that ufe it. Touching the Apoftles, he which gave them from above fuch power for miraculous confirmation of that which they taught, endued them alfo with wifdom from above to teach that which they fo did confirm. Our Saviour made choice of twelve fimple and unlearned men, that the greater their lack of natural wifdom was, the more admirable that might appear which God fupernaturally endued them with from heaven. Such therefore as knew the poor and filly eftate wherein they had lived, could not but won-der to hear the wifdom of their fpeech, and be fo much the more attentive unto their teaching. They ftudied for no tongue they fpake withall; of themfelves they were rude, and knew not fo much as how to premeditate; the Spirit gave them fpeech and eloquent utterance. But becaufe with S. *Paul* it was otherwife then with the reft, in as much as he never converfed with Chrift upon earth as they did; and his education had been fcholaftical altogether, which theirs was not: thereby occafion was taken by certain Malignants, fecretly to undermine his great authority in the Church of Chrift, as though the Gofpel had been taught him by others then by Chrift himfelf, and as if the

the caufe of the *Gentiles* converfion and belief through his means , had been the
learning and skill which he had by being converfant in their Books, which thing made
them fo willing to hear him, and him fo able to perfwade them ; whereas the reft of
the Apoftles prevailed becaufe God was with them, and by miracle from Heaven confirmed his Word in their mouthes. They were mighty in *deeds* : As for him,
being abfent, his writings had fome force ; in prefence, his power not like unto theirs.
In fum , concerning his preaching, their very by-word was λόγ⊙ ἐξουτενωθ⊙ , **2 Cor.10 10,**
addle fpeech, empty talk. His writings full of great words, but in the power of miraculous operations, his prefence not like the reft of the Apoftles. Hereupon it arifeth
that S. *Paul* was fo often driven to make his Apologies. Hereupon it arifeth, that
whatfoever time he had fpent in the ftudy of Humane Learning, he maketh earneft
proteftation to them of *Corinth,* that the Gofpel which he had preached amongft
them, did not by other means prevail with them, then with others the fame Gofpel
taught by the reft of the Apoftles of Chrift. *My preaching,* faith he, *hath not been in* **1 Cor.2, 4,**
the perfwafive fpeeches of Humane Wifdom, but in demonftration of the Spirit and power,
that your faith may not be in the wifdom of men, but in the power of God. What is it which
the Apoftle doth here deny ? Is it denied that his fpeech amongft them had been *per-*
fwafive ? No ; for of him the facred Hiftory plainly teftifieth, that for the fpace of a
year and a half he fpake in the *Synagogue* every Sabbath, and *perfwaded* both Jews **Acts 18.v.4.11;**
and Grecians. How then is the fpeech of men made perfwafive ? Surely there can be
but two ways to bring this to pafs, the one Humane, the other Divine. Either S. *Paul*
did *onely* by art and natural induftry caufe his own fpeech to be credited ; or elfe God
by miracle did authorize it, and fo bring credit thereunto, as to the fpeech of the reft of
the Apoftles. Of which two, the former he utterly denieth. For why ? If the preaching
of the reft had been effectual by miracle, his *only* by force of his own learning; fo great
inequality between him and the other Apoftles in this thing, had been enough to fubvert their faith. For might they not with reafon have thought, that if he were fent
of God as well as they, would God have furnifhed them and not him, with the power
of the Holy Ghoft ? Might not a great part of them being fimple haply have feared, left
their affent had been cunningly gotten unto his doctrine, rather through the weaknefs
of their own wits , then the certainty of that truth which he had taught them ?
How unequal had it been, that all believers through the preaching of other Apoftles,
fhould have their Faith ftrongly built upon the evidence of Gods own miraculous approbation , and they whom he had converted, fhould have their perfwafion
built onely upon his skill and wifdom who perfwaded them ? As therefore calling
from men may authorize us to teach, although it could not authorize him to teach as
other Apoftles did : fo although the wifdom of man had not been fufficient to enable
him fuch a Teacher as the reft of the Apoftles were, unlefs Gods miracles had ftreng-
thened both the one and the others Doctrine; yet unto our ability both of teaching and
learning the truth of Chrift, as we are but meer Chriftian men, it is not a little which
the wifdom of man may add. Sixthly, yea, whatfoever our hearts be to God and to his **6,**
truth, believe we, or be we as yet faithlefs, for our converfion or confirmation, the
force of natural reafon is great. The force whereof unto thofe effects is nothing without grace. What then ? To our purpofe it is fufficient, that whofoever doth ferve,
honour and obey God, whofoever believeth in him ; that man would no more do this
then innocents and infants do, but for the light of natural reafon that fhineth in him,
and maketh him apt to apprehend thofe things of God, which being by grace difcovered, are effectual to perfwade reafonable mindes, and none other, that honour, obedience and credit belong aright unto God. No man cometh unto God to offer him
Sacrifice, to pour out Supplications and Prayers before him, or to do him any fer- **Heb.11.6;**
vice, which doth not firft believe him both to be, and to be a rewarder of them who
in fuch fort feek unto him. Let men be taught this either by revelation from Heaven,
or by inftruction upon earth, by labour, ftudy and meditation, or by the onely fecret
infpiration of the Holy Ghoft ; whatfoever the mean be they know it by, if the knowledge thereof were poffible without difcourfe of natural reafon, why fhould none be
found capable thereof but only men, nor men till fuch time as they come unto ripe and
full ability to work by reafonable underftanding ? The whole drift of the Scripture of
God, what is it but onely to teach *Theologie ? Theologie,* what is it, but the Science of
things Divine ? What Science can be attained unto, without the help of natural

S 2 difcourfe

discourse and reason ? *Judge you of that which I speak*, saith the Apostle. In vain
it were to speak any thing of God, but that by reason men are able somwhat to
judg of that they hear, and by discourse to discerne how consonant it is to truth.
Scripture indeed teacheth things above nature, things which our reason by it self
could not reach unto. Yet those things also we believe, knowing by reason that the
Scripture is the Word of God. In the presence of *Festus* a Roman, and of King
Agrippa a Jew, S. *Paul* omitting the one, who neither knew the Jews Religion, nor
the Books whereby they were taught it, speaks unto the other of things foreshewed
by *Moses* and the Prophets, and performed in Jesus Christ, intending thereby to prove
himself so unjustly accused, that unless his judges did condemn both *Moses* and the
Prophets, him they could not choose but acquit, who taught only that fulfilled,
which they so long since had foretold. His cause was easie to be discerned ; what
was done, their eyes were witness : what *Moses* and the Prophets did speak, their
Books could quickly shew ; it was no hard thing for him to compare them, which
knew the one and believed the other ; *King Agrippa, believest thou the Prophets ? I
know thou dost.* The question is, how the books of the Prophets came to be credited of King *Agrippa.* For what with him did authorize the Prophets, the like with
us doth cause the rest of the Scripture of God to be of credit. Because we maintain,
that in Scripture we are taught all things necessary unto Salvation ; hereupon very
childishly it is by some demanded, What Scripture can teach us the Sacred Authority
of the Scripture, upon the knowledg whereof our whole Faith and Salvation dependeth ? As though there were any Kind of Science in the world, which leadeth men
unto knowledge, without presupposing a number of things already known. No
Science doth make known the first Principles whereon it buildeth ; but they are always
either taken as plain and manifest in themselves, or as proved and granted already,
some former knowledge having made them evident. Scripture teacheth all supernaturally revealed truth ; without the knowledge whereof Salvation cannot be attained.
The main principal whereupon our belief of all things therein contained dependeth,
is, That the Scriptures are the Oracles of God himself. This in it self we cannot
say is evident. For then all men that hear it, would acknowledg it in heart, as they do
when they hear that *every whole is more then any part of that whole*, because this in it
self is evident. The other we know that all do not acknowledge when they hear it.
There must be therefore some former knowledge presupposed, which doth herein
assure the hearts of all believers. Scripture teacheth us that saving Truth which God
hath discovered unto the World by Revelation : and it presumeth us taught otherwise that it self is Divine and Sacred. The question then being, by what means we are
taught this : some answer, that to learn it we have no other way then onely Tradition : as namely, that so we believe, because both we from our Predecessours, and
they from theirs have so received. But is this enough ? That which all mens experience teacheth them, may not in any wise be denyed. And by experience we all
know, that the first outward Motive leading men so to esteem of the Scripture, is
the authority of Gods Church. For when we know the whole Church of God hath
that opinion of the Scripture, we judg it even at the first an impudent thing for any
man bred and brought up in the Church, to be of a contrary mind without cause. Afterwards the more we bestow our labour in reading or hearing the Mysteries thereof,
the more we find that the thing it self doth answer our received opinion concerning it. So that the former inducements prevailing somwhat with us before,
do now much more prevaile, when the very thing hath Ministred further Reason. If Infidels or Atheists chance at any time to call it in question, this giveth us
occasion to sift what reason there is, whereby the testimony of the Church
concerning Scripture, and our own persvasion which Scripture it self hath confirmed, may be proved a truth infallible. In which case the ancient fathers being
often constrained to shew, what warrant they had so much to rely upon the Scriptures, endeavoured still to maintain the authority of the Books of God, by arguments, such as unbelievers themselves must needs think reasonable, if they judged
thereof as they should. Neither is it a thing impossible or greatly hard, even by
such kind of proofs so to manifest and clear that point, that no man living
shall be able to deny it, without denying some apparent Principle, such as all
men acknowledge to be true. Wherefore if I believe the Gospel, yet is rea-

son

1 Cor. 10. 15.

Acts 26. 22.

son of singular use, for that it confirmeth me in this my belief the more. If I do not as yet believe, neverthelefs to bring me into the number of Believers, except reason did fomewhat help, and were an inftrument which God doth use unto fuch purpofes, what fhould it boot to difpute with Infidels, or godlefs perfons for their converfion and perfwafion in that point? Neither can I think that when grave and learned men do fometime hold, that of this Principle there is no proof but by the teftimony of the fpirit, which affureth our hearts therein, it is their meaning to exclude utterly all force which any kind of reafon may have in that behalf: but I rather incline to interpret fuch their fpeeches, as if they had more exprefly fet down, that other motives and inducements, be they never fo ftrong and confonant unto reafon, are notwithftanding ineffectual of themfelves to work faith concerning this Principle, if the fpecial grace of the Holy Ghoft concur not to the inlightning of our minds. For otherwife, I doubt not but men of wifdom and judgment will grant, that the Church in this point efpecially is furnifhed with reafon, to ftop the mouths of her impious Adverfaries: and that as it were altogether bootlefs to alleadg againft them, what the Spirit hath taught us; fo likewife that even to our own felves it needeth caution and explication, how the teftimony of the Spirit may be difcerned, by what means it may be known, left men think that the Spirit of God doth teftifie thofe things which the fpirit of Error fuggefteth. The operations of the fpirit, efpecially thefe ordinary which be common unto all true Chriftian men, are, as we know, things fecret and undifcernable even to the very foul where they are, becaufe their nature is of another and an higher kind than that they can be by us perceived in this life. Wherefore albeit the fpirit lead us into all truth, and direct us in all goodnefs; yet becaufe thefe workings of the Spirit in us are fo privy and fecret, we therefore ftand on a plainer ground, when we gather by reafon from the quality of things believed or done, that the Spirit of God hath directed us in both; than if we fettle our felves to believe, or to do any certain particular thing, as being moved thereto by the Spirit. But of this enough. To go from the books of Scripture to the fenfe and meaning thereof, becaufe the Sentences which are by the Apoftles recited out of the *Pfalms* to prove the Refurrection of Jefus Chrift, did not prove it, if fo be the Prophet *David* meant them of himfelf; this Expofition, therefore they plainly difprove, and fhew by manifeft reafon, that of *David* the words of *David* could not poffibly be meant. Exclude the ufe of natural reafoning about the fenfe of Holy Scripture, concerning the Articles of our Faith, and then that the Scripture doth concern the Articles of our Faith, who can affure us? That which by right expofition buildeth up Chriftian Faith, being mifconftrued breedeth Error: between true and falfe conftruction, the difference reafon muft fhew. Can Chriftian men perform that which *Peter* requireth at their hands? Is it poffible they fhould both believe, and be able without the ufe of reafon, to render a reafon of their beliefe, a reafon found and fufficient to anfwer them that demand it, be they of the fame faith with us, or Enemies thereunto? May we caufe our faith without reafon to appear reafonable in the eyes of men? This being required even of learners in the School of Chrift, the duty of their Teachers in the bringing them unto fuch ripenefs, muft needs be fomewhat more, then only to read the Sentences of Scripture, and then Paraphraftically to fcholy them, to vary them with fundry forms of fpeech, without arguing or difputeing about any thing which they contain. This method of teaching may commend it felf unto the world by that eafinefs and facility which is in it: but a law or a pattern it is not, as fome do imagin, for all men to follow, that will do good in the the Church of Chrift. Our Lord and Saviour himfelf did hope by difputation to do fome good, yea by difputation not only of, but againft the truth, albeit whith purpofe for the truth. That Chrift fhould be the Son of *David*, was truth, yet againft this truth our Lord in the Gofpel objecteth, If Chrift be the Son of *David*, how doth *David* call him Lord? There is as yet no way known how to difpute, or to determine of things difputed, without the ufe of natural reafon. If we pleafe to adde unto Chrift their Example, who followed him as near in all things as they could, the Sermon of *Paul* and *Barnabas* fet down in the *Acts*, where the people would have offered unto them Sacrifice: in that Sermon what is there but only natural reafon to difprove their act? *O men, why do ye thefe things? We are men even fubject to the felf-fame paffions with you: we preach unto you to leave thefe vanities, and to turn*

Acts 13.36. & cap. 2.34.

1 Pet. 3. 15.

Mat. 21. 3.

Acts 14. 15.

turn to the living God, the God that hath not left himself without witness, in that he hath done good to the world, giving rain and fruitful seasons, filling our hearts with joy and gladness. Neither did they only use reason in winning such unto a Christian belief as were yet thereto unconverted, but with believers themselves they followed the self-same course. In that great and solemn Assembly of believing Jews, how doth *Peter* prove that the Gentiles were partakers of the grace of God as well as they, but by reason drawn from those effect, which were apparantly known amongst them? *God which knows the hearts hath born them witness in giving unto them the Holy Ghost as unto you.* The light therefore which the Star of natural reason and wisdom casteth, is too bright to be obscured by the mist of a word or two, uttered to diminish that opinion which justly hath been received concerning the force and vertue thereof, even in matters that touch more neerly the principal duties of men, and the glory of the eternal God. In all which hitherto hath been spoken, touching the force and use of mans reason in things Divine, I must crave that I be not so understood or construed, as if any such thing by vertue thereof could be done without the aid and assistance of Gods most blessed Spirit : The thing we have handled according to the question moved about it : which question is, whether the light of Reason be so pernicious, that in devising laws for the Church ; men ought not by it to search what may be fit and convenient. For this cause therefore we have endeavoured to make it appear, how in the nature of reason it self there is no impediment, but that the self-same Spirit, which revealeth the things that God hath set down in his Law, may also be thought to aid and direct men in finding out by the light of reason, what laws are expedient to be made for the guiding of his Church, over and besides them that are in Scripture, Herein therefore we agree with those men, by whom humane laws are defined to be Ordinances which such as have lawful Authority given them for that purpose, do probably draw from the Laws of Nature and God, by discourse of reason, aided with the influence of Divine grace. And for that cause it is not said amiss touching Ecclesiastical Canons, that by *instinct of the Holy* *Ghost they have been made, and consecrated by the reverend acceptation of the World.*

9. Laws for the Church are not made as they should be, unless the makers follow such direction as they ought to be guided by. Wherein that Scripture standeth not the Church of God in any stead, or serveth nothing at all to direct, but may be let pass as needless to be consulted with, we judge it profane, impious, and irreligious to think. For although it were in vain to make laws which the Scripture hath already made, because what we are already there commanded to do, on our parts there resteth nothing but only that it be executed : yet because both in that which we are commanded, it concerneth the duty of the Church by law to provide, that the loosenefs and slacknefs of men may not cause the Commandements of God to be unexecuted ; and a number of things there are for which the Scripture hath not provided by any law, but left them unto the careful discretion of the Church ; we are to search how the Church in these cases may be well directed, to make that provision by laws which is most convenient and fit. And what is so in these cases, partly Scripture, and partly reason must teach to discern. Scripture comprehending examples and laws ; laws some Natural, and some Positive ; examples neither are there for all cases which require Laws to be made, and when they are, they can but direct as presedents onely. Natural laws direct in such sort, that in all things we must for ever do according unto them; Positive so, that against them in no case we may do any thing, as long as the will of God is that they should remain in force. Howbeit when Scripture doth yeild us presidents, how far forth they are to be followed ; when it giveth Natural laws, what particular order is thereunto most agreeable ; when Positive, which way to make laws unrepugnant unto them ; yea, though all these should want, yet what kind of Ordinances would be most for that good of the Church which is aimed at, all this must be by reason found out. And therefore *To refuse the* *conduct of the light of nature,* saith St. *Augustine, is not folly alone, but accompa-* *nied with impiety.* The greatest amongst the School Divines studying how to set down by exact definition the nature of an humane law, (of which nature all the Churches Constitutions are) found not which way better to do it then in these words:

Out

*Out of the Preceps of the Law of nature, as out of certain common and undemonstrable Prin-
ciples, mans reason doth necessarily proceed unto certain
more perticular determinations: which particular determinations being found out according unto the reason
of man, they have the names of humane laws, so
that such other conditions be therein kept as the making
of laws doth require; that is, if they whose authori-*
ty is thereunto required do establish and publish
them as Laws. And the truth is, that all our con-

Tho. Aqui. 2. q. 91. art 3. *Ex praeceptis Legis naturalis,
quasi ex quibusdam principio is communibus, & indemonstrabi-
libus, necesse est quod ratio humana procedat ad aliqua magis
particulariter disponenda. Est ista particulares dispositiones
adinvenire secundum rationem humanam, dicuntur leges
humanae, observatis aliis conditionibus qua pertinent ad rationem legis.*

troversie in this cause concerning the orders of the Church, is, what particulars the
Church may appoint. That which doth find them out, is the force of mans reason. That
which doth guide and direct his reason, is the first general law of nature, which law of
nature, and the moral law of Scripture are in the substance of law all one. But because
there are also in Scripture a number of Laws particular and possitive, which being in
force may not by any law of man be violated, we are in making laws to have thereunto an especial eye. As for example, it might perhaps seem reasonable unto the Church
of God, following the general laws concerning the nature of Marriage, to ordain
in particular that Cozen Germans shall not marry. Which Law notwithstanding
ought not to be received in the Church, if there should be in the Scripture a law particular to the contrary, forbidding utterly the bonds of Marriage to be so far forth
abridged. The same *Thomas* therefore whose definition of humane laws we mentioned
before, doth add thereunto this caution concerning the rule and canon whereby to
make them: *Humane laws are measures* in respect of men whose actions they must
direct; howbeit such measures they are, as have also their higher rules to be measured by, *which rules are two, the Law of God, and the law of Nature.* So that laws humane
must be made according to the general Laws of nature, and without contradiction
unto any possitive law in Scripture; Otherwise they are ill made. Unto laws thus
made & received by a whole Church, they which live within the bosom of that Church
must not think it a matter indifferent either to yield or not to yield obedience. Is it
a small offence to despise the Church of God? *My son keep thy Fathers commandement,*
saith Solomon, *and forget not thy Mothers instruction, bind them both always about thine
heart.* It doth not stand with the duty which we ow to our heavenly Father, that to
the Ordinances of our Mother the Church we should shew our selves disobedient.
Let us not say we keep the Commandements of the one, when we break the Law of
the other: for unless we observe both, we obey neither. And what doth let, but that
we may observe both, when they are not the one to the other in any sort repugnant?
for of such laws onely we speak, as being made in form and manner already declared, can
have in them no contradiction unto the Laws of Almighty God. Yea, that which is
more, the Laws thus made, God himself doth in such sort authorize, that to despise
them, is to despise in them him. It is a loose and licentious opinion which the Anabaptists have imbraced, holding that a Christian mans liberty is lost, and the soul which
Christ hath redeemed unto himself, injuriously drawn into servitude under the yoke
of humane power, if any law be now imposed besides the Gospel of Jesus Christ: in
obedience whereunto the Spirit of God, and not the constraint of men is to lead us,
according to that of the blessed Apostle, *Such as are led by the Spirit of God are the Sons
of God, and not such as live in thraldom unto men.* Their judgment is therefore that
the Church of Christ should admit no Law-makers but the Evangelists. The Author
of that which causeth another thing to be, is Author of that thing also which thereby
is caused. The light of natural understanding, wit, and reason, is from God; he it
is which thereby doth illuminate every man entring into the world. If there proceed
from us any thing afterwards corrupt and naught, the mother thereof is our own darknes, neither doth it proceed from any such cause whereof God is the Author. He is
the Author of all that we think or do by vertue of that light which himself hath given.
And therefore the Laws which the very Heathens did gather to direct their actions by,
so far forth as they proceed from the light of nature, God himself doth acknowledg to
have proceeded even from himself, and that he was the Writer of them in the
Tables of their hearts. How much more then is he the Author of those Laws
which have been made by his Saints, endued further with the heavenly grace of
his Spirit, and directed as much as might be with such instruction as his sacred
Word

1.2 q. 91. art 3.

1.2 q. 95. art 3.

1 Cor. 11. 12.
Prov. 6. 20.

Rom. 8. 14.

John 1. 4.

Rom. 1. 9.
and 2. 15.

Word doth yield? Surely if we have unto those laws that dutiful regard which their dignity doth require, it will not greatly need, that we should be exhorted to live in obedience unto them. If they have God himself for their Author, contempt which is offered unto them cannot choose but redound unto him. The safest, and unto God the most acceptable way of framing our lives therefore, is, with all Humility, Lowliness and Singleness of heart to study, which way our willing obedience both unto God and *Man* may be yeilded even to the utmost of that wich is due.

That neither Gods being the Author of laws, nor his committing them to Scripture, nor the continuance of the end for which they were instituted, is any reason sufficient to prove that they are unchangable.

Deut. 22. 10. and 22. 11.

10. Touching the mutability of Laws that concern the Regiment and Polity of the Church, changed they are, when either altogether abrogated, or in part repealed, or augmented with farther additions. Wherein we are to note, that this question about the changing of Laws, concerneth onely such laws as are positive, and do make that now good or evil by being commanded or forbidden, which otherwise of it self were not simply the one or the other. Unto such laws it is expresly sometimes added, how long they are to continue in force. If this be no where exprest, then have we no light to direct our judgments concerning the changeableness or immutability of them, but by considering the nature and quality of such Laws. The nature of every law must be judged of by the end for which it was made, and by the aptness of things therein prescribed unto the same end. It may so fall out, that the reason why some laws of God were given, is neither opened nor possible to be gathered by the wit of man. As why God should forbid *Adam* that one tree, there was no way for *Adam* ever to have certainly understood. And at *Adams* ignorance of this point Satan took advantage, urging the more securely a false cause, because the true was unto *Adam* unknown. Why the Jews were forbidden to plow their ground with an Ox and an Ass, why to cloth themselves with mingled attyre of Wooll and Linnen, it was both unto them, and to us it remaineth obscure. Such laws perhaps cannot be abrogated, saving onely by whom they were made: because the intent of them being known unto none but the Author, he alone can judge how long it is requisite they should endure. But if the reason why things were instituted may be known and being known, do appear manifestly to be of perpetual necessity; then are those things also perpetual, unless they cease to be effectual unto that purpose for which they were at first instituted. Because when a thing doth cease to be availeable unto the end which gave it being, the continuance of it must then of necessity appear superfluous. And of this we cannot be ignorant, how sometimes that hath done great good, which afterwards when time hath changed the ancient course of things, doth grow to be either very hurtful, or not so greatly profitable and necessary. If therefore the end for which a law provideth, be perpetually necessary, and the way whereby it provideth perpetually also most apt, no doubt but that every such law ought for ever to remain unchangeable. Whether God be the Author of Laws, by authorising that power of men whereby they are made, or by delivering them made immediately from himself, by word onely, or in writing also, or howsoever; notwithstanding the authority of their Maker, the mutability of that end for which they are made, maketh them also changeable. The law of Ceremonies came from God. *Moses* had commandement to commit it unto the sacred Records of Scripture, where it continueth even unto this very day and hour; in force still as the Jew surmiseth, because God himself was Author of it; and for us to abolish what he hath established, were presumption most intolerable. But (that which they in the blindness of their obdurate hearts are not able to discern) sith the end for which that Law was ordained is now fulfilled, past and gone; how should it but cease any longer to be, which hath no longer any cause of being in force as before? *That which necessity of some special time doth cause to be enjoyned, bindeth no longer then during that time, but doth afterward become free.* Which thing is also plain, even by that law which the Apostles assembled at the councel of Jerusalem did from thence deliver unto the Church of Christ; the preface whereof to authorize it, was *To the Holy Ghost and to us it hath seemed good:* which stile they did not use as matching themselves in power with the holy Ghost but as testifying the holy Ghost to be the Author, and themselves but only utterers of that decree. This law thefore to have proceeded from God as the Author thereof, no faithful man will deny. It was of God, not onely because God gave them the power whereby they might make laws, but for that it proceeded even from the holy motion and suggestion of that secret divine Spirit, whose sentence they did but

onely

Quod procceffitate temporis flatutum eft, ceffante necessitate debet ceffare pariter quod urgebat. i. q. I.

Quod pro necest Acts 15.

only pronounce. Notwithstanding, as the law of *Ceremonies* delivered unto the Jews, so this very law which the Gentiles received from the mouth of the Holy Ghost, is in like respect abrogated by decease of the end for which it was given. But such as do not stick at this point, such as grant that what hath been instituted upon any special cause, needeth not to be observed, that cause ceasing, do notwithstanding herein fail; they judge the laws of God onely by the Author and main end for which they were made, so that for us to change that which he hath established, they hold it execrable pride and presumption, if so be the end and purpose for which God by that mean provideth be permanent. And upon this they ground those ample disputes concerning orders and offices, which being by him appointed for the Government of his Church, if it be necessary always that the Church of Christ be governed, then doth the end for which God provided remain still; and therefore in those means which he by law did establish as being fittest unto that end, for us to alter any thing, is to lift up our selves against God, and as it were to countermand him. Wherein they mark not, that Laws are instruments to rule by, and that instruments are not onely to be framed according unto the general end for which they are provided, but even according unto that very particular which riseth out of the matter whereon they have to work. The end wherefore Laws were made may be permanent, and those Laws nevertheless require some alteration, if there be any unfitness in the means which they prescribe as tending unto that end and purpose. As for example, a law that to bridle theft doth punish theeves with a quadruple restitution, hath an end which will continue as long as the world it self continueth. Theft will be always, and will always need to be bridled. But that the mean which this law provideth for that end, namely, the punishment of quadruple restitution, that this will be always sufficient to bridle and restrain that kind of enormity, no man can warrant. Insufficiency of Laws doth sometimes come by want of judgment in the makers. Which cause cannot fall into any law termed properly and immediately divine, as it may and doth into humane laws often. But that which hath been once most sufficient, may wax otherwise by alteration of time and place; that punishment which hath been sometimes forcible to bridle sin, may grow afterwards too weak and feeble. In a word, we plainly perceive by the difference of those three Laws which the Jews received at the hands of God, the moral, ceremonial, and judicial, that if the end for which, and the matter according whereunto God maketh his laws, continue always one and the same, his laws also do the like, for which cause the moral law cannot be altered : Secondly, that whether the matter whereon laws are made, continue or continue not, if their end have once ceased, they cease also to be of force; as in the Law ceremonial it fareth. Finally, that albeit that end continue, as in the law of theft specified, as in a great part of those ancient Judicials it doth; yet forasmuch as there is not in all respects the same subject or matter remaining, for which they were first instituted, even this is sufficient cause of change. And therefore laws, though both ordained of God himself, and the end for which they were ordained continuing, may notwithstanding cease, if by alteration of persons or times they be found unsufficient to attain unto that end. In which respect why may we not presume, that God doth even call for such change or alteration, as the very condition of things themselves doth make necessary ? They which do therefore plead the Authority of the Law-maker, as an argument wherefore it should not be lawful to change that which he hath instituted, and will have this the cause why all the ordinances of our Saviour are immutable; they which urge the wisdome of God as a proof, that whatsoever laws he hath made, they ought to stand, unless himself from Heaven proclaim them disanuld, because it is not in man to correct the ordinance of God; may know, if it please them to take notice thereof, that we are far from presuming to think that men can better any thing which God hath done, even as we are from thinking that men should presume to undo some things of men, which God doth know they cannot better. God never ordained any thing that could be bettered. Yet many things he hath, that have been changed, and that for the better. That which succeeded as better now when change is requisite, had been worse, when that which now is changed was instituted. Otherwise God had not then left this to choose that, neither would now reject that to choose this, were it not for some new-grown occasion, making that which hath been better worse. In this case therefore men do not presume to change Gods ordinance, but they yield thereunto, requiring it

Consultp. p. 8.

self

self to be changed. Against this it is objected, that to abrogate or innovate the Gospel of Christ if Men or Angels should attempt, it were most hainous and cursed sacriledge. And the Gospel, as they say, containeth not only doctrine but also precepts concerning the regiment of the Church.

Discipline therefore is a part of the Gospel; and God being the Author of the whole Gospel, as well of discipline as of Doctrine, it cannot be but that both of them have a common cause. So that as we are to believe for ever the Articles of Evangelical doctrine, so the precepts of discipline we are in like sort bound for ever to observe. Touching points of Doctrine, as for example, the Unity of God, the Trinity of Persons, Salvation by Christ, the Resurrection of the Body, Life everlasting, the Judgment to come, and such like, they have been since the first hour that there was a Church in the World, and till the last they must be believed. But as for matters of regiment, they are for the most part of another nature. To make new articles of faith and doctrine, no man thinketh it lawful; new laws of government, what Common-wealth or Church is there which maketh not either at one time or another? *The Rule of Faith*, saith *Tertullian*, *is but one, and that alone immoveable, and impossible to be framed or cast a new*. The law of outward order and polity not so. There is no reason in the world wherefore we should esteem it as necessary always to do, as always to believe the same things; seeing every man knoweth that the matter of faith is constant, the matter contrariwise of actions daily changeable, especially the matter of action belonging unto Church-Polity. Neither can I find that men of soundest judgment have any otherwise taught, then that articles of belief, and things which all men must of necessity do to the end they may be saved, are either expresly set down in Scripture, or else plainly thereby to be gathered. But touching things which belong to discipline and outward polity, the Church hath authority to make Canons, laws and decrees, even as we read that in the Apostles times it did. Which kind of laws (forasmuch as they are not in themselves necessary to salvation) may after they are made be also changed as the difference of times or places shall require. Yea it is not denied I am sure by themselves, that cerain things in discipline are of that nature, as they may be varied by times, places, persons, and other the like circumstances. Whereupon I demand, are those changeable points of discipline commanded in the Word of God, or no? If they be not commanded, and yet may be received in the Church, how can their former position stand, condemning all things in the Church which in the Word are not commanded? if they be commanded, and yet may suffer change; how can this latter stand, affirming all things immutable which are commanded of God? Their distinction touching matters of substance and of circumstance, though true, will not serve. For be they great things, or be they small, if God have commanded them in the Gospel, and his commanding them in the Gospel do make them unchangeable, there is no reason we should more change the one then we may the other. If the authority of the Maker do prove unchangeableness in the laws which God hath made; then must all laws which he hath made be necessarily for ever permanent, though they be but of circumstance onely and not of substance. I therefore conclude, that neither Gods being author of Laws for government of his Church, nor his committing them unto Scripture, is any reason sufficient, wherefore all Churches should for ever be bound to keep them without change. But of one thing we are here to give them warning by the way. For whereas in this discourse we have often times protest, that many parts of discipline or Church-Polity are delivered in Scripture, they may perhaps imagine that we are driven to confess their discipline to be delivered in Scripture, and that having no other means to avoid it, we are fain to argue for the changablenss of laws ordained even by God himself, as if otherwise theirs of necessity should take place, and that under which we live, be abandoned: there is no remedy therefore but to abate this errour in them, and directly to let them know, that if they fall into any such conceit, they do but a little flatter their own cause. As for us, we think in no respect so highly of it. Our perswasion is, that no age ever had knowledge of it but only ours; that they which defend it, devised it; that neither Christ nor his Apostles at any time taught it, but the contrary. If therefore we did seek to maintain that which most advantageth our own cause, the very best way for us, and the strongest against them, were to hold even as they do, that in Scripture there must needs be found some particular form of Church-Polity, which God hath instituted and

which

which ᵃ for that very cause belongeth to all Churches, to all times. But with any such partial eye to respect our selves, and by cunning to make those things seem the truest which are the fittest to serve our purpose, is a thing which we neither like nor mean to follow. Wherefore that which we take to be generally true concerning the mutability of laws, the same we have plainly delivered, as being perswaded of nothing more then we are of this, ᵇ that whether it be in matter of speculation or of practice, no untruth can possibly availe the patron and defender long, and that things most truly are likewise most behovefully spoken.

Diſciplina eſt chriſtiana Eccleſia politia, à Deo ejus recte adminiſtrande cauſa conſtituta, ac propterea ex ejus verbo petenda, & ob eandem cauſam

omnium Eccleſiarum communis & omnium temporum. l. 3. de Eccleſ. Diſcip. in Anala. ᵇ *Εὔλογον ἐκ δι ἀληθεῖς τῆς λόγοις, ἢ μόνον πρὸς τὸ εἰδέναι χρησιμώτατοι ὑϊ, ἀλλὰ ἢ πρὸς ἢ βίον. Συναθεῖ ἢ ἀντὶς ἄρρητις μαῖυοντω.* Ariſt. Et. l. 1. 10. c. 1.

11 This we hold and grant for truth, that those very laws which of their own nature are changeable, be notwithſtanding uncapable of change, if he which gave them being of authority ſo to do, forbid abſolutely to change them; neither may they admit alteration againſt the will of ſuch a Law-maker. Albeit therefore we do not find any cauſe why of right there ſhould be neceſſarily an immutable form ſet down in holy Scripture; neverthelesſ, if indeed there have been at any time a Church-Polity ſo ſet down, the change whereof the ſacred Scripture doth forbid, ſurely for men to alter thoſe Laws which God for perpetuity hath eſtabliſhed, were preſumption moſt intolerable. To prove therefore that the will of Chriſt was to eſtabliſh laws ſo permanent and immutable that in any ſort to alter them cannot but highly offend God, thus they reaſon. Firſt, If *Moſes* being but a ſervant in the houſe of God, did therein eſtabliſh laws of government for a perpetuity; laws, which they that were of the houſhold might not alter : ſhall we admit into our thoughts, that the Son of God hath in providing for this his houſhold declared himſelf less faithful then *Moſes*? *Moſes* delivering unto the Jews ſuch laws as were durable, if thoſe be changable which Chriſt hath delivered unto us, we are not able to avoid it, but (that which to think were heinous impiety) we of neceſſity muſt confeſs, even the Son of God himſelf to have been less faithful then *Moſes*. Which argument ſhall need no touchſtone to try it

Heb. 3. 6. Either that commendation of the Son before the ſervant is a falſe teſtimony, or this Son ordained a permanent government in the Church. If permanent, then not to be changed. What then do they that hold it may be changed at the Magiſtrates Pleaſure, but advise the Magiſtrate by his poſitive laws to proclaim that it is his will; that if there ſhall be a Church within his Dominions, he will maim and deform the ſame? *M. M. Pag. 16.* He that was as faithful as *Moſes*, left as clear inſtruction for the government of the Church. But Chriſt was as faithful as *Moſes*; ergo. *Demonſt. of Diſc. cap. 1.*

by, but ſome other of the like making: *Moſes* erected in the Wilderneſs a Tabernacle, which was moveable from place to place; *Salomon* a ſumptuous and ſtately Temple, which was not moveable; therefore *Salomon* was faithfuller then *Moſes*; which no man indued with reaſon will think. And yet by this reaſon it doth plainly follow. He that will ſee how faithful the one or the other was, muſt compare the things which they both did, unto the charg which God gave each of them. The Apoſtle in making compariſon between our Saviour and *Moſes*, attributeth faithfulneſs unto both, and maketh this difference between them; *Moſes in*, but *Chriſt over* the houſe of God; *Moſes* in that houſe which was *his by charge* and commiſſion, though to govern it, yet to govern it *as a ſervant*; but *Chriſt* over this houſe as being *his own intire poſſeſſion*. Our Lord and Saviour doth make proteſtation, *I have given unto them the words which thou gaveſt me.* Faithful therefore he was, and concealed not any part of his Fathers will. But did any part of that will require the immutability of Laws concerning Church-Polity? They anſwer, yea; For elſe God ſhould leſs favour us than the Jews. God would not have their Churches guided by any laws but his own. And ſeeing this did ſo continue even till Chriſt, now to eaſe God of that care, or rather to deprive the Church of his patronage what reaſon have we? Surely none, to derogate any thing from the ancient love which God hath born to his Church. An Heathen Philoſopher there is, who conſidering how many things beaſts have which men have not, how naked in compariſon of them, how impotent, and how much leſs able we are to ſhift for our ſelves a long time after we enter into this World, repiningly concluded hereupon, that Nature being a careful Mother for them, is towards us a hard-hearted Stepdame. No, we may not meaſure the affection of our gracious God towards his

Iohn 17.

Either God hath left a preſcript form of Government, or elſe he is I ſe consfull under the new Teſtament then under the old *Demonſt. of Diſc. cap. 1*

by

by such differences. For even herein shineth his wisdom, that though the wayes of his providence be many, yet the end which he bringeth all at the length unto, is one and the self-same. But if such kind of reasoning were good, might we not even as directly conclude the very same concerning laws of secular regiment? Their own words are these; *In the ancient Church of the Jews, God did command, and Moses commit unto writing, all things pertinent as well to the Civil as to the Ecclesiastical state.* God gave them laws of civil regiment, and would not permit their Commonweal to be governed by any other laws than his own. Doth God less regard our temporal estate in this world, or provide for it worse then theirs? To us notwithstanding he hath not as to them delivered any particular form of temporal regiment, unless perhaps we think, as some do, that the grafting of the Gentiles and their incorporating into *Israel*, doth import that we ought to be subject unto the rites and laws of their whole Polity. We see then how weak such disputes are, and how small they make to this purpose. That Christ did not mean to set down particular positive Laws for all things in such sort as *Moses* did, the very different manner of delivering the Laws of *Moses* and the Laws of Christ doth plainly shew. *Moses* had commandement to gather the ordinances of God together distinctly, and orderly to set them down according unto their several kinds; for each publique duty and office, the laws that belong thereto, as appeareth in the books themselves written of purpose for that end. Contrariwise the Laws of Christ we find rather mentioned by occasion in the writings of the Apostles, then any solemn thing directly written to comprehend them in legal sort. Again, the positive laws which *Moses* gave, they were given for the greatest part with restraint to the land of *Jury*; Behold, saith *Moses*, *I have taught you ordinances and Laws as the Lord my God commanded me, that ye should do so even within the land whither ye go to possess it.* Which Laws and Ordinances positive he plainly distinguished afterward from the laws of the two Tables which were moral; *The Lord spake unto you out of the midst of the fire, ye heard the voyce of the words, but saw no similitude, onely a voyce. Then he declared unto you his Covenant which he commanded you to do, the ten Commandements, and wrote them upon two Tables of stone. And the Lord commanded me that same time, that I should teach you ordinances and laws which ye should observe in the land whither ye go to possess it.* The same difference is again set down in the next Chapter following. For rehearsal being made of the ten Commandements, it followeth immediately; *These words the Lord spake unto all your multitude in the Mount out of the midst of the fire, the cloud and the darkness, with a great voice, and added no more, and wrote them upon two Tables of stone, and delivered them unto me.* But concerning other laws, the people give their consent to receive them at the hands of *Moses*; *Go thou neerer, and hear all that the Lord our God saith unto thee, and we will hear it and do it.* The peoples alacrity herein God highly commendeth with most effectual and hearty speech; *I have heard the voyce of the words of this people; they have spoken well: O that there were such an heart in them to fear me, and to keep all my Commandements always, that it might go well with them, and with their children for ever! Go, say unto them, Return you to your Tents; But stand thou here with me, and I will tell thee all the Commandements and Ordinances and the Laws which thou shalt teach them, that they may do them in the land which I have given them to possess.* From this latter kind the former are plainly distinguished in many things. They were not both at one time delivered, neither both after one sort, nor to one end. The former uttered by the voice of God himself in the hearing of six hundred thousand men; the former written with the finger of God; the former termed by the name of Covenant; the former given to be kept without either mention of time how long, or of that place where. On the other side, the latter given after, and neither written by God himself, nor given unto the whole multitude immediately from God, but unto *Moses*, and from him to them both by word and writing; The latter termed Ceremonies, Judgements, Ordinances, but nowhere Covenants; finally, the observation of the latter restrained unto the Land where God would establish them to inhabit. The Laws positive are not framed without regard had to the place and persons for the which they are made. If therefore Almighty God in framing their Laws, had an eye unto the nature of that people, and to the Countrey where they were to dwell; if these peculiar and proper considerations were respected in the making of their laws, and must be also regarded in the Positive laws of all other Nations besides; then

Ecclesiast. Disc. lib. 1.

Rom. 11. 16.
Ephes. 2. 12. 16.

Deut. 4. 5.

Vorse 12, 13, 14.

Deut. 5. 22.

27.
28.
29.

30.
31.

then seeing that Nations are not all alike, surely the giving of one kind of Positive laws unto one only people, without any liberty to alter them, is but a slender proof, and therefore one kind should in like sort be given to serve everlastingly for all. But that which most of all maketh for the clearing of this point, is, that the Jews who had laws so particularly determining and so fully instructing them in all affaires what to do, were notwithstanding continually inured with causes exorbitant, and such as their laws had not provided for. And in this point much more is granted as then we ask, namely, that for one thing which we have left to the order of the Church, they had twenty which were undecided by the express Word of God; and that as their Ceremonies and Sacraments were multiplied above ours, even so grew the number of those cases which were not determined by any express word. So that if we may devise one law, they by this reason might devise twenty: and if their devising so many were not forbidden, shall their example prove us forbidden to devise as much as one law for the ordering of the Church? We might not devise no not one, if their example did prove that our Saviour hath utterly forbidden all alteration of his laws, inasmuch as there can be no law devised, but needs it must either take away from his, or add thereunto more or less, and so make some kind of alteration. But of this so large a grant we are content not to take advantage. Men are oftentimes in a sudden passion more liberal, then they would be if they had leisure to take advice: And therefore so bountiful words of course and franck speeches we are contented to let pass, without turning them to advantage with too much rigour. It may be they had rather be listened unto, when they commend the Kings of Israel which attempted nothing in the government of the Church without the express Word of God; and when they urge that God left nothing in his Word undescribed, whether it concerned the Worship of God or outward Polity, nothing unset down, and therefore charged them strictly to keep themselves unto that, without any alteration. Howbeit seeing it cannot be denyed, but that many things there did belong unto the course of their publique affaires, wherein they had no express word at all to shew precisely what they should do; the difference between their condition and ours in these cases, will bring some light unto the truth of this present controversie. Before the fact of the Son of *Shelomith*, there was no law which did appoint any certain punishment for Blasphemers; That wretched creature being therefore deprehended in that impiety, was held in Ward, till the mind of the Lord was known concerning his case. The like practice is also mentioned upon occasion of a breach of the Sabbath Day. They find a poor silly creature gathering sticks in the Wilderness; they bring him unto *Moses* and *Aaron* and all the Congregation; they lay him in hold, because it was not declared what should be done with him, till God had said unto *Moses*, *this man shall dye the death.* The law required to keep the Sabbath Day: but for the breach of the Sabbath what punishment should be inflicted, it did not appoint. Such occasions as these are rare. And for such things as do fall scarce one in many ages of men, it did suffice to take such order as was requisite when they fell. But if the case were such as being not already determined by Law, were notwithstanding likely oftentimes to come into question, it gave occasion of adding laws that were not before. Thus it fell out in the case of those men polluted, and of the Daughters of *Zelophehad*, whose causes *Moses* having brought before the Lord, received laws to serve for the like in time to come. The Jews to this end had the Oracle of God, they had the Prophets. And by such means God himself instructed them from heaven what to do in all things that did greatly concern their state, and were not already set down in the law. Shall we then hereupon argue even against our own experience and knowledge? Shall we seek to perswade men, that of necessity it is with us as it was with them, that because God is ours in all respects as theirs, therefore either no such way of direction hath been at any time, or if it hath been, it doth still continue in the Church, or if the same do not continue, that yet it must be at the least supplied by some such means as pleaseth us to account of equal force? A more dutiful and religious way for us were to admire the wisdome of God, which shineth in the beautiful variety of all things? but most in the manifold and yet harmonious dissimilitude of those ways, whereby his Church upon Earth is guided from Age to Age throughout all generations of Men. The Jews were necessarily to continue till the comming of Christ in the flesh, and the gathering of Nations unto him. So much the promise made

[Marginal notes:]
T.C.l. pag.35. Where as you say that they had nothing, but it was either mined by the law, and we have many things undecided and left to the order of the Church: I will offer for one that you shall bring that we have left to the order of the Church, to shew you that they had twenty which were undecided by the express Word of God.

T.C. in the table of his second Book. *T.C.l.2.p.446.* If he will needs Separate the Worship of God from the external Polity; yet as the Lord setforth the one, so he left nothing undescribed in the other.

Levit. 24.11.
Num.15.34.

Num. 9.
Num. 17.

Gen 11. 18.

made unto *Abraham* did import. So much the Prophesie of *Jacob* at the hour of his death did foreshew. Upon the safety therefore of their very outward state and condition for so long, the after good of the whole world, and the salvation of all did depend. Unto their so long safety, for two things it was necessary to provide, namely, the preservation of their state against forreign resistance, and the continuance of their peace within themselves. Touching the one, as they received the promise of God to be the Rock of their defence, against which who so did violently rush, should but bruise and batter themselves; so likewise they had his commandment in all their affairs that way, to seek direction and counsel from him. Mens consultations are always perillous. And it falleth out many times that after long deliberation, those things are by their wit even resolved on, which by tryal are found most opposite to publique safety. It is no impossible thing for States, be they never so well established, yet by over-sight in some one act or treaty between them and their potent opposites, utterly to cast away themselves for ever. Wherefore lest it should so fall out to them, upon whom so much did depend; they were not permitted to enter into War, nor conclude any league of Peace, nor to wade through any act of moment between them and forreign States, unless the Oracle of God or his Prophets were first consulted with. And lest domestical disturbance should waste them within themselves, because there was nothing unto this purpose more effectual, then if the authority of their Laws and Governours were such, as none might presume to take exception against it, or to shew disobedience unto it, without incurring the hatred and detestation of all men that had any spark of the fear of God; therefore he gave them even their positive laws from Heaven, and as oft as occasion required, chose in like sort Rulers also to lead and govern them. Notwithstanding some desperately impious there were which adventured to try what harm it could bring upon them, if they did attempt to be Authors of Confusion, and to resist both Governors and Laws. Against such Monsters God maintained his own, by fearful execution of extraordinary judgement upon them. By which means it came to pass, that although they were a people infested and mightily hated of all others throughout the World, although by nature hard-hearted, querulous, wrathful, and impatient of rest and quietness, yet was there nothing of force either one way or other to work the ruine and subversion of their State, till the time before mentioned was expired. Thus we see that there was no cause of dissimilitude in these things, between that one onely people before Christ, and the Kingdoms of the World since. And whereas it is further alledged, that albeit *in Civil matters and things pertaining to this present life, God hath used a greater particularity with them then amongst us, framing laws according to the quality of that People and Countrey; yet the leaving of us at greater liberty in things civil, is so far from proving the like liberty in things pertaining to the Kingdom of Heaven, that it rather proves a straiter bond. For even as when the Lord would have his favour more appear by temporal blessings of this life towards the people under the Law then towards us, he gave also politick Laws most exactly, whereby they might both most easily come into, and most stedfastly remain in possession of those earthly benefits: even so at this time, wherein he would not have his favour so much esteemed by those outward commodities, it is required, that as his care in prescribing Laws for that purpose hath somewhat fallen, in leaving them to mens consultations, which may be deceived; so his care for conduct and government of the life to come, should (if it were possible) rise, in leaving less to the order of men then in times past.* These are but weak and feeble disputes for the inference of that conclusion which is intended. For saving onely in such consideration as hath been shewed, there is no cause wherefore we should think God more desirous to manifest his favour by temporal blessings towards them, then towards us. · Godliness had unto them, and it hath also unto us, the promises both of this life and the life to come. That the care of God hath fallen in earthly things, and therefore should rise as much in heavenly; that more is left unto mens consultations in the one, and therefore less must be granted in the other; that God having used a greater particularity with them then with us for matters pertaining unto this life, is to make amends by the more exact delivery of Laws for Government of the life to come; these are proportions, whereof if there be any rule, we must plainly confess that which truth is, we know it not. God which spake unto them by his Prophets, hath unto us spoke by his onely begotten Son; those Mysteries of Grace and Salvation which were but darkly

disclosed

T. C. l. 2. f. 4 ; 5. [margin note]

disclosed unto them, have unto us more clearly shined. Such differences between them and us the Apostles of Christ have well acquainted us withall. But as for matter belonging to the outward conduct or government of the Church; seeing that even in sense it is manifest, that our Lord and Saviour hath not by positive Laws descended so far into particularities with us, as *Moses* with them; neither doth by extraordinary means, Oracles and Prophets, direct us, as them he did, in those things which rising daily by new occasions, are of necessity to be provided for; doth it not hereupon rather follow, that although not to them, yet to us there should be freedom and liberty granted to make Laws? Yea, but the Apostle S. *Paul* doth fearfully charge Timothy, *even in the sight of God who quickneth all, and of Christ Jesus who witnessed that famous confession before Pontius Pilate, to keep what was commanded him, safe and sound till the appearance of our Lord Jesus Christ.* This doth exclude all liberty of changing the Laws of Christ, whether by abrogation or addition, or howsoever. For in *Timothy* the whole Church of Christ receiveth charge concerning her duty. And that charge is to keep the Apostles commandment: And his commandment did contain the Laws that concerned Church Government: And those Laws he straightly requireth to be observed without breach or blame, till the appearance of our Lord Jesus Christ. In Scripture we grant every mans lesson, to be the common instruction of all men, so far forth as their cases are like, and that religiously to keep the Apostles commandments in whatsoever they may concern us, we all stand bound. But touching that commandment which *Timothy* was charged with, we swerve undoubtedly from the Apostles precise meaning, if we extend it so largely that the arms thereof shall reach unto all things which were commanded him by the Apostle. The very words themselves do restrain themselves unto some special Commandment among many. And therefore it is not said, Keep *the Ordinances, Laws, and Constitutions which thou hast received;* but ἐντολὴν, *that great Commandment,* which doth principally concern thee and thy calling; that commandment which Christ did so often inculcate unto *Peter;* that commandment which the careful discharge whereof they of *Ephesus* are exhorted, *Attend to your selves, and to all the flock; wherein the Holy Ghost hath placed you Bishops to feed the Church of God, which he hath purchased by his own blood;* finally, that commandment which unto the same *Timothy* is by the same Apostle even in the same form and manner afterwards again urged, *I charge thee in the sight of God and the Lord Jesus Christ, which will judge the quick and dead at his appearance and in his Kingdom, preach the Word of God.* When *Timothy* was instituted in that Office, then was the credit and trust of this duty committed unto his faithful care. The Doctrine of the Gospel was then given him, *as the precious talent or treasure of Jesus Christ;* then received he for performance of this duty, the special gift of the Holy Ghost. To keep this commandment immaculate and blameless, *was to teach the Gospel of Christ without mixture of corrupt and unsound Doctrine,* such as a number even in those times intermingled with the mysteries of Christian Belief. *Till the appearance of Christ to keep it so,* doth not import the time wherein it should be kept, but rather the time whereunto the final reward for keeping it was reserved: according to that of S. *Paul* concerning himself, *I have kept the faith; for the residue, there is laid up for me a crown of Righteousness; which the Lord the righteous Judge shall in that Day render unto me.* If they that labour in this Harvest should respect but the present fruit of their painful travel, a poor encouragement it were unto them to continue therein all the days of their life. But their reward is great in Heaven; the Crown of Righteousness which shall be given them in that day is honorable. The fruit of their industry then shall they reap with full contentment and satisfaction, but not till then. Wherein the greatness of their reward is abundantly sufficient to countervail the tediousness of their expectation. Wherefore till then they that are in labour must rest in hope. O *Timothy*, keep that which is committed unto thy charge; that great Commandment which thou hast received, keep, till the appearance of our Lord Jesus Christ. In which sense, although we judge the Apostles words to have been uttered; yet hereunto we do not require them to yield, that think any other construction more sound. It therefore it be rejected, and theirs esteemed more probable, which hold that the last words do import perpetual observation of the Apostles Commandment imposed necessarily for ever upon the Militant Church of Christ; let them withall

Margin notes: 1 Tim 6.14. Iohn 18.37. Iohn 21.15. Acts 20.28. 1 Tim. 6. 1 Tim. 6.20. † παρακαταθήκην. 1 Tim. 4.14. 2 Tim. 4.7.

consider, that then his Commandment cannot so largely be taken, to comprehend whatsoever the Apostle did command *Timothy*. For themselves do not all binde the Church unto some things whereof *Timothy* received charge, and namely unto that Precept concerning the choice of Widows. So as they cannot hereby maintain, that all things positively commanded concerning the affairs of the Church, were commanded for perpetuity. And we do not deny that certain things were commanded to be, though positive, yet perpetual in the Church. They should not therefore urge against us places that seem to forbid change, but rather such as set down some measure of alteration; which measure if we have exceeded, then might they therewith charge us justly: whereas now they themselves both granting, and also using liberty to change, cannot in reason dispute absolutely against all change. Christ delivered no inconvenient or unmeet Laws. Sundry of ours they hold inconvenient. Therefore such Laws they cannot possibly hold to be Christs. Being not his, they must of necessity grant them added unto his. Yet certain of those very Laws so added, they themselves do not judge unlawful; as they plainly confess, both in matter of prescript attire, and of rites appertaining to burial.

Their own Protestations are, that they plead against the inconvenience, not the unlawfulness of Popish Apparel; and against the inconvenience, not the unlawfulness of Ceremonies in burial. Therefore they hold it a thing not unlawful to adde to the Laws of Jesus Christ; and so consequently they yield, that no Law of Christ forbiddeth addition unto Church Laws. The judgement of *Calvin* being alledged against them, to whom of all men they attribute most, whereas his words be plain, that for Ceremonies and external Discipline, the Church hath power to make Laws; the answer which hereunto they make, is, that indefinitely the speech is true, and that so it was meant by him, namely, that some things belonging unto External Discipline and Ceremonies, are in the power and arbitriment of the Church; but neither was it meant, neither is it true generally, that all external Discipline, and all Ceremonies are left to the Order of the

T. C. l 3. p. 141. My reasons do never conclude the unlawfulness of these ceremonies of Burial, but the inconvenience and inexpedience of them. *And in the Table.* Of the inconvenience, nor of the unlawfulness of Popish apparel and ceremonies in burial. *T. C. 4. p. 32.* Upon the indefinite speaking of *M. Calvin,* saying, Ceremonies and external discipline, without adding all or some, you go about subti'ly to make men believe, that Mr. *Calvin* had placed the whole external discipline in the power and arbitrement of the Church. For if all external discipline were arbitrary, and in the choice of the Church, Excommunication also, (which is a part of it) might be cast away, which I think you will not say. *And in the very next words before.* Where you will give to understand that ceremonies and external discipline are not prescribed particularly by the Word of God, and therefore left to the order of the Church: you must understand that all external discipline is not left to the orders of the Church, being particularly prescribed in the Scriptures, no more then all ceremonies are left to the order of the Church, or the Sacraments of Baptism, and the Supper of the Lord.

Church, in as much as the Sacraments of Baptism and the Supper of the Lord are Ceremonies, which yet the Church may not therefore abrogate. Again, Excommunication is a part of external Discipline; which might also be cast away, if all external Discipline were arbitrary, and in the choice of the Church. By which their answer it doth appear, that touching the names of Ceremony and external Discipline, they gladly would have us so understood, as if we did herein contain a great deal more then we do. The fault which we finde with them, is, that they over much abridge the Church of her power in these things. Whereupon they recharge us, as if in these things we gave the Church a liberty which hath no limits or bounds; as if all things which the name of Discipline containeth, were at the Churches free choice; so that we might either have Church-Governours and Government, or want them; either retain or reject Church Censures as we list. They wonder at us as at men which think it so indifferent what the Church doth in matters of Ceremonies, that it may be feared lest we judge the very Sacraments themselves to be held at the Churches pleasure. No; the name of Ceremonies we do not use in so large a meaning, as to bring Sacraments within the compass and reach thereof; although things belonging unto the outward form and seemly administration of them, are contained in that name, even as we use it. For the name of Ceremonies we use as they themselves do, when they speak *T. C. l. 2. p. 171.* after this sort: *The Doctrine and Discipline of the Church, as the weightiest things, ought especially to be looked unto; but the Ceremonies also, as Mint and Cummin, ought not to be neglected.* Besides, in the matter of External Discipline or Regiment

ment it self, we do not deny but there are some things whereto the Church is bound till the worlds end. So as the question is onely how far the bounds of the Churches liberty do reach. We hold that the power which the Church hath lawfully to make Laws and Orders for it self, doth extend unto sundry things of Ecclesiastical jurisdiction, and such other matters, whereto their opinion is, that the Churches authority and power doth not reach. Whereas therefore in disputing against us about this point, they take their compass a great deal wider then the truth of things can afford, producing reasons and arguments by way of generality, to prove that Christ hath set down all things belonging any way unto the form of ordering his Church, and hath absolutely forbidden change by addition or diminution great or small (for so their manner of disputing is:) we are constrained to make our defence, by shewing that Christ hath not deprived his Church so far of all liberty in making orders and laws for it self, and that they themselves do not think he hath so done. For are they able to shew that all particular customs, rites, and orders of reformed Churches, have been appointed by Christ himself? No; They grant that in matter of circumstance they alter that which they have received; but in things of substance they keep the laws of Christ without change. If we say the same in our own behalf (which surely we may do with a great deal more truth) then must they cancel all that hath been before alledged, and begin to enquire afresh, Whether we retain the Laws that Christ hath delivered concerning matters of substance, yea or no. For our constant perswasion in this point is as theirs, that we have nowhere altered the Laws of Christ, further then in such particulars onely, as have the nature of things changeable acording to the difference of times, places, persons, and other the like circumstances. Christ hath commanded prayers to be made, Sacraments be ministred, his Church to be carefully taught and guided. Concerning every of these, somewhat Christ hath commanded which must be kept till the worlds end. On the contrary side, in every of them somewhat there may be added, as the Church shall judge it expedient. So that if they will speak to purpose, all which hitherto hath been disputed of they must give over, and stand upon such particulars onely, as they can shew we have either added or abrogated, otherwise then we ought in the matter of Church Politie. Whatsoever Christ hath commanded for ever to be kept in his Church, the same we take not upon us to abrogate; and whatsoever our laws have thereunto added besides, of such quality we hope it is, as no law of Christ doth any where condemn. Wherefore that all may be laid together, and gathered into a narrow room. First, so far forth as the Church is the Mystical Body of Christ, and his invisible Spouse, it needeth no external Polity. That very part of the Law Divine which teacheth faith and works of righteousness, is it self alone sufficient for the Church of God in that respect. But as the Church is a visible Society and Body-Politique, laws of Polity it cannot want. Secondly, Whereas therefore it cometh in the second place to be inquired, what laws are fittest and best for the Church; they who first embraced that rigorous and strict opinion, which depriveth the Church of liberty to make any kinde of law for her self, inclined (as it should seem) thereunto, for that they imagined all things which the Church doth without commandment of Holy Scripture, subject to that reproof which the Scripture it self useth in certain cases, when Divine Authority ought alone to be followed. Hereupon they thought it enough for the cancelling of any kinde of order whatsoever to say, *The Word of God teacheth it not, it is a device of the brain of man, away with it therefore out of the Church.* S. *Augustine* was of another minde, who speaking of fasts on the Sunday, saith, *That he which would choose out that day to fast on, should give thereby no small offence to the Church of God, which had received a contrary custom. For in these things whereof the Scripture appointeth no certainty, the use of the people of God, or the Ordinances of our Fathers, must serve for a Law. In which case if we dispute, and condemn one sort by anothers custom; it will be but matter of endless contention; where, forasmuch as the labour of reasoning shall hardly beat into mens heads any certain or necessary truth, surely it standeth us upon to take heed, lest with the tempest of strife, the brightness of charity and love be darkned.* If all things must be commanded of God which may be practised of his Church, I would know what commandment the *Gileadites* had to erect that altar which is spoken of in the Book of *Joshua.* Did not congruity of reason induce them thereunto, and suffice for defence of their fact? I would know what Commandment

the

the Women of Ifrael had yearly to mourn and lament in the memory of *Jephthahs*
daughter; what commandment the *Jews* had to celebrate their feast of *Dedication* never
spoken of in the Law, yet folemnized even by our Saviour himfelf; what commandment finally they had for the ceremony of odors ufed about the bodies of the dead,
after which cuftom notwithftanding (fith it was their cuftom) our Lord was contented that his own moft precious body fhould be intombed. Wherefore to reject all
orders of the Church which men have eftablifhed, is to think worfe of the Laws of
men in this refpect, then either the judgement of wife men alloweth, or the Law
of God it felf will bear. Howbeit, they which had once taken upon them to condemn all things done in the Church, and not commanded of God to be done, faw it
was neceffary for them (continuing in defence of this their opinion) to hold that
needs there muft be in Scripture fet down a compleat particular form of Church-
Polity, a form prefcribing how all the affairs of the Church muft be ordered, a form
in no refpect lawful to be altered by mortal men. For reformation of which overfight and errour in them, there were that thought it a part of Chriftian love and charity to inftruct them better, and to open unto them the difference between matters
of perpetual neceffity to all mens falvation, and matters of Ecclefiaftical Polity : the
one both fully and plainly taught in holy Scripture; the other not neceffary to be in
fuch fort there prefcribed; the one not capable of any diminution or augmentation
at all by men, the other apt to admit both. Hereupon the Authors of the former
opinion were prefently feconded by other wittier and better learned, who being
loth that the form of Church-Polity which they fought to bring in, fhould be otherwife then in the higheft degree accounted of, took firft an exception againft the difference between Church-Polity and matters of neceffity to falvation. 2. Againft the
reftraint of Scripture, which (they fay) receiveth injury at our hands, when we teach
that it teacheth not as well matters of Polity as of Faith and Salvation. 3. Conftrained hereby we have been therefore, both to maintain that diftinction, as a thing
not onely true in it felf, but by them likewife fo acknowledged, though unawares.
4. And to make manifeft that from Scripture, we offer not to derogate the leaft thing
that truth thereunto doth claim, inafmuch as by us it is willingly confeft, that the
Scripture of God is a ftore-houfe abounding with ineftimable Treafures of wifdom
and knowledge in many kindes, over and above things in this one kinde barely neceffary; yea, even that matters of Ecclefiaftical Polity are not therein omitted, but
taught alfo, albeit not fo taught as thofe other things before mentioned. For fo perfectly are thofe things taught, that nothing ever can need to be added, nothing ever
ceafe to be neceffary : Thefe on the contrary fide, as being of a far other nature and
quality, not fo ftrictly nor everlaftingly commanded in Scripture, but that unto the
compleat form of Church-Polity much may be requifite which the Scripture teacheth not, and much which it hath taught, become unrequifite, fometime becaufe
we need not ufe it, fometimes alfo becaufe we cannot. In which refpect, for mine
own part, although I fee that certain Reformed Churches, the Scottifh efpecially
and French, have not that which beft agreeth with the facred Scripture, I mean
the Government that is by Bifhops, inafmuch as both thofe Churches are fallen
under a different kinde of Regiment; which to remedy it, is for the one altogether too late, and too foon for the other, during their prefent affliction and trouble : This their defect and imperfection I had rather lament in fuch cafe then exa-
gitate, confidering that men oftentimes without any fault of their own, may be
driven to want that kinde of Politie or Regiment which is beft ; and to content themfelves with that, which either the irremediable errour of former time, or the neceffity of the prefent hath caft upon them. 5. Now, becaufe that Pofition firft mentioned, which holdeth it neceffary that all things which the Church may lawfully do
in her own Regiment be commanded in Holy Scripture; hath by the latter Defenders thereof been greatly qualified; who, though perceiving it to be over-extream,
are notwithftanding loth to acknowledge any overfight therein, and therefore labour what they may to falve it by conftruction ; we have for the more perfpicuity
delivered what was thereby meant at the firft. 6. How injurious a thing it were
unto all the Churches of God for men to hold it in that meaning. 7. And
how imperfect their Interpretations are who fo much labour to help it, either
by dividing Commandments of Scripture into two kindes, and fo defending

Iudg. 11.40.
I Iohn 10.20.

Iohn 19.40.

1.

2.

3.

4.

5.

6.

7.

that

that all things must be commanded, if not in special, yet in general Precepts.

8. Or by taking it as meant that in case the Church do devise any new Order, she ought therein to follow the direction of Scripture onely, and not any Star-light of Mans Reason. 9. Both which evasions being cut off, we have in the next place declared after what sort the Church may lawfully frame to her self Laws of Polity, and in what reckoning such Positive Laws both are with God, and should be with men. 10. Furthermore, because to abridge the liberty of the Church in this behalf, it hath been made a thing very odious, that when God himself hath devised some certain Laws, and committed them to sacred Scripture, man by abrogation, addition, or any way, should presume to alter and change them; it was of necessity to be examined, Whether the authority of God in making, or his care in committing those his Laws unto Scripture, be sufficient argument to prove that God doth in no case allow they should suffer any such kinde of change. 11. The last refuge for proof that Divine Laws of Christian Church-Polity may not be altered, by extinguishment of any old, or addition of new in that kinde, is partly a marvellous strange Discourse, that Christ (unless he would shew himself not so faithful as *Moses*, or not so wise as *Lycurgus* and *Solon*) must needs have set down in Holy Scripture some certain compleat, and unchangeable form of Polity; and partly a coloured shew of some evidence, where change of that sort of Laws may seem expresly forbidden, although in truth nothing less be done. I might have added hereunto their more familiar and popular disputes, as, The Church is a City, yea, the City of the great King, and the life of a City is Polity: The Church is the House of the living God; and what house can there be without some order for the government of it? In the royal house of a Prince there must be Officers for government, such as not any servant in the house but the Prince, whose the house is, shall judge convenient: So the house of God must have orders for the Government of it, such as not any of the Houshold, but God himself hath appointed. It cannot stand with the love and wisdom of God, to leave such order untaken as is necessary for the due government of his Church. The numbers, degrees, orders, and attire of *Salomons* Servants did shew his wisdom; therefore he which is greater then *Salomon*, hath not failed to leave in his house such orders for government thereof, as may serve to be as a looking-glass for his providence, care, and wisdom to be seen in. That little spark of the light of nature which remaineth in us, may serve us for the affairs of this life; But as in all other matters concerning the Kingdom of Heaven, so principally in this which concerneth the very government of that Kingdom, needful it is we should be taught of God. ' As long as men are perswaded of any order that it is onely of men, they presume of their own understanding, ' and they think to devise another not onely as good, but better then that which they ' have received. By severity of punishment this presumption and curiosity may be re-' strained. But that cannot work such cheerful obedience as is yielded where the con-' science hath respect to God as the Author of Laws and Orders. This was it which ' countenanced the Laws of *Moses* made concerning outward Polity for the administra-' tion of Holy things. The like some Law-givers of the Heathen did pretend, but ' falsly; yet wisely discerning the use of this perswasion. For the better obedience ' sake therefore it was expedient, that God should be Author of the Polity of his ' Church. But to what issue doth all this come? A man would think that they which ' hold out with such discourses, were of nothing more fully perswaded then of this, ' that the Scripture hath set down a compleat form of Church-Polity, universal, per-' petual, altogether unchangeable. For so it would follow, if the premises were found and strong to such effect as is pretended. Notwithstanding, they which have thus formally maintained argument in defence of the first oversight, are by the very evidence of truth themselves constrained to make this in effect their conclusion, that the Scripture of God hath many things concerning Church-Polity; that of those many, some are of greater weight, some of less; that what hath been urged as touching immutability of laws, it extendeth in truth no further then onely to laws wherein things of greater moment are prescribed. Now those things of greater moment, what are they? Forsooth, *Doctors, Pastors, Lay-Elders, Elderships compounded of these three; Synods consisting of many Elderships, Deacons, Women Church-servants, or Widows; free consent of the people unto actions of greatest moment, after they be by Churches or Synods orderly resolved.* All *this form* of Polity (if yet we may term that a form of building, when men have

laid

a *Nisi Reip. sua statum omnem constituere magistratus ordinavit, singulorum munera potestatemq; descripsit, qua jud cio rumsorsq; ratio habenda quomodo civium siniende litis: non solum minus Ecclesie Christiana providit quam Moses olim Iudaica, sed quam a Lycurgo Solone, Numa, civitatibus, suis prospectum sit. l. ib. de Ecclesiast. Disc.*

The defence of godly Minist. against D. Bridges 133.

laid a few rafters together, and thofe not all of the foundeft neither) but howfoever, all *this form* they conclude is prefcribed in fuch fort, that to adde to it any thing as of like importance (for fo I think they mean) or to abrogate of it any thing at all, is unlawful. In which refolution if they will firmly and conftantly perfift, I fee not but that concerning the points which hitherto have been difputed of, they muft agree that they have molefted the Church with needlefs oppofition; and hencefor-ward, as we faid before, betake themfelves wholly unto the trial of particulars, whe-ther every of thofe things which they efteem as principal, be either fo efteemed of, or at all eftablifhed for perpetuity in Holy Scripture; and whether any particular thing in our Church-Politie be received other then the Scripture alloweth of, either in greater things or in fmaller. The matters wherein Church-Polity is converfant, are the publique religious duties of the Church, as the adminiftration of the Word and Sacraments, Prayers, fpiritual Cenfures, and the like. To thefe the Church ftand-eth always bound. Laws of Polity, are Laws which appoint in what manner thefe duties fhall be performed. In performance whereof, becaufe all that are of the Church cannot joyntly and equally work, the firft thing in Politie required, is, a difference of perfons in the Church, without which difference thofe funtions can-not in orderly fort be executed. Hereupon we hold, that Gods Clergy are a ftate which hath been and will be, as long as there is a Church upon Earth, neceffary by the plain Word of God himfelf; a ftate whereunto the reft of Gods people muft be fubject as touching things that appertain to their fouls health. For where Polity is, it cannot but appoint fome to be Leaders of others, and fome to be led by others. *If the*

Luke 6.39. *blinde lead the blinde, they both perifh.* It is with the Clergy, if their perfons be re-fpected, even as it is with other men; their quality many times far beneath that which the dignity of their place requireth. Howbeit, according to the order of Po-lity, they being the *lights of the World*, others (though better and wifer) muft that

Mat. 5.14. way be fubject unto them. Again, forafmuch as where the Clergy are any great mul-titude, order doth neceffarily require that by degrees they be diftinguifhed; we hold, there have ever been, and ever ought to be in fuch cafe, at leaftwife two forts of Eccle-fiaftical perfons, the one fubordinate unto the other; as to the Apoftles in the begin-ning, and to the Bifhops always fince, we finde plainly both in Scripture and in all Ecclefiaftical Records, other Minifters of the Word and Sacraments, have been. Moreover, it cannot enter into any mans conceit to think it lawful, that every man which lifteth, fhould take upon him change in the Church; and therefore a folemn admittance is of fuch neceffity, that without it there can be no Church-Polity. A number of particularities there are, which make for the more convenient being of thefe principal and perpetual parts in Ecclefiaftical Polity, but yet are not of fuch conftant ufe and neceffity in Gods Church. Of this kinde are, times and places appointed for the exercife of Religion; fpecialities belonging to the publike folemnity of the Word, the Sacraments and Prayer; the enlargement or abridgement of Functions minifterial de-pending upon thofe two principals before mentioned; to conclude, even whatfoever doth by way of formality and circumftance concern any publike action of the Church. Now although that which the Scripture hath of things in the former kinde be for ever per-manent; yet in the latter both much of that which the Scripture teacheth is not al-ways needful; and much the Church of God fhall always need which the Scripture teacheth not. So as the form of Polity by them fet down for perpetuity, is three ways faulty. Faulty in omitting fome things which in Scripture are of that nature, as namely the difference that ought to be of Paftors, when they grow to any great multitude; faulty in requiring Doctors, Deacons, Widows, and fuch like, as things of perpetual neceffity by the Law of God, which in truth are nothing lefs; faul-ty alfo in urging fome things by Scripture immutable: as their lay-Elders, which the Scripture neither maketh immutable, nor at all teacheth, for any thing either we can yet finde, or they have hitherto been able to prove. But hereof more in the Books that follow. As for thofe marvellous difcourfes, whereby they adventure to argue, that God muft needs have done the things which they imagine was to be done; I muft confefs, I have often wondred at their exceeding boldnefs herein. When the queftion is, Whether God have delivered in Scripture (as they af-firm he hath) a compleat particular immutable form of Church-Politie; why take they that other both prefumptuous and fuperfluous labour, to prove he fhould

have

have done it ; there being no way in this case to prove the deed of God, saving onely by producing that evidence wherewith he hath done it ? But if there be no such
thing apparent upon record, they do as if one should demand a Legacy by force and
vertue of some written Testament, wherein there being no such thing specified, he
pleadeth that there it must needs be, and bringeth arguments from the love or good
will, which always the Testator bore him, imagining that these or the like proofs
will convict a Testament to have that in it, which other men can nowhere by reading finde. In matters which concern the actions of God, the most dutiful way on
our part is to search what God hath done, and with meekness to admire that, rather
then to dispute what he in congruity of reason ought to do. The ways which he
hath whereby to do all things for the greatest good of his Church, are more in
number then we can search, other in nature then that we should presume to determine, which of many should be the fittest for him to chuse, till such time as we see he
hath chosen of many some one ; which one we then may boldly conclude to be the fit-
est, because he hath taken it before the rest. When we do otherwise, surely we exceed our bounds ; who and where we are we forget ; and therefore needful it is that
our pride in such cases be controld, and our disputes beaten back with those demands
of the blessed Apostle, *How unsearchable are his judgements, and his ways past finding* Rom.11.13.
out ? Who hath known the minde of the Lord, or who was his Counsellour ?

Of

OF THE

L A W S

O F

Ecclefiaftical Politie.

The fourth Book.

Concerning their third Affertion, *That our Form of Church-Politie is corrupted with Popiſh Orders, Rites, and Ceremonies, baniſhed out of certain Reformed Churches, whoſe example therein we ought to have followed.*

The matter contained in this fourth Book.

12. *The fourth, for that sundry of them have been (they say) abused unto Idolatry, and are by that mean become scandalous.*

13. *The fifth, for that we retain them still, notwithstanding the example of certain Churches reformed before us, which have cast them out.*

14. *A declaration of the proceedings of the* Church of England, *for the establishment of things as they are.*

Uch was the ancient simplicity and softness of spirit, which sometimes prevailed in the World, that they whole words were even as Oracles amongst men, seemed evermore loth to give sentence against any thing publiquely received in the Church of God, except it were wonderful apparently evil; for that they did not so much encline to that severity, which delighteth to reprove the least things it seeth amiss; as to that Charity, which is unwilling to behold any thing, that duty bindeth to reprove. The state of this present Age, wherein zeal hath drowned charity, and skill meekness, will not now suffer any man to marvel, whatsoever he shall hear reproved, by whomsoever. Those Rites and Ceremonies of the Church therefore, which are the self same now, that they were, when holy and vertuous men maintained them against profane and deriding Adversaries, her own children have at this day in derision. Whether justly or no, it shall then appear, when all things are heard, which they have to alledge against the outward received Orders of this Church. Which inasmuch as themselves do compare unto *Mint and Cummin,* granting them to be no part of those things, which in the matter of Polity are weightier, we hope that for small things their strife will neither be earnest nor long. The sifting of that which is objected against the Orders of the Church in particular, doth not belong unto this place. Here we are to discuss onely those general exceptions, which have been taken at any time against them. First therefore, to the end that their nature and use, whereunto they serve, may plainly appear, and so afterwards their quality the better be discerned; we are to note, that in every grand or main publique duty, which God requireth at the hands of his Church, there is, besides that matter and form wherein the essence thereof consisteth, a certain outward fashion, whereby the same is in decent sort administred. The substance of all religious actions is delivered from God himself in few words. For example sake in the Sacraments, *Unto the Element let the Word be added; and they do both make a Sacrament,* saith S. *Augustine.* Baptism is given by the Element of Water, and that prescript form of words, which the Church of Christ doth use; the Sacrament of the Body and Blood of Christ is administred in the Elements of Bread and Wine, if those mystical words be added thereunto: But the due and decent form of administring those holy Sacraments, doth require a great deal more. The end which is aimed at in setting down the outward form of all religious actions, is the edification of the Church. Now men are edified, when either their understanding is taught somewhat whereof in such actions it behoveth all men to consider, or when their hearts are moved with any affection suitable thereunto; when their mindes are in any sort stirred up unto that reverence, devotion, attention, and due regard, which in those cases seemeth requisite. Because therefore unto this purpose not onely speech, but sundry sensible means besides have always been thought necessary, and especially those means which being object to the eye, the liveliest and the most apprehensive sense of all other, have in that respect seemed the fittest to make a deep and strong impression; from hence have risen not only a number of Prayers, Readings, Questionings, Exhortings, but even of visible signs also, which being used in performance of holy actions; are undoubtedly most effectual to open such matter, as men when they know and remember carefully, must needs be a great deal the better informed to what effect such duties serve. We must not think but that there is some ground of reason even in nature, whereby it cometh to pass, that no Nation under Heaven either doth or ever did suffer publique actions which are of weight, whether they be Civil and Temporal, or else Spiritual and Sacred, to pass without some visible solemnity: The very strangeness whereof, and difference from that which is common doth

cause

How great use ceremonies have in the Church.

Mat.23.v.23. The Doctrine and Discipline of the Church, as the weightiest things ought especially to be looked unto: but the ceremonies also, as Mint and Cummin ought not to be negl. &c. T. C. l.3.p.171.

cause Popular eyes to obſerve and to mark the ſame. Words, both becauſe they are common, and do not ſo ſtrongly move the phanſie of man, are for the moſt part but ſlightly heard; and therefore with ſingular wiſdom it hath been provided, that the deeds of men which are made in the preſence of witneſſes, ſhould paſs not onely with words, but alſo with certain ſenſible actions, the memory whereof is far more eaſie and durable then the memory of ſpeech can be. The things which ſo long experience of all Ages hath confirmed and made profitable, let not us preſume to condemn as follies and toys, becauſe we ſometime know not the cauſe and reaſon of them. A wit diſpoſed to ſcorn whatſoever it doth not conceive, might ask where-

Gen.24.2.

fore *Abraham* ſhould ſay to his ſervant, *Put thy hand under my thigh, and ſwear:* was it not ſufficient for his ſervant to ſhew the Religion of an Oath, by naming the Lord God of Heaven and Earth, unleſs that ſtrange ceremony were added? In Contracts, Bargains and Conveyances, a mans word is a token ſufficient to expreſs his will. *Yet*

Ruth.4.7.

this was the ancient manner in Iſrael concerning redeeming and exchanging, to eſtabliſh all things; A man did pluck off his ſhooe, and gave it to his neighbour; and this was a ſure witneſs in Iſrael. Amongſt the Romans in their making of a Bond-man free, was it not wondred wherefore ſo great a do ſhould be made? The Maſter to preſent his Slave in ſome Court, to take him by the hand, and not onely to ſay in the hearing of the pub-like Magiſtrate, *I will that this man become free;* but after theſe ſolemn words uttered, to ſtrike him on the cheek, to turn him round, the hair of his head to be ſhaved off, the Magiſtrate to touch him thrice with a rod, in the end a cap and a white garment to

Exod.2.16.

be given him? To what purpoſe all this circumſtance? Among the *Hebrews* how ſtrange and in outward appearance almoſt againſt reaſon, that he which was minded to make himſelf a perpetual ſervant, ſhould not onely teſtifie ſo much in the preſence of the Judge, but for a viſible token thereof have alſo his ear bored thorow with an awl? It were an infinite labour to proſecute theſe things ſo far as they might be exemplified both in Civil and Religious actions. For in both they have their neceſſary uſe and

a Dionyſ.p.121.

force. [a] *Theſe ſenſible things which Religion hath allowed, are reſemblances framed according to things ſpiritually underſtood, whereunto they ſerve as a hand to lead, and a way to direct.* And whereas it may peradventure be objected, that to adde to religions duties ſuch rites and ceremonies as are ſignificant, is to inſtitute new Sacraments: ſure I am they will not ſay, that *Numa Pompilius* did ordain a ſacrament; a ſignificant ceremony he did ordain, in commanding the Prieſts [b] *to execute the work of their Divine Service with their hands as far as to the fingers covered; thereby ſignifying that ſidelity muſt be defended, and that mens right hands are the ſacred ſeat thereof.* Again, we are alſo to put them in minde, that themſelves do not hold all ſignificant ceremonies for ſacraments; inaſmuch as impoſition of hands they deny to be a Sacrament, and yet they give thereunto a forcible ſignification. For concerning it their words are theſe, (c) *The party ordained by this ceremony, was put in minde of his ſeparation to the work of the Lord, that remembring himſelf to be taken as it were with the hand of God from amongſt others, this might teach him not to account himſelf now his own, nor to do what himſelf liſteth; but to conſider that God hath ſet him about a work, which if he will diſcharge and accompliſh, he may at the hands of God aſſure himſelf of reward and; if otherwiſe, of revenge.* Touching ſignificant Ceremonies ſome of them are Sacraments, ſome as Sacraments onely. Sacraments are thoſe, which are ſigns and tokens of ſome general promiſed grace; which alwaies really deſcendeth from God unto the ſoul that duly receiveth them: other ſignificant tokens are only as Sacraments, yet no Sacraments. Which is not our diſtinction, but theirs. For concerning the Apoſtles impoſition of hands, theſe are their own words, *Magnum ſignum hoc & quaſi Sacramentum uſurparunt;* They uſed this ſign as it were a Sacrament.

b Liv. l.1. Manu ad digitos uſq, involutâ rem divinam facere; ſignificantes ſidem tutandam, ſedemque ejus etiam in dextris ſacratam eſſe.
c Eccleſ.diſci. fol.51.

Fol.25.

2. Concerning rites and ceremonies, there may be fault, either in the kinde, or in the number and multitude of them. The firſt thing blamed about the kinde of ours, is, that in many things we have departed from the ancient ſimplicity of Chriſt and his Apoſtles; we have embraced more outward ſtatelineſs, we have thoſe orders in the exerciſe of Religion, which they who beſt pleaſed God, and ſerved him moſt devoutly, never had. For it is out of doubt, that the firſt ſtate of things was beſt, that in the prime of Chriſtian Religion faith was ſoundeſt, the Scriptures of God were then beſt underſtood by all men, all parts of godlineſs did then moſt abound; and therefore it muſt needs follow, that Cuſtoms, Laws, and Ordinances deviſed ſince, are not ſo good for the Church

The firſt thing they blame in the kinde of our Ceremonies, is, that we have not in them ancient Apoſtolical ſimplicity, but a greater pomp and ſtatelineſs. Lib.Eccl ſdiſ. & T.C.l.3.p. 141.

Church of Chrift, but the beft way is to cut off later inventions, and to reduce things unto the ancient ftate wherein at the firft they were. Which Rule or Canon we hold to be either uncertain, or at leaft wife unfufficient, if not both For in cafe it be certain, hard it cannot be for then to fhew us, where we fhall find it fo exactly fet down, that we may fay without all controverfie; *Thefe were the orders of the Apoftles times, thefe wholly and onely, neither fewer nor more then thefe* True it is that many things of this nature be alluded unto, yea many things declared, and many things neceffarily collected out of the Apoftles writings But is it neceffary that all the orders of the Church which were then in ufe, fhould be contained in their books?Surely no For if the tenor of their writings be well obferved,it fhall unto any man eafily appear, that no more of them are there touched,then were needful to be fpoken of fometimes by one occafion,and fometimes by another.Will they allow then of any other Records befides? Well affured I am they are far enough from acknowledging that the Church ought to keep any thing as Apoftolical, which is not found in the Apoftles writings, in what other Records fo ever it be found. And therefore whereas St *Auguftine* affirmeth, that thofe things which the whole Church of Chrift doth hold, may well be thought to be Apoftolical,although they be not found written, this his judgment they utterly condemn I will not here ftand in defence of S. *Auguftines* opinion, which is, that fuch things are indeed Apoftolical, but yet with this exception, unlefs the Decree of fome general Council have haply caufed them to be received: for of Pofitive laws and orders received througho it the whole Chriftian world, S. *Auguftine* could imagine no other fountain fave thefe two. But to let pafs S. *Auguftine*, they who condemn him herein,muft needs confefs it a very uncertain thing what the orders of the Church were in the Apoftles times, feeing the Scriptures do not mention them all, and other Records thereof befides they utterly reject. So that in tying the Church to the orders of the Apoftles times, they tye it to a marvelous uncertain rule, unlefs they require the obfervation of no orders but onely thofe which are known to be Apoftolical by the Apoftles own writings But then is not this their rule of fuch fufficiency, that we fhould ufe it as a touchftone to try the orders of the Church by for ever ? Our end ought always to be the fame; our ways and means thereunto not fo. The glory of God and the good of his Church was the thing which the Apoftles aimed at, and therefore ought to be the mark whereat we alfo level But feeing thofe rites and orders may be at one time more, which at another are lefs available unto that purpofe: what reafon is there in thefe things to urge the ftate of our onely age, as a pattern for all to follow ? It is not, I am fure, their meaning, that we fhould now affemble our people to ferve God in clofe and fecret meetings ; or that common Brooks or Rivers fhould be ufed for places of Baptifm ; or that the Eucharift fhould be miniftred after meat; or that the cuftom of Church-feafting fho uld be renewed or that all kind of ftanding provifion for the Miniftry fhould beutterly taken away, and their eftate made again dependant upon the voluntary devotion of men.In thefe things they eafily perceive how unfit that were for the prefent, which was for the firft Age convenient enough. The faith, zeal, and godlinefs of former. times is worthily had in honour, but doth this prove that the order of the Church of Chrift muft be ftill the felf-fame with theirs, that nothing may be which was not then, or that nothing which then was may lawfully fince have ceafed? They who recal the Church unto that which was at the firft, muft neceffarily fet bounds and limits unto their fpeeches. If any thing have been received repugnant unto that which was firft delivered, the firft things in this cafe muft ftand, the laft give place unto them. But where difference is without repugnancy, that which hath been can be no prejudice to that which is. Let the ftate of the people of God when they were in the houfe of bondage, and their manner of Serving God in a ftrange land, be compared with that which *Canaan* and *Jerufalem* did afford,and who feeth not what huge difference there was between them? In Egypt, it may be, they were right glad to take fome corner of a poor Cottage, and there to ferve God upon their knees, peradventure covered in duft and ftraw fometimes. Neither were they therefore the lefs accepted of God, but he was with them in all their afflictions, and at the length by working their admirable deliverance, did teftifie that they ferved him not in vain. Notwithftanding in the very defert they are no fooner poffeft with fome little thing of their own, but a Tabernacle is required at their hands. Being planted in the land of *Canaan*, and having *David* to be their

Tom. 7. de bart. contra Donatift. libus ca. 13. *r. c. l. 1. p 31.* If this judgement of S. Auguftine be a good judgement & found; then there be fome things commanded of God, which are not in the Scripture, and ther. fore there is no fufficient Doctrine contained in fcripture, whereby we may be faved For all the Commandements of God and of the A. poftles, are needful for our falvation V de Epift. 118.

King; when the Lord had given him reſt from all his enemies, it grieved his religious mind to conſider the growth of his own eſtate and dignity, the affairs of religion continuing ſtill in the former manner : *Behold, now I dwell in an houſe of Cedar trees, and the Ark of God remaineth ſtill within Curtains.* What he did purpoſe, it was the pleaſure of God that *Solomon* his ſon ſhould perform, and perform it in manner ſutable unto their preſent, not their ancient eſtate and condition. For which cauſe *Solomon* writeth unto the King of *Tyrus : The houſe which I build is great and wonderful ; for great is our God above all gods.* Whereby it cleerly appeareth, that the orders of the Church of God may be acceptable unto him, as well being framed ſuitable to the greatneſs and dignity of latter, as when they keep the reverend ſimplicity of ancienter times. Such diſſimilitude therefore between us and the Apoſtles of Chriſt, in the order of ſome outward things, is no argument of default.

3. Yea, but we have framed our ſelves to the cuſtomes of the Church of *Rome*, our Orders and Ceremonies are Papiſtical. It is eſpied that our Church-founders were not ſo careful as in this matter they ſhould have been, but contented themſelves with ſuch diſcipline as they took from the Church of *Rome*. Their error we ought to reform by aboliſhing all Popiſh orders. There muſt be no communion nor fellow-ſhips with Papiſts, *neither in Doctrine, Ceremonies, nor Government.* It is not enough that we are divided from the Church of *Rome* by the ſingle wall of Doctrine, retaining as we do part of their Ceremonies, and almoſt their whole Government : but Government or Ceremonies, or whatſoever it be which is Popiſh, away with it. This is the thing they require in us, the utter relinquiſhment of all things Popiſh. Wherein to the end we may anſwer them according unto their plain direct meaning, and not take advantage of doubtful ſpeech, whereby controverſies grow alway ſendleſs; their main Poſition being this, that nothing *ſhould be placed in the Church but what God in his word hath commanded*, they muſt of neceſſity hold all for Popiſh, which the Church of *Rome* hath over and beſides this. By Popiſh Orders, Ceremonies, and Government they muſt therefore mean in every of theſe ſo much, as the Church of *Rome* hath embraced without Commandment of Gods word : ſo that whatſoever ſuch things we have, if the Church of *Rome* have it alſo, it goeth under the name of thoſe things that are Popiſh, yea, although it be lawful, although agreeable to the Word of God. For ſo they plainly affirm, ſaying: *Although the forms and ceremonies which they (the Church of Rome) uſed were not unlawful, and that they contained nothing which is not agreable to the Word of God, yet notwithſtanding neither the Word of God, nor reaſon, nor the examples of the eldeſt Churches both Jewiſh and Chriſtian, do permit us to uſe the ſame form and ceremonies, being neither commanded of God, neither ſuch as there may not as good as they and rather better be eſtabliſhed.* The queſtion therefore is, whether we may follow the Church of *Rome* in thoſe orders, Rites and ceremonies, wherein we do not think them blamable, or elſe ought to deviſe others, and to have no conformity with them, no not as much as in theſe things? In this ſenſe and conſtruction therefore as they affirm, ſo we deny, that whatſoever is Popiſh we ought to abrogate. Their Arguments to prove that generally all Popiſh Orders and Ceremonies ought to be clean aboliſhed, are in ſum theſe : Firſt, *whereas we allow the judgment of S.* Auguſtine, *that touching thoſe things of this kind which are not commanded or forbidden in the Scripture, we are to obſerve the cuſtome of the people of God, and decrees of our forefathers: how can we retain the cuſtomes and conſtitutions of the Papiſts in ſuch things, who were neither the people of God nor our forefathers ?* Secondly, *although the forms and ceremonies of the Church of* Rome *were not unlawful, neither did contain any thing which is not agreable to the Word of God, yet neither the Word of God, nor the example of the eldeſt Churches of God, nor reaſon, do permit us to uſe the ſame,* they being Hereticks and ſo neer about us, *and their orders being neither commanded of God, nor yet ſuch, but that as good or rather better may be eſtabliſhed. It is againſt the Word of God, to have conformity with the Church of* Rome *in ſuch things, as appeareth, in that the wiſdm of God hath thought it a good way to keep his people from infection of Idolatry and Superſtition by ſevering them from Idolaters in outward ceremonies, and therefore hath forbidden them to do things which are in themſelves very lawful to be done. And further, whereas the Lord was careful to ſever them by ceremonies from other Nations, yet was he not ſo careful to ſever them from any, as from the Egyptians amongſt whom they lived, and from thoſe Nations which were next neighbours to them, becauſe from them was the greateſt*
      fear

2 Sam. 7. 2.

2 Chron. 2. 5.

Our Orders and Ceremonies blamed, in that ſo many of them are the ſame which the Church of *Rome* uſeth. *Eccleſ. Diſcipl fol.* 12. T. C. *lii.* 1. *pag.* 131.
T. C. *l.* p. 2
T. C. *l.* 1, *p.* 15.

T. C. *lib* 1. *p.* 131.

T. C. *l.* 1. *p.* 30.

T. C. *l.* 1. *p.* 131.

fear of infection. So that following the course which the wisdom of God doth teach, it were more safe for us to conform our indifferent ceremonies to the Turks which are far off, then to the Papists which are so near. Touching the example of the eldest Churches of God, in one councel it was decreed, that Christians should not deck their houses with Bay-leaves and green boughs, because the Pagans did use so to do; and that they should not rest from their labours those days that the Pagans did, that they should not keep the first day of every moneth as they did. Another Councel decreed that Christians should not celebrate feasts on the birth days of the Martyrs, because it was the manner of the Heathen. O, saith Tertullian, better is the Religion of the Heathen: for they use no solemnity of the Christians, neither the Lords day, neither the Pentecost, and if they knew them, they would have nothing to do with them: for they would be afraid least they should seem Christians: but we are not afraid to be called heathens. The same Tertullian would not have Christians to sit after they had prayed, because the Idolaters did so. Whereby it appeareth, that both of particular men and of Counsels, in making or abolishing of ceremonies, heed had been taken that the Christians should not be like the Idolaters, no not in those things which of themselves are most indifferent to be used or not used. The same conformity is not less opposite unto reason, first inasmuch as contraries must be cured by their contraries, and therefore Popery being Antichristianity, is not healed by establishment of orders thereunto opposite. The way to bring a drunken man to sobriety, is to carry him as far from excess of drink as may be. To rectifie a crooked stick, we bend it on the contrary side, as far as it was at the first on that side from whence we draw it: and so it commeth in the end to a middle between both, which is perfect straightness. Utter inconformity thereof with the Church of Rome in these things, is the best and surest policy which the Church can use. While we use their ceremonies, they take occasion to blaspheme, saying that our religion cannot stand by it self, unless it lean upon the staff of their ceremonies. [a] They hereby conceive great hope of having the rest of their Popery in the end, which hope causeth them to be more frozen in their wickedness. Neither is it without cause that they have this hope, considering that which M. Bucer noteth upon the eighteenth of S. Matthew, that where these things have been left, Popery hath returned; but on the other part, in places which have been cleansed of those things, it hath not yet been seen that it hath had any entrance. [b] None make such clamors for these ceremonies, as the Papists, and those whom they suborn; a manifest token how much they triumph and joy in these things. They breed grief of mind in a number that are godly minded, and have Antichristianity in such detestation, that their minds are Martyred with the very sight of them in the Church. Such godly brethren we ought not thus to grieve with unprofitable ceremonies, yea, ceremonies wherein there is not only no profit but also danger of great hurt that may grow to the Church by infection, which Popish ceremonies are means to breed. This in effect is the sum and substance of that which they bring by way of opposition against those orders which we have common with the Church of Rome; these are the reasons wherewith they would prove our, Ceremonies in that respect worthy of blame.

4. Before we answer unto these things, we are to cut off that, whereunto they from whom these objections proceed, do oftentimes fly for defence and succour, when the force and strength of their Arguments is elided. For the Ceremonies in use amongst us, being in no other respect retained, saving onely for that to retain them is to our seeming, good and profitable, yea so profitable and so good, that if we had either simply taken them clean away, or else removed them so as to place in their stead others, we had done worse: the plain and direct way against us herein had been onely to prove, that all such Ceremonies as they require to be abolished, are retained by us with the hurt of the Church, or with less benefit then the abolishment of them would bring. But forasmuch as they saw how hardly they should be able to performe this; they took a more compendeous way, traducing the Ceremonies of our Church under the name of being Popish. The cause why this way seemed better unto them, was, for that the name of Popery is more odious then very Paganism amongst diverse of the more simple sort; so whatsoever they hear named Popish, they presently conceive deep hatred against it, imagining there can be

That whereas they who blame us in this behalf, when reason evicteth that all such Ceremonies are not to be abolished, make answer that when they condemn Popish Ceremonies, their meaning is of ceremonies unprofitable, or ceremonies, instead whereof as good or better may be demised: they cannot hereby get out of the bryers, but contradict and gainsay themselves: inasmuch as their usual manner is to prove, that ceremonies uncommanded in the Church of God and yet used in the Church of Rome, are for this very cause unprofitable to us, and not so good as others in their place would be.

nothing

nothing contained in that name, but needs it muſt be exceeding deteſtable. The ears of the people they have therefore filled with ſtrong clamors. *The Church of England is fraught with Popiſh Ceremonies : They that favour the cauſe of reformation, maintain nothing but the ſincerity of the Goſpel of* Jeſus Chriſt : *All ſuch as withſtand them, fight for the Laws of his ſworn enemy, uphold the filthy reliques of Antichriſt; and are defenders of that which is Popiſh.* Theſe are the notes wherewith are drawn from the hearts of the multitude ſo many ſighs; with theſe tunes their minds are exaſperated againſt the lawful Guides and Governours of their ſouls; theſe are the voices that fill them with general diſcontentment, as though the boſome of the famous Church, wherein they live, were more noyſome than any dungeon. But when the Authors of ſo ſcandalous incantations are examined and called to account, how they can juſtifie ſuch their dealings; when they are urged directly to anſwer, whether it be lawful for us to uſe any ſuch Ceremonies as the Church of *Rome* uſeth, although the ſame be not commanded in the Word of God; being driven to ſee that the uſe of ſome ſuch Ceremonies muſt of neceſſity be granted lawful, they go about to make us believe that they are juſt of the ſame opinion, and that they only think ſuch Ceremonies are not to be uſed when they are unprofitable, or when as good or beter may be eſtabliſhed. Which anſwer is both idle in regard of us, and alſo repugnant to themſelves. It is, in regard of us, very vain to make this anſwer, becauſe they know that what Ceremonies we retain common unto the Church of *Rome*, we therefore retain them, for that we judge them to be profitable, and to be ſuch that others inſtead of them would be worſe. So that when they ſay that we ought to abrogate ſuch Romiſh Ceremonies as are unprofitable, or elſe might have other more profitable in their ſtead, they trifle and they beat the Air about nothing which toucheth us, unleſs they mean that we ought to abrogate all Romiſh Ceremonies, which in their judgment have either no uſe, or leſs uſe than ſome other might have. But then muſt they ſhew ſome commiſſion, whereby they are authorized to ſit as Judges, and we required to take their judgment for good in this caſe. Otherwiſe, their ſentences will not be greatly regarded, when they oppoſe their *Me thinketh*, unto the Orders of the Church of *England*: as in the queſtion about Surpleſſes one of them doth; *If we look to the colour, black methinks is the more decent; if to the form, a garment down to the foot hath a great deal more comelineſs in it.* If they think that we ought to prove the Ceremonies commodious which we have retained, they do in this point very greatly deceive themſelves. For in all right and equity, that which the Church hath received and held ſo long for good, that which publique approbation hath ratified, muſt carry the benefit of preſumption with it to be accounted meet and convenient. They which have ſtood up as yeſterday to challenge it of defect, muſt prove their challenge. If we being defendants do anſwer, that the Ceremonies in queſtion are godly, comely, decent, profitable for the Church; their reply is childiſh and unorderly to ſay, that we demand the thing in queſtion, and ſhew the poverty of our cauſe, the goodneſs whereof we are fain to beg that our Adverſaries would grant. For on our parts this muſt be the anſwer, which orderly proceeding doth require. The burden of proving doth reſt on them. In them it is frivolous to ſay, we ought not to uſe bad Ceremonies of the Church of Rome, and preſume all ſuch bad as it pleaſeth them to diſlike, unleſs we can perſwade them the contrary. Beſides, they are herein oppoſite alſo to themſelves. For what one thing is ſo common with them, as to uſe the cuſtome of the Church of Rome for an argument to prove, that ſuch and ſuch Ceremonies cannot be good and profitable for us, inaſmuch as that Church uſeth them ? Which uſual kind of diſputing, ſheweth that they do not diſallow onely thoſe Romiſh Ceremonies which are unprofitable, but count all unprofitable, which are Romiſh, that is to ſay, which have been deviſed by the Church of Rome, or which are uſed in that Church and not preſcribed in the Word of God. For this is the onely limitation which they can uſe ſutable unto their other Poſitions. And therefore the cauſe which they yield, why they hold it lawful to retain in *Doctrine* and in *Diſcipline* ſome things as good, which yet are common to the Church of *Rome*, is, for that thoſe good things are perpetual commandements, in whoſe place no other can come : but Ceremonies are changeable. So that their judgement in truth, is, that whatſoever by the Word of God is not changeable in the Church of *Rome*, that Churches uſing is a cauſe why reformed Churches ought to change it, and not to think it good or profitable. And left

we

T.C. lib.3.p.171
What an open untruth is it, that this is one of our principles not to be lawful to uſe the ſame ceremonies which the Papiſts did, when as I have both before declared the contrary, and even here have expreſly added, that they are not to be uſed when as good or better may be eſtabliſhed ? Eccleſ. diſcip. fol. 100.

T.C.l.3, p.175. As for your often repeating that the ceremonies in queſtion are godly, comely, and decent : It is your old word of demanding the thing in queſtion, and an undoubted argument of your extream poverty.
T.C.l.3.p. 175.

we seem to father any thing upon them more than is properly their own, let them read even their own words, where they complain, that *we are thus constrained to be like unto the Papists in any their Ceremonies*, yea they urge that this cause, al'though it were alone, ought to move them to whom that belongeth, to do them away, *forasmuch as they are their Ceremonies*, and that the B. of *Salisbury* doth justifie this their complaint. The clause is untrue which they add concerning the B. of *Salisbury*; but the sentence doth shew, we do them no wrong in setting down the state of the question between us thus; Whether we ought to abolish out of the .Church of *England* all such orders, rites, and ceremonies, as are established in the Church of *Rome*, and are not prescribed in the Word of God For the affirmative whereof we are now to answer such proofs of theirs as have been before alleadged.

T·C.l.3.p.177. And that this complaint of ours is just, in that we are thus constrained to be like unto the Papists in any their ceremonies, and that this cause only ought to move them to whom tha. belongeth to do theirs away, for asmuch as they are their ceremonies the Reader may further see in the Bishop of *Salisbury*, who brings divers proofs thereof.

5. Let the Church of *Rome* be what it will, let them that are of it be the people of God and our fathers in the Christian faith, or let them be otherwise; hold them for Catholicks, or hold them for Hereticks, it is not a thing either one way or another in this present question greatly material. Our conformity with them in such things as have been proposed, is not proved as yet unlawful by all this. S *Augustine* hath said, yea and we have allowed his saying, *That the custome of the people of God and the decrees of our forefathers are to be kept, touching those things whereof the Scripture hath neither one way nor other given us any charge.* What then? Doth it here therefore follow, that they, being neither the people of God, nor our forefathers, are for that cause in nothing to be followed? This consequent were good, if so be it were granted, that only the custom of the people of God, and the decrees of our forefathers are in such case to be observed. But then should no other kind of latter laws in the Church be good, which were a grossabsurdity to think. S *Augustines* speech therefore doth import, that where we have no divine precept, if yet we have the custom of the people of God, or a decree of our forefathers, this is a law and must be kept. Notwithstanding it is not denied, but that we lawfully may observe the positive constitutions of our own Churches, although the same were but yesterday made by our selves alone. Nor is there any thing in this to prove, that the Church of *England* might not by law receive orders, rites, or customs from the Church of *Rome*, although they were neither the people of God, nor yet our forefathers. How much less, when we have received from them nothing but that which they did themselves receive from such, as we cannot deny to have been the people of God, yea such as either we must acknowledge for our own forefathers, or else disdain the race of Christ?

That our allowing the customes of our fathers to be followed, is no proof that we may not allow some customes which the Church of Rome hath, although we do not account of them as of our fathers.

6 The rites and orders wherein we follow the Church of *Rome*, are of no other kind than such as the Church of *Geneva* it self doth follow them in We follow the Church of *Rome* in moe things, yet they in some things of the same nature about which our present controversie is: so that the difference is not in the kind, but in the number of Rites only, wherein they and we do follow the Church of *Rome*. The use of Wafercakes, the custome of God-fathers and God-mothers in Baptism, are things not commanded nor forbidden in the Scripture, things which have been of old, and are retained in the Church of *Rome*, even at this very hour. Is conformity with *Rome* in such things a blemish unto the Church of *England*, and unto Churches abroad an ornament? Let them, if not for the reverence they owe unto this Church, in the bowels whereof they have received I trust that precious and blessed vigor, which shall quicken them to eternal life, yet at the leastwise for the singular affection which they do bear towards others, take heed how they strike, lest they wound whom they would not For undoubtedly it cutteth deeper then they are aware of; when they plead that even such ceremonies of the Church of *Rome*, as contain in then nothing which is not of it self agreeable to the word of God, ought nevertheless to be abolished, and that neither the Word of God, nor reason, nor the examples of the eldest Churches, do permit the Church of *Rome* to be therein followed. Hereticks they are, and they are our Neighbours. By us and amongst us, they lead their lives. But what then? therefore is no ceremonie of theirs lawful for us to use? We must yield and will, that none are lawful if God himself be a precedent against the use of any. But how appeareth it that God is so? Hereby, they say, it doth appear, in that *God severed*

That the course which the wisdome of God doth teach, make h not against our conformity with the Church of Rome in such things.

T.C.li.1.p.131 & l.1.

U 3

red his people from the heathens, but specially from the Egyptians, and such Nations as were nearest Neighbours unto them, by forbidding them to do those things, which were in themselves very lawful to be done, yea very profitable some, and incommodious to be forborn; such things it pleased God to forbid them, onely because those Heathens did them, with whom conformity in the same thing might have bred infection. Thus in shaving, cutting, apparel-wearing, yea in sundry kinds of meats also, Swines-flesh, Conies, and such like, they were forbidden to do so and so, because the Gentiles did so. And the end why God forbade them such things, was, to sever them, for fear of infection, by a great and an high wall from other Nations, as S. Paul teacheth. The cause of more careful separation from the nearest Nations, was, the greatness of danger to be especially by them infected. Now, *Papists* are to us as those Nations were unto *Israel.* Therefore if the wisdome of God be our guide, we cannot allow conformity with them, no not in any such indifferent Ceremony. Our direct answer hereunto is, that for any thing here alledged we may still doubt, whether the Lord in such indifferent Ceremonies as those whereof we dispute, did frame his people of set purpose unto any utter dissimilitude, either with *Egyptians*, or with any other Nation else. And if God did not forbid them all such indifferent Ceremonies, then our conformity with the Church of *Rome* in some such is not hitherto as yet disproved, although *Papists* were unto us as those Heathens were unto *Israel. After the doings of the Land of Egypt, wherein you dwelt, ye shall not do,* saith the Lord; *and after the manner of the Land of* Canaan, *whither I will bring you, shall ye not do, neither walk in their Ordinances : Do after my judgements, and keep my ordinances to walk therein : I am the Lord your God.* The speech is indefinite, *ye shall not be like them :* It is not general, *ye shall not be like them in any thing, or like unto them in any thing indifferent, or like unto them in any indifferent Ceremony of theirs.* Seeing therefore it is not set down how far the bounds of his speech concerning dissimilitude should reach, how can any man assure us, that it extendeth farther then to those things only, wherein the Nations there mentioned were Idolatrous, or did against that which the Law of God commanded ? Nay, doth it not seem a thing very probable, that God doth purposely add, *Do after my judgements,* as giving thereby to understand that his meaning in the former sentence was but to bar similitude in such things as were repugnant to the Ordinances, Laws, and Statutes, which he had given ? *Egyptians* and *Canaanites* are for example sake named unto them, because the customs of the one they had been, and of the other they should be best acquainted with: But that wherein they might not be like unto either of them, was such peradventure as had been no whit less unlawfull, although those Nations had never been. So that there is no necessity to think that God for fear of infection by reason of neerness, forbad them to be like unto the *Canaanites* or the *Egyptians*, in those things which otherwise had been lawful enough. For I would know what one thing was in those Nations, and is here forbidden, being indifferent it self, yet forbidden only because they used it ? In the Laws of *Israel* we find it written, *Ye shall not cut round the corners of your heads, neither shalt thou tear the tufts of thy beard.* These things were usual amongst those Nations, and in themselves they are indifferent. But are they indifferent being used as signes of immoderate and hopeless lamentation for the dead? In this sense it is that the law forbiddeth them. For which cause the very next words following are, *Ye shall not cut your flesh for the dead, nor make any print of a mark upon you ; I am the Lord.* The like in *Leviticus*, where speech is of mourning for the dead, *They shall not make bald parts upon their head, nor shave off the locks of their beard, nor make any cutting in their flesh.* Again, in *Deut. Ye are the Children of the Lord your God ; ye shall not cut your selves, nor make you baldness between your eyes for the dead.* What is this but in effect the same which the Apostle doth more plainly express, saying, *Sorrow not as they do which have no hope?* The very light of nature it self was able to see herein a fault; that which those Nations did use, having been also in use with others, the ancient *Roman* laws do forbid. That shaving therefore and cutting which the Law doth mention, was not a matter in it self indifferent, and forbidden only because it was in use amongst such Idolaters as were Neighbours to the people of God ; but to use it had been a crime, though no other people or Nation under heaven should have done it saving only themselves. As for those laws concerning attires, *There shall no garment of Linnen and wollen come upon thee ;* as also those touching food and diet, wherein *Swines-flesh* together with sundry other meats are forbidden; the use of these things had been indeed of it self harmless and indifferent:

Levit. 18. 3.

Levit. 19. 27.
and 19. 19.
Deut. 22. 11.
and 1. 7. &
Levit. 11.
Ephes. 2. 14.

Levit. 18. 3.

Levit. 19. 17.

Levit. 21. 5.

Deut. 14. 1.

1 Thes. 4. 13.

Levit. 19. 19.
Deut. 22. 11.

so

fo that hereby it doth appear , how the Law of God forbade in fome fpecial confideration, fuch things as were lawful enough in themfelves. But yet even here they likewife fail of that they intend. For it doth not appear that the confideration in regard
whereof the Law forbiddeth thefe things, was becaufe thofe Nations did ufe them.
Likely enough it is that the *Canaanites* ufed to feed as well on Sheep as on Swines-
flefh ; and therefore if the forbidding of the latter had no other reafon then diffimili-
tude with that people, they which of their own heads alleadge this for reafon, can fhew
I think fome reafon more then we are able to find, why the former was not alfo forbidden. Might there not be fome other myftery in this prohibition then they think of ?
Yes, fome other myftery there was in it by all likely-hood. For what reafon is there
which fhould but induce, and therefore much lefs inforce us to think, that care of diffi-
militude between the people of God and the Heathen Nations about them, was any more
the caufe of forbidding them to put on garments of fundry ftuff , then of chargeing
them withal not to fow their fields with Meflin; or that this was any more the caufe of
forbidding them to eat Swines-flefh, than of chargeing them withal not to eat the flefh
of *Eagles*, *Hawks*, and the like ; wherefore although the Church of *Rome* were to us,
as to *Ifrael* the *Egyptians* and *Canaanites* were of old ; yet doth it not follow that
the wifdome of God without refpect doth teach us to erect between us and
them a partition wall of difference ; in fuch things indifferent as have been hitherto
difputed of.

7 Neither is the example of the eldeft Churches a whit more availeable to this
purpofe. Notwithftanding fome fault undoubtedly there is in the very refemblance of
Idolaters. Were it not fome kind of blemifh to be like unto Infidels and Heathens, it
would not fo ufually be objected ; men would not think it any advantage in the caufes
of Religion, to be able therewith juftly to charge their Adverfaries as they do.
Wherefore to the end that it may a little more plainly appear , what force this hath,
and how far the fame extendeth, we are to note how all men are naturally defirous, that
they may feem neither to judge, nor to do amifs , becaufe every error and offence is a
ftain to the beauty of Nature, for which caufe it blufheth thereat, but glorieth in the
contrary; from whence it rifeth , that they which difgrace or deprefs the credit of
others ; do it either in both or in one of thefe. To have been in either directly by a
weak and unperfect rule, argueth imbecillity and imperfection. Men being either led
by reafon, or by imitation of other mens examples ; if their perfons be odious whofe
example we chufe to follow, as namely, if we frame our opinions to that which condemned Hereticks think, or direct our actions according to that which is practifed and
done by them ; it lies as an heavy prejudice againft us, unlefs fomewhat mightier then
their bare example, did move us to think or do the fame things with them. Chriftian men therefore having befides the common light of all men, fo great help of heavenly direction from above, together with the Lamps of fo bright examples as the Church
of God doth yield ; it cannot but worthily feem reproachful for us, to leave both the
one and the other, to become Difciples unto the moft hateful fort that live , to do as
they do, onely becaufe we fee their example before us, and have a delight to follow it.
Thus we may therefore fafely conclude , that it is not evil fimply to concur with the
Heathens either in opinion or action : and that conformity with them is onely then
a difgrace, when either we follow them in that they think and do amifs, or follow them
generally in that they do, without other reafon than only the likeing we have to the
pattern of their example : which likeing doth intimate a more univerfal approbation
of them than is allowable. *Fauftus* the Manichey therefore objecting againft the
Jews, that they forfook the Idols of the Gentiles ; but their Temples, and Oblations,
and Altars, and Prieft-hoods & all kind of Miniftry of holy things, they exercifed even
as the Gentiles did, yea more fuperftitioufly a great deal ; againft the Catholick Chriftians likewife, that between them and the Heathens there was in many things little
difference; *From them (faith Fauftus) ye have learned to hold that one onely God is the
Author of all , their facrifices ye have turned into feafts of charity , their Idols into Martyrs , whom ye honour with the like Religious offices unto theirs ; The Ghofts of the dead ye
appeafe with Wine and delicates, the feftival days of the Nations ye celebrate together with
them , and of their kind of life ye have utterly changed nothing.* S. *Auftines* defence in
behalf of both, is, that touching the matters of action , Jews and Catholick Chriftians were free from the Gentiles faultinefs , even in thofe things
which

Margin notes:
D ut 14. 7.
Levit. 11.

Levit. 15. 19.

Deut. 14.
Lev. t. 11.

Eph. c. 2. 14.

That the ex-
ample of the
eldeft Chur-
ches is not
herein againft
us.

T.C. l. 1. p 132
The Councels
although they
did not ob-
ferve them-
felves always
in making of
decrees this
Rule: yet have
kept this con-
fideration con-
tinually in ma-
king of their
laws, that they
would have
the Chriftians
differ from
others in their
Ceremonies.

Tom. 6. cont.
Fauft. Manich.
lib. 20. cap. 4.

T. C. l. 1. p. 131. Alſo it was decreed in another Councel, that they ſhould not deck their houſes with Bay-leaves and green Boughs, becauſe the Pagans did ſo; and that they ſhould not reſt from their labour thoſe days that the Pagans did, that they ſhould not keep the firſt day of every moneth as they did.

which were objected as tokens of their agreement with the Gentiles, and concerning their conſent in opinion, they did not hold the ſame with the Gentiles, becauſe Gentiles had ſo taught, but becauſe Heaven and Earth had ſo witneſſed the ſame to be truth, that neither the one ſort could err in being fully perſwaded thereof, nor the other but erre in caſe they ſhould not conſent with them. In things of their own nature indifferent, if either Councils or particular men have at any time with ſound judgment miſliked conformity between the Church of God and Infidels, the cauſe thereof hath been ſomewhat elſe then onely affectation of diſſimilitude. They ſaw it neceſſary ſo to do, in reſpect of ſome ſpecial accident, which the Church being not always ſubject unto, hath not ſtill cauſe to do the like. For example, in the dangerous days of trial,

T. C. l. 3. p. 131. Tertul. ſaith, Our faith he, better is the Religion of the Heathen: for they uſe no ſolemnity of the Chriſtians, neither the Lords day, neither &c. but we are not afraid to be called Heathen T. l. 3. p. 131. But having ſhewed this in general to be the Policy of God firſt, and of his people afterwards, to put as much difference as can be commodiouſly between the people of God and others which are not, I ſhall not &c.

wherein there was no way for the truth of Jeſus Chriſt to triumph over infidelity, but through the conſtancy of his Saints, whom yet a natural deſire to ſave themſelvs from the flame, might peradventure cauſe to joyn with Pagans in external cuſtoms, too far uſing the ſame as a cloak to conceale themſelves in, and a miſt to darken the eyes of Infidels withal: for remedy hereof thoſe laws it might be were provided, which forbad that Chriſtians ſhould deck their houſes with Boughs, as the Pagans did uſe to do, or reſt thoſe Feſtival days whereon the Pagans reſted, or celebrate ſuch feaſts as were, though not Heatheniſh, yet ſuch that the ſimpler ſort of Heathens might be beguiled in ſo thinking them. As for *Tertullians* judgement concerning the rites and Orders of the Church ; no man, having judgment, can be ignorant how juſt exceptions may be taken againſt it. His opinion touching the Catholick Church was as unindifferent, as touching our Church the opinion of them that favour this pretended reformation is. He judged all them who did not Montanize, to be but carnally minded; he judged them ſtill over-abjectly to fawn upon the *Heathens*, and to curry favour with *Infidels* ; Which as the Catholick Church did well provide that they might not do indeed, ſo *Tertullian* over-often through diſcontentment carpeth injurriouſly at them, as though they did it even when they were free from ſuch meaning. But if it were ſo that either the judgment of thoſe Councils before alledged, or of *Tertullian* himſelf againſt Chriſtians, are in no ſuch conſideration to be underſtood as we have mentioned ; if it were ſo, that men are condemned as well of the one as of the other, only for uſing the Ceremonies of a Religion contrary unto their own, and that this cauſe is ſuch as ought to prevaile no leſs with us than with them ; ſhall it not follow, that ſeeing there is ſtill between our Religion and Paganiſme the ſelf-ſame contrariety, therefore we are ſtill no leſs rebukeable, if we now deck our houſes with Boughs, or ſend New-years gifts unto our Friends ; or feaſt on thoſe days which the Gentiles then did, or ſit after prayer as they were accuſtomed? For ſo they inſer upon the premiſes, that as great difference as commodiouſly may be, there ſhould be in all outward Ceremonies between the people of God, and them which are not his people. Again, they teach as hath been declared, that there is not as great a difference as may be between them, except the one do avoid whatſoever Rites and Ceremonies uncommanded of God the other doth embrace. So that generally they teach, that the very difference of ſpiritual condition it ſelf between the Servants of Chriſt and others, requireth ſuch difference in Ceremonies between them, although the one be never ſo far disjoyned in time or place from the other. But in caſe the people of God and *Belial* do chance to be neighbours ; then as the danger of infection is greater, ſo the ſame difference they ſay, is thereby made more neceſſary. In this reſpect as the Jews were ſevered from the Heathen, ſo moſt eſpecially from the Heathen neareſt them. And in the ſame reſpect we, which ought to differ howſoever from the Church of *Rome*, are now, they ſay, by reaſon of our nearneſs more bound to differ from them in Ceremonies then from *Turks*. A ſtrange kind of ſpeech unto Chriſtian ears, and ſuch, as I hope, they themſelves do acknowledge unadviſedly uttered. *We are not ſo much to fear infection from Turks as from Papiſts.* What of that? we muſt remember that by conforming rather our ſelves in that reſpect to *Turks*, we ſhould be ſpreaders of a worſe infection into others, then any we are likely to draw from *Papiſts* by our conformity with them in ceremonies. If they did hate, as *Turks* do, the Chriſtian ; or as *Canaanites* did of old the Jewiſh Religion even in groſs ; the circumſtance of local nearneſs in them unto us, might haply inforce

ia

in us a duty of greater separation from them then from those other metioned. But forafmuch as Papifts are much in Chrift neerer unto us then Turks, is there any reasonable man, trow you, but will judge it meeter that our Ceremonies of Chriftian Religion fhould be Popifh that Turkifh, or Heatheniſh? Eſpecially conſidering that we were not brought to dwell amongft them (as *Ifrael* in *Canaan*) having not been of them. For even a very part of them we were. And when God did by his good Spirit put it into our hearts, firſt, to reform our felves (whence grew our ſeparation) and then by all good means to ſeek alſo their reformation; had we not onely cut off their corruptions, but alſo eſtranged our ſelves from them in things indifferent; who ſeeth not how greatly prejudicial this might have been to ſo good a cauſe, and what occaſion it had given them to think (to their greater obduration in evil) that through a froward or wanton deſire of innovation, we did conſtrainedly thoſe things, for which conſcience was pretended? Howſoever the caſe doth ſtand, as *Juda* had been rather to chooſe conformity in things indifferent with *Ifrael*, when they were neareſt oppoſites, then with the fartheſt removed Pagans: So we in like caſe, much rather with Papiſts than with *Turks*: I might add further for more full and complete anſwer, ſo much concerning the large odds between the caſe of the eldeſt Churches in regard of thoſe Heathens, and ours in reſpect of the Church of *Rome*, that very Cavillation it ſelf ſhould be ſatisfied, and have no ſhift to fly unto.

8. But that no one thing may detain us over-long, I return to their reaſons againſt our conformity with that Church. That extreme diſſimilitude which they urge upon us, is now commended as our beſt and ſafeſt policy for eſtabliſhment of ſound Religion. The ground of which politick Poſition is, that *Evils muſt be cured by their contraries*: and therefore the cure of the Church infected with the poyſon of Antichriſtianity, muſt be done by that which is thereunto as contrary as may be. A medled eſtate of the orders of Goſpel, and the Ceremonies of Popery, is not the beſt way to baniſh Popery. We are contrariwiſe of opinion, that he which will perfectly recover a ſick, and reſtore a diſeaſed body unto health, muſt not endeavour ſo much to bring it to a ſtate of ſimple contrariety, as of fit proportion in contrariety unto thoſe evils which are to be cured. He that will take away extreme heat, by ſetting the body in extremity of cold, ſhall undoubtedly remove the diſeaſe, but together with it the diſeaſed too. The firſt thing therefore in skilful cures, is the knowledge of the part affected; the next is of the evil which doth affect it; the laſt is not onely of the kind, but alſo of the meaſure of contrary things whereby to remove it. They which meaſure Religion by diſlike of the Church of *Rome*, think every man ſo much the more ſound, by how much he can make the corruptions thereof to ſeem more large. And therefore ſome there are, namely the *Arrians* in reformed Churches of *Poland*, which imagine the Canker to have eaten ſo far into the very bones and Marrow of the Church of *Rome*, as if it had not ſo much as a ſound belief; no not concerning God himſelf, but that the very belief of the Trinity were a part of Antichriſtian corruption; and that the wonderful providence of God did bring to paſs, that the Biſhop of the Sea of *Rome* ſhould be famous for his tripple Crown; a ſenſible mark whereby the world might know him to be that myſtical beaſt ſpoken of in the Revelation, to be that great and notorious Antichriſt in no one reſpect ſo much, as in this, that he maintaineth the Doctrine of the Trinity. Wiſdome therefore and skill is requiſite to know, what parts are ſound in that Church, and what corrupted. Neither is it to all men apparent which complain of unſound pars, with what kind of unſoundneſs every ſuch part is poſſeſſed. They can ſay; that in *Doctrine*, in *Diſcipline*, in *Prayers*, in *Sacraments*, the Church of *Rome* hath (as it hath indeed) very foul and groſs corruptions: the nature whereof notwithſtanding becauſe they have not for the moſt part exact skill and knowledge to diſcern, they think that amiſs many times which is not, and the ſalve of reformation they mightily call for; but where & what the ſores are which need it, as they wot full little, ſo they think it not greatly material to ſearch; ſuch mens contentment muſt be wrought by ſtratagem: the uſual method of art is not for them. But with thoſe that profeſs more than ordinary and common knowledg of good from evil, with them that are able to put a difference between things naught, and things indifferent in the Church of *Rome*, we are yet at controverſie about the manner of removing that which is naught: whether it may not be perfectly helpt, unleſs that alſo

which

Marginal notes:

That it is not our beſt policy for the eſtabliſhment of ſound Religion, to have in their things no agreement with the Church of Rome being unſound.

T. C. l. p. 132. Common reaſon alſo doth teach that contraries are cured by their contraries.

Now Chriſtianity and Antichriſtianity, the Goſpel and Popery, be contrary: and therefore Antichriſtianity muſt be cured, not by it ſelf, but by that which is (as much as may be) contrary unto it.

which is indifferent be cut off with it, so far till no rite or ceremony remain which the Church of *Rome* hath, being not found in the Word of God. If we think this too extreme, they reply, that to draw men from great excess, it is not amiss though we

T. C. l. 1. p. 132. If a man would bring a drunken man to sobriety, the best and nearest way is to carry him as far from his excess in drink as may be: and if a man could not keep a mean, it were better to fault in prescribing less, than he should drink, than to fault in giving him more then he ought. As we see, to bring a stick which is crooked to be straight, we do not onely bow it so far until it come to be straight, but we bend it so far until we make it to be so crooked on the other side, as it was before of the first side, to this end that at the last it may stand straight, and as it were in the mid way between both the crooks.

use them unto somewhat less then is competent; and that a crooked stick is not straightned, unless it be bent as far on the clean contrary side, that so it may settle it self at the length in a middle estate of evenness between both. But how can these comparisons stand them in any stead? When they urge us to extreme opposition against the Church of *Rome*, do they mean we should be drawn unto it onely for a time, and afterwards return to a mediocrity? or was it the purpose of those reformed Churches, which utterly abolished all Popish Ceremonies, to come in the end back again to the middle point of evenness, and moderation? Then have we conceived amiss of their meaning. For we have always thought their opinion to be, that utter inconformity with the Church of *Rome* was not an extremity whereunto we should be drawn for a time, but the very mediocrity it self wherein they meant we should ever continue. Now by these comparisons it seemeth clean contrary, that howsoever they have bent themselves at first to an extreme contrariety against the Romish Church, yet therein they will continue no longer, then onely till such time as some more moderate course for establishment of the Church may be concluded. Yea, albeit this were not at the first their intent, yet surely now there is great cause to lead them unto it. They have seen that experience of the former Policy; which may cause the authors of it to hang down their heads. When *Germany* had stricken off that which appeared corrupt in the Doctrine of the Church of *Rome*, but seemed nevertheless in Discipline still to retain therewith very great conformity: *France*, by that rule of policy, which hath been before mentioned, took away the Popish orders which *Germany* did retain. But process of time hath brought more light into the World; whereby men perceiving that they of the Religion in *France* have also retained some orders which were before in the Church of *Rome*, and are not commanded in the Word of God; there hath arisen a sect in England, which following still the very self-same Rule of policy, seeketh to reform even the *French* reformation, and purge out from thence also dregs of Popery. These have not taken as yet such root that they are able to establish any thing. But if they had what would spring out of their stock, and how far the unquiet wit of man might be carried with rules of such policy, God doth know. The trial

That we are not to abolish our Ceremonies either because Papists upbraid us as having taken from them, or for that they are said hereby to conceive, I know not what, great hopes.

which we have lived to see, may somewhat teach us what posterity is to fear. But our Lord, of his infinite mercy, avert whatsoever evil our swervings on the one hand or on the other may threaten unto the state of his Church.

9. That the Church of *Rome* doth hereby take occasion to blaspheme, and to say our Religion is not able to stand of it self, unless it lean upon the staff of their Ceremonies, is not a matter of so great moment, that it did need to be objected, or doth deserve to receive answer. The name of blasphemy in this place, is like the shoo of *Hercules* on a childs foot. If the Church of *Rome* do use any such kind of silly exprobration, it is no such ugly thing to the ear, that we should think the honour and credit of our Religion to receive thereby any great wound. They which hereof make so perillous a matter, do seem to imagine, that we have erected of late a frame of some new Religion; the furniture whereof we should not have borowed from our Enemies, lest they relieving us, might afterwards laugh and gibe at our poverty: whereas in truth the Ceremonies which we have taken from such as were before us, are not things that belong to this or that sect, but they are the ancient rites and customes of the Church of Christ; whereof our selves being a part, we have the self-same interest in them which our Fathers before us had, from whom the same are descended unto us. Again, in case we had been so much beholden privately unto them, doth the reputation of one Church stand by saying unto another, *I need thee not?* If some should be so vain and impotent, as to miar a benefit with reproachful upbraiding, where at the least they suppose themselves to have bestowed some good turn; yet surely a wise bodies part it were not, to put out his fire, because his fond and foolish Neighbour, from whom he borrowed peradventure wherewith to kindle it,

might

might haply cast him therewith in the teeth, saying, Were it not for me thou would-est freez, and not be able to heat thy self. As for that other argument derived from the secret affection of Papists, with whom our conformity in certain Ceremonies is said to put them in great hope, that their whole Religion in time will have rë-entrance ; and therefore none are so clamorous amongst us for the observation of these ceremonies, as Papists and such as Papists suborn to speak for them : whereby it clearly appeareth how much they rejoyce, how much they triumph in these things; our answer hereunto is still the same, that the benefit we have by such ceremonies overweigh even this also. No man which is not exceeding partial can well deny, but that there is most just cause wherefore we should be offended greatly at the Church of *Rome.* Notwithstanding at such times as we are to deliberate for our selves, the freer our minds are from all distempered affections, the founder and better is our judgement. When we are in a fretting mood at the Church of *Rome,* and with that angry disposition enter into any cogitation of the order and rites of our Church ; taking particular survey of them, we are sure to have always one eye fixed upon the countenance of our Enemies, and according to the blith or heavy aspect thereof, our other eye sheweth some other suitable token either of dislike or approbation towards our own orders. For the rule of our judgement in such case being onely that of *Homer , This is the thing which our Enemies would have*; what they seem contented with, even for that very cause we reject ; and there is nothing but it pleaseth us much the better, if we espie that it gauleth them. Miserable were the state and condition of that Church, the weighty affairs whereof should be ordered by those deliberations wherein such an humour as this were predominant. We have most heartily to thank God therefore, that thay amongst us, to whom the first consultations of causes of this kind fell, were men which aiming at another mark, namely, the glory of God and the good of this his Church, took that which they judged thereunto necessary, not rejecting any good or convenient thing, onely because the Church of *Rome* might perhaps like it. If we have that which is meet and right, although they be glad, we are not to envy them this their solace ; we do not think it a duty of ours, to be in every such thing their tormentors. And whereas it is said, that Poperie for want of this utter extir-pation hath in some places taken root and flourish-ed again, but hath not been able to re-establish it self in any place, after provision made against it by utter evacuation of all Romish Ceremonies, and therefore as long as we hold any thing like un-to them, we put them in some more hope, than if all were taken away, as we deny not but this may be true; so being of two evils to choose the less, we hold it better that the friends and fa-yourers of the Church of Rome, should be in some kind of hope to have a corrupt religion restored, then both we and they con-ceive just fear, lest under colour of rooting out Popery, the most effectual means to bear up the state of Religion be removed, and so away made either for Paganisme, or for extreme Barbarisme to enter. If desire of weakning the hope of others should turn us away from the course we have taken ; how much more the care of preventing our own fear, with-hold us from that we are urged unto ? Especially seeing that our own fear we know, but we are not so certain what hope the Rites and Orders of our Church have bred in the hearts of others. For it is no sufficient Argument therefore to say, that in maintaining and urging these Ceremonies, none are so clamorous as Papists, and they whom Papists suborn ; this speech being more hard to justifie than the former, and so their proof more doubtful then the thing it self, which they prove. He that were certain that this is true, must have marked who they be that speak for Ceremonies ; he must have noted, who amongst them do speak oftenest, or is most earnest : he must have been both acquainted thorowly with the Religion of such, and also privy what conferences or compacts are passed in secret between them and others ; which kinds of notice are not wont to be vulgar and common. Yet they which alleage this, would have it taken as a thing that needeth no proof, a thing which all men know and see. And if so be it were granted them as true, what gain

T. C. l. 3. p. 175. To prove the Papists tri-umph and joy in these things I alleadged fur-ther that there are none which make such clamors for these cere-monies, as the Papists and those which they suborn.

ΗΚΑΝ ἡ δ'ήισ'ιν Πριαμ-@ .II.

T. C. l. 3. p. 179. Thus they conceiving hope of having the rest of their Popery in the end, it causeth them to be more frozen in their wickedness, &c. For not the cause but the occasion also ought to be taken away, &c. Al-though let the Reader judge, whether they have cause given to hope, that the tale of Popery yet remayning, they shall the easilier hale in the whole body after : consi-dering also what Master *Bucer* noteth, that where these things have been left, there Popery have returned; but on the other part, in places which hath been cleansed of these dregs, it hath not been seen that it hath had any entrance.

they by it ? Sundry of them that be Popish, are eager in maintenance of Ceremonies. Is it so strange a matter to find a good thing furthered by ill men of a sinister intent and purpose, whose forwardness is not therefore a bridle to such as favour the same cause with a better and sincere meaning ? They that seek, as they say, the removing of all Popish Orders out of the Church, and reckon the state of Bishops in the number of those orders, do (I doubt not) presume that the cause which they prosecute, is holy. Notwithstanding it is their own ingenuous acknowledgment, that even this very cause which they term so often by an excellency, *The Lords cause*, is, gratissima, *must acceptable unto some which hope for prey and spoile by it*, *and that our Age hath store of such*, *and that such are the very Sectaries of* Dionysius the famous *Atheist.*

Ecclef. discf. 19.
Now if hereupon we should upbraid them with irreligious, as they do us, with superstitious favours ; if we should follow them in their own kind of pleading, and say, that the most clamorous for this pretended reformation, are either Atheists, or else Proctors suborned by Atheists ; the answer which herein they would make unto us, let them apply unto themselves, and there an end. For they must not forbid us to presume our cause in defence of our Church-orders to be as good as theirs against them, till the contrary be made manifest to the World.

The error of which, they say, godly *Brethren conceive in regard of such Ceremonies as we have common with the Church of Rome. T.C. l.1 p.131. There be numbers which have Antichristianisme in such detestation, that they cannot without grief of mind behold them.* And afterwards, *such godly Brethren are not easily to be grieved, which they seem to be, when they are thus Martyred in their minds, for Ceremonies, which (to speak the best of them) are unprofitable.*

10. In the mean while sorry we are, that any good and godly mind should be grieved with that which is done. But to remedy their grief, lyeth not so much in us as in themselves. They do not wish to be made glad with the hurt of the Church : and to remove all out of the Church, whereat they shew themselves to be sorrowful, would be, as we are perswaded, hurtful, if not pernicious thereunto. Till they be able to perswade the contrary, they must and will, I doubt not, find out some other good mean to cheer up themselves. Amongst which means the example of *Geneva* may serve for one. Have not they the old Popish custome of using God-fathers and God-mothers in Baptisme ; the old Popish custom of administring the blessed Sacrament of the holy Eucharist with wafer-cakes ? These things the godly there can digest. Wherefore should not the godly here learn to do the like, both in them and in the rest of the like nature ? Some further mean peradventure it might be to asswage their grief, if so be they did consider the revenge they take on them, which have been, as they interpret it, the workers of their continuance in so great grief so long. For if the maintenance of Ceremonies be a corrosive to such as oppugne them ; undoubtedly, to such as maintain them, it can be no great pleasure, when they behold how that which they reverence is oppugned. And therefore they that judge themselves Martyrs, when they are grieved, should think withal what they are whom they grieve. For we are still to put them in mind, that the cause doth make no difference ; for that it must be presumed as good at the least on our part as on theirs, till it be in the end decided, who have stood for truth, and who for error. So that till then the most effectual medicine, and withal the most sound, to ease their grief, must not be (in our opinion) the taking away of those things whereat they are grieved, but the altering of that perswasion which they have concerning the same : For this we therefore both pray and labour ; the more because we are also perswaded, that it is but conceit in them to think, that those *Romish* Ceremonies, whereof we have hitherto spoken, are like leprous clothes, infectious unto the Church ; or like soft and gentle Poysons, the venome whereof being insensibly pernicious, worketh death, and yet is never felt working. Thus they say : but because they say it only, and the World hath not as yet had so great experience of their art, in curing the diseases of the Church, that the bare authority of their word should perswade in a cause so weighty ; they may not think much if it be required at their hands to shew ; First, by what means so deadly infection can grow from similitude between us and the Church of *Rome* ; in these things indifferent : Secondly, for that it were infinite, if the Church would provide against every such evil as may come to pass, it is not sufficient that they shew possibility of dangerous event, unless there appear some likeli-hood also of the same to follow in us, except we prevent it. Nor is this enough, unless it be moreover made plain, that there is no good and sufficient way of prevention, but by evacuating

T.C.L. 1. p 171. Alt ough the corruptions in them so is not straight to the heart, yet as gentle poysons they consume by little and little.

-ciiating clean, and by emptying the Church of every such Rite and Ceremony, as is presently called in question. Till this be done, their good affection towards the safety of the Church is acceptable, but the way they prescribe us to preserve it by, must rest in suspence. And lest hereat they take occasion to turn upon us the speech of the Prophet *Jeremy* used against *Babylon*, *Behold we have done our endeavour to cure the diseases of Babylon*, but she through her wilfulness doth rest uncured : let them consider into what streights the Church might drive it self, in being guided by this their counsel. Their axiome is, that the sound beleiving Church of Jesus Christ, may not be like Heretical Churches in any of those indifferent things, which men make choice of, and do not take by prescript appointment of the Word of God. In the word of God the use of Bread is prescribed, as a thing without which the Eucharist may not be celebrated : but as for the kind of bread, it is not denyed to be a thing indifferent. Being indifferent of it self, we are by this axiome of theirs to avoid the use of unleavened Bread in the Sacrament, because such bread the Church of *Rome* being Heretical useth. But doth not the self-same axiome bar us even from leavened Bread also; which the Church of the *Grecians* useth : the opinions whereof are in a number of things the same, for which we condemn the Church of *Rome* ; and in some things erroneous, where the Church of *Rome* is acknowledged to be found : as namely in the Article of the Holy Ghosts proceeding ? and lest here they should say that because the Greek Church is farther off, and the Church of *Rome* nearer, we are in that respect rather to use that which the Church of *Rome* useth not ; let them imagine a reformed Church in the City of Venice, where a Greek Church and Popish both are. And when both these are equally near, let them consider what the third shall do. Without either leavened or unleavened bread, it can have no Sacrament : the word of God doth tye it to neither ; and their axiome doth exclude it from both. If this constraine them, as it must, to grant that their axiome is not to take any place, save in those things onely where the Church hath larger scope ; it resteth that they search out some stronger reason then they have as yet alleadged ; otherwise they constrain not us to think that the Church is tied unto any such rule or axiome, no not then when she hath the widest field to walk in, and the greater store of choice.

11 Against such Ceremonies generally as are the same in the Church of *England* and of *Rome*, we see what hath been hitherto alleadged. Albeit therefore we do not find the one Churches having of such things, to be sufficient cause why the other should not have them : nevertheless in case it may be proved, that amongst the number of Rites and Orders common unto both, there are particulars, the use whereof is utterly unlawful, in regard of some special bad and noysome quality ; there is no doubt but we ought to relinquish such Rites and orders, what freedom soever we have to retain the other still. As therefore we have heard their general exception against all those things, which being not commanded in the Word of God, were first received in the Church of *Rome*, and from thence have been derived into ours, so it followeth that now we proceed unto certain kinds of them, as being excepted against, not onely for that they are in the Church of *Rome*, but are besides either *Jewish* or abused unto Idolatry, and so grown scandalous. The Church of *Rome* they say being ashamed of the simplicity of the Gospel, did almost out of all Religions take what soever had any fair and gorgeous shew, borrowing in that respect from the *Jews* sundry of their abolished Ceremonies. Thus by foolish and ridiculous imitation, all their Massing furniture almost they took from the Law, lest having an Altar and a Priest, they should want Vestments for their Stage; so that whatsoever we have in common with the Church of *Rome*, if the same be of this kind, we ought to remove it. *Constantine* the Emperor *speaking of the keeping of the Feast of* Easter, saith, *That it is an unworthy thing to have any thing common with that most spiteful company of the Jews. And a little after he saith, That it is most absurd and against reason, that the Jews should vaunt and glory that the Christians could not keep those things without their Doctrine. And in another place it is said after this sort ; It is convenient so to order the matter, that we have nothing common with that Nation. The Councel of Laodicea, which was afterward confirmed by the first general Councel, decreed that the Christians should not take unleavened bread of the Jews, or communicate with their impiety.* For the easier manifestation of truth in this point, two things there are which must be considered, namely the causes wherefore the Church should decline from *Jewish* Ceremonies ; and how far it ought to to do. One cause is, that the Jews were the deadliest and spitefullest Enemies of

X   Chri-

Ier. 51. 5.

Their exception against such Ceremonies as we have received from the Church of *Rome*, that Church having taken them from the Iews.

Ecclef. difci. fol. 38. And *T. C. l. 3. p.* 181. Many of these Popish Ceremonies fault by reason of the pomp in them : where they should be agreeable to the simplicity of the Gospel of Christ crucified.

T. C. l. 1. p. 132. *Eufeb. li.* 3. *c.* 17. *Sozra. lib.* 1. *c.* 9. *So.* 1. *Concil. 1 ead.* Can. 38.

Christianity that were in the world, and in this respect their Orders so far to be shunned, as we have already set down in handling the matter of Heathenish Ceremonies. For no Enemies being so venemous against Christ as *Jews*, they were of all other most odious, and by that mean least to be used as fit Church patterns for imitation. Another cause is the solemne abrogation of the *Jews* ordinances ; which ordinances for us to resume, were to check our Lord himself which hath disanulled them. But how far this second cause doth extend, it is not on all sides fully agreed upon. And touching those things whereunto it reacheth not, although there be small cause wherefore the Church should frame it self to the *Jews* example, in respect of their persons which are most hateful ; yet God himself having been the Author of their laws, herein they are (notwithstanding the former consideration) still worthy to be honoured, and to be followed above others, as much as the state of things will bear. Jewish Ordinances had some things natural, and of the perpetuity of those things no man doubteth. That which was positive, we likewise know to have been by the comming of Christ partly necessary not to be kept, and partly indifferent to be kept or not. Of the former kind Circumcision and Sacrifice were. For this point *Stephen* was accused; and the Evidence which his accusers brought against him in judgement was, *This man ceaseth not to speak blasphemous words against this holy place and the law, for we have heard him say that this Jesus of Nazareth shall destroy this place, and shall change the Ordinances that Moses gave us.* True it is that this

Acts 6, 13, 14.

Doctrine was then taught, which unbeleevers condemning for blasphemy, did therein commit that which they did condemn. The Apostles notwithstanding from whom *Stephen* had received it, did not so teach the abrogation, no not of those things which were necessarily to cease, but that even the jews being Christians, might for a time continue in them. And therefore in *Jerusalem* the first Christian Bishop not circum-

Vide Niciph la c.25, Sulpiti. & Sever-p. 145, in Edit, Plant.

cised was *Mark*, and he not Bishop till the days of *Adrian* the Emperour, after the overthrow of *Jerusalem*, there having been fifteen Bishops before him which were all of the Circumcision. The Christian *Jews* did think at the first not only themselves, but the Christian Gentiles also bound, and that necessarily, to observe the whole law. There went forth certain of the Sect of *Pharises* which did believe, and

Acts 15.

they comming unto Antioch, taught that it was necessary for the Gentiles to be circumcised, and to keep the Law of *Moses*. Whereupon there grew dissention, *Paul* and *Barnabas* disputing against them. The determination of the Council held at *Jerusalem* concerning this matter, was finally this. *Touching the Gentiles which believe,*

Acts 21. 25.

we have written and determined that they observe no such thing ; Their protestation by

Acts 15. 24.

Letters is, *For as much as we have heard that certaine which departed from us have troubled you with words, and cumbred your minds, saying, Ye must be circumcised and keep the Law ; know, that we gave them no such commandement.* *Paul* therefore continued still teaching the Gentiles, not only that they were not bound to observe the Laws of *Moses*, but that observation of those laws which were necessary to be abrogated, was in them altogether unlawful. In which point his Doctrine was misreported, as though he had every where Preached this, not only concerning the Gentiles, but also touching the Jews. Wherefore comming unto *James* and the rest of the Clergie at *Jerusalem*,

Acts 13.

they told him plainly of it, saying, *Thou seest, brother, how many thousand Jews they are which beleive, and they are all zealous of the law, Now they are informed of thee, that thou teachest all the Jews which are amongst the Gentiles, to forsake Moses, and sayest that they ought not to circumcise their children, neither to live after the customes.* And hereupon they gave him counsel to make it apparent in the eyes of all men, that those flying reports were untrue, and that himself being a Jew, kept the Law, even as they did. In some things therefore we see the Apostles did teach, that there ought not to be conformity between the Christian Jews and Gentiles. How many things this law of inconformity did comprehend, there is no need we should stand to examine. This general is true, that the Gentiles were not made conformable unto the Jews, in that which was necessary

Acts 15. 28.

to cease at the comming of Christ. Touching things positive which might either cease or continue as occasion should require, the Apostles tendring the zeal of the Jews, thought it necessary to bind even the Gentiles for a time to abstain as the Jews did, from things offered unto Idols, from blood, from strang-

Acts 16. 4.

led. These Decrees were every where delivered unto the Gentiles to be straightly observed and kept. In the other matters where the Gentiles were free,

Rom. 14. 10.

and the Jews in their own opinion still tied the Apostles Doctrine unto the Jews, was

was, *Condemn not the Gentile*; unto the Gentile, *Despise not the Jew*: the one sort they warned to take heed that scrupulosity did not make them rigorous; in giving unadvised sentence against their brethren which were free; the other, that they did not become scandalous, by abusing their liberty and freedom to the offence of their weak Brethren which were scrupulous. From hence therefore two conclusions there are, which may evidently be drawn; the first, that whatsoever conformity of positive laws the Apostles did bring in between the Churches of the Jews and Gentiles, it was in those things onely, which might either cease or continue a shorter or longer time, as occasion did most require; the second, that they did not impose upon the Churches of the Gentiles, any part of the Jews Ordinances with bond of necessary and perpetual observation (as we all both by doctrine and practice acknowledge) but onely in respect of the conveniency and fitnefs for the present state of the Church as then it stood. The words of the Councels Decree concerning the Gentiles are, *It seemed good to the Holy Ghost and to us, to lay upon you no more burthen, saving onely those things of necessity, abstinence from Idol-offerings, from strangled, and blood, and from fornication.* So that in other things positive which the coming of Christ did not necessarily extinguish, the Gentiles were left altogether free. Neither ought it to seem unreasonable, that the Gentiles should necessarily be bound and tied to Jewish Ordinances, so far forth as that decree importeth. For to the Jew, who knew that their difference from other Nations which were Aliens and strangers from God, did especially consist in this, that Gods people had positive Ordinances given to them of God himself; it seemed marvellous hard, that the Christian Gentiles should be incorporated into the same Commonwealth with Gods own chosen people, and be subject to no part of his Statutes, more then onely the Law of Nature, which Heathens count themselves bound unto. It was an opinion constantly received amongst the Jews, that God did deliver to the sons of *Noah* seven Precepts: namely, to live in same form of Regiment under; First, publique Laws; Secondly; to serve and call upon the Name of God: Thirdly, to shun Idolatry: Fourthly, not to suffer effusion of blood: Fifthly, to abhor all unclean knowledge in the flesh: Sixthly, to commit no Rapine: Seventhly, and finally, not to eat of any living Creature whereof the the blood was out first let out. If therefore the Gentiles would be exempted from the Law of *Moses*, yet it might seem hard they should also cast off even those things positive which were observed before *Moses*, and which were not of the same kinde with Laws that were necessarily to cease. And peradventure hereupon the Councill faw it expedient to determine, that the Gentiles should according unto the third, the seventh and the fifth of those Precepts, abstain from things sacrificed unto Idols, from strangled and blood, and from fornication. The rest the Gentiles did of their own accord observe, Nature leading them thereunto. And did not Nature also teach them to abstain from fornication? No doubt it did. Neither can we with reason think, that as that as the former two ore positive; so likewise this, being meant as the Apostle doth otherwise usually understand it. But very Mariage within a number of degrees, being not onely by the Law of *Moses*, but also by the Law of the sons of *Noah* (for so they took it) an unlawful discovery of nakednefs; this discovery of nakednefs by unlawful Mariages, such as *Moses* in the Law reckoneth up, I think it for mine own part more probable to have been meant in the words of that Canon, then fornication according unto the sense of the Law of Nature. Words must be taken according to the matter whereof they are uttered. The Apostles command to abstain from blood. Construe this according to the Law of Nature, and it will seem that Homicide onely is forbidden. But construe it in reference to the law of the Jews about which the question was, and it shall easily appear to have a clean other sense, and in any mans judgement a truer, when we expound it of eating, and not of shedding blood: So if we speak of fornication, he that knoweth no law but onely the law of Nature, must needs make thereof a narrower construction, then he which measureth the same by a law wherein sundry kindes even of Conjugal Copulation are prohibited as impure, unclean, unhonest. Saint *Paul* himself doth term incestuous Marriage, Fornication. If any do rather think that the Christian Gentiles themselves through the loose and corrupt Custome of those times, took simple Fornication for no sinne, and were in that respect offensive unto believing Jewes which by the Law had been better taught; our proposing of another conjecture, is unto theirs no prejudice. Some things therefore we see there were, wherein

the

X 2

Margin notes:
Lib. qui Seders Olam inscribitur.

ת נינוו ı
ב כרבחתשו ב
ע ג
ד שפיכותהםים ד
ה ג'יל ירוייה ה
ה חנול ה
ת אגו סיו ההו ז

Heb. 3. 4.
1 Cor 5. 11.
Gal. 5. 19.

Levit. 18.

1 Cor. 1.

the Gentiles were forbidden to be like unto the Jews ; fome things wherein they were commanded not to be unlike. Again, fome things alfo there were, wherein no Law of God did let, but that they might be either like or unlike ; as occafion fhould require. And unto this purpofe *Leo* faith, *Apoftolical Ordinance (beloved) knowing that our Lord Jefus Chrift came not into this world to undo the Law, hath in fuch fort diftinguifhed the Myfteries of the Old Teftament, that certain of them it hath chofen out to benefit Evangelical knowledge withal, and for that purpofe appointed that thofe things which before were Jewifh, might now be Chriftian Cuftomes.* The caufe why the Apoftles did thus conform the Chriftians as much as might be, according to the pattern of the Jews, was to rein them in by this mean the more, and to make them cleave the better. The Church of Chrift hath had in no one thing fo many and fo contrary occafions of dealing, as about Judaifm ; fome having thought the whole Jewifh Law wicked and damnable in it felf ; fome not condemning it as the former fort abfolutely, have notwithftanding judged it either fooner neceffary to be abrogated, or further unlawful to be obferved then truth can bear ; fome of fcrupulous fimplicity urging perpetual and univerfal obfervation of the Law of *Mofes* neceffary, as the Chriftian Jews at the firft in the Apoftles times ; fome as Hereticks, holding the fame no lefs even after the contrary determination fet down by confent of the Church at *Jerufalem* ; finally, fome being herein refolute through meer infidelity, and with open profeft enmity againft Chrift, as unbelieving Jews. To controul flanderers of the Law and Prophets, fuch as Marcionites and Manichees were, the Church in her Liturgies hath intermingled with Readings out of the New Teftament, Leffons taken out of the Law and Prophets ; whereunto *Tertullian* alluding, faith of the Church of Chrift, *It intermingleth with Evangelical and Apoftolical Writings, the Law and the Prophets ; and from thence it drinketh in that Faith which with Water it fealeth, clotheth with the Spirit, nourifheth with the Euchariſt, with Martyrdom fetteth forward.* They would have wondred in thofe times to hear, that any man being not a Favourer of Herefie, fhould term this by way of difdain, *mangling of the Gofpels and Epiftles.* They which honour the Law as an Image of the Wifdom of God himfelf, are notwithftanding to know that the fame had an end in Chrift. But what ? Was the Law fo abolifhed with Chrift, that after his Afcention the Office of Priefts became immediately wicked, and the very name hateful, as importing the exercife of an ungodly function ? No, as long as the glory of the Temple continued, and till the time of that final defolation was accomplifhed, the very Chriftian Jews did continue with their Sacrifices and other parts of Legal Service. That very Law therefore which our Saviour was to abolifh, did not fo foon become unlawful to be obferved as fome imagine ; nor was it afterward unlawful fo far, that the very name of Altar, of Priefts, of Sacrifice it felf, fhould be banifhed out of the World. For though God do now hate Sacrifice, whether it be Heathenifh or Jewifh, fo that we cannot have the fame things which they had, but with impiety ; yet unlefs there be fome greater let then the onely evacuation of the Law of *Mofes*, the names themfelves may (I hope) be retained without fin, in refpect of that proportion which things eftablifhed by our Saviour have unto them, which by him are abrogated. And fo through all the writings of the ancient Fathers we fee that the words which were, do continue ; the onely difference is, that whereas before they had a literal, they now have a metaphorical ufe, and are as fo many notes of remembrance unto us, that what they did fignifie in the letter, is accomplifhed in the truth. And as no man can deprive the Church of this liberty, to ufe names whereunto the Law was accuftomed ; fo neither are we generally forbidden the ufe of things which the Law hath, though it neither command us any particulars, as it did the Jews a number ; and the weightieft which it did command them, are unto us in the Gofpel prohibited. Touching fuch as through fimplicity of errour did urge univerfal and perpetual obfervation of the Law of *Mofes* at the firft, we have fpoken already. Againft Jewifh Hereticks and falfe Apoftles teaching afterwards the felf fame, S. *Paul* in every Epiftle commonly either difputeth or giveth warning. Jews that were zealous for the Law, but withal Infidels in refpect of Chriftianity, and to the name of Jefus Chrift moft fpiteful enemies, did while they flourifhed no lefs perfecute the Church then Heathens, and after their eftate was overthrown, they were not that way fo much to be feared. Howbeit, becaufe they had their Synagogues in every famous City almoft throughout the World, and by that means great opportunity to withdraw from the Chriftian Faith, which to do

thy

they spared no labour ; this gave the Church occasion to make sundry Laws against them. As in the Council of Laodicea, *The Festival Presents which Jews or Hereticks use to send must not be received, nor Holy-days solemnized in their company.* Again, *From the Jews men ought not to receive their unleavened bread, nor to communicate with their impieties.* Which Council was afterwards indeed confirmed by the sixt general Council. But what was the true sense or meaning both of the one and the other? Were Christians here forbidden to communicate in unleavened bread, because the Jews did so, being Enemies of the Church ? He which attentively shall weigh the words, will suspect that they rather forbid communion with Jews, then imitation of them : much more, if with these two decrees be compared a third in the Council of *Constantinople* ; *Let no man either of the Clergy or Laity eat the unleavened of the Jews, nor enter into any familiarity with them, nor send for them in sickness, nor take physick at their hands, nor as much as go into the Bath with them. If any do otherwise, being a Clergy man, let him be deposed; if being a Lay person, let excommunication be his punishment.* If these Canons were any argument, that they which made them, did utterly condemn similitude between the Christians and Jews, in things indifferent appertaining unto Religion, either because the Jews were enemies unto the Church, or else for that their ceremonies were abrogated ; these reasons had been as strong and effectual against their keeping the Feast of *Easter* on the same day the Jews kept theirs, and not according to the custom of the west Church. For so they did from the first begining till *Constantines* time. For in these two things the east and west Churches did interchangeably both confront the Jews, and concur with them: the west Church using unleavened bread, as the Jews in their Passover did, but differing from them in the day whereon they kept the Feast of *Easter* ; contrariwise, the east Church celebrating the Feast of *Easter* on the same day with the Jews, but not using the same kinde of bread which they did. Now if be so the east Church in using leavened bread had done well, either for that the Jews were enemies to the Church, or because Jewish ceremonies were abrogated, how should we think but that *Victor* the Bishop of *Rome*, (whom all judicious men do in that behalf disallow) did well to be so vehement and fierce in drawing them to the like dissimilitude for the Feast of *Easter?* Again, if the west Churches had in either of those two respects affected dissimilitude with the Jews in the Feast of *Easter*, what reason had they to draw the eastern Church herein unto them, which reason did not enforce them to frame themselves unto it in the ceremony of leavened bread ? difference in Rites should breed no controversie between one Church and another ; but if controversie be once bred, it must be ended. The Feast of *Easter* being therefore litigious in the days of *Constantine*, who honored of all other Churches most the Church of *Rome*, which Church was the Mother from whose breasts he had drawn that food, which gave him nourishment to eternal life, sith agreement was necessary, and yet impossible, unless the one part were yielded unto ; his desire was, that of the two, the eastern Church should rather yield. And to this end he useth sundry perswasive speeches. When *Stephen* the Bishop of *Rome* going about to shew what the Catholick Church should do, had alledged what the Hereticks themselves did, namely, that they received such as came unto them, and offered not to baptize them anew. S. *Cyprian* being of a contrary minde to him about the matter at that time in question, which was, *Whether Hereticks converted ought to be rebaptized, yea or no*, answered the allegation of Pope *Stephen* with exceeding great stomach, saying, [a] *To this degree of wretchidness the Church of God and Spouse of Christ is now come, that her ways she frameth to the example of Hereticks; that to celebrate the Sacraments which heavenly instruction hath delivered, light it self doth borrow from darkness, and Christians do that which Antichrists do.* Now albeit *Constantine* have done that to further a better cause, which *Cyprian* did to countenance a worse, namely, the rebaptization of Hereticks; and have taken advantage at the odiousness of the Jews, as *Cyprian* of Hereticks, because the eastern Church kept their Feast of *Easter* always the fourteenth day of the moneth as the Jews did, what day of the week soever it fel; or howsoever *Constantine* did take occasion in the handling of that cause to say, [b] *It is unworthy to have any thing common with that spiteful Nation of the Jews*; shall every motive argument used in such kinde of conferences, be made a rule for other still to conclude the like by, concerning all things of like nature, when as probable inducements may lead them to the contrary ? Let both this and other allegations suitable unto it, cease to bark any longer idly against that truth, the course and passage whereof it is not in them to hinder.

tenentur irreciti istud festum sanctissimum ageremus. In nostra enim sinum est potestate ut illorum more rejecto, verio æ ac magis sincero instituto, quod quidem usq; à prima passionis die hactenus recolimus hujus festi celebrationem ad posterorum seculorum memoriam propagemus. Nihil ig tur sit nobis cum Iudæorum turba nimium odiosa maxime.

I 2. But.

Their exception againſt ſuch Ceremonies as have been abuſed by the Church of *Rome*, and are ſaid in that reſpect to be ſcandalous.

Mat. 18. 6.

1 Pet. 2. 8.
2 Sam. 11. 13.
Rom. 1. 24.
Ezek. 36. 20.
Tertull. lib. de virgin. veland.

Epiſt. ad Quadrum Hiſp.

12. But the weightieſt exception, and of all the moſt worthy to be reſpected, is againſt ſuch kinde of ceremonies, as have been ſo groſly and ſhamefully abuſed in the Church of *Rome*, that where they remain they are ſcandalous, yea, they cannot chooſe but be ſtumbling blocks and grievous cauſes of offence. Concerning this point therefore we are firſt to note, what properly it is to be ſcandalous or offenſive. Secondly, what kinde of ceremonies are ſuch; and thirdly, when they are neceſſarily for remedy thereof to be taken away, and when not. The common conceit of the vulgar ſort is, whenſoever they ſee any thing which they miſlike and are angry at, to think that every ſuch thing is ſcandalous, and that themſelves in this caſe are the men concerning whom our Saviour ſpake in ſo fearful manner, ſaying, *Whoſoever ſhall ſcandalize or offend any one of theſe little ones which believe in me* [that is, as they conſtrue it, whoſoever ſhall anger the meaneſt and ſimpleſt Artizan which carrieth a good minde, by not removing out of the Church ſuch Rites and Ceremonies as diſpleaſe him] *better he were drowned in the bottom of the Sea.* But hard were the caſe of the Church of Chriſt, if this were to ſcandalize. Men are ſcandalized when they are moved, led, and provoked unto ſin. At good things evil men may take occaſion to do evil; and ſo Chriſt himſelf was a rock of offence in *Iſrael*, they taking occaſion at his poor eſtate, and at the ignominy of his Croſs, to think him unworthy the name of that great & glorious *Meſſias*, whom the Prophets deſcribe in ſuch ample and ſtately terms. But that which we therefore term offenſive, becauſe it inviteth men to offend; and by a dumb kinde of provocation encourageth, moveth, or any way leadeth unto ſin, muſt of neceſſity be acknowledged actively ſcandalous. Now ſome things are ſo even by their very eſſence and nature, ſo that whereſoever they be found, they are not, neither can be without this force of provocation unto evil; of which kinde all examples of ſin and wickedneſs are. Thus *David* was ſcandalous, in that bloody act, whereby he cauſed the enemies of God to be blaſphemous: thus the whole ſtate of *Iſrael* was ſcandalous, when their publique diſorders cauſed the Name of God to be ill ſpoken of amongſt the Nations. It is of this kinde that *Tertullian* meaneth: *Offence or ſcandal, if I be not deceived,* ſaith he, *is when the example not of a good, but of an evil thing, doth ſet men forward unto ſin. Good things can ſcandalize none ſave onely evil mindes:* Good things have no ſcandalizing nature in them. Yet that which is of it own nature, either good, or at leaſt not evil; may by ſome accident become ſcandalous at certain times, and in certain places, and to certain men, the open uſe thereof nevertheleſs being otherwiſe without danger. The very nature of ſome Rites and Ceremonies therefore is ſcandalous, as it was in a number of thoſe which the Manichees did uſe, and is in all ſuch as the Law of God doth forbid. Some are offenſive onely through the agreement of men to uſe them unto evil, and not elſe; as the moſt of thoſe things indifferent which the Heathens did to the ſervice of their falſe gods; which another in heart condemning their Idolatry, could not do with them in ſhew and token of approbation, without being guilty of ſcandal given. Ceremonies of this kinde are either deviſed at the firſt unto evil; as the Eunomian Hereticks in diſhonour of the bleſſed Trinity, brought in the laying on of water but once, to croſs the cuſtom of the Church, which in Baptiſm did it thrice: or elſe having had a profitable uſe, they are afterwards interpreted and wreſted to the contrary; as thoſe Hereticks which held the Trinity to be three diſtinct, not perſons, but natures, abuſed the ceremony of three times laying on water in Baptiſm, unto the ſtrengthning of their Hereſie. The element of water in Baptiſm neceſſary, once to lay iron or twice is indifferent. For which cauſe *Gregory* making mention thereof, ſaith, *To dive an Infant either thrice or but once in Baptiſm, can be no way a thing reproveable, ſeeing that both in three times waſhing, the Trinity of perſons; and in one; the unity of the God-head may be ſignified.* So that of theſe two ceremonies, neither being hurtful in it ſelf, both may ſerve unto good purpoſe; yet one was deviſed, and the other converted unto evil. Now whereas in the Church of *Rome*, certain ceremonies are ſaid to have been ſhamefully abuſed unto evil, as the ceremony of croſſing at Baptiſm, of kneeling at the Euchariſt, of uſing Wafer-cakes, and ſuch like; the queſtion is, whither for remedy of that evil, wherein ſuch ceremonies have been ſcandalous, and perhaps may be ſtill unto ſome even amongſt our ſelves, whom the preſence and ſight of them may confirm in that former errour whereto they ſerved in times paſt, they are of neceſſity to be removed. Are theſe or any other ceremonies we have common with the Church of *Rome*, ſcandalous and wicked in their very nature? This no man objecteth. Are any ſuch, as have

been

been polluted from their very birth, and instituted even at the first unto that thing which is evil? That which hath been ordained impiously at the first, may wear out that impiety in tract of time; and then what doth let, but that the use thereof may stand without offence? The names of our Moneths and our days, we are not ignorant from whence they came, and with what dishonour unto God they are said to have been devised at the first. What could bespoken against any thing more effectual to stir hatred, then that which sometime the antient Fathers in this case spake? Yet those very names are at this day in use throughout Christendom, without hurt or scandal to any. Clear and manifest it is, that things devised by Hererickes, yea devised of a very heretical purpose even against Religion, and at their first devising worthy to have been withstood, may in time grow meet to be kept; as that custom, the inventers whereof were the *Eunomian* Hereticks. So that customes once established and confirmed by long use, being presently without harm, are not in regard of their corrupt original to be held scandalous. But concerning those our Ceremonies which they reckon for most Popish,

Hom. 11. de Pasch. Idololatri e consuetudo in tantum hominum occœcaverat, ut, Solis, Lunæ, Martis, mercurii, Iovis, Veneris, Saturni, & versis elementorum ac Dæmonum appellationibus dies vocitarent & lucis tenebrarum nomen imponerent Baca deratione temp.c.4. Octavus dies idem, Primus est, ad quem ditur, indeq̃ rursus Hebdomada inchoatur. His nomina a Plantiis Gentilitas indidit, habere sedentes a Sole Spiritum, a Lunatorpor, a Marte Sanguinem, a Mercurio ingenium & Linguam, a Iove Temperantiam, a Venere Voluptatem, a Saturno Tarditatem, Isid Hispal.5. Etymol. c. 30. Dies dicti a Dis, quorum nomina Romani quibusdam syderibus sacraverunt.

they are not able to avouch that any of them was otherwise instituted, than unto good, yea, so used at the first. It followeth then that they all are such as having served to good purpose, were afterwards converted unto the contrary. And sith it is not so much as objected against us, that we retain together with them the evil wherewith they have been infected in the Church of *Rome*: I would demand who they are whom we scandalize, by using harmless things unto that good end for which they were first instituted. Among our selves that agree in the approbation of good use, no man will say that one of us is offensive and scandalous unto another. As for the favourers of the Church of *Rome*, they know how far we herein differ and dissent from them; which thing neither we conclude, and they by their publique writings also profess daily how much it grieveth them: so that of them there will not many rise up against us, as witnesses unto the Inditement of scandal, whereby we might be condemned and cast, as having strengthened them in that evil wherewith they pollute themselves in the use of the same Ceremonies. And concerning such as withstand the Church of *England* herein, and hate it because it doth not sufficiently seem to hate *Rome*, they (I hope) are far enough from being by this mean drawn to any kind of Popish error. The multitude therefore of them, unto whom we are scandalous through the use of abused Ceremonies, is not so apparent, that it can justly be said in general of any one sort of men or other, we cause them to offend. If it be so that now or then some few are espied, who having been accustomed heretofore to the rites and Ceremonies of the Church of *Rome*, are not so scoured of their former rust, as to forsake their antient perswasion which they have had, howsoever they frame themselvs to outward obedience of laws & orders; because such may misconster the meaning of our Ceremonies and so take them as though they were in every sort the same they have been, shall this be thought a reason sufficient whereon to conclude, that some Law must necessarily be made to abolish all such ceremonies? They answer, that there is no law of God which doth bind us to retain them. And S. *Pauls* rule is, that in those things from which without hurt we may lawfully abstain, we should frame the usage of our liberty with regard to the weaknes and imbecillity of our brethren. Wherefore unto them which stood upon their own defence, saying, *All things are lawful unto me*; he replyeth, *But all things are not expedient* in regard of others. All things are clean, all meats are lawful; but evil unto that man that eateth offensively. If for thy meats sake thy brother be grieved, thou walkest no longer according to Charity. Destroy not him with thy meat, for whom Christ died. Dissolve not for foods sake the work of God. We that are strong, must bear the imbecillity of the impotent, and not please our selves. It was a weaknes in the Christian Jews, and a maym of judgment in them, that they thought the gentiles polluted by the eating of those meats, which themselves were afraid to touch, for fear of transgressing the Law of *Moses*; yea, hereat their hearts did so much rise, that the Apostles had just cause to fear, least they would rather forsake Christianity, then endure any fellowship with such, as made no conscience of that which was unto them abominable. And for this cause

1 Cor. 6.12.

Rom. 14.
and 15.1.

mention

mention is made of destroying the weak by meats, and of dissolving the work of God, which was his Church, a part of the living stones whereof were beleiving Jews. Now those weak brethren before mentioned are said to be as the Jews were, and our Ceremonies which have been abused in the Church of *Rome*, to be as the scandalous meats from which the Gentiles are exhorted to abstaine in the presence of Jews, for fear of averting them from Christian faith. Therefore as Charity did bind them to refrain from that for their brethrens sake, which otherwise was lawful enough for them; so it bindeth us for ourbrethrens sake likewise to abolish such Ceremonies, although we might lawfully else retain them. But between these two cases there are great odds. For neither are our weak brethren as the *Jews*, nor the Ceremonies which we use as the meats which the Gentiles used. The *Jews* were known to be generally weak in that respect; whereas contrariwise the imbecillity of ours is not common unto so many, that we can take any such certain notice of them. It is a chance if here and there some one be found; and therefore seeing we may presume men commonly otherwise, there is no necessity that our practice should frame it self by that which the Apostle doth prescribe to the Gentiles. Againe, their use of meats was not like unto our Ceremonies; that being a matter of private action in common life, where every man was free to order that which himself did; but this a publique constitution for the ordering of the Church: and we are not to look that the Church should change her publique laws and Ordinances, made according to that which is judged ordinarily and commonly fittest for the whole, although it chance that for some particular men the same be found inconvenient, especially when there may be other remedy also against the sores of particular inconveniences. In this case therefore where any private harm doth grow, we are not to reject instruction, as being an unmeet plaister to apply unto it; neither can we say that he which appointeth Teachers for Physicians in this kind of evil, is, as if a man *would set one to watch a child all day long lest he should hurt himself with a knife, whereas by taking away the knife from him, the danger is avoided, and the service of the man better imployed.* For a knife may be taken from a child, without depriving them of the benefit thereof which have years and discretion to use it. But the Ceremonies which Children do abuse, if we remove quite and clean, as it is by some required that we should; then are they not taken from children onely, but from others also; which is as though because Children may perhaps hurt themselves with knives, we should conclude, that therefore the use of knives is to be taken quite and clean from men also. Those particular Ceremonies which they pretend to be so scandalous, we shall in the next book have occasion more throughly to sift, where other things also traduced in the publique duties of the Church, whereunto each of these appertaineth, are together with these to be touched, and such reasons to be examined as have at any time been brought either against the one or the other. In the mean while against the conveniency of curing such evils by instruction, strange it is that they should object the multitude of other necessary matters, wherein Preachers may better bestow their time, then in giving men warning not to abuse Ceremonies; a wonder it is that they should object this, which have so many years together troubled the Church with quarrels concerning these things, and are even to this very hour so earnest in them, that if they write or speak publiquely but five words, one of them is lightly about the dangerous estate of the Church of *England*, in respect of abused Ceremonies. How much happier had it been for this whole Church, if they which have raised contention therein about the abuse of Rites and Ceremonies, had considered in due time that there is indeed store of matters fitter and better a great deal for Teachers to spend time and labour in? It is through their importunate and vehement asseverations, more than through any such experience which we have had of our own, that we are enforced to think it possible for one or other now and then, at leastwise in the prime of the Reformation of our Church, to have stumbled at some kind of Ceremonies, Wherein for as much as we are contented to take this upon their credit, and to think it may be; sith also they further pretend the same to be so dangerous a snare to their souls, that are at any time taken therein, they must give our Teachers leave for the saving of those souls (be they never so few) to intermingle sometime with other more necessary things admonition concerning these not unnecessary. Wherein they should in reason more easily yeild this leave, considering that hereunto we shall not need to use the hundreth part of that time, which themselves think very needful to bestow in making most bitter Invectives against the Ceremonies of the Church.

Vide Harme-kop. l. g. lib. 1 § 28.

T. C. l. 3 f. 178.

T. C. l. 3. p. 177. It is not so convenient that the Minister having so many necessary points to bestow his time in, should be driven to spend it in giving warning of not abusing them, of which (although they were used to the best) there is profit.

                                             13 But

13. But to come to the last point of all, the Church of *England* is grievously charged with forgetfulness of her duty, which duty had been to frame her self unto the pattern of their example, that went before her in the work of Reformation. For *as the Churches of Christ ought to be most unlike the Synagogue of Antichrist in their indifferent Ceremonies; so they ought to be most like one unto another, and for preservation of unity to have as much as possible may be all the same Ceremonies. And therefore S. Paul to establish this order in the Church of Corinth, that they should make their gatherings for the poor upon the first day of the Sabbath (which is our Sunday) alleadgeth this for a reason, that he had so ordained in other Churches. Again, as children of one father, and servants of one family, so all Churches should not only have one diet, in that they have one Word, but also wear as it were one Livery in using the same Ceremonies.* Thirdly, *this rule did the great Councel of Nice follow, when it ordained, that where certain at the Feast of Pentecost did pray kneeling, they should pray standing; the reason whereof is added, which is that one custom ought to be kept throughout all Churches. It is true that the diversity of Ceremonies ought not to cause the Churches to dissent one with another: but yet it maketh most to the avoiding of dissention, that there be amongst them an unity, not only in Doctrine, but also in ceremonies. And therefore our form of service is to be amended, not onely for that it commeth too near that of the Papists, but also because it is so different from that of the reformed Churches.* Being asked to what Churches ours should conform it self, and why other Reformed Churches should not as well frame themselves to ours? their answer is, *That if there be any Ceremonies which we have better then others, they ought to frame themselves to us: if they have better then we, then we ought to frame our selves to them : if the Ceremonies be alike commodious, the latter Churches should conform themselves to the first, as the younger daughter to the elder. For as S. Paul in the members, where all other things are equal, noteth it for a mark of honour above the rest, that one is called before another to the Gospel : so is it for the same cause amongst the Churches. And in this respect he pincheth the Corinths, that not being the first which received the Gospel, yet they would have their several manners from other Churches. Moreover where the Ceremonies are alike commodious, the fewer ought to conform themselves unto the mo.* Forasmuch therefore as all the Churches (so far as they know which plead after this manner) of our confession in Doctrine, agree in the abrogation of divers things which we retain : our Church ought either to shew that they have done evil, or else she is found to be in fault that doth not conform her self in that, which she cannot denie to be well abrogated. In this axiome, that preservation of peace and unity amongst Christian Churches should be by all good means procured, we joyn most willingly and gladly with them. Neither deny we, but that to the avoiding of dissention it availeth much, that there be amongst them an unity as well in Ceremonies as in Doctrine. The only doubt is about the manner of their unity, how far Churches are bound to be uniform in their Ceremonies and what way they ought to take for that purpose. Touching the one, the rule which they have set down, is, that in Ceremonies indifferent all Churches ought to be one of them unto another as like as possibly they may be. Which possibly, we cannot otherwise conster, then that it doth require them to be even as like as they may be, without breaking any possitive Ordinance of God. For the Ceremonies whereof we speak, being matter of possitive Law; they are indifferent, if God have neither commanded nor forbidden them, but left them unto the Churches discretion; so that if as great uniformity be required as is possible in these things, seeing that the Law of God forbiddeth not any one of them; it followeth, that from the greatest unto the least they must be in every Christian Church the same, except meer impossibility of so having it be the hindrance. To us this opinion seemeth over-extreme and violent : we rather incline to think it a just and reasonable cause for any Church, the state whereof is free and independent, if in these things it differ from other Churches, not to judge it so fit and expedient to be framed therein by the pattern of their example, as to be otherwise framed then they. That of *Gregory* unto *Leander* : is a charitable speech and a peaceable : *In una fide nil officit Ecclesiæ sanctæ consuetudo diversa, Where the Faith of the holy Churches is one, a diffe-*

Our Ceremonies excepted against, for that some Churches reformed before ours, have cast out those things which we, notwithstanding their example to the contrary, do retain still.

T.C.l.1.p. 133.

1 Cor. 16.1.

Can. 20. The Canon of that Councel which is here cited, doth provide against kneeling at Prayer on Sundays, or for list day after *Easter* on any day, and not at the Feast of Pentecost onely.

T.C.lib. 1 pag. 182, 183

Rom. 16. 5, 7

1 Cor. 14. 37

rence

rence in customes of the Church doth no harme. That of S. *Augustine* to *Casſulanus* is somewhat particular, and toucheth what kind of ceremonies they are wherin one Church may vary from the example of another without hurt: *Let the faith of the whole Church, how wide ſoever it hath ſpred it ſelf, be always one, although the unity of beliefe be famous for variety of certaine ordinances, whereby that which is rightly beleeved, ſuffereth no kind of let or impediment.* Calvin goeth further. *As concerning rites in particular, let the ſentence of* Augustine *take place, which leaveth it free unto all Churches to receive their own cuſtome. Yea, ſometime it profiteth and is expedient that there be difference, leſt men ſhould think that Religion is tyed to outward ceremonies. Always provided than there be not emulation, nor that Churches delighted with novelty, affect to have that which others have not.* They which grant it true that the diverſitie of Ceremonies in this kind ought not to cauſe diſſenſion in Churches, muſt either acknowledge that they grant in effect nothing by theſe words ; or if any thing bee granted, there muſt as much be yeilded unto, as we affirme againſt their former ſtrict Aſſertion. For if Churches be urged by way of duty to take ſuch Ceremonies as they like not of, how can diſſenſion be avoided? will they ſay that there ought to be no diſſenſion, becauſe ſuch as are urged, ought to like of that whereunto they are urged ? If they ſay this, they ſay juſt nothing. For how ſhould any Church like to be urged of duty, by ſuch as have no authority or power over it, unto thoſe things which being indifferent, it is not of duty bound unto them ? It is their meaning, that there ought to be no diſſenſion, becauſe that which Churches are not bound unto, no man ought by way of duty to urge upon them ? and if any man do, he ſtandeth in the ſight both of God and men moſt juſtly blameable, as a needleſs Diſturber of the Peace of Gods Church, and an Author of Diſſenſion ? In ſaying this, they both condemne their owne practice, when they preſs the Church of England, with ſo ſtrict a bond of duty in theſe things, and they overthrow the ground of their practice, which is, that there ought to be in all kinde of Ceremonies uniformity, unleſs impoſſibility hinder it. For proofe whereof it is not enough to alledge what S. *Paul* did about the matter of collections, or what noblemen do in the Liveries of their Servants, or what the Councell of Nice did for ſtanding in time of Prayer on certain days : becauſe though S. *Paul* did will them of the Church of Corinth, every man to lay up ſome-

T. C. l. 1. p. 122. And therefore S. *Paul*, to eſtabliſh this order in the Church of Corinth, that they ſhould make their gatherings for the Poore upon the firſt day of the Sabbath, (which is our Sunday) alledgeth this for a reaſon, that he had ſo ordained in other Churches.

what by him upon the Sunday, and to reſerve it in ſtore, till himſelfe did come thither, to ſend it unto the Church of Jeruſalem for reliefe of the poore there ; ſignifying withall that he had taken the like order with the Churches of Galatia ; yet the reaſon which he yeeldeth of this order taken

T. C. l. p. 31,123. So that as children of one Father, & ſervants of one Maſter, he will have all the Churches, not only have one diet, in that they have one word, but alſo we are as it were one livery in uſing the ſame ceremonies. *T. C. l. 3, p. 133.* This rule did the great Council of Nice follow, &c. *Die Dominico & per omnem Pentecoſtem. nec de geniculis adorare, &c. De. cero. Milit.*

both in one place and the other, ſheweth the leaſt part of his meaning to have been that, whereunto his words are writhed. *Concerning collection for the Saints* (he meaneth them of Jeruſalem) *as I have given order to the Church of Galatia, ſo likewiſe dʒye* (ſaith the Apoſtle) *that is, in every firſt day of the Weeke let each of you lay aſide by himſelf, and reſerve according to that which God hath bleſſed him with, that when I come, collections be not then to make ; and that when I come, whom you ſhall chooſe, them I may forth with ſend away by Letters, to carry your beneficence unto Jeruſalem.* Out of which words, to conclude the duty of uniformitie throughout all Churches in all manner of indifferent Ceremonies, will be very hard, and therefore beſt to give it over. But perhaps they are by ſo much the more loth to forſake this argument, for that it hath, though nothing elſe, yet the name of Scripture, to give it ſome kinde of countenance more than the pretext of Livery-coats affordeth them. For neither is it any mans duty to cloath all his children, or all his ſervants with one weed ; nor theirs to cloath themſelves ſo, if it were left to their own judgements, as theſe Ceremonies are left of God to the judgment of the Church. And ſeeing Churches are rather in this caſe like divers Families, than like divers ſervants of one Familie, becauſe every Church, the State whereof is independent upon any other, hath authority to appoint orders for it ſelf in things indifferent ; therefore of two we may rather inferre, that as one Familie is not abridged of libertie to be cloathed in Friers Gray, for that another doth wear Clay-Colour ; ſo neither are all Churches bound to the ſelfſame indifferent Ceremonies which it liketh ſundry to uſe. As for that Canon in the Council of Nice, let them but read it and weigh it well. The ancient uſe of the Church throughout

all

all Christendome, was, for fifty days after Easter (which fifty days were called Pentecost, though most commonly the last day of them which is Whitsunday be so called) in like sort on all the Sundays throughout the whole year their manner was to stand at Prayer : whereupon their meetings unto that purpose on those days, had the names of *Stations* given them. Of which custome *Tertullian* speaketh in this wise; *It is not with us thought fit either to fast on the Lords Day, or to pray kneeling. The same immunitie from fasting and kneeling wee keep all the time which is between the Feasts of Easter and Pentecost.* This being therefore an order generally received in the Church; when some began to be singular and different from all others, and that in a Ceremony which was then judged very convenient for the whole Church even by the whole, those few excepted which break out of the common pale ; the Council of *Nice* thought good to enclose them again with the rest, by a law made in this sort: *Because there are certain which will needs kneel at the time of Prayer on the Lords day, and in the fifty days after Easter ; the holy Synode judging it meet that a convenient custome be observed throughout all Churches, hath decreed, that standing we make our Prayers to the Lord.* Whereby it plainly appeareth, that in things indifferent, what the whole Church doth think convenient for the whole, the same if any part do wilfully violate, it may be reformed and intrayled again by that generall authority whereunto each particular is subject, and that the Spirit of singularity in a few ought to give place unto publick judgement; this doth cleerly enough appear : but not that all Christian Churches are bound in every indifferent Ceremony to be uniform; because where the whole Church hath not tyed the parts unto one and the same thing, they being therein left each to their own choice, may either do, as others do, or else otherwise, without any breach of duty at all. Concerning those indifferent things, wherein it hath been heretofore thought good that all Christian Churches should be uniform, the way which they now conceive to bring this to pass was then never thought on. For till now it hath been judged, that seeing the law of God doth not prescribe all particular Ceremonies which the Church of Christ may use, and so great variety of them as may be found out, it is not possible that the law of nature and reason should direct all Churches unto the same things, each deliberating by it self what is most convenient : the way to establish the same things indifferent throughout them all, must needs be the judgement of some judiciall authority drawn into one only sentence, which may be a rule for every particular to follow. And because such authority over all Churches, is too much to be granted unto any one mortall man ; there yet remaineth that which hath been alwayes followed, as the best, the safest, the most sincere and reasonable way ; namely the verdict of the whole Church orderly taken, and set down in the assembly of some generall Councell. But to maintain that all Christian Churches ought for unities sake to be uniform in all Ceremonies and then to teach that the way of bringing this to pass must be by mutuall imitation, so that where we have better Ceremonies than others, they shall be bound to follow us, and we them where theirs are better : how should we think it agreeable and consonant unto reason? For sith in things of this nature there is such variety of particular inducements, whereby one Church may be led to think that better, which another Church led by other inducements judgeth to be worse : (For example, the East Church did think it better to keep Easter day after the manner of the Jews, the West Church better to do otherwise ; the Greek Church judgeth it worse to use unleavened bread in the Eucharist, the Latine Church leavened: one Church esteemeth it not so good to receive the Eucharist sitting as standing, another Church not so good standing as sitting ; there being on the one side probable Motives as well as on the other) unless they adde somewhat else to define more certainly what Ceremonies shall stand for best, in such sort that all Churches in the world shall know them to be the best, and so know them, that there may not remain any question about this point, we are not a whit the nearer for that they have hitherto said. They themselves although resolved in their own judgements what Ceremonies are best, foreseeing that such as they are addicted unto, be not all so cleerly and so incomparably best, but others there are or may be, at leastwise when all things are well considered, as good ; knew not which way smoothly to rid their hands of this matter, without providing some more certain rule to be followed for establishment of uniformity in Ceremonies, when there are divers kinds of equall goodness; and therefore in this case they say, that the

later

T.C.l.3.p.188.
If the Ceremony be alike commodious, the later Churches should conform th mselves to the first &c.
And again,
The fewer ought to conform themselves unto the more.
Rom. 16. 5.
1 Cor. 14. 36.

latter Churches & the fewer should conform themselves unto the elder & if it no Iere-upon they conclude, that forasmuch as all the Reformed Churches (so far as they know) which are of our confession in Doctrine, have agreed already in the abrogation of divers things which we retain: our Church ought either to shew that they have done evil; or else she is found to be in fault for not conforming her self to those Churches, in that which she cannot deny to be in them well abrogated. For the authority of the first Churches, (and those they account to be the first in this cause which were first reformed) they bring the comparison of younger Daughters conforming themselves in attire to the example of their elder Sisters; wherein there is just as much strength of reason as in the Livery-Coats before mentioned. S. Paul, they say noteth it for a marke of speciall honour, that *Epænetus* was the first man in all Achaia which did imbrace the Christian faith; after the same sort he toucheth it also as a speciall preheminence of *Junius* and *Andronicus*; that in Christianity they were his Auncients? the *Corinthians* he pincheth with this demand, *Hath the Word of God gone out from you, or hath it lighted on you alone?* But what of all this? If any man should think that alacrity and forwardnes in good things doth adde nothing unto mens condemnation; the two former speeches of S. *Paul* might lead him to reforme his judgement. In like sort to take down the stomack of proud conceited men, that glory as though they were able to set all others to schoole, there can be nothing more fit than some such words as the Apostles third sentence doth contain; wherein he teacheth the Church of Corinth to know, that there was no such great ods between them and all the rest of their brethren, that they should think themselves to be Gold, and the rest to be but Copper. He therefore useth speech unto them to this effect: *Men instructed in the knowledge of Jesus Christ there both were before you, and are besides you in the world; ye neither are the Fountain from which first, nor yet the River into which alone the Word hath flowed.* But although as *Epænetus* was the first Man in all Achaia, so Corinth had been the first Church in the whole World that received Christ: the Apostle doth not shew that in any kinde of things indifferent whatsoever, this should have made their example a law unto all others. Indeed the example of sundry Churches for approbation of one thing doth sway much; but yet still as having the force of an example only, and not of a law. They are effectuall to move any Church unles some greater thing do hinder; but they binde none, no not though they be many; saving only when they are the Major part of a generall Assembly, and then their voices being moe in number, must over-sway their judgements who are fewer, because in such cases the greater half is the whole. But as they stand out single each of them by it self, their number can purchase them no such Authority that the rest of the Churches being fewer, should be therefore bound to follow them and to relinquish as good Ceremonies as theirs for theirs. Whereas therefore it is concluded out of these so weak Premises, that the retaining of divers things in the Church of *England*, which other reformed Churches have cast out, must needs argue that we do not well, unles we can shew that they have done ill; what needed this wrest to draw out from us an accusation of forain Churches? It is not proved as yet, that if they have done well, our duty is to follow them, and to forsake our own course, because it differeth from theirs, although indeed it be as well for us every way, as theirs for them. And if the proofs alleadged for confirmation hereof had been found, yet seeing they lead no further than only to shew, that where we can have no better Ceremonies, theirs must be taken; as they cannot with modesty think themselves to have found out absolutely the best which the wit of men may devise; so liking their own somewhat better than other mens, even because they are their own, they must in equity allow us to be like unto them in this affection: which if they do, they ease us of that uncourteous burden, whereby we are charged either to condemn them, or else to follow them. They grant we need not follow them, if our own ways already be better. And if our own be but equall, the law of common indulgence alloweth us to think them at the least half a thought the better, because they are our own; which we may very well do, and never draw any Inditement at all against theirs, but think commendably even of them also.

14 To leave reformed Churches therefore and their actions for him to judge of, in whose sight they are, as they are; and our desire is that they may even in his sight be found such, as we ought to endeavour by all meanes that our own may likewise
be

T.C.l.3.p.183.
Our Church ought either to shew that they have done evil, or else she is found to be in fault that doth not conform her self in that which she cannot deny to be well abrogated.

A Declaration of the proceedings of the Church of England, for establishment of things as they are.

be: somewhat we are enforced to speak by way of simple Declaration, concerning the proceedings of the Church of *England* in these affairs, to the end that men whose mindes are free from those partiall constructions, whereby the only name of difference from some other Churches is thought cause sufficient to condemn ours, may the better discern whether that we have done be reasonable, yea or no The Church of *England* being to alter her received laws concerning such Orders, Rites, and Ceremonies as had been in former times an hindrance unto Piety and Religious Service of God, was to enter into consideration first, that the change of laws, especially concerning matter of Religion, must be warily proceeded in. Laws, as all other things humane, are many times full of imperfection, and that which is supposed behoveful unto men, proveth oftentimes most pernicious. The wisdom which is learned by tract of time, findeth the laws that have been in former Ages establisht, needful in later to be abrogated. Besides, that which sometime is expedient, doth not always so continue: and the number of needless laws unabolisht, doth weaken the force of them that are necessary. But true withal it is, that alteration, though it be from worse to better, hath in it inconveniences, and those weighty : unless it be in such laws as have been made upon speciall occasions, which occasions ceasing, laws of that kind do abrogate themselves. But when we abrogate a law as being ill made, the whole cause for which it was made still remaining : do we not herein revoke our very own deed, and upbraid our selves with folly, yea, all that were makers of it with over-sight and with error ? Further, if it be a law which the custome and continual practice of many ages or years hath confirmed in the minds of men, to alter it, must needs be troublesome and scandalous. It amazeth them, it causeth them to stand in doubt, whether any thing be in it self by nature either good or evil, and not all things rather such as men at this or that time agree to account of them, when they behold even those things disproved, disanulled, rejected, which use had made in a manner natural. What have we to induce men unto the willing obedience and observation of laws, but the weight of so many mens judgments, as have with deliberate advice assented thereunto ; the weight of that long experience, which the world hath had thereof with consent and good liking ? So that to change any such law, must needs with the common sort impair and weaken the force of those grounds, whereby all laws are made effectual. Notwithstanding we do not deny alteration of laws to be sometimes a thing necessary ; as when they are unnatural, or impious, or otherwise hurtful unto the publique community of men, and against that good for which humane societies were instituted. When the Apostles of our Lord and Saviour were ordained to alter the laws of Heathenish Religion received throughout the whole world ; chosen I grant they were (S. *Paul* excepted) the rest ignorant, poor simple, un-schooled altogether and un-lettered men: howbeit extraordinarily indued with ghostly wisdom from above before they ever undertook this enterprize, yea, their authority confirmed by miracle, to the end it might plainly appear that they were the Lords Ambassadors, unto whose Sovereign power for all flesh to stoop, for all the Kingdoms of the earth to yeeld themselves willingly conformable in whatsoever should be required, it was their duty. In this case therefore their oppositions in maintenance of publique superstition against Apostolick endeavours, as that they might not condemn the ways of their ancient Predecessors, that they must keep *Religiones traditas*, the rites which from Age to Age had descended, that the Ceremonies of Religion had been ever accounted by so much holier as elder ; these and the like allegations in this case were vain and frivolous. Not to stay longer therefore in speech concerning this point, we will conclude, that as the change of such laws as have been specified is necessary, so the evidence that they are such must be great. If we have neither voice from heaven that so pronounceth of them ; neither sentence of men grounded upon such manifest and clear proof, that they in whose hands it is to alter them, may likewise infallibly even in heart and conscience judge them so ; upon necessity to urge alteration, is to trouble and disturbe without necessity. As for arbitrary alterations, when laws in themselves not simply bad or unmeet are changed for better and more expedient, if the benefit of that which is newly better devised be but small, sith the custome of easiness to alter and change is so evil, no doubt but to bear a tolerable sore, is better then to venter on a dangerous remedy. Which being generally thought upon, as a matter that touched neerly their whole enterprize; whereas change was notwithstanding concluded necessary, in regard of the great hurt which the Church did receive by a number of things then in use, whereupon a great deal of that which had been, was now to be taken away and removed out of the Church; yet sith there are divers ways of abrogating things established, they saw it best to cut off presently such things, as might in that sort be extinguished without danger, leaving the rest to be abolished by disusage through tract of time. And as this was done for the manner of abrogation; so touching the stint or measure thereof, Rites and Ceremonies, and other external things of like nature being hurtful unto the Church, either in respect of their quality, or in regard of their number; in the former there could be no doubt or difficulty what should be done; their deliberation in the latter was more hard. And therefore inasmuch as they did resolve to remove only such things of that kind as the Church might best spare, retaining the residue; their whole councel is in this point utterly condemned, as having either proceeded from the blindness of those times, or from negligence, or from desire of honour and glory, or from an erroneous opinion that such things might be tolerated for a while; or if it did proceed (as they which would seem most favourable, are content to think it possible) from a purpose *partly the easilier to draw Papists unto the Gospel*, by keeping so many orders still the same with theirs, *and partly to redeem peace thereby, the breach whereof they might fear would ensue upon more thorow alteration*; or howsoever it came to pass, the thing they did is judged evil.

T. C. l. 1. p. 29. It may well be, their purpose was by that temper of Popish Ceremonies with the Gospel, partly the easilier to draw the Papists to the Gospel, &c, partly to redeem peace thereby.

But such is the lot of all that deal in publique affairs, whether of Church or Common-wealth, that which men list to surmise of their doings, being it good or ill, they must beforehand patiently arme their minds to indure. Wherefore to let go private surmises, whereby the thing it self is not made either better or worse; if just and allowable reasons might lead them to do as they did, then are all these censures frustrate. Touching ceremonies harmeless therefore in themselves, and hurtful only in respect of number: was it amisse to decree, that those things which were least needful and newliest come, should be the first that were taken away, as in the abrogating of a number of Saints days, and of other the like customes it appeareth they did, till afterwards the form of common Prayer being perfected, Articles of sound Religion and Discipline agreed upon, Catechismes framed for the needful instruction of youth, Churches purged of things that indeed were burthensome to the people, or to the simple offensive and scandalous, all was brought at the length unto that wherein now we stand? Or was it amiss, that having this way eased the Church as they thought of superfluity, they went on till they had pluckt up even those things also which had taken a great deal stronger and deeper root, those things which to abrogate without constraint of manifest harm thereby arising, had been to alter unnecessarily (in their judgments) the antient received custome of the whole Church, the universal practice of the people of God, and those very decrees of our Fathers which were not only set down by agreement of general Councels, but had accordingly been put in ure, and so continued in use till that very time present? True it is that neither Councels nor customes, be they never so ancient and so general, can let the Church from taking away that thing which is hurtful to be retained. Where things have been instituted, which being convenient and good at the first, do afterward in process of time wax otherwise, we make no doubt but they may be altered, yea though Councels or Customes General have received them. And therefore it is but a needless kind of opposition which they make who thus dispute, *If in those things which are not expressed in the Scripture, that is to be observed of the Church, which is the custome of the people of God and decree of our forefathers; then how can these things at any time be varied, which heretofore have been once ordained in such sort?* Whereto we say, that things so ordained are to be kept, howbeit not necessarily, any longer then till there grow some urgent cause to ordain the contrary. For there is not any Positive Law of men, whether it be general or particular, received by formal express consent, as in Councels; or by secret approbation, as in customes it commeth to pass; but the same may be taken away if occasion serve. Even as we all know, that many things kept generally heretofore, are now in like sort generally unkept and abolished every where. Notwithstanding,

T. C. l. 3. p. 33.

T. C. l. 3. p. 30.

standing till such things be abolished, what exception can there be taken against the judgement of S. *Augustine*, who saith, that, Of things harmeless whatsoever there is which the whole Church doth observe throughout the world, to argue for any mans immunitie from observing the same, it were a point of most insolent madness? And surely, odious it must needs have been, for one Christian Church, to abolish that which all had received and held for the space of many ages, and that without any detriment unto Religion so manifest and so great, as might in the eyes of unpartiall men appear sufficient to cleere them from all blame of rash and inconsiderate proceeding, if in fervor of zeale they had removed such things. Whereas contrariwise so reasonable moderation herein used, hath freed us from being deservedly subject unto that bitter kind of obloquie, whereby as the Church of Rome doth under the colour of love towards those things which be harmless, maintaine extremly most hurtfull corruptions; so we peradventure might be opbraided, that under colour of hatred towards those things that are corrupt, we are on the other side as extreme, even against most harmless Ordinances, And as they are obstinate to retain that, which no man of any conscience is able well to defend. so we might be reckoned fierce and violent, to tear away that which if our own mouths did condemn, our consciences would storme and repine thereat. The Romans having banished *Tarquinius* the Proud, and taken a solemn oath that they never would permit any man more to reigne, could not herewith content themselves, or think that tyranny was throughly extinguished, till they had driven one of their Consuls to depart the City, against whom they found not in the world what to object, saving only that his name was *Tarquine*, and that the Common-wealth could not seem to have recovered perfect freedome, as long as a man of so dangerous a name was left remayning. For the Church of England to have done the like, in casting out Papall tyranny and superstition, to have shewed greater willingness of accepting the very Ceremonies of the Turke, Christs professed enemy, than of the most indifferent things which the Church of Rome approveth · to have left not so much as the names which the Church of Rome doth give unto things innocent · to have ejected whatsoever that Church doth make account of, be it never so harmless in it selfe, and of never so ancient continuance, without any other crime to charge it with, than only that it hath been the hap thereof to be used by the Church of Rome, & not to be commanded in the Word of God this kind of proceeding might haply have pleased some few men, who having begun such a course themselves, must needs be glad to see their example followed by us. But the Almightie which giveth wisdom, and inspireth with right understanding whomsoever it pleaseth him, he foreseeing that which mans wit had never bin able to reach unto ; namely, what Tragedies the attempt of so extream alteration would raise in some parts of the Christian World, did for the endless good of his Church (as we cannot chuse but interpret it) use the bridle of his provident restraining hand, to stay those eager affections in some, and to settle their resolution upon a course more calme and moderate ; left as in other most ample and heretofore most flourishing Dominions it hath since falne out, so likewise if in ours it had come to pass, that the adverse part being enraged, and betaking it selfe to such practices as men are commonly wont to embrace, when they behold things brought to desperate extremities, and no hope left to see any other end than only the utter oppression and clean extinuishment of one side ; by this mean Christendom flaming in all parts of greatest importance at once, they had all wanted that comfort of mutuall relief, whereby they are now for the time sustained (and not the least by this our Church which they so much impeach) till mutuall conbustions, blood-sheds and wastes (because no other inducements will serve) may enforce them through very faintness, after the experience of so endless miseries, to enter on all sides at the length into some such consultation, as may tend to the best re-establishment of the whole Church of Iesus Christ. To the singular good whereof it cannot but serve as a profitable direction, to teach men what is most likely to prove available, when they shall quietly consider the trial that hath bin thus long had of both kinds of Reformation, as well this moderate kind which the Church of England hath taken, as that other more extream and rigorous, which certain Churches elsewhere have better liked In the mean while it may be, that suspence of judgement and exercise of charity were safer and seemlier for Christian men, than the hot pursuite of these Controversies, wherein they that are more fervent to dispute, be not alwayes the most able to determin. But

who

Aug. Ep. 118.

T. C. l 17. 131. For indeed it were more fit for us to conforme our indifferent Ceremonies to the Turkes which are farther off, than to the Papists which are so neere.

who are on his fide and who againft him. our Lord in his good time fhall reveal. And fich thus far we have proceeded in opening the things that have been done, let not the principall doers themfelvs beforgotten. When the ruines of the houfe of God (that houfe which confifting of Religious Souls, is moft immediately the precious Temple of the Holy Ghoft) were become not in his fight alone, but in the eyes of the whole world fo exceeding great, that very Superftition began even to feel it felf too far grown the firft that with us made way to repaire the decayes thereof by beheading Super-ftition, was King *Henry* the Eighth; the Son and Succeffor of which famous King, as we know was *Edward* the Saint : in whom (for fo by the event we may gather) it pleafed God Righteous and Juft to let England fee, what a bleffing fin and iniquitie would not fuffer it to enjoyn. Howbeit that which the Wifeman hath faid concerning *Enoch* (whofe dayes were, though many in refpect of ours yet fcarce, as three to nine in com-parifon of theirs with whom he lived) the fame, to that admirable Child moft worthi-ly may be applied, *Though He departed this world foone, yet fulfilled He much time.* But what enfued ? That worke, which the own in fuch fort had begun, and the other fo farproceeded in , was in fhort fpace fo over-thrown , as if almoft it had never been : till fuch time as that God, whofe property is to fhew his mercies then. greateft when they are neareft to be utterly defpaired of, caufed in the depth of difcomfort and dark-nefs.a moft glorious Star to arife, and on her head fetled the Crown, whom himfelf had kept as a Lamb from the flaughter of thofe bloody times, that the experience of his goodnefs in her own deliverance, might caufe her mercifull difpofition to take fo much the more delight in faving others, whom the like neceffity fhould prefs. What in this behalf hath been done towards Nations abroad, the parts of Chriftendom moft afflicted can beft teftifie. That which efpecially concerneth our felves in the prefent matter we treat of, is, the ftate of reformed Religion, a thing at Her com-ming to the Crown, even raifed as it were by miracle from the dead; a thing which we fo little hoped to fee, that even they which beheld it done, fcarcely beleeved their own fences at the firft beholding. Yet being then brought to pafs, thus many years it hath continued ftanding by no other wordly mean but that one only hand which erected it, that hand, which as no kind of imminent danger could caufe at the firft to with-hold it felf, fo, neither have the practifes, fo many, fo bloody, fol-lowing fince, been ever able to make weary. Nor can we fay in this cafe fo juftly, that *Aaron* and *Hur*, the Ecclefiafticall and Civill States have fuftained the hand which did lift it felf to Heaven for them; as that Heaven it felf hath by this hand fuftained them, no aid or help having thereunto been miniftred for performance of the work of reformation, other than fuch kind of help or aid as the Angel in the Pro-phet *Zacharie* fpeaketh of, faying *Neither by an Army nor ftrength, but by my Spirit, faith the Lord of Hofts.* Which grace and favour of Divine affiftance having not in one thing or two fhewed it felf, nor for fome few days or yeers appeared, but in fuch fort fo long continued, our manifold fins and tranfgreffions ftriving to the contrary; what can we lefs thereupon conclude, than that God would at leaft wife by tract of time teach the World, that the thing which he bleffeth, defendeth, keeepeth fo ftrangely, cannot chufe but be of him ? Wherefore if any refufe to beleeve us dif-puting for the verity of Religion eftablifhed, let them beleive God himfelf thus miracu-loufly working for it, and wifh life even for ever and ever unto that Glorious and Sacred Inftrument whereby he worketh.

OF THE

LAWES

OF

Ecclesiastical Politie.

The Fifth Book.

Of their fourth Assertion, *That touching the several Publique Duties of Christian Religion, there is amongst us much Superstition retained in them ; and concerning Persons, which for performance of those Duties are endued with the Power of Ecclesiastical Order, our Laws and Proceedings according thereunto, are many ways herein also corrupted.*

The Matter contained in this Fifth Book.

A a

Few there are of so weak capacity, but publique evils they easily espy ; **True Religion is the root of all true vertues, and the stay of all well ordered Common-weals:** fewer so patient, as not to complain, when the grievous inconveniences thereof work sensible smart. Howbeit to see wherein the harm which they feel consisteth, the seeds from which it sprang, and the method of curing it, belongeth to a skill, the study whereof is so full of toyl, and the practise so beset with difficulties, that wary and respective men had rather seek quietly their own, and wish that the world may go well, so it be not long of them, than with pain and hazard make themselves advisers for the common good. We which thought it at the very first a signe of cold affection towards the Church of God, to prefer private ease before the labour of appeasing publique disturbance, must now of necessity refer events to the gracious providence of Almighty God, and in discharge of our duty towards him, proceed with the plain and unpartial defence of a common cause. Wherein our endeavour is not so much to overthrow them with whom we contend, as to yeild them just and reasonable causes of those things, which for want of due consideration heretofore, they misconceived, accusing laws for mens oversights, imputing evils grown through personal defects, unto that which is not evil, framing unto some sores unwholsome plaisters, and applying other some where no sore is. To make therefore our beginning that which to both parts is most acceptable, *We agree,* That pure and unstained Religion ought to be the highest of all cares appertaining to publique Regiment : as well in regard of that [a] aid and protection, which they, who faithfully serve God, confess they receive at his merciful hands ; as also for the force which Religion hath to qualifie all sorts of men, and to make them in publique affairs the more serviceable ; Governours, the apter to rule with conscience ; Inferiours, for conscience sake the willinger to obey. It is no peculiar conceit, but a matter of sound consequence, that all duties are by so much the better performed, by how much the men are more religious from whose Abilities the same proceed. For if [b] the course of publique affairs cannot in any good sort go forward without fit instruments, and that which fitteth them be their vertues ; let Politie acknowledge it self indebted to Religion, godliness being the chiefest top and well spring of all true vertues, even as God is of all good things, So natural is the union of Religion with Justice, that we may boldly deem there is neither, where both are not. For how should they be unfainedly just, whom Religion doth not cause to be such ; or they religious, which are not found such by the proof of their just actions ? If they, which employ their labour and travel about the publique administration of Justice, follow it only as a trade, with unquenchable and unconscionable thirst of gain, being not in heart perswaded that [d] Justice is God's own work, and themselves his agents in this business, the sentence of right, God's own verdict, and themselves his Priests to deliver it ; formalities of Justice do but serve to smother right, and that which was necessarily ordained for the common good, is through shameful abuse made the cause of common misery. The same piety, which maketh them that are in authority desirous to please and resemble God by Justice, inflameth every way men of action with zeal to do good (as far as their place will permit) unto all. For [e] that they know is most noble and divine. Whereby, if no natural nor casual inability cross their desires, they always delighting to inure themselves with actions most beneficial to others, cannot but gather great experience, and through experience the more wisdom, because conscience, and the fear of swarving from that which is right, maketh them diligent observers of circumstances, the loose regard whereof is the nurse of vulgar folly, no less then *Solomons* attention thereunto was of natural furtherances to the most effectual to make him eminent above others. For he [f] gave good heed, and pierced every thing to the very ground, and by that means became the Author of many parables. Concerning fortitude, such evils great and unexpected (the true touchstone of constant minds) do cause oftentimes even them to think upon Divine power, with [g] fearfullest suspicions, which have been otherwise the most secure despisers thereof, how should we look for any constant resolution of minde, in such cases, saving only where unfained affection to God-ward hath bred the most assured

consi-

Marginal notes:
[a] Psal. 144. C. Th. lib. 4. tit. 1. *Gaudere & gloriari ex fide semper volumus, scientes magis religionibus quam officiis & labore corporis vel sudore nostram rempublicam contineri.*
[b] *Εστι δ' ἤδη ἐν τοῖς πολιτικοῖς δυνατὸν πράξαι ἀνὰ ζ ποιοῦσιν. &c. λέγω ζ ὅτι αινάδιον. Τὸ ζ αινάδιον ἐν ζ ἐν τὰ ἀγε-λαῖα ἔχειν.* Arist. Magn. moral. lib. 1. c. 1.
[c] *Ἀρχὴ δ' δεῖσι παύλαν ὄντων θεὸς, ἀεῖ.*
[e] *Philo de dec. praecept.*
[d] 1 Chro. 19. 6.
[e] *Ἀγαπᾷ ζ μετ' μόνον, & ἐνὶ μόνον, κάλλιον ζ καὶ σφέτερον ἔργον ζ πόλεων.* Arist. Ethic. lib. 1 cap. 2.
[f] Eccles. 12. 10.
[g] Wisd. 17. 13.

confidence to be assisted by his hand ? For proof whereof, let but the Acts of the ancient Jews be indifferently weighed, from whose magnanimity, in causes of most extream hazard, those strange and unwonted resolutions have grown, which for all circumstances, no people under the roof of heaven did ever hitherto match. And that which did always animate them, was their meer Religion. Without which, if so be it were possible that all other ornaments of minde might be had in their full perfection, neverthelefs, the minde that should possess them, divorced from piety, could be but a spectacle of commiseration ; even as that body is, which adorned with sundry other admirable beauties, wanteth eye-fight, the chiefest grace that Nature hath in that kinde to bestow. They which commend so much the felicity of that innocent world, wherein it is said, that men of their own accord did embrace fidelity and honesty, not for fear of the Magistrate, or becaufe revenge was before their eyes, if at any time they should do otherwife, but that which held the people in awe, was the shame of ill doing, the love of equity, and right it self, a bar against all oppressions which greatnefs of power causeth ; they which describe unto us any such estate of happinefs amongst men, though they speak not of Religion, do notwithstanding declare that which is in truth her only working. For if Religion did possefs sincerely and sufficiently the hearts of all men, there would need no other restraint from evil. This doth not only give life and perfection to all endeavours wherewith it concurreth ; but what event soever ensues, it breedeth, if not joy and gladness alwaies, yet always patience, satisfaction, and reasonable contentment of minde. Whereupon it hath been set down as an axiome of good experience, that all things religiously taken in hand, are [h] prosperously ended ; because whether men in the end have that which Religion did allow them to desire, or that which it teacheth them contentedly to suffer, they are in neither event unfortunate. But left any man should here conceive, that in greatly skilleth not of what fort our Religion be, in as much as Heathens, Turks, and Infidels, impute to Religion a great part of the same effects, which our selves ascribe thereunto, they having ours in the same detestation that we theirs ; it shall be requisite to obferve well, how far forth there may be agreement in the effects of different Religions. First, by the bitter strife which riseth oftentimes from small differences in this behalf, and is by so much alwaies greater, as the matter is of more importance ; we see a general agreement in the secret opinion of men, that every man ought to embrace the Religion which is true, and to shun, as hurtful, whatsoever diffenteth from it, but that most, which doth farthest diffent. The generality of which perfwasion argueth, that God hath imprinted it by nature, to the end it might be a spur, to our industry, in searching and maintaining that Religion, from which as to fwerve in the least points, is errour ; so the capital enemies thereof God hateth as his deadly foes, aliens, and without repentance, children of endless perdition. Such therefore ; touching mans immortal state after this life, are not likely to reap benefit by their Religion, but to look for the clean contrary, in regard of so important contrariety between it and the true Religion. Neverthelefs, in as much as the errors of the most feduced this way have been mixed with fore truths, we are not to marvel, that although the one did turn to their endlefs wo and confusion, yet the other had many notable effects, as touching the affairs of this present life. There were in these quarters of the world, sixteen hundred years ago, certain speculative men, whose authority difposed the whole Religion of those times. By their means it became a received opinion, that the fouls of men departing this life, do flit out of one body into fome other. Which opinion, though false, yet entwined with a true, that the fouls of men do never perish, abated the fear of death in them which were fo resolved, and gave them courage unto all adventures. The Romans had a vain superstitious custome, in most of their enterprifes, to conjecture before hand of the event, by certain tokens which they noted in Birds, or in the Intrails of Beasts, or by other the like frivolous divinations. From whence notwithstanding as oft as they could receive any signe, which they took to be favourable, it gave them such hope, as if their gods had made them more then half a promife of prosperous fuccefs. Which many times was the greatest cause that they did prevail, especially being

Margin notes:

b Psal. 1. 3.

i Τὸν γὰ ἐ ἀληθῶς ἀγαθὸν ἐ ἔμφρονα πάσας οἰόμεθα τὰς τύχας εὐσχημόνως φέρειν ἐ ἐκ τῶν ὑπαρχόντων ἀεὶ τὰ κάλλισα πράττειν. Arist. Eth. l. 1. cap. 10.

k Cæf. de Bell. Gall. lib. 6.

being men of their own natural inclination, hopeful and strongly conceited, whatsoever they took in hand. But could their fond superstition have furthered so great attempts, without the mixture of a true perswasion, concerning the unresistable force of Divine power? Upon the wilful violation of oaths, execrable blasphemies, and like contempts, offered by Deriders of Religion, even unto false gods, fearful tokens of Divine revenge have been known to follow. Which occurrents the devouter sort did take for manifest Arguments, that the gods whom they worshipped, were of power to reward such as fought unto them, and would plague those that feared them not. In this they erred. For (as the *Wise man* rightly noteth concerning such) it was not the power of them by whom they sware, but the vengeance of them that sinned, which punished the offences of the ungodly. It was their hurt untruly to attribute so great power unto false gods. Yet the right conceit which they had, that to perjury vengeance is due, was not without good effect, as touching the course of their lives, who feared the wilful violation of oaths in that respect. And whereas we read so many of them so much commended, some for their milde and merciful disposition, some for their vertuous severity, some for integrity of life, all these were the fruits of true and infallible principles delivered unto us in the Word of God, as the axiomes of our Religion, which being imprinted by the God of Nature in their hearts also, and taking better root in some than in most others, grew, though not from, yet with and amidst the heaps of manifold repugnant errors, which errors of corrupt Religion had also their suitable effects in the lives of the self same parties. Without all controversie the purer and perfecter our Religion is, the worthier effects it hath in them who stedfastly and sincerely embrace it, in others not. They that love the Religion which they profess, may have failed in choise, but yet they are sure to reap what benefit the same is able to afford; whereas the best and soundest professed by them that bear it not the like affection, yeildeth them, retaining it in that sort, no benefit. *David* was a man after God's own heart, so termed, because his affection was hearty towards God. Beholding the like disposition in them which lived under him, it was his prayer to Almighty God, *m O keep this for ever in the purpose and thoughts of the heart of this people.* But when, after that *David* had ended his days in peace, they who succeeded him in place, for the most part followed him not in quality, when their Kings (some few excepted) to better their worldly estate (as they thought) left their own and their peoples ghostly condition uncared for, by woful experience they both did learn, that to forsake the true God of heaven, is to fall into all such evils upon the face of the earth, as men either destitute of grace divine may commit, or unprotected from above endure. Seeing therefore it doth thus appear, that the safety of all estates dependeth upon Religion; that Religion unfainedly loved, perfecteth mens abilities unto all kindes of vertuous services in the Common-wealth; that mens desire in general is to hold no Religion but the true; and that whatsoever good effects do grow out of their Religion, who embrace instead of the true, a false, the roots thereof are certain sparks of the light of truth intermingled with the darkness of errour, because no Religion can wholly and only consist of untruths, we have reason to think that all true vertues are to honour true Religion as their parent, and all well ordered Common-weals to love her as their chiefest stay.

2. They of whom God is altogether unapprehended, are but few in number, and for grosness of wit such, that they hardly and scarcely seem to hold the place of humane being. These we should judge to be of all others most miserable, but that a wretcheder fort there are, on whom, whereas nature hath bestowed riper capacity, their evil disposition seriously goeth about therewith to apprehend God, as being not God. Whereby it cometh to pass, that of these two sorts of men, both godless, the one having utterly no knowledge of God, the other study how to perswade themselves that there is no such thing to be known. The *n* Fountain and Well-spring of which impiety, is a resolved purpose of minde to reap in this world what sensual profit or pleasure soever the world yeildeth, and not to be barred from any whatsoever means available thereunto. And that this is the very radical cause of their Atheisme, no man (I think) will doubt, which considereth what pains they take to destroy those principall spurs and motives unto all Vertue, the crea-

l Wisd. 14. 13.

m 1 Chr. 29. 17.

The most extream opposite to true Religion, is effected Atheism.
n Wisd. 2. 21.
Such things they imagine, and go astray, because their own wickedness hath blinded them.
Ἔςι γὰρ ἡ κακία φθαρτικὴ ἀρχῆς. Arist. Ethic. l. 6. c. 5.

creation of the World, the providence of God, the resurrection of the Dead, the joyes of the Kingdom of Heaven, and the endless paines of the wicked, yea above all things, the authority of the Scripture, because on these points it evermore beareth, and the Souls immortality, which granted, draweth easily after it the rest, as a voluntary train. Is it not wonderfull, that base desires should so extinguish in men the sense of their own excellency, as to make them willing that their souls should be like to the souls of beasts, mortall and corruptible with their bodies? till some admirable or unusual accident happen (as it hath in some) to work the beginning of a better alteration in their mindes; disputation about the knowledge of God with such kinde of persons commonly prevaileth little. For how should the brightness of wisedom shine, where the windows of the soul are of ° very set purpose closed? True Religion hath many things in it, the only mention whereof gaulerh and troubleth their mindes. Being therefore loth, that enquiry into such matters should breed a perswasion in the end contrary unto that they embrace, it is their endeavour to banish, as much as in them lyeth, quite and clean from their cogitation whatsoever may sound that way. But it cometh many times to pass (which is their torment) that the thing they shun doth follow them; truth, as it were, even obtruding it self into their knowledg, and not permitting them to be so ignorant as they would be. Whereupon, inasmuch as the nature of man is unwilling to continue, doing that wherein it shall alwaies condemn it self, they continuing still obstinate, to follow the course which they have begun, are driven to devise all the shifts that wit can invent for the smothering of this light, all that may but with any the least shew of possibility stay their mindes from thinking that true, which they heartily wish were false, but ᵖ cannot think it so, without some scruple and fear of the contrary. Now because that judicious learning, for which we commend most worthily the ancient Sages of the World, doth not in this case serve the turn, these trenchermates (for such the most of them be) frame to themselves a way more pleasant, a new method they have of turning things that are serious into mockerie, an Art of Contradiction by way of scorn, a learning wherewith we were ᑫ long sithence forewarned, that the miserable times whereinto we are fallen should abound. This they study, this they practise, this they grace with a wanton superfluity of wit, too much insulting over the patience of more virtuously disposed mindes. For towards these so forlorn creatures we are (it must be confest) too patient. In zeal to the glory of God, *Babylon* hath exceeded *Sion*. We want that ʳ decree of *Nabuchodonosor*, the fury of this wicked brood hath the reins too much at liberty, their tongues walk at large, the spit-venom of their poisoned hearts breaketh out to the annoyance of others, what their untamed lust suggesteth, the same their licentious mouths do every where set abroach. With our contentions their irreligious humour also is much strengthened. Nothing pleaseth them better, than these manifold oppositions about the matter of Religion, as well for that they have hereby the more opportunity to learn on one side how another may be oppugned, and so to weaken the credit of all unto themselves; as also because by their hot pursuit of lower controversies amongst men professing religion, and agreeing in the principal foundations thereof, they conceive hope that about the higher principles themselves time will cause alteration to grow. For which purpose, when they see occasion, they stick not sometime in other mens persons, yea, sometime without any vizard at all, directly to try, what the most religious are able to say in defence of the highest points whereupon all Religion dependeth. Now for the most part it so falleth out touching things which generally are received, that although in themselves they be most certain, yet because men presume them granted of all, we are hardliest able to bring such proof of their certainty as may satisfie gain-sayers, when suddenly and besides expectation they require the same at our hands. Which impreparation and unreadiness when they finde in us, they turn it to the soothing up of themselves in that cursed phansie, whereby they would fain believe that the hearty devotion of such as indeed fear God, is nothing else but a kinde of harmless error, bred and confirmed in them by the sleights of wiser men. For a politique use of Religion they see there is, and by it they would also gather that Religion it self is a meer politique device, forged purposely to serve for that use.

ute. Men fearing God are thereby a great deal more effectually than by positive Laws restrain'd from doing evil, in as much as those Laws have no farther power than over our outward actions only, whereas unto mens' inward cogitations, unto the privie intents and motions of their hearts, religion serveth for a bridle. What more savage, wilde, and cruel than man, if he see himself able either by fraud to' over-reach, or by power to over-bear the Laws whereunto he should be subject? Where-fore in so great boldness to offend, it behoveth that the world should be held in awe, not by a vain surmise, but a true apprehension of somwhat, which no man may think himself able to withstand. This is the politique use of Religion. In which respect there are of these wise malignants, some who have vouchsafed it their marvellous favourable countenance and speech, very gravely affirming, that Religion honoured, addeth greatness; and contemned, bringeth ruine unto Common-weals; That Princes and States which will continue, are above all things to uphold the re-verend regard of Religion, and to provide for the same by all means in the making of their Laws. But when they should define what means are best for that purpose, behold, they extol the wisdom of Paganisme, they give it out as a mystical precept of great importance, that Princes, and such as are under them in most authority or credit with the people, should take all occasions of rare events, and, from what cause soever the same do proceed, yet wrest them to the strengthning of their Reli-gion, and not make it nice for so good a purpose to use, if need be, plain forgeries. Thus while they study how to bring to pass that Religion may seem but a matter made, they lose themselves in the very maze of their own discourses, as if reason did even purposely forsake them, who of purpose forsake God the Author thereof: For surely a strange kinde of madness it is, that those men, who though they be void of piety, yet, because they have wit, cannot chuse but know, that treachery, guil, and deceit, are things which may for a while, but do not use long to go un-espied, should teach that the greatest honour to a State is perpetuity; and grant, that alterations in the Service of God, for that they impair the credit of Religion, are therefore perillous in Common-weals, which have no continuance longer than Religion hath all reverence done unto it, and withal acknowledge (for so they do) that when people began to espy the falshood of Oracles, whereupon all Gentilism was built, their hearts were utterly averted from it; and notwithstanding counsel, Princes, in sober earnest for the strengthning of their states, to maintain Religion, and for the maintenance of Religion not to make choice of that which is true, but to authorize that they make choise of by those false and fraudulent means, which in the end must needs overthrow it. Such are the counsels of men godless, when they would shew themselves politique devisers, able to create God in man by Art.

3. Wherefore to let go this execrable crue, and to come to extremities on the contrary hand, two affections there are, the forces whereof, as they bear the great-er or lesser sway in mans heart, frame accordingly to the stamp and character of his Religion, the one zeal, the other fear. Zeal, unless it be rightly guided, when it endeavoureth most busily to please God, forceth upon him those unseasonable offices which please him not. For which cause, if they who this way swerve be compared with such sincere found and discreet as *Abraham* was in matter of Religion, the service of the one, is like unto flattery; the other like the faithful sedulity of ' friend-ship. Zeal, except it be ordered aright, when it bendeth it self unto conflict with all things, either in deed, or but imagined to be opposite unto Religion, u-seth the razor many times with such eagerness, that the very life of Religion it self is thereby hazarded, through hatred of tares the corn in the field of God is pluck'd up. So that Zeal needeth both ways a sober guide. Fear on the other side, if it have not the light of true understanding concerning God, wherewith to be mode-rated, breedeth likewise superstition. It is therefore dangerous that in things di-vine, we should work too much upon the spur either of zeal or fear. Fear is a good Solicitor to Devotion. Howbeit, sith fear in this kinde doth grow from an appre-hension of Deity endued with irresistable power to hurt, and is of all affections (anger excepted) the unaptest to admit any conference with reason, for which cause the " Wise man doth say of fear, that it is a betrayer of the forces of reasonable un-derstanding, therefore except men know before-hand what manner of service pleas-

eth

s *Vos scelera admissa puni-tis, apud nos & cogitare peccare est; vos conscios timetis, nos eti-am conscienti-am solam, sine qua esse non possumus. Minu. Fel. in Octav.*

Summum præsi-dium regni est justitia ob aper-tos tumultus & religio obser-cultos Cards. de Sapien. li. 3.

Of superstition and the root thereof, either misguided zeal, or ignorant fear of divine glory.

t *chron. 20. 7.* *Abraham thy friend.*

u *Wisd. 17. 1.*

eth God, while they are fearful, they try all things which fancy offereth. Many there are who never think on God, but when they are in extremity of fear: and then becaufe, what to think, or what to do they are uncertain, perplexity not fuffe-ring them to be idle; they think and do, as it were in a phrenfie, they know not what. Superftition neither knoweth the right kinde, nor obferveth the due meafure of actions belonging to the fervice of God, but is alwaies joyned with a wrong o-pinion touching things divine. Superftition is, when things are either abhorred or obferved, with a zealous or fearfull, but erronious relation to God. By means whereof, the fuperftitious do fometimes ferve, though the true God, yet with need-lefs offices, and defraud him of duties neceffary, fometime load others than him with fuch honours as properly are his. The one their overfight, who mifs in the choice of that wherewith they are affected; the other theirs, who fail in the election of him towards whom they fhew their devotion : this the crime of Idolatry; that, the fault of voluntary, either nicenefs or fuperfluity in Religion. The Chriftian world it felf being divided into two grand parts, it appeareth by the general view of both, that with matter of herefie the Weft hath been often and much troubled; but the Eaft part never quiet, till the deluge of mifery, wherein now they are, overwhelmed them. The chiefeft caufe whereof doth feem to have lyen in the reftlefs wits of the Grecians, evermore proud of their own curious and fubtile inventions, which when at any time they had contrived, the great facility of their Language ferved them rea-dily to make all things fair and plaufible to mens underftanding. Thofe grand here-tical impieties therefore, which moft highly and immediately touched God and the glorious Trinity, were all in a manner the monfters of the Eaft. The Weft bred fewer a great deal, and thofe commonly of a lower nature, fuch as more nearly and directly concerned rather men than God, the Latines being alwaies to capital here-fies lefs inclined, yet unto grofs fuperftition more. Superftition, fuch as that of the *Pharifees, was, by whom divine things indeed were left, becaufe other things were more divinely efteemed of than reafon would; the fuperftition that rifeth vo-luntarily, and by degrees, which is hardly difcerned, mingleth it felf with the rites even of very divine fervice done to the only true God, muft be confidered of, as a creeping and incroaching evil; an evil, the firft beginnings whereof are commonly harmlefs, fo that it proveth only then to be an evil, when fome farther accident doth grow unto it, or it felf come unto farther growth. For in the Church of God fome-times it cometh to pafs, as in over-battle grounds, the fertile difpofition whereof is good; yet becaufe it exceedeth due proportion, it bringeth forth abundantly, through too much ranknefs, things lefs profitable, whereby, that which principally it fhould yield, being either prevented in place, or defrauded of nourifhment, fai-leth. This (if fo large a difcourfe were neceffary) might be exemplified even by heaps of rites and cuftomes, now fuperftitious in the greateft part of the Chriftian world, which in their firft original beginnings, when the ftrength of virtuous, devout or charitable affection bloomed them, no man could juftly have condemned as evil.

a Mark 7.9.

Of the redrefs of fuperftition in God's Church, and concerning the queftion of this Book.

4. But howfoever fuperftition doth grow, that wherein unfounder times have done amifs, the better ages enfuing muft rectifie, as they may. I now come there-fore to thofe accufations brought againft us by pretenders of Reformation; the firft in the rank whereof is fuch, that if fo be the Church of *England* did at this day therewith as juftly deferve to be touched as they in this caufe have imagined it doth, rather would I exhort all forts to feek pardon even with tears at the hands of God, than meditate words of defence for our doings, to the end that men might think fa-vourably of them. For as the cafe of this world, efpecially now, doth ftand, what other ftay or fuccour have we to lean unto, fave the teftimony of our confcience, and the comfort we take in this, that we ferve the living God (as near as our wits can reach unto the knowledge thereof) even according to his own will, and do there-fore truft that his mercy fhall be our fafegard againft thofe enraged powers abroad, which principally in that refpect are become our enemies? But, fith no man can do ill with a good confcience, the confolation which we herein feem to finde, is but a meer deceitfull pleafing of our felves in errour, which at the length muft needs turn to our greater grief, if that which we do to pleafe God moft, be for the manifold de-fects thereof offenfive unto him. For fo it is judged, our Prayers, our Sacraments,

our

our Fasts, our times and places of Publick meeting together for the worship and service of God ; our Marriages, our Burials, our Functions, Elections and Ordinations Ecclesiastical, almost whatsoever we do in the exercise of our Religion according to lawes for that purpose established, all things are some way or other thought faulty, all things stained with superstition. Now although it may be, the wiser sort of men are not greatly moved hereat, considering how subject the very best things have been alwaies unto cavil, when wits possessed either with disdain or dislike thereof, have set them up as their mark to shoot at : safe notwithstanding it were not therefore to neglect the danger which from hence may grow, and that especially in regard of them, who desiring to serve God as they ought, but being not so skilfull as in every point to unwinde themselves where the snares of glosing speech do lie to intangle them, are in minde not a litt'e troubled, when they hear so bitter invectives against that which this Church hath taught them to reverence as holy, to approve as lawfull, and to observe as behovefull, for the exercise of Christian duty. It seemeth therefore, at least for their sakes, very meet, that such as blame us in this behalf, be directly answered, and they which follow us, informed plainly of the reasons of that we do. On both sides the end intended between us, is to have Laws and Ordinances, such as may rightly serve to abolish superstition, and to establish the service of God with all things thereunto appertaining, in some perfect form. There is an inward *reasonable, and there is a *solemn outward serviceable worship, *a* Rom.12.1. belonging unto God. Of the former kinde are all kinde of virtuous Duties, that *b* Luke 1.23. each man in reason and conscience to God-ward oweth. Solemn and serviceable worship we name for distinction sake, whatsoever belongeth to the Church or publick society of God by way of external adoration. It is the later of these two, whereupon our present question groweth. Again, this later being ordered, partly, and as touching principal matters, by none but precepts divine onely ; partly, and as concerning things of inferior regard, by Ordinances as well humane as divine, about the substance of Religion, wherein Gods onely Law must be kept, there is here no controversie ; the crime now intended against us, is, that our Laws have not ordered inferiour things as behoveth, and that our customs are either superstitious, or otherwise amiss, whether we expect the exercise of publick duties in Religion, or the functions of persons authorised thereunto.

5. It is with teachers of Mathematical Sciences usual, for us in this present question necessary, to lay down first certain reasonable demands, which in most particulars following are to serve as principles whereby to work, and therefore must be beforehand considered. The men whom we labour to inform in the truth, perceive that to proceed is requisite. For to this end they also propose, touching customes and rites indifferent, their general axioms, some of them subject unto just exceptions, and as we think, more meet by them to be farther considered, then assented unto by us. As that, *In outward things belonging to the Service of God, reformed Churches ought by all means to shun conformity with the Church of Rome* ; that, *The first reformed should be a pattern whereunto all that come after ought to conform themselves* ; that, *Sound religion may not use the things, which being not commanded of God, have been either devised or abused unto superstition.* These and the rest of the same consort we have in the Book going before examined. Other Canons they allege, and rules not unworthy of approbation ; as, *That in all such things the glory of God and the edification or ghostly good of his people must be sought ; that nothing should be undecently or unorderly done.* But forasmuch as all the difficulty is in discerning what things do glorifie God, and edifie his Church, what not ; when we should think them decent and fir, when otherwise : because these rules being too general, come not neer enough unto the matter which we have in hand ; and the former principles being nearer the purpose, are too farr from truth, we must propose unto all men certain petions incident and very material in causes of this nature, such as no man of moderate judgment hath cause to think unjust or unreasonable.

6. The first thing therefore which is of force to cause approbation with good

[margin: Four general Propositions demanding that which may reasonably be granted concerning matters of outward form in the exercise of true Religion. And firstly, of a Rule not safe nor reasonable in these cases.]

[margin: The first Proposition touching judgment, what things are convenient in the outward publick ordering of Church Affairs]

Consci-

conscience towards such customes or rites, as publickly are establish'd, is, when there ariseth from the due consideration of those customs and rites in themselves apparent reason, although not alwaies to prove them better than any other that might possibly be devised, (for who did ever require this in mans ordinances?) yet competent to shew their conveniency and fitness, in regard of the use for which they shou'd serve. Now touching the nature of religious Services, and the manner of their due performance, thus much generally we know to be most clear, that whereas the greatness and dignity of all manner of actions is measured by the worthiness of the subject form which they proceed, and of the object whereabout they are conversant, we must of necessity in both respects acknowledg, that this present world affordeth not any thing comparable unto the publick duties of Religion. For if the best things have the perfectest and best operations, it will follow, that seeing man is the worthiest creature upon earth, and every society of men more worthy than any man, and of societies that most excellent which we call the Church; there can be in this world no work performed equal to the exercise of true Religion, the proper operation of the Church of God. Again, forasmuch as Religion worketh upon him, who in majesty and power is infinite, as we ought we account not of it, unless we *a* John.4.24. esteem it even [a] according to that very height of excellency which our hearts Wisd.6.10. conceive, when Divine sublimity it self is rightly considered. In the powers and 1 Chron.29.17 faculties of our souls God requireth the uttermost which our unfeigned affection towards him is able to yield: So that if we affect him not farr above and before all things, our Religion hath not that inward perfection which it should have, neither do we indeed worship him as our God. That which inwardly each man should be, the Church outwardly ought to testifie. And therefore the duties of our Religion which are seen, must be such as that affection which is unseen ought to be. Signs must resemble the things they signifie. If Religion bear the greatest sway in our hearts, our outward religious duties must shew it as farr as the Church hath outward ability. Duties of Religion performed by whole Societies of men, ought to *b* 2 Chron.2.5. have in them according to our power a sensible excellency, [b] correspondent to the Majesty of him whom we worship. Yea then are the publick duties of Religion best *c* Ἐκκλησία ordered, when the Militant Church doth [c] resemble by sensible means, as it may in ἔστιν ὅτη εἴσ such cases, that hidden Dignity and Glory wherewith the Church Triumphant in εργώδης Gar- Heaven is beautified. Howbeit, even as the very heat of the Sun it self, which is the mus αθί τῆ life of the whole world, was to the people of God in the Desert a grievous annoy-ἔτερ γυθῶαν. ance, for ease whereof his extraordinary Providence ordained a Cloudy Pillar to Delectatio Do-over-shaddow them: So things of general use and benefit (for in this world what mini in Eccle-fia est, Ecclesia is so perfect that no inconvenience doth ever follow it?) may by some accident be verò est imago incommodious to a few. In which case, for such private evils, remedies there are of cælestium. Am-like condition, though publick Ordinances wherein the common good is respected, brol.de interpel. Dan. be not stirred. Let our first demand be therefore, that in the external form of Re-Facit in terris ligion such things as are apparently, or can be sufficient ly proved effectual and ge-opera cælorum, nerally fit to set forward Godliness, either as betokening the greatness of God, or Sidon Apol. Epist.l.b.6. as beseeming the dignity of Religion, or as concurring with celestial Impressions in the mindes of men may be reverently thought of; some few, rare, casual, and tolerable, or otherwise curable inconveniences notwithstanding.

The second Proposition.   7. Neither may we in his case lightly esteem what hath been allowed as fit in the judgment of antiquity, and by the long continued practice of the whole Church, from which unnecessarily to swerve, experience hath never as yet found it safe. For whsedoms sake we reverence them no less that are young, or not much less, then if they were stricken in years. And therefore of such it is rightly said, that the ripe-*d* Wisd.4.9. ness of understanding is [d] *gray hair*, and their virtues *old Age*. But because Wisdome and Youth are seldom joyned in one, and the ordinary course of the World *e* Job 10.12. is more according to *Jobs* observation, who giveth men advice to seek Wisdom *amongst the Ancient*, and in the *length of dayes* understanding; therefore if the comparison do stand between man and man, which shall hearken unto other, such the aged for the most part are best experienced, least subject to rash and unadvised passions, it hath been ever judged reasonable, that their sentence in matter of counsel should be better trusted, and more relyed upon than other mens. The good-

                                                                    ness

nefs of God having furnished man with two chief inftruments, both neceffary for this life, hands to execute, and a mind to devife great things ; the one is not profitable longer than the vigour of youth doth ftrengthen it, nor the other greatly, till age and experience have brought it to perfection. In whom therefore time hath not perfected knowledge, fuch muft be contented to follow them in whom it hath. For this caufe none is more attentively heard, than they whofe fpeeches are as *Davids* were, *I have been young and now am old* ; much I have feen and obferved in the world. Sharp and fubtile difcourfes of wit procure many times very great applaufe, but being laid in the ballance with that which the habit of found experience plainly delivereth, they are over-weighed. God may endue men extraordinarily with underftanding as it pleafeth him : but let no man prefuming thereupon neglect the inftructions, or defpife the ordinances of his elders, fith he, whofe gift wifdom is, hath faid, f *Aske thy Father, and he will fhew thee, thine Ancients, and they fhall tell thee.* It is therefore the voyce both of God and Nature, not of learning only, that efpecially in matters of action and policy, g *The fentences and judgements of men experienced, aged and wife, yea though they fpeak without any proof or demonftration, are no lefs to be hearkned unto, than as being demonftrations in themfelves, becaufe fuch mens long obfervation is as an eye, wherewith they prefently and plainly behold thofe principles which fway over all actions.* Whereby we are taught both the caufe wherefore wife mens judgements fhould be credited, and the mean how to ufe their judgements to the increafe of our own wifdome. That which fheweth them to be wife, is the gathering of principles out of their own particular experiments. And the framing of our particular experiments according to the rule of their principles, fhall make us fuch as they are. If therefore, even at the firft, fo great account fhould be made of wife mens counfels touching things that are publikely done, as time fhall adde thereunto continuance and approbation of fucceeding ages, their credit and authority muft needs be greater. They which do nothing but that which men of account did before them, are although they do amifs, yet the lefs faulty, becaufe they are not the Authors of harme. And doing well, their actions are freed from prejudice and novelty. To the beft and wifeft, h while they live, the world is continually a froward oppofite, a curious obferver of their defects and imperfections, their vertues it afterwards as much admireth. And for this caufe, many times that which moft deferveth approbation, would hardly be able to find favour, if they which propofe it, were not content to profefs themfelves therein Scholars and Followers of the Ancient. For the world will not endure to hear that we are wifer than any have been which went before. In which confideration there is caufe why we fhould be flow and unwilling to change, without very urgent neceffity, the ancient Ordinances, Rites, and long approved Cuftomes of our venerable Predeceffors. The love of things ancient doth argue ftayednefs ; but levity and want of experience maketh apt unto innovations. That which Wifdome did firft begin, and hath been with good men long continued, challengeth allowance of them that fucceed, although it plead for it felf nothing. That which is new, if it promife not much, doth fear condemnation before tryal ; till tryal, no man doth acquit or truft it, what good foever it pretend and promife. So that in this kind there are few things known to be good, till fuch time as they grow to be ancient. The vain pretence of thofe glorious names, where they could not be with any truth, neither in reafon ought to have been fo much alledged, hath wrought fuch a prejudice againft them in the minds of the common fort, as if they had utterly no force at all, whereas (efpecially for thefe obfervances which concern our prefent queftion) Antiquity, Cuftome, and Confent in the Church of God, making with that which k Law doth eftablifh, are themfelves moft fufficient reafons to uphold the fame, unlefs fome notable publick inconvenience inforce the contrary. For a k fmall thing in the eye of Law is as nothing. We are therefore bold to make our fecond petition this, that in things the fitnefs whereof is not of it felf apparent, nor eafie to be made fufficiently manifeft unto all, yet the judgement of antiquity concurring with that which is received, may induce them to think it not unfit, who are not able to alledge any known weighty inconvenience which it hath, or to take any ftrong exception againft.

f Deut. 32. 7.

g *Arift. Eth.* 6. *cap.* 11.

h Πρὸς τοὺς ἐκ ποδῶν φθόνος οὐδεὶς φύεται. *Philo*

Πᾶσα δυσμένεια τῶ θείω τούτω συναποτίθεται. S. *nef.*

Τὸ ἐκ ποδῶν οὐκ ἀντιπίπτη ἡ ζετίμωται ἀσθύνας. *Gregor. Naz.*

ἐν Στιχ.

i ἴσοι δὲ εὑρίσκων θεᾶιν τρόπων τὸ τᾶς ἀρχαιότητος σεμνὸν τὸ καινοπρεποὺς προαιρεῖ μυσαν ἡ ἀναβαπτιστὸν ἀεὶ παρέρων διαφύλαξαν ἀ παραδόσιν κατὰ τε χθ. φαν ἡ πόλιν ταύτη κέχρηνται τᾶ φανῆ. *Bafil. de Spirit. Sanct. cap.* 7.

k ὁ μὲν μικρὸν τὸ εὖ παρεκβαίνων οὐ ψέγεται. *Arift. Ethic. 2. cap* 9. *Medici nulla fere ratio habere folet. Tiraquel de jud. in reb. exig. cap.* 10.

8. All

The third Proposition.

8. All things cannot be of ancient continuance, which are expedient and needful for the ordering of spiritual affairs; but the Church being a body which dieth not, hath alwayes power, as occasion requireth, no less to ordain that which never was, than to ratifie what hath been before. To prescribe the order of doing in all things, is a peculiar prerogative which *Wisdome* hath as Queen or Soveraign Commandress over other vertues. This in every several mans actions of common life apperteineth unto *Morall*; in publick and politick secular-affairs unto *Civil* wisdome. In like manner, to devise any certain form for the outward administration of publick duties in the Service of God, or things belonging thereunto, and to find out the most convenient for that use, is a point of Wisdome *Ecclesiastical*. It is not for a man which doth know, or should know what order is, and what peaceable government requireth, to ask, *why we should hang our judgement upon the Churches sleeve,* and *why in matters of order more than in matters of doctrine.* The Church hath authority to establish that for an order at one time, which at another time it may abolish, and in both do well. But that which in doctrine the Church doth now deliver rightly as a truth, no man will say that it may hereafter recall, and as rightly avouch the contrary. Lawes touching matter of order are changeable, by the power of the Church; Articles concerning doctrine not so. We read often in the writings of Catholick and Holy men touching matters of doctrine, *This we believe, this we hold, this the Prophets and Evangelists have declared, this the Apostles have delivered, this Martyrs have sealed with their blood, and confessed in the midst of torments, to this we cleave, as to the anchor of our souls, against this, though an Angel from heaven should preach unto us, we would not believe.* But did we ever in any of them read touching matters of meer comeliness, order, and decency, neither commanded nor prohibited by any Prophet, any Evangelist, any Apostle, *Although the Church wherein we live do ordain them to be kept, although they be never so generally observed, though all the Churches in the world should command them, though Angels from heaven should require our subjection thereunto.* I would hold him accursed that *doth obey?* Be it in matter of the one kind or of the other, what Scripture doth plainly deliver, to that the first place both of credit and obedience is due; the next whereunto is whatsoever any man can necessarily conclude by force of reason; after these the voice of the Church succeedeth. That which the Church by her Ecclesiastical Authority shall probably think and define to be true or good, must in congruity of reason over-rule all other inferiour judgements whatsoever. To them which ask why we thus hang our judgement on the Churches sleeve, I answer with *Solomon*, Because [m] *two are better than one.* Yea *simply* (saith [n] *Basil*) and *universally, whether it be in works of Nature, or of voluntary choyce and counsel, I see not any thing done as it should be, if it be wrought by an agent singling it selfe from consorts.* The Jewes have a sentence of good advice, [o] *Take not upon thee to be a Judge alone, there is no sole Judge but one only; say not to others, Receive my sentence, when their authority is above thine.* The bare consent of the whole Church should it self in these things stop their mouths, who living under it, dare presume to bark against it. *There is* (saith [p] *Cassianus*) *no place of audience left for them, by whom obedience is not yielded to that which all have agreed upon.* Might we not think it more than wonderful, that Nature should in all communities appoint a predominant judgement to sway and over-rule in so many things; or that God himself should allow so much authority and power unto every poor family, for the ordering of all which are in it; and the City of the living God, which is his Church, be able neither to command, nor yet to forbid any thing, which the meanest shall in that respect, and for her sole authorities sake be bound to obey? We cannot hide or dissemble that evil, the grievous inconvenience whereof we feel. Our dislike of them, by whom too much heretofore hath been attributed unto the Church, is grown to an errour on the contrary hand, so that now from the Church of God too much is derogated. By which removal of one extremity with another, the world seeking to procure a remedy, hath purchased a meer exchange of the evil which before was felt. Suppose we that the Sacred Word of God can at their hands receive due honour, by whose increment the holy Ordinances of the Church endure every where open contempt? No, it is not possible they should observe as they ought the one, who from the other withdraw unnecessarily

Marginal notes:

In μὲν φρόνησις περὶ τὰ ποιητέα ὅπου αἱρεῖσθαι τ᾽ἐθμῖσα. *Philo. pag.* 35.

T. C. lib. 3. *pag.* 171.

[m] *Eccles.* 4. 9.
[n] *Basil. Ep.* 68. d.8 c. qua contra. Τὸ πῖς ἐστ᾽ ὅμοις πᾶσι παντῃ, ἐν φ᾽ ἐνὸς οἷ σῦνον congruens.
[o] *R. Ismael in Cap. Patr.*
[p] *Cassian. de incarn. lib.* 1. *ca.* 6.

necessarily their own , or their brethrens obedience. Surely the Church of God in this business is neither of capacity , I trust, so weak , nor so unstrengthened, I know, with authority from above , but that her lawes may exact obedience at the hands of her own children, and injoin gain-sayers silence, giving them roundly to understand, that where our duty is submission , weak oppositions betoken pride. We therefore crave thirdly to have it granted , that where neither the evidence of any Law Divine , nor the strength of any invincible argument otherwise found out by the light of reason , nor any notable publique inconvenience doth make against that which our own Lawes Ecclesiasticall have ; although but newly instituted , for the ordering of these affairs , the very authority of the Church it self, at the least in such cases , may give so much credit to her own Lawes , as to make their sentence as touching fitnes and conveniency weightier than any bare or naked conceit to the contrary ; especially in them who can owe no less than childlike obedience to her that hath more than motherly power.

9. There are ancient Ordinances, Lawes which on all sides are allowed to be just and good, yea Divine and Apostolique Constitutions, which the Church, it may be, doth not always keep , nor always justly deserve blame in that respect. For in evils that cannot be removed, without the manifest danger of greater to succeed in their rooms, wisdom (of necessity) must give place to necessity. All it can do in those cases, is to devise ; how that , which must be endured , may be mitigated, and the inconveniencies thereof countervailed as near as may be ; that when the best things are not possible, the best may be made of those that are. Nature, than which there is nothing more constant, nothing more uniform in all her ways, doth notwithstanding stay her hand, yea and change her course, when that which God by creation did command, he doth at any time by necessity countermand. It hath therefore pleased himself sometime to unloose the very tongues even of dumb creatures, and to teach them to plead this in their own defence, left the cruelty of man should persist to afflict them for not keeping their wounted course, when some invincible impediment hath hindred. If we leave nature, and look into art , the workman hath in his heart a purpose, he carrieth in mind the whole form which his work should have ; there wanteth not in him skill and desire to bring his labour to effect; onely the matter which he hath to work on is unframable. This necessity excuseth him , so that nothing is derogated from his credit, although much of his works perfection be found wanting. Touching actions of common life, there is not any defence more favourably heard than theirs, who alleage sincerely for themselves, that they did as necessity constrained them. For when the mind is rightly ordered and affected as it should be, in case some external impediment crossing well-advised desires, shall potently draw men to leave what they principally wish, and to take a course which they would not, if their choice were free ; what necessity forceth men unto, the same in this case it maintaineth , as long as nothing is committed simply in it self evil , nothing absolutely sinfull or wicked , nothing repugnant to that immutable Law , whereby, whatsoever is condemned as evil, can never any way be made good. The casting away of things profitable for the sustenance of mans life, is an unthankfull abuse of the fruits of Gods good providence towards mankind. Which consideration for all that did not hinder [b] S. *Paul* from throwing corn into the Sea, when care of saving mens lives made it necessary , to loose that which else had been better saved. Neither was this to do evil, to the end that good might come of it. For of two such evils, being not both evitable, the choice of the less is not evil. And evils must be in our constructions judged inevitable, if there be no apparent ordinary way to avoid them ; because where counsel and advice bear rule, of Gods extraordinary power, without extraordinary warrant we cannot presume. In Civil affairs to declare what sway necessity hath ever been accustomed to bear, were labour infinite. The laws of all States and Kingdoms in the world have scarcely of any thing more common use. Should then only the Church shew it self inhumane and stern, absolutely urge in a rigorous observation of spiritual ordinances, without relaxation or exception, what necessity soever happen ? We know the [c] contrary practise to have been commended by him, upon the warrant of whose judgment, the Church most of all delighted with mercifull & moderate courses, doth the ofter condescend unto like

The fourth Proposition.

[a] *Necessitas quicquid coegit defendit. Senec. Controv. lib. 9.*

[b] *Acts 27.18.*

[c] *Luc. 6. 4.*

Numb. 22. 28.

equity

a Caufa neceffi-
tatis & utilita-
tis aquiparan-
tur in jure.
Ab. Panor. ad
c. ut fuper. nu.
15. de reb. Ec-
clef. non alien.

equity, permitting in cafes of neceffity that, which otherwife it diſalloweth and forbiddeth. Cafes of neceffity being ſomtime but urgent, ſometime extream, the confideration of *a* publick utility is by very good advice judged at the leaft equivalent with
the eafier kind of neceffity. Now that which caufeth numbers to ſtorme againſt ſome
neceffary tolerations, which they ſhould rather let paſs with ſilence, confidering that
in Politie as well Ecclefiaftical as Civil, there are and will be always evils, which no
art of man can cure, breaches and leaks moe than mans wit hath hands to ſtop; that
which maketh odious unto them many things, wherein notwithſtanding the truth is,
that very juſt regard hath been had of the publick good; that which in a great part
of the weightieſt caufes belonging to this prefent controverfie, hath infnared the
judgments both of ſundry good, and of ſome well learned men, is the manifeſt truth
of certain general principles, whereupon the Ordinances that ſerve for ufual practiſe in
the Church of God are grounded. Which principles men knowing to be moſt ſound,
and that the ordinary practiſe according y framed is good, whatſoever is over and
befides that ordinary, the ſame they judge repugnant to thofe true principles. The
caufe of which errour is ignorance, what reftraints and limitations all fuch principles
have, in regard of ſo manifold varieties, as the *b* matter whereunto they are appliable, doth commonly afford. Thefe varieties are not known but by much experience,
from whence to draw the true bounds of all principles, to diſcern how far forth they
take effect, to fee where and why they fail, to apprehend by what degrees and means
they lead to the practiſe of things in ſhow, though not indeed repugnant and contrary one to another, requireth more ſharpneſs of wit, more intricate circuitions of
difcourfe, more induſtry and depth of judgement than common ability doth yield.
So that general Rules, till their limits be fully known (efpecially in matter of publick and Ecclefiafticall affairs) are, by reafon of the manifold ſecret exceptions
which lie hidden in them, no other to the eye of mans underftanding, than cloudy
mifts caft before the eye of common fenfe. They that walk in darkneſs know not
whither they go. And even as little is their certainty, whofe opinions generalities
only do guid. With groſs and popular capacities, nothing doth more prevail, than
unlimited generalities, becaufe of their plainneſs at the firſt ſight; nothing leſs
with men of exact judgement, becaufe ſuch Rules are not fafe to be trufted over-
far. General Lawes are like general Rules of Phyfick, according whereunto, as
no wife man will defire himſelf to be cured, if there be joined with his difeafe ſome
ſpecial accident, in regard whereof that whereby others in the fame infirmity, but
without the like accident, recover health, would be to him either hurtfull, or at the
leaft unprofitable: So we muſt not, under a colourable commendation of holy
Ordinances in the Church, and of reafonable caufes whereupon they have been
grounded for the common good, imagine that all mens cafes ought to have one
meafure. Not without ſingular wifdom therefore it hath been provided, that as
the ordinary courfe of common affaires is difpofed of by general Lawes, ſo likewife mens rarer incident neceffities and utilities ſhould be with ſpecial equity conſidered. From hence it is, that ſo many priviledges, immunities, exceptions,
and difpenfations have been always with great equity and reafon granted, not to
turn the edge of Juſtice, or to make void at certaine times, and in certaine men
through meer voluntary grace or benevolence, that which continually and univerfally ſhould be of force (as ſome underſtand it) but in very truth to practiſe general Lawes according to their right meaning. We fee in contracts and other dealings which dayly paſs between man and man, that, to the utter undoing of ſome,
many things by ſtrictneſs of Law may be done, which equity and honeſt meaning
forbiddeth. Not that the Law is unjuſt, but unperfect; nor equity againſt, but
above the Law; binding mens confciences in thinges which Lawe cannot
reach unto. Will any man fay, that the vertue of private equitie is oppoſite and repugnant to that Lawe, the ſilence whereof it ſupplieth in all ſuch
private dealing? No more is publique equity againſt the Lawe of publique
affaires, albeit the one permit unto ſome in ſpecial Confiderations, that
which the other agreeably with general Rules of Juſtice doth in generall ſort
forbid. For, ſith all good Lawes are the voices of right reafon, which is the
inſtrument wherewith God will have the world guided, and impoffible it is
                                            that

b Ἐν τοῖς περὶ
τῆς πράξεις
λόγοις, οἱ μὲν
καθόλου κενώ-
τεροί εἰσιν, οἱ
δ' ἐπὶ μέρους
ἀληθινώτεροι,
περὶ γὰρ τὰ
καθ' ἕκαστα αἱ
πράξεις. *Ariſt.*
Eth. lib. 2. c. 7.

that right should withstand right ; it must follow that principles and rules of Justice, be they never so generally uttered, do no less effectually intend, than if they did plainly express an exception of all particulars, wherein their literal practise might any way prejudice equity ; and because it is natural unto all men to wish their own extraordinary benefit, when they think they have reasonable inducements so to do ; and no man can be presumed a competent judge what equity doth require in his own case, the likeliest mean whereby the wit of man can provide, that he which useth the benefit of any special benignity above the common course of others, may injoy it with good conscience, and not against the true purpose of Laws, which in outward shew are contrary, must needs be to arme with authority some fit both for quality and place to administer that, which in every such particular shall appear agreeable with equity : wherein, as it cannot be denyed, but that sometimes the practise of such Jurisdiction may swarve through errour even in the very best, and for other respects, where less integrity is. So the watchfullest observers of inconveniences that way growing, and the readiest to urge them in disgrace of authorized proceedings, do very well know, that the disposition of these things resteth not now in the hands of Popes, who live in no worldly awe or subjection, but is committed to them whom Law may at all times bridle, and superiour power controll ; yea to them also in such sort, that Law it self hath set down to what persons, in what causes, with what circumstances, a most every faculty or favour shall be granted, leaving in a manner nothing unto them, more than only to deliver what is already given by Law. Which maketh it by many degrees less reasonable, that under pretence of inconveniences so easily stopped, if any did grow, and so well prevented, that none may, men should be altogether barred of the liberty that Law with equity and reason granteth. These things therefore considered, we lastly require that it may not seem hard, if in cases of necessitie, or for common utilities sake, certain profitable ordinances sometimes be released, rather than all men alwayes, strictly bound to the general rigor thereof.

10. Now where the word of God leaveth the Church to make choyce of her own Ordinances, if against those things which have been received with great reason, or against that which the ancient practise of the Church hath continued time out of mind, or against such Ordinances as the power and authority of that Church under which we live hath in it self devised, for the publique good, or against the discretion of the Church in mitigating sometimes with favourable equity, that rigour which otherwise the literal generality of Ecclesiastical Lawes hath judged to be more convenient and meet, if against all this it should be free for men to reprove, to disgrace, to reject at their own liberty what they see done and practised according to order set down, if in so great variety of ways, as the wit of man is easily able to find out towards any purpose, and in so great liking as all men especially have unto those inventions, whereby some one shall seem to have been more inlightned from above than many thousands, the Church did give every man licence to follow what himself imagineth that *Gods Spirit doth reveal* unto him, or what he supposeth that God is likely to have revealed to some special person, whose vertues deserve to be highly esteemed, what other effect could hereupon ensue, but the utter confusion of his Church, under pretence of being taught, led, and guided by his Spirit ? the gifts and graces whereof do so naturally all tend unto common peace, that where such singularity is, they whose hearts it possesseth, ought to suspect it the more, in as much as if it did come of God, and should for that cause prevail with others, the same God which revealeth it to them, wou'd also give them power of confirming it unto others, either with miraculous operation, or with strong and invincible remonstrancy of sound reason, such as whereby it might appear that God would indeed have all mens judgements give place unto it ; whereas now the errour and unsufficience of their Arguments doth make it on the contrary side against them a strong presumption, that God hath not moved their hearts to think such things, as he hath not inabled them to prove. And so from Rules of general Direction it resteth, that now we descend to a more distinct explication of particulars, wherein those Rules have their special efficacie.

11. Solemne Duties of publique service to bee done unto God, must

The rule of mens private spirits not safe in these cases to be followed.

Places for the publique service of God.
a *Gen.* 3.8.
b *Gen.* 4.3.
c *Gen.* 13.4.
d 22.1.
e 21.33.
f *Exod.* 16.
g *Deut.* 12.5.
h 2 *Chron.* 3.1.
i 1 *Chron* 6.7.
Psalm. 132.5.

have their places set and prepared in such sort, as beseemeth actions of that regard. *Adam* even during the space of his small continuance in *Paradise*, had ᵃ where to present himself before the Lord. *Adams* sons had out of *Paradise* in like sort ᵇ whither to bring their sacrifices. The Patriarks used ᶜ Altars, and ᵈ Mountains, and ᵉ groves, to the self same purpose. In the vast wildernes when the people of God had themselves no setled habitation, yet a moveable ᶠ Tabernacle they were commanded of God to make. The like charge was given them against the time they should come to settle themselves in the land which had been promised unto their fathers, ᵍ *Ye shall seek that place which the Lord your God shall chuse.* When God had chosen *Jerusalem*, and in *Jerusalem* Mount ʰ *Moria*, there to have his standing habitation made, it was in the chiefest of ⁱ *Davids* desires to have performed so good a work. His grief was no less, that he could not have the honour to build God a Temple, than their anger is at this day, who bite asunder their own tongues with very wrath, that they have not as yet the power to pull down the Temples which they never built, and to level them with the ground. It was no mean thing which he purposed. To perform a work so majesticall and stately was no small

k 2 *Chron.* 25.9.

charge. Therefore ᵏ he incited all men to bountifull contribution, and procured towards it with all his power, gold, silver, brass, iron, wood, precious stones,

l 1 *Chron.* 29.3.

in great abundance. Yea moreover, ˡ *because I have* (saith David) *a joy in the house of my God, I have of mine own gold and silver, besides all that I have prepared for the house of the Sanctuary, given to the house of my God three thousand Talents of Gold, even the Gold of Ophir, seven thousand Talents of fined silver.* After the overthrow of this first House of God, a second was in stead thereof erected, but with so great odds, that ᵐ they wept which had seen the former, and beheld how much

m *Ezr.* 3.12.
Agge. 2.4.

this later came behind it, the beauty whereof notwithstanding was such, that even this was also the wonder of the whole world. Besides which Temple, there were both in other parts of the Land, and even in *Jerusalem*, by process of time, no small number of Synagogues for men to resort unto. Our Saviour himself, and after him the Apostles frequented both the one and the other. The Church of Christ which was in *Jerusalem*, and held that profession which had not the publique allowance and countenance of Authority, could not so long use the exercise of Christian Religion but in ⁿ private only. So that as Jews they had access to

n *Act.* 1.19.
& 2.1.
& 2.46.

the Temple and Synagogues, where God was served after the custom of the Law, but for that which they did as Christians, they were of necessity forced otherwhere to assemble themselves. And as God gave increase to his Church, they sought out both there and abroad for that purpose not the fittest (for so the times wou'd not suffer them to do) but the safest places they could. In process of time somewhiles by sufferance, somewhiles by special leave and favour, they began to erect to themselves Oratories, not in any sumptuous or stately manner, which neither was possible by reason of the poor estate of the Church, and had been perilous in regard of the worlds envie towards them. At length, when it pleased God to raise up Kings and Emperours favouring sincerely the Christian truth, that which the Church before either could nor, or durst not do, was with all alacrity performed. Temples were in all places erected, No cost was spared, nothing judged too dear which that way should be spent. The whole world did seem to exult, that it had occasion of pouring out gifts to so blessed a purpose. That cheerful devotion which *David* this way did exceedingly delight to behold, and (o) wish that the same

o 1 *Chron.* 29. 17.18.

in the Jewish people might be perpetual, was then in Christian people every where to be seen. Their actions till this day always accustomed to be spoken of with great honour, are now called openly into question. They and as many as have been followers of their example in that thing; we especially that worship God, either in Temples which their hands made, or which other men sithence have framed

The solemnity of erecting Churches condemned by *Bar.* p.130. The hallowing & dedicating of them scorned p.141.

by the like pattern, are, in that respect charged no less than with the sin of Idolatry. Our Churches in the scorn of that good Spirit, which directeth such fiery tongues, they term spitefully the Temples of *Baal*, are idle Synagogues, abominable styes.

12. Wherein the first thing which moveth them thus to cast up their poyson, are certain solemnities usual at the first erection of Churches. Now although the same should be blame-worthy, yet this age (thinks be to God) hath reasonably well forborn to incur the danger of any such blame.   It

It cannot be laid to many mens charge at this day living, either that they have been so curious, as to trouble Bishops with placing the first stone in the Churches they built, or so scrupulous, as after the erection of them, to make any great ado for their dedication. In which kind notwithstanding as we do neither allow unmeet, nor purpose the stiff defence of any unnecessary custome [a] heretofore received: So we know no reason wherefore Churches should be the worse, if at the first erecting of them, at the making of them publique, at the time when they are delivered, as it were, into Gods own possession, and when the use whereunto they shall ever serve is established, Ceremonies fit to betoken such intents, and to accompany such actions be usual, as [b] in the purest times they have been. When [c] *Constantine* had finished an house for the service of God at *Jerusalem*, the dedication he judged a matter not unworthy, about the solemn performance whereof, the greatest part of the Bishops in Christendom should meet together. Which thing they did at the Emperours motion, each most willingly setting forth that action to their power, some with Orations, some with Sermons, some with the sacrifice of Prayers un to God for the peace of the world, for the Churches safety, for the Emperours and his childrens good. [d] By *Athanasius* the like is recorded concerning a Bishop of *Alexandria*, in a work of the like devout magnificence. So that whether Emperours or Bishops in those days were Church-founders, the solemn dedication of Churches they thought not to be a work in it self either vaine, or superstitious. Can we judge it a thing seemly for any man to go about the building of an house to the God of Heaven with no other appearance, than if his end were to rear up a kitchen, or a parlour for his own use? Or when a work of such nature is finished, remaineth there nothing but presently to use it, and so an end? It behoveth that the place where God shall be served by the whole Church, be a publick place, for the avoiding of privy Conventicles, which covered with pretence of Religion, may serve in to dangerous practises. Yea, though such assemblies be had indeed for Religions sake, hurtfull nevertheless they may easily prove, as well in regard of their fitness to serve the turn of Heretiques, and such as privily will soonest adventure to instil their poyson into mens minds; as also for the occasion, which thereby is given to malicious persons, both of suspecting, and of traducing with more colourable shew those actions, which in themselves being holy, should be so ordered, that no man might probably otherwise think of them. Which considerations have by so much the greater waight, for that of these inconveniencies the Church heretofore had so plain experience, when Christian men were driven to use secret meetings, because the liberty of publick places was not granted them. There are which hold, that the presence of a Christian multitude, and the duties of Religion performed amongst them, do make the place of their Assembly publique, even as the presence of the King and his Retinue maketh any mans house a Court. But this I take to be an errour, in as much as the onely thing which maketh any place publique, is the publique assignement thereof unto such duties. As for the multitude there assembled, or the duties which they perform, it doth not appear how either should be of force to infuse any such prerogative. Nor doth the solemn dedication of Churches serve onely to make them publique, but further also to surrender up that right which otherwise their founders might have in them, and to make God himself their owner. For which cause at the Erection and Consecration as well of the [e] Tabernacle, as of [f] the Temple, it pleased the Almighty to give a manifest signe that he took possession of both. Finally, [f] it notifieth in solemn manner the holy and religious use whereunto it is intended such houses shall be put. [g] These things the wisdom of *Solomon* did not account superfluous. He knew how easily that which was meant should be holy and sacred, might be drawn from the use whereunto it was first provided; he knew how bold men are to take even from God himself; how hardly that house would be kept from impious profanation, he knew; and right wisely therefore endeavoured by such solemnities to leave in the minds of men that [h] impression, which might somewhat restrain their boldness, and nourish a reverend affection towards the house of God. For which cause when the first house was destroyed, and a new in the stead thereof erected by the children of *Israel* after their return from captivity, they kept the [i] dedication even of this house also with joy.

The

Marginal notes:

a *Durand. rationel. lib. 1. cap 6. & de conser. d. 1. c. tabernaculum. Greg. Mag. lib. 10. epist. 12. & lib. 7. epist. 71. & 1. 8. ep. 63.*

b Ἐγκαίνια τιμάσθω πάλαι νόμῳ καὶ καλῶς ἔχων μάλλον δὲ τὰ νέα τιμάσθω δι’ ἐγκαίνιον. Καὶ τοῦτο ἀπαξ ἀλλά κỳ πολλάκις ἑκάστης τῆς ἐνιαυτῶ περι τροπῆς ὅτ’ αὐτὴν ἡμέραν ἐπαγούσης ἵνα μὴ ἐξίτηλα τῷ χρόνῳ γένοιτο τὰ καλὰ. *Greg. Nazian. orat. εἰς ῆ κυείαχην.*

c *Vide Euseb. de vita Constan. lib. 4. cap. 41. 43. 44. 45.*

d *Athanasius Apol. ad Constantium.*

e *Exod. 40. 34.*

f *1 Reg. 8. 11.*

f *Exo. 1. 49.*

g *1 Reg. 8.*

h *Levit. 16. 2. The place named holy.*

i *Ezr. 6. 16.*

a *Matth.* 21.13.
b *Jer.* 17.24.
c *Mark* 11.16.
d *Levit.* 26.2.
e 1 *Cor.* 11.22.
f *Pet. Cluniac.*

The argument which our Saviour useth against Prophaners of the Temple, he taketh from the use whereunto it was with solemnity consecrated. And as the Prophet *Jeremy* forbiddeth the carrying of burdens on the Sabbath, because that was a Sanctified day : So because the Temple was a place sanctified, our Lord would not suffer, no nor the carriage of a vessel through the Temple: These two Commandements therefore are in the Law conjoyned, *Ye shall keep my Sabbaths, and reverence my Sanctuary.* Out of those the Apostles words, *Have ye not houses to eat and drink?* albeit Temples, such as now, were not then erected for the exercise of Christian Religion, it hath been neverthelefs not abfurdly conceived, that he teacheth what difference should be made between house and house ; that what is fit for the dwelling place of God, and what for mans habitation he sheweth ; requireth that Christian men at their own home take common food, and in the house of the Lord none but that food which is heavenly ; he instructeth them, that as in the one place they use to refresh their bodies, so they may in the other learn to seek the nourishment of their souls ; and as there they sustain temporal life, so here they would learn to make provision for eternal. Christ could not suffer that the Temple should serve for a place of Mart, nor the Apostle of Christ, that the Church should be made an Inne. When therefore we sanctifie or hallow Churches, that which we do, is only to testifie that we make them places of publick resort, that we invest God himself with them, that we sever them from common uses. In which action, other solemnities than such as are decent and fit for that purpose we approve none. Indeed we condemn not all as unmeet, the like whereunto have been either devised or used haply amongst Idolaters. For why should conformity with them in matter of opinion be lawful, when they think that which is true, if in action, when they do that which is meet, it be not lawful to be like unto them ? Are we to forsake any true opinion, because Idolaters have maintained it ? or to shun any requisite action, only because we have in the practise thereof been prevented by Idolaters. It is no impossible thing, but that sometimes they may judge as rightly what is decent about external affairs of God, as in greater things what is true. Not therefore whatsoever Idolaters have either thought or done, but let whatsoever they have either thought or done *idolatrously, be so far forth* abhorred. For of that which is good even in evil things, God is Author.

Of the names whereby we distinguish our Churches.
g From Κυριακὴ Κυρε, and by adding letters of aspiration, *Church.*
h *V. Soc.l.1.c.* 6 *Ev. lib. 4. c.* 30.
Hist. Trip. l. 4. *cap.* 18.
i *V. Aug.l.8.de civ.Dei, c.27.l.* 22.*cap.*10.*Epi.* 49, *ad Deo gra.*
The duty which Christian men performed in keeping Festival dedications.
S. *Basil* termeth λατρείαν τ̂ν θεῶ acknowledging the same to have been withall τιμὴν εἰς τοὺς μάρτυρας. *Basil in Psal.* 114.

13. Touching the names of Angels and Saints, whereby the most of our Churches are called ; as the custome of so naming them is very ancient, so neither was the cause thereof at the first, nor is the use and continuance with us at this present hurtful. That Churches were consecrated unto none but the Lord only, the very general name it self doth sufficiently shew, in as much as by plain grammatical construction, *Church* doth signifie no other thing than *the Lords House.* And because the multitude, as of persons, so of things particular causeth variety of proper names to be devised for distinction sake, Founders of *Churches* did herein that which best liked their own conceit at the present time ; yet each intending, that as oft as those Buildings came to be mentioned, the name should put men in mind of some memorable thing or person. Thus therefore it cometh to pass, that all Churches have had their names, some as memorials of peace, some of wisdome, some in memory of the Trinity it self ; some of Christ under sundry titles ; of the blessed Virgin not of a few, many of one Apostle, Saint, or Martyr, many of all. In which respect their commendable purpose being not of every one understood, they have been in later ages construed as though they had superstitiously meant, either that those places which were denominated of Angels and Saints, should serve for the worship of so glorious creatures, or else those glorified creatures for defence, protection, and patronage of such places. A thing which the Ancients do utterly disclaim. To them faith Saint *Augustine,* we appoint no Churches, because they are not to us as Gods. Again, *The Nations to their Gods erected Temples, we not Temples unto our Martyrs as unto Gods, but memorials as unto dead men, whose spirits with God are still living.* Divers considerations there are, for which Christian Churches might first take their names of Saints : as either because by the Ministry of Saints it pleased God there to shew some rare effect of his power ; or else in regard of death, which those Saints having suffered for the testimony of Jesus Christ,

Christ, did thereby make the places where they dyed venerable; or thirdly, for that it liked good and vertuous men to give such occasion of mentioning them often, to the end that the naming of their persons might cause enquiry to be made, and meditation to be had of their vertues. Wherefore seeing that we cannot justly account it superstition, to give unto Churches those fore-rehearsed names, as memorials either of holy persons or things, if it be plain that their Founders did with such meaning name them, shall not we in otherwise taking them, offer them injury? Or if it be obscure or uncertain what they meant, yet this construction being more favourable, charity (I hope) constraineth no man which standeth doubtful of their minds, to lean to the hardest and worst interpretation that their words can carry. Yea, although it were cleer, that they all (for the error of some is manifest in this behalf) had therein a superstitious intent, wherefore should their fault prejudice us, (who as all men know) do use but by way of meer distinction the names which they of superstition gave? In the use of those names whereby we distinguish both dayes and moneths, are we culpable of superstition, because they were, who first invented them? The signe k *Castor* and *Pollux* superstitiously given unto that ship wherein the Apostle sailed, polluteth not the Evangelists pen, who thereby doth but distinguish that ship from others. If to *Daniel* there had been given no other name, but only l *Beltisbazzar*, given him in honour of the Babylonian Idol *Belti*, should their Idolatry, which were authors of that name, cleave unto every man which had so tearmed him by way of personal difference only? Were it not to satisfie the minds of the simpler sort of men, these nice curiosities are not worthy the labour which we bestow to answer them.

k Act. 28.11.

l Dan. 4. 5.
Vide Scal. de emendat. temp. lib.6.pag.277.

14. The like unto this is a fancy, which they have against the fashion of our Churches, as being framed according to the pattern of the Jewish Temple. A fault no less grievous, if so be it were true, than if some King should build his mansion house by the model of *Solomons* Palace. So far-forth as our Churches and their Temple have one end, what should lett, but that they may lawfully have one form? The Temple was for Sacrifice, and therefore had rooms to that purpose, such as ours have none. Our Churches are places provided, that the people might there assemble themselves in due and decent manner, according to their several degrees and orders. Which thing being common unto us with Jews, we have in this respect our Churches divided by certain partitions, although not so many in number as theirs. They had their several for Heathen Nations, their several for the people of their own Nation, their several for men, their several for women, their several for their Priests, and for the high Priest alone their several. There being in ours for local distinction between the Clergy and the rest (which yet we do not with any great strictness or curiosity observe neither) but one partition, the cause whereof at the first (as it seemeth) was, that as many as were capable of the holy mysteries, might there assemble themselves, and no other creep in amongst them; this is now made a matter so hainous, as if our Religion thereby were become plain Judaisme, and as though we retained a most holy place, whereinto there might not any but the high Priest alone enter, according to the custome of the Jewes.

Of the fashion of the Churches.

15. Some it highly displeaseth, that so great expences this way are imployed: *The mother of such magnificence* (they think) *is but only a proud ambitious desire to be spoken of far and wide. Suppose we that God himself delighted to dwell sumptuously, or taketh pleasure in chargeable pomp? No, then was the Lord most acceptably served, when his Temples were rooms borrowed within the houses of poor men. This was suitable unto the nakedness of Jesus Christ and the simplicity of his Gospel.* What thoughts or cogitations they had which were Authors of those things, the use and benefit whereof hath descended unto our selves, as we do not know, so we need not search. It cometh (we grant) many times to pass, that the works of men being the same, their drifts and purposes therein are divers. The charge of *Herod* about the Temple of God was ambitious, yet *Solomons* vertuous, *Constantines* holy. But howsoever their hearts are disposed by whom any such thing is done in the World, shall we think that i baneth the work which they leave behind them, or taketh away from others the use and benefit thereof? Touching God himself, hath he any where revealed, that it his delight to dwell beggerly? and that he taketh no

The sumptuousness of Churches.

pleasure

pleasure to be worshipped, saving onely in poor Cottages ? Even then was the Lord as acceptably honoured of his people as ever, when the stateliest places and things in the whole World were sought out to adorn his Temple. This is most

* Εϊσοντο με-ζαι, καλῶντι-μιον' ἢ γὰρ
Τοιῦτε ἢ θεω-εια θαυμαϛὴ
Ariſt. Eth. l. 4.
c. 3. τὰ διοθι-σει καλὰ ἡ, νό-ησει καλῶν ἐ-κὸνης. Philo.
Jul.
a Fælix thefu-ri imperialis quæſtor corſpi-catus ſacrorum vaſorum pretia. En inquit qua-libus vaſis mi-niſtratur Ma-riæ filio.
Theodoret.hiſt. Ecclel.l.3.c.12.
b Ecclef. 3 .34.
c Agge 2. 5.10.
d M nut Fal. in Octav.

* sutable, decent, and fit for the greatnefs of Jefus Chrift, for the fublimity of his Gofpel, except we think of Chrift and his Gofpel as * the Officers of *Julian* did. As therefore the fon of *Syrach* giveth verdict concerning thofe things, which God hath wrought, b *A man need not fay this is worfe than that, this more acceptable to God, that lefs, for in their feafon they are all worthy praife:* the like we may alfo conclude, as touching thefe two fo contrary ways of providing in mearer or in coftlier fort for the honour of Almighty God, *A man need not fay this is worfe than that, this more acceptab'e to God, that lefs, for with him they are in their feafon both allowable ;* the one, when the ftate of the Church is poor, the other, when God hath inriched it with plenty. When they, which had feen the beauty of the firft Temple, built by *Solomon* in the days of his great profperity and peace, beheld how far it excelled the fecond, which had not builders of like ability, the tears of their grieved eyes the Prophets c endeavoured with comforts to wipe away. Where-as if the Houfe of God were by fo much the more perfect, by how much the glory thereof is lefs, they fhould have done better to rejoyce than weep, their Prophets better to reprove than comfort. It being objected againft the Church in the times of univerfal perfecution, that her Service done to God was not folemnly perform-ed in Temples fit for the honour of Divine Majefty, their moft convenient anfwer was, that d *The beft Temples which we can dedicate to God, are our fanctified fouls and bodies.* Whereby it plainly appeareth, how the Fathers, when they were up-braided with that defect, con forted themfelves with the meditation of Gods moft gracious and merciful nature, who did not therefore the lefs accept of their hearty affection and zeal rather, than took any great delight, or imagined any high per-fection in fuch their want of external Ornaments, which when they wanted, the caufe was their only lack of ability ; ability ferving, they wanted them not. Be-

e Eufeb. lib. 8. cap.1.

fore the e Emperour *Conftantines* time, under *Severus, Gordian, Philip,* and *Galie-nus,* the ftate of Chriftian affairs being tolerable, the former buildings which were but of mean and fmall eftate contented them not, fpacious and ample Churches they erected throughout every City. No envy was able to be their hinderance, no practife of Satan or fraud of men availeable againft their proceedings herein, while they continued as yet worthy to feel the aid of the arme of God extended over them for their fafety. Thefe Churches *Dioclefian* f caufed by folemn Edict to be

f Eufeb.lib. 8. cap. 2.

afterwards overthrown. *Maximinus* with like authority giving leave to erect them, the hearts of all men were even wrapt with divine joy, to fee thofe places, which tyranno s impiety had laid wafte, recovered, as it were out of mortal cala-

g Eufeb.lib.10. cap.2.

mity, Churches g *reared up to an height immeafurable, and adorned with far more beauty in their reftauration than their Founders before had given them.* Whereby we fee how moft Chriftian minds ftood then affected, we fee how joyful they were to behold the fumptuous ftatelinefs of Houfes built unto Gods glory. If we fhould, over and befides this, alledge the care which was had, that all things about the Ta-bernacle of *Mofes* might be as beautiful, gorgeous, and rich, as Art could make them, or what travel and coft was beftowed, that the goodlinefs of the Temple might be a fpectacle of admiration to all the world ; this they will fay was figura-tive, and ferved by Gods appointment but for a time, to fhadow out the true ever-lafting glory of a more divine Sanctuary, whereinto Chrift being long fithence en-tred, it feemeth that all thofe curious exornations fhould rather ceafe. Which thing we alfo our felves would grant, if the ufe thereof had been meerly and only myftical. But fith the Prophet *David* doth mention a natural conveniency which fuch kind of bounteous expences have, as well for that we do thereby give unto

h 1 Chro.28.14

God a teftimony of our h cheerful affection, which thinketh nothing too deer to be beftowed about the furniture of his Service, as alfo becaufe it ferveth to the world

i 2 Chron. 2. 5.

for a witnefs of his i Almightinefs, whom we outwardly honour with the chiefeft of outward things, as being of all things himfelf incomparably the greateft. Be-fides, were it not alfo ftrange, if God fhould have made fuch ftore of glorious crea-tures on earth, and leave them all to be confumed in fecular vanity, allowing none
but

but the baſer ſort to be imployed in his own ſervice? To ſet forth the [a] Majeſty of
Kings his Vicegerents in this world, the moſt gorgeous and rare treaſures which
the world hath, are procured. We think, [b] beſike, that he will accept what the
meaneſt of them would diſdain. If there be great care to build and beautifie theſe
corruptible Sanctuaries, little or none, that the living Temples of the Holy Ghoſt,
the dearly redeemed Souls of the people of God may be edified; huge expences
upon Timber and Stone, but towards the relief of the poor ſmall devotion; Coſt
this way infinite, and in the mean while Charity cold; we have in ſuch caſe juſt occaſion to make complaint as [c] Saint *Jerom* did, *The walls of the Church there are
enow contented to build, and to underſet it with goodly pillars, the marbles are poliſhed,
the roofs ſhine with gold, the Altar hath precious ſtones to adorn it; and of Chriſts
Miniſters no choyce at all.* The ſame *Jerom* both in that place and [d] elſewhere de-
baſeth with like intent the glory of ſuch magnificence (a thing whereunto mens
affections in thoſe times needed no ſpurre) thereby to extoll the neceſſity ſometimes of charity and almes, ſometimes of other the moſt principal duties belonging unto Chriſtian men, which duties were neither ſo highly eſteemed as they
ought, and being compared with that in queſtion, the directeſt ſentence we can
give of them both, as unto me it ſeemeth, is this; *God who requireth the one as neceſſary, accepteth the other alſo as being an honourable work.*

16. Our opinion concerning the force and vertue which ſuch places have, is, I
truſt, without any blemiſh or ſtain of Hereſie. Churches receive, as every thing
elſe, their chief perfection from the end whereunto they ſerve. Which end being
the publick worſhip of God, they are, in this conſideration, houſes of greater dignity,
than any provided for meaner purpoſes. For which cauſe they ſeem after a ſort even
to mourn, as being injured and defrauded of their right, when places not ſanctified as they are, prevent them *unneceſſarily* in that preheminence and honour.
Whereby alſo it doth come paſs, that the Service of God hath not then it ſelf *ſuch
perfection of grace and comelineſs*, as when the dignity of place which it wiſheth for
doth concurre. Again, albeit the true worſhip of God be to God in it ſelf acceptable, who reſpecteth not ſo much in what place, as with what affection he is ſerved; and therefore *Moſes* in the midſt of the Sea, *Job* on the dunghil, *Ezechias* in
bed, *Jeremy* in mire, *Jonas* in the Whale, *Daniel* in the Den, the Children in the
Furnace, the Thief on the Croſs, *Peter* and *Paul* in Priſon, calling unto God,
were heard; as [e] S. *Baſil* noteth: manifeſt notwithſtanding it is, that the very
majeſty and holineſs of the place where God is worſhipped, hath *in regard of us*
great vertue, force and efficacy, for that it ſerveth as a ſenſible help to ſtirre up devotion, and *in that respect*, no doubt, *bettereth* even our holieſt and beſt actions in this
kind. As therefore we every where exhort all men to worſhip God, even ſo, for
performance of this Service by the people of God aſſembled, we think not any
place *ſo good* as the Church, neither any exhortation ſo fit as that of *David,* [f] *O
worſhip the Lord in the beauty of holineſs.*

17. For of our Churches thus it becometh us to eſteem, howſoever others rapt
with the pang of a furious zeal, do pour out againſt them devout blaſphemies, cry-
ing, [g] *Down with them, down with them, even to the very ground; For to Idolatry
they have been abuſed.* And the places where Idols have been worſhipped, are by [h] the
Law of God devote to utter deſtruction. For execution of which Law, the [i] *Kings
that were Godly, as* Aſa, Jehoſaphat, Ezechia, Joſia, *deſtroyed all the high places,*
Altars and Groves, which had been erected in Juda *and* Iſrael. *He that ſaid, Thou
ſhalt have no other gods before my face, hath likewiſe ſaid, Thou ſhalt utterly deface
and deſtroy all theſe Synagogues and places where ſuch Idols have been worſhipped.
This Law containeth the temporal puniſhment which God hath ſet down, and will that
men execute, for the breach of the other Law. They which ſpare them therefore, do
but reſerve, as the Hypocrite* Saul *did, execrable things, to worſhip God withall.*
The truth is, that as no man ſerveth God, and loveth him not; ſo neither can
any man ſincerely love God, and not extreamly abhorre that ſin, which is the
higheſt degree of treaſon againſt the ſupream Guide and Monarch of the whole
world, with whoſe divine authority and power it inveſteth others. By means
whereof the ſtate of Idolaters is two ways miſerable. Firſt, In that which they
worſhip

Side notes:
a *Matth.* 6. 29.
b *Malac.* 1. 8.
c *Ad Nepotian. de vita cleric.*
d *Ad Demetr. Epiſt.* 12. *ad Gaudentium.*
What Holineſs and Vertue we aſcribe to the Church, more than other places.
e *Exhort. ad bapt.& pœnitent.*
f *Pſal.* 96. 9.
Their pretence that would have Churches utterly razed.
g *Pſal.* 137. 7.
h *Deut.* 12. 2.
i 2 *Chron.* 17. 6.
2 *Chron.* 29.
2 *Chron.* 3.

a Isa.1.4.20.
Hos. 14.4.
Isa 41.24.
b Psal 115.8.
81.13.
Rom. 1.24.
c Judic. 6.13.
d Apoc. 21.8.
Isa 2.21.
e Acts 14.14.
f Deut. 28.20.
g Jer. 2. 17.

worship, they find no succour; and secondly, at his hands whom they ought to serve, there is no other thing to be looked for, but the effects of most just displeasure, the [b] withdrawing of graces, dereliction in this world, and in the world to come[d] confusion.[c] *Paul* & *Barnabas*, when Infidels admiring their vertues, went about to sacrifice unto them, rent their garments in token of horrour, and as frighted persons, ran crying thorow the press of the people, *O men, wherefore do ye these things?* They knew the force of that dreadful[f] curse whereunto Idolatry maketh subject. Nor is there cause why the guilty sustaining the same, should grudge or complain of injustice. For whatsoever evil befalleth in that respect, [g] themselves have made themselves worthy to suffer it. As for those things either *whereon*, or else *wherewith* superstition worketh, polluted they are by such *abuse*, and deprived of that dignity, which their nature delighteth in. For there is nothing which doth not grieve, and as it were, even loath it self, whensoever iniquity causeth it to serve unto vile purposes. Idolatry therefore maketh, whatsoever it toucheth, the worse. Howbeit sith creatures which have no understanding can shew no will; and where no will is, there is no sin; and only that which sinneth is subject to *punishment*; which way should any creature be *punishable* by the Law of God? There may be cause sometime to *abolish*, or to *extinguish* them. But surely never by way of punishment *to the things themselves*. Yea farther, howsoever the Law of *Moses* did punish Idolaters, we find not that God hath appointed for us any definite or *certain temporal judgment*, which the Christian Magistrate *is of necessity for ever* bound to execute upon *offenders* in that kind, much less upon *things* that way *abused* as meer *instruments*. For what God did command touching *Canaan*, the same concerneth not us any otherwise than only as a fearful pattern of his just displeasure and wrath against sinfull Nations. It teacheth us how *God thought good* to plague and afflict them, it doth not appoint in what form and manner *we ought* to punish the sin of Idolatry *in all others*. Unless they will say, that because the Israelites were commanded to make no covenant with the people of that Land, therefore Leagues and Truces made between superstitious persons, and such as serve God aright, are unlawful altogether; or because God commanded the Israelites to smite the inhabitants of *Canaan*, and to root them out, that therefore reformed Churches are bound to put all others to the edge of the sword. Now whereas [h] *Commandment* was also given to destroy all *places* where the Cananites had served their gods, and not to convert any of them to the honour of the true God: *this precept had reference unto a special intent* and purpose, which was that there should be *but one only place* in the whole Land, whereunto the people might bring such offerings, gifts, and sacrifices, as their *Levitical* Law did require. By which Law, severe charge was given them in that respect, not to convert *those places* to the worship of the living God, where Nations before them had served [i] Idols, *But to seek the place which the Lord their God should chuse out of their tribes*. Besides, it is reason we should likewise consider how great a difference there is between their proceedings, who erect a new Common-wealth, which is to have neither people nor Law, neither Regiment nor Religion the same that was; and theirs who only reform a decaied estate, by reducing it to that perfection from which it hath swarved. In this case we are to retain as much, in the other as little of former things as we may. Sith therefore examples have not *generally* the force of Lawes which all men ought to keep, but of counsels only and persuasions not amiss to be followed by them whose case is the like, surely where cases are so unlike as theirs and ours, I see not how that which they did, should induce, much less any way enforce us to the same practise, especially considering that *groves* and *hill-altars* were, while they did remain, both dangerous in regard of the secret access, which people superstitiously given, might have always thereunto with ease, neither could they remaining serve with any fitness unto better purpose, whereas our Temples (their former abuse being by order of Law removed) are not only free from such peril, but withall so conveniently framed for the people of God to serve and honour him therein; that no man beholding them, can chuse but think it exceeding great pitty, they should be ever any otherwise employed. Yea but the cattel of *Amalek* (you will say) were *fit* for sacrifice; and this was the very conceit which sometime deceived *Saul*. It was so. Nor do I any thing doubt, but that *Saul* upon this conceit

h Deut. 12.2.

i Deut. 12.4.5.

might

might even lawfully have offered to God those reserved spoils, had not the Lord *in that particular case* given *special charge* to the contrary. As therefore notwithstanding the commandement of *Israel* to destroy Cananites, Idolaters may be converted and live : so the Temples which have served Idolatry as Instruments, may be sanctified again and continue, albeit, to *Israel* commandement have been given that *they* should destroy all Idolatrous places *in their land*; and to the good Kings of *Israel* commendation for fulfilling, to the evil for disobeying the same commandement, sometimes punishment, always sharp and severe reproof hath even from the Lord himself befallen. Thus much it may suffice to have written in defence of those Christian Oratories, the overthrow and ruine whereof is desired, not now by Infidels, Pagans, or Turks, but by a special refined Sect of Christian Believers ; pretending themselves exceedingly grieved at our Solemnities in erecting Churches, at the names which we suffer them to hold, at their forme and fashion, at the stateliness of them and costliness, at the opinion which we have of them, and at the manifold superstitious abuses whereunto they have been put.

18. Places of publick resort being thus provided for, our repair thither is especially for mutual conference, and as it were commerce to be had between God and us. Because therefore want [a] of the knowledge of God is the cause of all iniquity amongst men, as contrariwise, the ground of all our happiness, and the seed of whatsoever perfect vertue groweth from us, is a right opinion touching things divine, this kind of knowledge we may justly set down for the first and chiefest thing which God imparteth unto his people, and our duty of receiving this at his merciful hands, for the first of those religious Offices wherewith we publickly honour him on earth. For the instruction therefore of all sorts of men to eternal life, it is necessary, that the sacred and saving truth of God be openly published unto them. Which open publication of *heavenly mysteries*, is by an excellency termed *preaching*. For otherwise there is not any thing *publickly notified*, but we may in that respect, rightly and properly say it is *preached*. So that when the school of God doth use it as *a word of Art*, we are [b] Luc 8. 39. accordingly to understand it with restraint to such special matter as that school is accustomed to publish. We find not in the world any people that hath lived altogether without Religion. And yet this duty of Religion, which provideth that publikely all sorts of men may be instructed in the fear of God, is to the Church of God, and hath been always so peculiar, that none of the Heathens, how [c] curious *Vide Tertul.* soever in searching out all kinds of outward Ceremonies like to ours, could ever *de præscr. ad-* once so much as endeavour to resemble *herein* the Churches care for the endless *vers. hær* good of her Children. Ways of teaching there have been sundry always usual in Gods Church. For the first introduction of youth, to the knowledge of God, [d] the [d] The Jewes Jews even till this day have their Catechismes. With Religion it fareth as with *Catech called* other Sciences, the first delivery of the Elements thereof must, for like considera- *Lekach, Tob.* tion, [e] be framed according to the weak and slender capacity of young beginners : unto which manner of teaching Principles in Christianity, the Apostle in the sixth to the *Hebrews* is himself understood to allude. For this cause therefore, as a Decalogue of *Moses* declareth summarily those things which we ought to do ; the Prayer of our Lord whatsoever we should request or desire : so either by the [f] Apostles, or at the least-wise out of their writings, we have the substance of Christian Belief compendiously drawn into few and short Articles, to the end that the weakness of no mans wit might either hinder *altogether* the knowledge, or excuse the utter ignorance of needful things.

Such

Of publick teaching, or preaching, and the first kind thereof, Catechizing.

[a] *Contraria fortia in quibus homines sibi invicem opponuntur secundum exercitia & desideria & opiniones omnia proveniunt ex ignorantia : sicut cæcus ex privatione sui visus vocatur ubique & læditur. Scientia veritatis tollit hominum inimicitiam & odium. Hoc promisit sancta Theologia dicens, Habitabis agnus cum lupo. Et assignat rationem, repleta est terra sapientia Domini,* Moses *Ægypt. in Mor. Hannebuch. lib. 3. c. 12.*

[e] *Incipientibus brevius ac simplicius tradi præcepta magis convenis. Aut enim difficultate institutionis tam numerosa atque perplexa deterreri solent, aut eo tempore quo præcipue alenda ingenia atq; indulgentia quædam cuntrienda sunt assertorum rerum tractatu atteruntur* Fab procem l. 1. *Incipientibus nobis exponere jura populi Romani, ita videntur posse tradi commodissime, si primo levi ac simplici via, post deinde diligentissima atq; exactissima interpretatione singula tradantur. Alioqui si statim ab initio rudem adhuc & infirmum animum studiosi multitudine ac varietate rerum oneraverimus duorum alterum, aut desertorem studiorum afficiemus, aut cum magno labore ejus, sæpe etiam cum diffidentia (qua plerumque juvenes avertit) serius ad id perducemus ad quod leviore via ductus, sine magno labore & sine ulla diffidentia maturius perduci potuisset* Institut. Imper. l. 1. tit. 1. [f] *Vide Ruff in Symb.*

Such as were trained up in these Rudiments, and were so made fit to be afterward by Baptism received into the Church, the Fathers usually in their Writings do term *g* Tert. de pœ- *Hearers*, as having no farther communion or fellowship with the Church, than nitent. *An ali-* only this, that they were admitted to hear the Principles of Christian Faith made *us est sinctus* plain unto them. Catechizing may be in Schools, it may be in private Families. *Christus? Ali-* But when we make it a kind of Preaching, we mean always the publick performance *us audientibus?* thereof in the open hearing of men, because things are preached not in that they *Audientes op-* *tare intinctio-* are taught, but in that they are published. *nem non præsu-* *mere opertet.* Cyprian. Epist. 17. lib. 3. *Audientibus vigilantia vestra non desit.* Rupert. de divin. offic. lib. 4. cap. 18. *Audiens quisque regulam fidei, Catechumenus dicitur. Catechumenus namque Auditor interpretatur.*

Of Preaching, 19. *Moses* and the Prophets, Christ and his Apostles were in their times all by reading Preachers of Gods Truth; some by word, some by writing, some by both. This publickly the they did partly as faithful *Witnesses*, making meer *relation* what God himself had *re-* Books of holy *vealed* unto them; and partly as careful *Expounders*, Teachers, Perswaders there-Scripture; and of. The Church in like case *Preacheth* still, first publishing by way of *Testimony* concerning or relation, the truth which from them she hath received, even in such sort as it supposed un-was received, *written in the sacred volumes of Scripture*: secondly, by way of *ex-* truths in those *plication*, discovering the mysteries which lie hid therein. The Church as a *wit-* translations of *plication*, discovering the mysteries which lie hid therein. The Church as a *wit-* Scripture which ness, preacheth his meer revealed Truth, by *reading* publikely the Sacred Scripture. we allow to be So that a second kind of preaching is the reading of holy Writ. For thus we may read, as also of the boldlier speak, being strengthned *h* with the example of so reverend a Prelate as the choice saith, that *Moses* from the time of ancient generations and ages long since past, had which we amongst the Cities of the very Gentiles them that preached him, *in that he was* make in *h* Acts 15.21. read every Sabboth day. For so of necessity it must be meant, in as much as we reading. know, that the Jews have always had their weekly readings of the *Law of Moses*; but that they always had in like manner their weekly *Sermons upon some part of the Law of Moses*, we no where find. Howbeit still we must here remember, that the Church, by her publick reading of the Book of God, preacheth only *as a witness*. Now the principal thing required in a witness is fidelity. Wherefore as we cannot excuse that Church, which either through corrupt translations of Scripture, delivereth instead of divine Speeches, any thing repugnant unto that which God speaketh; or, through falsified additions, proposeth that to the people of God as Scripture, which is in truth no Scripture: So the blame, which in both these re-spects hath been laid upon the Church of *England*, is surely altogether without cause. Touching Translations of Holy Scripture, albeit we may not disallow of their painful travels herein, who strictly have tied themselves to the very original letter, yet the judgement of the Church as we see by the practise of all Nations, *Greeks, Latines, Persians, Syrians, Æthiopians, Arabians,* hath been ever, that the fittest for publick audience are such, as following a middle course between the ri-gor of literal Translators, and the liberty of Paraphrasts, do with greatest shortness and plainness deliver the meaning of the Holy Ghost. Which being a labour of so great difficulty, the exact performance thereof we may rather wish than look for. So that, except between the *words of translation* and the *mind of Scripture* it self, there be *Contradiction*, every little difference should not seem an intolerable blemish *i* Psal. 105.28. necessarily to be spunged out. Whereas therefore the *i* Prophet *David* in a certain Psalm doth say concerning *Moses* and *Aaron*, that they *were* obedient to the word of God, and in the self-same place our allowed Translation saith, they *were not* obedient, we are for this cause challenged as manifest gain-sayers of Scripture, even in that which we read for Scripture unto the people. But for as much as words are resemblances of that which the mind of the speaker conceiveth, and conceits are images representing that which is spoken of, it followeth that they who will judge of words, should have recourse to the things themselves from whence they rise. In setting down that miracle, at the sight whereof *Peter* fell down astonished be-*k* Luc. 5. 6,7. fore the feet of Jesus, and cryed, *Depart, Lord, I am a sinner*, the *k* Evangelist St. *Luke* saith, the store of the fish which they took was such, that the net they took *l* John 11.11. it in *brake*, and the Ships which they loaded therewith sunk; *l* St. *John* recording the like miracle, saith, that albeit the fishes in number were so many, yet the net with

with so great a waight was *not broken.* Suppose they had written both of one miracle. Although there be in their words a manifest shew of jar; yet none; if we
look upon the difference of matter; with regard whereunto they might both have
spoken even of one miracle, the very same which they spake of divers, the one intending thereby to signifie that the greatness of the burden exceeded the natural
ability of the instruments which they had to bear it; the other, that the weakness
thereof was supported by a supernatural and miraculous addition of strength. The
Nets, as touching themselves *brake*, but through the power of God they *held.*
Are not the words of the [a] Prophet *Micheas* touching *Bethleem*, Thou *Bethleem
the least?* And doth not the very [b] Evangelist translate these words, Thou *Bethleem not the least?* the one regarding the quantity of the place, the other the dignity.
Micheas attributeth unto it smalness, in respect of circuit; *Matthew* greatness, in
regard of honour and estimation, by being the native soyle of our Lord and Saviour
Christ. Sith therefore speeches, which gain-say one another; must of necessity be applied both unto one and the self-same subject; sith they must also the one affirm, the
other deny the same thing: what necessity of contradiction can there be between
the letter of the Prophet *David* and our authorized translation thereof, if he understanding *Moses* and *Aaron* do say, *They were not disobedient*; we applying
our speech to *Pharo* and the *Ægyptians*, do say of them, *They were not obedient?*
Or (which the matter it self will easily enough likewise suffer) if the *Ægyptians*
being meant by both, it be said that *they* in regard of [c] their offer to let go the people, when they saw the fearfull darkness, *disobeyed not* the Word of the Lord; and
yet that they *did not obey* his Word, in as much as the sheep and cattel at the self-
same time they with-held. Of both Translations the better, I willingly acknowledge
that which cometh nearer to the very letter of the original verity: yet so, that the
other may likewise safely enough be read, without any peril at all of gain-saying,
as much as the least jot or syllable of Gods most sacred and precious truth. Which
truth as in this we do not violate, so neither is the same gain-sayed or crost, no
not in those very preambles placed before certain readings, wherein the steps of the
Latin Service-book have been somewhat too nearly followed. As when we say,
Christ spake [d] *to his Disciples*, that which the Gospel declareth he spake [e] *unto the
Pharisees.* For doth the Gospel affirm he spake to the *Pharisees only?* doth it
mean that they, and besides them, no man else was at that time spoken unto by our
Saviour Christ? If not, then is there in this diversity no contrariety. I suppose it
somewhat probable, that St. *John* and St. *Matthew*, which have recorded those
Sermons, heard them, and being hearers, did think themselves as well respected as
the *Pharisees* in that which their Lord and Master taught, concerning the Pastoral
care he had over his own flock, and his offer of grace made to the whole World,
which things are the matter whereof he treateth in those Sermons. Wherefore
as yet there is nothing found, wherein we read for the Word of God that which may
be condemned as repugnant unto his Word. Furthermore somewhat they are displeased, in that we follow not the method of reading which [f] in their judgement is most commendable, the method used in some forrain Churches, where
Scriptures are read *before* the time of divine Service, and without either *choyce* or
stint appointed by any *determinate* order. Nevertheless, till such time as they shall
vouchsafe us some just and sufficient reason to the contrary, we must by their patience, if not allowance, retain the [g] ancient received custome which we now observe. For with us the reading of Scripture in the Church is a part of our Church
Liturgie, a special portion of the Service which we do to God, and not an exercise
to spend the time when one doth wait for anothers coming, til the assembly of them
that shall afterward worship him be compleat. Wherefore as the form of our publick service is not voluntary, so neither are the parts thereof uncertain, but they are
all set down in such order, and with such choyce, as hath in the wisdom of the Church
seemed best to concur as well with the special occasions, as with the general purpose which we have to glorifie God.

20. Other publique readings there are of Books and Writings not Canonical,
whereby the Church doth also preach, or openly make known the Doctrine
of vertuous conversation; whereupon, besides those things, in regard whereof we

C c

Marginal notes:

[a] *Matth.* 5. 2.
[b] *Matth.* 2. 6.
[c] *Exod.* 10. 24;
[d] The Gospel on the second Sunday after Easter, and on the twentieth after Trinity.
[e] *John* 10, 11.
*T.C.l.1.p.*381. Although it be very convenient which is, used in some Churches, where before preaching time the Church assembled hath the Scriptures read; yet neither is this, nor any other order of bare publick reading in the Church necessary had.
[g] *Aug. de Civ. Dei.* lib. 22. c. 8. *Fasso silentio scripturarum sunt lecta divina solennia.* That for several times several pieces of Scripture were read as parts of the Service of the Greek Church the Fathers thereof in their sundry Homilies and other Writings do all testifie the like order in the Syrian Churches, is clear by the very inscriptions of Chapters throughout their translation of the New Testament. See the Edition at *Vienna*, *Park* and *Antwerp.*

Of preaching by the publique reading of other profitable in-structions; and concerning Books Apocry-phal.

are thought to read the Scriptures of God amiss, it is thought amiss, that we read in our Churches any thing at all besides the Scriptures. To exclude the reading of any such profitable instruction, as the Church hath devised for the better understanding of Scripture, or for the easier trayning up of the people in holiness and righteousness of life, they plead, that God in the Law would have *nothing* brought into the Temple, neither Besomes, nor Flesh-hooks, nor Trumpets, but those only which were sanctified; that for the expounding of darker places, we *ought to* follow the Jews * Politie, who under *Antiochus*, where they had not the commodity of Sermons, appointed always at their meetings somewhat out of the Prophets to be read together with the Law, and so by the one made the other plainer to be understood; that before and after our Saviours coming they neither read *Onkelos* nor *Jonathans* Paraphrase, though having both, but contented themselves b with the reading onely of Scriptures; that if in the Primitive Church there had been any thing read besides the monuments of the Prophets and Apostles, c *Justin Martyr* and *Origen*, who mention these, would have spoken of the other likewise; that d the most ancient and best Councels forbidde any thing to bee read in Churches, saving Canonicall Scripture onely; that when e other thinges were afterwards permitted f fault was found with it, it succeeded but ill, the Bible it self was thereby in time quite and clean thrust out. Which arguments, if they be only brought in token of the Authors good-will and meaning towards the cause which they would set forward, must accordingly be accepted of by them, who already are perswaded the same way. But if their drift and purpose be to perswade others, it would be demanded, by what rule the legall *hallowing* of besomes and flesh-hooks must needs exclude all other readings in the Church save Scripture. Things sanctified were thereby in such sort appropriated unto God, as that they might never afterwards again be made common. For which cause, the Lord, to signe and mark them as his own, g appointed oyl of holy oyntment, the like whereunto it was not lawful to make for ordinary and daily uses. Thus the h anoynting of *Aaron* and his sons tyed them to the Office of the Priest-hood for ever; the anoynting not of those silver Trumpets (which i *Moses* as well for secular as sacred uses was commanded to make, not to sanctifie) but the unction of the k Tabernacle, the Table, the Laver, the Altar of God, with all the instruments appertaining thereunto, this made them for ever holy unto him, in whose service they were imployed. But what of this? Doth it hereupon follow, that all things now in the Church, from the greatest *to the least*, are unholy, which the Lord hath not himself precisely instituted? For so l those rudiments, they say, do import. Then is there nothing holy, which the Church by her authority hath appointed, and consequently all positive Ordinances that ever were made by Ecclesiastical power, touching spiritual affairs, are prophane, they are unholy. I would not wish them to undertake a work so desperate as to prove, that for the peoples instruction no kind of reading is good, but only that which the Jews devised under *Antiochus*, although even that be also mistaken. For according to m *Elias* the Levite (out of whom it doth seem borrowed) the thing which *Antiochus* forbad, was the publique reading of the Law, and not *Sermons* upon the Law. Neither did the Jews read a portion of the Prophets, together with the Law, to serve for an interpretation thereof, because Sermons were not permitted them; But instead of the Law, which they might not read openly, they read of the Prophets that, which in likeness of matter came nearest to each Section of their Law. Whereupon, when afterwards the liberty of reading the n Law was restored, the self same Custome o as touching the Prophets did continue still. If neither the Jewes have used publiquely to read their Paraphrasis, p nor the Primitive Church of *Laodicea*, that nothing should be read in the Church but the Canonicall Books of the old and new Testament. Afterwards, as corruptions grew in the Church, the reading of Homilies and of Martyrs lives was permitted. But besides the evil success thereof, that use and custom was controled as may appear by the Council of *Colen*. albeit otherwise Popish. The bringing in of Homilies and Martyrs live, hath thrust the Bible clean out of the Church, or into a corner.

for:

Marginal notes:

a *T.C.l.1.pag.196.* Neither the Homilies nor the Apocrypha are at all to be read in the Church. Wherein first it is good to consider the order which the Lord kept with his people in times past, when he commanded *Exod.30.29.* that no vessel, nor no instrument, either besome or flesh-hook, or pan, should once come into the Temple, but those onely which are sanctified and set apart for that use. And in the Book of *Numbers* he will have no other Trumpets blown to call the people together, but those onely which were set apart for that purpose. *Numb 10.2.*

* *T.C.l.8.p.197.* Besides this, the Politie of the Church of God in times past is to be followed, &c. b *Acts 13.15. Acts 15.21.* c *Justin. Apol. 2. Origen. Hom.1. super Exod. & in Judic.* d *Concil. Laod. cap. 59.*

e *Concil. Vasenf. 2.* f *Concil. Colon. par. 2.*

g *Ex.30.25.32.* h *Exod. 40.15.* i *Numb. 10.2.*

k *Exod. 27.3. & 30.26,27,28* l *T.C.l.1.p.197.* The Lord would by these Rudiments and Pædagogies teach, that he would have nothing brought into the Church but that which he had appointed.

m *Elias Thesb. in verbo Patar.* n *Acts 15.21.* o *Acts 13.15.* p *T.C.l.1.197.* This practise continued still in the Churches of God after the Apostles times, as may appear by the second Apologie of *Justin. Martyr. Idem p.198.* It was decreed in the Council

for a longe time any other Writinges than Scripture, except the cause of
their not doing it, were some Law of God, or reason forbidding them to do that
which we do, why should the latter ages of the Church be deprived of the Liberty
the former had? Are we bound while the world standeth, to put nothing in practice,
but only that which was at the very first? Concerning the Councel of *Laodicea*;
as it forbiddeth the reading of those things which are not Canonical, so it maketh
*some things not Canonical which are. Their judgement in this we may not, and
in that we need not follow. We have by thus many years experience found, that
exceeding great good, not incumbred with any notable inconvenience, hath grown
by the custome which we now observe. As for the harm whereof judicious men
have complained in former times; it came not of this, that other things were
read besides the Scripture, but that so evil choyse was made. With us there is never any time bestowed in divine Service, without the reading of a great part of the
holy Scripture, which we account a thing most necessary. We dare not admit any
such form of Liturgie, as either appointeth no Scripture at all, or very little to be
read in the Church. And therefore the thrusting of the Bible out of the House of
God, is rather there to be feared, where men
esteem it a matter so indifferent, whether the
same be by solemn appointment read publikely, or not read, the bare text excepted, which
the Preacher happily chuseth out to expound.
But let us here consider what the Practice of
our Fathers before us hath been, and how far
forth the same may be followed. We find, that
in ancient times there was publiquely read first
the Scripture, as namely, something out of
the Books of the Prophets of God, which
were of old; something out of the Apostles
writings; and lastly out of the holy Evangelists, some things which touched the person
of our Lord Jesus Christ himself. The cause of
their reading first the old Testament, then the
new, and always somewhat out of both, is
most likely to have been that which *Justin
Martyr* and Saint *August.* observe in compa-
ring the two Testaments. *The Apostles* (saith the one) *hath taught us as themselves did learn, first the Precepts of the Law, and then the Gospels. For what else
is the Law, but the Gospel foreshewed? What other the Gospel than the Law fulfilled?*
In like sort the other, *What the old Testament hath, the very same the new containeth, but that which lieth there as under a shadow, is here brought forth into the open
Sun: Things there prefigured, are here performed.* Again, *in the old Testament
there is a close comprehension of the new, in the new an open discovery of the old.* To
be short, the method of their publike readings either purposely did tend, or at the
leastwise doth fitly serve, *That from smaller things the mind of the hearers may go
forward to the knowledge of greater, and by degrees climb up from the lowest to the
highest things.* Now besides the Scripture, the Books which they called *Ecclesiastical,* were thought not unworthy sometime to be brought into puplike audience,
and with that name they entituled the Books which we term *Apocryphal.* Under
the self-same name they also comprised certain, no otherwise annexed unto the
new, than the former to the old Testament, as a Book of *Hermes,* Epistles of
Clement, and the like. According therefore to the Phrase of Antiquity, these we
may term *the new,* and the other the *old Ecclesiastical* Books or Writings. For
we being directed by a sentence (I suppose) of Saint *Jerom,* who saith, that *All
writings not Canonical are Apochryphal,* use not now the title *Apochryphal,* as the
rest of the Fathers ordinarily have done, whose custome is so to name for the most
part only, such as might not publiquely be read or divulged. *Ruffinus* therefore
having rehearsed the self-same Books of Canonical Scripture, which with us are
held to be alone Canonical, addeth immediately by way of caution, *We must know
that other Books there are also, which our fore-fathers have used to name not Canonical,*

C c 2

Marginal notes:
a The Apocr.
b *T.C.l.* 2. *p.* 381. It is untrue, that *simple reading* is necessary in the Church. A number of Churches which have
no such order of simple reading, cannot be in this point
charged with breach of Gods Commandment, which they
might be if simple reading were *necessary.* [By simple reading
he meaneth the custom of bare reading more than the Preacher at the same time expoundeth unto the people] c *Coimus
ad divinarum literarum commemorationem.* Tertul. Apol.
*p.*692. d *Judaiarum Historiarum libri traditi sunt ab Apostolis legendi in Ecclesia.* Orig. in. Ios. Hom. 15.
e Παύλων χτι πόλεις ἤ ἄγρος μνάθησαν ὅτι τὸ αὐτὸ σωμ-
λάσσες γίνε]αι ἡ τὰ ἀπομνημονευμα]α τῶ Ἀποστόλων, ἤ
τὰ συγγράμμα]α τῶ Προφητῶ ἀναγινώσκε]αι. Justin.
Apol. 2. pag. 162. *Factum est ut ista die Dominica Pro-
phetica lectione jam lecta, ante altare ad. stant, equi lectionem S. Pauli proferret, beatissimus Antistes Ambrosius,&c.*
Sulpit. sever. lib. 3. de vita S. Mart. f Vide Concil. *Vase
2. habitum An. Dom.* 444. *to. Concil.* 2. *p.* 19. Item Synod
Laod. cap. 16. Cypr. lib. 2. epist. 5. & lib. 4. epist. 5. Amb
l.1. *Offic.ca.*8. & Epist.75. & lib. de Helia atque je junio.
cap. 10.
g Just. quest.
101.
h August. quest.
33, in Nume.
i Walls. strab.
derebus Ecele-
siast. cap. 22.
k Hieron. in
Prolog. Galeas.
l Ruffinus in
Symbol. Apost.
apud. Cypr.

call, but *Ecclefiaftical books*, *as the book of* Wifdom, Ecclefiafticus, Tobie, Judith, *the* Maccabees *in the old Teftament* ; *in the new, the book of* Hermes, *and fuch others* : *All which Books and Writings they willed to be read in Churches, but not to be alleaged, as if their authority did bind us to build upon them our Faith. Other writings they named Apocryphal, which they would not have read in Churches. Thefe things delivered unto us from the Fathers, we have in this place thought good to fet down.* So far, *Ruffinus.* He which confidereth notwithftanding what ftore of falfe and forged Writings, dangerous unto Chriftian belief, and yet bearing [a] glorious infcriptions, began foon upon the Apoftles times to be admitted into the Church, and to be honoured as if they had been indeed Apoftolique, fhall eafily perceive what caufe the Provincial Synod of [b] *Laodicea* might have *as then to prevent,* efpecially the danger of books made newly Ecclefiaftical, and for fear of the fraud of Hereticks, to provide, that fuch publique readings might be altogether taken out of Canonical Scripture. Which Ordinance refpecting, but that abufe that grew through the intermingling of leffons humane with facred, at fuch time as the one both affected the credit, and ufurped the name of the other (as by the Canon of [c] a later Councell providing remedy for the felf fame evil, and yet allowing the old Ecclefiafticall Books to be read, it doth more plainly and cleerly appear) neither can be conftrued, nor fhould be urged utterly to prejudice our ufe of thofe old Ecclefiafticall Writings ; much lefs of Homilies, which were a third kinde of readings ufual in former times, a moft commendable inftitution as well then [d] to fupply the cafual, as now the neceffary defect of Sermons.

In the heat of general perfecution whereunto Chriftian Belief was fubject, upon the firft promulgation thereof throughout the World, it much confirmed the courage and conftancy of weaker mindes, when publique relation was made unto them, after what manner God had been glorified through the fufferings of Martyrs, famous amongft them for holinefs during life, and at the time of their death admirable in all mens eyes, through miraculous evidence of grace divine affifting them from above. For which caufe the vertues of fome being thought expedient to be annually had in remembrance above the reft, this brought in [e] a fourth kinde of publique reading, whereby the lives of fuch Saints and Martyrs had at the time of their yearly memorials folemn recognition in the Church of God. The fond imitation of which laudable cuftome being in latter ages refumed, when there was neither the like caufe to do as the Fathers before had done ; nor any care, confcience, or wit, in fuch as undertook to perform that work, fome brainefs men have by great labour and travel brought to pafs, that the Church is now afhamed of nothing more than of Saints. If therefore Pope [f] *Gelafius* did fo long fithence fee thofe defects of judgement even then, for which the reading of the Acts of Martyrs fhould be, and was at that time forborn in the Church of *Rome* ; we are not to marvail, that afterwards Legends being grown in a manner to be nothing elfe but heaps of frivolous and fcandalous vanities, they have been even with difdaine thrown out, the [g] very nefts which bred them abhorring them. We are not therefore to except onely Scripture, and to make confufedly all the refidue of one fute, as if they, who abolifh Legends, could not without incongruity retain in the Church either Homilies, or thofe old *Ecclefiaftical Books :* Which books in cafe my felf did think, as fome others do, fafer and better to be left publikely unread ; neverthelefs as in other things of like nature, even fo in this, [h] my private judgement I fhould be loth to oppofe againft the force of their reverend authority, who rather confidering the divine excellency of fome things in all, and of all thi gs in certain of thofe *Apocrypha* which we publikely read, have thought it better to let them ftand as a lift or marginal border unto the old Teftament, and, though with divine, yet as humane compofitions to grant at the leaft unto certain of them publique audience in the houfe of God. For in as much as the due eftimation of heavenly truth dependeth wholly upon the known and approved authority of thofe famous Oracles of God, it greatly behoveth the Church to have alwayes moft efpecial care, left through confufed mixture at any time humane ufurp the room and title of divine writings. Wherefore albeit for the peoples [i] more plain inftruction (as the ancient ufe hath been) we read in our Churches certain Books befides the Scripture, yet as the Scripture we read them

not

not. All men know our profeſſed opinion touching the d fference whereby we ſever them from the Scripture. And if any where it be ſuſpected that ſome one or
other will haply miſtake a thing ſo manifeſt in every mans eye, there is no lett, but
that as often as thoſe Books are read, and need ſo requireth, the ſtile of their difference may expreſly be mentioned, to barre even all poſſibi.ity of error. It being then known, that we hold not the *Apocrypha* for ſacred (as we doe the holy
Scripture) but for humane compoſitions, the ſubject whereof are ſundry divine
matters; let there be reaſon ſhewed, why to read any part of them publiquely, it
ſhould be unlawful or hurtful unto the Church of God. I hear it ſaid, that *many* a T. C. lib. 2.
things in them are very *frivolous*, and unworthy of publique audience; yea, many pag. 400 401.
contrary, *plainly contrary to the holy Scripture*. Which hitherto is neither ſufficiently proved by him who ſaith it, and if the proofs thereof were ſtrong, yet the very
allegation it ſelf is weak. Let us therefore ſuppoſe (for I will not demand to
what purpoſe it is, that againſt our cuſtom of reading Books not Canonical, they
bring exceptions of matter in thoſe Books which we never uſe to read) ſuppoſe
(I ſay) that what faults ſoever they have obſerved throughout the paſſages of all
thoſe Books, the ſame in every reſpect were ſuch as neither could be conſtrued,
nor ought to be cenſured otherwiſe, than even as themſe ves pretend: Yet as
men, through too much haſt, oftentimes forget the errand whereabout they
ſhould go, ſo here it appeareth, that an eager deſire to rake together whatſoever
might prejudice or any way hinder the credit of Apocryphal Books, hath cauſed
the Collectors Pe. ſo to run as it were on wheels, that the minde which ſhould
guide it, had no leiſure to think, whether that which might haply ſerve to with-hold
from giving them the Authority which belongeth unto ſacred Scripture, and to cut
them off from the Canon, would as effectually ſerve to ſhut them altogether out
of the Church, and to withdraw from granting unto them that publique uſe, wherein they are onely held as profitable for inſtruction. Is it not acknowledged, that
thoſe Books are [b] *Holy*, that they are *Eccleſiaſtical* and *Sacred*, that to term them b Harm.Confeſ.
Divine, as being for their excellency next unto them which are properly ſo termed, ſect. 1. Bel.
is no way to honour them above deſert; yea, even that the whole Church of con.art. 6. Lu-
Chriſt, as well *at the firſt as ſithence* hath moſt worthily approved their fitneſs for bart. de princip.
the pub ique informations of life and manners: Is not thus much, I ſay, acknow- Chriſt. degm.
ledged, and that by them, who notwithſtanding receive not the ſame for *any part of* lib.1.c.5.
Canonical Scripture, by them who deny not but that they are *faulty*, by them who
are ready enough to give inſtances, wherein they ſeem to contain matter *ſcarce*
agreeable with holy Scripture ? So little doth ſuch their ſuppoſed faultineſs in moderate mens judgement inforce the removal of them out of the Houſe of God, that
ſtill they are judged to retain worthily thoſe very Titles of Commendation; than
which, there cannot greater be given to Writings, the Authors whereof are Men.
As in truth, if the Scripture it ſelf, aſcribing to the perſons of men righteouſneſs
in regard of their manifold vertues, may not rightly be conſtrued, as though it
did thereby clear them and make them quite free from faults, no reaſon we ſhould
judge it abſurd to commend their Writings as reverend, holy, and ſound, wherein
there are ſo many ſingular perfections, onely for that the exquiſite wits of ſome
few peradventure are able diſperſedly here and there to find now a word and then
a ſentence, which may be more probably ſuſpected than eaſily cleared of error by
us which have but conjectural knowledge of thei meaning. Againſt immodeſt c The Libell of
Invectives therefore whereby they are charged as being fraught with [c] *outragious* Metaphyſ.
lies, we doubt not but their more allowable cenſure will prevail, who without ſo Schoolp. art.34.
paſſionate terms of diſgrace, do note a difference great enough between Apo- d Joſeph. cont.
cryphal and other writings, a difference ſuch as [d] *Joſephus* and *Epiphanius* obſerve App. lib. 1.
the one declaring, that amonſt the Jews, Books written after the days of *Artax-* e Epiph.in An-
erxes, were not of equal credit with them which had gone before, in as much as the cyrot. χρόνει-
Jews ſithence that time had not the like exact ſucceſſion of Prophets; the [e] other μοι ηδη εισι
acknowledgi g that they are *profitable*, although denying them to be *divine*, in ſuch ἀλλ' εἰς ἀκεί-
conſtruction and ſenſe as the Scripture it ſelf is ſo termed. With what intent they μὲν εχτῶν εκ
were firſt publiſhed, thoſe words of the [f] *Nephew of Jeſus* do plainly enough αναπρόνίας.
ſignifie, *After that my Grand-Father Jeſus had given himſelfe to the* f Praef. ad lib.
Eccleſ.

reading

reading of the Law *and the* Prophets, *and* other Books of our Fathers, *and had gotten therein* sufficient judgement, *he purposed* also *to write* something *pertaining to* Learning *and* Wisdome, *to the intent,* that they which were desirous to learn, *and would give themselves to these things,* might profit *much more in living according to the* Law. Their end in writing, and ours in reading them, is the same. The Books of *Judith, Toby, Baruch, Wisdome,* and *Ecclesiasticus,* we read, as serving most unto that end. The rest we leave unto men in private. Neither can it be reasonably thought, because upon certain solemn occasions, some Lessons are chosen out of those Books, and of Scripture it self some Chapters not appointed to be read at all, that we thereby do offer disgrace to the Word of God, or lift up the Writings of men above it. For in such choice we do not think, but that *fitness* of speech may be more respected than *worthiness.* If in that which we use to read, there happen by the way any Clause, Sentence, or Speech, that soundeth towards error, should the mixture of a little dross constrain the Church to deprive her self of so much Gold, rather than learn how by art and judgement to make separation of the one from the other? To this effect very fitly, from the counsel that S. *Jerome* giveth *Læta,* of taking heed how she read the *Apocrypha,* as also by the help of other learned mens judgements delivered in like case, we may take direction. But surely, the arguments that should bind us not to read them, or any part of them publikely at all, must be stronger than as yet we have heard any.

Of preaching by Sermons & whether Sermons be the only ordinary way of Teaching, whereby men are brought to the saving knowledge of Gods Truth.

21. We marvell the less that our reading of Books not Canonical is so much impugned, when so little is attributed unto the reading of Canonical Scripture it self; that now it hath grown to be a question, whether the *Word of God* be any *ordinary mean* to save the souls of men, in that it is either privately studied, or publikely read, and so made known, or else only as the same is *preached,* that is to say, *explained by lively voice,* and *applied* to the peoples use, *as the speaker in his Wisdom* thinketh meet. For this alone is it which they use to call *Preaching.* The publick reading of the *Apocrypha* they condemn altogether as a thing effectual unto evil, the *bare* reading *in like sort* of whatsoever, yea even of Scriptures themselves, they mislike, as a thing *uneffectual* to do *that good,* which we are perswaded may grow by it. Our desire is in this present controversie, as in the rest, not to be carried up and down with the waves of uncertain arguments, but rather positively to lead on the minds of the simpler sort by plain and easie degrees, till the very nature of the thing it self do make manifest what is truth. First therefore, because whatsoever is spoken concerning the efficacy or necessity of *Gods Word,* the same they tie and restrain only unto *Sermons,* howbeit not Sermons read neither (for such they also abhorre in the Church) but Sermons without book, Sermons which spend their life in their birth, and may have publick audience but once: For this cause, to avoid ambiguities, wherewith they often intangle themselves, not marking what doth agree to the Word of God in it self, and what in regard of outward accidents which may befall it, we are to know that the Word of God is his heavenly Truth, touching matters of eternal life revealed and uttered unto Men, unto Prophets and Apostles by immediate Divine Inspiration, from them to us by their Books and Writings. We therefore have no *Word of God* but the Scripture. Apostolick Sermons were unto such as heard them, his Word, even as properly as to us their Writings are. Howbeit not so our own Sermons, the expositions which our discourse of wit doth gather and minister out of the Word of God. For which cause, in this present question we are, when we name the *Word of God,* alwayes to mean the *Scripture only.* The end of the Word of God is *to save,* and therefore we term it *the Word of Life.* The way for all men to be saved, is by the knowledge of that truth which the Word hath taught. And sith eternal Life is a thing of it self communicable unto all, it behooveth that the Word of God, the necessary meane thereunto, be so likewise. Wherefore the Word of Life hath been alwayes a Treasure, though precious, yet easie, as well to attain, as to find, lest any man desirous of life should perish through the difficulty of the way. To this end the Word of God no otherwise serveth, than only in the nature of a doctrinal Instrument. It saveth, because it maketh *wise to salvation.* Wherefore the ignorant it saveth not, they which live by the Word, must know it. And being it self the Instru-

2 Tim. 3. 15.

ment

ment which God hath purpofely framed, thereby to work the knowledge of falvation in the hearts of men, what caufe is there wherefore it fhould not of it felf be acknowledged a moft apt and a likely meane, to leave an *apprehenfion* of things divine in our underftanding, and in the mind an *affent* thereunto? For touching the one, fith God, who knoweth and difclofeth beft the rich treafures of his own wifdom, hath by delivering his Word, made choice of the Scriptures, as the moft effectual means, whereby thofe treafures might be imparted unto the world, it followeth, that to mans underftanding the Scripture muft needs be even of it felf intended as a full and perfect difcovery, fufficient to imprint in us the lively character of all things neceffarily required for the attainment of eternal Life. And concerning our affent to the Myfteries of heavenly Truth, feeing that the Word of God, for the Authors fake, hath credit with all that confefs it (as we all do) to be his Word, every Propofition of holy Scripture, every Sentence being to us a principle; if the principles of all kinds of knowledge elfe have that vertue in themfelves, whereby they are able to procure our affent unto fuch conclufions, as the induftry of right difcourfe doth gather from them, we have no reafon to think the principles of that Truth, which tendeth unto mans everlafting happinefs, lefs forcible than any other, when we know that of all other they are for their certainty the moft infallible. But as every thing of price, fo this doth require travel. We bring not the knowledge of God with us into the world. And the lefs our own opportunity or ability is that way, the more we need the help of other mens Judgements, to be our direction herein. Nor doth any man ever believe, into whom the doctrine of belief is not inftilled by inftruction, fome way received at the firft from others. Wherein whatfoever fit means there are to notifie the Myfteries of the Word of God, whether publikely (which we call *Preaching*) or in private howfoever, the Word by *every fuch meane* even *ordinarily* doth fave, and not only by being delivered unto men in Sermons. *Sermons* are not *the only preaching* which doth fave Souls. For concerning the ufe and fenfe of this word *Preaching*, which they fhut up in fo clofe a Prifon, although more than enough have already been fpoken, to redeem the liberty thereof, yet becaufe they infift fo much, and fo proudly infult thereon, we muft a little inure their ears with hearing, how others whom they more regard, are in this cafe accuftomed to ufe the felf-fame language with us, whofe manner of fpeech they deride. [a] *Juftin Martyr* doubteth not to tell the Grecians, that even in certain of their *Writings* the very Judgement to come is preached; nor the [b] Council of *Vaus* to infinuate, that Presbyters, abfent through infirmity from their Churches, might be faid to preach by thofe Deputies, who in their ftead did but read *Homilies*; nor the [c] Council of *Toledo*, to call the ufual publick reading of the Gofpels in the Church, preaching; nor [d] others, long before thefe our days to write, that by him who but readeth a *Leffon* in the folemn Affembly as part of Divine Service, the very Office of Preaching is fo far-forth executed. Such kind of fpeeches were then familiar, thofe phrafes feemed not to them abfurd, they would have marvelled to hear the [e] out-cries which we do, becaufe we think, that the Apoftles *in writing*, and others *in reading* to the Church thofe Books which the Apoftles wrote, are neither untruly nor unhtly faid to *preach*. For although mens *Tongues* and their *Pens* differ, yet to one and the felf-*fame* general, if not particular *effect*, they may both ferve. It is no good argument, St. *Paul* could not *write with his Tongue*, therefore neither could he *preach with his pen*. For preaching is a general end whereunto writing and fpeaking do both ferve. Men fpeak not with the inftruments of writing, neither write with the inftruments of fpeech, and yet things *recorded* with the one, and *uttered* with the other, may be [f] *preached* well enough with both. By their patience therefore be it fpoken, the Apoftles preached as well when they wrote as when they fpake the Gofpel of Chrift, and our ufual *publick reading* of the Word of God for the peoples inftruction, *is preaching*. Nor about words would we ever contend, were not their purpofe in fo reftraining the fame, injurious to Gods moft facred Word and Spirit. It is on both fides confeft, that the Word of God outwardly adminiftred (his [g] Spirit inwardly concurring therewith) converteth, edifieth, and faveth Souls. Now whereas the external adminiftration of his Word is as well by reading barely the Scripture,

a *Parænet. ad Gent. p. 17.*
b *Concil. Va-fen. 2. c. 2.*
c *Concil. Tol. 4. cap. 11.*
d *Rupert. de Divin. Offic. lib. 1. c. 12, 13. Ifid. de Ecclef. Offic. l. 1. c. 10.*
e The Libel of *Schoolspart. 11. T. C. lib. 2. Pag. 388.* Saint *Pauls* writing is no more preaching, than his pen or his hand is his Tongue: feeing they cannot be the fame, which cannot be made by the fame Inftruments.
f *Evangelixo manu & fcripfione. Raino. de Rom. Ecclef. Idolola. praf. ad Co. Effex.*
g *Fohn 6.46. Mat. 16.17. 2 Cor. 4.6. 1 Cor. 3.1.3. Acts 16.14.*

ture, as by explaining the same when Sermons thereon be made, in the one they deny, that the finger of God hath *ordinarily* certain *principal operations*, which we most stedfastly hold and believe that it hath in both.

What they attribute to Sermons only, and what we to Reading also.

22. So worthy a part of Divine Service we should greatly wrong, if we did not esteem Preaching as the blessed Ordinance of God, Sermons as Keyes to the Kingdom of Heaven, as Wings to the Soul, as Spurres to the good Affections of Man, unto the found and healthy as Food, as Physick unto diseased minds. Wherefore how highly soever it may please them with words of truth to extoll Sermons, they shall not herein offend us. We seek not to derogate from any thing which they can justly esteem, but our desire is to uphold the just estimation of that, from which it seemeth unto us they derogate more than becometh them. That which offendeth us, is, first the great disgrace which they offer unto *our Custome* of bare reading the Word of God, and to his gracious Spirit, the *principal* vertue whereof thereby manifesting it self, for the endless good of mens Souls, even the vertue which it hath to *convert*, to *edifie*, to *save* Souls ; this they mightily strive to obscure : and secondly, the shifts wherewith they maintain their opinion of Sermons, whereunto while they labour to appropriate the *saving* power of the Holy Ghost, they separate from all *apparent* hope of life and salvation, thousands whom the goodness of Almighty God doth not exclude. Touching therefore the use of Scripture even in that it is openly read, and the inestimable good which the Church of God by that very mean hath reaped ; there was, we may very well think, some cause, which moved the Apostle Saint *Paul* to [a] to require, that those things which any one Churches affairs gave particular occasion to write, might for the instruction of all be published, and that by *reading*. 1. When the very having of the Books of God was a matter of no small charge and difficulty, in as much as they could not be had otherwise than only in written Copies, it was the necessity not of preaching things agreeable with the Word, but of reading the Word it self at large to the people, which caused Churches throughout the world to have publick care, that the sacred Oracles of God being procured by common charge, might with great sedulity be kept both intire and sincere. If then we admire the providence of God in the same continuance of Scripture, notwithstanding the violent endeavours of Infidels to abolish, and the fraudulent of Hereticks always to deprave the same, shall we set light by that custome of reading, from whence so precious a benefit hath grown ? 2. The voice and testimony of the Church acknowledging Scripture to be the Law of the living God, is for the truth and certainty thereof no mean evidence. For if with reason we may presume upon things which a few mens depositions do testifie, suppose we that the minds of men are not both at their first accefs to the School of Christ exceedingly moved, yea and for ever afterwards also confirmed much when they consider the main consent of all the Churches in the whole World witnessing the sacred authority of Scriptures, ever sithence the first publication thereof, even till this present day and hour ? And that they all have always so testified, I see not how we should possibly wish a proof more palpable, than this manifest received and every-where continued custome of reading them publikely as the Scriptures. The reading therefore of the Word of God, as the use hath ever been, in open audience, is the plainest evidence we have of the Churches *assent* and *acknowledgement* that it is his Word. 3. A further commodity this custome hath, which is, to furnish the very *simplest* and *rudest* sort with such infallible *Axiomes* and *Precepts* of sacred Truth, delivered even in the *very letter* of the Law of God, as may serve them for [b] *Rules* whereby to judge the better *all other doctrines* and instructions which they hear. For which end and purpose, I see not how the Scripture could be possibly made familiar unto all, unless far more should be read in the peoples hearing, than by a Sermon can be opened. For whereas in a manner the whole Book of God is by reading every year published, a small part thereof, in comparison of the whole, may hold very well the readiest Interpreter of Scripture occupied many years. 4. Besides, wherefore should any man think, but that reading in it self is one of the *ordinary* means, whereby it pleaseth God of his gracious goodness to instill that celestial Verity, which being *but so* received is nevertheless effectual to *save* souls ? Thus much therefore we ascribe to the reading of

a 1 Thess. 5. 27.
Coloss. 4. 16.

b John 5. 39.
Isa. 8. 20.

of the Word of God, as the manner is in our Churches. And becaufe it were odious, if they on their part fhould altogether defpife the fame, they yield that reading may *fet forward*, but not begin the work of falvation; that [a] Faith may be
nourifhed therewith, but not bred; that [b] herein mens attention to the Scriptures,
and their fpeculation of the creatures of God have like efficacy, both being of power to *augment*, but neither to effect belief without Sermons; that if [c] any *believe*
by reading alone, we are to account it a miracle, an *extraordinary* work of God.
Wherein that which they grant, we gladly accept at their hands, and wifh that
patiently they would examine how little caufe they have to deny that which as yet
they grant not. The [d] Scripture witneffeth, that when the Book of the Law of
God had been fometime miffing, and was after found, the King, which heard it but
only read, tare his clothes, and with tears confeffed, *Great is the wrath of the Lord
upon us, becaufe our Fathers have not kept his Word, to do after all things which are
written in this Book.* This doth argue, that by bare reading (for of Sermons at
that time there is no mention) true repentance may be wrought in the hearts of
fuch as fear God, and yet incurre his difpleafure, the deferved effect whereof is
eternal death. So that their repentance (although it be not their firft entrance) is
notwithftanding the firft ftep of their re-entrance into life, and may be in them
wrought by the Word only read unto them. Befides, it feemeth that God would
have no man ftand in doubt, but that the reading of Scripture is effectual, as well
to lay even the firft foundation, as to adde degrees of farther perfection in the fear
of God. And therefore the [e] Law faith, Thou fhalt *read* this Law before all Ifrael,
that men, women and *children* may hear, yea, even that their children, which as yet
have not known it, may hear it, and by hearing it fo read, may *learn to fear* the Lord.
Our [f] Lord and Saviour was himfelf of opinion, that they which would not be
drawn to amendment of life by the teftimony which *Mofes* and the Prophets have
given, concerning the miferies that follow finners after death, were not likely to
be perfwaded by other means, although God from the very dead fhould have raifed
them up Preachers. Many hear the Books of God, and believe them not. Howbeit, their unbelief in that cafe we may not impute unto any weaknefs or infuffici-
ency in the meane which is ufed towards them, but to the wilful bent of their obftinate hearts againft it. With minds obdurate nothing prevaileth. As well they
that preach, as they that read unto fuch, fhall ftill have caufe to complain with the
Prophets which were of old, *Who will give credit unto our Teaching?* But with
whom ordinary means will prevail, furely the power of the Word of God, even
without the help of Interpreters in *Gods Church*, worketh mightily, not unto their
confirmation alone which are converted, but alfo to their converfion which are not.
It fhall not boot them who derogate from reading, to excufe it, when they fee no
other remedy, as if their intent were only to deny, that *Aliens* and Strangers
from the Family of God are won, or that belief doth ufe to be wrought at the firft
in *them*, without Sermons. For they know it is our cuftome of fimple reading, *not
for converfion of Infidels* eftranged from the Houfe of God, but for *inftruction of
men baptized*, bred and brought up *in the* bofom of the Church, which they defpife
as a thing uneffectual to fave *fuch* Souls. In *fuch* they imagine that God hath no
ordinary meane to work Faith without Sermons. The reafon, why no man can attain belief by the bare contemplation of Heaven and Earth, is, for that they neither are fufficient to give us as much as the leaft fpark of Light concerning the very
principal Myfteries of our Faith; and whatfoever we may learn by them, the fame
we can only attain to know, according to the manner of natural Sciences, which
meer difcourfe of Wit and Reafon findeth out, whereas the things which we properly believe, be only fuch, as are received upon the credit of Divine Teftimony.
Seeing therefore, that he which confidereth the creatures of God, findeth therein
both thefe defects, and neither the one nor the other in Scriptures, becaufe he that
readeth unto us the Scriptures, delivereth all the Myfteries of Faith, and not any
thing amongft them all more than the mouth of the Lord doth warrant: It followeth in thofe two refpects, that our confideration of Creatures and attention
unto Scriptures are not in themfelves, and without Sermons, things of like difabi-
lity to *breed* or *beget* Faith. Small caufe alfo there is, why any man fhould greatly

[a] *F. C. lib. 2.*
pag. 376.377.
395.
[b] *Pag.78.*
[c] *Pag. 383.*

[d] *2 Chro.34.18*
2 Chro.34.3.

[e] *Deut. 31.13.*

[f] *Luke 16.19.*

ly wonder as at an extraordinary work, if without Sermons, Reading be found to effect thus much. For I would know by some special instance, what one Article of Christian Faith, or what duty required necessarily unto all mens salvation there is, which the very reading of the Word of God is not *apt* to notifie. Effects are miraculous and strange, when they grow by unlikely means. But did we ever hear it accounted for a wonder, that he which doth read, should believe and live according to the will of Almighty God? [a] Reading doth convey to the mind that Truth, without addition or diminution, which Scripture hath derived from the Holy Ghost. And the end of all Scripture is the same which [b] St. *John* proposeth in the writing of that most Divine Gospel, namely, *Faith*, and through Faith *Salvation*. Yea, all Scripture is to this effect [c] *in it self* available, as they which wrote it were perswaded; unless we suppose, that the Evangelist, or others, in speaking of their own intent to instruct and to save by writing, had a secret conceit which they never opened to any, a conceit that no man in the World should ever be that way the better for any Sentence by them written, till such time as the same might chance to be preached upon, or alledged at the least in a Sermon. Otherwise, if he which writeth, do that which is forceable in it self, how should he which readeth, be thought to do that which in it self is of no force to work belief, and to save Believers ? Now, although we have very just cause to stand in some jealousie and fear, lest by thus overvaluing their Sermons, they make the price and estimation of Scripture, otherwise notified, to fall: Nevertheless, so impatient they are, that being but requested to let us know what causes they leave for mens incouragement to attend to the reading of the Scripture, if Sermons only be the power of God to save every one which believeth; that which we move for our better learning and instructions sake, turneth unto anger and choler in them, they grow altogether out of quietness with it, they answer fumingly, that they are [d] *ashamed to defile their Pens with making answer to such idle questions*: Yet in this their mood they cast forth somewhat, wherewith under pain of greater displeasure we must rest contented. They tell us, the profit of reading is singular, in that it serveth for a preparative unto Sermons; it helpeth prettily towards the nourishment of Faith, which Sermons have once ingendred; it is some stay to his mind which readeth the Scripture, when he findeth the same things there which are taught in Sermons, and thereby perceiveth how God doth concurre in opinion with the Preacher; besides, it keepeth Sermons in memory, and doth in that respect, although not feed the soul of man, yet help the retentive force of that stomack of the mind, which receiveth ghostly food at the Preachers hand. But the principal cause of *writing* the Gospel was, *that it might be preached* upon or interpreted by publick Ministers, apt and authorized thereunto. Is it credible, that a superstitious conceit (for it is no better) concerning Sermons, should in such sort both darken their eyes, and yet sharpen their wits with all, that the only true and weighty cause why Scripture was written, the cause which in Scripture is so often mentioned, the cause which all men have ever till this present day acknowledged, this they should clean exclude, as being no cause at all, and load us with so great store of strange concealed causes, which did never see light till now ? In which number the rest must needs be of moment, when the very chiefest cause of committing the Sacred Word of God unto Books, is surmized to have been, lest the Preacher should want a Text whereupon to schoolie. Men of Learning hold it for a slip in judgement, when offer is made to demonstrate that as proper to one thing, which reason findeth common unto moe. Whereas therefore they take from all kinds of teaching that which they attribute to Sermons, it had been their part to yield directly some strong reason, why between *Sermons alone* and *Faith* there should be *ordinarily* that coherence which causes have with their usual effects, why a Christian mans belief should so naturally grow from Sermons, and not possibly from any other kind of teaching. In belief there being but these two operations, *Apprehension* and *Assent*, do only Sermons cause belief; In that no other way is able to explain the mysteries of God, that the mind may rightly apprehend or conceive them as behoveth ? We all know, that many things are believed, although they be intricate, obscure, and dark, although they exceed the reach and capacity of our wits, yea although in this World they be no
way

Marginalia:
a *Exod.* 24. 7.
b *John* 20. 31.
c *Pro.* 1. 2,3,4.
Rom. 1. 16.
2 *Tim.* 3. 15.
d *T. G. l. 2. p. 376*

way possible to be understood. Many things believed are likewise so plain, that every common person may therein be unto himself a sufficient Expounder. Finally, to explain even those things which need and admit explication, many other usual ways there are besides Sermons. Therefore Sermons are not the only ordinary means whereby we *first* come to *apprehend* the mysteries of God. Is it in regard then of Sermons only, that apprehending the Gospel of Christ we yield thereunto our unfained assent as to a thing infallibly true ? They which rightly consider after what sort the heart of man hereunto is framed, must of necessity acknowledge, that who so assenteth to the words of eternal life, doth it in regard of his *authority* whose words they are. This is in mans conversion unto God τὸ ἴδεν ἡ ἀρχὴ τῆς κινήσεως, the first step whereat his race towards Heaven beginneth. Unless therefore, clean contrary to our own experience, we shall think it a miracle if any man acknowledge the divine authority of the Scripture, till some Sermon have perswaded him thereunto, and that otherwise neither conversation in the bosom of the Church, nor religious Education, nor the reading of learned mens Books, nor Information received by conference, nor whatsoever pain and diligence in hearing, studying, meditating day and night on the Law, is so far blest of God as to work this effect in any man, how would they have us to grant, that faith doth not come but only by *hearing Sermons* ? Fain they would have us to believe the Apostle S. *Paul* himself to be the Author of this their paradox, only because he said, that it pleaseth God by the [b] *foolishness of preaching,* to save them which believe ; and again, [c] *How shall they call on him in whom they have not believed ? How shall they believe in him of whom they have not heard ? How shall they hear without a Preacher ? How shall men preach except they be sent ?* To answer therefore both allegations at once, the very substance of that they contain is in few but this. Life and salvation God will have *offered unto all* ; his will is that *Gentiles* should be saved as well as *Jews.* Salvation belongeth unto none but such *as call upon the Name of our Lord Jesus Christ.* Which *Nations as yet unconverted* neither do *nor possibly can do till they believe.* What they are to believe, impossible it is they should know till they *hear it.* Their hearing requireth *our preaching* unto them. [d] *Tertullian,* to draw even *Paynimes* themselves unto Christian Belief, willeth *the Books* of the old Testament to be *searched,* which were at that time in *Ptolomies* Library. And if men did not list to travell so far, though it were for their endless good, he addeth, that in *Rome* and other places the *Jews* had Synagogues, whereunto every one which would might resort, that this kind of liberty they purchased by payment of a standing tribute, that there they did openly [e] *read* the Scriptures ; and whosoever *will hear,* (saith *Tertullian*) *he shall find God ; whosoever will study to know, shall be also fain to believe.* But sith there is no likelihood that ever voluntarily they will seek instruction at our hands, it remaineth that unless we will suffer them to perish, salvation it self must seek them, it behoveth God to *send* them Preachers as he did *his elect Apostles* throughout the World. There is *a knowledge* which God hath alwayes revealed unto them in the *works of Nature.* This they honour and esteem highly as profound *wisdome* ; howbeit this wisdom saveth them not. That which must save Believers, is *the knowledge of the Cross of Christ,* the *only subject of all our preaching.* And in their eyes what doth this seem as yet but *folly* ? It pleaseth God by the *foolishness of preaching* to save. These words declare how admirable force those Mysteries have, which the World doth deride as follies, they shew that the *foolishness of the Cross of Christ* is the *wisdom of true believers* ; they concern the *object* of our faith, the *matter preached* of and believed in by Christian men. This we know that the Grecians or Gentiles did account foolishness ; but that they ever did think it *a fond* or unlikely *way* to seek mens conversion by *Sermons,* we have not heard. Manifest therefore it is, that the Apostles applying the name of *foolishness* in such sort as they did, must needs, by the *foolishness of preaching,* mean the Doctrine of Christ, which we learn that we may be saved, but that Sermons are the only manner of teaching, whereby it pleaseth our Lord to save, se could not mean. In like sort, where the same Apostle proveth, that as well the *sending of the Apostles,* as their preaching *to the Gentiles,* was necessary, dare we affirm it was ever his meaning, that unto their Salvation, who even from their tender

der

a T. C. lib. 2.
pag. 375.
b 1 Cor.1.21.
c Rom.10.14.
d Apologet.cap.
18. in fine.
e This they did in a tongue which to all learned men amongst the Heathens, and to a great part of the simplest was familiarly known : as appeareth by a supplication offered unto the Emperour *Justinian,* wherein the Jews make request that it might be lawful for them to read the Greek Translation of the 70 Interpreters in their Synagogues, as their custom before had been. *Authent. 146. Col. 10. incipit. Æquum sane.* f The Apostle useth the word κήρυγμα and not κήρυξις.

der infancy never knew any other Faith or Religion than only Christian, *no kind of teaching* can be available, *saving that* which was so needful for the first universal convertion of Gentiles hating Christianity ; neither the *sending* of any sort allowable in the one case, except only of such as had been in the other also most fit and worthy Instruments ? *Belief in all sorts* doth come by hearkning and *attending to the Word of Life.* Which Word somtime proposeth and preacheth it self to the hearer ; somtime they deliver it, whom privately zeal and piety moveth to be Instructers of others by conference ; somtime of them it is taught, whom the Church hath called to the publick, either reading thereof, or interpreting. All these tend unto one effect, neither doth that which S. *Paul* or other Apostles teach, concerning the necessity of *such teaching* as theirs was, or of *sending such* as they were, for *that purpose unto the Gentiles,* prejudice the efficacy of *any other way* of publick instruction, or inforce the utter disability of any other mens Vocation thought requisite in this Church for the saving of souls, where means more effectual are wanting. Their only proper and direct proof of the thing in question had been to shew, in what sort, and how far mans Salvation doth necessarily depend upon the knowledge of the Word of God ; what conditions, properties, and qualities there are, whereby Sermons are distinguished from other kinds of administring the Word unto that purpose ; and what special property or quality that is, which being no where found but in Sermons, maketh them effectual to save souls, and leaveth all other Doctrinal means besides destitute of vital efficacy. These pertinent Instructions, whereby they might satisfie us, and obtain the cause it self for which they contend, these things which only would serve they leave, (and which needeth not) somtime they trouble themselves with fretting at the ignorance of such as withstand them in their opinion; somtime they [a] fall upon their poor Brethren which can but read, and against *them* they are bitterly eloquent. If we alledge what the Scriptures themselves do usual y speak for the saving force of the Word of God, not with restraint to any one certain kind of delivery, but howsoever the same shall chance to be made known, yet by one trick or other they always [b] restrain it unto Sermons. Our Lord and Saviour hath said, [c] *Search the Scriptures, in them ye think to have eternal life.* But they tell us, he spake to the Jews, which Jews before *had heard his Sermons* ; and that peradventure it was his mind they should search, not by reading, nor by hearing them read, but by attending, whensoever the Scriptures should happen to be alledged in Sermons. Furthermore, having received Apostolick Doctrine, [d] the Apostle Saint *Paul* hath taught us to esteem the same as the supream Rule, whereby all other doctrines must for ever be examined. Yea, but in as much as the Apostle doth there speak of *that he had preached,* he flatly maketh (as they strangely affirm) *his preachings* or Sermons *the Rule,* whereby to examine all. And then, I beseech you, what Rule have we thereby to judge or examine any ? For, if Sermons must be our rule, because the Apostles Sermons were so to their hearers ; then, sith we are not as they were, hearers of the Apostles Sermons, it resteth that either the Sermons which we hear should be our rule, or (that being absurd) there will (which yet hath greater absurdity) no rule at all be remaining for trial, what doctrines now are corrupt, what consonant with heavenly truth. Again, let [e] the same Apostle acknowledge all Scripture profitable to teach, to improve, to correct, to instruct in righteousness. Still notwithstanding we erre, if hereby we presume to gather, that Scripture read, will avail unto any one of all these uses ; they teach us the meaning of the words to be, that so much the Scripture can do, if the Minister that way apply it in his Sermons, otherwise not. Finally, they never hear sentence which mentioneth the Word of Scripture , but forthwith their Glosses upon it are, the Word preached, the Scripture explained or delivered unto us in Sermons. Sermons they evermore understand to be that Word of God, which alone hath vital operation, the dangerous sequel of which construction I wish they did more attentively weigh. For sith, speech is the very Image, whereby the mind and soul of the speaker conveyeth it self into the bosom of him which heareth, we cannot chuse but see great reason, wherefore the Word that proceedeth from God, who is himself very truth and life, should be (as the Apostle to the [f] *Hebrews* noteth) lively and mighty in operation, sharper than any two-edged sword. Now, if in this and the like places we did conceive, that our

own

a T. C. lib. 1. pag. 373. This style of Readers. The Bishops more than beggerly Presents. Those Rascall Ministrels.
b T. C. l. 2. p. 37.
c John 5. 39.
d Gal. 1. 9.

e 1 Tim. 3. 16.

f Heb. 4. 12.

own Sermons are that strong and forcible Word, should we not hereby impart even the most peculiar glorie of the Word of God, unto that which is not his word? For, touching our Sermons, that which giveth them their very being, is the wit of man, and therefore they oftentimes accordingly taste too much of that over-corrupt fountain from which they come. In our speech of most holy things, our most frail affections many times are bewrayed. Wherefore, when we read or recite the Scripture, we then deliver to the people properly the Word of God. As for our Sermons, be they never so sound and perfect, his Word they are not, as the Sermons of the Prophets were; no, they are but ambiguously termed his, because his Word is commonly the subject whereof they treat, and must be the rule whereby they are framed. Notwithstanding, by these and the like shifts they derive unto Sermons alone, whatsoever is generally spoken concerning the Word. Again, what seemeth to have been uttered concerning Sermons, and their efficacy or necessity, *in regard of divine matter*, and must consequently be verified in sundry other kinds of teaching, if *the matter* be the same in all, their use is to fasten every such speech unto that one only manner of teaching, which is by Sermons, that still Sermons may be all in all. [a] Thus, because *Solomon* declareth that the people decay or *perish* for want of knowledg; where [b] no *prophecying* at all is, they gather that the hope of life and salvation is cut off, where Preachers are not which *prophecy by Sermons*, how many soever they be in number that read daily the Word of God, and deliver, though in other sort, the selfsame matter which Sermons do. The people which have no way to come to the knowledg of God, no *prophecying*, no teaching, perish. But that they should of necessity perish, where any one way of knowledg lacketh, is more then the words of *Solomon* import. [c] Another usual point of their art in this present question, is to make very large and plentiful discourses, how Christ is by Sermons [d] lifted up *higher*, and made more [e] apparent to the eye of Faith; how the [f] savour of the Word is more sweet being brayed, and more able to nourish being divided by preaching, then by onely reading proposed; how Sermons are the keys of the Kingdom of Heaven, and do open the Scriptures, which being but read, remain *in comparison* still clasped; how [g] God giveth richer increase of grace to the ground that is planted and watered by preaching, then by bare and simple reading. Out of which premises declaring how attainment unto life is easier where Sermons are, they conclude an [h] *impossibility* thereof where Sermons are not. *Alcidimas* the Sophister hath many arguments, to prove that voluntary and extemporal far excelleth premeditated speech. The like whereunto, & in part the same, are brought by them, who commend Sermons, as being (which all men, I think, will acknowledg) sundry [i] peculiar and proper vertues, such as no other way of teaching hath. Aptnes to follow particular occasions presently growing, to put life into words by countenance, voice and gesture, to prevail mightily in the sudden affections of men, this Sermons may challenge. Wherin notwithstanding so eminent properties whereof Lessons are happily destitute, yet Lessons being free from some inconveniences, whereunto Sermons are more subject, they may in this respect no less take, then in other they must give the hand which betokneth preeminence. For there is nothing which is not some way excell'd, even by that which it doth excel. Sermons therefore and Lessons may each excel other in some respects, without any prejudice unto either, as touching that vital force which they both have in the work of our salvation. To which effect when we have endeavoured as much as in us doth lie, to find out the strongest causes, wherefore they should imagine that reading is it self so unavailable, the most we can learn at their hands, is, that Sermons are [k] *the Ordinance of God*; the Scriptures dark, and the labour of reading *easie*. First, therefore as we know that God doth aide with grace, and by his special providence evermore bless with happy success those things which himself appointeth, so his Church, we perswade our selves, he hath not in such sort given over to a reprobate sence, that whatsoever it deviseth for the good of the souls of men, the same he doth still accurse and make frustrate. Or if he always did defeat the Ordinances of his Church, [l] is not reading the Ordinance of God? Wherefore then should we think that the force of his secret grace is accustomed to bless the labour of dividing his Word, according unto each mans private discretion in publike Sermons, and to withdraw it self from concurring with the publike delivery thereof by such selected portions of Scripture, as the whole Church hath solemnly appointed to be read for the peoples good, either by ordinary course, or otherwise, according to the exigence of

special

Side notes:

a T. C. lib. 2. pag. 381.
b Prov. 29. 18.
c T. C. lib. 2. pag. 379.
d 2 Cor. 2. 16.
e 2 Tim. 2. 15.
f Math. 16. 19.
g 1 Cor. 3. 6.
h T. C. lib. 2. pag. 380. No salvation to be looked for, where no Preaching is.
i T. C. lib. 2. pag. 394.
k T. C. lib. 2. pag. 396.
l Deut. 31. 13.

a *De Eccles. offic. lib.1.c.10.*
b *Psal. 1. 2.*
c *Psal.119. 16.*
d *Aug. in Ps. 66.*
e *Cyprian lib.1. Epist. 5.Lector. personat.verba sublimia, Evangelium Christi legis à fratribus conspicitur, cum gaudio fraternitatis auditur.*
f *Ps.119.33.35*
g *T.C.l.2.p. 383,384,392.*
h *Acts 8. 31.*
i *Apoc. 1. 3?*
k *T.C. l.2. 363. pag. 373.*

special occasions ? Reading (saith a *Isidore*) is to the hearers no small edifying: To them whose delight and meditation is in the Law, seeing that happiness and bliss belongeth, it is not in us to deny them the benefit of heavenly grace. And I hope we may presume, that a rare thing it is not in the Church of God, even for that very Word which is read to be both presently their c joy, and afterwards their study that heat it. d Saint *Augustin* speaking of devout men, noteth, how they daily frequented the Church, how attentive ear they gave unto the Lessons and Chapters read, how careful they were to remember the same, and to muse thereupon by themselves. e St. *Cyprian* observeth, that reading was not without effect in the hearts of men. Their joy and alacrity was to him an argument, that there is in this Ordinance a blessing, such as ordinarily doth accompany the administration of the Word of life. It were much if there should be such a difference between the hearing of Sermons preached and of Lessons read in the Church, that he which presenteth himself at the one, and maketh his Prayer with the Prophet f *David, Teach me, O Lord, the way of thy Statutes*, *direct me in the path of thy Commandments* might have the ground of usual experience whereupon to build his hope of prevailing with God, and obtaining the grace he seeketh; they contrariwise not so, who crave the like assistance of his Spirit, when they give ear to the reading of the other. In this therefore preaching and reading are equal, that both are approved as his Ordinances, both assisted with his grace. And if his grace do assist them both to the nourishment of Faith already bred, we cannot, without some very manifest cause yeilded, imagine that in breeding or begetting Faith, his grace doth cleave to the one, and utterly forsake the other. Touching g *hardness*, which is the second pretended impediment, as against Homilies being plain and popular instructions, it is no bar, so neither doth it infringe the efficacy, no not of Scriptures, although but read. The force of reading, how small soever they would have it, must of necessity be granted sufficient to notifie that which is plain or easie to be understood. And of things necessary to all mens salvation we have been hitherto accustomed to hold (especially sithence the publishing of the Gospel of Jesus Christ, whereby the simplest having now a Key unto knowledg, which the h *Eunuch* in the *Acts* did want) our children may of themselves by reading understand that, which he without an Interpreter could not) they are in Scripture plain and easie to be understood. As for those things which at the first are obscure and daily, when memory hath laid them up for a time, judgement afterwards growing explaineth them. Scripture therefore is not *so hard*, but that the *only reading* thereof may give life unto willing hearers. The easie performance of which holy labour, is in like sort a very cold objection, to prejudice the vertue thereof. For what though an *Infidel* ; yea, though *a child* may be able to read ; there is no doubt, but the meanest and worst amongst the people under the Law, had been as able as the Priests themselves were to offer Sacrifice. Did this make Sacrifice of no effect unto that purpose for which it was instituted? In Religion some duties are not commended so much by the hardness of their execution, as by the worthiness and dignity of that acceptation wherein they are held with God. We admire the goodness of God in nature, when we consider how he hath provided that things most needfull to preserve this life, should be most prompt and easie for all living creatures to come by. Is it not as evident a sign of his wonderful providence over us, when that food of eternal life, upon the *utter want* whereof our endless death and destruction necessarily ensueth, is prepared and always set in such a readiness, that those very means than which nothing is more easie may suffice to procure the same ? Surely, if we perish, it is not the lack of Scribes and learned Expounders that can be our just excuse. The Word which saveth our souls is near us, we need for knowledg but i to read and live. The man which readeth the Word of God, the Word it self doth pronounce blessed, if he also observe the same. Now all these things being well considered, it shall be no intricate matter for any man to judge with indifferency on which part the good of the Church is most conveniently sought ; whether on ours, whose opinion is such as hath been shewed, or else on k theirs, who leaving no ordinary way of salvation for them unto whom the Word of God is but only read, do seldom name them but with great disdain and contempt who execute that service in the Church of Christ. By means whereof it hath come to pass, that Churches, which cannot enjoy the benefit of usual Preaching, are judged, as it were even forsaken of God, forlorne, and without either hope or comfort: Contrariwise, those places which every day for the most part are at Sermons as the flowing Sea, do both by their emptinets at times of reading, and by other apparent tokens shew. to the voice of the living God, this way sounding in the ears of men a great deal less reverence then were meet. - But if no other evil were known to grow thereby, who can choose but think them cruel which do hear them so boldly teach, that [a] if God (as to him there is nothing impossible) do happily save any such as continue where they have all other means of instruction, but are not taught by continual preaching, yet this is miraculous, and more then the fitness of so poor instruments can give any man cause to hope for; that [b] Sacraments are not effectual to salvation, except men be instructed by *preaching before* they be made partakers of them; yea, that both [c] Sacraments and Prayers also, where Sermons are not, *Do not only not feed, but are ordinarily to further condemnation?* What mans heart doth not rise at the mention of these things? It is true that the weakness of our wits and the dulness of our affections do make us for the most part, even as our Lords own Disciples were for a certain time, hard and slow to beleive what is written. For help whereof expositions and exhortations are needful, and that in the most effectual manner. The principal Churches throughout the Land, and no small part of the rest being in this respect by the goodness of God so abundantly provided for, they which want the like furtherance unto knowledge, wherewith it were greatly to be desired that they also did abound, are yet, we hope, not left in so extream destitution, that justly any man should think the ordinary means of eternal life taken from them because their teaching is in publique for the most part but by reading. For which cause amongst whom there are not those helps that others have to set them forward in the way of life, such to dishearten with fearful sentences, as though their salvation could hardly be hoped for, is not in our understanding so consonant with Christian Charity. We hold it safer a great deal and better to give them [d] incouragement; to put them in mind that it is not the deepness of their knowledge, but the [e] singleness of their belief which God accepteth; that they which [f] hunger and thirst after righteousness, shall be satisfied; that no [g] imbecility of means can prejudice the truth of the promise of God herein; that the weaker their helps are, the more their need is to sharpen the edge of their own [h] industry; and that [i] painfulness by feeble means shall be able to gain that, which in the plenty of more forcible instruments is through sloth and negligence lost. As for the men, with whom we have thus far taken pains to confer, about the force of the Word of God, either read by it self or opened in Sermons; their speeches concerning both the one and the other are in truth such, as might give us very just cause to think, that the reckoning is not great which they make of either. For howsoever they have been driven to devise some odde kind of blind uses, whereunto they may answer that reading doth serve, yet the reading of the Word of God in publique more then their Preachers bare Text, who will not judge, that they deem needless, when if we chance at any time to term it necessary as being a thing which God himself did institute amongst the Jewes for purposes that touch as well us as them; a thing which the Apostles commend under the old and ordain under the New Testament; a thing wherof the Church of God hath ever sithence the first beginning reaped singular Commodity; a thing which without exceeding great detriment no Church can omit? they only are the men that ever were heard of, by whom this hath been crost and gain-said, they only the men which have given their peremptory sentence to the contrary, [k] *It is untrue that simple reading is necessary in the Church.* And why untrue? *Because although it be very convenient which is used in some Churches, where before preaching time the Church assembled hath the Scriptures read in such order, that the whole Canon thereof is oftentimes in one year run thorough: yet a number of Churches which have no such order of simple reading, cannot be in this point charged with breach of Gods Commandment, which they might be if simple reading were necessary.* A poor, a cold and an hungry cavil. Shall we therefore to p'ealee them change the Word *Necessary,* and say that it hath been a commendable order, a custom very expedient, or an ordinance most (profitable whereby they know right well that we mean exceedingly behoofull) to read the Word of God at large in the Church, whether it be as our manner is, or as theirs is whom they prefer before us? It is not this that will content or satisfie their minds.

They have against it a marvellous deep and profound axiome, [l] that *Two things*
to

D d 2

[a] *Pag.*364.375. 380. 383, 384.

[b] *Pag.*392.

[c] *Pag.*364.

[d] *Eccles.*51. 16 27.
*Matth.*12,20.
[e] 1 *Tim.*1.5.
*Rom.*14. 1.
1 *Thes.*3.10.
[f] *Matth.*5.6.
[g] *Phil.*1.6.
1 *Pet.*5, 10.
Matth 3.9.
[h] 1 *Thes.*4.18.
Heb 10. 24.
Iude verse 20.
1 *Pet.*4.10.
[i] *Luke,* 11.31

[k] *T.C.lib.*2. pag. 381.

[l] *T.C.lib.*2. pag. 372.

to one and the same end cannot but very improperly be said most profitable. And therefore if preaching be most profitable to mans salvation, then is not reading ; if reading be, then preaching is not. Are they resolved then at the leastwise, if preaching be the onely ordinary mean whereby it pleaseth God to save our souls, what kind of preaching is it which doth save ? Vnderstand they how or in what respect there is that force and vertue in preaching ? We have reason wherefore to make these demands, for that although their pens run all upon *Preaching* and *Sermons*, yet when themselves do practise that whereof they write, they change their Dialect, and those words they shun, as if there were in them some secret sting. It is not their phrase to say they *preach*, or to give to their own instructions and exhortations the name of Sermons ; the paine they take themselves in this kind is either *opening* or Lecturing, or Reading, or Exercising, but in no case *preaching*. [a] And in this present question they also warily protest that what they ascribe to the vertue of preaching, they still mean it of good preaching : Now one of them saith that a good Sermon [b] must expound and apply a large portion of the Text of Scripture at one time.

a T. C. lib. 2. pag. 385.
b Complaint of the Communaltie.

Another giveth us to understand, that sound preaching [c] *is not to do as one did at London, who spent most of his time in invectives against good men, and told his audience how the Magistrate should have an eye to such as troubled the peace of the Church.* The [d] best of them hold it for no good preaching, *when a man endeavoureth to make a glorious shew of eloquence and learning, rather then to apply himself to the capacity of the simple.* But let them shape us out a good Preacher by what pattern soever pleaseth them best, let them exclude and inclose whom they will with their definitions, we are not desirous to enter into any contention with them about this, or to abate the conceit they have of their own ways, so that when once we are agreed what Sermons shall currantly pass for good, we may at length understand from them what that is in a good Sermon which doth make it the Word of life unto such as hear. If substance of matter, evidence of things, strength and validity of arguments and proofs, or if any other vertue else which words and sentences may contain, of all this what is there in the best Sermons being uttered, which they loose by being read? But they utterly deny that the reading either of Scriptures, or Homilies and Sermons can ever by the ordinary grace of God save any soul. So that, although we had all the Sermons word for word which *James, Paul, Peter*, and the rest of the Apostles made, some one of which Sermons was of power to convert thousands of the hearers unto Christian faith ; yea although we had all the instructions, exhortations, consolations which came from the gracious lips of our Lord Jesus Christ himself, and should read them ten thousand times over, to faith and salvation. No man could hereby hope to attain. Whereupon it must of necessity follow, that the vigour and vital efficacy of Sermons doth grow from certain accidents which are not in them but in their Maker ; his vertue, his gesture, his countenance, his zeal, the motion of his body, and the inflection of his voice, who first uttereth them as his own, is that which giveth them the form, the nature, the very essence of instruments available to eternal life. If they like neither that nor this, what remaineth but that their final conclusion be, *Sermons we know are the only ordinary means to salvation, but why or how we cannot tell ?* Wherefore to end this tedious controversie, wherein the too great importunity of our over eager Adversaries hath constrained us much longer to dwell, then the barrennes of so poor a cause could have seemed at the first likely either to require or to admit, if they which without partialities and passions are accustomed to weigh all things, and accordingly to give their sentence, shall here sit down to receive our Audit, and to cast up the whole reckoning on both sides, the summe which truth amounteth unto will appear to be but this, that that as medicines provided of nature, and applied by art for the benefit of bodily health, take effect sometime under and sometime above the natural proportion of their vertue, according as the mind and fancy of the patient doth more or less concur with them : So whether we barely read unto men the Scriptures of God ; or by Homilies concerning matter of belief and conversation seek to lay before them the duties which they owe unto God and man ; whether we deliver them Books to read and consider of in private at their own best leasure, or call them to the hering of Sermons publikely in the house of God; albeit every of these & the like unto these means

c Doct. *semes.* Painter, pag. 21.
d T. C. lib. 2. pag. 385.

do

do truly and daily effect that in the hearts of men for which they are each and all meant, yet the operation which they have in common being most sensible and most generally noted in one kind above the rest, that one hath in some mens opinions drowned altogether the rest, and injuriously brought to pass that they have been thought not less effectual than the other, but without the other uneffectual to save souls. Whereas the cause why Sermons only are observed to prevail so much while all means else seem to sleep and do nothing, is in truth but that singular affection and attention which the people sheweth every where towards the one, & their cold disposition to the other, the reason hereof being partly the art which our Adversaries use for the credit of their Sermons, to bring men out of conceit with all other teaching besides; partly; a custom which men have to let those things carelessly pass by their ears which they have oftentimes heard before, or know they may hear again whenever it pleaseth themselves; partly, the special advantages which Sermons naturally have to procure attention, both in that they come always new, and because by the hearer it is still presumed that if they be let slip for the present, what good soever they contain is lost, and that without all hope of recovery. This is the true cause of oddes between Sermons and other kinds of wholesome instruction. As for the difference which hath been hitherto so much defended on the contrary side, making Sermons the only ordinary means unto faith and eternal life, sith this hath neither evidence of Truth, nor proof sufficient to give it warrant, a cause of such quality may with far better grace and conveniency ask that pardon which common humanity doth easily grant, then claim in challenging manner that assent which is as unwilling when reason guideth it to be yeilded where it is not, as with-held where it is apparantly due. All which notwithstanding, as we could greatly wish that the rigor of this their opinion were alayed and mitigated so because we hold it the part of religious ingenuity to honour vertue in whomsoever; therefore it is our most hearty desire, and shall be always our Prayer unto Almighty God, that in the self-same fervent zeal wherewith they seem to effect the good of the Souls of men, and to thirst after nothing more then that all men might by all means be directed in the way of life, both they and we may constantly persist to the Worlds end. For in this we are not their Adversaries, though they in the other hitherto have been ours.

23. Between the Throne of God in Heaven, and his Church upon earth here militant, if it be so that Angels have their continual intercourse, where should we find the same more verified then in those two ghostly Exercises, the one *Doctrine*, the other *Prayer*? For what is the Assembling of the Church to learn, but the receiving of Angels descended from above? What to pray, but the sending of Angels upward? His Heavenly Inspirations, and our holy desires are as so many Angels of entercourse and commerce between God and us. As teaching bringeth us to know that God is our supream truth; so prayer testifieth that we acknowledge him our soverain good. Besides, sith on God as the most high all inferiour causes in the world are dependant, and the higher any cause is, the more it covereth to impart vertue unto things beneath it, how should any kind of service we do or can do, find greater acceptance then Prayer, which sheweth our concurrence with him, in desiring that wherewith his very nature doth most delight? Is not the name of Prayer usual to signifie even all the service that ever we do unto God? And that for no other cause, as I suppose, but to shew that there is in Religion no acceptable duty which devout invocation of the name of God doth not either presuppose or infer. *a Ose.14.3.* Prayers are those [a] calves of mens lips; those most gracious and sweet [b] odours; *b Revel.5,8.* those rich presents and gifts, which being [c] carryed up into Heaven, do best testifie *c Acts 10.4.* our dutifull affection, and are, for the purchasing of all favour at the hands of God, the most undoubted means we can use. On others what more easily, and yet what more fruitfully bestowed then our Prayers? If we give counsell, they are the simpler only that need it; if almes the poorer only are releived; but by Prayer we do good to all. And whereas every other duty besides is but to shew it self as time and *d Rom. 1.9.* opportunity require, for this [d] all times are convenient: when we are not able to do *1 Thes.5.17.* any other thing for mens behoof, when through maliciousness or unkindness they *Luke 18.1.* vouchsafe not to accept any other good at our hands, Prayer is that which we always have in our power to bestow, and they never in theirs to refuse. Wherfore God

for-

forbid, faith * *Samuel*, speaking unto a moſt unthankfull people, a people weary of the benefit of his moſt vertuous government over them, God forbid that I ſhould ſin againſt the Lord, and ceaſe to pray for you. It is the firſt thing wherewith a righteous life beginneth, and the laſt wherewith it doth end. The knowledg is ſmall which we have on earth concerning things that are done in Heaven. Notwithſtanding thus much we know even of Saints in Heaven that they pray. And therefore Prayer being a work common to the Church as well Triumphant as Militant, a work common unto men with Angels, what ſhould we think, but that ſo much of our lives is celeſtial and divine as we ſpend in the exerciſe of Prayer? for which cauſe we ſee that the moſt comfortable [a] viſitations, which God hath ſent men from above, have taken eſpecially the times of Prayer as their moſt natural opportunities.

a Dan. 9. 20.
Acts 10. 13.

Of publique Prayer.
b Pſal. 55. 18.
Dan. 9. 3.
Acts 10. 9.

24. This holy and religious duty of ſervice towards God concerneth us one way in that we are men, and another way in that we are joined as parts to that viſible myſticall body which is his Church. As men, we are at our own [b] choice, both for time, and place, and form, according to the exigence of our own occaſions in private: But the ſervice, which we do as members of a publique body, is publique, and for that cauſe muſt needs be accompted by ſo much worthier than the other, as a whole ſociety of ſuch condition exceedeth the worth of any one. In which conſideration unto Chriſtian Aſſemblies, there are [c] moſt ſpecial promiſes made.

c Mat. 18. 20.
d 2 Cor. 1. 11.

[d] S. *Paul*, though likely to prevail with God as much as any one, did notwithſtanding think it much more, both for Gods glory and his own good, if Prayers might be made and thanks yeilded in his behalf by a number of men. The [e] Prince and people of *Nineveh* aſſembling themſelves as a main army of Suppliants, it was not in the power of God to withſtand them. I ſpeak no otherwiſe concerning the force of publique Prayer in the Church of God, then before me [f] *Tertullian* hath done, *We come by Troops to the place of Aſſembly, that being banded as it were together, we may be ſupplicants enough to beſiege God with our Prayers. Theſe forces are unto him acceptable.* When we publiquely make our Prayers it cannot be but that we do it with much more comfort than in private, for that the things we ask publiquely are approved as needful and good in the judgement of all, we hear them ſought for and deſired with common conſent. Again, thus much help and furtherance is more yeelded in that if ſo be our zeal and devotion to God-ward be ſlack, [g] the alacrity and fervor of others ſerveth as a preſent ſpur. [h] *For even Prayer it ſelf* (ſaith St. *Baſil*) *when it hath not the conſort of many voyces to ſtrengthen, it is not it ſelf,* Finally, the good which we do by publique Prayer, is more than in private can be done, for that beſides the benefit which here is no leſs procured to our ſelves, the whole Church is much bettered by our good example, and conſequently whereas ſecret neglect of our duty in this kind is but only our own hurt, one mans contempt of the Common Prayer of the Church of God may be and oftentimes is moſt hurtfull unto many. In which conſiderations the [i] Prophet *David* ſo often voweth unto God the ſacrifice of Praiſe and Thankſgiving in the Congregation; ſo earneſtly exhorteth others to ſing praiſes unto the Lord in his Courts, in his Sanctuary, before the memorial of his holineſs, and ſo much complaineth of his own uncomfortable exile, wherein although he ſuſtained many moſt grievous indignities, and indured the want of ſundry both pleaſures and honours before injoyed, yet as if [k] this one were his only grief and the reſt not felt, his ſpeeches are all of the heavenly benefit of publique aſſemblies, and the happineſs, of ſuch as had free acceſs thereunto.

e Jonah 4. 11.

f Apolog. 1. 39.
Ambroſ. lib. de Poe. Multi minimi dum congregantur unanimes ſunt magni & multorum preces impoſſibile eſt conſemni.
g Pſal. 122. 1.
h Καὶ αὐτῆ ἡ προσευχὴ μὴ ἦχουσα τοὺς συμφωνούντας ἀπανδρεύεται πολλῷ ἑαυτῆς.
i Pſal. 16. 11.
34. 18.
Pſal. 30. 4. 96. 5.

k Pſal. 27. 4. 42. 4. 84. 1.

Of the form of Common-Prayer.
l Matth. 6. 5, 6.

25. A great part of the cauſe, wherefore religious minds are ſo inflamed with the love of publique devotion, is that vertue, force and efficacy, which by experience they find that the very form and reverend ſolemnity of Common Prayer du'y ordered hath, to help that imbecility and weakneſs in us, by means whereof we are otherwiſe of our ſelves the leſs apt to perform unto God ſo heavenly a ſervice, with ſuch affection of heart, and diſpoſition in the powers of our ſouls as is requiſite. To this end therefore all things hereunto appertaining, have been ever thought convenient to be done with the moſt ſolemnity and majeſty that the wiſeſt could deviſe, It is not with publique as with private Prayer. In this [l] rather ſecreſie is commanded than outward ſhew, whereas that being the publique act of a whole ſociety,

ciety, requireth accordingly more care to be had of external appearance. The very assembling of men therefore unto this service hath been ever solemn. And concerning the place of assembly, although it serve for other uses as well as this, yet seeing that our Lord himself hath to this as to the chiefest of all other plainly sanctified his own Temple, by entituling it [a] *the house of Prayer*, what preheminence of dig- a *Mat.* 21, 13. nity soever hath been either by the Ordinance, or through the special favour and providence of God annexed unto his Sanctuary, the principal cause thereof must needs be in regard of *Common Prayer*. For the honour and furtherance whereof, if it be as the gravest of the [b] ancient Fathers seriously were perswaded, and do often- b *Chryf. Hom.* times plainly teach, affirming that the house of Prayer is a Court, beautified with 15. *ad Hebræ.* the presence of celestial powers, that there we stand, we pray, we found forth *& 24 in Act.* Hymnes unto God, having his Angels intermingled as our Associates; and that with reference hereunto [c] the Apostle doth require so great care to be had of decen- c *1 Cor.* 11.10. cy for the Angels sake; how can we come to the house of Prayer, and not be moved with the [d] very glory of the place it self, so to frame our affections praying, as d *Pfal.* 96.6. doth best beseem them, whose sutes the Almighty doth there fit to hear, and his Power and Angels attend to further? When this was ingrafted in the minds of men, there beauty are in needed no penal Statutes to draw them unto publick Prayer. The warning sound his Sanctuary. was no sooner heard, but the [e] Churches were presently filled, the pavements cove- e *Ad domos fig-* red with bodies prostrate, and washt with their tears of devout joy. And as the *tim Dominicas* place of publick Prayer is a circumstance in the outward forme thereof, which hath *currimus, corpo-* moment to help devotion; so the person much more with whom the people of *ra humi fterni-* God do joyn themselves in this action, as with him that standeth and speaketh in *fletu gaudiis,* the presence of God for them. The authority of his place, the fervour of his zeal, *fupplicamus.* the piety and gravity of his whole behaviour, must needs exceedingly both grace Salvia de and set forward the service he doth. The authority of his calling is a furtherance, *Prov.* l. 7. because if God have so far received him into favour, as to impose upon him by the hands of men that office of blessing the people in his Name, and making intercession to him in theirs, which Office he hath sanctified with his own most gracious [f] promise, and ratified that promise by manifest actual performance thereof, when f *Num.* 6. 23. [g] others before in like place have done the same, is not his very ordination a seal, g *2 Chro.* 30.17 as it were to us, that the self same divine love which hath chosen the instrument to work with, will by that instrument effect the thing whereto he ordained it, in blessing his people, and accepting the Prayers which his servant offereth up unto God for them? It was in this respect a comfortable title which the ancients used to give unto Gods Ministers, terming them usually [h] *Gods most beloved*, which were ordain- h *Cod.* l.1.tit.3. ed to procure by their Prayers his love and favour towards all. Again, if there be *de Epi.& Cler.* not zeal and fervency in him which proposeth for the rest those sutes and sup- 43. *& 44 fæpe.* plications, which they by their joyful acclamations must ratifie; if he praise not God with all his might; if he pour not out his soul in Prayer; if he take not their causes to heart, or speak not as *Mofes, Daniel*, and *Ezra*, did for their people; how should there be but in them frozen coldnes, when his affections seem benummed from whom theirs should take fire? Vertue and godlines of life are required at the hands of the Minister of God, not only in that he is to teach and instruct the people, who for the most part are rather led away by the ill example, then directed aright by the wholesome instruction of them, whose life swarveth from the rule of their own doctrine; but also much more in regard of this other part of his functi- on; whether we respect the weaknes of the people, apt to loath and abhorre the *Sanctuary*, when they which perform the service thereof are such as the sonnes of *Heli* were; or else consider the [i] inclination of God himself, who requireth the i *1 Tim.* 2. 8 lifting up of pure hands in prayers, and hath given the World plainly to understand, *John* 9. 31. that the wicked, although they cry, shall not be heard. They are no fit Supplicants *Fer.* 11. 11. to seek his mercy in the behalf of others, whose own un-repented sins provoke his *Ezech.* 8. 18. just indignation. [k] Let thy Priests therefore, O Lord, be evermore clothed with k *Pfal.* 132.9. righteousnes, that thy Saints may thereby with more devotion rejoyce and sing. But of all helps for due performance of this Service, the greatest is that very set and standing order it self, which framed, with common advice, hath both for matter and form prescribed whatsoever is herein publikely done. No doubt, from God it

hath

hath proceeded, and by us it muſt be acknowledged a work of his ſingular care and providence, that the Church hath evermore held a preſcript form of Common Prayer, although not in all things every where the ſame, yet for the moſt part retaining ſtill the ſame analogie. So that if the Liturgies of all ancient Churches throughout the World be compared amongſt themſelves, it may be eaſily perceived they had all one original mold, and that the publick Prayers of the people of God in Churches throughly ſetled, did never uſe to be voluntary Dictates, proceeding from any mans extemporal wit. To him which conſidereth the grievous and ſcandalous inconveniencies, whereunto they make themſelves daily ſubject, with whom any blind and ſecret corner is judged a fit houſe of Common Prayer ; the manifold confuſions which they fall into, where every mans private ſpirit and gift (as they term it) is the only Biſhop that ordaineth him to this Miniſtry ; the irkſome deformities whereby through endleſs and ſenſeleſs effuſions of indigeſted Prayers, they oftentimes diſgrace in moſt unſufferable manner, the worthieſt part of Chriſtian duty towards God, who herein are ſubject to no certain order, but pray both what and how they liſt ; to him, I ſay, which weigheth duly all theſe things the reaſons

a 2 *Chro. 6.20.*
b *Joel 2.* 17.
c 2 *Chro.* 29.30.

cannot be obſcure, why God doth in publick Prayer ſo much reſpect the [a] ſolemnity of places, [b] where the authority and calling of perſons by whom, and the [c] preciſe appointment even with what words or ſentences his Name ſhould be called on amongſt his people.

Of them which like not to have any ſet forme of Common Prayer.

26. No man hath hitherto been ſo impious, as plainly and directly to condemn Prayer: The beſt ſtratageme that Satan hath, who knoweth his Kingdom to be no one way more ſhaken, than by the publick devout Prayers of Gods Church, is by traducing the form and manner of them, to bring them into contempt, and ſo to ſhake the force of all mens devotion towards them. From this, and from no other

d *Num.* 6.23.

forge, hath proceeded a ſtrange conceit, that to ſerve God with any ſet form of Common Prayer, is ſuperſtitious. As though [d] God himſelf did not frame to his Prieſts the very ſpeech, wherewith they were charged to bleſs the people ; or as if our Lord, even of purpoſe to prevent this fancy of extemporal and voluntary Prayers, had not left us of his own framing one, which might both remain as a part of the Church Liturgy, and ſerve as a pattern whereby to frame all other Prayers with efficacy, yet without ſuperfluity of words. If Prayers were no otherwiſe accepted of God, then being conceived always new, according to the exigence of preſent occaſions ; if it be right to judge him by our own bellies, and to imagine that he doth loath to have the ſelf-ſame ſupplications often iterated, even as we do to be every day fed without alteration or change of diet ; if Prayers be actions which ought to waſte away themſelves in the making ; if being made to remain that they may be reſumed and uſed again as Prayers, they be but inſtruments of Superſtition ; ſurely, we cannot excuſe *Moſes*, who gave ſuch occaſion of ſcandal to the World, by not being contented to praiſe the Name of Almighty God, according to the uſual naked ſimplicity of Gods Spirit, for that admirable victory given them againſt *Pharoah*, unleſs ſo dangerous a preſident were left for the caſting of Prayers into certain Poetical moulds, and for the framing of Prayers which might be repeated often, although they never had again the ſame occaſions which brought

e *Mat.* 26. 30.
ὑμνήσαντες, having ſung the Pſalmes which were uſual at that Feaſt, thoſe Pſalms which the Jews call the great *Halleluja*, beginning at the 113. and continuing to the end of the 118. See *Paul. Burgenſ. in Pſ. 112 Edit.* 1. and *Scal. de emendat. tempo.*

them forth at the firſt. For that very Hymne of *Moſes* grew afterwards to be a part of the ordinary Jewiſh Liturgy ; nor only that, but ſundry other ſithence invented. Their books of Common Prayer contained partly Hymns taken out of the Holy Scripture, partly Benedictions, Thankſgivings, Supplications, penned by ſuch as have been, from time to time, The Governours of that Synagogue. Theſe they ſorted into their ſeveral times and places, ſome to begin the Service of God with, and ſome to end, ſome to go before, and ſome to follow, and ſome to be interlaced between the divine Readings of the Law and Prophets. Unto their cuſtom of finiſhing the Paſſeover with certain Pſalmes, there is not any thing more probable, then that the holy Evangeliſt doth evidently allude, ſaying, That after the Cup delivered by our Saviour unto his Apoſtles, [e] *they ſung*, and went forth to the Mount of Olives. As the Jews had their Songs of *Moſes*, and *David*, and the reſt, ſo the Church of Chriſt from the very beginning hath both uſed the ſame, and beſides them other alſo of like nature, the Song of the Virgin *Mary*, the Song of

Zachary,

Zachary, the Song of *Simeon*, such Hymnes as the Apostle doth often speak of, saying, [a] *I will pray and sing with the Spirit*, Again, [b] *In Psalmes, Hymnes, and Songs, making melody unto the Lord, and that heartily.* Hymnes and Psalms are such kinds of Prayer as are not wont to be conceived upon a sudden ; but are framed by Meditation before hand, or else by prophetical illumination are inspired, as at that time it appeareth they were, when God by extraordinary gifts of the Spirit, inabled men to all parts or service necessary for the edifying of his Church.

[a] 1 Cor. 14.15
[b] Ephes. 5.19

27. Now, albeit the admonitioners did seem at the first to allow no prescript form of prayer at all, but thought it the best that their Minister should always be left at liberty to pray, as his own discretion did serve, yet because this opinion upon better advice they afterwards retracted, their defender and his Associates have sithence proposed to the World a form, such as themselves like, and to shew their dislike of ours, have taken against it those exceptions, which, whosoever doth measure by number, must needs be greatly out of love with a thing that hath so many faults ; whosoever by weight, cannot chuse but esteem very highly of that, wherein the of so scrupulous Adversaries hath not hitherto observed any defect which themſ can seriously think to be of moment. Gross Errours and manifest Impiety they grant we have taken away. Yet ' many things in it they say are amiss, many instances they give of things in our Common Prayer, not agreeable as they pretend with the Word of God. It hath in their eye too great affinity with the form of the Church of *Rome* ; it differeth too much from that which Churches elsewhere reformed allow and observe ; our Attire disgraceth it ; it is not orderly read nor gestured as beseemeth ; it requireth nothing to be done, which a Child may not lawfully do ; it hath a number of short cuts or shreddings, which may be better called wishes than Prayers ; it intermingleth Prayings and Readings in such manner, as if Supplicants should use in proposing their Sutes unto mortal Princes, all the World would judge them mad ; it is too long, and by that meane abridgeth preaching ; it appointeth the people to say after the Minister , it spendeth time in singing and reading the *Psalmes* by course, from side to side ; it useth the Lords Prayer too oft, the Songs of *Magnificat, Benedictus,* and *Nunc Dimittis* it might very well spare ; it hath the *Letany*, the Creed of *Athanasius*, and *Gloria Patri* ; which are superfluous ; it craveth earthly things too much ; for deliverance from those evils against which we pray, it giveth no thanks : some things it asketh unseasonably when they need not to be prayed for, as deliverance from Thunder and Tempest when no danger is nigh , some in too abject and diffident manner ; as that God would give us that which we for our unworthiness dare not ask ; some which ought not to be desired, as the deliverance from sudden death, riddance from all adversity, and the extent of saving mercy towards all men. These and such like are the imperfections, whereby our form of Common Prayer is thought to swerve from the Word of God. A great favourer of that part, but yet (his errour that way excepted) a learned, a painful, a right vertuous and a good man did not fear sometime to undertake, against Popish Detractors, the general maintenance and defence of our whole Church Service, as having in it nothing repugnant to the Word of God. And even they which would file away most from the largeness of that offer, do notwithstanding in more sparing terms acknowledge little less. For when those opposite judgements which never are wont to construe things doubtful to the better, those very tongues which are always prone to aggravate whatsoever hath but the least shew whereby it may be suspected to favour of, or to sound towards any evil, do by their own voluntary sentence cleerly free us from *gross Errours*, and from *manifest Impiety* herein ; who would not judge us to be discharged of all blame, which are confest to have no great fault, even by their very word and testimony, in whose eyes no fault of ours hath ever hitherto been accustomed to seem small ? Nevertheless, what they seem to offer us with the one hand, the same with the other they pull back again. They grant we erre not in palpable manner, we are not openly and notoriously impious, yet Errors we have, which the sharp insight of their wisest men do espie, there is hidden impiety, which the profounder sort are able enough to disclose. Their skilful ears perceive certain harsh and unpleasant discords in the sound of our Common Prayer, such as the Rules of Divine Harmony, such as the Laws of God cannot bear. 28. Touch-

Of them who allowing a set forme of Prayer, yet allow not ours.

[c] T.C.l.1.p.131 afterwards pag. 135. Whereas M.Doctor affirmeth that there can be nothing in the whole Book which is not agreeable unto the Word of God: I am very loth, &c. Notwithstanding, my duty of defending the truth and love which I have first towards God, and then towards my Countrey, constraineth me being thus provoked, to speak a few words more particularly of the forme of Prayer, that when the blemishes thereof do appear, it may please the Queens Majesty, and her Honourable Council, with those of the Parliament, &c.

The forme of
our . Liturgie
too neer the
Papifts, too
farre different
from that of
other reformed
Churches, as
they pretend.

28. Touching our Conformity with the Church of *Rome*, as alſo of the difference between ſome Reformed Churches and ours, that which generally hath been
already anſwered, may ſerve for anſwer to that exception, which in theſe two reſpects they take particularly againſt the form of our Common Prayer. To ſay,
that in nothing they may be followed, which are of the Church of *Rome*, were violent and extream. Some things they do, in that they are men, in that they are
wiſe men, and Chriſtian men ſome things, ſome things in that they are miſ-
led and blinded with Errour. As far as they follow Reaſon and Truth, we fear not
to tread the ſelf-ſame ſteps wherein they have gone, and to be their Followers.
Where *Rome* keepeth that which is ancienter and better ; others whom we much
more affect leaving it for newer, and changing it for worſe, we had rather follow
the perfections of them whom we like not, than in defects reſemble them whom
we love. For although they profeſs they agree with us touching [a] *a preſcript forme*

a *T.C.l.1 p.135*
b A Book of
the forme of
Common
Prayer tende-
red to the Par-
lament, *pag.46.*

of Prayer to be uſed in the Church, yet in that very form which they ſay, is [b] *agreeable to Gods Word, and the uſe of Reformed Churches*, they have by ſpecial proteſtation declared, that their meaning is not it ſhall be preſcribed as a thing whereunto
they will tie their Miniſter. *It ſhall not* (they ſay) *be neceſſary for the Miniſter daily
to repeat all theſe things before mentioned, but beginning with ſome like confeſſion, to
proceed to the Sermon, which ended, he either uſeth the Prayer for all ſtates before
mentioned*, or prayeth as the Spirit of God ſhall move his heart. Herein therefore we hold it much better with the Church of *Rome* to appoint a preſcript forme
which every man ſhall be bound to obſerve, than with them to ſet down a kind of
direction, a forme for men to uſe if they liſt, or otherwiſe to change as pleaſeth
themſelves. Furthermore, the Church of *Rome* hath rightly alſo conſidered, that
publick Prayer is a duty intire in it ſelf, a duty requiſite to be performed, much
oftner than Sermons can poſſibly be made. For which cauſe, as they, ſo we have
likewiſe a publick form how to ſerve God both Morning and Evening, whether Sermons may be had or no. On the contrary ſide, their form of Reformed Prayer

c *Pag. 22.*
d 24.

ſheweth only what ſhall be done [c] *upon the dayes appointed for the preaching of the
Word* ; with what words the Miniſter ſhall begin, [d] *when the hour appointed for
Sermon is come* ; what ſhall be ſaid or ſung before Sermon, and what after. So that
according to this form of theirs, it muſt ſtand for a Rule, *No Sermon, No Service.*
Which overſight, occaſioned the French ſpitefully to term Religion in that ſort exerciſed, a meer Preach. Sundry other more particular defects there are, which I
willingly forbear to rehearſe, in conſideration whereof, we cannot be induced to
preferre their Reformed form of Prayer before our own, what Church ſoever we
reſemble therein.

Attire belong-
ing to the Ser-
vice of God.
T.C.l.1.p.71.
We think the
Surplice eſpe-
cially unmeet
for a Miniſter
of the Goſpel
to wear,*pag.75.*
It is eaſily ſeen
by Solomon Ec-
cleſ.8.9. that to
weat a white
Garment was
greatly eſteem-
ed in the Eaſt
parts,and was
ordinary to
thoſe that were
in any eſtima-
tion,as black
with us, and
therefore was
no ſeveral Apparel

29. The Attire which the Miniſter of God is by order to uſe at times of Divine
Service, being but a matter of meer formality, yet ſuch as for comelineſs ſake hath
hitherto been judged by the wiſer ſort of men not unneceſſary to concurre with
other ſenſible notes, betokening the different kind or quality of perſons and actions whereto it is tyed, as we think not our ſelves the holier, becauſe we uſe it, ſo
neither ſhould they with whom no ſuch thing is in uſe, think us therefore unholy,
becauſe we ſubmit our ſelves unto that, which in a matter ſo indifferent the wiſdom
of Authority and Law have thought comely. To ſolemn actions of Royalty and
Juſtice, their ſutable Ornaments are a beauty. Are they on y in Religion a ſtain ?
Divine Religion, ſaith Saint *Jerome* (he ſpeaketh of the Prieſtly attire of the Law)
*hath one kind of habit wherein to miniſter before the Lord, another for ordinary uſes
belonging unto common life.* *Pelagius* having carped at the curious neatneſs of mens
apparel in thoſe days, and through the ſowreneſs of his diſpoſition ſpoken ſomewhat too hardly thereof, affirming, that *the glory of Clothes and Ornaments was a
thing contrary to God and godlineſs* ; S. *Jerome* whoſe cuſtome is not to pardon over-
eaſily his Adverſaries, if any where they chance to trip, preſſeth him as thereby making all ſorts of men in the world *Gods enemies*. *Is it enmity with God* (ſaith he) *if I
wear my Coat ſomewhat handſome ?* If a Biſhop, a Prieſt, Deacon, and the reſt of the
Eccleſiaſtical Order *come to adminiſter the uſual Sacrifice in a [f] white Garment*, are

for the Miniſters to execute their Miniſtry in. e Hierom. 44. Ezech. f Hiero. Adver. Pelag.lib.1.c.9.
g *T.C.l.1.p.77.* By a white garment, is meant a comely Apparel, and not ſlovenly.

they

they hereby Gods Adverſaries ? *Clarks, Monks, Widows, Virgins, take heed, it is dan-gerous for you to be otherwiſe ſeen than in foul and ragged clothes. Not to ſpeak any thing of Secular men, which are proclaimed to have war with God as oft as ever they put on precious and ſhining clothes.* By which words of *Jerome* we may take it at the leaſt for a probable collection, that his meaning was to draw *Pelagius* into hatred, as condemning by ſo general a ſpeech even the neatneſs of that very Garment it ſelf, wherein the Clergy did then uſe to adminiſter publikely the holy Sacrament of Chriſts moſt bleſſed Body and Blood. For that they did then uſe ſome ſuch Orna-ment, the words of [a] *Chryſoſtome* give plain teſtimony, who ſpeaking to the Cler-gy of *Antioch*, telleth them that if they did ſuffer notorious Malefactors to come to the Table of our Lord and not put them by, it would be as heavily revenged up-on them, as if themſelves had ſhed his blood, that for this purpoſe God had called them to the rooms which they held in the Church of Chriſt, that this they ſhould reckon was *their dignity, this their ſafety, this their whole Crown and Glory*; and therefore this they ſhould carefully intend, and not when the Sacrament is admini-ſtred, imagine themſelves called only *to walk up and down in a white and ſhining Garment.* Now, whereas theſe ſpeeches of *Jerom* and *Chryſoſtome* do ſeem plainly to allude unto ſuch Miniſterial Garments as were then in uſe, to this they anſwer, that by *Jerom* nothing can be gathered, but only that the Miniſters came to Church in handſome holiday apparel, and that himſelf did not think them bound by the Law of God to go like Slovens; but the Weed which we mean he defendeth not; that [b] *Chryſoſtome* meaneth indeed the ſame which we defend, but ſeemeth rather to re-prehend than to allow it as we do. Which anſwer wringeth out of *Jerome* and Chry-ſoſtome that which their words will not gladly yield. They both ſpeak of the ſame perſons, namely, the Clergy; and of their Weed at the ſame time when they admi-niſter the bleſſed Sacrament; and of the ſelf-ſame kind of Weed, a white Garment, ſo far as we have wit to conceive; and for any thing we are able to ſee, their man-ner of ſpeech is not ſuch as doth argue either the thing it ſelf to be different where-of they ſpeak, or their judgements concerning it different; although the one do on-ly maintain it againſt *Pelagius*, as a thing not therefore unlawful, becauſe it was fair or handſome, and the other make it a matter of ſmall commendation in it ſelf, if they which wear it, do nothing elſe but aire the Robes which their place requireth. The honeſty, dignity, and eſtimation of white apparel in the Eaſtern part of the World, is a token of greater fitneſs for this Sacred uſe, wherein it were not conveni-ent that any thing baſely thought of ſhould be ſuffered. Notwithſtanding, I am not bent to ſtand ſtiffely upon theſe probabilities, that in *Jeroms* and *Chryſoſtoms* time any ſuch attire was made ſeveral to this purpoſe. Yet ſurely the words of *Solomon* are very impertinent to prove it an Ornament, therefore not ſeveral for the Min-ſters to execute their Miniſtery in, becauſe men of credit and eſtimation wore their ordinary apparel white. For we know that when *Solomon* wrote thoſe words, the ſe-veral apparel for the Miniſters of the Law, to execute their Miniſtry in was ſuch? The [c] Wiſe man which feared God from his heart, and honoured the Service that was done unto him, could not mention ſo much as the Garments of holineſs; but with effectual ſignification of moſt ſingular reverence and love. Were it not better that the love which men bear to God, ſhould make the leaſt things that are imp oyed in his Service amiable, than that their over-ſcrupulous diſlike of ſo mean a thing as a Veſtment, ſhould from the very ſervice of God withdraw their hearts and affecti-ons? I term it rather a mean thing, a thing not much to be reſpected, becauſe even they ſo account now of it, whoſe firſt Diſputations againſt it were ſuch, as if Religi-on had ſcarcely any thing of greater wright. Their [d] allegations were then, that *if a man were aſſured to gain a thouſand by doing that which may offend any one Brother, or be unto him a cauſe of falling, he ought not to do it*; *that this Popiſh apparel the Sur-plice eſpecially hath been by Papiſts abominably abuſed*; *that it hath been a mark and a very Sacrament of abomination*; *that remaining it ſerveth as a Monument of Idola-try*, and not only edifieth not, but as a dangerous and ſcandalous Ceremony, doth exceeding much harm *to them of whoſe good we are commanded to have regard, that it cauſeth men to periſh, and make ſhip-wrack of conſcience*, for ſo themſelves profeſs they mean, when they ſay the weak are offended herewith, that it hardneth Papiſts, hin-dreth the weak, from profiting in the knowledge of the Goſpel, grieveth godly minds, and

giveth

Marginal notes:

[a] *Chryſoſt. ad popul. Antioch. To. 5. Serm. 60.*

[b] *T.C. l. 1. p. 3⸗* It is true; *Chry-ſoſtom* maketh mention of a white garment, but not in com-mendation of it, but rather to the contra-ry: for hee ſheweth that the dignity of their Miniſte-ry was in ta-king heed that none unmeet were admitted to the Lords. Suppers not in going about the Church with a white Garment.

[c] *Eccleſ. 45. 74*

[d] *T.C. l. 1. p. 79.*

71, 75.

T.C. l. 2. p. 403. lib. 1. p. 73. Page 73. Page 76. Lib. 2. p. 403.

giveth them occasion to think hardly of their Ministers; that if the Magistrate may command, or the Church appoint Rites and Ceremonies, yet seeing our abstinence from things in their own nature indifferent, if the weak Brother should be offended, is a flat Commandement of the Holy Ghost, which no Authority either of Church or Commonwealth can make void, therefore neither may the one nor the other lawfully ordain this Ceremony, which hath great incommodity and no profit, great offence and no edifying; that by the Law it should have been burnt and consumed with fire as a thing infected with Leprosie; that the Example of Ezechias beating to powder the brazen Serpent, and of Paul abrogating those abused Feasts of Charity, inforceth upon us the duty of abolishing altogether a thing which hath been and is so offensive; Finally, that God by his Prophet hath given an express Commandement, which in this case toucheth us, no less then of old it did the Jews, " Ye shall pollute the covering of the Images of silver, and the rich ornament of your Images of gold, and cast them away as a stained ragge, thou shalt say unto it, Get thee hence. These and such like were their first Discourses, touching that Church Attire, which with us for the most part is usual in publick Prayer; our Ecclesiastical Laws so appointing, as well because it hath been of reasonable continuance, and by special choice was taken out of the number of those holy Garments, which (over and besides their mystical reference) served for comeliness under the Law, and is in the number of those Ceremonies, which may with choice and discretion be used to that purpose in the Church of Christ; as also for that it suteth so fitly with that lightsome affection of joy, wherein God delighteth when his Saints praise him; and so lively resembleth the glory of the Saints in Heaven, together with the beauty wherein Angels have appeared unto men, that they which are to appear for men in the presence of God, as Angels, if they were left to their own choice, and would chuse any, could not easily devise a Garment of more decency for such a Service. As for those fore-rehearsed vehement allegations against it, shall we give them credit, when the very Authors from whom they come, confess they believe not their own sayings? For when once they began to perceive how many, both of them in the two Universities, and of others, who abroad having Ecclesiastical charge, do favour mightily their cause, and by all means set it forward, might by persisting in the extremity of that opinion hazard greatly their own estates, and so weaken that part which their places do now give them much opportunity to strengthen, they asked counsel as it seemeth from some abroad, who wisely considered, that the body is of far more worth than the raiment. Whereupon for fear of dangerous inconveniences, it hath been thought good to adde, that sometimes authority must and may with good conscience be obeyed, even where Commandement is not given upon good ground; that the duty of preaching is one of the absolute Commandements of God, and therefore ought not to be forsaken, for the bare inconvenience of a thing which in the own nature is indifferent; that one of the foulest spots in the Surplice, is the offence which it giveth in occasioning the weak to fall, and the wicked to be confirmed in their wickedness, yet hereby there is no unlawfulness proved, but only an inconveniency, that such things should be established, howbeit no such inconveniency neither, as may not be born with; that when God doth flatly command us to abstain from things in their own Nature indifferent, if they offend our weak brethren, his meaning is not we should obey his Commandement herein, unless we may do it, and not leave undone that which the Lord hath absolutely commanded. Alwayes provided, that whosoever will enjoy the benefit of this Dispensation, to wear a scandalous Badge of Idolatry, rather than forsake his Pastoral charge, do (as occasion serveth) teach nevertheless still the incommodity of the thing it self, admonish the weak Brethren, that they be not, and pray unto God so to strengthen them that they may not be offended thereat. So that whereas before, they which had authority to institute Rites and Ceremonies, were denyed to have power to institute this, it is now confest, that this they may also lawfully, but not so conveniently appoint; they did well before, and as they ought, who had it in utter detestation and hatred as a thing abominable; they now do well, which think it may be both borne and used with a very good conscience; before, he which by wearing it were sure to win thousands unto Christ, ought not to do it if there were but one which might be offended; now, though it be with the offence of thousands, yet it may be done rather than that should be given over, whereby notwith-

notwithstanding we are not certain we shall gain one ; the Examples of *Ezechias* and of *Paul*, the Charge which was given to the Jews by *Esay*, the strict Apostolical prohibition of things indifferent, whensoever they may be scandalous, were before so forcible Laws against our Ecclesiastical Attire, as neither Church nor Commonwealth could possibly make void, which now one of far less authority than either, hath found how to frustrate by dispencing with the breach of inferiour Commandments, to the end that the greater may be kept. But it booteth them not, thus to soder up a broken Cause, whereof their first and last discourses will fall asunder, do what they can. Let them ingenuously confess that their Invectives were too bitter, their Arguments too weak, the matter not so dangerous as they did imagine. If those alledged testimonies of Scripture did indeed concern the matter to such effect as was pretended, that wch they should infer were unlawfulness, because they were cited as Prohibitions of that thing which indeed they concern. If they prove not our Attire unlawfull, because in truth they concern it not, it followeth that they prove not any thing against it, and consequently, not so much as uncomliness or inconveniency. Unless therefore they be able throughly to resolve themselves, that there is no one Sentence in all the Scriptures of God, which doth controul the wearing of it in such manner, and to such purpose as the Church of *England* alloweth ; unless they can fully rest and settle their minds in this most sound perswasion, that they are not to make themselves the only competent Judges of decency in these cases, and to despise the solemn judgment of the whole Church, preferring before it their own conceit, grounded only upon uncertain suspitions and fears, whereof if there were at the first some probable cause, when things were but raw and tender, yet now very tract of time hath it self worn that out also ; unless, I say, thus resolved in mind they hold their Pastoral charge with the comfort of a good Conscience, no way grudging at that which they do, or doing that which they think themselves bound of duty to reprove, how should it possibly help or further them in their course, to take such occasions as they say are requisite to be taken, and in pensive manner to tell their Audience ; " *Brethren, our hearts desire is ; that we might injoy the full liberty* " *of the Gospel, as in other reformed Churches they do else-where, upon whom the heavy* " *hand of Authority hath imposed no grievous burthen. But such is the misery of* " *these our days, that so great happiness we cannot look to attain unto: Were it so, that* " *the equity of the Law of* Moses *could prevail ; or the zeal of Ezechias be found in* " *the hearts of those Guides and Governours under whom we live ; or the voice of Gods* " *own Prophets be duly heard ; or the Example of the Apostles of Christ be followed,* " *yea or their Precepts be answered with full and perfect obedience, these abominable* " *rags, polluted garments, marks and Sacraments of Idolatry, which Power as you see* " *constraineth us to wear, and conscience to abhor, had long ere this day been removed* " *both out of sight and out of memory. But as now things stand, behold to what narrow* " *streights we are driven ; On the one side we fear the words of our Saviour Christ,* " *Woe be to them by whom scandal and offence cometh : on the other side, at the* " *Apostles speech, we cannot but quake and tremble,* If I preach not the Gospel, woe be " *unto me. Being thus hardly beset, we see not any other remedy, but to hazzard your* " *Souls the one way, that we may the other way endeavour to save them. Touching the* " *offence of the weak therefore, we must adventure it. If they perish, they perish. Our* " *Pastoral charge is Gods absolute commandment. Rather then that shall be taken from* " *us, we are resolved to take this filth, and to put it on, although we judge it to be so* " *unfit and inconvenient, that as oft as ever we pray or preach so arrayed before you,* " *we do as much as in us lieth, to cast away your souls that are weak minded, and* " *to bring you unto endless perdition. But we beseech you, Brethren, have care of* " *your own safety, take heed to your steps, that ye be not taken in those snares which we* " *lay before you. And our Prayer in your behalf to Almighty God is, that the poyson* " *which we offer you, may never have the power to do you harm.* Advice and counsell is best sought for at their hands, which either have no part at all in the cause whereof they instruct ; or else are so far ingaged, that themselves are to bear the greatest adventure in the success of their own counsels. The one of which two considerations maketh men the less respective, and the other the more circumspect. Those good and learned men which gave the first direction to this course, had reason to wish that their own proceedings at home might be favoured abroad also, and that the good affection of such as inclined towards them might be kept alive. But if themselves had gone under those sails which they require to be hoised up , if they had been themselves to execute their own Theory in this Church , I doubt not but easily they would have seen, being nearer at hand , that the way was not good which they took of advising men, first, to wear the apparel, that thereby they might be free to continue their preaching , and then, of requiring them so to preach as they might be sure they could not continue , except they imagine that Laws which permit them not to do as they would , will endure them to speak as they list , even against that which themselves do by constraint of Laws ; they would have easily seen that our people being accustomed to think evermore that thing evil which is publikely under any pretence reproved, and the men themselves worse which reprove it and use it too, it should be to little purpose for them to salve the wound, by making protestations in disgrace of their own actions, with plain acknowledgement that they are scandalous, or by using fair intreaty with the weak Brethren ; they would easily have seen how with us it cannot be endured , to hear a man openly profess that he putteth fire to his Neighbours house, but yet so halloweth the same with Prayer, that he hopeth it shall not burn.   It had been therefore perhaps safer and better for ours to have observed [a] St. *Basils* advice , both in this

a *Basil. Ascet. responf. ad inter. 47.* and in all things of like nature.   *Let him which approveth not his Governours Ordinances, either plainly (but privately always) shew his dislike if he have λόγον ἰχυρον , strong and invincible reason against them , according to the true will and meaning of Scripture, or else let him quietly with silence do that which is enjoyned.*   Obedience with profest unwillingness to obey, is no better than manifest disobedience.

Of gesture in praying, and of different places chosen to that purpose. *T.C.l.1.p.134.*   30 Having thus disputed , whether the Surplice be a fit garment to be used in the service of God, the next question whereinto we are drawn, is, whether it be a thing allowable or no, that the Minister should say Service in the Chancel, or turn his face at any time from the people, or before Service ended remove from the place where it was begun ? By them which trouble us with these doubts, we would more willingly be resolved of a greater doubt ; whether it be not a kind of taking Gods Name in vain, to debase Religion with such frivolous disputes, a sin to bestow time and labour about them ? Things of so mean regard and quality , although necessary to be ordered, are notwithstanding very unsavoury when they come to be disputed of ; because disputation presupposeth some difficulty in the matter which is argued, whereas in things of this nature they must be either very simple or very froward, who need to be taught by disputation what is meet. When we make profession of our Faith, we stand ; when we acknowledg our sins, or seek unto God for favour, we fall down, because the gesture of constancy becometh us best in the one, in the other the behaviour of humility.   Some parts of our Liturgy consist in the reading of the word of God , and the proclaiming of his Law , that the people may thereby learn what their duties are towards him ;some consist in words of praise and thanksgiving, whereby we acknowledge unto God what his blessings are towards us; some are such as albeit they serve to singular good purpose, even when there is no Communion administred ; neverthelefs, being devised at the first for that purpose, are at the Table of the Lord for that cause also commonly read ; some are uttered as from the people, some as with them unto God, some as from God unto them, all as before his sight, whom we fear, and whose presence to offend with any the least unseemliness, we would be surely as loath as they, who most reprehend or deride that we do.

b *T.C.l.1.p.203*   [b] Now, because the Gospels which are weekly read, do all historically declare something which our Lord Jesus Christ himself either spake, did, or suffered in his own person, it hath been the custom of Christian men then especially in token of the greater reverence to stand, to utter certain words of acclamation, and at the name of Jesus to bow. Which harmless Ceremonies, as there is *no man constrained to use* ; so we know no reason wherefore any man should yet imagine it an unsufferable evil. It

c *Mark 11. 6.*   sheweth a reverend [c] regard to the Son of God above other Messengers , although speaking as from God also. And against Infidels, Jews, Arrians, who derogate from the honour of Jesus Christ, such ceremonies are most profitable. [d] As for any erro-

d *T.C.l.1.p.115*   neous *estimation,* advancing the Son *above the Father and the holy Ghost,* seeing that the truth of his equality with them, is a mystery so hard for the wits of mortal men to rise unto, of all Heresies , that which may give him superiority above them , is least to be feared. But to let go this as a matter scarce worth the speaking of, whereas if fault be in these things any where justly found, Law hath referred the whole dis-

disposition and redress thereof to the Ordinary of the place; *they which elsewhere complain, that disgrace and *injury* is offred even to the meanest Parish Minister, when the Magistrate appointeth him what to wear, & leaveth not so small a matter as that to his own discretion, being presumed a man discreet, & trusted with the care of the peoples souls, do think the gravest Prelates in the Land no competent Judges, to discern and appoint where it is fit for the Minister to stand, or which way convenient to look praying. From their Ordinary therefore they appeal to themselves, finding great fault that we neither reform the thing against the which they have so long sithence given sentence, nor yet make answer unto that they bring, which is, that St. *Luke* declaring, how *Peter stood up in the midst of the Disciples,* did thereby deliver an *unchangeable* rule, that *whatsoever* is done in the Church, *ought to be done* in the midst of the Church, and therefore not Baptism to be administred in one place, Marriage solemnized in another, the Supper of the Lord received in a third, in a fourth Sermons, in a fift Prayers to be made; that the custom which we use is Levitical, absurd, and such as hindreth the understanding of the People; that if it be meet for the Minister, at some time to look towards the people, if the body of the Church be a fit place for some part of Divine Service, it must needs follow that whensoever his face is turned any other way, or any thing done any other where, it hath absurdity. *All these reasons,* they say, have been brought, and were hitherto never answered; besides a number of merriments and jests unanswered likewise, wherewith they have pleasantly moved much laughter at our manner of serving God. Such is their evil hap to play upon dull-spirited men. We are still perswaded that a bare denial is answer sufficient to things which meer fancy objecteth; and that the best Apologie to words of scorn and petulancy, is *Isaacks* Apologie to his brother *Ismael,* the Apologie which patience and silence maketh. Our answer therefore to their reasons, is no; to their scoffs, nothing.

31. When they object that our Book requireth nothing to be done, which a child may not doe as *lawfully and as well as that man wherewith the Book contenteth it self,* is it their meaning that the Service of God ought to be a matter of great difficulty, a labour which requireth great learning and deep skill, or else that the Book containing it should teach what men are fit to attend upon it, and forbid other men unlearned or children to be admitted thereunto? In setting down the form of Common Prayer, there was no need that the Book should mention either the learning of a fit, or the unfitness of an ignorant Minister, more than that he which describeth the manner how to pitch a field, should speak of moderation & sobriety in diet. And concerning the duty it self, although the hardness thereof be not such as needeth such Art, yet surely they seem to be very far carried besides themselves, to whom the dignity of publike Prayer doth not discover somwhat more fitness in men of gravity and ripe discretion, than in children of *ten years of age,* for the decent discharge & performance of that office. It cannot be that they who speak thus, should thus judge. At the boord and in private it very well becometh childrens innocency to pray, and their Elders to say, *Amen.* Which being a part of their vertuous education, serveth greatly both to nourish in them the fear of God, and to put us in continual remembrance of that powerful grace which openeth the mouths of Infants to sound his praise. But publike Prayer, the service of God in the solemne Assembly of Saints, is a work though easie, yet withal so weighty and of such respect, that the great facility thereof is but a slender argument to prove, it may be as well and as lawfully committed to children as to men of years, howsoever their ability of learning be but only to do that in decent order wherewith the Book contenteth it self. The Book requireth but orderly reading. As in truth, what should any prescript form of Prayer framed to the Ministers hand require, but onely so to be read as behoveth? We know that there are in the world certain voluntary Over-seers of all books, whose censure in this respect would fall as sharp on us as it hath done on many others, if delivering but a form of Prayer, we should either express or include any thing, more than doth properly concern Prayer. The Ministers greatness or meanness of knowledge to do other things, his aptness or insufficiency otherwise than by reading to instruct the Flock, standeth in this place as a stranger, with whom our form of Common Prayer hath nothing to do. Wherein their exception against easiness, as if that did nourish ignorance, proceedeth altogether of a needless jealousie. I have of-

Marginal notes:
* *T.C.l.1.p.74.*
a *T.C.l.1.p.134. lib.3. pag.187.*
b *Acts 1. 15. c T.C.l.1.p.134 lib.3. pag.187.*

Easiness of praying after our form.
d *T.C.l.1.p.135 & l.3. p.184.* Another fault in the whole Service or Liturgy of *England,* is, for that it maintaineth an unpreaching Ministry in requiring nothing to be done by the Minister which a child of ten years old cannot do as well, and as lawfully, as that man wherewith the Book contenteth it self.

ten

ten heard it inquired of by many, how it might be brought to pass that the Church should every where have able Preachers to instruct the people; what impediments there are to hinder it, and which were the speediest way to remove them. In which consultations the multitude of Parishes, the Paucity of Schools, the manifold discouragements which are offered unto mens inclinations that way, the penury of the Ecclesiastical estate, the irrecoverable loss of so many Livings of principal value, clean taken away from the Church long sithence by being appropriated, the daily bruizes that Spiritual promotions use to take by often falling, the want of somewhat in certain statutes which concern the state of the Church, the too great facility of many Bishops, the stony hardness of too many Patrons hearts not touched with any feeling in this case: such things oftentimes are debated, and much thought upon by them that enter into discourse concerning any defect of knowledge in the Clergie. But whosoever be found guilty, the Communion Book hath surely deserved least to be called in question for this fault. If all the Clergie were as learned as themselves are that most complain of ignorance in others, yet our Book of Prayer might remain the same; and, remaining the same it is, I see not how it can be a let unto any mans skill in preaching. Which thing we acknowledge to be Gods good gift, howbeit no such necessary element, that every act of Religion should be thought imperfect and lame, wherein there is not somewhat exacted that none can discharge but an able Preacher.

32. Two faults there are, which our Lord and Saviour himself especially reproved in Prayer; the one, when ostentation did cause it to be open; the other, when superstition made it long. As therefore prayers the one way are faulty, not whensoever they be openly made, but when Hypocrisie is the cause of open praying: so the length of Prayer is likewise a fault, howbeit not simply, but where errour and superstition causeth more than convenient repetition or continuation of speech to be used. It is not, as some do imagine, (saith St. *Augustine*) that long praying is that fault of much speaking in prayer which our Saviour did reprove; for then would not he himself in prayer have continued a whole nights.

The length of our Service.
T.C.l.1.p.133.
& lib.3.p.184.

Aug.Ep. 121.
a Luk.6. 12.

Use in prayer no vain superfluity of words, as the Heathens do, for they imagine that their much speaking will cause them to be heard: whereas in truth the thing which God doth regard is, how vertuous their minds are, and not how copious their tongues in prayer; how well they think, and not how long they talk, who come to present their supplications before him. Notwithstanding for as much as in publike prayer we are not only to consider what is needful in respect of God, but there is also in men that which we must regard; we somewhat the rather incline to length, leftover-quick dispatch of a duty so important should give the world occasion to deem, that the thing it self is but little accounted of, wherein but little time is bestowed. Length thereof is a thing which the gravity and weight of such actions doth require. Beside, this benefit also it hath, that they whom earnest lets and impediments do often hinder from being partakers of the whole, have yet through the length of Divine Service, opportunity left them, at the least, for access unto some reasonable part thereof. Again, it should be considered, how it doth come to pass that we are so long. For if that very service of God in the Jewish Synagogues, which our Lord did approve and sanctifie with the presence of his own person, had so large portions of the Law and Prophets, together with so many Prayers and Psalms read day by day, as equal in a manner the length of ours, and yet in that respect was never thought to deserve blame, is it now an offence that the like measure of time is bestowed in the like manner? Peradventure the Church hath not now the leisure which it had then, or else those things whereupon so much time was then well spent, have sithence that lost their dignity and worth. If the reading of the Law, the Prophets and Psalmes, be a part of the Service of God, as needful under Christ as before, and the adding of the New Testament, as profitable as the ordaining of the Old to be read; if therewith instead of Jewish Prayers it be also for the good of the Church to annex that variety which b the Apostle doth commend; seeing that the time which we spend is no more than the orderly performance of these things necessarily requireth, why are we thought to exceed in length; words, be they never so few, are too many when they benefit not the Hearer. But he which speaketh

b 1 Tim.2.1.

speaketh

speaketh no more than edifieth, is undeservedly reprehended for much speaking. That as [a] *the Devil under colour of long Prayer drave preaching out of the Church* [a T.C.l.3.p.184] heretofore, *so we in appointing so long Prayers and Readings, whereby the less can be spent in preaching, maintain an unpreaching Ministry*, is neither advisedly nor truly spoken. They reprove long Prayer, and yet acknowledge it to be in it self a thing commendable. For so it must needs be, if the Devil have used it as a colour to hide his malicious practises. When malice would work that which is evil, and in working avoyd the suspition of an evil intent, the colour wherewith it overcasteth it self, is always a fair and plausible pretence of seeking to further that which is good. So that if we both retain that good which Satan hath pretended to seek, and avoid the evil which his purpose was to effect, have we not better prevented his malice, then if, as he hath under colour of long prayer, driven preaching out of the Church, so we should take the quarrel of Sermons in hand, and revenge their cause by requital, thrusting Prayer in a manner out of doors under colour of long preaching? In case our Prayers being made at their full length, did necessarily inforce Sermons to be the shorter, yet neither were this to uphold and maintain an *unpreaching* Ministerie, unless we shall say that those ancient Fathers, *Chrysostom*, *Augustine*, *Leo*, and the rest, whose Homilies in that consideration were shorter for the most part than our Sermons are, did then not preach when their speeches were not long. The necessity of shortness causeth men to cut off impertinent Discourses, and to comprize much matter in few words. But neither doth it maintain inability, nor at all prevent opportunity of preaching, as long as a competent time is granted for that purpose. *An hour and a half* is, they say, in reformed Churches *ordinarily* thought reasonable, for *their whole Liturgy or Service*. Do we then continue as [a] *Ezra* did in reading the Law from morning till midday? [b] or as the Apostle St. *Paul* did in [b Neh. 8.3.] Prayer and preaching, till men through weariness be taken up dead at our feet? [c] [c Acts 20.9.] The huge length whereof they make such complaint, is but this, that if our whole form of Prayer be read, and besides an hour allowed for a Sermon, we spend ordinarily in both more time than they do by half an hour. Which half hour being such a matter, as the *age of some*, *and infirmity of other some are not able to bear*; if we have any sense of the *common imbecility*, if any care to preserve mens wits from being broken with the very *bent of so long attention*, if any love or desire to provide that things most holy be not with hazard of mens souls abhord and lothed, this half hours tediousness must be remedied, and that onely by cutting off the greatest part of our Common Prayer. For no other remedy will serve to help so dangerous an inconvenience.

33. The Brethren in *Ægypt* (saith St. *Augustine*, *Epist.* 121.) are reported to have [Instead of such many Prayers, but every of them very short, as if they were Darts thrown out with a [Prayers as the kind of sudden quickness, lest that vigilant and erect attention of mind, which in [Primitive Prayer is very necessary, should be wasted or dulled through continuance, if their [Churches have Prayers were few and long. But that which St. *Augustine* doth allow, they con- [used, and those demn. Those Prayers whereunto devout minds have added a piercing kind of bre- [ed now use; we vity, as well in that respect which we have already mentioned, so also thereby the [have (they say) better to express that quick and speedy expedition, wherewith ardent affections, [divers short cuts the very wings of Prayer, are delighted to present our suites in Heaven, even soon- [or shreddings, er than our tongues can devise to utter them, they in their mood of contradiction [rather wishes spare not openly to deride, and that with so base terms as do very ill beseem men of [than Prayers. their gravity. Such speeches are scandalous, they savour not of God in him that [T.C.l.1.p. 135. useth them, and unto vertuously disposed minds they are grievous corrosives. Our [& lib.3. pag. case were miserable, if that wherewith we most endeavour to please God, were in [210. 211. his sight so vile and despicable, as mens disdainful speech would make it.

34. Again, for as much as effectual Prayer is joined with a vehement in- [Lessons inter-tention of the inferiour powers of the soul, which cannot therein long continue [mingled with without paine, it hath been therefore thought good so by turns to interpose still [our Prayers. somewhat for the higher part of the mind, the understanding to work upon, that both being kept in continual exercise with variety, neither might feel any great weariness, and yet each be a spurre to other. For Prayer kindleth our desire to behold God by speculation; and the minde delighted

E e 3　　　　　　　　　　　　　　　　　　　　　with

with that contemplative sight of God, taketh every where new inflammations to pray, the riches of the Mysteries of heavenly Wisdom continually stirring up in us correspondent desires towards them. So that he which prayeth in due sort, is thereby made the more attentive to hear, and he which heareth, the more earnest to pray, for the time which we bestow as well in the one as the other. But for what cause soever we do it, this intermingling of Lessons with Prayers is * in their tast a thing as unsavorie, and as unseemly in their sight, as if the like should be done in Sutes and Supplications before some mighty Prince of the World. Our speech to worldly Superiors we frame in such sort as serveth best to inform and perswade the minds of them, who otherwise neither could nor would greatly regard our necessities: Whereas, because we know that God is indeed a King, but *a great* King; who understandeth all things beforehand, which no other King besides doth, a King which needeth not to be informed what we lack, a King readier to grant than we to make our requests; therefore in Prayer we do not so much respect what Precepts Art delivereth touching the method of perswasive utterance in the presence of great men, as what doth most avail to our

Note in left margin:
* We have no such forms in Scripture as that we should pray in two or three lines, and then after having read a while some other thing, come and pray as much more, and so the 20. or the 30. time, with pauses between. If a man should come to a Prince and having very many things to demand, after he had demanded one thing, would stay a long time, and then demand another, and so the third, the Prince might well think that either he came to ask before he knew what he had need of, or that he had forgotten some piece of his Suit, or that he were distracted in his understanding, or some other like cause of the disorder of his Supplication. *T. C. l. 1. p. 138.* This kind of reason the Prophet in the matter of Sacrifices doth use. *T. C. l. 3. p. 210.*

own edification in piety and godly zeal. If they on the contrary side do think that the same rules of decency which serve for things done unto terrene Powers, should universally decide what is fit in the service of God, if it be their meaning to hold it for a maxime, that the Church must deliver her publique Supplications unto God in no other form of speech than such as were decent, if sute should be made to the great Turk, or some other Monarch, let them apply their own rule unto their own form of Common-Prayer. Suppose that the people of a whole Town with some chosen man before them did continually twice or thrice in a week resort to their King, and every time they come, first acknowledg themselves guilty of rebellions and treasons, then sing a Song, after that explain some Statute of the Land to the standers by, and therein spend at the least an hour, this done, turn themselves again to the King and for every sort of his Subjects crave somewhat of him, at the length sing him another Song, and so take their leave: Might not the King well think, that either they knew not what they would have, or else that they were distracted in mind, or some other such like cause of the disorder of their Supplication? This form of suing unto Kings were absurd. This form of Praying unto God they allow. When God was served with Legal Sacrifices, such was the miserable and wretched disposition of some mens minds, that the best of every thing they had being culled out for themselves, if there were in their flocks any poor starved or diseased thing not worth the keeping, they thought it good enough for the Altar of God, pretending (as wise hypocrites do when they rob God to inrich themselves) that the fatnes of Calves doth benefit him nothing, to us the best things are most profitable, to him all as one if the mind of the Offerer be good, which is the only thing he respecteth. In reproof of which their devout fraud, the Prophet *Malachy* alledgeth, that gifts are offered unto God not as ᵃ supplies of his want indeed, but yet as testimonies of that affection wherewith we acknowledge and honour his greatnes. For which cause, sith the greater they are whom we honour, the more regard we have to the quality and choice of those presents which we bring them for honours sake, it must needs follow, that if

Note in left margin:
a Μέμνη τιμῆς τἀδίθεα, τἀ γἀρ ἐκάτοις τίμια. Καὶ γἀρ τὸ δ῀ωρον ἔςι χ῀ῆμα]ωρ δόσις κὶ τιμῆς σημεῖον Διὸ κὶ οἱ φιλοχρήμα]οι κὶ οἱ φιλότιμαι ἐςέενˁιαι αὐτῶν. Ἀμφοτέροις γἀρ ἐγεῖων δῖονˁαι. Καὶ γἀρ χ῀ῆμα ἐςιν οὗ ἐςέενˁιαι οἱ φιλοχρήμα]οις, χ῀τιμˁὼ ἔχει οἳ οἱ φιλότιμοι. Arist. Rhet. lib. 1. cap. 5.

we dare not disgrace our worldly Superiours with offering unto them such refuse as we bring unto God himself, we shew plainly that our acknowledgement of his Greatnes is but fained, in heart we fear him not so much as we dread them. ᵇ *If ye offer the blind for sacrifice, is it not evil? Offer it now unto thy Prince; Will he be content or accept thy person, saith the Lord of Hosts? Cursed be the Deceiver which hath in his Flock a Male, and having made a Vow, sacrificeth unto the Lord a corrupt thing: For I am a great King saith the Lord of Hosts.* Should we hereupon frame a Rule, that what form of speech or behaviour soever is fit for Suters in a Princes

Note in left margin: b Mal: 1. 8. 14.

Court,

Court, the same and no other beseemeth us in our Prayers to Almighty God?

35. But in vain we labour to perswade them that any thing can take away the tediousness of Prayer, except it be brought to the very same both measure and forme which themselves assigne. Whatsoever therefore our Liturgy hath more than theirs, under one devised pretence or other they cut it off. We have of Prayers for earthly things in their opinion too great a number; so oft to rehearse the Lords Prayer in so small a time, is as they think a loss of time, the peoples praying after the Lords Prayer.

The number of our Prayers for earthly things, and our oft rehearsing of the Lords Prayer.

Minister, they say, both wasteth time, and also maketh an unpleasant sound; the *Psalmes*, they would not have to be made (as they are) a part of our Common Prayer, not to be sung or said by turns, nor such Musick to be used with them; those Evangelical *Hymns* they allow not to stand in our Liturgy; the *Letany*, the *Creed of Athanasius*, the *Sentence of Glory*, wherewith we use to conclude *Psalmes*, these things they cancell, as having been instituted in regard of occasions peculiar to the times of old, and as being therefore now superfluous. Touching Prayers for things earthly, we ought not to think that the Church hath set down so many of them without cause. They peradventure, which find this fault, are of the same affection with *Solomon*, so that if God should offer to grant them whatsoever they ask, they would neither crave riches, nor length of dayes, nor yet victory over their Enemies, but only an understanding heart, for which cause themselves having Eagles wings, are offended to see others flye so neer the ground. But the tender kindness of the Church of God it very well beseemeth, to

I can make no Geometrical and exact measure, but verily I believe there shall be found more than a third part of the Prayers, which are not *Psalmes* and Texts of Scripture, spent in praying for, and praying against the commodities and incommodities of this life, which is contrary to all the Arguments or Contents of the Prayers of the Church set down in the Scripture, and especially of our Saviour Christs Prayer, by the which ours ought to be directed. *T.C. lib.1. p.* 136. What a reason is this, we must repeat the Lords Prayer oftentimes, therefore oftentimes in halfe an houre, and one in the neck of another? Our Saviour Christ doth not there give a prescript Forme of Prayer whereunto he bindeth us: but giveth us a Rule and Square to frame all our Prayers by. I know it is necessary to Pray, and Pray often. I know also that in a few words it is impossible for any man to frame so pithy a Prayer, and I confess that the Church doth well in concluding their prayers with the Lords Prayer: But I stand upon this, that there is no necessity laid upon us to use these very words and no more. *T.C. l.1. p.219.*

help the weaker sort which are by so great oddes moe in number, although some few of the perfecter and stronger may be therewith for a time displeased. Ignorant we are not, that of such as resorted to our Saviour Christ being present on earth, there came not any unto him with better success for the benefit of their souls everlasting happiness, than they whose bodily necessities gave them the first occasion to seek relief, where they saw willingness and ability of doing every way good unto all. The graces of the Spirit are much more precious than worldly benefits; our ghostly evils of greater importance than any harm which the body feeleth. Therefore our desires to heaven-ward should both in measure and number no less exceed, than their glorious Object doth every way excell in value. These things are true and plain in the eye of a perfect judgement. But yet it must be withal considered, that the greatest part of the world are they which be farthest from perfection. Such being better able by sense to discern the wants of this present life, than by spiritual capacity to apprehend things above sense, which tend to their happiness in the world to come, are in that respect the more apt to apply their minds even with hearty affection and zeal at the least unto those branches of publick prayer, wherein their own particular is moved. And by this mean there stealeth upon them a double benefit; first, because that good affection, which things of smaller account have once set on work, is by so much the more easily raised higher; and secondly, in that the very custome of seeking so particular aid and relief at the hands of God, doth by a secret contradiction withdraw them from endeavouring to help themselves by those wicked shifts, which they know can never have his allowance, whose assistance their prayer seeketh. These multiplyed petitions of worldly things in prayer have therefore, besides their direct use, a Service whereby the Church under-hand, through a kind of heavenly fraud, taketh therewith the souls of men as with certain baites. If then their calculation be true (for so they reckon) that a full third of our prayers be allotted unto earthly benefits, for which our Saviour in his platforme hath appointed but one petition amongst seven, the difference is without any great disagreement; we respecting what men are, and doing that which is meet in regard of the common imperfection, our Lord contrariwise proposing the most absolute

a *Præmiſſa le-gitima & or-dinaria oratio-ne, quaſi funda-mento, acciden-tium jus eſt de-ſideriorum, jus eſt ſuperſtruen-di extrinſecus petitiones. Ter-tul. de Orat.

abſolute proportion that can be in mens deſires, the very higheſt marke whereat we are able to aime. For which cauſe alſo our cuſtome is both to place it in the font of our prayers as a Guide, and to adde it in the end of ſome principal limbs or parts, as a complement which fully perfecteth whatſoever may be defective in the reſt. Twice we rehearſe it ordinarily, and oftner as occaſion requireth more ſo-lemnity or length in the forme of Divine Service, not miſtruſting, till theſe new curioſities ſprang up, that ever any man would think our labour herein miſ-ſpent, the time waſtfully conſumed, and the office it ſelf made worſe, by ſo repeating that which otherwiſe would more hardly be made familiar to the ſimpler ſort; for the good of whoſe Souls there is not in Chriſtian Religion any thing of like continual uſe and force throughout every hour and moment of their whole lives. I mean not only becauſe prayer, but becauſe this very prayer is of ſuch efficacy and neceſſity: for that our Saviour did but ſet men a bare example how to contrive or deviſe pray-ers of their own, and no way binde them to uſe this, is no doubt an Error, b *John* the *Baptiſts* Diſciples, which had been always brought up in the boſom of Gods Church from the time of their firſt Infancy, till they came to the School of *John*, were not ſo brutiſh, that they could be ignorant how to call upon the Name of God, but of their Maſter they had received a forme of Prayer amongſt themſelves, which forme none did uſe ſaving his Diſciples, ſo that by it as by a mark of ſpecial difference they were known from others. And of this the Apoſtles having taken notice, they requeſt that as *John* had taught his, ſo Chriſt would likewiſe teach them to pray. *Tertullian* and S. *Auguſtin* do for that cauſe terme it, *Orationem legi-timam*, the Prayer which Chriſts own Law hath tyed his Church to uſe in the ſame preſcript forme of words wherewith he himſelf did deliver it, and therefore what part of the World ſoever we fall into, if Chriſtian Religion have been there recei-ved, the ordinary uſe of this very Prayer hath with equal continuance accompanied the ſame, as one of the principal and moſt material duties of honour done to Jeſus Chriſt. Seeing *that we have* (ſaith S. *Cyprian*) *an Advocate with the Father for our ſins, when we that have ſinned come to ſeek for pardon, let us alledge unto God the words which our Advocate hath taught. For ſith his promiſe is our plain warrant, that in his Name what we ask we ſhall receive, muſt we not needs much the rather obtain that for which we ſue, if not only his Name do countenance, but alſo his ſpeech preſent our requeſts?* Though men ſhould ſpeak with the tongues of Angels, yet words ſo pleaſing to the ears of God, as thoſe which the Son of God himſelf hath compoſed, were not poſſible for men to frame. He therefore which made us to live, hath alſo taught us to pray, to the end that ſpeaking unto the Father in the Sonnes own preſcript form without ſcholy or gloſs of ours, we may be ſure that we utter nothing which God will either diſallow or deny. Other Prayers we uſe many be-ſides this, and this oftner than any other; although not tyed ſo to do by any Com-mandement of Scripture, yet moved with ſuch conſiderations as have been before ſet down: the cauſeleſs diſlike whereof which others have conceived, is no ſuffici-ent reaſon for us, as much as once to forbear in any place: a thing which uttered with true devotion and zeal of heart, affordeth to God himſelf that glory, that aid to the weakeſt ſort of men, to the moſt perfect, that ſolid comfort which is un-ſpeakable.

b *Luke* 11. 1.

c *Cypr. in Orat. Dom.*

The peoples ſaying after the Miniſter. Ano-ther fault is, that all the peo-ple are appoint-ed in divers pla-ces to ſay after the Miniſter, whereby not only the time is unprofitably waſted, and a

36. With our Lords Prayer they would find no fault, ſo that they might per-ſwade us to uſe it before or after Sermons only (becauſe ſo their manner is) and not (as all Chriſtian people have been of old accuſtomed) inſert it ſo often into the Li-turgie. But the peoples cuſtome to repeat any thing after the Miniſter, they utter-ly miſlike. Twice we appoint that the words which the Miniſter firſt pronounceth, the whole Congregation ſhall repeat after him. As firſt in the publick Confeſſion of ſins, and again in rehearſal of our Lords Prayer, preſently after the bleſſed Sa-crament of his Body and Bloud received. A thing no way offenſive, no way unfit or unſeemly to be done, although it had been ſo appointed oftner than with us it is. confuſed noiſe of the people (one ſpeaking after another) cauſed, but an Opinion bred in their heads that thoſe only be their Prayers which they pronounce with their own mouths after the Miniſter, otherwiſe than the order which is left to the Church doth bear, 1 *Cor.* 14. 16. and otherwiſe than *Juſtin Martyr* ſheweth the cuſtome of the Church to have been in his time. T. C. *lib.* 1. *pag.* 139. and *Lib.* 3. *pag.* 211, 212, 213.

But

But surely with so good reason it standeth in those two places, that otherwise to order it were not in all respects so well. Could there be any thing devised better, than that we all at our first access unto God by Prayer, should acknowledge meekly our sins, and that not only in heart, but with tongue, all which are present being made eare-witnesses, even of every mans distinct and deliberate assent unto each particular branch of a common Indictment drawn against our selves? How were it possible, that the Church should any way else with such ease and certainty provide, that none of her Children may as *Adam* dissemble that wretchedness, the penitent confession whereof is so necessary a Preamble, especially to Common Prayer? In like manner, if the Church did ever devise a thing fit and convenient, what more than this, that when together we have all received those Heavenly Mysteries wherein Christ imparteth himself unto us, and giveth visible testification of our blessed Communion with him, we should in hatred of all Heresies, Factions and Schismes, the Pastor as a Leader, the people as willing followers of him step by step, declare openly our selves united as Brethren in one, [a] by offering up with all our hearts and tongues that most effectual Supplication, wherein he unto whom we offer it, hath himself not only comprehended all our necessities, but in such sort also framed every Petition, as might most naturally serve for many, and doth though not alwayes require, yet alwayes import a multitude of speakers together? For which cause Communicants have ever used it, and we at that time by the form of our very utterance do shew we use it; yea, every word and syllable of it, as Communicants. In the rest we observe that custome whereunto [b] S. *Paul* alludeth, and whereof the Fathers of the Church in their Writings make often mention, to shew indefinitely what was done, but not universally to binde for ever all Prayers unto one only fashion of utterance. The reasons which we have alledged, induce us to think it still *a good work,* which they in their pensive care for the well bestowing of time account *waste.* As for unpleasantness of sound, if it happen, the good of mens Souls doth either deceive our ears that we note it not, or arme them with patience to endure it. We are not so nice as to cast away a sharp Knife, because the edge of it may sometimes grate. And such subtile opinions as few but Utopians are likely to fall into, we in this Climate do not greatly fear.

37. The complaint which they make about Psalms and Hymns, might as well be over-past without any answer, as it is without any cause brought forth. But our desire is to content them if it may be, and to yield them a just reason even of the least things wherein undeservedly they have but as much as dreamed or suspected that we do amiss. They seem sometimes so to speak, as if it greatly offended them, that such Hymns and Psalms as are Scripture, should in Common Prayer be otherwise used than the rest of the Scripture is wont; sometime displeased they are at the artificial Musick which we adde unto Psalms of this kind or of any other nature else; sometime the plainest and the most intelligible rehearsal of them yet they favour not, because it is done by Interlocution, and with a mutual return of Sentences from side to side. They are not ignorant what difference there is between other parts of Scripture and Psalms. The choice and flower of [*] all things profitable in other Books, the Psalms do both more briefly contain, and more movingly also express, by reason of that Poetical Forme wherewith they are written. The ancients when they speak of the Book of Psalms, use to fall into large Discourses, shewing how this part above the rest doth of purpose set forth and celebrate all the considerations and operations which belong to God; it magnifieth the holy meditations and actions of divine men, it is of things heavenly an universal declaration, working in them whose hearts God inspireth with the due consideration thereof, an habit or disposition of mind whereby they are made fit Vessels both for receipt and for delivery of whatsoever spiritual perfection. What is there necessary for man to know which the Psalms are not able to teach? They are to beginners an easie and familiar Introduction, a mighty augmentation of all vertue and knowledge in such as are entred before, a strong confirmation to the most perfect amongst others. Heroical Magnanimity, exquisite Justice, grave Moderation, exact Wisdom, Repentance unfained, unwearied Patience, the Mysteries of God, the Sufferings of Christ,

T. C. l. 3. p. 206. [*] ἡ πνευματικὴ τῆς πανιέρων ὑμνολογία. *Dionys. Hierar. Eccles. c. 3.*

the

Sidenotes:
[a] Τίς γὰρ ἔτι ἐχθρὸν ἡγήσεται τὸν κοινωνίας ταύτης μεθ᾽ οὗ μίαν ἀφῆκε πρὸς Θεὸν τὴν φωνήν. Basil. Praef. in Psal.

[b] 1 *Cor.* 14.16.

Our manner of reading the Psalms otherwise than the rest of the Scripture. They have alwayes the same prefit to be studied in, to be read, and preached upon, which other Scriptures have, and this above the rest, that they are to be sung. But to make daily Prayers of them handsomely over-head, or otherwise than the present estate wherein we be doth agree with the matter contained in them, is an abusing of them,

the Terrors of Wrath, the Comforts of Grace, the Works of Providence over this World, and the promised Joyes of that World which is to come, all good necessarily to be either known, or done, or had, this one Celestial Fountain yieldeth. Let there be any grief or disease incident to the soul of man, any wound or sickness named, for which there is not in this Treasure-house a present comfortable remedy at all times ready to be found. Hereof it is that we covet to make the Psalms especially familiar unto all. This is the very cause why we iterate the Psalms oftner than any other part of Scripture besides, the cause wherefore we inure the people together with their Minister, and not the Minister alone, to read them as other parts of Scripture he doth.

Of Musick with Psalms. 38. Touching Musical Harmony, whether by Instrument or by Voyce, it being but of high and low in sounds a due proportionable disposition, such notwithstanding is the force thereof, and so pleasing effects it hath in that very part of man which is most divine, that some have been thereby induced to think that the soul it self by nature is, or hath in it harmony. A thing which delighteth all Ages and beseemeth all States; a thing as seasonable in grief as in joy; as decent being added unto actions of greatest weight and solemnity, as being used when men most sequester themselves from action. The reason hereof is an admirable facility which Musick hath to express and represent to the mind, more inwardly than any other sensible mean, the very standing, rising, and falling, the very steps and inflections every way, the turns and varieties of all passions whereunto the mind is subject: yea, so to imitate them, that whether it resemble unto us the same state wherein our minds already are, or a clean contrary, we are not more contentedly by the one confirmed, than changed and led away by the other. In Harmony the very Image and Character even of Vertue and Vice is perceived, the mind delighted with their Resemblances, and brought, by having them often iterated, into a love of the things themselves. For which cause there is nothing more contagious and pestilent than some kinds of Harmony; than some nothing more strong and potent unto good. And that there is such a difference of one kind from another, we need no proof but our own experience, in as much as we are at the hearing of some more inclined unto sorrow and heaviness: of some more modified and softned in mind; one kind apter to stay and settle us, another to move and stir our affections; there is that draweth to a marvellous grave and sober mediocrity, there is also that carrieth as it were into extasies, filling the mind with an heavenly joy, and for the time, in a manner, severing it from the body. So that although we lay altogether aside the consideration of Ditty or Matter, the very harmony of sounds being framed in due sort, and carried from the ear to the spiritual faculties of our souls, is by a native puissance and efficacy greatly available to bring to a perfect temper whatsoever is there troubled, apt as well to quicken the spirits, as to allay that which is too eager, sovereign against melancholy and despair, forcible to draw forth tears of devotion, if the mind be such as can yield them, able both to move and to moderate all affections. The Prophet *David* having therefore singular knowledge not in Poetry alone but in Musick also, judged them both to be things most necessary for the House of God, left behind him to that purpose a number of divinely indited Poems, and was farther the Author of adding unto Poetry melody in publick prayer, melody both vocal and instrumental for the raising up of mens hearts, and the sweetning of their affections towards God. In which considerations the Church of Christ doth likewise at this present day retain it as an ornament to Gods service, and an help to our own devotion. They which under pretence of the Law Ceremonial abrogated require the abrogation of instrumental Musick, approving nevertheless the use of vocal melody to remain, must shew some reason wherefore the one should be thought a Legal Ceremony, and not the other. In Church-Musick curiosity and ostentation of Art, wanton, or light, or unsutable harmony, such as only pleaseth the ear, and doth not naturally serve to the very kind and degree of those impressions which the matter that goeth with it leaveth, or is apt to leave in mens minds, doth rather blemish and disgrace that we do, than adde either beauty or furtherance unto it. On the other side these faults prevented, the force and efficacy of the thing it self, when it drowneth not utterly, but fitly suteth with mat-

ter

ter altogether founding to the praise of God, is in truth most admirable, and doth much edifie, if not the understanding, because it teacheth not, yet surely the Affection, because therein it worketh much. They must have hearts very dry and tough, from whom the melody of Psalms doth not sometime draw that wherein a mind religiously affected delighteth. Be it as *Rabanus Maurus* observeth, that at the first the Church in this exercise was more simple and plain than we are, that their singing was little more than only a melodious kind of pronunciation, that the custome which we now use was not instituted so much for their cause which are spiritual, as to the end that into grosser and heavier minds whom bare words do not easily move, the sweetness of melody might make some entrance for good things. Saint *Basil* himself acknowledging as much, did not think that from such inventions the least jot of estimation and credit thereby should be derogated : " *For* (saith he) *whereas the Holy Spirit saw that mankind is unto vertue hardly drawn, and that righteousness is the less accounted of, by reason of the proneness of our affections to that which delighteth, it pleased the wisdome of the same Spirit to borrow from melody that pleasure, which mingled with Heavenly mysteries, causeth the smoothness and softness of that which toucheth the ear, to convey as it were by stealth the treasure of good things into mans mind. To this purpose were those harmonious tunes of Psalms devised for us, that they which are either in years but young, or touching perfection of vertue as yet not grown to ripeness, might, when they think they sing, learn. O the wise conceit of that Heavenly Teacher, which hath by his skill found out a way, that by doing those things wherein we delight, we may also learn that whereby we profit!*

39 And if the Prophet *David* did think that the very meeting of men together, and their accompanying one another to the House of God, should make the bond of their love insoluble, and tie them in a league of inviolable amity, *Psalm* 54. 14. how much more may we judge it reasonable to hope, that the like effects may grow in each of the people towards other, i them all towards their Pastor, and in their Pastor towards every of them, between whom there daily and interchangeably pass in the hearing of God himself, and in the presence of his Holy Angels, so many Heavenly Acclamations, Exultations, Provocations, Petitions, Songs of comfort, Psalms of praise and thanksgiving, in all which particulars, as when the Pastor maketh their sutes, and they with one voice testifie a general assent thereunto ; or when he joyfully beginneth, and they with like alacrity follow, dividing between them the sentences wherewith they strive which shall much shew his own, and stir up others zeal to the glory of that God whose name they magnifie ; or when he proposeth unto God their necessities, and they their own requests for relief in every of them ; or when he lifteth up his voice like a trumpet, to proclaim unto them the Laws of God, they adjoyning, though not as *Israel* did, by way of generality a cheerful promise, ⁿ *All that the Lord hath commanded we will do*, yet that which God doth no less approve, that which savoreth more of meekness, that which testifieth rather a feeling knowledge of our common imbecility, unto the several branches thereof, several, lowly, and humble requests for grace at the merciful hands of God, to perform the thing which is commanded ; or when they wish reciprocally each others ghostly happiness ; or when he by exhortation raiseth them up, and they by protestation of their readiness declare, he speaketh not in vain unto them ; these interlocutory formes of speech what are they but most effectual, partly testifications, and partly inflammations of all piety ? When and how this custom of singing by course came up in the Church, it is not certainly known. ᶜ *Socrates* maketh *Ignatius* the Bishop of *Antioch* in *Syria* the first beginner thereof, even under the Apostles themselves.

But

Of singing or saying Psalms and other parts of Common Prayer, wherein the people and Minister answer one another by course. For the singing of Psalms by course and side after side, although it be very ancient, yet it is not commendable, and so much the more to be suspected, for that the Devil hath gone about to get it so great authority, partly by deriving it from *Ignatius* time, and partly in making the world believe that this came from H aven, and that the Angels were heard to sing after this sort. Which as it is a meer fable, so is it confuted by Historiographers, whereof some ascribe the beginning of this to *Damasus* some other unto *Flavianus* and *Diodorus. T. C. lib.* 1. p. 203.

ᵇ *Exod.* 19.8. 24. 3. *Deut.* 5. 17. 26.17. *Josh.* 24. 16.

ᶜ *Socrat. Hist. Eccles. l.6.c.8.*

ᵃ Ἐπειδὴ γὰρ εἶδε τὸ πνεῦμα τὸ ἅγιον δυσάγωγον πρὸς ἀρετὴν τὸ γένος τῶν ἀνθρώπων ; καὶ διὰ τὸ πρὸς ἡδονὴν ἐπιρρεπῶς τὸ ὀρθὸ βί8 καταμελοῦντας ἡμᾶς, τί ποιεῖ ; τὸ ἐκ τῆς μελωδίας τερπνὸν τοῖς δόγμασιν ἐγκατέμιξεν ἵνα τῷ προσηνεῖ καὶ λείῳ τῆς ἀκοῆς τὸ ἐκ τῶν λόγων ὠφέλιμον λανθανόντως ὑποδεξώμεθα. Διὰ τῦτο τὰ ἐναρμόνια ταῦτα μέλη τῶν ψαλμῶν ἡμῖν ἐπινενόηται, ἵνα οἱ παῖδες τὴν ἡλικίαν ἢ καὶ ὅλως οἱ νεαροὶ τὸ ἦθο τῷ μὲν δοκεῖν μελωδῶσι τῇ δὲ ἀληθείᾳ τὰς ψυχὰς ἐκπαιδεύωνται· ὧ τῆς σοφῆς ἐπινοίας τῦ διδασκάλου ὁμῦ τε ᾄδειν ἡμᾶς καὶ τὰ λυσιτελῆ μανθάνειν μηχανωμένε. *Basil. in Psal.*

a *Theod. lib. 2. cap. 24.*

b *Platin. in vita Damasi.*

c *Bene mari plerunque comparatur Ecclesia, qua primo ingredientis populi agmine totius vestibulis undas vomit; deinde in oratione totius plebis tanquam undis undarum fragor resultat.* Hexam. l.2.c.5.

d *Basil.Epi.63.*

e *Plin.secund. Epist.*

f *Exod.*15.1.21

g *Isai.* 6. 3.

But against *Socrates* they set the authority of a *Theodoret*, who draweth the original of it from *Antioch*, as *Socrates* doth; howbeit ascribing the invention to others, *Flavian* and *Diodore*, men which constantly stood in defence of the Apostolick Faith, against the Bishop of that Church, *Leontius*, a favourer of the Arrians. Against both *Socrates* and *Theodoret*, b *Platina* is brought as a witness, to testifie that *Damasus* Bishop of *Rome* began it in his time. Of the Latine Church it may be true which *Platina* saith. And therefore the eldest of that Church which maketh any mention thereof, is c Saint *Ambrose*, Bishop of *Millan* at the same time when *Damasus* was of *Rome*. Amongst the Grecians d Saint *Basil* having brought it into his Church before they of *Neocasarea* used it, *Sabellius* the Heretick and *Marcellus* took occasion thereat to incense the Churches against him, as being an Author of new devices in the Service of God. Whereupon, to avoid the opinion of novelty and singularity, he alledgeth for that which he himself did, the example of the Churches of *Egypt, Lybia, Thebes, Palestina, Tharabians, Phenicians, Syrians, Mesopotamians*, and in a manner all that reverenced the custome of singing of Psalms together. If the *Syrians* had it then before *Basil, Antioch* the Mother-Church of those parts must needs have used it before *Basil*, and consequently before *Damasus*. The question is then how long before, and whether so long that *Ignatius*, or as ancient as *Ignatius*, may be probably thought the first Inventors. *Ignatius* in *Trajan's* days suffered Martyrdom. And e of the Churches in *Pontus* and *Bithynia*, to *Trajane* the Emperour his own Vicegerent there affirmeth, that the only crime he knew of them, was, they used to meet together at a certain day, and to praise Christ with Hymnes as a God, *secum invicem*, one to another amongst themselves. Which for any thing we know to the contrary, might be the self-same forme which *Philo Judaus* expresseth, declaring how the *Essens* were accustomed with Hymnes and Psalms to honour God, sometime all exalting their voices together in one, and sometime one part answering another, wherein, as he thought, they swerved not much from the pattern of *Moses* and f *Miriam*. Whether *Ignatius* did at any time hear the Angels praising God after that sort, or no, what matter is it? If *Ignatius* did not, yet one which must be with us of greater authority did. g *I saw the Lord* (saith the Prophet *Esay*) *on an high Throne, The Seraphims stood upon it*, one cryed to another, *saying, Holy, Holy, Holy, Lord God of Hosts, the whole world is full of his glory*. But whosoever were the Author, Whatsoever the Time, whensoever the Example of beginning this custome in the Church of Christ, sith we are wont to suspect things only before tryal, and afterwards either to approve them as good, or if we find them evil, accordingly to judge of them, their counsel must needs seem very unseasonable, who advise men now to suspect that wherewith the World hath had, by their own account, twelve hundred years acquaintance, and upwards, enough to take away suspition and jealousie. Men know by this time, if ever they will know, whether it be good or evil which hath been so long retained. As for the Devil, which way it should greatly benefit him to have this manner of singing Psalms accounted an invention of *Ignatius*, or an imitation of the Angels of Heaven we do not well understand. But we very well see in them who thus plead, a wonderful celerity of discourse. For perceiving at the first but only some cause of suspition, and fear lest it should be evil, they are presently in one and the self-same breath resolved, that h *what beginning soever it had, there is no possibility it should be good*. The potent arguments which did thus suddenly break in upon them and overcome them, are, first, that it is not unlawful for the people all joyntly to praise God in singing of Psalms: secondly, that they are not any where forbidden by the Law of God to sing every Verse of the whole Psalm, both with heart and voice quite and clean throughout: thirdly, that it cannot be understood what is sung after our manner. Of which three, for as much as lawfulness to sing one way proveth not another way inconvenient, the former two are true allegations, but they lack strength to accomplish their desire; the third

h From whence soever it came, it cannot be good, considering that when it is granted that all the people may praise God (as it is in singing of Psalms) then this ought not to be restrained unto a few; and where it is lawful both with heart and voice to sing the whole Psalm, there it is not meet that they should sing but the one half with their heart and voice, and the other with their heart only. For where they may both with heart and voice sing, there the heart is not enough. Therefore besides the incommodity which cometh this way, in that being tossed after this sort, men cannot understand what is sung, those other two inconveniences come of this forme of singing, and therefore it is banished in all reformed Churches. T.C. lib.1.pag.203.

so strong that it might perswade, if the truth thereof were not doubtful. And shall this inforce us to banish a thing which all Christian Churches in the World have received, a thing which so many ages have held; a thing which the most approved Councels and Laws have so oftentimes ratified; a thing which was never found to have any inconvenience in it; a thing which always heretofore the best men and wisest Governours of Gods people did think they could never commend enough; a thing which as *Basil* was perswaded, did both strengthen the Meditation of those holy words which were uttered in that sort, and serve also to make attentive, and to raise up the hearts of men; a thing whereunto Gods people of old did resort with hope and thirst, that thereby especially their souls might be edified; a thing which filleth the mind with comfort and heavenly delight, stirreth up flagrant desires and affections correspondent unto that which the words contain, allayeth all kind of base and earthly cogitations, banisheth and driveth away those evil secret suggestions which our invisible Enemy is always apt to minister, watreth the heart to the end it may fructifie, maketh the vertuous in trouble full of magnanimity and courage, serveth as a most approved remedy against all doleful and heavy accidents which befall men in this present life: To conclude, so fitly accordeth with the Apostles own exhortation, *Speak to your selves in Psalms and Hymns, and Spiritual Songs, making melody, and singing to the Lord in your hearts;* that surely there is more cause to fear least the want thereof be a mayme, than the use a blemish to the Service of God. It is not our meaning, that what we attribute unto the Psalms should be thought to depend altogether on that only form of singing or reading them by course, as with us the manner is; but the end of our speech is to shew, that because the Fathers of the Church, with whom the self-same custome was so many ages ago in use, have uttered all these things concerning the fruit which the Church of God did then reap, observing that another form, it may be justly avouched that we our selves retaining it, and besides it also the other more newly and not unfruitfully devised, do neither want that good which the later intention can afford, nor lose any thing of that for which the Ancients so oft and so highly commend the former. Let novelty therefore in this give over endless contradictions, and let ancient custome prevail. ^a *a Ephes.5.19.*

40. We have already given cause sufficient for the great conveniency and use of reading the Psalms oftner than other Scriptures. Of reading or singing likewise *Magnificat, Benedictus,* and *Nunc dimittis,* oftner than the rest of the Psalms, the causes are no whit less reasonable; so that if the one may very well monethly, the other may as well even daily be iterated. They are Songs which concern us so much more than the Songs of *David,* as the Gospel toucheth us more than the Law, the New Testament than the Old. And if the Psalms for the excellency of their use, deserve to be oftner repeated than they are, but that the multitude of them permitteth not any oftner repetition, what disorder is it if these few Evangelical Hymns which are in no respect less worthy, and may be by reason of their paucity imprinted with much more ease in all mens memories, be for that cause every day rehearsed? In our own behalf it is convenient and orderly enough, that both they and we make day by day prayers and supplications the very same; why not as fit and convenient to magnifie the Name of God day by day with certain the very self-same Psalms of praise and thanksgiving? Either let them not allow the one, or else cease to reprove the other. For the ancient received use of intermingling Hymns and Psalms with divine readings, enough hath been written. And if any may fitly serve unto that purpose, how should it better have been devised, than that a competent number of the Old being first read, these of the New should succeed in the place where now they are set? In which place notwithstanding there is joyned with *Benedictus* the hundredth Psalm; with *Magnificat,* the ninety eight, the sixty seventh with *Nunc dimittis,* and in every of them the choice left free for the Minister to use indifferently the one or the other. Seeing therefore they pretend no quarrel at other Psalms, which are in like manner appointed also to be daily read, why do these so much offend and displease their taste? They are the first gratulations wherewith our Lord and Saviour was joyfully received at his entrance into the world, by such as in their hearts, arms, and very bowels imbraced him; being prophetical discoveries of

Of Magnificat, Benedictus, and Nunc dimittis. These thanksgivings were made by occasion of certain particular benefits, and are no more to be used for ordinary Prayers, than the Ave-Maria. So that both for this cause and the other before alledged of the Psalms, it is not convenient to make ordinary prayers of them. T.C.l.3.p.108.

Chrift already prefent, whofe future coming the other Pfalms did but fore-fignifie; they are againft the obftinate incredulity of the Jews, the moft luculent teftimonies that Chriftian Religion hath; yea the only facred Hymns they are that Chriftianity hath peculiar unto it felf, the other being Songs too of praife and thankfgiving, but Songs wherewith as we ferve God, fo the Jew likewife. And whereas they tell us thefe Songs were fit for that purpofe, when *Simeon* and *Zachary*, and the bleffed *Virgin* uttered them, but cannot fo be to us which have not received like benefit; fhould they not remember how exprefly *Ezechias* amongft many other good things is commended for this alfo, * that the praifes of God were through his appointment daily fet forth, by ufing in publique divine Service the Songs of *David* and *Afaph* unto that very end? Either there wanted wife men to give *Ezechias* advice, and to inform him of that which in his cafe was as true as it is in ours, namely that without fome inconvenience and diforder he could not appoint thofe Pfalms to be ufed as ordinary Prayers, feeing that a'though they were Songs of thankfgiving, fuch as *David* and *Afaph* had fpecial occafion to ufe, yet not fo the whole Church and people afterwards, whom like occafions did not befall: or elfe *Ezechias* was perfwaded as we are, that the praifes of God in the mouths of his Saints, are not fo reftrained to their own particular, but that others may both conveniently and fruitfully ufe them, firft, becaufe the myftical communion of all faithfull men is fuch as maketh every one to be interefted in thofe precious bleffings, which any one of them receiveth at Gods hands: Secondly, becaufe when any thing is fpoken to extol the goodnefs of God, whofe mercy indureth for ever, albeit the very particular occafion whereupon it rifeth do come no more, yet the Fountain continuing the fame, and yeilding other new effects which are but only in fome fort proportionable, a fmall refemblance between the benefits which we and others have received may ferve to make the fame words of praife and thankfgiving fit, though not equally in all circumftances fit for both; a cleer demonftration whereof we have in all the Ancient Fathers Commentaries and Meditations upon the Pfalms: laft of all, becaufe even when there is not as much as the fhew of any refemblance, neverthelefs by often ufing their words in fuch manner, our minds are daily more and more inured with their affections.

* 1 Chron. 29.30.

Of the Letany. 41 The publique eftate of the Church of God amongft the Jews hath had many, rare and extraordinary Occurrents, which alfo were occafions of fundry *open folemnities and offices, whereby the people, did with general confent make fhew of correfpondent affection towards God. The like duties appear ufual in the ancient Church of Chrift, by that which *Tertullian* fpeaketh of Chriftian women matching themfelves with Infidels. *She cannot content the Lord with performance of his difcipline, that hath at her fide a Vaffal whom Satan hath made his vice-agent to crofs whatfoever the faithful fhould do. If her prefence be required at the time of Station or ftanding prayer, he chargeth her at no time but that to be with him in his baths; if a fafting day come, he hath on that day a banquet to make; if there be caufe for the Church to go forth in folemn Proceffion, his whole family have fuch bufinefs come upon them that no one can be fpared.* Thefe *Proceffions,* as it feemeth, were firft begun for the interring of holy Martyrs, and the vifiting of thofe places where they were in ombed. Which thing the name it felf applyed by *Heathens unto the office of Exequies, and partly the fpeeches of fome of the ancients delivered concerning

We pray for the avoiding of thofe dangers which are nothing nea us; as from Lightning and Thundring in the miaft of Winter, from Storm and Tempeft when the weather is moft fair and the Seas moft calm. It is true that upon fome urgent calamity a prayer may, and ought to be framed, which may beg either the commodity, for want whereof the Church is in diftrefs, or the turning away of that mifchief which either approcheth, or is a ready upon it: but to make thofe prayers which are for the prefent time and danger, ordinary and daily prayers, I cannot hitherto fee any, either Scripture, or example of the Primitive Church. And here for the fimples fake I will fet down after what this abufe crept into the Church. There was one *Mamercus* Bifhop of *Vienna*, which in the time of great Earthquakes, which were in *France*, inftituted certain fupplications, which the Grecians (and we of them) call the Letany. which concerned that matter: there is no doubt; but as other difcommodities rofe in other Countries; they likewife had prayers accordingly. Now Pope Gregory either made himfelf, or gathered the Supplications that were made againft the calamities of every Country, and made of them a great Letany or Supplication, as *Platina* calleth it, and gave it to be ufed in all Churches: which thing albeit all Churches might do for the time, in refpect of the cafe of the calamity which the Churches fuffered, yet there is no caufe why it fhould be perpetual that was ordained but far a time; and why all Lands fhould pray to be delivered from the incommodities that fome Land hath been troubled with.

T C l .p 127. a Exod.15.20. Wifd.10.20. 2 Sam. 6.2. 1 Chr.13.5. 2 Chr.20.3. Joel 2.15. b Tertul. lib. 2. ad Uxor. c Terent. And.

cerning

cerning ª Chriſtian Proceſſions, partly alſo the very droſs which ſuperſtition thereunto added, I mean, the Cuſtom of invocating Saints in Proceſſions heretofore uſual, do ſtrongly inſinuate. And as things invented to one purpoſe are by uſe eaſily
converted to ᵇ more, it grew, that Supplications, wᵗʰ this ſolemnity for the appeaſing of Gods wrath, and the averting of publike evils, were of the Greek Church
termed ᶜ *Litanies Rogations* of the Latine. To the people of *Vienna* (*Mamercus* being their Biſhop above 450 years after Chriſt) there befell many things, the ſudden-
neſs and ſtrangeneſs whereof ſo amazed the hearts of all men, that the City they began to forſake as a place which Heaven did threaten with imminent ruine. It beſeemed not the perſon of ſo grave a Prelate to be either utterly without counſel, as
the reſt were, or in a common perplexity to ſhew himſelf alone ſecure. Wherefore
as many as remained, he earneſtly exhorteth to prevent portended calamities, uſing
thoſe virtuous and holy means wherewith others in like caſe have prevailed with
God. To which purpoſe he perfecteth the *Rogations* or *Letanies* before in uſe, and
and addere unto them that which the preſent neceſſity required. Their good ſucceſs moved ᵈ *Sidonius* Biſhop of *Averna* to uſe the ſame ſo corrected *Rogations* at
ſuch time as he and his people were after afflicted with Famine, and beſieged with potent Adverſaries. For till the empty name of the Empire came to be ſetled in *Charles*
the great, the fall of the Romans huge Dominion concurring with other univerſal
evils, cauſed thoſe times to be dayes of much affliction and trouble throughout the
world. So that *Rogations* or *Litanies* were then the very ſtrength, ſtay, and comfort
of Gods Church. Whereupon in the year five hundred and ſix, it was by the ᵉ Councel of *Aurelia* decreed, that the whole Church ſhould beſtow yearly at the Feaſt of
Pentecoſt three days in that kind of proceſſionary ſervice. About half an hundred years
after, to the end that the Latine Churches, which all obſerved this cuſtom, might not
vary in the order and form of thoſe great *Litanies* which were ſo ſolemnly every
where exerciſed; it was thought convenient by *Gregory* the firſt, and the beſt of that
name, to draw the flower of them all into one. But this iron began at length to gather ruſt; Which thing the ᶠ *Synod* of *Colen* ſaw, and in part redreſt within that Province, neither denying the neceſſary uſe for which ſuch *Litanies* ſerve, wherein Gods
clemency and mercy is deſired by publike ſuit, to the end that plagues, deſtructions,
calamities, famines, wars, and all other the like adverſities, which for our manifold
ſins we have alwaies cauſe to fear, may be turned away from us and prevented
through his grace; nor yet diſſembling the great abuſe whereunto as ſundry other
things, ſo this had grown by mens improbity and malice; to whom that which was
deviſed for the appeaſing of Gods diſpleaſure, gave opportunity of committing
things which juſtly kindled his wrath. For remedy whereof it was then thought better, that theſe and all other ſupplications or proceſſions ſhould be no where uſed but
only within the wals of the Houſe of God, the place ſanctified unto prayer. And
by us not only ſuch inconveniences being remedied, but alſo whatſoever was otherwiſe amiſs in form or matter, it now remaineth a work, the abſolute perfection
whereof upbraideth with errour, or ſomewhat worſe, them whom in all parts it doth
not ſatiſfie. As therefore *Letanies* have been of longer continuance than that we
ſhould make either *Gregory* or *Mamercus* the Author of them, ſo they are of more
permanent uſe than that now the Church ſhould think it needeth them not. What
dangers at any time are imminent, what evils hang over our heads, God doth know
and not we. We find by daily experience, that thoſe calamities may be neareſt at
hand, readieſt to break in ſuddenly upon us, which we in regard of times or circumſtances may imagine to be fartheſt off. Or if they do not in deed approach, yet ſuch
miſeries as being preſent all men are apt to bewail with tears, the wiſe by their prayers ſhould rather prevent. Finally, if we for our ſelves had a priviledge of immunity,
doth not true Chriſtian Charity require that whatſoever any part of the World, yea
any one of all our brethren elſewhere, doth either ſuffer or fear, the ſame we account
as our own burthen? What one petition is there found in the whole *Letany*, whereof we ſhall ever be able at any time to ſay, that no man living needeth the grace or
benefit therein craved at Gods hands? I am not able to expreſs how much it doth
grieve me, that things of principal excellency ſhould be thus bitten at, by men whom
God hath indued with graces both of wit and learning for better purpoſes.

Ff 2 42 We

Marginal notes:

a *Hier. Epiſt.*
22. ad Euſt.
Martyres tibi
quærantur in
cubiculo tuo.
Nunquam cau-
ſa deerit proce-
dendi ſi ſemper
quando nec eſſe
eſt proceſſura
ſir.

b *Socrat lib. 6.*
Soʒom.
cap. 8. Soʒom.
lib. 8. cap. 8.
Theod. lib. 16.
lib. 30. Lib. 3.
cap. 10. Noveli
68. 51.

c *Baſil. Ep. 63.*
Niceph. lib. 14.
cap. 3. Codren.
in Theodoſ.

d *Sidon. lib. 7.*
Epiſt. 1.

e *Concil. tom. 2.*
pag. 513.

f *Concil. tom. 5.*
Anno 1536.

42. We have from the Apoftles of our Lord Jefus Chrift received that brief Confeffion of Faith, which hath been always a badge of the Church, a mark whereby to difcern Chriftian men from Infidels and Jews, *That Faith received from the Apoftles and their Difciples* (faith *Irenæus*) *the Church though difperfed throughout the World, doth notwithftanding keep as fafe as if it dwelt within the walls of fome one houfe, and as uniformely hold, as if it had but one only heart and foul; this as confonantly it preacheth, teacheth, and delivereth, as if but one tongue did fpeak for all. As one Sun fhineth to the whole world, fo there is no faith but this one publifhed, the brightnefs whereof muft enlighten all that come to the knowledge of the truth.* b *This rule* (faith *Tertullian*) *Chrift did inftitute, the ftream and current of this rule hath gone as far, it hath continued as long as the very promulgation of the Gofpel.* c Under *Conftantine* the Emperour, about three hundred years and upward after Chrift, *Arrius* a Prieft in the Church of *Alexandria*, a fubtile-witted and a marvellous fair-fpoken man, but difcontented that one fhould be placed before him in honour, whofe fuperiour he thought himfelf in defert, became through envy and ftomack prone unto contradiction, and bold to broach at the length that Herefie wherein the Deity of our Lord Jefus Chrift, contained, but not opened in the former Creed, the coequality and coeternity of the Son with the Father was denyed. Being for this impiery deprived of his place by the Bifhop of the fame Church, the punifhment which fhould have reformed him did but increafe his obftinacy, and give him occafion of labouring with greater earneftnefs elfewhere, to intangle unwary minds with the fnares of his damnable opinion. *Arrius* in fhort time had won to himfelf a number both of Followers and of great Defenders, whereupon much difquietnefs on all fides enfued. The Emperour, to reduce the Church of Chrift unto the unity of found belief, when other means, whereof tryal was firft made, took no effect, gathered that famous affembly of 318 Bifhops in the Council of *Nice*, where befides order taken for many things which feemed to need redrefs, there was with common confent for the fetling of all mens minds, that other Confeffion of Faith fet down, whereunto we call the Nicene Creed, whereunto the Arrians themfelves which were prefent fubfcribed alfo: not that they meant fincerely, and indeed to forfake their errour, but only to efcape deprivation and exile which they faw they could not avoid, openly perfifting in their former opinions when the greater part had concluded againft them, and that with the Emperours Royal Affent. Referving therefore themfelves unto future opportunities, and knowing that it would not boot them to ftir again in a matter fo compofed, unlefs they could draw the Emperour firft, and by his means the chiefeft Bifhops unto their part; till *Conftantines* death, and fomewhat after they always profeffed love and zeal to the Nicene Faith, yet ceafed not in the mean while to ftrengthen that part which in heart they favoured, and to infeft by all means under colour of other quarrels their greateft Adverfaries in this caufe: Amongft them *Athanafius* efpecially, whom by the fpace of 46 years, from the time of his Confecration to fuceed *Alexander* Arch-bifhop in the Church of *Alexandria*, till the laft hour or his life in this world, they never fuffered to enjoy the comfort of a peaceable day. The heart of *Conftantine* ftoln from him. *Conftantius Conftantines* fucceffor, his fcourge and torment by all the ways that malice armed with foveraign authority could devife and ufe. Under *Julian* no reft given him. And in the daies of *Valentinian* as little. Crimes there were laid to his charge many, the leaft whereof being juft, had bereaved him of eftimation and credit with men while the world ftandeth. His Judges evermore the felf-fame men by whom his accufers were fuborned. Yet the iffue always on their part fhame; on his, triumph. Thofe Bifhops and Prelates, who fhould have accounted his caufe theirs, and could not many of them, but with bleeding hearts, and with watred cheeks, behold a perfon of fo great place and worth conftrained to indure fo foul indignities, were fure by bewraying their affection towards him, to bring upon themfelves thofe moleftations, whereby if they would not be drawn to feem his Adverfaries, yet others fhould be taught how unfafe it was to continue his friends. Whereupon it came to pafs in the end, that (very few excepted) all became fubject to the fway of time; other odds there was none amongft them, faving only that fome fell fooner away, fome later from the foundnefs of belief; fome were Leaders in the Hoft of Impiety,

Impiety, and the rest as common Souldiers, either yeilding through fear, or brought under with penury, or by flattery insnared, or else beguiled through simplicity, which is the faireist excuse that well may be made for them. Yea (that which all men did wonder at) *Osius* the ancientest Bishop that Christendom then had, the most forward in defence of the Catholike cause, and of the contrary part most feared, that very *Osius*, with whose hand the Nicene Creed it self was set down and framed for the whole Christian World to subscribe unto, so far yeilded in the end, as even with the same hand to ratifie the Arrians confession, a thing which they neither hoped to see, nor the other part ever feared, till with amazement they saw it done. Both were perswaded, that although there had been for *Osius* no way but either presently subscribe or dye, his answer and choice would have been the same that *Eleazar's* was, *It doth not become our age to dissemble, whereby many young persons might think, that Osius an hundred years old and upward, were now gone to another Religion, and so through mine hypocrisie [for a little time of transitory life] they might be deceived by me, and I procure malediction and reproach to my old age. For though I were now delivered from the torments of men, yet could I not escape the hand of the Almighty, neither alive nor dead.* But such was the stream of those times, that all men gave place unto it, which we cannot but impute, partly, to their own over-sight. For at the first the Emperour was theirs, the determination of the Councel of Nice was for them, they had the *Arrians* hands to that Councel: So great advantages are never changed so far to the contrary, but by great errour. It plainly appeareth that the first thing which weakened them, was their security. Such as they knew were in heart still affected towards *Arrianisme*, they suffered by continual nearness to possess the minds of the greatest about the Emperour, which themselves might have done with very good acceptation, and neglected it. In *Constantines* life-time to have setled *Constantius*, the same way had been a duty of good service towards God, a mean of peace and great quietness to the Church of Christ, a labour easie, and how likely we may conjecture, when after that so much pains was taken to instruct and strengthen him in the contrary course, after that so much was done by himself to the furtherance of Heresie, yet being touched in the end voluntarily with remorse, nothing more grieved him than the memory of former proceedings in the cause of Religion, and that which he now foresaw in *Julian*, the next Physician into whose hands the body that was thus distempered mutt fall. Howbeit this we may somewhat excuse, in as much as every mans particular care to his own Charge was such, as gave them no leasure to heed what others practised in Princes Courts. But of the two Synods of *Arimine* and *Seleucia*, what should we think? *Constantius* by the Arrians suggestion had devised to assemble all the Bishops of the whole World about this controversie; but in two several places, the Bishops of the West at *Arimine* in *Italy*, the Eastern at *Seleucia* the same time. Amongst them of the East there was no stop, they agreed without any great ado, gave their sentence against Heresie, excommunicated some chief maintainers thereof, and sent the Emperour word what was done. They had at *Arimine* about four hundred which held the truth, scarce of the adverse part four-score, but these obstinate, and the other weary of contending with them: whereupon by both it was resolved to send to the Emperour, such as might inform him of the cause, and declare what hindred their peaceable agreement. There are chosen for the Catholique side, such men as had in them nothing to be noted but boldness, neither gravity, nor learning, nor wisedom. The *Arrians* for the credit of their faction take the eldest, the best experienced, the most warie, and the longest practised *Veterans* they had amongst them. The Emperour conjecturing of the rest on either part by the quality of them whom he saw, sent them speedily away, and with them a certain Confession of faith, ambiguously and subtilly drawn by the *Arrians*, whereunto unless they all subscribed, they should in no case be suffered to depart from the place where they were. At the length it was perceived, that there had not been in the Catholikes either at *Arimine*, or at *Seleucia*, so much foresight, as to provide that true intelligence might pass between them what was done. Upon the advantage of which errour, their Adversaries abusing each with perswasion that other had yeilded, surprized both. The Emperour the more desirous and glad of such events, for that besides all other things wherein they hindred themselves,

Margin notes:
a 2 *Mac.* 6. 24.
b *Major contenario. Sulpit. Sever. hist. l.2.*

c *Ex parte nostra leguntur homines adolescentes, parùm docti & parùm cauti. Ab Arrianis autem missi senes, callidi & ingenio valentes veterano, perfidia imbuti, qui apud Regem facile superiores extiterunt. Sulpit. lib. 1.*
d *Eisdemque conscriptis ab improbis filcm tradit verbis fallentibus involutam quæ Catholicam disciplinam perfidia latente loqueretur. Ibid.*

the

the gall and bitterness of certain mens writings, who spared him little for honours sake, made him for their sakes the less inclinable to that truth, which he himself should have honoured and loved. Only in *Athanasius* there was nothing observed throughout the course of that long Tragedy, other than such as very well became a wise man to do, and a righteous to suffer. So that this was the plain condition of those times, the whole World against *Athanasius*, and *Athanasius* against it; half an hundred of years spent in doubtful trial which of the two in the end would prevail, the side which had all, or else the part which had no friend but God and death; the one a Defender of his innocency, the other a finisher of all his troubles. Now although these contentions were cause of much evil, yet some good the Church hath reaped by them, in that they occasioned the learned and sound in faith to explain such things as Heresie went about to deprave. And in this respect the Creed of *Athanasius* first exhibited unto *Julius* Bishop of *Rome*, and afterwards (as we may probably gather) sent to the Emperour *Jovinian*, for his more full information concerning that truth which *Arrianisme* so mightily did impugne, was both in the East and the West Churches accepted as a treasure of inestimable price,

_b by as many as had not given up even the very ghost of belief.

b Ταύτην μο͂ δοκῶσιν αἰδώ-μενοι τῶ ὁμο-λογίαν ὅ͂τε Τῆς ἰσ σ͂είας ἰ Τῆς τοίκς ἑσσν βιόσ ιισν. Greg. de Atha.

Then was the Creed of *Athanasius* written, howbeit not then so expedient to be publickly used as now in the Church of God, because while the heat of division lasteth, truth it self enduring opposition, doth not so quietly and currantly pass throughout all mens hands, neither can be of that account which afterwards it hath, when the World once perceiveth the vertue thereof not only in it self, but also by the conquest which God hath given it over Heresie. That which Heresie did by sinister interpretations go about to pervert in the first and most ancient Apostolick Creed, the same being by singular dexterity and plainness cleared from those heretical corruptions, partly by this Creed of *Athanasius*, written about the year three hundred and forty, and partly by ^c that other set down in the Synod of *Constantinople* forty years after, comprehending together with the *Nicene* Creed an addition of other Articles which the *Nicene* Creed omitted, because the controversie then in hand needed no mention to be made of them; these Catholick Declarations of our belief delivered by them which were so much neerer than we are unto the first publication thereof, and continuing needful for all men at all times to know, these Confessions as testimonies of our continuance in the same faith to this present day, we rather use than any other gloss or paraphrase devised by our selves, which though it were to the same effect, notwithstanding could not be of the like authority and credit. For that of ^d *Hilary* unto S. *Augustin* hath been ever, and is likely to be always true, *Your most religious wisdome knoweth how great their number is in the Church of God, whom the very authority of mens names doth keep in that opinion which they hold already, or draw unto that which they have not before held.* Touching the Hymne of *Glory*, our usual conclusion to Psalms, the ^e glory of all things is that wherein their highest perfection doth consist: and the glory of God that divine excellency whereby he is eminent above all things, his omnipotent, infinite, and eternal being, ^f which Angels and glorified Saints do intuitively behold, we on earth apprehend principally by Faith, in part also by that kind of knowledge which groweth from experience of those effects, the greatness whereof exceedeth the powers and abilities of all creatures both in Heaven and Earth. God is ^g glorified when such his excellency above all things is with due admiration acknowledged, which dutiful acknowledgement of Gods excellency by occasion of special effects, being the very proper subject and almost the only matter purposely treated of in all Psalms, if that joyful Hymne of Glory have any use in the Church of God, whose Name we therewith extoll and magnifie, can we place it more fitly then where now it serveth as a close or conclusion to Psalms? Neither is the forme thereof newly or unnecessarily invented. *We must* (saith ^h Saint *Basil*) *as we have received, even so baptize, and as we baptize even so believe, and as we believe even so give glory.* Baptizing we use the Name of the Father, of the Son, and of the Holy Ghost; Confessing the Christian Faith we declare our belief in the Father, and in the Son, and in the Holy Ghost; ascribing glory unto God, we give it to the Father, and to the Son, and to the Holy Ghost. It is ἀπόδειξις τῆ ὀρθῦ φρονήματος, *the token of a true and sound understanding*

c That Creed which in the Book of Common Prayer, followeth immediately after the reading of the Gospel.

d Hilar. Arcla. Epist. ad Aug.

e 1 Cor. 15. 40. Exod. 33. 8. Heb. 1. 3.

f Mat. 18. 10.

g Jos. 7. 19. Psal. 21. 23.

h Basil. Ep. 78.

underftanding for matter of doctrine about the Trinity, when in miniftring Baptifme, and making Confeffion, and giving glory, there is a conjunction of all three, and no one of the three fevered from the other two. Againft the *Arrians* affirming the Father to be greater then the Son in honour, excellency, dignity, majefty, this forme and manner of glorifying God was not at that time firft begun, but received long before, and alledged at that time as an argument for the truth. *If (faith Fœ-* [Fœbad. lib.] *badius) there be that inequality which they affirm, then do we every day blafpheme* contr. Arrian. *God, when in Thanksgivings and Offerings of Sacrifice we acknowledge thofe things common to the Father and the Son.* The *Arrians* therefore, for that they perceived how this did prejudice their caufe, altered the Hymne of Glory, whereupon enfued in the Church of *Antioch* about the year 349. that jarre which [Theod.lib.2.] *Theodoret* and *Sozo-* cap.24. *mon* mention. *In their Quires while they praifed God together, as the manner was, at* Sozomon, lib.4. *the end of the Pfalms which they fung, it appeared what opinion every man held, for as* cap. 19. *much as they glorified fome the Father,* And the Son, And the Holy Ghoft; *fome the Father* By the Son, In the Spirit; *the one fort thereby declaring themfelves to embrace the Sons equality with the Father, as the Council of* Nice *had defined; the other fort againft the Council of* Nice *his inequality.* Leontius their Bifhop, although an enemy to the better part, yet wary and fubtile, as in a manner all the Heads of the *Arrians* Faction were, could at no time be plainly heard to ufe either forme, perhaps left his open contradiction of them whom he favoured not might make them the more eager, and by that mean the lefs apt to be privately wonne; or peradventure for that though he joyned in opinion with that fort of *Arrians*, who denied the Son to be equal with the Father; yet from them he diffented, which thought the Father and the Son not only unequal, but unlike, as *Arius* did upon a frivolous and falfe furmife, that becaufe the Apoftle hath faid, *one God of whom, one Lord by* 1 Cor.8.6. *whom,* one Spirit in whom, his different manner of fpeech doth argue a different m 1 Cor.12.3 Nature and Being in them of whom he fpeaketh: Out of which blind collection, it 4.13. feemeth that this their new devifed forme did firft fpring. But in truth even that very forme which the *Arrians* did then ufe (faving that they chofe it to ferve as their fpecial mark of recognifance, and gave it fecretly within themfelves a finifter conftruction) hath not otherwife as much as the fhew of any thing which foundeth towards impiety. For albeit if we refpect Gods glory within it felf, it be the equal right and poffeffion of all three, and that without any oddes, any difference, yet touching his manifeftation thereof unto us by continual effects, and our perpetual acknowledgement thereof unto him likewife by vertuous offices, doth not every tongue both ways confefs, that the brightnefs of his glory hath fpred it felf throughout the World By the Miniftery of his only begotten Son, and is *In* the manifold graces of the Spirit every way marvellous; Again, that whatfoever we do to his glory, it is done *In* the power of the Holy Ghoft, and made acceptable *By* the merit and mediation of Jefus Chrift? So that glory to the Father *And* the Son, or glory to the Father *By* the Son, faving only where evil minds do abufe and pervert moft holy things, are not elfe the voices of errour and fchifme, but of found and fincere Religion. It hath been the cuftome of the Church of Chrift to end fometimes Prayers, and Sermons always, with words of glory, wherein, as long as the bleffed Trinity had due honour, and till *Arrianifme* had made it a matter of great fharpnefs and fubtilty of wit to be a found believing Chriftian, men were not curious what fyllables or particles of fpeech they ufed. Upon which confidence and truft notwithftanding, when Saint *Bafil* began to practife the like indifferency, and to conclude publick prayers, glorifying fometime the Father with the Son and the Holy Ghoft, fometime the Father by the Son in the Spirit, whereas long cuftome had enured them unto the former kind alone, by means whereof the latter was new and ftrange in their ears, this needlefs experiment brought afterwards upon him a neceffary labour of excufing himfelf to his friends, and maintaining his own act againft them, who becaufe the light of his candle too much drowned theirs, were glad to lay hold on fo colourable matter, and exceeding forward to traduce him as an author of fufpicious innovation. How hath the world forfaken that courfe which it fometime held? How are the judgements, hearts, and affections of men altered? May we not wonder that a man of St. *Bafils* authority and quality,

an

an Arch-prelate in the House of God, should have his Name far and wide called in
question, and be driven to his painful Apologies, to write in his own defence whole
Volumns, and yet hardly to obtain with all his endeavour a pardon, the crime laid
against him being but only a change of some one or two syllables in their usual
Church-Liturgy? It was thought in him an unpardonable offence to alter any
thing; in us as intolerable, that we suffer any thing to remain unaltered. The
very Creed of *Athanasius* and that sacred Hymne of Glory, than which nothing doth
found more heavenly in the ears of faithful men, are now reckoned as superfluities,
which we must in any case pare away, lest we cloy God with too much service. Is
there in that Confession of Faith any thing which doth not at all times edifie and
instruct the attentive hearer? Or is our Faith in the blessed Trinity a matter needless to be so oftentimes mentioned and opened in the principal part of that duty
which we owe to God, our publick Prayer? Hath the Church of Christ from the
first beginning, by a secret universal instinct of Gods good Spirit, always tied it
self to end neither Sermon nor almost any speech of moment which hath concerned
matters of God, without some special words of honour and glory to that Trinity
which we all adore; and is the like conclusion of Psalms become now at length an
eye-sore or a galling to their ears that hear it? Those flames of *Arrianisme* they
say are quenched, which were the cause why the Church devised in such sort to confess and praise the glorious Deity of the Son of God. Seeing therefore the sore is,
whole, why retain we as yet the playster? When the cause why any thing was ordained doth once cease, the thing it self should cease with it, that the Church being
eased of unprofitable labours, needful offices may the better be attended. For
the doing of things unnecessary, is many times the cause why the most necessary
are not done. But in this case so to reason will not serve their turns. For first, the
ground whereupon they build, is not certainly their own, but with special limitations. Few things are so restrained to any one end or purpose, that the same being
extinct they should forthwith utterly become frustrate. Wisdome may have framed one and the same thing to serve commodiously for divers ends, and of those
ends any one be sufficient cause for continuance, though the rest have ceased; even
as the tongue, which Nature hath given us for an instrument of speech is not idle
in dumb persons, because it also serveth for taste. Again, if time have worne out,
or any other meane altogether taken away what was first intended, uses not thought
upon before may afterwards spring up, and be reasonable causes of retaining that
which other considerations did formerly procure to be instituted. And it cometh
sometime to pass, that a thing unnecessary in it self as touching the whole direct
purpose whereto it was meant or can be applied, doth notwithstanding appear convenient to be still held even without use, left by reason of that coherence which it
hath with somewhat most necessary, the removal of the one should indammage the
other; and therefore men which have clean lost the possibility of sight, keep still
their eyes nevertheless in the place where Nature set them. As for these two branches whereof our question groweth, *Arrianisme* was indeed some occasion of the
one, but a cause of neither, much less the only intire cause of both. For albeit conflict with *Arrians* brought forth the occasion of writing that Creed, which long
after was made a part of the Church-liturgy, as Hymns and Sentences of glory
were a part thereof before; yet cause sufficient there is why both should remain in
use, the one as a most divine explication of the chiefest Articles of our Christian
belief, the other as an heavenly acclamation of joyful applause to his praises in
whom we believe; neither the one nor the other unworthy to be heard sounding
as they are in the Church of Christ, whether Arrianisme live or dye. Against which
poyson likewise if we think that the Church at this day needeth not those ancient
preservatives, which ages before us were so glad to use, we deceive our selves
greatly. The weeds of Heresie being grown unto such ripeness as that was, do
even in the very cutting down scatter, oftentimes those seeds which for a while lie
unseen and buried in the earth, but afterward freshly spring up again no less pernicious than at the first. Which thing they very well know, and I doubt not will
easily confess, who live to their great, both toil and grief, where the blasphemies
of *Arrians, Samosatenians, Tritheits, Eutychians,* and *Macedonians* are renewed by
                                                                                        them,

them, who to hatch their Herefie, have chofen thofe Churches as fitteſt netts where *Athanaſius* Creed is not heard; by them I fay renewed, who following the courfe of extream reformation, were wont in the pride of their own proceedings to glory, that whereas *Luther* did but blow away the roof, and *Zwinglius* batter but the walls of Popifh Superſtition, the laſt and hardeſt work of all remained, which was, to raze up the very ground and foundation of Popery, that doctrine concerning the Deity of Chriſt, which *Satanaſius* (for fo it pleaſed thoſe impious forſaken Miſcreants to fpeak) hath in this memorable Creed explained. So manifeſtly true is that which one of the [a] Ancients hath concerning Arrianiſme, *Mortuis authoribus hujus veneni, ſcelerata tamen eorum doctrina non moritur*, the authors of this venom being dead and gone, their wicked doctrine notwithſtanding continueth.

a Fœbad. contra Arr.

43 Amongſt the heaps of theſe exceſſes and fuperfluities there is eſpied the want of a principal part of duty, *There are no thankſgivings for the benefits for which there are Petitions* in our Book of Prayer. This they have thought a point material to be objected. Neither may we take it in evil part to be admoniſhed what ſpecial duties of thankfulneſs we owe to that merciful God, for whoſe unfpeakable graces the only requital which we are able to make, is a true, hearty, and ſincere acknowledgement, how precious we eſteem ſuch benefits received, and how infinite in goodneſs the Author from whom they come. But that to every Petition we make, for things needful there fhould be fome anſwerable fentence of thanks provided particularly to follow ſuch requeſts obtained; either it is not a matter fo requiſite as they pretend; or if it be, wherefore have they not then in ſuch order framed their own Book of Common Prayer? Why hath our Lord and Saviour taught us a forme of Prayer containing fo many petitions of thoſe things which we want, and not delivered in like fort as many ſeveral forms of thankſgiving, to ſerve when any thing we pray for is granted? What anſwer foever they can reaſonably make unto theſe demands, the ſame ſhall difcover unto them how cauſeleſs a cenſure it is, that there are not in our Book thankſgivings for all the benefits for which there are petitions. For concerning the bleffings of God, whether they tend unto this life or the life to come, there is great cauſe why we ſhould delight more in giving thanks, than in making requeſts for them, in as much as the one hath penſiveneſs and fear, the other always joy annexed: the one belongeth unto them that ſeek, the other unto them that have found happineſs; they that pray do but yet fow, they that give thanks declare they have reaped. Howbeit, becauſe there are fo many graces whereof we ſtand in continual need, graces for which we may not ceaſe daily and hourly to fue, graces which are in beſtowing always, but never come to be fully had in this preſent life; and therefore when all things here have an end, endleſs thanks muſt have their beginning in a State which bringeth the full and final ſatisfaction of all ſuch perpetual deſires; again, becauſe our common neceſſities, and the lack which we all haye, as well of ghoſtly as of earthly favours is in each kind fo eaſily known, but the gifts of God according to thoſe degrees and times which he in his ſecret wiſdom ſeeth meet, are fo diverſly beſtowed, that it ſeldome appeareth what all receive, what all ſtand in need of it ſeldome lieth hid, we are not fo marvell though the Church do oftner concurre in ſuits than in thanks unto God for particular benefits. Nevertheleſs, leſt God ſhould be any way unglorified, the greateſt part of our daily Service, they know, confiſteth according to [b] the bleſſed Apoſtles own preciſe rule, in much variety of Pſalms and Hymns, for no other purpoſe, but only that out of fo plentiful a treaſure there might be for every mans heart to chuſe of it his own Sacrifice, and to offer unto God by particular fecret inſtinct, what fitteth beſt the often occaſions which any ſeveral either party or Congregation may ſeem to have. They that would clean take from us therefore the daily uſe of the very beſt means we have to magnifie and praiſe the Name of Almighty God for his rich bleſſings, they that complain of our reading and ſinging fo many Pſalms for fo good an end, they I fay that find fault with our ſtore, ſhould of all men be leaſt willing to reprove

our

Our want of particular thankſgiving. As ſuch prayers are needful whereby we beg releaſe from our diſtreſſes; ſo there ought to be as neceſſary prayers of thankſgiving, when we have received thoſe things at the Lords hand which we asked. T.C. lib. 1. pag. 138. I do not ſimply require a ſolemn and expreſs thankſgiving for ſuch benefits; but only upon a ſuppoſition, which is, that if it be expedient that there ſhould be expreſs prayers againſt ſo many of their earthly miſeries, that then alfo it is meet that upon the deliverance there ſhould be an expreſs thankſgiving. T.C. l. 3. p. 209.

The default of the Book, for that there are no formes of Thankſgiving for the releaſe from thoſe common calamities from which we have petitions to be delivered. T.C. l. 3. p. 208.

b Ephef. 5. 9. Coloſ. 3. 16.

our scarcity of thanksgivings. But becaufe peradventure they fee it is not either *gene-rally* fit or poffible that Churches fhould frame thankfgivings anfwerable to each pe-tition, they fhorten fomewhat the reins of their cenfure ; there are no forms of thankfgiving, they fay, for releafe of thofe *common calamities,* from which we have petitions to be delivered. *There are Prayers fet forth to be faid in the common cala-mities and univerfal fcourges of the Realm, as* Plague, Famine, &c. *And indeed fo it ought to be by the Word of God. But as fuch Prayers are needful,* whereby we beg releafe from our diftreffes, fo there ought to be as neceffary prayers of thankfgiving, when we have received thofe things at the Lords hand which we asked in our pray-ers. As oft therefore as any publike or univerfal fcourge is removed, as oft as we are delivered from thofe either imminent or prefent calamities, againft the ftorm & tem-peft whereof we all inftantly craved favour from above, let it be a queftion what we fhould render unto God for his bleffings univerfally, fenfibly, and extraordinarily beftowed. A prayer of three or four lines inferted into fome part of our Church Liturgie ? No, we are not perfvaded that when God doth in trouble injoin us the duty of invocation, and promife us the benefit of deliverance, and profefs that the thing he expecteth after at our hands, is to glorifie him as our mighty and only Sa-viour, the Church can difcharge in manner convenient a work of fo great importance by fore-ordaining fome fhort Collect wherein briefly to mention thanks. Our cuftom therefore whenfoever fo great occafions are incident, is by publike authori-ty to appoint throughout all Churches fet and folemn forms as well of fupplication as of thankfgiving, the preparations and intended complements whereof may ftir up the minds of men in much more effectual fort, than if only there fhould be added to the Book of Prayer that which they require. But we erre in thinking that they require any fuch matter. For albeit their words to our underftanding be very plain, that in our book *there are Prayers fet forth* to be faid when *common cala-mities* are felt, as *Plague, Famine,* and fuch like ; again, that *indeed fo it ought to be by the Word of God :* that likewife *there ough: to be as neceffary prayers of thankf-giving when we have received thofe things :* finally, that the want of fuch forms of thankfgiving for the releafe from thofe common calamities from which we have petitions to be delivered, is the *default of the Book of Common Prayer:*yet all this they mean but only by way of *fuppofition of exprefs Prayers* againft fo many earthly mife-ries were convenient, *that then* indeed as many exprefs and particular thankfgivings fhould be likewife neceffary. Seeing therefore we know that they hold the one fuperfluous, they would not have it fo underftood as though their minds were that any fuch addition to the book is needfull, whatfoever they fay for arguments fake concerning this pretended defect. The truth is, they wave in and out, no way fuffi-ciently grounded, no way refolved what to think, fpeak or write, more than only that becaufe they have taken it upon them, they muft (no remedy now) be oppo-fite.

In fome things the matter of our Prayer, as they affirm, unfound.   44 The laft fuppofed fault concerneth fome few things, the very matter whereof is thought to be much amifs. In a Song of praife to our Lord Jefus Chrift, we have thefe words, *When thou hadft overcome the fharpnefs of death, thou didft open the Kingdom of Heaven to all beleevers.* Which maketh fome fhew of giving counte-nance to their errour, who think that the faithful which departed this life before the coming of Chrift, were never till then made partakers of joy, but remained all in that place which they term the *Lake of the Fathers.* In our *Liturgy* requeft is made that we may be preferved from fudden death. This feemeth frivolous, be-caufe the godly fhould be always prepared to die. Requeft is made that God would give thofe things which we for our unworthinefs dare not ask. This they fay, *car-ryeth with it the note of popifh fervile fear, and favoureth not of that confidence and re-verent familiarity that the children of God have through Chrift with their heavenly Father.* Requeft is made that we may evermore be defended from all adverfity. For this *there is no promife in Scripture,* and therefore *it is no prayer of Faith, or of the which we can affure our felves that we fhall obtain it.* Finally, requeft is made that God wo ld have mercy upon all men. This is impoffible, becaufe fome are the veffels of wrath, to whom God will never extend his mercy.

45 As Chrut hath purchased that Heavenly Kingdom, the att perfection whereof is *glory in the life to come*, grace in this life a preparation thereunto ; so the same he hath *opened* to the world in such sort; that whereas none can possibly without him attain salvation, by him *all that believe* are saved. Now whatsoever he did or suffered, the end thereof was to open the doors of the Kingdom of Heaven which our iniquities had *shut up*. But because by *ascending after that the sharpness of death* was overcome, he took the very *local possession* of glory, and that *to the use of all that are his*, even as himself before had witnessed, [a] *I go to prepare a place for you* ; And again, *Whom thou hast given me, O Father,* [b] *I will that where I am, they be also with me, that my glory which thou hast given me they may behold:* it appeareth that *when Christ did ascend,* he then most *liberally opened* the Kingdome of Heaven, *to the end that* with him and by him all believers might raign. In what estate the Fathers rested which were dead before, it is not hereby either one way or other determined. All that we can rightly gather is, that as touching their souls what degree of joy or happiness soever it pleased God to bestow upon them, *his Ascension* which succeeded *procured* theirs, and theirs concerning the body must eeds be *not only of,* but after his. As therefore [c] *Helvidius*, against whom S. *Jerome* writeth, abused greatly those words of *Matthew* concerning *Joseph* and the mother of our Saviour Christ, *He knew her not till she had brought forth her first born,* thereby gathering, against the honour of the blessed Virgin, that a thing denied with special circumstance doth import an opposite affirmation when once that circumstance is expired: After the self-same manner it should be a weak Collection, if whereas we say that *when* Christ had overcome the sharpness of death, he *then opened* the Kingdome of Heaven to all Believers, a thing in such sort affirmed with circumstance were taken as insinuating an opposite denial before that circumstance be accomplished, and consequently, that because when the sharpness of death was overcome, he then opened Heaven *as well to believing Gentiles as Jews,* Heaven till then was no receptacle to the souls of either. Wherefore be the Spirits of the just and righteous before Christ truly or falsly thought excluded out of heavenly joy, by that which we in the words alledged before do attribute to Christs Ascension, there is to no such opinion, nor to the [d] favourers thereof any countenance at all given. We cannot better interpret the meaning of their words then Pope *Leo* himself expoundeth them, whose speech concerning our Lords Ascension may serve instead of a marginal gloss, [e] *Christs exaltation is our promotion, and whither the glory of the head is already gone before, thither the hope of the body also is to follow. For at this day we have not only the possession of Paradise assured unto us, but in Christ we have entred the highest of the Heavens.* His opening the Kingdom of Heaven and his entrance thereinto was not only to his own use, but for the benefit of all Believers.

46. Our good or evil estate after death dependeth most upon the quality of our lives. Yet somewhat there is why a vertuous mind should rather wish to depart this world with a kind of treatable dissolution, than to be suddenly cut off in a moment ; rather to be taken then snatched away from the face of the earth. Death is that which all men suffer, but not all men with one mind, neither all men in one manner. For being of necessity a thing common, it is through the manifold perswasions, dispositions and occasions of men, with equal desert both of praise and dispraise shunned by some, by others desired. So that absolutely we cannot discommend, we cannot absolutely approve either willingness to live or forwardness to dye. And concerning the ways of death, albeit the choice thereof be only in his hands, who alone hath power over all flesh, and unto whose appointment we ought with patience meekly to submit our selves (for to be agents voluntarily in our own destruction, is against both God and Nature) yet there is no doubt but in so great variety, our desires will and may lawfully preferre one kind before another. Is there any man of worth and vertue, although not instructed in the School of Christ, or ever taught what the soundness of Religion meaneth, that had not rather end the days of this transitory life as *Cyrus* in *Xenophon*, or in *Plato*, *Socrates* are described, then to sink down with them of whom [f] *Elihu* hath said, *Momento moriuntur*, there is scarce an instant between their flourishing and their not being ? But let us which know what it is to die as *Absalon* or *Ananias* and *Sapphira* died, let

us

Margin notes:

When thou hadst overcome the sharpness of death, thou didst open the Kingdome of Heaven unto all Believers.
a *John* 14. 2.
b *John* 17.24.

c *Hieron: cont. Helu.*
Aug. har. 84.

d *Lyr. super. Gen.* 19.
Th.p 3.q 52.
t *Leo ser.* 1. *de Ascens.*

Touching Prayer for deliverance from sudden death.

f *Job* 34.20.

- a Heb. 11. 21.
Deut. 33.
Josh. 14.
- Reg. 2.

us beg of God that when the hour of our rest is come, the patterns of our dissolution may be [a] *Jacob, Moses, Joshua, David*, who leasurably ending their lives in peace, prayed for the mercies of God to come upon their posterity; replenished the hearts of the neerest unto them with words of memorable Consolation; strengthned men in the fear of God, gave them wholesome instructions of Life, and confirmed them in true Religion; in summe, taught the World no less vertuously how to dye, then they had done before how to live. To such as judge things according to the sense of natural men, and ascend no higher, suddenness because it shortneth their grief should in reason be most acceptable. That which causeth bitterness in death, is the languishing attendance and expectation thereof ere it come. And therefore Tyrants use what Art they can to increase the slowness of death. Quick riddance out of life is often both requested and bestowed as a benefit. Commonly therefore it is for vertuous considerations, that Wisdom so far prevaileth with men as to make them desirous of slow and deliberate death against the stream of their sensual inclination, content to indure the longer grief and bodily pain, that the soul may have time to call it self to a just accompt of all things past, by means whereof Repentance is perfected, there is wherein to exercise patience, the joys of the Kingdom of Heaven have leasure to present themselves, the pleasures of sinne and this Worlds vanities are censured with uncorrupt judgement, Charity is free to make advised choice of the soyl wherein her last Seed may most fruitfully be bestowed, the mind is at liberty to have due regard of that disposition of worldly things which it can never afterwards alter, and because [b] the neerer we draw unto God, the more we are oftentimes enlightened with the shining beams of his glorious presence, as being then even almost in sight, a leasurable departure may in that case bring forth for the good of such as are present, that which shall cause them for ever after from the bottom of their hearts to pray, *O let us dye the death of the righteous, and let our last end be like theirs.* All which benefits and opportunities are by sudden death prevented. And besides, for as much as death howsoever is a general effect of the wrath of God against sin, and the suddenness thereof a thing which happeneth but to few; The World in this respect feareth it the more as being subject to doubtful constructions, which as no man willingly would incurre, so they whose happy estate after life is of all mens the most certain, would especially wish that no such accident in their death may give uncharitable minds occasion of rash, sinister, and suspitious verdicts, whereunto they are over-prone; so that whether evil men or good be respected, whether we regard our selves or others, to be preserved from sudden death is a blessing of God. And our Prayer against it importeth a two-fold desire, first, that death when it cometh may give us some convenient respite; or secondly, if that be denied us of God, yet we may have wisdome to provide always before-hand, that those evils overrake us not, which death unexpected doth use to bring upon careless men; and that although it be sudden in it self, nevertheless in regard of our prepared minds it may not be sudden.

b Cypr. de mortal.

Prayer that those things which we for our unworthiness dare not aske, God for the worthiness of his Son would vouchsafe to grant. This request carrieth with it still the note of the Popish servile fear, and favoureth not of that confidence and reverent familiarity that the Children of God have through Christ with their heavenly Father. *T. C. lib.* 1. page 136.

47. But is it credible that the very acknowledgement of our own unworthiness to obtain, and in that respect our professed fearfulness to ask any thing otherwise than only for his sake to whom God can deny nothing, that this should be noted for a Popish Errour, that this should be termed baseness, abjection of mind, or *servility*, is it credible? That which we for our unworthiness are afraid to crave, our Prayer is, that God for the worthiness of his Son would notwithstanding vouchsafe to grant. May it please them to shew us which of these words it is that carrieth the note of Popish and servile fear? In reference to other Creatures of this inferiour World, mans worth and excellency is admired. Compared with God, the truest Inscription wherewith we can circle so base a coyne is that of *David*, [c] *Universa vanitas est omnis homo*, whosoever hath the name of a mortal man, there is in him whatsoever the name of vanity doth comprehend. And therefore what we say of our own *unworthiness*, there is no doubt but Truth will ratifie, alledged in Prayer it both becometh and behoveth Saints. For as humility is

c Psal. 39. 5.

in

in Suiters a decent vertue, so the testification thereof by such effectual acknowledgements not only [a] argueth a sound apprehension of his supereminent Glory and Majesty before whom we stand, but putteth also into his hands a kind of pledge or bond for security against our unthankfulness, the very natural Root whereof is always either Ignorance, Dissimulation, or Pride; Ignorance, when we know not the Author from whom our good cometh; Dissimulation, when our hands are more open than our eyes, upon that we receive; Pride, when we think our selves *worthy* of that which meer grace and undeserved mercy bestoweth. In Prayer therefore to abate so vain imaginations with the *true conceit of unworthiness*, is rather to prevent than commit a fault. It being no Errour thus to think, no fault thus to speak of our selves when we pray, is it a fault that the consideration of our unworthiness maketh us *fearful* to open our mouths by way of Suite? While *Job* had prosperity and lived in honour, men feared him for his authorities sake, and in token of their fear when they saw him they [b] hid themselves. Between *Elihu* and the rest of *Jobs* Familiars the greatest disparity was but in years. And he, though riper than they in judgement, doing them reverence in regard of age, stood long [c] *doubtful*, and very loth to adventure upon speech in his Elders hearing. If so small inequality between man and man make their modesty a commendable vertue, who respecting Superiours *as Superiours*, can neither speak nor stand before them without fear: That the Publican approacheth not more boldly to God; that when Christ in mercy draweth neer to *Peter*, he in humility and fear craveth distance; that being to stand, to speak, to sue in the presence of so great Majesty, we are afraid, let no man blame us. [d] In which consideration notwithstanding, because to flie altogether from God, to despair that creatures unworthy shall be able to obtain any thing at his hands, and under that pretence to surcease from Prayers as bootless or fruitless offices, were to him no less injurious than pernicious to our own souls, even that which we tremble to do we do, we ask those things which we dare not ask. The knowledge of our own unworthiness is not without belief in the merits of Christ. With that true fear which the one causeth there is coupled true boldness, and encouragement drawn from the other. The very silence which our unworthiness putteth us unto, doth it self make request for us, and that in confidence of his grace. Looking inward we are stricken dumb, looking upward we speak and prevail. O happy mixture wherein things contrary do so qualifie and correct the one the danger of the others excess, that neither boldness can make us presume as long as we are kept under with the sense of our own wretchedness; nor, while we trust in the mercy of God through Jesus Christ, fear be able to tyrannize over us! As therefore our fear excludeth not that [e] boldness which becometh Saints; so if their *familiarity* with God do not savour of this fear, it draweth too near that irreverend confidence wherewith true Humility can never stand.

48 Touching continual deliverance in the world from all adversity, their conceit is, that we ought not to ask it of God by Prayer, forasmuch as in Scripture there is no promise that we shall be evermore free from vexations, calamities, and troubles. Minds rigorously affected are wont in every thing of weight and moment which they do or see, to examine according unto rules of Piety, *what dependency* it hath on God, what reference to themselves, what coherence with any of those duties whereunto all things in the World should lead, and accordingly they frame the inward disposition of their minds sometime to admire God, sometimes to bless him and give him thanks, sometime to exult in his love, sometime to implore his mercy. All which different elevations of spirit unto God are contained in the name of Prayer. Every good and holy desire though it lack the form, hath notwithstanding in it self the substance, and with him the force of a Prayer, who regardeth the very moanings, groans, and signes of the heart of man. Petitionary Prayer belongeth only to such as are in themselves impotent, and stand in need of relief from others. We thereby declare unto God what our own desire is that he by his power should effect. It presupposeth therefore in us, First, the want of that which we pray for; Secondly, a feeling of that want; Thirdly, an earnest willingness of mind to be eased therein; Fourthly, a declaration of this our desire in the sight of God, not as if he should be otherwise ignorant of our necessities, but because we this

Marginal notes (right column):
a Μεμνημένος ᾗ τῆς Ἰδίας παρ' αὐτῷς ἀσενείας μεμνηται ᾗ τῆς τὰ θεῷ παρ' αὐτῷς ὑπεροχῆς. Philo. de sacrif. Abel. & Cain.

b *Job* 29. 8. Amongst the parts of honour *Aristotle* reckoneth προσκύνησις and εὐλάβεια. Reth. l. 1. c. 5.
c *Job* 32. 6.

d The Publican did indeed not lift up his eyes: So that if by his Example we should lay we dare ask nothing, we ought also to ask nothing, otherwise in stead of teaching true humility, we open a School to hypocrisie, which the Lord detesteth.
T.C. l.3. p.103. e Ro. 5.2;8;15. Heb. 10.19.

Prayer to be evermore defired from all adversity. For as much as there is no promise in the Scripture that we should be free from all adversity, and that evermore it seemeth that this Prayer might have been better conceived being no Prayer of Faith, or of the which we can assure our selves that we shall obtain it. this T.C. l.1. p.136.

this way fhew that we honour him as our God, and are verily perfwaded that no good thing can come to pafs which he by his Omnipotent power effecteth nor. Now becaufe there is no mans Prayer acceptable, whofe perfon is odious, neither any mans perfon gracious without faith, it is of neceffity required that they which pray do believe. The Prayers which our Lord and Saviour made were for his own worthinefs accepted; as God accepteth not but with this condition, if they be joyned with ^a belief in Chrift. The Prayers of the Juft are accepted always, but not always thofe things granted for which they pray. For in Prayer if faith and affurance to obtain were both one and the fame thing, feeing that the effect of not obtaining is a plain teftimony that they which prayed were not fure they fhould obtain, it would follow that their Prayer being without certainty of the event, was alfo made unto God without faith, and confequently that God abhorred it. Which to think of fo many Prayers of Saints as we find have failed in particular requefts, how abfurd were it? His faithful people have this comfort, that whatfoever they right'y afk, the fame (no doubt, but) they fhall receive, fo far as may ftand with the glory of God, and their own everlafting good; unto either of which two it is no virtuous mans purpofe to feek or defire to obtain any thing prejudicial, and therefore that claufe which our Lord and Saviour in the Prayer of his Agony did exprefs, we in petitions of like nature do always imply, *Pater, fi poffibile eft*; if it may ftand with thy will and pleafure. Or if not, but that there be fecret impediments and caufes in regard whereof the thing we pray for is denied us, yet the Prayer it felf which we make is a pleafing Sacrifice to God, who both accepteth and rewardeth it fome other way. So that finners in very truth are denyed when they ^b feem to prevail in their Supplications, becaufe it is not for their fakes or to their good that their Sutes take place; the faithful contrariwife, becaufe it is for their good oftentimes that their Petitions do not take place, prevail even then when they moft (c) feem denied. *Our Lord God in anger hath granted fome impenitent mens requefts, as on the other fide the Apoftles fute he hath of favour and mercy not granted* (faith Saint *Auguftine*.) To think we may pray unto God for nothing but what he hath promifed in holy Scripture we fhall obtain, is perhaps an errour. For of Prayer there are two ufes. It ferveth as a mean to procure thofe things which God hath promifed to grant when we afke, and i. ferveth as a mean to exprefs our lawful defires, alfo towards that, which whether we fhall have or no we know not till we fee the event. Things in themfelves unholy or unfeemly we may not afk; we may whatfoever, being not forbidden, either Nature or Grace fhall reafonably move us to wifh as importing the good of men, albeit God himfelf have no where by promife affured us of that particular which our Prayer craveth. To pray for that which is in it felf and of its own nature apparently a thing impoffible, were not convenient. Wherefore though men do without offence wifh daily that the affairs which with evil fuccefs are paft, might have fallen out much better, yet to pray that they may have been any other than they are, this being a manifeft impoffibility in it felf, the Rules of Religion do not permit. Whereas contrariwife when things of their own nature contingent and mutable are by the fecret determination of God appointed one way, though we the other way make our Prayers, and confequently afk thofe things of God which are *by this fuppofition* impoffible, we notwithftanding do not hereby in Prayer tranfgrefs our lawful bounds. That Chrift, as the only begotten Son of God, having no Superior, and therefore owing honour unto none, neither ftanding in any need fhould either give thanks, or make petition unto God, were moft abfurd. As man, what could befeem him better, whether we refpect his affection to God-ward, or his own neceffity, or his charity and love towards men? Some things he knew fhould come to pafs, and notwithftanding prayed for them, becaufe he alfo knew that the neceffary means to effect them, were his prayers. As in the Pfalm it is faid, ^d *Afk of me, and I will give thee the Heathen for thine Inheritance, and the ends of the Earth for thy poffeffion.* Wherefore that which here God promifeth his Son, the fame in the 17. of *John* he prayeth for, ^e *Father, the hour is now come, glorifie thy Son, that thy Son alfo may glorifie thee, according as thou haft given him power over all flefh.* But had Chrift the like promife concerning the effect of every particular for which he prayed? That which was not effected could not be promifed

a *Oratio quæ non fit per Chriftum, non fatùm non poteft delere peccatum, fed etiam ipfa fit peccatum. Aug.evar.1. in Pfal.108.*

b *Num. 11.33. 1 Sam. 8.7. Job 1.12. & 2.6. Luke 8.52.*
c *2 Cor.12.7; 8,9. Aug.Epi.121. ad probam viduam.*

d *Pfal. 2.8.*

e *John 17.1,2.*

miled. And we know in ª what sort he prayed for removal of that bitter cup, which cup he tasted notwithstanding his Prayer. To shift off this Example they answer first, that ᵇ *as other children of God, so Christ had a promise of deliverance, as far as the glory of God in the accomplishment of his vocation would suffer.* And if we our selves have not also in that sort the promise of God to be evermore delivered from all adversity, what meaneth the Sacred Scripture to speak in so large terms, *Be obedient, and the Lord thy God will make thee plenteous in* ᶜ *every work of thy hand, in the fruit of thy body, and in the fruit of thy Cattel, and in the fruit of the Land for thy wealth.* Again, *Keep his Laws, and thou shalt be blest above all people, the Lord shall take from thee* ᵈ *all infirmities.* The man whose delight is in the Law of God, ᵉ *whatsoever he doth it shall prosper.* For the ungodly there are *great plagues remaining;* but whosoever putteth his trust in the Lord, mercy imbraceth him ᶠ *on every side.* Not only that mercy which keepeth from being over-laid or opprest, but mercy which saveth from being *touched with grievous miseries,* mercy which turneth away the course of ᵍ *the great water-flouds,* and permitteth them not to come *neer.* Nevertheless, because the Prayer of Christ did concern but one calamity, they are still bold to deny the lawfulness of our Prayer for deliverance out of all, yea, though we pray with the same exception that he did, *If such deliverance may stand with the pleasure of Almighty God, and not otherwise.* For they have, secondly, found out a Rule that Prayer ought only to be made for deliverance ʰ *from this or that particular adversity, whereof we know not, but upon the event, what the pleasure of God is.* Which quite overthroweth that other principle, wherein they require unto every Prayer which is of Faith an assurance to obtain the thing we pray for. At the first to pray against all adversity was unlawful, because we cannot assure our selves that this will be granted. Now we have licence to pray against any particular adversity, and the reason given, because we know not but upon the event what God will do. If we know not what God will do, it followeth that for any assurance we have, he may do otherwise than we pray, and we may faithfully pray for that which we cannot assuredly presume that God will grant. Seeing therefore neither of these two Answers will serve the turn, they have a third, which is, that to pray in such sort, is but idly miss-spent labour, because God hath already revealed his Will touching this request, and we know that the sute we make is denyed before we make it. Which neither is true, and if it were, was Christ ignorant what God had determined touching those things which himself should suffer? To say ⁱ *he knew not what weight of sufferances his heavenly Father had measured unto him,* is somewhat hard, harder, that although *he knew them,* notwithstanding for the present time they were *forgotten, through the force of those unspeakable pangs which he then was in.* The one against the plain express words of the holy Evangelist, ᵏ *He knew all things that should come upon him;* the other less credible, if any thing may be of less credit than what the Scripture it self gain-sayeth. Doth any of them which wrote his sufferings, make report that memory failed him? Is there in his words and speeches any sign of defect that way? Did not himself declare before whatsoever was to happen in the course of that whole tragedy? Can we gather by any thing after taken from his own mouth either in the place of publike judgment, or upon the Altar of the Cross, that through the bruising of his Body, some part of the treasures of his soul were scattered and slipt from him? If that, which was perfect both before and after did fail at this only middle instant, there must appear some manifest cause how it came to pass. True it is, that the pangs of his heaviness and grief were *unspeakable:* and as true, that because the minds of the afflicted do never think they have fully conceived the weight or measure of their own woe, they use their affection as a whetstone both to wit and memory; these as Nurses do feed grief, so that the weaker his conceit had been touching that which he was to suffer, the more it must needs in that hour have helped to the mitigation of his anguish. But his anguish we see was then at the very highest whereunto it could possibly rise; which argueth his deep apprehension even to the last drop of the gall which that Cup contained, and of every circumstance wherein there was any force to augment heaviness; but above all things, the resolute determination of God, and his own unchangeable purpose which he at that time could not forget. To what intent then was his Prayer,

Marginal notes:

a *Mat.* 26. 39.
Mark 14. 36.
Luke 22. 42.
d Neither did our Saviour Christ pray without promise: for as other the Children of God to whose condition he had humbled himself have, so had he a promise of deliverance so far as the glory of God in that accomplishment of his vocation would suffer. *T.C.l.3.p.* 200
c *Deut.* 30. 9.
d *Deut.* 7. 15.
e *Psal.* 1. 4.
f *Psal.* 32. 11. 17.
g *T.C.l.3.p.*101, h We ought not to desire to be free from all adversity, if it be his will, considering that he hath already declared his will therein. *T. C.l.3. p.*201.
i *T.C.l.3.p.*101,
k *John* 18. 4.

which

which plainly teſtifieth ſo great willingneſs to avoid death? Will, whether it be in God or man, belongeth to the eſſence or nature of both. The nature therefore of God being one, there are not in God divers wils, although the God-head be in divers perſons, becauſe the power of willing is a natural, not a perſonal propriety. Contrariwiſe, the perſon of our Saviour Chriſt being but one, there are in him two wils, becauſe two natures, the nature of God, and the nature of man, which both do imply this faculty and power. So that in Chriſt there is a divine, and there is an humane will, otherwiſe he were not both God and man. Hereupon the Church hath of old condemned Monothelites as Heretikes, for holding that Chriſt had but one will. The works and operations of our Saviours humane will were all ſubject to the Will of God, and framed according to his Law, [a] *I deſire to do thy will, O God, and thy Law is within mine heart.* Now as mans will, ſo the Will of Chriſt hath two ſeveral kinds of operation, the one natural or neceſſary, whereby it deſireth ſimply whatſoever is good in it ſelf, and ſhunneth generally all things which hurt; the other deliberate, when we therefore imbrace things as good, becauſe the eye of underſtanding judgeth them good to that end which we ſimply deſire. Thus in it ſelf we deſire health, phyſick only for healths ſake. And in this ſort ſpecial reaſon oftentimes cauſeth the will by choice to prefer one good thing before another, to leave one for anothers ſake, to forego meaner for the attainment of higher deſires, which our Saviour likewiſe did. Theſe different inclinations of the will conſidered, the reaſon is eaſie how in Chriſt there might grow deſires ſeeming, but being not indeed oppoſite either the one or the other, or either of them to the will of God. For let the manner of his ſpeech be weighed, [b] *My ſoul is now troubled, and what ſhould I ſay? Father ſave me out of this hour. But yet for this very cauſe I am come into this hour.* His purpoſe herein was moſt effectually to propoſe to the view of the whole world two contrary objects, the like whereunto in force and efficacy were never preſented in that manner to any but only to the Soul of Chriſt. There was preſented before his eyes in that fearful hour, on the one ſide Gods heavy indignation and wrath towards mankind as yet unappeaſed, death as yet in full ſtrength, Hell as yet never maſtered by any that came within the confines and bounds thereof, ſomewhat alſo peradventure more than is either poſſible or needful for the wit of man to find out; finally himſelf fleſh and blood [c] left alone to enter into conflict with all theſe; on the other ſide, a World to be ſaved by One, a pacification of wrath through the dignity of that ſacrifice which ſhould be offred, a conqueſt over death through the power of that Deity which would not ſuffer the Tabernacle thereof to ſee corruption, and an utter diſappointment of all the forces of infernal powers, through the purity of that ſoul which they ſhould have in their hands and not be able to touch. Let no man marvail that in this caſe the ſoul of Chriſt was much troubled. For what could ſuch apprehenſions breed, but (as their nature is) inexplicable paſſions of mind, deſires abhorring what they imbrace, and imbracing what they abhor? in which Agony *how ſhould the tongue go about to expreſs* what the ſoul indured? When the griefs of *Job* were exceeding great, his words accordingly to open them were many; howbeit, ſtill unto his ſeeming they were undiſcovered; [d] *Though my talk* (ſaith *Job*) *be this day in bitterneſs, yet my plague is greater than my groaning.* But here to what purpoſe ſhould words ſerve, when nature hath more to declare than grones and ſtrong cries, more than ſtreams of bloody ſweats, more than his doubled and tripled prayers can expreſs, who thrice putting forth his hand to receive that Cup, beſides which there was no other cauſe of his coming into the World, he thrice pulleth it back again, and as often even with tears of bloud craveth, if it be poſſible, O Father, or if not, *even what thine own good pleaſure is,* for whoſe ſake the Paſſion that hath in it a bitter, and bloudy conflict, even with Wrath and Death and Hell, is moſt welcome. Whereas therefore we find in God a will reſolved that Chriſt ſhall ſuffer; and in the humane will of Chriſt two actual deſires, the one avoiding, and the other accepting death; is that deſire which firſt declareth it ſelf by prayer, againſt that wherewith he concludeth prayer, or either of them againſt his mind to whom prayer in this caſe ſeeketh? We may judge of theſe diverſities in the will, by the like in the underſtanding. For as the intellectual part doth not croſs it ſelf, by conceiving man juſt & unjuſt, when it meaneth not the ſame man, nor by imagi-

a Pſal. 40. 8.

b Joh. 12. 21.
c Matth. 27. 46.
Non potuit divinitas humanitatem & ſecundum aliquid deſcruiſſe, & ſecundum aliquid non deſeruiſſe? Subtraxit protectionem, ſed non ſeparavit unionem. Sic ergo dereliquit ut non adjuvaret, ſed non dereliquit ut recederet. Sic ergo humanitas a divinitate in paſſione derelicta eſt. Quam tamen mortem quia non pro ſua iniquitate, ſed pro noſtra redemptione ſuſtinuit, quare ſit derelicta requirit, non quaſi adverſus Deum de pœna murmurans, ſed nobis innocentiam ſuam in pœna demonſtrans. Hug. de Sacra. lib. 2. par. 1. c. 10 Deus meus, ut quid dereliqui. nec ignorantiæ, nec diffidentiæ, nec querelæ, ſed admirationis tantum, quæ aliis inveſtigandæ cauſæ ardorem & diligentiam acuat.
d Job 23. 8.

imagining the same man learned and unlearned, if learned in one skill, and in another kind of learning unskilfull, because the parts of every true opposition do always both concern the same subject, and have reference to the same thing, sith otherwise they are but in shew opposite, and not in truth: So the will about one and the same thing may in contrary respects have contrary inclinations, and that without contrariety. The Minister of justice may, for publike example to others, virtuously will the execution of that party, whose pardon another for consanguinities sake as virtuously may desire. Consider death in it self, and nature teacheth Christ to shun it. Consider death as a mean to procure the salvation of the world, and mercy worketh in Christ all [a] willingness of mind towards it. Therefore in these two desires there can be no repugnant opposition. Again, compare them with the will of God, and if any opposition be, it must be only between his appointment of Christs death, and the former desire which wisheth deliverance from death. But neither is this desire opposite to the will of God. The will of God was that Christ should suffer the pains of death. Not so his will, as if the torment of innocency did in it self please and delight God, but such was his will, in regard of the end whereunto it was necessary that Christ should suffer. The death of Christ in it self therefore God willeth not, which to the end we might thereby obtain life, he both alloweth and appointeth. In like manner the Son of man indureth willingly to that purpose those grievous pains, which simply not to have shunned had been against nature, and by consequent against God. I take it therefore to be an errour, that Christ either knew not what himself was to suffer, or else had forgotten the things he knew. The root of which error was an over-restrained consideration of Prayer, as though it had no other lawful use but only to serve for a chosen mean, whereby the will resolveth to seek that which the understanding certainly knoweth it shall obtain: whereas prayers, in truth, both ours are, and his were, as well sometime a presentation of meer desires, as a mean of procuring desired effects at the hands of God. We are therefore taught by his example, that the presence of dolorous and dreadful objects, even in minds most perfect, may as clouds over-cast all sensible joy; that no assurance touching future victories can make present conflicts so sweet and easie, but nature will shun and shrink from them, nature will desire ease and deliverance from oppressive burthens; that the contrary determination of God is oftentimes against the effect of this desire; yet not against the affection it self, because it is naturally in us; that in such case our prayers cannot serve us as means to obtain the thing we desire; that notwithstanding they are unto God most acceptable sacrifices, because they testifie we desire nothing but at his hands, and our desires we submit with contentment to be over-ruled by his will; and in general they are not repugnant unto the natural will of God, which wisheth to the works of his own hands, in that they are his own handy-work, all happiness, although perhaps for some special cause in our own particular, a contrary determination have seemed more convenient; finally, that thus to propose our desires which cannot take such effects as we specifie, shall notwithstanding otherwise procure us his heavenly grace, even as this very prayer of Christ obtained [b] Angels to be sent him as comforters in his Agony. And according to this example we are not afraid to present unto God our prayers for those things, which that he will perform unto us we have no sure nor certain knowledge. [c] St. *Pauls* Prayer for the Church of *Corinth* was, that they might not do any evil, although he knew that no man liveth which sinneth not, although he knew that in this life we always must pray, [d] *Forgive us our sins.* It is our frailty, that in many things we all do amiss; but a virtue, that we would do amiss in nothing; and a testimony of that virtue, when we pray, that what occasion of sin soever do offer it self, we may be strengthned from above to withstand it. They pray in vain to have sin pardoned, which seek not also to prevent sin by prayer, even every particular sin, by prayer against all sin, except men can name some transgression wherewith we ought to have truce. For in very deed although we cannot be free from all sin collectively, in such sort that do part thereof shall be found inherent in us, yet distributively at the least all great and grievous actual offences, as they offer themselves one by one, both may and ought to be by all means avoided. So that in this sense to be preserved from all sin is not impossible. Finally, concerning deliverance it

a Esa. 53. 10. & Iob 10. 15.

b Luke 22.12.
c 2 Cor. 13. 7.

d We may not pray in this life to be free from all sin, because we must always pray, Forgive us our sins. e T.C.l.3.p.200

self

self from all adversity, we are not to say men are in adversity whensoever they feel any small hinderance of their wel-fare in this World, but when some notable affliction or cross, some great calamity or trouble befalleth them. Tribulation hath in it divers circumstances, they mind sundry faculties; to apprehend them: It offereth sometime it self to the lower powers of the soul as a most unpleasant spectacle to the higher, sometimes as drawing after it a train of dangerous inconveniences; sometime as bringing with it remedies for the curing of sundry evils, as Gods instrument of revenge and fury sometime, sometime as a rod of his just, yet moderate ire and displeasure, sometime, as matter for them that spitefully hate us to exercise their poysioned malice, sometime as a furnace of tryal for vertue to shew it self, and through conflict to obtain glory. Which different contemplations of adversity do work for the most part their answerable effects. Adversity either apprehended by sense as a thing offensive and grievous to nature; or by reason conceived as a snare, an occasion of many mens falling from God, a sequel of Gods indignation and wrath, a thing which Satan desireth, and would be glad to behold; tribulation thus considered being present causeth sorrow, and being imminent breedeth fear. For moderation of which two affections growing from the very natural bitterness and gall of adversity, the Scripture much alledgeth contrary fruits, which affliction likewise hath whensoever it falleth on them that are tractable, the grace of Gods holy Spirit concurring therewith. But when the Apostle Saint *Paul* teacheth, that every one which will live godly in Christ Jesus must suffer persecution, and by many tribulations we enter into the Kingdome of Heaven, because in a forrest of many Wolves Sheep cannot choose but feed in continual danger of life; or when Saint *James* exhorteth to account it a matter of exceeding joy when we fall into divers temptations, because by the tryal of faith, patience is brought forth; was it, suppose we, their meaning to frustrate our Lords admonition, *Pray that ye enter not into temptation*? When himself pronounceth them blessed that should for his Name sake be subject to all kinds of ignominy and opprobrious malediction, was it his purpose that no man should ever pray with *David*, *Lord, remove from me, shame and contempt*? In those tribulations, saith Saint *Augustine, which may hurt as well as profit, we must say with the Apostle, What we should ask as we ought, we know not; yet because they are tough, because they are grievous, because the sense of our weakness flieth them, we pray according to the general desire of the will of man, that God would turn them away from us, owing in the mean while this devotion to the Lord our God, that if he remove them not, yet we do not therefore imagine our selves in his sight despised, but rather with godly sufferance of evils, expect greater good at his merciful hands. For thus is vertue in weakness perfected.* To the flesh (as the Apostle himself granteth) all affliction is naturally grievous. Therefore nature which causeth to fear, teacheth to pray against all adversity. Prosperity in regard of our corrupt inclination to abuse the blessings of Almighty God, doth prove for the most part a thing dangerous to the souls of men. Very ease it self is death to the wicked, and the prosperity of fools slayeth them. Few men there are which long prosper and sin not. Howbeit even as these ill effects, although they be very usual and common, are no barre to the hearty prayers, whereby most vertuous minds wish peace and prosperity always where they love, because they consider that this in it self is a thing naturally desired: So because all adversity is in it self against nature, what should hinder to pray against it, although the providence of God turn it often unto the great good of many men? Such Prayers of the Church to be delivered from all adversity, are no more repugnant to any reasonable disposition of mens minds towards death, much less to that blessed patience and meek contentment which Saints by heavenly inspiration have to endure, (what cross or calamity soever it pleaseth God to lay upon them) then our Lord and Saviours own Prayer before his Passion was repugnant unto his most gracious resolution to dye for the sins of the whole World.

49. In praying for deliverance from all adversitie, wee seek that which nature doth wish to it self; but by intreating for mercy towards all, wee declare that affection wherewith Christian Charity thirsteth after the good
of

a *Psal.* 119.71.
b 1 *Tim.* 3.12.
To pray against persecution is contrary to that word which saith, that every one which will live godly in Christ Jesus, must suffer persecution.
T.C. l.3. p.200.
c *James* 1.3.
d *Psal.* 110.22.
e *Aug. Epist.* 121. cap. 14.

f *Prov.* 1.32.

Prayer that all men may find mercy, and of the will of God that all men might be saved.

of the whole World, we discharge that duty which the [a] Apostle himself doth im- [a 1 *Tim.*2.3.] pose on the Church of Christ as a *commendable* office, a sacrifice *acceptable* in Gods sight, a service according to his heart, whose *desire* is to have all men saved; a work most suteable with his purpose, who gave himself to be the price of redemption *for all*, and a forcible meane to *procure the conversion* of all such as are not yet acquainted with the mysteries of that truth which must save their souls. Against it there is but the bare shew of this one impediment, that all mens salvation, and many mens eternal condemnation or death, are things the one repugnant to the other, that both cannot be brought to pass; that we know there are vessels of wrath to whom God will never extend mercy, and therefore that wittingly we ask an impossible thing to be had. The truth is, that as life and death, mercy and wrath, are matters of meer understanding or knowledge, all mens salvation and some mens endless perdition are things so opposite, that whosoever doth affirm the one, must necessarily deny the other; God himself cannot effect both, or determine that both shall be. There is in the knowledge both of God and man this certainty, that life and death have divided between them the whole body of mankind. What portion either of the two hath, God himself knoweth; for us he hath left no sufficient means to comprehend, and for that cause neither given any leave to search in particular who are infallibly the heirs of the Kingdom of God, who cast-aways. Howbeit concerning the state of all men with whom we live (for only of them our prayers are meant) we may till the Worlds end, *for the present*, always presume, that *as far as in us there is power to discern* what others are, and as far as any duty of ours dependeth upon the notice of their condition in respect of God, the safest axiomes for Charity to rest it self upon are these; *He which believeth already, is*; and *He which believeth not as yet, may be the Child of God.* [b] It becometh not us *during* [b *Sidon. Apol. lib.* 6. *Epist.*] *life altogether to condemn any man, seeing that* (for any thing we know) *there is hope of every mans forgiveness, the possibility of whose repentance is not yet cut off by death.* And therefore charity which [c] *hopeth all things*, prayeth also for all men. Where- [c 1 *Cor.*14.7.] fore to let go personal knowledge touching vessels of wrath and mercy, what they are inwardly in the sight of God it skilleth not, for us there is cause sufficient in all men whereupon to ground our prayers unto God in their behalf. For whatsoever the mind of man apprehendeth as good, the will of charity and love is to have it inlarged in the very uttermost extent, that all may enjoy it to whom it can any way adde perfection. Because therefore the farther a good thing doth reach, the nobler and worthier we reckon it, our prayers for all mens good, no less than for our own, the Apostle with very fit terms commendeth as being καλὸν, a work commendable for the largeness of the affection from whence it springeth, even as theirs, [d] which [d *Rom.*9.3. *&*] have requested at Gods hands the salvation of many with the loss of their own [10.1.] souls, drowning as it were and over-whelming themselves in the abundance of their love towards others, is proposed as being in regard of the rareness of such affections ὑπέρκαλον, more than excellent. But this extraordinary height of desire after other mens salvation is no common mark. The other is a duty which belongeth unto all and prevaileth with God daily. For as it is in it self good, so God accepteth and taketh it in very good part at the hands of faithful men. Our prayers for all men do include both them that shall find mercy, and them also that shall find none. For them that shall, no man will doubt but our prayers are both accepted and granted. Touching them for whom we crave that mercy which is not to be obtained, let us not think that our Saviour did miss-instruct his Disciples, willing them to pray for the peace even of such as should be uncapable of so great a blessing; or that the Prayers of the [e] Prophet *Jeremy* offended God, because the an- [e *Mat.*10.11.12] swer of God was a resolute denial of favour to them for whom supplication was [f *Jer.*15.1.] made. And if any man doubt how God should accept such prayers in case they be opposite to his Will, or not grant them if they be according unto that which himself willeth, our answer is, that such sures God accepteth,in that they are conformable unto his *general inclination*, which is that all men might be saved; yet always he granteth them not, for as much as there is in God sometimes a more private *occasioned will* which determineth the contrary. So that the other being the rule of our actions; and not this, our requests for things opposite to this Will of God are

not

not therefore the lefs gracious in his fight. There is no doubt but we ought in all things to frame our wils to the Will of God, and that otherwife in whatfoever we do we fin. For of our felves being fo apt to erre, the only way which we have to ftreighten our paths, is by following the rule of his will, whofe footfteps naturally are right. If the eye, the hand, or the foot, do that which the will commandeth, though they ferve as inftruments to fin, yet is fin the Commanders fault and not theirs, becaufe Nature hath abfolutely and without exception made them fubjects to the wil of man which is Lord over them. As the body is fubject to the will of man, fo is mans will to the Will of God; for fo it behoveth that the better fhould guide and command the worfe. But becaufe the fubjection of the body to the wil is by natural neceffity, the fubjection of the will unto God voluntary; we therefore ftand in need of direction after what fort our wills and defires may be rightly conformed to his. Which is not done by willing always the felf-fame thing that God intendeth. For it may chance that his purpofe is fometime the fpeedy death of them, whofe long continuance in life if we fhould not wifh we were unnatural. When the object or matter therefore of our defires is (as in this cafe) a thing both good of it felf, and not forbidden of God; when the end for which we defire it is virtuous and apparently moft holy; when the root from which our affection towards it proceedeth, is Charity; piety that which we do in declaring our defire by pray'r; yea over and befides all this, fith we know that to pray for all men living, is but to fhew the fame affection which towards every of them our Lord Jefus

a Propterea nihil contrariciatik erat,fi Chriftus homo fecundum affectum pietatik quam in humanitate fua affumpferat aliquid volebat, quod tamen fecundum voluntatem divinam, in qua cum patre omnia difponebat futurum non effe prafciebat,quia &hoc ad veram humanitatem pertinebat, ut pictate moveretur, & hoc ad veram divinitatem,ut à fua difpofitione,non moveretur. Hug.de quat. b Profp. de vocat.Gen.l.i.c.4 inter opera Ambrof.

Chrift hath born, who knowing only as God who are his, did[*] as man tafte death for the good of all men; furely to that will of God which ought to be and is the known rule of all our actions, we do not herein oppofe our felves, although his fecret determination haply be againft us; which if we did underftand, as we do not, yet to reft contented with that which God will have done, is as much as he requireth at the hands of men. And concerning our felves what we earneftly crave in this cafe, the fame, as all things elfe of like condition, we meekly fubmit unto his moft gracious will and pleafure. Finally, as we have caufe fufficient why to think the practice of our Church allowable in this behalf, fo neither is ours the firft which hath been of that mind. For to end with the words b of *Profper*, *This Law of fupplication for all men* (faith he) *the devout zeal of all Priefts and all faithful men doth hold with fuch full agreement, that there is not any part of all the World where Chriftian people do not ufe to pray in the fame manner. The Church every where maketh prayers unto God not only for Saints, and fuch as already in Chrift are regenerated, but for all Infidels and enemies of the Crofs of Jefus Chrift, for all Idolaters, for all that perfecute Chrift in his followers, for Jews to whofe blindnefs the light of the Gofpel doth not yet fhine, for Heretiques and Schifmatiques,who from the unity of faith and charity are eftranged. And for fuch what doth the Church ask of God but this, that leaving their errors they may be converted unto him, that faith and charity may be given them, and that out of the darknefs of ignorance they may come to the knowledge of his truth? Which becaufe they cannot themfelves doe in their own behalf, as long as the fway of evil cuftom over-beareth them, and the chains of Satan detain them bound, neither are they able to break thorough thofe errours wherein they are fo determinately fetled, that they pay unto falfity the whole fum of whatfoever love is owing unto Gods Truth, our Lord merciful and juft requireth to have all men prayed for, that when we behold innumerable multitudes drawn up from the depth of fo bottomlefs evils; we may not doubt but (in part) God hath done the thing we requefted; nor defpair, but that being thankfull for them towards whom already he hath fhewed mercy, the reft which are not as yet enlightened, fhall before they pafs out of life be made partakers of the like grace. Or if the grace of him which faveth [for fo we fee it falleth out] over-pafs fome, fo that the Prayer of the Church for them be not received, this we may leave to the hidden Judgments of Righteoufnefs, and acknowledge that in that fecret there is a Gulf, which while we live we fhall never found.*

Of the name, the Author, and the force 50 Inftruction and Praye, whereof we have hitherto fpoken, are duties which ferve as Elements, Parts or Principles to the reft that follow, in which number the of Sacraments, which force confifteth in this; that God hath ordained them as means to make us partakers of him in Chrift, and of life through Chrift.

Sacra-

Sacraments of the Church are chief. The Church is to us that very [a] Mother of our new Birth, in whose Bowels we are all bred, at whose breasts we receive nourishment. As many therefore as are apparently to our judgement born of God, they have the seed of Regeneration by the Ministery of the Church, which useth to that end and purpose not only the Word, but the Sacraments, both having generative force and vertue. As oft as we mention a Sacrament properly understood (for in the Writings of the ancient Fathers, all Articles which are peculiar to Christian Faith, all duties of Religion containing that which sense or natural reason cannot of it self discern, are most commonly named Sacraments) our restraint of the Word to some few principal divine Ceremonies, importeth in every such Ceremony two things, the substance of the Ceremony it self which is visible, and besides that somewhat else more secret, in reference whereunto we conceive that Ceremony to be a Sacrament. For we all admire and honour the holy Sacraments, not respecting so much the Service which we do unto God in receiving them, as the dignity of that sacred and secret gift which we thereby receive from God. Seeing that Sacraments therefore consist altogether in relation to some such gift or grace supernatural, as only God can bestow, how should any but the Church administer those Ceremonies as Sacraments, which are not thought to be Sacraments by any but by the Church? There is in Sacraments to be observed their force and their forme of administration. Upon their force their necessity dependeth. So that how they are necessary we cannot discern, till we see how effectual they are. When Sacraments are said to be visible Signs of invisible Grace, we thereby conceive how grace is indeed the very end for which these Heavenly Mysteries were instituted; and besides sundry other properties observed in them, the matter whereof they consist is such as signifieth, figureth, and representeth their end. But still their efficacy resteth obscure to our understanding, except we search somewhat more distinctly what grace in particular, that is, whereunto they are referred, and what manner of operation they have towards it. The use of Sacraments is but only in this life, yet so, that here they concern a far better life than this, and are for that cause accompanied with *grace which worketh Salvation.* Sacraments are the powerful Instruments of God to eternal life. For as our natural life consisteth in the Union of the body with the Soul; so our life supernatural in the Union of the Soul with God. And for as much as there is no Union of God with man, without that [b] meane between both which is both, it seemeth requisite that we first consider how God is in Christ, then how Christ is in us, and how the Sacraments do serve to make us partakers of Christ. In other things we may be more brief, but the weight of these requireth largeness.

Margin notes: a Gal. 4. 26: Esay 54. 1.

b *Oportebat Deum carnem fieri ut in seipso concordiam constabularet, terrenorum pariter atque cælestium, dum utriusque partis in se connectens pignora, & Deum pariter homine, & hominem Deo copularet.* Tertul. de Trinit.

51. The Lord our God is but one God. In which indivisible unity notwithstanding we adore the Father as being altogether of himself, we glorifie that Consubstantial Word which is the Son, we bless and magnifie that Co-essential Spirit eternally proceeding from both, which is the Holy Ghost. Seeing therefore the Father is of none, the Son is of the Father, and the Spirit is of both, they are by these their several properties really distinguishable each from other. For the substance of God with this property *to be of none,* doth make the person of the Father; the very self same substance in number with this property *to be of the Father,* maketh the person of the Son: the same substance having added unto it the property of *proceeding from the other two,* maketh the person of the Holy Ghost. So that in every person there is implied both the substance of God which is one, and also that propriety which causeth the same person really and truly to differ from the other two. Every [c] person hath his own subsistence, which no other besides hath, although there be others besides that are of the same substance. As no man but *Peter* can be the person which *Peter* is, yet *Paul* hath the self-same Nature which *Peter* hath. Again, Angels have every of them the nature of pure and invisible Spirits, but every Angel is not that Angel which appeared in a Dream to *Joseph.*

Margin notes: That God is in Christ by the personal Incarnation of the Son, who is very God. Isaiah 9. 6. Jer. 23. 6. Rom. 9. 5. John 16. 15. John 5. 21. Colos. 2. 9. 1 John 5. 20:

c Πρόσωπον ἢ γοῦν ὑπόστασις ὅτι χ[?] τὸς ἰδίας πατέρας τὸ ἴδιον παρὰ τὸ κοινόν. Κοινότης δὲ ἐστιν ἡ φύσις ἑκάστι προσήκα[?], ἰδιάς δὲ εἰσιν ὑποστάσεις. Suid. ἡ ουσία καθ᾽ ἑαυτὴν ὑφίσταται ἀλλ᾽ ἐν ταῖς ὑποστάσεσι θεωρεῖται· τὸ δὲ κοινὸν μεθ᾽ τῶ ἰδιαζούσης ἔχει ἡ πρόσταξις κ[?] τὸ καθ᾽ ἑαυτὴν ὑπάρξαι Dam: de Orthod. fide lib. 3. cap. 6.

Now

Now when God became man, left we should erre in applying this to the person of the Father, or of the Spirit, Saint *Peters* Confession unto Christ was, Thou art the

a Match.16.16. *Son* of the Living God; and Saint *Johns* Exposition thereof was made plain, and that it is the *b Word* which was made flesh. *The*

b John 1. Ignat. Epist. ad Magnes. Ὃς ἐςιν αὐτος λόγΘ̔ ἐ μ πος ἀλλ᾽ ἐνεςώδης. Ὀυ γὸ εξι λαλιας ἐναρθρυ ἀλλ᾽ ἐνεργειας θεικης ἐσία γεννητη̇. c Κατ᾽ εθεια λόγον κεκοινώνηκεν ὁ πατηρ κ̄ το αγιον πνευμα τη σαρκωσει τυ λόγυ, εἰ μη κατ᾽ ευδοκιαν κ̄ βολησιν. Damasc.

Father, and the holy Ghost (saith *Damascen*) *have no communion with the Incarnation of the Word, otherwise than onely by approbation and assent.* Notwithstanding, forasmuch as the Word and Deity are one subject, wee must beware wee exclude not the Nature of God from incarnation, and so make the Son of God incarnate not

d *In illo divinitas est unigeniti facta particeps mortalitatis nostrae, ut & nos participes ejus immortalitatis essemus.* Aug. Epist. 57. to be very God. For undoubtedly even *d* the Nature of God it self in the onely person of the Son is incarnate, and hath taken to it self flesh. Wherefore Incarnation may neither be granted to any person but onely one, nor yet denied to that nature which is common unto all three. Concerning the cause of which incomprehensible Mystery, for as much as it seemeth a thing unconsonant, that the world should honour any other person as the Saviour, but him whom it honoureth as the Creatour of the World, and in the Wisdom of God it hath not been thought convenient to admit any way of saving man but by man himself, though nothing should be spoken of the love and mercy of God towards man, which this way are become such a spectacle, as neither men nor Angels can behold without a kind of heavenly astonishment, we may hereby perceive there is cause sufficient why divine Nature should assume

e 2 Cor. 5. 19. Humane, that so *e* God might be in Christ reconciling to himself the World. And if some cause be likewise required, why rather to this end and purpose the Son, than either the Father, or the Holy Ghost, should be made man, could we which are born the children of wrath, be adopted the Sons of God through grace, any other

f Heb. 2. 16. than the natural Son of God being Mediatour between God and us? It *f* became therefore him by whom all things are to be the way of salvation to all, that the institution and restitution of the World might be both wrought by one hand. The Worlds Salvation was without the Incarnation of the Son of God a thing impossible; not simply impossible, but impossible, it being presupposed that the Will of God was no otherwise to have it saved than by the death of his own Son. Wherefore taking to himself our flesh, and by his Incarnation making it his own flesh, he had now of his own, although from us, what to offer unto God for us. And as Christ took Manhood, that by it he might be capable of death whereunto he humbled himself, so because Manhood is the proper subject of compassion and feeling pity, which maketh the Scepter of Christs Regency even in the Kingdome of Heaven amiable, he which without our Nature could not on Earth suffer for the sins of the

g Heb. 4. 15. World, doth now also *g* by means thereof both make intercession to God for sinners, and exercise dominion over all men with a true, a natural, and a sensible touch of mercy.

The mis-interpretations which Heresie hath made of the manner how God and man are united in one Christ. 52. It is not in mans ability either to express perfectly, or conceive the manner how this was brought to pass. But the strength of our Faith is tryed by those things wherein our wits and capacities are not strong. Howbeit because this Divine Mystery is more true than plain, divers having framed the same to their own conceits and fancies, are found in their expositions thereof more plain than true: In so much that by the space of five hundred years after Christ, the Church was almost troubled with nothing else, saving only with care and travel to preserve this Article from the sinister construction of Hereticks. Whose first mists when the light of

h An.Dom.325 the *h Nicene* Council had dispelled, it was not long ere *Macedonius* transferred unto Gods own Holy Spirit the same blasphemy, wherewith *Arrius* had already dishonoured his coeterna ly begotten Son; not long ere *Apollinarius* began to *i* pare

i Μηδε̇ ,δ̄ Ἀ. ηθλωαι φησι̇ τλ̄υ σαρκα ε̇κτινην ανθρωπινω ποθς ηγεμονευομενην απο τη̇ ζωτλ̄υ ενδεδυκότΘ̔ Θε̇υ̇. Suid. away from Christs humanity. In refutation of which impieties when the Fathers of the Church, *Athanasius, Basil,* and the two *Gregories,* had by their painful travels sufficiently cleered the truth, no less for the Deity of the Holy Ghost, than for the compleat humanity of Christ, there followed hereupon a final conclusion, whereby those Controversies, as also the rest which *Paulus Samosatenus, Sabellius, Photinus, Ætius, Eunomius,* together with the whole swarme of pestilent *Demi-arrians,* had from time to time stirred up sithence the Council of *Nice,* were both privately, first

at

at *Rome* in a smaller Synod, and then at *Constantinople* in a general famous Assembly brought to a peaceable and quiet end, seven-score Bishops and ten agreeing in that Confession, which by them set down, remaineth at this present hour, a part of our Church Liturgy, a Memorial of their fidelity and zeal, a soveraign preservative of Gods people from the venemous infection of heresie. Thus in Christ the verity of God, and the compleat substance of man, were with full agreement established throughout the World, till such time as the Heresie of *Nestorius* broached it self, dividing Christ into two persons, the Son of God, and the Son of man, the one a person begotten of God before all Worlds, the other also a person born of the Virgin Mary, and in special favour chosen to be made intire to the Son of God above all men, so that whosoever will honour God, must together honour Christ, with whose person God hath vouchsafed to joyn himself in so high a degree of gracious respect and favour. But that the self-same person, which verily is man, should properly be God also, and that by reason not of two persons linked in amity, but of two natures, Humane and Divine, conjoyned in one and the same Person, the God of glory may be said as well to have suffered death, as to have raised the dead from their graves; the Son of man as well to have made, as to have redeemed the World, *Nestorius* in no case would admit. That which deceived him, was want of heed to the first beginning of that admirable combination of God with man. The Word (saith S. *John*) was made flesh, and dwelt *in us*. The Evangelist useth the plural number, Men for Manhood, us for the nature whereof we consist, even as the Apostle denying the Assumption of *Angelical nature*, saith likewise in the plural number, he took not *Angels*, but the seed of *Abraham*. It pleased not the *Word* or Wisdom of God, to take to it self some one person amongst men, for then should that one have been advanced which was assumed, and no more; but Wisdom, to the end she might save many, built her House of that *nature* which is common unto all, she made not *this or that* man her Habitation, but dwelt *in us*. The Seeds of Herbs and Plants at the first are not in act, but in possibility, that which they afterwards grow to be. If the Son of God had taken to himself a man now made and already perfected, it would of necessity follow that there are in Christ two persons, the one assuming, and the other assumed, whereas the Son of God did not assume a mans person unto his own, but a mans nature to his own person, and therefore took *semen*, the seed of *Abraham*, the very first original Element of our nature, before it was come to have any personal Humane subsistence. The flesh and the conjunction of the flesh with God began both at one instant; his making, and taking to himself our flesh was but one act, so that in Christ there is no personal subsistence but one, and that from everlasting. By taking onely the nature of man, he still continueth one person, and changeth but the manner of his subsisting, which was before in the meer glory of the Son of God, and is now in the habit of our flesh. For as much therefore as Christ hath no personal subsistence but one whereby we acknowledge him to have been eternally the Son of God, we must of necessity apply to the *person* of the Son of God, even that which is spoken of Christ according to his humane nature. For example, according to the flesh he was born of the Virgin *Mary*, baptized of *John* in the River *Jordan*, by *Pilate* adjudged to dye, and executed by the Jews. We cannot say properly that the Virgin bore, or *John* did baptize, or *Pilate* condemn, or the Jews crucifie the nature of man, because these are all personal Attributes, his person is the subject which receiveth them, his nature that which maketh his person capable or apt to receive. If we should say that the person of a man in our Saviour Christ was the subject of these things, this were plainly to intrap our selves in the very snare of the *Nestorians* Heresie, between whom and the Church of God there was no difference, saving only that *Nestorius* imagined in Christ as well a personal Humane subsistence, as a Divine, the Church acknowledging a substance both Divine and Humane, but no other personal subsistence than Divine, because the Son of God took not to himself a mans person, but the nature onely of a man. Christ is a person both Divine and Humane, howbeit not therefore two persons in one, neither both these in one sence, but a person Divine, because he is *personally* the Son of God, Humane, because *he hath* really *the nature* of the children of men. In Christ therefore God and Man, *there is* (saith *Paschasius*) *a two-fold substance, not*

Margin notes:
a *Anno D.*381
b *O'υκ ετι την ενωσιν ομολο-γει μεθ' ημων.* Cyril. Epist. ad Eulog.
O'υκ ελαβε γδ ενωσιν τε λογε τε θεε προς ανθρωπον, αλλα δυο υποστασεις ελαβε, διαιρεσιν. Ετ δε η ανθρω-πον κ θεον απεκαλει την προσον αλλ εν ετι ως ημιας αλλα τη σγκισει κ τη οικειωσει καθα το ταυτα αλ-ληλοις αφερο-κειν διαιρετω υπερβολην της φιλιας.
c Leont. de Sect.
c *John* 1. 14.
d *Heb.* 2. 16.
e *η ληρωσιας φυσις δ πρω-τηγχε της λητρεως.* Theod. Dial.
Ατρεπτω.
f *Paschas.* lib. de Spir. sancto

not a two fold perfon, becaufe one perfon diftinguisheth another, whereas one nature cannot in another become extinct. For the perfonal being which the Son of God already had, fuffered not the fubftance to be perfonal which he took, although together with the nature which he had, the nature alfo which he took continueth. Whereupon it followeth againft *Neftorius*, that no perfon was born of the Virgin but the Son of God, no perfon but the Son of God baptized, the Son of God condemned, the Son of God and no other perfon crucified, which one onely point of Chriftian Belief, *the infinite worth of the Son of God*, is the very ground of all things believed concerning life and falvation, by that which Chrift either did or fuffered as man in our behalf. But for as much as Saint *Cyril*, the chiefeft of thofe two hundred Bifhops affembled in the [a] Council of *Ephefus* where the Herefie of *Neftorius* was condemned, had in his Writings againft the Arrians avouched, that *the Word or Wifdome* of God hath *but one nature* which is eternal, and whereunto he affumed flefh (for the Arrians were of opinion, that befides Gods own eternal Wifdome there is a Wifdome which God created before all things, to the end he might thereby create all things elfe, and that this created Wifdome was the Word which took flefh.) Again, for as much as the fame *Cyril* had given inftance in the body and the foul of man no farther than onely to enforce by example againft *Neftorius*, that a vifible, and an invifible, a mortal and an immortal fubftance may unired make *one perfon*, the words of *Cyril* were in procefs of time fo taken, as though it had been his drift to teach, that even as in us the body and the Soul, fo in Chrift, God and man make but *one nature*. Of which error, fix hundred and thirty Fathers in the [b] Council of *Chalcedon* condemned *Eutiches*. For as *Neftorius* teaching rightly that God and man are diftinct Natures, did thereupon mif-inferre that in Chrift thofe natures can by no conjunction make one perfon; fo *Eutiches* of found belief, as touching their true perfonal copulation became unfound, by denying the difference which ftill continueth between the one and the other nature. We muft therefore keep warily a middle courfe, fhunning both that diftraction of perfons wherein *Neftorius* went awry, and alfo this later confufion of natures which deceived *Eutiches*. [c] Thefe natures from the moment of their firft combination have been and are for ever infeparable. For even when his Soul forfook the Tabernacle of his Body, his Deity forfook neither Body nor Soul. If it had, then could we not truly hold either that the perfon of Chrift was buried, or that the perfon of Chrift did raife up it felf from the dead. For the Body feparated from the Word, can in no true fence be termed the Perfon of Chrift; nor is it true, to fay that the Son of God in raifing up that Body did raife up himfelf, if the Body were not both with him and of him, even during the time it lay in the Sepulchre. The like is alfo to be faid of the Soul, otherwife we are plainly and inevitably *Neftorians*. The very perfon of Chrift therefore for ever one and the felf-fame, was onely touching bodily fubftance concluded within the Grave, his Soul onely from thence fevered, but by perfonal union, his Deity ftill infeparably joyned with both.

53. The fequel of which conjunction of natures in the perfon of Chrift, is no abolifhment of natural properties appertaining to either fubftance, no tranfition or tranfmigration thereof out of one fubftance into another; finally, no fuch mutual infufion as really caufeth the fame natural operations or properties to be made common unto both fubftances; but whatfoever is natural to Deity, the fame remaineth in Chrift uncommunicated unto his Manhood, and whatfoever natural to Manhood, his Deity thereof is uncapable. The true properties and operations of his Deity are, to know that which is not poffible for *created natures* to comprehend: to be fimply the higheft caufe of all things, the well-fpring of immortality and life; to have neither end nor beginning of dayes; to be every where prefent, and inclofed no where, to be fubject to no alteration nor paffion; to produce of it felf thefe effects which cannot proceed but from infinite Majefty and Power. The true properties and operations of his Manhood are fuch, as [d] *Irenæus* reckoneth up, *If Chrift* (faith he) *had not taken flefh from the very earth, he would not have coveted thofe earthly nourifhments wherewith bodies which be taken from thence are fed. This was the nature which felt hunger after long fafting, was defirous of reft after travel, teftified compaffion and love by tears, groaned in heavinefs, and with extremity of grief*

even

à *Anno D.* 431.

b *Anno D.* 451.

c Ἀχώριϲον προσπαϲι τῆς σαρκὸς εἶναι τῦ Θεῖαν οὗϲιν ὁμολογεῖν κἂν τῆ ϲαυρᾶ κἂν τῶ ταϕῶ. Theodor. Dial. Ἀπαθῆς.

d Ταῦῖα πάνῖα ϲύμϲολα σαρκὸς τῆς ἀπὸ γῆς εἰλημμένης. Iren. lib. 3. ad-verf. bæref.

That by the union of the one with the other nature in Chrift, there groweth neither gain nor lofs of effential properties to either.

even melted away it self into bloudy sweats. To Christ we ascribe both working of Wonders and suffering of pains, we use concerning him, speeches as well of Humility as of Divine Glory, but the one we apply unto that nature which he took of the Virgin *Mary*, the other to that which was in the beginning. We may not therefore imagine that the properties of the weaker nature have vanisht with the presence of the more glorious, and have been therein swallowed up as in a Gulf. We dare not in this point give ear to them, who over-boldly affirm, that [a] *The nature which Christ took weak and feeble from us by being mingled with Deity became the same which Deity is, that the assumption of our substance unto his was like the blending of a drop of Vinegar with the huge Ocean, wherein although it continue still, yet not with those properties which severed it hath, because sithence the instant of their conjunction, all distinction and difference of the one from the other is extinct; and whatsoever we can now conceive of the Son of God, is nothing else but meer Deity:* which words are so plain and direct for *Eutiches,* that I stand in doubt they are not his whose name they carry. Sure I am they are far from truth, and must of necessity give place to the better advised sentences of other men. [b] *He which in himself was appointed* (saith *Hilary*) *a Mediator to save his Church, and for performance of that mystery of mediation between God and Man is become God and Man, doth now being but one, consist of both those natures united, neither hath he through the union of both incurred the damage or loss of either, lest by being born a Man, we should think he hath given over to be God; or that because he continued God, therefore he cannot be Man also; whereas the true belief which maketh a man happy, proclaimeth joyntly God and Man, confesseth the Word and Flesh together.* Cyril more plainly, [c] *His two natures have knit themselves the one to the other, and are in that neerness as uncapable of confusion, as of distraction. Their coherence hath not taken away the difference between them, Flesh is not become God, but doth still continue flesh, although it be now the flesh of God.* Yea, of each substance (saith [d] *Leo*) *the properties are all preserved and kept safe.* These two natures are as causes and original grounds of all things which Christ hath done. Wherefore some things he doth as God, because his Deity alone is the well-spring from which they flow; some things as Man, because they issue from his meer humane nature, some things joyntly as both God and Man, because both natures concurre as principles thereunto. For albeit the properties of each *nature* do cleave only to that nature whereof they are properties, and therefore Christ cannot *naturally be* as God, the same which he *naturally* is as Man, yet both natures may very well concur unto *one effect,* and Christ in that respect be truly said to *work* both as God and as Man, one and the self-same thing. Let us therefore set it down for a rule or principle so necessary, as nothing more, to the plain deciding of all doubts and questions about the union of natures in Christ, that of both natures there is a *co-operation* often, an *association* always, but never any mutual *participation,* whereby the properties of the one are infused into the other. Which rule must serve for the better understanding of that which [e] *Damascene* hath touching cross and circulatory speeches, wherein there are attributed to God such things as belong to Manhood, and to Man such as properly concern the Deity of Christ Jesus, the cause whereof is the *association* of natures in one subject. A kind of mutual commutation there is, whereby those concrete names, *God* and *Man,* when we speak of *Christ,* do take interchangeably one anothers room; so that for truth of speech it skilleth not whether we say that the Son of God hath created the World, and the Son of man by his death hath saved it, or else that the Son of man did create, and the Son of God die to save the World. Howbeit, as oft as we attribute to God what the Man-hood of Christ claimeth, or to Man what his Deity hath right unto, we understand by the name of God, and the name of Man, neither the one nor the other nature, but the whole person of Christ in whom both natures are. When the Apostle saith of the Jews, that they crucified the Lord of glory, and when the Son of man, being on earth, affirmeth that the Son of Man was in Heaven at the same instant, there is in these two speeches that mutual circulation before mentioned.

suas alteri proprietates impartire, enunciando videlicet, idque non in abstracto sed in concreto solùm, non humanitati humanas, non Deitati sed Deo tribui. Cujus hæc est ratio, quia cum suppositum prædicationis sit ejusmodi ut utramque naturam in se contineat, sive ab una sive ab altera denominetur, nihil refert.

H h

Christ did all these ἀνθρωπίνως σώματος ύμως. Greg.Nazian. orat. 2. de filio. τὰς μὲν ταπεινὰς λόγους τῷ ἐκ Μαρίας ἀνθρώπω, τὰς δὲ ἀνυμηλοτέρας καὶ θεοπρεπεῖς τῷ ἐν ἀρχῇ ὄντι λόγω Theodor. Dial. Ασύγχυτ.

a Gregor. Nyss. Epist. ad Theophil. Alexandr.

b Hilar. de Trilib. 9.

c Cypr. Epist. ad Nest.

d salva proprietate utriusque natura, suscepta est a majestate humilitas, a virtute infirmitas, ab aternitate mortalitas, Leo. Epist. ad Flavia.

e Οὗτος ἐστιν ὁ τρόπος τῆ ἀντιδόσεως ἑκατέρας φύσεως ἀντιδιδούσης τῇ ἑκαλέρᾳ τὰ ἰδία, διὰ τὴν τῆς ὑποσάσεως ταυτότητα, καὶ τὴν εἰς ἀλληλα αὐτῶν περιχώρησιν. Damasc. de Orthod. fid. lib.3. c. 4. Verum est duarum in Christo naturarum, alteram divinas homini,

mentioned.

* 1 Cor. 2. 8.
a John 3. 13.

mentioned. In the one there is attributed to God, or the * Lord of glory, death, whereof divine nature is not capable ; in the other ubiquitie unto a Man, which humane nature admitteth not. Therefore by the Lord of glory we must needs understand the whole person of Christ, who being Lord of glory was indeed crucified, but not in that nature for which he is termed the Lord of glory. In like manner, by the Son of man the whole person of Christ must necessarily be meant, who being man upon earth, filled Heaven with his glorious presence, but not according to that nature for which the title of man is given him. Without this caution the Fathers whose belief was sincere, and their meaning most sound, shall seem in their writings one to deny what another constantly doth affirm. *Theodoret* disputeth with great earnestness, that *God* cannot be said to suffer. But he thereby meaneth Christs *divine nature* against b *Apollinarius*, which held even Deity it self passible. *Cyril* on the other side against *Nestorius* as much contendeth, that whosoever will deny *very God* to have suffered death, doth forsake the faith. Which notwithstanding to hold, were heresie, if the name of God in this assertion did not import, as it doth, the person of Christ, who being verily God suffered death, but in the flesh, and not in that substance for which the name of God is given him.

b Θυητὺυ τῦ
ίυ καὶαωκι-
αζωι τ̃ θεό-
τητα. Greg.
Nyſſ.de ſecta-
tor.
Apollinar. Ep.
ad Flaviā.

What Christ hath obtained according to the flesh, by the union of his flesh with Deity.

54 If then both natures do remain with their properties in Christ thus distinct as hath been shewed, we are for our better understanding what either nature receiveth from other, to note, that Christ is by three degrees a receiver ; first, in that he is the Son of God ; secondly, in that his humane nature hath had the honour of union with Deity bestowed upon it ; thirdly, in that by means thereof sundry eminent graces have flowed as effects from Deity into that nature which is coupled with it. On Christ therefore is bestowed the gift of eternal Generation, the gift of Union, and the gift of unction. By the gift of eternal Generation Christ hath received of the Father one & in number the self same substance, which the Father hath of himself, unreceived from any other. For every i *beginning is a Father* unto that which cometh of it ; and every *Off-spring is a Son* unto that out of which it groweth. Seeing therefore the Father alone is e originally that Deity which Christ f originally is not (for Christ is God g by being of God, light h by issuing out of light) it followeth hereupon, that whatsoever Christ hath i common unto him with his heavenly Father, the same of necessity must be *given* him, but naturally and k eternally given ; not bestowed by way of benevolence and favour, as the other gifts both are. And therefore l where the Fathers give it out for a rule, that whatsoever Christ is said in Scripture to have *received*, the same we ought to apply only to the Manhood of Christ : their Assertion is true of all things which Christ hath received *by grace* ; but to that which he hath received of the Father by eternal nativity or birth, it reacheth not. Touching union of Deity with Man-hood, it is by grace, because there can be no greater grace shewed towards man, then that God should vouchsafe to unite to mans nature the Person of his only begotten Son. Because the Father m loveth the Son as Man ; he hath by uniting Deity with Man-hood, *given* all things into his hands. It hath n *pleased* the Father that in him all fulness should dwell. The name which he hath o above all names is o *given* him. As the Father hath life in himself, the Son in himself hath life also by the p *gift* of the Father. The gift whereby God hath made Christ a Fountain of life, is, that q *conjunction of the nature of God with the nature of Man*, in the person of Christ, r *which gift* (faith Christ to the Woman of *Samaria*) if thou didst know, and in *that respect* understand, *who it is which asketh water of thee*

d *Nativitas Dei non potest non eam ex qua profecta est tenere naturam. Neq; enim aliud quàm Deus subsistit qui non aliunde quàm ex Deo Deus subsistit* Hilar. de Trinit. lib. 5. *Cum sit gloria, sempiternitate, virtute, regno, potestate hoc quod pater est, omnia tamen hæc non sine auctore sicut pater, seu ex patre tanquam filius sine initio & æqualis habet.* Ruffin. in Symb. Apost. cap. 9. *Filium aliunde non deduco, sed de substantia patris omnem à patre consecutum potestatem,* Tertul. Contra. Prax. d Ephes. 1. 15. πᾶσα πατρὶα, *quicquid alteri quovismodo dat esse.* e loc. 1. 17. *Pater luminum* υἱὸς τε καὶ πνεῦματ Gʼ δηλονότι Pachym. in Dionys. de Cœl. Hieror. c. 1. *Pater est principium totius divinitatis quia ipsa à nullo est. Non enim habet de quo procedat, sed ab eo & filius est genitus, & Spiritus sanctus procedit,* Aug. de Trin. lib. 4. c. 20. *Hinc Christus deitatis loco nomen ubique patris usurpat; quia pater nimirum est πρηγαία θεότης.* f *Pater tota substantia est, filius vero derivatio totius & propagatio.* Tert. cont. Prax. g *Quod enim Deus est ex Deo est,* Hilar. de Trin. lib. 5. *Nihil nisi natum habet filius.* Hilar. lib. 4. h Ἀπαύγασμα δόξης Heb. 1. 2. Ἐςìυ ἀτόῤῥοιά τῆς τῦ παντοκρατορος δόξης εἰλικρινὴς, ἀπαύγασμα φωτὸς ἀιδίε. Sap. 7. 25, 26. i *Nihil in se diversum ac dissimile habent natus & generans.* Hil. de Syn. A ivert. Aria. *In Trinitate alius atque alius, non aliud atq; aliud,* Vincent Lyr. c. 19. k *Ubi author æternus est, ibi & nativitatis æternitas est: quia sicut nativitas ab authore est, ità & ab æterni authore æterna nativitas est,* Hil. de Trin. lib. 12. *sicut naturam præstat filio sine initio generatio: ità spiritui sancto præstat essentiam sine initio processio,* Aug. de Trin. lib. 5. cap. 15. l Ὅσα λέγη ὁ Χριστὸς ὅτι ἔλαβεν ὁ υἱὸς καὶ ἐδοξάσθη, διὰ τὴν ἀνθρωπότητα αυτῦ λέγη ἀ τὴν θεότητα, Theodoret. fol. 42. & ex Greg. Naz. Orat. 2. de ill. ibid. 44.

m Iohn 3. 35.
n Eph. 1. 5.
o Phil. 2. 9.
p Iohn 5. 26.
q Iohn. 5. 20.
Hic est verus Deus, & vita æterna.
r Iohn 4. 10.

thee, thou wouldest ask of him, that he might give thee living Water. The Union therefore of the Flesh with Deity, is to *that flesh* a gift of principal grace and favour. For by virtue of this grace, Man is really made God, a creature is exalted above the dignity of all creatures, and hath all creatures else under it. This admirable union of God with Man can inforce in that higher nature no alteration, because unto God there is nothing more natural than not to be subject to any change. Neither is it a thing impossible, that the Word being made flesh, should be that which it was not before, as touching the manner of subsistence, and yet continue in all qualities or properties of nature the same it was, because the Incarnation of the Son of God consisteth *meerly in the union* of Natures, which union doth adde perfection to the Weaker, to the Nobler no alteration at all. If therefore it be demanded what the Person of the Son of God hath attained by assuming Manhood; surely, the whole sum of all is this, to be as we are, truly, really, and naturally man, by means whereof he is made capable of meaner offices, than otherwise his Person could have admitted, the only gain he thereby purchased for himself, was to be capable of loss and detriment for the good of others. But may it rightly be said concerning the Incarnation of Jesus Christ, that as our nature hath in no respect changed his, so from his to ours as little alteration hath ensued? The very cause of his taking upon him our nature, was to change it, to better the quality, and to advance the condition thereof, although in no sort to abolish the substance which he took; nor to infuse into it the natural forces and properties of his Deity. As therefore we have shewed how the Son of God by his Incarnation hath changed the manner of that personal subsistence which before was solitary, and is now in the association of flesh, no alteration thereby accruing to the nature of God; so neither are the *properties of mans nature*, in the person of Christ, by force and virtue of the same conjunction so much altered, as not to stay within those limits which our substance is bordered withal; nor the *state and quality* of our substance so unalter'd, but that there are in it many glorious effects proceeding from so near copulation with Deity. God from us can receive nothing, we by him have obtained much. For albeit the natural properties of Deity be not communicable to mans nature, the supernatural gifts, graces, and effects thereof are. The honour which our flesh hath by being the flesh of the Son of God, is in many respects great. If we respect but that which is common unto us with him, the glory provided for him and his in the Kingdom of Heaven, his Right and Title thereunto even in that he is man, differeth from other mens, because he is that Man of whom God is himself a part. We have right to the same inheritance with Christ, but not the same right which he hath, his being such as we cannot reach, and ours such as he cannot stoop unto. Furthermore, to be the Way, the Truth, and the Life; to be the Wisdom, Righteousness, Sanctification, Resurrection; to be the Peace of the whole world, the Hope of the righteous, the Heir of all things; to be that supream Head whereunto all power both in Heaven and in earth is given; these are not honours common unto Christ with other men; they are Titles above the dignity and worth of any which were but a meer man, yet true of Christ, even in that he is man. But man with whom Deity is personally joined, and unto whom it hath added those excellencies which makes him more than worthy thereof. Finally, sith God hath deified our nature, though not by turning it into himself, yet by making it his own inseparable habitation, we cannot now conceive how God should without man either [b] exercise divine power, or receive the glory of divine praise. For Man is in [c] both an associate of Deity. But to come to the grace of *Unction*; Did the parts of our nature, the Soul and Body of Christ receive by the influence of Deity, wherewith they were matcht, no ability of operations, no virtue, or quality above nature? Surely, as the sword which is made fiery, doth not only cut by reason of the sharpness which simply it hath, but also burn by means of that heat which it hath from fire; so, there is no doubt, but the Deity of Christ hath enabled that nature which it took of man, to do more than man in this world hath power to comprehend, forasmuch as (the bare essential properties of Deity excepted) he hath imparted unto it all things, he hath re-

ἀ ὥσπερ τῶν ἀνθρώπων κοινὸν ἔςι τὸ θνητὸν, οὕτω τῆς ἁγίας τρίαδος κοινὸν τὸ ἀτρεπτον τε ᾗ ἀναλλοίωτον. Theod. Dial.

Ἄτρεπτ@. Periculum status sui Deo nullum est. Tertul. de car.

Chr. Majestati filii Dei corporea nativitas nihil contulit, nihil abstulit. Leo de Nativ. Ser. 8.

Μένει ὃν λῶ ἀπαρχῆς, Θεὸς μένει, ᾗ τὴν ἡμῶν ἐν ταυ]ῷ περισκευάζων ὑπαρξιν. Theophil. In formam servi transisse, non est naturam perdidisse Dei, Hilar. de Trin. lib. 12.

[b] Μετέχειν ἀνθρωπίνην τῆς θείας ἐνεργείας. Theod.

[c] ἡ δεξιὰ τῶ Θεῶ ἢ ποιήτικὴ τῷ ὄντων ᾗ πάντων ἢ τις ἐστὶν ἐκλεκτη ος δὲ τὰ πάντα ἐξάνητος.

ζωὴ τὸν ἑνωθέντα πρὸς αὐτὴν ἄνθρωπον εἰς τὸ ἴδιον ἀνήγαγεν ὕψος διὰ τῆς ἑνώσεως. Gregor. Nyssa. apud Theod.

Ἀπὸ τῆς φύσεως τῆς σῆς λαβὼν ἀπαρχὴν ἰκάθισεν ἐπάνω πάσης ἀρχῆς ᾗ ἐξουσίας. Chry. in Psa. 41.

plentihe

a Luk. 2. 47.
b ἡσυχάζευ-
ἴ© ἀδὲ τὸ λό-
γης ἐν τῷ ασε-
εϛ ἑαυτὸ, κὴ ἑαυ-
ἐϳῦ αὶ κὴ ἀ-
ποθνήσκειν,
συζγιτεμένες ἡ
τῶ ἀνθρωπω
ἐν τῷ νικᾶν κὴ
ὑποτεμένεν κὴ
χεηϛευεῖς κὴ
ἀνίϛαϛ κὴ ἀ-
ναλαμβανειτ.
Theod. & Iren.
lib. 3. adverf.
hæref. Mat. 27.
46.
c Ifai. 11. 2:
d Ifai. 11. 2.
Luke 2. 18.
Acti 4. 17.
e Heb. 1. 9.
f 2 Cor. 1. 21.
1 Ioh. 2. 20. 27.
h Iohn 20. 7.

ſleniſhe it with all ſuch perfections as the ſame is any way apt to receive, [a] at the leaſt, according to the exigence of that œconomy or ſervice, for which it pleaſed him in love and mercy to be made man. For as the parts, degrees, and offices of that myſtical adminiſtration did require, which he voluntarily undertook, the beams of Deity did in operation always accordingly either [b] reſtrain or inlarge themſelves: From hence we may ſomewhat conjecture, how the powers of that Soul are illuminated, which being ſo inward unto God cannot chuſe but be privy unto all things which God worketh, and muſt therefore of neceſſity be indued with knowledge ſo far forth [c] univerſal, though not with infinite knowledge peculiar to Deity it ſelf. The Soul of Chriſt that ſaw in this life the face of God, was here, through ſo viſible preſence of Deity, filled with all manner [d] of graces and virtues in that unmatchable degree of perfection, for which of him we read it written, *That God with the Oyl of gladneſs anointed* [e] *him* [f] *above his* [g] *fellows.* And as God hath in Chriſt unſpeakably glorified the Nobler, ſo likewiſe the meaner part of our nature, the very bodily ſubſtance of man. Where alſo that muſt again be remembred which we noted before, concerning the degrees of the influence of Deity proportionable unto his own purpoſes, intents, and counſels. For in this reſpect his body which by natural condition was corruptible, wanted the [i]gift of everlaſting immunity from death, paſſion, and diſſolution, till God which gave it to be ſlain for ſin, had for righteouſneſs ſake reſtored it to life with certainty of endleſs continuance. Yea, in this reſpect the very glorified Body of Chriſt retained in it the [h] skars and marks of former mortality. But ſhall we ſay, that in Heaven his glorious Body by virtue of the ſame cauſe, hath no power to preſent it ſelf in all places, and to be every where at once preſent ? We nothing doubt, but God hath many ways above the reach of our capacities exalted that Body which it hath pleaſed him to make his own, that Body wherewith he hath ſaved the world, that Body which hath been, and is the root of eternal Life, the inſtrument wherewith Deity worketh, the Sacrifice which taketh away ſin, the Price which hath ranſomed Souls from death, the Leader of the whole Army of bodies that ſhall riſe again. For though it had a beginning from us, yet God hath given it vital efficacy, Heaven hath indowed it with celeſtial power, that virtue it hath from above, in regard whereof all Angels of Heaven adore it. Notwithſtanding, [i] a Body ſtill it continueth, a Body conſubſtantial with our bodies, a Body of the ſame both nature and meaſure which it had on earth.

i Μετὰ τὴ
ἀνάϛασιν διά-
ναỊον μὲν ἐϛὶ
κὴ ἄρθαρτον κὴ
ϑείας δόξης
μιϛθωτομα ἡ
ὅμως τὴ οἰ-
κείαν ἔχον
περιϛραφὴν.
Theod. fol. 80.

To gather therefore into one ſum all that hitherto hath been ſpoken touching this point, there are but four things which concur to make compleat the whole ſtate of our Lord Jeſus Chriſt ; his Deity, his Manhood, the conjunction of both, and the diſtinction of the one from the other, being joined in one. Four principal Hereſies there are which have in thoſe things withſtood the truth ; *Arrians*, by bending themſelves againſt the Deity of Chriſt ; *Apollinarians*, by maiming and miſ-interpreting that which belongeth to his humane nature ; *Neſtorians*, by renting Chriſt aſunder, and dividing him into two perſons ; the followers of *Eutiches*, by confounding in his perſon thoſe natures which they ſhould diſtinguiſh. Againſt theſe there have been four moſt famous ancient general Councels ; the Council of *Nice*, to define againſt *Arrians* ; againſt *Apollinarians*, the Councel of *Conſtantinople* ; the Council of *Epheſus* againſt *Neſtorians* ; againſt *Eutichians*, the *Calcedon* Councel. In four words, ἀληθῶς, τελέως, ἀδιαιρέτως, ἀσυγχύτως, *truly, perfectly, indiviſibly, diſtinctly,*, the firſt applyed to be his being God ; and the ſecond to his being Man ; the third to his being of both One, and the fourth to his ſtill continuing in that One both; we may fully by way of abridgement comprize whatſoever antiquity hath at large handled, either in declaration of Chriſtian belief, or in refutation of the foreſaid Hereſies. Within the compaſs of which four heads, I may truly affirm, that all Hereſies which touch but the perſon of Jeſus Chriſt, (whether they have riſen in theſe later days, or in any Age heretofore,) may be with great facility brought to confine themſelves. We conclude therefore, that to ſave the world, it was of neceſſity the Son of God ſhould be thus incarnate, and that God ſhould ſo be in Chriſt as hath been declared.

Of the Perſonall preſence 55 Having thus farre proceeded in ſpeech concerning the perſon of Jeſus
of Chriſt everywhere, and in what ſence it may be granted he is every where preſent according to the fleſh,

Chriſt

Christ, his two natures, their conjunction, that which he either is or doth in respect of both, and that which the one receiveth from the other; sith God in Christ is general y the medicine, which doth cure the world, and Christ in us is that receipt of the same medicine, whereby we are every one particularly cured. In as much as Christs Incarnation and Passion can be available to no mans good which is not made partaker of Christ, neither can we participate him without his presence, we are briefly to consider how Christ is present, to the end it may thereby better appear how we are made partakers of Christ, both otherwise, and in the Sacraments themselves. All things are in such sort divided into finite and infinite, that no one substance, nature, or quality, can be possibly capable of both. The world and all things in the world are stinted, all effects that proceed from them, all the powers and abilities whereby they work, whatsoever they do, whatsoever they may, and whatsoever they are, is limited. Which limitation of each creature is both the perfection and also the preservation thereof. Measure is that which perfecteth all things, because every thing is for some end; neither can that thing be available to any end which is not proportionable thereunto; and to proportion as well excesses, as defects are opposite. Again, for as much as nothing doth perish but only through excess or defect of that, the due proportioned measure whereof doth give perfection, it followeth, that measure is likewise the preservation of all things. Out of which premises we may conclude, not only that nothing created can possibly be unlimited, or can receive any such accident, quality, or property, as may really make it infinite (for then should it cease to be a creature) but also that every creatures limitation is according to his own kind, and therefore as oft as we note in them any thing above their kind, it argueth that the same is not properly theirs, but groweth in them from a cause more powerful than they are. Such as the substance of each thing is, such is also the presence thereof. Impossible it is that God should withdraw his presence from any thing, because the very substance of God is infinite. He filleth Heaven and Earth, although he take up no room in either, because his substance is immaterial, pure, and of us in this World so incomprehensible, that albeit [b] no part of us be ever absent from him, who is present whole unto every particular thing, yet his presence with us we no way discern further than only that God is present, which partly by reason, and more perfectly by Faith we know to be firm and certain. Seeing therefore that presence every where is the sequel of an infinite and incomprehensible substance, (for what can be every where, but that which can no where be comprehended?) to inquire whether Christ be every where, is to inquire of a natural property, a property that cleaveth to the Deity of Christ. Which Deity being common unto him with none, but only the Father, and the Holy Ghost, it followeth, that nothing of Christ which is limited, that nothing created, that neither the Soul nor the Body of Christ, and consequently, not Christ as man, or Christ according to his humane nature, can possibly be every where present, because those phrases of limitation and restraint do either point out the principal subject whereunto every such attribute adhereth, or else they intimate the radical cause out of which it groweth. For Example, when we say that Christ as man, or according to his humane nature suffered death, we shew what nature was, the proper subject of mortality; when we say that as God, or according to his Deity, he conquered death, we declare his Deity to have been the cause, by force and virtue whereof he raised himself from the Grave. But neither is the Manhood of Christ that subject whereunto universal presence agreeth, neither is it the cause original by force whereof his Person is inabled to be every where present. Wherefore Christ is essentially present with all things, in that he is very God, but not present with all things as man; because Manhood and the parts thereof can neither be the cause, nor the true subject of such presence. Notwithstandg, in somwhat more plainly to shew a true immediate reason wherefore the Manhood of Christ can neither be every where present, nor cause the Person of Christ so to be, we acknowledge that of Saint *Augustine* concerning Christ most true, [c] *In that he is personally the Word, he created all things; in that he is naturally man, he himself is created of God*; and it doth not appear that any one creature hath power to be present with all creatures.

Wherupon, nevertheless it will not follow, that Christ cannot therfore be thus present,

[marginal notes:]
Psal. 133. 7, 8.
Jer. 23. 24.
[b] *Ideo Deus ubique esse dicitur, quia, nulli parti rerum absens est; idea tota, quia non parti rerum partem sui præsentem præbet, & alteri parti, alteram partem, sed non solùm, universitati creatura verum etiam cuilibet parti ejus totus pariter adest. Aug. Epist. 57.*
[c] *Quod ad verbum attinet, Creator est; quod ad hominem, creatura est. Aug. Ep. 57. Deus qui semper est, & semper erat, fit creatura Leo de Nativ. Multi timore trepidant ne Christum esse creaturam dicere compellantur, nos proclamamus non esse periculum dicere Christum esse creaturam. Hieron. in Epist. ad Ephes. 2.*

sent,becaufe he is himfelf a creature,forafmuch as only infinite prefence is that which cannot poffibly ftand with the effence or being of any creature ; as for prefence with all things that are,fith the whole race, mafs, and body of them is finite, Chrift by being a *creature*,is not *in that refpect* excluded from poffibility of prefence with them. That which excludeth him therefore as man from fo great largenefs of prefence, is only his being *Man*, a creature *of this particular kind*,whereunto the God of Nature hath fet thofe bounds of reftraint and limitation, beyond which to attribute unto it any thing more than a creature *of that fort* can admit, were to give it another nature, to make it a creature of fome other kind than in truth it is. Furthermore, if Chrift in that he is man be every where prefent, feeing this cometh not by the nature of Man-hood it felf, there is no other way how it fhould grow, but either by the grace of union with Deity, or by the grace of unction received from Deity. It hath been already fufficiently proved, that by force of union the properties of both natures are imparted *to the perfon only* in whom they are, and not what belongeth to the one nature really conveyed or tranflated into the other ; it hath been likewife proved, that natures united in Chrift continue the very fame which they are where they are not united. And concerning the grace of unction, wherein are contained the gifts and virtues which Chrift as man hath above men, they make him really and habitually a man more excellent than we are, they take not from him the nature and fubftance that we have, they caufe not his foul nor body to be of another kind than ours is. Supernatural endowments are an advancement, they are no extinguifhment of that nature whereto they are given. The fubftance of the body of Chrift hath no prefence, neither can have,but only local. It was not therefore every where feen, nor did it every where fuffer death, every where it could not be intombed, it is not every where now being exalted into Heaven. There is no proof in the world ftrong to inforce that Chrift had a true body, but by the true and natural properties of his body. Amongft which properties, definite or local prefence is chief, [a] *How is it true of Chrift* (faith *Tertullian*) *that he died, was buryed, and rofe again, if Chrift had not that very flefh, the nature whereof is capable of thefe things, flefh mingled with blood, fupported with bones, woven with finews, imbroidred with veins ?* If his majeftical body have now any fuch new property, by force whereof it may every where really even *in fubftance* prefent it felf, or may at once be in many places: then hath the Majefty of his eftate extinguifhed the verity of his nature. [b] *Make thou no doubt or queftion of it* (faith St. *Auguftine*) *but that the man Chrift Jefus is now in that very place from whence he fhall come in the fame form and fubftance of flefh, which he carryed thither, and from which he hath not taken nature, but given thereunto immortality. According to this form he fpreadeth not out himfelf into all places. For it behoveth us to take great heed, left while we go about to maintain the glorious Deity of him which is man,we leave him not the true bodily fubftance of a man.* According to St. *Auguftines* opinion therefore, that Majeftical body which we make to be every where prefent, doth thereby ceafe to have the fubftance of a true body. To conclude, we hold it in regard of the fore-alleadged proofs a moft infallible Truth, that Chrift as man is not every where prefent. There are which think it as infallibly true, that Chrift is every where prefent as man, which peradventure in fome fence may be well enough granted. His humane fubftance in it felf is naturally abfent from the earth, his foul and body not on earth, but in Heaven only. Yet becaufe this fubftance is infeparably joined to that perfonal Word which by his very divine effence is prefent with all things, the nature which cannot have in it felf univerfal prefence, hath it *after a fort* by being *no where fevered* from that which every where is prefent. For inafmuch as that infinite Word is not divifible into parts, it could not in part, but muft needs be wholly incarnate, and confequently wherefoever the Word is,it hath with it Man-hood,elfe fhould the Word be in part or fomewhere God only, and not man, which is impoffible. For the *perfon of Chrift is whole*, perfect God and perfect man, wherefoever, although the parts of his Man-hood,being finite,and his Deity infinite, we cannot fay that the *whole of Chrift* is fimply every where,as we may fay that his Deity is, & that his perfon is by force of Deity.For *fomewhat of the perfon of Chrift* is not every where in that fort, namely, his Man-hood,the *only conjunction* whereof with Deity is extended as far as Deity,the

actual

actual *position* restrained and tyed to a certain place; yet presence *by way of conjunction* is in some sort presence.

Again, as the Manhood of Christ may after a sort be every where said to be present, because that Person is every where present, from whose divine substance Manhood is no where severed: So the same Universality of presence may likewise seem in another respect appliable thereunto, namely, by *co-operation* with Deity, and that *in all things*. The light created of God in the beginning did first by it self illuminate the World, but after that the Sun and Moon were created, the World sithence hath *by them* always enjoyed the same. And that Deity of Christ which before our Lords Incarnation wrought all things without man, doth now work nothing wherein the nature which it hath assumed is either absent from it or idle. Christ as man hath [a] all power both in Heaven and Earth given him. He hath as man, not as God only, [b] a supreme dominion over quick and dead, for so much his Ascension into Heaven and his Session at the right hand of God do import. The Son of God which did first humble himself by taking our flesh upon him, descended afterwards much lower, and became according to the flesh obedient so far as to suffer death, even the death of the Cross, for all men, because such was his Fathers will. The former was an humiliation of Deity, the later an humiliation of Manhood, [c] for which cause there followed upon the later an exaltation of that which was humbled; for with power he created the world, but restored it by obedience. In which obedience as according to his Manhood he had glorified God on earth, so God hath glorified in Heaven that nature which yielded him obedience; and hath given unto Christ even in that he is Man, such fulness of power over the whole World, that he which before fulfilled in the state of humility and patience whatsoever God did require, doth now [d] reign in glory till the time that all things be restored. He which came down from Heaven, and descended into the lowest parts of the Earth, is ascended far above all Heavens, that sitting at the right hand of God, he might from thence fill all things with the gracious and happy fruits of his saving presence. Ascension into Heaven is a plain local translation of Christ according to his Manhood from the lower to the higher parts of the World. Session at the right hand of God, is the actual exercise of that Regency and Dominion wherein the Manhood of Christ is joyned and matched with the Deity of the Son of God. Not that his Manhood was before without the possession of the same power, but because the full use thereof was suspended, till that humility which had been before as a vail to hide and conceal Majesty were laid aside. [e] After his rising again from the dead then did God set him at his right hand in Heavenly places far above all principality and power, and might, and domination, and every name that is named, not in this World only, but also in that which is to come, and hath [f] put all things under his feet, and hath appointed him over all the head to the Church which is his body, the fulness of him that filleth all in all. The [g] scepter of which spiritual Regiment over us in this present World is at the length to be yielded up into the hands of the Father which gave it, that is to say, the use and exercise thereof shall cease, there being no longer on earth any Militant Church to govern. This government therefore he exerciseth both as God and as man; as God, by essential presence with all things; as man, by co-operation with that which essentially is present. Touching the manner how he worketh as man in all things, the principal powers of the soul of man are the will and Understanding, the one of which two in Christ assenteth unto all things, and from the other nothing which Deity doth work is hid; so that by knowledge and assent the soul of Christ is present with all things which the Deity of Christ worketh. And even the body of Christ it self, although the definite limitation thereof be most sensible, doth notwithstanding admit in some sort a kind of infinite and unlimited presence likewise. For his body being a part of that nature, which whole nature is presently joyned unto Deity wheresoever Deity is, it followeth that his bodily substance hath every where a presence of true conjunction with Deity. And for as much as it is by vertue of that conjunction made the body of the Son of God, by whom also it was made a Sacrifice for the sins of the whole World, this giveth it a *presence of force and efficacy* throughout all generations of men. Albeit therefore nothing be *actually* infinite *in substance*, but God only in that he is God, nevertheless

[a] *Mat.* 28.
[b] *Rom.* 14: 9.
[c] *Philip.* 2. 9.
[Heb.] 2. 9.
[Rev.] 5. 12.
[d] *Luke* 21. 27.
[Acts] 3. 21.
[Ephes.] 4. 9.
[e] *Ephes.* 1. 20.
[f] *Psal.* 8. 6.
[Heb.] 2. 8:
[g] 1 *Cor.* 15.

verthelels as every number is infinite by poffibility of addition, and every line by poffibility of extenfion infinite, fo there is no flint which can be fet to the value or merit of the facrificed Body of Chrift, it hath no meafured certainty of limits, bounds of efficacy unto life it knoweth none , but is alfo it felf infinite in *poffibility of application.* Which things indifferently every way confidered, that gracious promife of our Lord and Saviour Jefus Chrift concerning prefence with his to the very end of the World, I fee no caufe but that we may well and fafely interpret he doth perform, both as God, by effential prefence of Deity, and as man, in that order, fence, and meaning which hath been fhewed.

56. We have hitherto fpoken of the perfon and of the prefence of Chrift. Participation is that mutual inward hold which Chrift hath of us, and we of him, in fuch fort that each poffeffeth other by way of fpecial intereft, property, and inherent coputation. For plainer explication whereof, we may from that which hath been before fufficiently proved, affume to our purpofe thefe two Principles, that *every original caufe imparteth it felf unto thofe things which come of it, and whatfoever taketh being from any other, the fame is after a fort in that which giveth it being.* It followeth hereupon that the Son of God being light of light, muft needs be alfo light in light. The perfons of the God-head, by reafon of the unity of their fubftance, do as neceffarily remain one within another, as they are of neceffity to be diftinguifhed one from another, becaufe two are the iffue of one, and one the off-fpring of the other two, only of three one not growing out of any other. And fith they all are but one God in number, one indivifible Effence or Subftance, their diftinction cannot poffibly admit Separation. For how fhould that fubfift *folitarily* by it felf which hath no fubftance, but *individually* the very fame whereby others fubfift with it; feeing that the Multiplication of fubftances *in particular* is neceffarily required to make thofe things fubfift apart, which have the felf-fame general Nature, and the perfons of that Trinity are not three particular fubftances, to whom one *General Nature* is common, but three that fubfift by one fubftance , *which it felf is particular,* yet they all three have it, and their feveral ways of having it are that which maketh their perfonal diftinction ? The Father therefore is in the Son, and the Son in him, they both in the Spirit, and the Spirit in both them. So that the Fathers firft Off-fpring which is the Son, remaineth eternally in the Father ; the Father eternally alfo in the Son, no way fevered or divided by reafon of the fole and fingle unity of their fubftance. The Son in the Father as light in that light, out of which it floweth without feparation ; the Father in the Son as light in that light which it caufeth and leaveth not. And becaufe in this refpect his eternal being is of the Father, which eternal being is his life, therefore he by the Father liveth. Again, fith all things do accordingly love their Off-fpring as themfelves are more or lefs contained in it, he which is thus the only begotten, muft needs be in this degree the only Beloved of the Father. He therefore which is in the Father by eternal derivation of being and life from him , muft needs be in him through an eternal affection of love. His Incarnation caufeth him alfo as man to be now in the Father, and the Father to be in him. For in that he is man, he receiveth Life from the Father as from the Fountain of that ever-living Deity, which in the perfon of the Word hath combined it felf with Manhood, and doth thereunto impart fuch life as to no other Creature befides him is communicated. In which confideration likewife the [b] love of the Father towards him is more than it can be towards any other, neither can any attain unto that perfection of love which he beareth towards his Heavenly Father. Wherefore God is not fo in any, nor any fo in God as Chrift, whether we confider him as the perfonal Word of God, or as the natural Son of Man. All other things that are of God have God in them, and he them in himfelf likewife. Yet becaufe their fubftance and his wholly differeth, their coherence and communion either with him or amongft themfelves is in no fort like unto that before mentioned. God hath his influence into the very Effence of all things, without which influence of Deity fupporting them, their utter annihilation could not chufe but fo low. Of him all things have both received their firft being, and their continuance to be that which they are. All things are therefore partakers of God, they are his off-fpring, his influence is in them, and the perfonal Wifdom of God is for that very caufe faid

to

The union or mutual participation which is between Chrift and the Church of Chrift in this prefent world.

a *In the bofome of the Father. Joh. 1. 18. Eo ordine alium effe patrem, & alium filium, & alium fpiritum, non divifione alium, fed diftinctione Tertul. contra Prax. Nec in numerum pluralem defluit incorporea generatio, nec in divifionem cadit, ubi qui nafcitur nequaquam à generante feparatur. Ruffin. in Symbol.*

b *Luk. 3. 22. Joh. 3. 34, 35. 5. 20. 10. 17. 14. 31. 15. 10.*

to excell in nimblenefs or agility, to [a] pierce into all intellectual, pure and fubtile
fpirits, to go through all, and to reach unto every thing which is. Otherwife, how
fhould the fame wifdom be that which fupporteth, [b] beareth up, and fuftaineth all? Whatfoever God doth work, the hands of all three Perfons are jointly and equally
in it, according to *the order of that connexion*, whereby they each depend upon o-
ther: And therefore albeit in that refpect the Father be firft, the Son next, the Spirit laft, and confequently neereft unto every effect which groweth from all three,
neverthelefs, they all being of one effence, are likewife all of one efficacy. Dare
any man, unlefs he be ignorant altogether how infeparable the Perfons of the Trinity are, perfwade himfelf that every of them may have their fole and feveral Pof-
feffions, or that [c] we being not partakers of all, can have fellowfhip with any one? The Father as Goodnefs, the Son as Wifdom, the Holy Ghoft as Power, do all concur in every particular, outwardly iffuing from that one only glorious Deity which
they all are. For that which moveth God to work, is Goodnefs; and that which
ordereth his Work, is Wifdom; and that which perfecteth his Work, is Power.
All things which God in their times and feafons hath brought forth, were eternally
and before all times in God, as a work unbegun is in the Artificer, which afterward
bringeth it unto effect. Therefore whatfoever we do behold now in this prefent
World, it was inwrapped within the Bowels of divine Mercy, written in the Book
of eternal Wifdom, and held in the hands of Omnipotent Power, the firft Foundations of the World being as yet unlaid. So that all things which God hath made
are in that refpect the [d] Off-fpring of God, they are in him as effects in their higheft caufe; he likewife actually is in them, the affiftance and influence of his Deity
is their life. Let hereunto faving efficacy be added, and it bringeth forth a fpecial
off-fpring amongft men, containing them to whom God hath himfelf given the
gracious and amiable name of [e] Sons. We are by Nature the Sons of *Adam.*
When God created *Adam* he created us; and as many as are defcended from *Adam*,
have in themfelves the Root out of which they fpring. The Sons of God we neither are all, nor any one of us, otherwife than only by grace and favour. The Sons
of God have Gods own natural Son as a [f] fecond *Adam* from Heaven, whofe Race
and Progenie they are by Spiritual and Heavenly Birth. God therefore loving eternally his Son, he muft needs eternally, [*] in him have loved and preferred before all
others them which are fpiritually fithence defcended and fprung out of him. Thefe
were in God as in their Saviour, and not as in their Creatour only. It was the purpofe of his *faving* Goodnefs, his *faving* Wifdom, and his *faving* Power, which inclined it felf towards them. They which thus were in God eternally by their intended admiffion to life, have by vocation or adoption God actually now in them,
as the Artificer is in the Work which his hand doth prefently frame. Life as all
other gifts and benefits groweth originally from the Father, and cometh not to us
but [g] by the Son, nor by the Son to any of us in particular, but [h] through the Spirit.
For this caufe the Apoftle wifheth to the Church of *Corinth* [i] the grace of our Lord
Jefus Chrift, and the love of God, and the Fellowfhip of the Holy Ghoft. Which
three Saint *Peter* comprehendeth in one, [k] the *participation of divine Nature*. We
are therefore in God through Chrift eternally according to that intent and purpofe,
whereby we are chofen to be made his in this prefent World, before the World it
felf was made; we are in God through the knowledge which is had of us, and the
love which is born towards us from everlafting. But in God we actually are no
longer than only from the time of our actual Adoption into the body of his true
Church, into the fellowfhip of his children. For his Church he knoweth and loveth;
fo that they which are in the Church, are thereby known to be in him. Our being
in Chrift by Eternal fore-knowledge faveth us not, without our actual and real A-
doption into the fellowfhip of his Saints in this prefent World. For in him we actually are by our actual [l] incorporation into that fociety which hath him for their
Head; and doth make together with him one body (he and they in that refpect
having [m] one name) for which caufe by vertue of this Myftical conjunction, we are
of him, and in him, even [n] as though our very flefh and bones fhould be made con-
tinuate with his. We are in Chrift, becaufe he [o] knoweth and loveth us even as parts
of himfelf. No man actually is in him but they [p] in whom he actually is. For he

which

Marginal notes:
a *Sap.* 7. 23.
b *Heb.* 1. 3.
c *John* 14. 23.
d *Acts* 17. 28, 29.
John 1. 1. 4. 10.
Ifai. 40. 26.
e 1 *John* 3. 1.
f 1 *Cor.* 15. 47.
* *Ephef.* 1. 3. 4.
g 1 *John* 5. 11.
h *Rom.* 8. 10.
i 1 *Cor.* 13. 13.
k 1 *Pet.* 1. 4.
l *Col.* 2. 10.
m 1 *Cor.* 12. 12.
n *Ephef.* 5. 30.
o *John* 15. 9.
p 1 *John* 5. 12.

a *John* 15.5,6. which hath not the Son of God, hath not life : ᵃ *I am the Vine, and you are the branches : He which abideth in me, and I in him, the same bringeth forth much Fruit:* but the branch severed from the Vine withereth. We are therefore adopted Sons of God to Eternal Life by participation of the only begotten Son of God, whose Life b *John* 14.19.
Ephes. 5.23. is the ᵇ Well-spring and cause of ours. It is too cold an interpretation, whereby some men expound our being in Christ to import nothing else, but only that the self-same Nature which maketh us to be men, is in him, and maketh him man as we are. For what man in the World is there which hath not so far forth communion with Jesus Christ ? It is not this that can sustain the weight of such sentences as c *John* 14. 20.
John 15. 4. speak of the mystery of our ᶜ coherence with Jesus Christ. The Church is in Christ, as *Eve* was in *Adam.* Yea by grace we are every of us in Christ and in his Church, as by nature we are in those our first Parents. God made *Eve* of the rib of *Adam,* and his Church he frameth out of the very flesh, the very wounded and bleeding side of the Son of Man. His body crucified and his blood shed for the life of the d 1 *Cor.* 15. 48. World, are the true Elements of that Heavenly being, which maketh us ᵈ such as himself is of whom we come. For which cause the words of *Adam* may be fitly the words of Christ concerning his Church, *Flesh of my flesh, and bone of my bones,* a true native extract out of my own body. So that in him even according to his Manhood, we according to our Heavenly Being, are as branches in that root out of which e *John* 1.
f *John* 6. 57. they grow. To ᵉ all things he is life, and to men light, *as the Son of God* ; to the Church both life and light, ᶠ eternal by being made the Son of man for us, and by being in us a Saviour, whether we respect him as God, or as Man. *Adam* is in us as an original cause of our nature, and of that corruption of nature which causeth g *Heb.* 5. 9. death ; Christ as the ᵍ cause original of restauration to life ; The person of *Adam* is not in us, but his nature, and the corruption of his nature derived into all men by propagation ; Christ having *Adams* nature, as we have, but incorrupt, deriveth not nature but incorruption, and that immediately from his own person, into all that belong unto him. As therefore we are really partakers of the body of sin and death received from *Adam* ; so except we be truly partakers of Christ, and as really pos-h 1 *Cor.* 15. 45.
51. sessed of his Spirit, all we speak of eternal life is but a dream. That which ʰ quickneth us, is the Spirit of the second *Adam,* and his flesh that wherewith he quickneth. That which in him made our nature uncorrupt, was the union of his Deity with our nature. And in that respect the sentence of death and condemnation, which only taketh hold upon sinful flesh, could no way possibly extend unto him. This caused his voluntary death for others to prevail with God, and to have the force of an expiatory Sacrifice. The bloud of Christ, as the Apostle witnesseth, doth i *Heb.* 9. 14. therefore take away sin, because ⁱ *through the eternal Spirit he offered himself unto God without spot.* That which sanctified our nature in Christ, that which made it a sacrifice available to take away sin, is the same which quickeneth it, raised it out of the grave after death, and exalted it unto glory. Seeing therefore that Christ is in us as a quickning Spirit, the first degree of Communion with Christ must needs consist k *Cypr. de cœna Dom. cap.* 6. in the participation of his Spirit, which *Cyprian* in that respect well termeth ᵏ *germanissimam societatem,* the highest and truest society that can be between man and l *Cyril in Joan. lib.* 10. *cap.* 13. him, which is both God and Man in one. These things ˡ Saint *Cyril* duly considering, reproveth their speeches, which taught that only the Deity of Christ is the Vine whereupon we by Faith do depend as branches, and that neither his flesh nor our bodies are comprised in this resemblance. For doth any man doubt but that even from the flesh of Christ our very bodies do receive that life which shall make them glorious at the later day, and for which they are already accounted parts of his blessed Body ? Our corruptible bodies could never live the life they shall live, were it not that here they are joyned with his Body which is incorruptible, and that his is in ours as a cause of immortality, a cause by removing through the death and me-m *Nostra quippe & ipsius conjunctio nec miscet personas nec unit substantias,* rit of his own flesh that which hindered the life of ours. Christ is therefore both as God and as Man, that true Vine whereof we both spiritually and corporally are branches. The mixture of his bodily substance with ours is a thing which the ancient Fathers ᵐ disclaim. Yet the mixture of his flesh with ours they ⁿ speak of, to

sed affectus consociat & confœderat voluntates. Cypr. de Cœn. Dom. n *Quomodo dicunt carnem in corruptionem devenire, & non percipere vitam, quæ à corpore Domini & sanguine alitur ?* Iræn. lib. 4. adverf. hæref. cap. 34.

signifie

signifie what our very bodies through mystical conjunction receive from that vital efficacy which we know to be in his, and from bodily mixtures they borrow divers [a] similitudes, rather to declare the truth, than the manner of coherence between his sacred and the sanctified bodies of Saints. Thus much no Christian man will deny, that when Christ sanctified his own flesh, giving as God, and taking as man the Holy Ghost, he did not this for himself only, but for our sakes, that the grace of sanctification and life which was first received in him, might pass from him to his whole Race, as malediction came from *Adam* unto all mankind. Howbeit,

[margin] a *Unde considerandum est non solam σχέσει seu conformitate affectionum Christum in nobis esse, verum etiam participatione naturali (id est, reali & vera) quemadmodum si quis igne liquefactam ceram alii ceræ similiter liquefacta ita miscuerit ut unum quid ex utrisque factum videatur, sic communicatione Corporis & Sanguinis Christi ipse in nobis est, & nos in ipso.* Cyril. in Joan. lib. 10. cap. 13.

because the work of his Spirit to those effects is in us prevented by sin and death possessing us before, it is of necessity that as well our present sanctification unto newness of life, as the future restauration of our bodies should presuppose a participation of the grace, efficacy, merit or vertue of his Body and Bloud, without which foundation first laid there is no place for those other operations of the Spirit of Christ to ensue. So that Christ imparteth plainly himself by degrees. It pleaseth him in mercy to account himself incompleat and maimed [b] without us. But most assured we are that we all receive of his fulness, because he is in us as a moving and working cause, from which many blessed effects are really found to ensue, and that in sundry both kinds and degrees, all tending to eternal happiness. It must be confest that of Christ, working as a Creatour, and a Governour of the World by providence, all are partakers ; not all partakers of that grace whereby he inhabiteth whom he saveth. Again, as he dwelleth not by grace in all, so neither doth he equally work in all them in whom he dwelleth. [c] *Whence is it* (saith Saint *Augustin*) *that some be holier than others are, but because God doth dwell in some more plentifully than in others ?* And because the divine substance of Christ is equally in all, his humane substance equally distant from all, it appeareth that the participation of Christ, wherein there are many degrees and differences, must needs consist in such effects as being derived from both natures of Christ really into us, are made our own, and we by having them in us, are truly said to have him from whom they come ; CHRIST also more or less to inhabit and impart himself as the graces are fewer or more, greater or smaller, which really flow into us from Christ. Christ is whole with the whole Church, and whole with every part of the Church, as touching his person which can no way divide it self, or be possest by degrees and portions. But the participation of Christ importeth, besides the presence of Christs person, and besides the mystical copulation thereof with the parts and members of his whole Church, a true actual influence of grace whereby the [d] life which we live according to godliness is his, and from him we receive those perfections wherein our eternal happiness consisteth. Thus we participate Christ partly by imputation, as when those things which he did and suffered for us are imputed unto us for righteousness ; partly by habitual and real infusion, as when grace is inwardly bestowed while we are on earth, and afterwards more fully both our souls and bodies made like unto his in glory. The first thing of his so infused into our hearts in this life is the [f] Spirit of Christ, whereupon because the rest, of what kind soever, do all both necessarily depend and infallibly also ensue, therefore the Apostles term it sometime [g] the seed of God, sometime the [h] pledge of our Heavenly Inheritance, sometime the [i] hansell or earnest of that which is to come. From hence it is, that they which belong to the mystical body of our Saviour Christ, and be in number as the stars of Heaven, divided successively by reason of their mortal condition into many generations, are notwithstanding coupled [k] every one to Christ the Head, and [l] all unto every particular person amongst themselves, in as much as the same Spirit, which anointed the blessed soul of our Saviour Christ, doth so formalize, unite, and actuate his whole race, as if both he and they were so many limbs compacted into one body, by being quickned all with one and the same soul. That wherein we are partakers of Jesus Christ by imputation, agreeth equally unto all that have it. For it consisteth in such acts and deeds of his, as could not have longer continuance than while they were in doing, nor at that very time belong unto any other but

[margin notes, right column]
b *Ephes.* 1. 23. *Ecclesia complementum ejus qui implet omnia in omnibus.* Τὸ πλήρωμα τοῦ κατὰ πάντα ἐν πᾶσιν πληρουμένου. c *Aug. Epist.* 57.

d *Gal.* 2. 20.

e *Isa.* 53. 5. *Ephes.* 1. 7.

f *Rom.* 8. 9. *Gal.* 4. 6. g 1 *John* 3. 9. h *Eph.* 1. 14. i *Rom.* 8. 23.

k 1 *Cor.* 12. 12. *Ephes.* 4. 15. l *Rom.* 12. 5. *Ephes.* 4. 25.

τὸ

to him trom whom they come , and therefore how men either then , or before, or sithence, should be made partakers of them , there can be no way imagined, but only by imputation. Again, a deed must either not be imputed to any, but rest altogether in him whose it is, or if at all it be imputed, they which have it by imputation, must have it such as it is, whole. So that degrees being neither in the personal presence of Christ, nor in the participation of those effects which are ours by imputation only, it resteth that we wholly apply them to the participation of Christs infused grace, although even inth is kind also the first beginning of life, the seed of God, the first fruits of Christs Spirit be without latitude. For we have hereby only the being of the Sons of God, in which number how far soever one may seem to excel another, yet touching this that all are Sons, they are all equals, some haply better sons than the rest, but none any more a son than another. Thus therfore we see how the Father is in the Son, and the Son in the Father, how both are in all things, and all in them, what communion Christ hath with his Church, how his Church and every member thereof, is in him by original derivation, and he personally in them by way of mystical association wrought through the gift of the holy Ghost, which they that are his receive from him, and together with the same, what benefit soever the vital force of his body and blood may yeild, yea by steps and degrees they receive the compleat measure of all such divine grace as doth sanctifie and save throughout, till the day of their final exaltation to a state of fellowship in glory with him , whose partakers they are now in those things that tend to glory. As for any mixture of the subtance of his flesh with ours, the participation which we have of Christ includeth no such kind of gross surmize.

The necessity of Sacraments unto the participation of Christ,

57 It greatly offendeth, that some, when they labour to shew the use of the holy Sacraments, assigne unto them no end but only *to teach* the mind , by other senses , that which the Word doth teach by hearing. Whereupon, how easily neglect and carelef regard of so Heavenly mysteries may follow , we see in part by some experience had of those men with whom that opinion is most strong. For where the Word of God may be heard, which teacheth with much more expedition and more full Explication any thing we have to learn ; if all the benefit we reap by Sacraments be instruction , they which at all times have opportunity of using the better mean to that purpose, will surely hold the worse in less estimation. And unto Infants which are not capable of instruction, who would not think it a meer superfluity that any Sacrament is administred , if to administer the Sacraments be but to teach receivers what God doth for them ? There is of Sacraments therefore undoubtedly some other more excellent and Heavenly use. Sacraments, by reason of their mixt nature, are more diversly interpreted and disputed of, than any other part of Religion besides , for that in so great store of properties belonging to the self-same thing , as every mans Wit hath taken hold of some special consideration above the rest , so they have accordingly seemed one to cross another as touching their several opinions about the necessity of Sacraments ; whereas in truth their disagreement is not great. For let respect be had to the duty which every communicant doth undertake, and we may well determine concerning the use of Sacraments, that they serve as bonds of obedience to God, strict obligations to the mutual exercise of Christian Charity, provocations to godliness, preservations from sin, memorials of the principal benefits of Christ ; respect the time of their institution , and it thereby appeareth that God hath anexed them for ever unto the New Testament, as other Rites were before with the Old ; regard the weakness which is in us, and they are warrants for the more security of our belief ; compare the receivers of them with such as receive them not, and Sacraments are marks of distinction to separate Gods own from strangers ; so that in all these respects they are found to be most necessary. But their chiefest force and virtue consisteth not herein so much, as in that they are Heavenly Ceremonies, which God hath sanctified and ordained to be administred in his Church ; first, as marks whereby to know when God doth impart the vital or saving grace of Christ unto all that are capable thereof ; and secondly , as means conditional, which God requireth in them unto whom he imparteth grace. For sith God in himself is invisible, and cannot by us be discerned working , therefore when it seemeth good in the eyes of his Heavenly Wisdom, that men for some special intent and purpose should take notice of his glorious presence,

he

,he giveth some plain and sensible token whereby to know what they cannot see. For *Moses* to see God and live was impossible, yet [a] *Moses* by fire knew where the glory of God extraordinarily was present. The [b] Angel, by whom God indued the waters of the Pool called *Bethesda* with supernatural virtue to heal, was not seen of any, yet the time of the Angels presence known by the troubled motions of the waters themselves. The Apostles [c] by fiery tongues which they saw, were admonished when the Spirit, which they could not behold, was upon them. In like manner it is with us. Christ and his Holy Spirit with all their blessed effects, though entring into the soul of man we are not able to apprehend or express how, do notwithstanding give notice of the times when they use to make their access, because it pleaseth A mighty God to communicate by sensible means those blessings which are incomprehensible. Seeing therefore that grace is a consequent of Sacraments, a thing which accompanieth them as their end, a benefit which they have received from God himself the Author of Sacraments, and not from any other natural or supernatural quality in them, it may be hereby both understood that Sacraments are necessary, and that the manner of their necessity to life supernatural is not in all respects as food unto natural life, because they contain *in themselves* no vital force or efficacy; they are not physical but *moral instruments* of salvation, duties of service and worship, which unless we perform as the Author of grace requireth, they are unprofitable. For all receive not the grace of God which receive the Sacraments of his grace, Neither is it *ordinarily* his will to bestow the grace of Sacraments on any, but by the Sacraments; which grace also they that receive by Sacraments or with Sacraments, receive it from him, and not from them. For of Sacraments the very same is true which *Solomons* wisdom observeth in the brazen Serpent: [d] *He that turned towards it, was not healed by the thing he saw, but by thee, O Saviour of all.* This is therefore the necessity of Sacraments. That saving grace which Christ originally is, or hath for the general good of his whole Church, by Sacraments he severally deriveth into every member thereof. Sacraments serve as the instruments of God to that end and purpose; moral instruments, the use whereof is in our own hands, the effect in his; for the use we have his express commandment, for the effect his conditional promise; so that without our obedience to the one there is of the other no apparent assurance; and contrariwise where the signs and Sacraments of his grace are not either through contempt unreceived, or received with contempt, we are not to doubt but that they really give what they promise, and are what they signifie. For we take not Baptisme nor the Eucharist for bare *resemblances* or memorials of things absent, neither for *naked signs* and testimonies assuring us of grace received before, but (as they are indeed and in verity) for means effectual, whereby God, when we take the Sacraments, delivereth into our hands that grace available unto eternal life, which grace the Sacraments [d] represent or signifie. There have grown in the doctrine concerning Sacraments many difficulties for want of distinct explication what kind or degree of grace doth belong unto each Sacrament. For by this it hath come to pass, that the true immediate cause why Baptisme, and why the Supper of our Lord is necessary, few do rightly and distinctly consider. It cannot be denied but sundry the same effects and benefits which grow unto men by the one Sacrament, may rightly be attributed unto the other. Yet then doth Baptisme challenge to it self but the inchoation of those graces, the consummation whereof dependeth on mysteries ensuing. We receive Christ Jesus in Baptisme once as the first beginner, in the Eucharist often, as being by continual degrees the finisher of our faith. By Baptisme therefore we receive Christ Jesus, and from him that saving grace which is proper unto Baptisme. By the other Sacrament we receive him also, imparting therein himself and that grace which the Eucharist properly bestoweth. So that each Sacrament having both that which is general or common, and that also which is peculiar unto it self, we may hereby gather that the participation of Christ, which properly belongeth to any one Sacrament, is not otherwise to be obtained but by the Sacrament whereunto it is proper.

58 Now even as the Soul doth organize the body, and give unto every member thereof, that substance, quantity, and shape which nature seeth most expedient, so the rites or solemnities thereunto belonging, and that the substance therof being kept, other things in Baptism may give place to necessity.

a *Exod. 3. 2.*
b *John 5. 4.*
c *Acts 2. 3.*
d *Wisd. 16. 17.*

Spiritus Sancti munus est gratiam implere mysterii, Ambr. in Luc. cap. 3. Sanctificatis elementis effectum non propria ipsarum natura prabet, sed virtus divina potentia operatur. Cypr. de Chrism. Dum homini bonum invisibile redditur, forte ei ejusdem significatio per species visibiles adhibetur: ut foris excitetur & intus reparetur. In ipsa vasis specie virtus exprimitur medicina. Hugo de Sacram. li. 1. cap. 3. Si ergo vasa sunt spiritualis gratia sacramenta, non ex suo sanant, quia vasa agrotum non curant, sed medicina. Idem. lib. 1. cap. 4.

The substance of Baptism; the

the inward grace of Sacraments may teach what serveth best for their outward form; a thing in no part of Christian Religion, much less here to be neglected. Grace intended by Sacraments was a cause of the choice, and is a reason of the fitness of the Elements themselves. Furthermore, seeing that the grace which here we receive doth no way depend upon the natural force of that which we presently behold, it was of necessity that words of express declaration taken from the very mouth of our Lord himself should be added unto visible Elements; that the one might infallibly teach what the other do most assuredly bring to pass. In writing and speaking of the blessed Sacrament, we [a] use for the most part under the name of their *substance*, not only to comprise that whereof they outwardly and sensibly consist, but also the secret grace which they signify and exhibit. This is the reason wherefore commonly in [b] definitions, whether they be framed larger to augment, or stricter to abridge the number of Sacraments, we find grace expressly mentioned as their true essential forme; Elements as the matter whereunto that forme doth adjoyn it self. But if that be separated which is secret, and that considered alone which is seen, as of necessity it must in all those speeches that make distinction of Sacraments from Sacramental grace, the name of a Sacrament in such speeches can imply no more than what the *outward substance thereof* doth comprehend. And to make compleat the outward substance of a Sacrament, there is required an outward form, which form Sacramental Elements receive from Sacramental words. Hereupon it groweth that [c] many times there are three things said to make up the substance of a Sacrament; namely, the grace which is thereby offered, the Element which shadoweth or signifieth grace, and the Word which expresseth what is done by the Element. So that whether we consider the outward by it self alone, or both the outward and inward substance of any Sacraments, there are in the one respect but two essential parts, and in the other but three that concurre to give Sacraments their full being. Furthermore, because definitions are to express but the most immediate and neerest parts of nature, whereas other principles farther off, although not specified in defining, are notwithstanding in nature implyed and presupposed, we must note that in as much as Sacraments are actions religious and mystical, which nature they have not unless they proceed from a serious meaning; and what every mans private mind is, as we cannot know, so neither are we bound to examine: therefore always in these cases the known intent of the Church generally doth suffice, and where the contrary is not [d] manifest; we may presume that he which outwardly doth the work, hath inwardly the purpose of the Church of God. Concerning all other Orders, Rites, Prayers, Lessons, Sermons, Actions, and their Circumstances whatsoever, they are to the outward substance of Baptism but things accessorie, which the wisdom of the Church of Christ is to order according to the exigence of that which is principal. Again, considering that such Ordinances have been made to adorn the Sacrament, [e] not the Sacrament to depend upon them; seeing also that they are not of the substance of Baptism, and that Baptism is far more necessary then any such incident Rite or Solemnity ordained for the better administration thereof, [f] if the case be such as permitteth not Baptism to have the decent Complements of Baptism, better it were to enjoy the body without his Furniture, then to wait for this, till the opportunity of that for which we desire it be lost. Which Premises standing, it seemeth to have been no absurd collection, that in cases of necessity which will not suffer delay till Baptism be administred, with usual solemnities, (to speak the least) it may be tolerably given without them, rather than any man without it should be suffered to depart this life.

a *Eucharistia duabus ex rebus constat, terrena & cælesti.* Iren. adverf. hæref. l.4. c.34. *Arcanarum rerum symbola non nudis signis, sed signis simul & rebus constant.* Helvet. confef. prior. Art. 2. b *Sacramentum est cum res gesta visibilis longè aliud invisibile intus operatur.* Isid. Etym. l. 1. *Sacramentum est per quod sub tegumento rerum visibilium divina virtus salutem secretius operatur.* Gregor. mag. *Sacramentum est signum significans efficaciter effectum Dei gratuitum.* Occa. sent. l.4. d 1. *Sacramentum propriè non est signum cujuslibet rei sacra, sed tantum rei sacra sanctificantis homines.* Th. 12. q. 101.4 & q.102.5. *Sacramentum est signum passionis Christi gratia & gloria. Ideo est commemoratio praeteriti, demonstratio praesentis, & prognosticon futuri.* Th 3. q.60. 3. *Sacramenta sunt signa & symbola visibilia rerum internarum & invisibilium, per quæ, seu per media Dei virtute spiritus sancti in nobis agit.* Cōf. Belg. Art. 33. Item Bar. Conf. c. 11. c *Sacramenta constant verbo, signis, & rebus significatis.* Confef. Helvet. post. cap. 19.

d *Si aliud Ministri agere intendunt, puta sacris illudere mysteriis, vel aliud quod Ecclesia non consentiat, nihil agitur; sine fide enim spiritualis potestas exerceri quidem potest, sine Ecclesia intentione non potest.* Lancel. inst. j π. Can. lib. 2. tit. 2. 5. hoc tamen. e *Accessorium non regulat principale sed ab eo regulatur.* 42. De regul. jur. in Sext. l. 3: ff. quod jussu. f *Etsi nihil facile mutandum est ex solennibus, tamen ubi aquitas evidens poscit subveniendum est.* Lib. 183. de reg. jur.

59 They which deny that any such case of necessity can fall, in regard whereof the Church should to erate Baptisme without the decent Rites and So emnities thereunto belonging, pretend that such tolerations have risen from a false interpretation which *certain men* have made of the Scripture, grounding a necessity of external Baptisme upon the words of our Saviour Christ: *Unless a man be born again of Water and of the Spirit, he cannot enter into the Kingdom of Heaven.* For by *Water and the Spirit*, we are in that place to understand (as they imagine) no more than if the Spirit alone had been mentioned, and Water not spoken of. Which they think is plain, because elsewhere it is not improbable, that *the Holy Ghost and Fire*, do but signifie the Holy Ghost in operation resembling Fire. Whereupon they conclude, that seeing Fire in one place may be, therefore Water in another place is but a Metaphor; Spirit, the interpretation thereof; and so the words do only mean, *That unless a man be born again of the Spirit, he cannot enter into the Kingdom of Heaven.* I hold it for a most unfallible rule in Expositions of sacred Scripture, that where a literal construction will stand, the farthest from the letter is commonly the worst. There is nothing more dangerous than this licentious and deluding Art, which changeth the meaning of words, as Alchymie doth or would do the substance of Metals, maketh of any thing what it listeth, and bringeth in the end all Truth to nothing. Or howsoever such voluntary exercise of wit might be born with otherwise; yet in places which usually serve, as this doth, concerning Regeneration by Water and the Holy Ghost, to be alledged for grounds and principles, less is permitted. To hide the general consent of Antiquity agreeing in the literal interpretation, they cunningly affirm, that *certain* have taken those words as meant of material Water, when they know, that of all the Ancients there is not one to be named, that ever did otherwise either expound or alledge the place, than as implying external Baptisme. Shall that which hath always received this and no other construction, be now disguised with a toy of novelty? Must we needs at the only shew of Critical conceit without any more deliberation, utterly condemn them of errour, which will not admit that Fire in the words of *John* is quenched with the Name of the Holy Ghost; or with the name of the Spirit, Water dryed up in the words of Christ? When the letter of the Law hath two things plainly and expresly specified, *Water* and the *Spirit*; Water as a duty required on our parts, the Spirit as a gift which God bestoweth; there is danger in presuming so to interpret it, as if the clause which concerneth our selves were more than needeth. We may by such rare expositions attain perhaps in the end to be thought witty, but with ill advice. Finally, if as at [b] the time, when that Baptisme which was meant by *John*, came to be really and truly performed by Christ himself, we find the Apostles, that had been, as we are, before bapt'zed, new baptized with the Holy Ghost, and in this their latter Baptisme as well a [c] visible descent of fire, as a secret miraculous infusion of the Spirit; if on us he accomplish likewise the Heavenly work of our new-birth, not with the Spirit alone, but with Water thereunto adjoyned, sith the faithfullest expounders of his words are his own deeds, let that which his hand hath manifestly wrought, declare what his speech did doubtfully utter.

60 To this they adde, That as we erre by following a wrong construction of the place before alledged; so our second over-sight is, that we thereupon infer a necessity over-rigorous and extream. The true necessity of Baptisme, a few Propositions

Margin notes:

The ground in Scripture whereupon a necessity of outward Baptisme hath been built. *T.C.l.1.p 143.*

Private Baptisme first rose upon a false interpretation of the place of St. *John* 3. 5. *Unless a man be born again of Water, and of the Spirit*; and where certain do interpret the word *Water* for the material and elemental Water, when as our Saviour Christ taketh Water there by a borrowed speech, for the Spirit of God, the effect whereof it shadoweth out. For even as in another place, *Mat.* 3. 11. by Fire and the Spirit, he meaneth nothing but the Spirit of God, which purgeth and purifieth as the Fire doth: So in this place by Water and the Spirit, he meaneth nothing else but the Spirit of God which cleanseth the filth of sin, and cooleth the broyling heat of an unquiet Conscience, as Water washeth the thing which is foul, and quencheth the heat of the fire.

a *Minimè sunt mutanda quæ inter relationem certam semper habuerunt.*

b *Acts* 1. 3; *John* baptized with Water, but you shall within few days be baptized with the Holy Ghost.

c *Acts* 2. 3.

gathered by the words of our Saviour Christ, and what the true necessity thereof indeed is *T.C.l.1.p.143.* Secondly, this errour [of private Baptisme] came by a false and unnecessary conclusion drawn from that place. For although the Scripture should say, that none can be saved but those which have the Spirit of God, and are baptized with material and elemental Water; yet ought it to be understood of those which can conveniently and orderly be brought to Baptisme; as the Scripture, saying, that who so doth not believe the Gospel, is condemned already, *John* 3. 18. meaneth this sentence of those which can hear the Gospel, and have discretion to understand it when they hear it; and cannot here shut under this condemnation, either those that be born deaf, and so remain, or little Infants or natural Fools, that have no wit to conceive what is preached.

What kind of necessity in outward Baptisme hath been

Ii 2   positions

positions considered will soon decide. All things which either are known * Causes or set *Means*, whereby any great good is usually procured, or men delivered from grievous evil, the same we must needs confess necessary. And if *Regeneration* were not in this very sence a thing necessary to eternal life, would Christ himself have taught *Nicodemus* that to see the Kingdom of God is * impossible, saving only for those men which are born from above? His words following in the next sentence, are a proof sufficient, that to our regeneration *his Spirit* is no less † necessary, than Regeneration it self necessary unto life. Thirdly, unless as the Spirit is a necessary inward cause, so *Water* were a necessary outward meane to our Regeneration, what construction should we give unto those words wherein we are said to be new-born, and that ἐξ ὕδατος, even of *Water*? Why are we taught that with water God doth purifie and cleanse his Church? Wherefore do the Apostles of Christ term Baptism [b] a bath of Regeneration? What purpose had they in giving men advice to receive outward Baptism, and in perswading them it did avail to remission of sins? If outward Baptism were a cause in it self possessed of that power either natural or supernatural, without the present operation whereof no such effect could possibly grow, it must then follow, that seeing effects do never prevent the necessary causes out of which they spring, no man could ever receive grace before Baptism: Which being apparently both known and also confest to be otherwise in many particulars, although in the rest we make not Baptism a cause of grace, yet the grace which is given them with their [d] Baptism, doth so far forth depend on the very outward Sacrament, that God will have it imbraced not onely as a sign or token what we receive, but also as an instrument or meane whereby we receive grace, because Baptism is a Sacrament which God hath instituted in his Church, to the end that they which receive the same, might thereby be [e] incorporated into Christ, and so through his most precious Merit obtain as well that saving grace of imputation which taketh away [f] all former guiltiness, as also that [g] infused Divine vertue of the Holy Ghost, which giveth to the powers of the Soul their first disposition towards future newness of life.

There are that elevate too much the ordinary and immediate means of life, relying wholly upon the bare conceit of that eternal Election, which notwithstanding includeth a subordination of means, without which we are not actually brought to enjoy what God secretly did intend, and therefore to build upon Gods Election, if we keep not our selves to the ways which he hath appointed for men to walk in, is but a self-deceiving vanity. When the Apostle saw men called to the participation of Jesus Christ, after the Gospel of God embraced, and the Sacrament of life received, he feareth not [h] then to put them in the number of Elect Saints, he [i] then accounteth them delivered from death, and clean purged from all sin. Till then, notwithstanding their preordination unto life, which none could know of, saving God, what were they in the Apostles own [k] account but children of wrath, as well as others plain Aliens, altogether without hope, strangers utterly without God in this present world? So that by Sacraments and other sensible tokens of grace, we may boldly gather that he, whose mercy vouchsafeth now to bestow the means, hath also long sithence intended us that whereunto they lead. But let us never think it safe to presume of our own last end, by bare conjectural collections of his intent and purpose, the means failing that should come between. Predestination bringeth not to life, without the grace of external [l] vocation, wherein our Baptism is implyed.

plyed. For as we are not naturally men without birth, so neither are we Christian men in the eye of the Church of God but by new birth, nor according to the manifest ordinary course of Divine Dispensation new born, but by that Baptism which both declareth and maketh us Christians. In which respect we justly hold it to be the door of our actual entrance into Gods house, the first apparent [m] beginning of life, a seal perhaps to the [n] grace of *Election* before received, but to our Sanctification here, a step that hath not any before it. There were of the old *Valentinian* Hereticks some, which had knowledge in such admiration, that to it they ascribed all, and so despised the Sacraments of Christ, pretending that as ignorance had made us subject to all misery, so the full Redemption of the inward man, and the work of our Restauration, must needs belong unto [o] *Knowledge onely.* They draw very neer unto this errour, who fixing wholly their minds on the known necessity of Faith, [p] imagine that nothing but Faith is necessary for the attainment of all Grace. Yet is it a branch of Belief, that Sacraments are in their place no less required then Belief it self. For when our Lord and Saviour promiseth eternal Life, is it any otherwise then as he promised restitution of health unto *Naaman* the Syrian, namely, with this condition, [q] *Wash and be clean ?* or as to them which were stung of Serpents, health by [r] beholding the brazen Serpent ? If Christ himself which giveth Salvation do [s] require Baptism, it is not for us that look for salvation, to found and examine him whether unbaptized men may be saved, but seriously to [s] do that which is required, and religiously to fear the danger which may grow by the want thereof. Had Christ only declared his will to have all men baptized, and not acquainted us with any cause why Baptism is necessary, our ignorance in the reason of that he enjoyneth, might perhaps have hindered somewhat the forwardness of our obedience thereunto : whereas now being taught, that Baptism is necessary to take away sin, how have we the fear of God in our hearts, if care of delivering mens Souls from sin do not move us to use all means for their Baptism ? [t] *Pelagius* which denyed utterly the guilt of original sin, and *in that respect* the necessity of Baptism, did notwithstanding both baptize Infants, and acknowledge their Baptism necessary for *entrance into the Kingdom of God.* Now the Law of Christ, which in these considerations maketh Baptism necessary, must be construed and understood according to rules of [x] natural equity. Which rules if they themselves did not follow in expounding the Law of God, they would never be able to prove that [y] the Scripture in saying, *Whoso believeth not the Gospel of Christ, is condemned already* ; meaneth this sentence of those which can hear the Gospel, and have discretion when they hear to understand it, neither ought it to be applyed unto Infants, Deaf men and Foo's. That which teacheth them thus to interpret the Law of Christ is natural equity. And (because equity so teacheth) it is on all parts gladly confest that *there may be in divers cases* life by vertue of inward Baptism, even where outward is not found. So that if any question be made, it is but about the bounds and limits of this possibility. For example, to think that a man whose Baptism the Crown of Martyrdom preventeth, doth lose, in that case, the happiness which so many thousands enjoy, that onely have had the grace to believe, and not the honour to seal the testimony thereof with death, were almost barbarous. Again, when [z] some certain opinative men in Saint *Bernards* time began privately to hold that, because our Lord hath said, *Unless a man be born again of water,* therefore life, without either actual Baptism, *or Martyrdome* in stead of Baptism, cannot *possibly* be obtained at the hands of God : *Bernard* considering that the same equity which had moved them to think of the necessity of Baptism no bar against the happy estate of unbaptized Martyrs ; is as forcible for the warrant of their Salvation, in whom, although there be not the Sufferings of Holy Martyrs, there are the vertues which sanctified those Sufferings and made them precious in Gods sight, professed himself an enemy to that severity and strictness which admitteth no exception but of Martyrs only. For, saith he, if a man desirous of Baptism be suddenly cut off by death, in whom there wanted neither sound Faith, devout Hope, nor sincere Charity (God

propter vitam, sed propter regnum Cœlorum Baptismum parvulis conferendum. Euseb. Emiss. Hom. 5. de Pasch. x *Benignius leges interpretandæ sunt, quo voluntas earum conservetur.* L. Benign. D. de legib. & Senatule. y T. C. l. 1. p. 143. z *Bern. Epist. 70. ad Hugonem.*

Marginal notes:

m 'Αρχὴ μοι ζωῆς τὸ Βάπτισμα. Basil.
n Sp. S. c. 10.
n T. C. l. 3. p. 134. He which is not a Christian before he come to receive Baptism, cannot be made a Christian by Baptism, which is only the seal of the grace of God before received.
o Iren. contra Hæres. l. 1. c. 18.
p *Hic sceleftissimi illi provocant quæstiones. Adeo dicunt, baptismus non est necessarius quibus fide satis est.* Tert. de baptismo.
Huic nulla proderit fides, quæ cum possit non percipit sacramentum. Bern. Epist. 70. ad Hugon.
q 1 Reg. 5. 14.
r Num. 21. 8.
s Marc. 16. 16.
t *Institutio Sacramentorum quantum ad Deum authorem dispensationis est, quantum vero ad hominem obedientem necessitatis. Quoniam In potestate Dei est præter ista hominem salvare, sed in potestate hominis non est sine iste ad salutem pervenire.* Hug. de Sacr. lib. 1. cap. 5.
u P. Isagius asserit arrepta rere impietate præficeis non

be merciful unto me, and pardon me if I erre) but verily of such a ones Salvation, in whom there is no other defect besides his faultlesse lack of Baptisme, despair I cannot, nor induce my mind to think his Faith void, his Hope confounded, and his Charity fain to nothing, only because he hath not that which not contempt but impossibility with-holdeth. *Tell me I beseech you* (saith *Ambrose*) *what there is in any of us more then to will, and to seek for our own good. Thy Servant* Valentinian, *O Lord, did both.* For *Valentinian* the Emperour dyed before his purpose to receive Baptisme could take effect.) *And is it possible that he which had purposely thy Spirit given him to desire grace, should not receive that grace which that Spirit did desire? Doth it move you that the outward accustomed Solemnities were not done? As though Converts that suffer Martyrdome before Baptisme, did thereby forfeit their right to the Crown of eternal glory in the Kingdom of Heaven. If the blood of Martyrs in that case be their Baptisme, surely his religious desire of Baptisme standeth him in the same stead.* It hath been therefore constantly held as well touching other Believers as Martyrs, that Baptisme taken away by necessity, is supplyed by desire of Baptisme, because with [b] equity this opinion doth best stand.

b *Quid ad tolerandam omnem Dei gloria injuriam semet dicavit animum in Martyrium mihi videtur implesse, Summi ergo meriti est semel fixisse sententiam, atq; ideo, ut dixi, ratio principatum obtinet passionis; & si fors perstiendi degener facultatem, persulit tamen cuncta qua voluit pati.* Josep. l. de imper. ratio.

c Gers. Serm. in Nativit. Beata Maria Cajetan. in 3. Theo, q 68. art. 1 & 2. Biel. in 4. Senten. d. 4. q. 2. Tilman. Segeberg. de sacr. c. 1. Elisius Neapol. in Cly. adverf. harese. c. de bapt.

d 1 Cor. 7. 12.

Touching Infants which dye unbaptized, sith they neither have the Sacrament it self, nor any sense or conceit thereof, the judgement of many hath gone hard against them. But yet seeing grace is not absolutely tyed unto Sacraments, and besides, such is the lenity of God, that unto things altogether impossible he bindeth no man, but where we ca not do what is injoined us, accepteth our will to do in stead of the deed it self; Again, forasmuch as there is in their Christian Parents and in the Church of God a presumed desire that the Sacrament of Baptisme might be given them, yea a purpose also that it shall be given; remorse of equity hath moved divers of the [c] School-Divines in these considerations ingenuously to grant, that God all merciful to such as are not in themselves able to desire Baptisme, imputeth the secret desire that others have in their behalf, and accepteth the same as theirs, rather than casteth away their Souls for that which no man is able to help. And of the Will of God to impart his grace unto Infants without Baptisme, in that case the very circumstance of their natural birth may serve as a just Arugment, whereupon it is not to be misliked that men in charitable presumption do gather a great likelihood of their Salvation, to whom the benefit of Christian parentage being given, the rest that should follow is prevented by some such casualty as man hath himself no power to void. For, we are plainly taught of God. [d] That the Seed of faithful Parentage is holy from the very birth. Which albeit we may not so understand, as if the Children of beleiving Parents were without sin, or grace from baptized Parents derived by Propagation, of God by Covenant and Promise tyed to save any in meer regard of their Parents Belief: yet seeing that to all professors of the name of Christ, this preeminence above Infidels is freely given, the fruit of their bodies bringeth into the World with it a present interest and right to those means wherewith the Ordinance of Christ is that his Church shall be sanctified, it is not to be thought that he which as it were from Heaven hath nominated and designed them unto holiness by special priviledge of their very birth, will himself deprive them of Regeneration and inward grace, only because necessity depriveth them of outward Sacraments. In which case, it were the part of Charity to hope, and to make men rather partial than cruel Judges, if we had not those fair apparancies which here we have. Wherefore a necessity there is of receiving, and a necessity of administring the Sacrament of Baptisme; the one peradventure not so absolute as some have thought, but out of all peradventure the other more Straight and narrow, than that the Church which is by office a Mother unto such as crave at their hands the Sacred Mystery of their new-Birth, should repel them, and see them dye unsatisfied of these their Ghostly desires, rather than give them their Souls Rites, with omission of those things which serve [e] but only for the more convenient and orderly Administration thereof. For as on the one side we grant that those sentences of Holy Scripture which make Sacraments most necessary to eternal life, are no prejudice to their Salvation that want them by some inevitable necessity, and without any fault of their own; so it ought in reason to be likewise acknowledged, that forasmuch as our Lord himself maketh Baptisme necessary, necessary whether we respect the good

e T. C. l. 3. p. 218 It is in question whether there be any such necessity of Baptisme, as that for the ministring thereof, the common decent orders should be broken.

good received by Baptisme, or the Testimony thereby yielded unto God of that humility and meek obedience, which reposing wholly it self on the absolute authority of his Commandment, and on the truth of his Heavenly Promise, doubteth not but from Creatures despicable in their own condition and substance to obtain grace of inestimable value, or rather not from them, but from him, yet by them as by his appointed means, howsoever he hy the secret ways of his own incomprehensible mercy may be thought to save without Baptisme, this cleareth not the Church from guiltiness of blood, if through her superfluous scrupulosity, lets and impediments of less regard should cause a grace of so great moment to be with-held, wherein our mercyless strictness may be our own harm, although not theirs towards whom we shew it; and we for the hardness of our hearts may perish, albeit they through Gods unspeakable mercy do live. God which did not afflict that innocent, whose Circumcision *Moses* had over-long deferred, took revenge upon [t] *Moses* himself for the [t Exod. 4. 24.] injury which was done through so great neglect, giving us thereby to understand, that they whom Gods own mercy saveth without us, are on our parts notwithstanding, and as much as in us lieth, even destroyed, when under unsufficient pretences, we defraud them of such ordinary outward helps as we should exhibit. We have for Baptisme no day set as the Jews had for Circumcision, neither have we by the Law of God, but only by the Churches discretion, a place thereunto appointed. Baptisme therefore, even in the meaning of the Law of Christ, belongeth unto Infants capable thereof, from the [g] very instant of their birth. Which if they have not, howsoever, rather then lose it by being put off, because the time, the place, or some such like circumstance, doth not solemnly enough concur, the Church as much as in her lyeth, wilfully casteth away their souls. *[g In omnibus obligationibus in quibus dies non ponitur, presenti die debetur, lib. 14. D. de Reg. Jur.]*

61 The ancients it may be were too severe, and made the necessity of Baptisme more absolute then reason would, as touching Infants. But will [b] any man say that they, notwithstanning their too much rigour herein, did in that respect sustain and tolerate defects of local or of personal solemnities, belonging to the Sacrament of Baptism? The Apostles themselves did neither use nor appoint for Baptisme any certain time. The Church for general Baptisme heretofore made choice of two chief days in the year; the Feast of Easter, and the Feast of Pentecost. Which custome, when certain Churches in *Sicily* began to violate without cause, they were by [i] *Leo* Bishop of *Rome* advised, rather to conform themselves to the rest of the World in things so reasonable, then to offend mens minds through needless singularity: howbeit, always providing that nevertheless in apparent peril of death, danger of siege, streights of persecution, fear of shipwrack, and the like exigents, no respect of times should cause this singular defence of true safety to be denyed unto any. This of *Leo* did but confirm that sentence which [k] *Victor* had many years before given, extending the same exception as well unto *places* as times. That which Saint *Augustine* speaketh of women, hasting to bring their children to the Church when they saw danger, is a weak proof, that *when necessity did not leave them so much time*, it was not then permitted them neither to make a Church of their own home: Which answer dischargeth likewise their example of a sick Jew, carried in bed to the place of Baptisme, and not baptized at home in private. The cause why such kind of Baptism barred men afterwards from entring into holy orders, the reason wherefore it was objected against *Novatian*, in what respect, and how far forth it did disable, may be gathered by the twelfth Canon, set down in the Council of *Neocæsarea*, after this manner. *A man which hath been baptized in sickness, is not after to be ordained Priest.* For it may be thought, *that such do rather at that time, because they see no other remedy, than of a voluntary mind, lay hold on the Christian faith, unless their*

[What things in Baptisme have been dispenced with by the Fathers respecting necessity. h T. C. l p. 146. The Authours themselves of that errour that they cannot be saved which are not baptized, did never seek no remedy of the mischief in Womans or private Baptisme. T. C. li. 3. p. 219. What plainer testimony can there be then that of Augustine; which noteth the use of the Church to have been, to come to the Church with their children in danger of death, and that when some had opinion, that their children could not be saved if they were not baptized, Cont. lit. Parm. lib. 2. cap. 13. I would also know of him what he will answer to that; which is noted of a Christian Jew desperately sick of the Palsie, that was with his bed carried to the place of Baptisme, Socr. lib. 7. cap. 4. What will he answer to this, That those which were baptized in their beds, were thereby made unapt to have any place amongst the Clergy as they call them] doth it not leave a note of infamy in those, which had procured that Baptisme should be ministred in private houses? Euseb. lib. 6. cap. 43. What unto the Emperous Decree, which upon authority of the ancient Laws, and of the Apostles, forbiddeth that the holy things should be administred in any private mans house? Just. Novel. 57. i Leo Epist. 4. ad Episc. Cicil. k Vict. Epist. ad Theoph. Alexand. in Pontif. Damas.]

true

true and sincere meaning be made afterwards the more manifest, or else the scarcity of others inforce the Church to admit them. They bring in *Justinians* Imperial Constitution, but to what purpose, seeing it only forbiddeth men to have the mysteries of God administred in their private Chappels, left under that pretence Hereticks should do secretly those things which were unlawful? In which consideration he therefore commandeth, that if they would use those private Oratories otherwise than only for their private Prayers, the Bishop should appoint them a Clerk, whom they might entertain for that purpose. This is plain by later Constitutions, made in the time of *Leo*: * *It was thought good* (saith the Emperour) *in their judgement* *which have gone before, that in private Chappels none should celebrate the holy Communion, but Priests belonging unto greater Churches. Which Order they took as it* *seemeth for the custody of Religion, lest men should secretly receive from Hereticks,* *in stead of the food, the bane of their Souls, pollution in place of expiation.* † Again, *Whereas a sacred Canon of the sixth reverend Synod requireth Baptism, as others have* *likewise the holy Sacrifices and Mysteries to be celebrated only in Temples hallowed* *for publick use, and not in private Oratories; which strict Decrees appear to have* *been made hertofore in regard of Hereticks, which eared closely into such mens houses* *as favoured their opinions, whom, under colour of performing with them such religious* *Offices, they drew from the soundness of true Religion: Now that perverse opinions* *through the grace of Almighty God are extinct and gone, the cause of former re-* *straints being taken away, we see no reason but that private Oratories may hence for-* *ward enjoy that liberty, which to have granted them heretofore, had not been safe.* In sum, all these things alledged are nothing, nor will it ever be proved while the world doth continue, but that the practice of the Church in cases of extream necessity, hath made for private Baptism always more than against it. Yea, *Baptism* *by any man in the case of necessity,* was the ᵃ voice of the whole world heretofore. Neither is *Tertullian, Epiphanius, Augustine,* or any other of the ancient against it. The boldness of such as pretending *Teclaes* example, took openly upon them both Baptism, and all other publick Functions of Priesthood, *Tertullian* severely controlleth, saying: ᵇ *To give Baptism is in truth the Bishops Right. After him it* *belongeth unto Priests and Deacons; but not to them without authority from him recei-* *ved. For so the honour of the Church requireth, which being kept, preserveth peace.* *Were it not in this respect, the Laity might do the same, all sorts might give even as all* *forts receive. But because Emulation is the mother of Schismes, Let it content thee* (which art of the order of Lay-men) *to do it in necessity when the state of time, or* *place, or person thereunto compelleth. For then is their boldness priviledged that help,* *when the circumstance of other mens dangers craveth it.* What he granteth generally to Lay-persons of the House of God, the same we cannot suppose he denyeth to any sort or sex contained under that name, unless himself did restrain the limits of his own speech; especially seeing that *Tertullians* rule of interpretation is ᶜ else-where, *Specialties are signified under that which is general, because they are therein* *comprehended.* All which *Tertullian* doth ᵈ deny, is, that women may be called to bear, or publickely take upon them to execute Offices of Ecclesiastical Order, whereof none but men are capable. As for *Epiphanius,* he striketh on the very self-fame Anvil with *Tertullian.* And in necessity if S. *Augustine* alloweth as much unto Lay-men as *Tertullian* doth, his *not mentioning* of women, is but a slender proof that his meaning was to exclude women. Finally, the Council of *Carthage* likewise, although it make no express submission, may be very well presumed willing to stoop, as other Positive Ordinances do, to the countermands of necessity. Judge therefore what the Ancients would have thought, if in their days it had been heard which is published in ours, ᵉ *that because, The substance of the Sacrament doth chie-*

a *T. C. lib.* 1. pag. 145. To allow of Womens baptizing, is not onely contrary to the learned Writers now, but also contrary to all learned Antiquity, and contrary to the practise of the Church whilest there was any tolerable estate. *Tertul. de Virgin. ve-land. & lib. de Baptis.* *Epiphan. lib.* 1. & *lib. 2. contra Haret.* S. *Augustine,* although he seem to allow of a Lay-mans Baptisme in time of necessity *Cont. Epist. Parmen. lib.* 2. c. 13. yet there he menticneth not Womens Baptism: and in the fourth Council of

Carthage, cap. 100. It is simply without exception decreed, that a woman ought not to baptize. b *Tertul. de Baptis.* c *Subjectum est generali speciale. In ipso significatur, quia in ipso continetur* Tert. de velan. Virg. *Pessio genere suppo-* *nitur species, Azo in* l. 1. c. de T ansact. d *Non permittitur mulieri in Ecclesia loqui, sed nec docere, nec tingere, nec of-* *ferre, nec ulla virilis munerh nedum Sacerdotalis officii sortem sibi vendicare,* Tertul. de veland. Vir. e *T.C.* l.1. p. 144. The substance of the Sacrament dependeth chiefly on the Institution and Word of God, which is the forme, and as it were the life of the Sacrament. *T. C. lib.* 1. p. 144. Although part of the Institution be observed, yet if the whole Institution b not, it is no Sacrament. *T.C. lib.* 1. p. 145. The orders which God hath set, are, that it should be done in the Congregation, and by the Minister. *T.C. lib.* 1. 146. And I will further say, that although the Infants which dye without Baptisme should be assuredly damned, (which is most false) yet ought not the orders which God hath set in his Church be broken after this sort.

fly depend on the institution of God, which is the form, and as it were the life of the Sacrament ; therefore first, *if the whole Institution be not kept, it is no Sacrament* ; and secondly, if Baptism be private his institution is broken, in as much as *according to the orders which he hath set for Baptism, it should be done in the Congregation,* from whose Ordinance in this point *we ought not to swerve, although we know that Infants should be assuredly damned without Baptism.* O Sir, you that would spurn thus at such, as in case of so dreadful extremity should lye prostrate before your feet ; you that would turn away your face from them at the hour of their most need ; you that would damme up your ears, and harden your hearts as Iron, against the unresistable cryes of Supplicants, calling upon you for mercy with terms of such invocation, as that most dreadful perplexity might minister, if God by miracle did open the mouths of Infants, to express their supposed necessity, should first imagine your self in their case, and them in yours. This done, let their supplications proceed out of your mouth, and your answer out of theirs. Would you then contentedly hear, *My Son, the Rites and Solemnities of Baptism must be kept, we may not do* ill that good may come of it, neither are souls to be delivered from eternal death and condemnation, by breaking Orders which Christ hath set ; would you in their case your self be shaken off with these answers, and not rather embrace, inclosed with both your arms, a sentence, which now is no Gospel unto you, ᵍ *I will have mercy and not Sacrifice* ? To acknowledge Christs Institution the ground of both Sacraments, I suppose, no Christian man will refuse : For it giveth them their very nature, it appointeth the matter whereof they consist, the form of their administration it teacheth, and it blesseth them with that grace whereby to us they are both pledges and instruments of life. Nevertheless, seeing Christs Institution containeth, besides that which maketh compleat the Essence or Nature, other things that only are parts as it were of the furniture of Sacraments, the difference between these two must unfold that which the general terms of indefinite speech would confound. If the place appointed for Baptism be a part of Christs Institution, it is but his Institution as *sacrifice,* Baptism his Institution as *mercy,* in this case. He which requireth both Mercy and Sacrifice, rejecteth his own Institution of Sacrifice, where the offering of Sacrifice would hinder mercy from being shewed ; External Circumstances even in the holiest and highest actions, are but the ʰ *lesser things of the Law,* whereunto those actions themselves being compared are *the greater* ; and therefore as the greater are of such importance that they *must be done,* so in that extremity before supposed, if our account of the lesser which are *not to be omitted,* should cause omission of that which is more to be accounted of, were not this our strict obedience to Christs Institution touching *Mint and Cummin,* a disobedience to his Institution concerning love ? But sith no Institution of Christ hath so strictly tyed Baptism to publick Assemblies, as it hath done all men unto Baptism, away with these merciless and bloudy Sentences, let them never be found standing in the Books and Writings of a Christian man, they savour not of Christ, nor of his most gracious and meek Spirit, but under colour of exact obedience, they nourish cruelty and hardness of heart.

62. To leave private Baptism therefore, and to come unto Baptism by women , which ⁱ they say , is no more a Sacrament, then any other ordinary washing or bathing of a mans body ; the reason whereupon they ground their opinion herein is such , as making Baptism by Women void , because Women are no Ministers in the Church of God, must needs generally annihilate the Baptism of all unto whom their conceit shall apply this exception, whether it be in regard of sex, of quality, or insufficiency, or whatsoever. For if want of Calling do frustrate Baptism, they that baptize without Calling do nothing, be they Women or Men. To make Women Teachers in the House of God, were a gross absurdity, seeing the Apostle hath said, ᵏ *I per-mit not a Woman to teach* : And again, ˡ *Let your Women in Churches be silent.* Those extraordinary gifts of speaking with tongues and prophecying, which God at that
time

Marginal notes:

f *Nostro peccato alterius saluti consulere non debemus.* Aug. lib. cont. Mend. cap. 17.

g *Math.* 9.13.

h *Math.* 23.23.

Whether baptism by Women be true baptism, good and effectual to them that receive it.

i *T.C. lib.* 1. *pag.* 144. On this point, whether he be a Minister or no, dependeth not only the dignity, but also the being of the Sacrament. So that I take the baptism of Women to be no more the holy Sacrament of baptism, then any other daily or ordinary washing of the child.

k 1 *Tim.* 1.12.

l 1 *Tim.* 14.34.

time did not only bestow upon Men, but on Women also, made it the harder to hold them confined with private bounds. Whereupon the Apostles Ordinance was necessary against Womens publique admission to teach. And because when Law hath begun some one thing or other well, it giveth good occasion either to draw by judicious exposition out of the very Law it self, or to annex to the Law by authority and jurisdiction things of like conveniency; therefore * Clement extendeth this Apostolike Constitution to Baptism. For (saith he) *If we have denyed them leave to teach, how should any man dispense with nature, and make them Ministers of holy things, seeing this unskilfulness is a part of the Grecians impiety, which for the service of women goddesses, have women Priests?* I somewhat marvel, that men which would not willingly be thought to speak or write, but with good conscience, dare hereupon openly avouch Clement for a † witness, that *as when the Church began not only to decline, but to fall away from the sincerity of Religion, so it borrowed a number of other prophanations of the Heathens, so it borrowed this, and would needs have women Priests, as the Heathens had; and that this was an occasion of bringing Baptism by Women into the Church of God.* Is it not plain in their own eyes, that first by an evidence which forbiddeth Women to be Ministers of Baptism, they endeavour to shew how Women were admitted unto that Function in the wain and declination of Christian piety: Secondly, that by an evidence rejecting the Heathens, and condemning them of impiety, they would prove such affection towards Heathens, as ordereth the affairs of the Church by the pattern of their example: And Thirdly, that out of an evidence which nameth the Heathens, as being in some part a reason why the Church had no Women Priests, they gather, the Heathens to have been one of the first occasions why it had. So that throughout every branch of this testimony their issue is, *Yea*, and their evidence directly *Noe*. But to Womens Baptism in private by occasion of urgent necessity, the reasons that only concern ordinary Baptism in publick, are no just prejudice; neither can we by force thereof disprove the practice of those Churches which (necessity requiring) allow Baptism in private to be administred by Women.

We may not from Laws that prohibit any thing with restraint, conclude absolute and unlimited prohibitions: Although we deny not but they which utterly forbid such Baptisme, may have perhaps wherewith to justifie their orders against it. For, even things lawful are a well prohibited, when there is fear left they make the way too unlawful more easie. And it may be, the liberty of Baptisme by Women at such times, doth sometimes embolden the rasher sort to do it where no such necessity is. But whether of permission besides Law, or in presumption against Law they do it, it is thereby altogether frustrate, void, and as though it were never given. They which have not at the first their right Baptisme, must of necessity be re-baptized, because the Law of Christ tyeth all men to receive Baptisme. Iteration of Baptisme once given hath been always thought a manifest contempt of that ancient Apostolick Aphorisme, b *One Lord, One Faith, One Baptisme*; Baptisme not only one inasmuch as it hath every where the same substance, and offereth unto all men the same grace, but one also for that it ought not to be received by any one man above once. We serve that Lord which is but one, because no other can be joined with him: we embrace that Faith which is but one, because it admitteth no innovation: that Baptisme we receive which is but one, because it cannot be received often: For how should we practise Iteration of Baptisme, and yet teach that we are by Baptisme born anew; that by Baptisme we are admitted into the Heavenly society of Saints, that those things be really and effectually done by Baptisme, which are no more possible to be often done, than a man can naturally be often born, or civilly be often adopted into any ones Stock and Family? This also is the cause why they that present us unto Baptisme, are intituled for ever after, our Parents in God; and the reason why there we receive new names, in token that by Baptisme we are made new creatures. As Christ hath therefore dyed and risen again from the dead but once, so the Sacrament which both extinguisheth in him our former sin, and beginneth in us a new condition of life, is by one only actual administration for ever available, according to that in the Nicene Creed, *I beleeve one Baptisme for the remission of sins.* And because second Baptisme was ever d abhorred in the Church of God

* Clem. Const.
Apostol.lib. 2.
cap. 9.

†T.C l.1 p.144

a Licita prohibentur,ne si permitterentur,eorum occasione peruenitur ad illicita. Just. de Asueth.tit.l.Officium, D. de rei vind.

b Ephes. 4. 5.
c una est natiuitas de terra, alia de cœlo; una de carne, alia de spiritu; una de aeternitate, alia de mortalitate: una de masculo & foemina,alia deDeo &Ecclesia. Sed ipsa dua singulares sunt. Quomodo enim uterus non potest repeti, sic nec Baptismus iterari, Prosp. Sent. 331. Eja fratres, lacteum genialis fontis ad laticem conuolito,ut semper uobis aqua sufficiat, hoc ante omnia scientes quia hinc nec effundere licet nec rursus haurire. Zeno. Invit. ad font.
d August. de Baptij. cont. Don.l.1.c. 14.

God as a kind of inceſtuous birth, they that iterate Baptiſme, are driven under ſome pretence or other to make the former Baptiſme void. ' *Tertullian* the firſt that propoſed to the Church ; ' *Agrippinus* the firſt in the Church that accepted, and againſt the uſe of the Church ; *Novatian* the firſt that publikely began to practiſe re-baptization, did it therefore upon theſe two grounds ; a true perſwaſion that Baptiſme is neceſſary ; and a falſe, that the Baptiſme which others adminiſtred was not Baptiſme. *Novatians* his conceit was , that none can adminiſter true Baptiſme but the true Church of Jeſus Chriſt ; that he and his followers alone were the Church ; and for the reſt he accounted them wicked and prophane perſons , ſuch as by Baptiſme could cleanſe no man, unleſs they firſt did puriſie themſelves, and reform the faults wherewith he charged them. At which time ° St. *Cyprian* with the greateſt part of Affrican Biſhops, becauſe they likewiſe thought that none but only the true Church of God can baptize ; and were of nothing more certainly perſwaded, than that Hereticks are as rotten branches cut off from the life and body of the true Church, gathered hereby that the Church of God born may with good conſideration, and ought to reverſe that Baptiſme which is given by Hereticks. Theſe held and practiſed their own opinion, yet with great proteſtations often made that they neither loved awhit the leſs, nor thought in any reſpect the worſe of them that were of a contrary mind. In requital of which ingenuous moderation, the reſt that withſtood them , did it in peaceable ſort , with very good regard had of them as of men in errour, but not in Hereſie. The Biſhop of *Rome* againſt their novelties, upheld, as beſeemed him, the ancient and true Apoſtolick cuſtomes, till they which unadviſedly before had erred,

became in a manner all [h] reconciled friends unto Truth, and ſaw that Hereſie in the Miniſters of Baptiſm, could no way evacuate the force thereof ; [i] ſuch Hereſie alone excepted, as by reaſon of unſoundneſs in the higheſt Articles of Chriſtian Faith, preſumed to change, and by changing to maim the ſubſtance, the form of Baptiſm. In which reſpect the Church did neither ſimply diſanul, nor abſolutely ratiſie Baptiſm by Hereticks. For the Baptiſm which Novatianiſts gave, ſtood firm ; whereas they whom [k] Samoſotenians had baptized, were rebaptized. It was likewiſe ordered in the [l] Councel of *Arles*, that if any Arian did reconcile himſelf to the Church, they ſhould admit him without new Baptiſm, unleſs by examination they found him not baptized in the Name of the Trinity. *Dionyſius* Biſhop of *Alexandria* [m] maketh report how there lived under him a man of good reputation, and of very ancient continuance in that Church, who being preſent at the Rites of Baptiſm , and obſerving with better conſideration than ever before, what was there done, came, and with weeping ſubmiſſion craved of his Biſhop not to deny him Baptiſm, the due of all which profeſs Chriſt, ſeeing it had been ſo long ſithence his evil hap to be deceived by the fraud of Hereticks, and at their hands (which till now he never throughly and duely weighed) to take a Baptiſm in full fraught with blaſphemous impieties ; a Baptiſm in nothing like unto that which the true Church of Chriſt uſeth. The Biſhop greatly moved thereat, yet durſt not adventure to re-beptize, but did the beſt he could to put him in good comfort, uſing much perſwaſion with him not to trouble himſelf with things that were paſt and gone , nor after ſo long continuance in the fellowſhip of Gods people, to call now in queſtion his firſt entrance. The poor man that ſaw himſelf in this ſort anſwered, but not ſatiſfied, ſpent afterwards his life in continual perplexity, whereof the Biſhop remained fearful to give releaſe : perhaps too fearful , if the Baptiſm were ſuch as his own Delaration importeth. For that the ſubſtance whereof was rotten at the very firſt , is never by tract of time able to recover ſoundneſs. And where true Baptiſm was not before given , the caſe of re-baptization is clear. But by this it appeareth that Baptiſm is not void in regard of Hereſie ; and therefore much leſs through any *other moral* defect in the Miniſter thereof. Under which ſecond pretence, Donatiſts notwithſtanding , took upon them to make fruſtrate

the

e *Tert. de Bapt.*
f *Cypr. Epiſt. 72.*

g *Euſeb. lib.7. cap. 12, 3.*
Cyp. Epiſt. 70, 71,72,73,74, 75,76.

h *Illi ipſi Epiſcopi qui rebaptizandos Hæreticos cum Cypriano ſtatuerant, ad antiquam conſuetudinem revoluti, novum emiſere decretum,* Hieron. Cont. Lucifer. *Vide & * Auguſt. conc. Creſcon. lib. 3. cap. 2. 3. *& * Epiſt. 48. i *Dixiſti fieri non poſſe ut in falſo baptizmate inquinatus abluat, immundm emundet , ſupplantatus erigas perditus liberet, reus veniam tribuat, damnatus abſolvat. Bene hæc omnia poterunt ad ſolos Hæreticos pertinere, qui falſaverunt ſymbolum, dum alter dixerit duos Deos, cum Deus unus ſit , alter Patrem vult in perſona Filii cognoſci; alter carnem ſubducens Filio Dei , per quam Deo reconciliatus eſt mundus: & cæteri hujuſmodi , qui à Sacramentis Catholicis alieni noſcuntur.* Optat. lib. 1.

k *Synod. Nicen. cap. 19.*
l *Synod.* 1. *Arelat. cap. 8.*

m *Euſeb. Eccl. Hiſt. l. 7. c. 8.*

the Churches Baptism, and themselves to re-baptize their own fry. For whereas some forty years after the Martyrdom of blessed *Cyprian*, the Emperour *Dioclesian*
Circa an. 300.
began to ⁿ persecute the Church of Christ ; and for the speedier abolishment of their Religion, to burn up their sacred Books, there were in the Church it self *Traditors*, content to deliver up the Books of God by composition, to the end their own lives might be spared. Which men growing thereby odious to the rest, whose constancy was greater ; it fortuned that after, when one *Cecilian* was ordained Bishop in the Church of *Carthage*, whom others endeavoured in vain to defeat by excepting against him as a *Traditor*, they whose accusations could not prevail, desperately joined themselves in one, and made a Bishop of their own crue, accounting from that day forward their Faction the only true and sincere Church. The first Bishop on that part was *Majorinus*, whose Successor *Donatus*, being the first that wrote in defence of their Schism, the Birds that were hatched before by others, have their names from him. Arrians and Donatists began both about one time: Which Heresies according to the different strength of their own sinews, wrought as hope of success led them, the one with the choicest wits, the other with the multitude, so far, that after long and troublesome experience the perfectest view men could take of both was hardly able to induce any certain determinate resolution, whether Errour may do more by the curious subtilty of sharp Discourse, or else by the meer appearance of zeal and devout affection; the later of which two aids, gave Donatists, beyond all mens expectation, as great a sway as ever any Schism or Heresie had within that reach of the Christian world where it bred and grew : the rather perhaps, because the Church which neither greatly feared them, and besides had necessary cause to bend it self against others that aimed directly at a far higher mark, the Deity of Christ, was contented to let Donatists have their course by the space of three-score years and above, even from ten years before *Constantine*, till the time
b *Circa an.370.*
that ᵇ *Optatus* Bishop of *Milevis* published his books against *Parmenian*. During which term, and the space of that Schismes continuance afterwards, they had, besides many other Secular and worldly means to help them forward, these special advantages. First, the very occasion of their breach with the Church of God, a just hatred and dislike of *Traditors*, seemed plausible, they easily perswaded their hearers that such men cou dnot be holy as held communion and fellowship with them that betray Religion. Again, when to dazle the eyes of the simple, and to prove that it can be no Church which is not holy,they had in shew and found of words the glorious pretence of the Creed Apostolick, *I beleeve the holy Catholick Church* ; we need not think it any strange thing that with the multitude they gain credit. And avouching that such as are not of the true Church can administer no true Baptism, they had for this point whole Volumns of St. *Cyprians* own writing, together with the judgment of divers *African* Synods, whose sentence was the same with his. Whereupon, the Fathers were likewise in defence of their just cause very greatly prejudiced, both for that they could not inforce the duty of mens communion with a Church confest to be in many things blame-worthy, unless they should oftentimes seem to speak as half defenders of the faults themselves, or at the least not so vehement accusers thereof as their adversaries ; and to withstand iteration of Baptism, the other branch of the Donatists Heresie was impossible, without manifest and profest rejection of *Cyprian*, whom the world universally did in his life time admire as the greatest amongst Prelates, and now honour as the lowest in the Kingdom of Heaven. So true we find it by experience of all Ages in the Church of God, that the teachers errour is the peoples tryal, harder and heavier by so much to bear, as he is in worth and regard greater, that mis-perswadeth them. Although there was odds between *Cyprians* cause and theirs, he differing from others of sounder understanding in that point, but not dividing himself from the body of the Church by Schism,
c *Vincent. Liren. adverf. hæref. cap.* 11.
d *Vide C. Theo. lib.* 16.*tit.*6.*l. Adverfarios & l. Nullus circa an.* 405.
as did the Donatists. For which cause, ᶜ saith *Vincentius*, *Of one and the same opinion we judge (which may seem strange) the Authors Catholick, and the followers heretical ; we acquit the Masters, and condemn the Scholars ; they are Heirs of Heaven which have written those Books, the defendors whereof are troden down to the pit of Hell.* The invectives of Catholick Writers therefore against them are sharp ; the the words of ᵈ Imperial Edicts by *Honorius* and *Theodosius* made to bridle them ve-

ry

ry bitter, the punishments severe in revenge of their folly. Howbeit for fear (as we may conjecture) lest much should be derogated from the Baptism of the Church, and Baptism by Donatists be more esteemed of than was meet, if on the one side that which Hereticks had done ill should stand as good, on the other side that be reversed, which the Catholick Church had well and religiously done, divers better minded than advised men, thought it fittest to meet with this inconvenience, by re-baptizing Donatists as well as they re-baptized Catholicks. For stay whereof, the * same Emperours saw it meet to give their Law a double edge, whereby it might equally on both sides cut off not only Hereticks which re-baptized whom they could pervert; but also Catholick and Christian Priests which did the like unto such as before had taken Baptism at the hands of Hereticks, and were afterwards reconciled to the Church of God. Donatists were therefore in process of time, though with much ado, wearied, and at the length worn out by the constancy of that Truth which teacheth, that evil Ministers of good things are as Torches, a light to others, a waste to none but themselves only, and that the foulness of their hands can neither any whit impair the vertue, nor stain the glory of the Mysteries of Christ. Now that which was done amiss by vertuous and good men, as *Cyprian* carried aside with hatred against Heresie, and was secondly followed by Donatists, whom Envy and Rancor, covered with shew of Godliness, made obstinate to cancel whatsoever the Church did in the Sacrament of Baptism, hath of later days, in another respect, far different from both the former, been brought freshly again into practice. For the Anabaptist re-baptized, because, in his estimation the Baptism of the Church is frustrate, for that we give it unto Infants which have not Faith, whereas, according unto Christs Institution, as they conceive it, true Baptism should always presuppose actual belief in Receivers, and is otherwise no Baptism. Of these three Errours, there is not any but hath been able at the least to alledge in defence of it self many fair probabilities.

Notwithstanding, sith the Church of God hath hitherto always constantly maintained, that to re-baptize them which are known to have received true Baptism is unlawful; that if, Baptism seriously be administred in the same Element, and with the same form of words which Christs Institution teacheth, there is no other defect in the World that can make it frustrate, or deprive it of the nature of a true Sacrament; And lastly, that Baptism is only then to be re-administred, when the first delivery thereof is void, in regard of the fore-alledged imperfections and no other, shall we now in the case of Baptism, which having both for matter and form the substance of Christs Institution, is by a fourth sort of men voided, for the only defect of Ecclesiastical Authority in the Minister, think it enough that they blow away the force thereof with the bare strength of their very breath, by saying, *We take such Baptism to be no more the Sacrament of Baptism, than any other ordinary bathing to be a Sacrament?* [a] It behoveth generally all sorts of men to keep themselves within the limits of their own vocation. And seeing God, from whom mens several degrees and preeminences do proceed, hath appointed them in his Church, at whose hands his pleasure is that we should receive both Baptism, and all other publick medicinable helps of Soul, perhaps thereby the more to settle our hearts in the love of our ghostly Superiors, they have small cause to hope that with him their voluntary Services will be accepted, who thrust themselves into Functions, either above their capacity or besides their place, and over-boldly intermeddle with Duties, whereof no charge was ever given them. They that in any thing exceed the compass of their own order, do as much as in them lyeth to dissolve that Order which is the harmony of Gods Church. Suppose therefore that in these and the like considerations the Law did utterly prohibit Baptism to be administred by any other than persons thereunto solemnly consecrated, what necessity soever happen. Are not [b] many things firm being done, although in part done otherwise than Positive rigour and strictness did require? Nature as much as is possible inclineth unto validities and preservations. Dissolutions and Nullities of things done are not only not favoured, but hated, when either urged without cause, or extended beyond their reach: If therefore at any time it come to pass, that in teaching publickly or privately, in delivering this blessed Sacrament of Regeneration, some unsanctified

hand,

Marginal notes:
* *si quis C. Nt. sanct. Baptism. circa an. 413.*
a *Numb. 16. 10. Levit. 10. 1. 1 Sam. 13. 11. 2 Sam. 6. 6. 2 Chron. 26. 16. Heb. 5. 4.*
b *Seq. 306. Lugdunensis ex literis Decret. de matrim. contract. Damas. Burchar. Reg. 109. Prohibita fieri si fiant non tenent. In prohibitionibus autem circa res favourabiles contrarium obtinet.*

K k

hand, contrary to Chrifts fuppofed Ordinance, do intrude it felf to execute that, whereupon the Laws of God and his Church have deputed others, which of thefe two opinions feemeth more agreeable with Equity, ours that difallow what is done amifs, yet make not the force of the Word and Sacraments, much lefs their nature and very fubftance to depend on the Minifters authority and calling, or elfe theirs which defeat, difanull, and annihilate both, in refpect of that one only perfonal defect, there being not any Law of God which faith, that if the Minifter be incompetent, his Word fhall be no Word, his Baptifm no Baptifm? He which teacheth and is not fent, lofeth the reward, but yet retaineth the name of a Teacher; his ufurped actions have in him the fame nature which they have in others, although they yield him not the fame comfort. And if thefe two cafes be peers, the cafe of Doctrine and the cafe of Baptifm both alike, fith no defect in their vocation that teach the Truth, is able to take away the benefit thereof from him which heareth, wherefore fhould the want of a lawful calling in them that baptize, make Baptifm to be vain? [b] They grant that the matter and the form in Sacraments are the only parts of fubftance, and that if thefe two be retained, albeit other things befides be ufed which are inconvenient, the Sacrament notwithftanding is adminiftred but not fincerely. Why perfift they not in this opinion? when by thefe fair fpeeches they have put us in hope of agreement, wherefore fip they up their words again, interlacing fuch frivolous Interpretations and Gloffes as difgrace their Sentence? What fhould move them, having named the *matter* and the *form* of the Sacrament, to give us prefently warning, [c] that they mean by the *form* of the Sacrament *the inftitution*, which expofition darkeneth whatfoever was before plain? For whereas in common underftanding, that *form*, which added to the Element doth make a Sacrament, and is of the outward fubftance thereof, containeth onely the words of ufual application, they fet it down (left common Dictionaries fhould deceive us) that *the form* doth fignifie in their Language *the inftitution*, which inftitution in truth comprehendeth both form and matter. Such are their fumbling fhifts to inclofe the Minifters vocation within the compafs of fome effential part of the Sacrament. A thing that can never ftand with found and fincere conftruction. For what if the [d] Minifter be *no circumftance*, but *a fubordinate efficient caufe in the* work of Baptifm? What if the Minifters vocation be a matter [e] *of perpetual neceffity, and not a Ceremony variable as times and occafions require? What if his calling be a principal part of the Inftitution of Chrift?* Doth it therefore follow that the Minifters authority is [f] *of the fubftance of the Sacrament*, and as incident into the nature thereof as the matter and the form it felf, yea, more incident? For whereas in cafe of neceffity the greateft amongft them profeffeth the change of the Element of Water lawful, and others which like nor fo well this opinion, could be better content that voluntarily the *words* of Chrifts Inftitution were altered, and men baptized in *the Name of Chrift*, without either mention made of the Father or the Holy Ghoft, neverthelefs, in denying that Baptifm adminiftred by private perfons ought to be reckoned of as a Sacrament, they both agree. It may therefore pleafe them both to confider, that Baptifm is an action in part Moral, in part Ecclefiaftical, and in part Myftical: Moral, as being a duty which men perform towards God; Ecclefiaftical, in that it belongeth unto Gods Church as a publike duty; finally, Myftical; if we refpect what God doth thereby intend to work. The greateft Moral perfection of Baptifm confifteth in mens devout obedience to the Law of God, which Law requireth both the outward act or thing done, and alfo that Religious affection which God doth fo much regard, that without it whatfoever we do is hateful in his fight, who therefore is faid to refpect *Adverbs* more than *Verbs*, becaufe the end of his Law in appointing what we fhall do is our own perfection, which perfection confifteth chiefly in the virtuous difpofition of the mind, and approveth it

Bez. Epift. 2. *Defit aqua, & tamen Baptifmus alicujus differri cum ædificatione non poffit nec debeat, ego certè quovis alio liquore non minus ritè quàm aqua baptizarim.* [T] C.l.3.p.138. Shew me why the breach of the Inftitution in the form fhould make the Sacrament unavaileable, and not the breach of this part (which concerneth the Minifter) T.C. *ibid.* Howfoever fome learned and godly give fome liberty in the change of the Elements of the holy Sacrament, yet I do not fee how that can ftand. Idem p.137. I would rather judge him baptized into the Name of Chrift, without adding the Father and the Holy Ghoft, when the Element of water is added, than when the other words being duly kept, fome other liquor is ufed.

self to him not by *doing*, but by doing *well*. Wherein appeareth also the difference between Humane and Divine Laws, the one of which two are content with *opus operatum*, the other require *opus operantis*, the one do but claim the deed, the other especially the mind. So that according to Laws which principally respect the heart of men, works of Religion being not religiously performed cannot morally be perfect. Baptism as an Ecclesiastical work, is for the manner of performance ordered by divers Ecclesiastical Laws, providing that as the Sacrament it self is a gift of no mean worth, so the Ministery thereof might in all circumstances appear to be a Function of no small regard. All that belongeth to the Mystical perfection of Baptism outwardly, is the Element, the Word, and the serious application of both unto him which receiveth both; whereunto if we adde that secret reference which this action hath to life and remission of sins, by virtue of Christs own compact solemnly made with his Church, to accomplish fully the Sacrament of Baptism, there is not any thing more required.

Now put the question whether Baptism administred to Infants without any Spiritual calling, be unto them both a true Sacrament and an effectual instrument of grace, or else an act of no more account than the ordinary Washings are. The sum of all that can be said to defeat such Baptism, is, that those things which have no being, can work nothing; and that Baptism without the power of Ordination, is as a judgement without sufficient Jurisdiction, void, frustrate, and of no effect. But to this we answer, that the fruit of Baptism dependeth only upon the Covenant which God hath made; that God by Covenant requireth in the elder sort, Faith and Baptism; in Children the Sacrament of Baptism alone, whereunto he hath also given them right by special priviledge of birth, within the bosom of the holy Church; that Infants therefore, which have received Baptism compleat, as touching the Mystical perfection thereof, are by vertue of his own Covenant and Promise cleansed from all sin, for as much as all other Laws concerning that which in Baptism is either Moral or Ecclesiastical, do bind the Church which giveth Baptism, and not the Infant which receiveth it of the Church. So that if any thing be therein amiss, the harm which groweth by violation of holy Ordinances, must altogether rest where the bonds of such Ordinances hold. For that in actions of this Nature it fareth not as in Jurisdictions, may somewhat appear by the very opinion which men have of them. The nullity of that which a Judge doth by way of authority without authority, is known to all men, and agreed upon with full consent of the whole World, every man receiveth it as a general Edict of Nature; whereas the nullity of Baptism in regard of the like defect, is only a few mens new ungrounded and as yet unapproved imagination. Which difference of generality in mens perswasions on the one side, and their paucity whose conceit leadeth them the other way, hath risen from a difference easie to observe in the things themselves. The exercise of unauthorized Jurisdiction is a grievance unto them that are under it, whereas they that without authority presume to baptize, offer nothing but that which to all men is good and acceptable. Sacraments are food, and the Ministers thereof, as Parents or as Nurses, at whose hands when there is necessity, but no possibility of receiving it, if that which they are not present to do in right of their Office, be of pity and compassion done by others, shall this be thought to turn Celestial Bread into gravel, or the medicine of Souls into poyson? Jurisdiction is a yoke which Law hath imposed on the necks of men in such sort, that they must endure it for the good of others, how contrary soever it be to their own particular appetites and inclinations: Jurisdiction bridleth men against their wills, that which a Judge doth prevail by vertue of his very power; and therefore not without great reason, except the Law hath given him authority, whatsoever he doth, vanisheth. Baptism on the other side being a favour which it pleaseth God to bestow, a benefit of soul to us that receive it, and a grace which they that deliver are but as meer Vessels, either appointed by others or offered of their own accord to this Service, of which two if they be the one, it is but their own honour, their own offence to be the other; can it possibly stand with equity and right, that the faultiness of their presumption in giving Baptism should be able to prejudice us, who by taking Baptism have no way offended? I know there are many sentences found in the Books and Writings of the ancient Fathers, to prove both Ecclesiastical and also

Moral

a Factum alterius alii nocere non debet Ulp.l. de pupillo. Si plurimum. Item Alphen. l. Pater-familias. De Haere.instit. Maleficia tenent Authores suos non alios. L.Sancimus 22 C. de poen.

Moral defects in the Minister of Baptism, a bar to the heavenly benefit thereof. Which sentences we always so understand, as [a] *Augustin* understood in a case of like nature the words of *Cyprian*. When Infants baptized were after their Parents revolt carried by them in arms to the stewes of Idols, those wretched creatures, as Saint *Cyprian* thought, were not only their own ruine, but their childrens also ; *Their children*, whom this their Apostasie profaned, *did lose what Christian Baptism had given them being newly born*. They lost (saith S. *Augustin*) the grace of Baptism, *if we consider to what their Parents impiety did tend*, although the mercy of God preserved them, and will also in that dreadful day of account give them favourable audience pleading in their own behalf ; *The harm of other mens persidiousnefs it lay not in us to avoid*. After the same manner, whatsoever we read written, if it found to the prejudice of Baptism through any either Moral or Ecclesiastical defect therein, we construe it, as Equity and Reason teacheth, with restraint to the offender only, which doth, as far as concerneth himself, and them which wittingly concur with him, make the Sacrament of God fruitless. S. *Augustines doubtfulnefs*, [b] whether Baptism by a Lay-man may stand, or ought to be re-administred, should not be mentioned by them which presume to define peremptorily of that, wherein he was content to profess himself unresolved. Albeit in very truth his opinion is plain enough, but the manner of delivering his judgement being modest, they make of a vertue an imbecility , and impute his calmness of speech to an irresolution of mind. His Disputation in that place is against *Parmenian*, which held, that a Bishop or a Priest if they fall into any Heresie, do thereby lose the Power which they had before to baptize, and that therefore Baptism by Hereticks is meerly void. For answer whereof he first denyeth, that Heresie can more deprive men of power to baptize others, than it is of force to take from them their own Baptism ; and in the second place he farther addeth, that if Hereticks did lose the power which before was given them by Ordination, and did therefore unlawfully usurp as oft as they took upon them to give the Sacrament of Baptism, it followeth not that Baptism, by them administred without authority, is no Baptism. For then what should we think of Baptism by Lay-men, to whom authority was never given ? I doubt (saith S. *Augustine*) whether any man which carrieth a vertuous and godly mind will affirm, that the Baptism which Lay-men do in case of necessity administer should be iterated. For to do it *unnecessarily, is to execute another mans office ; necessity urging, to do it is then either no fault at all* (much less so grievous a crime that it should deserve to be termed by the name of [c] *facriledge*) *or if any, a very pardonable fault. But suppose it even of very purpose usurped and given unto any man by every man that listeth, yet that which is given cannot possibly be denyed to have been given, how truly foever we may say it hath not been given lawfully. Unlawful usurpation a penitent affection must redress. If not, the thing that was given shall remain to the hurt and detriment of him which unlawfully either administred or received the same, yet so that in this respect it ought not to be reputed, as if it had not at all been given*. Whereby we may plainly perceive, that Saint *Augustine* was not himself uncertain what to think, but doubtful, whether any well-minded man in the whole World, could think otherwise then he did. Their [d] Argument taken from a stoln seal, may return to the place out of which they had it, for it helpeth their cause nothing. That which men give or grant to others, must appear to have proceeded of their own accord. This being manifest, their Gifts and Grants are thereby made effectual, both to bar themselves from revocation, and to assecure the right they have given. Wherein, for further prevention of mischiefs, that otherwise might grow by the malice, treachery, and fraud of men, it is both equal and meet that the strength of mens deeds, and the instruments which declare the same, should strictly depend upon divers solemnities, whereof there cannot be the like reason in things that pass between God and us, because sith we need not doubt, lest the treasures of his Heavenly grace should without his consent be past by forged conveyances, nor lest he should deny at any time his own acts, and seek to revoke what hath been consented unto before : As there is no such fear of danger through deceit and falshood in this case, so neither hath the circumstance of mens persons that weight in Baptism, Which for good and just considerations in the custody of seals of Office it ought to have.

a *Aug. Epi.* 23.

b *T.C.l.* 1 *p.* 136 *Augustin* standeth in doubt, whether Baptism by a Lay-man be available or no. *Cont. lit. Parm. l.* 2. *c.* 13. where by all likelihood he was out of doubt, that that which was ministred by a Woman, whose unaptness herein is double to that of a Lay-man, was of no effect.

c *T.C.l.* 1. *p.* 116 The sacriledge of private persons, Women especially, in administring the holy Sacrament of Baptism.

d *T.C.l.* 3 *p.* 139 As by the seal which the Prince hath set apart to seale his Grants with, when it is stolln and set to by him that hath no authorkie, there groweth no assurance to the party that hath it : So if it were possible to be the seale of God which a woman should set to, yet for that she hath stolln it and put it to, not only without, but contrary to the Commandment of God, I see not how any can take any assurance by reason thereof.

haye.. The grace of Baptifm commeth by donation from God alone. That God hath committed the Miniftery of Baptifm unto fpecial men; it is for orders fake in his Church, and not to the end that their authority might give being, or adde force to the Sacrament it felf. That Infants have right to the Sacrament of Baptifm, we all acknowledge. Charge them we cannot as guilful and wrongful poffeffors of that, whereunto they have right by the manifeft will of the Donor, and are not parties unto any defect or diforder in the manner of receiving the fame. And if any fuch diforder be, we have fufficiently before declared, that *delictum cum capite femper ambulat*, mens own faults are their own harms. Wherefore to countervail this and the like mifchofen refemblances with that, which more truly and plainly agreeth, the Ordinance of God concerning their vocation that minifter Baptifm, wherein the myftery of our regeneration is wrought, hath thereunto the fame Analogy which laws of wedlock have to our firft nativity and birth. So that if Nature do effect procreation, notwithftanding the wicked violation and breach even of Natures law, made that the entrance of all mankind into this prefent World might be without blemifh, may we not juftly prefume that grace doth accomplifh the other, although there be faultinefs in them that transgrefs the Order which our Lord Jefus Chrift hath eftablifhed in his Church? Some light may be borrowed from Circumcifion, for explication, what is true in this queftion of Baptifm.

Seeing then that even they, which [a] condemn *Zipporah* the wife of *Mofes*, for taking upon her to circumcife her fon, a thing neceffary at that time for her to do, and as I think very hard to reprove in her, confidering how *Mofes*, becaufe himfelf had not done it fooner, was therefore ftricken by the hand of God, neither could in that extremity perform the office; whereupon, for the ftay of Gods indignation, there was no choice, but the action muft needs fall into her hands; whofe fact therin whether we interpret, as fome have done, that being a Midianite, and as yet not fo throughly acquainted with the Jewifh Rites, it much difcontented her, to fee her felf through her hufbands over-fight, in a matter of his own Religion brought unto thofe perplexities & ftraits, that either fhe muft now indure him perifhing before his eyes, or elfe wound the flefh of her own Child, which fhe could not do but with fome indignation fhewed, in that fhe fumingly both threw down the fore-skin at his feet, and upbraided him with the cruelty of his Religion: or if we better like to follow their more judicious Expofition, which are not inclinable to think that *Mofes* was match't like *Socrates*, nor that Circumcifion could now in *Eleazar* be ftrange unto her, having had *Gerfom* her elder fon before circumcifed, nor that any occafion of choler could rife from a fpectacle of fuch mifery, as doth [b] naturally move compaffion and not wrath, nor that *Zipporah* was fo impious, as in the vifible prefence of Gods deferved anger, to ftorm at the Ordinance and Law of God, nor that the words of the hiftory it felf can inforce any fuch affection, but do only declare how after the act performed, fhe *touched* the feet of *Mofes*, faying, [c] *Sponfus tu mihi es fanguinnus; Thou art unto me an hufband of blood*, which might be very well, the one done, and the other fpoken, even out of the flowing abundance of commiferation and love, to fignifie with hands laid under his feet, that her tender affection towards him, had caufed her thus to forget woman-hood, to lay all motherly affection afide; and to redeem her hufband out of the hands of Death with effufion of blood; the fequel thereof, take it which way you will, is a plain argument that God was fatisfied with that fhe did, as may

[a] *Exod.* 4. 14. *T.C.l. 1. p. 144.* I fay that the unlawfulnefs of that fact doth appear fufficiently, in that fhe did it before her hufband *Mofes* which was a Prophet of the Lord, to whom that office of circumcifion did appertain. Befides, that fhe did cut off the fore-skin of the Infant, not of mind to obey the Commandment of God, or for the falvation of the Child, but in a choler only, to the end that her hufband might be eafed and have releafe: which mind appeareth in her both by her words, and by cafting away in anger the fore-skin which fhe had cut off. And if it be faid, that the event declared that the act pleafed God, becaufe that *Mofes* forthwith waxed better, and was recovered of his ficknefs, I have fhewed before that if we meafure things by the event, we fhall oftentimes juftifie the wicked, and take the righteoufnefs of the righteous from them.

[b] *Mala paffis non irafcimur, fed compatimur,* Boet. de Confol.

[c] Where the ufual tranflation hath *Exod.* 4. 25. She cut away the fore-skin of her fon, and caft it at his feet, and faid, Thou art indeed a bloody hufband unto me. So he departed from him. Then fhe faid, O bloody hufband, becaufe of the Circumcifion: the words as they lie in the original, are rather thus to be interpreted: And fhe cut off the fore-skin of her fon. Which being done, fhe touched his feet (the feet of *Mofes*) and faid, Thou art to me an hufband of blood (in the plural number, thereby fignifying effufion of blood.) And the Lord withdrew from him at the very time, when fhe faid, A hufband of blood in regard of Circumcifion.

appear

appear by his own testimony, declaring how there followed in the person of *Moses* present release of his grievous punishment upon her speedy discharge of that duty, which by him neglected, had offended God, even as after execution of Justice by the hands of *Phineas*, the plague was immediately taken away, which former impunity of sin had caused ; in which so manifest and plain cases, not to make that a reason of the event, which God himself hath set down as a reason, were falsly to accuse whom he doth justifie, and without any cause to traduce what we should allow : yet seeing they which will have it a breach of the Law of God, for her to circumcise in that necessity, are not able to deny, but Circumcision being in that very manner performed, was to the innocent childe which received it true Circumcision ; why should that defect whereby Circumcision was so little weakned be to Baptism a deadly wound ? These premises therefore remaining, as hitherto they have been laid, because the Commandment of our Saviour Christ, which committeth jointly to publick Ministers both Doctrine and Baptism, doth no more by linking them together import, that the nature of the Sacrament dependeth on the Ministers authority and power to preach the Word, than the force and virtue of the Word doth on licence to give the Sacrament ; and considering that the work of external ministery in Baptism is only a preeminence of honour, which they that take to themselves and are not thereunto called as *Aaron* was, do but themselves in their own persons, by means of such usurpation, incur the just blame of disobedience to the Law of God, farther also in as much as it standeth with no reason ; that errours grounded on a wrong interpretation of other mens deeds, should make frustrate whatsoever is misconceived, and that Baptism by Women should cease to be Baptism, as oft as any man will thereby gather that children which dye unbaptized are damned ; which opinion if the act of Baptism administred in such manner did inforce, it might be sufficient cause of disliking the same, but none of defeating or making it altogether void; last of all, whereas general and full consent of the godly-learned in all ages, doth make for validity of Baptism, yea, albeit administred in private, and even by Women, which kinde of Baptisme, in case of necessity, divers reformed Churches do both allow and defend, some others which do not defend, tolerate ; few, in comparison, and they without any just cause, do utterly disanul and annihilate : surely, however part, licence soever through defect on either side, the Sacrament may be without fruit, as well in some cases to him which receiveth, as to him which giveth it ; yet no disability of either part can so far make it frustrate and without effect, as to deprive it of the very nature of true Baptism, having all things else which the Ordinance of Christ requireth. Whereupon we may consequently infer, that the administration of this Sacrament by private persons, be it lawful or unlawful, appeareth not as yet to be meerly void: which none can take unto him, but he which is called unto it, as was *Aaron* : and further, forasmuch as the baptizing by private persons, and by women especially, confirmeth the dangerous errour of the condemnation of young children, which die without Baptism ; last of all, seeing we have the consent of the godly learned of all times against the Baptism by women, and of the Reformed Churches now, against the Baptism by private men, we conclude that the administration of this Sacrament by private persons, and especially by women, is meerly both unlawful and void.

a Psal. 106.30.

b T.C.l.b.3.p. 142. Seeing they only are bidden in the Scripture to administer the Sacraments, which they are bidden to preach the Word, and that the publick Ministers have only this charge of the word ; and seeing that the administration of both these are linked together, that the denyal of licence to do one, is a denyal to do the other; as of the contrary part, licence to one, is licence to the other ; considering also, that to minister the Sacraments, is an honour in the Church,

63 All that are of the race of Christ, the Scripture nameth them *Children of the promise*, which God hath made. The promise of eternal Life is the seed of the Church of God. And because there is no attainment of life, but through the only begotten Son of God, nor by him otherwise than being such as the Creed Apostolick describeth, it followeth that the Articles thereof are principles, necessary for all men to subscribe unto, whom by Baptism the Church receiveth into Christs School. All points of Christian doctrine are either demonstrable Conclusions, or demonstrative Principles. Conclusions have strong and invincible proofs, as well in the School of Jesus Christ, as elsewhere. And Principles be grounds, which require no proof in any kind of Science, because it sufficeth, if either their certainty be evident in it self, or evident by the light of some higher knowledge, and in it self such as no mans knowledge is ever able to overthrow. Now the principles whereupon we build our souls, have their evidence where they had their original ; and as received from thence we adore them, we hold them in reverend admiration, we neither argue nor dispute above them, we give unto them that assent which the Oracles of God require.

Interrogatories in Baptism touching Faith, and the purpose of a Christian life.

quire. We are not therefore ashamed of the Gospel of our Lord Jesus Christ, because miscreants in scorn have upbraided us, that the highest point of our wisdom is a *Belief*. That which is true, and neither can be discerned by sense, nor concluded by meer natural principles, must have principles of revealed Truth whereupon to build it self, and an habit of Faith in us wherewith principles of that kind are apprehended. [b] The mysteries of our Religion are above the reach of our understanding, above discourse of mans reason, above all that any creature can comprehend. Therefore the first thing required of him, which standeth for admission into Christs Family, is belief. Which belief consisteth not so much in knowledge, as in acknowledgement of all things that Heavenly wisdom revealeth; the affection of Faith is above her reach, her love to God-ward above the comprehension which she hath of God. And because only for Believers all things may be done, he which is goodness it self, loveth them above all. Deserve we then the love of God, because we believe in the Son of God? What more opposite than Faith and Pride? When God had created all things, he looked upon them, and loved them, because they were all as himself had made them. So the true reason wherefore Christ doth love Believers, is, because their belief is [c] the gift of God, a gift than which flesh and blood in this world cannot possibly receive a greater. And as love to them of whom we receive good things, is duty, because they satisfie out desires in that which else we should want, so to love them on whom we bestow, is nature, because in them we behold the effects of our own virtue. Seeing therefore no Religion enjoyeth Sacraments the signes of Gods love, unless it have also that Faith whereupon the Sacraments are built, could there be any thing more convenient than that our first admittance to the actual receit of his grace in the Sacrament of Baptism, should be [d] consecrated with profession of belief, which is to the Kingdom of God as a key, the want whereof excludeth Infidels both from that and from all other saving grace? We find by experience, that although Faith be an intellectual habit of the mind, and have her seat in the understanding, yet an evil moral disposition obstinately wedded to the love of darkness, dampeth the very light of heavenly illumination, and permitteth not the mind to see what doth shine before it. Men are lovers of pleasure more then lovers of God. Their assent to his saving Truth is many times with-held from it, not that the Truth is too weak to perswade, but because the stream of corrupt affection carrieth them a clean contrary way. That the mind therefore may abide in the light of Faith, there must abide in the will as constant a resolution to have no fellowship at all with the vanities and works of darkness. Two Covenants there are which Christian men (saith [e] *Isidor*) do make in Baptism, the one concerning relinquishment of Satan, the other touching obedience to the Faith of Christ. In like sort [f] Saint *Ambrose*, *He which is baptized*, forsaketh the intellectual *Pharaoh*, the Prince of this world, saying, *Abrenuncio; Thee, O Satan, and thy Angels, thy works and thy mandates, I forsake utterly.* [g] *Tertullian* having speech of wicked spirits: *These* (saith he) *are the Angels which we in Baptism renounce.* The declaration of [h] *Justin* the *Martyr* concerning Baptism, sheweth how such as the Church in those days did baptize, made profession of Christian belief, and undertook to live accordingly. Neither do I think it a matter easie for any man to prove that ever Baptism did use to be administred without Interrogatories of these two kinds. Whereunto [i] S. *Peter* (as it may be thought) alluding, hath said, that the Baptism *which saveth us*, is not (as Legal Purifications were) a cleansing of the flesh from outward impurity, but ἐπερώτημα, *an interrogative tryal of a good conscience toward God.*

χεὸς τε χαιῖεν υκεύονϊες πάεος τῦ θεῦ ΣΩ πεϛμαϛλνμίενων ἀϛεον διδάσκοιϊαι, ἔπειϊα ἀγονῆαι ὑφ' ἡμῶν ἔνϑα ὕδωρ ὅϛι κỷ τρόπον ἀναγεννήσιως ὁν κỷ ἡμεῖς αὐϊοι ἀνεγεννήθημεν ἀναγεννῶϊαι. Juftin. Apol. 1 1 Pet. 3.21.

Margin notes:
- a *Apoftata ma-ledictum.*
- ὐδὲν ὑπὲρ τὸ πίϛευσον τῆς ὑμῖλέρας ὑπ' σοφίας. Nazia. Ora.1.cont.Jul.
- b ὑπὲρ νοῦν, ὑπὲρ λόγον, ὑπὲρ κατάλη-ψιν κϊίσηῆς φύσεως τὰ πάνϊα· eg. Juft.Mart. Expof.Fid.
- c *Mat.*16.17. *John* 1.12.
- d *Spiritus Sanctus habitator ejus Templi non efficitur, quod Antiftitem non habet veram fidem.* Hieron. adver. Lucifer. cap.4.
- e *Ifid. de Offic. Ecclef.li.2.c.24.*
- f *Ambrof. Hexam.l.1.c.4.*
- g *Tertul. de Spectac.*
- h Ὅσοι ἂν πεισϑῶσι κỷ πιϛεύωσιν ἀληϑῆ ταῦτα τὰ ἀφ' ἡμῶν διδασκόμενα κỷ λε-γόμενα εἶναι κỷ βιοῦν ὕτως δυνατὸς ἐπαϊγνῶϊαι, ἐυ-χεϑαι τε κỷ κτλ.

64. Now the fault which they find with us concerning Interrogatories, is our moving of these questions unto *Infants* which cannot answer them, and the answering

Margin note: Interrogatories proposed unto Infants in baptism.

tism, and answered as in their names by god-fathers. They prophane holy baptism in toying foolishly, for that they ask questions of an Infant which cannot answer, and speak unto them, as was wont to be spoken unto men, and unto such as being converted answered for themselves, and were baptized. Which is but a mockery of God, and therefore against the holy Scripture; *Gal.*6.7 Admon. to the Parlia. The same defended in *T.C.lib.1.pag.*168.

swering

swering of them by others as in their names. The Anabaptist hath many pretences to scorn at the Baptism of children : First, because the Scriptures, he saith, do no where give commandment to baptize Infants : Secondly, for that as there is no commandment, so neither any manifest example shewing it to have been done either by Christ or his Apostles : Thirdly, in as much as the Word preached and the Sacraments must go together, they which are not capable of the one, are not fit receivers of the other : Last of all, sith the Order of Baptism continued from the first beginning, hath in it those things which are unfit to be applied unto sucking children, it followeth in their conceit, that the Baptism of such is no Baptism, but plain mockery. They with whom we contend are no enemies to the Baptism of Infants ; it is not their desire that the Church should hazard so many Souls, by letting them run on till they come to ripeness of understanding, that so they may be converted and then baptized, as Infidels heretofore have been ; they bear not towards God so unthankful minds, as not to acknowledge it even amongst the greatest of his endless mercies, that by making us his own possession so soon, many advantages which Satan otherwise might take are prevented, and (which should be esteemed a part of no small happiness) the first thing whereof we have occasion to take notice is, how much hath been done already to our great good, though altogether without our knowledge ; the Baptism of Infants they esteem as an Ordinance which Christ hath instituted, even in special love and favour to his own people ; they deny not the practice thereof accordingly to have been kept, as derived from the hands, and continued from the days of the Apostles themselves unto this present. Only it pleaseth them not, that to Infants there should be Interrogatories proposed in Baptism. This they condemn as foolish, toyish, and prophane mockery. But are they able to shew that ever the Church of Christ had any publick Form of Baptism without Interrogatories ; or that the Church did ever use at the solemn Baptism of Infants, to omit those questions as needless in this case ?

[a] *Boniface* a Bishop in S. *Augustines* time, knowing that the Church did universally use this custom of baptizing Infants with Interrogatories, was desirous to learn from S. *Augustine* the true cause and reason thereof : *If* (saith he) *I should set before thee a young Infant, and should ask of thee whether that Infant when he cometh unto riper age, will be honest and just or no ; thou wouldest answer (I know) that to tell in these things what shall come to pass, is not in the power of a mortal man. If I should ask, what good or evil such an Infant thinketh, thine answer hereunto must needs be again with the like uncertainty. If thou neither canst promise for the time to come, nor for the present pronounce any thing in this case, how is it that when such are brought unto Baptism, their Parents there undertake what the child shall afterwards do ; yea they are not doubtful to say it doth that which is impossible to be done by Infants ? At the least there is no man precisely able to affirm it done. Vouchsafe me hereunto some short answer, such as not only may press me with the bare authority of custom, but also instruct me in the cause thereof.* Touching which difficulty, whether it may truly be said for Infants at the time of their Baptism that they do believe, the effect of Saint *Augustines* answer is yea, but with this distinction, [b] a present *actual habit of Faith there is not* in them, there is delivered unto them that Sacrament, a part of the due celebration whereof consisteth in answering to the Articles of Faith, *because* the habit of Faith, which afterwards doth come with years, is but *a farther* building up of the same edifice, *the first foundation whereof was laid by the Sacrament of Baptism.* For that which there we professed without any understanding, when we afterwards come to acknowledge, do we any thing else but only bring unto ripeness the very seed that was sown before ? We are *then believers, because then we begin to be* that which process of time doth make perfect. And till we come to actual belief, the very Sacrament of Faith is a shield as strong as after this the Faith of the Sacrament against all contrary Infernal Powers. Which whosoever doth think impossible, is undoubtedly farther off from Christian Belief, though he be baptized, then are these Innocents, which at their Baptism albeit they have no conceit or cogitation of Faith, are notwithstanding pure and free from all opposite cogitations, whereas the other is not free. If therefore without any fear or scruple we may account them and term them believers only for their outward professions sake,

which

which inwardly are farther from Faith then Infants, why not Infants much more at the time of their solemn initiation by Baptism the Sacrament of Faith, whereunto they not only conceive nothing opposite, but have also that ᶜ grace given them which is the first and most effectual cause out of which our belief groweth? In sum, the whole Church is a multitude of Believers, all honoured with that title, even Hypocrites for their professions sake as well as Saints, because of their inward sincere perswasion, and *Infants as being in the first degree of their ghostly motion toward the actual habit of Faith* ; the first sort are faithful in the eye of the World, the second faithful in the sight of God ; the last in the ready direct way to become both, if all things after be sutable to these their present beginnings. *This* (saith Saint *Augustine*) *would not haply content such persons as are uncapable or unquiet, but to them which having knowledge are not troublesome, it may suffice. Wherein I have not for ease of my self objected against you that custome onely, than which nothing is more firm, but of a custome most profitable I have done that little which I could to yield you a reasonable cause.* Were Saint *Augustine* now living, there are which would tell him for his better instruction, that to say ᵈ of a child *it is elect*, and to say it doth believe, are all one ; for which cause sith no man is able precisely to affirm the one of any Infant in particular, it followeth that *precisely* and *absolutely* we ought not to say the other. Which *precise* and *absolute* terms are needless in this case. We speak of Infants *as the rule of piety* alloweth both to speak and think. They that can take to themselves in ordinary talk a charitable kind of liberty to name men of their own sort *Gods dear children* (notwithstanding the large reign of Hypocrisie) should not methinks be so strict and rigorous against the Church for presuming as it doth of a Christian Innocent. For when we know how Christ in general hath said, that *of such* is the Kingdom of Heaven, which Kingdom is the Inheritance of Gods Elect, and do withal behold how his providence hath called them unto the first beginnings of eternal life, and presented them at the well-spring of new birth, wherein original sin is purged, besides which sin there is no hinderance of their Salvation known to us, as themselves will grant, hard it were that having so many fair inducements whereupon to ground, we should not be thought to utter at the least a truth as probable and allowable in terming any such particular Infant an elect Babe, as in presuming ᵉ the like of others, whose safety nevertheless we are not *absolutely* able to warrant. If any troubled with these scruples be only for Instructions sake desirous to know yet some farther reason why Interrogatories should be ministred to Infants in Baptism, and be answered unto by others as in their names, they may consider that Baptism implyeth a Covenant or League between God and Man, wherein as God doth bestow presently remission of sins and the Holy Ghost, binding also himself to adde in process of time what grace soever shall be farther necessary for the attainment of everlasting life ; so every baptized Soul receiving the same grace at the hands of God, tieth likewise it self for ever to the observation of his Law no less than the Jews ᶠ by Circumcision bound themselves to the Law of *Moses.* The Law of Christ requiring therefore Faith and newness of Life in all men by vertue of the Covenant which they make in Baptism, is it toyish that the Church in Baptism exacteth at every mans hands an express profession of Faith, and an irrevocable promise of obedience by way of ᵍ solemn stipulation? That Infants may contract and covenant with God, ʰthe Law is plain. Neither is the reason of the Law obscure. For sith it tendeth, we cannot sufficiently express how much, to their own good, and doth no way hurt or endanger them to begin the race of their lives herewith, they are, as equity requireth, admitted hereunto, and in favour of their tender years such formal complements of stipulation as being requisite are impossible by themselves in their own persons to be performed, leave is given that they may ⁱ sufficiently discharge by others. Albeit therefore neither deaf nor dumb men, neither furious persons, nor children can receive any civil stipulation, yet this kind of ghostly stipulation they may through his indulgence who re-

Marginal notes:

ᶜ *Multum mirabilis res est quemadmodum quorundam nondum cognoscentium sit inhabitator Deus, & quorundam cognoscentium non sit. Nec illi enim ad Templum Dei pertinent, qui cognoscunt Deum non sicut Deum glorificaverunt: & ad templum Dei pertinent parvuli sanctificati sacramento Christi regenerati spiritu sancto qui per ætatem nondum possunt cognoscere Deum. Unde quem potuerunt illi nosse nec habere isti potuerunt habere antequam nosse.* August. Epist. 57.

ᵈ *T.C.l.1.p 169* If Children could have faith yet they that present the child cannot precisely tell whether that particular child hath faith or no ; we are to think charitably, and to hope it is one of the Church, but it can be no more precisely said that it hath faith, than it may be said precisely elected.

ᵉ 2 *John* 1.

ᶠ *Gal.* 5.3.

ᵍ *Stipulatio est verborum conceptio, quibus is qui interrogatur daturum facturumve se quod interrogatus est respondet; l. 5. sect. 1. ff. de oblig. & act. In hac re olim talia verba tradita fuerunt. Spondes? Spondeo. Promittis? Promitto. Fide promittis? Fide promitto. Fide jubes? Fide jubeo. Dabis? Dabo. Facies? Faciam. Instit.de verb:obl.lib.3.tit.15.* ʰ Gen.17.14. ⁱ *Accommodat illis mater Ecclesia aliorum pedes ut veniant, aliorum cor ut credant, aliorum linguam ut fateantur, ut quoniam quod ægri sunt alio peccante præ, gravantur, sic sum sani fiant alio pro eis confitente salvantur.* Aug. Serm. 10. de verb. Apost.

specting

specting the singular benefit thereof, accepteth Children brought unto him for that end, entreth into Articles of Covenant with them, and in tender commiseration granteth that other mens professions and promises in Baptism made for them shall avail no less than if they had been themselves able to have made their own. None more fit to undertake this office in their behalf than such as present them unto Baptism. A wrong conceit that none may receive the Sacrament of Baptism, but they whose Parents, at the least the one of them, are by the soundness of their Religion and by their vertuous demeanour, known to be men of God, hath caused ^a some to repell Children whosoever bring them, if their Parents be mis-perswaded in Religion, or for other mis-deserts excommunicated; some likewise for that cause to with-hold Baptism, unless the Father, albeit no such exception can justly be taken against him, do notwithstanding make profession of his Faith, and avouch the child to be his own. Thus whereas God hath appointed the Ministers of holy things, they make themselves Inquisitours of mens persons a great deal farther than need is. They should consider that God hath ordained Baptism in favour of mankind. To restrain favours is an odious thing, to enlarge them acceptable both to God and Man. Whereas therefore the Civil Law gave divers immunities to them which were Fathers of three children and had them living, those immunities they held although their children were all dead, if war had consumed them, because it seemed in that case not against reason to repute them by a courteous construction of Law as ^b live-men, in that the honour of their Service done to the Common-wealth would remain always. Can it hurt us in exhibiting the graces which God doth bestow on men, or can it prejudice his glory if the self-same equity guide and direct our hands? When God made his Covenant with such as had *Abraham* to their Father, was onely *Abrahams* immediate issue, or onely his lineal posterity according to the flesh, included in that Covenant? Were not Proselytes as well as Jews always taken for the Sons of *Abraham?* Yea because the very Heads of Families are Fathers in some sort, as touching providence and care for the meanest that belong unto them, the servants which *Abraham* had bought with money were as capable of Circumcision, being newly born, as any natural child that *Abraham* himself begat. Be it then that Baptism belongeth to none but such as either believe presently, or else being Infants are the children of *believing parents.* In case the Church do bring children to the holy Font whose natural parents are either unknown, or known to be such as the Church accurseth; but yet forgetteth not in that severity to take compassion upon their off-spring (for ^c it is the Church which doth offer them to Baptism by the Ministry of Presenters) were it not against both equity and duty to refuse the Mother of believers her self, and not to take her in this case for a faithful Parent? It is not the vertue of our fathers, nor the Faith of any other that can give us the true holiness which we have by vertue of our new birth. Yet even through the common faith and spirit of Gods Church (a thing which no quality of Parents can prejudice) I say through the Faith of the Church of God undertaking the motherly care of our souls, so far forth we may be, and are in our Infancy sanctified, as to be thereby made sufficiently capable of Baptism, and to be interessed in the Rites of our new birth for their pieties sake that offer us thereunto. It cometh sometime to pass (saith Saint *Augustine*) *that the children of bond-slaves are brought to Baptism by their Lord; sometime the Parents being dead, the friends alive undertake that office; sometime strangers or Virgins consecrated unto God, which neither have nor can have children of their own, take up Infants in the open streets, and so offer them unto Baptism, whom the cruelty of unnatural Parents casteth out and leaveth to the adventure of uncertain pity.* As therefore he which did the part of a Neighbour, was a Neighbour to that wounded man whom the parable of the Gospel describeth: so they are fathers, although strangers, that bring Infants to him which maketh them the Sons of God. In the Phrase of some kind of men they use to be termed *witnesses*, as if they came but to see and testifie what is done. It savoureth more of piety to give them their old accustomed name of Fathers and Mothers in God, whereby they are well put in mind what affection they ought to bear towards those Innocents, for whose religious education the Church accepteth them as pledges. This therefore is their own duty. But because the answer which they make to the usual demands of stipula-

tion

tion proposed in Baptism is not their own, the Church doth best to receive it of them in that form which best sheweth whose the act is.

That which a Guardian doth in the name of his Guard or Pupil standeth by natural equity forcible for his benefit, though it be done without his knowledge. And shall we judge it a thing unreasonable, or in any respect unfit, that infants by words which others utter, shou'd though unwittingly, yet truly and forcibly, bind themselves to that whereby their estate is so assuredly bettered? Herewith [a] *Nestorius* the Heretick was charged as having fallen from his first profession, and broken the promise which he made to God in the arms of others. Of such as profaned themselves being Christians with irreligious delight in the Ensigns of Idolatry, heathenish spectacles, shows, and Stage-plays, [b] *Tertullian*, to strike them the more deep, claimeth the promise which they made in Baptism. Why were they dumb being thus challenged? Wherefore stood they not up to answer in their own defence, that such professions and promises made in their names were frivolous; that all which others undertook for them was but mockery and prophanation? That which no Heretick, no wicked liver, no impious despiser of God, no miscreant or malefactor, which had himself been baptized, was ever so desperate as to disgorge in contempt of so fruitful received customes; is now their voice that restore, as they say, the ancient purity of Religion.

[a] *Si Arianæ aut Sabellianæ hereseos adsertor esses, & non tuo ipsius symbolo tecum niteris, convinceremtte tamen testimoniorum sacrorum auctoritate; quid tandem si apud se agerem, quid diceres? quid responderes? nonne obsecro illud in eo te*

baptisatum, in eo te renatum esse? Et verè in negotio quamvis improbo non importuna defensio, & quæ non absurde causam erroris diceres, si pertinaciam non sociares errori. Nunc autem cùm in Catholica urbe natus, Catholica fide institutus, Catholico baptismate regeneratus sis, nunquid agere tecum quasi cum Arriano aut Sabelliano possim? quod utinam fuisses. Minus dolerem in malis editum quàm de bonis lapsum, minus fidem non habitam quàm amissam. Nonniquidem autem, hæretice, non iniquum aut grave aliquid postulo. Hoc fac in Catholica fide editus quod fueras pro perversitate facturus. Cassiad. de incarn. lib. 6. cap. 5. [b] Tertul. lib. de spectac.

65 In Baptism many things of very antient continuance are now quite and clean **Of the Cross in Baptism.** abolisht, for that the virtue and grace of this Sacrament had been therewith overshadowed as with too great abundance of leaves. Notwithstanding to them which think it always imperfect reformation that doth but shear and not flea, our retaining certain of those former Rites, especially the *dangerous* sign of the Cross, hath seemed almost an impardonable over-sight. *The Cross* (they say) *sith it is but a meer invention of man, should not therefore at all have been added to the Sacrament of Baptism. To sign childrens fore-heads with a Cross, in token that hereafter they shall not be ashamed to make profession of the Faith of Christ, is to bring into the Church a new word, whereas there ought to be no Doctor heard in the Church, but our Saviour Christ. That reason which moved the Fathers to use, should move us not to use the sign of the Cross. They lived with Heathens which had the Cross of Christ in contempt, we with such as adore the Cross; and therefore we ought to abandon it even as Ezechias did of old the brasen Serpent.* These are the causes of displeasure conceived against the Cross; a Ceremony, the use whereof hath been profitable although we observe it not as the Ordinance of God but of man. For, saith [c] *Tertullian, If of this and* **Tertul. de** *the like customs thou shouldest require some commandment to be shewed thee out of Scri-* **Coro. Milit.** *tures, there is found.* What reason there is to justifie tradition, use or custome in [d] *Traditiones, non scriptas, si* this behalf, either thou mayest of thy self perceive, or else learn of some other that doth. *doctrinam re* Lest therefore the name of tradition should be offensive to any, considering how far *spicias, cum* by some it hath been abused, we mean by [d] traditions, or ordinances made in the *doctrina scripta* prime of Christian Religion, established with that authority which Christ hath left *convenire debe* to his Church for matters indifferent; and in that consideration requisite to be ob- *ra dicimus.* served, till like authority see just and reasonable cause to alter them. So that tradi- *Quod ad ritua* tions Ecclesiastical are not rudely and in gross to be shaken off, because the Inven- *les & Ecclesi* tors of them were men. Such as say, they allow no [e] invention of man to be ming- *asticus attinet,* led with the outward administration of Sacraments, and under that pretence con- *ordini & ædi* demn our using the signe of the Cross, have belike some special dispensation them- *ficationis Ec* selves to violate their own rules. For neither can they indeed decently, nor do they *semper habenda* *ratio est; inu-*

tiles autem & noxias, nempe ineptas & superstitiosas patronis suis relinquamus. Goulart. Genevens. in Epist. Cypr. 74. [e] T. C. l. 1. p. 171. They should not have been so bold as to have brought it into the holy Sacrament of Baptism; and so mingle the ceremonies and inventions of men with the Sacraments and Institutions of God.

ever

ever baptize any without manifest breach of this their profound axiome, that *Mens inventions should not be mingled with Sacraments and Institutions of God.* They seem [*] to like very well in Baptim the custome of God-fathers, [*] *because so generally the Churches have received it.* Which custome being of God no more instituted then the other (howsoever they pretend the other hurtful, and this profitable) it followeth that even in their own opinion, if their words do shew their minds, there is no necessity of stripping Sacraments out of all such attire of Ceremonies as mans wisdom hath at any time clothed them withal, and consequently that either they must reform their speech as over-general, or else condemn their own practice as unlawful. Ceremonies have more in weight then in sight, they work by commonness of use much, although in the several acts of their usage we scarcely discern any good they do. And because the use which they have for the most part is not perfectly understood, Superstition is apt to impute unto them greater vertue then indeed they have. For prevention whereof, when we use this Ceremony we always plainly express the end whereunto it serveth, namely, for a sign of remembrance to put us in mind of our duty.

[*]*T.C.l.1.p.170*

^a*T.C.l.1.p.170* The profitable signification of the Cross maketh the thing a great deal worse, and bringeth in a new word into the Church, whereas there ought to be no Doctor heard in the Church but only our Saviour Christ. For although it be the Word of God that we should not be ashamed of the Cross of Christ, yet is it not the Word of God that we should be kept in remembrance of that by two lines drawn across one over another in the childs forehead. b *Luke* 7. 44.

But by this mean they say we make it a great deal ^a worse. For why? Seeing God hath no where commanded to draw two lines in token of the duty which we owe to Christ, our practice with this exposition publisheth a new *Gospel*, and causeth another *Word* to have place in the Church of Christ, where no voice ought to be heard but his. By which good reason the Authors of those grave admonitions to the Parliament are well holpen up, which held that *sitting at Communions betokeneth rest and full accomplishment of legal Ceremonies in our Saviour Christ.* For although it be the Word of God that such Ceremonies are expired, yet seeing it is not the word of God that men to signifie so much should sit at the Table of our Lord, these have their doom as well as others, *Guilty of a new devised Gospel in the Church of Christ.* Which strange imagination is begotten of a special dislike they have to hear, that Ceremonies now in use should be thought significant, whereas in truth such as are not significant must needs be vain. Ceremonies destitute of signification are no better then the idle gestures of men, whose broken wits are not Masters of that they do. For if we look but into secular and civil complements, what other cause can there possibly be given why to omit them where of course they are looked for; for where they are not so due, to use them, bringeth mens secret intents oftentimes into great jealousie: I would know I say what reason we are able to yield why things so light in their own nature should weigh in the opinions of men so much, saving only in regard of that which they use to signifie or betoken? Doth not our Lord Jesus Christ [b] himself impute the omission of some courteous Ceremonies even in domestical entertainment to a colder degree of loving affection, and take the contrary in better part, not so much respecting what was less done, as what was signified less by the one then by the other? For to that very end he referreth in part those gracious expostulations, *Simon, seest thou this woman? since I entred into thine house thou gavest me no water for my feet, but she hath washed my feet with tears, and wiped them with the hairs of her head; thou gavest me no kiss, but this woman since the time I came in hath not ceased to kisse my feet; mine head with oyl thou didst not anoint, but this woman hath anointed my feet with oyntment.* Wherefore as the usual dumb Ceremonies of common life are in request or dislike according to that they import, even so Religion having likewise her silent Rites, the chiefest rule whereby to judge of their quality is that which they mean or betoken. For if they signifie good things (as somewhat they must of necessity signifie, because it is of their very nature to be signs of intimation presenting both themselves unto outward sense, and besides themselves some other thing to the understanding of beholders) unless they be either greatly mischosen to signifie the same, or else applyed where that which they signifie agreeth not, there is no cause of exception against them as against evil and unlawful Ceremonies, much less of excepting against them only in that they are not without sense. And if every religious Ceremony which hath been invented of men to signifie any thing that God himself alloweth, were the publication of another Gospel in the Church of Christ, seeing that no Christian Church which men have in the World, is, or can be without continual use of some Ceremonies which men have instituted, inftituted, and that to fignifie good things (unlefs they be vain and frivolous Ceremonies) it would follow that the World hath no Chriftian Church which doth not daily proclaim new Gofpels, a fequel, the manifeft abfurdity whereof argueth the rawnefs of that fuppofal out of which it groweth.

Now the [a] caufe why antiquity did the more *in actions of common life* honour the Ceremony of the Crofs, might be for that they lived with Infidels. But that which they did in the Sacrament of Baptifm was for the felf-fame good of Believers which is therby intended ftill. The Crofs is for us an admonition no lefs neceffary then for them to glory in the fervice of Jefus Chrift, and not to hang down our heads as men afhamed thereof, although it procure us reproach and obloquie at the hands of this wretched World. Shame is a kind of fear to incur difgrace and ignominy. Now whereas fome things are worthy of reproach, fome things ignominious only through a falfe opinion which men have conceived of them, nature that generally feareth opprobrious reprehenfion muft by reafon and Religion be [b] taught what it fhould be afhamed of, and what not. But be we never fo well inftructed what our duty is in this behalf, without fome prefent admonition at the very inftant of practife, what we know is many times not called to mind till that be done whereupon our juft confufion enfueth. To fupply the abfence of fuch as that way might do us good when they fee us in danger of fliding, there are [c] judicious and wife men which think we may greatly relieve our felves by a bare imagined prefence of fome, whofe authority we fear and would be loath to offend, if indeed they were prefent with us. Witneffes at hand are a bridle unto many offences. Let the mind have always fome whom it feareth, fome whofe authority may keep even fecret thoughts under awe. Take *Cato*, or if he be too harfh and rugged, chufe fome other of a fofter mettal, whofe gravity of life and fpeech thou loveft, his mind and countenance carry with thee, fet him always before thine eyes either as a watch or as a pattern. That which is crooked we cannot ftreighten but by fome fuch level. If men of fo good experience and infight in the maims of our weak flefh, have thought thefe fancied remembrances available to awaken fhamefaftnefs, that fo the boldnefs of fin may be ftayed ere it look abroad, furely the wifdom of the Church of Chrift which hath to that ufe converted the Ceremony of the Crofs in Baptifm, it is no Chriftian mans part to defpife, efpecially feeing that by this mean, where nature doth earneftly import aid, Religion yiledeth her that ready affiftance, than which there can be no help more forcible, ferving only to relieve memory, and to bring to our cogitation that which fhould moft make afhamed of fin. The mind while we are in this prefent life [d] whether it contemplate, meditate, deliberate, or howfoever exercife it felf, worketh nothing without continual recourfe unto imagination the only ftore-houfe of wit, and peculiar chair of memory. On this anvile it ceafeth not day and night to ftrike, by means whereof, as the pulfe declareth how the heart doth work, fo the very [e] thoughts and cogitations of mans mind, be they good or bad, do no where fooner bewray themfelves, than through the creveffes of that wall wherewith nature hath compaffed the Cels and Clofets of fancy. In the forehead nothing more plain to be feen than the fear of contumely

[a] *T.C. lib.* 1. p. 170. It is known to all that have read the Ecclefiaftical ftories, that the Heathen did object to Chriftians in times paft in reproach that the God which they believed on was hanged upon a Crofs. And they thought good to teftifie that they were not afhamed therefore of the Son of God, by the often ufing of the figne of the Crofs. Which carefulnefs and good mind to keep amongft them an open profeffion of Chrift crucified although it be to be commended, yet is not this means fo. For they might otherwife have kept it, and with lefs danger then by this ufe of croffing. And as it was brought in upon no good ground, fo the Lord left a mark of his curfe of it, and whereby it might be perceived to come out of the forge of mens brain, in that it began forthwith while it was yet in the fwadling clouts to be fuperftitioufly abufed. The Chriftians had fuch a fuperftition in it, that they would do nothing without Croffing. But if it were granted that upon this confideration which I have before mentioned, the ancient Chriftians did well, yet it followeth not that we fhould fo do. For we live not amongft thofe Nations which do caft us in the teeth or reproach us with the Crofs of Chrift. Now that we live amongft Papifts that do not contemn the Crofs of Chrift, but which efteem more of the wooden Crofs, then of the true Crofs, which is his fufferings, we ought now to do clean contrariwife to the old Chriftians, and abolifh all ufe of thefe Croffes. For contrary difeafes muft have contrary remedies. If therefore the old Chriftians to deliver the Crofs of Chrift from contempt did often ufe the Crofs, the Chriftians now to take away the fuperftitious eftimation of it ought to take away the ufe of it. [b] *Ephef.* 5. 12. *Rom.* 6. 21.

[c] *Sen. Epift.* 11 *lib.* 1.

[d] Τὸ νοεῖν ἢ φαντασία τίς ἢ ἐκ ἀνευ φαντασίας. *Arift. de anim. lib.* 1. c. 1 Ἡ μὲν αἰσθητικὴ φανlασία ἡ ἐν τοῖς ἀλόγοις ὑπάρχει, ἢ δὲ

Ἐνλευτικὴ ἐν τοῖς λογιστικοῖς *lib.* 3. c. 11. Τὰ μὲν οὐν εἴδη τὸ νοητικὸν ἐν τοῖς φαντάσμασι νοεῖ. &c. τὸ δὲ ἀιστανὀμενον ὁρᾷ. *lib.* 3. c. 8. [e] *Frons hominis triftitiæ, hilaritatis, clementiæ, feveritatis index eft. Plin. lib.* 11.

and diſgrace. For which cauſe the Scripture (as with great probability it may be thought) deſcribeth them [a] marked of God in the forehead, whom his mercy hath undertaken to keep from final confuſion and ſhame. Not that God doth ſet any corporal mark on his choſen, but to note that he giveth his elect ſecurity of preſervation from reproach , the fear whereof doth uſe ſhew it ſelf [b] in that part. Shall I ſay that the ſigne of the Croſs (as we uſe it) is in ſome ſort a mean to work our preſervation from reproach ? Surely the mind which as yet hath not hardened it ſelf in ſin is ſeldom provoked thereunto in any groſs and grievous manner, but natures ſecret ſuggeſtion objected againſt it ignominy as a bar. Which conceit being entred into that Palace of mans fancy, the gates whereof have imprinted in them that holy ſigne which bringeth forthwith to mind whatſoever Chriſt hath wrought and we vowed again ſt ſin, it cometh hereby to paſs, that Chriſtian men never want a moſt effectual though a ſilent teacher to avoid whatſoever may deſervedly procure ſhame. So that in things which we ſhould be aſhamed of we are by the Croſs admoniſhed faithfully of our duty at the very moment when admonition doth moſt need. Other things there are which deſerve honour and yet do purchaſe many times our diſgrace in this preſent World, as of old the very truth of Religion it ſelf, till God by his own out-ſtretched arm made the glory therof to ſhine over all the earth. Whereupon [d] St. *Cyprian* exhorting to martyrdome in times of heatheniſh perſecution and cruelty, thought it not vain to alleage unto them with other arguments the very Ceremony of that Croſs whereof we ſpeak. Never let that hand offer ſacrifice to Idols which hath already received the body of our Saviour Chriſt,and ſhall hereafter the Crown of his glory ; *arm your fore-heads* unto all boldneſs, that *the ſigne of God* may be kept ſafe. Again, when it pleaſed God that the fury of their enemies being bridled the Church had ſome little reſt and quietneſs, (if ſo ſmall a liberty but on y to breathe between troubles may be termed quietneſs and reſt) to ſuch as fell not away from Chriſt through former perſecutions, he giveth due and deſerved praiſe in the ſelf-ſame manner , [e] *You that were ready to indure impriſonment, and were reſolute to ſuffer death ; you that have couragiouſly withſtood the world, ye have made your ſelves both a glorious ſpectacle for God to behold,and a worthy example for the reſt of your brethren to follow. Thoſe mouths which had ſanctified themſelves with food coming down from Heaven,loathed after Chriſts own body and blood to taſte the poyſoned and contagious ſcraps of Idols; thoſe fore-heads which the ſigne of God had purified, kept themſelves to be crowned by him, the touch of the garlands of Satan they abhorred.* Thus was the memory of that ſigne which they had in Baptiſm a kind of bar or prevention to keep them even from apoſtaſie, whereunto the frailty of fleſh and blood over-much fearing to indure ſhame , might peradventure the more eaſily otherwiſe have drawn them. We have not now through the gracious goodneſs of Almighty God , thoſe extream conflicts which our fathers had with blaſphemous contumelies every where offered to the Name of Chriſt, by ſuch as profeſſed themſelves infidels and unbeleevers. Howbeit , unleſs we be ſtrangers to the age wherein we live, or elſe in ſome partial reſpect diſſemblers of that we hourely both heat and ſee,there is not the ſimpleſt of us but knoweth with what diſdain and ſcorn Chriſt is honoured far and wide. Is there any burden in the world more heavy to bear than contempt ? Is there any contempt that grieveth as theirs doth, whoſe quality no way making them leſs worthy than others are of reputation, only the ſervice which they do to Chriſt in the daily exerciſe of Religion treadeth them down? Doth any contune y which we ſuſtain for Religion ſake , pierce ſo deeply as that which would ſeem of meer conſcience religiouſly ſpiteful ? when they that honour God are deſpiſed ; when the chiefeſt ſervice of Honor that man can do unto him is the cauſe why they are deſpiſed ; when they which pretend to honour him , and that with greateſt ſincerity , do with more than heatheniſh petulancy trample under foot almoſt whatſoever either we or the whole Church of God by the ſpace of ſo many ages have been accuſtomed unto for the comlier and better exerciſe of our Religion, according to the ſoundeſt rules that wiſdom, directed by the Word of God , and by long experience confirmed, hath been able with common advice, with much deliberation and exceeding great diligence to comprehend ; when no man fighting under Chriſts banner can be always exempted from ſeeing

or

a Ezek. 9. 4:
Apoc.7.3 9.4.

b Ἐπυθειvoíſαι
γὰρ δὲ αίσχυ-
vóμεvοι.Ariſt.
Eth. 4. c.9.
c Caro ſignatur
ut & anima
munitur.Tert.
de reſur. car.

d Cypr. Epiſt.
56. ad Thibari-
tanos.

e Cypr. de laps.

f Erant enim
ſupplices coro-
narii. Tert. lib.
de coro. mil.
In the ſervice
of Idols the
doors of their
Temples, the
ſacrifices, the
Altars, the
Prieſts, and the
Suppliants that
were preſent
wore Garlands.

or suftaining those indignities, the fting whereof not to feel, or feeling, not to be moved thereat; is a thing impoffible to flefh and blood : if this be any object for patience to work on, the ftricteft bond that thereunto tyeth us is our vowed obedience to Chrift ; the folemneft vow that we ever made to obey Chrift and to suffer willingly all reproaches for his fake was made in Baptifm : and amongft other memorials to keep us mindful of that vow, we cannot think that the figne which our new baptized fore-heads did there receive is either unfit or unforcible, the reafons hitherto alleaged being weighed with indifferent ballance. It is not (you will fay) the Crofs in our fore-heads, but in our hearts the faith of Chrift that armeth us with patience, conftancy and courage. Which as we grant to be moft true, fo neither dare we defpife, no not the meaneft helps that ferve, though it be but in the very loweft degree of furtherance towards the higheft fervices that God doth require at our hands. And if any man deny that fuch Ceremonies are available at the leaft as memorials of duty, or do think that himfelf hath no need to be fo put in mind what our duties are, it is but reafonable that in the one the publike experience of the World overweigh fome few mens perfwafion, and in the other the rare perfection of a few condefcend unto common imbecility. Seeing therefore that to fear fhame which doth worthily follow fin, and to bear undeferved reproach conftantly is the general duty of all men profeffing Chriftianity ; seeing alfo that our weaknefs while we are in this prefent World doth need towards fpiritual duties the help even of corporal furtherance, and that by reafon of natural intercourfe between the higheft and the loweft powers of mans mind in all actions, his fancy or imagination carrying in it that fpecial note of remembrance than which there is nothing more forcible, where either too weak or too ftrong a conceit of infamy and difgrace might do great harm, ftandeth always ready to put forth a kind of neceffary helping hand, we are in that refpect to acknowledge the [a] good and profitable ufe of this Ceremony, and not to think it fuperfluous that Chrift hath his mark applied [b] unto that part where bafhfulnefs appeareth, in token that they which are Chriftians fhould be at no time afhamed of his ignominy. But to prevent fome inconveniencies which might enfue, if the over-ordinary ufe thereof (as it fareth with fuch rites when they are too common) fhould caufe it to be of lefs obfervation or regard where it moft availeth, we neither omit it in that place, nor altogether make it fo vulgar as the cuftome heretofore hath been : although to condemne the whole Church of God when it moft flourifhed in zeal and piety, to mark that age with the brand of errour and fuperftition, only becaufe they had this Ceremony more in ufe than we now think needful, boldly to affirm that this their practife grew fo foon through a fearful malediction of God upon the Ceremony of the Crofs, as if we knew that his purpofe was thereby to make it manifeft in all mens eyes how execrable thofe things are in his fight which have proceeded from humane invention, is as we take it a cenfure of greater zeal than knowledge. Men whofe judgements in thefe cafes are grown more moderate, although they retain not as we do the ufe of this Ceremony, perceive notwithftanding very well fuch cenfures to be out of fquare, and do therefore not only [c] acquit the Fathers from fuperftition therein, but alfo think it fufficient to anfwer in excufe of themfelves, [d] *This Ceremony which li*. ad Demetr. *was but a thing indifferent even of old, we judge not at this day a matter neceffary for all Chriftian men to obferve.* As for their laft upfhot of all towards this mark, they are of opinion that if the ancient Chriftians to deliver the Crofs of Chrift from contempt did well and with good confideration ufe often the figne of the Crofs in teftimony of their faith and profeffion before Infidels which upbraided them with Chrifts fufferings, now that we live with fuch as contrariwife adore the figne of the Crofs (becaufe contrary difeafes fhould always have contrary remedies) we ought to take away all ufe thereof. In which conceipt they both wayes greatly feduce themfelves; firft, for that they imagine the Fathers to have had no ufe of the Crofs, but with reference unto Infidels, which mif-perfwafion we have before difcovered at large ; and fecondly, by reafon that they think there is not any other way befides univerfal extirpation to reform fuperftitious abufes of the Crofs. Wherein becaufe there are that ftand very much upon the example of *Ezechias*, as if his [e] *breaking to pieces that Serpent* of brafs whereunto the children of Ifrael had burnt *incenfe*

[a] Ἐγὼ δὴ αἰσθὸν χ̀ τὸ φυλακτιχὸν τῶν τοιούτων χ̀ ἐξ ἀκολουθεῖ τὰ τοιαῦτα χ̀ τὰ κωλυτικὰ τῶν ἐναντίων χ̀ τὰ φθαρτικά. Arift. Rhet. lib. 1. cap. 6.

[b] Ozias Rex lepræ varietate in fronte maculatus eft, ea parte corporis notatus offenfo Domino ubi fignantur qui Dominum promerentur. Cypr. de unit. Ecclef. cap. 16.

[c] Goulart. Annot. in Cypr.

[d] Quamvis veteres Chriftiani externo figno crucis ufi funt, id tamen fuit fine fuperftitione, & doctrina de Chrifti merito ab errore, quipoftea irreppfit pios fervavit immunes.

[d] Idem annot. in Cypr. li. 56. cap. 7.

[e] Reg. 18. 3.

incenfe, did enforce the utter abolition of this Ceremony, the fact of that virtuous Prince is by fo much the more attentively to be confidered. Our lives in this world are partly guided by rules, and partly directed by examples. To conclude out of general rules and axioms by difcourfe of wit our duties in every particular action, is both troublefome and many times fo full of difficulty, that it maketh deliberations hard and tedious to the wifeft men. Whereupon we naturally all incline to obferve examples, to mark what others have done before us, and in the favour of our own eafe rather to follow them than to enter into new confultation, if in regard of their virtue and wifdom we may but probably think they have waded without errour. So that the willingnefs of men to be led by example of others both difcovereth and helpeth the imbecility of our judgment. Becaufe it doth the one, therefore infolent and proud wits would always feem to be their own guids; and becaufe it doth the other, we fee how hardly the vulgar fort is drawn unto any thing for which there are not as wel examples as reafons alleaged. Reafons proving that which is more particular by things more general and farther from fenfe are with the fimpler fort of men lefs trufted, for that they doubt of their own judgement in thofe things; but of examples which prove unto them one doubtful particular by another more familiarly and fenfibly known, they eafily perceive in themfelves fome better ability to judge. The force of examples therefore is great, when in matter of action being doubtful what to do, we are informed what others have commendably done whofe deliberations were like. But whofoever doth perfwade by example, muft as well refpect the fitnefs as the goodnefs of that he alleageth. To *Ezechias* God himfelf in this fact giveth teftimony of well-doing. So that nothing is here queftionable but only whether the example alleaged be pertinent, pregnant and ftrong. The Serpent fpoken of was firft erected for the extraordinary and *miraculous cure* of the Ifraelites in the Defart. This ufe having prefently an end when the caufe for which God ordained it was removed, the thing it felf they notwithftanding kept for a *monument of Gods mercy,* as in like confideration they did the pot of Manna, the Rod of *Aaron,* and the Sword which *David* took from *Goliah.* In procefs of time they made a monument of divine power a plain Idol, they burnt incenfe before it contrary to the Law of God, and did it the fervices of honour due unto God only. Which grofs and grievous abufe continued till *Ezechias* reftoring the purity of found Religion, deftroyed utterly that which had been fo long and fo generally a fnare unto them.

a Diff. 6, 3, c. Quiz.

It is not amifs which the [a] Canon Law hereupon concludeth, namely, that *if our Predeceffors have done fome things which at that time might be without fault, and afterward be turned to Errour and Superftition, we are taught by* Ezechias *breaking the brazen Serpent, that Pofterity may deftroy them without any delay, and with great authority* But may it be fimply and without exception hereby gathered, that Pofterity *is bound to deftroy* whatfoever hath been either at the firft invented, or but afterwards turned to like fuperftition and errour? No, it cannot be. The Serpent therefore and the figne of the Crofs although feeming equal in this point, that fuperftition hath abufed both, yet being herein alfo unequal, that neither they have been both fubject to the like degree of abufe, nor were in hardnefs of redrefs alike, it may be that even as the one for abufe was religioufly taken away, fo now, when Religion hath taken away abufe from the other, we fhould by utter abolition thereof deferve hardly his commendation, whofe example there is offered us no fuch neceffary caufe to follow. For by the words of *Ezechias* in terming the Serpent but *a lump of brafs,* to fhew that the beft thing in it now was the metal or matter whereof it confifted, we may probably conjecture, that the people whofe errour is therein control'd, had the felf-fame opinion of it which the Heathens had of Idols, they thought that the power of Deity was with it, and when they faw it diffolved, haply they might to comfort themfelves, imagine as *Olympius* the Sophi-

b Sozom. lib. 7. cap. 15.

fter did beholding the diffipation of Idols, [b] *Shapes, and counterfeits they were, fafhioned of matter fubject unto corruption, therefore to grind them to duft was eafie, but thofe celeftial powers which dwelt and refided in them are afcended into Heaven.* Some difference there is between thefe opinions of palpable Idolatry, and that which the Schools in fpeculation have boulted out concerning the Crofs. Notwithftanding forafmuch as the Church of *Rome* hath hitherto practifed, and doth pro-

fefs

sess the same adoration to the signe of the Cross, and neither less nor other than is due unto Christ himself, howsoever they varnish and qualifie their sentence, pretending that the Cross, which to outward sense presenteth visibly it self alone, is not by them apprehended alone, but hath in their secret surmise or conceit a reference to the Person of our Lord Jesus Christ; so that the honour which they jointly do to both, respecteth principally his Person, and the Cross but only for his Persons sake, the people not accustomed to trouble their wits with so nice and subtle differences in the exercise of Religion, are apparently no less insnared by adoring the Cross, than the Jews by burning incense to the brazen Serpent. It is by [a] *Tho-* *mas* ingenuously granted, that because unto reasonable creatures a kind of reverence is due for the excellency which is in them, and whereby they resemble God, therefore if reasonable Creatures, Angels, or Men should receive at our hands holy and divine honour, as the signe of the Cross doth at theirs, to pretend that we honour not them alone, but we honour God with them, would not serve the turn, neither would this be able to prevent the errour of men, or cause them always to respect God in their adorations, and not to finish their intents in the object next before them. But unto this he addeth, that no such errour can grow by adoring in that sort a dead Image, which every man knoweth to be void of excellency in it self, and therefore will easily conceive that the honour done unto it hath an higher reference. Howbeit, seeing that we have by over-true experience been taught how often, especially in these cases, the light event of common understanding faileth, surely their usual adoration of the Cross is not hereby freed. For in actions of this kinde we are more to respect what the greatest part of men is commonly prone to conceive, than what some few mens wits may devise in construction of their own particular meanings. Plain it is, that a false opinion of some personal divine excellencie to be in those things which either Nature or Art hath framed, causeth always religious adoration. And as plain, that the like adoration applyed unto things sensible, argueth to vulgar capacities, yea leaveth imprinted in them the very same opinion of Deity from whence all idolatrous worship groweth. Yea the meaner and baser a thing worshipped is in it self, the more they incline to think that every man which doth adore it, knoweth there is in it or with it a presence of divine power: Be it therefore true that Crosses purposely framed or used for receipt of divine honour, be even as scandalous as the brazen Serpent it self, where they are in such sort adored. Should we hereupon think our selves in the sight of God, and in conscience charged to abolish utterly the very *Ceremony* of the Cross, neither meant at the first, nor now converted unto any such offensive purpose? Did the Jewes which could never be perswaded to admit in the City of *Jerusalem* that [b] Image of *Cæsar* which the *Romans* were accustomed to [c] adore, make any scruple of [d] *Cæsars* Image in the Coin which they knew very well that men were not wont to worship? Between the Cross which Superstition honoureth as Christ, and that Ceremony of the Crosse which serveth onely for a signe of remembrance, there is as plain and as great a difference, as between those [e] brazen Images which *Solomon* made to bear up the Cesterne of the Temple, and (sith both were of like shape, but not of unlike use) [f] that which the Israelites in the Wildernesse did adore; or between the [g] Altars which *Josias* destroyed because they were instruments of meer Idolatry, and [h] that which the Tribe of *Reuben* with others erected near to the River Jordan, for which also they grew at the first into some dislike, and were by the rest of their brethren suspected, yea hardly charged with open breach of the Law of God, accused of backwardnesse in Religion, upbraided bitterly with the fact of *Peor*, and the odious example of *Achan*, as if the building of their Altar in that place had given manifest shew of no better than intended Apostasie, till by a true declaration made in their own defence, it appeared that such as misliked mis-understood their enterprize, in as much as they had no intent to build any Altar for Sacrifice, which God would have no where offered saving in *Jerusalem* onely, but to a farre other end and purpose, which being opened, satisfied all parties, and so delivered them from causeless blame. In this particular suppose the worst, imagine that the immateriall Ceremony of the Crosse had been the subject of as grosse po-

[a] *Tho. p. 3.q.25.* *art.3. resp. ad. teri.*

[b] *Joseph. Anti. lib.17.c.8. & l. 18.c.3. & de bell. lib.2.c.8.*
[c] Their Eagles their Ensigns, and the Images of their Princes they carried with them in all their Armies, and had always a kind of Chappel wherein they placed and adored them as Gods. *Dio. lib. 40.*
[d] *Mat.22.20.*
[e] 2 *Chron. 4:3.* *Herod.in.l.4.*
[f] *Exod.32. 4.*
[g] 2 *Chron.34.7*
[h] *Josh. 22,10.*

lution

lution as any Heathenish or prophane Idol. If we think the example of *Ezechias*
a proof, that things which Errour and Superstition hath abused, may in no confideration be tolerated, although we presently finde them not subject to so vile abuse,
the plain example of *Ezechias* proveth the contrary. The Temples and Idols which
under *Solomon* [a] had been of very purpose framed for the honour of forrain Gods,
Ezechias destroyed not, because they stood as forlorn things and did now no harm,
although formerly they had done harm. [b] *Josias*, for some inconvenience afterwards, razed them up. Yet to both there is one commendation given even from
God himself, that touching [c] matter of Religion, they walked in the steps of *David*, and did no way displease God. Perhaps it seemeth that by force and virtue
of this example, although it bare detestation and hatred of Idolatry, all things which
have been at any time worshipped, are not necessarily to be taken out of the World,
neverthelesse for remedy and prevention of so great offences, wisdom should judge
it the safest course to remove altogether from the eyes of men that which may put
them in mind of evil. Some kinds of evil, no doubt, there are very quick in working on those affections that most easily take fire, which evils should in that respect
no oftner than need requireth be brought in presence of weak minds. But neither is the Cross any such evil, nor yet the brazen Serpent it self: so strongly poysoned, that our eyes, ears, and thoughts, ought to shun them both, for fear of
some deadly harm to ensue the onely representation thereof by gesture, shape,
sound, or such like significant means. And for mine own part, I most assuredly
perswade my self, that had *Ezechias* (till the days of whose most virtuous Reign
they ceased not continually to burn Incense to the brazen Serpent) had he found
the Serpent, though sometime adored; yet at that time recovered from the evil of so
grosse abuse, and reduced to the same that was before in the time of *David*, at which
time they esteemed it only as a memorial, signe, or monument of Gods miraculous goodness towards them, even as we in no other sort esteem the Ceremony of
the Cross, the due consideration of an use so harmless, common to both, might no
lesse have wrought their equal preservation, than different occasions have procured,
notwithstanding the ones extinguishment, the others lawful continuance. In all
perswasions, which ground themselves upon example, we are not so much to respect
what is done, as the causes and secret inducements leading thereunto. The question being therefore, whether this Ceremony supposed to have been *sometimes scan-*
dalous and offensive, ought for that cause to be *now* removed, there is no reason we
should forthwith yeild our selves to be carried away with example, no not of them
whose acts the highest judgment approveth for having reformed in that manner any
publike evil: but before we either attempt any thing or resolve, the state and condition as well of our own affairs as theirs whose example presseth us, is advisedly to
be examined, because some things are of their own nature scandalous, and cannot
chuse but breed offence, as those [d] Sinks of execrable filth which *Josias* did over-
whelm; some things, albeit not by nature and of themselves, are notwithstanding so
generally turned to evil, by reason of an evil corrupt habit grown, and through long
continuance incurably setled in the minds of the greatest part, that no redress can
be well hoped for, without removal of that wherein they have ruined themselves,
which plainly was the state of the Jewish people, and the cause why *Ezechias* did
with such sudden indignation destroy what he saw worshipped; finally, some things
are as the signe of the Cross, though subject either almost or altogether to as great
abuse, yet curable with more facility and ease. And to speak as the truth is, our
very nature doth hardly yield to destroy that which may be fruitfully kept, and without any great difficulty clean scowred from the rust of evil, which by some accident
hath grown into it. Wherefore to that which they build in this question upon the
example of *Ezechias*, let this suffice. When Heathens despised Christian Religion,
because of the sufferings of Jesus Christ, the Fathers, to testifie how little such contumelies and contempts prevailed with them, chose rather the sign of the Cross, than
any other outward mark, whereby the world might most easily discerne alwayes
what they were. On the contrary side now, whereas they which do all professe
the Christian Religion are divided amongst themselves, and the fault of the
one part is, that the zeal to the sufferings of Christ they admire too much, and
over-

a 1 Reg. 11. 17.

b 2 Reg. 23. 13.

c 2 Reg. 18. 3. 6.
2 Reg. 22. 2.

d 2 Reg. 23. 7.

ever-superstitiously adore the Visible sign of his Cross, if you ask, what we that mislike them, should do, we are here advised to cure one contrary by another. Which Art or Method is not yet so current as they imagine. For if, as their practice for the most part sheweth, it be their meaning that the scope and drift of Reformation, when things are faulty, should be to *settle* the Church in the contrary, it standeth them upon to beware of this rule, because seeing Vices have not only Vertues, but other Vices also in nature opposite unto them, it may be dangerous in these cases to seek but that which we find contrary to present evils. For in sores and sicknesses of the mind we are not simply to measure good by distance from evil, because one Vice may in some respect be more opposite to another, then either of them to that Vertue which holdeth the mean between them both. Liberality and Covetousness, the one a Vertue and the other a Vice, are not so contrary as the Vices of Covetousness and Prodigality; Religion and Superstition have more affiance, though the one be Light and the other Darkness, then Superstition and Prophaneness, which are vicious extremities. By means whereof it cometh also to pass, that the meane, which is Vertue, seemeth in the eyes of each extream an extremity; the liberal hearted man is by the opinion of the Prodigal miserable, and by the judgement of the Miserable lavish; Impiety for the most part upbraideth Religion as superstitious, which Superstition often accuseth as impious, both so conceiving thereof because it doth seem more to participate each extream, then one extream doth another, and is by consequent less contrary to either of them, then they mutually between themselves. Now, if he that seeketh to reform Covetousness or Superstition, should but labour to induce the contrary, it were but to draw men out of Lime into Cole-dust. So that their course which will remedy the superstitious abuse of things profitable in the Church is not still to abolish utterly the use thereof, because not using at all is most opposite to ill using, but rather if it may be, to bring them back to a right perfect and religious usage, which albeit less contrary to the present sore, is notwithstanding the better and by many degrees the sounder way of recovery. And unto this effect that very precedent it self which they propose may be best followed. For as the Fathers, when the Cross of Christ was in utter contempt, did not superstitiously adore the same, but rather declare that they so esteemed it as was meet: In like manner where we find the Cross to have that honour which is due to Christ, is it not as lawful for us to retain it in that estimation which it ought to have, and in that use which it had of old without offence, as by taking it clean away to seem Followers of their Example, which cure wilfully by abscission that which they might both preserve and heal? Touching therefore the Sign and Ceremony of the Cross, we no way find our selves bound to relinquish it, neither because the first Inventors thereof were but mortal men, nor left the sence and signification we give unto it should burthen us as Authors of a new Gospel in the House of God, nor in respect of some cause which the Fathers had more then we have to use the same, nor finally for any such offence or scandal as heretofore it hath been subject unto by errour now reformed in the minds of men.

66. The ancient custome of the Church was, after they had baptized, to adde thereunto Imposition of hands, with effectual Prayer for the [a] illumination of Gods most Holy Spirit, to confirm and perfect that which the grace of the same Spirit had already begun in Baptism. For our means to obtain the graces which God doth bestow, are our Prayers. Our Prayers to that intent are available as well for others as for our selves. To pray for others, is *to bless* them for whom we pray, because Prayer procureth the blessing of God upon them, especially the Prayer of such as God either most respecteth for their Piety and Zeal that way, or else regardeth for that their place and calling bindeth them above others unto this duty, as it doth both natural and spiritual Fathers. With Prayers of spiritual and personal Benediction, the manner hath been in all Ages to use *Imposition of hands*, as a Ceremony betokening our *restrained desires* to the party, whom we present unto God by Prayer. Thus when [b] *Israel blessed Ephraim* and *Manasses, Josephs* Sons, he *imposed* upon them his hands and prayed, *God in whose sight my Fathers* Abraham *and* Isaac *did walk, God which hath fed me all my life long unto this day, and the Angel which hath delivered me from all evil, bless these Children.* The Prophets which healed diseased

Of Confirmation after Baptism.

a *Caro manus imponitione adumbratur, ut & anima spiritu illuminetur.* Tertul. de Resurrect. car.

b Gen. 48.14.

diseases by Prayer, used therein the self-same Ceremony. And therefore when *Elizeus* willed *Naaman* to wash himself seven times in *Jordan* for cure of his foul disease, it much offended him: *I thought* (saith he) *with my self, Surely the man will come forth and stand and call upon the Name of the Lord his God, and put his hand on the place, to the end he may so heal the Leprosie.* In Consecrations and Ordinations of men unto rooms of divine calling, the like was usually done from the time of *Moses* to Christ. Their sutes that came unto Christ for help were also tendred oftentimes, and are expressed in such formes or phrases of speech, as shew that he was himself an observer of the same custome. He which with Imposition of Hands and Prayer did so great Works of Mercy for restauration of bodily health, was worthily judged as able to effect the infusion of Heavenly grace into them, whose age was not yet depraved with that malice which might be supposed a bar to the goodness of God towards them. They brought him therefore young children to put his hands upon them and *pray*. After the Ascension of our Lord and Saviour Jesus Christ, that which he had begun continued in the daily practice of his Apostles, whose Prayer and Imposition of Hands, were a mean whereby thousands became partakers of the wonderful gifts of God; The Church had received from Christ a promise, that such as believed in him, these signs and tokens should follow them, *To cast out Devils, to speak with tongues, to drive away Serpents, to be free from the harm which any deadly poyson could work, and to cure diseases by Imposition of Hands.* Which power, common at the first in a manner unto *all Believers*, all Believers had not power to derive or communicate unto all other men, but whosoever was the instrument of God to instruct, convert and baptize them, the gift of miraculous operations by the power of the Holy Ghost they had not, but only at the Apostles own hands. For which cause *Simon Magus* perceiving that power to be in none but them, and presuming that they which had it might sell it, sought to purchase it of them with money. And as miraculous graces of the Spirit continued after the Apostles times (for saith *Irenæus*) *They which are truly his Disciples, do in his Name and through grace received from him, such works for the benefit of other men, as every of them is by him inabled to work; Some cast out Devils, insomuch as they which are delivered from wicked spirits have been thereby won unto Christ, and do constantly persevere in the Church and society of faithful men; Some excell in the knowledge of things to come, in the grace of Visions from God, and the gift of Prophetical Predictions; Some by laying on their hands, restore them to health which are grievously afflicted with sickness; yea there are that of dead have been made alive, and have afterwards many years conversed with us; What should I say? the gifts are innumerable wherewith God hath inriched his Church throughout the World, and by vertue whereof in the Name of Christ crucified under* Pontius Pilate, *the Church every day doth many Wonders for the good of Nations, neither fraudulently nor in any respect of lucre and gain to her self, but as freely bestowing as God on her hath bestowed his divine Graces:* So it no where appeareth, that ever any did by Prayer and Imposition of Hands sithence the Apostles times, make others partakers of the like *miraculous* gifts and graces as long as it pleased God to continue the same in his Church; but only Bishops the Apostles Successors for a time, even in that power. Saint *Augustine* acknowledgeth, that such gifts were not permitted to last always, lest men should wax cold with the commonness of that, the strangeness whereof at the first inflamed them. Which words of Saint *Augustine* declaring how the vulgar use of these Miracles was then expired, are no prejudice to the like extraordinary graces more rarely observed in some, either then or of later days. Now whereas the Successors of the Apostles had but only for a time such power as by Prayer and Imposition of Hands to bestow the Holy Ghost; The reason wherefore Confirmation, nevertheless, by Prayer and Laying on of hands hath hitherto always continued, is for other very special benefits which the Church thereby enjoyeth. The Fathers every where impute unto it that gift of grace of the Holy Ghost, not which maketh us first Christian men, but when we are made such, assisteth us in all vertue, armeth us against temptation and sin. For after Baptism administred, *there followeth* (saith *Tertullian*) *Imposition of hands with invocation and invitation of the Holy Ghost, which willingly cometh down from the Father to rest upon the purified and blessed bodies,*

c 2 Reg.5.11.

d Numb.27.18.

e Mat.9. 18.
Mar.5.23,8.22.

f Mat.19.13.
Marke 10. 13.
Luke 18.15.

g Marke 16.17

h Acts 19. 6.

i Acts 8.17,18.

k Iren.l.2.c.57.

l Aug.de vera Relig. cap.15.

m Tertul.de Baptif.

bodies, as it were acknowledging the waters of Baptism a fit seat. S. [n] *Cyprian* in more particular manner alluding to that effect of the Spirit which here especially was respected, *How great* (saith he) *is that power and force wherewith the mind is here* (he meaneth in Baptism) *inabled, being not only withdrawn from that pernicious hold which the World before had of it, nor only so purified and made clean that no stain, or blemish of the Enemies invasion doth remain, but over and besides* (namely, through Prayer and Imposition of Hands) *becometh yet greater, yet mightier in strength, so far as to raign with a kind of Imperial dominion over the whole Band of that roming and spoiling Adversary.* As much is signified by [o] *Eusebius Emissenus,* saying, *The Holy Ghost which descendeth with saving influence upon the waters of Baptism, doth there give that fulness which sufficeth for innocency, and afterwards exhibiteth in Confirmation an augmentation of further grace.* The Fathers therefore being thus perswaded, held Confirmation as [p] an Ordinance Apostolick *always profitable in Gods Church,* although not always accompanied with equal largeness of those external effects which gave it countenance at the first. The cause of severing Confirmation from Baptism (for most commonly they went together) was sometimes in the Minister, which being of inferiour degree might baptize but not confirm, as in [q] their case it came to pass whom *Peter* and *John* did confirm, whereas *Philip* had before baptized them ; and in theirs of whom [r] S. *Jerome* hath said, *I deny not but the custome of the Churches is that the Bishop should go abroad, and imposing his hands, pray for the gift of the Holy Ghost on them whom Presbyters and Deacons far off in lesser Cities have already baptized.* Which ancient custom of the Church, S.*Cyprian* groundeth upon the Example of *Peter* and *John* in the eight of the *Acts* before alledged. The [s] faithful in *Samaria* (saith he) *Had already obtained Baptism : Only that which was wanting,* Peter and John *supplyed by Prayer and Imposition of Hands, to the end the Holy Ghost might be poured upon them: Which also is done amongst our selves, when they which be already baptized are brought to the Prelates of the Church, to obtain by our Prayer and Imposition of Hands the Holy Ghost.* By this it appeareth that when the Ministers of Baptism were persons of inferiour degree, the Bishops did after confirm whom such had before baptized. Sometimes they which by force of their Ecclesiastical calling might do as well the one as the other, were notwithstanding men whom Heresie had dis-joyned from the Fellowship of true Believers. Whereupon when any man by them baptized and confirmed, came afterwards to see and renounce their errour, there grew in some Churches very hot contention about the manner of admitting such into the bosome of the true Church, as hath been declared already in the question of re-baptization. But the general received custom was only to admit them with Imposition of Hands and Prayer. Of which custom while some imagined the reason to be for that Hereticks might give remission of sins by Baptism, but not the Spirit by Imposition of Hands, because themselves had not Gods Spirit, and that therefore their Baptism might stand, but Confirmation must be given again : the imbecility of this ground gave *Cyprian* occasion to oppose himself against the practice of the Church herein, labouring many ways to prove that Hereticks could do neither, and consequently, that their Baptism in all respects, was as fruitrate as their Christm ; for the manner of those times was in Confirming to use anointing. On the other side, against *Luciferians* which ratified only the Baptism of Hereticks, but disnulled their Confirmations and Consecrations, under pretence of the reason which hath been before specified, *Hereticks cannot give the Holy Ghost.* Saint *Jerome* proveth at large, that if Baptism by Hereticks be granted available to remission of sins, which no man receiveth without the Spirit, it must needs follow that the reason taken from disability of bestowing the Holy Ghost, was no reason wherefore the Church should admit Converts with any new Imposition of Hands. Notwithstanding, because it might be objected, that if the gift of the Holy Ghost do always joyn it self with true Baptism, the Church, which thinketh the Bishops Confirmation after other mens Baptism needful for the obtaining of the Holy Ghost, should hold an errour ; Saint *Jerom* hereunto maketh answer, that the cause of this observation is not any absolute impossibility of receiving the Holy Ghost by the Sacrament of Baptism, unless a Bishop adde after it the Imposition of Hands, but rather a certain congruity and fitness

n *Cyp. Epist.* 2. ad *Donat. cap.*2.

o *Euseb. Emis. Ser. de Penit.*

p *Aug. de Trin. lib.*15.*cap.*16. *Heb.* 6. 2.

q *Acts* 8.12.15
r *Hieron. adver. Lucif. cap.*4.

s *Cyp. Epist.*73. ad *Jubajanum.*

fitnefs to honour Prelacy with fuch preeeminences , becaufe the fafety of the Church dependeth upon the dignity of her chief Superiours, to whom if fome eminent Offices of power above others fhould not be given, there would be in the Church as many Schifms as Priefts. By which anfwer it appeareth his opinion was, that the Holy Ghoft is received in Baptifm ; that Confirmation is only a Sacramental complement ; that the reafon why Bifhops alone did ordinarily confirm, was not becaufe the benefit, grace, and dignity thereof is greater then of Baptifm, but rather for that by the Sacrament of Baptifm men being admitted into Gods Church, it was both reafonable and convenient that if he baptize them not unto whom the chiefeft authority and charge of their fouls belongeth, yet for honour fake, and in token of his fpiritual fuperiority over them, becaufe to [a]blefs is an act of authority, the performance of this annexed Ceremony fhould be fought for at his hands. Now what effect their Impofition of hands hath, either after Baptifm adminiftred by Hereticks or otherwife. S. *Jerome* in that place hath made no mention, becaufe all men underftood that in Converts it tendeth to the fruits of Repentance, and craveth in behalf of the Penitent , fuch grace as [b]*David* after his fall defired at the hands of God ; in others the fruit and benefit thereof is that which hath been before fhewed. Finally, fometime the caufe of fevering Confirmation from Baptifm, was in the parties that received Baptifm being Infants, at which age they might be very well admitted to live in the Family ; but becaufe to fight in the Army of God, to difcharge the duties of a Chriftian man, to bring forth the fruits, and to do the Works of the Holy Ghoft, their time of ability was not yet come (fo that Baptifm were not deferred) there could by ftay of their Confirmation no harm enfue but rather good. For by this means it came to pafs that Children in expectation thereof, were feafoned with the principles of true Religion, before malice and corrupt examples depraved their minds, a good foundation was laid betimes for direction of the courfe of their whole lives, the feed of the Church of God was preferved fincere and found, the Prelates and Fathers of Gods Family, to whom the cure of their fouls belonged , faw by tryal and examination of them a part of their own heavy burthen difcharged, reaped comfort by beholding the firft beginnings of true goodinefs in tender years, glorified him whofe praife they found in the mouths of Infants, and neglected not fo fit opportunity of giving every one Fatherly encouragement and exhortation. Whereunto Impofition of hands and prayer being added, our warrant for the great good effect thereof is the fame which Patriarks, Prophets, Priefts, Apoftles, Fathers, and Men of God have had for fuch their particular Invocations and Benedictions, as no man, I fuppofe, profeffing truth of Religion, will eafily think to have been without fruit. No, there is no caufe we fhould doubt of the benefit, but furely great caufe to make complaint of the deep neglect of this Chriftian duty, almoft with all them to whom by right of their place and calling the fame belongeth. Let them not take it in evil part, the thing is true, their fmall regard hereunto hath done harm to the Church of God. That which [c]errour rafhly uttereth in difgrace of good things may peradventure be fpunged out, when the print of thofe evils which are grown through neglect

a *Heb.*6.3.

b *Pfal.*51.10. 11, 12.

c *T.C.l.*1.*p.*199. Tell me why there fhould be any fuch

confirmation in the Church, being brought in by the fained Decretal Epiftles of the Popes (this is retracted by the fame, *T. C. lib.* 3. *pag.* 23 . That it is ancienter than the fained Decretal Epiftles, I yield unto) and no one tittle thereof being once found in the Scripture, and feeing that it hath been fo horribly abufd, and not neceffary, why ough. it not to be utterly abolifhed ? And thirdly, this Confirmation hath many dangerous points in it. The firft ftep of Popery in this Confirmation, is in the laying of Hands upon the Head of the Child, whereby the opinion of it that it is a Sacrament, is confirmed, efpecially when as the Prayer doth fay, that it is done according to the Example of the Apoftles, which is a manifeft untruth, and taken indeed from the Popifh Confirmation. The fecond is, for that the Bifhop, as he is called, muft be the only Minifter of it, whereby the Popifh opinion, which efteemeth it above Baptifm, is Confirmed. For whileft Baptifm may be miniftred of the Minifter, and not Confirmation but only of the Bifhop, there is great caufe of fufpition given to think that Baptifm is not fo precious a thing as Confirmation, feeing this was one of the principal reafons whereby that wicked opinion was eftablifhed in Popery. I do not here fpeak of the inconvenience, that men are conftrained with charges to bring their children oftentimes half a fcore miles for that, which if it were needfu, might be as well done at home in their own Parifhes. The third is, for that the Bookfaith, a caufe of ufing Confirmation is, that by Impofition of Hands and Prayer, the Children may receive ftrength and defence againft all temptations , whereas there is no promife, that by the laying on of Hands upon Children any fuch gift fhall be given ; and it maintaineth the Popifh diftinction, that the Spirit of God is given at Baptifm, unto remiffion of fins, and in Confirmation, unto ftrength.

will remain behind. Thus much therefore generally spoken, may serve for answer
unto their demands that require us to tell them, *Why there should be any such confirmation* in the Church, seeing we are not ignorant how earnestly they have protested against it, and how directly (although untruly, for so they are content to acknowledge) it hath by some of them been said, to be *first brought in by the fained Decretal Epistles of the Popes*; or why it should not be *utterly abolished, seeing that no one title thereof can be once found in the whole Scripture*, except the Epistle to the [a] *Hebrews* be Scripture; and again, seeing that how free soever it be now from a-
buse, if we look back to the times past, which wise men do always more respect
than the present, it *hath been* abused, and is found at the length *no* such *profitable
Ceremony* as the whole silly Church of Christ for the space of these sixteen hundred
years hath through want of experience imagined: Last of all, *seeing* also besides the
cruelty which is shewed towards poor Country people, who are fain sometimes to
let their Ploughs stand still, and with incredible wearisome toyl of their feeble bodies, to wander over Mountains and through Woods; it may be now and then little less then a whole *half score of miles* for a Bishops blessing, *which if it were needful, might as well be done at home in their own Parishes*, rather than they to purchase
it with so great loss and intolerable pain: There are, they say, in Confirmation besides this, *three terrible points*. The first is, *laying on of hands with pretence that the
same is done to the example of the Apostles*, which is not only, as they suppose, *a
manifest untruth* (for all the World doth know that the Apostles did never after
Baptism lay hands on any, and therefore [b] *S. Luke* which saith they did was much
deceived) but farther also we thereby teach men to think *imposition of Hands a Sacrament*, belike because it is a principle ingrafted by common light of Nature in the
minds of men, that all things done by Apostolick example must needs be Sacraments: The second high point of danger is, that by *tying Confirmation to the Bishop alone, there is great cause of suspition given to think that Baptism is not so precious a thing as Confirmation*; for will any man think that a velvet Coat is of no more
price then a linen Coif, knowing the one to be an ordinary garment, the other an
ornament which only Sergeants at Law do wear? Finally, to draw to an end of perils, the last and the weightiest hazard is, where the Book it self doth say that children by *imposition* of hands and prayer may receive *strength* against all temptation;
which speech as a two-edged sword doth both ways dangerously wound; partly, because it ascribeth grace to imposition of hands, whereby we are able no more to assure our selves in the warrant of *any promise from God* that his Heavenly grace shall
be given, then the Apostle was that himself should obtain grace by the 'bowing
of his knees to God; and partly, because by using the very word *strength* in this
matter, a word so apt to spread infection, we *maintain* with Popish Evangelists, an'
old forlorn *distinction* of the Holy Ghost, [d] bestowed upon Christs Apostles before
his Ascension into Heaven, and [e] *augmented* upon them afterwards, a distinction
of *grace* infused into Christian men by degrees, planted in them *at the first* by Baptism, *after* cherished, watred, and (be it spoken without offence) *strengthened* as by
other vertuous offices which Piety and true Religion teacheth, even so by this very
special Benediction whereof we speak, the Rite or Ceremony of Confirmation.

67. The grace which we have by the holy Eucharist, doth not begin but continue life. No man therefore receiveth this Sacrament before Baptism, because no
dead thing is capable of nourishment. That which groweth must of necessity first
live. If our bodies did not daily waste, food to restore them were a thing superfluous. And it may be that the grace of Baptism would serve to eternal life, were it
not that the state of our spiritual being is daily so much hindered and impaired after
Baptism. In that life therefore where neither body nor soul can decay, our souls
shall as little require this Sacrament as our bodies corporal nourishment. But as
long as the days of our warfare last, during the time that we are both subject to diminution and capable of augmentation in grace, the Words of our Lord and Saviour Christ will remain forceable, [f] *Except ye eat the Flesh of the Son of man, and
drink his Bloud, ye have no life in you.* Life being therefore proposed unto all men
as their end, they which by Baptism have laid the foundation and attained the first
beginning of a new life, have here their nourishment and food prescribed for *continuance*

[a] Heb. 6. 3.

[b] Acts 8. 15. 17

[c] Ephes. 3. 14.

[d] John 20. 22.
[e] Acts 1. 8.

Of the Sacra-
ment of the
Body and
Bloud of
Christ.

[f] Iohn 6. 53.

tinuance of life in them. Such as will live the life of God, muſt eat the Fleſh and drink the Bloud of the Son of man, becauſe this is a part of that dyet, which if we want, we cannot live. Whereas therefore in our Infancy we are incorporated into Chriſt, and by Baptiſm receive the grace of his Spirit without any ſenſe or feeling of the gift which God beſtoweth, in the Euchariſt we ſo receive the gift of God, that we know by grace what the grace is which God giveth us, the degrees of our own increaſe in holineſs and virtue we ſee and can judge of them, we underſtand that the ſtrength of our life begun in Chriſt is Chriſt, that his Fleſh is meat, and his Bloud drink, not by ſurmiſed imagination, but truly, even ſo truly, that through Faith we perceive in the Body and Bloud ſacramentally preſented the very taſte of eternal life, the grace of the Sacrament is here as the food which we eat and drink. This was it that ſome did exceedingly fear, leſt *Zwinglius* and *OEcolampadius* would bring to paſs, that men ſhould account of this Sacrament but only as of a ſhadow, deſtitute, empty, and void of Chriſt. But ſeeing that by opening the ſeveral opinions which have been he'd, they are grown, for ought I can ſee, on all ſides at the length to a general agreement, concerning that which alone is material, namely, the *real participation* of Chriſt, and of life in his Body and Bloud *by means of this Sacrament*, wherefore ſhould the World continue ſtill diſtracted and rent with ſo manifold contentions, when there remaineth now no Controverſie ſaying only about the ſubject *where* Chriſt is ? Yea, even in this point no ſide denieth, but that *the ſoul of man* is the receptacle of Chriſts preſence. Whereby the queſtion is yet driven to a narrower iſſue, nor doth any thing reſt doubtful but this, whether when the Sacrament is adminiſtred, Chriſt be whole *within man only*, or elſe his Body and Bloud be alſo externally ſeated in the very conſecrated Elements themſelves : which opinion they that defend, are driven either to *Conſubſtantiate* and incorporate Chriſt with Elements Sacramental, or to *Tranſubſtantiate* and change their ſubſtance into his ; and ſo the one to hold him real y but inviſibly moulded up with the ſubſtance of thoſe Elements, the other to hide him under the only viſible ſhew of Bread and Wine, the ſubſtance whereof, as they imagine, is aboliſhed, and his ſucceeded in the ſame room. All things conſidered and compared with that ſucceſs, which truth hath hitherto had by ſo bitter conflicts with errours in this point, ſhall I wiſh that men would more give themſelves to meditate with ſilence what we have, by the Sacrament, and leſs to diſpute of the manner how ? If any man ſuppoſe that this were too great ſtupidity and dulneſs, let us ſee whether the Apoſtles of our Lord themſelves have not done the like. It appeareth by many examples, that they of their own diſpoſition were very ſcrupulous and inquiſitive, yea, in other caſes of leſs importance and leſs difficulty always apt to move queſtions. How cometh it to paſs that ſo few words of ſo high a myſtery being uttered, they receive with gladneſs the gift of Chriſt, and make no ſhew of doubt or ſcruple ? The reaſon hereof is not dark to them which have any thing at all obſerved how the powers of the mind are wont to ſtir, when that which we infinitely long for, preſenteth it ſelf above and beſides expectation. Curious and intricate ſpeculations do hinder, they abate, they quench ſuch inflamed motions of delight and joy, as divine graces uſe to raiſe when extraordinarily they are preſent. The mind therefore feeling preſent joy, is always marvellous unwilling to admit any other cogitation, and in that caſe caſteth off thoſe diſputes whereunto the intellectual part at other times eaſily draweth. A manifeſt effect whereof may be noted, if we compare with our Lords Diſciples in the twentieth of *John*, the people that are ſaid in the ſixth of *John* to have gone after him to *Capernaum*. Theſe leaving him on the one ſide the Sea of *Tiberias*, and finding him again as ſoon as themſelves by ſhip were arrived on the contrary ſide, whither they knew that by ſhip he came not, and by Land the journey was longer then according to the time he could have to travel, as they wondered, ſo they asked alſo, *Rabbi, when cameſt thou hither ?* The Diſciples, when Chriſt appeared to them in far more ſtrange and miraculous manner, moved no queſtion, but rejoyced greatly in that they ſaw. For why ? The one ſort beheld only that in Chriſt which they knew was more then natural, but yet their affection was not rapt therewith through any great extraordinary gladneſs ; the other when they looked on Chriſt, were not ignorant that they ſaw the Well-ſpring of their own everlaſting

John 6. 16.

everlasting felicity, the one, because they enjoyed not, disputed; the other dispu-
red not, because they enjoyed. If then the presence of Christ with them did so
much move, judge what their thoughts and affections were at the time of this new
presentation of Christ, not before their eyes, but within their Souls. They had
learned before, that his Flesh and Bloud are the true cause of eternal Life, that
this they are not by the bare force of their own substance, but through the dignity
and worth of his Person, which offered them up by way of Sacrifice for the life of
the whole World, and doth make them still effectual thereunto; Finally, that to
us they are life in particular, by being particularly received. Thus much they knew,
although as yet they understood not perfectly to what effect or issue the same would
come, till at the length being assembled for no other cause which they could imagine, but to have eaten the Passeover only that *Moses* appointed, when they saw
their Lord and Master with hands and eyes lifted up to Heaven first bless and consecrate for the endless good of all generations till the Worlds end, the chosen Elements of Bread and Wine, which Elements made for ever the instruments of life
by vertue of his Divine Benediction, they being the first that were commanded to
receive from him, the first which were warranted by his promise, that not only unto them at the present time, but to whomsoever they and their Successors after them
did duely administer the same, those mysteries should serve as conduits of life and
conveyances of his Body and Bloud unto them, was it possible th.y should hear
that voice, *Take, eat, this is my Body, drink ye all of this, this is my Bloud*; possible that doing what was required, and believing what was promised, the same
should have present effect in them, and not fill them with a kind of fearful admiration at the Heaven which they saw in themselves? They had at that time a Sea of
comfort and joy to wade in, and we by that which they did are taught, that this
Heavenly Food is given for the satisfying of our empty souls, and not for the exercising of our curious and subtile wits. If we doubt what those admirable words
may import, let him be our Teacher for the meaning of Christ, to whom Christ was
himself a School-master, let our Lords Apostle be his Interpreter, content we our
selves with his explication, My Body, *The communion of my Body*; My Bloud, *The
communion of my Bloud*. Is there any thing more expedite, cleer and easie, then
that as Christ is termed our life, because through him we obtain life, so the parts of
this Sacrament are his Body and Bloud, for that they are so to us, who receiving
them, receive that by them which they are termed? The Bread and Cup are his
Body and Bloud, because they are causes instrumental, upon the receit whereof the
participation of his Body and Bloud ensueth. For that which produceth any certain
effect, is not vainly nor improperly said to be that very effect wh. reunto it tendeth.
Every cause is in the effect which groweth from it. Our souls and bodies quickened
to eternal Life are effects, the cause whereof is the Person of Christ, his Body and
Bloud are the true Well-spring out of which this life floweth. So that his Body
and Bloud are in that very subject whereunto they minister life, not only by effect
or operation, even as the influence of the Heavens is in Plants, Beasts, Men, and
in every thing which they quicken, but also by a far more divine and mystical kind
of Union, which maketh us one with him, even as He and the Father are one. The
real presence of Christs most blessed Body and Bloud, is not therefore to be sought
for in the Sacrament, but in the worthy Receiver of the Sacrament. And with
this the very order of our Saviours words agreeth, first, *Take and eat*; then, *This
is my Body which was broken for you*: first, *Drink ye all of this*, then followeth, *Marke* 14. 22.
*This is my Bloud of the New Testament, which is shed for many for the remission of
sin*, I see not which way it should be gathered by the Words of Christ, when and
where the Bread is his Body, or the Cup his Bloud, but only in the very heart and
soul of him which receiveth them. As for the Sacraments they really exhibite, but
for ought we can gather out of that which is written of them, they are not really,
nor do really contain in themselves that grace which with them or by them it pleaseth God to bestow. If on all sides it be confest, that the grace of Baptism is poured into the soul of man, that by Water we receive it, although it be neither seated
in the Water, nor the Water changed into it, what should induce men to think that
the grace of the Eucharist must needs be in the Eucharist, before it can be in us that

M m   receive

receive it ? The fruit of the Eucharist is the participation of the Body and Bloud of Christ. There is no sentence of Holy Scripture which saith, that we cannot by this Sacrament be made partakers of his Body and Bloud, except they be first contained in the Sacrament, or the Sacrament converted into them. *This is my Body,* and *This is my Bloud,* being words of promise, sith we all agree, that by the Sacrament Christ doth really and truly in us perform his promise, why do we vainly trouble our selves with so fierce contentions, whether by Consubstantiation, or else by Transubstantiation the Sacrament it self be first possessed with Christ or no ? A thing which no way can either further or hinder us howsoever it stand, because our participation of Christ in this Sacrament dependeth on the co-operation of his Omnipotent Power, which maketh it his Body and Bloud to us, whether with change or without alteration of the Element such as they imagine, we need not greatly to care not inquire. Take therefore that wherein all agree, and then consider by it self what cause why the rest in question should not rather be left as superfluous than urged as necessary. It is on all sides plainly confest, first, That this Sacrament is a true and a real participation of Christ, who thereby imparteth himself, even his whole intire Person, *as a mystical head,* unto every soul that receiveth him, and that every such Receiver doth thereby incorporate or unite himself unto Christ as *a mystical member* of him, yea of them also whom he acknowledgeth to be his own : Secondly, That to whom *the Person of Christ* is thus communicated, to them he giveth by the same Sacrament his holy Spirit to sanctifie them, as it sanctifieth him which is their Head : Thirdly, That what *merit, force, or vertue soever there is in his sacrificed body and bloud,* we freely, fully, and wholly have it by this Sacrament : Fourthly, That *the effect thereof in us is a real transmutation of our souls and bodies* from sin to righteousness, from death and corruption to immortality and life : Fifthly, That because the Sacrament being of it self but a corruptible and earthly Creature, must needs be thought an unlikely Instrument to work so admirable effects in Man, we are therefore to rest our selves altogether upon *the strength of his glorious power,* who is able and will bring to pass that the Bread and Cup which he giveth us shall be truly the thing he promiseth. It seemeth therefore much amiss, that against them whom they term Sacramentaries, so many invective Discourses are made, all running upon two points, that the Eucharist is not a bare sign or figure only, and that the efficacy of his Body and Bloud is not all we receive in this Sacrament. For no man, having read their Books and Writings which are thus traduced, can be ignorant that both these Assertions they plainly confess to be most true. They do not so interpret the Words of Christ as if the name of his Body did import but the figure of his Body, and to be, were only to signifie his Bloud. They grant that these holy Mysteries received in due manner, do instrumentally both make us partakers of the grace of that Body and Bloud which were given for the life of the World, and besides also impart unto us even in true and real, though mystical manner, the very Person of our Lord himself, whole, perfect, and intire, as hath been shewed. Now whereas all three opinions do thus far accord in one, that strong conceit which two of the three have imbraced as touching a Literal, Corporal, and Oral manducation of the very substance of his Flesh and Bloud, is surely an opinion no where delivered in Holy Scripture, whereby they should think themselves bound to believe it, and (to speak with the softest terms we can use) greatly prejudiced in that when some others did so conceive of eating his Flesh, our Saviour to abate that errour in them, gave them directly to understand how his Flesh so eaten could profit them nothing, because the words which he spake were Spirit, that is to say, they had a reference to a mystical participation, which mystical participation giveth life. Wherein there is small appearance of likelihood, that his meaning should be only to make them Marcionites by inversion, and to teach them that as *Marcion* did think, Christ seemed to be man, but was not, so they contrariwise should believe that Christ in truth would so give them as they thought his flesh to eat ; but yet left the horrour thereof should offend them, he would not seem to do that he did. When they which have this opinion of Christ in that blessed Sacrament go about to explain themselves, and to open after what manner things are brought to pass, the one sort lay the Union of Christs Deity with his Man-hood, as their

first

first foundation and ground ; from thence they inferre a power which the Body of Christ hath thereby to present it self in all places ; out of which ubiquity of his Body they gather the presence thereof with that sanctified Bread and Wine of our Lords Table ; the conjunction of his Body and Bloud with those Elements they use as an Argument, to shew how the Bread may as well in that respect be termed a *Acceptum pancm & di-* his Body, because his Body is therewith joyned, as the Son of God may be named *stributum Dif-* Man, by reason that God and Man in the person of Christ are united ; to this they *cipulis corpus* adde, how the Words of Christ commanding us to eat, must needs import, that as *suum illum fe-* he hath coupled the substance of his Flesh, and the substance of Bread together, so *cit, hoc est cor-* we together should receive both ; Which Labyrinth as the other sort doth justly *pus meum di-* shun, so the way which they take to the same Inne is somewhat more short, but no *cendo, id est,* whit more certain. For through Gods Omnipotent Power they imagine that Tran- *figura corporis* substantiation followeth upon the words of Consecration, and upon Transubstantia- *mei. Figura* tion the participation of Christs both Body and Bloud, in the only shape of Sacra- *autem non fu-* mental Elements. So that they all three do plead Gods Omnipotency, Sacramenta- *isset nisi veri-* ries to that alteration, which the rest confess he accomplisheth ; the Patrons of *tatis esset cor-* Transubstantiation over and besides that to the change of one substance into ano- *pus, cum vacua* ther ; the Followers of Consubstantiation, to the kneading up of both substances, *res quod est* as it were, into one lump: Touching the sentence of Antiquity in this cause : First, for *guram capere* as much as they knew that the force of this Sacrament doth necessarily pre-suppose *non posset.* the Verity of Christs both Body and Bloud, they used oftentimes the same as an Ar- Tertul. contra gument to prove that Christ hath as truly the substance of Man as of God, because *Marc. l.4. c.40.* here we receive Christ and those graces which flow from him in that he is Man. So *b secundum* that if he have no such being, neither can the Sacrament have any such meaning as *hac* (that is to we all confess it hath. Thus *Tertullian*, thus *Ireny*, thus *Theodoret* disputeth. say, if it should Again, as evident it is how they teach that Christ is *personally* there present whole, be true which albeit a part of Christ be *corporally* absent from thence, that *Christ assisting this* Hereticks have Heavenly Banquet with his personal and true presence, *doth by his own Divine* taught, denying Power adde to the natural substance thereof supernatural efficacy, which addition *that Christ* to the nature of those consecrated Elements, changeth them and maketh them th t *of man) nec* unto us, which otherwise they could not be , that to us they are thereby made such *Dominus san-* instruments, as *mystically, yet truly ; invisibly, yet really work our communion *guine suo re-* or fellowship with the person of Jesus Christ, as well in that he is Man as God, *charistia com-* our participation also in the fruit, grace and efficacy of his Body and Bloud ; where- *municatio san-* upon there ensueth a kind of Transubstantiation in us , a true change both of soul *guinis ejus* *erit , nec*

panis quem frangimus communicatio corporis ejus est. Sanguis enim non est, nisi à venis & carnibus & à reliqua quæ est secundum hominem substantia. Irenæus lib.5.cap.1. c *Ei τόνυν τὸ ὁν◌̄ σωμα◌τ◌ ἀλήτυπ◌̄ τὰ θεῖα μυςήϱιæ, σῶμα ἄρα ὁτι ᾖ νυ◌̃ τὸ δεσπότ◌ τὸ σω̃μα. ὐκ ἐις θεότητος φύσιν μεταςκλύθη ἀλλὰ θείας ἀ◌̇ξίης ἀναπλεσθέν.*Theod. Dialog. *Ασύγχυτος.* d *Sacramenta quidem quantum in se est sine propria virtute esse non possunt, neu ullo modo se absentat majestas mysteriis.* Cypr. de Cœn.cap.7. e *Sacramento visibili ineffabiliter divina in se infudit essentia ut esset Religioni circa Sacramenta devotio.* Idem cap. 6. *Invisibilis Sacerdos visibiles creaturas in substantiam corporis & san-guinis sui verbo suo secreta potestate convertit.* In spiritualibus Sacramentis verbi præcipit virtus & servit effectus. Euf. Emissen.hom.5.de Pasch. f *Τὰ σύμβολα τᾳ δεσποτικ◌ σώμα◌τος τε ◌̃ αἵματος ἀλλα μὲν εἰσι πϱὸ τῆς ἱεϱατικῆς ἐπι-κλήσεως, με̌α δὲ ◌̃ τὴν ἐπίκλησιν με̌αβάλλεσι ◌̃ ἕτεϱα γίνεται. Ἀλλ᾽ ἐκ οἰκείας ἐξίςαται φύσεως. Μένει ◌̃ ἐπι τῆς πϱοτέϱας οὐσίας ◌̃ τῆς χήμα◌ιος ◌̃ τῆ εἰδᵳς, ◌θεϱατά ◌̃ ἀπὰ οἷα ◌̃ πϱότεϱον ιω voεῖται δὲ ἃ ◌εϱ ἐγένετο ◌̃ πιςεύεται ◌̃ πϱοσκυνεῖται ὡς ἐκεῖνα ὄν◌α ἅ◌εϱ πιςεύεται.* Theodor. Ex quo à Domino dictum est, Hoc facite in *meam commemorationem, hac est caro mea, & hic est sanguis meus, quotiescunque his verbis & hac fide actum est, panis iste supersubstantialis, & calix benedictione solenni sacratus, ad totius hominis vitam salutemque proficit.* Cypr. de Cœn. cap.3. *Immortalitatis alimonia datur, à communibus cibis differens, corporalis substantia retinens speciem, sed virtutis divinæ invisibili efficientia probans adesse præsentiam.* Ibid.cap.2. g *Sensibilibus Sacramentis inest vita æternæ effectus, & non tam corporali quam spirituali transitione Christo unimur.Ipse enim & panis & caro, & sanguis idem c busq; substantia & vita factus est Ecclesia suæ quam corpus suum appellat, dans ei participationem spiritus.* Ibidem cap.5. *Nostra & ipsius conjunctio nec mi◌ cet personas, nec unit substantias , sed effectu conjociat & cor fæderat voluntat◌s,* cap. 6. *Mansio nostra in ipso est manducatio, & potus quasi quædam incorporatio* cap 9. *Ille est in patre per naturam divinitatis, nos in eo per corporalem ejus Nativitatem, ille rursus in nobis per Sacramentorum mysterium.* Hier. de Trin. 8. h *Panis hic æzymus cibus verus & sincera per speciem & Sacramentum nos tactu sanctificat, fide illuminat, veritate Christo conformat.*Cypr.de Cœn.cap.6. No ι aliud agit participatio corporis & sanguinis Christi, quàm ut in id *quod sumimus transeamus, & in quo mortui & sepulti & correscuscitati sumus, ipsum per omnia & spiritu & carne ge-stemus.* Leo de Pass.Serm.14. *Quemadmodum qui est à terra panis percipiens Dei vocationem* (idest tacta invec◌ one di-vini numinis) *jam non communis panis est, sed Eucharistia ex duabus rebus conflans, terrena & cælesti : sic & corpora nostra percipientia Eucharistiam, jam non sunt corruptibilia spem resurrectionis habentia,* Iren. l.4. c.3. *Qu niam ja u-taris caro verbo Dei quod naturaliter vita est conjuncta, vivifica affecta est quando eam comedimus, tunc vita◌ h b◌mus in nobis illi carni conjuncti, quæ vita effecta est.* Cyril. in Johan.lib.4.cap.14.

and

and body, an alteration from death to life. In a word, it appeareth not, that of all the ancient Fathers of the Church, any one did ever conceive or imagine other than only a myſtical participation of Chriſts both Body and Bloud in the Sacrament, neither are their ſpeeches concerning the change of the Elements themſelves into the Body and Bloud of Chriſt ſuch, that a man can thereby in conſcience aſſure himſelf it was their meaning to perſwade the world either of a corporal Conſubſtantiation of Chriſt with thoſe Sanctified and Bleſſed Elements before we receive them, or of the like Tranſubſtantiation of them into the Body and Bloud of Chriſt. Which both to our myſtical Communion with Chriſt are ſo unneceſſary, that the Fathers, who plainly hold but this myſtical Communion, cannot eaſily be thought to have meant any other change of Sacramental Elements, then that which the ſame Spiritual Communion did require them to hold. Theſe things conſidered, how ſhould that mind, which loving Truth, and ſeeking Comfort out of Holy Myſteries, hath not perhaps the leiſure, perhaps not the wit nor capacity to tread out ſo endleſs Mazes, as the intricate Diſputes of this cauſe have led men into, how ſhould a vertuouſly diſpoſed mind better reſolve with it ſelf then thus ? " Variety of judge-
" ments and opinions argueth obſcurity in thoſe things whereabout they differ.
" But that which all parts receive for Truth, that which every one having ſifted, is
" by no one denyed or doubted of, muſt needs be matter of infallible certainty.
" Whereas therefore there are but three Expoſitions made of, *This is my Body*, the
" firſt, This is in it ſelf before participation *really and truly the natural ſubſtance of*
" *my Body, by reaſon of the coexiſtence which my Omnipotent Body hath with the ſan-*
" *ctified Element of Bread, which is the Lutherans Interpretation:* The ſecond, This is
" in it ſelf and before participation *the very true and natural ſubſtance of my Body,*
" *by force of that Deity which with the words of conſecration aboliſheth the ſubſtance*
" *of Bread, and ſubſtituteth in the place thereof my Body, which is the Popiſh con-*
" *ſtruction:* The laſt, *This hallowed food through concurrence of divine power, is in*
" *verity and truth, unto faithful Receivers, inſtrumentally a cauſe of that myſtical*
" *participation, whereby as I make my ſelf wholly theirs, ſo I give them in hand an*
" *actual poſſeſſion of all ſuch ſaving grace as my ſacrificed body can yield, and as their*
" *ſouls do preſently need: this is* to them, and in them *my Body:* Of theſe three re-
" hearſed Interpretations, the laſt hath in it nothing but what the reſt do all ap-
" prove and acknowledge to be moſt true, nothing but that which the words of
" Chriſt are on all ſides confeſt to inforce, nothing but that which the Church of
" God hath always thought neceſſary, nothing but that which alone is ſufficient for
" every Chriſtian man to believe concerning the uſe and force of this Sacrament;
" finally, nothing but that wherewith the writings of all Antiquity are conſonant,
" and all Chriſtian Confeſſions agreeable. And as truth in what kind ſoever is by
" no kind of truth gain-ſaid, ſo the mind which reſteth it ſelf on this, is never
" troubled with thoſe perplexities which the other do both find, by means of ſo
" great contradiction between their opinions, and true principles of reaſon ground-
" ed upon Experience, Nature and Senſe. Which albeit with boyſtorous courage
" and breath they ſeem oftentimes to blow away, yet whoſo obſerveth, how again
" they labour and ſweat by ſubtilty of wit to make ſome ſhew of agreement be-
" tween their peculiar conceits, and the general Edicts of Nature, muſt needs per-
" ceive they ſtruggle with that which they cannot fully maſter. Beſides, ſith of that
" which is proper to themſelves, their Diſcourſes are hungry and unpleaſant, full
" of tedious and irkſome labour, heartleſs and hitherto without fruit; on the other
" ſide read we them, or hear we others, be they of our own or of ancienter times,
" to what part ſoever they be thought to incline touching that whereof there is
" controverſie, yet in this where they all ſpeak but one thing, their Diſcourſes are
" Heavenly, their words ſweet as the Honey-comb, their tongues melodiouſly tu-
" ned Inſtruments, their ſentences meer conſolation and joy: Are we not hereby
" almoſt even with voice from Heaven admoniſhed which we may ſafelieſt cleave
" unto ? He which hath ſaid of the one Sacrament, *Waſh and be clean*, hath ſaid con-
" cerning the other likewiſe, *Eat and Live*. If therefore without any ſuch particu-
" lar and ſolemn warrant as this is, that poor diſtreſſed Woman coming unto Chriſt
" for health, could ſo conſtantly reſolve her ſelf, *May I but touch the ſkirt of his*
                                                      " *garment,*

" *garment, I shall be whole*, what moveth us to argue of the manner how life should
" come by bread, our duty being here but to take what is offered, and most assu-
" redly to rest perswaded of this, that can we but eat we are safe ? when I behold
" with mine eyes some small and scarce discernable Grain or Seed whereof Nature
" maketh a promise that a tree shall come, and when afterwards of that tree any
" skilful Artificer undertaketh to frame some exquisite and curious Work, I look for
" the event, I move no question about performance either of the one or of the o-
" ther. Shall I simply credit Nature in things natural, shall I in things artificial re-
" lye my self on Art, never offering to make doubt, and in that which is above
" both Art and Nature refuse to believe the Author of both, except he acquaint me
" with his wayes, and lay the secret of his skill before me ? Where God himself
" doth speak those things which either for height and sublimity of matter, or else
" for secresie of performance we are not able to reach unto, as we may be ignorant
" without danger, so it can be no disgrace to confess we are ignorant. Such as love
" Piety will, as much as in them lieth, know all things that God commandeth, but
" especially the duties of service which they owe to God. As for his dark and hid-
" den works, they preferre, as becometh them in such cases, simplicity of Faith be-
" fore that knowledge, which curiously sifting what it should adore, and disputing
" too boldly of that which the wit of man cannot search, chilleth for the most part
" all warmth of zeal, and bringeth soundness of belief many times into great ha-
" zard. Let it therefore be sufficient for me presenting my self at the Lords Ta-
" ble, to know what there I receive from him, without searching or enquiring of
" the manner how Christ performeth his promise ; let disputes and questions, ene-
" mies to Piety, abatements of true devotion, and hitherto in this cause but over-
" patiently heard, let them take their rest ; let curious and sharp-witted men beat
" their heads about what Questions themselves will, the very letter of the Word of
" Christ giveth plain security, that these mysteries do as nails fasten us to his very
" Cross, that by them we draw out, as touching efficacy, force and vertue, even the
" bloud of his gored side ; in the wounds of our Redeemer we there dip our tongues,
" we are died red both within and without, our hunger is satisfied and our thirst for
" ever quenched, they are things wonderful which he feeleth, great which he seeth,
" and unheard of which he uttereth, whose soul is possest of this Pascall Lamb,
" and made joyful in the strength of this new wine, this bread hath in it more than
" the substance which our eyes behold, this Cup hallowed with solemn Benediction,
" availeth to the endless life and welfare both of Soul and Body, in that it serveth
" as well for a Medicine to heal our infirmities and purge our sins, as for a Sacrifice
" of Thanksgiving, which touching it sanctifieth, it enlightneth with belief, it tru-
" ly conformeth us unto the Image of Jesus Christ ; what these Elements are in
" themselves it skilleth not, it is enough that to me which take them, they are the
" Body and Bloud of Christ, his promise in witness hereof sufficeth, his Word he
" knoweth which way to accomplish, why should any cogitation possess the mind
of a faithful Communicant but this, *O my God thou art true, O my soul thou art hap-*
py. Thus therefore we see, that howsoever mens opinions do otherwise vary, neverthelefs touching Baptism and the Supper of the Lord, we may with consent of
the whole Christian world conclude they are necessary, the one to initiate or begin,
the other to consummate or make perfect our life in Christ.

68. In administring the Sacrament of the Body and Blood of Christ, the supposed faults of the Church of *England* are not greatly material, and therefore it shall
suffice to touch them in few words. *The first is, that we do not use in a generality*
once for all to say to Communicants, Take, eat, and drink, *but unto every particular*
person, Eat thou, drink thou, *which is according to the Popish manner, and not the*
form that our Saviour did use. Our second oversight is by gesture. For in kneeling
there hath been Superstition ; sitting agreeth better to the action of a Supper ; and our
Saviour using that which was most fit, did himself not kneel. A third accusation is
for not examining all Communicants, whose knowledge in the mystery of the Gospel
should that way be made manifest, a thing every where, they say, used in the Apostles
times, because all things necessary were used, and this in their opinion is necessary, yea,
it is commanded, in as much as the [a] *Levites are commanded to prepare the people for*

Of faults no-
ted in the
form of ad-
ministring the
holy Commu-
nion.

[a] 2 Chro. 35. 6.

M m 3   *the*

the *Passeover, and examination is a part of their preparation, our Lords Supper in place of the Passeover. The fourth thing misliked is, that against the Apostles* pro-hibition *to have any familiarity at all with notorious Offenders, Papists being not of the Church are admitted to our very Communion, before they have by their Religious and Gospel-like behaviour purged themselves of that suspition of Popery which their for-mer life hath caused. They are Dogs, Swine, unclean Beasts, Forreigners and Stran-gers from the Church of God, and therefore ought not to be admitted though they offer themselves. We are fitly condemned, in as much as when there have been store of peo-ple to hear Sermons and Service in the Church, we suffer the Communion to be mini-stred to a few. It is not enough that our Book of Common Prayer hath godly Exhorta-tions to move all thereunto which are present. For it should not suffer a few to Commu-nicate, it should by Ecclesiastical Discipline and Civil punishment provide, that such as would with-draw themselves, might be brought to Communicate according both to the* c *Law of God and the ancient Church Canons. In the sixth and last place cometh the enormity of imparting this Sacrament privately unto the sick.* Thus far accused, we answer briefly to the first, that seeing God by Sacraments doth apply in parti-cular unto every mans person the grace which himself hath provided for the benefit of all Man-kind, there is no cause, why administring the Sacraments we should for-bear to express that in our forms of speech, which he by his Word and Gospel tea-cheth all to believe. In the one Sacrament, *I baptize thee* displeaseth them not. If *Eat thou* in the other offend them, their fancies are no Rules for Churches to fol-low. Whether Christ at his last Supper did speak generally once to all, or to every one in particular, is a thing uncertain. His words are recorded in that form which serveth best for the setting down with historical brevity what was spoken, they are no manifest proof that he spake but once unto all which did then Communicate, much less that we in speaking unto every Communicant severally do amiss, although it were cleer that we herein do otherwise than Christ did. Our imitation of him con-sisteth not in tying scrupulously our selves unto his syllables, but rather in speaking by the Heavenly direction of that inspired Divine Wisdom, which teacheth divers ways to one end, and doth therein controul their boldness, by whom any profita-ble way is censured as reproveable, only under colour of some small difference from great Examples going before, to do throughout every the like Circumstance, the same which Christ did in this action, were by following his foot-steps in that sort to erre more from the purpose he aimed at, than we now do by not following them with so nice and severe strictness. They little weigh with themselves how dull, how heavy, and almost how without sense the greatest part of the common multi-tude every where is, who think it either unmeet or unnecessary to put them, even man by man, especially at that time, in mind whereabout they are. It is true that in Sermons we do not use to repeat our sentences severally to every particular hea-rer, a strange madness it were if we should. The softness of wax may induce a wise man to set his stamp or image thereon; it perswadeth no man that because Wooll hath the like quality, it may therefore receive the like impression. So the reason taken from the use of Sacraments in that they are Instruments of grace unto every particular man, may with good congruity lead the Church to frame accord-ingly her words in administration of Sacraments, because they easily admit this form, which being in Sermons a thing impossible, without apparent ridiculous ab-surdity, agreement of Sacraments with Sermons in that which is alledged as a rea-sonable proof of conveniency; for the one proveth not the same allegation imper-tinent, because it doth not inforce the other to be administred in like sort. For equal principles do then avail unto equal conclusions, when the matter whereunto we ap-ply them is equal, and not else. Our kneeling at Communions is the gesture of Piety. If we did there present our selves but to make some shew or dumb resem-blance of a Spiritual Feast, it may be that sitting were the fitter Ceremony; but coming as Receivers of inestimable grace at the hands of God, what doth better beseem our bodies at that hour, than to be sensible Witnesses of minds unfainedly humbled? Our Lord himself did that which custom and long usage had made fit; we, that which fitness and great decency hath made usual. The tryal of our selves before we eat of this Bread and drink of this Cup, is by express Commandment eve-

Marginal notes:

b 1 *Cor.*5.11.

c *Numb.* 3. 13. *Can.* 9. *Apost.* *Concil.* 2. *Bras.* cap. 83.

d *T.C.l.*3.*p.*166 Besides that it is good to leave the Po-pish forme in those things, which we may so convenient-ly do, it is best to come as neer the man-ner of celebra-tion of the Supper which our Saviour Christ used as may be. And if it be a good Argument to prove that therefore we must rather say, *Take thou,* than *Take ye,* because the Sacrament is an application of the benefits of Christ, it be-hoveth that the Preacher should direct his Admoniti-ons particular-ly one after a-nother unto all those which hear his Ser-mon, which is a thing absurd.

e *T.C.l.*1 *p.*165 Kneeling car-rieth a shew of worship, sitting agreeth better with the action of the Supper, Christ and his Apostles knee-led not.

ry mans precise duty. As for necessity of calling others unto account besides our selves, albeit we be not thereunto drawn by any great strength which is in their Arguments, who first press us with it as a thing necessary, by affirming that the Apostles did use it, and then prove the Apostles to have used it, by affirming it to be necessary; again, albeit we great'y muse how they can avouch, that God did command the Levites to prepare their Brethren against the Feast of Passeover, and that the Examination of them was a part of their preparation, when the place alledged to this purpose doth but charge the Levite, saying, *Make ready Laahhechem for your Brethren*, to the end they may do according to the Word of the Lord by *Moses*. Wherefore in the self-same place it followeth how Lambs, and Kids, and Sheep, and Bullocks were delivered unto the Levites, and that thus *the service was made ready*: It followeth likewise how the Levites having in such sort provided for the people, they made provision for *themselves, and for the Priests, the Sons of Aaron*; so that confidently from hence to conclude the necessity of Examination, argueth their wonderful great forwardness in framing all things to serve their turn, nevertheless the Examination of Communicants when need requireth, for the profitable use it may have in such cases, we reject not. Our fault in admitting Popish Communicants, is it in that we are forbidden to eat, and therefore much more to communicate, with notorious Malefactors? The name of a Papist is not given unto any man for being a notorious Malefactor. And the crime wherewith we are charged, is suffering of Papists to communicate, so that be their life and conversation whatsoever in the sight of man, their Popish opinions are in this case laid as bars and exceptions against them, yea those opinions which they have held in former times, although they now both profess by word, and offer to shew by fact the contrary. All this doth not justifie us which ought not (they say) to admit them in any wise, till their Gospel-like behaviour have removed all suspition of Popery from them, because Papists are *Dogs, Swine, Beasts, Forreigners and Strangers* from the House of God, in a word, they are *not of the Church*. What the terms of Gospel-like behaviour may include, is obscure and doubtful. But of the *visible Church of Christ* in this present World, from which they separate all Papists, we are thus perswaded: *Church* is a word which Art hath devised, thereby to sever and distinguish that society of men, which professeth the true Religion from the rest which profess it not. There have been in the world from the very first foundation thereof, but they would three Religions, *Paganism*, which lived in the blindness of corrupt and depraved Nature; *Judaism*, imbracing the Law which reformed Heathenish Impiety, and taught Salvation to be looked for through One, whom God in the last days would send and exalt to be Lord of all; finally, *Christian Belief*, which yieldeth obedience to the Gospel of Jesus Christ, and acknowledgeth him the Saviour whom God did promise. Seeing then that *the Church* is a name, which Art hath given to *Professours of true Religion*, as they which will define a man, are to pass by those qualities wherein one man doth excell another, and to take only those essential properties, whereby a man doth differ from creatures of other kinds: So he that will teach what *the Church* is, shall never rightly perform the work whereabout he goeth, till that *in matter of Religion* he touch that difference which severeth the *Churches Religion* from theirs who are not the Church. *Religion* being therefore a matter partly of *contemplation*, partly of *action*, we must define the Church, which is a religious society, by such differences as do properly explain the essence of such things, that is to say, by the object or matter whereabout the contemplations and actions of the Church are properly conversant. For so all knowledges and all vertues are defined. Whereupon, because the *only object* which separateth ours from other Religions, is *Jesus Christ*, in whom none but the Church doth believe, and whom none but the Church doth worship, we find that accordingly the Apostles do every where distinguish hereby the Church from Infidels and from Jews, accounting *them which call upon the name of our Lord Jesus Christ to be his Church*. If we go lower, we shall but adde unto this certain casual and variable accidents, which are not properly of the being, but make only for the happier and better being of the Church of God, either indeed, or in mens opinions and conceits. This is the errour of all Popish definitions that hitherto have been brought. They define not the Church by that which

the

Marginal notes:

a *T.C.l.1.p.*164 All things necessary were used in the Churches of God in the Apostles times, but examination was a necessary thing, therefore used. In the Book of *Chronicles*, 2 *Chron.* 35, 6. the Levites were commanded to prepare the people to the receiving of the Passeover, in place whereof we have the Lords Supper. Now Examination being a part of preparation, it followeth that here is commandment of the Examination.

b 1 *Cor.*5.11. *T.C. L.1, p.*167. c Although they would receive the communion, yet they ought to be kept back until such time as by their Religious and Gospel-like behaviour, they have purged themselves of that suspition of Poperie, of which their former life and conversation hath caused to be conceived. *T.C. L.1, p.*167.

the Church effentially is, but by that wherein they imagine their own more perfect then the reft are. Touching parts of eminency and perfection, parts likewife of imperfection and defect in the Church of God, they are infinite, their degrees and differences no way poffible to be drawn unto any certain account. There is not the leaft contention and variance, but it blemifheth fomewhat the Unity that ought to be in the Church of Chrift, which notwithftanding may have not only without offence or breach of concord her manifold varieties in Rites and Ceremonies of Religion, but alfo her ftrifes and contentions many times, and that about matters of no fmall importance ; yea, her fchifms, factions, and fuch other evils whereunto the Body of the Church is fubject, found and fick remaining both of the fame body, as long as both parts retain by outward profeffion that vital fubftance of truth, which maketh Chriftian Religion to differ from theirs which acknowledge not our Lord Jefus Chrift the bleffed Saviour of Mankind, give no credit to his glorious Gofpel, and have his Sacraments, the feals of eternal life, in derifion. Now the priviledge of the vifible Church of God (for of that we fpeak) is to be herein like the Ark of *Noah*, that, for any thing we know to the contrary, all without it are loft fheep ; yet in this was the Ark of *Noah* priviledged above the Church, that whereas none of them which were in the one could perifh, numbers in the other are caft away, becaufe to eternal life our profeffion is not enough. Many things exclude from the Kingdom of God, although from the Church they feparate not. In the Church there arife fundry grievous ftorms, by means whereof whole Kingdomes and Nations profeffing Chrift, both have been heretofore, and are at this prefent day divided about Chrift. During which divifions and contentions amongft men, albeit each part do juftifie it felf, yet the one of neceffity muft needs erre, if there be any contradiction between them, be it great or little, and what fide foever it be that hath the truth, the fame we muft alfo acknowledge alone to hold *with the true Church in that point*, and confequently, reject the other as an enemy, *in that cafe fallen away from the true Church*. Wherefore of Hypocrites and Diffemblers whofe profeffion at the firft was but only from the teeth outward, when they afterwards took occafion to oppugne certain principal Articles of Faith, the Apoftles which defended the truth againft them, pronounce them *gone out* from the Fellowfhip of found and fincere Believers, when as yet the Chriftian Religion they had not utterly caft off. In like fence and meaning throughout all ages, *Hereticks* have juftly been hated, as branches cut off from the body of the true Vine, yet only fo far forth cut off as their Herefies have extended. Both Herefie and many other crimes, which *wholly fever from God*, do fever from God the Church of God in part only. The Myftery of Piety, faith the Apoftle, is without peradventure great, *God hath been manifefted in the Flefh, hath been juftified in the Spirit, hath been feen of Angels, hath been preached to Nations, hath been believed on in the World, hath been taken up into Glory.* The Church a pillar and foundation of this truth, which no where is known or profeft, but only within the Church, and they all of the Church that profefs it. In the mean while it cannot be denyed, that many profefs this, who are not therefore cleered fimply from all either faults or errours which make feparation between us and the Well-fpring of our happinefs. Idolatry fevered of old the Ifraelites ; Iniquity, thofe Scribes and Pharifees from God, who notwithftanding were a part of the Seed of *Abraham*, a part of that very Seed which God did himfelf acknowledge to be his Church. The Church of God may therefore contain both them which indeed are not his, yet muft be reputed his by us that know not their inward thoughts, and them whofe apparent wickednefs teftifieth even in the fight of the whole world that God abhorreth them. For to this and no other purpofe, are meant thofe Parables, which our Saviour in the Gofpel hath concerning mixture of Vice with Vertue, Light with Darknefs, Truth with Errour, as well and openly known and feen as a cunningly cloked mixture. That which feparateth therefore *utterly*, that which cutteth off *clean* from the vifible Church of Chrift, is plain Apoftafie, *direct* denial, utter rejection of the whole Chriftian Faith, as far as the fame is profeffedly different from Infidelity. Hereticks, as touching thofe points of doctrine wherein they fail: Schifmaticks, as touching the quarrels for which, or the duties wherein they divide themfelves from their Brethren : Loofe, licentious

and

Rom. 15. 5.
1 Cor. 1. 10.

3 John 2. 19.

1 Tim. 3. 16.

Mat. 13. 24. 47.

and wicked persons, as touching their several offences or crimes, have all forsaken the true Church of God, the Church which is found and sincere in the doctrine that they corrupt ; the Church that keepeth the bond of Unity, which they violate ; the Church that walketh in the Laws of Righteousness, which they transgress ; this very true Church of Christ they have left, howbeit not altogether left, nor forsaken simply the Church upon the main foundations whereof they continue built , notwithstanding those breaches whereby they are *rent at the top* asunder. Now because for redress of professed Errours and open Schisms, it is, and must be the Churches care that all may in outward conformity be one, as the laudible Politie of former Ages , even so our own to that end and purpose hath established divers Laws , the moderate severity whereof is a mean both to stay the rest, and to reclaim such as heretofore have been led awry. But seeing that the offices which Laws require, are always definite, and when that they require is done, they go no farther, whereupon sundry ill affected persons to save themselves from danger of Laws, pretend obedience, albeit inwardly they carry still the same hearts which they did before, by means whereof it falleth out, that receiving unworthily the blessed Sacrament at our hands, they eat and drink their own damnation ; it is for remedy of this mischief [a] here determined, that whom the Law of the Realm doth punish unless they communicate, such if they offer to obey Law, the Church notwithstanding should not admit without probation before had of their Gospel-like behaviour. Wherein they first set no time how long this supposed probation must continue ; again, they nominate no certain judgement, the verdict whereof shall approve mens behaviour to be Gospel-like ; and that which is most material, whereas they seek to make it more hard for dissemblers to be received into the Church, than Law and Politie as yet hath done, they make it in truth more easie for such kind of persons, to wind themselves out of the Law, and to continue the same they were. The Law requireth at their hands that duty which in conscience doth touch them neerest, because the greatest difference between us and them is the Sacrament of the Body and Bloud of Christ, whose name in the service of our Communion we celebrate with due honour, which they in the errour of their Mass prophane. As therefore on our part to hear Mass, were an open departure from that sincere profession whefein we stand , so if they on the other side receive our Communion , they give us the strongest pledge of fidelity that man can demand. What their hearts are, God doth know. But if they which mind treachery to God and man , shall once apprehend this advantage given them, whereby they may satisfie Law, in pretending themselves conformable (for what can Law with Reason or Justice require more ?)and yet be sure the Church will accept no such offer, till their Gospel-like behaviour be allowed, after that our own simplicity hath once thus fairly eased them from sting of Law ; it is to be thought they will learn the mystery of Gospel-like behaviour when leisure serveth them. As also while without any cause we fear to profane Sacraments, we shall not only defeat the purpose of most wholesome Laws, but lose or wilfully hazard those Souls, from which the likeliest means of full and perfect recovery, are by our indiscretion with-held. For neither doth God thus bind us to dive into mens consciences, nor can their fraud and deceit hurt any man but themselves. To him they seem such as they are; but of us they must be taken for

a *T. C. l. 1. p. 167.* If the place of the fifth to the *Corinthians*, do forbid that we should have any familiarity with notorious offenders , it doth much more forbid that they should be received to the Communion: And therefore Papists being such as which are notoriously known to hold heretical opinions, ought not to be admitted, much less compelled to the Supper. For seeing that our Saviour Christ did institute his Supper amongst his Disciples, and those only which were, as S. *Paul* speaketh, within ; it is evident, that the Papists being without, and Forreigners and Strangers from the Church of God, ought not to be received if they would offer themselves : and that Minister that shall give the Supper of the Lord to him, which is known to be a Papist, and which hath never made any cleer renouncing of Popery, with which he hath been defiled, doth profane the table of the Lord, and doth give the meat that is prepared for the children, unto Dogs, and he bringeth into the pasture, which is provided for the Sheep, Swine, and unclean Beasts, contrary to the faith and trust that ought to be in a Steward of the Lords House, as he is. For albeit that I doubt not but many of those which are now Papists, pertain to the Election of God, which God also in his good time will call to the knowledge of his truth: yet notwithstanding they ought to be unto the Minister and unto the Church, touching the ministring of Sacraments, as strangers and as unclean beasts. The ministring of the holy Sacraments unto them, is a declaration and seal of Gods favour and reconciliation with them, and a plain preaching partly, that they be washed already from their sin, partly, that they are of the houshold of God, and such as the Lord will fred to eternal life, which is not lawful to be done unto those which are not of the houshold of Faith. And therefore I conclude, that the compelling of Papists unto the Communion and the dismissing and letting of them go, when as they be to be punished for their stubbo ness in Popery (with this condition, if they will receive the Communion) is very unlawful, when as although they would receive, yet they ought to be kept back till such time as by their Religious and Gospel-like behaviour, &c.

such

such as they seem. In the eye of God they are against Christ, that are not truely and sincerely with him ; in our eyes they must be received as with Christ, that are not to outward shew against him. The case of impenitent and notorious sinners is not like unto theirs, whose only imperfection is Errour, severed from pertinacy, Errour in appearance content to submit it self to better instruction, Errour so far already cured, as to crave at our hands that Sacrament, the hatred and utter refusal whereof was the weightiest point wherein heretofore they swerved and went astray. In this case therefore they cannot reasonably charge us with remiss dealing, or with carelessness to whom we impart the Mysteries of Christ, but they have given us manifest occasion to think it requisite, that we earnestly advise rather and exhort them to consider as they ought, their sundry over-sights ; first, in equalling undistinctly crimes with errours, as touching force to make uncapable of this Sacrament. Secondly, in suffering indignation at the faults of the Church of *Rome*, to blind and with-hold their judgements from seeing that which withal they should acknowledge, concerning so much nevertheless still due to the same Church, as to be held and reputed a part of the House of God, a limb of the visible Church of Christ : Thirdly, in imposing upon the Church a burthen to enter farther into mens hearts, and to make a deeper search of their consciences, than any Law of God or reason of man inforceth : Fourthly and lastly, in repelling under colour of longer tryal such from the Mysteries of heavenly grace, as are both capable thereof by the Laws of God, for any thing we hear to the contrary, and should in divers considerations be cherished according to the merciful examples and precepts whereby the Gospel of Christ hath taught us towards such to shew compassion, to receive them with lenity and all meekness, if any thing be shaken in them to strengthen it, not to quench with delays & jealousies that feeble smoke of conformity which seemeth to breathe from them, but to build wheresoever there is any foundation, to adde perfection unto slender beginnings, and that as by other offices of piety, even so by this very food of Life, which Christ hath left in his Church, not only for preservation of strength, but also for relief of weakness : But to return to our own selves, in whom

T.C.l.1.p.147. the next thing severely reproved is the paucity of Communicants, if they require 2 *Chron.*30.13. at Communions frequency, we wish the same, knowing how acceptable unto God such service is, when multitudes cheerfully concur unto it ; if they encourage men *Psal.*122.1. thereunto, we also (themselves acknowledge it) are not utterly forgetful to do the like ; if they require some publick coaction for remedy of that, wherein by milder and softer means little good is done, they know our Laws and Statutes provided in that behalf, whereunto whatsoever convenient help may be added more by the wisdome of man, what cause have we given the World to think that we are not ready *Luke* 14.23. to hearken to it, and to use any good means of sweet compulsion, to have this high and Heavenly Banquet largely furnished ? Only we cannot so far yield as to judge it convenient, that the ho y desire of a competent number should be unsatisfied, because the greater part is careless and undisposed to joyn with them. Men should not (they say) be permitted a few by themselves to communicate, when so many are gone away, because this Sacrament is a token of our conjunction with our Brethren, and therefore by communicating apart from them, we make an apparent shew of distraction: I ask then, on which side Unity is broken, whether on theirs that depart, or on theirs who being left behind do communicate ? First, in the one it is not denyed, but that they may have reasonable causes of departure, and that then even they are delivered from just blame. Of such kind of causes two are allowed, namely, danger of impairing health, and necessary business requiring our presence otherwhere. And may not a third cause, which is *unfitness* at the present time, detain us as lawfully back as either of these two ? True it is, that we cannot hereby altogether excuse our selves, for that we ought to prevent this and do not. But if we have committed a fault in not preparing our minds before, shall we therefore aggravate the same with a worse, the crime of unworthy participation ?, He that abstaineth, doth want for the time that grace and comfort which religious Communicants have, but he that eateth and drinketh unworthily, receiveth death ; that which is life to others, turneth in him to poyson. Notwithstanding whatsoever the cause be for which men abstain, were it reason that the fault of one part

should

should any way abridge their benefit that are not faulty? There is in all the Scripture of God no one syllable which doth condemn communicating amongst a few, when the rest are departed from them. As for the last thing, which is our imparting this Sacrament privately unto the sick, whereas there have been of old (they grant) two kinds of necessity, wherein this Sacrament might be privately administred, of which two, the one being erroniously imagined, and the other (they say) continuing no longer in use, there remaineth unto us no necessity at all, for which that custome should be retained. The falsly surmised necessity is that, whereby some have thought all such excluded from possibility of salvation, as did depart this life, and never were made partakers of the holy Eucharist. The other case of necessity was, when men, which had fallen in time of persecution, and had afterwards repented them, but were not as yet received again unto the fellowship of this Communion, did at the hour of their death request it, that so they might rest with greater quietness and comfort of mind, being thereby assured of departure in unity of Christs Church, which virtuous desire the Fathers did think it great impiety not to satisfie. This was *Serapions* case of necessity. *Serapion* a faithful aged person, and always of very upright life, till fear of persecution in the end caused him to shrink back, after long sorrow for his scandalous offence, and sure oftentimes made to be pardoned of the Church, fell at length into grievous sickness, and being ready to yield up the Ghost, was then more instant than ever before to receive the Sacrament. Which Sacrament was necessary in this case, not that *Serapion* had been deprived of everlasting Life without it, but that his end was thereby to him made the more comfortable. And do we think that all cases of *such necessity* are clean vanished? Suppose that some have by mispersuasion lived in Schism, withdrawn themselves from holy and publike Assemblies, hated the Prayers, and lothed the Sacraments of the Church, falsly presuming them to be fraught with impious and Antichristian corruptions, which errour the God of mercy and truth opening at the length their eyes to see, they do not only repent them of the evil which they have done, but also in token thereof desire to receive comfort by that whereunto they have offered disgrace (which may be the case of many poor seduced souls even at this day) God forbid we should think that the Church doth sin, in permitting the wounds of such to be suppled with that Oyl, which this gracious Sacrament doth yield, and their bruised minds not only need but beg. There is nothing which the soul of man doth desire in that last hour so much, as comfort against the natural terrours of death, and other scruples of conscience, which commonly do then most trouble and perplex the weak, towards whom the very Law of God doth exact at our hands all the helps that Christian lenity and indulgence can afford. Our general consolation departing this life, is the hope of that [a] glorious and blessed Resurrection, which the Apostle [b] St. *Paul* nameth ἐξανάστασιν, [c] to note that as all men shall have their ἀνάστασιν, and be raised again from the dead, so the just shall be taken up and exalted above the rest, whom the power of God doth but raise and not exalt. This Life [d] and this Resurrection our Lord Jesus Christ is for all men, as touching the sufficiency of that he hath done, but that which maketh us partakers thereof, is our particular communion with Christ, and this Sacrament a principal mean, as well to strengthen the bond, as to multiply in us the fruits of the same Communion; for which cause [d] Saint *Cyprian* termeth it a joyful solemnity of expedite and speedy Resurrection; [e] *Ignatius*, a medicine which procureth immortality and preventeth death; [f] *Irenæus*, the nourishment of our bodies to eternal life, and their preservative from corruption. Now because that Sacrament, which at all times we may receive unto this effect, is then most acceptable and most fruitful, when any special extraordinary occasion, nearly and presently urging, kindleth our desires towards it, their severity, who cleave unto that alone which is generally fit to be done, and this so make all mens conditions alike, may adde much affliction to divers troubled and grieved minds, of whose particular estate, particular respect being had, according to the charitable order of the Church wherein we live, there injueth unto God that glory, which his righteous Saints comforted in their greatest distresses do yield, and unto them which have their reasonable Petitions satisfied, the same contentment, tranquility and joy, that others before them by means of like satisfaction have reaped

a 1 *Cor.* 15.21.
b *Philip.* 3.11.
c Διὰ τῶ ἐκ τῆς γῆς ἐξαναστήσεσθαι, *Theophil.* πάντες οἱ ἄνθρωποι ἀνιστάμενοι σῶμα ζανται ἀναζωμένοι τε περὶ ἐξετάζεται ἐπὶ τῆς ἀναστάσεως, *Ammon*; vide. 1 *Thess.* 4. 17.
d *Maturata resurrectionis lætabunda solemnia.* Cypr. de Cœn. Dom. cap. 10.
e Φάρμακον ἀθανασίας ἀντίδοτον μὴ ἀποθανεῖν. *Ignat.* Epist. ad Ephe. Item. l. 4. c. 34. f *Etsi nihil sæ-tite mutandum est ex solemnibus, tamen ubi aquitas evident poscit subvenit. rhanm est,* Lib. 183. ff. de Reg. Jur.

reaped

reaped, and wherein we all are or should be desirous finally to take our leave of the World, whensoever our own uncertain time of most assured departure shall come. Concerning therefore both Prayers and Sacraments, together with our usual and received form of administring the same in the Church of *England*, let thus much suffice.

Of Festivall Days, and the natural causes of their convenient institution.

69 As the substance of God alone is infinite, and hath *no kind* of limitation, so likewise his continuance is from everlasting to everlasting, and knoweth neither beginning nor end. Which demonstrable conclusion being presupposed, it followeth necessarily, that besides him all things are finite, both in substance and in continuance. If in substance all things be finite, it cannot be, but that there are bounds without the compass whereof their substance doth not extend; if in continuance also limited, they all have, it cannot be denied, their set and their certain terms, before which they had no being at all. This is the reason, why first we do most admire those things which are greatest; and secondly, those things which are ancientest, because the one are least distant from the infinite substance; the other from the infinite continuance of God. Out of this we gather, that only God hath true immortality or eternity, that is to say, continuance wherein there groweth no difference by addition of hereafter unto now, whereas the noblest and perfectest of all things besides, have continually through continuance the time of former continuance lengthened, so that they could not heretofore be said to have continued so long as now, neither now so long as hereafter. Gods own eternity is the hand which leadeth Angels in the course of their Perpetuity; their Perpetuity the hand that draweth out celestial Motion, the Line of which Motion, and the Threed of Time are spun together. Now as Nature bringeth forth Time with Motion, so we by Motion have learned how to divide Time, and by the smaller parts of Time, both to measure the greater, and to know how long all things else endure. For Time considered in it self, is but the flux of that very instant, wherein the Motion of the Heaven began; being coupled with other things, it is the quantity of their continuance measured by the distance of two instants: As the time of a man is a mans continuance from the instant of his first breath, till the instant of his last gasp. Hereupon, some have defined Time to be the Measure of the Motion of Heaven; because the first thing which Time doth measure, is that Motion wherewith it began, and by the help whereof it measureth other things, as when the Prophet *David* saith, that a mans continuance doth not commonly exceed threescore and ten years, he useth the help both of Motion and Number to measure Time. They which make Time an effect of Motion, and Motion to be in Nature before Time, ought to have considered with themselves, that albeit we should deny as *Melissus* did, all Motion, we might notwithstanding acknowledge Time, because Time doth but signifie the quantity of continuance, which continuance may be in things that rest and are never moved. Besides, we may also consider in rest both that which is past, and that which is present, and that which is future; yea, farther, even length and shortness in every of these, although we never had conceit of Motion. But to *define* without Motion, *how* long or *how* short such continuance is, were impossible. So that herein we must of necessity use the benefit of Years, Days, Hours, Minutes, which all grow from Celestial Motion. Again, for as much as that Motion is Circular, whereby we make our divisions of Time, and the Compass of that Circuit such, that the Heavens which are therein continually moved, and keep in their Motions uniform celerity, must needs touch often the same points, they cannot chuse but bring unto us by equal distances frequent returns of the same times. Furthermore whereas Time is nothing but the meer quantity of that continuance which all things have that are not as God is, without beginning, that which is proper unto all quantities agreeth also to this kind, so that Time doth but measure other things, and neither worketh in them any real effect, nor is it self ever capable of any. And therefore when commonly we use to say, that Time doth eat or fret our all things, that Time is the wisest thing in the World, because it bringeth forth all Knowledge, and that nothing is more foolish then Time, which never holdeth any thing long, but whatsoever one Day learneth, the same another day forgetteth again; that some men see prosperous and happy Days, and that some mens Days are miserable;

in-

in all thefe and the like fpeeches, that which is uttered of the Time is not verified of Time it felf, but agreeth unto thofe things which are in Time, and do by means of fo near conjunction either lay their burthen upon the back, or fet their Crown upon the head of Time. Yea the very *opportunities which we afcribe to Time do in truth cleave to the things themfelves wherewith Time is joyned: as for Time it neither caufeth things nor opportunities of things, although it comprize and contain both. All things whatfoever having their time, the Works of God have always that time which is feafonableft and fitteft for them. His Works are, fome ordinary, fome more rare, all worthy of obfervation, but not all of like neceffity to be often remembred; they all have their times, but they all do not adde the fame eftimation and glory to the times wherein they are. For as God by being every where, yet doth not give unto all places one and the fame degree of holinefs, fo neither one and the fame dignity to all times by working in all. For if all either places or times were in refpect of God alike, wherefore was it faid unto *Mofes* by particular defignation, *That very place wherein thou ftandeft is holy ground?* Why doth the Prophet *David* chufe out of all the days of the year but one, whereof he fpeaketh by way of principal admiration, *This is the day the Lord hath made?* No doubt, as Gods extraordinary prefence hath hallowed and fanctified certain places, fo they are his extraordinary works that have truly and worthily advanced certain times, for which caufe they ought to be with all men that honour God, more holy then other days. The Wifeman therefore compareth herein not unfitly the times of God with the perfons of men. If any fhould ask how it cometh to pafs, that one day doth excel another, feeing the light of all the days in the year proceedeth from one Sun, to this he anfwereth, that, *The knowledge of the Lord hath parted them afunder, he hath by them difpofed the times and folemne Feafts, fome he hath chofen out and fanctified, fome he hath put among the days, to number: even as Adam and all other men are of one fubftance, all created of the Earth: but the Lord hath divided them by great knowledge, and made their ways divers; fome he hath bleffed and exalted, fome he hath fanctified and appropriated unto himfelf, fome he hath curfed, humbled, and put them out of their dignity.* So that the caufe being natural and neceffary, for which there fhould be a difference in days, the folemne obfervation whereof declareth Religious thankfulnefs towards him whofe works of principal reckoning we thereby admire and honour, it cometh next to be confidered what kinds of duties and fervices they are wherewith fuch times fhould be kept holy.

70 The fanctification of days and times is a token of that thankfulnefs, and a part of that publike honour which we owe to God for admirable benefits, whereof it doth not fuffice that we keep a fecret Kalender, taking thereby our private occafions as we lift our felves, to think how much God hath done for all men, but the dayes which are chofen out to ferve as publike Memorials of fuch his mercies, ought to be clothed with thofe outward Robes of holinefs, whereby their difference from other dayes may be made fenfible. But becaufe time in it felf, as hath been already proved, can receive no alteration, the hallowing of Feftival Dayes muft confift in the fhape or countenance which we put upon the affairs that are incident into thofe Days. *This is the Day which the Lord hath made,* faith the Prophet *David, Let us rejoyce and be glad in it.* So that generally offices and duties of [b] religious joy, are they wherein the hallowing of Feftival times confifteth. The moft natural teftimonies of our rejoycing in God, are firft his Praifes fet forth with cheerful alacrity of mind: Secondly, our comfort and delight expreffed by a [c] charitable largenefs of fomewhat more then common bounty: Thirdly, Sequeftration from ordinary labours, the toyls and cares whereof are not meet to be companions of fuch gladnefs. Feftival folemnity therefore is nothing but the due mixture as it were of thefe three Elements, praife, bounty and reft.

Touching praife, forafmuch as the Jews, who alone knew the way how to magni-

Margin notes:
a χρόνΘ· έσιν έν ὧ καιρός, καὶ καιρὸς ἐν ὧ χρόνΘ· ε πολύς. Hippo. lib. qui Præceptiones infcribitur.

Exod. 3. 5.

Pfal. 118. 24.

Pfal. 118. 14.

Ecclu. 33. 7.

The manner of celebrating feftival Days. b *Grande videlicet officium focos & choros in publicum educere vicatim epulari, civitatem taberna babitu obolefcere, vino lutum cogere, cateruatim curfitare ad injurias, ad impudicitias, ad libidinis illecebras.* c *ficcine expritmitur publicum gautium per publicum dedecus?* Tert. Apol c. 35. *Dies feftos Majeftati altiffima dedicatos nulli volumus voluptatibus occupari.* Cl. 12. tit. 12. l. 1.

jeftati altiffima dedicatos nulli volumus voluptatibus occupari. Cl. 12. tit. 12. l. 1. Ἀντὶ τῆς πάλαι πομπείας ᾳ ᾳισχρουργίας ᾳ ᾳισχρορρημοσύνης σώφρονες ἑορτάζονται πανηγύρεις, ε μέθην ἔχεσαι ᾳ κώμον ᾳ γέλωτα, ἀλλ᾽ ὕμνυς θεῖυς ᾳ ἱερῶν λογίων ἀκρόασιν, ᾳ προσῦχὴν ἀξιεπαίνοις κοσμυμένην δακρύοις; Theod. ad Grac. Infidel. Scr. 9. c Τῆς γὰρ αὖ τῆς φύσεως ἐσιν εὐσεβῆτε ἔιναι ᾳ φιλανθρωπον. Philo. lib. de Abraha.

fie God aright, did commonly (as appeared by their wicked lives) more of custom and for fashion sake execute the services of their Religion, then with heartie & true devotion (which God especially requireth) he therefore protesteth against their Sabbaths and solemn Days, as being therewith much offended, Plentifull & liberall expence is required in them that abound, partly as a sign of their ownjoy in the goodnes of God towards them, and partly as a mean whereby to refresh those poorand needy, who being especially at these times made partakers of relaxation and joy with others

Deut. 16. 14.
Nehem. 8. 9.

do the more religiously blesse God, whose great mercies were a cause thereof, & the more contentedly indure the burthen of that hard estate wherein they continue. Rest is the end of all Motion, and the last perfection of all things that labour. Labours in us are journeys, and even in them which feele no wearinesse by any worke, yet they are but wayes whereby to come unto that which bringeth not happinesse til it do bring rest. For as long as any thing which we desire is unattained, we rest not. Let us not here take rest for idlenesse. They are idle, whom the painfulnesse of action causeth to avoid those labours, whereunto both God and Nature bindeth them; they rest, which either cease from their worke when they have brought it unto perfection, or else give over a meaner labour, because a worthier and better is to be undertaken. God hath created nothing to be idle or ill imployed. As therefore, man doth consist of different and distinct parts, every part indued with manifold abilities, which all have their severall ends and actions thereunto referred; so there is in this great variety of duties which belong to men, that dependency and order, by means whereof the lower sustaining alwaies the more excellent, and the higher perfecting the more base, they are in their times and seasons continued with most exquisite correspondence; labours of bodily and daily toile purchase freedome for actions of religious joy, which benefit these actions require with the gift of desired rest: a thing most naturall and fit to accompany the solemne Festivall duties of honour which are done to God. For if those principall works of God, the memory whereof we use to celebrate at such times, be but certain tastes and sayes, as it were, of that finall benefit, wherein our perfect felicitie and blisse lieth folded up, seeing that the presence of the one doth direct our cogitations, thoughts and desires towards the other, it giveth surely a kind of life, and addeth inwardly no small delight to those so comfortable expectations, when the very outward countenance of that we presently doe, representeth after a sort that also whereunto we tend; as Festival rest doth that Celestiall estate

a Οὐδ᾽ ἔςιν ὁ-
δενὸς ὑδεμία
μεταβολὴ ὁ
ὑπὲρ ἐξατάτω
φερμένην φο-
ερὸν ἀλλ᾽ ἀναλ-
λοίωτα κỳ α-
παθῆ τλῶ ἀ-
είς ἥν ἔχοντα
ξῶην κỳ τλῶ
αὐταρκις άτην
διατελεῖ τε
ἅπαντα αἰῶ-
να. Arist.

whereof the very [a] Heathens themselves which had not the meanes whereby to apprehend much, did notwithstanding imagine that it needs must consist in rest, and have therefore taught, that above the highest moveable Sphere there is nothing which feeleth alteration, motion or change, but all things immutable, unsubject to passion, blest with eternall continuance in a life of the highest perfection, and of that compleat abundant sufficiency within it self, which no possibilitie of want, maime or defect can touch. Besides, whereas ordinary labours are both in themselves painfull, and base in comparison of Festivall Services done to God, doth not the natural difference between them shew, that the one as it were by way of submission and homage should surrender themselves to the other, wherewith they can neither easily concur, because painfulnesse and joy are opposite, nor decently, because while the minde hath just occasion to make her abode in the House of gladnesse, the Weed of ordinary toyle and travel becometh her not? Wherefore even Nature hath taught the Heathens, and God the Jews, and Christ us, first, that Festivall Solemnities are a part of the publike exercise of Religion; secondly, that Praise, Liberalitie, and rest are as naturall Elements whereof Solemnities consist.

But these things the Heathens converted to the honour of their false gods; and as they failed in the end it selfe, so neither could they discerne rightly what form and measure Religion therein should observe. Whereupon, when the Israelites impiously followed so corrupt example, they are in every degree noted to have done amiss; their Hymnes or Songs of praise were Idolatrie, their bountie excesse, and their rest wantonnesse. Therefore the Law of God which appointed them daies of Solemnitie, taught them likewise in what manner the same should be celebrated: According to the pattern of which Institution, *David* establishing the state of Religion

ordai-

ordained praise to be given unto God in the Sabbaths, Moneths, and appointed 1 *Chron.*23.30
times, as their cuftome had been always before the Lord. Now, befides the times
which God himfelf in the Law of *Mofes* particularly fpecified, there were, through
the wifedome of the Church, certain other devifed by occafion of like occurrents to
thofe whereupon the former had rifen, as namely, that which *Mardocheus* and *Eft-* *Heft.* 9. 27.
her did firft celebrate in memory of the Lords moft wonderful protection, when *Ha-*
man had laid his inevitable plot, to mans thinking, for the utter extirpation of the
Jews even in one day. This they call the Feaft of *Lots*, becaufe *Haman* had caft their
life and their death, as it were upon the hazard of a Lot. To this may be added, that
other alfo of *Dedication*, mentioned in the tenth of Saint *Johns* Gofpel, the inftitu- *Ioh.* 10. 22.
tion whereof is declared in the Hiftory of *Maccabees*. But forafmuch as their Law 1 *Mac.* 4. 53,
by the coming of Chrift is changed, and we thereunto no way bound, Saint *Paul*
although it were not his purpofe to favour invectives againft the fpecial fanctification of days and times to the fervice of God, and to the honour of Jefus Chrift, doth
notwithftanding bend his forces againft that opinion, which impofed on the Gentiles the yoke of Jewifh Legal obfervations, as if the whole world ought for ever,
and that upon pain of condemnation, to keep and obferve the fame. Such as in this
perfwafion hallowed thofe Jewifh Sabbaths, the Apoftle fharply reproveth, faying,
Te obferve dayes and monoths, and times and years, I am in fear of you, left I have a *Gal.* 4. 10.
beftowed upon you labour in vain. Howbeit, fo far off was [b] *Tertullian* from imagin- b *Si omnem in*
ing how any man could poffible hereupon call in queftion fuch days as the Church *totum devotio-*
of Chrift doth obferve, that the obfervation of thefe days he ufeth for an Argument *nem temporum*
whereby to prove, it could not be the Apoftles intent and meaning to condemn *& dierum &*
fimply all obferving of fuch times. Generally therefore touching Feafts in the *menfium & an-*
Church of Chrift, they have that profitable ufe whereof St. *Auguftine* fpeaketh, *By* *norum crafit A-*
Feftival Solemnities and fet-days, we dedicate and fanctifie to God the memory of his *poftolus, cur*
benefits, left unthankful forgetfulnefs thereof fhould creep upon us in courfe of time. *Pafcha celebra-*
And concerning particulars, their Sabbath the Church hath changed into our Lords *mus annuo cir-*
Day, that is, as the one did continually bring to mind the former world finifhed by *culo in menfe*
creation, fo the other might keep us in perpetual remembrance of a far better world, *primo?*
begun by him which came to reftore all things, to make both Heaven and Earth new. *Cur quinqua-*
For which caufe they honoured the laft day, we the firft, in every feven, throughout *ginta exinde*
the year. The reft of the days and times which we celebrate, have relation all un- *diebus in omni*
to one head. We begin therefore our Ecclefiaftical year with the glorious [c] Annun- *exultatione de-*
tiation of his birth by Angelical Embaffage. There being hereunto added his blef- *currimus? Lib.*
fed Nativity it felf, the myftery of his legal [d] Circumcifion; the teftification of his *adverf. Pfych.*
true Incarnation by the Purification of her which brought him into the world, his Aug. de Civit.
Refurrection, his Afcenfion into Heaven, the admirable fending down of his Spi- Dei, lib. 16. c. 4.
rit upon his chofen, and (which confequently enfued) the notice of that incompre- c *Luke* 1. 16,
henfible Trinity thereby given to the Church of God; again, forafmuch as we know d *Luke* 2. 21,
that Chrift hath not only been manifefted great in himfelf, but great in other his
Saints alfo, the days of whofe departure out of the world are to the Church of Chrift,
as the Birth and Coronation days of Kings or Emperours, therefore efpecial choice
being made of the very flower of all occafions in this kind, there are annual felect-
ed times to meditate of Chrift glorified in them which had the honour to fuffer for
his fake, before they had age and ability to know him; glorified in them which
knowing him as *Stephen*, had the fight of that before death, whereinto fo acceptable
death did lead; glorified in thofe Sages of the Eaft, that came from far to adore him,
and were conducted by ftrange light; glorified in the fecond *Elias* of the world,
fent before him to prepare his way; glorified in every of thofe Apoftles, whom it
pleafed him to ufe as Founders of his Kingdom here; glorified in the Angels, as in
Michael; glorified in all thofe happy fouls that are already poffeffed of Heaven.
Over and befides which number not great, the reft be but four other days heretofore annexed to the Feaft of Eafter and Pentecoft, by reafon of general Baptifme u-
fual at thofe two Feafts, which alfo is the caufe why they had not, as other days, any
proper name given them. Their firft inftitution was therefore through neceffity,
and their prefent continuance is now for the greater honour of the principals,
whereupon they ftill attend. If it be then demanded, whether we obferve thefe
N n 2
times

times as being thereunto bound by force of Divine Law, or else by the only Pofitive Ordinances of the Church, I anfwer to this, that the very Law of Nature it felf, which all men confefs to be Gods Law, requireth in general no lefs the fanctification of times than of places, perfons and things unto Gods honour. For which caufe it hath pleafed him heretofore, as of the reft, fo of times likewife to exact fome parts by way of perpetual homage, never to be difpenfed withal, nor remitted; again, to require fome other parts of time with as ftrict exaction, but for lefs continuance; and of the reft which were left arbitrary, to accept what the Church fhall in due confideration confecrate voluntarily unto like Religious ufes. Of the firft kind amongft the Jewes was the Sabbath-day; of the fecond, thofe Feafts which are appointed by the Law of *Mofes*; the Feaft of Dedication invented by the Church, ftandeth in the number of the laft kind. The Moral Law requiring therefore a feventh part throughout the age of the whole world to be that way imployed, although with us the day be changed in regard of a new revolution begun by our Saviour Chrift, yet the fame proportion of time continueth which was before, becaufe in reference to the benefit of Creation, and now much more of Renovation thereunto added by him which was Prince of the world to come, we are bound to accompt the fanctification of one day in feven, a duty which Gods immutable Law doth exact for ever. The reft, they fay, we ought to abolifh, becaufe the continuance of them doth nourifh wicked fuperftition in the minds of men, befides, they are all abufed by Papifts, the enemies of God, yea, certain of them, as Eafter and Pentecoft, even by the Jews.

Exceptions againft our keeping of other Feftival dayes befides the Sabbath. *T.C. l.1. p.* 151. If they had been never abufed, neither by the Papifts, nor by the Jews, as they have been, and are dayly, yet fuch making of Holy days is never without fome great danger of bringing in fome evil and corrupt opinions into the minds of men. I will ufe an example in one, and that the chief of Holy days, and moft generally, and of longeft time obferved in the Church, which is the Feaft of Eafter, which was kept of fome more days, of fome fewer. How many thoufands are there, I will not fay of the ignorant Papifts, but of thofe alfo which profefs the Gofpel, which when they have celebrated thofe days with diligent heed taken unto their life, and with fome earneft devotion in praying, and hearing the Word of God, and think that they have well celebrated the Feaft of Eafter, and yet have they thus notably deceived themfelves. For Saint *Paul* teacheth, 1 *Cor.* 5. 8. that the celebrating of the Feaft of the Chriftians Eafter, is not as the Jews was, for certain days, but fheweth that we muft keep this Feaft all the days of our life in the unleavened bread of fincerity and of truth. By which we fee that the obferving of the Feaft of Eafter for certain dayes in the year doth pull out of our minds, ere ever we be aware, the Doctrine of the Gofpel, and caufeth us to reft in that neer confideration of our duties, for the fpace of a few days, which fhould be extended to all our life.

71 Touching Jewes, their Eafter and Pentecoft have with ours as much affinity, as *Philip* the Apoftle with *Philip* the Macedonian King. As for *imitation of Papifts*, and the *breeding of fuperftition*, they are now become fuch common guefts, that no man can think it difcourteous to let them go as they came. The next is a rare Obfervation and ftrange: You fhall find, if you mark it (as it doth deferve to be noted well) that many thoufands there are, who if they have vertuoufly during thofe times behaved themfelves, if their devotion and zeal in prayer have been fervent, their attention to the Word of God fuch as all Chriftian men fhould yield, imagine that herein they have performed a good duty, which notwithftanding to think is a very dangerous errour, inafmuch as the Apoftle Saint *Paul* hath taught, that we ought not to keep our Eafter as the Jews did for certain days, but in the unleavened bread of fincerity and of truth to feaft continually, whereas the reftraint of Eafter to a certain number of days caufeth us to reft for a fhort fpace in that near confideration of our duties, which fhould be extended throughout the courfe of our whole lives, and fo pulleth out of our minds the Doctrine of Chrifts Gofpel ere we be aware. The Doctrine of the Gofpel which here they mean or fhould mean, is, that Chrift having finifhed the Law, there is no Jewifh Pafchal Solemnity, nor abftinence from fowr Bread now required at our hands; there is no Leaven which we are bound to caft out, but malice, fin and wickednefs; no Bread but the food of fincere Truth, wherewith we are tied to celebrate our Paffeover. And feeing no time of fin is granted us, neither any intermiffion of found belief, it followeth that this kind of feafting ought to endure always. But how are ftanding Feftival Solemnities againft this? That which the Gofpel of Chrift requireth, is the perpetuity of vertuous duties, not perpetuity of exercife or action, but difpofition perpetual, and practice as oft as times and opportunities require. Juft, valiant, liberal, temperate, and holy men are they, which can whenfoever they will, and will whenfoever they

they ought, execute what their several perfections import. If virtues did always cease to be, when they cease to work, there should be nothing more pernicious to Virtue than sleep: neither were it possible that men, as *Zachary* and *Elizabeth* should in all the Commandments of God walk unreprovable, or that the Chain of our conversation should contain so many links of divine Virtues, as the Apostles in divers places have reckoned up, if in the exercise of each virtue perpetual continuance were exacted at our hands. Seeing therfore all things are done in time, and many offices are not possible at one and the same time to be discharged, duties of all sorts must have necessarily their several successions and seasons, in which respect the School-men have well and soundly determined, that Gods affirmative Laws and Precepts, the Laws that injoyn any actual duty, as Prayer, Alms, and the like, do bind us *ad semper velle*, but not *ad semper agere*, we are tyed to iterate and resume them when need is, howbeit not to continue them without any intermission. Feasts, whether God himself hath ordained them, or the Church by that Authority which God hath given, they are of Religion such publike services, as neither can, nor ought to be continued otherwise than only by iteration. Which iteration is a most effectual mean to bring unto full maturity and growth those seeds of godlinesse, that these very men themselves do grant to be sown in the hearts of many thousands, during the while that such Feasts are present. The constant habit of well-doing is not gotten without the custome of doing well, neither can virtue be made perfect, but by the manifold works of virtue often practised. Before the powers of our minds be brought unto some perfection, our first essays and offers towards virtue must needs be raw, yet commendable, because they tend unto ripeness. For which cause the Wisdom of God hath commanded especially this circumstance amongst others in solemn Feasts, that to Children and Novices in Religion, they minister the first occasion to ask and inquire of God. Whereupon if there follow but so much piety as hath been mentioned, let the Church learn to further imbecillity with prayer, *Preserve, Lord, these good and gracious beginnings, that they suddenly dry not up as the morning dew, but may prosper and grow as the trees which rivers of waters keep always flourishing*; let all mens acclamations be, *Grace, Grace unto it*, as to that first laid corner stone in *Zerubbabels* buildings. For who hath despised the day of those things which are small? Or how dare we take upon us to condemne that very thing which voluntarily we grant, maketh us of nothing somewhat, seeing all we pretend against it is only, that as yet this somewhat is not much? The days of solemnity which are but few, cannot chuse but soon finish that outward exercise of godlinesse, which properly appertaineth to such times, howbeit mens inward disposition to virtue, they both augment for the present, and by their often returns bring also the same at the length unto that perfection which we most desire. So that although by their necessary short continuance, they abridge the present exercise of piety in some kind, yet because by repetition they enlarge, strengthen and confirm the habits of all virtue, it remaineth that we honour, observe and keep them as Ordinances, many ways singularly profitable in Gods Church. This exception being taken against Holy days, for that they restrain the praises of God unto certain times, another followeth condemning restraint of men from their ordinary Trades and labours at those times. It is not they say in the power of the Church to command rest, because God hath left it to all men at liberty, that if they think good to bestow six whole days in labour, they may, neither is it more lawful for the Church to abridge any man of that liberty which God hath granted, then to take away the yoke which God hath laid upon them, and to countermand what he doth expresly injoyn. They deny not but in times of publike calamity, that men may the better assemble themselvs to fast and pray, the Church, *because it*

a *T. C. l. 1. p. 152.* I confess that it is in the power of the Church to appoint so many days in the Week, or in the Year (in the which the Congregation shall assemble to hear the Word of God, and receive the Sacraments, and offer up Prayers unto God) as it shall think good, according to those Rules which are before alleaged. But that it hath power to make so many *Holy days* as we have, wherein men are commanded to cease from their daily vocations of ploughing, and exercising their Handy-crafts, that I deny to be in the power of the Church. For proof whereof, I will take the fourth Commandment, and no other interpretation of it then M. Doct. alloweth of, which is, That God licenseth and leaveth it at the liberty of every man, to work six days in the Week, so that he rest the Seventh Day. Seeing therefore that the Lord hath left it to all men at liberty, that they might labour, if they think good, six days; I say, the Church, nor no man can take this liberty away from them, and drive them to a *necessary* neceffary reft of the body. And it it be lawful to abridge the liberty of the Church in this point, and inftead that the Lord faith, fix days thou maift labour if thou wilt, to fay, thou fhalt not labour fix days : I do not fee why the Church may not as well, whereas the Lord faith, *Thou fhalt reft the Seventh Day*, command that thou fhalt not reft the Seventh Day. For if the Church may reftrain the liberty which God hath given them, it may take away the yoke alfo which God hath put upon them. And whereas you fay, that notwithftanding this fourth Commandment, the Jews had certain other Feafts which they obferved; indeed the Lord which gave this general Law, might make as many exceptions as he thought good, and fo long as he thought good. But it followeth not, becaufe the Lord did it, that therefore the Church may do it, unlefs it hath Commandment and Authority from God fo to do. As when there is any general Plague or Judgement of God either upon the Church, or coming towards it, the Lord commandeth in fuch a cafe, *Ioel* 2.15. that they fhould fanctifie a general Faft, and proclaim *Ghnatfarah*, which fignifieth a Prohibition, or forbidding of ordinary works, and is the fame Hebrew word wherewith thofe Feaft days are noted in the Law wherein they fhould reft. The reafon of which Commandment of the Lords was, that they abftained that day as much as might be conveniently from meats, fo they might abftain from their daily works, to the end they might beftow the whole day in hearing the Word of God, and humbling themfelves in the Congregation, confeffing their faults, and defiring the Lord to turn away from his fierce wrath. In this cafe the Church having Commandment to make a Holy day, may and ought to do it, as the Church which was in *Babylon*, did during the time of their Captivity : but where it is deftitute of a Commandment it may not prefume by any Decree to reftrain that liberty which the Lord hath given.

hath received *Commandment* from God to proclaim a Prohibition from ordinary works, ftandeth bound to do it, as the Jewes afflicted did in *Babylon*. But without fome exprefs Commandment from God, there is no power, they fay, under Heaven which may prefume by any Decree to reftrain the liberty that God hath given. Which opinion, albeit applied here no farther then to this prefent caufe, fhaketh univerfally the Fabrick of Government, tendeth to Anarchie and meer confufion, diffolveth Families, diffipateth Colledges, Corporations, Armies, overthroweth Kingdomes, Churches, and whatfoever is now, through the providence of God, by authority and power upheld. For whereas God hath foreprized things of the greateft weight, and hath therein precifely defined, as well that which every man muft perform, as that which no man may attempt, leaving all forts of men in the reft, either to be guided by their own good difcretion, if they be free from fubjection to others, or elfe to be ordered by fuch Commandments and Laws as proceed from thofe Superiours under whom they live; the Patrons of liberty have here made Solemn Proclamation, that all fuch Laws and Commandments are void, in as much as every man is left to the freedom of his own mind, in fuch things as are not either exacted or prohibited by the Law of God; and becaufe onely in thefe things the Pofitive Precepts of men have place, which Precepts cannot poffibly be given without fome abridgement of their liberty, to whom they are given : therefore if the Father command the Son, or the Husband the Wife, or the Lord the Servant, or the Leader the Souldier, or the Prince the Subject, to go or ftand, fleep or wake; at fuch times as God himfelf in particular commandeth neither, they are to ftand in defence of the freedom which God hath granted, and to do as themfelves lift, knowing that men may as lawfully command them things utterly forbidden by the Law of God, as tye them to any thing which the Law of God leaveth free. The plain contradictory whereunto is unfallibly certain. Thofe things which the Law of God leaveth arbitrary and at liberty, are all fubject to the pofitive Laws of men, which Laws for the common benefit abridge particular mens liberty in fuch things, as far as the Rules of equity will fuffer. This we muft either maintain, or elfe over-turn the world, and make every man his own Commander. Seeing then that labour and reft upon any one day of the fix throughout the year, are granted free by the Law of God, how exempt we them from the force and power of Ecclefiaftical Law, except we deprive the world of power to make any Ordinance or Law at all ? Befides, is it probable that God fhould not only allow, but command concurrencie of reft, with extraordinary occafions of doleful events, befalling peradventure fome one certain Church, or not extending unto many, and not as much as permit or licenfe the like; when Piety triumphant with joy and gladnefs, maketh folemne commemoration of Gods moft rare & unwonted mercies, *fuch efpecially as the whole race of Mankind* doth or might participate ? Of vacation from labour in times of forrow, the only caufe is, for that the general publike prayers of the whole Church, and our own private bufineffes, cannot both be followed at once; whereas of reft in the famous folemnities of pub.ique joy, there is both this confideration the fame, and alfo farther a kind of natural repugnancy, which maketh labours (as hath been proved) much more unfit to accompany Feftival praifes of God, then offices of

humilia-

humiliation and grief. Again, if we sift what they bring for proof and approbation of rest with fasting, doth it not in all respects as fully warrant, and as strictly command rest, whensoever the Church hath equal reason by feasts, and gladsome solemnities to testifie publique thankfulness towards God? I would know some cause, why those words of the Prophet *Joel, Sanctifie a Fast, call a solemne Assembly,* which words were uttered to the Jewes, in misery and great distress, should more bind the Church to do at all times after the like, in their like perplexities, then the words of *Moses,* to the same people, in a time of joyful deliverance from misery, *Remember this day,* may warrant any annual celebration of benefits, no less importing the good of men; and also justifie as touching the manner and form thereof, what circumstance soever they imitate only in respect of natural fitness or decency, without any Jewish regard to Ceremonies, such as were properly theirs, and are not by us expedient to be continued. According to the Rule of which general directions, taken from the Law of God, no less in the one then the other, the practice of the Church commended unto us in holy Scripture, doth not only make for the justification of black and dismal days (as one of the Fathers termeth them) but plainly offereth it self to be followed by such Ordinances (if occasion require) as that which *Mardocheus* did sometimes devise, *Hesther* what lay in her power help forward, and the rest of the Jewes establish for perpetuity, namely, That the fourteenth and fifteenth days of the moneth *Adar,* should be every year kept throughout all Generations, as days of feasting and joy, wherein they would rest from bodily labour, and what by gifts of charity bestowed upon the poor, what by other liberal signs of amity and love, a I testifie their thankful minds towards God, which almost beyond possibility had delivered them all, when they all were as men dead.

Joel. 2. 15.

Exod. 13. 3.

Hest. 9.

But this decree, they [a] say, was Divine, not Ecclesiastical, as may appear in that there is another decree in another Book of Scripture, which decree is plain, not to have proceeded from the Churches Authority, but from the mouth of the Prophet onely; and as a poor simple man sometime was fully perswaded, that if *Pontius Pilate* had not been a Saint, the Apostles would never have suffered his name to stand in the Creed, so these men have a strong opinion, that because the Book of *Hesther* is Canonical, the decree of *Hesther* cannot be possibly Ecclesiastical: If it were, they ask how the Jews could bind themselves always to keep it, seeing Ecclesiastical Laws are mutable? As though the purposes of men might never intend constancy in that, the nature whereof is subject to alteration. Doth the Scripture it self make mention of any divine Commandment? Is the Scripture

[a] *T.C. l. 3. p. 193.* The example out of *Hesther* is no sufficient warrant for these Feasts in question. For first, as in other cases, so in this case of days, the estate of Christians, under the Gospel, ought not to be so ceremonious, as was theirs under the Law. Secondly, that which was done there, was done by a special direction of the Spirit of God, either through the ministry of the Prophets, which they had, or by some other extraordinary means, which is not to be followed by us. This may appear by another place, *Zach. 8.* where the Jews changed their Fasts into Feasts, only by the mouth of the Lord, through the ministry of the Prophet. For further proof whereof, first, I take the 28. verse, where it appeareth, that this was an order to endure always, even as long as the other Feast days, which were instituted by the Lord himself. So that what abuses soever were of that Feast, yet as a perpetual Decree of God, it ought to have remained, whereas our Churches can make no such Decree, which may not upon change of times, and other circumstances, be altered. For the other proof hereof I take the last Verse: For the Prophet contenteth not himself with that, that he had rehearsed the Decree, as he doth sometimes the decree of prophane Kings, but addeth precisely, that as soon as ever the Decree was made, it was registred in this Book of *Hesther,* which is one of the books of Canonical Scripture, declaring thereby in what esteem they had it. If it had been of no further Authority then our decrees, or then a Canon of one of the Councels, it had been presumption to have brought it into the Library of the holy Ghost. The sum of my Answer is, That this Decree was Divine, and not Ecclesiastical only.

witness of more, then only that *Mardocheus* was the Author of this custome, that by Letters written to his brethren the Jews, throughout all Provinces under *Darius* the King of *Persia,* he gave them charge to celebrate yearly those two days, for perpetual remembrance of Gods miraculous deliverance and mercy, that the Jewes hereupon undertook to do it, and made it with general consent an order for perpetuity; That *Hesther* secondly, by her Letters confirmed the same which *Mardocheus* had before decreed; and that finally, the Ordinance was written to remain for ever upon record? Did not the Jewes in Provinces abroad observe at the first the fourteenth day, the Jewes in *Susis* the fifteenth? Were they not all reduced to an uniform order by means of those two Decrees, and so every where three days kept, the first with fasting, in memory of danger; the rest, in token of deliverance, as

festival

festival and joyful days? Was not the first of those three, afterwards the day of sorrow and heaviness, abrogated, when the same Church saw it meet that a better day, a day in memory of like deliverance, out of the bloudy hands of *Nicanor*, should succeed in the room thereof? But for as much as there is no end of answering fruitless oppositions, let it suffice men of sober minds, to know that the Law both of God and Nature alloweth generally, days of rest and festival solemnity, to be observed by way of thankful and joyful remembrance, if such miraculous favours be shewed towards mankind as require the same; that such graces God hath bestowed upon his Church, as well in latter as in former times, that in some particulars, when they have fallen out, himself hath demanded his own honour, and in the rest hath left it to the wisdom of the Church, directed by those precedents, and enlightned by other means, always to judge when the like is requisite. About questions therefore concerning Days and Times, our manner is not to stand at bay with the Church of God, demanding wherefore the memory of [a] *Paul* should be rather kept than the memory of [b] *Daniel*; we are content to imagine, it may be perhaps true that the least in the Kingdom of Christ, is greater than the greatest of all the Prophets of God that have gone before; we never yet saw cause to despair, but that the simplest of the people might be taught the right construction of as great mysteries as the [d] name of a Saints day doth comprehend, although the times of the year go on in their wonted course; we had rather, glorifie and bless God, for the fruit we daily behold, reaped by such Ordinances as his gracious Spirit maketh the ripe wisdom of this National Church to bring forth, than vainly boast of our own peculiar and private inventions, as if the skill of [e] profitable Regiment had left her publick habitation, to dwell in retired manner with some few men of one livery; we make not our childish [f] appeals sometimes from our own to forreign Churches, sometime from both unto Churches ancienter than both are, in effect always from all others to our own selves, but as becometh them that follow with all humility the ways of peace, we honour, reverence and obey, in the very next degree unto God, the voice of the Church of God wherein we live. They, whose wits are too glorious to fall to so low an ebbe, they which have risen and swollen so high, that the walls of ordinary Rivers are unable to keep them in, they whose wanton contentions in the cause whereof we have spoken, do make all where they go, a Sea, even they at their highest float, are constrained both to see and [g] grant, that what their fancy will not yield to like, their judgement cannot with reason condemn. Such is evermore the final victory of all truth, that they which have not the hearts to love her, acknowledge, that to hate her they have no cause.

Touching those festival Days therefore which we now observe, their number being no way felt [h] discommodious to the Common-wealth, and their grounds such as hitherto hath been shewed, what remaineth, but to keep them throughout, all generations holy, severed by manifest notes of difference from other times, adorned with that which most may betoken true, virtuous, and celestial joy? To which intent, because surcease from labour is necessary, yet not so necessary, no not on the Sabbath or Seventh Day it self, but that rarer occasions in mens particular Affairs subject to manifest detriment, unless they be presently followed, may with very good conscience draw them sometimes aside from the ordinary rule, considering the favourable dispensation which our Lord and Saviour grounded on this Axiome,

2 *Mac.* 15. 36.

1 *Mac.* 4. 55.

a *Commemoratio Apostolica passionis totius Christianitatis magistra à cunctis jure celebratur.* Cod. l. 3. tit. 12. l. 7.   b *T. C. l.* 1. 153. For so much as the old people did never keep any Feast or Holy day for remembrance either of *Moses*, &c.   c *T. C. l.* 1. p. 153. The people, when it is called S. *Pauls* day, or the blessed Virgin *Maries* day, can understand nothing thereby, but that they are instituted to the honour of Saint *Paul*, or the Virgin *Mary*, unless they be otherwise taught. And if you say, let them so be taught; I have answered, that the teaching in this Land, cannot by any order which is yet taken, come to the most part of those, which have drunk this poyson, &c.   d *Scilicet ignorant nos nec Christum unquam relinquere, qui pro totius servandorum mundi salute passus est, nec alium quempiam colere posse. Nam hunc quidem tanquam filium Dei adoramus, Martyres verò tanquam Discipulos & Imitatores Domini dignè propter insuperabilem in Regem ipsorum ac Praeceptorem benevolentiam diligimus, quorum & nos consortes & discipulos fieri optamus.* Euseb. Hist. Eccles. lib. 4. cap. 15.

e *T. C. l.* 1. p. 153. As for all the commodities, &c.

f *T. C. l.* 1. p. 154.

g *T. C. l.* 1. p. 154. We condemn not the Church of England, neither in this, nor in other things, which are meet to be reformed. For it is one thing to mislike, another thing to condemn, and it is one thing to condemn something in the Church, and another thing to condemn the Church for it.

h Πολλὰς μὲν θυσίας πολλαὶ ἦ χ ἱερομηνίαι ἄς ἕπανσε τὸ τῆ ⟨ϖ⟩ πλεῖσον τῶ ἔτσς τις αὐταὶ ἀνηλίσκετο χ τῶ δ'ημοσίω ζημία ἐκ ἐλαχίση ἐγίγνετο. de Claudio dictû apud Dion. l. 60

ome, *Man was not made for the Sabbath, but the Sabbath ordained for man*, so far Mark 2. 27.
forth as concerneth Ceremonies annexed thereof and to the principal Sanctification thereof, Numb. 15.32.
howsoever the rigour of the Law of *Moses* may be thought to import the contrary,
if we regard with what severity the violation of Sabbaths hath been sometime punished, a thing perhaps the more requisite at that instant, both because the Jews
by reason of their long abode in a place of continual servile toil, could not suddenly be wained and drawn unto contrary offices, without some strong impression of
terrour; and also for that there is nothing more needful, then to punish with extremity the first transgressions of those Laws, that require a more exact observation
for many Ages to come; therefore as the Jews superstitiously addicted to their Sab- a *Hi vacare*
baths rest for a long time, not without danger to themselves, and [b] obloquie to their *consueti sunt*
very Law, did afterwards perceive and amend wisely their former errour, not doubt- *septima die, &*
ing that bodily labours are made by [b]   *neq; arma por-*
necessity venial, though otherwise espe-   *tare in prædictis diebus, neque terræ culturam contingere, neq; al-*
cially on that day, rest be more conveni-   *terius cujuspiam curam habere patiuntur, sed in templis extenden-*
ent, so at all times the voluntary scanda-   *tes manus adorare usq; ad vesperam soliti sunt. Ingrediente verò*
lous contempt of that rest from labour,   *in civitatem* Ptolomæo Lago *cum exercitu & multis hominibus,*
wherewith publickly God is served, we   *cum custodire debuerint civitatem, ipsis stultitiam observantibus*
                                             provincia qnidem Dominum suscepit amarissimum, lex verò mani-
cannot too severely correct and bridle.   *festata est, malam habere solennitatem.* Agatharchid. apud Joseph.
The Emperour [a] *Constantine* having with   lib. 1. cont. Appion. vide & Dion. l. 37. b 1 Mac. 2.40.
over-great facility licensed Sundays labours in Country Villages, under that pre-   c *Neh.* 13. 15.
tence, whereof there may justly no doubt sometime consideration be had, namely,   d *Cod. l.* 3. *tit.*
left any thing which God by his providence hath bestowed, should miscarry, not   12. l. 3.
being taken in due time. *Leo*, which afterwards saw that this ground would not
bear so general and large indulgence as had been granted, doth, by a contrary Edict,
both reverse and severely censure his Predecessours remissness, saying, *We ordain*   e *Leo consti.* 54.
according to the true meaning of the Holy Ghost, and of the Apostles thereby directed,
that on the sacred Day, wherein our own integrity was restored, all do rest and surcease
labour, that neither Husband-man nor other on that day put their hands to forbidden
works. For if the Jews did so much reverence their Sabbath, which was but a shad-
dow of ours, are not we which inhabit the light and truth of grace, bound to honour that
day which the Lord himself hath honoured, and hath therein delivered us both from
dishonour and from death? are we not bound to keep it singular and inviolable, well
contenting our selves with so liberal a grant of the rest, and not incroaching upon that
one, which God hath chosen to his own honour? Were it not wretchless neglect of Reli-
gion, to make that very day common, and to think we may do with it as with the rest?
Imperial Laws which had such care of hallowing, especially, our Lords Day, did not
omit to provide that [f] other Festival times might be kept with vacation from labour, f *T.C.l.* 3. *tit.* 11
whether they were days appointed on the sudden, as extraordinary occasions fell   *Dies festos.*
out, or days which were celebrated yearly, for Politick and Civil considerations;
or finally, such days as Christian Religion hath ordained in Gods Church. The joy
that setteth aside labour, disperseth those things which labour gathereth. For gladness doth always rise from a kind of fruition and happiness, which happiness banisheth the cogitation of all want, it needeth nothing but only the bestowing of that
it hath, inasmuch as the greatest felicity that felicity hath, is to spread and enlarge
it self; it cometh hereby to pass, that the first effect of joyfulness is to rest, because it seeketh no more; the next, because it aboundeth, to give. The root of both
is the glorious presence of that joy of mind which riseth from the manifold considerations of Gods unspeakable mercy, into which considerations we are led by occasion of sacred times. For how could the Jewish Congregations of old be put in mind
by their weekly Sabbaths, what the World reaped through his goodness, which did
of nothing creat the World; by their yearly Passover, what farewell they took of
the Land of *Ægypt*; by their Pentecost, what Ordinances, Laws, and Statutes,
their Fathers received at the hands of God; by their Feast of Tabernacles, with
what protection they journeyed from place to place, through so many fears and
hazards, during the tedious time of forty years travel in the Wilderness; by their
Annual solemnity of Lots, how near the whole seed of *Israel* was unto utter extirpation, when it pleased that great God which guideth all things in Heaven and
                                                                              Earth,

Earth, fo to change the councils and purpofes of men, that the fame hand which had figned a Decree in the opinion both of them that granted, and of them that procured it, irrevocable, for the general maffacre of Man, Woman, and Child, became the Buckler of their prefervation, that no one hair of their heads might be toucht; the fame days which had been fet for the pouring out of fo much innocent blood, were made the days of their execution, whofe malice had contrived the plot thereof; and the felf-fame perfons that fhould have endured whatfoever violence and rage could offer, were imployed in the juft revenge of cruelty, to give unto [a] bloud-thirfty men the tafte of their own Cup: or how can the Church of Chrift now indure to be fo much called on and preached unto by that which every [a] Dominical Day throughout the year, that which year by year fo many Feftival times, [b] if not commanded by the Apoftles themfelves, whofe care at that time was of greater things, yet inftituted either by fuch [c] univerfal authority, as no man, or at the leaft fuch as we, with no reafon may defpife, do as fometime the holy Angels did from Heaven, fing, [d] *Glory be unto God on high, peace on earth, towards men good will* (for this in effect is the very Song that all Chriftian Feafts do apply as their feveral occafions require) how fhould the days and times continually thus inculcate what God hath done, and we refufe to agnize the benefit of fuch remembrances; that very benefit which caufed *Mofes* to acknowledge thofe Guides of Day and Night, the Sun and Moon which enlighten the World, not more profitable to nature by giving all things life, then they are to the Church of God, by occafion of the ufe they have, in regard of the appointed Feftival Times? That which the head of all Philofophers hath faid of Women, if they be good, the half of the Common-wealth is happy, wherein they are; the fame we may fitly apply to times; well to celebrate thefe religious and facred days, is to fpend the flower of our time happily. They are the fplendor and outward dignity of our Religion, forcible Witneffes of ancient Truth, provocations to the exercifes of all Piety, fhadows of our endlefs felicity in Heaven, on Earth everlafting Records and Memorials, wherein they which cannot be drawn to hearken unto that we teach, may only by looking upon that we do, in a manner read whatfoever we beleive.

72. The matching of contrary things together is a kind of illuftration to both. Having therefore fpoken thus much of Feftival Days, the next that offer themfelves to hand, are days of penfive humiliation and forrow. Faftings are either of mens own free and voluntary accord, as their particular devotion doth move them thereunto; or elfe they are publickly injoyned in the Church, and required at the hands of all men. There are which altogether difallow not the former kinde; and the latter they greatly commend, fo that it be upon extraordinary occafions only, and after one certain manner exercifed. But yearly or weekly Fafts, fuch as ours in the Church of *England*, they allow no farther, then as the Temporal State of the Land doth require the fame, for the maintenance of Sea-faring-men, and prefervation of Cattel, becaufe the decay of the one, and the wafte of the other, could not well be prevented but by a Politick order, appointing fome fuch ufual change of Diet as ours is. We are therefore the rather to make it manifeft in all mens eyes, that fet times of Fafting appointed in fpiritual confideration to be kept by all forts of men, took not their beginning either from *Montanus*, or any other, whofe Herefies may prejudice the

Marginal notes:

a Mat. 28. 1.
Mark 16. 1.
Luke 24. 1.
John 20. 1.
1 Cor. 16. 2.
Apoc. 1. 10.

b *Apoftolis propofitum fuit non ut leges de feftis diebus celebrandis fancirent, fed ut, recta vivendi rationis & pietatis nobis authores effent. Socrat. Hift. lib. 5. cap. 25.* c *Quæ toto terrarum orbe fervantur, vel ab ipfis Apoftolis vel Confiliis generalibus quorum eft faluberrima in Ecclefia authoritas, ftatuta effe intelligere licet: ficuti quod Domini Paffio & Refurrectio, & in Cælum Afcenfus; & Adventus fpiritus fancti anniverfaria folennitate celebrantur. Aug. Ep. 118.* d *Luke 1. 14.*

Of Dayes appointed as well for ordinary, as for extraordinary Fafts in own free and voluntary accord, as their particular devotion doth move them thereunto; or elfe they are publickly injoyned in the Church of God.

T. C. l. 1. p. 30. I will not enter now to difcufs whether it were well done to faft in all places according to the cuftome of the place. You oppofe *Ambrofe* and *Auguftine*, I could oppofe *Ignatius* and *Tertullian*, whereof the one faith, it is *nefas*, a deteftable thing to faft upon the Lords Day; the other, that it is to kill the Lord. *Tertul. de Coron. mil. Ignatius, Epift. ad Philippen.* And although *Ambrofe* and *Auguftine* being private men of *Rome* would have fo done, yet it followeth not, but they had been Citizens and Minifters there, that they would have done it. And if they had done fo, yet it followeth not, that if they would have fpoken againft that appointment of Days, and *nomotefian* of Fafting, whereof *Eufebius* faith, that *Montanus* was the firft Author. I fpeak of that which they ought to have done. For otherwife I know, they both thought corruptly of Fafting, when as the one faith, it was a remedy or reward to faft other days, but in Lent not to faft, was fin: and the other asketh, what falvation we can obtain, if we blot not out our fins by Fafting, feeing that the Scripture faith, that Fafting and Almes doth deliver from fin, and therefore calleth them new Teachers, that fhut out the merit of Fafting. *Aug. de temp. 62. Ser. Amb. lib. 10. Ep.*

the credit and due eſtimation thereof, but have their ground in the Law of Nature, are allowable in Gods ſight, were in all Ages heretofore, and may till the Worlds end be obſerved, not without ſingular uſe and benefit. Much hurt hath grown to the Church of God, through a falſe imagination, that Faſting ſtandeth men in no ſtead for any ſpiritual reſpect, but only to take down the franckneſs of Nature, and to tame the wildeneſs of fleſh. Whereupon the World being bold to ſurfeit, doth now bluſh to faſt; ſuppoſing that men when they faſt, do rather bewray a Diſeaſe, then exerciſe a Virtue. I much wonder what they who are thus perſwaded do think, what conceit they have concerning the Faſts of the Patriarks, the Prophets, the Apoſtles, our Lord Jeſus Chriſt himſelf. The affections of *Joy* and *Grief* are ſo knit unto all the actions of mans life, that whatſoever we can do, or may be done unto us, the ſequel thereof is continually the one or the other affection. Wherefore conſidering that they which grieve and joy as they ought, cannot poſſibly otherwiſe live then as they ſhould, the Church of Chriſt, the moſt abſolute and perfect School of all virtue, hath by the ſpecial direction of Gods good Spirit hitherto always inured men from their infancy, partly with days of Feſtival Exerciſe, for the framing of the one affection; and partly with times of a contrary ſort, for the perfecting of the other. Howbeit over and beſides this, we muſt note, that as reſting, ſo faſting likewiſe attendeth ſometimes no leſs upon the Actions of the higher, than upon the affections of the lower part of the mind. Faſting, ſaith *Tertullian*, is a work of reverence towards God. The end thereof ſometimes elevation of mind; ſometime the purpoſe thereof quite contrary. The cauſe why *Moſes* in the Mount did ſo long faſt, was meer divine ſpeculation; the cauſe why *David*, [a] humiliation. Our life is [b] a mixture of good with evil. When we are partakers of good things, we joy, neither can we but grieve at the contrary. If that befall us which maketh glad, our Feſtival Solemnities declare our rejoycing to be in him whoſe meer undeſerved mercy is the Author of all happineſs; if any thing be either imminent or preſent which we ſhun, our Watchings, Faſtings, Cryes, and Tears, are unfained reſtimonies, that our ſelves we condemne as the only cauſes of our own miſery, and do all acknowledge him no leſs inclinable than able to ſave. And becauſe as the memory of the one, though paſt, reneweth gladneſs; ſo the other called again to mind doth make the wound of our juſt remorſe to bleed a-new, which wound needeth often touching the more, for that we are generally more apt to Kalender Saints then ſinners days, therefore there is in the Church a care not to iterate the one alone, but to have frequent repetition of the other. Never to ſeek after God, ſaving only when either the Crib or the Whip doth conſtrain were bruitiſh ſervility, and a great derogation to the worth of that which is moſt predominant in man, if ſometime it had not a kind of voluntary acceſs to God, and of conference as it were with God, all theſe inferiour conſiderations laid aſide. In which ſequeſtration foraſmuch as [c] higher cogitations do naturally drown and bury all inferior cares, the mind may as well forget natural both food and ſleep, by being carried above it ſelf with ſerious and heavenly Meditation, as by being caſt down with heavineſs, drowned and ſwallowed up of ſorrow. Albeit therefore concerning Jewiſh Abſtinence from certain kinds of meats, as being unclean, the Apoſtle doth teach that [d] the Kingdom of Heaven is not meat nor drink, that food commendeth us not unto God, whether we take it, or abſtain from it; that if we eat, we are not thereby the more acceptable in his ſight, nor the leſs if we eat not; his purpoſe notwithſtanding was far from any intent to derogate from that Faſting, which is no ſuch ſcrupulous Abſtinence, as only refuſeth ſome kinds of meats and drinks, leſt they make them unclean that taſte them; but an Abſtinence whereby we either interrupt or otherwiſe abridge the care of our bodily ſuſtenance, to ſhew by this kind of outward exerciſe, the ſerious intention of our minds, fixed on Heavenſier and better deſires, the earneſt hunger and thirſt whereof depriveth the body of thoſe uſual contentments, which otherwiſe are not denied unto it. Theſe being in Nature the firſt cauſes that induce faſting, the next thing which followeth to be conſidered, is the ancient practice therof amongſt the Jews. Touching whoſe private voluntary Faſts, the Precept our Saviour gave them, was, *When ye faſt, look not ſowr, as Hypocrites: For they disfigure their faces, that they might ſeem to men to faſt: Verily I ſay unto you, they have their reward. When thou faſteſt, anoint thy head; & waſh thy face, that thou ſeem not*

unto

[a] *Tertul. de jejun. Neque enim cibi tempus in periculo: ſemper inedia mœroris ſequela eſt.*

[b] Μεᾶδεῖς δ᾽ ὖ-πολαβέτω τꞷ ἄκρατον κ᾽ ἀμιγῆ λύπης χάᾳε ἀπ᾽ ὀυεργꞷ κατάβαινειν ἐπὶ τꞷ γꞷ, ἀλλ᾽ ἐγκέκρωται ἐξ ἀμφοῖν, ὀυ γᾳ ἵλαςⴱ ὁ πατὴρ τὸ ἀνθρώπων γένος λυπαῖς κ᾽ ὀ-δύναις κ᾽ ἀχθεσιν ἀνιάϊσι ἐμφερεσⴱ, ᴃ τꞷ-ρεμιζⴳε δὲ κ᾽ Τῆς ἀμεινονος φύσεως, ἐυδιάσᴂ ποτ᾽ κ᾽ ναλωιάσαι τꞷ ψυχꞷ δικαιώϊⴲ. *Philo. lib. de Abrah.*

[c] *John* 4. 34.

[d] *Rom.* 14. 17.

Mat. 6. 16.

unto men to faſt, but unto thy Father which is in ſecret, and thy Father which ſeeth in ſecret will reward thee openly. Our Lord and Saviour would not teach the manner of doing, much leſs propoſe a reward for doing that, which were not both holy and acceptable in Gods ſight. The Phariſees weekly bound themſelves unto double Faſts, neither are they for this reproved. Often faſting, which was a virtue in *Johns* Diſciples, could not in them of it ſelf be a vice ; and therefore not the oftenneſs of their faſting, but their hypocriſie therein was blamed. Of [a] publick injoined Faſts, upon cauſes extraordinary, the examples of Scripture are ſo far frequent, that they need no particular rehearſal. Publick extraordinary Faſtings were ſometimes for [b] one only day, ſometimes for [c] three, ſometimes for [d] ſeven. Touching Faſts not appointed for any ſuch extraordinary cauſes, but either yearly, or monethly, or weekly obſerved and kept ; Firſt, upon the [e] ninth day of that moneth, the tenth whereof was the Feaſt of Expiation, they were commanded of God, that every ſoul, year by year, ſhould afflict it ſelf. Their yearly Faſts every fourth moneth, in regard of the City of *Jeruſalem*, entred by the Enemy ; every fifth, for the memory of the overthrow of their Temple ; every ſeventh, for the treacherous deſtruction and death of *Gedaliah*, the very laſt ſtay which they had to lean unto in their greateſt miſery ; every tenth, in remembrance the time when ſiege began firſt to be laid againſt them ; all theſe not commanded by God himſelf, but ordained by a publick Conſtitution of their own ; the Prophet [f] *Zachary* expreſly toucheth, That Saint *Jerome*, following the tradition of the Hebrews, doth make the firſt, a memorial of the breaking of thoſe two Tables, when *Moſes* deſcended from Mount Sinai ; the ſecond a memorial as well of Gods indignation, condemning them to forty years travel in the Deſart, as of his wrath in permitting Chaldeans to waſte, burn and deſtroy their City ; the laſt, a heavy tydings, brought out of *Jury* to *Ezechiel* and the reſt, which lived as Captives in forrain parts, the difference is not of any moment, conſidering that each time of ſorrow is naturally evermore a Regiſter of all ſuch grievous events as have hapned, either in, or near about the ſame time. To theſe I might adde [g] ſundry other Faſts, above twenty in number, ordained amongſt them by like occaſions, and obſerved in like manner, beſides their weekly Abſtinence, Mundays and Thurſdays, throughout the whole year. When men faſted, it was not always after one and the ſame ſort, but either by depriving themſelves wholly of all food, during the time that their Faſts continued, or by abating both the quantity and kind of Diet. We have of the one a plain Example in the Ninivites Faſting, and as plain a preſident for the other in the Prophet *Daniel, I was* (ſaith he) *in heavineſs for three weeks of days, I eat no pleaſant bread, neither taſted fleſh nor wine.* Their tables, when they gave themſelves to faſting, had not that uſual furniture of ſuch Diſhes as do cheriſh blood with blood, but [h] for food they had bread, for ſuppage, ſalt, and for ſawce, hearbs. Whereunto the Apoſtle may be thought to allude, ſaying, *One beleeveth he may eat all things, another which is weak* (and maketh a conſcience of keeping thoſe cuſtomes which the Iewes obſerve) *eateth herbs.* This auſtere repaſt they took in the Evening, after abſtinence the whole day. For, to forfeit a noons Meale, and then to reccompence themſelves at night, was not their uſe. Nor did they ever accuſtome themſelves on Sabbaths or Feſtival days to faſt. And yet it may be a queſtion whether in ſome ſort they did not always faſt the Sabbath. Their Faſtings were partly in token of penitency, humiliation, grief and ſorrow, partly in ſigne of devotion and reverence towards God. Which ſecond conſideration (I dare not peremptorily and boldly affirm any thing) might induce to abſtain till noon, as their manner was on faſting days to do till night. May it not very well be thought that hereunto the ſacred [i] Scripture doth give ſome ſecret kind of Teſtimony? *Joſephus* is plain, that the ſixth hour (the day they divided into twelve) was wont on the Sabbath always to call them home unto meat. Neither is it improbable but that the [k] Heathens did therfore ſo often upbraid them with Faſting on that day. Beſides, they which found ſo great fault with our Lords Diſciples, for rubbing a few ears of corn in their hands on the Sabbath Day,

Mat. 6. 16.
a 2 Chron. 20.
Ier. 36. Ezra 8.
1 Sam. 7.
b Iudg. 20. 12.
c 2 Mac. 13. 12.
d 1 Sam. 31. 13.
1 Chron. 10. 12
e Levit. 13.
Levit. 16.
Philo de hujus feſti jejunio ita loquitur.
Οὐ σῖτον ἐν πόλῳ ἔξεσι προσενέγκαϑ καϑαρᾶις ὅπως διανοίαις μεδενὸς ἐνοχλουντος μηδὲ ἐμποδίζοντ σωμα-τικᾶ παϑους ὁποῖα φιλεῖ συμβαίνειν ἐκ πλησμονῆς ἐορτάζουσιν ἱλασκόμενοι τὸν παντῆρα τῶ παντὸς ὁσίαις εὐχᾶις διῶν ἀμνηςείαν μὲν παλαιῶν ἁμαρτημάτων κτῆσιν δὲ ἀπόλαυσιν νεων ἀγαϑῶν ἱλάςαςιν αἰτῆςαι.pag. 447.
f Zac. 8. 16.
Exod. 31.
Numb. 14.
g Vide Riber. l. 5. c. 21.
Dan. 10. 23.
h *Puram & ſine animalibus cœnam. Apul. in Aſclep. in fine Paſtum & potum purum noſſe, non ventris ſcilicet ſed anima cauſa.* Tertul. de pœnit. vide Phil. lib. de vita contempl.
Rom. 14. 2.

Hieron. lib. 2. cont. Jovinian. Judith 8. 6. R. Moſ. in Miſne. Tora. lib. 3. *qui eſt de tempor.* cap. de Sab. & cap. de Jejun. i Neh. 8. 3. 12. *Hora ſexta qua Sabbatè noſtrû ad prandium vocare ſolet ſuper venit. Ioſeph. lib. de vita ſua.* k *Sabbata Iudæorum à Moſe in omne ævum jejunio dicata.* Iuſtin. lib. 36. *Ne Iudæus quidem, mi Tiberi, tam libenter Sabbati jejunium ſervat, quàm ego hodie ſervavi.* Sutton. in Octav. cap. 76. Acts 2, 15.

etc.

are not unlikely to have aimed at the same mark. For neither was the bodily pain so great that it should offend them in that respect, and the very manner of defence which our Saviour there useth, is more direct and literal to Justifie the breach of the Jewish custome in Fasting, than in working at that time. Finally, the Apostles afterwards themselves when God first gave them the gift of Tongues, whereas some in disdain and spight termed grace drunkenness, it being then the day of Pentecost, and but only a fourth part of the day spent, they use this as an argument against the other cavil; *These men*, saith *Peter*, *are not drunk as you suppose, since as yet the* **Acts 2. 15.** *third hour of the day is not over-past.* Howbeit, leaving this in suspence, as a thing not altogether certainly known, and to come from Jews to Christians, we finde that of private voluntary Fastings the Apostle S. *Paul* speaketh [a] more then once. **a 1 Cor. 7. 5.** And (saith *Tertullian*) they are sometime commanded throughout the Church, *ex* **2 Cor. 11. 27.** *aliqua sollicitudinis Ecclesiastica causa,*the care and fear of the Church so requiring. **Col. 4. 4.** It doth not appear that the Apostles ordained any set and certain days to be generally kept of all. Notwithstanding, forasmuch as Christ hath fore-signified, that when himself should be taken from them, his absence would soon make them apt to fast, it seemeth that even as the first Festival Day appointed to be kept of the Church was the Day of our Lords return from the dead; so the first sorrowful and mourning day was that we now observe in memory of his departure out of this World. And because there could be no abatement of grief, till they saw him raised whose death was the occasion of their heaviness; therefore the day he lay in Sepulchre hath been also kept and observed as a weeping day. The custome of fasting these two days before Easter, is undoubtedly most ancient, in so much that *Igna-* **Ignat. Ep. ad** *tius* not thinking him a Catholique Christian man which did not abhor (and as the **Philip.** state of the Church was then) avoid fasting on the Jews Sabbath, doth notwithstanding except for ever that one Sabbath or Satturday which falleth out to be the Easter-eve, as with us it always doth, and did sometimes also with them which kept at that time their Easter the fourteenth day of *March*, as the custom of the Jews was. It came afterward to be an order, that even as the day of Christs Resurrection, so the other two, in memory of his death and burial, were weekly. But this when St. *Ambrose* lived, had not as yet taken place throughout all Churches, no not in *Millan*, where himself was Bishop. And for that cause he saith, that although at *Rome* he observed the Saturdays-fast, because such was then the custome in *Rome*, neverthelefs in his own Church at home he did otherwise. The Churches which did not observe that day, had another instead thereof, which was the Wednesday, for that when they judged it meet to have weekly a day of humiliation, besides that whereon our Saviour suffered death, it seemed best to make their choice of that day especially, whereon the Jews are thought to have first contrived their treason together with *Judas* against Christ. So that the instituting and ordaining both of these and of all other times of like exercise, is as the Church shall judge, expedient for mens good. And concerning every Christian mans duty herein, surely that which *Augustine* and *Ambrose* are before alleadged to have done, is such, as all men savouring equity must needs allow, and follow, if they affect peace. As for specified errours, I will not in this place dispute, whether voluntary fasting with a vertuous purpose of mind, be any medicinable remedy of evil, or a duty acceptable unto God, and in the world to come even rewardable, as other offices are which proceed from Christian piety; whether wilfully to break and dispose the wholesome Laws of the Church herein, be a thing which offendeth God; whether truly it may not be said, that penitent both weeping and fasting, are means to blot out sin, means whereby through Gods unspeakable and undeserved mercy we obtain or procure to our selves pardon; which attainment unto any gracious benefit by him bestowed, the Phrase of antiquity useth to express by the name of merit; but if either Saint *Augustine*, or Saint *Ambrose* have taught any wrong opinion, seeing they which reprove them are not altogether free from errour, I hope they will think it no errour in us so to censure mens smaller faults, that their vertues be not thereby generally prejudiced. And if in Churches abroad, where we are not subject to power or jurisdiction, discretion should teach us for peace and quietness sake to frame our selves to other mens example, is it meet that at home

where

where our freedom is iefs, our boldnefs fhould be more? Is it our duty to oppugne, in the Churches whereof we are Minifters, the rites and cuftomes which
in forrain Churches piety and mod fly did teach us as ftrangers not to oppugne, but
to keep without fhew of contradiction or diflike? Why oppofe they the name of
a Mi ifter in this cafe unto the ftate of a private man? Doth their order exempt
them from obedience to Laws? That which their Office and place requireth, is
to fhew themfelves patterns of reverend fubjection, not Authours and Mafters
of contempt towards Ordinances, the ftrength whereof when they feek to weak-
en, they do but in truth difcover to the world their own imbecilities, which a
great deal wifelier they might conceal. But the practice of the Church of Chrift
we fhall by fo much the better both underftand and love, if to that which hitherto
hath been fpoken, there be fomewhat added for more particular declaration, how
Hereticks have partly abufed Fafts, and partly bent themfelves againft the lawful ufe thereof in the Church of God. Whereas therefore *Ignatius* hath faid, If
any keep Sundays or Saturdays Fafts (one only Saturday in the year excepted) that
man is no better then a murtherer of Chrift; the caufe of fuch his earneftnefs at
that time was the impiety of certain Hereticks, which thought [a] that this world
being corruptible, could not be made but a very evil Author. And therefore as
the Jews did by the Feftival Solemnity of their Sabbath, rejoyce in the God that
created the world, as in the Author of all goodnefs: fo thofe Hereticks in hatred
of the Maker of the world, forrowed, wept, and fafted on that day, as being the
birth-day of all evil. And as Chriftian men of found belief, did folemnize the Sunday, in joyful memory of Chrifts Refurrection, fo likewife at the felf-fame time
fuch hereticks as denied his refurrection, did the contrary to them which held it;
when the one fort rejoyced, the other fafted. Againft thofe hereticks, which have
urged perpetual abftinence from certain meats, as being in their very nature unclean,
the Church hath ftill bent her felf as an enemy; Saint *Paul* giving charge to take
heed of them, which under any fuch opinion, fhould utterly forbid the ufe of meats
or drinks. The Apoftles themfelves forbad fome, as the order taken at *Jerufalem* declareth. But the caufe of their fo doing, we all know. Again, when *Tertullian*, together with fuch as were his followers, began to Montanize, and pretending to perfect the feverity of Chriftian Difcipline, brought in fundry unaccuftomed
days of fafting, continued their Fafts a great deal longer, and made them more rigorous then the ufe of the Church had been; the minds of men being fomewhat moved at fo great, and fo fudden novelty, the caufe was prefently inquired into. After
notice taken how the Montanifts held thefe additions to be fupplements of the
Gofpel, whereunto the Spirit of Prophefie did now mean to put, as it were, the laft
hand, and was therefore newly defcended upon *Montanus*, whofe orders all Chriftian men were no lefs to obey, then the Laws of the Apoftles themfelves; this
abftinence the Church abhorred likewife, and that juftly. Whereupon *Tertullian*
proclaiming even open war to the Church, maintained Montanifme, wrote a
Book in defence of the new Faft, and intituled the fame; *A Treatife of Fafting
againft the opinion of the carnal fort.* In which Treatife neverthelefs, becaufe fo
much is found and good, as doth either generally concern the ufe, or in particular
declare the cuftome of the Churches fafting in thofe times, men are not to reject
whatfoever is alledged out of that book, for confirmation of the truth. His errour
difclofeth it felf in thofe places, where he defendeth Fafts to be duties neceffary for
the whole Church of Chrift to obferve as commanded by the holy Ghoft, and
that with the fame authority from whence all other Apoftolical ordinances came,
both being the Laws of God himfelf, without any other diftinction or difference,
faving only that he which before had declared his will by *Paul* and *Peter*, did now
farther reveal the fame by *Montanus* alfo. *Againft us ye pretend,* faith *Tertullian,
that the publick orders which Chriftianity is bound to keep, were delivered at the firft,
and that no new thing is to be added thereunto. Stand if you can upon this point; For behold, I challenge you for fafting more than at Eafter your felves. But in fine ye anfwer,
that thefe things are to be done as eftablifhed by the voluntary appointment of men, and
not by virtue or force of any divine Commandment. Well then* (he addeth) *Ye have
removed your firft footing, and gone beyond that which was delivered, by doing more*
than

'Ἐι τις κυείξ,
κλω̃ ἢ σάββα-
τον νηςεύει
σπλω̃ ἑνὸς
σαββάτε ὅτος
χειροκτόν@,
ἔ]. Epiſt. ad
Philip.
a Vide Irenæ.
l.1.c.20,21,22,
23,24,25. Epi.
harcf.23,22,23
24,27,28, &
41, 42.
Vide Canon.
Apoſt. 55.

than was at the first imposed upon you. You say, you must do that which your own judg-
ments have allowed: we require your obedience to that which God himself doth insti-
tute. Is it not strange that men to their own will should yield that which to Gods Com-
mandment they will not grant? Shall the pleasure of men prevail more with you than
the power of God himself? These places of *Tertullian* for fasting, have worthily been
put to silence. And as worthily *Aerius* condemned for opposition against fasting. The
one endeavoured to bring in such fasts as the Church ought not to receive; the o-
ther, to overthrow such as already it had received and did observe; the one was plausible unto many by seeming to hate carnal looseness and riotous excess much more
than the rest of the world did; the other drew hearers, by pretending the maintenance of Christian liberty; the one thought his cause very strongly upheld by making
invective declamations with a pale and a withered countenance against the Church,
by filling the ears of his starved hearers with speech sutable to such mens humours,
and by telling them, no doubt to their marvellous contentment and liking, *Our new*
Prophesies are refused, they are despised. Is it because Montanus *doth preach some*
other god, or dissolve the Gospel of Jesus Christ, or overthrow any Canon of faith and
hope? No, our crime is, we teach that men ought to fast more often then marry, the best
feast-maker is with them the perfectest Saint, they are assuredly meer Spirit, and there-
fore these our carporal devotions please them not: thus the one for *Montanus* and his
Superstition. The other in a clean contrary tune against the Religion of the Church.   Epiph. Hær. 75.
These set-fasts away with them, for they are Jewish, and bring men under the yoke of
servitude: if I will fast let me chuse my time, that Christian liberty be not abridged:
Hereupon their glory was to fast especially upon the Sunday, because the order of
the Church was on that day not to fast. *On Church fasting-days, & especially the week*
before Easter, when with us (saith Epiphanius) *custome admitteth nothing but lying*
down upon the earth, abstinence from fleshly delights and pleasures, sorrowfulness, dry and
unsavoury diet, prayer, watching, fasting, all the medicines which holy affections can
minister, they are up betimes to take in of the strongest for the belly; and when their
veins are well swoln, they make themselves mirth with laughter at this our service,
wherein we are perswaded we please God. By this of *Epiphanius* it doth appear, not only what fastings the Church of Christ in those times used, but also what other
parts of Discipline were together therewith in force, according to the ancient use
and custome of bringing all men at certain times to a due consideration and an open
humiliation of themselves. Two kinds there were of publick penitency; the one
belonging to notorious offenders, whose open wickedness had been scandalous;
the other appertaining to the whole Church, and unto every several person whom
the same containeth. It will be answered, that touching this latter kind it may be
exercised well enough by men in private. No doubt, but penitency is as Prayer,
a thing acceptable unto God, be it in publick or in secret. How if as in the one, if
men were wholly left to their own voluntary Meditations in their Closets, and not
drawn by Laws and Orders unto the open Assemblies of the Church, that there they
may joyn with others in Prayer, it may be soon conjectured, what Christian devotion that way would come unto in a short time: even so in the other, we are by
sufficient experience taught, how little it booteth to tell men of washing away their
sins with tears of Repentance, and so to leave them altogether unto themselves. O
Lord, what heaps of grievous transgressions have we committed, the best, the perfectest, the most righteous amongst us all, and yet can pass them over unsorrowed
for, and unrepented of; only because the Church hath forgotten utterly how to bestow her wonted times of Discipline, wherein the publick example of all was unto
every particular person, a most effectual mean to put them often in mind, and even
in a manner to draw them to that which now we all quite and clean forget, as if penitency were no part of a Christian mans duty. Again, besides our private offences
which ought not thus loosely to be over-slipt, suppose we the body and corporation
of the Church so just, that at no time it needeth to shew it self openly cast down in
regard of those faults and transgressions, which though they do not properly be long
unto any one, had notwithstanding a special Sacrifice appointed for them in the Law
of *Moses*, & being common to the whole society which containeth all, must needs
so far concern every man in particular, as at sometime in solemn manner to require

acknowledgment

ment with more then daily and ordinary rectifications of grief. There could not hereunto a fitter preamble be devised, then that memorable commination set down in the Book of Common-Prayer, if our practice in the rest were sutable. The head already so well drawn, doth but wish a proportionable body. And by the Preface to that very part of the English Liturgy, it may appear how at the first setting down thereof, no less was intended. For so we are to interpret the meaning of these words, wherein restitution of the Primitive Church Discipline is greatly for, touching the manner of publique penance in time of Lent. Wherewith some being not much acquainted, but having framed in their minds the conceit of a new Discipline, far unlike to that of old, they make themselves believe, it is undoubtedly this their Discipline, which at the first was so much desired. They have long pretended that the whole Scripture is plain for them. If now the Communion Book make for them too (I well think the one doth as much as the other) it may be hoped that being found such a well-willer unto their cause, they will more favour it than they have do e. Having therefore hitherto spoken, both of Festival days, and so much of solemne Fasts, as may reasonably serve to shew the ground thereof in the Law of Nature, the practice partly appointed, and partly allowed of God in the Jewish Church, the like continued in the Church of Christ, together with the sinister oppositions, either of Hereticks erroneously abusing the same, or of others thereat quarrelling without cause, we will only collect the chiefest points as well of resemblance, as of difference between them, and so end. First, in this they agree, that because nature is the general root of both, therefore both have been always common to the Church with Infidels and Heathen men. Secondly, they also herein accord, that as oft as joy is the cause of the one, and grief the wel-spring of the other, they are [a] incompatible. A third degree of affinity between them, is, that neither being acceptable to God in it self, but both tokens of that which is acceptable, their approbation with him must necessarily depend on that which they ought to import and signifie; so that if herein the mind dispose not it self aright, whether we [b] rest or [c] fast we offend. A fourth thing common unto them is, that the greatest part of the world hath always grosly and palpably offended in both; Infidels because they did all in relation to false gods; godless, sensual, and careless minds, for that there is in them no constant, true and sincere affection towards those things which are pretended by such exercise; yea, certain flattering oversights they are, wherewith sundry, and they not of the worst sort, may be easily in these cases led awry, even through abundance of love and liking to that which must be imbraced by all means, but with caution, inasmuch as the very admiration of Saints, whether we celebrate their glory, or follow them in humility, whether we laugh or weep, mourn or rejoyce with them, is (as in all things the affection of love) apt to deceive, and doth therefore need the more to be directed by a watchful guide, seeing there is manifestly both ways, even in them whom we honour, that which we are to observe and shun. The best have not still been sufficiently mindful, that Gods very Angels in Heaven are but Angels, and that bodily exercise considered [d] in it self is no great matter. Finally, seeing that both are Ordinances well devised for the good of man, and yet not man created purposely for them; as for [e] other Offices of vertue whereunto Gods immutable Law for ever tyeth, it is but equity to wish or admonish that, where by uniform order they are not as yet received, the example of [f] Victors extremity in the one, and of [g] Johns Disciples curiosity in the other, be not followed; yea, where they are appointed by Law, that notwithstanding [h] we avoid Judaisme, and as in Festival days, mens necessities for matter of labour; so in times of Fasting, regard be had to their imbecillities, lest they should suffer harm, doing good. Thus therefore we see how these two customes are in divers respects equal. But of Fasting the use and exercise, though less pleasant, is by so much more requisite than the other, as grief of necessity is a more familiar guest then the contrary passion of mind, albeit gladness to all men be naturally more welcom. For first, we our selves do many moe things amiss than well, and the fruit of our own ill doing is remorse, because nature is conscious to it self that it should do the contrary. Again, forasmuch as the world over-aboundeth with malice, and few are delighted in doing good unto other men, there is no man so

a *Con. Laod. cap. 51. 52. vel 52. Nata itia Martyrum in Quadragessima celebrari.*
b *Esay. 1. 13.*
c *Esay. 58. 3.*

d *1 Tim. 4. 8.*
e *Eccles 11. 13. Esay. 58. 6, 7. Rom. 14. 17. Iac. 1. 27. Heb. 13. 14. Ephes. 2. 4.*
f *Euseb. Eccles. Hist. l.c.5.c.23.*
g *Matth. 9. 14.*
h *Col. 2. 16.*

seldome

feldome croft as pleafured at the hands of others, whereupon it cannot be chofen, but every mans woes muft dou'le in that refpect the number and meafure of his delights. Befides, concerning the very choice which oftentimes we are to make, our corrupt inclination well confidered, there is no caufe why our Saviour fhould account **Mat. 6. 4.** them happieft that do moft mourn, and why *Solomon* might judge it better to fre- **Ecclef. 7. 4.** quent mourning then feafting-houfes ; not better fimply and in it felf (for then would Nature that way incline) but in regard of us and our common weaknefs better. *Job* was not ignorant that his Childrens Banquets, though tending to amity, **Job 1. 5.** needed Sacrifice. Neither doth any of us all need to be taught that in things which delight, we [a] eafily fwarve from mediocrity, and are not eafily led by a right **a** 'Εν παντί δὲ direct line. On the other fide, the fores and difeafes of mind which inordinate μάλιςα φι- pleafure breedeth, are by dolour and grief cured. For which caufe as all offences ufe λαχτέον τὸ to feduce by pleafing, fo all punifhments endeavour by vexing to reform tranf- ἡδὺ κ, τὼ ἡ- greffions. We are of our own accord apt enough to give entertainment to things δονὴν κ, 'ὃ α- delectable, but patiently to lack what flefh and blood doth defire, and by vertue μεν αὐτὼ. to forbear what by nature we covet: this no man attaineth unto, but with labour **Arift. Eth. 2,** and long practice. From hence it rifeth, that in former Ages, abftinence and faft- **c. p. 13.** ing more then ordinary, was always a fpecial branch of their praife, in whom it could be obferved and known, were they fuch as continually gave themfelves to auftere life, or men that took often occafions in private vertuous refpects to lay *So-* *lomons* counfel afide, [b] *Eat thy Bread with joy,* and to be followers of *Davids* ex- **b Ecclef. 9. 7.** ample, which faith, [c] *I humbled my foul with fafting* ; or but they who otherwife **c Pfal. 35. 13.** worthy of no great commendation, have made of hunger, fome their gain, fome their Phyfick, fome their Art, that by maftering fenfual appetites without conftraint, they might grow able to indure hardnefs whenfoever need fhould require. For the body accuftomed to emptinefs pineth not away fo foon as having ftill ufed to fill it felf. Many fingular effects there are which fhould make fafting even in publick confiderations the rather to be accepted. For I prefume we are not altogether without experience how great their advantage is in martial enterprizes, that lead Armies of men trained in a School of abftinence. It is therefore noted at this day in fome, that patience of hunger and thirft hath given them many victories ; in others that becaufe if they want, there is no man able to rule them, nor they in plenty to moderate themfelves : he which can either bring them to hunger or overcharge them, is fure to make them their own overthrow. What Nation foever doth feel thefe dangerous inconveniencies, may know that floth and fulnefs in peaceable times at home is the caufe thereof, and the remedy a ftrict obfervation of that part of Chriftian Difcipline, which teacheth men in practice of ghoftly welfare againft themfelves, thofe things that afterwards may help them, juftly affaulting or ftanding in lawful defence of themfelves againft others. The very purpofe of the Church of God, both in the number and in the order of her Fafts, hath been not only to preferve thereby throughout all Ages, the remembrance of miferies heretofore fuftained, and of the caufes in our felves out of which they have rifen, that men confidering the one, might fear the other the more, but farther alfo to temper the mind, left contrary affections coming in place fhould make it too profufe and diffolute, in which refpect it feemeth that Fafts have been fet as Ufhers of Feftival Days, for prevention of thofe diforders, as much as might be ; wherein, notwithftanding, the World always will deferve, [d] as it hath done, blame ; becaufe fuch evils being not **d Valde abfur-** poffible to be rooted out, the moft we can doe, is in keeping them low ; and (which **dum eft nimia** is chiefly the fruit we look for) to create in the minds of men a love towards frugal **faturitate velle** and fevere life, to undermine the palaces of wantonnefs, to plant Parfimony as Na- **honorare marty-** ture, where Riotoufnefs hath been ftudied, to harden whom pleafure would melt, **rem quem fciss** and to help the tumours which always fulnefs breedeth, that children as it were in **Deo placuiffe** the Wool of their Infancy died with hardnefs, may never afterwards change colour; **jejuniis, Hier.** that the poor, whofe perpetual Fafts are of neceffity, may with better contentment **Epift. ad Euft.** endure the hunger, which Vertue caufeth others fo often to chufe ; and by advice of Religion it felf fo far to efteem above the contrary ; that they, which for the moft part do lead fenfual and eafie lives ; they which, as the Prophet *David* defcribeth **Pfal. 73. 5.** them, are not plagued like other men, may by the publick fpectacle of all be ftill

pu-

put in mind what themselves are ; finally, that every man may be every mans daily guide and example, as well by falling to declare humility, as by praise to expreſs joy in the ſight of God, although it have herein befaln the Church as ſometimes David ; ſo that the ſpeech of the one may be truly the voice of the other, *My ſoul faſted, and even that was alſo turned to my reproof.*

Pſal. 69. 10.

73 In this world there can be no ſociety durable, otherwiſe then only by propagation. Albeit therefore ſingle Life be a thing more Angelical and Divine, yet ſith the repleniſhing firſt of Earth with bleſſed Inhabitants, and then of Heaven with Saints everlaſtingly praiſing God, did depend upon conjunction of Man and Woman, he which made all things compleat and perfect, ſaw it could not be good to leave men without any Helper, unto the foreſalleaged end : In things which ſome farther end doth cauſe to be deſired, choice ſeeketh rather proportion, then abſolute perfection of goodneſs. So that woman being created for mans ſake to be his Helper, in regard of the end before mentioned, namely, the having and bringing up of Children, whereunto it was not poſſible they could concur, unleſs there were ſubalternation between them, which ſubalternation is naturally grounded upon inequaity, becauſe things equal in every reſpect are never willingly directed one by another. Woman therefore was even in her firſt eſtate framed by Nature, not only after in time, but inferiour in excellency alſo unto man, howbeit in ſo due and ſweet proportion, as being preſented before our eyes, might be ſooner perceived then defined. And even herein doth lie the reaſon, why that kind of love which is the perfecteſt ground of Wedlock is ſeldome able to yeild any reaſon of it ſelf. Now, that which is born of Man muſt be nouriſhed with far more travel, as being of greater price in Nature, and of ſlower pace to perfection, then the Offſpring of any other Creature beſides. Man and Woman being therefore to join themſelves for ſuch a purpoſe, they were of neceſſity to be linked with ſome ſtraight and inſoluble knot. The bond of Wedlock hath been always more or leſs eſteemed of, as a thing religious and ſacred. The title which the very Heathens themſelves do oftentimes give, is [a] *Holy.* Thoſe Rites and Orders which were inſtituted in the ſolemnization of Marriage, the Hebrews term by the name of conjugal [b] *ſanctification.* Amongſt our ſelves, becauſe ſundry things appertaining unto the publique order of Matrimony, are called in queſtion, by ſuch as know not from whence thoſe Cuſtomes did firſt grow, to ſhew briefly ſome true and ſufficient reaſon of them ſhall not be ſuperfluous; although we do not hereby intend, to yield ſo far unto Enemies of all Church Orders ſaving their own, as though every thing were unlawful, the true cauſe and reaſon whereof at the firſt might hardly perhaps be now rendred. Wherefore, to begin with the times wherein the liberty of Marriage is reſtrained ; *There is,* ſaith *Solomon, a time for all things; a time to laugh, and a time to mourn.* The duties belonging unto Marriage, and Offices pertaining to Penance, are things unſuitable and unfit to be matched together ; the Prophets and Apoſtles themſelves do witneſs. Upon which ground, as we might right well think it marvellous abſurd to ſee in a Church a Wedding on the day of a publick Faſt, ſo likewiſe in the ſelf-ſame conſideration, our Predeceſſors thought it not amiſs to take away the common liberty of Marriages, during the time which was appointed for preparation unto, and for exerciſe of general humiliation by faſting and praying, weeping for ſins. As for the delivering up of the woman, either by her Father or by ſome other, we muſt note, that in ancient times, [c] all women which had not husbands nor fathers to govern them, had their Tutors [d] without whoſe authority there was no act which they did warrantable. And for this cauſe, they were in marriage delivered unto their husbands by others. Which cuſtome retained, hath ſtill this uſe, that it putteth women in mind of a duty, whereunto the very imbecility of their nature and ſex doth bind them, namely, to be always directed, guided and ordered by others, although our Poſitive Laws do not tie them now as Pupils. The cuſtome of laying down money ſeemeth to have been derived from the Saxons, whoſe manner was to buy their wives. But, ſeeing there is not any great cauſe, wherefore the memory of that cuſtome ſhould remain, it skilleth not much, although we ſuffer it to lie dead, even as we ſee it in a manner already worn out. The Ring hath been always uſed as an eſpecial Pledge of faith and fidelity. Nothing

The celebration of Matrimony.
T. C. l. 1. p. 199.

a Τὰς ἱεροὺς γάμους. Dionyſ. Halicar. ant. l. 2.
b Kidduſchin. in Rituali Heb. de benedictione nuptiaruua. Eccleſ. 3. 1. Ioel. 1. 16.
1 Cor. 7. 5.
c Mulieres antiquo jure tutela perdetua continebat Recede. bant verò à tutoris poteſtate, quæ in manum conveniſſent. Boet. in Topic. Cic.
d Nullam ne privatim quidem rem ſeminas ſine auctore agere majores noſtri voluerunt. Liv. lib. 44.
The reaſon yeilded by Tully, this, Propter infirmitatem conſilii. Cic. pro Mur. Vide leges. Sixon. tit. 6. & 17.

thing more fit to serve as a Token of our purposed endless continuance in that which we never thought to revoke. This is the cause wherefore the Heathens themselves did in such cases use the Ring, whereunto *Tertullian* alluding, saith, that in ancient times ; [a] *No woman was permitted to wear gold, saving only upon one finger, which her husband had fastned unto himself, with that Ring which was usually given for assurance of future marriage.* The cause why the Christians use it, as some of the Fathers think, is [b] either to testifie mutual love, or rather to serve for a pledge of conjunction in heart and mind agreed upon between them. But what right and custome is there so harmless, wherein the wit of man bending it self to derision, may not easily find out somewhat to scorn and jest at ? He that should have beheld the Jews when they should with [c] a four-cornered Garment, spred over the heads of espoused couples, while their Espousals were in making ; he that should have beheld their [d] praying over a Cup, and their delivering the same at the Marriage Feast with set forms of Benediction, as the order amongst them was, might being lewdly affected, take thereat as just occasion of scornful cavil, as at the use of the Ring in Wedlock amongst Christians. But of all things the most hardly taken, is the uttering of these words, *With my body I thee worship;* in which words when once they are understood, there will appear as little cause as in the rest, for any Wise man to be offended. First therefore, inasmuch as unlawful copulation doth pollute and [e] dishonour both parties, this protestation that we do worship and honour another with our bodies, may import a denial of all such lets and impediments to our knowledge, as might cause any stain, blemish, or disgrace that way ; which kind of construction being probable, would easily approve that speech to a peaceable and quiet mind. Secondly, in that the Apostle doth so expresly affirm, that parties unmarried have not any longer entire power over themselves, but each hath interest in others person, it cannot be thought an absurd construction to say, that worshipping with the body, is the imparting of that interest in the body unto another, which none before had, save only our selves. But if this were the natural meanings the words should perhaps be as requisite to be used on the one side as on the other ; and therefore a third sense there is, which I rather rely upon. Apparent it is, that the ancient difference between a lawful Wife and a Concubine was only [f] in the different purpose of man betaking himself to the one or the other. If his purpose were only fellowship, there grew to the Woman by this mean no worship at all, but the contrary. In professing that his intent was to adde by his person, honour and worship unto hers, he took her plainly and cleerly to Wife. This is it which the Civil Law doth mean, when it maketh a Wife to differ from a Concubine in [g] dignity ; a Wife to be taken where [h] Conjugal honour and affection do go before. The worship that grew unto her being taken with declaration of this intent, was that her Children became by this mean legitimate and free ; her self was made a Mother over his Family ; last of all, she received such advancement of state as things annexed unto his person might augment her with, yea, a right of participation was thereby given her both in him, and even in all things which were his. This doth somewhat the more plainly appear, by adding also that other Clause, *With all my worldly Goods I thee endow.* The former branch having granted the principal, the latter granted that which is annexed thereunto. To end the publick Solemnity of Marriage, with receiving the blessed Sacrament, is a custome so Religious and so Holy, that if the Church of *England* be blameable in this respect, it is not for suffering it to be so much, but rather for not providing that it may be more put in ure. The Laws of *Romulus* concerning Marriage are therefore extolled above the rest amongst the Heathens which were before, in that they established the use of certain special Solemnities, whereby the minds of men were drawn to make the greater conscience of wedlock, and to esteem the bond thereof, a thing which could not be without impiety dissolved. If there be any thing in Christian Religion strong and effectual to like purpose, it is the Sacrament of the holy Eucharist, in regard of the force whereof *Tertullian* breaketh out into these words, concerning Matrimony therewith sealed ; *Unde suf-*

a Aurum nulla norat praeter unico digito quem sponsa oppignorasset pronubo annulo. Tertul. Apol. c. 6.
b Isidor. de Ecclef. Offic. lib. 2. cap. 19.
c Elias Thesb. in dict. Hhupha.
d In Ritual. de benedict. nuptiarum.
e Rom. 4.14. 1 Cor. 7. 4.
f L. penul. D. de concub.
g L. item legate sect pendit. D. de legat.3.
h L. donationes D. de donationibus.

Ὅυτ@ ὁ νόμ@ τὰς τε γυναῖκας ἠνάκατε τὰς γαμητὰς δια μεδεμίαν ἐχόσαι ἑτέραν ἀποςροφὴν πρὸς ἕνα τὸν τε γαμηκότε ζῆν τρόπον, ἢ τοὺς ἄνδρας ὡς ἀναγκαίαν τε ἢ ἀναφαιρέτε χρῆμαι@ ἢ γυναῖκ@ κρατεῖν. Dion. Hal. Antiq. lib. 2.

Churching of
Women.
T.C. l.1. p.150.

sufficiam ad enarrandam fœlicitatem ejus Matrimonii quod Ecclesia conciliat & confirmat oblatio? I know not which way I should be able to shew the happiness of that Wedlock, the knot whereof the Church doth fasten, and the Sacrament of the Church confirm. Touching Marriage therefore, let thus much be sufficient.

74. The fruit of Marriage is Birth, and the companion of Birth travel, the grief whereof being so extream, and the danger always so great, dare we open our mouths against the things that are holy, and presume to censure it, as a fault in the Church of Christ, that women after their deliverance do publickly shew their thankful minds unto God? But behold what reason there is against it: Forsooth, *if there should be solemn and express giving of thanks in the Church for every benefit, either equal, or greater then this, which any singular person in the Church doth receive, we should not only have no preaching of the Word, nor ministring of the Sacraments, but we should not have so much leisure as to do any corporal or bodily work, but should be like those Massilian Hereticks which do nothing else but pray.* Surely better a great deal to be like unto those Hereticks which do nothing else but pray, then those which do nothing else but quarrel. Their heads it might haply trouble somewhat more then as yet they are aware of, to find out so many benefits greater then this, or equivalent thereunto, for which if so be out Laws did require solemn and express thanksgiving in the Church, the same were like to prove a thing so greatly cumbersome as is pretended. But if there be such store of mercies, even inestimable, poured every day upon thousands (as indeed the earth is full of the blessings of the Lord, which are day by day renewed without number and above measure) shall it not be lawful to cause solemn thanks to be given unto God for any benefit, then which greater or whereunto equal are received, no Law binding men in regard thereof to perform the like duty? Suppose that some bond there be that tieth us at certain times to mention publickly the names of sundry our Benefactors. Some of them it may be are such, that a day would scarcely serve to reckon up together with them the Catalogue of so many men besides, as we are either more or equally beholden unto: Because no Law requireth this impossible labour at our hands, shall we therefore condemn that Law whereby the other being possible and also dutiful is enjoyned us? So much we owe to the Lord of Heaven, that we can never sufficiently praise him nor give him thanks for half those benefits for which this Sacrifice were most due. Howbeit, God forbid we should cease performing this duty, when publick Order doth draw us unto it, when it may be so easily done, when it hath been so long executed by devout and vertuous people; God forbid, that being so many ways provoked in this case unto so good a duty, we should omit it, only because there are other cases of like nature, wherein we cannot so conveniently, or at least wise do not perform the same most vertuous Office of Piety. Wherein we trust that as the action it self pleaseth God, so the order and manner thereof is not such as may justly offend any. It is but an over-flowing of Gall, which causeth the Womans absence from the Church, during the time of her lying in, to be traduced and interpreted as though she were so long judged *unholy*, and were thereby shut out or sequestred from the House of God, according to the ancient Levitical Law. Whereas the very Canon Law it self doth not so hold, but directly [a] professeth the contrary; she is not barred from thence in such sort as they interpret it, nor in respect of any unholiness forbidden entrance into the Church, although her abstaining from publick Assemblies, and her abode in separation for the time be [b] most convenient. To scoffe at the manner of attire, than which there could be nothing devised for such a time more grave and decent, to make it a token of some folly committed, for which they are loth to shew their faces, argueth

a Dist. 5. c. Hæc quæ. In lege præcipiebatur ut mulier si masculum pareret 40 si fœminam 80. diebus à templi leisure ingressu Nunc autem statim post partum Ecclesiam ingredi non prohibetur. b Leo. Cont. 17. *Quod profecto non tam propter muliebrem immunditiem, quam ob alias causas in intima legis ratione reconditas, & veteri prohibitum esse lege, & gratiæ tempus traditionis loco suscepisse puto. Existimo siquidem sacram legem id præscripsisse, quo protervam eorum qui intemperanter viverent concupiscentiam castigaret, quemadmodum & alia multa per alia præcepta ordinantur & præscribuntur, quo indomitus quorundam in mulieres stimulus retundatur. Quin & hæc providentia quâ legem constituit voluntas est ut parius à depravatione liberi sint. Quia enim quicquid naturæ supervacaneum est idem corruptivum est & inutile, quod hic sanguis superfluus sit, quæ illi obnoxia essent in immundtie ad id temporis vivere illa lex jubet, quo ipso etiam nomine sono lascivi concupiscentia ad temperantiam redigatur, ne ex inutili & corrupta materia ipsum animans coagmentetur.*

gueth that great Divines are sometime more merciful, then wise. As for the Women themselves, God accepting the service which they faithfully offer unto him, it is no great disgrace though they suffer pleasant witted men, a little to intermingle with zeal scorn. The name of *Oblations* applied not only here to those small and petite payments which yet are a part of the Ministers right, but also generally given unto all such allowances as serve for their needful maintenance, is both ancient and convenient. For as the life of the Clergy is spent in the Service of God, so it is sustained with his Revenue. Nothing therefore more proper then to give the name of Oblations to such payments, in token that we offer unto him whatsoever his Ministers receive.

75. But to leave this, there is a duty which the Church doth owe to the faithful departed, wherein for as much as the Church of *England* is said to do those things which are, though *not unlawful*, yet *inconvenient*, because it appointeth a prescript form of Service at Burials, suffereth mourning Apparel to be worn, and permitteth Funeral Sermons, a word or two concerning this point will be necessary, although it be needless to dwell long upon it. The end of Funeral Duties is, first, to shew that love towards the party deceased which Nature requireth; then to do him that honour which is fit both generally for man, and particularly for the quality of his person; last of all, to testifie the care which the Church hath to comfort the living, and the hope which we all have concerning the Resurrection of the dead. For signification of love towards them that are departed, mourning is not denied to be a thing convenient, as in truth the Scripture every where doth approve lamentation made unto this end. The Jews by our Saviours tears, therefore, gathered in this case, that his love towards *Lazarus* was great. And that as mourning at such times is fit, so likewise that there may be a kind of Attire sutable to a sorrowful affection, and convenient for Mourners to wear; how plainly doth *Davids* example shew, who being in heaviness went up to the Mount with his head covered, and all the people that were with him in like sort? White garments being fit to use at Marriage-Feasts, and such other times of joy; whereunto *Solomon* alluding, when he requireth continual cheerfulness of mind, speaketh in this sort, *Let thy garments be always white*: which doth hinder the contrary from being now as convenient in grief, as this heretofore in gladness hath been? *If there be no sorrow*, they say, *it is hypocritical to pretend it, and if there be, to provoke it* by wearing such attire, is *dangerous*. Nay, if there be, to shew it is natural, and if there be not, yet the signs are meet to shew what should be, especially, sith it doth not come oftentimes to pass, that men are fain to have their mourning Gowns pull'd off their backs, for fear of killing themselves with sorrow that way nourished. The honour generally due unto all men, maketh a decent interring of them to be convenient even for very humanities sake. And therefore so much as is mentioned in the Burial of the Widows Son, the carrying of him forth upon a Bier, and the accompanying of him to the earth, hath been used even amongst Infidels, all men accounting it a very extream destitution, not to have at the least this honour done them. Some mans estate may require a great deal more; according as the fashion of the Country where he dyeth doth afford. And unto this appertained the ancient use of the Jews, to embalm the Corps with sweet Odours, and to adorn the Sepulchres of certain. In regard of the quality of men, it hath been judged fit to commend them unto the world at their death, amongst the Heathen in Funeral Orations, amongst the Jews in sacred Poems; and why not in Funeral Sermons also amongst Christians? Us it sufficeth that the known benefit hereof doth countervail Millions of such inconveniences as are therein surmised, although they were not surmised only but found therein. The life and the death of Saints is precious in Gods sight: Let it not seem odious in our eyes, if both the one and the other be spoken of, then especially, when the present occasion doth make mens minds the more capable of such speech. The care no doubt of the living, both to live and to dye well must needs be somewhat increased, when they know that their departure shall not be folded up in silence, but the ears of many be made acquainted with it. Moreover when they hear how mercifully God hath dealt with their Brethren in their last need, besides the praise which they give to God, and the joy which they have or should have by reason of their Fellowship and

Of the Rites of Burial.
T.C.l.3. p.236.

Iohn 11.36.
2 Sam.15.30.
Ecclef.9.8.

Luke 7.12.

Psal. 79.3.
Iohn 19.40.
Mat. 23.27.
1 Sam.1.19.

and Communion with Saints , is not their hope also much confirmed against the day of their own diffolution ? Again , the found of thefe things doth not fo pafs the ears of them that are moft loofe and diffolute in life , but it caufeth them one time or other to wifh, *O that I might dye the death of the Righteous , and that my end might be like his* ! Thus much peculiar good there doth grow at thofe times by fpeech concerning the dead, befides the benefit of publick inftruction common unto Funeral with other Sermons. For the comfort of them whofe minds are through natural affection penfive in fuch cafes , no man can juftly miflike the cuftome which the Jews had to end their Burials with Funeral Banquets , in reference whereunto the Prophet *Jeremy* fpake, concerning the people which God had appointed unto a grievous manner of deftruction, faying, that men fhould not *give them the Cup of confolation to drink for their Father or for their Mother*, becaufe it fhould not be now with them as in peaceable times with others, who bringing their Anceftors unto the Grave with weeping eyes , have notwithftanding means wherewith to be re-comforted. *Give wine*, faith *Solomon*, *unto them that have grief of heart*. Surely, he that miniftreth unto them comfortable fpeech , doth much more then give them wine. But the greateft thing of all other about this duty of Chriftian Burial, is an outward teftification of the hope which we have touching the Refurrection of the dead. For which purpofe let any man of reafonable judgement examine , whether it be more convenient for a company of men , as it were in a dumb fhow , to bring a Corfe to the place of burial , there to leave it covered with earth, and fo end, or elfe to have the Exequies devoutly performed with folemn recital of fuch Lectures, Pfalms and Prayers , as are purpofely framed for the ftirring up of mens minds unto a careful confideration of their eftate, both here and hereafter. Whereas therefore it is objected, that neither the people of God under the Law, nor the Church in the Apoftles times did ufe any form of fervice in burial of their dead , and therefore that this order is taken up without any good example or precedent followed therein ; Firft, while the world doth ftand, they fhall never be able to prove , that all things which either the one or the other did ufe at Burials , are fet down in holy Scripture, which doth not any where of purpofe deliver the whole manner and form thereof, but toucheth only fometime one thing , and fometime another which was in ufe , as fpecial occafions require any of them to be either mentioned or infinuated. Again, if it might be proved that no fuch thing was ufual amongft them , hath Chrift fo deprived his Church of judgement, that what Rites and Orders foever the latter Ages thereof have devifed, the fame muft needs be inconvenient ? Furthermore, that the Jews befor o r Saviours coming had any fuch form of fervice , although in Scripture it be not affirmed ; yet neither is it there denyed (for the forbidding of Priefts to be prefent at burials, letteth not but that others might difcharge that duty, feeing a J were not Priefts which had rooms of publick Function in their Synagogues) and if any man be of opinion , that they had no fuch form of fervice , thus much there is to make the contrary more probable. The Jews at this day have, as appeareth in their form of Funeral Prayers , and in certain of their Funeral Sermons publifhed ; neither are they fo affected towards Chriftians, as to borrow that order from us ; befides, that the form thereof is fuch as hath in it fundry things, which the very words of the Scripture it felf do feem to allude unto, as namely, after departure from the Sepulchre unto the houfe whence the dead was brought , it fheweth the manner of their burial-Feaft, and a confolatory form of prayer, appointed for the Mafter of the Synagogue thereat to utter ; albeit I may not deny, but it hath alfo fome things whic are not perhaps fo ancient as the Law and the Prophets. But whatfoever the Jews cuftome was before the days of our Saviour Chrift, hath it once at any time been heard of, that either Church or Chriftian man of found belief did ever judge this a thing unmeet, undecent, unfit for Chriftianity, till thefe miferable days, wherein under the colour of removing fuperftitious abufes, the moft effectual means, both to teftifie and to ftrengthen true Religion, are plucked at, and in fome places even pul'ed up by the very roots ? Take away this which was ordained to fhew at Burials the peculiar hope of the Church of God concerning the dead, and in the manner of thofe dumb Funerals, what one thing is there whereby the World may perceive we are Chriftian men ?

Jer. 16. 7.

Prov. 31. 6.
1 Chron. 19. 2.
Job 2. 11.

76. I come now unto that Function which undertaketh the publick Ministry of holy things, according to the Laws of Christian Religion. And because the nature of things consisting, as this doth, in action, is known by the object whereabout they are conversant, and by the end or scope whereunto they are referred, we must know that the object of this Function is both God and Men; God, in that he is publickly worshipped of his Church; and Men, in that they are capable of happiness, by means which Christian Discipline appointeth. So that the summe of our whole labour in this kind, is to honour God, and to save men. For whether we severally take, and consider men one by one, or else gather them into one society and body, as it hath been before declared, that every mans Religion is in him the Well-spring of all other sound and sincere vertues, from whence both here in some sort, and hereafter more abundantly, their full joy and felicity ariseth, because while they live, they are blessed of God, and when they dye, their works follow them: So at this present we must again call to mind how the very wordly peace and prosperity, the secular happiness, the temporal and natural good estate both of all Men, and of all Dominions, hangeth chiefly upon Religion, and doth evermore give plain testimony, that as well in this as in other considerations the Priest is a pillar of that Common-wealth, wherein he faithfully serveth God. For if these Assertions be true, first, that nothing can be enjoyed in this present world against his will which hath made all things: secondly, that albeit God doth sometime permit the impious to *have*, yet impiety permitteth them not to *enjoy*, no not temporal blessings on earth: thirdly, that God hath appointed those blessings to attend as Hand-maids upon Religion: and fourthly, that without the work of the Ministry, Religion by no means can possibly continue, the use and benefit of that sacred Function, even towards all mens wordly happiness, must needs be granted. Now the [a] first being a Theoreme both understood and consest of all, to labour in proof thereof were superfluous. The second perhaps may be called in question, except it be perfectly understood. By good things temporal therefore we mean length of days, health of body, store of friends and well-willers, quietness, prosperous success of those things we take in hand; riches with fit opportunities to use them during life, reputation following us both alive and dead, children, or such as instead of children, we wish to leave Successors and Partakers of our happiness. These things are naturally every mans desire, because they are good. And on whom God bestoweth the same, them we confess he graciously blesseth. Of earthly blessings the meanest is wealth, reputation the chiefest. For which cause we esteem the gain of honour an ample recompence for the loss of all other worldly benefits. But for as much as in all this there is no certain perpetuity of goodness, nature hath taught to affect these things, not for their own sake, but with reference and relation to somewhat independantly good, as is the exercise of vertue and speculation of truth. None, whose desires are rightly ordered, would wish to live, to breathe, and move, without performance of those actions which are beseeming mans excellency. Wherefore having not how to employ it, we wax weary even of life it self. Health is precious, because sickness doth breed that pain which disableth action. Again, why do men delight so much in the multitude of friends, but for that the actions of life being many, do need many helping hands to further them? Between troublesome and quiet days we would make no difference, if the one did not hinder and interrupt, the other uphold our liberty of action. Furthermore, if those things we do, succeed, it rejoyceth us not so much for the benefit we thereby reap, as in that [b] it probably argueth our actions to have been orderly and well guided. As for riches, to him which hath and doth nothing with them, they are a contumely. Honour is commonly presumed a sign of more then ordinary vertue and merit, by means whereof when ambitious minds thirst after it, their endeavours are testimonies how much it is in the eye of nature to possess that body, the very shadow whereof is set at so high a rate. Finally, such is the pleasure and comfort which we take in doing, that when life forsaketh us, still our desires to continue action, and to work, though not by our selves, yet by them whom we leave behind us, causeth us providently to resign into other mens hands, the helps we have gathered for that purpose, devising also the best we can to make them perpetual. It appeareth therefore,

[a] Si creatura Dei, merito & dispensatione Dei sumus: Qui enim mā-gis diligit, quam ille qui fecit? Quis autem ordina-tius regit quam & qui & fecit & diligit? Quis vero sa-pientius & suo-tius ordinare & regere saffa potest quam qui & facienda providit & provisa perfe-cit? Quapropter omnem po-testatem à Deo esse omnemque ordinationem, & qui non le-gerunt senti-unt, & qui le-gerunt cognos-cunt. Paul O-ros. Hist. adverf. Pagan. lib. 2. [b] Οὗτοι τὰ χρήματ᾽ ἴσια ἀκίνδυνα βεό-Τοι τὰ μεῖς Se-ῶν δ᾽ ἔχοντες ὀπημελήμεθα. Eurip. Phœnis. [b] Οἰόμεσθα τὸν ἐντυχοῦν τα ὀρθῶς ἐπι-σαμῶς κακῶς. Eurip. Hersel.

fore, how all the parts of temporal felicity are only good in relation to that which useth them as instruments, and that they are no such good as wherein a right desire doth ever stay or rest it self. Now temporal blessings are enjoyed of those which have them, know them, *esteem them according to that they are in their own nature.* Wherefore of the wicked whom God doth hate, his usual and ordinary speeches are, That bloud-thirsty and deceitful men shall not live out half their days; that God shall cause a pestilence to cleave unto the wicked, and shall strike them with consuming grief, with Fevers, burning diseases and sores which are past cure; that when the impious are fallen, all men shall tread them down, and none shew countenance of love towards them, as much as pitying them in their misery; that the sins of the ungodly shall bereave them of peace; that all counsels, complots, and practices against God shall come to nothing; that the lot and inheritance of the unjust is beggery; that the name of unrighteous persons shall putrifie, and the posterity of Robbers starve. If any think that Iniquity and Peace, Sin and Prosperity can dwell together, they erre, because they distinguish not aright between the matter, and that which giveth it the form of happiness, between possession and fruition, between the having and the enjoying of good things. The impious cannot enjoy that they have, partly because they receive it not as at Gods hands, which only consideration maketh temporal blessings comfortable; and partly because through errour, placing it above things of far more price and worth, they turn that to poyson which might be food, they make their prosperity their own snare, in the nest of their highest growth they lay foolishly those Egges, out of which their woful over-throw is afterwards hatcht. Hereby it cometh to pass, that wise and judicious men observing the vain behaviours of such as are risen to unwonted greatness, have thereby been able to prognosticate their ruine. So that in very truth no impious or wicked man doth prosper on earth, but either sooner or later the world may perceive easily, how at such time as others thought them most fortunate, they had but only the good estate which fat Oxen have above lean; when they appeared to grow, their climbing was towards ruine. The gross and bestial conceit of them which want understanding, is only, that the fullest bellies are happiest. Therefore the greatest felicity they wish to the Common-wealth wherein they live, is that it may but abound and stand, that they which are riotous may have to pour out without stint; that the poor may sleep and the rich feed them; that nothing unpleasant may be commanded, nothing forbidden men which themselves have a lust to follow; that Kings may provide for the ease of their Subjects, and not be too curious about their manners; that wantonness, excess, and lewdness of life may be left free, and that no fault may be capital, besides dislike of things setled in so good terms. But be it far from the just to dwell either in or neer to the Tents of these so miserable felicities. Now whereas we thirdly affirm, that Religion and the Fear of God, as well induceth secular prosperity as everlasting bliss in the world to come, this also is true. For otherwise godliness could not be said to have the promises of both lives, to be that ample Revenue, wherein there is always sufficiency, and to carry with it a general discharge of want, even so general, that *David* himself should protest, he never saw the just forsaken. Howbeit to this we must adde certain special limitations; as first, that we do not forget how crazed and diseased minds (whereof our heavenly Physitian must judge) receive oftentimes most benefit by being deprived of those things which are to others beneficially given, as appeareth in that which the Wise-man hath noted concerning them whose lives God mercifully doth abridge, lest wickedness should alter their understanding; again, that the measure of our outward prosperity be taken by proportion with that which every mans estate in this present life requireth. External abilities are instruments of action. It contenteth wise Artificers to have their instruments proportionable to their work, rather fit for use, than huge and goodly to please the eye: Seeing then the actions of a servant do not need that which may be necessary for men of calling and place in the world, neither men of inferiour condition many things which greater Personages can hardly want, surely they are blessed in worldly respects, that have wherewith to perform [a] sufficiently what their station and place asketh, though they have no more. For by reason of mans imbecillity and
proneness

Psal.55.23.
Deut.28.22.

Prov.10.

Prov.16.18.
Ante ruinam claūo.
φιλεῖ ὁ Θεὸς πάντα τὰ ὑπερέχοντα κολ λύειν· ὁ γὰρ ἐᾷ φρονεῖν μέγα ἢ ἑαυτὸν. Hero-dot.lib.7.

a Ἐπεὶ τὰν ἀρκοῦνθ' ἱκανὰ τοῖς γε σώφρο-σιν. Eurip. Phœnif.

pronenefs to elation of mind, too high a flow of prosperity is dangerous, too low an ebbe again as dangerous ; for that the vertue of patience is rare , and the hand of necessity stronger,than ordinary vertue is able to withstand; *Solomons* discreet and moderate desire we all know: *Give me, O Lord, neither riches nor penury.* Men over-high exalted either in honour, or in power, or in nobility, or in wealth ; they likewise that are much on the contrary hand sunk either with beggery, or through dejection, or by bafeness, do not easily give ear to reason , but the one exceeding apt unto outrages , and the other to petty mischiefs. For greatness delighteth to shew it self by effects of power, and bafeness to help it self with shifts of malice. For which cause,a moderate, indifferent temper, between fulness of bread, and emptiness hath been evermore thought and found (all circumstances duly considered) the safest and happiest for all Estates, even for King and Princes themselves. Again, we are not to look,that these things should always concur,no not in them which are accounted happy, neither that the course of mens lives, or of publick affairs should continually be drawn out as an even thred (for that the nature of things will not suffer) but a just survey being made,as those particular men are worthily reputed good, whose vertues be great , and their faults tolerable, so him we may register for a man fortunate, and that for a prosperous or happy State, which having flourished, doth not afterwards feel any tragical alteration, such as might cause them to be a spectacle of mifery to others. Besides,whereas true felicity consisteth in the highest operations of that nobler part of man , which sheweth sometime greatest perfection, not in using the benefits which delight nature, but in suffering what nature can hardliest indure, there is no cause why either the loss of good, if it tend to the purchase of better,or why any misery,the issue whereof,is their greatest praise and honor that have sustained it,should be thought to impeach that temporal happiness,wherewith Religion,we say,is accompanied,but yet in such measure,as the several degrees of men may require by a competent estimation,and unless the contrary do more advance,as it hath done those most Heroical Saints,whom afflictions have made glorious. In a word, not to whom no calamity falleth,but whom neither misery nor prosperity is able to move from a right mind,them we may truly pronounce fortunate, and whatsoever doth outwardly happen without that precedent improbitie, for w^c it appeareth in the eyes of found and unpartial Judges to have proceeded from Divine revenge, it passeth in the number of humane casualties whereunto we are all alike subject. No misery is reckoned more then common or humane, if God so dispose that we pass thorow it,and come safe to shore,even as contrariwise, men do not use to think those flourishing days happy,which do end In tears.It standeth therefore with these cautions firm and true, yea, ratified by all mens unsained confessions drawn from the very heart of experience, that whether we compare men of note in the world with others of like degree and state,or else the same men with themselves, whether we confer one Dominion with another, or else the different times of one and the same Dominion, the manifest odds between their very outward condition, as long as they stedfastly were observed to honour God, and their success being faln from him,are remonstrances more then sufficient, how all our welfare even on earth dependeth wholly upon our Religion.Heathens were ignorant of true Religion.Yet such as that little was which they knew,it much impaired,or bettered their worldly affairs,as their love and zeal towards it did wain or grow. Of the Jews,did not even their most malicious and mortal Adversaries all acknowledge, that to strive against them, it was in vain, as long as their amity with God continued, that nothing could weaken them but Apostasie ? In the whole course of their own proceedings, did they ever find it otherwise , but that during their faith and fidelity towards God, every man of them was in war as a thousand strong, and as much as a grand Senate for counsel in peaceable deliberations; contrariwise that if they swarved, as they did often, their wonted courage and magnanimity forsook them utterly; their Souldiers and Military men trembled at the sight of the naked sword ; when they entered into mutual conference, and sate in counsel for their own good, that which children might have seen, their gravest Senators could not discern ; their Prophets faw darkness instead of Visions ; the wise and prudent were as men bewitcht,even that which they knew (being such as might stand them in stead) they had not the

[right margin:] ^a τα περιοτέρωυ ὁ λογισμός ἴσως ἀλλ᾽ ἐν ἀραλεσερων , ἴσου απεχειν χρ ὕψει χ πλανματ@ Greg. Naz: Apol.3. They may seem haply the most dejeɛt, but they are the wisest for their own safety, which fear clyming; no less then falling. *Arist. Polit. lib. 4. cap. 11.*

grace

grace to utter, or if any thing were well proposed, it took no place, it entered not into the minds of the rest to approve and follow it, but as men confounded with strange and unusual amazements of Spirit, they attempted tumultuously they saw not what; and by the issues of all attempts, they found no certain conclusion but this, *God and Heaven are strong against us in all we do.* The cause whereof was secret fear, which took heart and courage from them, and the cause of their fear, an inward guiltiness that they all had offered God such apparent wrongs as were not pardonable. But it may be, the case is altogether changed, and that in Christian Religion there is not like force towards temporal felicity. Search the ancient Records of time, look what hath happened by the space of these sixteen hundred years, see if all things to this effect be not luculent and clear, yea, all things so manifest, that for evidence and proof herein, we need not by uncertain dark conjectures surmise any to have been plagued of God for contempt, or blest in the course of faithful obedience towards true Religion, more then only them, whom we find in that respection the one side, guilty by their own confessions, and happy on the other side by all mens acknowledgment, who beholding the prosperous estate of such as are good and vertuous, impute boldly the same to Gods most especial favour, but cannot in like manner pronounce, that whom he afflicteth above others, with them he hath cause to be more offended. For Vertue is always plain to be seen, rareness causeth it to be observed, and goodness to be honoured with admiration. As for iniquity and sin, it lieth many times hid, and because we be all offenders, it becometh us not to incline towards hard and severe sentences touching others, unless their notorious wickedness did sensibly before proclaim that which afterwards came to pass. Wherefore the sum of every Christian mans duty is, to labour by all means towards that which other men seeing in us may justifie; and what we our selves must accuse, if we fall into it, that by all means we can, to avoid, considering especially, that as hitherto upon the Church there never yet fell tempestuous storm, the vapours whereof were not first noted to rise from coldness in affection, and from backwardness in duties of service towards God; so if that which the tears of Antiquity have uttered concerning this point should be here set down, it were assuredly enough to soften and to mollifie a heart of Steel. On the contrary part, although we confess with Saint *Augustine* most willingly, that the chiefest happiness for which we have some Christian Kings in so great admiration above the rest, is not because of their long Raign; their calm and quiet departure out of this present life; the setled establishment of their own flesh and blood, succeeding them in Royaltie and power; the glorious overthrow of forrain enemies, or the wise prevention of inward danger, and of secret attempts at home; all which solaces and comforts of this our unquiet life, it pleaseth God oftentimes to bestow on them which have no society or part in the joys of Heaven, giving thereby to understand, that these in comparison are toys and trifles far under the value and price of that which is to be looked for at his hands: but in truth the reason wherefore we most extoll their felicity, is, if so be they have virtuously reigned, if honour have not filled their hearts with pride, if the exercise of their power have been service and attendance upon the Majesty of the most High, if they have feared him as their own inferiours and subjects have feared them, if they have loved neither pomp nor pleasure more than Heaven, if revenge have slowly proceeded from them, and mercy willingly offered it self, if so they have tempered rigour with lenity, that neither extream severity might utterly cut them off in whom there was manifest hope of amendment, nor yet the easiness of pardoning offences imbolden offenders, if knowing that whatsoever they do, their potency may bear it out, they have been so much the more careful not to do any thing but that which is commendable in the best, rather than usual with greatest parsonages, if the true knowledge of themselves have humbled them in Gods sight, no less than God in the eyes of men hath raised them up; I say, albeit we reckon such to be the happiest of them that are mightiest in the world, and albeit those things alone are happiness, nevertheless, considering what force there is even in outward blessings, to comfort the minds of the best disposed, and to give them the greater joy, when Religion and Peace, Heavenly and Earthly happiness are wreathed in one Crown, as to the
worthiest

worthiest of Christian Princes it hath by the providence of the Almighty hitherto befallen, let it not seem unto any man a needless and superfluous waste of labour, that th.re hath been thus much spoken, to declare how in them especially it hath been so observed, and withal universally noted even from the highest to the very meanest, how this peculiar benefit, this singular grace and preeminence Religion hath, that either it guardeth as an heavenly shield from all calamities, or else conducteth us safe through them, and permitteth them not to be miseries; it either giveth honours, promotions, and wealth, or else more benefit by wanting them than if we had them at will; it either filleth our houses with plenty of all good things, or maketh a Sallad of green herbs more sweet than all the sacrifices of the ungodly. Our fourth Proposition before set down was, that Religion without the help of spiritual Ministery is unable to plant it self, the fruits thereof not possible to grow of their own accord. Which last Assertion is herein as the first, that it needeth no farther confirmation. If it did, I could easily declare, how all things which are of God, he hath by wonderful art and wisdom sodered, as it were, together with the glue of mutual assistance, appointing the lowest to receive from the nearest to themselves, what the influence of the highest yieldeth. And therefore the Church being the most absolute of all his works, was in reason to be also ordered with like harmony, that what he worketh, might no less in grace than in nature be effected by hands and instruments duly subordinated unto the power of his own Spirit. A thing both needful for the humiliation of man, which would not willingly be debtor to any, but to himself, and of no small effect to nourish that divine love, which now maketh each embrace other, not as Men, but as Angels of God. Ministerial actions tending immediately unto Gods honour, and mans happiness, are either as contemplation, which helpeth forward the principal work of the Ministery, or else they are parts of that principal work of administration it self, which work consisteth in doing the service of Gods house, and in applying unto men the soveraign medicines of grace already spoken of the more largely, to the end it might thereby appear, that we *owe to the guides of our souls even as much as our souls are worth, although the debt of our temporal blessings should be stricken off.

Luke 12.42.
1 Cor.4.1.
Tit. 1. 7.
1 Pet.4.10.
Ephes.3.2.
ᵃ ᾗ σεαυτόν μοι προσοφείλεις Epist.ad Philem.

77. The Ministery of things divine is a function, which as God did himself institute; so neither may men undertake the same but by authority and power given them in lawful manner. That God which is no way deficient or wanting unto Man in necessities, and hath therefore given us the light of his heavenly Truth, because without that inestimable benefit we must needs have wandered in darkness, to our endless perdition and woe, hath in the like abundance of mercies ordained certain to attend upon the due execution of requisite parts and offices therein prescribed for the good of the whole world, which men, thereunto assigned, do hold their authority from him, whether they be such as himself immediately, or as the Church in his name investeth, it being neither possible for all, nor for every man without distinction convenient to take upon him a charge of so great importance. They are therefore Ministers of God, not only by way of subordination as Princes and civil Magistrates, whose execution of judgement and justice, the supream hand of divine providence doth uphold, but Ministers of God, as from whom their authority is derived, and not from men. For in that they are Christs Embassadours and his Labourers, who should give them their Commission, but he whose most inward affairs they manage? Is not God alone the Father of Spirits? Are not souls the purchase of Jesus Christ? What Angel in Heaven could have said to man, as our Lord did unto *Peter, Feed my sheep? Preach? Baptize? Do this in remembrance of me? Whose sins ye retain, they are retained, and their offences in Heaven pardoned, whose faults you shall on earth forgive?* What think we? Are these terrestrial sounds, or else are they voices uttered out of the clouds above? The power of the Ministery of God translateth out of darkness into glory; it raiseth men from the earth, and bringeth God himself down from Heaven; by blessing visible Elements it maketh them invisible grace; it giveth daily the Holy Ghost, it hath to dispose of that flesh which was given for the life of the World, and that bloud which was poured out to redeem souls; when it poureth malediction upon the heads of the wicked, they perish; when it revoketh the same, they revive.

Of power given unto man to execute that heavenly Office; of the gift of the Holy Ghost in Ordination; and whether conveniently the power of Orders may be sought or sued for.

O wretched blindness, if we admire not so great power, more wretched if we consider it aright, and notwithstanding, imagine that any but God can bestow it! To whom Christ hath imparted power, both over that mystical Body which is the society of souls, and over that natural, which is himself for the knitting of both in one, (a work which antiquity doth call the making of Christs Body) the same power is in such not amiss both termed a kind of mark or Character, and acknowledged to be indelible. Ministerial power is a mark of separation, because it severeth them that have it from other men, and maketh them a special *order* consecrated unto the service of the most High, in things wherewith others may not meddle. Their difference therefore from other men, is in that they are a distinct *order*. So *Tertullian* calleth them. And Saint *Paul* himself dividing the body of the Church of Christ into two Moyeties, nameth the one part ἰδιώτας, which is as much as to say, the order of the Laity, the opposite part whereunto we in like sort term the order of Gods Clergy, and the spiritual power which he hath given them, the power of their *order*, so far forth as the same consisteth in the bare execution of holy things, called properly the affairs of God. For of the Power of their jurisdiction over mens persons we are to speak in the books following. They which have once received this power, may not think to put it off, and on, like a Cloke, as the weather serveth, to take it, reject and resume it as oft as themselves list, of which prophane and impious contempt these latter times have yeilded, as of all other kinds of iniquity and Apostasie, strange examples; but let them know which put their hands unto this Plough, that once consecrated unto God, they are made his peculiar inheritance for ever. Suspensions may stop, and degradations utterly cut off the use or exercise of power before given; but voluntarily it is not in the power of man to separate and pull asunder what God by his authority coupleth. So that although there may be through misdesert degradation, as there may be cause of just separation after Matrimony; yet if (as sometime it doth) restitution to former dignity, or reconciliation after breach doth happen, neither doth the one nor the other ever iterate the first knot. Much less is it necessary, which some have urged, concerning the reordination of such, as others in times more corrupt did consecrate heretofore. Which errour already que.'d by St. *Jerome*, doth not now require any other refutation. Examples I grant there are which make for restraint of those men from admittance again into rooms of spiritual function, whose fall by heresie, or want of constancy in professing the Christian Faith, hath been once a disgrace to their calling. Nevertheless, as there is no Law which bindeth, so there is no cause that should always lead to shew one and the same severity towards persons culpable. Goodness of nature it self more inclineth to clemency than rigour. And we in other mens offences do behold the plain image of our own imbecility. Besides also them that wander out of the way, [a] it cannot be unexpedient to win with all hopes of favour, lest strictness used towards such as reclaim themselves should make others more obstinate in errour. Wherefore [c] after that the Church of *Alexandria* had somewhat recovered it self from the tempests and storms of Arrianisme, being in consultation about the re-establishment of that which by long disturbance had been greatly decayed and hindered, the fervent sort gave quick sentence, that touching them which were of the Clergy, and had stained themselves with heresie, there should be none so received into the Church again, as to continue in the order of the Clergy. The rest which considered how many mens cases it did concern, thought it much more safe and consonant to bend somewhat down towards them which were fallen, to shew severity upon a few of the chiefest leaders, and to offer to the rest a friendly reconciliation, without any other demand saving only the abjuration of their errour; as in the Gospel that wastfull young man which returned home to his Fathers house, was with joy admitted and honoured, his elder brother hardly thought of for repining thereat, neither commended so much for his own fidelity and vertue, as blamed for not embracing him freely, whose unexpected recovery ought to have blotted out all remembrance of mis-demeanors and faults past. But of this sufficient. A thing much stumbled at in the manner of giving Orders, is our using those memorable words of our Lord and Saviour Christ, *Receive the Holy Ghost*. The Holy Ghost they say we cannot give,

and

Tertul. de Adhort. Castit.

Heb. 2. 17.

Matth. 19.

a In 12. tabulis cautem est, ut idem juris esset sanantibus quod sontibus, id est, bonis & qui nunquam defecerunt à populo Romano. Fest. in ver. Samnites.

b Ruffin. Hist. Eccl. lib. cap. 28.

and therefore we *foolishly* bid men receive it. Wise men for their authorities fake must have leave to befool them whom they are able to make wise by better instruction. Notwithstanding, if it may please their wisdom as well to hear what fools can say, as so controul that which they do ; thus we have heard some wise men teach, namely, That the *holy Ghost* may be used to signifie not the person alone , but the gifts of the holy Ghost ; and we know that spiritual gifts are not only abilities to do things miraculous, as to speak with tongues which were never taught us, to cure diseases without art , and such like ; but also that the very authority and power which is given men in the Church to be Ministers of holy things, this is contained within the number of those gifts whereof the holy Ghost is Author ; and therefore he which giveth this power may say without absurdity or folly, *Receive the holy Ghost* ; such power as the Spirit of Christ hath indued his Church withal ; such power as neither Prince nor Potentate, King nor *Cæsar* on earth can give. So that if men alone had devised this form of speech, thereby to express the heavenly wellspring of that power which Ecclesiastical Ordinations do bestow , it is not so foolish but that wise men might bear with it. If then our Lord and Saviour himself have used the self-same form of words, and that in the self-same kind of action , although there be but the least shew of probability, yea, or any possibility, that his meaning might be the same which ours is, it should teach sober and grave men not to be too venturous in condemning that of folly, which is not impossible to have in it more profoundness of wisdom than flesh and blood should presume to control. Our Saviour after his Resurrection from the dead gave his Apostles their Commission, saying ; *All power is given me in Heaven and in Earth : Go therefore and teach all Nations, baptizing them in the Name of the Father and the Son, and the holy Ghost, teaching them to observe all things whatsoever I command you.* In summe, *As my Father sent me, so send I you.* Whereunto St. *John* doth adde farther, that *having thus spoken, he breathed on them and said, Receive the holy Ghost.* By which words he must of likelyhood understand some gift of the Spirit which was presently at that time bestowed upon them, as both the speech of actual delivery in saying *Receive,* and the visible signe thereof, his breathing did shew. Absurd it were to imagine our Saviour did both to the ear, and also to the very eye express a real donation, and they at that time receive nothing. It resteth then that we search what special grace they did at that time receive. Touching miraculous power of the Spirit , most apparent it is , that as then they received it not , but the promise thereof was to be shortly after performed. The words of Saint *Luke* concerning that power, are therefore set down with signification of the time to come, *Behold I will send* the promise of my Father upon you , but tarry you in the City of *Jerusalem,* until ye be indued with power from on high. Wherefore, undoubtedly, it was some other effect of the Spirit, the holy Ghost in some other kind which our Saviour did then bestow. What other likelyer than that which himself doth mention , as it should seem of purpose to take away all ambiguous constructions, and to declare that the Holy Ghost, which he then gave, was an holy and a ghostly authority, authority over the souls of men ; authority, a part whereof consisteth in power to remit and retain sins ? Receive the holy Ghost, *Whose sins soever ye remit, they are remitted ; whose sins ye retain, they are retained.* Whereas therefore the other Evangelists had set down , that Christ did before his suffering promise to give his Apostles the Keys of the Kingdom of Heaven , and being risen from the dead promised moreover at that time a miraculous power of the holy Ghost : Saint *John* addeth, that he also invested them even then with the power of the holy Ghost for castigation and relaxation of sin, wherein was fully accomplished that which the promise of the Keys did import. Seeing therefore that the same power is now given, why should the same form of words expressing it be thought foolish ? The cause why we breath not as Christ did on them unto whom he imparted power, is, for that neither Spirit nor spiritual authority may be thought to proceed from *us,* which are but delegates or assignes to give men possession of his graces. Now besides that the power and authority delivered with those words is it self χαείσμα, a gracious donation which the Spirit of God doth bestow , we may most assuredly perswade our selves, that the hand which imposeth upon us the function of our

a *Papisticus quidem ritus, stulte quidem ab illis & sine ullo Scripturæ fundamento institutus & a disciplinæ nostra autoribus (pace illorum dixerim) non magno primum judicio acceptus minore adhuc in Ecclesia nostra retinetur. Ecclesiast.disscip. p. 53.*
b *Ecclef. disscip. fol.52.p 1.8.*

Matth.28.18.

Iohn 20. 21.

Luke 24.47.

Iohn 20. 33.

Ministry, doth under the same form of words so tie it self thereunto, that he which receiveth the burthen, is thereby for ever warranted to have the Spirit with him, and in him for his assistance, aid, countenance and support in whatsoever he faithfully doth to discharge duty. Knowing therefore that when we take Ordination, we also receive the presence of the holy Ghost, partly to guid, direct, and strengthen us in all our ways, and partly to assume unto it self for the more authority, those actions that appertain to our place and calling, can our ears admit such a speech uttered in the reverend performance of that solemnity ; or can we at any time renew the memory, and enter into serious cogitation thereof, but with much admiration and joy ? Remove what these foolish words do imply, and what hath the Ministry of God besides wherein to glory ? Whereas now forasmuch as the holy Ghost, which our Saviour in his first Ordinations gave, doth no less concur with spiritual vocations throughout all ages, than the Spirit which God derived from *Moses* to them that assisted him in his government, did descend from them to their successors in like authority and place, we have for the least and meanest duties performed by virtue of Ministerial power, that, to dignifie, grace, and authorize them, which no other offices on earth can challenge. Whether we Preach, Pray, Baptize, Communicate, Condemn, give Absolution, or whatsoever, as disposers of Gods mysteries ; our words, judgments, acts, and deeds, are not ours but the holy Ghosts. Enough if unfainedly and in heart we did believe it, enough to banish whatsoever may justly be thought corrupt, either in bestowing, or in using, or in esteeming the same otherwise than is meet. For prophanely to bestow, or loosely to use, or vilely to esteem of the holy Ghost, we in all shew and profession abhor. Now because the Ministery is an office of dignity and honour ; some are doubtful whether any man may seek for it without offence, or to speak more properly, doubtful they are not, but rather bold to accuse our Discipline in this respect, as not only permitting, but requiring ambitious suits and other oblique ways or means whereby to obtain it. Against this they plead, that our Saviour did stay till his Father sent him, and the Apostles till he them ; that the ancient Bishops in the Church of Christ were examples and patterns of the same modesty. Whereupon in the end they infer, *Let us therefore at the length amend that custome of repairing from all parts unto the Bishop at the day of Ordination, and of seeking to obtain Orders; let the custome of bringing commendatory Letters be removed ; let men keep themselves at home, expecting there the voice of God, and the authority of such as may call them to undertake charge.* Thus severely they censure and control ambition, if it be ambition which they take upon them to reprehend. For of that there is cause to doubt. Ambition, as we understand it, hath been accounted a vice which seeketh after honours inordinately, Ambitious minds esteeming it their greatest happiness to be admired, reverenced, and adored above others, use all means lawful and unlawful which may bring them to high rooms. But as for the power of order considered by it self, and as in this case it must be considered, such reputation it hath in the eye of this present World, that they which affect it, rather need encouragement to bear contempt, than deserve blame as men that carry aspiring minds. The work whereunto this power serveth is commended, and the desire thereof allowed by the Apostle for good. Nevertheless because the burthen thereof is heavy, and the charge great, it cometh many times to pass, that the minds even of virtuous men are drawn into clean contrary affections, some in humility declining that by reason of hardness, which others in regard of goodness only do with fervent alacrity covet. So that there is not the least degree in this service, but it may be both in b reverence shunned, and of very devotion longed for. If then the desire thereof may be holy, religious, and good, may not the profession of that desire be so likewise? We are not to think it so long good as it is dissembled, & evil if once we begin to open it. And allowing that it may be opened without ambition, what offence, I beseech you, is there in opening it, there where it may be furthered and satisfied, in case they to whom it appertaineth think meet ?

a Et si necessarium est trepidare de merito, religiosum est tamen gaudere de dono: quoniā qui mihi oneris est autor, ipse fiet administrationis adjutor; & ne magnitudine gratiæ succumbat infirmus, dabit virtutem qui contulis dignitatē. Leo. ser. 1. in Anniver. die A. τὸ πνεῦμα τὸ ἅγιον ἔθε]ο ἡμᾶς εἰς τὴν διακονίαν ταύτην. Greg. Nazian. Num. 11. 17. Author. libel. discipl. Ecclesiast.

b τῶν παλαιῶν τοὺς εὐδοκιμω]άτας ἀναχοτῶν εὐείσκω ὅσους πώποτε ἔις ἱπασασίαν ἢ προφητείαν ἢ

1 Tim. 3. 1.

χάεις πρεσβάλε]ο τοὺς μὴ ἕιξαντας προθύμως τῷ κλάσει τὸ δὲ ἀναβαλλομένες τὸ χάεισμα κ] ὐδ έτέρων μεμπ]ω ᾶτε τῆ̈ ὑποχωρησάντων τὴν δειλίαν, ᾶτε τῆ̈ ὁρμησάντων τὴν προθυμίαν, ὁι μετὰ τὸ τ διακονία, τὸ μέγιθ⊙ ἐνλαβήθησαν, ὁι δὲ τῷ καλῦντι πιςεύσαν]ες ἠκολόθησαν, Greg. Nazian. Apologet.

In

In vain are those desires allowed, the accomplishment whereof it is not lawful for men to seek. Power therefore of Ecclesiastical order may be desired, the desire thereof may be professed, they which profess themselves that way inclined, may endeavour to bring their desires to effect, and in all this no necessity of evil. Is it the bringing of testimonial Letters wherein so great obliquity consisteth? What more simple, more plain, more harmless, more agreeable with the law of common humanity, then that men where they are not known, use for their easier access the credit of such as can best give testimony of them? Letters of any other construction our Church-Discipline alloweth not, and these to allow, is neither to require ambitious suings, nor to approve any indirect or unlawful act. The Prophet *Esay* receiving his message at the hands of God, and his charge by heavenly vision, heard the voice of the Lord, saying, *Whom shall I send? Who shall go for us?* Whereun- *Esay 6. 8.* to he recordeth his own answer, *Then I said, Here Lord I am, send me.* Which in effect is the Rule and Canon whereby touching this point the very order of the Church is framed.

The appointment of times for solemn ordination, is but the publick demand of the Church in the name of the Lord himself, *Whom shall I send, Who shall go for us?* The confluence of men, whose inclinations are bent that way, is but the answer *Heb. 10. 8.* thereunto, whereby the labours of sundry being offered, the Church hath freedom to take whom her agents in such case think meet and requisite. As for the example of our Saviour Christ who took not to himself this honour to be made our high Priest, but received the same from him which said; *Thou art a Priest for ever after the order of Melchisedec,* his waiting, and not attempting to execute the office till *Heb. 5. 5.* God saw convenient time, may serve in reproof of usurped honours, for as much as we ought not of our own accord to assume dignities, whereunto we are not called as Christ was. But yet it should be withal considered, that a proud usurpation without any orderly calling is one thing, and another the bare declaration of willingness to obtain admittance; which willingness of mind, I suppose, did not want in him whose answer was to the voice of his heavenly calling, *Behold I am come to do thy will.* And had it been for him, as it is for us, expedient to receive his commission signed with the hands of men, to seek it, might better have beseemed his humility, then it doth our boldness, to reprehend them of Pride and Ambition, that make no worse kind of sutes then by letters of information. Himself in calling his Apostles prevented all cogitations of theirs that way, to the end it might truly be said of them, *Ye chose not me, but I of mine own voluntary motion made choice of you.* Which kind of undesired nomination to Ecclesiastical places befell divers of the most famous amongst the ancient Fathers of the Church in a clean contrary consideration. For our Saviours election respected not any merit or worth, but took them which were farthest off from likelihood of fitness: that afterwards their supernatural ability and performance, beyond hope, might cause the greater admiration; whereas in the other, meer admiration of their singular and rare vertues was the reason why honours were inforced upon them, which they of meekness and modesty did what they could to avoid. But did they ever judge it a thing unlawful to wish or desire the office, the only charge and bare Function of the Ministery? Towards which labour, what doth the blessed Apostle else but encourage, saying, *He which desireth it, is desirous of a good work?* What doth he else by such sentences but stir, kindle and inflame ambition, if I may term that desire ambition, which coveteth more to testifie love by painfulness in Gods service, than to reap any other benefit? Although of the very honour it self, and of other emoluments annexed to such labours, for more encouragement of mans industry, we are not so to conceive neither, as if no affection could be cast towards them without offence. Only as the Wiseman giveth counsel: *Seek not to be made a Judge, lest thou be not able to take Ecclef. 7. 6. away iniquity, and lest thou fearing the person of the mighty, shouldst commit an offence against thine uprightness;* so it always behoveth men to take good heed, lest affection to that, which hath in it as well difficulty as goodness, sophisticate the true and sincere judgement which before-hand they ought to have of their own ability, for want whereof, many forward minds have found in stead of contentment repentance. But for as much as hardness of things in themselves most excellent cooleth

the

the fervency of mens defires, unlefs there be fomewhat naturally acceptable to incite labour (for both the method of fpeculative knowledge doth by things which we fenfibly perceive conduct to that which is in nature more certain though lefs fenfible, and the method of vertuous actions is alfo to train beginners at the firft by things acceptable unto the tafte of natural appetite, till our minds at the length be fetled to embrace things precious in the eye of reafon, meerly and wholly for their own fakes) howfoever inordinate defires do hereby take occafion to abufe the Politie of God, and Nature, either affecting without worth, or procuring by unfeemly means that which was inftituted, and fhould be referved for better minds to obtain by more approved courfes, in which confideration the Emperours *Anthemius* and *Leo* did worthily oppofe againft fuch ambitious practices that ancient and famous Conftitution, wherein they have thefe fentences ; *Let not a Prelate be ordained for reward or upon requeft, who fhould be fo far fequeftred from all ambition, that they which advance him might be fain to fearch where he hideth himfelf, to entreat him drawing back, and to follow him till importunity have made him yield, let nothing promote him but his excufes to avoid the burthen, they are unworthy of that vocation which are not thereunto brought unwillingly* ; notwithftanding, we ought not therefore with the odious name of ambition, to traduce and draw into hatred every poor requeft or fute wherein men may feem to affect honour ; feeing that ambition and modefty do not always fo much differ in the mark they fhoot at, as in the manner of their profecutions. Yea even in this may be errour alfo, if we ftill imagine them leaft ambitious, which moft forbear to ftir either hand or foot towards their own preferments. For there are that make an Idol of their great fufficiency, and becaufe they furmize the place fhould be happy that might enjoy them, they walk every where like grave Pageants, obferving whether men do not wonder why fo fmall account is made of fo rare worthinefs ; and in cafe any other mans advancement be mentioned, they either fmile or blufh at the marvellous folly of the world, which feeth not where dignities fhould offer themfelves. Seeing therefore that futes after fpiritual Functions may be as ambitioufly forborn as profecuted, it remaineth that the a eveneft line of moderation between both, is neither to follow them, *without confcience* ; nor of *pride*, to withdraw our felves utterly from them.

78. It pleafeth Almighty God to chufe to himfelf, for difcharge of the b legal Miniftery, one only Tribe out of twelve others, the Tribe of *Levi*, not all unto every divine fervice, but *Aaron* and his fons to one charge, the reft of that fanctified Tribe to another. With what folemnities they were admitted into their Functions, in what manner *Aaron* and his fucceffors the high Priefts afcended every Sabbath and feftival day, offered, and miniftred in the Temple ; with what fin-offering once every year they reconciled firft themfelves and their own houfe, afterwards the people unto God ; how they confeffed all the iniquities of the children of *Ifrael*, laid all their trefpaffes upon the head of a facred Goat, and fo carried them out of the City ; how they purged the holy place from all uncleannefs ; with what reverence they entred within the Vail, prefented themfelves before the Mercy-Seat, and confulted with the Oracle of God : What fervice the other Priefts did continually in the Holy Place, how they miniftred about the Lamps Morning and Evening ; how every Sabbath they placed on the Table of the Lord thofe twelve loaves with pure Incenfe, in perpetual remembrance of that mercy which the Fathers, the twelve Tribes had found by the providence of God for their food, when hunger caufed them to leave their natural foil, and to feek for fuftenance in *Egypt* ; how they imployed themfelves in facrifice day by day ; finally, what offices the Levites difcharged, and what duties the reft did execute, it were a labour too long to enter into, if I fhould collect that which Scriptures and other ancient Records do mention. Befides thefe, there were indifferently out of all Tribes from time to time fome call'd of God as Prophets, fore-fhewing them things to come, and giving them counfel in fuch particulars as they could not be directed in by the Law ; fome chofen of men to read, ftudy, and interpret the Law of God, as the Sons or Scholars of the old Prophets ; in whofe room afterwards Scribes and Expounders of the Law fucceeded. And becaufe where fo great variety is, if there fhould be equality,

lity,

lity, confusion would follow, the Levites were in all their service at the appointment and direction of the Sons of *Aaron*, or Priests, they subject to the principal guides and leaders of their own Order, and they all in obedience under the High Priest. Which difference doth also manifest it self in the very titles, that men for honours sake gave unto them, terming *Aaron* and his Successors, High or Great; the ancients over the companies of Priests, Arch-Priests, Prophets, Fathers; Scribes and Interpreters of the Law, Masters. Touching the Ministery of the Gospel of Jesus Christ, the whole body of the Church being divided into Laity and Clergy, the Clergy are either Presbyters or Deacons. I rather term the one sort Presbyters than Priests, because in a matter of so

small moment I would not willingly offend their ears, to whom the name of Priesthood is odious, though without cause. For as things are distinguished one from another by those true essential forms, which being really and actually in them, do not only give them the very last and highest degree of their natural perfection, but are also the knot, foundation and root whereupon all other inferiour perfections depend: so if they that first do impose names, did always understand exactly the nature of that which they nominate, it may be that then by hearing the terms of vulgar speech,

a *T. C. l. 1. p. 198.* For so much as the common and usual speech of *England* is to note by the word *Priest* not a Minister of the Gospel, but a *Sacrificer*, which the Minister of the Gospel is not, therefore we ought not to call the Ministers of the Gospel *Priests*. And that this is the English speech, it appeareth by all the English Translations, which translate always ἱερεύς, which were sacrificers, *Priests*, and do not of the other side, for any that ever I read, translate πρεσβύτερον a *Priest*. Seeing therefore a Priest with us, and in our Tongue, doth signifie both by the Papists Judgement, in respect of their abominable *Mass*, and also by the Judgement of the Protestants, in respect of the Beasts which were offered in the Law, *a sacrificing Office*, which the Minister of the Gospel neither doth nor can execute; it is manifest that it cannot be without great offence so used.

we should still be taught what the things themselves most properly are. But because words have so many Artificers by whom they are made, and the things whereunto we apply them are fraught with so many varieties, it is not always apparent, what the first Inventers respected, much less what every mans inward conceit is which useth their words. For any thing my self can discern herein, I suppose that they which have bent their study to search more diligently such matters, do for the most part find that names advisedly given, had either regard unto that which is naturally most proper; or if perhaps, to some other speciality, to that which is sensibly most eminent in the thing signified; and concerning popular use of words, that which the wisdom of their Inventors did intend thereby, is not commonly thought of, but by the name the thing altogether conceived in gross, as may appear in that if you ask of the common sort what any certain word, for example, what a Priest doth signifie, their manner is not to answer, a Priest is a Clergy-man which offereth sacrifice to God, but they shew some particular person, whom they use to call by that name. And if we list to descend to Grammar, we are told by Masters in those Schools, that the word *Priest* hath his right place ἐπὶ τῶ φιλῶ πρεσβύτε- τῆς θεραπείας τῶ θεῶ, in him whose meer function or charge is the service of God. Howbeit because the most eminent part both of *Heathenish* and *Jewish* service did consist in sacrifice, when learned men declare what the word Priest doth properly signifie, *according to the mind of the first imposer* of that name, their ordinary b Schools do well expound it to imply sacrifice. Seeing then that sacrifice is now no part of the Church-Ministery, how should the name of Priesthood be thereunto rightly applyed? Surely even as S. *Paul* applyeth the name of c *flesh* unto that very substance of fishes which hath a proportionable correspondence to flesh, although it be in nature another thing. Whereupon when Philosophers will speak warily, they d make a difference between flesh in one sort of living creatures, and that other substance in the rest which hath but a kind of analogie to flesh: the Apostle contrariwise having matter of great importance whereof to speak, nameth indifferently both flesh. The Fathers of the Church of Christ with like security of speech call usually the Ministery of the Gospel *Priesthood*, in regard of that which the Gospel hath proportionable to ancient sacrifices, namely the *Communion* of the blessed body and blood of Christ, although it hath properly now no sacrifice. As for the people, when they hear the name, it draweth no more *their minds* to any cogitation of sacrifice, than the name of a Senator or of an Alderman causeth them to think upon old age, or to imagine that every one so termed must needs be ancient, because years were re-

Etymol. mag.

b ἱερεῦσαι, θυσιάσαι. H.ly. *Christus homo dicitur, quia natus est, Propheta quia futura revela- vit; sacerdos, quia pro nobis hostiam se obtu- lit.* Isid. Orig. lib. 7. cap. 2.

c 1 *Cor.* 15.39.

d ᾿Εχει δ᾿ ἀ- νάλον τινα [τῷ] αἱματι τὸ τῶν ἀναίμα- των πτερον ἢ σάρξ ἢ ἐν τοῖς ἄλλοις τὸ ἀνά- λογον ἢ ἐν. Arist. de Anim. lib. 2. c. 11.

spected

spected in the first nomination of both. Wherefore to pass by the name, let them use what dialect they will, whether we call it a Priesthood, a Presbytership, or a Ministery, it skilleth not : Although in truth the word *Presbyter* doth seem more fit, and in propriety of speech more agreeable then *Priest* with the drift of the whole Gospel of Jesus Christ. For what are they that embrace the Gospel but Sons of God ? What are Churches but his families ? Seeing therefore we receive the Adoption and state of Sons by their Ministery whom God hath chosen out for that purpose ; seeing also that when we are the Sons of God, our continuance is still under their care which were our Progenitors, what better title could there be given them than the reverend name of *Presbyters*, or fatherly guides ? The Holy Ghost throughout the body of the New Testament, making so much mention of them, doth not any where call them Priests. The Prophet *Esay*, I grant, doth, but in such sort as the ancient Fathers, by way of analogie. *A Presbyter*, according to the proper meaning of the new Testament, *is he, unto whom our Saviour Christ hath communicated the power of spiritual procreation.* Out of the twelve Patriarks issued the whole multitude of *Israel* according to the flesh. And according to the mystery of heavenly birth, our Lords Apostles we all acknowledge to be the Patriarks of his whole Church. S. *John* therefore beheld sitting about the throne of God in heaven [a] four and twenty Presbyters, the one half Fathers of the old, [b] the other of the new *Jerusalem*. In which respect the Apostles likewise gave themselves the same title, albeit that name were not proper, but common unto them with others. For of Presbyters, some were greater, some less in power, and that by our Saviours own appointment ; the greater they which received fulness of spiritual power, the less they to whom less was granted. The Apostles peculiar charge was to publish the Gospel of Christ unto all Nations, and to deliver them his Ordinances received by [c] *immediate revelation from himself.* Which preeminence excepted, to all other offices and duties incident into their order, it was in them to ordain and consecrate whomsoever they thought meet, even as our Saviour did himself assign seventy others of his own Disciples inferiour Presbyters, whose commission to preach and baptize was the same which the Apostles had. Whereas therefore we find, that the very first Sermon which the Apostles did publickly make was the conversion of above three thousand souls, unto whom there were every day more and more added, they having no open place permitted them for the exercise of Christian Religion, think we that twelve were sufficient to teach and administer Sacraments in so many private places, as so great a multitude of people did require ? This harvest, our Saviour (no doubt) foreseeing, provided accordingly Labourers for it before hand. By which mean it came to pass, that the growth of that Church being so great and so sudden, they had notwithstanding in a readiness Presbyters enough to furnish it. And therefore the history doth make no mention by what occasion Presbyters were instituted in *Jerusalem*, only we read of things which they did, and how the like were made afterwards elsewhere. To these two degrees appointed of our Lord and Saviour Christ, his Apostles soon after annexed Deacons ; Deacons therefore must know, saith *Cyprian*, that our Lord himself did elect Apostles, but Deacons after his ascension into Heaven the Apostles ordained, Deacons were Stewards of the Church, unto whom at the first was committed the distribution of Church-goods, the care of providing therewith for the poor, and the charge to see that all things of expence might be religiously and faithfully dealt in. A part also of their Office, was attendance upon their Presbyters at the time of Divine Service. For which cause *Ignatius*, to set forth the dignity of their calling, saith, that they are in such case to the Bishop, as if Angelical powers did serve him. These only being the uses for which Deacons were first made, if the Church have sithence extended their Ministery further than the circuit of their labour at the first was drawn, we are not herein to think the Ordinance of Scripture violated, except there appear some prohibition, which hath abridged the Church of that liberty. Which I note chiefly in regard of them to whom it seemeth a thing so monstrous, that Deacons should sometime be licensed to preach, whose institution was at the first to another end. To charge them for this as men not contented with their own vocations, and as breakers into that which appertaineth unto others, it is very hard. For when

they

Esay 66. 21.

a *Revel.*4.4.
b *Rev.*20.14.
*Mat.*19.28.
1 *Pet.*5.1.

c οἱ τῶν ἱερῶν Θεοπαράδοτοι νομοθεσίαι.Dionyl.Areop. pag. 110.
*Act.*2.41,47.

*Cyp.*Ep.9 l.3.
ad Rogatianum

Ignat.Epist.
ad Trall.

they are thereunto once admitted, it is a part of their own vocation, it appertaineth now unto them as well as others; neither is it intrusion for them to do it being in such sort called, but rather in us it were temerity to blame them for doing it. Suppose we the office of teaching to be so repugnant unto the office of Deaconship, that they cannot concur in one and the same person? What was there done in the Church by Deacons, which the Apostles did not first discharge being Teachers? Yea, but the Apostles found the burthen of Teaching so heavy, that they judged it meet to cut off that other charge, and to have Deacons, which might undertake it. Be it so. The multitude of Christians increasing in *Jerusalem,* and waxing great, it was too much for the Apostles to teach, and to minister unto Tables also. The former was not to be slacked, that this latter might be followed. Therefore unto this they appointed others. Whereupon we may rightly ground this axiome, that when the subject wherein one mans labours of sundry kinds are imployed, doth wax so great, that the same men are no longer able to manage it sufficiently as before, the most natural way to help this, is, by dividing their charge into slipes, and ordaining of under-officers, as our Saviour under twelve Apostles, seventy Presbyters, and the Apostles by his example seven Deacons to be under both. Neither ought it to seem less reasonable, that when the same men are sufficient both to continue in that which they do, and also to undertake somewhat more, a combination be admitted in this case; as well as division in the former. We may not therefore disallow it in the Church of *Geneva,* that *Calvin* and *Beza* were made both Pastors and Readers in Divinity, being men so able to discharge both. To say they did not content themselves with their Pastoral vocations, but brake into that which belongeth to others; to alledge against them, *He that exhorteth in exhortation,* as against Rom. 12.8. us, *He that distributeth in simplicity,* is alledged in great dislike of granting licence for Deacons to preach, were very hard. The ancient custome of the Church, was to yield the poor much relief, especially Widows. But as poor people are always querelous and apt to think themselves less respected then they should be, we see that when the Apostles did what they could without hinderance to their weightier business, yet there were which grudged that others had too much, and they too little, the Grecian Widows shorter Commons then the Hebrews. By means whereof the Apostles saw it meet to ordain Deacons. Now tract of time having clean worn out those first occasions, for which the Deaconship was then most necessary, it might the better be afterwards extended to other Services, and so remain as at this present day, a degree in the Clergy of God which the Apostles of Christ did institute. That the first seven Deacons were chosen out of the seventy Disciples, is an errour in *Epiphanius.* For to draw men from places of weightier, unto rooms of Epiph.l.1.c.21. meaner labour, had not been fit. The Apostles, to the end they might follow teaching with more freedom, committed the Ministery of Tables unto Deacons. And shall we think they judged it expedient to chuse so many out of those seventy to be Ministers unto Tables, when Christ himself had before made them Teachers? It appeareth therefore, how long these three degrees of Ecclesiastical Order have continued in the Church of Christ, the highest and largest, that which the Apostles, the next that which Presbyters, and the lowest that which Deacons had. Touching Prophets, they were such men as having otherwise learned the Gospel, had from above bestowed upon them a special gift of expounding Scriptures, and of foreshewing things to come. Of this sort *Agabus* was, and besides him in *Jerusalem* Acts 21.10. sundry others, who notwithstanding are not therefore to be reckoned with the Acts 11.27. Clergy, because no mans gifts of qualities can make him a Minister of holy things, unless Ordination do give him power. And we no where find Prophets to have been made by Ordination, but all whom the Church did ordain, were either to serve as Presbyters or as Deacons. Evangelists were Presbyters of principal sufficiency, whom the Apostles sent abroad, and used as Agents in Ecclesiastical affairs wheresoever they saw need. They whom we find to have been named in Scripture, Evan- a Acts 9.18. gelists, [a] *Ananias,* [b] *Apollos,* [c] *Timothy,* and others were thus employed. And con- b Acts 18.24. cerning Evangelists, afterwards in *Trajans* days, the History Ecclesiastical noteth c 2 Tim.4.5.9. that many of the Apostles, Disciples and Scholars which were then alive, and did 1 Tim.3.15,5. with singular love of Wisdom affect the Heavenly Word of God, to shew their Euseb.Ecclef. hist.l.3.c.34.

willing

willing minds in executing that which Christ first of all required at the hands of men, they sold their Possessions, gave them to the poor, and betaking themselves to travel, undertook the labour of Evangelists, that is, they painfully preached Christ, and delivered the Gospel to them, who as yet had never heard the Doctrine of Faith. Finally, whom the Apostle nameth Pastors and Teachers, what other were they than Presbyters also, howbeit setled in some certain charge, and thereby differing from Evangelists ? I beseech them therefore which have hitherto troubled the Church with question, about Degrees & Offices of Ecclesiastical calling, because they principally ground themselves upon two places, that all partiality laid aside, they would sincerely weigh and examine whether they have not mis-interpreted both places, and all by surmising incompatible Offices, where nothing is meant but sundry graces, gifts and abilities which Christ bestowed. To them of *Corinth,* his words are these, *God placed in the Church, first of all, some Apostles ; Secondly, Prophets ;*

1 *Cor.* 2. 18.

Thirdly, Teachers ; after them powers, then gifts of Cures, Aides, Governments, kinds of Languages. Are all Apostles ? Are all Prophets ? Are all Teachers ? Is there power in all ? Have all grace to cure ? Do all speak with Tongues ? Can all interpret ? But be you desirous of the better graces. They which plainly discern first, that some *one general* thing there is which the Apostle doth here divide into all these branches, and do secondly conceive that general to be Church-offices, besides a number of other difficulties, can by no means possibly deny but that many of these might concur in one man, and peradventure, in some one all, which mixture notwithstanding, their form of Discipline doth most shun. On the other side, admit that *Communicants of special infused grace,* for the benefit of members knit into one body, the Church of Christ, are here spoken of, which was in truth the plain drift of that whole Discourse, and see if every thing do not answer in due place with that fitness, which sheweth easily what is likeliest to have been meant. For why are Apostles the first, but because unto them was granted the Revelation of all Truth from Christ immediately ? Why Prophets the second, but because they had of some things knowledge in the same manner ? Teachers the next, because whatsoever was known to them it came by hearing, yet God withal made them able to instruct, which every one could not do that was taught. After Gifts of Edification there follow general abilities to work things above Nature, Grace to cure men of bodily Diseases, Supplies against occurrent defects and impediments, Dexterities to govern and direct by counsel ; Finally, aptness to speak or interpret forreign tongues. Which Graces not poured out equally, but diversly sorted and given, were a cause why not only they all did furnish up the whole Body, but each benefit and help other. Again, the same Apostle other-where in like sort. *To every one of us is*

Ephes. 4. 7.
Psal. 68. 18.

given grace, according to the measure of the gift of Christ. Wherefore he saith, When he ascended up on high, he led Captivity captive, and gave gifts unto men. He therefore gave some Apostles, and some Prophets, and some Evangelists, and some Pastors and Teachers, for the gathering together of Saints, for the work of the Ministery, for the edification of the Body of Christ. In this place none but gifts of Instruction are exprest. And because of Teachers some were Evangelists which neither had any part of their knowledge by Revelation as the Prophets, and yet in ability to teach were far beyond other Pastors, they are, as having received one way less then Prophets, and another way more then Teachers, set accordingly between both. For the Apostle doth in neither place respect what any of them were by Office or Power given them through Ordination, but what by Grace they all had obtained through miraculous infusion of the Holy Ghost. For in Christian Religion, this being the ground of our whole Belief, that the promises which God of old had made by his Prophets concerning the wonderful Gifts and Graces of the Holy Ghost, wherewith the Reign of the true *Messias* should be made glorious, were immediately after our Lords Ascension performed, there is no one thing whereof the Apostles did take more often occasion to speak. Out of men thus indued with gifts of the Spirit upon their Conversion to Christian Faith, the Church had her Ministers chosen, unto whom was given Ecclesiastical power by Ordination. Now, because the Apostle in reckoning degrees and varieties of Grace, doth mention Pastors and Teachers, although he mention them not in respect of their Ordination to exercise the Ministery,

stery, but as examples of men especially enriched with the gifts of the Holy
Ghost, divers learned and skilful men have so taken it, as if those places did intend
to teach what Orders of Ecclesiastical persons there ought to be in the Church of
Christ, which thing we are not to learn from thence but out of other parts of holy
Scripture, whereby it clearly appeareth, that Churches Apostolick did know but
three degrees in the power of Ecclesiastical Order ; at the first Apostles, Presbyters,
and Deacons, afterwards in stead of Apostles, Bishops, concerning whose Order
we are to speak in the seventh Book. There is an errour which beguileth many
who much intangle both themselves and others by not distinguishing *Services, Offices* and *Orders* Ecclesiastical, the first of which three, and in part the second may
be executed by the Laity, whereas none have, or can have the third but the Clergy. Catechists, Exorcists, Readers, Singers, and the rest of like sort, if the nature
only of their labours and pains be considered, may in that respect seem Clergy-
men, even as the Fathers for that cause term them usually Clerks, as also in regard
of the end whereunto they were trained up, which was to be ordered when years
and experience should make them able. Notwithstanding, in as much as they no
way differed from others of the Laity longer then during that work of Service,
which at any time they might give over, being thereunto but admitted, not tied by
irrevocable Ordination, we find them always exactly severed from that body, whereof those three before rehearsed Orders alone are natural parts. Touching Widows,
of whom some men are perswaded, that if such as Saint *Paul* describeth may be
gotten, we ought to retain them in the Church for ever, certain mean Services
there were of Attendance; as about Women, at the time of their Baptism, about
the bodies of the sick and dead, about the necessities of Travellers, Wayfaring men
and such like, wherein the Church did commonly use them when need required,
because they lived of the Alms of the Church, and were fittest for such purposes ;
Saint *Paul* doth therefore, to avoid scandal, require that none but Women well experienced and vertuously given, neither any under threescore years of age should
be admitted of that number. Widows were never in the Church so highly esteemed
as Virgins. But seeing neither of them did or could receive Ordination, to make
them Ecclesiastical persons were absurd. The ancientest therefore of the Fathers
mention those three degrees of Ecclesiastical Order specified, and no moe. *When
your Captains* (saith *Tertullian*) *that is to say, the Deacons, Presbyters and Bishops flye,
who shall teach the Laity, that they must be constant ?* Again, *What should I mention
Lay-men* (saith *Optatus*) *yea, or divers of the Ministery it self ? To what purpose Deacons, which are in the third, or Presbyters in the second degree of Priesthood, when the
very Heads and Princes of all, even certain of the Bishops themselves* were content to
redeem life with the loss of Heaven ? Heaps of Allegations in a case so evident and
plain are needless. I may securely therefore conclude, that there are at this day in
the Church of *England*, no other then the same degrees of Ecclesiastical Order,
namely, Bishops, Presbyters, and Deacons, which had their beginning from Christ,
and his blessed Apostles themselves. As for Deans, Prebendaries, Parsons, Vicars,
Curates, Arch-deacons, Chancellors, Officials, Commissaries, and such other the
like names, which being not found in holy Scripture, we have been thereby through
some mens errour thought to allow of Ecclesiastical Degrees not known, nor ever
heard of in the better Ages of former times ; all these are in truth but Titles of Office, whereunto partly Ecclesiastical persons, and partly others are in sundry forms
and conditions admitted, as the state of the Church doth need Degrees of Order,
still continuing the same they were from the first beginning. Now what habit or
attire doth beseem each order to use in the course of common life, both for the gravity of his place, and for example sake to other men, is a matter frivolous to be disputed of. A small measure of wisdom may serve to teach them how they should cut
their coats. But seeing all well ordered Polities have ever judged it meet and fit by
certain special distinct Ornaments to sever each sort of men from other
when they are in publick, to the end that all may receive such. Complements of Civil Honour, as are due to their Rooms and Callings, even
where their persons are not known, it argueth a disproportioned mind in
them whom so decent orders displease.

Q q

79. We

79 We might somewhat marvel, what the Apostle Saint *Paul* should mean to

say that Covetousness is Idolatry, if the daily practice of men did not shew, that whereas Nature requireth God to be honoured with wealth, we honour for the most part wealth as God. Fain we would teach our selves to believe, that for worldly goods it sufficeth frugally and honestly to use them to our own benefit, without detriment and hurt of others; or if we go a degree farther, and perhaps convert some small contemptible Portion thereof to Charitable uses, the whole duty which we owe unto God herein is fully satisfied. But for as much as we cannot rightly honour God, unless both our Souls and Bodies be sometime imployed in his Service; Again, sith we know that Religion requireth at our hands the taking away of so great a part of the time of our lives quite and clean from our own business, and the bestowing of the same in his, suppose we that nothing of our wealth and substance is immediately due to God, but all our own to bestow and spend as our selves think meet? Are not our riches as well his, as the days of our life are his? Wherefore, unless with part we acknowledge his Supream Dominion, by whose benevolence we have the whole, how give we Honour to whom Honour belongeth, or how hath God the things that are Gods? I would know what Nation in the World did ever honour God, and not think it a point of their duty to do him honour with their very goods. So that this we may boldly set down as a principle clear in Nature, an Axiome which ought not to be called in question, a Truth manifest and infallible, that men are eternally bound to honour God with their substance, in token of thankfull acknowledgment that all they have is from him. To honour him with our worldly goods, not only by spending them in lawful manner, and by using them without offence, but also by alienating from our selves some reasonable part or portion thereof, and by offering up the same to him as a signe that we gladly confess his Sole and Soveraign Dominion over all, is a duty which all men are bound unto, and a part of that very Worship of God, which as the Law of God and Nature it self requireth, so we are the rather to think all men no less strictly bound thereunto than to any other natural duty, in as much as the hearts of men do so cleave to these earthly things, so much admire them for the sway they have in the World, impute them so generally either to Nature or to Chance and Fortune, so little think upon the Grace and Providence from which they come, that unless by a kind of continual tribute we did acknowledge Gods Dominion, it may be doubted that in short time men would learn to forget whose Tenants they are, and imagine that the World is their own absolute, free and independent inheritance. Now, concerning the kind or quality of gifts which God receiveth in that sort, we are to consider them, partly as first they proceed from us, and partly as afterwards they are to serve for divine uses. In that they are testimonies of our affection towards God, there is no doubt, but such they should be as beseemeth most His Glory to whom we offer them. In this respect the fatness of *Abels* sacrifice is commended; the flower of all mens increase assigned to God by *Solomon*; the gifts and donations of the people rejected as oft as their cold affection to God-ward made their presents to be little worth. Somewhat the Heathens saw touching that which was herein fit, and therefore they unto their gods did not think they might consecrate any thing which was *impure* or

unsound, or *already given*, or else *not truly their own to give*. Again, in regard of use, forasmuch as we know that God hath himself no need of worldly commodities, but taketh them because it is our good to be so exercised, and with no other intent accepteth them, but to have them used for the endless continuance of Religion; there is no place left of doubt or controversie, but that we in the choice of our gifts are to level at the same mark, and to frame our selves to his known intents and purposes. Whether we give unto God therefore that which himself by commandment requireth; or that which the publick consent of the Church thinketh good to allot, or that which every mans private devotion doth best like, in as much as the gift which we offer, proceedeth not only as a testimony of our affection towards God, but also as a mean to uphold Religion, the exercise whereof cannot stand without the help of temporal commodities: if all men be taught of Nature to wish, and as much as in them lieth, to procure the perpetuity of good things;

if

if for that very cause we honour and admire their wisdom, who having been founders of Common-weals, could devise how to make the benefit they left behind them
durable; if especially in this respect we prefer *Lycurgus* before *Solon*, and the
Spartan before the *Athenian* Politie, it must needs follow, that as we do unto God
very acceptable service in honouring him with our substance, so our service that way
is then most acceptable, when it tendeth to perpetuity. The first permanent donations of honour in this kind are Temples. Which works do so much set forward
the exercise of Religion, that while the World was in love with Religion, it
gave to no sort greater reverence than to whom it could point and say, *These are
the men that have built us Synagogues.* But of Churches we have spoken sufficiently heretofore. The next things to Churches are the ornaments of Churches, memorials which mens devotion hath added to remain in the treasure of Gods house,
not only for uses wherein the exercise of Religion presently needeth them, but
also partly for supply of future casual necessities, whereunto the Church is on earth
subject, and partly to the end that while they are kept they may continually serve
as testimonies, giving all men to understand, that God hath in every Age and Nation, such as think it no burthen to honour him with their substance. The riches first
of the Tabernacle of God; and then of the Temple of *Jerusalem*, arising out of
voluntary gifts and donations, were, as we commonly speak, a *Nemo scit*, the
value of them above that which any man would imagine. After that the Tabernacle was made, furnished with all necessaries, and set up, although in the wilderness their ability could not possibly be great, the very mettle of those vessels which *Num. 7. 8 5, 86.*
the Princes of the twelve Tribes gave to God for their first presents, amounted even
then to two thousand and four hundred shekels of Silver, an hundred and twenty *1 Chron. 29.*
shekels of Gold, every shekel weighing half an ounce. What was given to the *Exod. 25. 28.*
Temple which *Solomon* erected, we may partly conjecture, when over and be- *& 37. 24.*
sides Wood, Marble, Iron, Brass, Vestments, precious Stones, and Money; the *Ezra 2. 68, 69.*
sum which *David* delivered into *Solomons* hands for that purpose, was of Gold in *Hag. 2. 4.*
Masse eight thousand, and of Silver seventeen thousand Cichars, every Cichar con- *Ezr. 8. 24.*
taining a thousand and eight hundred shekels, which riseth to nine hundred Ounces
in every one Cichar: whereas the whole charge of the Tabernacle did not amount
unto thirty Cichars. After their return out of *Babylon*, they were not presently in
case to make their second Temple of equal magnificence and glory with that which
the enemy had destroyed. Notwithstanding what they could they did. Insomuch
that the building finished, there remained in the Coffers of the Church, to uphold
the fabrick thereof, six hundred and fifty Cichars of Silver, one hundred of Gold.
Whereunto was added by *Nehemias* of his own gift a thousand drams of Gold, fifty *Nehem. 7. 70.*
vessels of Silver, five hundred and thirty Priests vestments; by other the Princes
of the fathers twenty thousand dram's of Gold, two thousand and two hundred pieces of Silver; by the rest of the people twenty thousand of Gold, two thousand
of Silver, threescore and seven attires of Priests. And they furthermore bound *Nehem. 10. 32.*
themselves towards other charges to give by the Poll in what part of the World so- *a Cic. orat. pro*
ever they should dwell, the third of a shekel, that is to say, the sixt part of an ounce *L. Flac. Cum*
yearly. This out of fortain Provinces, they always sent in Gold. Whereof [b] *Mi-* *aurum Iudæo-*
thridaies is said to have taken up by the way before it could pass to *Jerusalem* from *rum nomine*
Asia, in one adventure eight hundred talents; *Crassus* after that to have borrowed *quotannis ex*
of the Temple it self eight thousand: at which time *Eleazar* having both many *Italia & ex*
other rich ornaments, and all Tapestry of the Temple under his custody, thought *omnibus vestris*
it the safest way to grow unto some composition, and so to redeem the residue by *provinciis His-*
parting with a certain beam of Gold about seven hundred and a half in weight, a prey *rosolymam ex-*
sufficient for one man, as he thought, who had never bargained with *Crassus* till then, *portari soleret*
and therefore upon the confidence of a solemne oath that no more should be look- *Flaccus Sanxit*
ed for, he simply delivered up a large morsel, whereby the value of that which re- *edisto, ne ex*
mained was betrayed, and the whole lost. Such being the casualties whereunto *Asia exportari*
moveable treasures are subject, the Law of *Moses* did both require eight and *liceret.*
twenty Cities together with their fields and whole Territories in the Land of *Ju-* *b Joseph. Anti.*
ry, to be reserved to God himself; and not only provide for the liberty of farther *lib. 14 cap. 12.*
additions, if men of their own accord should think good, but also for the safe *c Every talent in value 600.*
Num. 35.
Levit. 25. 34.
& 7. 38.

preser-

preſervation thereof unto all poſterities, that no mans avarice or fraud, by defeating ſo vertuous intents, might diſcourage from like purpoſes. Gods third indowment did therefore of old conſiſt in lands. Furthermore, ſome cauſe no doubt there is, why beſides ſundry other more rare donations on uncertain rate, the tenth ſhould be thought a revenue ſo natural to be allotted out unto God. For of the ſpoils which *Abraham* had taken in war, he delivered unto *Melchiſedeck* the Tithes. The

Gen. 14. 20.
Gen. 28, 20.

vow of *Jacob*, at ſuch times as he took his journey towards *Haran*, was, *If God will be with me, and will keep me in this voyage which I am to go, and will give me bread to eat, and clothes to put on, ſo that I may return to my fathers houſe in ſafety, then ſhall the Lord be my God; and this ſtone which I have ſet up as a pillar, the ſame ſhall be Gods Houſe, and of all thou ſhalt give me I will give unto thee the Tithe.* And as *Abraham* gave voluntarily, as *Jacob* vowed to give God Tithes, ſo the Law of *Moſes* did require

Deut. 84. 22.

at the hands of all men the ſelf-ſame kind of Tribute, the tenth of their Corn, Wine, Oyl, Fruit, Cattle, and whatſoever increaſe his heavenly Providence ſhould ſend. In ſo much that Panyms being herein followers of their ſteps, paid Tithes likewiſe:

Plin. hiſt. nat.
lib. 12. *cap.* 14.

Imagine we that this was for no cauſe done, or that there was not ſome ſpecial inducements to judge the tenth of our worldly profits the moſt convenient for Gods portion? Are not all things by him created in ſuch ſort, that the forms which give them their diſtinction are number, their operations meaſure, & their matter weight? *Three* being the myſtical number of Gods unſearchable perfection within himſelf; *ſeven* the number whereby our own perfections through grace are moſt ordered;

a Δεκὰς ἀριθ-
μῶν τῶν ἀπὸ
μονάδ Θ· ἐϛὶ
τέρας τελεό-
τατον. Philo.
περὶ Ἀποικ.

and *ten* the number of natures perfections (for the beauty of nature is order, and the foundation of order number, and of number the higheſt we can riſe unto without iteration of numbers under it) could nature better acknowledge the power of the God of nature then by aſſigning unto him that quantity which is the continent of all ſhe poſſeſſeth? There are in *Philo* the Jew, many arguments to ſhew the great congruity and fitneſs of this number in things conſecrated unto God. But becauſe over-nice and curious ſpeculations become not the earneſtneſs of holy things, I omit what might be farther obſerved, as well out of others as out of him, touching the quantity of this general ſacred tribute; whereby it cometh to paſs, that the meaneſt and the very pooreſt amongſt men, yeilding unto God as much in proportion as the greateſt, and many times in affection more, have this as a ſenſible token always aſſuring their minds, that in his ſight, from whom all good is expected, they are concerning acceptation, protection, divine priviledges and preheminencies whatſoever, equals and peers with them unto whom they are otherwiſe in earthly reſpects inferiours, being furthermore well aſſured that the top as it were thus preſented to God is neither loſt, nor unfruitfully beſtowed, but doth ſanctifie to them again the whole Maſs, and that he by receiving a little undertaketh to bleſs all. In which conſideration the Jews were accuſtomed to name their

b *Maſſoreth (e-*
pes eſt legis;
divitiarum ſe-
pes decima. R.
A. quiba in
Pirk. Aboth.

Tithes the b *hedge* of their riches. Albeit a hedge do only fence and preſerve that which is contained, whereas their Tithes and offerings did more, becauſe they procured increaſe of the heap out of which they were taken. God demandeth no ſuch debt for his own need, but for their only benefit that owe it. Wherefore detaining the ſame, they hurt not him whom they wrong; and themſelves whom they think they relieve, they wound; except men will haply affirm, that God did by fair ſpeeches, and large promiſes, delude the world in ſaying, *Bring ye all the*

Mal. 3.

Tithes into the ſtore-houſe, that there may be meat in mine houſe, (deal truly, defraud not God of his due) *and prove if I will not open unto you the Windows of Heaven, and pour down upon you an immeaſurable bleſſing.* That which Saint *James* hath concerning the effect of our prayers unto God, is for the moſt part of like moment in our gifts: We pray and obtain not, becauſe he which knoweth our hearts, doth ſee our deſires are evil. In like manner we give, and we are not the more accepted, becauſe he beholdeth how unwiſely we ſpill our gifts in the

c *Nemo liben-*
ter dedit quod
non accepit
ſed expreſſit.
Sen. de Benef.
lib. 1. cap. 1.

' bringing. It is to him which needeth nothing, all one whether any thing or nothing be given him. But for our own good, it always behoveth that whatſoever we offer up into his hands, we bring it ſeaſoned with this cogitation, *Thou Lord art worthy of all honour.* With the Church of Chriſt touching theſe matters, it ſtandeth as it did with the whole World before *Moſes.* Whereupon for many years men-
being

being defirous to honour God in the fame manner, as other vertuous and holy perfonages before had done, both during the time of their life, and if farther ability did
ferve, by fuch device as might caufe their works of piety to remain always, it came
by thefe means to pafs that the Church from time to time, had treafure proportionable unto the poorer or wealthier eftate of Chriftian men. And affoon as the ftare
of the Church could admit thereof, they eafily condefcended to think it moft natural and moft fit, that God fhould receive, as before, of all men his ancient accuftomed revenues of Tithes. Thus therefore both God and Nature have
taught to convert things temporal to eternal ufes, and to provide for the perpetuity of Religion, even by that which is moft tranfitory. For to the end that in
worth and value there might be no abatement of any thing once affigned to fuch
purpofes, the Law requireth precifely the beft of that we poffefs; and to prevent
all damages by way of commutation, were in ftead of natural commodities, or
other rights, the price of them might be taken, the Law of *Mofes* determined
their rates, and the payments to be always made by the Sicle of the Sanctuary, *Levit.27.25.*
wherein there was great advantage of weight above the ordinary currant Sicle. The
trueft and fureft way for God to have always his own, is by making him payment in
kind out of the very felf-fame riches, which through his gracious benediction the
earth doth continually yield. This where it may be without inconvenience, is for
every mans confcience fake. That which cometh from God to us, by the natural
courfe of his providence, which we know to be innocent and pure, is perhaps beft
accepted, becaufe leaft fpotted with the ftain of unlawful, or indirect procurement.
Befides, whereas prices daily change, Nature which commonly is one, muft
needs be the moft indifferent and permanent ftandard between God and Man.
But the main foundation of all, whereupon the fecurity of thefe things dependeth,
as far as any thing may be afcertained amongft men, is, that the Title and Right
which man had in every of them before Donation, doth by the Act, and from
the time of any fuch Donation, Dedication, or Grant, remain the proper poffeffion of God till the worlds end, unlefs himfelf renounce or relinquifh it. For
if equity have taught us, that every one ought to enjoy his own; that what is ours
no other can alienate from us, but with our [a] own [b] deliberate confent; finally, a *Lib.* 11. *de*
that no man having paft his confent or deed, may [c] change it to the prejudice of any *Reg. Jur.*
other, fhould we prefume to deal with God worfe then God hath allowed any man b *Cujus per er-*
to deal with us? Albeit therefore we be now free from the Law of *Mofes*, and *rorem dati re-*
confequently, not thereby bound to the payment of Tithes; yet becaufe Nature *petitio eft. ejus*
hath taught men to honour God with their fubftance, and Scripture hath left us *confulto dati*
an example of that particular proportion, which for moral confiderations hath been *D. de cond.*
thought fitteft by him whofe wifdom could beft judge; furthermore, feeing that the *indeb.*
Church of Chrift hath long fithence entred into obligation, it feemeth in thefe days This the
a queftion altogether vain and fuperfluous, whether Tithes be a matter of divine ground of *Con-*
Right: becaufe howfoever at the firft, it might have been thought doubtful, our *fideration* ina-
cafe is clearly the fame now with theirs, unto whom St. *Peter* fometime fpake, fay- lienations from
ing, *While it was whole, it was whole thine.* When our Tithes might have pro- man to man.
bably feemed our own, we had colour of liberty to ufe them as we our felves faw c Nemo poteft
good. But having made them his whofe they are, let us be warned by other mens um fuum in al-
example what it is νοσφίσασθαι, to wafh or clip that coine which hath on it the mark cium,lib.75 de
of God. For that all thefe are his poffeffions, and that he doth himfelf fo reckon them, Reg. Jur.
appeareth by the form of his own fpeeches. Touching Gifts and Oblations, *Thou* Acts 5. 4.
fhalt give them *me*; touching Oratories and Churches, *My houfe* fhall be called the Exod.32.29,30.
Houfe of Prayer; touching Tithes, *Will a man fpoil God?* Yet behold, even me Matth.21.13.
your God ye have [d] *fpoiled*, notwithftanding ye ask wherein, as though ye were d Non videntur
ignorant, what injury there hath been offered in *Tithes*: ye are heavily accurfed, rem admittere
becaufe with a kind of publike confent ye have joined your felves in one to rob me, quibus propria
imagining the commonnefs of your offence to be every mans particular juftification; non fuit 83.
touching Lands, *Ye fhall offer to the Lord a facred portion of ground, and that facred* de Reg. Jur.
portion fhal belong to the Priefts Neither did God on y thus ordain amongft the Jews, Ezech.45.1.4.
but the very purpofe, intent, and meaning of all that have honoured him with
their fubftance, was to inveft him with the property of thofe benefits, the ufe whereof

muft

Mag.Char.c. 1.

Capitul.Carn. lib.6.cap.284.

a *Nullius autem sunt res sacra & religiosa & sancta. Quod enim divini juris est,id nullius in bonis est* Inst.l.2.tit.1 b *Soli cum Diis sacrilegi pugnant,* Curt.l.7. *Sacrum sacrove commendatum qui dempserit rapseritve, parricida esto,* Leg. 12. tab. Capitul. Caroli.6.c.285 c *Deposita pietatis,* Tertul. Apologet. Prudent. Peristeph.

must needs be committed to the hands of men. In which respect the stile of ancient Grants and Charters,is, *We have given unto God both for Us and our Heirs for ever, Yea, We know,* saith *Charls* the Great, *that the goods of the Church are the sacred indowments of God, to the Lord our God we offer and dedicate whatsoever we deliver unto his Church.* Whereupon the Laws Imperial do likewise divide all things in such sort, that they make some to belong by right of Nature indifferently unto every man, some to be the certain goods and possessions of Common-weals, some to appertain unto several Corporations or Companies of men, some to be privately mens own in particular, and some to be separated quite a from all men; which last branch comprizeth things sacred and holy, because thereof God alone is owner. The sequel of which received opinion, as well without as within the Walls of the House of God touching such possessions hath been ever, that there is not an act more honourable, then by all means to amplifie and defend the patrimony of Religion, not any more b impious and hateful, than to impair those possessions which men in former times, when they gave unto holy uses, were wont at the Altar of God,and in presence of their ghostly Superiours,to make as they thought, inviolable, by words of fearful execration, saying, *These things we offer to God, from whom if any take them away* (which we hope no man will attempt to do) *but if any shall, let his account be without favour in the last day, when he cometh to receive the doom which is due for sacrilege against that Lord and God unto whom we dedicate the same.* The best and most renowned Prelates of the Church of Christ have in this consideration rather sustained the wrath, then yielded to satisfie the hard desire of their greatest Commanders on earth, coveting with ill advice and counsel that which they willingly should have suffered God to injoy. There are of Martyrs,whom posterity much honour, for that having under their hands the custody of such c treasures,they could by vertuous delusion invent how to save them from prey, even when the safety of their own lives they gladly neglected,as one, somtime an Archdeacon under *Xistus* the Bishop of *Rome*,did, whom when his Judge understood to be one of the Church Stewards; thirst of blood began to slake, and another humour to work, which first by a favourable countenance, and then by quiet speech did thus calmly discloseth it self, *You that profess the Christian Religion, make great complaint of the wonderful cruelty we shew towards you. Neither peradventure altogether without cause. But for my self, I am far from any such bloody purpose. Ye are not so willing to live, as I unwilling that out of these lips should proceed any capital sentence against you. Your Bishops are said to have rich vessels of gold and silver, which they use in the exercise of their Religion; besides, the fame is, that numbers sell away their Lands and Livings, the huge prices whereof are brought to your Church coffers; by which means the devotion that maketh them and their whole posterity poor, must needs mightily enrich you, whose God we know was no Coyner of money, but left behind him many wholesome and good Precepts, as namely, that Crist should have of you the things that are fit for,and due to Cæsar. His wars are costly and chargeable unto him. That which you suffer to rust in corners,the affairs of the Common wealth do need. Your profession is not to make account of things transitory. And yet if ye can be contented but to foregoe that which ye care not for, I dare undertake to warrant you both safety of life,and freedome of using your conscience, a thing more acceptable to you than wealth.* Which fair parly the happy Martyr quietly hearing, and perceiving it necessary to make some shift for the safe concealment of that which being now desired was not unlikely to be more narrowly afterwards sought,he craved respite for three days, to gather the riches of the Church together, in which space against the time the Governour should come to the doors of the Temple,big with hope to receive his prey,a miserable rank of the poor,lame,and impotent persons was provided,their names delivered him up in writing as a true Inventory of the Churches goods, & some few words used to signifie how proud the Church was of these treasures.If men did not naturally abhor sacrilege, to resist or defeat so impious attempts would deserve small praise. But such is the general detestation of rapine in this kind, that wheras nothing doth in peace or war more uphold mens reputation then prosperous success, because in common construction,unless notorious improbity be join'd with prosperity,it seemeth to argue favour with God,they which once have stained their hands with these
odious

odious spoils, do thereby fasten unto all their actions an eternal prejudice, in respect whereof, for that it passeth through the world as an undoubted rule and principle, that sacriledge is open defiance to God, whatsoever they afterwards undertake, if they prosper in it, men reckon it but *Dionysius* his Navigation; and if any thing befall them otherwise, it is not, as commonly, so in them ascribed to the great uncertainty of casual events, wherein the providence of God doth controul the purposes of men oftentimes, much more for their good then if all things did answer fully their hearts desire, but the censure of the world is ever directly against them both [a] bitter and peremptory. To make such actions therefore less odious, and to mitigate the envy of them, many colourable shifts and inventions have been used, as if the world did hate only Wolves, and think the Fox a goodly creature. The [b] time it may be will come, when they that either violently have spoiled or thus smoothly defrauded God, shall find they did but deceive themselves. In the mean while there will be always some skilful persons, which can teach a way how to grind treatably the Church with jawes that shall scarce move, and yet devour in the end more then they that come ravening with open mouth, as if they would worry the whole in an instant; others also who having wastfully eaten out their own patrimony, would be glad to repair, if they might, their decayed estates, with the ruine they care not of what nor of whom, so the spoil were theirs, whereof in some part if they happen to speed, yet commonly they are men born under that constellation which maketh them, I know not how, as unapt to enrich themselves, as they are ready to impoverish others; it is their lot to sustain during life both the misery of beggers, and the infamy of robbers. But though no other plague and revenge should follow sacrilegious violations of holy things, the natural secret disgrace and ignominy, the very turpitude of such actions in the eye of a wise understanding heart, is it self a [c] heavy punishment. Men of vertuous quality are by this sufficiency moved to beware how they answer and require the mercies of God with injuries, whether openly or indirectly offered. I will not absolutely say concerning the goods of the Church, that they may in no case be seized on by men, or that no Obligation, Commerce and Bargain made between man and man, can ever be of force to alienate the property which God hath in them. Certain cases I grant there are wherein it is not so dark what God himself doth warrant, but that we may safely presume him as willing to forgoe for our benefit, as always to use and convert to our benefit whatsoever our Religion hath honoured him withal. But surely under the name of that which may be, many things that should not be are often done. By means whereof the Church most commonly for go'd hath suffered; and whereas the usual Saw of old was *Glaucus his change*, the Proverb is now *A Church bargain*. And for fear lest covetousness alone should linger out the time too much, and not be able to make havock of the House of God with that expedition, which the mortal enemy thereof did vehemently wish, he hath by certain strong inchantments so deeply bewitcht Religion it self, as to make it in the end an earnest Sollicitor, and an eloquent Perswader of sacriledge, urging confidently, that the very best service which men of power can do to Christ, is without any more Ceremony, to sweep all, and to leave the Church as bare as in the day it was first born; that fulness of bread having made the children of the houshold wanton, it is without any scruple to be taken away from them, and thrown to Dogs; that they which laid the prices of their Lands as offerings at the Apostles feet, did but sow the seeds of superstition; that they which indowed Churches with Lands, poysoned Religion; that Tithes and Oblations are now in the sight of God as the sacrificed bloud of Goats; that if we give him our hearts and affections, our goods are better bestowed otherwise; that *Irenæus Polycarp*'s Disciple should not have said, *We offer unto God our goods as tokens of thankfulness for that we receive*; neither *Origen*, *He which worshippeth God, must by Gifts and Oblations acknowledge him the Lord of all*; in a word, that to give unto God is errour; reformation of errour, to take from the Church that which the blindness of former Ages did unwisely give: By these or the like suggestions, received with all joy, and with like sedulity practised in certain parts of the Christian world, they have brought to pass, that as *David* doth say of man, so it is in hazard to be verified concerning the whole Religion and Service of God: *The time thereof may per ad.*

Marginal notes:

a Novimus multa regna, & reges eorum propterea cecidisse, quia Ecclesias spoliaverunt, resq;earum vastaverunt,alienaverunt vel diripuerunt, Episcopis q;& Sacerdotibus, atq; quod majus est, Ecclesiis eorum abstulerunt, & pugnantibus dederunt. Quasi in proelio stabiles fuerunt, nec victores extiterunt, sed terga mulți vulnerati & plures interfecti verterunt, regnaq; & regiones, & quod pejus est, regna coelestia perdiderunt, atq; propriis hæreditatibus caruerunt & hactenus carent. *Verba Caroli.Ma.in Capitu. Caru. l. 7. c. 104.*

b Turno tempus erit magno cum optaverit emptum Intactum Pallanta, & cum spolia ista diemq;ode rit. *Virg. Æn. lib. 10.*

c ... τῶν πραγμάτων αισχύνη έσομένη ελάττων ζημία τοῖς γε ούφρονοῦσι. Demost. Pœnam non dico legum quas sæpe pertumpunt, sed ipsius turpitudinis quæ scerbissima est non vident. *Cic. Offic.lib.3.* Impunita tu credes else quæ invisa sunt? aut ullum supplicii gravius existimas publico odio? *Sen. de Benef. lib.3. c17.* Orig.in 18. *Num.hom.11.*

Pſal. 90. 10.

per adventure fall out to be threescore and ten years, or if strength do serve, unto four-score, what followeth, is likely to be small-joy for them whosoever they be that behold it. Thus have the best things been overthrown, not so much by puissance and might of Adversaries; as through defect of counsel; in them that should have upheld and defended the same.

Of Ordinations lawful without title, and without any popular election precedent, but in no case without regard of due information what their quality is, that enter into holy Orders.

80. There are in a Minister of God these four things to be considered, his Or-dination which giveth him power to meddle with things sacred, the charge or por-tion of the Church allotted unto him for exercise of his Office; the performance of his duty, according to the exigence of his charge; and lastly, the maintenance which in that respect he receiveth. All Ecclesiastical Laws and Canons which ei-ther concern the bestowing or the using of the power of Ministerial Order, have re-lation to these four. Of the first we have spoken before at large. Concerning the next, for more convenient discharge of Ecclesiastical duties, as the body of the peo-ple must needs be severed by divers precincts, so the Clergy likewise accordingly distributed. Whereas therefore Religion did first take place in Cities, and in that respect was a cause why the name of Pagans, which properly signifieth Country people, came to be used in common speech for the same that Infidels and Unbelie-vers were; it followed thereupon that all such Cities had their Ecclesiastical Col-ledges, consisting of Deacons and of Presbyters, whom first the Apostles or their Delegates the Evangelists, did both ordain and govern. Such were the Colledges of *Jeruſalem, Antioch, Epheſus, Rome, Corinth,* and the rest, where the Apostles are known to have planted our Faith and Religion. Now because Religion and the cure of souls was their general charge in common over all that were neer about them, neither had any one Presbyter his several Cure apart, till *Evariſtus* Bishop in the See of *Rome,* about the year 112 began to assign precincts unto every Church, or Title, which the Christians held, and to appoint unto each Presbyter a certain compass, whereof himself should take charge alone; the commodiousness of this invention caused all parts of Christendom to follow it, and at the length a-mongst the rest our own Churches, about the year 636. became divided in like manner. But other distinction of Churches there doth not appear any in the Apostles Writings, save only, according to those [a] Cities wherein they planted the Gospel of Christ, and erected Ecclesiastical Colledges. Wherefore to ordain [b] κατὰ πόλιν throughout every City, and [c] κατὰ ἐκκλησίαν throughout every Church, do in them signifie the same thing. Churches then neither were, nor could be in so con-venient sort limited as now they are; first, by the bounds of each state, and then within each state by more particular precincts, till at the length we descend unto several Congregations termed *Pariſhes,* with far narrower restraint, than this name at the first was used. And from hence hath grown their errour, who as oft as they read of the duty which Ecclesiastical persons are now to perform towards the Church, their manner is always to understand by that Church, some particular Congregation, or Parish Church. They suppose that there should now be no man of Ecclesiastical Order, which is not tyed to some certain Parish. Because the names of all Church-Officers are words of relation, because a Shepherd must have his Flock, a Teacher his Scholars, a Minister his company which he ministreth unto, therefore it seemeth a thing in their eyes absurd and unreasonable, that any man should be ordained a Minister, otherwise, than only for some particular Congrega-tion. Perceive they not, how by this meane they make it unlawful for the Church to imploy men at all, in converting Nations? For if so be the Church may not lawfully admit to an Ecclesiastical Function, unless it tie the party admitted unto some particular Parish, then surely, a thankless labour it is, whereby men seek the Conversion of Infidels, which know not Christ, and therefore cannot be as yet divided into their special Congregations and Flocks: But to the end it may appear how much this one thing amongst many more hath been mistaken, there is first no Precept, requiring that Presbyters and Deacons be made in such sort, and not other-wise. Albeit therefore the Apostles did make them in that order, yet is not their Example such a Law, as without all exception bindeth to make them in no other order but that. Again, if we will consider that which the Apostles themselves did, surely, no man can justly say that herein we practise any thing repugnant to their

example,

a *Acts* 8.15:36
Apoc. 1.20.
b *Tit.* 1.5.
c *Acts* 14.23.

example. For by them there was ordained only in each Christian City a Colledge of Presbyters and Deacons to administer holy things. *Evaristus* did a hundred years after the birth of our Saviour Christ begin the distinction of the Church into Parishes. Presbyters and Deacons having been ordained before to exercise Ecclesiastical Functions in the Church of *Rome* promiscuously, he was the first that tied them each one to his own station. So that of the two, indefinite Ordination of Presbyters and Deacons doth come more neer the Apostles Example, and the tying of them to be made only for particular Congregations, may more justly ground it self upon the Example of *Evaristus* than of any Apostle of Christ. It hath been the opinion of wise and good men heretofore, that nothing was ever devised more singularly beneficial unto Gods Church, than this which our honourable Predecessors have to their endless praise found out by erecting such Houses of Study, as those two most famous Universities do contain, and by providing that choice Wits, after reasonable time spent in contemplation, may at the length either enter into that holy Vocation, for which they have been so long nourished and brought up, or else give place and suffer others to succeed in their rooms, that so the Church may be always furnished with a number of men, whose ability being first known by publick tryal in Church-labours there where men can best judge of them, their calling afterwards unto particular charge abroad may be according. All this is frustrate, those worthy Foundations we must dissolve, their whole device and religious purpose which did erect them is made void, their Orders and Statutes are to be cancelled and disanulled, in case the Church be forbidden to grant any power of Order, unless it be with restraint to the party ordained unto some particular Parish or Congregation. Nay, might we not rather affirm of Presbyters and of Deacons, that the very nature of their Ordination is unto necessary local restraint a thing opposite and repugnant? The Emperour *Justinian* doth say of Tutors, *Certæ rei vel causæ tutor dari non potest, quia personæ non causæ vel rei tutor datur.* He that should grant a Tutorship, restraining his grant to some one certain thing or cause, should do but idlely, because Tutors are given for personal defence generally, and not for managing of a few particular things or causes. So he that ordaining a Presbyter or a Deacon, should in the form of Ordination restrain the one or the other to a certain place, might with much more reason be thought to use a vain and frivolous addition, than they reasonably to require such local restraint, as a thing which must of necessity concur evermore with all lawful Ordinations. Presbyters and Deacons are not by Ordination consecrated unto places, but unto Functions. In which respect, and in no other it is, that sith they are by vertue thereof bequeathed unto God, severed and sanctified to be imployed in his Service, which is the highest advancement that mortal creatures on Earth can be raised unto, the Church of Christ hath not been acquainted in former Ages with any such prophane and unnatural custom, as doth hallow men with Ecclesiastical Functions of Order only for a time, and then dismiss them again to the common Affairs of the World. Whereas, contrariwise, from the place or charge where that power hath been exercised, we may be by sundry good and lawful occasions translated, retaining nevertheless the self-same power which was first given. It is some grief to spend thus much labour in refuting a thing that hath so little ground to uphold it, especially sith they themselves that teach it do not seem to give thereunto any great credit, if we may judge their minds by their actions. There are amongst them that have done the work of Ecclesiastical persons, sometime in the Families of Noble men, sometime in much more publick and frequent Congregations; there are that have successively gone through perhaps seven or eight particular Churches after this sort; yea, some that at one and the same time have been, some which at this present hour are, in real obligation of Ecclesiastical duty, and possession of commodity thereto belonging, even in sundry particular Churches within the Land; some there are amongst them which will not so much abridge their liberty, as to be fastened or tied unto any place; some which have bound themselves to one place, only for a time, and that time being once expired, have afterwards voluntarily given other places the like experience and tryal of them. All this I presume they would not do, if their perswasion were as strict as their words pretend. But for the avoiding of these and such other the like confusi-

Just.lib.1.tit. 14. sect. 4.

ons as are incident into the cause and question whereof we presently treat, there is not any thing more material, then first to separate exactly the nature of the Ministery from the use and exercise thereof ; Secondly, to know that the only true and proper Act of Ordination is, to invest men with that power which doth make them Ministers by consecrating their persons to God, and his Service in holy things during term of life, whether they exercise that power or no ; Thirdly, that to give them a title or charge where to use their Ministery, concerneth not the making, but the placing of Gods Ministers ; and therefore the Laws which concern only their Election or Admission unto that place of charge, are not appliable to infringe any way their Ordination ; Fourthly, that as oft as any ancient Constitution, Law or Canon is alledged, concerning either Ordinations or Elections, we forget not to examine whether the present case be the same which the ancient was, or else do contain some just reason for which it cannot admit altogether the same Rules which former Affairs of the Church, now altered, did then require. In the question of making Ministers without a *Title*, which to do they say is a thing unlawful, they should at the very first have considered what the name of *Title* doth imply, and what affinity or coherence Ordinations have with Titles, which thing observed would plainly have shewed them their own errour. They are not ignorant that when they speak of a Title, they handle that which belongeth to the placing of a Minister in some charge, that the place of charge wherein a Minister doth execute his Office, requireth some House of God for the people to resort unto, some definite number of Souls unto whom he there ad ministreth holy things, and some certain allowance whereby to sustain life ; that the Fathers at the first named *Oratories*, and Houses of Prayer, Titles, thereby signifying how God was interessed in them, and held them as his own Possessions. But because they know that the Church had Ministers before Christian Temples and Oratories were, therefore some of them understand by a Title, a *definite Congregation* of people only, and so deny that any Ordination is lawful which maketh Ministers, that have no certain Flock to attend, forgetting how the Seventy whom Christ himself did ordain Ministers, had their calling in that manner, whereas yet no certain charge could be given them. Others referring the name of a Title, especially to the *maintenance* of the Minister, infringe

*Unlawful to ordain a Minister without a Title. Abstr. p.243.& p.246. The Law requireth that every one admitted unto Orders having for his present Relief some Ecclesiastical Benefice, should also have some other title unto some annual rent or pension whereby he might be relieved in case he were not able through infirmity, sickness, or other lawful impediment to execute his Ecclesiastical Office and Function.

all Ordinations made, [a] except they which receive Orders be first intituled to a competent Ecclesiastical Benefice, and (which is most ridiculously strange) except besides their present Title to some such Benefice, they have likewise some other Title of Annual Rent or Pension whereby they may be relieved, in case through infirmity, sickness, or other lawful impediment they grow unable to execute their Ecclesiastical Function. So that every man lawfully ordained must bring a bow which hath two strings, a Title of present Right, and another to provide for future possibility or chance. Into these absurdities and follies they slide by mis-conceiving the true purpose of certain Canons, which indeed have forbidden to ordain a Minister without a Title, not that simply it is unlawful so to ordain, but because it might grow to an inconvenience, if the Church did not somewhat restrain that liberty. For seeing they which have once received Ordination, cannot again return into the World, it behoveth them that ordain, to fore-see how such shall be afterwards able to live, lest their poverty and destitution should redound to the disgrace and discredit of their calling. Which evil prevented, those very Laws which in that respect forbid, do expresly admit Ordinations to be made at large, and without Title ; namely, if the party so ordained have of his own for the sustenance of this life, or if the Bishop which giveth him Orders will find him competent allowance, till some place of Ministration, from whence his maintenance may arise, be provided for him, or if any other fit and sufficient means be had against the danger before mentioned. Absolutely therefore it is not true, that any ancient Canon of the Church which is, or ought to be with us in force, doth make Ordinations at large unlawful, and as the state of the Church doth stand, they are most necessary. If there be any conscience in men touching that which they write or speak, let them consider as well what the present condition of all things doth now suffer, as what the Ordinances of former Ages did appoint, as well the weight of those causes, for which our Affairs have altered, as the reasons in regard whereof our Fathers and

Predecessors

Predecessors did sometime strictly and severely keep that, which for us to observe now, is neither meet nor always possible. In this our present Cause and Controversie, whether any not having Title or Right to a Benefice may be lawfully ordained a Minister, is it not manifest in the eyes of all men, that whereas the name of a Benefice doth signifie some standing Ecclesiastical Revenue, taken out of the Treasure of God, and allotted to a spiritual Person, to the end he may use the same, and enjoy it as his own for term of life, unless his default cause Deprivation? The Clergy for many years after Christ had no other Benefices, but only their Canonical Portions, or monethly Dividends allowed them according to their several degrees and qualities, out of the common Stock of such Gifts, Oblations and Tithes, as the fervour of Christian Piety did then yield. Yea, that even when Ministers had their Churches and Flocks assigned unto them in several, yet for maintenance of life, their former kind of allowance continued, till such time as Bishops and Churches Cathedral being sufficiently endowed with Lands, other Presbyters enjoyed in stead of their first Benefices, the Tithes and Profits of their own Congregations whole to themselves? Is it not manifest that in this Realm, and so in other the like Dominions, where the tenure of Lands is altogether grounded on Military Laws, and held as in Fee under Princes which are not made Heads of the people by force of voluntary Election, but born the Soveraign Lords of those whole and intire Territories, which Territories their famous Progenitors obtaining by way of Conquest, retained what they would in their own hands, and divided the rest to others with reservation of Soveraignty and Capital Interest; the building of Churches, and consequently the assigning of either Parishes or Benefices was a thing impossible without consent of such as were principal Owners of Land; in which consideration, for their more encouragement hereunto, they which did so far benefit the Church, had by common consent granted (as great equity and reason was) a right for them and their Heirs till the Worlds end, to nominate in those Benefices men whose quality the Bishop allowing might admit them thereunto? Is it not manifest, that from hence inevitably such inequality of Parishes hath grown, as causeth some through the multitude of people which have resort unto one Church, to be more than any one man can weild, and some to be of that nature by reason of Chappels annex'd, that they which are Incumbents should wrong the Church, if so be they had not certain Stipendaries under them, because where the Corps of the profit or Benefice is but one; the Title can be but one mans, and yet the charge may require more? Not to mention therefore any other reason whereby it may clearly appear how expedient it is, and profitable for this Church to admit Ordinations without Title, this little may suffice to declare, how impertinent their allegations against it are out of ancient Canons, how untrue their confident asseverations, that only through negligence of Popish Prelates the custom of making such kind of Ministers hath prevailed in the Church of *Rome* against their Canons, and that with us it is expresly against the Laws of our own Government, when a Minister doth serve as a Stipendary Curate, which kind of service nevertheless the greatest Rabbins of that part do altogether follow. For howsoever they are such peradventure to be named Curates, Stipendaries they are, and the labour they bestow is in other mens cures, a thing not unlawful for them to do, yet unseemly for them to condemn which practise it. I might here discover the like over-sight throughout all their Discourses, made in behalf of the peoples pretended right to elect their Ministers before the Bishop may lawfully ordain. But because we have other where at large disputed of popular Elections, and of the Right of Patronage, wherein is drowned whatsoever the people under any pretence of colour may seem to challenge about admission and choice of the Pastors that shall feed their Souls, I cannot see what one duty there is which always ought to go before Ordination, but only care of the parties worthiness, as well for integrity and vertue, as knowledge, yea, for vertue more, in as much as defect of knowledge may sundry ways be supplyed, but the scandal of vicious and wicked life is a deadly evil.

81 The truth is, that of all things hitherto mentioned, the greatest is that three- Of the learning that should be in Ministers, their residence, and the number of their Livings: fold

fold blot or blemish of notable ignorance, unconscionable absence from the Cures whereof men have taken charge, and unsatiable hunting after spiritual preferments without either care or conscience of the publick good. Whereof, to the end that we may consider as in Gods own sight and presence with all uprightness, sincerity and truth, let us particularly waigh and examine in every of them ; First, how far forth they are reproveable by Reasons and Maximes of common right ; Secondly, whether that which our Laws do permit, be repugnant to those Maximes, and with what equity we ought to judge of things practised in this case, neither on the one hand defending that which must be acknowledged out of square, nor on the other side condemning rashly whom we list, for whatsoever we disallow. Touching Arguments therefore, taken from the principles of common right, to prove that Ministers should

a T. C.l.1.p.70.
b 66.
c 69.
1 Tim. 3. 2.
Tit. 1. 9.
2 Tim. 2. 15.
Hof. 4. 6.
Mat. 15. 14.
Luke 1. 8.
Acts 20. 2.
1 Sam. 1. 19.
1 Tim. 4. 12.
Iohn 10. 4.
1 Pet. 5. 2.
Acts 20. 28.
1 Thes. 1. 17.
Concil. Nic. c.
15.
Mat. 6. 14.
1 Cor. 7. 24.

be [a] learned, that they ought to be [b] Resident upon their Livings, and that [c] more then one only Benefice or Spiritual Living may not be granted unto one man; the first, because St. *Paul* requireth in a Minister ability to teach, to convince, to distribute the Word rightly, because also the Lord himself hath protested, they shall be no Priests to him which have rejected knowledge, and because if the Blind lead the Blind, they must both needs fall into the Pit ; the second, because Teachers are Shepherds, whose Flocks can be at no time secure from danger ; they are Watchmen whom the Enemy doth always besiege, their labours in the Word and Sacraments admit no intermission ; their duty requireth instruction and conference with men in private ; they are the living Oracles of God, to whom the people must resort for counsel ; they are commanded to be Patterns of Holiness, Leaders, Feeders, Supervisors amongst their own ; it should be their grief, as it was the Apostles, to be absent, though necessarily, from them over whom they have taken charge ; finally, the last, because Plurality and Residence are opposite, because the placing of one Clark in two Churches is a point of Merchandize and filthy gain, because no man can serve two Masters, because every one should remain in that Vocation whereto he is called ; what conclude they of all this ? Against Ignorance, against Non-residence, and against Plurality of Livings, is there any man so raw and dull, but that the Volumes which have been written, both of old and of late, may make him in so plentiful a cause eloquent ? For if by that which is *generally* just and requisite, we measure what knowledge there should be in a Minister of the Gospel of Christ ; the Arguments which Light of Nature offereth ; the Laws and Statutes which Scripture hath ; the Canons that are taken out of ancient Synods ; the Decrees, and Constitutions of sincerest Times ; the Sentences of all Antiquity ; and in a word, even every mans full consent and conscience is against Ignorance in them that have charge and cure of Souls. Again, what availeth it if we be Learned and not Faithful ? or what benefit hath the Church of Christ, if there be in us sufficiency without endeavour, or care to do that good which our place exacteth ? Touching the pains and industry therefore, wherewith men are in conscience bound to attend the work of their Heavenly Calling, even as much as in them lieth, bending thereunto their whole endeavour, without either fraud, sophistication or guil ; I see not what more effectual Obligation or Bond of Duty there should be urged, then their own only Vow and Promise made unto God himself, at the time of their Ordination. The work which they have undertaken requireth both care and fear. Their sloth that negligently perform it maketh them subject to malediction. Besides, we also know that the fruit of our pains in this Function is life both to our selves and others. And do we yet need incitements to labour ? Shall we stop our ears both against those conjuring exhortations which Apostles, and against the fearful comminations which Prophets have uttered out of the mouth of God ; the one for prevention, the other for reformation of our sluggishness in this behalf ?

Acts 20. 17. St. *Paul*, *Attend to your selves, and to all the flock, whereof the holy Ghost hath made you over seers, to feed the Church of God, which he hath purchased with his own blood. Again, I charge thee before God and the Lord Jesus Christ, which shall judge the quick and the dead at his coming, preach the Word; be instant.* Jeremiah, *Wo unto* Jer. 23. 1. *the Pastors that destroy and scatter the sheep of my pasture ; I will visit you for the wickedness of your works, saith the Lord ; the remnant of my sheep I will gather together out of all Countries, and will bring them again to their folds, they shall grow*

and

and increase, and I will set up shepherds over them which shall feed them. Ezechiel, Ezek. 34. 2. *Should not the shepherds, should they not feed the flocks ? Ye eat the fat, and ye clothe your selves with the wool; but the weak ye have not strengthened, the sick ye have not cured, neither have ye bound up the broken, nor brought home again that which was driven away; ye have not inquired after that which was lost, but with cruelty and rigor ye have ruled.* And verse 8. *Wherefore, as I live,* &c. Nor let us think to excuse our selves, if happily we labour, though it be at randome, and sit not altogether idle abroad. For we are bound to attend that part of the flock of Christ, whereof the Holy Ghost hath made us over-seers. The residence of Ministers upon their own peculiar charge, is by so much the rather necessary ; for that absenting themselves from the place where they ought to labour, they neither can do the good which is looked for at their hands, nor reap the comfort which sweetneth life to them that spend it in these travels upon their own. For it is in this, as in all things else, which are through private interest dearer, than what concerneth either others wholly, or us but in part, and according to the rate of a general regard. As for plurality, it hath not only the same inconveniencies which are observed to grow by absence ; but over and besides, at the least in common construction, a shew of that worldly humour which men do think should not raign so high. Now from hence their Collections are as followeth ; first, a repugnancy or contradiction between the Principles of common right, and that which our Laws in special considerations have allowed : secondly, a nullity or frustration of all such acts, as are by them supposed opposite to those Principles, an invalidity in all ordinations of men unable to preach, and in all dispensations which mitigate the Law of common right for the other two. And why so ? Forsooth, because whatsoever we do in these three cases, Abstract.p. 117. and not by vertue of common right, we must yield it of necessity done by warrant of peculiar right or priviledge. Now a priviledge is said to be that, that for favour of certain persons cometh forth *against* common right ; things *prohibited* are dispensed with, because things *permitted* are dispatched by common right, but things *forbidden* require dispensations. By which descriptions of a priviledge and dispensation it is (they say) apparent, that a priviledge must licence and authorize the same, which the Law against ignorance, non-residence and plurality doth infringe ; and so be a Law contrariant or repugnant to the Law of Nature, and the Law of God, because all the reasons whereupon the Positive Law of man against these three was first established, are taken and drawn from the Law of Nature and the Law of God. For answer whereunto we will but lead them to answer themselves. First therefore if they will grant (as they must) that all direct oppositions of speech require one and the self-same subject, to be meant on both parts where opposition is pretended, it will follow that either the maximes of common right do inforce *the very same things* not to be good which we say are good, grounding our selves on the reasons, by vertue whereof our priviledges are established ; or if the one do not reach unto that *particular subject* for which the other have provided, then is there no contradiction between them. In all contradictions, if the one part be true, the other eternally must be false. And therefore if the Principles of common right, do at any time truly inforce *that particular* not to be good, which priviledges make good, it argueth invincibly, that such priviledges have been grounded upon errour. But, to say, that every priviledge is opposite unto the principles of common right, because it dispenseth with that which common right doth prohibit, hath gross absurdity. For the voice of Equity and Justice is, that a general Law doth never derogate from a special Priviledge ; whereas if the one were contrariant to the other, a general Law being in force should always dissolve a Priviledge. The reason why many are deceived by imagining that so it should do, and why men of better insight conclude directly it should not, doth rest in the *subject or matter* it self, which matter *indefinitely* considered in Laws of common right, is in Priviledges considered as *beset and limited with special circumstances,* by means whereof to them which respect it, but by way of generality,it seemeth one and the same in both, although it be not the same, if once we descend to particular consideration thereof. Precepts do always propose perfection, not such as none can attain unto, for then in vain should we ask or require it at the hands of men, but such perfection as all men must aim at ; to the end that as largely as humane providence and care can extend it, it

R r may

may take place. Moral Laws are the rules of Politick, those Politick, which are made to order the whole Church of God, Rules unto all particular Churches, and the Laws of every particular Church, Rules unto every particular man, within the body of the same Church; Now because the higher we ascend in these rules, the further still we remove from those specialties, which being proper to the subject, whereupon our actions must work are therefore chiefly considered by us, by them least thought upon that wade altogether in the two first kinds of general directions, their judgment cannot be exact and sound, concerning either Laws of Churches, or Actions of men in particular, because they determine of effects by a part of the causes on y out of which they grow, they judge conclusions by demi-premises and half principles, they lay them in the balance stript from those necessary material circumstances which should give them weight, and by shew of falling uneven with the scale of most universal and abstracted rules, they pronounce that too light which is not, if they had the skill to weigh it. This is the reason why men altogether conversant in study do know how to teach, but not how to govern; men experienced contrariwise govern well, yet know not which way to set down orderly the Precepts and Reasons of that they do. He that will therefore judge rightly of things done, must join with his forms and conceits of general speculation, the matter wherein our actions are conversant. For by this shall appear what equity there is in those Priviledges and peculiar grants or Favours, which otherwise will seem repugnant to justice, and because in themselves considered they have [a] a shew of repugnancy, this deceiveth those great Clerks, which hearing a priviledge defined to be *an especial right brought in by their power and authority, that make it for some publick benefit against the general course of reason*, are not able to comprehend how the word *against* doth import *exception*, without any *opposition* at all. For inasmuch as the hand of justice must distribute to every particular what is due, and judge what is due with respect had, no less of particular circumstances then of general rules and axiomes, it cannot fit all sorts with one measure, the wills, counsels, qualities and states of men being divers. For example, the Law of common right bindeth all men to keep their promises, perform their compacts, and answer the Faith they have given either for themselves, or in. Notwithstanding he which bargaineth with one under years, can have no benefit by this allegation, because he bringeth it against a person which is exempt from the common rule. Shall we then conclude, that thus to exempt certain men from the Law of common right, is against God, against Nature, against whatsoever may avail to strengthen and justifie that Law before alledged, or else acknowledge (as the truth is) that special causes are to be ordered by special rules, that if men grown unto ripe age, disadvantage themselves by bargaining, yet what they have wittingly done, is strong, and in force against them, because they are able to dispose and manage their own affairs, whereas youth for lack of experience and judgment, being easily subject to circumvention, is therefore justly exempt from the Law of common right, whereunto the rest are justly subject? This plain inequality between men of years, and under years, is a cause why Equity and Justice cannot apply equally the same general Rule to both, but ordereth the one by common right, and granteth to the other a special [b] priviledge. Priviledges are either transitory or permanent. [b] Transitory, such as serve only some one turn, or at the most extend no farther than to this or that man, with the end of whose natural life they expire; Permanent, such as the use whereof doth continue still, for that they belong unto certain *kinds* of men and causes which never die. Of this nature are all immunities and preeminences, which for just considerations one sort of men injoyeth above another, both in the Church and Commonwealth, no man suspecting them of contrariety to any branch of those Laws or Reasons, whereupon the general right is grounded. Now there being general Laws and Rules whereby it cannot be denied, but the Church of God standeth bound to provide that the Ministry may be learned, that they which have charge may reside upon it, and that it may not be free for them in scandalous manner to multiply Ecclesiastical livings; it remaineth in the next place to be examined, what the Laws of the Church of *England* do admit, which may be thought repugnant to any thing hitherto alledged, and in what special consideration they seem to admit the same. Considering

ing therefore, that to furnish all places of Cure in this Realm, it is not an Army of twelve thousand learned men that would suffice, nor two Universities that can always furnish as many as decay in so great a number, nor a fourth part of the livings with Cure, that when they fall are able to yield sufficient maintenance for learned men, is it not plain, that unless the greatest part of the people should be left utterly without the publick use and exercise of Religion, there is no remedy but to take into the Ecclesiastical order, a number of men meanly qualified in respect of learning? For whatsoever we may imagine in our private Closets, or talk for Communication sake at our Boords, yea, or write in our Books, through a notional conceit of things needful, for performance of each mans duty, if once we come from the Theory of learning, to take out so many learned men, let them be diligently viewed, out of whom the choice shall be made, and thereby an estimate made, what degree of skill we must either admit, or else leave numbers utterly destitute of guides; and I doubt not but that men indued with sense of common equity, will soon discern, that besides eminent and competent knowledge, we are to descend to a lower step, receiving knowledge in that degree which is but tolerable. When we commend any man for learning, our speech importeth him to be more than meanly qualified that way; but when Laws do require learning as a quality, which maketh capable of any function, our measure to judge a learned man by, must be some certain degree of learning, beneath which we can hold no man so qualified. And if every man that listeth may set that degree himself, how shall we ever know when Laws are broken, when kept, seeing one man may think a lower degree sufficient, another may judge them unsufficient that are not qualified in some higher degree. Wherfore of necessity either we must have some Judge, in whose conscience they that are thought and pronounced sufficient, are to be so accepted and taken, or else the Law it self is to set down the very lowest degree of fitness that shall be allowed in this kind. So that the question doth grow to this issue. Saint *Paul* requireth learning in Presbyters, yea such learning as doth inable them to exhort in doctrine which is sound, and to disprove them that gain-say it. What measure of ability in such things shall serve to make men capable of that kind of Office, he doth not himself precisely determine, but referreth it to the conscience of *Titus*, and others, which had to deal in ordaining Presbyters. We must therefore of necessity make this demand, whether the Church lacking such as the Apostle would have chosen, may with good conscience take out of such as it hath in a meaner degree of fitness, them that may serve to perform the service of publick Prayer, to minister the Sacraments unto the People, to solemnize Marriage, to visit the Sick, and bury the Dead, to instruct by reading, although by preaching he be not as yet so able to benefit and feed Christs flock. We constantly hold, that in this case the Apostles Law is not broken. He requireth more in Presbyters than there is found in many whom the Church of *England* alloweth. But no man being tyed unto impossibilities, to do that we cannot, we are not bound. It is but a stratagem of theirs therefore, and a very indirect practice, when they publish large declamations to prove that learning is required in the Ministry, and to make the silly people believe that the contrary is maintained by the Bishops, and upheld by the Laws of the Land; whereas the question in truth is not whether learning be required, but whether a Church wherein there is not sufficient store of learned men to furnish all Congregations, should do better to let thousands of souls grow savage, to let them live without any publick service of God, to let their children dye unbaptized, to with-hold the benefit of the other Sacrament from them, to let them depart this world like Pagans, without any thing as much as read unto them concerning the way of life, then as it doth in this necessity, to make such Presbyters as are so far forth sufficient, although they want that ability of preaching which some others have. In this point therefore we obey necessity, and of two evils we take the less; in the rest a publick utility is sought, and in regard thereof some certain inconveniencies tolerated, because they are recompenced with greater good. The Law giveth liberty of non-Residence for a time to such as will live in Universities, if they faithfully there labour to grow in knowledge, that so they may afterwards the more edifie and the better instruct their Congregations. The Church in their absence is not destitute, the

Tit. 1. 9.

peoples

peoples salvation not neglected for the present time, the time of their absence is in the intendment of Law bestowed to the Churches great advantage and benefit, those necessary helps are procured by it, which turn by many degrees more to the peoples comfort in time to come, than if their Pastors had continually a sidden with them. So that the Law doth hereby provide in some part to remedy and help that evil which the former necessity hath imposed upon the Church. For compare two men of equal meaneness, the one perpetually resident, the other absent for a space, in such sort as the Law permitteth. Allot unto both some nine years continuance with Cure of souls. And must not three years absence in all probability and likelihood make the one more profitable than the other unto Gods Church, by so much as the increase of his knowledge, gotten in those three years, may adde unto six years travel following ? For the greater ability there is added to the instrument, wherewith it pleaseth God to save Souls, the more facility and expedition it hath to work that which is otherwise hardlier effected. As much may be said touching absence granted to them that attend in the families of Bishops, which Schools of gravity, discretion and wisdom, preparing men against the time that they come to reside abroad, are in my poor opinion even the fittest places that any ingenious mind can wish to enter into, between departure from private study and access to a more publick charge of Souls ; yea no less expedient, for men of the best sufficiency and most maturity in knowledge, than the very Universities themselves are for the ripening of such as be raw. Imployment in the families of Noble men, or in Princes Courts, hath another end, for which the self-same leave is given, not without greater respect to the good of the whole Church. For assuredly whosoever doth well observe, how much all inferiour things depend upon the orderly courses and motions of those greater Orbes, will hardly judge it either meet or good, that the Angels assisting them should be driven to betake themselves unto other Stations, although by nature they were not tyed where now they are, but had charge also elsewhere, as long as their absence from beneath might but tolerably be supplyed, and by descending their rooms above should become vacant. For we are not to dream in this case of any platform, which bringeth equally high and low unto Parish Churches, nor of any constraint to maintain at their own charge men sufficient for that purpose ; the one so repugnant to the Majesty and Greatness of English Nobility, the other so improbable and unlikely to take effect, that they which mention either of both, seem not indeed to have conceived what either is. But the eye of Law is the eye of God, it looketh into the hearts and secret dispositions of men, it beholdeth how far one star differeth from another in glory, and as mens several degrees require, accordingly it guideth them, granting unto principal Personages priviledges correspondent to their high estates, and that not only in Civil, but even in Spiritual affairs, to the end they may love that Religion the more, which no way seeketh to make them vulgar, no way diminisheth their dignity and greatness, but to do them good doth them honour also, and by such extraordinary favours teacheth them to be in the Church of God the same which the Church of God esteemeth them, more worth than thousands. It appeareth therefore in what respect the Laws of this Realm have given liberty of non-residence to some, that their knowledge may be increased, and their labours by that mean be made afterwards the more profitable to others, lest the houses of great men should want that daily exercise of Religion, wherein their example availeth as much, yea many times peradventure more than the Laws themselves, with the common sort. A third thing respected both in permitting absence, and also in granting to some that liberty of addition or plurality, which necessarily inforceth their absence, is a meer both just and conscionable regard, that as men are in quality, and as their services are in weight for the publick good, so likewise their rewards and encouragements by special priviledge of Law might somewhat declare how the State it self doth accept their pains, much abhorring from their bestial and savage rudeness, which think that Oxen should only labour, and Asses feed. Thus to Readers in Universities, whose very paper and book expences their ancient allowances and stipends at this day do either not or hardly sustain ; to Governors of Colledges, lest the great overplus of charges necessarily inforced upon them, by reason of their place,

and

and very slenderly supplied, by means of that change in the present condition of things, which their Founders could not fore-see; to men called away from their Cures, and implyed in weightier business, either of the Church or Common-wealth, because to impose upon them a burthen which requireth their absence, and not to release them from the duty of Residence, were a kind of cruel and barbarous injustice; to Residents in Cathedral Churches, or upon dignities Ecclesiastical, forasmuch as these being rooms of greater Hospitality, places of more respect and consequence then the rest, they are the rather to be furnished with men of best quality, and the men for their qualities sake to be favoured above others; I say unto all these in regard of their worth and merit, the Law hath therefore given leave while themselves bear weightier burthens, to supply inferiour by deputation; and in like consideration partly, partly also by way of honour to learning, Nobility and Authority permitteth, that men which have taken Theological degrees in Schools, the Suffraganes of Bishops, the houshold Chaplains of men of honour, or in great Office, the brethren and sons of Lords temporal, or of Knights, if God shall move the hearts of such to enter at any time into holy Orders, may obtain to themselves a faculty or licence to hold two Ecclesiastical Livings though having cure; any Spiritual Person of the Queens Councel three such Livings; her Chaplains, what number of promotions her self in her own Princely wisdom thinketh good to bestow upon them. But, as it fareth in such cases, the gap which for just considerations we open unto some, letteth in others through corupt practices, to whom such favours were neither meant, nor should be communicated. The greatness of the Harvest, and the scarcity of able Workmen hath made it necessary, that Law should yield to admit numbers of men but slenderly and meanly qualified. Hereupon because whom all other worldly hopes have forsaken, they commonly reserve Ministerial Vocation, as their last and surest refuge ever open to forlorn men; the Church that should nourish them, whose service she needeth, hath obtruded upon her, their service, that know not otherwise how to live and sustain themselves. These finding nothing more easie then means to procure the writing of a few lines to some one or other which hath authority; and nothing more usual than too much facility in condescending unto such requests, are often received into that Vocation whereunto their unworthiness is no small disgrace. Did any thing more aggravate the crime of *Jeroboams* prophane Apostasie, than that he chose to have his Clergy the scum and refuse of his who'e Land? Let no man spare to tell it them, they are not faithful towards God, that burthen wilfully his Church with such swarms of unworthy creatures. I will not say of all degrees in the Ministry, that which S. *Chrysostom* doth of the highest, *He that will undertake so weighty a charge,* Chrysost. de Sa- *had need to be a man of great understanding, rarely assisted with Divine grace,* for cerd.l.3.c.15. *integrity of manners, purity of life, and for all other vertues, to have in him more then a man;* but surely this I will say with *Chrysostom, We need not doubt whether God be highly displeased with us, or what the cause of his anger, is if things of so great fear and holiness as are the least and lowest duties of his service, be thrown wilfully on them whose not only mean, but bad and scandalous quality doth defile whatsoever they handle.* These eye-sores and blemishes, in continual attendants about the Service of Gods Sanctuary, do make them every day fewer that willingly resort unto it, till at length all affection and zeal towards God be extinct in them through a wearisom contempt of their persons; which for a time only live by Religion, and are for recompence, in fine, the death of the Nurse that feedeth them. It is not obscure, how incommodious the Church hath found both this abuse of the liberty, which Law is enforced to grant; and not only this, but the like abuse of that favour also, which Law in other considerations already mentioned, affordeth touching Residence and plurality of spiritual Livings. Now that which is practised corruptly to the detriment and hurt of ᵃ ὥτε γεωργὸν the Church, against the purpose of those very Laws, which notwithstanding are ἔτε βάναυσον pretended in defence and justification thereof, we must needs acknowledge no less ἱερέα καὶ ὡς a- repugnant to the grounds and principles of common right, than the fraudulent pro- τέον ἀπὸ γὸ ceedings of Tyrants to the principles of just Soveraignty. Howbeit not so those τῶν πολιτικῶν special priviledges which are but instruments wrested and forced to serve malice. πρέπει τιμᾶ- There is in the Petriark of Heathen Philosophers this precept, ᵃ *Let no husbandman* Arist.Po.7.c.6.

nor

nor no Handy-craftſman be a Prieſt. The reaſon whereupon he groundeth,is a maxime in the Law of Nature. It importeth greatly the good *of all men that God be reverenced,* with whoſe honour it ſtandeth not that they which are publickly imployed in his ſervice ſhould live of baſe and manuary Trades. Now compare herewith the Apoſtles words, ^b *Ye know theſe hands have miniſtred to my neceſſities, and them that are with me.* What think we ? Did the Apoſtle any thing oppoſite herein, or repugnant to the Rules and Maximes of the Law of Nature ? The ſelf-ſame reaſons that accord his actions with the Law of Nature. ſhall declare our Priviledges and his Laws no leſs conſonant. Thus therefore we ſee, that although they urge very colourably the Apoſtles own ſentences, requiring that a Miniſter ſhould be able to divide rightly the Word of God, that they who are placed in charge ſhould attend unto it themſelves,which in abſence they cannot do, and that they which have divers Cures muſt of neceſſity be abſent from ſome, whereby the Law Apoſtolick ſeemeth apparently broken, which Law requiring attendance cannot otherwiſe be underſtood, than ſo as to charge them with perpetual Reſidence : again,though in every of theſe cauſes,they infinitely heap up the Sentences of Fathers,the Decrees of Popes,the ancient Edicts of Imperial authority,our own National Laws & Ordinances prohibiting the ſame,and grounding evermore their prohibitions,partly on the Laws of God and partly on reaſons drawn from the light of Nature, yet hereby to gather and infer contradiction between thoſe Laws which forbid indefinitly, and ours which in certain caſes have allowed the ordaining of ſundry Miniſters, whoſe ſufficiency for learning is but mean; again,the licenſing of ſome to be abſent from their Flocks,and of others to hold more than one only Living which hath cure of ſouls, I ſay,to conclude repugnancy between theſe eſpecial permiſſions,and the former general prohibitions, which ſet not down their own limits, is erroneous, and the manifeſt cauſe thereof ignorance in differences of matter which both ſorts of Law concern. If then the conſiderations be reaſonable, juſt and good, whereupon we ground whatſoever our Laws have by ſpecial right permitted ; if only the effects of abuſed Priviledges be repugnant to the Maximes of common right, this main foundation of repugnancy being broken, whatſoever they have built thereupon falleth neceſſarily to the ground. Whereas therefore, upon ſurmiſe or vain ſuppoſal of oppoſition between our ſpecial , and the principles of common right , they gather that ſuch as are with us ordained Miniſters , before they can preach , be neither lawful, becauſe the Laws already mentioned forbid generally to create ſuch, neither are they indeed Miniſters, although we commonly ſo name them, but whatſoever they execute by vertue of ſuch their pretended vocation is void ; that all our grants and tolerations, as well of this as the reſt are fruſtrate and of no effect ; the perſons that enjoy them poſſeſs them wrongfully, and are deprivable at all hours ; finally, that other juſt and ſufficient remedy of evils there can be none beſides the utter abrogation of theſe our mitigations , and the ſtrict eſtabliſhment of former Ordinances, to be abſolutely executed whatſoever follow , albeit the anſwer already made in diſcovery of the weak and unſound foundation whereupon they built theſe erroneous collections may be thought ſufficient, yet becauſe our deſire is rather to ſatisfie, if it be poſſible, than to ſhake them off, we are with very good will contented to declare the cauſes of all particulars more formally and largely than the equity of our own defence doth require.

There is crept into the minds of men, at this day, a ſecret pernicious and peſtilent conceit, that the greateſt perfection of a Chriſtian man doth conſiſt in diſcovery of other mens faults , and in wit to diſcourſe of our own profeſſion. When the World moſt abounded with juſt, righteous and perfect men, their chiefeſt ſtudy was the exerciſe of piety , wherein for their ſafeſt direction , they reverently hearkened to the readings of the Law of God, they kept in mind the Oracles and Aphoriſms of wiſdom, which tended unto vertuous life ; if any ſcruple of conſcience did trouble them for matter of Actions which they took in hand, nothing was attempted before counſel and advice were had, for fear leſt raſhly they might offend. We are now more confident, not that our knowledge and judgment is riper, but becauſe our deſires are another way.

Their ſcope was obedience, ours is skill ; their endevour was reformation of life,

our

b *Acts* 20.34.
1 *Cor.*4.12.
1 *Theſ* 2.9.
2 *Theſ.*3.8.

our vertue nothing but to hear gladly the reproof of vice; they in the practice of their Religion wearied chiefly their knees and hands, we especially our ears and tongues. We are grown, as in many things else, so in this, to a kind of intemperancy, which (only Sermons excepted) hath almost brought all other duties of Religion out of taste. At the least they are not in that account and reputation which they should be. Now because men bring all Religion in a manner to the only office of hearing Sermons, if it chance that they who are thus conceited do imbrace any special opinion different from other men, the Sermons that relish not that opinion, can in no wise please their appetite. Such therefore as preach unto them, but hit not the string they look for, are rejected as unprofitable, the rest as unlawful, and indeed no Ministers, if the faculty of Sermons want. For why? A Minister of the Word should, they say, be able rightly to *divide* the Word. Which Apostolick Canon many think they do well observe, when in opening the sentences of holy Scripture, they draw all things favourably spoken unto one side, but whatsoever is reprehensive, severe, and sharp, they have others on the contrary part whom that must always concern, by which their over-partial and unindifferent proceeding while they thus labour amongst the people to divide the Word, they make the Word a meane to divide and distract the people. *Ορθοτομειν to divide aright*, doth note in the Apostles Writings, soundness of doctrine only, and in meaning standeth opposite to *καινοτομειν the broaching of new opinions against that which is received* For questionless the first things delivered to the Church of Christ, were pure and sincere Truth. Which whosoever did afterwards oppugne, could not chuse but divide the Church into two moities; in which division, such as taught what was first believed, held the truer part, the contrary side in that they were teachers of noyelty, erred. For prevention of which evil there are in this Church many singular and well devised remedies, as namely the use of subscribing to the Articles of Religion before admission to degrees of learning, or to any Ecclesiastical living, the custom of reading the same Articles and of approving them in publick Assemblies wheresoever men have Benefices with cure of Souls, the order of testifying under their hands allowance of the Book of Common-Prayer, and the Book of ordaining Ministers; finally, the Discipline and moderate severity which is used either in other wise correcting or silencing them that trouble and disturbe the Church with Doctrines which tend unto Innovation; it being better that the Church should want altogether the benefit of such mens labours, than endure the mischief of their inconformity to good Laws; in which case if any repine at the course and proceedings of Justice, they must learn to content themselves with the answer of *M. Curius*, which had sometime occasion to cut off one from the Body of the Common-wealth, in whose behalf because it might have been pleaded that the party was a man serviceable, he therefore began his judicial sentence with this preamble, *Non esse opus Reip. eo cive qui parere nesciret; The Common-wealth needeth men of quality, yet never those men which have not learned how to obey.* But the ways which the Church of *England* hath taken to provide that they who are Teachers of others may do it soundly, that the Purity and Unity as well of ancient Discipline as Doctrine may be upheld, that avoiding singularities, we may all glorifie God with one heart and one tongue, they of all men do least approve, that most urge the Apostles Rule and Canon. For which cause they alledge it not so much to that purpose, as to prove that unpreaching Ministers (for so they term them) can have no true nor lawful calling in the Church of God. Saint *Augustine* hath said of the will of man, that *simply to will proceedeth from Nature, but our well-willing is from Grace.* We say as much of the Minister of God *publickly to teach and instruct the Church; is necessary in every Ecclesiastical Minister, but ability to teach by Sermons is a Grace which God doth bestow on them whom he maketh sufficient for the commendable discharge of their duty.* That therefore wherein a Minister differeth from other Christian men, is not as some have childishly imagined, the *sound preaching of the Word of God*, but as they are lawfully and truly Governours to whom authority or regiment is given in the Common-wealth, according to the order which Politie hath set, so Canonical Ordination in the Church of Christ is that which maketh a lawful Minister, *as touching the validity of any Act which appertaineth to that vocation.* The

cause

a Αλλ᾽ οι πολλοι ταυτα μεν ου πραττουσιν, επι δε τον λογον καταφευγοντες οιονται φιλοσοφειν, και ουτως εσεσθαι σπουδαιοι ὁμοιον τι ποιουν-τες τοις καμ-νουσιν οι των ιατρων ακουουσι μεν επιμελως, ποιουσι δε ουδεν των προσταττο-μενων ωσπερ ουν ουδ᾽ εκεινοι ευ εξουσι το σωμα ουτω θε-ραπευομενοι, ουδ᾽ ουτοι την ψυχην ουτω φι-λοσοφουντες.

A. iii. E.h. ib. 2. cap. 5.

Valer. l. 6. e. 3.

Oxman. p. 21.

cause why Saint *Paul* willed *Timothy* not to be over-hasty in ordaining Ministers, was (as we very well may conjecture) because imposition of hands doth consecrate and make them Ministers, whether they have gifts and qualities fit for the laudable discharge of their duties or no. If want of learning and skill to preach did frustrate their Vocation, Ministers ordained before they be grown unto that maturity should receive new Ordination, whensoever it chanceth that study and industry doth make them afterwards more able to perform the office, than which what conceit can be more absurd? Was not S. *Augustine* himself contented to admit an Assistant in his own Church, a man of small Erudition, considering that what he wanted in knowledge was supplied by those vertues which made his life a better Orator, than more learning could make others whose conversation was less Holy ? Were the Priests, sithence *Moses*, all able and sufficient men, learnedly to interpret the Law of God ? Or was it ever imagined, that this defect should frustrate what they executed, and deprive them of right unto any thing they claimed by vertue of their Priesthood? Surely, as in Magistrates, the want of those gifts which their Office needeth, is cause of just imputation of blame in them that wittingly chuse unsufficient and unfit men when they might do otherwise, and yet therefore is not their choice void, nor every action of Magistracy frustrate in that respect. So whether it were of necessity, or even of very carelesness, that men unable to preach should be taken in Pastors rooms, neverthelesss, it seemeth to be an errour in them, which think that the lack of any such perfection defeateth utterly their Calling. To wish that all men were so qualified, as their Places and Dignities require, to hate all sinister and corrupt dealings which hereunto are any lett, to covet speedy redress of those things whatsoever, whereby the Church sustaineth detriment, these good and vertuous desires cannot offend any but ungodly minds. Notwithstanding, some in the true vehemency, and others under the fair pretence of these desires, have adventured that which is strange, that which is violent and unjust. There are which in confidence of their general allegations concerning the knowledge, the Residence and the single Livings of Ministers, presume not only to annihilate the solemn Ordinations of such as the Church must of force admit, but also to urge a kind of universal proscription against them, to set down Articles, to draw Commissions, and almost to name themselves of the *Quorum*, for inquiry into mens estates and dealings, whom at their pleasure they would deprive and make obnoxious to what punishment themselves list, and that not for any violation of Laws, either Spiritual or Civil, but because men have trusted the Laws too far, because they have held and enjoyed the liberty which Law granteth, because they had not the wit to conceive as these men do, that Laws were made to intrap the simple, by permitting those things in shew and appearance, which indeed should never take effect, for as much as they were but granted with a secret condition to be put in practice; *If they should be profitable and agreeable with the Word of God*, which condition failing in all Ministers that cannot preach, in all that are absent from their Livings, and in all that have divers Livings (for so it must be presumed, though never as yet proved) therefore as men which have broken the Law of God, and Nature, they are depriveable at all hours. Is this the Justice of that Discipline whereunto all Christian Churches must stoop and submit themselves ? Is this the equity wherewith they labour to reform the World ? I will no way diminish the force of those Arguments whereupon they ground. But if it please them to behold the visage of these collections in another Glass, there are Civil as well as Ecclesiastical Unsufficiencies, Non-residences, and Pluralities ; yea the reasons which Light of Nature hath ministred against both are of such affinity, that much less they cannot inforce in the one than in the other. When they that bear great Offices be persons of mean worth, the contempt whereinto their authority groweth, [a] weakneth the sinews of the whole State. Notwithstanding, where many Governours are needful, and they not many, whom their quality can commend, [b] the penury of worthier must needs make the meaner sort of men capable : Cities in the absence of their Governours, are as ships wanting Pilots at Sea. But were it therefore [c] Justice to punish whom superiour Authority pleaseth to call from home, or alloweth to be employed elsewhere ? In committing [d] many Offices to one man, there are apparently these inconveniences ; the-

Common-

The Author of the *Abstract*.
a μεγάλων κινδύνων καθεστῶσι ἐν εὐτελέσι ὧσι μεγάλα ἔλαθται. Arlsto. Polit. 2. cap. 11.
b Nec ignoro maximos honores ad parum dignos penuria meliorum solere deferri. Mamertin. paneg. ad Julian.
c Neque enim æquum visum est absentem reipub. causa inter reos referri dum reipub. operatur. Ulpian. l. 15. si maritus ad legem Julian. de adulter.
d Arist. Polit. lib....cap. 11.
See the like Preamble framed by the Author of the *Abstract*, where he fancieth a Bishop depsing one unapt to preach, whom himself had before ordained.

Common-wealth doth lose the benefit of serviceable men, which might be trained up in those rooms ; it is not easie for one man to discharge many mens duties well, in service of Warfare and Navigation, were it not the overthrow of whatsoever is undertaken, if one or two should ingross such Offices as being now divided into many hands, are discharged with admirable both perfection and expedition ? Nevertheless, be it far from the mind of any reasonable man to imagine, that in these considerations Princes either ought of duty to revoke all such kind of grants, though made with very special respect to the extraordinary merit of certain men , or might in honour demand of them the resignation of their Offices, with speech to this or the like effect. *For as much as you A. B. by the space of many years, have done us that faithful service in most important affairs , for which we always judging you worthy of much honour, have therefore commuted unto you from time to time, very great and weighty Offices, which hitherto you quietly enjoy: we are now given to understand, that certain grave and learned men have found in the books of ancient Philosophers, divers Arguments drawn from the common light of Nature, and declaring the wonderful discommodities which use to grow by Dignities thus heaped together in one: For which cause, at this present, moved in conscience and tender care for the publick good, we have summoned you hither , to dis-possess you of those places, and to depose you from those rooms , whereof indeed by vertue of our own grant , yet against reason, you are possessed. Neither ought you, or any other to think us rash, light, or inconstant , in so doing: For we tell you plain, that herein we will both say and do that thing which the noble and wise Emperour sometime both said and did, in a matter of far less weight than this ;* Quod inconsulto fecimus, consulto revocamus, *That which we unadvisedly have done, we advisedly will revoke and undo.* Now for mine own part, the greatest harm I would wish them who think that this were consonant with equity and right, is, that they might but live where all things are with such kind of Justice ordered, till experience have taught them to see their errour. As for the last thing which is incident into the cause whereof we speak, namely, what course were the best and safest whereby to remedy such evils as the Church of God may sustain, where the present liberty of Law is turned to great abuse, some light we may receive from abroad, not unprofitable for direction of Gods own sacred house and family. The Romanes being a people full of generosity, and by nature courteous, did no way more shew their gentle disposition, than by easie condescending to set their bond-men at liberty. Which benefit in the happier and better times of the Common-wealth, was bestowed for the most part as an ordinary reward of vertue, some few now and then also purchasing freedom with that which their just labours could gain, and their honest frugality save. But as the Empire daily grew up, so the manners and conditions of men decayed, wealth was honoured, and vertue not cared for, neither did any thing seem opprobious out of which there might rise commodity and profit, so that it could be no marvel in a State thus far degenerated, if when the more ingenious sort were become base, the baser laying aside all shame and face of honesty, did some by robberies, burglaries, and prostitutions of their bodies gather wherewith to redeem liberty ; others obtain the same at the hands of their Lords, by serving them as vile instruments in those attempts , which had been worthy to be revenged with ten thousand deaths. A learned, judicious, and polite Historian, having mentioned so foul disorders , giveth his judgement and censure of them in this sort: *Such eye-sores in the Common-wealth have occasioned many vertuous minds to condemn altogether the custome of granting liberty to any bond slave, for as much as it seemed a thing absurd, that a people which commanded all the world should consist of so vile refuse. But neither is this the only custome wherein the profitable inventions of former are depraved by later Ages ; and for my self I am not of their opinion that wish the abrogation of so grosly used customes, which abrogation might peradventure be cause of greater inconveniences ensuing ; but as much as may be I would rather advise that redress were sought, through the careful providence of chief Rulers and Overseers of the Common-wealth , by whom a yearly survay being made of all that are manumised, they which seem worthy might be taken and divided into Tribes with other Citizens, the rest dispersed into Colonies abroad, or otherwise disposed of, that the Common-wealth might sustain neither harm nor disgrace by them.* The ways

Dionys. Halica. Rom. antiq. l. 4.

to

to meet with diforders growing by abufe of Laws, are not fo intricate and fecret, efpecially in our cafe, that men fhould need either much advertifement or long time for the fearch thereof. And if counfel to that purpofe may feem needful, this Church (God be thanked) is not deftitute of men endued with ripe judgement, whenfoever any fuch thing fhall be thought neceffary. For which end at this prefent to propofe any fpecial inventions of mine own, might argue in a man of my place and calling more prefumption perhaps than wit. I will therefore leave it intire unto graver confideration, ending now with requeft only and moft earneft fute ; firft, that they which give Ordination, would, as they tender the very honour of Jefus Chrift, the fafety of men, and the endlefs good of their own fouls, take heed, left unneceffarily, and through their default the Church be found worfe, or lefs furnifhed than it might be : fecondly, that they which by right of Patronage have power to prefent unto fpiritual Livings , and may in that refpect much damnifie the Church of God, would, for the eafe of their own account in that dreadful day , fomewhat confider what it is to betray for gain the Souls which Chrift hath redeemed with bloud, what to violate the facred bond of fidelity and folemn promife, given at the firft to God and his Church by them, from whole original intereft together with the felf-fame Title of right, the fame Obligation of duty likewife is defcended: Thirdly, that they unto whom the granting of Difpenfations is committed, or which otherwife have any ftroke in the difpofition of fuch preferments as appertain unto learned men , would bethink themfelves what it is to refpect any thing either above or befides merit , confidering how hardly the world taketh it , when to men of commendable note and quality there is fo little refpect had, or fo great unto them whofe deferts are very mean, that nothing doth feem more ftrange than the one fort, becaufe they are not accounted of, and the other becaufe they are, it being every mans hope and expectation in the Church of God, efpecially that the only purchafe of greater rewards fhould be always greater deferts, and that nothing fhould ever be able to plant a Thorn where a Vine ought to grow: Fourthly, that honourable Perfonages, and they, who by vertue of any principal office in the Common-wealth are inabled to qualifie a certain number, and make them capable of favours or facu ties above others, fuffer not their names to be abufed , contrary to the true intent and meaning of wholfome Laws, by men in whom there is nothing notable befides covetoufnefs and ambition : Fifthly, that the graver and wifer fort in both Univerfities, or whofoever they be, with whofe approbation the marks and recognifances of all learning are beftowed, would think the Apoftles caution againft unadvifed Ordinations not impertinent or unneceffary to be born in mind, even when they grant thofe degrees of Schools , which degrees are not *gratie gratis date*, kindneffes beftowed by way of humanity, but they are *gratie gratum facientes*, favours which always imply a teftimony given to the Church and Common-wealth, concerning mens fufficiency for manners and knowledge ; a teftimony, upon the credit whereof fundry Statutes of the Realm are built, a teftimony fo far available, that nothing is more refpected for the warrant of divers mens ability to ferve in the affairs of the Realm ; a teftimony wherein if they violate that Religion wherewith it ought to be always given, and do thereby induce into errour fuch as deem it a thing uncivil to call the credit thereof in queftion , let them look that God fhall return back upon their heads , and caufe them in the ftate of their own Corporations to feel either one way or other the punifhment of thofe harms, which the Church through their negligence doth fuftain in that behalf: Finally, and to conclude, that they who enjoy the benefit of any fpecial Indulgence or Favour which the Laws permit, would as well remember what in duty towards the Church, and in confcience towards God they ought to do, as what they may do by ufing to their own advantage whatfoever they fee tolerated, no man being ignorant that the caufe why abfence in fome cafes hath been yielded unto, and in equity thought fufferable, is the hope of greater fruit through induftry elfewhere; the reafon likewife wherefore pluralities are allowed unto men of note, a very foveraign and fpecial care, that as Fathers in the ancient world did declare the preeminence of priority in birth , by doubling the worldly portions of their firft born ; fo the Church by a courfe not unlike in affigning mens rewards, might teftifie an eftimation had proportionably of their

vertues;

vertues, according to the ancient rule Apoſtolick, *They which excell in labour,*
ought to excell in honour ; and therefore unleſs they anſwer faithfully the expectation of the Church herein, unleſs ſincerely they bend their wits day and night, both
to ſow becauſe they reap, and to ſow as much more abundantly as they reap more
abundantly than other men, whereunto by their very acceptance of ſuch benignities
they formally bind themſelves, let them be well aſſured that the honey which they For the main
eat with fraud ſhall turn in the end into true gall, for as much as Laws are the ſa- Hypotheſis or
cred image of his wiſdom who moſt ſeverely puniſheth thoſe colourable and ſubtile foundation of
crimes that ſeldom are taken within the walk of humane Juſtice : I therefore con- ons, let that be-
clude, that the grounds and maximes of common right whereupon Ordinations of fore ſet down in
Miniſters unable to preach, tolerations of abſence from their Cures, and the multi- the 9. be read
plications of their ſpiritual livings are diſproved, do but indefinitely enforce them together with
unlawful, not unlawful univerſally and without exception ; that the Laws which Paragraph.
indefinitely are againſt all theſe things, and the Priviledges which make for them in
certain caſes are not the one repugnant to the other, that the Laws of God and
Nature are violated through the effects of abuſed Priviledges ; that neither our Ordinations of men unable to make Sermons, nor our diſpenſations for the reſt, can
be juſtly proved fruſtrate by vertue of any ſuch ſurmiſed oppoſition between the
ſpecial Laws of this Church which have permitted, and thoſe general which are alledged to diſprove the ſame ; that when priviledges by abuſe are grown incommodious, there muſt be redreſs ; that for remedy of ſuch evils, there is no neceſſity the
Church ſhould abrogate either in whole or in part the ſpecialties before mentioned ;
and that the moſt to be deſired were a voluntary reformation thereof on all hands
which may give paſſage unto any abuſe.

FINIS.

OF THE
LAWES
OF
Ecclesiastical Policy:

The sixth Book.

Containing their fifth Assertion.

That our Lawes are corrupt and repugnant to the Lawes of God, in matter belonging to the power of Ecclesiastical Jurisdiction, in that we have not throughout all Churches certain Lay-Elders established for the exercise of that Power.

THe same men which in heat of contention, do hardly either speak or give ear to reason, being after sharp and bitter conflicts, retired to a calm remembrance of all their former proceedings; the causes that brought them into quarrell, the course which their striving affections have followed, and the issue whereunto they are come, may peradventure as troubled waters, in small time of their own accord, by certain easie degrees settle themselves again, and so recover that clearnesse of well advised judgement, whereby they shall stand at the length indifferent, both to yeild and admit any reasonable satisfaction, where before they could not endure with patience to be gain-said. Neither will I despair of the like successe in these unpleasant controversies touching Ecclesiastical Policy, the time of silence which both parts have willingly taken to breath, seeming now as it were a pledge of all mens quiet contentment, to hear with more indifferency the weightiest and last remains of that Cause, Jurisdiction, Dignity, Dominion Ecclesiastical. For, let any man imagine, that the bare and naked difference of a few Ceremonies could either have kindled so much fire, or have caused it to flame so long; but that the parties which herein laboured mightily for change, and (as they say) for Reformation, had somewhat more then this mark whereat to aim?

Having therefore drawn out a compleat Form, as they suppose, of publick service to be done to God, and set down their plot for the Office of the Ministry in that behalf; they very well knew, how little their labours so far forth bestowed, would availe them in the end, without a claim of Jurisdiction to uphold the Fabrick which they had erected; and this neither likely to be obtained, but by the strong hand of the people, nor the people unlikely to favour it, the more, if overture were made of their own interest, right and title thereunto. Whereupon there are many which have conjectured this to be the cause, why in all the projects of their Discipline, (it being manifest that their drift is, to wrest the Key of Spiritual Authority out of the hands of

The question between us, whether all Congregations, or Parishes ought to have Lay-Elders invested with power of Jurisdiction in spiritual causes.

Lib. 6.
Lib. 7.
Lib. 8.

former

former Governours, and equally to poffeffe therewith the Paftors of all feveral Congregations) the people firft for furer accomplifhment, and then for better defence thereof, are pretended neceffary Actors in thofe things, whereunto their ability for the moft part is as flender, as their title and chanlenge unjuft.

Notwithftanding (whether they faw it neceffary for them to perfwade the people, without whofe help they could do nothing, or elfe (which I rather think) the affection which they bear towards this new Form of Government, made them to imagine it Gods own Ordinance,) Their Doctrine is, that by the Law of God, there muft be for ever in all Congregations certain Lay-Elders, Minifters of Ecclefiaftical Jurifdiction, in as much as our Lord and Saviour by Teftament (for fo they prefume) hath left all Minifters or Paftors in the Church Executors equally to the whole power of fpiritual Jurifdiction, and with them hath joyned the people as Colleagues. By maintenance of which affertion, there is unto that part apparently gained a twofold advantage, both becaufe the people in this refpect are much more eafily drawn to favour it, as a matter of their own intereft; and for that, if they chance to be croffed by fuch as oppofe againft them, the colour of Divine Authority, affumed for the grace & countenance of that power in the vulgar fort, furnifheth their Leaders with great abundance of matter behoveful for their encouragement, to proceed alwayes with hope of fortunate fucceffe in the end, confidering their caufe to be as *Davids* was, a juft defence of power given them from above, and confequently their Adverfaries quarrel the fame with *Sauls* by whom the Ordinance of God was withftood.

Now on the contrary fide, if this their furmife prove falfe; if fuch, as in Juftification whereof no evidence fufficient either hath been or can be alleadged (as I hope it fhall clearly appear after due examination and trial) let them then confider whether thofe words of *Corah, Dathan* and *Abiram* against *Mofes* and againft *Aaron, it is too much that ye take upon you, you feeing all the Congation is holy*, be not the very true abftract and abridgment of all their publifhed Admonitions, Demonftrations, Supplications, and Treatifes whatfoever, whereby they have laboured to void the rooms of their fpiritual Superiours, before Authorized, and to advance the new fancied Scepter of Lay-Presbyterial Power.

Numb. 16.

The nature of Spiritual Jurifdiction.

But before there can be any fetled Determination, whether Truth do reft on their part, or on ours, touching Lay-Elders, we are to prepare the way thereunto, by Explication of fome things requifite, and very needful to be confidered, as firft how befides that fpiritual power, which is of Order, and was inftituted for performance of thofe duties, whereof there hath been fpeech already had, there is in the Church no lefs neceffary, a fecond kind, which we call the power of Jurifdiction. When the Apoftle doth fpeak of ruling the Church of God, and of receiving accufations, his words have evident reference to the power of Jurifdiction. Our Saviours words to the power of Order, when he giveth his Difciples charge, faying, *Preach, Baptize: Do this in remembrance of me.* τὴς μὲν τὸι Θεῖ ὅς εἴσιν τὴι ἄυτ ἢ ἡμῖν. Καλντι ἢ εἰ ἀργαλα Θεῖ αὐτὰ μόνων, καὶ μὴ τὴ ἔχητι Θεῖ, εἰ δὴ καὶ ἰματίοις Χριστῖ. *Epift. ad Smyrn.* A Bifhop faith. (*Ignatius*) doth bear the Image of God and of Chrift, of God in ruling, of Chrift in adminiftring holy things: By this therefore we fee a manifeft difference acknowledged between the power of Ecclefiaftical Order, and the power of Jurifdiction Ecclefiaftical.

Acts 20. 28.
1 Tim. 5. 19.
Marc. 6. 15
Mat. 28. 19.
1 Cor. 11. 24.

The fpiritual power of the Church, being fuch as neither can be challenged by right of nature, nor could by humane authority be inftituted, becaufe the forces and effects thereof are fupernatural and Divine, we are to make no doubt or queftion, but that from him which is the Head, it hath defcended unto us that are the Body now invefted therewith. He gave it for the benefit and

and good of souls, as a mean to keep them in the Path which leadeth unto endlesse felicity, a bridle to hold them within their due and convenient bounds, and if they do go astray, a forcible help to reclaim them. Now although there be no kind of Spiritual Power, for which our Lord Jesus Christ did not give both Commission to exercise, and direction how to use the same, although his Laws in that behalf recorded by the holy Evangelists be the onely ground and foundation, whereupon the practice of the Church must sustain it self: yet as all multitudes once grown to the form of societies are even thereby naturally warranted, to enforce upon their own subjects particularly those things, which publick wisdom shall judge expedient for the common good: so it were absurd to imagine the Church it self the most glorious amongst them abridged of this liberty, or to think that no Law, Constitution or Canon, can be further made, either for Limitation or Amplification, in the practice of our Saviours Ordinances, whatsoever occasion be offered through variety of times, and things, during the state of this inconstant world, which bringeth forth daily such new evils, as must of necessity by new remedies be redrest, did both of old enforce our venerable Predecessor, and will always constrain others, sometime to make, sometime to abrogate, sometime to augment, and again to abridge sometime; in sum, often to vary, alter and change customes, incident into the manner of exercising that Power which doth it self continue alwayes one and the same: I therefore conclude, that Spiritual Authority is a Power which Christ hath given to be used over them which are subject unto it for the eternal good of their souls according to his own most Sacred Laws, and the wholsome positive Constitutions of his Church.

In Doctrine referred unto Action and Practice, as this is, which concerns Spiritual Jurisdiction, the first sound and perfect understanding is the knowledge of the end, because thereby both use doth frame, and contemplation judge all things.

Of Penitency, the chiefest end propounded by Spiritual Jurisdiction. Two kinds of Penitency; the one a Private Duty toward God, the other a Duty of external Discipline. Of the vertue of Repentance from which the former Duty proceedeth: And of Contrition the first part of that Duty.

SEing that the chiefest cause of Spiritual Jurisdiction, is to provide for the health and safety of mens Souls, by bringing them to see and repent their grievous offences committed against God, as also to reform all injuries offered with the breach of Christian Love and Charity toward their brethren, in matters of Ecclesiastical cognizance; the use of this power, shall by so much the plainlier appear, if first the nature of Repentance it self be known.

We are by Repentance to appease whom we offend by sin. For which cause, whereas all sin deprives us of the favour of Almighty God, our way of Reconciliation with him, is the inward secret Repentance of the heart; which inward Repentance alone sufficeth, unlesse some special thing, in the quality of sin committed, or in the party that hath done amisse, require more. For besides our submission in Gods sight, Repentance must not onely proceed to the private contentation of men, if the sin be a crime injurious; but also farther, where the wholsome Discipline of Gods Church exacteth a more exemplary and open satisfaction. Now the Church being satisfied with outward repentance, as God is with inward, it shall not be amisse, for more perspicuity to term this latter alwayes the Vertue, that former the Discipline of Repentance: Which Discipline hath two sorts of Penitents to work upon, in as much as it hath been accustomed to lay the Offices of Repentance on some, seeking others,

Pænitentia secunda, & unius quanto in actu negotium est, tanto potior probatio est ut no sola conscientia profera-tur, sed aliquo etiam actu administretur.

S f 2   others,

others, shunning them, on some at their own voluntary request, on others altogether against their wills, as shall hereafter appear by store of ancient examples. Repentance being therefore either in the sight of God alone, or else with the notice also of men: Without the one, sometime throughly performed, but alwayes practised more or lesse, in our daily devotions and prayers, we have no remedy for any fault: Whereas the other is onely required in sins of a certain degree and quality; the one necessary for ever, the other so far forth as the Laws and Orders of Gods Church shall make it requisite, the nature, parts and effects of the one alwayes the same; The other limited, extended, varied by infinite occasions.

Second penitency following that before Baptisin, and being not more then once admitted in one man, requireth by so much the greater labour to make it manifest, for that it is not a work which can come again in tryal, but must be therefore with some open solemnity executed, and not left to be discharged with the privity of conscience alone *Tertul. de pæ.*

The vertue of Repentance in the heart of man is Gods handy work, a fruit or effect of Divine Grace, which Grace continually offereth it self, even unto them that have forsaken it, as may appear by the words of Christ in St. *Johns* Revelation, *I stand at the door and knock:* Nor doth he only knock without, but also within assist to open, whereby accesse and entrance is given to the heavenly presence, of that saving power, which maketh man a repaired Temple for Gods good Spirit again to inhabit. And albeit the whole traine of vertues which are implied in the name of Grace be infused at one instant; yet because when they meet and concur unto any effect in man, they have their distinct operations rising orderly one from another; It is no unnecessary thing that we note the way or method of the Holy Ghost, in framing mans sinful heart to repentance: A work, the first foundation whereof is laid by opening and illuminating the eye of faith, because by faith are discovered the principles of this action, whereunto unlesse the understanding do first assent, there can follow in the will towards penitency no inclination at all: Contrariwise the Resurrection of the dead, the Judgement of the World to come, and the endlesse misery of sinners being apprehended, this worketh fear, such as theirs was, who feeling their own distresse and perplexity in that passion, besought our Lords Apostles earnestly to give them counsel what they should do. For fear is impotent and unable to advise it self; yet this good it hath, that men are thereby made desirous to prevent, if possibly they may, whatsoever evil they dread:: The first thing that wrought the *Ninivites* repentance, was fear of destruction within fourty dayes; signes and miraculous works of God, being extraordinary representations of Divine power, are commonly wont to stir any the most wicked with terrour, left the same power should bend it self against them: And because tractable minds, though guilty of much sin, are hereby moved to forsake those evil wayes, which make his power in such sort their astonishment and fear; Therefore our Saviour denounced his curse against *Corahzin* and *Bethsaida*, saying, that if *Tyre* and *Sidon* had seen that which they did, those signes which prevailed little with the one, would have brought the others repentance. As the like thereunto did in the men given to curious Arts, of whom the Apostolick History saith, that *Feare came upon them, and many which had followed vain sciences, burnt openly the very books out of which they had learned the same*; As fear of contumely and disgrace amongst men, together with other civil punishments, are a bridle to restrain from any hainous acts, whereinto mens outrage would otherwise break; So the fear of Divine revenge and punishment where it taketh place, doth make men desirous to be rid likewise from that inward guiltinesse of sin, wherein they would else securely continue. Howbeit, when Faith hath wrought a fear of the event of sin, yet repentance hereupon ensueth not, unlesse our belief conceive both the possibility and means to avert evil: The possibility in as much as God is merciful, and most willing to have sin cured; The means, because he hath plainly taught what is requisite, and shall suffice unto that purpose. The

nature

nature of all wicked men, is, for fear of revenge to hate whom they most wrong; The nature of hatred, to wish that destroyed which it cannot brook; And from hence ariseth the furious endeavours of godlesse, and obdurate sinners, to extinguish in themselves the opinion of God because they would not have him to be, whom execution of endlesse wo doth not suffer them to love.

Every sin against God abateth, and continuance in sin extinguisheth our love towards him: It was therefore said to the Angel of *Ephesus* having sinned, *Thou art fallen away from thy first love*; so that, as we never decay in love till we sin, in like sort neither can we possibly forsake sin, unless we first begin again to love. What is love towards God, but a desire of union with God? And shall we imagine a sinner converting himself to God, in whom there is no desire of union with God presupposed? I therefore conclude, that fear worketh no mans inclination to repentance, till somewhat else have wrought in us love also: Our love and desire of union with God ariseth from the strong conceit wch we have of his admirable goodnes: The goodness of God which particularly moveth unto repentance, is his mercy towards mankind, notwithstanding sin: For let it once sink deeply into the mind of man, that howsoever we have injuried God, his very nature is averse from revenge, except unto sin we add obstinacy, otherwise alwayes ready to except our commission, as a full discharge or recompence for all wrongs; And can we chuse but begin to love him whom we have offended, or can we but begin to grieve that we have offended him whom we love? Repentance considereth sin as a breach of the Law of God; an act obnoxious to that revenge, which notwithstanding may be prevented, if we pacifie God in time.

The root and beginning of penitency therefore, is the consideration of our own sin, as a cause which hath procured the wrath, and a subject which doth need the mercy of God: For unto mans understanding, there being presented on the one side, tribulation and anguish upon every soul that doth evil: On the other, eternal life unto them which by continuance in well doing, seek Glory, and Honour, and Immortality; On the one hand, a curse to the children of disobedience; On the other, to lovers of righteousnesse, all grace and benediction; Yet between these extreams, that eternal God from whole unspotted justice and undeserved mercy, the lot of each inheritance proceedeth, is so inclinable, rather to shew compassion then to take revenge, that all his speeches in holy Scripture are almost nothing else but entreaties of men to prevent destruction by amendment of their wicked lives; All the works of his providence little other then meer allurements of the just to continue stedfast, and of the unrighteous to change their course; All his dealings and proceedings towards true Converts, as have even filled the grave writings of holy men, with these and the like most sweet sentences: *Repentance (if I may so speak) stoppeth God in his way, when being provoked by crimes past, he cometh to revenge them with most just punishments; Yea, it tieth as it were the hands of the Avenger, and doth not suffer him to have his will. Again,

The merciful eye of God towards men, hath no power to withstand penitency, at what time soever it comes in presence. And again,

God doth not take it so in evil part, though we wound that which hehath required us to keep whole, as that after we have taken hurt, there should be in us no desire to receive his help. Finally, least I be carried too far in so large a Sea, there was never any man condemned of God but for neglect; Nor justified, except he had care of repentance.

From these considerations, setting before our eyes our inexcusable, both unthankfulnesse in disobeying so merciful, foolishnesse in provoking so powerful a God; there ariseth necessarily a pensive and corrosive desire that we had done otherwise; a desire which suffereth us to follow no time,

* *Cassia Col.* 20 c.4.
* *Basil. Epist.* Se eur. p.196.
φιλάνθρωπον ἔλεμιαι πρὸς ἀμαρτίαν ἡ μανϊιϊαν. *Chry.* in 1 *Cor. hom.* 8 ὃ τὸ Τροθυῶσι ὅτα ἀεινϊ, οἷς τὸ Τριωϊωτα καὶ ἐνλιὸς θερα πίνεϊθαι. *Marc. Erem.* ἰδὺς κατηρίσθη εἰ μὴ μετανοίας κρατηρὶ στασι, καὶ εἰλὶς ἐλεγχθισα εἰ μὴ πωνϊΐ ι. μεϊλὶ.

time, to feel no quietnesse within our selves, to take neither sleep nor food with contentment, never to give over supplications, confessions, and other penitent duties, till the light of Gods reconciled favour, shine in our darkned soul.

Ful. de remi. peccat. lib. 2. cap. 1 5.
Fulgentius asking the question, why *David*'s confession should be held for effectuall penitence and not *Sauls*; answereth, that the one hated sin, the other feared onely punishment in this world : *Saul*'s acknowledgement of sin was fear, *David*'s both fear and also love.

This was the fountain of *Peters* tears, this the life and spirit of *Davids* eloquence, in those most admirable Hymns intituled *Penitentiall*, where the words of sorrow for sin, do melt the very bowels of God remitting it, and the comforts of grace in remitting sin, carry him which sorrowed, rapt as it were into heaven with extacies of joy and gladnesse. The first motive of the *Ninivites* unto repentance was their belief in a sermon of fear, but
Jona c. 3. 9. the next and most immediate, an axiom of love; *Who can tell whether God will turn away his fierce wrath, that we perish not*: No conclusion such as theirs, let every man turn from his evil way, but out of premisses such as theirs were, fear and love: Wherefore the well-spring of repentance is faith, first breeding fear, and then love, which love causeth hope, hope resolution of attempt, *I will go to my Father, and say, I have sinned against heaven and against thee*; that is to say, I will do what the duty of a Convert requireth.

Now in a Penitents or Converts duty, there are included; first, the aversion of the will from sin; secondly, the submission of our selves to God, by supplication and prayer; thirdly, the purpose of a new life, testified with present works of amendment: Which three things do very well seem to be comprised in one definition, by them which handle repentance, as a vertue that hateth, bewaileth, and sheweth a purpose to amend sin: We offend God in thought, word, and deed. To the first of which three, they make contrition; to the second, confession; and to the last, our works o satisfaction, answerable.

Contrition doth not here import these sudden pangs and convulsions of the mind, which cause sometimes the most forsaken of God, to retract their own doings; it is no naturall passion or anguish, which riseth in us against our wills, but a deliberate aversion of the will of man from sin, which being alwaies accompanied with grief, and grief oftentimes partly with tears, partly with other external signes; it hath been thought, that in these things, contrition doth chiefly consist: whereas the chiefest thing in contrition, is that alteration whereby the will which was before delighted with sin, doth now abhor and shun nothing more. But forasmuch as we cannot hate sin in our selves without heavinesse and grief, that there should be in us a thing of such hateful quality, the will averted from sin must needs make the affection suitable; yea, great reason why it should so do: For since the will by conceiving sin hath deprived the soul of life; and of life there is no recovery without repentance the death of sin; repentance not able to kill sin, but by withdrawing the will from it, the will unpossible to be withdrawn, unlesse it concur with a contrary affection to that which accompanied it before in evil: Is it not clear, that as an inordinate delight did first begin sin, so repentance must begin with a just sorrow, a sorrow of heart, and such a sorrow as renteth the heart; neither a feigned nor slight sorrow; not feigned, least it increase sin; nor slight, least the pleasures of sin over-match it.

Wherefore of Grace, the highest cause from which mans penitency doth proceed, of Faith, Fear, Love, Hope, what force and efficiency they have in repentance: of parts and duties thereunto belonging, comprehended in the Schoolemens definitions; finally, of the first among those duties, Contrition which disliketh and bewaileth iniquity, let this suffice.

And

And because God will have offences by repentance, not onely abhorred within our selves, but also with humble supplication displayed before him, and a testimony of amendment to be given, even by present works, worthy repentance, in that they are contrary to those we renounce and disclaim: Although the vertue of Repentance do require, that her other two parts, Confession and Satisfaction should here follow; yet seeing they belong as well to the Discipline as to the vertue of Repentance, and onely differ for that in the one they are performed to man; in the other to God alone; I had rather distinguish them in joynt handling, then handle them apart, because in quality and manner of practise, they are distinct.

Of the Discipline of Repentance instituted by Christ, practised by the Fathers, converted by the School-men into a Sacrament; and of confession, that which belongeth to the vertue of Repentance, that which was used among the Jews, that which the Papacy imagineth a Sacrament, and that which Ancient Discipline practiced.

1. OUr Lord and Saviour in the 16th. of St. *Matthews* Gospel, giveth his Apostles regiment in general over Gods Church. For they that have the Keyes of the Kingdom of Heaven, are thereby signified to be Stewards of the House of God under whom they guide, command, judge, and correct his Familie. The souls of men are Gods treasure, committed to the trust and fidelity of such, as must render a strict account for the very least which is under their custody. God hath not invested them with power to make a revenue thereof; but to use it for the good of them whom Jesus Christ hath most dearly bought. *Mat.16.19.*

And because their Office therein consisteth of sundry functions, some belonging to Doctrine, some to Discipline, all contained in the name of the Keyes, they have for matters of Discipline, as well litigious as criminal, their Courts and Consistories erected by the heavenly Authority of his most sacred voice, who hath said, *Dic Ecclesiæ,* Tell the Church, against rebellious and contumacious persons, which refuse to obey their sentence; armed they are with power to eject such out of the Church, to deprive them of the honours, rights, and priviledges of Christian men, to make them as Heathens and Publicans, with whom society was hatefull? *Mat.18.17.*

Furthermore, lest their acts should be slenderly accounted of, or had in contempt, whether they admit to the Fellowship of Saints or seclude from it, whether they bind Offenders, or set them again at liberty, whether they remit, or retain sins, whatsoever is done by way of orderly and lawful proceeding, the Lord himself hath promised to ratifie. This is that grand Original Warrant, by force whereof the Guides and Prelates in Gods Church, first his Apostles, and afterwards others following them successively, did both use and uphold that Discipline, the end whereof is to heal mens Consciences, to cure their sins, to reclaim Offenders from iniquity, and to make them by repentance just. *Mat.18,18. Jo.20 23. 1 Cor.5 3. 2 Cor.2.6. 1 Tim 1,20.*

Neither hath it of Ancient time, for any other respect been accustomed to bind by Ecclesiastical Censures, to retain so bound, till tokens of manifest Repentance appeared, and upon apparent Repentance to release, saving onely because this was received as a most expedient method for the cure of sin.

The course of Discipline in former Ages reformed open Transgressors, by putting them unto Offices of open penitence; especially Confession, whereby they declared their own crimes in the hearing of the whole Church, and were not from the time of their first convention capable of the holy Mysteries of Christ, till they had solemnly discharged this duty.

Offenders

Offenders in secret knowing themselves altogether as unworthy to be admitted to the Lords Table, as the other which were with-held, being also perswaded that if the Church did direct them in the offices of their penitency, and assist them with publike prayer, they should more easily obtain that they sought, then by trusting wholly to their own endeavours; finally, having no impediment to stay them from it but bashfulnesse, which countervailed not the former inducements; and besides, was greatly eased by the good construction, which the charity of those times gave to such actions, wherein mens piety and voluntary care to be reconciled to God, did purchase then much more love, then their faults (the testimonies of common frailty) were able to procure disgrace, they made it not nice to use some one of the Ministers of God, by whom the rest might take notice of their faults, prescribe them convenient remedies, and in the end after publick Confession, all joyn in prayer unto God for them.

The first beginner of this custome, had the more Followers by meanes of that special favour which alwayes was with good consideration shewed towards voluntary penitents above the rest.

But as Professors of Christian belief, grew more in number, so they waxed worse, when Kings and Princes had submitted their Dominions unto the Scepter of Jesus Christ, by means whereof Persecution ceasing, the Church immediately became subject to those evils which peace and security bringeth forth; there was not now that love which before kept all things in tune, but every where Schismes, Discords, Dissentions amongst men, Conventicles of Hereticks, bent more vehemently against the sounder and better sort then very Infidels and Heathens themselves; faults not corrected in charity, but noted with delight, and kept for malice, to use when the deadliest opportunities should be offered.

Whereupon, forasmuch as publick Confessions became dangerous and prejudicial to the safety of well-minded men, and in divers respects advantagious to the enemies of Gods Church; it seemed first unto some, and afterwards generally requisite, that voluntary Penitents should surcease from open Confession.

In stead whereof, when once private and secret Confession had taken place with the *Latins*, It continued as a profitable Ordinance, till the *Lateran* Council had Decreed, that all men once in a year at the least, should confesse themselves to the Priest.

So that being a thing thus made both general and also necessary, the next degree of estimation whereunto it grew, was to be honoured and lifted up to the nature of a Sacrament, that as Christ did institute Baptisme to give life, and the Eucharist to nourish life, so Penitence might be thought a Sacrament, ordained to recover life, and Confession a part of the Sacrament.

They define therefore their private Penitency, to be a Sacrament of remitting sins after Baptism: The vertue of Repentance, a detestation of wickednesse, with full purpose to amend the same, and with hope to obtain pardon at Gods hands.

Wheresoever the Prophets cry *Repent*, and in the Gospel S. *Peter* maketh the same Exhortation to the Jews, as yet unbaptized, they will have the vertue of Repentance only to be understood. The Sacrament, where he adviseth *Simon Magus* to repent, because the sin of *Simon Magus*, was after Baptism.

Now although they have onely external Repentance for a Sacrament, internal for a Vertue; yet make they Sacramental Repentance neverthelesse to be composed of three parts, Contrition, Confession, and Satisfaction; which is absurd; because Contrition being an inward thing, belongeth to the Vertue, and not to the Sacrament of Repentance; which must consist of external parts, if the nature thereof be external.

Besides,

Besides, which is more abfurd, they leave out Abfolution, whereas fome of their School Divines, handling Penance in the nature of a Sacrament, and being not able to efpie the leaft refemblance of a Sacrament, fave only in Abfolution (for a Sacrament by their doctrine muft both fignifie and alfo confer, or beftow fome fpecial Divine Grace) refolved themfelves, that the duties of the Penitent could be but meer preparations to the Sacrament, and that the Sacrament it felf was wholly in Abfolution. And albeit *Thomas* with his Followers have thought it fafer, to maintain as well the fervices of the Penitent, as the words of the Minifter, neceffary unto the effence of their Sacrament; the fervices of the Penitent, as a caufe material; the words of Abfolution, as a formal; for that by them all things elfe are perfected to the taking away of fin: which opinion, now reigneth in all their Schools, fince the time that the Councel of *Trent* gave it folemn approbation, feeing they all make Abfolution, if not the whole effence, yet the very form whereunto they afcribe chiefly the whole force and operation of their Sacrament; furely to admit the matter as a part, and not to admit the form, hath fmall congruity with reafon.

Again, for as much as a facrament is complear, having the matter and form which it ought, what fhould lead them to fet down any other parts of Sacramental repentance, then Confeffion and Abfolution, as *Durandus* hath done? For touching Satisfaction, the end thereof, as they underftand it, is a further matter, which refteth after the Sacrament adminiftred, and therefore can be no part of the Sacrament.

Will they draw in Contrition with fatisfaction, which are no parts, and exclude Abfolution (a principal part,) yea, the very complement, form and perfection of the reft as themfelves account it? But for their breach of precepts in art, it fkilleth not, if their Doctrine otherwife concerning Penitency, and in Penitency touching Confeffion might be found true.

Wefay, Let no man look for pardon, which doth fmother and conceal fin, where in duty it fhould be revealed.

The caufe why God requireth Confeffion to be made to him, is that thereby teftifying a deep hatred of own iniquity, the only caufe of his hatred and wrath towards us, we might becaufe we are humble, be fo much the more capable of that compaffion and tender mercy, which knoweth not how to condemn finners that condemn themfelves.

If it be our Saviours own principle, that the conceit we have of our debt forgiven, proportioneth our thankfulneffe and love to him, at whofe hands we receive pardon; doth not God fore-fee, that they which with ill advifed modefty feek to hide their fin like *Adam*, that they which rake it up under afhes, and confeffe it not, are very unlikely to requite with offices of love afterwards, the grace which they fhew themfelves unwilling to prize at the very time when they fue for it, in as much as their not confeffing what crimes they have committed, is a plain fignification how loth they are that the benefit of Gods moft gracious pardon fhould feem great. Nothing more true, then that of *Tertullian. Confeffion doth as much abate the weight of mens offences, as concealment doth make them heavier.* For he which confeffeth, hath a purpofe to appeafe God; he, a determination to perfift and continue obftinate, which keeps them fecret to himfelf. St. *Chryfoftome* almoft in the fame words, *Wickedneffe is by being acknowledged, leffened, and doth but grow by being hid.* If men having done amiffe, let it flip, as though they knew no fuch matter, what is there to ftay them from falling into one and the fame evil? To call our felves finners availeth nothing, except we lay our faults in the ballance, and take the weight of them one by one. Confeffe thy crimes to God, difclofe thy tranfgreffions before thy Judge, by way of humble fupplication and fuit, if not with tongue, at the leaft with heart, and in this fort feek mercy. A general perfwafion that thou art a finner, will neither fo humble, nor bridle thy foul, as if the Catalogue of thy fins examined feverally, be continuall, kept in mind. This fhall make thee lowly in thine eyes, this fhall preferve thy feet

T t

from

Marginal notes:
Scot. fent. l. 4. d. 147. 4.

Seff. 14. c. 3. Decet Sanctæ Synodus Sacramenti pœnitentiæ formam in qua præcipue ipfius vis fita eft, in illis Miniftri verbis pofitam effe, Ego te abfolvo. Sunt autem quafi materia hujus Sacramenti ipfius pœnitentis actus, nempe Contritio, Confeffio, & Satisfactio.

Luk. 7. 47.

Tantum relevat Conceffio delictorum quantum diffimulatio exaggerat. Confeffio autem fatisfactionis confilium eft, diffimulatio contumaciæ. Tert. de pen. Chrys. hom. 30. in Epiff. ad Heb.

from falling, and sharpen thy desires towards all good things. The mind I know doth hardly admit such unpleasant remembrances, but we must force it, we must constrain it thereunto. It is safer now to be bitten with the memory, then hereafter with the torment of sin.

The Jews with whom no repentance for sin is available without Confession, either conceived in mind or uttered; which latter kind they call usually וְדֻי Confession delivered by word of mouth, had first that general Confession which once every year was made, both severally by each of the people for himself, upon the day of expiation, and by the Priest for them all. On the day of expiation, the high Priest maketh three expresse confessions, acknowledging unto God the manifold transgressions of the whole Nation, his own personal offences likewise, together with the sins, as well of his Family, as of the rest of his rank and order.

They had again their voluntary Confessions, at the times and seasons, when men bethinking themselves of their wicked conversation past, were resolved to change their course, the beginning of which alteration was still Confession of sins.

Thirdly, over and besides these, the Law imposed upon them also that special Confession, which they in their book call וְדֻי עַל עָךְ כִּיהֵחֵר.

Confession of that particular fault, for which we namely seek pardon at Gods hands. The words of the Law concerning Confession in this kind are as followeth : When a man or woman shall commit any sin, that men commit, and transgresse against the Lord, their sin which they have done (that is to say the very deed it self in particular) they shall acknowledge. In *Leviticus* after certain transgressions there mentioned, we read the like: When a man hath sinned in any one of these things, he shall then confesse, how in that thing he hath offended. For such kind of special sins, they had also special Sacrifices, wherein the manner was that the Offender should lay his hands on the head of the Sacrifice which he brought, and should there make Confession to God, saying, *Now O Lord, that I have offended, committed sin, and done wickedly in thy sight, this or this being my fault, behold, I repent me, and am utterly ashamed of my doings; my purpose is never to return more to the same crime.*

None of them, whom neither the house of judgement had condemned to die, or of them which are to be punished with stripes, can be clear by being executed or scourged, till they repent and confess their faults.

Finally, there was no man amongst them at any time, either condemned to suffer death, or corrected, or chastized with stripes, none ever sick and near his end, but they called upon him to repent and confesse his sins.

Of Malefactors convict by witnesses, and thereupon either adjudged to die, or otherwise chastized, their custom was to exact, as *Joshua* did of *Achan*, open confession, *My son, now give glory to the Lord God of Israel, confesse unto him, and declare unto me what thou hast committed, conceal it not from me,* Jos. 7. 19.

Concerning injuries and trespasses which happen between men, they highly commend such as will acknowledge before many.

It is in him which repenteth, accepted as an high Sacrifice, if he will confesse before many, make them acquainted with his over-sights, and reveal the transgressions which have passed between him and any of his brethren; saying, I have verily offended this man, thus and thus I have done unto him, but behold I do now repent and am sorry. Contrariwise, whosoever is proud and will not be known of his faults, but cloaketh them, is not yet come to perfect repentance; for so it is written, *He that hides his sins shall not prosper,* which words of *Solomon* they do not further extend, then only to sins committed against men, which are in that respect meet before men to be acknowledged particularly. But in sins between man and God, there is no necessity that man should himself make any such open and particular recital of them; to God they are known, and of us it is required, that we
                                                                cast

Levit. 16.21.

All *Israel* is bound on the day of expiation to repent and confesse, R. *Mos. in lib. Mitsworth biggadol. par. 2. prae. 16.*

Num. 5. 6.

Lev. 5. 5.

Misne Tora Tractatu Teshuba, cap. 1. & R M. in. lib. Mishnoth, par. 2. chap. 16. Mos. in Mishnoth. par. 2. pra. 16. To him which is sick, and draweth towards death, they say confesse. Idem.

caft not the memory of them, carelefly and loofly behind our backs, but keep in mind as near as we can, both our own debt, and his grace which remitteth the fame.

Wherefore to let paffe Jewifh confeffion, and to come unto them which hold Confeffion in the ear of the Prieft commanded; yea, commanded in the nature of a Sacrament, and thereby fo neceffary, that fin without it cannot be pardoned, let them find fuch a Commandment in holy Scripture, and we ask no more. *John* the *Baptift* was an extraordinary perfon, his birth, his actions of life, his Office extraordinary. It is therefore recorded for the ftrangneffe of the act, but not fet down as an everlafting Law for the World; *That to him* Mat. 3. 6. *Jerufalem and all Judea made confeffion of their fins:* Befides, at the time of this confeffion, their pretended facrament of repentance, as they grant, was not yet inftituted, neither was it fin after Baptifm, which Penitents did there confeffe; When that which befel the feven fons of *Sceva,* for ufing the name of Act. 19. 18: our Lord Jefus Chrift in their conjurations, was notified to Jews and Grecians in *Ephefus,* it brought an univerfal fear upon them, in fo much that divers of them which had believed before, but not obeyed the Laws of Chrift as they fhould have done, being terrified by this example, came to the Apoftle, and confeffed their wicked deeds. Which good and vertuous act, no wife man, as I fuppofe will difallow, but commend highly in them, whom Gods good Spirit fhall move to do the like when need requireth.

Yet neither hath this example the force of any general commandment, or law to make it neceffary for every man, to pour into the ears of the Prieft whatfoever hath been done amiffe, or elfe to remain everlaftingly culpable and guilty of fin; in a word, it proveth confeffion practized as a vertuous act, but not commanded as a Sacrament.

Now concerning St. *James* his Exhortation, whether the former branch be confidered, which faith, *Is any fick among you? let him call for the Ancients of the* Jam. 5 16. *Church, and let them make their prayers for him;* or the latter, which ftirreth up all Chriftian men unto mutual acknowledgement of faults amongft themfelves; *Lay open your minds, make your confeffions one to another;* is it not plain, that the one hath relation to that gift of healing, which our Saviour promifed Mar. 16. 18. his Church, faying, *They fhall lay their hands on the fick, and the fick fhall recover health?* relation to that gift of healing, whereby the Apoftle impofed his hands on the Father of *Publius,* and made him miraculoufly a found man; Act. 28. 8. relation finally to that gift of healing, which fo long continued in practice after the Apoftles times, that whereas the *Novatianifts* denyed the power of the Church of God, in curing fin after Baptifm, St. *Ambrofe* asked them again, *Why it might not as well prevail with God for fpiritual, as for corporal and bodily health; yea, wherefore (* faith he *) do ye your felves lay hands on the difeafed and believe it* Amb. de pœn. *to be a work of benediction or prayer, if haply the fick perfon be reftored to his former* l. 1. c. 7. *fafety?* And of the other member which toucheth mutual confeffion, do not fome of themfelves, as namely, *Cajetan* deny, that any other Confeffion is meant, then only that, *which feeketh either affociation of prayers, or reconciliation, or pardon of wrongs?* Is it not confeffed by the greateft part of their own reti- Annot. Rhem. nue, that we cannot certainly affirm Sacramental Confeffion to have been in Jac. 5. meant or fpoken of in this place? Howbeit *Bellarmaine* delighted to run a courfe by himfelf where colourable fhifts of wit will but make the way paffible, ftandeth as formally for this place, and not leffe for that in St. *John,* then for this. St. *John* faith, *If we confeffe our fins, God is faithful and juft to forgive our fins,* 1 John 1. 9. *and to cleanfe us from all unrighteoufneffe;* doth St. *John* fay, If we confeffe to the Prieft, God is righteous to forgive, and if not, that our fins are unpardonable? No, but the titles of God *juft* and *righteous* do import, that he pardoneth fin only for his promife fake; *And there is not (* they fay *) any promife of forgiveneffe upon confeffion made to God without the Prieft;* Not any promife, but with this condition, and yet this condition no where expreft.

Is it not ftrange that the Scripture fpeaking fo much of repentance, and of the several duties which appertain thereunto, should ever mean, and no where mention that one condition, without which all the rest is utterly of none effect; or will they say, because our Saviour hath said to his Ministers, *Whose sins ye retain, &c.* and because they can remit no more, then what the offenders have contest, that therefore by vertue of his promise, it standeth with the Righteousnesse of God, to take away no mans sins, until by auricular confession they be opened unto the Priest?

They are men that would seem to honour Antiquity, and none more to depend upon the reverend judgement thereof. I dare boldly affirm, that for many hundred years after Christ, the Fathers held no such opinion; they did not gather by our Saviours words, any such necessity of seeking the Priests Absolution from sin, by secret and (as they now term it) sacramental confession: Publick confession they thought necessary by way of Discipline, not private confession, as in the nature of a Sacrament necessary.

For to begin with the purest times it is unto them which read and judge without partiality a thing most clear, that the ancient Ἐξ, ὁμολογία or confession, defined by *Tertullian* to be a Discipline of humiliation, and submission, framing mens behaviour in such sort as may be fittest to move pity, the confession which they use to speak of in the exercise of repentance, was made openly in the hearing of the whole both Ecclesiastical Consistory and Assembly.

Plerosq, hoc opus ut publicationem sui aut sufugere, aut de die in diem d sterre, prasumo pudoris magis re mores quam salutis, velut thou avoid them, as likely to insult over thee, whom thou knowest subject to the same ili qui in per tibus re cun dio. Sui cer, orus contracta This is the reason wherefore he perceiving, that divers were better content their sores should secretly fester, and eat inward, then be laid so open to the eyes of many, blameth greatly their unwise bashfulnesse, and to reform the same, perswadeth with them saying, *Amongst thy brethren and fellow servants, which are partakers with thee of one and the same nature, fear, joy, grief, sufferings (for of one common Lord and Father, we have all received one spirit) why shouldest thou not think with thy self, that they are but thine own self ? wherefore dost haps? At that which grieveth any one part, the whole body cannot rejoyce, t must needs be that the whole will labour and strive to help that wherewith a part of it self is molested.*

vexatione con se en. sa me dentium ti tant, & ita cum erupe, en tra sua ser eunt. Tert de pœn. St. *Cyprian* being grieved with the dealings of them, who in time of persecution had through fear betrayed their faith, and notwithstanding thought by shift to avoid in that case the necessary Discipline of the Church, wrote for their better instruction, the book intituled *De lapsis* ; a Treatise concerning such, as had openly forsaken their Religion, and yet were loth openly to confesse their fault, in such manner as they should have done: In which book he compareth with this sort of men, certain others which had but a purpose only to have departed from the Faith ; and yet could not quiet their minds, till this very secret and hidden fault was confest, *How much both greater in faith* (saith St. Cyprian) *and also as touch ng their fear, better, are those men who although neither sacrifice, nor libel could be objected against them, yet because they thought to have done that which they should not, even this their intent they dolefully open unto Gods Priests ? They confesse that whereof their conscience accuseth them, the burthen that presseth their minds they discover, they foreslow not of smaller and slighter evils, to seek remedy.* He saith they declared their fault, not to one only man in private, but revealed it to Gods Priests, they confest it before the whole Consistory of Gods Ministers.

Qui necessita te in sacrifican di pecunia a pud Magistra tum red m - bant accepta securitatis Syngrapha libeilati ci di cebantur.

Him i de m io quadragesi m.d. *Salvianus* (for I willingly embrace their conjecture, who ascribe those Homilies to him which have hitherto by common error past under the counterfeit name of *Eusebius Emesenus*,) I say, *Salvianus*, though coming long after Cyprian in time, giveth neverthelesse the same evidence for his truth, in a case very little different from that before alleadged; his words are these, *Whereas (most dearly beloved) we see that penitance oftentimes is sought and sued for by holy soules, which even from their youth have bequeathed themselves a precious treasure unto God, let us know that the inspiration of Gods good Spirit moveth them so to do for the benefit of his Church, and let such as are wounded, learn to enquire for that remedy, whereunto the very soundest do thus offer and obtrude*

as

as it were themselves, that if the vertuous do bewaile small offences, the others cease not to lament great. And surely, when a man that hath lesse need, performeth *sub oculis Ecclesiæ,* in the view, sight, and beholding of the whole Church, an office worthy of his faith and compunction for sin, the good which others thereby reap is his own harvest, the heap of his rewards groweth by that which another gaineth, and through a kind of spiritual usury from that amendment of life which others learn by him, there returneth lucre into his coffers. The same *Salvianus* in another of his Homilies, *If faults haply be not great and grievous (for example, if a man have offended in word, or in desire, worthy of reproof, if in the wantonnesse of his eye, or the vanity of his heart, the stains of words and thoughts are by daily prayer to be cleansed, and by private compunction to be scoured out : But if any man examining inwardly his own Conscience, have committed some high and capital offence, as if by bearing false witnesse, he have quelled and betrayed his faith, and by rashnesse of perjury have violated the sacred name of Truth, if with the mire of lustfull uncleannesse he have sullied the vail of Baptism, and the gorgeous robe of Virginity, if by being the cause of any mans death, he have been the death of the new man within himself, if by conference with South-sayers, Wizards, and Charmers, he hath enthralled himself to Satan, These and such like committed crimes, cannot throughly be taken away with ordinary, moderate, and secret satisfaction, but greater causes do require greater and sharper remedies, they need such remedies as are not onely sharp, but solemn, open, and publick.* Again, *Let that soul (saith he) answer me, which through pernicious shamefastnesse is now so abasht to acknowledge his sin in conspectu fratrum, before his brethren, as he should have been before abasht to commit the same, what he will do in the presence of that Divine Tribunal where he is to stand arraigned in the Assembly of a glorious and celestial host ?* I will hereunto adde but St. *Ambrose*'s testimony : For the places which I might alleadge, are more then the cause it self needeth ; *There are many (saith he) who fearing the judgement that is to come, and feeling inward remorse of conscience, when they have offered themselves unto penitency, are enjoyned what they shall do, give back for the onely skar which they think that publick supplication will put them unto.* He speaketh of them which sought voluntarily to be penanced, and yet withdrew themselves from open confession, which they that were penitents for publick crimes could not possibly have done, and therefore it cannot be said he meaneth any other then secret sinners in that place. *Gennadius* a Presbyter of *Marsiles* in his book touching Ecclesiastical assertions, maketh but two kinds of confession necessary, the one in private to God alone for smaller offences, the other open, when crimes committed are hainous and great, *Although (saith he) a man be bitten with conscience of sin, let his will be from thenceforward to sin no more ; let him before he communicate, satisfie with tears and prayers, and then putting his trust in the mercy of Almighty God (whose wont is, to yeild to godly confessions) let him boldly receive the Sacrament. But I speak this of such as have not burthened themselves with capital sins. Then I exhort to satisfie, first by publick penance, that so being reconciled by the sentence of the Priest, they may communicate safely with others.* Thus still we hear of publick confessions, although the crimes themselves discovered were not publick ; we hear that the cause of such confessions was not the openesse, but the greatnesse of mens offences ; finally, we hear that the same being now held by the Church of *Rome* to be Sacramental, were the onely penitential confessions used in the Church for a long time, and esteemed as necessary remedies against sin.

They which will find Auricular confessions in *S. Cyprian*, therefore must seek out some other passage, then that which *Bellarmine* alledgeth, *Whereas in smaller faults which are not committed against the Lord himself, there is a competent time assigned unto penitency, and that confession is made, after that observation and tryal had been had of the Penitents behaviour, neither may any communicate till the Bishop and Clergy have laid their hands upon him ; how much more ought all things to be warily and stayedly observed, according to the Discipline of the Lord, in these most grievous and extream crimes ? S. Cyprians* speech is against rashnes in admitting
Idolaters

Hom. 10. Ad Monachos.

Graviores & actiores, & publicas curas requirunt. Hom. 8. ad Monach.

Lib. 2. de pæn. cap 9.

Cypr. Epist. 12

Inspecta vita ejus qui agit pœnitentiam.

Idolaters to the holy Communion, before they had shewed sufficient Repentance, considering that other offenders were forced to stay out their time, and that they made not their publick confession, which was the last act of penitency, till their Life and Conversation had been seen into, not with the eye of Auricular Scrutiny, but of Pastoral Observation, according to that in the Councel of *Nice*, where thirteen years, being set for the penitency of certain offenders, the severity of this Decree is mitigated with special caution:

Con. Nic. par. 2. c. 12. Pro fide & conversatione Pænitentium. *That in all such cases, the mind of the penitent and the manner of his repentance is to be noted, that as many as with fear and tears, and meeknesse, and the exercise of good works, declared themselves to be Converts indeed, and not in outward appearance only, towards them the Bishop at his discretion might use more lenity.* If the Councel of *Nice* suffice not, let *Gratian* the Founder of the Canon Law expound *Cyprian,* who sheweth that the stint of time in penitency, is either to be abridged or enlarged, as the Penitents faith and behaviour shall give occasion; *I have*

De pæn. dist. 1. cap. Men'uram Ambr. de pæn. lib. 2. c. 10. Greg. Niss. orat In eos qui alios acerbe judicant. *easilier found out men* (Saith S. *Ambrose*) *able to keep themselves free from crimes, then conformable to the rules which in penitency they should observe.* S. *Gregory* Bishop of *Nice* complaineth and enveigheth bitterly against them, who in the time of their penitency, lived even as they had done alwayes before ; *Their countenance as chearful, their attire as neat, their dyet as costly, and their step as secure as ever, their worldly businesse purposely followed, to exile pensive thoughts from their minds, repentance pretended, but indeed nothing lesse exprest ;* These were the inspections of life whereunto S. *Cyprian* alludeth; as for Auricular Examinations he knew them not.

Were the Fathers then without use of private Confession as long as publick was in use ? I affirm no such thing. The first and ancientest that mentioneth this Confession, is *Origen,* by whom it may seem that men being loth to present rashly themselves and their faults unto the view of the whole Church, thought it best to unfold first their minds to some one special man of the Clergy, which might either help them himself, or referre them to an

Orig. in Psal. 37. higher Court if need were ; *Be therefore circumspect* (saith *Origen*) *in making choise of the party, to whom thou mean'st to confesse thy sin; know thy Physitian before thou use him ; I, be find thy malady, such as needeth to be made publick, that other may be the better by it, and thy self sooner helpt, his counsel must be obeyed.* That which moved sinners thus voluntarily to detect themselves both in private and in publick, was fear to receive with other Christian men the mysteries of heavenly grace, till Gods appointed Stewards and Ministers did judge them

Amb. l. 2. de pæn. c. 9. worthy : It is in this respect that S. *Ambrose* findeth fault with certain men which sought imposition of penance, and were not willing to wait their time,

Si non tam se solvere cupiunt quam Sacerdotem ligare. Aug. in hom. de pæn. but would be presently admitted Communicants. *Such people* (saith he) *do seek by so rash and preposterous desires, rather to bring the Priest into bonds then to loose themselves:* In this respect it is that S. *Augustine* hath likewise said, *When the wound of sin is so wide, and the disease so far gone that the medicinable body and bloud of our Lord may not be touched, men are by the Bishops authority to sequester themselves from the Altar, till such time as they have repented, and be after reconciled by the same authority.* Furthermore, because the knowledge how to handle our own sores, is no vulgar and common art, but we either carry towards our selves for the most part an over-soft and gentle hand, fearfull of touching too near the quick, or else endeavouring not to be partial, we fall into timorous scrupulosities, and sometime into those extream discomforts of mind, from which we hardly do ever lift up our heads again, men thought it the safest way to disclose their secret faults, and to crave imposition of penance from them whom our Lord Jesus Christ hath left in his Church to be spiritual and ghostly Physitians, the guides and Pastors of redeemed souls, whose office doth not onely consist in general perswasions unto amendment of life, but also in the private particular cure of diseased minds.

Hom de pæn. Ninir. Howsoever the *Novatianists* presume to plead against the Church (saith *Salvianus*) *that every man ought to be his own penitentiary, and that it is a part of our duty to exercise, but not of the Churches Authority to impose or prescribe repentance;* the

the truth is otherwise, the belt and ſtrongeſt of us may need in ſuch caſes direction : *What doth the Church in giving penance, but ſhew the remedies which ſin requireth ? or what do we in receiving the ſame but fulfill her precepts ? what elſe but ſue unto God with tears, and faſts, that his merciful ears may be opened ?* S. *Auguſtines* exhortation is directly to the ſame purpoſe ; *Let every man whilſt he hath time judge himſelf, and change his life of his own accord, and when this is reſolved, Let him from the diſpoſers of the holy Sacraments, learn in what manner he is to pacifie Gods diſpleaſure* ; But the greateſt thing which made men forward and willing upon their knees to confeſſe whatſoever they had committed againſt God, and in no wiſe to be with-held from the ſame, with any fear of diſgrace, contempt, or oblique, which might enſue, was their fervent deſire to be helped and aſſiſted with the prayers of Gods Saints. Wherein as St. *James* doth exhort unto mutual confeſſion, alledging this onely for a reaſon, *that juſt mens devout prayers are of great avail with God* ; ſo it hath been heretofore the uſe of Penitents for that intent to unburthen their minds, even to private perſons, and to crave their prayers. Whereunto *Caſſianus* alluding, counſelleth, That *if men poſſeſt with dulneſſe of ſpirit be themſelves unapt to do that which is required, they ſhould in meek affection ſeek health at the leaſt by good and vertuous mens prayers unto God for them.* And to the ſame effect *Gregory* Biſhop of *Niſſe, Humble thy ſelf, and take unto thee ſuch of thy brethren as are of one mind, and do bear kind affection towards thee, that they may together mourn and labour for thy deliverance. Show me thy bitter and abundant tears, that I may blend mine own with them.*

But becauſe of all men there is or ſhould be none in that reſpect more fit for troubled and diſtreſſed minds to repair unto then Gods Miniſters, he proceedeth further, *Make the Prieſt, as a Father partaker of thine affection and grief, be bold to impart unto him the things that are moſt ſecret, he will have care both of thy ſafety, and of thy credit.*

Confeſſion (ſaith *Leo*) *is firſt to be offered to God, and then to the Prieſt, as to one which maketh ſupplication for the ſins of penitent offenders.* Suppoſe we, that men would ever have been eaſily drawn, much leſſe of their own accord have come unto publick confeſſion, whereby they know they ſhould ſound the trumpet of their own diſgrace, would they willingly have done this, which naturally all men are loth to do, but for the ſingular truſt and confidence which they had in the publick prayers of Gods Church? *Let thy mother the Church weep for thee* (ſaith *Ambroſe*) *let her waſh and bathe thy faults with her tears: Our Lord doth love that many ſhould become ſuppliant for one* ; In like ſort long before him, *Tertullian, Some few aſſembled make a Church; and the Church is as Chriſt himſelf* ; *When thou doſt therefore put forth thy hands to the knees of thy brethren, thou toucheſt Chriſt* ; *it is Chriſt unto whom thou art a ſupplicant* ; *ſo when they pour out tears over them, it is even Chriſt that taketh compaſſion* ; *Chriſt which prayeth when they pray: Neither can that eaſily be denyed, for which the Son is himſelf contented to become a ſuitor.*

Whereas in theſe conſiderations therefore, voluntary Penitents had been long accuſtomed for great and grievous crimes, though ſecret, yet openly both to repent and confeſſe as the Canons of Ancient Diſcipline required, the Greek Church firſt, and in proceſſe of time the Latine altered this order, judging it ſufficient and more convenient that ſuch offenders ſhould do penance and make confeſſion in private onely. The cauſe why the Latins did, *Leo* declareth, ſaying: *Although that ripeneſſe of faith be commendable, which for the fear of God doth not fear to incur ſhame before all men, yet becauſe every ones crimes are not ſuch, that it can be free and ſafe for them to make publication of all things, wherein repentance is neceſſary, let a cuſtome ſo unfit to be kept, be abrogated, leaſt many forbear to uſe remedies of penitency, whilſt they either bluſh or are afraid to acquaint their enemies with thoſe acts for which the Laws may take hold upon them. Beſides, it ſhall win the more repentance, if the conſciences of ſinners be not emptied into the peoples ears;* And to this onely cauſe doth *Sozomen* impute the change, which the *Grecians* made, by ordaining throughout all Churches certain Penitentiaries

Aug. hom. de pœn. citatur a Grat. diſt.1. c. judicet.
A præpoſitis Sacramentorum accipiat ſatisfactionis ſuæ modam.

Jam. 5.16.

Caſſia.col 20. c.8.
Greg. Niſſ. oratione in eos qui alioſacerbe judicant.

Leo 1. Ep.78. ad Epiſc. Campan. citat. a Grat.de pœn. d 1.c. ſufficit.

Ambr.l. 2. de pœn.c.10.

Tertul. de pœn.

Leo 1. Ep.78.

tentiaries to take the Confessions, and appoint the penances of secret offenders. *Socrates* (for this also may be true that more inducements then one, did set forward an alteration so generally made) affirmeth the *Grecians* (and not unlikely) to have specially respected therein the occasion, which the *Novatianists* took at the multitude of publick Penitents, to insult over the Discipline of the Church, against which they still cryed out, wheresoever they had time and place, *He that sheweth sinners favour, doth but teach the innocent to sin*: And therefore they themselves admitted no man to their Communion upon any repentance, which once was known to have offended after Baptism, making sinners thereby not the fewer, but the closer, and the more obdurate, how fair soever their pretence might seem.

The *Grecians* Canon for some one Presbyter in every Church to undertake the charge of penitency, and to receive their voluntary Confessions, which had sinned after Baptism, continued in force for the space of above some hundred years, till *Nectarius*, and the Bishops of Churches under him begun a second alteration, abolishing even that confession which their *Penitentiaries* took in private. There came to the *Penitentiary* of the Church of *Constantinople*, a certain Gentlewoman, and to him she made particular confession of her faults committed after Baptism, whom thereupon he advised to continue in fasting and prayer, that as with tongue she had acknowledged her sins, so there might appear likewise in her some work worthy of repentance: But the Gentlewoman goeth forward, and detecteth her self of a crime, whereby they were forced to dis-robe an Ecclesiastical person, that is, to degrade a Deacon of the same Church. When the matter by this mean came to publick notice, the people were in a kind of tumult offended, not onely at that which was done, but much more, because the Church should thereby endure open infamy and scorn. The Clergy perplexed and altogether doubtfull what way to take, till one *Eudemon* born in *Alexandria*, but at that time a Priest in the Church of *Constantinople*, considering that the causes of voluntary Confession whether publick or private, was especially to seek the Churches aid, as hath been before declared, least men should either not communicate with others, or wittingly hazard their souls, if so be they did communicate, and that the inconvenience which grew to the whole Church was otherwise exceeding great, but especially grievous by means of so manifold offensive detections, which must needs be continually more, as the world did it self wax continually worse: for Antiquity together with the gravity and severity thereof (saith *Sozomen*) had already begun by little and little to degenerate into loose and carelesse living, whereas before offences were lesse, partly through bashfulnesse in them which open their own faults, and partly by means of their great austerity, which thought as judges in this businesse; these things *Eudemon* having weighed with himself, resolved easily the mind of *Nectarius*, that the *Penitentiaries* office must be taken away, and for participation in Gods holy mysteries every man be left to his own Conscience, which was as he thought, the onely means to free the Church from danger of Obloquie and Disgrace. *Thus much* (saith *Socrates*) *I am the bolder to relate, because I received it from Eudæmons own mouth, to whom mine answer was at that time; Whether your counsel, Sir, have been for the Churches good, or otherwise, God knoweth: But I see, you have given occasion whereby we shall not now any more reprehend one anothers faults, nor observe that Apostolick precept, which saith, Have no Fellowship with the unfruitful works of darknesse, but rather be ye also reprovers of them.* With *Socrates*, *Sozomon* both agreeth in the occasion of abolishing *Penitentiaries*; and moreover testifieth also, that in his time living with the younger *Theodosius*, the same abolition did still continue, and that the Bishops had in a manner every where followed the example given them by *Nectarius*.

Wherefore to implead the truth of this History, Cardinal *Baronius* alledgeth that *Socrates*, *Sozomen* and *Eudæmon* were all *Novatianists*, and that
                                                                    they

they falsifie in saying, (for so they report) that as many as held the Con-
substantiall being of Christ, gave their assent to the abrogation of the
fore-hearsed Canon. The sum is, he would have it
taken for a fable, and the world to be perswaded that
Nectarius did never any such thing. Why then should
Socrates first and afterwards *Sozomen* publish it? To
please their pew-fellows the Disciples of *Novatian.* A
poor gratification, and they very silly friends, that
would take lyes for good turns. For the more acceptable the matter was, being deemed true, the lesse
they must needs (when they found the contrary)
either credit, or affect him which had deceived them.
Notwithstanding we know that joy and gladnesse, rising from false information, do not onely make men
so forward to believe that which they first hear, but
also apt to scholie upon it, and to report as true
whatsoever they wish were true. But so far is *Socrates*
from any such purpose, that the fact of *Nectarius*
which others did both like and follow, he doth disallow and reprove. His speech to *Eudæmon* before set
down, is proof sufficient that he writeth nothing, but
what was famously known to all, and what himself

did wish had been otherwise. As for *Sozomen*'s correspondency with Hereticks,
having shewed to what end the Church did first ordain *Penitentiaries*, he addeth
immediately that *Novatianists*, which had no care of repentance, could have
no need of this office. Are these the words of a friend or enemy? Besides, in
the entrance of that whole narration : *Not to sin* (saith he) *at all would require
a nature more divine then ours is; But God hath commanded to pardon sinners; yea, although they transgresse and offend often.* Could there be any thing spoken more
directly opposite to the Doctrine of *Novatian ? Eudæmon* was Presbyter under
Nectarius.

To *Novatianists* the Emperor gave liberty of using their Religion quietly by
themselves, under a Bishop of their own, even within the City, for that they
stood with the Church in defence of the Catholick faith against all other Hereticks besides. Had therefore *Eudæmon* favoured their heresie, their Camps were
not pitched so far off, but he might at all times have found easie accesse unto
them. Is there any man that lived with him and hath touched him that way?
if not, why suspect we him more then *Nectarius?* Their report touching Grecian Catholick Bishops, who gave approbation to that which was done, and did
also the like themselves in their own Churches, we have no reason to discredit
without some manifest and clear evidence brought against it. For of Catholick
Bishops, no likelihood but that their greatest respect to *Nectarius*, a man honored in those parts no lesse then the Bishop of *Rome* himself in the western Churches, brought them both easily and speedily unto conformity with him, *Arrians, Eunomians, Apollinarians,* and the rest that stood divided from the Church,
held their *Penitentiaries* as before. *Novatianists* from the beginning had never
any; because their opinion touching penitency was against the practice of the
Church therein; and a cause why they severed themselves from the Church; so
that the very state of things as they then stood, giveth great shew of probability to his speech, who hath affirmed, that *they only which held the Son consubstantial with the Father, and Novatianists which joyned with them in the same opinion, had
no Penitentiaries in their Churches, the rest retained them.* By this it appeareth therefore how *Baronius* finding the relation plain, that *Nectarius* did abolish even
those private secret confessions which the people had been before accustomed
to make to him, that was *Penitentiary*, laboureth what he may to discredit the
Authors of the report, and to leave it imprinted in mens minds, that whereas
Nectarius did but abrogate publick confession, *Novatianists* have maliciously forged the abolition of private, as if the ods between these two were so great in the

ballance

ballance of their judgment, which equally hated and contemned both; or, as if it were not more clear then light that the first alteration which established *Penitentiaries,* took away the burthen of publick confession in that kind of penitents, and therefore the second must either abrogate private, or nothing.

Cardinal *Bellarmine* therefore finding that against the Writers of the History, it is but in vain to stand upon so doubtful terms, and exceptions, endeavoureth mightily to prove even by their report, no other confession taken away then publick used in private to impose upon publick offenders; For why? It is (saith he) *very certain that the name of Penitents in the Fathers writings signifieth onely publick penitents; certain, that to hear the confessions of the rest was more then one could possibly have done; certain, that Sozomen, to shew how the Latine Church retained in his time what the Greek had clean cast off, declareth the whole order of publick penitency used in the Church of Rome, but of private he maketh no mention.* And in these considerations *Bellarmine* will have it the meaning both of *Socrates* and *Sozomen,* that the former Episcopal constitution, which first did erect *Penitentiaries,* could not concern any other offenders, then such as publickly had sinned after Baptisn. That onely they, were prohibited to come to the holy Communion, except they did first in secret confesse all their sins to the *Penitentiary,* by his appointment openly acknowledge their open crimes and do publick penance for them: that whereas before *Novatians* uprising, no man was constrainable to confesse publickly any sin, this Canon enforced publick offenders thereunto, till such time as *Nectarius* thought good to extinguish the practice thereof.

Let us examine therefore these subtile and fine conjectures, whether they be able to hold the touch, *It seemed good* (saith *Socrates*) *to put down the Office of these Priests which had charge of Penitency; what charge that was, the kinds of penitency then usual must make manifest.* There is often speech in the Fathers Writings, in their Books frequent mention of Penitency, exercised within the chambers of our heart and seen of God, and not communicated to any other, the whole charge of which penitency is imposed of God, and doth rest upon the sinner himself. But if Penitents in secret being guilty of crimes whereby they knew they had made themselves unfit guests for the Table of our Lord, did seek direction for their better performance of that which should set them clear; it was in this case the *Penitentiaries* office to take their confessions, to advise them the best way he could for their souls good, to admonish them, to counsel them, but not to lay upon them more then private penance. As for notorious wicked persons, whose crimes were known, to convict, judge, and punish them, was the office of the Ecclesiastical Consistory; *Penitentiaries* had their institution to another end: But unlesse we imagine that the ancient time knew no other repentance then publick, or that they had little occasion to speak of any other repentance, or else that in speaking thereof they used continually some other name, and not the name of repentance, wherby to expresse private penitency, how standeth it with reason, that whensoever they write of Penitents, it should be thought they meant onely publick Penitents? The truth is, they handle all three kinds, but private and voluntary repentance much oftner, as being of far more general use, whereas publick was but incident unto few, and not ofter then once incident unto any. Howbeit, because they do not distinguish one kind of penitency from another by difference of names, our safest way for construction, is to follow circumstance of matter, which in this Narration will not yeild it self appliable onely unto publick penance, do what they can, that would so expound it.

They boldly and confidently affirm that no man being compellable to confesse publickly any sin, before *Novatians* time, the end of instituting *Penitentiaries* afterward in the Church, was that by them, men might be constrained unto publick confession. Is there any record in the world which doth testifie this to be true? There is that testifieth the plain contrary; For *Sozomen* declaring purposely the cause of their institution, saith. *that whereas men openly craving pardon at Gods hands (for publick confession the last act of penitency was alwaies*

made

made in the form of a contrite prayer unto God,) it could not be avoided, but they must with a l confesse what their offences were; This in the opinion of their Prelate seemed, from the first beginning (as we may probably think) to be somewhat burthensome, that men whose crimes were unknown, should blaze their own faults, as it were on the Stage, acquainting all the people with whatsoever they had done amisse. And therefore to remedy this inconvenience, they laid the charge upon one onely Priest, chosen out of such as were of best conversation, a silent and a discreet man, to whom they which had offended, might resort and lay open their lives. He according to the quality of every ones transgressions, appointed what they should do or suffer, and left them to execute it upon themselves. Can we with a more direct and evident testimony, that the office here spoken of, was to ease voluntary penitents from the burthen of publick confessions, and not to constrain notorious offenders thereunto? That such offenders were not compellable to open confessions till *Novatians* time, that is to say, till after the dayes of persecution under *Decius* the Emperour, they of all men should not so peremptorily avouch; which whom, if *Fabian* Bishop of *Rome*, who suffered Martyrdom the first year of *Decius*, be of any authority and credit, it must enforce them to reverse their sentence, his words are so plain and clear against them. For *such as commit those crimes whereof the Apostle hath said, They that do them shall never inherit the Kingdom of heaven, must* (saith he) *be forced unto amendment, because they slip down to hel, if Ecclesiastical Authority stay them not* Their conceit of impossibility that one man should suffice to take the general charge of penitency in such a Church as *Constantinople,* hath risen from a meer erroneous supposal, that the Ancient manner of private confession was like the shrift at this day usual in the Church of *Rome,* which tyeth all men at one certain time to make confession, whereas confession was then neither looked for till men did offer it, nor offered for the most part by any other, then such as were guilty of hainous transgressions, nor to them any time appointed for that purpose. Finally, the drift which *Sozomen* had in relating the Discipline of *Rome,* and the form of publick penitency there retained even till his time, is not to signifie that onely publick confession was abrogated by *Nectarius,* but that the West or Latine Church held still one and the same order from the very beginning, and had not, as the Greek, first cut off publick voluntary confession, by ordaining, and then private by removing *Penitentiaries.* Wherefore to conclude, it standeth I hope very plain and clear, first against the one Cardinal, that *Nectarius* did truly abrogate confession in such sort as the Ecclesiastical History hath reported; and secondly, as clear against them both, that it was not publick confession onely which *Nectarius* did abolish.

Fab. Decreta Ep. 2. Tom. 1. Conc p. 358.

The paradox in maintenance whereof *Hessels* wrote purposely a book touching this Argument to shew that *Nectarius* did but put the *Penitentiary* from his office, and not take away the office it self, is repugnant to the whole advice which *Eudæmon* gave, of leaving the people from that time forward to their own Consciences, repugnant to the conference between *Socrates* and *Eudæmon,* wherein complaint is made of some inconvenience, which the want of the office would breed; finally, repugnant to that which the History declareth concerning other Churches which did as *Nectarius* had done before them, not in deposing the same man (for that was impossible) but in removing the same office out of their Churches, which *Nectarius* had banished from his. For which cause *Bellarm.* doth well reject the opinion of *Hessels,* howsoever it please *Pamelius* to admire it as a wonderful happy invention. But in sum, they are all gravelled, no one of them able to go smoothly away, and to satisfie either others, or himself, with his own conceit concerning *Nectarius.*

Nec est quod sibi blandiantur illi de facto Nectarii cum id potius secretorum pec-catorum confessionem concernat, & non probet, & non aliud quam Presbyterum pænitentialem tilo officio suo moverit, uti amplissime deducit D. Iones Hessellus Pamel. in Cypr. lib. de annot. 58. & in lib. Tertul. de pœn. annot. a

Onely in this they are stiffe, that Auricular Confession *Nectarius* did not abrogate, least if so much should be acknowledged, it might enforce them to grant that the Greek Church at that time held not confession, as the Latin now doth, to be the part of a Sacrament instituted by our Saviour Jesus Christ, which therefore the Church till the worlds end hath no power to alter. Yet

X n 2   *seeing*

seeing that as long as publick voluntary confeſſion of private crimes did continue in either Church (as in the one it remained not much above 200. years,
in the other about 400) the only acts of ſuch repentance were; firſt, the offenders intimation of thoſe crimes to ſome one Presbyter, for which impoſition of
penance was ſought; ſecondly, the undertaking of penance impoſed by the
Biſhop; thirdly, after the ſame performed and ended, open confeſſion to God
in the hearing of the whole Church; whereupon fourthly, enſued the prayer
of the Church; fifthly, then the Biſhops impoſition of hands; and ſo ſixthly,
the parties reconciliation or reſtitution to his former right in the holy Sacrament. I would gladly know of them which make only private confeſſion a part
of their Sacrament of penance, how it could be ſo in thoſe times: For where
the Sacrament of penance is miniſtred, they hold that confeſſion to be Sacramental which he receiveth who muſt abſolve; whereas during the fore-re-
hearſed manner of penance, it can no where be ſhewed, that the Prieſt to whom
ſecret information was given, did reconcile, or abſolve any: for, how could he
when publick confeſſion was to go before reconciliation, and reconciliation
likewiſe in publick thereupon to enſue? ſo that if they did account any confeſſion Sacramental, it was ſurely publick, which is now aboliſht in the Church
of *Rome*; and as for that which the Church of *Rome* doth ſo eſteem, the Ancient neither had it in ſuch eſtimation, nor thought it to be of ſo abſolute neceſſity for the taking away of ſin: But (for any thing that I could ever obſerve
out of them) although not onely in crimes open and notorious, which made
men unworthy and uncapable of holy myſteries, their Diſcipline required, firſt
publick penance, and then granted that which S. *Hierom* mentioneth, ſaying,
*The Prieſt layeth his hand upon the penitent, and by invocation intreateth that the holy
Ghoſt may return to him again, and ſo after having enjoyned ſolemnly all the people to
pray for him, reconcileth to the Altar him who was delivered to Satan for the deſtruction of his fleſh, that his Spirit might be ſafe in the day of the Lord.* Although I ſay
not onely in ſuch offences being famouſly known to the world, but alſo if
the ſame were committed ſecretly, it was the cuſtom of thoſe times, both that
private intimation ſhould be given, and publick confeſſion made thereof, in
which reſpect whereas all men did willingly the one, but would as willingly
have withdrawn themſelves from the other, had they known how: *Is it tolerable,* (ſaith S. *Ambroſe*) *that to ſue to God thou ſhouldſt be aſhamed, which bluſh-
eſt not to ſeek and ſue unto man? ſhould it grieve thee to be a ſuppliant to him from
whom thou canſt not poſſible hide thy ſelf, when to open thy ſins to him, from whom,
if thou wouldſt, thou mighteſt conceal them, it doth not any thing at all trouble thee?
This thou art loath to do in the Church, where all being ſinners, nothing is more
opprobrious indeed then concealment of ſin, the moſt humble the beſt thought of, and
the lowlieſt accounted the juſteſt.* All this notwithſtanding, we ſhould do them
very great wrong, to father any ſuch opinion upon them, as if they did teach
it a thing impoſſible for any ſinner to reconcile himſelf unto God, without
confeſſion unto the Prieſt.

Would *Chryſoſtom* thus perſwaded have ſaid, *Let the enquiry and puniſhment of
thy offences be made in thine own thoughts, let the Tribunal whereat thou arraigneſt
thy ſelf be without witneſſe, Let God and onely God ſee thee and thy confeſſion.*

Would *Caſſianus* ſo believing have given counſell, *That if any were with-
held with baſhfulneſſe from diſcovering their faults to men, they ſhould be ſo much
the more inſtant and conſtant in opening them by ſupplication to God himſelf, whoſe
wont is to help without publication of mens ſhame, and not to upbraid them when he
pardoneth?*

Finally, would *Proſper* ſetled in this opinion have made it, as touching reconciliation to God, a matter indifferent, *Whether men of Eccleſiaſtical order did
detect their crimes by confeſſion, or leaving the world ignorant thereof, would ſeparate voluntarily themſelves for a time from the Altar, though not in affection, yet in execution*

of

Sacerdos impo-
nit manum
ſubjecto, redi-
tum ſpiritus
ſancti invocat,
atque ita eum
qui traditus
fuerat Satanæ
in interitum
carnis, ut ſpi-
ritus ſalvus
fieret, indicta
in populum o-
ratione altari
reconciliat.
Hier. adverſ.
Lucif.
Ambr. de pæn.
l. 2. c. 10.

Chryſ. hom:
περὶ μετανοίας
ἐξετασμός ἔστω
περὶ τῆς δια-
νοίας ἀμάρτυρον ἔστω τὸ δικαστήριον, ὁ Θεὸς ὁράτω μόνος τὴν ἐξομολόγησιν.

Caſſian. Collat.
20 c. 8.

Proſper. de
vita contempl.
lib. 2. c. 7.

f their Ministry, and so bewail their corrupt life? *Would he haue willed them as he doth, to make bold of it, that the favour of God being either way recovered by ruits of forcible repentance, they should not only receive whatsoever they had lost by sin, but also after this their new enfranchisement, aspire to the endlesse joyes of that supernal City?* To conclude, we every where find the use of confession, especially publick, allowed of, and commended by the Fathers, but that extream and rigorous necessity of Auricular and private confession, which is at this day so mightily upheld by the Church of *Rome*, we find not. First, it was not then the Faith and Doctrine of Gods Church, as of the Papacy at this present. Secondly, that the only remedy for sin after Baptism, is Sacramental penitency. Thirdly, that confession in secret is an essential part thereof. Fourthly, That God himself cannot now forgive sin without the Priest. That because forgivenesse at the hands of the Priest must arise from confession in the offenders; Therefore to confesse unto him, is a matter of such necessity, as being not either in deed, or at the least in desire performed, excludeth utterly from all pardon, and must consequently in Scripture be commanded, wheresoever any promise of forgivnesse is made. No, no; these opinions have youth in their countenance, Antiquity knew them not, it never thought nor dreamed of them.

But to let passe the Papacy. For as much as Repentance doth import alteration within the mind of a sinful man, whereby through the power of Gods most gracious and blessed Spirit, he seeth, and with unfained sorrow acknowledgeth former offences committed against God, hath them in utter detestation, seeketh pardon for them in such sort as a Christian should do, and with a resolute purpose settleth himself to avoid them, leading as near as God shall assist him for ever after an unspotted life; And in the order (which Christian Religion hath taught for procurment of Gods mercy towards sinners) confession is acknowledged a principal duty; Yea, in some cases, confession to man, not to God only; It is not in reformed Churches denied by the Learneder sort of Divines, but that even this confession, cleared from all errours, is both lawful and behoveful for Gods people.

Calv Instit: lib: 3, cap.4. sect 7.

Confession by man being either private or publick, private confession to the Minister alone touching secret crimes, or absolution thereupon ensuing, as the one, so the other is neither practised by the French Discipline, nor used in any of those Churches, which have bin cast by the French mould. Open confession to be made in the face of the whole Congregation by notorious Malefactors, they hold necessary; Howbeit not necessary towards the remission of sins; But only in some sort to content the Church, and that one mans repentance may seem to strengthen many, which before have weakned by one mans fall.

Sed tantum ut Ecclesia sit aliqua ratione satisfactum, & omnes unius pœnitentia confirmentur, qui fuerant unius peccatis & scandalis vulnerati. Sadeel in ps. 32 v. 5

Saxonians and *Bohemians* in their Discipline constrain no man to open confession: Their Doctrine is, that whose faults have been publick and thereby scandalous unto the world, such when God giveth them the spirit of repentance, ought as solemnly to return, as they have openly gone astray. First, for the better testimony of their own unfained conversion unto God. Secondly, the more to notifie their reconcilement unto the Church: And lastly, that others may make benefit of their example.

But concerning confession in private; the Churches of *Germany*, as well the rest, as *Lutherans* agree, that all men should at certain times confesse their offences to God in the hearing of Gods Ministers, thereby to shew how their sins displease them, to receive instruction for the warier carriage of themselves hereafter, to be soundly resolved, if any scruple or snare of conscience do entangle their minds, and which is most material, to the end that men may at Gods hands seek every one his own particular pardon, through the power of those Keyes, which the Minister of God using according to our blessed Saviours Institution in that case, it is their part to accept the benefit thereof as Gods most merciful Ordinance for their good,

Harm Confess. Sect. 8 ex. 5. cap confess. Bohem.

and

and without any diftruft or doubt, to embrace joyfully his grace fo given them, according to the word of our Lord, which hath faid, *Whofe fins ye remit are remitted.* So that grounding upon this affured belief, they are to reft with minds encouraged and perfwaded concerning the forgiveneffe of all their fins, as out of Chrifts own word and power by the Miniftry of the Keyes.

Cap. 5. Confeff. Bohem.

It ftandeth with us in the Church of *England*, as touching publick confeffion thus :

Firft, feeing day by day we in our Church begin our publick Prayers to Almighty God, with publick acknowledgement of our fins, in which confeffion every man proftrate as it were before his glorious Majefty, cryeth againft himfelf, and the Minifter with one fentence pronounceth univerfally all clear, whofe acknowledgement fo made hath proceeded from a true penitent mind; What reafon is there, every man fhould not under the general terms of confeffion reprefent to himfelf his own particulars whatfoever, and adjoyning thereunto that affection which a contrite fpirit worketh, embrace to as full effect the words of Divine grace, as if the fame were feverally and particularly uttered with addition of prayers, impofition of hands, or all the ceremonies and folemnities that might be ufed for the ftrengthening of mens affiance in Gods peculiar mercy towards them ? Such complements are helps to fupport our weakneffe, and not caufes that ferve to procure or produce his gifts, as *Davids* fpeaketh, the difference of general and particular Forms in confeffion and abfolution is not fo material, that any mans fafety or ghoftly good fhould depend upon it. And for private confeffion and abfolution, it ftandeth thus with us.

As for private confeffion, abufes and errors fet apart, we condemn it not, but leave it at liberty. *Iewel defen. part.* 156.

The Minifters power to abfolve is publickly taught and profeffed, the Church not denyed to have authority either of abridging, or enlarging the ufe and exercife of that power; upon the people no fuch neceffity impofed of opening their tranfgreffions unto men, as if remiffion of fins otherwife were impoffible, neither any fuch opinion had of the thing it felf, as though it were either unlawful or unprofitable, faving only for thefe inconveniences, which the world hath by experience obferved in it heretofore. And in regard thereof, the Church of *England* hitherto hath thought it the fafer way to refer mens hidden crimes unto God and themfelves only ; Howbeit not without fpecial caution for the admonition of fuch as come to the holy Sacrament, and for the comfort of fuch as are ready to depart the world. Firft, becaufe there are but few that confider how much that part of Divine Service which confifts in partaking the holy Eucharift doth import their fouls, what they loofe by neglect thereof, and what by devout practice they might attain unto, therefore leaft carelefneffe of general confeffion fhould as commonly it doth extinguifh all remorfe of mens particular enormous crimes. Our cuftom (whenfoever men prefent themfelves at the Lords Table) is folemnly to give themfelves fearful admonition, what woes are perpendicularly hanging over the heads of fuch as dare adventure to put forth their unworthy hands to thofe admirable myfteries of life, which have by rare examples been proved conduits of irremediable death to impenitent Receivers, whom therefore as we repel being known, fo being not known we can but terrifie. Yet with us, the Minifters of Gods moft holy Word and Sacraments, being all put in truft with the cuftody and difpenfation of thofe myfteries, wherein our Communion is and hath been ever accounted the higheft grace that men on earth are admitted unto, have therefore all equally the fame power to with-hold that facred myftical food from notorious evil livers, from fuch as have any way wronged their neighbours, and from parties between whom there doth open hatred and malice appear, till the firft fort have reformed their wicked lives, the fecond recompenfed them unto whom they were injurious, and the laft condefcended unto fome courfe of Chriftian reconciliation, whereupon their mutual accord may enfue. In which cafes for the firft branch

of

f wicked life, and the laſt which is open enmity, there can ariſe no great
difficulty about the exerciſe of his power: In the ſecond, concerning
wrongs, there may if men ſhall preſume to define or meaſure injuries, according to their own conceits depraved oftentimes; aſwel by error, as par-
iality, and that no leſſe in the Miniſter himſelf, then in another of the
people under him.

The knowledge therefore which he taketh of wrongs muſt riſe as it doth
in the other two, not from his own opinion or con-
cience, but from the evidence of the fact which is
committed; Yea, from ſuch evidence as neither
doth admit denial nor defence. For if the offender
having either colour of Law to uphold, or any
other pretence to excuſe his own uncharitable and
wrongful dealings, ſhall wilfully ſtand in defence
thereof, it ſerveth as a bar to the power of the Mi-
niſter in this kind. Becauſe (as it is obſerved by men of very good judgement in theſe affairs,) although in this ſort our ſeparating of them be not
to ſtrike them with the mortal wound of Excommunication, but to ſtay them
rather from running deſperately headlong into their own harm, yet it is not
in us, to ſever from the holy Communion, but ſuch as are either found culpable by their own confeſſion, or have been convicted in ſome publick, ſecular, Eccleſiaſtical Court. For, who is he, that
dares take upon him to be any mans both accuſer and
judge? Evil perſons are not raſhly, and as we liſt to
be thruſt from Communion with the Church, inſo-
much that if we cannot proceed againſt them by any
orderly courſe of judgement, they rather are to be
ſuffered for the time then moleſted. Many there are
reclaimed, as *Peter*; Many as *Judas* known well enough,
and yet tollerated; Many which muſt remain un-
deſcried till the day of his appearance, by whom the ſecret corners of dark-
neſſe ſhall be brought into open light.

Leaving therefore unto his judgement, them, whom we cannot ſtay from
caſting their own ſouls into ſo great hazard, we have in the other part of
penitential Juriſdiction in our power, and Authority to releaſe ſin, joy on
all ſides, without trouble or moleſtation unto any. And if to give, be a
thing more bleſſed then to receive, are we not infinitely happier in being authorized to beſtow the Treaſure of God, then when neceſſity doth conſtrain
to with-draw the ſame.

They which during life and health are never deſtitute of wayes to delude
repentance, do notwithſtanding oftentimes when their laſt hour draweth on,
both feel that ſting which before lay dead in them, and alſo thirſt after ſuch
helps as have been alwayes till then unſavoury; St. *Ambros* words touching
late repentance are ſomewhat hard, I *a man be penitent and receive abſolution*
(which cannot in that caſe be denied him) even at the very point of death, and ſo
depart, I dare not affirm he goeth out of the world well; I will counſel no man to
truſt to this, becauſe I am loth to deceive any man, ſeeing I know not what to think of
it; ſhall I judge ſuch a one a caſt away? Neither I will avouch him ſafe: *All I am*
able to ſay, is, Let his eſtate be left to the will and pleaſure of Almighty God: Wilt
thou be therefore delivered of all doubt? Repent while yet thou art healthy and
ſtrong: If thou defer it till time give no longer poſſibility of ſinning, thou canſt not be
thought to have left ſin, but rather ſin to have forſaken thee. Such admonitions
may in their time and place be neceſſary, but in no wiſe prejudicial to the
generality of Gods own high and heavenly promiſe, *Whenſoever a ſinner doth*
repent from the bottom of his heart, I will put out all his iniquity. And of this,
although it have pleaſed God not to leave to the world any multitude of examples, leaſt the careleſſe ſhould too far preſume, yet one he hath given,
and that moſt memorable to with-hold from deſpair in the mercies of God,

Non à communione quemquam prohibere
non poſſumus, quamvis hæc prohibitio non-
dum ſit mortalis, ſed medicinalis, niſi aut
ſponte confeſſum, aut aliquo ſive ſeculari, ſi-
ve Eccleſiaſtico judicio accuſatum atq; con-
victum. Quis enim ſibi utrumq; audet aſſu-
mere ut cuiquam ipſe ſit & accuſator & ju-
dex?

Non enim temere & quodammodo libet,
ſed propter judicium ab Eccleſia communione
ſeparandi ſunt mali, ut ſi propter judicium
auferri non poſſint, tolleventur potius, velut
palea cum tritico Multi corriguntur, ut Pe-
trus; mu'ri tolerantur, ut Iudas; multi neſ-
ciuntur, donec veniat Dominus, & illumi-
nabit abſcondita tenebrarum. Rhenàn.
admonit. de dogmat. Tercul.

Lib. 3 de
pœn.

at what instant so ever mans unfained conversion be wrought. Yea, because to countervail the fault of delay, there are in the latest repentance oftentimes the surest tokens of sincere dealing; Therefore upon special confession made to the Minister of God, he presently absolveth in this case the sick party from all sins by that Authority which Jesus Christ hath committed unto him, knowing that God respecteth not so much what time is spent, as what truth is shewed in repentance.

In sum, when the offence doth stand only between God and mans conscience, the Council is good, which St. *Chrysostome* giveth, *I wish thee not to bewray thy self publickly, nor to accuse thy self before others. I wish thee to obey the Prophet who saith, Disclose thy way unto the Lord, confesse thy sins before him, Tell thy sins to him that he may blot them out. If thou be abashed to tell unto any other, wherein thou hast offended, rehearse them every day between thee and thy soul, I wish thee not to confesse them to thy fellow servant, who may upbraid thee with them; Tell them to God, who will cure them; There is no need for thee in the presence of witnesses to acknowledge them; Let God alone see thee at thy Confession; I pray and beseech you that you would more often then you do, confesse to God eternal, and reckoning up your trespasses, desire his pardon: I carry you not into a Theatre or open Court of many your fellow servants, I seek not to detect your crimes before men; Disclose your conscience before God, unfold your selves to him, Lay forth your wounds before him, the best Physitian that is, and desire of him salve for them.* If hereupon it follow, as it did with David, I thought, *I will confesse against my self my wickedness unto thee O Lord, and thou forgavest me the plague of my sin,* we have our desire, and there remaineth only thankfulnesse accompanied with perpetuity of care to avoid that which being not avoided, we know we cannot remedy without new perplexity and grief. Contrariwise, if peace with God do not follow the paines we have taken in seeking after it, if we continue disquieted, and not delivered from anguish, mistrusting whether that we do be sufficient, it argueth that our soar doth exceed the power of our own skill, and that the wisdom of the Pastor must bind up those parts, which being bruised, are not able to be recured of themselves.

Non dico tibi, ut te prodas in publicum, neque ut te apud alios accuses, sed obedire te volo Phophetæ dicenti, Revela Domino viam tuam. Ante Deum confitere peccata tua; Peccata tua dicito ut ea deleat; Si confunderis alicui dicere quæ peccasti, dicito ea quotidie in anima: Non dico ut confitearis conservo qui exprobret; Deo dicito qui ea curat; Non necesse est præsentibus testibus confiteri, solus te Deus confitentem videat. Rogo & oro ut crebrius Deo immortali, confiteamini, & enumeratis vestris delectis veniam petatis. Non te in Theatrum conservorum duco, non hominibus peccata tua conor detegere. Repete coram Deo conscientiam tuam, te explica, ostende medico præstantissimo vulnera tua, & pete ab eo medicamentum, Christ. hom. 31. al Hebr. & in Psal. 59. Hom. de pæn. & confess. & hom 5. de incor. Die natura, homil. item que de Lazare.

Of Satisfaction.

There resteth now Satisfaction only to be considered; A point which the Fathers do often touch, albeit they never aspire to such mysteries as the Papacy hath found, enwrapped within the folds, and plaits thereof: And it is happy for the Church of God that we have the Writings of the Fathers, to shew what their meaning was. The name of satisfaction, as the Ancient Fathers meant it, containeth whatsoever a Penitent should do in the humbling himself unto God, and testifying by deeds of contrition, the same which confession in words pretendeth; *He which by Repentance for sins* (saith Tertullian speaking of fickle minded men) *had a purpose to satisfie the Lord, will now by repenting his repentance make Satan satisfaction, and be so much more hateful to God, as he is unto Gods enemy more acceptable.* Is it not plain that satisfaction doth here include the whole work of penitency, and that God is satisfied, when men are restored through sin into favour by Repentance? *How canst thou* (saith Chrysostom) *move God to pitty thee, when thou wilt not seem as much as to know that thou hast offended?* By appealing, pacifying, and moving God to pitty. St. *Chrysostom* meaneth the very same with the Latin Fathers, when they speak of satisfying God. *We feel* (saith Cyprian) *the bitter smart*

Tertul. de. poenit.

Chry. in 1. Cor. hom 8. de Obir isti adi ou.

{mart of this rod and scourge, because there is in us neither care to please him with our good deeds, nor to satisfie him for our evil. Again, Let the eyes which have looked on Idols sponge out of their unlawful acts with those sorrowful tears, which have power to satisfie God.* The Master of sentences alleadgeth out of St. *Augustine,* that which is plain enough to this purpose. *Three things there are in perfect penitency, Compunction, Confession, and Satisfaction ; that as we three wayes offend God, namely in heart, word, and deed : So by three duties we may satisfie God.*

Cypr. Ep. 3,
Cypr. Ep. 26.
Sentent l. 4.
dist. 16.

Satisfaction, as a part, comprehendeth only that which the Papists meant by *worthy of Repentance ;* and if we speak of the whole work of repentance it self, we may in the phrase of antiquity term it very well satisfaction.

Satisfaction is a work which Justice requireth to be done for contentment of persons injured : Neither is it in the eye of Justice a sufficient satisfaction, unlesse it fully equal the injury for which we satisfie. Seeing then that sin against God Eternal and Infinite, must needs be an infinite wrong : Justice in regard thereof doth necessarily exact an infinite recompense, or else inflict upon the offender infinite punishment. Now because God was thus to be satisfied, and man not able to make satisfaction, in such sort his unspeakable love and inclination to save mankind from eternal death ordained in our behalf a Mediator to do that which had been for any other impossible : Wherefore all sin is remitted in the only faith of Christs passion, and no man without belief thereof justified ; *Bonavent. in sentent.* 4. *dist.* 15. 9. 9. Faith alone maketh Christs satisfaction ours, howbeit that faith alone which after sin maketh us by conversion his.

For in as much as God will have the benefit of Christs satisfaction, both thankfully acknowledged and duly esteemed, of all such as enjoy the same, he therefore imparteth so high a treasure unto no man whose faith hath not made him willing by repentance to do even that which of it self, how unavailable soever, yet being required, and accepted with God, we are in Christ thereby made capable, and fit vessels to receive the fruits of his satisfaction : Yea, we so far please and content God, that because when we have offended, he looketh but for repentance at our hands ; our repentance and the works thereof are therefore termed satisfactory, not for that so much is thereby done as the justice of God can exact, but because such actions of grief and humility in man after sin, are *ilices divinæ misericordiæ* (as *Tertullian* speaketh of them) they draw that pity of Gods towards us, wherein he is for Christs sake contented upon our submission to pardon our rebellion against him; and when that little which his Law appointeth is faithfully executed, it pleaseth him in tender compassion and mercy to require no more.

Repentance is a name which noteth the habit and operation of a certain grace, or vertue in us : Satisfaction, the effect which it hath, either with God or man. And it is not in this respect said amisse, that satisfaction importeth acceptation, reconciliation & amity ; because that through satisfaction on the one part made, and allowed on the other, they which before did reject are now content to receive, they to be won again which were lost, and they to love unto whom just cause of hatred was given. We satisfie therefore in doing that which is sufficient to this effect, and they towards whom we do it are satisfied, if they accept it as sufficient and require no more : Otherwise we satisfie not, although we do satisfie : For so between man and man it oftentimes falleth out, but between man and God, never ; It is therefore true that our Lord Jesus Christ by one most precious and propitiatory sacrifice, which was his body, a gift of infinite worth, offered for the sins of the whole world, hath thereby once reconciled us to God, purchased his general free pardon, and turned away divine indignation from mankind. But we are not for that cause to think, any office of penitence, either needlesse or fruitlesse, on our own behalf. For then would not God require any such duties at our hands; Christ doth remain everlastingly a gracious Intercessour, even for every particular penitent. Let this assure us, that God how highly soever

X x   displeased

displeased and incensed with our sins, is notwithstanding for his sake by our tears pacified, taking that for satisfaction, which is due by us, because Christ hath by his satisfaction made it acceptable. For, as he is the high Priest of our salvation, so he hath made us Priests likewise under him, to the end we might offer unto God praise and thankfulnesse while we continue in the way of life; and when we sin, the satisfactory or propitiatory sacrifice of a broken and a contrite heart. There is not any thing that we do that could pacifie God, and clear us in his sight from sin, if the goodnesse, and mercy of our Lord Jesus Christ were not, whereas now beholding the poor offer of our religious endeavours, meekly to submit our selves as often as we have offended, he regardeth with infinite mercy those services which are as nothing, and with words of comfort reviveth our afflicted minds, saying, *It is I, even I that take away thine iniquities for mine own sake.* Thus doth repentance satisfie God, changing his wrath and indignation unto mercy.

Anger and mercy are in us, passions; but in him not so.

God (saith St. Basil) *is no wayes passionate, but because the punishments which his judgements do inflict, are like effects of indignation severe and grievous to such as suffer them, therefore we term the revenge which he taketh upon sinners anger; and the withdrawing of his plagues, mercy.* His wrath (saith St. Augustine) *is not as ours, the trouble of a mind disturbed and disquieted with things amisse, but a calm, unpassionate, and just assignation of dreadful punishment to be their portion which have disobeyed; his mercy a free determination of all felicity and happinesse unto men, except their sins remain as a bar between it and them.* So that when God doth cease to be angry with sinful men, when he receiveth them into favour; when he pardoneth their offences, and remembreth their iniquities no more, (for all these signifie but one thing) it must needs follow that all punishments before due in revenge of sin, whether they be temporal or eternal are remitted.

For how should Gods indignation import only mans punishment; and yet some punishment remain unto them towards whom there is now in God no indignation remaining ? God (saith Tertullian) *takes penitency at mens hands, and men at his in lieu thereof receive impunity;* which notwithstanding doth not prejudice the chastisements which God after pardon hath laid upon some offenders, as on *a* the people of Israel, on *b* Moses, on *c* Miriam, on *d* David, either for their own *e* more sound amendment, or for *f* example unto others in this present world (for in the world to come, punishments have unto these intents no use; the dead being not in case to be better by correction, nor to take warning by executions of Gods Justice there seen) but assuredly to whomsoever he remitteth sin, their very pardon is in it self a full, absolute and perfect discharge for revengeful punishment, which God doth now here threaten, but with purpose of revocation, if men repent, no where inflict but on them whom impenitency maketh obdurate.

Of the one therefore it is said, *Though I tell the wicked, Thou shalt die the death, yet if he turneth from his sin, and do that which is lawful and right, he shall surely live and not die.* Of the other, *Thou according to thy hard burdnesse, and heart that will not repent, treasurest up to thy self wrath against the day of wrath, and evident appearance of the judgement of God.* If God be satisfied and do pardon sin, our justification restored is as perfect as it was at the first bestowed : For so the Prophet Isaiah witnesseth, *Though your sins were as crimson, they shall be made as white as snow, though they were as scarlet, they shall be as white as wooll.* And can we doubt concerning the punishment of revenge, which was due to sin, but that if God be satisfied, and have forgotten his wrath, it must be even as St. Augustine reasoneth, *g What God hath covered, he will not observe, and what he observeth not, he will not punish.* The truth of which doctrine is not to be shifted off by restraining it unto eternal punishment alone : For then would not David have said, *They are blessed to whom God imputeth not sin;* blessednesse having no part or fellowship at all with malediction : Whereas to be subject to revenge for sin, although the punishment be but temporal, is to be under

Apoc. 1. 6.

Cassia.coll. 20. c. 8.

Bas. hom in Psal 37. καιτ Θ· γὲ τωδεςμὸς τοιο, τὸ Θῖιι.

Cum Deus irascitur, non eius significatur perturbatio qualis est in animo irascentis hominis sed ex humanis motibus translato vocabulo, vindicta eius quae non nisi justa est, ira nomen accepit. Aug.tom.3, Ench c.33.

Poenitentiae compensatione redimendam proponit impunitatem Deus, Tertull. de poen.

aNum 14.11
bNum.20 12
cNum 12.14
d:Sam 12.14
e Cui Deus vera propitius est non solum condonat peccata ne noceant ad futurum seculum, sed etiam castigat nescienter peccare desinet. Aug. in Psal 98.
f Eliguntur quidam quorum corriguntur exempla sunt omnium, eximuntur pauciorum. Cypr. de lapsis.

Ezec. 33. 14. Rom. 2. 5 Es. 1. 18.
g Si texit Deus peccata, noluit advertere, si noluit advertere noluit animadvertere.

under the curse of the Law; wherefore, as one and the same fire consumeth stubble and refineth gold, so if it please God to lay punishment on them whose sins he hath forgiven; yet is not this done for any destructive end of wasting and eating them out, as in plagues inflicted upon the impenitent, neither is the punishment of the one as of the other proportioned by the greatnesse of sin past, but according to that future purpose, whereunto the goodnesse of God referreth it, and wherein there is nothing meant to the sufferer, but furtherance of all happinesse, now in grace, and hereafter in glory; St. *Augustine*, to stop the mouths of *Pelagians*, arguing, *That if God had imposed death upon Adam and Adams posterity, as a punishment of sin, death should have ceased when God had procured sinners their pardon .* Answereth first, *It is no marvel, either that bodily death should not have happned to the first man, unlesse he had first sinned, (death as a punishment following his sin) or that after sin is forgiven, death notwithstanding befalleth the faithful, to the end that the strength of righteousnesse might be exercised, by overcomming the fear thereof.* So that justly God did inflict bodily death on man for committing sin, and yet after sin forgiven, took it not away; that his righteousnesse might still have whereby to be exercised. He fortifieth this with *Davids* example, whose sin he forgave, and yet afflicted him for exercise and tryal of his humility. Briefly, a general axiome he hath for all such chastisements, *Before forgivenesse, they are the punishment of sinners, and after forgivenesse, they are exercises and trials of righteous men.* Which kind of proceeding is so agreeable with Gods nature and mans comfort, that it sheweth even injurious to both, if we should admit those surmised reservations of temporall wrath, in God appeased towards reconciled sinners. As a Father he delights in his childrens conversion, neither doth he threaten the penitent with wrath, or them with punishment which already mourn; but by promise assureth such of indulgence and mercy; yea, even of plenary pardon which taketh away all both faults and penalties: There being no reason why we should think him the lesse just because he sheweth him thus merciful, when they which before were obstinate labour to appease his wrath with the pensive meditation of contrition, the meek humility which confession expresseth, and the deeds wherewith repentance declareth it self to be an amendment as well of the rotten fruits, as the dried leaves and withered root of the tree. For with these duties by us performed and presented unto God in heaven by Jesus Christ, whose blood is a continual sacrifice of propitiation for us, we content, please, and satisfie God. Repentance therefore, even the sole vertue of Repentance without either purpose of shrift or desire of absolution from the Priest ; Repentance the secret conversion of the heart, in that it consisteth of these three; and doth by these three pacifie God ; may be without hyperbolical terms most truly magnified, as a recovery of the soul of man from deadly sicknesse, a restitution of glorious light to his darkned mind, a comfortable reconciliation with God, a spiritual nativity, a rising from the dead, a day spring from out the depth of obscurity, a redemption from more then the *Egyptian* thraldom, a grinding of the old *Adam*, even into dust and powder, a deliverance out of the prisons of hell, a full restauration of the Seat of Grace, and Throne of Glory, a triumph over sin, and a saving Victory.

Amongst the works of satisfaction, the most respected have been alwayes these three, Prayers, Fasts, and Almes deeds; by prayers, we lift up our souls to him from whom sin and iniquity hath withdrawn them ; by fasting, we reduce the body from thraldom under vain delights, and make it serviceable for parts of vertuous conversation; by Almes, we dedicate to charity those worldly goods and possessions, which unrighteousnesse doth neither get, nor bestow well : The first a token of pity intended towards God; the second a pledge of moderation and sobriety in the carriage of our own persons; the last, a testimony of our meaning to do good to all men. In which three, the Apostle by way of abridgement comprehendeth whatsoever may appertain to sanctimony, holinesse, and good life : As contrariwise the very masse of general cor-

X x 2   ruption

ruption throughout the world, what is it but only forgetfulnefs of God, carnal pleasure, immoderate desire after worldly things, prophanefs, licentioufnefs, coveteoufnefs? All offices to repentance have thefe two properties; there is in performance of them painfulneffe, and in their nature a contrariety unto fin. The one confideration, caufeth them both in holy Scripture and elfewhere to be termed judgement or revenges taken voluntarily on our felves, and to be furthermore alfo prefervatives from future evils, in as much we commonly ufe to keep with the greater care that which with pain we have recovered. And they are in the other refpect contrary to fin committed, contrition, contrary to the pleafure; confeffion, to the errour, which is mother of fin; and to the deeds of fin, the works of fatisfaction contrary; therefore they are the more effectual to cure the evil habit thereof: Hereunto it was that S. *Cyprian* referred his earneft and vehement exhortations, *That they which had fallen, fhould be inftant in prayer, reject bodily ornaments, when once they had ftripped themfelves out of Chrifts attire, abhor all food after Satans morfels tafted, follow works of righteoufneffe, which wafh away fin, and be plentiful in alms deeds wherewith fouls are delivered from death. Not, as if God did according to the manner of corrupt Judges, take fome money to abate fo much in the punifhment of Malefactors.* Thefe duties muft be offered (faith Salvianus) *not in confidence to redeem or buy out fin, but as tokens of meek fubmiffion; neither are they with God accepted, becaufe of their value, but for the affections fake, which doth thereby fhew it felf.* Wherefore concerning fatisfaction made to God by Chrift only, and of the manner how repentance generally, particularly alfo, how certain fpecial works of penitency, both are by the Fathers in their ordinary phrafe of fpeech called fatisfactory, and may be by us very well fo acknowledged, enough hath been fpoken.

Our offences fometimes are of fuch nature as requireth that particular men be fatisfied, or elfe repentance to be utterly void, & of none effect. For, if either through open repine or cloaked fraud, if through injurious; or unconfcionable dealing a man have wittingly wronged others to enrich himfelf, the firft thing evermore in this cafe required (ability ferving) is reftitution: For let no man deceive himfelf, from fuch offences we are not difcharged, neither can be, till recompence and reftitution to man, accompany the penitent confeffion we have made to Almighty God. In which cafe the Law of *Mofes* was direct and plain, *If any fin and commit a trefpaffe againft the Lord, and deny unto his neighbours that which was given him to keep, or that which was put unto him of truft, or doth by robbery, or by violence oppreffe his neighbour; or hath found that which was loft and denyeth it, and fwear falfly, for any of thefe things that a man doth wherein he finneth, he that doth thus offend and trefpaffe, fhall reftore the robbery that he hath taken, or the thing he hath gotten by violence, or that which was delivered him to keep, or the loft thing which he found; and for whatfoever he hath fworn falfly; adding perjury to injury, he fhall both reftore the whole fum and fhall adde thereunto a fift part more, and deliver it unto him, unto whom it belongeth, the fame day wherein he offereth for his trefpaffe.* Now becaufe men are commonly overflack to perform this duty, and do therefore defer it fometime, till God have taken the party wronged out of the world, the Law providing that trefpaffers might not under fuch pretence gain the reftitution which they ought to make, appointeth the kindred furviving to receive what the dead fhould, if they had continued. But (faith Mofes) *if the party wronged have no kinfman to whom this damage may be reftored, it fhall then be rendered to the Lord himfelf for the Priefts ufe.* The whole order of proceeding herein is in fundry traditional writings fet down by their great Interpreters and Scribes, which taught them that a trefpaffe between a man and his neighbour, can never be forgiven till the offender have by reftitution made recompence for wrongs done; yea, they hold it neceffary that he appeafe the party grieved by fubmitting himfelf unto him, or, if that will not ferve, by ufing the help and mediation of others; in this cafe (fay they) *for any man to fhew himfelf unappeafable and cruel, were a fin moft grievous, confidering that the people of God fhould be eafie to relent, as Jofeph was
towards*

2 Cor 7. 11.
Cypr. de lapfis
Salv. ad Eccl. Cath. lib. 1.
Levit. 6. 2.
Numb. 5. 8.

towards his brethren; finally, if so it fall out that the death of him which was injured, prevent his submission which did offend, let him then (for so they determine that he ought) go accompanied with ten others unto the Sepulchre of the dead, and there make confession of the fault, saying, *I have sinned against the Lord God of Israel, and against this man, to whom I have done such or such injury; and if money be due, let it be restored to his heirs, or in case he have none known, leave it with the house of judgement.* That is to say, with the Senators, Ancients and Guides of *Israel*; we hold not Christian people tyed unto Jewish orders, for the manner of restitution; but surely restitution, we must hold necessary as well in our own repentance as theirs, for sins of wilfull oppression and wrong.

Quandiu enim res propter quam peccatum est, non redditur, si reddi potest, non agitur pœnitentia sed fingitur. Sent. 4.d.15.

Now although it suffices, that the offices wherewith we pacifie God or private men, be secretly done; yet in cases where the Church must be also satisfied, it was not to this end and purpose unnecessary, that the ancient Discipline did farther require outward signes of contrition to be shewed, confession of sins to be made openly, and those works to be apparent which served as testimonies for conversion before men. Wherein, if either hypocrisie did at any time delude their judgement, they knew, that God is he whom masks and mockeries cannot blind, that he which seeth mens hearts would judge them according unto his own evidence, and as Lord, correct the sentence of his servants, concerning matters beyond their reach; Or if such as ought to have kept the rules of Canonical satisfaction, would by sinister means and practices undermine the same, obtruding presumptuously themselves to the participation of Christs most sacred mysteries, before they were orderly readmitted thereunto, the Church for contempt of holy things, held them uncapable of that grace, which God in the Sacrament doth impart to devout Communicants; and no doubt but he himself did retain bound, whom the Church in those cases refused to loose.

Cypr. Ep.l.52.

The Fathers, as may appear by sundry Decrees and Canons of the Primitive Church, were (in matter specially of publick scandal) provident that too much facility of pardoning might not be shewed. *He that casteth off his lawful wife* (saith S. *Basil*) *and doth take another, is adjudged an adulterer by the verdict of our Lord himself; and by our Fathers it is Canonically ordained, that such for the space of a year shall mourn, for two years space hear, three years be prostrate, the seventh year assemble with the faithful in prayer, and after that be admitted to communicate, if with tears they bewail their fault.*

Basil Ep. ad Amphil. c. 26.

Of them which had fallen from their faith in the time of Emperour *Licinius*, and were not thereunto forced by any extream usage, the *Nicen* Synod, under *Constantine* ordained, *That earnestly repenting, they should continue three years Hearers, seven years be prostrate, and two years communicate with the people in prayer, before they came to receive the oblation.* Which rigor sometimes they tempered neverthelesse with lenity, the self same Synod having likewise defined, *That whatsoever the cause were, any man desirous at the time of departure out of this life to receive the Eucharist might (with examination and tryal) have it granted him by the Bishop.* Yea, besides this case of special commiseration, there is a Canon more large which giveth alwayes liberty to abridge, or extend out the time, as the parties meek, or sturdy disposition should require.

Concil. Nycen. can. 11.

By means of which Discipline, the Church having power to hold them many years in suspence, there was bred in the minds of the penitents, thorough long and daily practice of submission, a contrary habit unto that which before had been their ruine, and for ever afterwards warinesse not to fall into those snares, out of which they knew they could not easily wind themselves. Notwithstanding, because there was likewise hope, and possibility of shortning the time, this made them in all the parts and offices of their repentance the more fervent. In the first station, while they only beheld others passing towards the Temple of God, whereunto for themselves to approach, it was not lawfull, they stood as miserable forlorn men, the very patterns of perplexity and woe. In the second, when they had the favour to wait at the doors of

Cant. 13.

God,

God, where the found of his comfortable word might be heard, none received it with attention like to theirs: thirdly, being taken and admitted to the next degree of proſtrates, at the feet, yet behind the back of that Angel repreſenting God, whom the reſt ſaw face to face; their tears, and entreaties both of Paſtor and People were ſuch as no man could reſiſt. After the fourth ſtep which gave them liberty to hear and pray with the reſt of the people, being ſo near the haven, no diligence was then ſlacked which might haſten admiſſion to the heavenly Table of Chriſt their laſt deſire. It is not therefore a thing to be marvelled at, though S. *Cyprian* took it in very ill part, when open backſliders from the faith and ſacred Religion of Chriſt, laboure'd by ſiniſter practice to procure from impriſoned Saints, thoſe requeſts for preſent abſolution, which the Church could neither yield unto with ſafety of Diſcipline, nor in honour of Martyrdom eaſily deny. For, what would thereby enſue, they needed not to conjecture, when they ſaw how every man which came ſo commended to the Church by letters, thought that now he needed not to crave, but might challenge of duty his peace; taking the matter very highly, if but any little forbearance, or ſmall delay was uſed. *He which is overthrown* (ſaith *Cyprian*) *menaceth them that ſtand, the wounded them that were never toucht ; and becauſe preſently he hath not the body of our Lord, in his ſoul imbrued hands, nor the blood within his polluted lips, the miſcreant fumeth at Gods Prieſts; Such is thy madneſſe, O thou furious man ; thou art angry with him, which laboureth to turn away Gods anger from thee; him thou threatneſt which ſueth unto God for grace, and mercy on thy behalf.*

*Jacens ſtanti-
bus, & inte-
gris vulneratus
minatur.*
Ex.12.31.
Jer.7.15.
Ezech.14.14.

Touching Martyrs, he anſwereth, *That it ought not in this caſe to ſeem offenſive, though they were denied, ſeeing God did himſelf refuſe to yeild to the piety of his own righteous Saints, making ſuit for obdurate Jewes.*

As for the parties in whoſe behalf ſuch ſhifts were uſed, to have their deſire, was in very truth, a way to make them the more guilty. Such peace granted contrary to the rigour of the Goſpel, contrary to the Law of our Lord and God, doth but under colour of merciful relaxation deceive ſinners; and by ſoft handling deſtroy them, a grace dangerous for the giver, and to him which receiveth it, nothing at all available. The patient expectation that bringeth health, is by this means not regarded; recovery of ſoundneſſe not ſought for by the onely medicine available, which is ſatisfaction, penitency thrown out of mens hearts, the remembrance of that heavieſt and laſt judgement clean baniſht ; the wounds of dying men, which ſhould be healed, are covered ; the ſtroke of death, which hath gone as deep as any bowels are to receive it, is overcaſt with the ſlight ſhew of a cloudy look. From the Altar of Satan to the holy of the Lord, men are not afraid to come even belching in a manner the ſacrificed morſels they have eaten, yea, their jaws yet breathing out the irkſome ſavour of their former contagious wickedneſſe, they ſeize upon the bleſſed body of our Lord, nothing terrified with that dreadful commination, which ſaith, *Whoſoever eateth and drinketh unworthily, is guilty of the body and blood of Chriſt.* They vainly think it to be peace which is gotten before they be purged of their faults, before their crime be ſolemnly confeſt, before their Conſcience be cleared by the ſacrifice and impoſition of the Prieſts hands, and before they have pacified the indignation of God. Why term they that a favour which is an injury? wherefore cloak they impiety with the name of charitable indulgence? Such facility giveth not, but rather taketh away peace; and is it ſelf another freſh perſecution or tryal, whereby that fraudulent enemy maketh a ſecret havock of ſuch as before he had overthrown; and now to the end he may clean ſwallow them, he caſteth ſorrow in a dead ſleep, putteth grief to ſilence, wipeth away the memory of faults newly done, ſmothereth the ſighs that ſhould riſe from a contrite Spirit, dryeth up eyes, which ought to ſend forth rivers of tears, and permitteth not God to be pacified with full repentance, whom hainous and enormous crimes have diſpleaſed.

1 Cor.11.27.

By this then we ſee that in S. *Cyprians* judgement all abſolutions are void, fruſtrate

fruſtrate and of no effect, without ſufficient repentance firſt ſhewed; Whereas contrariwiſe, if true and full ſatisfaction have gone before, the ſentence of man here given is ratified of God in Heaven, according to our Saviours own ſacred Teſtimony, *Whoſe ſins ye remit, they are remitted.*

By what works in the vertue, and by what in the diſcipline of repentance, we are ſaid to ſatisfie either God or men, cannot now be thought obſcure; As for the Inventers of Sacramental ſatisfaction, they have both altered the natural order heretofore kept in the Church, by bringing in a ſtrange preſterous courſe, to abſolve before ſatisfaction be made, and moreover by this their miſordered practice, are grown into ſundry errours concerning the end whereunto it is referred.

The end of ſatisfaction.

They imagine beyond all conceit of Antiquity, that when God doth remit ſin, and the puniſhment eternal thereunto belonging, he reſerveth the torments of hell fire to be neverthereſſe endured for a time, either ſhorter or longer, according to the quality of mens crimes. Yet ſo that there is between God and man, a certain compoſition (as it were) or contract, by vertue whereof works aſſigned by the Prieſt to be done after abſolution, ſhall ſatisfie God, as touching the puniſhment which he otherwiſe would inflict for ſin pardoned and forgiven.

Now becauſe they cannot aſſure any man, that if he performeth what the Prieſt appointeth, it ſhall ſuffice; This (I ſay) becauſe they cannot do, in as much as the Prieſt hath no power to determine or define of equivalency between ſins and ſatisfactions; And yet if a Penitent depart this life, the debt of ſatisfaction being either in whole or in part undiſcharged, they ſtedfaſtly hold, that the ſoul muſt remain in unſpeakable torment till all be paid; Therefore for help and mitigation in this caſe, they adviſe men to ſet certain copeſmates on work, whoſe prayers and ſacrifices may ſatisfie God for ſuch ſouls as depart in debt. Hence have ariſen the infinite penſions of their Prieſts, the building of ſo many Altars and Tombs, the enriching of Churches with ſo many glorious coſtly gifts, the bequeathing of lands, and ample poſſeſſions to Religious Companies, even with utter forgetfulneſſe of friends, parents, wife and children, all natural affection giving place unto that deſire; which men doubtful of their own eſtate, have to deliver their ſouls from torment after death.

The way of ſatisfying by others.

' Yet, behold even this being done, how far forth it ſhall avail; they are not ſure; And therefore the laſt upſhot unto all their former inventions, is, that as every action of Chriſt, did both merit for himſelf, and ſatisfie partly for the eternal, and partly for the temporal puniſhment due unto men for ſin; So his Saints have obtained the like priviledge of Grace, making every good work they do, not only meritorious in their own behalf, but ſatisfactory too for the benefit of others; Or if, having at any time grievouſly ſinned, they do more to ſatisfie God, then he in juſtice can exact, or look for at their hands, the ſurpluſage runneth to a common ſtock, out of which treaſury, containing whatſoever Chriſt did by way of Satisfaction for temporal puniſhment, together with the ſatisfactory force which reſideth in all the vertuous works of Saints; And in their Satisfactions whatſoever doth abound, (I ſay) *From hence they hold God ſatisfied for ſuch arrereges, as men behind in accompt diſcharge not by other means, and for diſpoſition hereof, as it is their Doctrine, that Chriſt remitteth not eternal death without the Prieſts Abſolution, ſo without the grant of the Pope, they cannot but teach it alike unpoſſible, that Souls in Hell ſhould receive any temporal releaſe of pain. The Sacrament of Pardon from him being to this effect no leſſe neceſſary, than the Prieſts Abſolution to the other.* So that by this poſtern gate cometh in the whole mark of Papal Indulgences, a gain uneſtimable unto him, to others a ſpoil, a ſcorn both to God and Man. So many works of ſatisfaction pretended to be done by Chriſt, by Saints, and Martyrs; So many vertuous acts poſſeſſed with ſatisfactory force and vertue, ſo many ſupererogations in ſatisfying beyond the exigence of their own neceſſity; And this that the Pope might make a

Menopolie

Monopolie of all, turning all to his own gain, or at least to the gain of those which are his own. Such facilitie they have to convert a pretended Sacrament into a Revenue.

Of Absolution of Penitents.

SIn is not helped but by being assecured of Pardon: It resteth therefore to be considered what warrant we have concerning Forgivenesse, when the Sentence of man absolveth us from sin committed against God. At the words of our Saviour, saying, to the sick of the Palsey, *Son, thy sins are forgiven thee,* Exception was taken by the Scribes, who secretly reasoned against him, *Is any able to forgive sins, but only God ?* Whereupon they condemned his speech as blasphemy, the rest which believed him to be a Prophet sent from God, saw no cause wherefore he might not as lawfully say; and as truly, To whomsoever amongst them, *God hath taken away thy sins,* as *Nathan* (they all knew) had used the very like speech, to whom *David* did not therefore impute blasphemy, but imbraced, as became him, the words of truth, with joy and reverence.

Now there is no Controversie, but as God in that special case did authorize *Nathan,* so Christ more generally his Apostles, and the Ministers of his Word, in his Name to absolve sinners. Their power being equal, all the difference between them can be but only in this, that whereas the one had prophetical evidence, the other have the certainty, partly of Faith, and partly of Humane experience, whereupon to ground their sentence; Faith, to assure them of Gods most gracious Pardon in Heaven unto all Penitents, and touching the sincerity of each particular parties repentance as much, as outward sensible tokens or signes can warrant.

It is not to be marvailed that so great a difference appeareth between the Doctrine of *Rome* and *Ours,* when we teach Repentance. They, imply in the Name of Repentance much more than we do ; We stand chiefly upon the due inward Conversion of the Heart, they more upon Works of external shew ; We teach above all things, that Repentance which is one and the same from the beginning to the Worlds end ; They a Sacramental Penance of their own devising and shaping : We labour to instruct men in such sort, that every Soul which is wounded with sin, may learn the way how to cure it self, they clean contrary would make all Soars seem incurable, unlesse the Priests have a hand in them.

sins pœnitẽtis actio nē est pars sacramenti, quatenus tessari Sacdotalisubtur & a erdote igitur vel e-ur- Bell. Pœn. l. t. 16.

riftus inuit Sadotes Judæs super ram cum nor estare, fui i psorum sententia, nemo post Baptum lapsus reconciliari possit. Bell. c. t. De pœnit.

Touching the force of whose Absolution they strangely hold, that whatsoever the Penitent doth, His Contrition, Confession, and Satisfaction have no place of right to stand, as material parts in this Sacrament, nor consequently any such force as to make them available for the taking away of sin, in that they proceed from the Penitent himself without the privity of the Minister, but onely, as they are enjoyned by the Ministers Authority and Power. So that no contrition or grief of heart, till the Priest exact it, no acknowledgement of sins, but that which he doth demand, no praying, no fasting, no alms, no recompence, or restitution for whatsoever we have done, can help, except by him, it be first imposed. It is the chain of their own Doctrine, no remedie for mortal sin committed after Baptisme, but the Sacrament of Penance only : No Sacrament of Penance, if either matter or form be wanting ; No wayes to make those duties a material part of the Sacrament, unlesse we consider them, as required and exacted by the Priest. Our Lord and Saviour, they say, hath ordained his Priests, Judges in such sort, that no man which sinneth after Baptisme, can be reconciled unto God, but by their sentence. For why ? If there were any other way of Reconciliation, the very promise of Christ should be false in saying,

Mat. 9 2
Mark. 5. 22.
Luc. 5. 25.

What-

Whatsoever ye bind on Earth, shall be bound in Heaven, and whose sins soever yo retain, are retained. Except therefore the Priest be willing, God hath by promise hampred himself so, that it is not now in his own power to pardon any man. Let him which hath offended crave as the Publican did, *Lord be thou merciful to me a sinner;* Let him, as *David* make a thousand times his supplication, *Have mercy upon me, O God, according to thy loving kindnesse, according to the multitude of thy compassion put away mine iniquities.* All this doth not help till such time as the pleasure of the Priest be known, till he have signed us a pardon, and given us, our *quietus est.* God himself hath no answer to make but such as that of his Angel unto *Lot,* I can do nothing.

Quod si possent ei sine sacerdotum sententia absolvi, enim esset vera Christi promissio, Quæcunque &c. Bellarm. ibid.

It is true, that our Saviour by these words, *whose sins ye remit, they are remitted,* did ordain Judges over our sinful Souls, give them Authority to absolve from sin, and promise to ratifie in Heaven whatsoever they should do on Earth, in execution of this their Office; to the end that hereby, as well his Ministers might take encouragement to do their duty with all Faithfulness, as also his people admonition, gladly, with all reverence, to be ordered by them, both parts knowing that the Functions of the one towards the other have his perpetual assistance and approbation. Howbeit all this with two restraints which every jurisdiction in the world hath, the one, that the practice thereof proceed in due order, the other that it do not extend it self beyond due bounds, which bounds or limits have so confined penitential jurisdiction, that although there be given unto it power of remitting sin, yet not such soveraignty of power that no sin should be pardonable in man without it: Thus to enforce our Saviours words, is as though we should gather, that because, *Whatsoever Joseph* did command in the Land of *Egypt, Pharaohs* grant is, it should be done, therefore, he granteth that nothing should be done in the Land of *Ægypt,* but what *Joseph* did command, and so consequently, by enabling his servant *Joseph,* to command under him, disableth himself to command any thing without *Joseph.*

Christus ordinariam suam potestatem in Apostolos transtulit, extraordinariam sibi reservavit.

But by this we see how the Papacy maketh all sin unpardonable, which hath not the Priests Absolution, except peradventure in some extraordinary case, where albeit absolution be not had, yet, it must be desired.

Ordinaria enim remedia in Ecclesia ad remittanda peccata sunt ab eo instituta, Sacramenta: sine quibus peccata remittere Christus potest, sed extraordinarie & multo varius, hoc fecit quàm per Sacramenta. Noluit igitur eos extraordinariis remissionis peccatorum confidere, quæ, & rara sunt & incerta, sed ordinaria, ut ita dicam, visibilia Sacramentorum quærere remedia. Maldon in Mat. 16. 19.

What is then the force of absolution? What is it which the act of Absolution worketh in a sinful man? doth it by any operation derived from it self alter the state of the Soul? Doth it really take away sin, or but ascertain us of Gods most gracious and merciful pardon? The latter of which two is our assertion, the former theirs.

Mat. 9. 2.
Mar. 2. 7.
Luc. 5. 21.
Cypr. de laps. c. 14.
Clem. Alex.
Pædag. lr. 1.

At the words of our Lord and Saviour Jesus Christ, saying unto the sick of the palsie, *Son, thy sins are forgiven thee,* the Pharisees which knew him not to be *Son of the living God,* took secret exception, and fell to reasoning with themselves against him: *Is any able to forgive sin, but God only? The sins* (saith St. Cyprian) *that are committed against him, he alone hath power to forgive, which took upon him our sins, he which sorrowed and suffered for us, he whom the Father delivered unto death for our offences.* Whereunto may be added that which *Clemens Alexandrinus* hath, *Our Lord is profitable every way, every way beneficial, whether we respect him as Man, or as God, as God forgiving, as Man instructing and learning how to avoid sin.* For it is I, even I that putteth away thine iniquities for mine own sake, and will not remember thy sins, saith the Lord.

τοῖς τὰ θῖνον Κύριος ᾠφέλει, πάντα ᾠφελεῖ, ἡ δὲ ἄνθρωπος, ᾖ δὲ Θεὸς, τὰ ἁμαρτήματα, οἷε Θεὸς ἀφιεὶς εἰς τὸ δὲ μὴ ἐξαμαρτάνειν παιδαγωγῶν δὲ ἀνθρωπος. Esa. 43. 25.

Y y   Now

Now albeit we willingly confeſſe with St. *Cyprian*, *The ſins that are commit-* *ted againſt him, he onely hath power to forgive, who hath taken upon him our ſins, he* *which hath ſorrowed and ſuffered for us, he, whom God hath given for our offences.* Yet neither did St. *Cyprian* intend to deny the power of the Miniſter, otherwiſe then if he preſume beyond his Commiſſion to remit ſin, where Gods own will is it ſhould be retained ; For, againſt ſuch Abſolutions he ſpeaketh (which being granted to whom they ought to have been denyed are of no validitie,) and if rightly it be conſidered, how higher cauſes in operation uſe to concur with inferiour means, his grace with our Miniſterie, God really performing the ſame, which man is authorized to act as in his name, there ſhall need for deciſion of this point no great labour.

Veniam pec-
catis quæ in
ipſum com-
miſſa ſunt ſo-
lus poteſt ille
largiri, qui
peccata no-
ſtra portavit,
qui pro nobis
doluit, quem
Deus tradidit
pro peccatis
noſtris.

To remiſſion of ſins, there are two things neceſſary, Grace, as the only cauſe which taketh away iniquity, and Repentance as a duty or condition required in us. To make repentance ſuch as it ſhould be, what doth God demand but inward ſincerity, joyned with fit and convenient offices for that purpoſe, the one referred wholly to our own conſciences, the other beſt diſcerned by them whom God hath appointed Judges in this Court. So that having firſt the promiſes of God for pardon generally unto all offenders penitent, and particularly for our own unfained meaning, the unfallible teſtimony of a good conſcience, the ſentance of Gods appointed Officer and Vicegerent to approve with unpartial judgement the quality of that we have done, and, as from his tribunal in that reſpect to aſſoil us of any crime : I ſee no cauſe but that by the rules of our Faith and Religion we may reſt our ſelves very well aſſured touching Gods moſt merciful pardon & grace, who eſpecially for the ſtrengthning of weak, timorous and fearful minds, hath ſo far indued his Church with power to abſolve ſinners. It pleaſeth God that men ſometimes ſhould by miſſing this help perceive how much they ſtand bound to him for ſo precious a benefit enjoyed. And ſurely ſo long as the world lived in any awe or fear of falling away from God, ſo dear were his Miniſters to the People, chiefly in this reſpect, that being through tyrannie, and perſecution deprived of Paſtors, the doleful rehearſal of heir loſt felicities hath not any one thing more eminent, then that ſinners diſtreſt ſhould not now know, how or where to unlade their burthens. Strange it were unto me that the Fathers who ſo much every where extol the grace of Jeſus Chriſt in leaving unto his Church this Heavenly and Divine power, ſhould as men whoſe ſimplicity had univerſally been abuſed, agree all to admire and magnifie a needleſſe Office.

Victor. de per-
ſecutum Van-
dal.

The ſentence therefore of Miniſterial abſolution hath two effects, touching ſin it only declareth us freed from the guiltineſs thereof, and reſtored into Gods favours ; but concerning right in ſacred and divine myſteries whereof through ſin we were made unworthy, as the power of the Church did before effectually bind and retain us from acceſſe unto them, ſo upon our apparent repentance, it truly reſtoreth our liberty, looſeth the chains wherewith we were tied, remitteth all whatſoever is paſt, and accepteth us no leſſe returned then if we never had gone aſtray.

For in as much as the power which our Saviour gave to his Church, is of two kinds, the one to be exerciſed over voluntary penitents only; the other over ſuch as are to be brought to amendment by Eccleſiaſtical cenſures, the words wherein he hath given this Authority muſt be ſo underſtood as the ſubject or matter whereupon it worketh, will permit. It doth not permit that in the former kind (that is to ſay) in the uſe of power over voluntary Converts to bind or looſe, remit or retain ſhould ſignifie any other, then only to pronounce of ſinners according to that which may be gathered by outward ſigns, becauſe really to effect the removal or continuance of ſin in the ſoul of any offender, is no Prieſtly act, but a work which far exceedeth their ability. Contrarywiſe in the latter kind of ſpiritual Juriſdiction, which by cenſures conſtraineth men to amend their lives: It is true that the Miniſter of God doth then more declare and ſignifie what God hath wrought. And this power, true it is, that the Church hath inveſted in it.

Howbeit,

Howbeit, as other truths, so this hath by errour been oppugned and depraved through abuse. The first of name, that openly in writing withstood the Churches authority, and power to remit sin, was *Tertullian*, after he had combined himself with *Montanists*, drawn to the liking of their Heresie, through the very sowernesse of his own nature, which neither his incredible skill and knowledge otherwise, nor the Doctrine of the Gospel it self, could but so much alter as to make him favour any thing, which carried with it the taste of lenitie. A spung steeped in Worm-wood and Gall, a man through too much severity mercilesse, and neither able to endure, nor to be endured of any. His book entitled concerning Chastity, and written professedly against the Discipline of the Church, hath many fretful and angry sentences, declaring a mind very much offended with such as would not perswade themselves that of sins, some be pardonable by the Keys of the Church, some uncapable of forgivenesse; That middle and moderate offences having received chastizment, may by spiritual authority afterwards be remitted: But greater transgressions must (as touching indulgence) be left to the only pleasure of Almighty God in the World to come: That as Idolatry and Blood-shed, so likewise Fornication and sinful Lust are of this nature; that they which so far have fallen from God, ought to continue for ever after barred from accesse unto his Sanctuary, condemned to perpetual profusion of tears, deprived of all expectation and hope to receive any thing at the Churches hands, but publication of their shame. For (saith he) *who will fear to waste out that which he hopeth he may recover ? Who will be careful for ever to hold that, which he knoweth cannot for ever be withheld from him ? He which slacketh the bridle to sin, doth thereby give it even the spur also.* Take away fear, and that which presently succeedeth in stead thereof is licentious desire. Greater offences therefore are punishable, but not pardonable by the Church. If any Prophet or Apostle be found to have remitted such transgressions, they did it, not by the ordinary course of discipline, but by extraordinary power. For they also raised the dead, which none but God is able to do; they restored the Impotent and Lame men, a work peculiar to Jesus Christ; Yea, that which Christ would not do, because executions of such severity beseemed not him, who came to save and redeem the World by his sufferings, they by their power strook *Elymus* and *Ananias*, the one blind, and the other dead. Approve first your selves to be as they were Apostles or Prophets, and then take upon you to pardon all men. But if the authority you have be only Ministerial, and no way Soveraign, over-reach not the limits which God hath set you; know that to pardon capital Sin, is beyond your Commission.

Securitas delecti etiam liberi est ejus.

Howbeit, as oftentimes the vices of wicked men do cause other their commendable qualities to be abhorred, so the honour of great mens vertues is easily a Cloak of their errours: In which respect *Tertullian* hath past with much lesse obloquie and reprehension than *Novatian*, who broached afterwards the same opinion, had not otherwise wherewith to countervail the offence he gave, and to procure it the like toleration. *Novatian* at the first a Stoical Philosopher (which kind of men hath alwayes accounted stupidity the highest top of wisdom, and commiseration the deadliest sin) became by Institution and Study the very same which the other had been before, thorow a secret natural distemper upon his conversion to the Christian Faith and recovery from sicknesse, which moved him to receive the Sacrament of Baptisme in his Bed. The Bishop contrary to the Canons of the Church, would needs in special love towards him ordain him Presbyter, which favour satisfied not him, who thought himself worthy of greater place and dignity. He closed therefore with a number of well minded men, and not suspicious what his secret purposes were, and having made them sure unto him by fraud, procureth his own consecration to be their Bishop. His Prelacy now was able as he thought to countenance what he intended to publish, and therefore his letters went presently abroad to sundry Churches, advising them never to admit to the fellowship of holy Mysteries, such as had after Baptism offered sacrifice to Idols.

Concil. Neocasar. c. 12.

There was present at the Councel of *Nice*, together with other Bishops, one

Socrat. l. 4. c. 23.

one *Acesius* a *Novatianist*, touching whose diversity in opinion from the Church, the Emperour desirous to here some reason, asked of him certain questions, for answer whereunto *Acesius* weaveth out a long History of things that hapned in the persecution under *Decius*. And of men, which to save life, forsook Faith, but the end was a certain bitter Canon framed in their own School, *That men which fall into deadly sin after holy Baptisme, ought never to be again admitted to the Communion of Divine Mysteries: That they are to be exhorted unto repentance, howbeit not to be put in hope that pardon can be had at the Priests hands, but with God, which hath Soverain Power and Authority in himself, to remit sins, it may be in the end they shall find Mercy.* These followers of *Novatian*, which gave themselves the title of καθαροι, clean, pure and unspotted men, had one point of *Montanisme* more then their Master did professe; for amongst sins unpardonable, they reckoned second Marriages, of which opinion *Tertullian* making (as his usual manner was) a salt Apologie, *Such is (saith he) our stony hardnesse, that defameing our Comforter with a kind of enormity in discipline, we dam up the doors of the Church, no lesse against twice married men, then against Adulterers and Fornicators.* Of this sort therefore it was ordained by the *Nycene* synod, that, if any such did return to the Catholick and Apostolick unity, they should in writing bind themselves to observe the Orders of the Church, and Communicate aswel with them which had been often married, or had fallen in time of persecution, as with other sort of Christian people. But further to relate, or, at all to refel the errour of mis-believing men, concerning this point, is not now to our present purpose greatly necessary.

The Church may receive no small detriment by corrupt practice, even there where Doctrine concerning the substance of things practized is free from any great or dangerous corruption. If therefore that which the Papacy doth in matter of Confessions and Absolution, be offensive, if it palpably serve in the use of the keyes, howsoever, that, which it teacheth in general concerning the Churches power to retain and forgive sins be admitted true, have they not on the one side as much whereat to be abasht, as on the other wherein to rejoyce?

They bind all men upon pain of everlasting condemnation and death, to make confession to their Ghostly Fathers of every great offence they know, and can remember that they have committed against God. Hath Christ in his Gospel so delivered the Doctrine of Repentance unto the World? Did his Apostles so preach it to Nations? Have the Fathers so believed, or so taught? Surely *Novatian* was not so mercilesse in depriving the Church of power to Absolve some certain offenders, as they in imposing upon all a necessity thus to confesse. *Novatian* would not deny but God might remit that which the Church could not, whereas in the Papacy it is maintained that what we conceal from men, God himself shall never pardon. By which oversight; as they have here surcharged the World with multitude, but much abated the weight of confession, so the carelesse manner of their Absolution hath made discipline for the most part amongst them a bare formality: Yea, rather a mean of embolding unto vicious and wicked life, then either any help to prevent future, or medicine to remedie present evils in the Soul of Man. The Fathers were slow and always fearful to absolve any before very manifest tokens given of a true penitent and contrite spirit. It was not their custome to remit sin first, and then to impose works of satisfaction, as the fashion of *Rome* is now, in so much that this their preposterous course and misordered practises hath bred also in them an errour concerning the end and purpose of these works. For against the guiltinesse of sin and the danger of everlasting condemnation thereby incurred, Confession and Absolution succeeding, the same are as they take it, a remedy sufficient, and therefore what their penitentiaries do think to enjoyn farther, whether it be a number of *Ave-Maries* dayly to be scored up, a Journey of Pilgrimage to be undertaken, some few dishes of ordinary diet to be exchanged, offerings to be made at the shrines of Saints, or a little to be scraped off from mens superfluities for relief of poor people,

all

all is in lieu or exchange with God, whose Justice notwithstanding our par-don, yet oweth us still some temporal punishment; Either in this or in the life to come, except we quit it our selves here with works of the former kind, and continued till the ballance of Gods most strict severity shall find the paines we have taken equivalent, with the plagues which we should en-dure, or else the mercy of the Pope relieve us. And at this postern gate cometh in the whole Mart of Papal Indulgences so infinitely strewed that the pardon of sin, which heretofore was obtained hardly, and by much suit, is with them become now almost impossible to be escaped.

To set down then the force of this sentence in Absolving Penitents; There are in sin these three things; The act which passeth away and vanisheth; .The Pollution wherewith it leaveth the Soul defiled; And the punishment whereunto they are made subject that have committed it. The act of sin, is every deed, word, and thought against the Law of God. For *sin is the transgression of the Law*, and although the deed it self do not continue, yet is that bad quality permanent, whereby it maketh the soul unrighteous and deformed in Gods sight. *From the Heart, come evil Cogitations, Murthers, Adulteries, Fornications, Thefts, false Testimonies, Slanders; These are things which defile a man.* They do not only as effects of impurity argue the nest to be unclean, out of which they came, but as causes they strengthen that disposition unto wickednesse, which brought them forth; They are both fruits and seeds of uncleannesse, they nourish the root out of which they grow, they breed that iniquity, which bred them. The blot therefore of sin abideth, though the act be transitory. And out of both ariseth a present debt, to endure what punishment soever the evil which we have done, deserveth, an obligation, in the chains whereof sinners by the Justice of Almighty God continue bound till Repentance loose them. *Repent this thy wickednesse* (saith *Peter*) unto *Simon Magus*, beseech God, that, if it be possible, the thought of thine heart may be pardoned; For I see thou art in the gall of bitternesse, and in the bond of iniquity. In like manner *Solomon*; *The wicked shall be held fast in the cords of his own sin.*

Nor doth God, only bind sinners hand a foot by the dreadful determination of his own unsearchable judgement against them; But sometime also the Church bindeth by the Censures of her discipline: So that when offenders upon their repentance are by the same discipline absolved, the Church looseth but her own bonds, the chains wherein she had tyed them before.

The act of sin God alone remitteth, In that his purpose is never to call it to account, or to lay it unto mens charge; The stain he washeth out by the sanctifying grace of his spirit; And concerning the punishment of sin, as none else hath power to cast body and soul into hell fire, so none power to deliver either besides him.

As for the Ministerial sentence of private Absolution, it can be no more than a Declaration what God hath done; It hath but the force of the Prophet *Nathans* Absolution, *God hath taken away thy sin*: Then which construction, especially of words judicial, there is not any thing more vulgar. For example, the Publicans are said in the Gospel to have justified God, The Jews in *Malachi* to have blessed proud men, which sin and prosper not that the one did make God righteous, or the other the wicked happy: But to blesse, to justifie and to absolve, are as commonly used for words of judgement, or declaration, as of true and real efficacie; Yea, even by the opinion of the Master of sentences; It may be soundly affirmed and thought that God alone doth remit and retain sins, although he have given power to the Church to do both; But he one way, and the Church another. He only by himself forgiveth sin, who cleanseth the soul from inward blemish, and looseth the debt of eternal death. So great a Priviledge he hath not given unto his Priests, who notwithstanding are authorized

thorized

In peccato, tria funt, actio mala, inter or macula, & sequela Bon. sent l. 4. d.

17 q 3.
Job 3.4.
Mat. 15. 19.

Act. 8. 23.

Prov 5 22.

Sacerdotes opus Justitia exercent in peccatores cum eos justa pæna ligant, opus misericordiæ cum de ea aliquid relaxant, vel Sacramentorum communioni conciliant; alia opera in peccatores exercere nequeunt. Sent. l. 4. dist. 18.

Act 7 60
Mich 7.19
1 Cor 6.11
Tit. 3.5
Luc 12.5
Mat. 10.28

2 Sam. 12. 13
Luc. 7. 7
Malach. 3.15
Sent. l. 4 dis. 18

thorized to loose and bind, that is to say, declare who are bound, and who are loosed. For albeit a man be already cleared before God, yet he is not in the Church of God so taken, but by the vertue of the Priests sentence, who likewise may be said to bind by imposing satisfaction, and to loose by admitting to the holy Communion.

Hier. tom.6. comment. in 16. Mat.

Saint *Hierome* also, whom the Master of the Sentences alleadgeth for more countenance of his own opinion, doth no lesse plainly and directly affirm ; *That as the Priests of the Law could only discern, and neither cause nor remove Leprosies , So the Ministers of the Gospel when they retain or remit sin, do but in the one judge how long we continue guilty, and in the other declare when we are clear or free.* For there is nothing more apparent, then that the discipline of Repentance both publick and private was ordained as an outward mean to bring men to the vertue of inward conversion : So that when this by manifest tokens did seem effected, Absolution ensuing (which could not make) served only to declare men innocent.

But the cause wherefore they are so stiffe and have forsaken their own Master in this point, is for that they hold the private discipline of Penitency to be a Sacrament : Absolution an external sign in this Sacrament ; the signs external of all Sacraments in the New Testament, to be both causes of that which they signifie, and, signes of that which they truly cause.

To this opinion concerning Sacraments, they are now tied by expounding a Canon in the *Florentine* Councel, according to the former Ecclesiastical invention received from *Thomas*. For his devise it was, that the mercy of God, which useth Sacraments as instruments whereby to work, indueth them at the time of their Administration with supernatural force and abilitie to induce grace into the souls of men ; Even as the Ax and Saw doth seem to bring Timber into that fashion which the mind of the Artificer intendeth.

Scot. sent. l. 4 solut. ad 4 quæst & quintam. Occam in 1. qu. quent. Alliac. quæst. 1. in 4. sent.

His concept *Scotus, Occam, Petrus Alliancensis,* with sundry others, do most earnestly and strongly impugne, shewing very good reason, wherefore no Sacrament of the new Law can either by vertue which it self hath, or by force supernatural given it, be properly a cause to work grace ; but Sacraments are therefore said to work or conferr grace, because the will of Almighty God is, although not to give them such efficacy, yet himself to be present in the Ministry of the working that effect, which proceedeth wholly from him without any real operation of theirs, such as can enter into mens Souls.

In which construction, seeing that our book and writings have made it known to the World how we joyn with them, it seemeth very hard and injurious dealing, that *Bellarmine* throughout the whole course of his second book *de Sacramentis in genere,* should so boldly face down his Adversaries, as if their opinion were that Sacraments are naked, empty, and uneffectual signes ; wherein there is no other force then only such as in pictures to stir up the mind, that so by theorie and speculation of things represented, Faith may grow ; finally, that all the operation which Sacraments have, is a sensible and divine Instruction. But had it pleased him not to bud-wink his own knowledge, I nothing doubt but he fully saw how to answer himself, it

Lutherani de hac re interdum ita scribunt ut videantur à Catholicis non dissentire ; interdum autem apertissime scribunt contraria, at semper in eadem sententia manent, Sacramenta non habere immediate illam efficientiam respectu gratiæ, sed esse nuda signa, tamen mediate aliquid efficere quatenus excitant & alunt fidem, quod ipsum non faciunt nisi representandæ ut Sacramenta per usum excitant fidem, quemadmodum prædicatio verbi per auditum. Bellarm. de Sacr. in genere l. 2. c. 2.
Quædam signa sunt theorica, non ad alium finem instituta, quam ad significandum, alia ad significandum & efficiendum, quæ ob id practica dici possunt. Controversia est inter nos & hæreticos, quod illi faciunt Sacramenta signa prioris generis. Quare si ostendere poterimus esse signa posterioris generis, obtinuimus causam, cap. 8.
Semper memoria repetendum est Sacramenta nihil aliud quam instrumentales esse conferendæ nobis gratiæ causas. Calv. in Ant. con. Frid. se. 7 c. 5.
Si quis sint qui negent Sacramentis contineri gratiam quam figurant, illos improbamus, ibid. can. 6
Ille modus non transcendit rationem signi, cum Sacramentum novæ legis non solum significent, sed causent gratiam. part. 3. q. 6 : act 1. Alexan. par. 4. q. 8, memb. 3. act. 5. 5. 1. & 2. Th. de verit. q. 27. act. 3 Alliac. in quar. sent. 5. 1. Capr. in 4. d. 1. q. 1 Palud. tom. Ferrar. lib. 4 cont. Gent. c. 57.

it being a matter very ſtrange and credible, that one which with ſo great diligence hath winowed his adverſaries writings, ſhould be ignorant of their minds. For, even as in the perſon of our Lord Jeſus Chriſt both God and Man, when his humane nature is by it ſelf conſidered, we may not attribute that unto him, which we do and muſt a-

Neceſſe eſt ponere aliquam virtutem ſupernaturalem in Sacramentis. Sent. 4. d. 1. q. 1. act. 4.
Sacramentum conſequitur ſpiritualem virtutem cum benedictione Chriſti, & applicatione Miniſteri ad uſum Sacramenti. par. 3. q. 62. art. 4. concil.
Victus Sacramentalis habet eſſe tranſiens, ex unio in aliud & incompletum, Ibidem.
Ex Sacramentis duo conſequuntur in anima, unum eſt caracbter, ſive aliquis ornatus ; aliud eſt gratia. Reſpectu primo Sacramenta ſunt cauſa aliquo modo efficientes ; reſpectu ſecundo ſunt diſponentes. Sacramenta cauſant diſpoſitionem ad formam ultimam, ſed ultimam perfectionem non inducunt, Sent. 4. d. 1. q 1. art. 4.

ſcribe as oft as reſpect is had unto both natures combined ; ſo becauſe in Sacraments there are two things diſtinctly to be conſidered, the outward ſigne, and the ſecret concurrance of Gods moſt bleſſed Spirit, in which reſpect our Saviour hath taught that water and the Holy Ghoſt are combined, to work the myſterie of new birth ; Sacraments therefore as ſignes have only thoſe effects before mentioned ; but of Sacraments, in that by Gods own will and Ordinance they are ſignes aſſiſted alwayes with the power of the Holy Ghoſt ; we acknowledge whatſoever either the places of the Scripture, or the authority of Councels and Fathers, or the proofs and arguments of reaſon which he alleadgeth, can ſhew to be wrought by them. The Elements and words have power of infallible ſignification, for which they are called Seals of Gods Truth ; The Spirit affixed unto thoſe Elements and Words, power of operation within the Soul, moſt admirable, divine, and impoſſible to be expreſt. For ſo God hath inſtituted and ordained that together with due adminiſtration and receit of Sacramental ſigns, there ſhall proceed from himſelf, grace effectual, to Sanctifie, to Cure, to Comfort, and whatſoever is elſe for the good of the Souls of Men. Howbeit this opinion *Thomas* rejecteth, under pretence that it maketh Sacramental Words and Elements to be in themſelves no more then ſigns, whereas they ought to be held as cauſes of that they ſignifie. He therefore reformeth it with this addition, that the very ſenſible parts of the Sacraments do Inſtrumentally effect and produce, not grace, (for the Schoolmen both of theſe times, and long after, did for the moſt part maintain it untrue, and ſome of them unpoſſible, that ſanctifying grace ſhould efficiently proceed but from God alone, and that by immediate creation, as the ſubſtance of the Soul doth) but the phantaſie which *Thomas* had, was that ſenſible thing through Chriſt & the Prieſts Benediction, receive a certain ſupernatural tranſitory force, which leaveth behind it a kind of preparative quality or beauty within the Soul, whereupon immediately from God doth enſue the grace that juſtifieth.

Now they which pretend to follow *Thomas*, differ from him in two points. For firſt, they make grace an immediate effect of the outward ſigne, which he for the dignitie and excellency thereof was afraid to do. Secondly, whereas he to produce but a preparative quality in the Soul, did imagine God to create in the inſtrument, a ſupernatural gift, or hability ; they confeſſe that nothing is created, infuſed, or any way inherent either in the word, or in the elements ; nothing that giveth them inſtrumental efficacie, but Gods meer motion, or application. Are they able to explain unto us, or themſelves to conceive what they mean when they thus ſpeak ? For example, let them teach us, in the Sacrament of Baptiſm, what it is for water to be moved, till it bring forth grace. The application thereof by the Miniſter is plain to ſenſe ; the force which it hath in the mind, as a mortal inſtrument of information, or inſtruction, we know by reaſon, and by faith we underſtand how God doth aſſiſt it with his Spirit ; whereupon enſueth the grace which Saint *Cyprian* did in himſelf obſerve, ſaying, *After the bath of regeneration having ſcowred out the ſtained foulneſſe of former life, ſupernatural light had entrance into the breſt which was purified and cleanſed for it ; after that a ſecond nativity had made another man, by inward receipt of the Spirit from Heaven ;*

Solus Deus eſficit gratiam adeo quod nec Angelis qui ſunt nobiliores ſenſibilibus creaturis, hoc communicetur. Sent. 4. d. 1. q. 1. art. 4. Eph. 1.

Heaven ; things doubtful began in marvellous manner to appear certain that to be open which lay hid, darknesse to shine like the clear light, former hardnesse to be made facility, impossibilitie easinesse : Insomuch as it might be discerned how that was earthly, which before had been carnally bred and lived, given over unto sins : That now Gods own, which the holy Ghost did quicken.

Our opinion is therefore plain unto every mans understanding. We take it for a very good speech which *Bonaventure* hath uttered in saying, Heed must be taken that while we assigne too much to the bodily signes in way of their commendation, we withdraw not the honour which is due to the cause which worketh in them, and the Soul which receiveth them : Whereunto we conformably teach, that the outward sign applyed, hath of it self no natural efficacie towards grace, neither doth God put into it any supernatural inherent vertue ; And, as I think, we thus far avouch no more than they themselves confesse to be very true.

Cavendum enim ne dum nimis damus corporalibus signis ad laudem, subtrahamus honorem causæ curanti & animæ suscipienti.

If any thing displease them, it is because we add to these premisses another assertion ; that with the outward sign, God joyneth his holy Spirit ; and so the whole instrument of God bringeth that to passe, whereunto the baser and meaner part could not extend. As for operations through the motions of signs, they are dark, intricate and obscure, perhaps possible ; Howbeit, not proved either true or likely, by alleadging that the touch of our Saviours garment restored health, clay sight, when he applyed it. Although ten thousand such examples should be brought, they overthrow not this one principle ; that, where the instrument is without inherent, the effect must necessarily proceed from the only agents adherent power.

Luk. 8 Jo. 9.

It passeth a mans conceit how water should be carried into the Soul with any force of divine motion, or grace proceed but meerly from the influence of Gods Spirit : Notwithstanding if God himself teach his Church in this case to believe that which he hath not given us capacity to comprehend, how incredible soever it may seem, yet our wits should submit themselves, and reason give place unto faith therein. But they yield it to be no question of faith, how grace doth proceed from Sacraments ; if in general they be acknowledged true instrumental causes, by the Ministry whereof men receive divine grace : And that they which impute grace to the only operation of God himself, concurring with the external sign, do no lesse acknowledge the true efficacie of the Sacrament, then they that ascribe the same to the quality of the sign applyed, or to the motion of God applying, and so far carrying it, till grace be not created but extracted, out of the natural possibility of the soul. Neverthelesse this last Philosophical imagination (if I may call it Philosophical,) which useth the terms, but overthroweth the rules of Philosophy, and hath no article of Faith to support it, but whatsoever it be, they follow it in a manner all, they cast off the first opinion wherein is most perspicuity and strongest evidence of certain truth. The Councel of *Florence* and *Trent* defining that Sacraments contain and confer grace, the sense whereof (if it liked them) might so easily conform it self with the same opinion which they drew without any just cause quite and clean the other way, making grace the issue of bare words, in such Sacraments as they have framed destitute of any visible Element, and holding it the off-spring as well of Elements as of words in those Sacraments where both are ; but in no Sacrament acknowledging grace to be the fruit of the Holy Ghost working with the outward signe, and not by it, in such sort, as *Thomas* himself teacheth ; that the Apostles Imposition of Hands caused not the comming of Holy Ghost, which notwithstanding was bestowed together with the exercise of that Ceremony ; Yea by it, (saith the Evangelist)to wit, as by a mean, which came between the true Agent and the Effect, but not otherwise.

Bel. de Sacr. in gen. l. 2. c. 1.

Dicimus gratiam non creari à Deo, sed produci ex aptitudine & potentia naturali animæ, sicut cætera omnia quæ producuntur in subjectis talibus quæ sunt apta nata ad suscipiendam accidentia. Allen de Sacram. in gen. c. 37.

Tho. de Verit. q. 27. art. 3. resp. ad 16. Art. 8. 18.

Many

Many of the Ancient Fathers prefuppofing that the Faithful before Chrift had not till the time of his coming, that perfect Life and Salvation which they looked for and we poffeffe, thought likewife their Sacraments to be but prefigurations of that which ours in prefent do exhibit. For which caufe the *Florentine* Councel comparing the one with the other, faith, *that the old did onely fhaddow grace, which was afterward to be given through the paffion of Jefus Chrift.* But the after-wit of latter dayes hath found out another more exquifite diftinction that Evangelical Sacraments are caufes to effect grace, through motions of fignes legal according to the fame fignification and fenfe wherein Evangelical Sacraments are held by us to be Gods Inftruments for that purpofe. For howfoever *Bellar.* hath fhrunk up the *Lutherans* finews, and cut off our doctrin by the skirts; *Allen,* although he term us Heretiques, according to the ufual bitter venome of his firft ftile; doth yet ingenioufly confeffe, that the old Schoolmens doctrine and ours is one concerning Sacramental efficacie, derived from God himfelf affifting by promife thofe outward figns of Elements and words, out of which their School-men of the newer mint are fo defirous to hatch grace. Where God doth work and ufe thefe outward means, wherein he neither findeth nor planteth force and aptneffe towards his intended purpofe, fuch means are but figns to bring men to the confideration of his omnipotent power, which without the ufe of things fenfible, would not be marked. At the time therefore when he giveth his heavenly grace, he applyeth by the hands of his Minifters, that which betokeneth the fame, nor only betokeneth, but being alfo accompanied for ever with fuch power as doth truly work, is in that

Quod ad circumcifionem fequebatur remiffio, fiebat ratione rei adjunctæ & ratione pacti divini, eodem plane modo quo non folum hæretici fed etiam aliquot vetuftiores Scholaftici voluerunt nova Sacramenta conferre gratiam. *Allen de Sacra, in gen. c. 39.*

Bonaventura, Scotus, Durandus, Richardus, Occamus, Maffilius, Gabriel, volunt folum Deum producere gratiam ad præfentiam Sacramentorum. Bellarm. de Sacr. in gen. lib. 2 c. 11.

Puto longe probatiorem & tutiorem fententiam quæ dat Sacramentis veram efficientiam: Primò, quia doctores paffim docent Sacramenta non agere nifi prius à Deo virtutem feu benedictionem, feu fanctificationem accipiant: & referunt effectum Sacramentorum ad omnipotentiam Dei, & conferunt cum veris caufis efficientibus. Secundò quia non effet differentia inter modum agendi Sacramentorum, & fignorum Magicorum. Tertio, quia tunc non effet hinc Dei Minifter in ipfa actione Sacramenti, fed homo præbeiet fignum actione fua, & Deus alia actione vifo eo figno infunderet gratiam, ut cum unus oftendit fyngrapham Mercatori, & ille dat pecunias. At Scriptura docent quod Deus baptizat per hominem. Bel. l. a cap. 11.

refpect, termed Gods inftrument a true efficient caufe of Grace; a caufe not in it felf, but only by connexion of that which is in it felf a caufe, namely Gods own ftrength and power. Sacraments, that is to fay, the outward figns in Sacraments, work nothing till they be bleffed and fanctified by God. But what is Gods heavenly benediction and fanctification, faving only the affociation of his fpirit? fhall we fay that Sacraments are like Magical figns, if thus they have their effect? Is it magick for God to manifeft by things fenfible what he doth, and to do by his moft glorious fpirit really, what he manifefteth in his Sacraments? The delivery and adminiftration whereof, remaineth in the hands of mortal men, by whom, as by perfonal inftruments, God doth apply figns, and with figns infeparably joyn his fpirit, and through the power of his fpirit work grace. The firft is by way of concomitance and confequence to deliver the reft alfo that either accompany, or enfue. It is not here, as in cafes of mutual commerce, where divers perfons have divers acts to be performed in their own behalf; a creditor to fhew his bill, and a debtor to pay his money. But God and man do here meet in one action upon a third, in whom, as it is the work of God to create grace, fo it is his work by the hand of the Minifter to apply a fign which fhould betoken, and his work to annex that fpirit which fhall effect it. The action therefore is but one, God the Author thereof, and man a copartner by him affigned to work for, with, and under him. God the giver of grace, by the outwards Miniftery of man, fo far forth as he authorizeth man to apply the Sacraments of grace in the foul, which he alone worketh, without either inftrument or coagent.

Whereas therefore with us the remiffion of fin is afcribed unto God, as a thing which proceedeth from him only, and prefently followeth upon the vertue of true repentance appearing in man; that which we attribute to the

vertue,

they do not onely impute to the Sacrament of Repentance ; but having made Repentance a *Sacrament*, and thinking of Sacraments as they do, they are enforced to make the Miniftry of his Priefts, and their Abfolution a caufe of that which the fole Omnipotency of God worketh. And yet for my own part, I am not able well to conceive how their Doctrine, That humane Abfolution is really a caufe out of which our deliverance from fin doth

Conc. Trid. feff. 14. c 4.

ensue, can cleave with the Council of *Trent*, defining, *That contrition perfected with Charity doth at all times it felf reconcile offenders to God, before they come to receive actually the Sacrament of Penance.* How it can ftand with thofe Difcourfes

Bellarm. de. 1æ it.l.2.c.13.

of the learned Rabbies, which grant, *That whofoever turneth unto God with his whole heart, hath immediately his fins taken away ; that if a man be truly converted, his pardon can neither be denyed nor delayed ;* It doth not ftay for the Priefts Abfolution, but prefently followeth. *Surely if every contrite finner in whom there is charitie, and a fincere converfion of heart, have remiffion of fins given him, before he feek it at the Priefts hands, if reconciliation to God be a prefent and immediate fequel, upon every fuch converfion or change ; it muft of neceffitie follow, feeing no man can be a true Penitent or Contrite, which doth not both love God and fincerely abhor fin ; that therefore they all before Abfolution attain forgivenefe ; whereunto notwithftanding Abfolution is pretended a caufe fo neceffary, that fin without it, except in fome rare extraordinary cafe, canno: poffibly be remitted.* Shall Abfolutely be a caufe producing and working that effect, which is always brought forth without it, and had before Abfolution be thought ? But when they which are thus before hand pardoned of God, fhall come to be alfo affoiled by the Brieft, I would know what force his Abfolution hath in this cafe ? Are they able to fay here that the Prieft doth remit any thing ? Yet, when any of ours afcribeth the work of Remiffion to God, and interpreteth the Priefts fentence to be but a folemn declaration of that which God himfelf hath already performed, they fcorn at it ; they urge againft it, that if this were true, our Saviour Chrift fhould rather have faid, *What is loofed in Heaven, ye fhall loofe on earth,* then as he doth, *Whatfoever ye loofe on Earth, fhall in Heaven be loofed.* As if he were to learn of us how to place his words, and not we to crave rather of him a found and right underftanding ; leaft to his difhonour, and our own hurt we mif-expound them. It fufficeth I think both againft their conftructions to have proved that they ground an untruth on his fpeech ; and in behalf of our own, that his words without any fuch tranfpofition do very well admit the fenfe we give them; which is, that he taketh to himfelf the lawful proceedings of Authority in his name, and that the Act of Spiritual Authority in this cafe, is by fentence to acquit or pronounce them free from fin, whom

Hæc expofitio, Ego te abfolvo, id eft, Abfolutum oftendo, partim quidem vera eft, non vamen perfecta. Sacramenta quippe novæ legis non folum fignificant, fed efficiunt quod fignificant. Soto. fent. l. 4. dift. 14. q. 1. art. 3.

they judge to be fincerely and truly penitent ; which Interpretation they themfelves do acknowledge though not fufficient, yet very true.

Abfolution they fay, declareth indeed ; but this is not all, for it likewife maketh innocent ; which addition, being an untruth proved, our truth granted, hath I hope fufficiency without it ; and confequently our opinion therein, neither to be challenged as untrue, nor as unfufficient.

To rid themfelves out of thefe Bryars, and to make Remiffion of fins an effect of Abfolution, notwithftanding that which hitherto hath been faid, they have two fhifts; at firft, that in many penitents, there is but attrition of heart,

Attritio folum dicit dolorem propter pænas inferni ; dum quis accedit attritus per gratiam Sacramentalem, fit contritus Soto. fent. 4. dift. 14. q. 1. art. 1.

which attrition they define to be grief proceeding from fear without love ; and to thefe they fay Abfolution doth give that contrition whereby men are really purged from fin. Secondly, that even where contrition or inward repentance doth cleanfe without ab-

Dum accedit vere contritus propter Deum, illi etiam contritio non eft contritio, nifi quatenus prius natura informetur gratia per Sacramentum in voto. Soto fent. 4. dift. 14. q. 1. art. 1.

folution;the reafon why it cometh fo to pafs, is,becaufe fuch contrites intend and defire Abfolution, though they have it not. Which two things granted : The one, that Abfolution given, maketh them contrite that are not; the other, even in them wch are contrite; the caufe why God remitteth fin,

is

s the purpose or desire they have to receive Absolution : we are not to stand against a sequel so clear and
manifest as this, that alwayes remission of sin proceedeth from Absolution either had or desired. But
should a reasonable man give credit to their bare con-
ceit, and because their Positions have driven them to imagine Absolving of
unsufficiently disposed penitents, to be a real creating of further vertue in
them, must all other men think it due ? Let them
cancel hence forward and blot out all their Books,
those old Cautions touching necessity of Wisdom, least
Priests should inconsiderately absolve any man in
whom there were not apparent tokens of true Repentance ; which to do, was in *Cyprians* judgement *Pestilent Deceit and Flattery, not onely not available, but
hurtful to them that had transgrest ; a frivolous, frustrate
and false peace ; such as caused the unrighteous to trust
to a lie, and destroyed them unto whom it promised
safety.* What needeth observation whether Penitents have worthinesse and bring contrition,
if the words of Absolution do infuse contriti-
on ? Have they born us all this while in hand, that contrition is a part of
the matter of their Sacrament ; a Condition or Preparation of the Mind towards Grace to be received by Absolution in the form of their Sacrament ?
And must we now believe that the form doth give the matter ? That Absolution bestoweth contrition, and that the words do make presently of *Saul,
David,* of *Judas, Peter?* For what was the penitency of *Saul* and *Judas,* but
plain attrition, honour of sin through fear of punishment, without any loving sense, or tast of Gods Mercy ?
   Their other fiction, imputing remission of sin to desire of Absolution from
the Priest, even in them which are truly contrite, is an evasion somewhat
more witty, but no whit more possible for them to prove. Belief of the
World and Judgement to come, Faith in the Promises, and Sufferings of
Christ for Mankind, Fear of his Majestie, Love of his Mercy, Grief for Sin,
Hope for Pardon, Suit for Grace ; These we know to be the Elements of
true Contrition ; suppose that besides all this God did also command that
every penitent should seek his Absolution at the Priests hands, where so many causes are concurring unto one effect ; Have they any reason to impute
the whole effect unto one, any reason in the choice of that one to passe by
Faith, Fear, Love, Humility, Hope, Prayer, whatsoever else, and to en-
thronize above them all a desire of Absolution from the Priest, as if in the
whole work of mans Repentance, God did regard and accept nothing but
for and in consideration of this ? Why do the *Tridentine* Counsel impute it
to Charitie, *That contrites are reconciled in Gods sight, before they receive the Sacrament of Penance, if desired Absolution be the true Cause ?* But let this passe how
it will, seeing the question is not what vertue God may accept in penitent
sinners, but what grace Absolution actually given doth really bestow upon
them. If it were as they will have it, that God regarding the humiliation
of a contrite Spirit, because there is joyned therewith a lowly desire of the
Sacrament of Priestly Absolution, pardoneth immediately, and forgiveth
all offences : Doth this any thing help to prove that Absolution received afterward from the Priest, can more then declare him already pardoned which
did desire it ? To desire Absolution, presupposing it commanded, is obedience :
and obedience in that case is a Branch of the vertue of Repentance, which
vertue being thereby made effectual to the taking away of sins without
the Sacrament of Repentance, Is it not an Argument that the Sacrament
of Absolution hath here no efficacie, but the vertue of Contrition worketh all ?
For how should any effect ensue from causes which actually are not ? The
Sacrament must be applyed wheresoever any grace doth proceed from it.

*Legitima contritio votum Sacramenti pro suo
tempore debet inducere, atque adeo in virtute futuri Sacramenti peccata remittit. Id.
art. 3.*

*Tunc sententia Sacerdotis judicio Dei, &
totius coelestis Curiæ approbatur, & con-
firmatur, cum ita ex discretione procedit,
ut reorum merita non contradicant. sent.
l. 4. d. 18.*

*Non est periculosum sacerdoti dicere,
Ego te absolvo, illis in quibus signa
contritionis videt, quæ sunt dolor de
præteritis, & propositum de cætero non
peccandi ; alias, absolvere non debet.
Tho. Opusc. 22.*
Cypr. de lapsis.

So

A reatu mortis æternæ absolvitur homo à Deo per contritionem ; manet autem reatus ad quandam pœnam temporalem, & Minister Ecclesiæ quicunque virtute clavium tollit reatum cujusdam partis pœnæ illius. *Abul. in defenf. per.* 1. *c.* 7.

So that where it is but defired onely, whatfoever may follow upon Gods acceptation of this defire, the Sacrament afterwards received, can be no caufe thereof. Therefore the further we wade, the better we fee it ftill appear, that the Prieft doth never in Abfolution, no not fo much as by way of Service and Miniftry, really either forgive them, take away the uncleannefſe, or remove the punifhment of fin ; but if the party penitent come contrite, he hath by their own grant, Abfolution before Abfolution ; if not contrite, although the Prieft fhould feem a thoufand times to Abfolve him, all were in vain. For which caufe, the Antients and better fort of their School Divines, *Abulenfis, Alexander Hales, Bonaventure*, afcribe the real abolition of fin, and eternal punifhment, to the meer pardon of Almighty God, without dependency upon the Priefts Abfolution, as a caufe to effeſt the fame. His Abfolution hath in their Doſtrine certain other effeſts fpecified, but this denyed ; Wherefore having hitherto fpoken of the vertue of Repentance required ; of the Difcipline of Repentance which Chrift did eftablifh ; and of the Sacrament of Repentance invented fithence, againft the pretended force of Humane Abfolution in Sacramental penitency ; *Let it fuffice thus far to have fhewed how God alone doth truly give, the vertue of Repentance alone procure, and private Minifterial Abfolution, but declare remiffion of fins.*

Signum hujus Sacramenti eft caufa effeſtiva gratiæ five remiffionis peccatorum, non fimpliciter ficut ipfa prima pœnitentia, fed fecundum quid, quia eft caufæ efficaciæ gratiæ qua fit remiffio peccati, quantum ad aliquem effeſtum in pœnitente, ad minus quantum ad remiffionem fequelæ ipfius peccati, fcilicet pœnæ, *Alex. p.* 4. *q.* 14. *memb.* 2.

Poteftas clavium propriè loquendo non fe extendit fupra culpam ; ad illud quod objicitur To. 22. Quorum remiferitis peccata, dicendum quod vel illud de remiffione dicitur quantum ad oftenfionem vel folum quantum ad pœnam. *Bon. fent.* 1. 1. *d.* 18. *q.* 1.

Ab æterni pœna nullo modo folvit facerdos, fed à purgatoria ; neque hoc per fe, fed per accidens, quod cum in pœnitente virtute clavium minuitur debitum pœnæ temporalis, non ita acriter punietur in purgatorio ficut fi non effet abfolutus. *Sent. fib.* 4. *d.* 18. *q.* 2.

Now the laft and fometimes hardeft to be fatisfied by Repentance, are our Minds ; and our Minds we have then fatisfied, when the Confcience is of guilty become clear. For, as long as we are in our felves privy to our own moft hainous crimes, but without fenfe of Gods Mercy and Grace towards us, unlefſe the heart be either brutifh for want of Knowledge, or altogether hardned by wilful Atheifme ; the remorfe of fin is in it, as the deadly fting of a Serpent : which point fince very Infidels and Heathens have obferved in the nature of fin, (for the difeafe they felt, though they knew no remedy to help it) we are not rafhly to defpife thofe fentences, which are the teftimonies of their experience touching this point. They knew that the eye of a Mans own Confcience is more to be feared by evil doers, then the prefence of a thoufand Witneffes, in as much as the mouths of other accufers are many wayes ftopt, the ears of the accufed not alwayes fubjeſt to glowing with contumely and exprobration ; whereas a guilty Mind being forced to be ftill both a Martyr and a Tyrant it felf, muft of neceffity endure perpetual Anguifh and Grief. For, as the Body is rent with ftripes, fo the mind with guiltineffe of Cruelty, Luft, and wicked Refolutions. Which furies brought the Emperour *Tyberius* fometimes into fuch perplexity, that writing to the Senate, his wonted art of diffimulation failed him utterly in this cafe ; And whereas it had been ever his peculiar delight fo to fpeak, that no man might be able to found his meaning, he had not the power to conceal what he felt through the fecret fcourge of an evil Confcience, though no neceffity did now enforce him to difclofe the fame. *What to write, or how to write, at this prefent, if I know* (faith Tyberius) *let the Gods and Goddeffes, who thus continually eat me, onely be worfe to me then they are.* It was not his Imperial Dignity and Power, that could provide a way to proteſt him againft himfelf ; the fears and fufpition which improbriety had bred, being ftrengthned

ned by every occasion, and those vertues clean banished which are the onely foundation of sound tranquility of minde. For which cause, it hath been truly said, and agreeably with all mens experience, that if the vertuous did excell in no other priviledge, yet far happier they are then the contrary sort of men, for that their hopes be always better. Neither are we to marvel that these things known unto all, do stay so few from being Authors of their own wo. For we see by the ancient example of *Josephs* unkind brethren, how it cometh to remembrance easily when crimes are once past, what the difference is of good from evil, and of right from wrong. But such considerations when they should have prevented sin, were over matcht by inordinate desires. Are we not bound then with all thankfulnesse to acknowledge his infinite goodnesse and mercy, which hath revealed unto us the way how to rid our selves of these mazes; the way how to shake off that yoke, which no flesh is able to beare; the way how to change most grisly horror into a comfortable apprehension of heavenly joy?

Whereunto there are many which labour with so much the greater difficulty, because imbecillity of mind doth not suffer them to censure rightly their own doings: Some fearful least the enormity of their crimes be so impardonable that no repentance can do them good; some, least the imperfection of their Repentance make it uneffectual to the taking away of sin. The one drive all things to this issue, whether they be not men that have sinned against the *Holy Ghost*; the other to this, what Repentance is sufficient to clear sinners, and to assure them that they are delivered. Such as by error charge themselves of unpardonable sin, must think it may be they deem that impardonable which is not. Our Saviour speaketh indeed of Blasphemy which shall never be forgiven. But have they any sure and infallible knowledge what that Blasphemy is? If not, why are they unjust and cruel to their own Souls, imagining certainty of guiltinesse in a Crime concerning the very nature whereof they are uncertain? For mine own part, although where this Blasphemy is mentioned, the cause why our Saviour spake thereof, was the Pharisees Blasphemy, which was not afraid to say, *He had an unclean Spirit, and did cast out Spirits by the Power of Beelzebub*; Neverthelesse I dare not precisely deny but that even the Pharisees themselves might have repented and been forgiven, and that our Lord Jesus Christ peradventure might but take occasion at their Blasphemy, which as yet was pardonable, to tell them further of an unpardonable Blasphemy, whereinto he foresaw that the Jews would fall. For it is plain that many thousands at the first, professing Christian Religion, became afterwards wilful Apostates, moved with no other cause of revolt, but meer indignation that the Gentiles should enjoy the benefit of the Gospel as much as they, and yet not be burthened with the yoak of *Moses* Law. The Apostles by Preaching had wone them to Christ, in whose Name they embraced with great alacrity the full remission of their former sins and iniquities, they received by the Imposition of the Apostles hands, *that Grace and Power of the Holy Ghost* whereby they cured Diseases, Prophesied, spake with Tongues; and yet in the end after all this they fell utterly away, renounced the Mysteries of Christian Faith, Blasphemed in their formal Abjurations that most Glorious and Blessed Spirit, the Guifts whereof themselves had possest; and by this means sunk their Souls in the Gulf of that unpardonable sin; whereof, as our Lord JESUS CHRIST had told them before hand; so the Apostle at the first appearance of such their revolt, putteth them in mind again, that falling now to their former Blasphemies, their Salvation was irrecoverably gone: it was for them in this case impossible to be renewed by any repentance; because they were now in the state of *Satan* and his Angels; the Judge of quick and dead had passed his irrevocable sentence against them. So great difference there is between Infidels unconverted and back-sliders in this manner fallen away, that alwayes we have hope to reclaim the one, which onely hate whom they never knew; but to the other which know and Blaspheme, to them that with more then

Mat. 11. 31.
Mar. 3. 30.

Acts 2. 38.

Heb. 6. 6.

infernal

infernal malice accurse both the seen brightnesse of Glory which is in him, and in themselves, the tasted goodnesse of Divine Grace, as those execrable Miscreants did, who first received in extraordinary miraculous manner, and then in outragious sort blasphemed the *Holy Ghost*, abusing *both it and the whole Religion*, which God by it did confirm and magnifie; to such as willfully thus sin, after so great light of the Truth, and Gifts of the Spirit, there remaineth justly no fruit or benefit to be expected by Chrifts Sacrifice.

Heb. 10. 16.

For all other offenders without exception or stint, whether they be strangers that seek accesse, or followers that will make return unto God, upon the tender of there Repentance, the grant of his grace standeth everlastingly signed with his blood in the book of eternal life. That which in this case overterrifieth fearful Souls, is, a misconceit whereby they imagine every act which they do knowing that they do amisse, and every wilful Breach or Transgression of Gods Law, to be meer sin against the Holy Ghost; forgetting that the Law of *Moses* it self ordained Sacrifices of Expiation, aswel for faults presumptuously commited, as things wherein men offend by errour.

Now there are on the contrary side others, who doubting not of Gods Mercy toward all that perfectly repent, remain notwithstanding scrupulous and troubled with continual fear, least defects in their own Repentance be a bar against them.

Jer. 6. 26.
Mich. 1. 8,9.
Lament. 2, 18.

These cast themselves first into very great, and peradventure needlefs Agonies through misconstruction of things spoken about proportioning our griefs to our sins, for which they never think they have wept and mourned enough; yea, if they have not alwayes a stream of Tears at Command, they take it for a heart congealed and hardned in sin, when to keep the wound of contrition bleeding, they unfold the circumstances of their Transgressions, and endeavour to leave nothing which may be heavy against themselves. Yet do what they can, they are still fearful, least herein also they do not that which they ought and might. Come to prayer, their coldnesse taketh all heart and courage from them with fasting; albeit their flesh should be withered, and their Blood clean dried up, would they ever the lesse object, What is this to *Davids* humiliation? Wherein notwithstanding there was not any thing more then necessary. In works of Charity and Almf-deeds? It is not all the world can perswade them they did ever reach the poor bounty of the widdows two Mites, or by many Milions of Leagues come near to the mark which *Cornelius* touched; so far they are off from the proud surmise of any Penitential Supererogation in miserable wretched worms of the earth. Notwithstanding for as much as they wrong themselves with over-rigorous and extream exactions, by means whereof they fall sometimes into such perplexities as can hardly be allayed: it hath therefore pleased Almighty God in tender commiseration over these imbecilities of men, to ordain for their Spiritual and Ghostly comfort, consecrated persons, which by sentence of Power and Authority given from above, may as it were out of his very mouth ascertain timerous and doubtful minds in their own particular, ease them of all their scrupulosities, leave them setled in Peace, and satisfied touching the Mercy of God towards them. To use the benefit of this help for the better satisfaction in such cases, is so natural that it can be forbidden no man, but yet not so necessary that all men should be in case to need it.

Quam magna deliquimus, tam granditer defleamus. Alto vulneri diligens & longa medicina non defit, pœnitentia crimina minor non fit. Cypr. de lapsis— *Non levi agendum est contritione, ut debita illa redimantur, quibus mors æterna debetur; nec transitoria opus est satisfactione per malis illis propter quæ paratus est ignis æternus.* Euseb. Emissenus, vel potius Salv. f. 106.

Psal. 6. 6.
Mar. 12. 42.
Acts 10. 31.

They are of the two the happier therefore that can content and satisfie themselves by judging discreetly what they perform, and soundly what God doth require of them. For having that which is most material, the substance of Penitency rightly bred touching signs and tokens thereof, we may bouldly affirm that they do which imagine for every offence a certain

propor-

proportionable degree in the Passions and Griefs of Mind, whereunto whosoever aspireth not, repenteth in vain. That to frustrate mens Confessions and Considerations of sin, except every circumstance which may aggravate the same, be unript and laid in the Ballance, is a mercilesse extremity, although it be true, that, as neer as we can, such wounds must be searched to the very bottom; last of all to set down the like stint, and to shut up the doors of Mercy against penitents which come short thereof in the devotion of their Prayers, in the continuance of their Fasts, in the largenesse and bounty of their Almes, or in the course of any other such like duties, is more then God himself hath thought meet, and consequently more then mortal men should presume to do. That which God doth chiefly respect in mens penitency, is their hearts. *The Heart is it which maketh Repentance sin-*cere, sincerity that which findeth favour in Gods sight, and the favour of God that which supplieth by Gracious acceptation whatsoever may seem defective in the faithful, hearty and true offices of his Servants. Take it (saith *Chrys.*) upon my credit, *Such is Gods merciful inclination towards men, that repentance offered with a single and sincere mind, he never refuseth, no, not although we be come to the very top of Iniquity.* If there be a will and desire to return, he receiveth, imbraceth, omitteth nothing which may restore us to former happinesse; yea, that which is yet above all the rest, albeit we cannot in the duty of satisfying him, attain what we ought, and would, but come far behind our mark, he taketh neverthelesse in good worth that little which we do; be it never so mean, wee loose not our labour therein. The least and lowest step of Repentance in Saint *Chrysostoms* judgement severeth and setteth us above them that perish in their sin. I therefore will end with Saint *Augustines* conclusion. *Lord, in thy Book and Volume of Life all shall be written, as well the least of thy Saints, as the chiefest.* Let not therefore the unperfect fear; Let them onely proceed and go forward.

Jer. 29. 13.
Joel 2. 12.

Chrys. de repar. lapf. lib. ad Theodor. Depofit. dift. 3. c. Talis.

Aug. in Pf. 138.

O F

OF THE

LAWES

OF

Ecclefiaftical Policy:

The eighth Book.

Containing their feventh Affertion.

That to no civil Prince or Governour, there may be given fuch power of Ec-clefiaftical Dominion as by the Laws of this Land belongeth unto the fupreme Regent thereof.

Maccab. 14.

E come now to the laft thing whereof there is controver-fie moved, namely *the power of fupreme jurifdiction*, which for diftinction fake we call *the power of EcclefiafticalDomi-nion*. It was not thought fit in the *Jews Common-wealth*, that the exercife of *Supremacy Ecclefiaftical* fhould be de-nied unto him, to whom the exercife of *Chiefty Civil* did appertain; and therefore their Kings were invefted with both. This power they gave unto *Simon*, when they confented that he fhould be their Prince, not only to fet men over their works, and countrey, and wea-pons, but alfo to provide for the holy things; and that he fhould be obeyed of every man, and that the writings of the countrey fhould be made in his name; and that it fhould not be lawfull for any of the people or Priefts to withftand his words, or to call any congregation in the countrey without him. And if happily it be furmifed that thus much was given to *Simon*, as being both Prince and high Prieft; which otherwife (being their *Civil Governor*) he could not lawfully have enjoyned : we muft note, that all this is no more then the ancient Kings of that People had, being Kings and not Priefts. By this power, *David*, *Afa*, *Iehofaphat*, *Iofias*, and the reft, made thofe Laws and Orders which facred Hiftory fpeaketh of, concerning matters of meer Reli-gion, the affaires of the Temple, and fervice of God. Finally had it not been by the vertue of this power, how fhould it poffibly have come to pafs, that the piety or impiety of the Kings did alwayes accordingly change the publick face of Religion; which things the Prophets by themfelves never did, nor at any time could hinder from being done : had the Priefts alone been poffeft of all power in Spiritual affairs, how fhould any thing concerning matter of Religion have been made but only by them; in them it had been and not in the King to change the face of Religion at any time ; the altering of Religion, the making of Ecclefiaftical Laws, with other the like actions belonging unto the Power of Dominion, are ftill termed *the deeds of the King*: to fhew, that in him was placed the fupremacy of power in this kind over all ;

and

OF THE
LAWS
OF
Ecclesiastical Politie.

The Seventh BOOK.

Their Sixth Assertion, *That there ought not to be in*
the Church, Bishops indued with such Authority
and Honour as ours are.

The Matter contained in this Seventh Book.

1. THe state of Bishops although sometime oppugned, and that by such as therein would most seem to please God, yet by his providence upheld hitherto, whose glory it is to maintain that whereof himself is the Author.

2. What a Bishop is, what his name doth import, and what doth belong unto his office as he is a Bishop.

3. In Bishops two things traduced; of which two, the one their Authority, and in it the first thing condemned, their superiority over other Ministers: What kinde of superiority in Ministers it is which the one part holdeth, and the other denieth lawful.

4. From whence it hath grown that the Church is governed by Bishops.

5. The time and cause of instituting every where Bishops with restraint.

6. What manner of power Bishops from the first beginning have had.

7. After what sort Bishops, together with Presbyters have used to govern the Churches which were under them.

8. How far the power of Bishops hath reached from the beginning in respect of territory, or local compass.

9. In what respects Episcopal Regiment hath been gainsaid, of old by Aerius.

10. In what respect Episcopal Regiment is gainsaid by the Authors of pretended Reformation at this day.

The state of Bishops although somtime oppugned, and that by such as therein would most seem to please God, yet by his providence upheld hitherto, whose glory it is to maintain that whereof himself is the Author.

1. Have heard that a famous Kingdom in the world being sollicited to reform such disorders as all men saw the Church exceedingly burthened with, when of each degree great multitudes thereunto inclined, and the number of them did every day so encrease that this intended work was likely to take no other effect then all good men did wish and labour for: A principal actor herein (for zeal and boldness of spirit) thought it good to shew them betimes what it was which must be effected, or else that there could be no work of perfect Reformation accomplished. To this purpose, in a solemn Sermon, and in a great Assembly he described unto them the present quality of their publique Estate, by the parable of a tree, huge and goodly to look upon, but without that fruit which it should and might bring forth; affirming that the onely way of redress was a full and perfect establishment of Christs Discipline (for so their manner is to entitle a thing hammered out upon the forge of their own invention) and that to make way of entrance for it, there must be three great limbs cut off from the body of that stately tree of the Kingdom: Those three limbs were three sorts of men; Nobles, whose high Estate would make them otherwise disdain to put their necks under that yoke: Lawyers, whose Courts being not pulled down, the new Church Consistories were not like to flourish: Finally, Prelates, whose ancient Dignity, and the simplicity of their intended Church Discipline, could not possibly stand together. The proposition of which device being plausible to active spirits, restless through desire of innovation, whom commonly nothing doth more offend then a change which goeth fearfully on by slow and suspicious paces; the heavier and more experienced sort began presently thereat to pull back their feet again, and exceedingly to fear the stratagem of Reformation for ever after. Whereupon ensued those extream conflicts of the one part with the other, which continuing and encreasing to this very day, have now made the state of that flourishing Kingdom even such, as whereunto we may most fitly apply those words of the Prophet *Jeremiah, Thy breach is great, like the Sea, who can heal thee?* Whether this were done in truth, according to the constant affirmation of some avouching the same, I take not upon me to examine;

That

That which I note therein is, How with us that policie hath been corrected. For to the Authors of pretended Reformation with us, it hath not seemed expedient to offer the edge of the axe unto all three boughs at once, but rather to single them, and strike at the weakest first; making show that the lop of that one shall draw the more abundance of sap to the other two, that they may thereby the better prosper. All prosperity, felicity and peace we wish multiplied on each Estate, as far as their own hearts desire is: But let men know that there is a God, whose eye beholdeth them in all their ways, a God, the usual and ordinary course of whose justice, is to return upon the head of malice the same devices which it contriveth against others. The foul practices which have been used for the overthrow of Bishops, may perhaps wax bold in process of time to give the like assault even there, from whence at this present they are most seconded. Nor let it over-dismay them who suffer such things at the hands of this most unkind world, to see that heavenly estate and dignity thus conculcated, in regard whereof so many their Predecessors were no lesse esteemed then if they had not been men but Angels amongst men. With former Bishops it was as with *Job* in the days of that prosperity, which at large he describeth, saying, *Unto me men gave ear, they waited and held their tongue at my counsel, after my words they replied not, I appointed out their way and did sit as chief, I dwelt as it had been a King in an Army.* At this day the case is otherwise with them; and yet no o-therwise then with the self same *Job* at what time the alteration of his estate wrested these contrary speeches from him, *But now they that are younger then I mock at me, the children of fools, and off-spring of slaves, creatures more base then the earth they tread on, such as if they did show their heads young and old would shout at them and chase them thorow the streets with a cry, their sing I am, I am a theam for them to talk on.* An injury lesse grievous if it were not offered by them whom Satan hath through his fraud and subtilty so far beguiled as to make them imagine herein they do unto God a part of most faithful service. Whereas the Lord in truth, whom they serve herein, is as St. *Cyprian* telleth them, like, not Christ (for he it is that doth appoint and protect Bishops) but rather Christs adversary and enemy of his Church. A thousand five hundred years and upward the Church of Christ hath now continued under the sacred Regiment of Bishops. Neither for so long hath Christianity been ever planted in any Kingdom throughout the world but with this kind of government alone, which to have been ordained of God, I am for mine own part even as resolutely perswaded, as that any other kind of Government in the world whatsoever is of God. In this Realm of *England*, before *Normans*, yea before *Saxons*, there being Christians, the chief Pastors of their souls was Bishops. This order from about the first establishment of Christian Religion which was publiquely begun through the vertuous disposition of King *Lucie* not fully two hundred years after Christ, continued till the coming in of the *Saxons*; By whom Paganism being every where else replanted, onely one part of the Island, whereinto the ancient, natural inhabitants the *Britains* were driven, retained constantly the faith of Christ, together with the same form of spiritual Regiment, which their Fathers had before received. Wherefore in the Histories of the Church we find very ancient mention made of our own Bishops. At the Council of *Ariminum* about the year 359 Britain had three of her Bishops present. At the arrival of *Augustine* the Monk, whom *Gregory* sent hither to reclaim the Saxons from Gentility about six hundred years after Christ, the Britains he found observers still of the self same Government by Bishops over the rest of the Clergy; under this form Christianity took root again, where it had been exiled; Under the self same form it remained * till the days of the *Norman* Conqueror. By him and his successors thereunto † sworn, it hath from that time till now, by the space of above five hundred years more been upheld. O Nation utterly without knowledge, without sence! We are not through error of mind deceived, but some wicked thing hath undoubtedly bewitched us, if we forsake that Government; the use whereof universal experience hath for so many years approved, and betake our selves unto a Regiment, neither appointed of God himself, as they who favour it pretend, nor till yesterday ever heard of among men. By the Jews *Festus* was much complained of, as being a Governor marvellous corrupt, and almost intolerable: Such notwithstanding were they who came after him, that men which thought the publique condition most afflicted under *Festus*, began to wish they had

Marginal notes:
Cyp.l.3.ep.3.

Sulpit. Sever. lib.2.

Beda Eccl. hist.l.2.c.2.
An.1066.
† alpidus tho-race sit Archie-piscopus Guliel-mum cogno-mento Nothum serrantem adnuc minarum & ca-dic in populum mittens reddidit & nigusti pro caaf rwanda re-tus.tuendaq, ec-clesiast. d.sc. sa-cram. obstrinxi.
Nubrig.l.1.c 1.

had him again, and to esteem him a Ruler commendable. Great things are hoped for at the hands of these new Presidents, whom Reformation would bring in: Notwithstanding the time may come, when Bishops whose Regiment doth now seem a yoke so heavy to bear, will be longed for again even by them that are the readiest to have it taken from off their necks. But in the hands of Divine Providence we leave the ordering of all such events; and come now to the Question it self which is raised concerning Bishops. For the better understanding whereof we must before hand set down what is meant, when in this Question we name a Bishop.

What a Bishop is, what his name doth import, and what doth belong to his Office: as he is a Bishop.

II. For whatsoever we bring from Antiquity by way of defence in this cause of Bishops, it is cast off as impertinent matter, all is wiped away with an odd kind of shifting Answer, *That the Bishops which now are, be not like unto them which were*. We therefore beseech all indifferent Judges to weigh sincerely with themselves how the case doth stand. If it should be at this day a controversie whether Kingly Regiment were lawful or no; peradventure in defence thereof, the long continuance, which it hath had sithence the first beginning might be alledged; mention perhaps might be made what Kings there were of old even in *Abrahams* time, what Soveraign Princes both before and after. Suppose that herein some man purposely bending his wit against Sovereignty, should think to elude all such allegations by making ample discovery through a number of particularities, wherein the Kings that are, do differ from those that have been, and should therefore in the end conclude, That such ancient examples are no convenient proofs of that Royalty which is now in use. Surely for decision of truth in this case there were no remedy, but only to shew the nature of Sovereignty, to sever it from accidental properties, make it clear that ancient and present Regality are one and the same in substance, how great odds soever otherwise may seem to be between them. In like manner, whereas a Question of late hath grown, whether Ecclesiastical Regiment by Bishops be lawful in the Church of Christ or no: In which Question, they that hold the Negative, being pressed with that general received order, according whereunto the most renowned Lights of the Christian World, have governed the same in every age as Bishops; seeing their manner is to reply, that such Bishops as those ancient were, ours are not: There is no remedy but to shew, that to be a Bishop is now the self same thing which it hath been; that one definition agreeth fully and truly as well to those elder, as to these latter Bishops. Sundry dissimilitudes we grant there are, which notwithstanding are not such that they cause any equivocation in the name, whereby we should think a Bishop in those times to have had a clean other definition then doth rightly agree unto Bishops as they are now: Many things there are in the state of Bishops, which the times have changed; Many a Parsonage at this day is larger then some ancient Bishopricks were; many an ancient Bishop poorer then at this day sundry under them in degree. The simple hereupon lacking judgement and knowledge to discern between the nature of things which changeth not, and these outward variable accidents, are made beleeve that a Bishop heretofore and now are things in their very nature so distinct that they cannot be judged the same. Yet to men that have any part of skill, what more evident and plain in Bishops, then that augmentation or diminution in their precincts, allowances, priviledges, and such like, do make a difference indeed, but no essential difference between one Bishop and another? As for those things in regard whereof we use properly to term them Bishops; those things whereby they essentially differ from other Pastors, those things which the natural definition of a Bishop must contain, what one of them is there more or less appliable unto Bishops now then of old? The name Bishop hath been borrowed from the (*a*) Grecians, with whom it signifieth one which hath principal charge to guide and oversee others. The same word in Ecclesiastical writings being applied unto Church-governors, at the first unto (*b*) all and not unto the chiefest

(*a*) Οι παρ Ἀθηναίοις εἰς χαρμε το guide and oversee others. τοις επισκόπε ποδεις οπισκέψα.

Ὃς τα παρ δεδοτις συμ-beroi Επισκοτει η φυλακας εκαλουντο ἐς ἐν Ἀλακωνι ἑρμοσαις ἱκτερον. *Suid.* Κατιστοιν ἰφ' ἑκαστὲ τῶν πτησιν ἀρχοντα οπιτασεῖν τε η ποιτασεων ὁ ἴδιας μεθεας Διουῖς. *Halicar. de Numa Pompilio, Antiq. l. 2.* Viut me Pompo es esse quem tota hec comparito & maritima ora habeat Επισκοπον ad quem del: Cur: & negotii summa referatur. *Cic. ad Attic. lib. 7. ep. 11.* (*b*) Acts 20 Phil. 1.1.

onely, grew in fhort time peculiar and proper to fignifie fuch Epifcopal Authority alone, as the chiefeft Governors exercifed over the reft. For with all names this is ufual, that in as much as they are not given till the things whereunto they are given have been fome time firft * obferved, therefore generally things are ancienter then the names whereby they are called.

Again, fith the firft things that grow into general obfervation, and do thereby give men occafion to find names for them, are thofe which being in many fubjects, are thereby the eafier, the oftner, and the more univerfally noted; it followeth that names impofed to fignifie common qualities or operations are ancienter, then is the reftraint of thofe names, to note an excellency of fuch qualities or operations in fome one or few amongft others. For example, the name Difciple being invented to fignifie generally a learner, it cannot choofe but in that fignification be more ancient then when it fignifieth as it were by a kinde of appropriation, thofe Learners who being taught of Chrift were in that refpect termed Difciples by an excellency. The like is to be feen in the name Apoftle, the ufe whereof to fignifie a Meffenger, muft needs be more ancient then that ufe which reftraineth it unto Meffengers fent concerning Evangelical affairs: Yea this ufe more ancient then that whereby the fame word is yet reftrained farther to fignifie onely thofe whom our Saviour himfelf immediately did fend. After the fame manner the Title or Name of a Bifhop having been ufed of old to fignifie both an Ecclefiaftical Overfeer in general, and more particularly alfo a Principal Ecclefiaftical Overfeer; it followeth, that this latter reftrained fignification is not fo antient as the former, being more common. Yet becaufe the things themfelves are always ancienter then their names; therefore that thing which the reftrained ufe of the word doth import; is likewife ancienter then the reftraint of the word is; and confequently that power of chief Ecclefiaftical Overfeers, which the term of a Bifhop importeth, was before the reftrained ufe of the name which doth import it. Wherefore a lame and an impotent kind of reafoning it is, when men go about to prove that in the Apoftles times there was no fuch thing as the reftrained name of a Bifhop doth now fignifie; becaufe in their writings there is found no reftraint of that name, but onely a general ufe whereby it reacheth unto all fpiritual Governors and Overfeers.

But to let go the name, and to come to the very nature of that thing which is thereby fignified in all kindes of Regiment whether Ecclefiaftical or Civil: as there are fundry operations publique, fo likewife great inequality there is in the fame operations, fome being of principal refpect, and therefore not fit to be dealt in by every one to whom publique actions, and thofe of good importance, are notwithftanding well and fitly enough committed. From hence have grown thofe different degrees of Magiftrates or publique perfons, even Ecclefiaftical as well as Civil. Amongft Ecclefiaftical Perfons therefore Bifhops being cheif ones; a Bifhops function muft be defined by that wherein his Cheifty confifteth. A Bifhop is a Minifter of God, unto whom with permanent continuance, there is given not onely power of adminiftring the Word and Sacraments, which power other Presbyters have; but alfo a further power to ordain Ecclefiaftical perfons, and a power of Cheifty in Government over Presbyters as well as Lay men, a power to be by way of jurifdiction a Paftor even to Paftors themfelves. So that this Office, as he is a Presbyter or Paftor, confifteth in thofe things which are common unto him with other Paftors, as in miniftring the Word and Sacraments: But thofe things incident unto his Office, which do properly make him a Bifhop, cannot be common unto him with other Paftors. Now even as Paftors, fo likewife Bifhops being principal Paftors, are either at large or elfe with reftraint. At large, when the fubject of their Regiment is indefinite, and not tyed to any certain place: Bifhops with reftaint are they whofe regiment over the Church is contained within fome definite, local compafs, beyond which compafs their jurifdiction reacheth not. Such therefore we always mean when we fpeak of that regiment by Bifhops which we hold a thing moft lawful, divine and holy in the Church of Chrift.

Marginal notes:

* And God brought them unto *Adam*, that *Adam* might fee or confider what names it was meet he fhould give unto them, G:n.2.19.

So alfo the name *Deacons*, a Minifter, appropriated to a certain order of Minifters.

The name likewife of a Minifter was common to divers degrees, which now is peculiarly among our felves given onely to Paftors, and not as anciently to Deacons alfo.

III. In our present regiment by Bishops two things there are complained of, the one their great Authority, and the other their great Honor. Touching the Authority of our Bishops, the first thing which therein displeaseth their Adversaries, is their Superiority which Bishops have over other Ministers. They which cannot brook the superiority which Bishops have, do notwithstanding themselves admit that some kind of difference and inequality there may be lawfully amongst Ministers: Inequality as touching gifts and graces they grant, because this is so plain that no mist in the world can be cast before mens eyes so thick, but that they needs must discern thorow it, that one Minister of the Gospel may be more learneder, holier and wiser, better able to instruct, more apt to rule and guide them then another: Unless thus much were confest, those men should lose their fame and glory whom they themselves do entitle the Lights and grand Worthies of this present age. Again, a priority of Order they deny not, but that there may be, yea such a priority as may been one man amongst many a principal Actor in those things whereunto sundry or them must necessarily concur, so that the same be admitted only during the time of such actions and no longer; that is to say just so much superiority, and neither more nor less may be liked of, then it hath pleased them in their own kind of regiment to set down. The inequality which they complain of is, *That one Minister of the Word and Sacraments should have a permanent superiority above another, or in any sort a superiority of power mandatory, judicial and coercive over other Ministers.* By us on the contrary side, inequality, *even such inequality as unto Bishops being Ministers of the Word and Sacraments granteth a superiority permanent above Ministers, yea a permanent superiority of power mandatory, judicial and coercive over them,* is maintained a thing allowable, lawful and good. For superiority of power may be either above them or upon them, in regard of whom it is termed superiority. One Pastor hath superiority of power above another, when either some are authorised to do things worthier then are permitted unto all, some are preferred to be principal Agents, the rest Agents with dependency and subordination. The former of these two kinds of superiority is such as the High-Priest had above other Priests of the Law, in being appointed to enter once a year the holy place, which the rest of the Priests might not do. The latter superiority such as Presidents have in those actions which are done by others with them, they nevertheless being principal and chief therein. One Pastor hath superiority of power, not onely above but upon another, when some are subject unto others commandment and judicial controlment, by vertue of publique jurisdiction. Superiority in this last kinde is utterly denied to be allowable, in the rest it is onely denied that the lasting continuance and setled permanency thereof is lawful. So that if we prove at all the lawfulness of superiority in this last kind, where the same is simply denied, and of permanent superiority in the rest where some kind of superiority is granted, but with restraint to the term and continuance of certain actions, with which the same must, as they say, expire and cease; If we can show these two things maintainable, we bear up sufficiently that which the adverse party endeavoureth to overthrow. Our desire therefore is, that this issue may be strictly observed, and those things accordingly judged of, which we are to alleadge. This we boldly therefore set down, as a most infallible truth, *That the Church of Christ is at this day lawfully, and so hath been sithence the first beginning, governed by Bishops, having permanent superiority, and ruling power over other Ministers of the Word and Sacraments.*

For the plainer explication whereof, let us briefly declare first, The birth and original of the same power, whence and by what occasion it grew. Secondly, What manner of power antiquity doth witness Bishops to have had more then Presbyters, which were no Bishops. Thirdly, After what sort Bishops together with Presbyters have used to govern the Churches under them, according to the like testimonial evidence of antiquity. Fourthly, How far the same Episcopal power hath usually extended, unto what number of persons it hath reached, what bounds and limits of place it hath had. This done, we may afterwards descend unto those by whom the same either hath been heretofore, or is at this present hour gainsaid.

IV. The

IV. The first Bishops in the Church of Christ were his blessed Apostles, for the Office whereunto *Matthias* was chosen the sacred History doth term Ἐπισκοπὴν an Episcopal Office. Which being spoken expresly of one, agreeth no less unto them all then unto him. For which cause St. *Cyprian* speaking generally of them all doth call them * Bishops. They which were termed Apostles, as being sent of Christ to publish his Gospel throughout the world, and were named likewise Bishops, in that the care of Government was also committed unto them, did no less perform the offices of their Episcopal Authority by governing, then of their Apostolical by teaching. The word Ἐπισκοπὴ, expressing that part of their office which did consist in regiment, proveth not (I grant) their chiefty in regiment over others; because as then that name was common unto the function of their inferiors, and not peculiar unto theirs. But the History of their actions sheweth plainly enough how the thing it self which that name appropriated importeth, that is to say, even such spiritual chiefty as we have already defined to be properly Episcopal, was in the holy Apostles of Christ. Bishops therefore they were at large. But was it lawful for any of them to be a Bishop with restraint? True it is their charge was indefinite: yet so, that in case they did all, whether severally or joyntly discharge the Office of proclaiming every where the Gospel, and of guiding the Church of Christ, none of them casting off his part in their (a) burthen which was laid upon them; there doth appear no impediment but that they having received their common charge indefinitely might in the execution thereof notwithstanding restrain themselves, or at leastwise be restrained by the after commandment of the Spirit, without contradiction or repugnancy unto that charge more indefinite and general before given them; especially if it seemed at any time requisite, and for the greater good of the Church, that they should in such sort tye themselves unto some special part of the flock of Jesus Christ, guiding the same in several as Bishops. For first, notwithstanding our Saviours commandment unto them all to go and preach unto all Nations: Yet some restraint we see there was made, when by agreement between *Paul* and *Peter* moved with those effects of their labours which the providence of God brought forth; the one betook himself unto the Gentiles, the other unto the Jews, for the exercise of that Office of every where preaching. A further restraint of their Apostolical labours as yet there was also made, when they divided themselves into several parts of the world; (a) *John* for his charge taking *Asia*, and so the residue other quarters to labour in. If nevertheless it seem very hard that we should admit a restraint so particular, as after that general charge received, to make any Apostle notwithstanding the Bishop of some one Church, what think we of the Bishop of *Jerusalem* (b) *James*, whose consecration unto that other Sea of the world, because it was not meet that it should at any time be left void of some Apostle doth seem to have been the very cause of St. *Pauls* miraculous vocation to make up the (c) number of the Twelve again, for the gathering of nations abroad, even as the (d) martyrdom of the other *James* the reason why *Barnabas* in his stead was called. Finally, Apostles whether they did settle in any one certain place, as *James*, or else did otherwise as the Apostle *Paul*; Episcopal Authority either at large or with restraint they had and exercised: Their Episcopal power they sometimes gave unto others to exercise as agents onely in their stead, and as it were by commission from them. Thus (e) *Titus*, and thus *Timothy* at the first, though (f) afterwards indued with Apostolical power of their own. For in process of time the Apostles gave Episcopal Authority, and that to continue always with them which had it.

We are able to number up them, saith Ireneus, who by the Apostles were made Bishops. In Rome he affirmeth that the Apostles themselves made Linus the first Bishop. Again of Polycarp he saith likewise, that the Apostles made him Bishop of the Church of Smyrna. Of Antioch they made Evodius Bishop as Ignatius witnesseth, exhorting that

Marginal notes:

From whence it hath grown that the Church is governed by Bishops. *meminisse Dia coni, debere quoniam Apostolos id est Episco, or propositos Dominus elegit. cyp.l.1.ep.9.*

Rom. 2.14,15 1 Cor. 9.16. Joh. 21.15,16

Gal. 2.8.

a Him *Eusebius* doth name the Governour of the Churches in Asia *Lib. 3. Hist. Eccles. cap 26. Tertullian* calleth the same Churches St. *Johns* Foster daughters *Lib. 3. adversus Marcion.*

b *Iacobus qui appellatur frater Domini cognomento iustus post passionem Domini statim ab Apostolis Hierosol. marum Episcopus ordinatus est. Hieron de script. Ecclef. Eodem tempore iacobum primum sedem Episcopalem Ecclesia quae est Hierosolymis obtinuisse memoriae traditur, Euseb. Hist. ecclef. lib 2. cap. 1.* The same seemeth to be intimated Acts 15, 13. and Acts 21.18. c Acts 12.2. a Acts 13.2.

e Tit 1.5. f This appeareth by those subscriptions which are set after the Epistle to *Titus*, and the second to *Timothy*, and by *Eusebius Ecclesiast lib. 3. c. 4.*

Iren. lib. 3. cap 3.

In Ep. ad Antioc.

that Church to tread in his holy steps, and to follow his vertuous example. The Apostles therefore were the first which had such authority, and all others who have it after them in orderly fort are their lawful Successors, whether they succeed in any particular Church, where before them some Apostle hath been seated, As Simon succeeded James in Jerusalem; or else be otherwise endued with the same kind of Bishoply power, although it be not where any Apostle before hath been. For to succeed them, is after them to have that Episcopal kind of power which was first given to them. All Bishops are, saith Jerome, the Apostles successors. In like fort Cyprian doth term Bishops, Prepositos qui Apostolis vicaria ordinatione succedunt. From hence it may happily seem to have grown, that they whom now we call Bishops * were usually termed at the first Apostles, and so did carry their very names in whose rooms of spiritual authority they succeeded. Such as deny Apostles to have (a) any successors at all in the office of their Apostleship, may hold that opinion without contradiction to this of ours, if they well explain themselves in declaring what truly and properly Apostleship is: In some things every Presbyter, in some things onely Bishops, in some things neither the one nor the other are the Apostles Successors. The Apostles were sent as special chosen (b) eye-witnesses of Jesus Christ, from whom (c) immediately they received their whole Embassage, and their Commission to be the principal (d) first founders of an House of God consisting as well of (e) Gentiles as of Jews: In this there are not after them any other like unto them; And yet the Apostles have now their successors upon earth, their true successors, if not in the largeness, surely in the kind of that Episcopal function, whereby they had power to sit as spiritual ordinary Judges, both over Laity and over Clergy where Churches Christian were established.

V. The Apostles of our Lord did according unto those directions which were given them from above, erect Churches in all such Cities as received the Word of Truth, the Gospel of God: All Churches by them erected, received from them the same Faith, the same Sacraments, the same form of publick regiment. The form of Regiment by them established at first was, That the Laity or people should be subject unto a Colledge of Ecclesiastical persons, which were in every such City appointed for that purpose. These in their writings they term sometime Presbyters, sometime Bishops. To take one Church out of a number for a pattern what the rest were, the Presbyters of Ephesus, as it is in the History of their departure from the Apostle Paul at Miletum, are said to have wept abundantly all, which speech doth shew them to have been many. And by the Apostles exhortation it may appear, that they had not each his several flock to feed, but were in common appointed to feed that one flock the Church of Ephesus; for which cause the phrase of his speech is this, Attendite gregi, Look all to that one flock over which the Holy Ghost hath made you Bishops. These persons Ecclesiastical being termed as then, Presbyters and Bishops both, were all subject unto Paul as to an higher Governor appointed of God to be over them. But for as much as the Apostles could not themselves be present in all Churches, and as the Apostle St. Paul foretold the Presbyters of the Ephesians that there would rise up from amongst their own selves, men speaking perverse things, to draw Disciples after them; there did grow in short time amongst the Governors of each Church, those emulations, strifes, and contentions, whereof there could be no sufficient remedy provided, except according unto the order of Jerusalem already begun, some one were indued with Episcopal Authority over the rest, which one being resident might keep them in order, and have preheminence or principality in those things, wherein the equality of many agents was the cause of disorder and trouble. This one President or Governour amongst the rest had his known Authority established a long time before that settled difference of name and title took place, whereby such alone were named Bishops. And therefore in the book of St. Johns Revelation we find that they are entituled Angels. It will perhaps be answered, That the Angels of those Churches were onely in every Church a Minister of the Word and Sacraments.

Sacraments : But then we ask, Is it probable that in every of these *Churches*, even in *Ephesus* it self, where many such Ministers were long before, as ath been proved, there was but one such when *John* directed his speech to the Angel of that Church? If there were many, surely St. *John* in naming but onely one of them an Angel, did behold in that one somewhat above the rest. Nor was this order peculiar unto some few Churches, but the whole world universally became subject thereunto ; insomuch as they did not account it to be a Church, which was not subject unto a Bishop. It was the general received perswasion of the ancient Christian world , that *Ecclesia est in Episcopo*, the outward being of a Church consisteth in the having of a Bishop : That where Colledges of Presbyters were, there was at the first, equality amongst them, St. *Jerome* thinketh it a matter clear; but when the rest were thus equal, so that no one of them could command any other as inferiour unto him, they all were controleable by the Apostles, who had that Episcopal authority abiding at the first in themselves, which they afterwards derived unto others. The cause wherefore they under themselves appointed such Bishops as were not every where at the first, is said to have been those strifes and contentions, for remedy whereof, whether the Apostles alone did conclude of such a regiment, or else they together with the whole Church judging it a fit and a needful policy did agree to receive it for a custom ; no doubt but being established by them on whom the Holy Ghost was powred in so abundant measure for the ordering of Christs Church, it had either Divine appointment beforehand, or Divine approbation afterwards, and is in that respect to be acknowledged the Ordinance of God, no less then that ancient Jewish regiment, whereof though *Jethro* were the Deviser, yet after that God had allowed it, all men were subject unto it, as to the Polity of God, and not of *Jethro*. That so the ancient Fathers did think of Episcopal Regiment , that they held this order as a thing received from the blessed Apostles themselves, and authorized even from heaven, we may perhaps more easily prove, then obtain that they all shall grant it who see it proved. St. *Augustine* setteth it down for a principle, that whatsoever positive order the whole Church every where doth observe, the same it must needs have received from the very Apostles themselves, unless perhaps some general Councel were the Authors of it. And he saw that the ruling superiority of Bishops was a thing universally established, not by the force of any Councel, (for Councels do all presuppose Bishops , nor can there any Councel be named so antient , either general , or as much as provincial, sithence the Apostles own times, but we can shew that Bishops had their Authority before it , and not from it.) Wherefore St. *Augustine* knowing this , could not chuse but reverence the Authority of Bishops , as a thing to him apparently and most clearly apostolical. But it will be perhaps objected that Regiment by Bishops was not so universal nor antient as we pretend; and that an Argument hereof may be *Jeroms* own Testimony , who living at the very same time with St. *Augustine* , noteth this kind of Regiment as being no where antient , saving onely in *Alexandria*; his words are these, *It was for a remedy of Schism that one was afterwards chosen to be placed above the rest, least every mans pulling unto himself , should rend asunder the Church of Christ. For (that which also may serve for an Argument or token hereof)* at Alexandria *from Mark the Evangelist, unto Heraclas and Dionysius, the Presbyters always chose one* OF THEMSELVES, *whom they placed in higher degree , and gave unto him the Title of Bishop.* Now St. *Jerom* they say would never have picked out that one Church from amongst so many , and have noted that in it there had been Bishops from the time that St. *Mark* lived , if so be the self same order were of like antiquity every where ; his words therefore must be thus scholied ; In the Church of *Alexandria*, Presbyters indeed had even from the time of St. *Mark* the Evangelist , always a Bishop to rule over them for a remedy against Divisions , Factions and Schismes. Not so in other Churches, neither in that very Church any longer then *usq; ad Heraclam & Dionysium*, till *Heraclas* and his Successor *Dionysius* were Bishops. But this construction doth bereave the words construed, partly of wit, and partly of truth, it maketh them both absurd and false. For if the meaning be that Episcopal Government in that Church was then expired , it must have expired with the end of some one , and not of two several Bishops days, unless perhaps it fell sick under *Heraclas* , and with *Dionysius* gave up the Ghost. Besides it is clearly untrue that the Presbyters of that Church did then cease to be under a Bishop. Who doth not know that after *Dionysius* ,
　　　　　　　　　　　　　　　　　　　　　　　　　　　　　Maximus

* B

Cypr. l. 4. Epist. 9.

Hieron. Ep. ad Evag.

Exod. 18. 19.

Epist. ad Ianuar.

Epist. ad Evag.

T. C. l. 2. p. 82. It is to be observed that *Ierom* saith, it was so in *Alexandria*, signifying that in other Churches it was no so.

Socrat.l. cap.3

Maximus was Bishop of *Alexandria*, after him *Theonas*, after him *Peter*, after him *Achillas*, after him *Alexander*, of whom *Socrates* in this sort writeth; it fortuned on a certain time that this *Alexander* in the presence of the Presbyters which were under him, and of the rest of the Clergy there, discoursed somewhat curiously and subtilly of the holy Trinity, bringing high Philosophical proofs, that there is in the Trinity an Unity. Whereupon *Arius* one of the Presbyters which were placed in that degree under *Alexander*, opposed eagerly himself against those things which were uttered by the Bishop. So that thus long Bishops continued even in the Church of *Alexandria*. Nor did their Regiment here cease; but these also had others their Successors till St. *Jeroms* own time, who living long after *Heraclas*, and *Dionysius* had ended their days, did not yet live himself to see the Presbyters of *Alexandria*, otherwise then subject unto a Bishop. So that we cannot with any truth, so interpret his words, as to mean, that in the Church of *Alexandria* there had been Bishops indued with Superiority over Presbyters from St. *Marks* time, onely till the time of *Heraclas* and of *Dionysius*; Wherefore that St. *Jerom* may receive a more probable interpretation then this, We answer, that generally of Regiment by Bishops, and what term of continuance it had in the Church of *Alexandria*, it was no part of his mind to speak, but to note one onely circumstance belonging to the manner of their election, which circumstance is, that in *Alexandria* they used to chuse their Bishops altogether out of the colledge of their own Presbyters, and neither from abroad nor out of any other inferior order of the Clergy, whereas oftentimes (a) elsewhere

Vnto greeting Bishop of Antioch, Hero a
Deacon there
was made
Successor,
Chrysostom be-
ing a Presby-
ter of that ch.
was chosen
to succeed
Nectarius in
the Bishop-
rick of Con-
stantinople.

the use was to chuse as well from abroad as at home, as well inferior unto Presbyters as Presbyters when they saw occasion. This custome, saith he, the Church of *Alexandria* did always keep, till in *Heraclas* and *Dionysius*, they began to do otherwise. These two were the very first not chose out of their Colledge of Presbyters.

The drift and purpose of St. *Jeromes* speech doth plainly show what his meaning was; for whereas some did over-extol the Office of the Deacon in the Church of *Rome*, where Deacons being grown great, through wealth, challenged place above Presbyters: St. *Jerom* to abate this insolency, writing to *Evagrius*, diminisheth by all means the Deacons estimation, and lifteth up Presbyters as far as possible the truth might bear. *An attendant*, saith he, *upon Tables and Widows proudly to exalt himself above them, at whose prayers is made the body and blood of Christ; above them, between whom and Bishops there was at the first for a time no difference neither in authority nor in title. And whereas afterward schisms and contentions made it necessary that some one should be placed over them, by which occasion the title of Bishop became proper unto that one, yet was that one chosen out of the Presbyters, as being the chiefest, the highest, the worthiest degree of the Clergie, and not out of Deacons; in which consideration also it seemeth that in Alexandria even from St. Mark to Heraclas and Dionysius, Bishops there, the Presbyters evermore have chosen one of themselves, and not a Deacon at any time, to be their Bishop. Nor let any man think that Christ hath one Church in Rome and another in the rest of the world; that in Rome he alloweth Deacons to be honoured above Presbyters, and otherwhere will have them to be in the next degree to the Bishop. If it be deemed that abroad where Bishops are poorer, the Presbyters under them may be the next unto them in honour; but at Rome where the Bishop hath ample revenues, the Deacons whose estate is nearest for wealth, may be also for estimation the next unto him: We must know that a Bishop in the meanest City is no less a Bishop then he who is seated in the greatest; the countenance of a rich, and the meanness of a poor estate doth make no odds between Bishops; and therefore if a Presbyter at Engubium be the next in degree to a Bishop, surely, even at Rome it ought in reason to be so likewise; and not a Deacon for wealths sake only to be above, who by order should be, and elsewhere is, underneath a Presbyter. But ye will say that according to the custom of Rome a Deacon presenteth unto the Bishop him which standeth to be ordained Presbyter; and upon the Deacons testimony given concerning his fitness, he receiveth at the Bishops hands Ordination: So that in Rome the Deacon having this special preheminence, the Presbyter ought there to give place unto him. Wherefore is the custom of one City brought against the practice of the whole World? The paucity of Deacons in the Church of Rome hath gotten the credit, as unto Presbyters their multitude hath been cause of contempt: Howbeit even in the Church of Rome, Presbyters sit and Deacons stand; an Argument as strong against the superiority of Deacons, as the forealleaged reason doth seem for it. Besides, whosoever is promoted must needs be raised from a*
lower

lower degree to an higher; wherefore either let him which is Presbyter be made a Deacon, that so the Deacon may appear to be the greater; or if of Deacons Presbyters be made, let them know themselves to be in regard of Deacons, though below in gain, yet above in Office. And to the end we may understand that those Apostolical Orders are taken out of the Old Testament, what Aaron and his Sons and the Levites were in the Temple, the same in the Church may Bishops and Presbyters and Deacons challenge unto themselves. This is the very drift and substance, this the true construction and sence of St. *Jeroms* whole discourse in that Epistle: Which I have therefore endeavoured the more at large to explain, because no one thing is less effectual or more usual to be alleaged against the antient Authority of Bishops; concerning whose Government St. *Jeroms* own words otherwhere are sufficient to show his opinion, that this order was not onely in *Alexandria* so ancient, but even as ancient in other Churches. We have before alleadged his testimony touching *James* the Bishop of *Jerusalem*. As for Bishops in other Churches on the first of the Epistle to *Titus*, thus he speaketh, *Till through instinct of the devil there grew in the Church factions, and among the people it began to be profest, I am of* Paul, *I of* Apollo, *and I of* Cephas, *Churches were governed by the common advice of Presbyters; but when every one began to reckon those whom himself had baptized his own and not* Christs, *it was decreed* IN THE WHOLE WORLD *that one chosen out of the Presbyters should be placed above the rest, to whom all care of the Church should belong, and so the seeds of schism be removed.* If it be so, that by St. *Jeroms* own confession this order was not then begun when people in the Apostles absence began to be divided into factions by their Teachers, and to rehearse, I am of Paul, but that even at the very first appointment thereof was agreed upon and received thorowout the world; how shall any man be perswaded that the same *Jerom* thought it so ancient no where saving in *Alexandria*, one only Church of the whole world. A sentence there is indeed of St. *Jeroms* which being not throughly considered and weighed may cause his meaning so to be taken, as if he judged Episcopal regiment to have been the Churches invention long after, and not the Apostles own institution; as namely, when he admonisheth Bishops in this manner; *As therefore Presbyters do know that the custom of the Church makes them subject to the Bishop which it set over them; so let (b)t Bishops know*

that custom rather then the truth of any Ordinance of the Lords maketh them greater then the rest, and that with common advice they ought to govern the Church. To clear the sence of these words therefore, as we have done already the former: Laws which the Church from the beginning universally hath observed were some delivered by Christ himself, with a charge to keep them till the worlds end, as the law of baptizing and administring the holy Eucharist; some brought in afterwards by the Apostles, yet not with-

(b) Bishops he meaneth by restraint; For Episcopal power was always in the Church instituted by Christ himself, the Apostles being in government Bishops at large; as no man will deny having received from Christ himself that Episcopal Authority. For which cause Cyprian hath said of them. *Meminisse Diaconi debent quoniam Apostolos id est episcopos & praepositos Dominus elegit: Diacones autem post ascensum Domini in caelos Apostoli sibi constituerunt & episcopatus sui & Ecclesia ministros.* Lib. 3. Ep. 9.

out the special direction of the Holy Ghost, as occasions did arise. Of this sort are those Apostolical orders and laws whereby Deacons, Widows, Virgins were first appointed in the Church.

This answer to Saint *Jerom*, seemeth dangerous, I have qualified it as I may, by addition of some words of restraint; yet I satisfie not my self, in my judgment it would be altered. Now whereas *Jerom* doth term the Government of Bishops by restraint, an Apostolical tradition, acknowledging thereby the same to have been of the Apostles own institution, it may be demanded how these two will stand together; namely, that the Apostles by divine instinct, should be as Jerom confesseth the *Authors* of that regiment, and yet the custome of the Church be accompted (for so by Jerom it may seem to be in this place accompted) the chiefest prop that upholdeth the same? To this we answer, That for as much as the whole body of the Church, hath power to alter with general consent and upon necessary occasions, even the positive laws of the Apostles, if there be no commandment to the contrary, and it manifestly appears to her, that change of times have clearly taken away the very reason of Gods first institution, as by sundry examples may be most clearly proved; What laws the universal Church might change, and doth not; if they have long continued without any alteration; it seemeth that St. Jerom ascribeth the continuance of such positive laws, though instituted by God himself, to the judgement of the Church. For

they

they which might abrogate a Law and do not, are properly said to uphold, to establish it, and to give it being. The Regiment therefore whereof Jerom speaketh being positive, and consequently, not absolutely necessary, but of a changeable nature, because there is no Divine voice which in express words forbiddeth it to be changed, he might imagine hath that it came by the Apostles by very Divine appointment at the first, and not withstanding be after a sort, said to stand in force, rather by the custome of the Church, chosing to continue in it, then by the necessary constraint of any Commandment from the Word, requiring perpetual continuance thereof. So that St. Jeromes admonition is reasonable, sensible, and plain, being contrived to this effect ; The ruling superiority of one Bishop over many Presbyters, in each Church, is an order descended from Christ to the Apostles, who were themselves Bishops at large, and from the Apostles to those whom they in their steads appointed Bishops over particular Countries and Cities, and even from those antient times, universally established, thus many years it hath continued throughout the World; for which cause Presbyters must not grudge to continue subject unto their Bishops, unless they will proudly oppose themselves against that which God himself ordained by his Apostles, and the whole Church of Christ approveth and judgeth most convenient. On the other side Bishops albeit they may avouch with conformity of truth, that their Authority hath thus descended even from the very Apostles themselves, yet the absolute and everlasting continuance of it, they cannot say that any Commandment of the Lord doth injoyn ; *And therefore must acknowledge that the Church hath power by universal consent upon urgent cause to take it away, if thereunto she be constrained through the proud, tyrannical, and unreformable dealings of her Bishops, whose Regiment she hath thus long delighted in, because she hath found it good and requisite to be so governed. Wherefore least Bishops forget themselves, as if none on earth had Authority to touch their states, let them continually bear in mind, that it is rather the force of custome, whereby the Church having so long found it good to continue under the Regiment of her vertuous Bishops, doth still uphold, maintain, and honour them, in that respect, then that any such true and heavenly Law, can be showed, by the evidence whereof, it may of a truth appear that the Lord himself hath appointed Presbyters for ever to be under the Regiment of Bishops, in what sort soever they behave themselves ; let this consideration be a bridle unto them, let it teach them not to disdain the advice of their Presbyters, but to use their authority with so much the greater humility and moderation, as a Sword which the Church hath power to take from them.* In all this there is no let why St. Jerom might not think the Authors of Episcopal Regiment to have been the very blessed Apostles themselves, directed therein by the special motion of the Holy Ghost, which the ancients all before, and besides him and himself also elsewhere, being known to hold, we are not without better evidence then this, to think him in judgment divided both from himself and from them. Another Argument that the Regiment of Churches by one Bishop over many Presbyters, hath been always held Apostolical, may be this. We find that throughout all those Cities where the Apostles did plant Christianity, the History of times hath noted succession of pastors in the seat of one, not of many (there being in every such Church evermore many Pastors) and the first one in every rank of succession, we find to have been if not some Apostle, yet some Apostles Disciple. By *Epiphanius* the Bishops of *Jerusalem* are reckoned down from *James* to *Hilarion* then Bishop. Of them which boasted that they held the same things which they received of such as lived with the Apostles themselves, *Tertullian* speaketh after this sort, let them therefore shew the beginnings of their Churches, let them recite their Bishops one by one, each in such sort succeeding other, that the first Bishop of them have had, for his Author and Predecessour, some Apostle, or at least some Apostolical Person, who persevered with the Apostles. For so Apostolical Churches are wont to bring forth the evidence of their estates. So doth the Church of *Smyrna*, having *Polycarp* whom *John* did consecrate; Catalogues of Bishops in a number of other Churches, Bishops and succeeding one another, from the very Apostles times are by *Eusebius* and *Socrates* collected, whereby it appeareth so clear, as nothing in the World more, that under them and by their appointment this order began, which maketh many Presbyters subject unto the Regiment of some one Bishop. For as in *Rome* while the civil ordering of the Commonwealth, was joyntly and equally in the hands of two Consuls, *Historical* Records concerning them, did evermore mention them both, and note which two as Collegues

Lib 2. to 2.
H cer f.66.

De prescrip.
adver. heret.

legues fuceeded from time to time; So there is no doubt but Ecclesiastical antiquity had done the very like, had not one Pastors place and calling been always so eminent above the rest in the same Church. And what need we to seek far for proofs that the Apostles who began this order of Regiment by Bishops, did it not but by divine instinct, when without such direction things of far less weight and moment they attempted not? *Paul* and *Barnabas* did not open their mouthes to the Gentiles, till the Spirit had said, separate me *Paul* and *Barnabas* for the work whereunto I have sent them. The Eunuch by *Philip* was nither baptized nor instructed before the Angel of God was sent to give him notice that so it pleased the most High. In *Asia*, *Paul* and the rest were silent, because the spirit forbad them to speak. When they intended to have seen *Bythinia* they stayed their journey, the Spirit not giving them leave to go. Before *Timothy* was imployed in those Episcopal affairs of the Church, about which the Apostle St. *Paul* used him, the Holy Ghost gave special charge for his Ordination, and prophetical intelligence more then once, what success the same would have. And shall we think that *James* was made Bishop of *Jerusalem*, *Evodius* Bishop of the Church of *Antioch*, the Angels in the Churches of *Asia* Bishops, that Bishops every where were appointed to take away factions, contentions and Schisms, without some like divine instigation and direction of the Holy Ghost? Wherefore let us not fear to be herein bold and peremptory; that if any thing in the Churches Government, surely the first institution of Bishops was from Heaven, was even of God, the Holy Ghost was the Author of it.

Acts. 13.
Acts 8.
Acts 16.
1 Tim. 1. 18.

VI. A Bishop, saith St. *Augustin*, is a Presbyters Superior, but the question is now wherein that superiority did consist. The Bishops preeminence we say therefore was twofold. First he excelled in latitude of the power of order, secondly in that kind of power which belongeth unto jurisdiction. Priests in the law had authority and power to do greater things then *Levites*, the high Priest greater then inferiour Priests might do, therefore *Levites* were beneath Priests, and Priests inferiour to the high Priest, by reason of the very degree of dignity, and of worthiness in the nature of those functions which they did execute, and not onely for that the one had power to command and controul the other. In like sort Priests having a waightier and a worthier charge then Deacons had, the Deacon was in this sort the Presbyters inferior, and where we say that a Bishop was likewise ever accompted a Presbyters superior, even according unto his very power of order, we must of necessity declare what principal duties belonging unto that kind of power a Bishop might perform, and not a Presbyter. The custome of the primitive Church in confecrating holy Virgins, and Widows, unto the service of God and his Church, is a thing not obscure, but easie to be known, both *by that which* St. Paul *himself concerning them hath, and by the letter consonant evidence of other mens writings*. Now a part of the preeminence which Bishops had in their power of order, was that by them onely such were confecrated. Again, the power of ordaining both Deacons and Presbyters, the power to give the power of order unto others, this also hath been always peculiar unto Bishops. It hath not been heard of, that inferiour Presbyters were ever authorized to ordein. And concerning ordination so great force and dignity it hath, that whereas Presbyters by such power as they have received for Administration of the Sacraments, are able onely to beget Children unto God; Bishops having power to Ordain, do by vertue thereof create fathers to the people of God, as *Epiphanius* fitly disputeth. There are which hold that between a Bishop and a Presbyter, touching power of order, there is no difference: The reason of which conceipt is for that they see Presbyters no less then Bishops Authorized to offer up the prayers of the Church, to Preach the Gospel, to Baptize, to Administer the holy Eucharist, but they considered not with all as they should, that the Presbyters authority to do these things is derived from the Bishops which doth ordein him thereunto, so that even in those things which are common unto both, yet the power of the one, is as it were a certain light borrowed from the others lamp. The Apostles being Bishops at large, Ordeined every where Presbyters. *Titus* and *Timothy* having received Episcopal power, as Apostolique Embassadors or Legates, the one in *Greece*, the other in *Ephesus*, they both did by vertue thereof, likewise ordein throughout all Churches

What manner of power Bishops from the first beginning have had.

Aug. Ep. 19. ad Hierom. & de hæres. 53.

1 Cor. 7. 25.
1 Tim. 5. 9.
Tertul. de. vel. virg.

Epiph. 3. l. to. 1. hær. 7.

Acts 14. 23.

Tim. 1. 5.
1 Tim 5. 22.

Deacons

Apud Æ gyp-
tum Presbyteri
consignant e
pratens ron fit
t prf opus com,
q. vulgo Arb.
dic. in 4. F p ad
Ephef.

Deacons and Presbyters within the circuits allotted unto them. As for Bishops by restraint, their power this way incommunicable unto Presbyters, which of the antients do not acknowledge? I make not confirmation any part of that power which hath always belonged onely unto Bishops; because in some places the custom was that Presbyters might also confirm in the absence of a Bishop; albeit for the most part none but onely Bishops were thereof the allowed Ministers.

Here it will be perhaps objected that the power of Ordination it self was not every where peculiar and proper unto Bishops, as may be seen by a Council of Carthage, which sheweth their Churches Order to have been. That Presbyters should together with the Bishop lay hands upon the ordained. But the Answer hereunto is easie; For doth it hereupon follow that the power of Ordination was not principally and originally in the Bishop? Our Saviour hath said unto his Apostles, *With me ye shall sit and judge the Twelve Tribes of Israel*; yet we know that to him alone it belongeth to judge the World, and that to him all judgement is given. With us even at this day Presbyters are licensed to do as much as this Council speaketh of, if any be present. Yet will not any man thereby conclude that in this Church others then Bishops are allowed to ordain : The association of Presbyters is no sufficient proof that the power of Ordination is in them; but rather that it never was in them, we may hereby understand, for that no man is able to shew either Deacon or Presbyters ordained by Presbyters only, and his Ordination accounted lawful in any antient part of the Church; every where examples being found both of Deacons and of Presbyters ordained by Bishops alone oftentimes, neither ever in that respect thought unsufficient. Touching that other chiefty, which is of Jurisdiction; amongst the Jews he which was highest through the worthiness of peculiar duties incident into his function in the legal service of God, did bear always in Ecclesiastical jurisdiction the chiefest sway. As long as the glory of the Temple of God did last, there were in it sundry orders of men consecrated unto the service thereof; one sort of them inferior unto another in dignity and degree; the Nathiners subordinate unto the Levites, the Levites unto the Priests, the rest of the Priests to those twenty four, which were cheif Priests, and they all to the High Priest. If any man surmise that the difference between them was onely by distinction in the former kind of power, and not in this latter of jurisdiction, are not the words of the Law manifest which make *Eleazar*

Numb. 3 32
the Son of *Aaron* the Priest cheif Captain of the Levites, and overseer of them, unto whom the charge of the Sanctuary was committed? Again at the commandment of *Aaron* and his Sons, are not the Gersonites themselves required to do all their
Numb. 4 27.
2 Chron. 19.11
service in the whole charge belonging unto the Gersonites being inferiour Priests as *Aaron* and his Sons were High Priests? Did not *Jehoshaphat* appoint *Amarias* the Priest to be cheif over them who were Judges for the cause of the Lord in *Jerusalem*? Priests, saith Josephus, *Worship God continually, and the eldest of the stock*
Josph. ant q.
p 612.
are governors over the rest, He doth sacrifice unto God before others, he hath care of the Laws, judgeth controversies, correcteth offendors, and whosoever obeyeth him not is convict of impiety against God. But unto this they answer, That the reason thereof was because the High-Priest did prefigure Christ, and represent to the people that cheifty of our Saviour which was to come; so that Christ being now come there is no cause why such preheminence should be given unto any one. Which fancy pleaseth so well the humour of all sorts of rebellious spirits that they all seek to shroud themselves under it. Tell the *Anabaptist* which holdeth the use of the sword unlawful for a Christian man, that God himself did allow his people to make wars; they have their answer round and ready, *Those antient wars were figures of the spiritual wars of Christ.* Tell the Barrowist what sway *David*, and others the Kings of *Israel* did bear in the ordering of spiritual affairs, the same answer again serveth, namely, *That David and the rest of the Kings of Israel prefigured Christ.* Tell the Martinist of the High-Priests great authority and jurisdiction amongst the Jews, what other thing doth serve his turn but the self-same shift; *By the power of the High-Priest the universal supreme Authority of our Lord Jesus Christ was shadowed.* The thing is true, that indeed High-Priests were figures of Christ, yet this was in things belonging unto their power of Christ; they figured Christ by entring into the holy place, by offering for the sins of all the people once a year, and by other the like duties : But that to govern and to maintain order amongst those that were subject

to

to them, is an office figurative and abrogated by Chrift coming in the Miniftry; that their exercife of jurifdiction was figurative, yea figurative in fuch fort, that it had no other caufe of being inftituted, but onely to ferve as a reprefentation of fomewhat to come, and that herein the Church of Chrift ought not to follow them; this Article is fuch as muft be confirmed, if any way by miracle, otherwife it will hardly enter into the heads of reafonable men, why the High-Prieft fhould more figure Chrift in being a Judge, then in being whatfoever he might be befides. St. Cyprian deemed it no wrefting of Scripture to challenge as much for Chriftian Bifhops, as was given to the High-Prieft amongft the Jews, and to urge the Law of Mofes as being moft effectual to prove it. St. Jerome likewife thought it an argument fufficient to ground the Authority of Bifhops upon. *To the end, faith he, we may underftand Apoftolical traditions to have been taken from the Old Teftament, that which Aaron, and his Sons, and the Levites were in the Temple; Bifhops, and Presbyters and Deacons in the Church may lawfully challenge to themfelves.* In the Office of a Bifhop Ignatius obferveth thefe two functions ἱεραπεύειν ϰỳ ἄρχειν, concerning the one fuch is a preheminence of a Bifhop, that he onely hath the heavenly myfteries of God committed originally unto him, fo that otherwife then by his Ordination, and by authority received from him, others befides him are not licenfed therein to deal as ordinary Minifters of Gods Church. And touching the other part of their facred Function, wherein the power of their jurifdiction doth appear, firft how the Apoftles themfelves, and fecondly how *Titus* and *Timothy* had rule and jurifdiction over Presbyters, no man is ignorant. And had not Chriftian Bifhops afterward the like power? *Ignatius* Bifhop of *Antioch* being ready by bleffed martyrdom to end his life, writeth unto his Presbyters the Paftors under him in this fort, οἱ πρεσβύτεροι ποιμάνατε τὸ ἐν ὑμῖν ποίμνιον, ἕως ἀναδείξῃ ὁ Θεὸς τὸν μέλλοντα ἄρχειν ὑμῶν. Ἐγὼ ϰỳ ἤδη ἀνέθεμαι. After the death of *Fabian* Bifhop of *Rome*, there growing fome trouble about the receiving of fuch perfons into the Church, as had fallen away in perfecution, and did now repent their fall; the Presbyters and Deacons of the fame Church advertifed St. *Cyprian* thereof, fignifying *That they muft of neceffity defer to deal in that caufe, till God did fend them a new Bifhop which might moderate all things.* Much we read of extraordinary fafting ufually in the Church. And in this appeareth alfo fomewhat concerning the chiefty of Bifhops. The cuftome is, faith *Tertullian*, that Bifhops do appoint when the people fhall all faft. Yea, it is not a matter left to our own free choice whether Bifhops fhall rule or no, but the will of our Lord and Saviour is, faith *Cyprian*; that every act of the Church, be governed by her Bifhops. An Argument it is of the Bifhops high preeminence, rule and Government over all the reft of the Clergy, even that the Sword of perfecution did ftrike, efpecially, always at the Bifhop as at the head, the reft by reafon of their lower eftate, being more fecure, as the felf-fame *Cyprian* noteth; the very manner of whofe fpeech unto his own, both Deacons and Presbyters who remained fafe, when himfelf then Bifhop was driven into exile, argueth likewife his eminent authority and rule over them, *By thefe letters,* faith he, *I both exhort and COMMAND, that ye whofe prefence there is not envied, nor fo much befet with dangers, fupply my room in doing thofe things which the exercife of Religion doth require.* Unto the fame purpofe ferve moft directly thofe comparifons, then which nothing is more familiar in the books of the ancient Fathers, who as oft as they fpeak of the feveral degrees in Gods Clergy, if they chance to compare Presbyters with *Levitical* Priefts of the law; the Bifhop (a) they compare unto *Aaron* the High Prieft; if they compare the one with the Apoftles, the other they compare (although in a lower proportion) fometime (b) to Chrift, and fometime to God himfelf, evermore fhewing that they placed the Bifhop in an eminent degree of ruling authority and power above other Presbyters. (c) *Ignatius* comparing Bifhops with Deacons, and with fuch Minifters of the word and Sacrament as were but Presbyters, and had no Authority over Presbyters; *What is* faith he, *the Bifhop but one which hath all principality and power over all, fo far forth as man may have it; being to his power, a follower even of Gods own Chrift;* Mr. (d) *Calvin* himfelf, though an enemy unto Regiment by Bifhops, doth notwithftanding confefs, that in old time the Minifters which had charge to teach, chofe of their Company one in every City, to whom they appropriated the Title of Bifhop, leaft equality fhould breed diffenfion. He added farther, that look what duty the *Roman* Confuls did execute

ecute

Cypr. l. 3. ep. 9. ad Rogatianum

Hieron. Ep. 85.

Epift. ad Smyr.

1 Tim. 5. 19. Againft a Presbyter receive no accufation under two or three witneffes. Ignat. Epift. ad Antioch. Apud Cypr. Ep. l. ep. 7.

Tertul. adverf. Pfychic. Epifcopi univerfe plebi mandare jejunia affolent. Cypr. Ep. 27.

Cypr. Ep. 39.
Vide Ignat. ad Magnef.
(a) Quod Aaron & filios ejus boc Epifcopum & Presbyteros effe noverimus, Hier. Ep. 2. ad Nepotianum.
(b) Ita eft ut in Epifcopis omnium in Presbyteris Apoftolos recognofcas Audor opufc. de 7. ordini.
Eccl. inter opera Hieron.
(c) Ignat Ep. ad Tra.
(d) Inftit l. 4. cap. 4. Sect. 2.

ecute in proposing matters unto the Senate, in asking their opinions, in directing them by advise, admonition, exhortation, in guiding actions by their Authority, and in seeing that performed which was with common consent agreed on, the like charge had the Bishop in the assembly of other Ministers. Thus much *Calvin* being forced by the evidence of truth to grant, doth yet deny the Bishops to have been so in Authority at the first as to bear rule over other Ministers, Wherein what rule he doth mean I know not. But if the Bishops were so far in dignity, above other Ministers as the Consuls of *Rome*, for their year above other Senators, it is as much as we require. And undoubtedly if as the Consul of *Rome*, so the Bishops in the Church of Christ had such authority, as both to direct other Ministers, and to see that every of them should observe that which their common consent had agreed on, how this could be done by the Bishop not bearing rule over them, for mine own part I must acknowledge that my poor conceipt is not able to comprehend. One objection there is of some force to make against that which we have hitherto endeavoured to prove, if they mistake it not who alledge it. St. *Jerom* comparing other

Presbyters with him, unto whom the name of Bishop was then appropriate, asketh *what a Bishop by virtue of his place and calling may do more then a Presbyter, except it be onely to Ordein?* In like sort *Chrysostome* having moved a question, wherefore St. *Paul* should give *Timothy* precept concerning the quality of Bishops, and descend from them to Deacons, omitting the Order of Presbyters between, he maketh there-

unto this answer, *What things he spake concerning Bishops, the same are also meet for Presbyters, whom Bishops seem not to excell in any thing but onely in the power of Ordination.* Wherefore seeing this doth import no ruling superiority, it follows that Bishops were as then no rulers over that part of the Clergy of God. Whereunto we answer that both St. *Jerom* and St. *Chrysostom* had in those their speeches, an eye no farther then onely to that function, for which Presbyters and Bishops were consecrated unto God. Now we know that their Consecration had reference to nothing but onely that which they did by force and virtue of the power of order, wherein sith Bishops received their charge, onely by that one degree to speak of, more ample then Presbyters did theirs, it might be well enough said that Presbyters were that way authorized to do, in a manner even as much as Bishops could do, if we consider what each of them did by virtue of solemn consecration; for as concerning power of regiment and jurisdiction, is was a thing withal added unto Bishops for the necessary use of such certain persons and people, as should be thereunto subject in those particular Churches whereof they were Bishops, and belonged to them onely, as Bishops of such or such a Church, whereas the other kind of power had relation indefinitely unto any of the whole society of Christian men, on whom they should chance to exercise the same, and belonged to them absolutely, as they were Bishops, wheresoever they lived, St. *Jeroms* conclusion therefore is, *that seeing in the one kind of power, there is no greater difference between a Presbyter and a Bishop, Bishops should not because of their preeminence in the other, too much lift up themselves, above the Presbyters under them.* St. *Chrysostomes* collection, *that whereas the Apostle doth set down the qualities, whereof regard should be had in the Consecration of Bishops, there was no need to make a several discourse how Presbyters ought to be qualified when they are Ordained, because there being so little difference in the functions, whereunto the one and the other receive Ordination, the same precepts might well serve for both, at least-wise by the vertues required in the greater, what should need in the less might be easily understood.* As for the difference of jurisdiction, the truth is the Apostles yet living, and themselves where they were resident, exercising the jurisdiction in their own persons, it was not every where established in Bishops. When the Apostles prescribed those laws; and when *Chrysostom* thus spake concerning them, it was not by him at all respected, but his eye was the same way with *Jeroms*, his cogitation was wholly fixed on that power which by Consecration is given to Bishops, more then to Presbyters,

and not on that which they have over Presbyters by force of their particular accessory jurisdiction. Wherein if any man suppose that *Jerom* and *Chrysostom* knew no difference at all between a Presbyter and a Bishop, let him weigh but one or two of their sentences. The pride of insolent Bishops, hath not a sharper enemy then *Jerom*, for which cause he taketh often occasions most severely to inveigh against them, sometimes for * shewing disdain and contempt of the Clergy

under

under them; sometime for not(*b*) suffering themselves to be told of their faults, and admonished of their duty by inferiors; sometime for not (*c*) admitting their Presbyters to teach, if so be themselves were in presence; sometimes for not vouchsafing to use any conference with them, or to take any counsel of them. Howbeit never doth he in such wise bend himself against their disorders, as to deny their Rule and Authority over Presbyters: Of *Vigilantius* being a Presbyter he thus writeth (*d*) *Miror sanctum Episcopum in cujus parochia Presbyter esse dicitur, acquiescere furori ejus & non virga Apostolica virgaq; ferrea confringere vas inutile.* I marvel that the holy Bishop under whom Vigilantius is said to be a Presbyter, doth yield to his fury, and not break that unprofitable vessel with his Apostolick and iron rod. With this agreeth most fitly the grave advice he giveth to Nepotian, *Be thou subject unto thy Bishop, and receive him as the father of thy soul. This also I say that Bishops should know themselves to be Priests and not* (*f*) *Lords, that they ought to honor the Clergie as beseemeth the Clergie to be honoured, to the end their Clergie may yeeld them the honour which is Bishops they ought to have: That of the Orator Domitius is famous, Wherefore should I esteem of thee as of a Prince, when thou makest not of me that reckoning which should in reason be made of a Senator? Let us know the Bishop and his Presbyters to be the same which Aaron sometime and his Sons were.* Finally writing against the Heretiques which were named *Luciferians,* The very safety of the Church, saith he, dependeth on the dignity of the chief Priest, to whom unless men grant an exceeding and an eminent power, there will grow in Churches even as many Schisms as there are persons which have authority.

Touching *Chrysostom,* to shew that by him there was also acknowledged a ruling superiority of Bishops over Presbyters, both then usual, and in no respect unlawful; what need we alleage his words and sentences, when the history of his own Episcopal actions in that very kind, is till this day extant for all men to read that will? For St. *Chrysostom* of a Presbyter in *Antioch,* grew to be afterwards Bishop of *Constantinople,* and in process of time when the Emperors heavy displeasure had through the practice of a powerful faction against him effected his banishment: *Innocent* the Bishop of *Rome* understanding thereof wrote his Letters unto the Clergy of that Church, *That no successor ought to be chosen in Chrysostoms room, Nec ejus clerum alii parere pontifici, nor his Clergie O B E Y any other Bishop then him.* A fond kind of speech if so be there had been as then in Bishops no ruling superiority over Presbyters. When two of *Chrysostoms* Presbyters had joyned themselves to the faction of his mortal enemy *Theophilus,* Patriarch in the Church of *Alexandria;* the same *Theophilus* and other Bishops which were of his Conventicle, having sent those two amongst others to cite *Chrysostom* their lawful Bishop, and to bring him into publique judgement, he taketh against this one thing special exception, as being contrary to all order, *That those Presbyters should come as Messengers, and call him to judgement who were a part of that Clergy whereof himself was Ruler and Judge.* So that Bishops to have had in those times a ruling superiority over Presbyters, neither could *Jerom* nor *Chrysostom* be ignorant; and therefore hereupon it were superfluous that we should any longer stand.

VII. Touching the next point, How Bishops together with Presbyters have used to govern the Churches, which were under them: It is by *Zonaras* somewhat plainly and at large declared, that the Bishop had his seat on high in the Church above the residue which were present; that a number of Presbyters did always there assist him; and that in the oversight of the people those Presbyters were (*b*) after a sort the Bishops Coadjutors. The Bishops and Presbyters, who, together with him, governed the Church, are for the most part by *Ignatius* joyntly mentioned. In the Epistle to them of *Trallis,* he saith of Presbyters that they are *συμβουλοι & συνεδρευται τῶ ἐπισκόπω, Counsellors and Assistants of the Bishop,* and concludeth in the end, *He that should disobey these were a plain Atheist, and an irreligious person, and one that did set Christ himself and his own Ordinances at nought.* Which order making Presbyters or Priests the

* C

Marginal notes:

(*b*) *Nemo peccantibus Episcopis audet contradicere: Nemo audet accusare majorem propterea quasi sancti & beati & in praeceptis Domini ambulantes augent eccata peccatis. Difficilis est accusatio in presbyterum. S enim peccaverit, non creditur, & si convictus fuerit non punitur.* In cap 8. ecclesiast.

(*c*) *Pessime consuetudinis est in quibusdam ecclesiis tacere Presbyteros & praesentibus Episcopis non loqui quasi aut invideant aut non dignentur audire.* Ep. ad Nepotian.

d Ep. 54. ad Ripar.

Hieron. ad Nepot.

f No Bishop may be a Lord in reference unto the Presbyters which are under him, if we take that name in the worse part, as Ierome here doth, For a Bishop is to rule his Presbyters, not as Lords do their slaves, but as Fathers do their children. *in vita Chrys. & Cassiod. sen.*

Pallad. in vita Chrysostom.

After what sort Bishops together with Presbyters have used to govern the Churches which were under them. *& παρ. συμ...* *in Can. Apost. 5.*

Cum episcopo presbyteri sacerdotali honore conjuncti, ep.18 Ego et compresbyteri nostri qui nobis adsidebant, ep.27.

the Bishops Assistants doth not import that they were of equal authority with him, but rather so adjoyned that they also were subject, as hath been proved. In the Writings of St. *Cyprian* nothing is more usual then to make mention of the Colledge of Presbyters subject unto the Bishop, although in handling the common affairs of the Church they assisted him. But of all other places which open the ancient order of Episcopal Presbyters the most clear is that Epistle of *Cyprian* unto *Cornelius*, concerning certain *Novatian* Heretiques received again upon their conversion into the unity of the Church: *After that* Urbanus *and* Sidonius *Confessors had come and signified unto our Peesbyters that* Maximus *a Confessor and Presbyter, did together with them desire to return into the Church, it seemed meet to hear from their own mouths and confessions that which by message they had delivered. When they were come, and had been called to accompt by the Presbyters touching those things they had committed; their answer was, That they had been deceived, and did request that such things as there they were charged with might be forgotten. It being brought unto me what was done, I took order that the Presbytery might be assembled. There were also present five Bishops, that upon setled advice it might be, with consent of all, determined what should be done about their persons.* Thus far St. *Cyprian.* Wherein it may be peradventure

Cyp. ep. 93.

demanded, Whether he and other Bishops did thus proceed with advice of their Presbyters in all such publique affairs of the Church, as being thereunto bound by Ecclesiastical Canons; or else that they voluntarily so did, because they judged it in discretion as then most convenient. Surely the words of *Cyprian* are plain, that of his own accord he chose this way of proceeding. *Unto that,* saith he, *which* Donatus, *and* Fortunatus, *and* Novatus, *and* Gordius *our Compresbyters have written, I could by my self alone make no answer, forasmuch as at the very first entring into my Bishoprick I resolutely determined not to do any thing of mine own private judgement, without your counsel and the peoples consent.* The reason whereof he rendreth in the same Epistle saying, *When by the grace of God my self shall come unto you* (for St. *Cyprian* was now in exile) *of things which either have been, or must be done we will consider,* sicut honor mutuus poscit, *as the law of courtesie which one doth owe to another of us requireth.* And at this very mark doth St. *Jerom* evermore aim in telling Bishops that Presbyters were at the first their equals, that in some Churches for a long time no Bishop was made but only such as the Presbyters did choose out amongst themselves, and therefore no cause why the Bishop should disdain to consult with them, and in weighty affairs of the Church to use their advice; sometime to countenance their own actions, or to repress the boldness of proud and insolent spirits, that which Bishops had in themselves sufficient authority and power to have done, notwithstanding they would not do alone, but craved therein the aid and assistance of other Bishops, as in the case of those *Novatian* Hereticks, before alleaged, *Cyprian* himself

Cyp. ep. 38.

did. And in *Cyprian* we finde of other the like practice. *Rogatian* a Bishop, having been used contumeliously by a Deacon of his own Church wrote thereof his complaint unto *Cyprian* and other Bishops. In which case their answer was, *That although in his own cause, he did of humility rather shew his grievance, then himself take revenge, which by the vigor of his Apostlical Office, and the authority of his Chair he might have presently done, without any further delay: Yet if the party should do again as before, their judgements were,* Fungaris circa eum potestate honoris tui, & eum vel deponas vel abstineas : *Use on that power which the honour of thy place giveth thee, either to depose him or exclude him from access unto holy things.* The Bishop for his assistance and ease had under him to guide and direct, Deacons in their charge his Archdeacon so termed in respect of care over Deacons, albeit himself were not Deacon but Presbyter, For the guidance of Presbyters in their function the Bishop had likewise under him one of the selfsame order with them, but above them in authority, one whom the antient termed usually an * Arch-Presbyter, we at this day name him Dean For most certain truth it is that Churches Cathedral, and the Bishops of them are as glasses wherein the face and very countenance of Apostolical antiquity remaineth even as yet to be seen, notwithstanding the alterations which tract of time and the course of the world hath brought. For defence and maintenance of them we are most earnestly bound to strive, even as the Jews were for their Temple, and the High-Priest of God therein : The overthrow and ruine of the one, if ever the sacrilegious avarice of Atheists should prevail so far, which God of his infinite

* Such a one was that Peter whom Cassiodor writing the life of Chrysostom d the call the Archpresbyter of the Church of Alexandria under Theophilus at that time Bishop.

infinite mercy forbid, ought no otherwiſe to move us then the people of God were
moved, when having beheld the ſack and combuſtion of his Sanctuary in moſt lamentable manner flaming before their eyes, they uttered from the bottom of their
grieved ſpirits thoſe voices of doleful ſupplication, *Exurge Domine & miſerearis Sion,* Pſal. 141.
ſervi tui diligunt lapides ejus, pulveris ejus miſeret eos.

How far the
power of Biſhops hath
reached
from the beginning in
reſpect of
territory or
localcompaſs

VIII. How far the power which Biſhops had did reach, what number of perſons
was ſubject unto them at the firſt, and how large their territories were, it is not for
the queſtion we have in hand, a thing very greatly material to know : For if we prove
that Biſhops have lawfully of old ruled over other Miniſters, it is enough, how few
ſoever thoſe Miniſters have been, how ſmall ſoever the circuit of place which hath
contained them. Yet hereof ſomewhat, to the end we may ſo far forth illuſtrate
Church antiquities ; a *(a)* law imperial there is,
which ſheweth that there was great care had to provide for every Chriſtian City a Biſhop as neer as
might be, and that each City had ſome territory belonging unto it, which territory was alſo under the
Biſhop of the ſame City ; that becauſe it was not
univerſally thus, but in ſome Countries, one Biſhop
had ſubject unto him many Cities and their territories ; the law which provided for eſtabliſhment
of the other orders, ſhould not prejudice thoſe
Churches wherein this contrary cuſtome had before
prevailed. Unto the Biſhop of every ſuch City, not
onely the Presbyters of the ſame City, but alſo of the territory thereunto belonging,
were from the firſt beginning ſubject. For we muſt note that when as yet there were
in Cities no pariſh Churches ; but onely Colledges of Presbyters under their Biſhops
Regiment, yet ſmaller Congregations and Churches there were even then abroad,
in which Churches there was butſome one onely Presbyter to perform amongſt them
Divine duties. Towns and Villages abroad receiving the faith of Chriſt from Cities
whereunto they were adjacent, did as ſpiritual and heavenly Colonies by their ſubjection, honour thoſe ancient mother Churches, out of which they grew. And
in the Chriſtian Cities themſelves, when the mighty increaſe of beleivers made it
neceſſary to have them divided into certain ſeveral companies, and over every of
thoſe companies one onely paſtor to be appointed for the miniſtry of holy things :
between the firſt ; and the reſt after it, there could not but be a natural inequality,
even as between the Temple and Synagognes in *Jeruſalem.* The Clergy of Cities
were termed *Urbici,* to ſhew a difference between them and the Clergies of the
Towns, of Villages, of Caſtles abroad. And how many ſoever theſe Pariſhes or
Congregations were in number, which did depend on any one principal City
Church unto the Biſhop of that one Church they and their ſeveral ſole Presbyters
were all ſubject.

For if ſo be as ſome imagine every petty Congregation or Hamlet had had his own
particular Biſhop, what ſence could there be in thoſe words of *Jerom,* concerning
Caſtles, Villages, and other places abroad, which having onely Presbyters, to teach
them, and to miniſter unto them the Sacraments, were reſorted unto by Biſhops
for the Adminiſtration of that wherewith their Presbyters were not licenſed to meddle. To note a difference of that one Church where the Biſhop hath his ſeat, and the
reſt which depend upon it ; that one hath uſually been termed Cathedral, according
to the ſame ſence wherein *Ignatius* ſpeaking of the Church of *Antioch,* termeth it
his throne, and *Cyprian* making mention of *Evariſtus* who had been Biſhop, and
was now depoſed, termeth him *cathedræ extorrem,* one that was thruſt beſides his
chair. The Church where the Biſhop is ſet with his Colledge of Presbyters about
him, we call a Sea ; the Local compaſs of his authority we term a Dioceſs. Unto
a Biſhop within the compaſs of his own both Sea and Dioceſs, it hath by right of his
place evermore appertained ✱ to ordein Presbyters, to make Deacons, and with

(a) L. 36. c. de Epiſ. ad cler. Ἔκάςη πόλις
ἴδιον ἐπίσκοπον ἐχέτω· Καὶ καὶ διὰ δείας ἀπηγόρευος τολμάειη τις ἀφελέῶαι πόλιν τῦ ἰδία ὑποκώσω ἤ τῆς μετοικιᾷ αὐτῆς ἢ τινὸς ἄλλα διζμοῦ γυμνῦται ἐπ ὄντος κ ἀπεμῦναι· Ἐξήρηται ἢ ἡ τόμιος Σκυθῶι πόλις. Ὁ γὰρ ἐπίσκοπος αὐτῆς κ ἐπ λοιπᾶν προνοεῖ· Καὶ ἡ Λεοντίκων λις Ἰουυλίας ὑπὸ ἢ ἐπίσκοπον ὄψι Ἰουυρφόλεως·

Beſides *Cyprian* ep 52. *Cum jam pridem per omnes provincias & per urbes ſingulas ordinati ſunt Epiſcopi.*

Ubi eccleſiaſti ordinuon eſt con ſeſſu, & offert & tingit ſacerdos qui eſt ibi ſolus. Tuſt.
exhort. ad caſtit.

Cypr. Ep. 25.

Hieron. ad ver Lucifer.

Cypr. Ep. 45.

✱ Con Anti. och Cap. 9.

Ἀκλύτας ἢ ἐπισκόπας νᾶρ ἐτολήσειν μὴ ἐπιτάλειν ὑδὶ χειροτονία ἤ τινὶ ἄλλαις δικονεμίαις ἐκκλησιαςικοῖς. Con. Conſtant. c. 2. τᾶτο γὰρ πρότερον διαφὲ διωγμᾶς ἐγίνετο ἀδιαφόρως· Sicr. Lib. 5. cap. 8.

C   judge-

judgement, to difpofe of all things of waight. The Apoftle St. *Paul* had Epifcopal Authority, but fo a large that we cannot affign unto him any one certain Diocefs. His *(a)* pofitive orders and conftitutions, Churches every where did obey. Yea, a charge and a care, faith he, I *(b)* have even of all Churches. The walks of *Titus* and *Timothy* was limited within the bounds of a narrow precinct, as for other Bifhops, that which *Chryfoftom* hath concerning them, *if they be evil, could not poffibly agree unto them, unlefs their Authority had reached farther then to fome one onely Congregation?* The danger being fo great as it is, to him that fcandalizeth one foul, what fhall he faith *(c) Chryfoftom*, fpeaking of a Bifhop, what fhall he deferve, by whom fo many fouls, yea even whole Cities and peoples, men, women and children, citizens, pefants, inhabitants, both of his own City, and of other Towns, fubject unto it are offended? A thing fo unufual it was for a Bifhop not to have ample jurifdiction, that *Theophilus*, patriark of *Alexandria*, for making one a Bifhop of a fmall Town, is noted as a proud defpifer of the commendable orders of the Church with this cenfure, *(d)* fuch novelties *Theophilus* prefumed every where to begin, taking upon him as it had been another *Mofes*. Whereby is difcovered alfo their error, who think that fuch as in Ecclefiaftical writings they find termed *Chorepifcopos* were the fame in the Country which the Bifhop was in the City: Whereas the old *Chorepifcopi* are they, that were appointed of the Bifhops to have, as his vicegerent, fome overfight of thofe Churches abroad, which were fubject unto his Sea, in which Churches they had alfo power to make Sub-Deacons, Readers and fuch like petty Church Officers. With which power fo ftinted, they not contenting themfelves, but adventuring at the length, to Ordain even Deacons and Presbyters alfo, as the Bifhop himfelf did, their prefumption herein was controlled and ftaied by the antient edict of Councils. For example that of *Antioch*, it hath feemed good to the holy Synod that fuch in Towns and Countries as are called *Chorepifcopi* do know their limits and govern the Churches under them, contenting themfelves with the charge thereof, and with Authority to make Readers, Sub-Deacons, Exorcifts, and to be Leaders or Guiders of them, but not to meddle with the Ordination either of a Presbyter or of a Deacon, without the Bifhop of that City, whereunto the *Chorepifcopus* and his territory alfo is fubject. The fame Synod appointeth likewife that thofe *Chorepifcopi* fhal be made by none but the Bifhop of that City, under which they are. Much might hereunto be added, if it were further needful to prove that the Local compafs of a Bifhops authority and power was never fo ftraightly limited, as fome men would have the World to imagine. But to go forward, degrees there are and have been of old even amongft Bifhops, alfo themfelves: One fort of Bifhops being fuperiors unto Presbyters onely, another fort having preeminence alfo above Bifhops. It cometh here to be confidered in what refpect inequality of Bifhops was thought at the firft a thing expedient for the Church, and what ods there hath been between them, by how much the power of one hath been larger, higher, and greater then of another. Touching the caufes for which it hath been efteemed meet that Bifhops themfelves fhould not every way be equals; they are the fame for which the wifdom both of God and Man hath evermore approved it as moft requifite, that where many Governors muft of neceffity concur for the ordering of the fame affairs, of what naturefoever they be, one fhould have fome kind of fway or ftroke more then all the refidue. For where number is, there muft be order, or elfe of force there will be confufion. Let there be divers agents, of whom each hath his private inducements, with refolute purpofe to follow them, (as each may have) unlefs in this cafe fome had preeminence above the reft, a chance it were if ever any thing fhould be either begun, proceeded in, or brought unto any conclufion by them, deliberations and Councels would feldom go forward, their meetings would always be in danger, to break up with jarrs and contradictions In an Army a number of Captains, all of equal power, without fome higher to overfway them; what good would they do? In all Nations where a number are to draw any one way, there muft be fome one principal Mover. Let the practife of our very Adverfaries themfelves herein be confidered, are the Presbyteries able to determine of Church affairs, unlefs their paftors do ftrike the chiefeft ftroke and have power above the reft? Can their Paftoral Synod do any thing, unlefs they have fome Prefident amongft them? in Synods they are forced to give

one

o 1 Cor. 16. As I have ordained in the Churches of *Galatia*, the fame do ye alfo.

b 2 Cor. 11. 28

c Chryf. in ead 2 it.

d Palladin vita Chryfoft.

Concil. Anaode tan. 10.

one Pastor preheminence and superiority above the rest. But they answer, That he who being a Pastor according to the order of their Discipline, is for the time some little deal mightier then his brethren, doth not continue so longer then only during the Synod. Which answer serveth not to help them out of the briars : for by their practice they confirm our principle touching the necessity of one mans preheminence wheresoever a concurrency of many is required unto any one solemn action, this nature teacheth, and this they cannot chuse but acknowledge. As for the change of his person to whom they give this preheminence, if they think it expedient to make for every Synod a new Superior, there is no law of God which bindeth them so to, neither any that telleth them that they might suffer one and the same man being made President, even to continue so during life, and to leave his preheminence unto his Successors after him, as by the antient order of the Church, Archbishops, Presidents amongst Bishops have used to do. The ground therefore of their preheminence above Bishops is the necessity of often concurrency of many Bishops about the publick affairs of the Church, as consecrations of Bishops, consultations of remedy of general disorders, audience judicial, when the actions of any Bishop should be called in question, or appeals are made from his sentence by such as think themselves wronged. These and the like affairs usually requiring, that many Bishops should orderly assemble, begin, and conclude somewhat, it hath seemed, in the eyes of reverend Antiquity a thing most requisite, that the Church should not onely have Bishops, but even amongst Bishops some to be in Authority chiefest. Unto which purpose, the very state of the whole World, immediately before Christianity took place, doth seem by the special Providence of God to have been prepared : For we must know, that the Countreys where the Gospel was first planted, were for the most part subject to the Roman Empire. The Romans use was commonly, when by war they had subdued Forreign Nations, to make them Provinces, that is, to place over them Roman Governors, such as might order them according to the Laws and Customs of *Rome*. And to the end that all things might be the more easily and orderly done, a whole Countrey being divided into sundry parts, there was in each part some one City, whereinto they about did resort for justice. Every such part was termed a (*a*) Diocess. Howbeit, the name Diocess is sometime so generally taken, that it containeth not onely mo such parts of a Province, but even moe Provinces also then one; as the Diocess of *Asia* contained eight, the Diocess of *Africa* seven. Touching Diocesses according unto a stricter sense, whereby they are taken for part of a Province, the words of *Livy* do plainly shew, what order the Romans did observe in them. For at what time they had brought the Macedonians into subjection, the Roman Governor, by order from the Senate of *Rome*, gave charge that *Macedonia* should be divided into four Regions or Diocesses. *Capita regionum ubi concilia fierent prima sedis Amphipolim, secunda Thessalonicen, tertia Pellam, quarta Pelagoniam fecit. Eo concilia sua cujusque regionis indici, pecuniam conferri, ibi Magistratus creari jussit.* This being before the days of the Emperors, by their appointment *Thessalonica* was afterwards the chiefest, and in it the highest Governor of *Macedonia* had his seat : Whereupon the other three Diocesses were in that respect inferior unto it, as Daughters unto a Mother City ; for not unto every town of justice was that title given, but was peculiar unto those Cities wherein principal Courts were kept. Thus in *Macedonia*, the Mother City was *Thessalonica* : In *Asia* (*b*) *Ephesus*; in *Africa Carthage*; For so (*c*) *Justinian* in his time made it. The Governors, Officers and Inhabitants of these Mother Cities were termed for difference sake *Metropolites*, that is to say, *Mother-city-men*; then which, nothing could possible have been devised more fit to suit with the nature of that form of spiritual Regiment under which afterward the Church should live. Wherefore if the Prophet saw cause to acknowledge unto the Lord that the light of his gracious providence did shine no where more

a *Cic. Fam. Ep 52. lib 13. Si quid habebis eum a-lquo teli sponsio controversia ut in illam solutionis repetas. The suit which ... maketh was this, that the party in whose behalf he wrote to the Proprætor, might have his causes put over to that Court which was held in the Diocess of Hellespont, where the man did abide, and not to his trouble be forced to follow them at Ephesus, which was the chiefest Court in that Province.*

b *Cic. ad Attic. lib. 5 ep. 13 Ison l. deserv. D. de officio Proconsulis & legati.*

c *Libri ... Sancimus ... ilicut Orien ... q. Illyricum ita & Africa præmiana mox in potestate specialiter à nostra clementia decretur. Cu ut fidem jubemus isse Carthaginem ... ab ea auxiliante Deosepim pro-vinci. cum suis judicibus disponantur.*

apparently

apparently to the eye then in preparing the Land of *Canaan* to be receptacle for that Church which was of old, *Thou hast brought a Vine out of Egypt, thou hast cast out the Heathen and planted it, thou madest room for it , and when it had taken root it filled the Land.* How much more ought we to wonder at the handy-work of Almighty God, who to settle the Kingdom of his dear Son did not cast out any one people, but directed in such fort the politick councils of them who ruled far and wide over all, that they throughout all Nations, people and Countries upon earth should unwittingly prepare the field wherein the vine which God did intend, that is to fay, the Church of his dearly beloved Son was to take root. For unto nothing else can we attribute it, faving onely unto the very incomprehensible force of Divine providence, that the world was in fo marvellous fit fort divided, levelled and laid out before hand? whofe work could it be but his alone to make fuch provifion for the direct implantation of his Church? wherefore inequality of Bishops being found a thing convenient for the Church of God, in fuch confideration as hath been fhewed, when it came fecondly in queftion which Bishops should be higher and which lower, it feemed herein not to the civil Monarch only, but to the moft, expedient, that the dignity and celebrity of (*a*) Mother-cities should be refpected. They which dream that if civil Authority had not given fuch preheminence unto one City more then another, there had never grown an inequality among Bishops, are deceived; fuperiority of one Bishop over another would be requifite in the Church although that civil diftinction were abolished; other caufes having made it neceffary even amongft Bishops to have fome in degree higher then the reft, the civil dignity of place was confidered onely as a reafon wherefore this Bishop should be preferred before that : Which deliberation had been likely enough to have raifed no fmall trouble, but that fuch was the circumftance of place, as being followed in that choyce, befides the manifeft conveniency thereof, took away all fhow of partiality, prevented fecret emulations, and gave no man occafion to think his perfon difgraced in that another was preferred before him.

(*a*)Concil.*Antioc.c.*9. Τὰς καθ᾽ ἑκά-
sἱω ἐπαρχίαν ὁπικόπως εἰδέναι χρὴ τῇ πρη μητρόπολει προεςῶτα ὁπίσκοπον, κ᾽ ᾗ φροντίδα ἀναδιχεδαι πάσης τῆς ἐπαρχίας διὰ τὸ ἐν τῇ μητρόπολει παντα χόδεν συντρέχειν πάντας τὸς τὰ πράγματα ἔχοντας, ὅθεν ἔδοξε κ᾽ τῇ τιμῇ προηγείδαι αὐτόν.

Thus we fee upon what occafion Metropolitan Bishops became Archbishops. Now while the whole Chriftian world in a manner ftill continued under one civil Government, there being oftentimes within fome one more large Territory divers and fundry mother Churches, the *Metropolitans* whereof were Archbishops, as for orders fake, it grew hereupon expedient, there should be a difference alfo amongft them, fo no way feemed in thofe times more fit then to give preeminence unto them whofe *Metropolitan* Seas were of fpecial defert or dignity : for which caufe thefe as being Bishops in the chiefeft Mother Churches were termed Primates, and at the length by way of excellency, *Patriarks.* For ignorant we are not, how fometimes the Title of *Patriark* is generally given to all *Metropolitan* Bishops. They are mightily therefore to blame which are fo bold and confident, as to affirm, that for the fpace of above four hundred and thirty years after Chrift, all *Metropolitan* Bishops were in every respect equals, till the fecond council of *Conftantinople* exalted certain *Metropolitans* above the reft. True it is, they were equals as touching the exercife of fpiritual power within their Diocefes, when they dealt with their own flock. For what is it that one of them might do within the compafs of his own precinct, but another within his might do the fame? But that there was no fubordination at all, of one of them unto another, that when they all or fundry of them were to deal in the fame caufes, there was no difference of firft and fecond in degree, no diftinction of higher and lower in authority acknowledged amongft them, is moft untrue. The great Council of *Nice*, was after our Saviour Chrift but three hundred twenty four years, and in that Council, certain *Metropolitans* are faid even then to have had ancient preeminence and dignity above the reft, namely the Primate of *Alexandria*, of *Rome*, and of *Antioch*. Threefcore years after this there were Synods under the Emperor *Theodofius*, which Synod was the firft at *Conftantinople*, whereat one hundred and fifty Bishops were affembled : at which council it was decreed that the Bishop of *Conftantinople* should not onely be added unto the former Primates, but alfo that his place should be fecond amongft them, the next to the Bishop of *Rome* in dignity. The fame decree

Ubiervius de ftatu primitivæ Eccesfiæ.

Socrat.l 3.*c.*8.

again

again renewed concerning *Constantinople*, and the reason thereof laid open in the Can. 28.
Councel of *Chalcedon*: At the length came that second of *Constantinople*, whereat
were six hundred and thirty Bishops for a third conformation thereof: Laws impe- Can. 36.
rial there are likewise extant to the same effect. Herewith the Bishop of *Constantino-*
ple being over much puffed up, not onely could not indure that Sea to be in estimation higher, whereunto his own had preferment to be the next, but he challenged more then ever any Christian Bishop in the World before either had
or with reason could have. What he challenged, and was therein as then refused
by the Bishop of *Rome*; the same the Bishop of *Rome* in procels of time, obtained
for himself, and having gotten it by bad means, hath both up held and augmented it, and
upholdeth it by acts and practises much worse. But Primates according to their first in- Novel. 13,
stitution, were all in relation unto Archbishops, the some by prerogative, which
Archbishops were being compared unto Bishops. Before the councel of *Nice*, albeit
there were both *Metropolitans* and *Primates*, yet could not this be a means forcible
enough to procure the peace of the Church, but all things were wonderful tumultuous and troublesome, by reason of one special practise common unto the Heretiques of those times; which was, That when they had been condemned and cast out
of the Church by the sentence of their own Bishops, they contrary to the antient
received orders of the Church, had a custome to wander up and down, and to insinuate themselves into favour where they were not known, imagining themselves to
be safe enough, and not to be clean cut off from the body of the Church, if they could
any where find a Bishop which was content to communicate with them; whereupon
ensued, as in that case there needs must, every day quarrels and jars unappeasable
amongst Bishops. The *Nicene* Councel for redres hereof considered the bounds of Con. Nic.
every Archbishops Ecclesiastical jurisdiction, what they had been in former times,
and accordingly appointed unto each grand part of the Christian World some one
Primate, from whose judgement no man living within his territory might appeal, unless it were to a Councel general of all Bishops. The drift and purpose of which order
was, that neither any man opprest by his own particular Bishop might be destitute of
a remedy through appeal unto the more indifferent sentence of some other ordinary
judge, nor yet every man be left at such liberty as before, to shift himself out of their Con.
hands, for whom it was most meet to have the hearing and determining of his cause.
The evil, for remedy whereof this order was taken, annoyed at that present, especially the Church of *Alexandria* in *Egypt*, where *Arianisme* begun. For which cause
the state of that Church is in the *Nicene* Canons, this matter mentioned
before the rest. The words of their sacred edict are these, Let those customs remain Concil. Nic.
in force which have been of old, the customes of *Egypt* and *Libya*, and *Pentapolis*; c. 6.
by which customes the Bishop of *Alexandria* hath authority over all these, the rather
for that this hath also been the rule of the Bishop of *Rome*, yea the same hath been
kept in *Antioch*, and in other Provinces. Now because the custome likewise had Ejusd. Con.
been that great honour should be done to the Bishop of *Ælia* or *Jerusalem*, there- cap 7.
fore least their decree concerning the Primate of *Antioch*, should any whit prejudice
the dignity and honour of That Sea, speciall provision is made, that although it were
inferior in degree, not onely unto *Antioch* the chief of the *East*, but even unto *Cesaria*
too, yet such preeminence it should retain as belonged to a Mother City, and enjoy
whatsoever special prerogative or priviledge it had besides. Let men therefore
hereby judge of what continuance this order which upholdeth degrees of Bishops
must needs have been, when a general Council of three hundred and eighteen Bishops
living themselves within three hundred years after Christ doth reverence the same
for antiquities sake, as a thing which had been even then of old observed in the most
renowned parts of the Christian World. Wherefore needles altogether are those T. C. l. 2. p. 526.
vain and wanton demands, no mention of an Archbishop in *Theophilus Bishop of* What? no
Antioch? none in *Ignatius*? none in *Clemens* of *Alexandria*? none in *Justin Mar-* mention of
tyr, *Irenæus*, *Tertullian*, *Cyprian*? none in all those old *Historiographers*, out of him in *Theo-*
philus, Bishop

of *Antioch*: none in *Clemens Alexandrinus*? none in *Ignatius*? none in *Justin Martyr*? in *Irenæus*? in *Tertull.* in *Origen*
in *Cyprian*? in those old Historiographers, out of which *Eusebius* gathered his story? was it for his baseness and
smalness that he could not be seen among the Bishops, Elders and Deacons, being the cheif and principal
of them all? Can the Cedar of Lebanon be hidden amongst the Box trees?

which

which *Eusebius* gathereth his story? none till the time of the Council of *Nice* three hundred and twenty years after Christ? As if the mention which is thereof made in that very Council, where so many Bishops acknowledge Archiepiscopal dignity even their antient were, not of far more weight and value then if every of those Fathers had written large discourses thereof. But what is it which they will blush at, who dare so confidently set it down, that in the Council of *Nice* some Bishops being termed Metropolitans, no more difference is therby meant to have been betwen one Bishop and another, then is shewed between one Minister and another, when we say such a one is a Minister in the City of *London*, and such a one Minister in the town of *Newington*. So that to be termed a Metropolitan Bishop did in their conceit, import no preheminence above other Bishops, then we mean that a Girdler hath over others of

T. C. l. 1. ubi supra. A Metropolitan Bishop was nothing else but a Bishop of that place which it pleased the Emperor or Magistrate to make the chief of the Diocess or Shire, and as for this name it makes no more difference between Bishop and a bishop, then when I say a Minister of London and a Minister of Newington.

the same trade, if we term him which doth inhabit some Mother-city, for difference sake a Metropolitan Girdler. But the truth is too manifest to be so deluded; a Bishop at that time had power in his own Diocess over all other Ministers there, and a Metropolitan Bishop sundry preheminences above other Bishops, one of which preheminences was in the ordination of Bishops, to have κύρος τῆς χειροτονίας, the chief power of ordering all things done. Which preheminence that Council it self doth mention, as also a greater belonging unto the Patriach or Primate of *Alexandria*,

Con Nic. ca.6. Illud autem omnino manifestum, quod Metropolitani sententia sit episc. hinc magna & nodus definivit Episc. esse non oportere.

concerning whom it is there likewise said, that to him did belong ἐξουσία, authority and power over all *Egypt*, *Pentapolis* and *Lybia* : within which compass sundry Metropolitan Seas, to have been there is no man ignorant, which in those antiquities have any knowledge. Certain prerogatives there are wherein Metropolitans excelled other Bishops, certain also wherein Primates excelled other Metropolitans. Archiepiscopal or Metropolitan prerogatives are those mentioned in old Imperial constitutions, (a) to convocate the holy Bishops under them within the compass of their own Provinces, when need

Can. 4.
a Novel 123.
can 10
b Nov.123 c.9
c Novel 79 2.
d Novel 123. can. 22
e Novel. 123. ca. 23.
f Can.9.

required their meeting together for inquisition and redress of publick disorders; (b) to grant unto Bishops under them leave and faculty of absence from their own Diocess, when it seemed necessary that they should otherwhere converse for some reasonable while; (c) to give notice unto Bishops under them of things commanded by supream Authority; (d) to have the hearing and first determining of such causes as any man had against a Bishop; (e) To receive the appeals of the inferior Clergy, in case they found themselves overborn by the Bishop their immediate Judge. And least happily it should be imagined that Canons Ecclesiastical we want to make the self same thing manifest: In the Council of *Antioch* it was thus decreed, (f) *The Bishops in every Province must know, that he which is Bishop in the Mother-city, hath not onely charge of his own Parish or Diocess, but even of the whole Province also.* Again, *It hath seemed good that other Bishops without him should do nothing more then onely that which concerneth each ones Parish and the places underneath it.* Further by the self

g Can. 16.

same Council (g) all Councils provincial are reckoned void and frustrate, unless the Bishop of the mother City within that province, where such Councils should be, were present at them. So that the want of his presence, and in Canons for Church government, want of his approbation also, did disanul them. Not so the want of any others. Finally concerning elections of Bishops, the Council of *Nice* hath this general rule, that the chief ordering of all things here, is in every Province committed to the Metropolitan. Touching them, who amongst Metropolitans were also Primates, and had of sundry united Provinces, the chiefest Metropolitan See, of such

h Can. 4. & 5. pag. Εβ. προχειρισθῆναι.

that Canon, in the Council of *Carthage*, was eminent, whereby a Bishop is forbidden to go beyond Seas, without the licence of the highest Chair within the same Bishops own Country; and of such which beareth the name of Apostolical, is that antient Canon likewise, which chargeth the Bishops of each NATION to know,

Can. 23.

him which is FIRST amongst them, and to esteem of him as an HEAD, and to do no extraordinary thing but with his leave. The chief Primates of the Christian World, were the Bishop of *Rome*, *Alexandria*, and *Antioch*. To whom

Can. 34.

the Bishop of *Constantinople* being afterwards added, St. *Chrysostom* the Bishop of that Sea, is in that respect said to have had the care and charge not onely of the City of *Constantinople*, *sed etiam totius Thraciæ quæ sex præfecturis est divisa, & Asiæ totius*

Cassiod. in vita Chrysost.

quæ

quæ ab undecim præsidibus regitur. The rest of the East was under *Antioch*, the *South* under *Alexandria*, and the *West* under *Rome*. Whereas therefore *John* the Bishop of *Jerusalem* being noted of Herefie, had written an Apology for himself unto the Bishop of *Alexandria*, named *Theophilus*; St. *Jerom* reproveth his breach of the order of the Church herein, saying, *Tu qui regulas quæris Ecclesiasticas, & Niceni concilii canonibus uteris, responde mihi, ad Alexandrinum Episcopum Palæstina quid pertinet? Ni fallor hoc ibi decernitur ut Palæstine Metropolis Cæsarea sit, & totius Orientis Antiochia. Aut igitur ad Cæsariensem Episcopum referre debueras, aut si procul expetendum judicium erat, Antiochiam potius literæ dirigendæ.* ❧hus much concerning that Local Compass which was antiently set out to Bishops, within the bounds and limits whereof we find that they did accordingly exercise that Episcopal Authority and power which they had over the Church of Christ.

Hieron.ep.91.

IX. The first whom we read to have bent themselves against the Superiority of Bishops, were *Aerius* and his followers. *Aerius* seeking to be made a Bishop, could not brook that *Eustathius* was thereunto preferred before him. Whereas therefore he saw himself unable to rise to that greatness which his ambitious pride did affect, his way of revenge was to try what wit being sharpned with envy and malice could do, in raising a new seditious opinion that the Superiority which Bishops had, was a thing which they should not have, that a Bishop might not ordain, and that a Bishop ought not any way to be distinguished from a Presbyter: For so doth * St. *Augustine* deliver the opinion of *Aerius: Epiphanius* not so plainly nor so directly, but after a more Rhetorical sort. His speech was rather furious then convenient for man to use, *What is*, saith he, *a Bishop more then a Presbyter? The one doth differ from the other nothing. For their order is one, their honour one, one their dignity. A Bishop imposeth his hands, so doth a Presbyter. A Bishop Baptizeth, the like doth a Presbyter. The Bishop is a Minister of Divine service, a Presbyter is the same. The Bishop sitteth as Judge in a Throne, Even the Presbyter sitteth also. A Presbyter therefore doing thus far the self-same thing which a Bishop did, it was by Aerius inferred that they ought not in any thing to differ.* Are we to think *Aerius* had wrong in being judged an Heretique for holding this opinion? Surely if heresie be an errour, falsely fathered upon Scriptures, but indeed repugnant to the truth of the Word of God, and by the consent of the universal Church, in the councels, or in her contrary uniform practise throughout the whole World, declared to be such, and the opinion of *Aerius* in this point be a plain error of that nature, there is no remedy, but *Aerius* so Schismatically, and stiffly maintaining it, must even stand where *Epiphanius* and *Augustine* have placed him. An errour repugnant unto the truth of the Word of God is held by them whosoever they be, that stand in defence of any conclusion drawn erroneously out of Scripture, and untruely thereon fathered. The opinion of *Aerius* therefore being falsly collected out of Scripture, must needs be acknowledged an errour repugnant to the truth of the word of God. His opinion was that there ought not to be any difference between a Bishop and a Presbyter. His grounds and reasons for this opinion, were sentences of Scripture. Under pretence of which sentences, whereby it seemed that Bishops and Presbyters at the first did not differ, it was concluded by *Aerius* that the Church did ill in permitting any difference to be made. The Answer which *Epiphanius* maketh unto some part of the proofs by *Aerius* alledged, was not greatly studied or laboured, for through a contempt of so base an errour, for this himself did perceive and profess, yeildeth, he thereof expresly this reason, Men that have wit do evidently see that all this is meer foolishness. But how vain and ridiculous soever his opinion seemed unto wise men; with it *Aerius* deceived many, for which cause, somewhat was convenient to be said against it. And in that very extemporal slightness which *Epiphanius* there useth, albeit the answer made to *Aerius* be * in part but raw, yet ought not

In what respects Episcopal regiment hath bin gainsaid of old by Aerius.

Aug.de ber. ad quod vult deu.
* *Aerius ab de-rio quædam sunt nominati qui quum esset Pres-byter docuisse sertur quod E-piscopum non potest ordinare. Dicebat Episco-pum a presbyte-ro nulla ratione debere discerni. Aug.de hær.*

Ἐν τούτῳ πλάνης ἡγανάκτησε * As in that he saith the

the Apostle doth name sometime Presbyters and not Bishops, 1 Tim. 4. 14. Sometime Bishops and not Presbyters, Phil 1.1. because all Churches had not both, for want of able and sufficient men. In such Churches therefore as had but the one, the Apostle could not mention the other. Which answer is nothing to the latter place above mentioned: For that the Church of *Philippi* should have more Bishops then one, and want a few able men to be Presbyters under the regiment of one Bishop, how shall we think it probable or likely?

* D   hereby

hereby the truth to finde any less favour then in other causes it doth, where we do not therefore judge Heresie to have the better, because now and then it alledgeth that for it self, which Defenders of Truth do not always so fully answer. Let it therefore suffice, that *Aerius* did bring nothing unanswerable. The weak Solutions which the one doth give, are to us no prejudice against the cause, as long as the others oppositions are of no greater strength and validity. Did not *Aerius*, trow you, deserve to be esteemed as a new *Apollos*, mighty and powerful in the Word, which could for maintenance of his cause, bring forth so plain Divine Authorities, to prove by the Apostles own Writing, that Bishops ought not in any thing to differ from other Presbyters? for example, where it is said that Presbyters made *Timothy* Bishop, is it not clear that a Bishop should not differ from a Presbyter, by having power of Ordination? again, if a Bishop might by order be distinguished from a Presbyter, would the Apostle have given, (*a*) as he doth unto Presbyters, the title of Bishops? These were the invincible demonstrations wherewith *Aerius* did so fiercely assault Bishops. But the sentence of *Aerius* perhaps was onely, that the difference between a Bishop and a Presbyter, hath grown by the order and custom of the Church, the Word of God not appointing that any such difference should be. Well, let *Aerius* then finde the favour to have his sentence so construed; yet his fault in condemning the order of the Church, his not submitting himself unto that order, the Schism which he caused in the Church about it, who can excuse? No, the truth is, that these things did even necessarily ensue, by force of the very opinion which he and his followers did hold. His conclusion was, That there ought to be no difference between a Presbyter and a Bishop. His proofs, those Scripture sentences which make mention of Bishops and Presbyters, without any such distinction or difference. So that if between his conclusion and the proofs whereby he laboured to strengthen the same, there be any shew of coherence at all, we must of necessity confess, that when *Aerius* did plead, There is by the Word of God no difference between a Presbyter and a Bishop, his meaning was not onely, that the Word of God it self appointeth not, but that it enforceth on us, the duty of not appointing nor allowing that any such difference should be made.

1 Tim. 4.14. with the imposition of the Presbyteries hands. Of which Presbytery S. *Paul* was chief 2 Tim. 1. 6. And I think no man will deny that S. *Paul* had more then a simple Presbyter was Author to.

Phil. 1. 1. To all the Saints at *Philippi*, with the Bishops and Deacons. For as yet in his time there was no one which had Authority besides the Apostles but their Presbyters or Bishops, were all both in title and in power received.

X. And of the self same minde are the Enemies of Government by Bishops, even at this present day. They hold as *Aerius* did, that if Christ and his Apostles were obeied, a Bishop should not be permitted to ordain; that between a Presbyter and a Bishop the Word of God alloweth not any inequality or difference to be made; that their Order, their Authority, their Power, ought to be one; that it is but by usurpation and corruption, that the one sort are suffered to have rule of the other, or to be any way Superior unto them. Which opinion having now so many Defenders, shall never be able while the World doth stand, to finde in some, believing antiquity, as much as one which hath given it countenance, or born any friendly affection towards it. Touching these men therefore, whose desire is to have all equal, three ways there are, whereby they usually oppugn the received Order of the Church of Christ. First, by disgracing the inequality of Pastors, as a new and meer Humane invention, a thing which was never drawn out of Scripture, where all Pastors are found (they say) to have one and the same power, both of Order and Jurisdiction. Secondly, by gathering together the differences between that power which we give to Bishops, and that which was given them of old in the Church: So that a bit even the ancient took more then was warrantable, yet so far they swerved not as ours have done. Thirdly, by endeavouring to prove, that the Scripture directly forbideth, and that the judgement of the wisest, the holiest, the best in all Ages, condemneth utterly the inequality which we allow.

In what respect Episcopal Regiment is gainsaid by the Authors of pretended Reformation at this day.

XI. That

XI. That inequality of Pastors is a meer Humane invention, a thing not found in the Word of God, they prove thus:

1. *All the places of Scripture where the word* Bishop *is used, or any other derived of that name, signifie an oversight in respect of some particular Congregation onely, and never in regard of Pastors committed unto his oversight. For which cause the names of Bishops, and Presbyters, or Pastoral Elders are used indifferently, to signifie one and the self same thing. Which so indifferent and common use of these words, for one and the self same Office, so constantly and perpetually in all places declareth, that the word* Bishop *in the Apostles Writing, importeth not a Pastor of higher Power and Authority over other Pastors.*

2. *All Pastors are called to their Office by the same means of proceeding; the Scripture maketh no difference in the manner of their Tryal, Election, Ordination, which proveth their Office and Power to be by Scripture all one.*

3. *The Apostles were all of equal power; and all Pastors do alike succeed the Apostles in their Ministery and Power, the Commission and Authority whereby they succeed, being in Scripture but one and the same that was committed to the Apostles, without any difference of committing to one Pastor more, or to another less.*

4. *The power of the Censures and Keys of the Church, and of Ordaining and ordering Ministers (in which two points especially this Superiority is challenged) is not committed to any one Pastor of the Church, more then to another; but the same is committed as a thing to be carried equally in the guidance of the Church. Whereby it appeareth, that Scripture maketh all Pastors, not onely in the Ministery of the Word and Sacraments, but also in all Ecclesiastical Jurisdiction and Authority equal.*

5. *The Council of* Nice *doth attribute this difference, not unto any Ordination of God, but to an ancient Custom used in former times, which judgement is also followed afterward by other Councils,* Concil. Antioch. cap. 9.

6. *Upon these premises, their summary collection and conclusion is, That the Ministery of the Gospel, and the functions thereof, ought to be from Heaven, and of God,* Joh. 1. 23. *that if they be of God, and from Heaven, then are they set down in the Word of God; that if they be not in the Word of God (as by the premises it doth appear (they say) that our kinde of Bishops are not) it followeth, they are invented by the brain of men, and are of the Earth, and that consequently they can do no good in the Church of Christ, but harm.*

from Heaven: From Heaven, I say, and Heavenly, because although it be executed by Earthly men, and Ministers are chosen also by men like unto themselves, yet because it is done by the Word and Institution of God, it may well be accounted to come from Heaven, and from God.

Our Answer hereunto is, first, That their proofs are unavailable to shew, that Scripture affordeth no evidence for the inequality of Pastors. Secondly, That albeit the Scripture did no way insinuate the same to be Gods Ordinance, and the Apostles to have brought it in, albeit the Church were acknowledged by all men to have been the first beginner thereof, a long time after the Apostles were gone, yet is not the Authority of Bishops hereby disanulled, it is not hereby proved unfit, or unprofitable for the Church:

1. That the Word of God doth acknowledge no inequality of power amongst Pastors of the Church, neither doth it appear by the signification of this word *Bishop*, nor by the indifferent use thereof. For concerning signification, first it is clearly untrue, that no other thing is thereby signified, but onely an oversight in respect of a particular Church and Congregation. For I beseech you of what Parish, or particular Congregation was *Matthias* Bishop? His Office Scripture doth term Episcopal: which being no other then was common unto all the Apostles of Christ; forasmuch as in that number there is not any to whom the oversight of many Pastors did not belong, by force and vertue of that Office; it followeth that the very word doth sometimes even in Scripture signifie an oversight, such as includeth charge over Pastors themselves. And if we look to the use of the word, being applied with reference unto some one Church, as *Ephesus, Philippi,* and such like, albeit the Guides of those Churches be interchangeably in Scripture termed sometime Bishops, sometime

* D 2

Side notes:

Their Arguments in disgrace of Regiment by Bishops, as being a meer invention of man, and not found in Scripture, Answered.
Tit. 1. 5.
1 Tim. 3. 5.
Phil. 1. 1.
1 Pet. 5. 1, 2.

T. C. l. 1 p. 13. So that it appeareth that the Ministery of the Gospel, and the functions thereof, ought to be

Answer

Acts 1. 10.

Revel. 2.

time Presbyters, to fignifie men having overfight and charge, without relation at all unto other then the Chriftian Laity alone; yet this doth not hinder, but that Scripture may in fome place have other names, whereby certain of thofe Presbyters o: Bifhops, are noted to have the overfight and charge of Paftors, as out of all peradventure they had, whom S. *John* doth intitle Angels.

2. As for thofe things which the Apoftle hath fet down concerning Tryal, Election, and Ordination of Paftors, that he maketh no difference in the manner of their calling, this alfo is but a filly argument to prove their Office and their Power equal by the fcripture. The form of admitting each fort unto their Offices, needed no particular inftruction : There was no fear but that fuch matters of courfe would eafily enough be obferved. The Apoftle therefore toucheth thofe things wherein Judgement, Wifdom and Confcience is required, he carefully admonifheth of what quality Ecclefiaftical perfons fhould be, that their dealing might not be fcandalous in the Church. And forafmuch as thofe things are general, we fee that of Deacons there are delivered in a manner the felf fame Precepts, which are given concerning Paftors, fo far as concerneth their Tryal, Election and Ordination. Yet who doth hereby collect, that Scripture maketh Deacons and Paftors equal ? If notwithftanding it be yet demanded, *wherefore he which teacheth what kinde of perfons Deacons and Presbyters fhould be, hath nothing in particular about the quality of chief Presbyters, whom we call Bifhops?* I anfwer briefly, that there it was no fit place for any fuch difcourfe to be made, inafmuch as the Apoftle wrote unto *Timothy* and *Titus,* who having by Commiffion Epifcopal Authority, were to exercife the fame in ordaining, not Bifhops (the Apoftles themfelves yet living, and retaining that power in their own hands) but Presbyters, fuch as the Apoftles at the firft did create throughout all Churches. Bifhops by reftraint (onely *James* at *Jerufalem* excepted) were not yet in being.

3. About equality amongft the Apoftles, there is by us no Controverfie moved. If in the room of the Apoftles, which were of equal Authority, all Paftors do by Scripture fucceed alike, where fhall we finde a Commiffion in Scripture which they fpeak of, which appointed all to fucceed in the felf fame equality of power, except that Commiffion which doth authorize to preach and baptize fhould be alledged, which maketh nothing to the purpofe, for in fuch things all Paftors are ftill equal : We muft I fear me, wait very long before any other will be fhewed. For howfoever the Apoftles were equals amongft themfelves, all other Paftors were not equals with the Apoftles while they lived, neither are they any where appointed to be afterward each others equal. Apoftles had, as we know, authority over all fuch as were no Apoftles, by force of which their Authority, they might both command and judge. It was for the fingular good and benefit of thofe Difciples whom Chrift left behinde him, and of the Paftors which were afterwards chofen : For the great good, I fay, of all forts, that the Apoftles were in power above them. Every day brought forth fomewhat wherein they faw by experience, how much it ftood them in ftead to be under controulment of thofe Superiors and higher Governors of Gods Houfe. Was it a thing fo behoveful that Paftors fhould be fubject unto Paftors in the Apoftles own times ? and is there any commandment that this fubjection fhould ceafe with them ? and that the Paftors of the fucceeding ages fhould be all equals? No, no, this ftrange and abfurd conceit of equality amongft Paftors (the mother of Schifm, and of confufion) is but a dream newly brought forth, and feen never in the Church before.

4. Power of Cenfure and Ordination appeareth even by Scripture marvellous probable , to have been derived from Chrift to his Church, without this furmifed equality in them, to whom he hath committed the fame. For I would know whether *Timothy* and *Titus* were commanded by S. *Paul* to do any thing, more then Chrift hath authorized Paftors to do ; And to the one it is Scripture which faith, *Againft a Presbyter receive T H O U no accufation, faving under two or three witneffes :* Scripture which likewife hath faid to the other, *For this very caufe left I T H E E in Crete, that T H O U fhouldft redrefs the things that remain, and fhou'dft O R D A I N Presbyters in every City, as I appointed T H E E.* In the former place the power of Cenfure is fpoken of, and the power of Ordination in the latter. Will they fay that every Paftor there was equal to *Timothy,* and *Titus* in thefe things ? If they do

1 Tim. 5. 19.

Tit. 1. 5.

do, the Apostle himself is against it, who saith that of their two very persons he had made choise, and appointed in those places them, for performances of those duties; whereas if the same had belonged unto others, no less then to them, and not principally unto them above others, it had been fit for the Apostle accordingly to have directed his Letters concerning these things in general unto them all which had equal interest in them; even as it had been likewise fit to have written those Epistles in St. *Johns* Revelation, unto whole Ecclesiastical Senates, rather then onely unto the Angels of each Church, had not some one been above, the rest in Authority to order the affairs of the Church. Scripture therefore doth most probably make for the inequality of Pastors, even in all Ecclesiastical affairs, and by very express mention as well in Censures as Ordinations.

5. In the *Nicene* Council there are confirmed certain prerogatives and dignitysbelonging unto Primates or Archbishops, and of them it is said that the antient custom of the Church, had been to give them such preeminence, but no syllable whereby any man should conjecture that those fathers did not honour the superiority which Bishops had over other Pastors, onely upon ancient custome, and not as a true Apostolical heavenly and divine ordinance.

6. Now although we should leave the general received perswasion, held from the first beginning; that the Apostles themselves, left Bishops, invested with power above other Pastors; although I say, we should give over this opinion, and imbrace that other conjecture which so * many have taught good to follow, and which my self did sometimes judge a great deal more probable then now I do, meerly that after the Apostles were deceased, Churches did agree amongst themselves for preservation of peace and order, to make one Presbyter in each City chief over the rest, and to translate into him that power, by force and vertue whereof the Apostles while they were alive, did preserve and uphold order in the Church, exercising spiritual jurisdiction, partly by themselves and partly by Evangelists, because they could not always every where themselves be present: This order taken by the Church it self (for so let us suppose that the Apostles did neither by word nor deed appoint it) were notwithstanding more warrantable then that it should give place and be abrogated; because the Ministry of the Gospel and the functions thereof ought to be from Heaven: There came chief Priests and Elders unto our Saviour Christ as he was teaching in the Temple, and the Question which they moved unto him was this, *By what authority dost thou these things, and who gave thee this authority?* their question he repelled with a Counterdemand, *The Baptisme of* John *whence was it, from Heaven or of men?* Hereat they paused, secretly disputing within themselves, *If we shall say from Heaven, he will ask, wherefore did ye not then beleive him? And if we say of men, we fear the people,* for all hold *John* a Prophet. What is it now which hereupon these men would inter? That all functions Ecclesiastical, ought in such sort to be from Heaven, as the function of *John* was! No such matter here contained. Nay doth not the contrary rather appear most plainly by that which is here set down? For when our Saviour doth ask concerning the Baptism that is to say the whole spiritual function of *John*, whether it were from Heaven or of men, he giveth clear to understand that men give Authority unto some, and some God himself from Heaven doth Authorize. Nor is it said, or in any sort signified that none have lawful authority which have it not in such manner as, *John*, from Heaven. Again when the Priests and Elders were loth to say that *John* had his calling from men, the reason was not because they thought that so *John* should not have had any good or lawful calling, but because they saw that by this means they should somewhat embase the calling of *John*, whom all men knew to have been sent from God, according to the manner of Prophets, by a meer celestial vocation. So that out of the evidence here a'ledged, these things we may directly conclude, first that whoso doth exercise any kind of function in the Church, he cannot lawfully so do except authority be given him; Secondly that if authority be not given him from men, as the Authority of teaching was given unto *Scribes* and *Pharisees*, it must be given him from Heaven, as Authority was given unto *Christ, Elias, John Baptist* and the Prophets. For these two onely ways there are to have Authority. But a strange conclusion it is, God himself did from Heaven authorize *John* to bear witness of the light, to prepare a way for the promised *Messias*, to publish the neerness of the

They of Walden, Abu. Syl bish. Boem. Marsilius, Defens pac. Nic. Them. Wald. c. 1. La. ca. 60. Calvin coment in 1. ad Tit. Bullinger, Decad 5. Ser. 3. Incl, Defens. apol par 2. Ca. 9. Di. 1. Fulk. Ans, to the Test. Tit. 1. 5. Ioh. 1. 15. Mat. 21. 23.

the Kingdom of God, to Preach repentance and to baptize (for by this part which was in the function of *John* most noted, all the rest are together signified) Therefore the Church of God hath no power upon new occurrences to appoint, to ordein an Ecclesiastical function, as *Moses* did upon *Jethroes* advice devise a civil. All things we grant which are in the Church ought to be of God. But for as much as they may be two ways accompted such, one, if they be of his own institution, and not of ours, another if they be of ours, and yet with his approbation, this latter way there is no impediment but that the same thing which is of men, may be also justly and truely said to be of God, the same thing from heaven which is from earth. Of all good things God himself is Author and consequently an approver of them. The rule to discern when the actions of men are good when they are such as they ought to be, is more ample and large then the law which God hath set particular down in his holy Word, the Scripture is but a part of that rule as hath been heretofore at large declared. If therefore all things be of God which are well done, and if all things be well done, which are according unto the rule of well doing; and if the rule of well-doing be more ample then the Scripture, what necessity is there, that every thing which is of God, should be set down in holy Scripture? true it is in things of some one kind, true it is, that what we are now of necessity for ever bound to beleive or observe in the special mysteries of salvation, Scripture must needs give notice of it unto the World; yet true it cannot be, touching all things that are of God. Sufficient it is for the proof of lawfulness in any thing done, if we can shew that God approveth it. And of his approbation, the evidence is sufficient if either himself have by revelation in his word warranted it, or we by some discourse of reason, find it good of it self, and unrepugnant unto any of his revealed laws and ordinances. Wherefore injurious we are unto God, the Author and giver of humane capacity, judgement and wit, when because of somethings wherein he precisely forbiddeth men to use their own inventions, we take occasion to disauthorize and disgrace the works which he doth produce by the hand, either of nature or of grace in them. We offer contumely, even unto him, when we scornfully reject what we list without any other exception then this; *the brain of man hath devised it.* Whether we look into the Church or Common-weal, as well in the one as in the other, both the Ordination of Officers, and the very institution of their Offices may be truely derived from God, and approved of him, although they be not always of him in such sort as those things are which are in Scripture. Doth not the Apostle term the law, of nature even as the Evangelist doth the law of Scripture, *Δικαίωμα τῶ Θεῦ* Gods own righteous ordinance? The law of nature then being his law, that must needs be of him which it hath directed men unto. Great ods, I grant, there is between things devised by men, although agreeable with the law of nature, and things in Scripture set down by the finger of the holy Ghost. Howbeit the dignity of these is no hinderance, but that those be also reverently accompted of in their place. Thus much they very well saw, who although not living themselves under this kind of Church Polity, yet being through some experience more moderate, grave and circumspect in their judgment, have given hereof their founder and better advised sentence. That which the holy fathers (saith *Zanchius*) have by common consent without contradiction of Scripture received, for my part I neither will nor dare with good conscience disallow. And what more certain then that the ordering of Ecclesiastical persons, one in authority above another, was received into the Church by the common consent of the Christian World. What am I that I should take upon me to control the whole Church of Christ in that which is so well known to have been lawfully, religiously and to notable purpose instituted? *Calvin* making mention even of Primates that have authority above Bishops, *It was,* saith he, *the institution of the ancient Church, to the end that the Bishops might by this bond of concord, continue the faster linked amongst themselves.* And least any man should think that as well he might allow the papacy it self, to prevent this he addeth, *Aliud est moderatum gerere & honorem, quam totum terrarum orbem immenso imperio complecti.* These things standing as they do, we may conclude that albeit the Offices which Bishops execute, had been committed unto them onely by the Church, and that the superiority which they have over other Pastors, were not first by Christ himself given to the Apostles, and from them descended to others, but afterwards in such consideration brought in and agreed upon as is pretended; yet could not this be a just or lawful exception against it.   XII. But

Lib. 1.

Rom. 1. 32.
Luk. 1. 6.

Confes. 169.

Epist. 190.

12. But they will say, *There was no necessity of instituting Bishops, the Church might have stood well enough without them, they are as those superfluous things which neither while they continue do good, nor do harm when they are removed, because there is not any profitable use whereunto they should serve. For first, in the primitive Church their Pastors were all equal, the Bishops of those days were the very same which Pastors of Parish Churches at this day are with us, no one at commandment or controulment by any others Authority amongst them. The Church therefore may stand and flourish without Bishops: If they be necessary, wherefore were they not sooner instituted? Again, if any such thing were needful for the Church, Christ would have set it down in Scripture, as he did all kinde of Officers needful for Jewish Regiment. He which prescribed unto the Jews so particularly the least thing pertinent unto their Temple, would not have left so weighty Offices undetermined of in Scripture, but that he knew the Church could never have any profitable use of them. 3 Furthermore, it is the judgement of* Cyprian, *that equity requireth every mans cause to be heard, where the fault he is charged with was committed. And the reason he alledgeth is, forasmuch as there they may have both accusers and witnesses in their cause. Sith therefore every mans cause is meetest to be handled at home by the Judges of his own Parish, to what purpose serveth their devise, which have appointed Bishops unto whom such causes may be brought, and Archbishops to whom they may be also from thence removed.*

The Arguments to prove there was no necessity of instituting Bishops in the Church.

Ep. 3. lib. 1.

13 What things have necessary use in the Church, they of all others are the most unfit to judge, who bend themselves purposely against whatsoever the Church useth, except it please themselves to give it the grace and countenance of their favourable approbation, which they willingly do not yield unto any part of Church Polity, in the forehead whereof there is not the mark of that new devised stamp. But howsoever men like or dislike, whether they judge things necessary or needless in the house of God, a Conscience they should have touching that which they boldly affirm or deny. 1. *In the primitive Church no Bishops, no Pastors having power over other Pastors, but all equals, every man supreme Commander and Ruler within the Kingdom of his own Congregation or Parish? The Bishops that are spoken of in the time of the Primitive Church, all such as Parsons or Rectors of Parishes are with us?* If thus it have been in the prime of the Church, the question is, how far they will have that prime to extend? and where the latter spring of this new supposed disorder to begin? That primative Church wherein they hold that amongst the Fathers, all which had pastoral charge were equal, they must of necessity so far enlarge, as to contain some hundred of years, because for proof hereof they alleage boldly and confidently S. Cyprian, who suffered Martyrdom about two hundred and threescore years after our blessed Lords Incarnation. A Bishop they say, such as Cyprian doth speak of, had onely a Church or Congregation, such as the Ministers and Pastors with us, which are appointed unto several Towns. Every Bishop in Cyprians time was Pastor of one onely Congregation, assembled in one place, to be taught of one man. A thing impertinent, although it were true. For the question is about personal inequality amongst Governors of the Church. Now to shew there was no such thing in the Church at such time as Cyprian lived, what bring they forth? forsooth, that Bishops had then but a small circuit of place for the exercise of their Authority. Be it supposed, that no one Bishop had more then one onely Town to govern, one onely Congregation to rule: Doth it by Cyprian appear, that in any such Town or Congregation, being under the cure and charge of some one Bishop, there were not besides that one Bishop, others also Ministers of the Word and Sacraments, yet subject to the power of the same Bishop? If this appear not, how can Cyprian be alleaged for a witness, that in those times there were no Bishops which did differ from other Ministers, as being above them in degree of Ecclesiastical power? But a gross and a palpable untruth it is, *That Bishops with Cyprian, were as Ministers are with us in Parish Churches.*

The fore-alledged arguments answered.

T. C. lib. 1. p. 99. & 100. The Bishop which Cyprian speaketh of, is nothing else but such as we call Pastor, or as the common name with us is, Parson, and his Church whereof he is Bishop is neither Diocess nor Province, but a Congregation which met together in one place, and to be taught of one man.

Churches; and that each of them did guide some Parish without any other Pastors under him. S. *Cyprians* own Person may serve for a manifest disproof hereof. *Pontius* being Deacon under *Cyprian* noteth, that his admirable vertues caused him to be Bishop with the soonest, which advancement therefore himself endeavoured for a while to avoid. It seemed in his own eyes too soon for him to take the title of so great Honor, in regard whereof a Bishop is termed *Pontifex, Sacerdos, Antistes Dei*. Yet such was his quality, that whereas others did hardly perform that duty, whereunto the Discipline of their Order, together with the Religion of the Oath they took at their entrance into the Office even constrained them, him the Chair did not make, but receive such a one, as behoved that a Bishop should be. But soon after followed that prescription, whereby being driven into exile, and continuing in that estate for the space of some two years, he ceased not by Letters to deal with his Clergy, and to direct them about the publique affairs of the Church. They unto whom those Epistles were written, he commonly entituleth the Presbyters and Deacons of that Church. If any man doubt, whether those Presbyters of *Carthage* were Ministers of the Word and Sacraments or no, let him consider but that one onely place of *Cyprian*, where he giveth them his careful advice, how to deal with circumspection in the perilous times of the Church, that neither they which were for the truths sake imprisoned, might want those Ghostly comforts which they ought to have, nor the Church by ministring the same unto them, incur unnecessary danger and peril. In which Epistle it doth expresly appear, that the Presbyters of whom he speaketh, did offer, that is to say, administer the Eucharist, and that many there were of them in the Church of *Carthage*, so as they might have every day change for performance of that duty. Nor will any man of sound judgement I think deny, that *Cyprian* was in Authority and Power above the Clergy of that Church, above those Presbyters unto whom he gave direction. It is apparently therefore untrue, that in *Cyprians* time Ministers of the Word and Sacraments were all equal, and that no one of them had either title more excellent then the rest, or Authority and Government over the rest. *Cyprian* being Bishop of *Carthage*, was clearly Superior unto all other Ministers there : Yea, *Cyprian* was, by reason of the Dignity of his Sea an Archbishop, and so consequently Superior unto Bishops. Bishops we say there have been always, even as long as the Church of Christ it self hath been. The Apostles who planted it, did themselves rule as Bishops over it, neither could they so well have kept things in order during their own times, but that Episcopal Authority was given them from above, to exercise far and wide over all other Guides and Pastors of Gods Church. The Church indeed for a time continued without Bishops by restraint, everywhere established in Christian Cities: But shall we thereby conclude, that the Church hath no use of them, that without them it may stand and flourish ? No, the cause wherefore they were so soon universally appointed was, for that it plainly appeared, that without them the Church could not have continued long. It was by the special Providence of God no doubt so disposed, that the evil whereof this did serve for remedy, might first be felt, and so the reverend Authority of Bishops be made by so much the more effectual, when our general experience had taught men what it was for Churches to want them. Good Laws are never esteemed so good, nor acknowledged so necessary, as when precedent crimes are as seeds out of which they grow. Episcopal Authority was even in a manner sanctified unto the Church of Christ, by that little better experience which it first had of the pestilent evil of Schisms. Again, when this very thing was proposed as a remedy, yet a more suspicious and fearful acceptance it must needs have found, if the self-same provident Wisdom of Almighty God, had not also given beforehand sufficient tryal thereof in the Regiment of *Jerusalem*, a Mother Church, which having received the same order even at the first, was by it most peaceably governed, when other Churches without it had trouble. So that by all means, the necessary use of Episcopal Government is confirmed, yea strengthened it is and ratified, even by the not establishment thereof in all Churches every where

tesi fratres pro dilectione sua cupidi sunt ad conveniendum & visitandam confessores bonos, quos illustravit jam gloriosis initiis divina dignatio, tamen caute hoc & non glomeratim nec per multitudinem simul junctim introisse facie: dum nec ex hoc ipso invidia concitetur, & introeundi aditus denegetur, & dum insatibiles multum volumus, totum perdamus consulite ergo & providete ut cum temperamento hoc agi tutius possit: ita ut Presbyteri quoque qui illic apud confessores offerunt singuli cum singulis diaconis per vices alternent, quia & mutatio personarum & vicissitudo convenientium minuit invidiam, Ep. 5.

at the first. 2. When they further dispute, *That if any such thing were needful, Christ would in Scripture have set down particular Statutes and Laws, appointing that Bishops should be made, and prescribing in what order, even as the Law doth for all kinde of Officers which were needful in the Jewish Regiment*; might not a man that would bend his wit to maintain the fury of the *Petrobrusian* Hereticks, in pulling down Oratories, use the self same argument, with as much countenance of reason? *If it were needful that we should assemble our selves in Churches, would that God which taught the Jews so exactly the frame of their sumptuous Temple, leaves no particular instructions in writing, no not so much as which way to lay any one stone?* Surely such kinde of Argumentation doth not so strengthen the sinews of their cause, as weaken the credit of their judgement which are led therewith. 3. And whereas thirdly, in disproof that use which Episcopal Authority hath in judgement of spiritual causes, they bring forth the verdict of *Cyprian*, who saith, *That equity requireth every mans cause to be heard, where the fault he was charged with was committed, forasmuch as there they may have both accusers and witnesses in the cause* : This Argument grounding it self on principles no less true in Civil, then in Ecclesiastical causes, unless it be qualified with some exception or limitations, overturneth the highest Tribunal Seats both in Church and Commonwealth, it taketh utterly away all appeal, it secretly condemneth even the blessed Apostle himself, as having transgressed the Law of Equity, by his appeal from the Court of *Judea*, unto those higher which were in *Rome*. The generality of such kinde of axiomes deceiveth, unless it be construed with such cautions as the matter whereunto they are appliable doth require. An usual and ordinary transportation of causes out of *Africa* into *Italy*, out of one Kingdom into another, as discontented persons list, which was the thing that *Cyprian* disalloweth, may be unequal and unmeet, and yet not therefore a thing unnecessary to have the Courts erected in higher places, and judgement committed unto greater persons, to whom the meaner may bring their causes either by way of appeal, or otherwise, to be determined according to the order of Justice; which hath been always observed every where in Civil States, and is no less requisite also for the State of the Church of God. The Reasons which teach it to be expedient for the one, will shew it to be for the other, at leastwise not unnecessary. Inequality of Pastors is an Ordinance both Divine and profitable : Their exceptions against it in these two respects we have shewed to be altogether causless, unreasonable, and unjust

Cypr. lib. 1 Ep. 3.

Acts 25.

XIV. The next thing which they upbraid us with, is the difference between that inequality of Pastors which hath been of old, and which now is : For at length they grant, *That the superiority of Bishops and of Archbishops is somewhat ancient, but no such kind of Superiority as ours have.* By the Laws of our Discipline a Bishop may ordain without asking the peoples consent, a Bishop may excommunicate and release alone, a Bishop may imprison, a Bishop may bear civil office in the Realm, a Bishop may be a Counsellor of State, these things, antient Bishops neither did nor might do. Be it granted that ordinarily neither in elections nor deprivations, neither in excommunicating nor in releasing the excommunicate, in none of the weighty affairs of Government, Bishops of old were wont to do any thing without consultation with their Clergy, and consent of the people under them. Be it granted that the same Bishops did neither touch any man with corporal punishment, nor meddle with secular affairs and Offices, the whole Clergy of God being then tied by the strict and severe Canons of the Church, to use no other then ghostly power, to attend no other business then heavenly. *Tarquinius* was in the Roman Commonwealth deservedly hated, of whose unorderly proceedings the History speaketh thus, *Hic regum primus traditum a prioribus morem de omnibus Senatum consulendi solvit, domesticis consiliis rempub. administravit, bellum, pacem, foedera, societates, per se ipsum cum quibus voluit injussu populi ac Senatus fecit dirimitq;* Against Bishops the like is objected, *That they are invaders of other mens right, and by intolerable usurpation take upon them to do that alone wherein ancient Laws have appointed that others, not they onely, should bear sway.* Let the case of Bishops be put, not in such sort as it is, but even as their very heaviest adversaries would devise it : Suppose that Bishops at the first had encroached upon the Church, that by sleights and cunning practices they had appropriated ecclesiastical, as *Augustus* did, imperial power; that they had taken the advantage of mens inclinable affections, which did not suffer them for revenue sake

An Answer unto those things which are objected, concerning the difference between that power which Bishops now have, and that which ancient Bishops had more then other Presbyters.

Liv.lib.1.

*E

to

to be fufpected of ambition; that in the mean while their ufurpation had gone forward by certain eafie and unfenfible degrees; that being not difcerned in the growth, when it was thus far grown, as we now fee it hath proceeded, the world at length perceiving there was juft caufe of complaint, but no place of remedy left, had affented unto it by a general fecret agreement to bear it now as an helplefs evil; all this fuppofed for certain and true, yet furely a thing of this nature, as for the Superiour to do that alone, unto which of right the confent of fome other Inferiours fhould have been required by them: though it had an indirect entrance at the firft, muft needs through continuance of fo many ages as this hath ftood be made now a thing more natural to the Church, then that it fhould be oppreft with the mention of contrary orders worn fo many ages fince quite and clean out of ure. But with Bifhops the cafe is otherwife; for in doing that by themfelves, which others together with them have been accuftomed to do, they do not any thing, but that whereunto they have been upon juft occafions authorized by orderly means. All things natural, have in them naturally more or lefs the power of providing for their own fafety: And as each particular man hath this power, fo every politick Society of men muft needs have the fame, that thereby the whole may provide for the good of all parts therein. For other benefit we have not any, by forting our felves into Politique Societies, faving onely that by this mean each part hath that relief, which the vertue of the whole is able to yield it. The Church therefore being a Politique Society or Body, cannot poffibly want the power of providing for it felf: And the chiefeft part of that power confifteth in the Authority of making Laws. Now forafmuch as Corporations are perpetual, the Laws of the ancienter Church cannot choofe but binde the latter, while they are in force. But we muft note withal, that becaufe the body of the Church continueth the fame, it hath the fame Authority ftill, and may abrogate old Laws, or make new, as need fhall require. Wherefore vainly are the ancient Canons and Conftitutions, objected as Laws, when once they are either let fecretly to dye by difufage, or are openly abrogated by contrary laws. The Ancient had caufe to do no otherwife then they did; and yet fo ftrictly they judged not themfelves in confcience bound to obferve thofe Orders, but that in fundry cafes they eafily difpenfed therewith, which I fuppofe they would never have done, had they efteemed them as things whereunto everlafting, immutable, and undifpenfable obfervation did belong. The Bifhop ufually promoted none, which were not firft allowed as fit, by conference had with the reft of his Clergy, and with the people: Notwithftanding, in the cafe of *Aurelius*, S. *Cyprian* did otherwife. In matters of deliberation and counfel, for difpofing of that which belongeth generally to the whole body of the Church, or which being more particular, is neverthelefs of fo great confequence, that it needeth the force of many judgements conferred, in fuch things the common faying muft neceffarily take place, *An eye cannot fee that which eyes can.* As for Clerical Ordinations, there are no fuch reafons alledged againft the Order which is, but that it may be efteemed as good in every refpect, as that which hath been; and in fome confiderations better; at leaftwife (which is fufficient to our purpofe) it may be held in the Church of Chrift, without tranfgreffing any Law, either ancient or late, Divine or Humane, which we ought to obferve and keep. The form of making Ecclefiaftical Officers, hath fundry parts, neither are they all of equal moment. When Deacons having not been before in the Church of Chrift, the Apoftles faw it needful to have fuch ordained, They firft affemble the multitude, and fhew them how needful it is that Deacons be made. Secondly, they name unto them what number they judge convenient, what quality the men muft be of, and to the people they commit the care of finding fuch out. Thirdly, the people hereunto affenting, make their choice of *Stephen* and the reft, thofe chofen men they bring and prefent before the Apoftles: Howbeit, all this doth not endue them with any Ecclefiaftical power. But when fo much was done, the Apoftles finding no caufe to take exception, did with prayer and impofition of hands, make them Deacons. This was it which gave them their very being, all other things befides were onely preparations unto this. Touching the form of making Presbyters, although it be not wholly of purpofe any where fet down in the Apoftles Writings, yet fundry fpeeches there are, which infinuate the chiefeft things that belong unto that action: As when *Paul* and *Barnabas* are faid

to

to have fasted, prayed, and made Presbyters: When *Timothy* is willed to lay hands *Acts* 14. 13. suddenly on no man, for fear of participating with other mens sins. For this cause *1 Tim* 5. 22. the Order of the Primitive Church was, between Choice and Ordination to have some space for such Probation and Tryal as the Apostle doth mention in Deacons, saying, *Let them first be proved, and then minister, if so be they be found* *1 Tim.* 3. 10. *blameless.*

Alexander Severus beholding in his time how careful the Church of Christ was, *Lamprid. in A-* especially for this point; how after the choice of their Pastors, they used to pub- *lex. Sever.* lish the names of the parties chosen, and not to give them the final act of Approbation, till they saw whether any let or impediment would be alleaged; he gave Commandment, That the like should also be done in his own Imperial Elections, adding this as a Reason wherefore he so required, namely, *For that both Christians and Jews being so wary about the Ordination of their Priests, it seemed very unequal for him not to be in like sort circumspect, to whom he committed the Government of Provinces, containing power over mens both Estates and Lives.* This the Canon Law it self doth provide for, requiring before Ordination scrutiny: *Let them diligently be examined three days together before the Sabbath, and on* *D.ca.quando* *the Sabbath let them be presented unto the Bishop.* And even this in effect al- *Epis.Sigitur,* so is the very use of the Church of *England,* at all Solemn Ordaining of Misters; and if all Ordaining were Solemn, I must confess it were much the better.

The pretended disorder of the Church of *England* is, That Bishops Ordain them, to whose Election the people give no voyces, and so the Bishops make them alone, that is to say, they give Ordination without popular Election going before, which ancient Bishops neither did nor might do. Now in very truth, if the multitude have hereunto a right, which right can never be translated from them for any cause, then is there no remedy but we must yield, that unto the lawful making of Ministers, the voyce of the people is required; and that according unto the Adverse Parties Assertion, Such as make Ministers without ask- *Eccl.dis.p.34.* ing the peoples consent, do but exercise a certain Tyrannie.

At the first Erection of the Commonwealth of *Rome,* the people (for so it was then fittest) determined of all affairs: Afterwards this growing troublesome, their Senators did that for them, which themselves before had done: In the end all came to one mans hands, and the Emperor alone was instead of many Senators.

In these things the experience of time may breed both Civil and Ecclesiastical change from that which hath been before received, neither do latter things always violently exclude former, but the one growing less convenient then it hath been, giveth place to that which is now become more. That which was fit for the people themselves to do at the first, might afterwards be more convenient for them to do by some other: Which other is not thereby proved a Tyrant, because he alone doth that which a multitude were wont to do, unless by violence he take that Authority upon him, against the Order of Law, and without any publique appointment; as with us if any did, it should (I suppose) not long be safe for him so to do.

This Answer (I hope) will seem to be so much the more reasonable, in that themselves, who stand against us, have furnisht us therewith. For whereas against the making of Ministers by Bishops alone, their use hath been to object, What sway the people did bear when *Stephen* and the rest were ordained Deacons: They begin to espy how their own Platform swerveth not a little from that example wherewith they controul the practice of others. For touching the form of the peoples concurrence in that action, they observe it not; no, they plainly profess that they are not in this point bound to be followers of the Apostles. The Apostles Ordained whom the people had first chosen. They hold, that their Ecclesiastical Senate ought both to choose, and also to Ordain. Do not themselves then take away that which the Apostles gave the people, namely, the priviledge of choosing Ecclesiastical Officers? They do. But behold in what sort they answer it.

Ecclef.Difcipl.
fol.41.

By the sixth and the fourteenth of the Acts (say they) it doth appear, that the people had the chiefest power of choosing. Howbeit that, as unto me it seemeth, was done upon special cause, which doth not so much concern us, neither ought it to be drawn unto the ordinary and perpetual form of governing the Church : For as in establishing Commonweals, not onely if they be popular, but even being such as are ordered by the power of a few the chiefest, or as by the sole Authority of one, till the same be established, the whole sway is in the peoples hands, who voluntarily appoint those Magistrates by whose Authority they may be governed; so that afterward not the multitude it self, but those Magistrates which were chosen by the multitude, have the ordering of publique Affairs : After the self same manner it fared in establishing also the Church : When there was not as yet any placed over the people, all Authority was in them all ; but when they all had chosen certain to whom the Regiment of the Church was committed, this power is not now any longer in the hands of the whole multitude, but wholly in theirs who are appointed Guides of the Church. Besides, in the choice of Deacons, there was also another special cause wherefore the whole Church at that time should choose them. For inasmuch as the Grecians murmured against the Hebrews, and complained, that in the daily distribution which was made for relief of the poor, they were not indifferently respected, nor such regard had of their widows as was meet, this made it necessary that they all should have to deal in the choice of those unto whom that care was afterwards to be committed, to the end that all occasion of jealousies and complaints might be removed. Wherefore that which was done by the people for certain causes, before the Church was fully settled, may not be drawn out and applied unto a constant and perpetual form of ordering the Church.

Let them cast the Discipline of the Church of *England* into the same scales where they weigh their own, let them give us the same measure which here they take, and our strifes shall soon be brought to a quiet end. When they urge the Apostles as presidents, when they condemn us of Tyrannie because we do not, in making Ministers the same which the Apostles did, when they plead, *That with us one alone doth ordain, and that our Ordinations are without the peoples knowledge, contrary to that example which the blessed Apostles gave ;* We do not request at their hands allowance as much as of one word we speak in our own defence, if that which we speak be of our own ; but that which themselves speak, they must be contented to listen unto. To exempt themselves from being over far prest with the Apostles example, they can answer, *That which was done by the people once upon special causes, when the Church was not yet established, is not to be made a rule for the constant and continual ordering of the Church.* In defence of their own election, although they do not therein depend on the people so much as the Apostles in the choice of Deacons, they think it a very sufficient Apology, that there were special considerations why Deacons at that time should be chosen by the whole Church, but not so now. In excuse of dissimilitudes between their own and the Apostles Discipline, they are contented to use this answer, *That many things were done in the Apostles times, before the setling of the Church, which afterward the Church was not tied to observe.* For countenance of their own proceedings, wherein their Governors do more then the Apostles, and their people, less then under the Apostles the first Churches are found to have done, at the making of Ecclesiastical Officers, they deem it a marvellous reasonable kinde of pleading to some, *That even as in Commonweals, when the multitude have once chosen many, or one to rule over them, the right which was at the first in the whole body of the people, is now derived into those many, or that one which is so chosen ; and that this being done, it is not the whole multitude, to whom the administration of such Publique affairs any longer appertaineth, but that which they did, their Rulers may now do lawfully without them ; after the self same manner it standeth with the Church also.*

How easie and plain might we make our defence ? how clear and allowable even unto them, if we could but obtain of them to admit the same things consonant unto equity in our mouthes, which they require to be so taken from their own ? If that which is truth, being uttered in maintenance of *Scotland* and *Geneva*, do not cease to be truth when the Church of *England* once alledgeth it, this great crime of Tyrannie wherewith we are charged, hath a plain and an easie defence ? Yea, but we do not at all ask the peoples approbation, which they do, whereby they shew themselves more indifferent and more free from taking away the peoples right. Indeed, when their lay-Elders have chosen whom they think good, the peoples consent thereunto is asked, and if they give their approbation, the thing ſtandeth warranted for ſound and good. But if not, is the former choice overthrown? No, but the people is to yield to reaſon, and if they which have made the choice, do ſolike the peoples reaſon, as to reverſe their own deed at the hearing of it, then a new election to be made, otherwiſe the former to ſtand, notwithſtanding the peoples negative and diſlike. What is this elſe but to deal with the people, as thoſe Nurſes do with Infants, whoſe mouthes they beſmear with the backſide of the ſpoon, as though they had fed them, when they themſelves devour the food. They cry in the ears of the people, that all mens conſent ſhould be had unto that which concerns all; they make the people believe we wrong them, and deprive them of their right in making Miniſters, whereas with us, the people have commonly far more ſway and force then with them. For inaſmuch as there are but two main things obſerved in every Eccleſiaſtical function, Power to exerciſe the duty it ſelf, and ſome charge of people whereon to exerciſe the ſame; the former of theſe is received at the hands of the whole viſible Catholick Church: For it is not any one particular multitude that can give power, the force whereof may reach far and wide indefinitely; as the power of Order doth, which whoſo hath once received, there is no action which belongeth thereunto, but he may exerciſe effectually the ſame in any part of the World, without iterated Ordination. They whom the whole Church hath from the firſt beginning uſed as her Agents, in conferring this power, are not either one or moe of the Laity, and therefore it hath not been heard of, that ever any ſuch were allowed to ordain Miniſters: Onely perſons Eccleſiaſtical, and they in place of calling, Superiors both unto Deacons, and unto Presbyters, onely ſuch perſons Eccleſiaſtical have been authorized to ordain both, and to give them the power of Order, in the name of the whole Church. Such were the Apoſtles, ſuch was *Timothy*, ſuch was *Titus*, ſuch are Biſhops. Not that there is between theſe no difference, but that they all agree in pre-eminence of place above both Presbyters and Deacons, whom they otherwiſe might not ordain. Now whereas hereupon ſome do infer, that no Ordination can ſtand, but onely ſuch as is made by Biſhops, which have had their Ordination likewiſe by other Biſhops before them, till we come to the very Apoſtles of Chriſt themſelves. In which reſpect it was demanded of *Beza* at *Poiſſie*, *By what Authority he could adminiſter the holy Sacraments, being not thereunto ordained by any other then* Calvin, *or by ſuch as to whom the power of Ordination did not belong, according to the ancient Orders and Cuſtoms of the Church, ſith* Calvin, *and they who joyned with him in that action, were no Biſhops:* And *Athanaſius* maintaineth the fact of *Macarius* a Presbyter, which overthrew the holy Table, whereat one *Iſchyras* would have miniſtred the bleſſed Sacrament, having not been conſecrated thereunto by laying on of ſome Biſhops hands, according to the Eccleſiaſtical Canons; as alſo *Epiphanius* inveigheth ſharply againſt divers for doing the like, when they had not Epiſcopal Ordination. To this we anſwer, That there may be ſometimes very juſt and ſufficient reaſon to allow Ordination made without a Biſhop. The whole Church viſible being the true original ſubject of all power, it hath not ordinarily allowed any other then Biſhops alone to ordain: Howbeit, as the ordinary courſe is ordinarily in all things to be obſerved, ſo it may be in ſome caſes not unneceſſary that we decline from the ordinary ways. Men may be extraordinarily, yet allowably two ways admitted unto Spiritual Functions in the Church. One is, when God himſelf doth of himſelf raiſe up any, whoſe labour he uſeth without requiring that men ſhould Authorize them. But then he doth ratifie their calling by manifeſt ſigns and tokens himſelf from Heaven. And thus even ſuch as believed not our Saviours teaching, did yet acknowledge him a lawful Teacher ſent from God: *Thou art a Teacher ſent from God, otherwiſe none could do thoſe things which thou doſt.* Luther did but reaſonably therefore, in declaring that the Senate of *Mulheuſe* ſhould do well to aſk of *Minicer* from whence he received power to teach, who it was that had called him, and if his anſwer were that God had given him his charge, then to require at his hands ſome evident ſign thereof for mens ſatisfaction, becauſe ſo God is wont, when he himſelf is the Author of any extraordinary calling. Another extraordinary kinde of vocation is, when the exigence of neceſſity doth conſtrain to leave the uſual ways of the Church, which otherwiſe we would willingly keep: Where the Church muſt needs have ſome ordained, and neither hath nor can have poſſibly a Biſhop to ordain; in caſe

Ecclef. Diſcipl. f.41.

Neque enim fas erat aut licebat ut inferior ordinaret majorem. Coment. q. Ambroſ. tribuuntur, in 1 Tim.3.

Ἐπισκοπῆς χειροθεσίαν.

case of such necessity, the ordinary Institution of God hath given oftentimes, and may give place. And therefore we are not simply without exception, to urge a lineal descent of power from the Apostles by continued succession of Bishops, in every effectual Ordination. These cases of inevitable necessity excepted, none may ordain but onely Bishops: By the Imposition of their hands it is, that the Church giveth power of Order, both unto Presbyters and Deacons. Now when that power so received is once to have any certain subject whereon it may work, and whereunto it is to be tied, *here cometh in the peoples consent, and not before.* The power of Order I may lawfully receive, without asking leave of any multitude; but that power I cannot exercise upon any one certain people utterly against their wills ; Neither is there in the Church of *England* any man, by order of Law, possessed with Pastoral charge over any Parish, but the people in effect do chuse him thereunto. For albeit they chuse not by giving every man personally his particular voyce, yet can they not say that they have their Pastors violently obtruded upon them, inasmuch as their ancient and original interest therein, hath been by orderly means derived into the Patron who chooseth for them. And if any man be desirous to know how Patrons came to have such interest, we are to consider, that at the first erection of Churches, it seemed but reasonable in the eyes of the whole Christian World, to pass that right to them and their Successors, on whose soil, and at whose charge the same were founded. This all men gladly and willingly did, both in honor of so great Piety, and for encouragement of many others unto the like, who peradventure else, would have been as slow to erect Churches, or to endow them, as we are forward both to spoil them, and to pull them down.

Its no true assertion therefore in such sort as the pretended Reformers mean it, *That all Ministers of Gods Word ought to be made by consent of many, that is to say, by the peoples suffrages ; that ancient Bishops neither did nor might ordain otherwise, and that ours do herein usurp a far greater power then was, or then lawfully could have been granted unto Bishops which were of old.* Furthermore, as touching spiritual Jurisdiction, our Bishops, they say, do that which of all things is most intollerable, and which the Ancient never did. *Our Bishops excommunicate and release alone, whereas the Censures of the Church neither ought, nor were wont to be administred otherwise, then by consent of many.* Their meaning here when they speak of *many,* is not as before it was: when they hold that Ministers should be made with consent of many, they understand by *many* the multitude, or common people ; But in requiring that many should ever more joyn with the Bishop in the administration of Church Censures, they mean by *many,* a few lay-Elders, chosen out of the rest of the people to that purpose. This they say is ratified by Ancient Councils, by Ancient Bishops this was practised. And the reason hereof, as *Beza* supposeth was, *Because if the power of Ecclesiastical Censures did belong unto any one, there would this great inconveniency follow, Ecclesiastical Regiment should be changed into meer Tyrannie, or else into a Civil Royalty: Therefore no one, either Bishop or Presbyter, should or can alone exercise that Power, but with his Ecclesiastical Consistory he ought to do it, as may appear by the old Discipline.*

And is it possible, that one so grave and judicious should think it in earnest Tyrannie for a Bishop to excommunicate, whom Law and Order hath authorized so to do? or be perswaded that Ecclesiastical Regiment degenerateth into Civil Regality, when one is allowed to do that which hath been at any time the deed of moe? Surely, far meaner witted men then the World accompteth Mr. *Beza,* do easily perceive, that Tyrannie is power violently exercised against Order, against Law ; and that the difference of these two Regiments, Ecclesiastical and Civil, consisteth in the matter about which the actions of each are conversant ; and not in this, that Civil Royalty admitteth but one, Ecclesiastical Government requireth many supreme Correctors. Which Allegation, were it true, would prove no more then onely, that some certain number is necessary for the assistance of the Bishop : But that a number of such as they do require is necessary, how doth it prove ? Wherefore albeit Bishops should now do the very same which the Ancients did, using the Colledges of Presbyters under them as their Assistants, when they administer Church Censures, yet should they still swerve utterly from that which these men so busily labour for, because the Agents whom they require to assist in those cases, are a sort of lay-Elders, such as no ancient Bishop ever was assisted with.

Shall

Shall these fruitless jars and janglings never cease? shall we never see end of them? How much happier were the world if those eager Taskmasters whose eyes are so curious and sharp in discerning what should be done by many and what by few, were all changed into painful doers of that which every good Christian man ought either onely or chiefly to do, and to be found therein doing when that great and glorious Judge of all mens both deeds and words shall appear? In the mean while, be it one that hath this charge, or be they many that be his assistants, let there be careful provision that justice may be administred, and in this shall our God be glorified more then by such contentious Disputes.

XV. Of which nature that also is, wherein Bishops are over and besides all this accused *to have much more excessive power then the antient, in as much as unto their Ecclesiastical authority, the Civil Magistrate for the better repressing of such as contemn Ecclesiastical censures, hath for divers ages annexed Civil.* The crime of Bishops herein is divided into these two several branches, the one that in causes Ecclesiastical, they strike with the sword of secular punishments; the other, that offices are granted them, by vertue whereof they meddle with Civil affairs. Touching the one, it reacheth no farther then onely unto restraint of liberty by imprisonment (which yet is not done but by the Laws of the Land, and by vertue of authority derived from the Prince.) A thing which being allowable in Priests amongst the Jews, must needs have received some strange alteration in nature since, if it be now so pernicious and venemous to be coupled with a spiritual vocation in any man which beareth office in the Church of Christ. *Shemaia* writing to the Colledge of Priests which were in *Jerusalem,* and to *Zephania* the Principal of them, told them they were appointed of *God, that they might be Officers in the house of the Lord, for every man which raved, and did make himself a Prophet,* to the end that they might by the force of this their authority *put such in prison and in the stocks.* His malice is reproved, for that he provoketh them to shew their power against the innocent. But surely, when any man justly punishable had been brought before them, it could be no unjust thing for them even in such sort then to have punished As for Offices by vertue whereof Bishops have to deal in civil affairs, we must consider that Civil Affairs are of divers kinds, and as they be not all fit for Ecclesiastical persons to meddle with; so neither is it necessary, nor at this day happily convenient, that from medling with any such thing at all they all should without exception be secluded. I will therefore set down some few causes, wherein it cannot but clearly appear unto reasonable men, that Civil and Ecclesiastical Functions may be lawfully united in one and the same person.

First therefore, in case a Christian Society be planted amongst their professed enemies, or by toleration do live under some certain State whereinto they are not incorporated, whom shall we judge the meetest men to have the hearing and determining of such meer civil controversies as are every day wont to grow between man and man? Such being the state of the Church of *Corinth,* the Apostle giveth them this direction, *Dare any of you having business against another be judged by the unjust, and not under Saints? Do ye not know that the Saints shall judge the world? If the world then shall be judged by you, are ye unworthy to judge the smallest matters? Know yee not that we shall judge the Angels? How much more things that appertain to this life? If then ye have judgement of things pertaining to this life, set up them which are least esteemed in the Church. I speak it to your shame; Is it so that there is not a wise man amongst you? no not one that can judge between his brethren, but a brother goeth to law with a brother and that under the Infidels? Now therefore there is utterly a fault among you, because ye go to law one with another; why rather suffer ye not wrong, why rather sustain ye not harm?* In which speech there are these degrees; Better to suffer and to put up injuries, then to contend; better to end contention by arbitrement, then by judgement; better by judgement before the wisest of their own, then before the simpler; better before the simplest of their own, then the wisest of them without: So that if judgement of secular affairs should be committed unto wise men, unto men of chiefest credit and accompt amongst them, when the Pastors of their souls are such, who more fit to be also their Judges for the ending of strifes? The wisest in things divine, may be also in things humane the most skilful.

[margin notes:] Concerning the civil power and authority which our Bishops have. / Jer. 29. 26. / 1 Cor. 6. / Vid Barnab. Brisson. antiq. jur. lib. 5. c. 16.

skilful. At leastwise they are by likelihood commonly more able to know right from wrong then the common unlettered fort. And what *St. Augustine* did hereby gather, his own words do sufficiently show. *I call God to witness upon my soul, saith he, that according to the order which is kept in well ordered Monasteries, I could wish to have every day my hours of labouring with my hands, my hours of reading and of praying, rather then to endure these most tumultuous perplexities of other mens causes, which I am forced to bear while I travel in secular businesses, either by judging to discuss them, or to cut them off by intreaty: Unto which toils that Apostle, who himself sustained them not, for any thing we read, hath notwithstanding tied us not of his own accord, but being thereunto directed by that Spirit which speaks in him. His own Apostleship which drew him to travel up and down, suffered him not to be any where setled for this purpose ; wherefore the wise, faithful and holy men which were seated here and there, and not them which travelled up and down to preach, he made examiners of such businesses. Whereupon of him it is no where written, that he had leasure to attend these things, from which we cannot excuse our selves although we be simple ; because even such he requireth, if wisemen cannt be had, rather then the affairs of Christians should be brought into publick judgement. Howbeit not without comfort in our Lord are these travels undertaken by us, for the hopes sake of eternal life, to the end that with patience we may reap fruit.* So far is St. *Augustine* from thinking it unlawful for Paitors in such sort to judge civil causes, that he plainly collecteth out of the Apostles words, a necessity to undertake that duty; yea himself he comforteth with the hope of a blessed reward, in lieu of travel that way sustained.

Again, even where whole Christian Kingdoms are, how troublesome were it for Universities and other greater Collegiate Societies, erected to serve as Nurseries unto the Church of Christ, if every thing which civilly doth concern them, were to be carried from their own peculiar Governors, because for the most part they are (as fittest it is they should be) persons of Ecclesiastical calling ? It was by the wisdom of our famous Predecessors foreseen how unfit this would be, and hereupon provided by grant of special Charters that it might be as now it is in the Universities; where their Vice-Chancellors, being for the most part Professors of Divinity, are nevertheless Civil Judges over them in the most of their ordinary causes.

And to go yet farther degrees further, A thing impossible it is not, neither altogether unusual, for some who are of royal blood to be consecrated unto the Ministry of Jesus Christ, and so to be Nurses of Gods Church, not onely as the Prophet did foretel, but also as the Apostle St. *Paul* was. Now in case the Crown should by this mean descend unto such persons, perhaps when they are the very last, or perhaps the very best of their Race, so that a greater benefit they are not able to bestow upon a Kingdom then by accepting their right therein ; shall the sanctity of their Order deprive them of that honour whereunto they have right by blood ? or shall it be a bar to shut out the publick good that may grow by their vertuous Regiment ? If not, then must they cast off the Office which they received by divine imposition of hands ; or if they carry a more religious opinion concerning that heavenly function ; it followeth, that being invested as well with the one as the other, they remain Gods lawfully anointed both ways. With men of skill and mature judgement there is of this so little doubt, that concerning such as at this day are under the Archbishops of *Ments, Colen,* and *Trevers,* being both Archbishops and Princes of the Empire; yea such as live within the Popes own Civil Territories, there is no cause why any should deny to yeild them civil obedience in any thing which they command, not repugnant to Christian piety; yea even that civilly, for such as are under them, not to obey them, were the part of seditious persons : Howbeit for persons Ecclesiastical, thus to exercise Civil Dominion of their own, is more then when they onely sustain some publick Office, or deal in some business Civil, being thereunto even by supream Authority required. As Nature doth not any thing in vain, so neither Grace : Wherefore if it please God to bless some principal attendants on his own Sanctuary, and to endue them with extraordinary parts of excellency, some in one kind and some in another, surely a great derogation it were to the very honour of him who bestoweth so precious graces, except they on whom he hath bestowed them should accordingly be imployed that the fruit of those heavenly Gifts might extend it self unto the body of the Commonwealth
wherein

wherein they live; which being of purpose instituted (for so all Commonwealths are) to the end, that all might enjoy whatsoever good it pleaseth the Almighty to endue each one man with, must needs suffer loss, when it hath not the gain which eminent civil hability in Ecclesiastical persons is now and then found apt to afford. Shall we then discommend the people of *Milan* for using *Ambrose* their Bishop as an Ambassador about their publick and politick Affairs; the Jews for electing their Priests sometimes to be leaders in War; *David* for making the High-priest his chiefest Counsellor of State; finally, all Christian Kings and Princes which have appointed unto like services, Bishops or other of the Clergy under them? No, they have done in this respect that which most sincere and religious wisdom alloweth. Neither is it allowable onely, when either a kind of necessity doth cast civil offices upon them, or when they are thereunto preferred in regard of some extraordinary fitness, but further also when there are even of right annexed unto some of their places, or of course imposed upon certain of their persons functions of dignity and accompt in the Commonwealth, albeit no other consideration be had therein, save this, that their credit and countenance may by such means be augmented. A thing if ever to be respected, surely most of all now, when God himself is for his own sake generally no where honoured, religion almost no where, no where religiously adored, the Ministry of the Word and Sacraments of Christ a very cause of disgrace in the eyes both of high and low, weere it hath not somewhat besides it self to be countenanced with. For unto this very pass things are come, that the glory of God is constrained even to stand upon borrowed credit, which yet were somewhat the more tolerable, if there were not that dissuade to lend it him. No practice so vile, but pretended holiness is made somtime as a cloak to hide it.

The French King *Philip Valoie* in his time made an Ordinance that all Prelates and Bishops should be clean excluded from Parliaments where the Affairs of the Kingdom were handled; pretending that a King with good conscience cannot draw Pastors, having cure of Souls, from so weighty a business, to trouble their heads with Consultations of State. But irreligious intents are not able to hide themselves, no not when holiness is made their cloak. This is plain and simple truth That the councels of wicked men hate always the presence of them, whose vertue, though it should not be able to prevail against their purposes, would notwithstanding be unto their minds a secret corrosive, and therefore, till either by one shift or another they can bring all things to their own hands alone, they are not secure. Ordinances holier and better there stand as yet in force by the grace of Almighty God, and the works of his Providence amongst us. Let not envy so far prevail, as to make us account that a blemish, which if there be in us any spark of sound Judgement, or of religious Conscience, we must of necessity acknowledge to be one of the chiefest Ornaments unto this Land: By the antient Laws whereof, the Clergy being held for the chief of those Three Estates, which together make up the entire body of this Commonwealth, under one Supream Head and Governour, it hath all this time ever born a sway proportionable in the weighty affairs of the Land, wise and vertuous Kings condescending most willingly thereunto, even of reverence to the Most High, with the flower of whose sanctified Inheritance, as it were with a kind of Divine presence, unless their chiefest Civil Assemblies were so far forth beautified as might be without any notable impediment unto their heavenly Functions, they could not satisfie themselves as having showed towards God an Affection most dutiful.

Thus first, in defect of other Civil Magistrates; Secondly, for the ease and quietness of Scholastical Societies; Thirdly, by way of political necessity; Fourthly, in regard of quality, care, and extraordinancy; Fifthly, For countenance unto the Ministry; And lastly, even of devotion and reverence towards God himself, there may be admitted at least wise in some particulars well and lawfully enough a conjunction of Civil and Ecclesiastical Power; except there be some such Law or Reason to the contrary, as may prove it to be a thing simply in it self naught.

Against it many things are objected, as first, *That the matters which are noted in the holy Scripture to have belonged to the ordinary Office of any Minister of Gods holy*
F*Word*

Word and Sacraments, are these which follow, with such like, and no other, namely, The watch of the Sanctuary, the business of God, the Ministry of the Word and Sacraments, Over-sight of the House of God, Watching over his Flock, Prophesie, Prayer, Dispensations of the Mysteries of God, (harge and care of mens souls. If a man would shew what the offices and duties of a Chyrurgeon or Physician are; I suppose it were not his part, as much as to mention any thing belonging unto the one or the other, in case either should be also a Souldier or a Merchant, or an House-keeper, or a Magistrate; Because the Functions of these are different from those of the former, albeit one and the same man may happily be both. The case is like, when the Scripture teacheth what duties are required in an Ecclesiastical Minister; in describing of whose office, to touch any other thing then such as properly and directly toucheth his office that way were impertinent.

Yea, But in the Old Testament the two Powers Civil and Ecclesiastical were distinguished, not onely in nature, but also in person, the one committed unto Moses, and the Magistrates joyned with him, the other to Aaron and his Sons. Jehosaphat in his Reformation doth not onely distinguish causes Ecclesiastical from Civil, and erecteth divers Courts for them, but appointeth also divers Judges. With the Jews these two Powers were not so distinguished, but that sometimes they might and did concur in one and the same person: Was not *Ely* both Priest and Judge? After their return from captivity, *Esdras* a Priest, and the same their chief Governor even in Civil Affairs also? These men which urge the necessity of making always a personal distinction of these two Powers, as it by *Jehosaphats* example the same person ought not to deal in both causes, yet are not scrupulous to make men of Civil place and calling, Presbyters and Ministers of spiritual jurisdiction in their own spiritual Consistories.

If it be against the Jewish precedents for us to give Civil power unto such as have Ecclesiastical, is it not as much against the same for them to give Ecclesiastical power unto such as have Civil? They will answer perhaps, That their Position is onely against conjunction of Ecclesiastical Power of order, and the power of Civil Jurisdiction in one person. But this Answer will not stand with their proofs, which make no less against the power of Civil and Ecclesiastical Jurisdiction in one person, for of these two Powers *Jehosaphats* example is: Besides the contrary example of *Hely* and of *Ezra*, by us alledged do plainly shew that amongst the Jews, even the power of order Ecclesiastical and Civil Jurisdiction were sometimes lawfully united in one and the same person. Pressed further we are with our Lord and Saviours example, who *denieth his Kingdom to be of this world, and therefore as not standing with his calling refused to be made a King, to give sentence in a criminal cause of Adultery, and in a civil of dividing an Inheritance.*

The Jews imagining that their Messiah should be a Potent Monarch upon earth, no marvail, though when they did otherwise wonder at Christs greatness, they sought so to with to have him invested with that kinde of Dignity, to the end he might presently begin to reign; Others of the Jews, which likewise had the same imagination of the Messiah, and did somewhat incline to think that peradventure this might be he, thought good to try whether he would take upon him that which he might do, being a King, such as they supposed their true Messiah should be. But Christ refused to be a King over them, because it was no part of the Office of their Messiah, as they did falsely conceive, and to intermeddle in those acts of civil judgement he refused also, because he had no such Jurisdiction in that Commonwealth, being in regard of his Civil person, a man of mean and low calling. As for repugnancy between Ecclesiastical and Civil Power, or any inconvenience that these two Powers should be united, it doth not appear that this was the cause of his resistance either to reign or else to judge.

2 Tim. 2. 4. What say we then to the blessed Apostles, who teach, *that Souldiers intangle not themselves with the business of this life, but leave them to the end they may please him who hath chosen them to serve, and that so the good Souldiers of Christ ought to do.*

The

The Apoftles which taught this, did never take upon them any place or Office of Civil power. No, they gave over the Ecclefiaftical care of the poor, that they might wholly attend upon the Word and Prayer. S. *Paul* indeed doth exhort *Timothy* after this manner, *Suffer thou evil as a noble Souldier of Jefus Chrift : no man warring is entangled with the affairs of life, becaufe he muft ferve fuch as have preffed him unto Warfare.* The fenfe and meaning whereof is plain, that Souldiers may not be nice and tender, that they muft be able to endure hardnefs, that no man betaking himfelf unto Wars, continueth entangled with fuch kinde of bufineffes as tend onely unto the eafe and quiet felicity of this life, but if the fervice of him who hath taken them under his banner, require the hazard, yea, the lofs of their lives, to pleafe him, they muft be content and willing with any difficulty, any peril, be it never fo much againft the natural defire which they have to live in fafety. And at this point the Clergy of God muft always ftand, thus it behoveth them to be affected as oft as their Lord and Captain leadeth them into the field, whatfoever conflicts, perils or evils they are to endure. Which duty being not fuch, but that therewith the Civil Dignities which Ecclefiaftical perfons amongft us do enjoy may enough ftand ; The Exhortation of *Paul* to *Timothy*, is but a flender Allegation againft them. As well might we gather out of this place, that men having children, or wives, are not fit to be Minifters (which alfo hath been collected, and that by fundry of the Ancient) and that it is requifite the Clergy be utterly forbidden marriage. For as the burthen of Civil Regiment doth make them who bear it, the lefs able to attend their Ecclefiaftical charge ; even fo S. *Paul* doth fay, that the married are careful for the World, the unmarried freer to give them-

Convenit hujufmodi eligi & ordinari facerdotes quibus nec liberi funt nec nepotes. Etenim fieri vix poteft ut vacaut hujus vitæ quotidianæ curis quas liberi creant parentibus maxima, omne ftudium omnemq; cogitationem circa divinam liturgiam & res Ecclefiafticas confumat, l. 4*. §. r. C. de Epifc. & Cler.*

felves wholly to the fervice of God. Howbeit, both experience hath found it fafer, that the Clergy fhould bear the cares of honeft marriage, then be fubject to the inconveniencies which fingle life, impofed upon them, would draw after it. And as many as are of found judgement know it to be far better for this prefent age, that the detriment be born, which happily may grow through the leffening of fome few mens fpiritual labours, then that the Clergy and Commonwealth fhould lack the benefit which both the one and the other may reap through their dealing in Civil affairs. In which confideration, that men confecrated unto the fpiritual fervice of God, be licenfed fo far forth to meddle with the fecular affairs of the World, as doth feem for fome fpecial good caufe requifite, and may be without any grievous prejudice unto the Church. Surely there is not in the Apoftles, being rightly underftood, any let. That no Apoftle did ever bear Office, may it not be a wonder, confidering the great devotion of the age wherein they lived, and the zeal of *Herod*, of *Nero* the great Commander of the known World, and of other Kings of the earth, at that time to advance by all means Chriftian Religion ? Their deriving unto others that fmaller charge of diftributing of the goods which were laid at their feet, and of making provifion for the poor, which charge, being in part Civil, themfelves had before (as I fuppofe lawfully) undertaken, and their following of that which was weightier, may ferve as a marvellous good example, for the dividing of one mans Office into divers flips, and the fubordinating of inferiors to difcharge fome part of the fame, when by reafon of multitude encreafing, that labour waxeth great and troublefome, which before was eafie and light : but very fmall force it hath to infer a perpetual divorce between Ecclefiaftical and Civil power in the fame perfons. The moft that can be faid in this cafe is , *That fundry eminent Canons, bearing the name of Apoftolical, and divers Councils likewife there are, which have forbidden the Clergy to bear any Secular Office ; and have enjoyned them to attend altogether upon reading, preaching, and prayer : Whereupon the moft of the ancient Fathers, have fhewed great diflikes that thefe two powers fhould be united in one perfon.*

For a full and final Anfwer whereunto, I would firft demand, Whether the commixtion and feparation of thefe two powers, be a matter of meer pofitive Law, or elfe a thing fimply with or againft the Law immutable of God and Nature ? That which is fimply againft this latter Law, can at no time be allowable in any perfon, more then Adultery, Blafphemy, Sacriledge, and the like. But conjunction of power Ecclefiaftical and Civil, what law is there which hath not at fome time or other al-

*F 2 lowed,

lowed as a thing convenient and meet ? In the Law of God we have examples sundry, whereby it doth most manifestly appear, how of him the same hath oftentimes been approved. No Kingdom or Nation in the World, but hath been thereunto accustomed, without inconvenience a d hurt. In the prime of the World, Kings and Civil Rulers were Priests for the most part all. The (a) Romans note it as a thing beneficial in their own Commonwealth, and even to (b) them apparently forcible for the strengthening of the Jews Regiment, under *Moses* and *Samuel*. I deny not, but sometime there may be, and hath been perhaps just cause to ordain otherwise. Wherefore we are not to to urge those things, which heretofore have been either ordered or done as thereby to prejudice those Orders, which upon contrary occasion, and the exigence of the present time, by like Authority have been established. For what is there which doth let, but that from contrary occasions, contrary Laws may grow, and each be reasoned and disputed for by such as are subject thereunto, during the time they are in force; and yet neither so opposite to other, but that both may laudably continue, as long as the ages which keep them, do see no necessary cause which may draw them unto alteration. Wherefore in these things, Canons, Constitutions, and Laws which have been at one time meet, do not prove that the Church should always be bound to follow them. Ecclesiastical persons were by ancient Order forbidden to be Executors of any mans Testament, or to undertake the Wardship of children. Bishops by the Imperial Law are forbidden to bequeath by Testament or otherwise to alienate any thing grown unto them after they were made Bishops. Is there no remedy but that these or the like Orders must therefore every where still be observed ? The reason is not always evident, why former Orders have been repealed, and other established in their room: Herein therefore we must remember the axiome used in the Civil Laws, *That the Prince is always presumed to do that with reason, which is not against reason being done, although no reason of his deed be exprest.* Which being in every respect as true of the Church, and her Divine Authority in making Laws, it should be some bridle unto those malapert and proud spirits, whose wits not conceiving the reason of Laws that are established, they adore their own privatenancy, as the supreme Law of all, and accordingly take upon them to judge that whereby they should be judged. But why labour we thus in vain ? For even to change that which now is, and to establish instead thereof, that which themselves would acknowledge the very self same which hath been, to what purpose were it, sith they protest, *That they utterly condemn as well that which hath been, as that which is; as well the ancient, as the present Superiority, Authority, and Power of Ecclesiastical persons ?*

a *Cum multa divinitus pontifices à majorè nostris inventa atq; instituta sint, cum nihil præclarius quam quod vos eosdem & Religionibus Deorum immortalium & summæ reipu. præesse voluerunt. Cic. pro domo sua ad pontif.*

b *Honor sacerdotii firmamen um potentiæ assumebatur.* Tacit. hist. lib. 5 He sheweth the reason wherefore their Rules were also Priests. The joyning of these two powers, as now, so then likewise profitable for the publique State but in respects clean opposite and contrary. For whereas then Divine things being more esteemed, were used as helps for the countenance of Secular power, the case in these latter ages is turned upside down, earth hath now brought Heaven under foot, and in the curse of the World, hath of the two the greater credit. Priesthood was then a strengthening to Kings, which now is forced to take strength and credit from far meaner degrees of Civil Authority.

Hic mos apud Indos suit ut eisdem reges & sacerdotes huberent, quoniam justa a religus permixta incredibile quantum valuere. Just. hist. lib. 36.

Lib. 41. S...... de Epi.

XVI. Now where they lastly alledge, *That the Law of our Lord Jesus Christ, and the judgement of the best in all ages, condemn all ruling Superiority of Ministers over Ministers;* they are in this, as in the rest, more bold to affirm, then able to prove the things which they bring for support of their weak and feeble cause. *The bearing of Dominion, or the exercising of Authority* (they say) *is that wherein the Civil Magistrate is severed from the Ecclesiastical Officer, according to the words of our Lord and Saviour,* Kings of Nations bear rule over them, but it shall not be so with you : *Therefore bearing of Dominion doth not agree to one Minister over another.* This place hath been, and still is, although most falsly, yet with far greater shew and likelihood of truth, brought forth by the Anabaptists, to prove that the Church of Christ ought to have no Civil Magistrates; but ordered onely by Christ. Wherefore they urge the opposition between Heathens, and them unto whom our Saviour speaketh. For sith the Apostles were opposite to Heathens, not in that they were Apostles, but in that

they

they were Christians, The Anabaptists inference is, *That Christ doth here give a Law, to be for ever observed by all true Christian men, between whom and Heathens there must be always this difference, that whereas Heathens have their Kings and Princes to rule, Christians ought not in this thing to be like unto them.* Wherein their construction hath the more shew, because that which Christ doth speak to his Apostles, is not found always agreeable unto them as Apostles, or as Pastors of mens souls, but oftentimes it toucheth them in generality, as they are Christians; so that Christianity being common unto them with all Believers, such speeches must be so taken, that they may be applied unto all, and not onely unto them. They which consent with us, in rejecting such Collections as the Anabaptist maketh with more probability, must give us leave to reject such as themselves have made with less: For a great deal less, likely it is, that our Lord should here establish an everlasting difference, not between his Church and Pagans, but between the Pastors of his Church and Civil Governors. For if herein they must always differ, that the one may not bear rule, the other may; How did the Apostles themselves observe this difference, the exercise of whose Authority, both in commanding, and in controuling others, the Scripture hath made so manifest, that no gloss can overshadow it? Again, it being, as they would have it, our Saviours purpose to withhold his Apostles, and in them all other Pastors from bearing rule, why should Kingly Dominion be mentioned, which occasions men to gather, that not all Dominion and Rule, but this one onely form was prohibited, and that Authority was permitted them, so it were not Regal? Furthermore, in case it had been his purpose to withhold Pastors altogether from bearing rule, why should Kings of Nations be mentioned, as if they were not forbidden to exercise, no not Regal Dominion it self, but onely such Regal Dominion as Heathen Kings do exercise? The very truth is, our Lord and Saviour did aim at a far other mark then these men seem to observe: The end of his speech was to reform their particular misperswasion to whom he spake: And their misperswasion was, that which was also the common fancy of the Jews at that time, that their Lord being the Messias of the World, should restore unto *Israel* that Kingdom, whereof the Romans had as then bereaved them; they imagined that he should not onely deliver the State of *Israel,* but himself reign as King in the Throne of *David,* with all Secular Pomp and Dignity; that he should subdue the rest of the World, and make *Jerusalem* the seat of an universal Monarchy. Seeing therefore they had forsaken all to follow him, being now in so mean condition, they did not think, but that together with him, they also should rise in state, that they should be the first, and the most advanced by him.

? Of this conceit it came that the mother of the Sons of *Zebedee* sued for her childrens preferment; of this conceit it grew that the Apostles began to question amongst themselves which of them should be greatest: And in controlement of this conceit it was that our Lord so plainly told them, *that the thoughts of their hearts were vain;* the King of Nations have indeed their large and ample Dominions, they reign far and wide, and their servants they advance unto honour in the world, they bestow upon them large and ample secular Preferments, in which respect they are also termed many of them Benefactors, because of the liberal hand which they use in rewarding such as have done them service: But was it the meaning of the ancient Prophets of God, that the Messias the King of *Israel* should be like unto these Kings, and his retinue grow in such sort as theirs? wherefore ye are not to look for at my hands such preferments as Kings of Nations are wont to bestow upon their Attendants, *With you not so.* Your reward in Heaven shall be most ample, on earth your chiefest honour must be to suffer persecution for righteousness sake; submission, humility and meekness are things fitter for you to inure your mindes withal, then these aspiring cogitations; if any amongst you be greater then other, let him shew himself greatest in being lowliest, let him be above them in being under them, even as a servant for their good. These are Affections which you must put on; as for degrees of preferment and honour in this world, if ye expect any such thing at my hands, ye deceive your selves; for in the world your portion is rather the clear contrary. Wherefore they who alledge this place against Episcopal Authority abuse it, they many ways deprave and wrest it, clean from the true understanding wherein our Saviour himself did utter it.

For

For Firſt, whereas he by way of meer negation had ſaid, *With you it ſhall not be ſo*, foretelling them onely that it ſhould not ſo come to paſs, as they vainly ſurmiſed; theſe men take his words in the plain nature of a prohibition, as if Chriſt had thereby forbidden all inequality of Eccleſiaſtical power. Secondly, Whereas he did but cut off their idle hope of ſecular advancements, all ſtanding ſuperiority amongſt perſons Eccleſiaſtical theſe men would raſe off with the edge of his ſpeech. Thirdly, whereas he in abating their hope even of ſecular advancements ſpake but onely with relation unto himſelf, informing them that he would be no ſuch munificent Lord unto them in their temporal dignity and honor, as they did erroneouſly ſuppoſe, ſo that any Apoſtle might afterwards have grown by means of others to be even Emperor of *Rome*, for any thing in thoſe words to the contrary; theſe men removing quite and clean the hedge of all ſuch reſtraints, enlarge ſo far the bounds of his meaning, as if his very preciſe intent and purpoſe had been not to reform the error of his Apoſtles, conceived as touching him, and to teach what himſelf would not be towards them; but to preſcribe a ſpecial law both to them and their Succeſſors for ever; a Law determining what they ſhould not be in relation of one to another, a law forbidding that any ſuch title ſhould be given to any Miniſter as might import or argue in him a Superiority over other Miniſters. Being thus defeated of that ſuccour which they thought their cauſe might have had out of the words of our Saviour Chriſt, they try their adventure in ſeeking what aid

T. C. l. 1. ſ. 1.
ſag. 95.

Ὅτε τ̃ ἀρώ-
Ἰυς καθέδρας
ἐπίσκοπον μὴ
λέγεϛ̄ ἐξαρ-
χον τ̃ ἱερέων
ἢ ἄκρον ἱερέα
ἢ τοιούτότεςὶν
τι ῥοῖϛ̄ ἀλλὰ
μόνον ἐπίσκοπον
τ̃ πρώτης κα-
θέδϛ̄ϛϛ̄. Can. 39.

mans teſtimony will yield them: Cyprian *objecteth it to* Florentinus, *as a proud thing, that by believing evil reports, and miſ-judging of* Cyprian, *he made himſelf Biſhop of a Biſhop, and Judge over him, whom God had for the time appointed to be Judge, lib. 4. ep. 9.* The endeavour of godly men to ſtrike at theſe inſolent names, may appear in the *Council of* Carthage, *where it was decreed, That the Biſhop of the chief Sea ſhould not be entituled the Exarch of Prieſts, or the higheſt Prieſt, or any other thing of like ſenſe, but onely the Biſhop of the chiefeſt Sea; whereby are ſhut out the name of Archbiſhop, and all other ſuch haughty titles.* In theſe Allegations it fareth, as in broken reports ſnatched out of the Authors mouth, and broached before they be half either told on the one part, or on the other underſtood. The matter which *Cyprian* complaineth of in *Florentinus* was thus, *Novatus* miſliking the eaſineſs of *Cyprian* to admit men into the fellowſhip of Believers, after they had fallen away from the bold and conſtant confeſſion of Chriſtian faith, took thereby occaſion to ſeparate himſelf from the Church, and being united with certain excommunicate perſons, they joyned their wits together, and drew out againſt *Cyprian* their lawful Biſhop ſundry grievous accuſations; the crimes ſuch, as being true, had made him uncapable of that Office whereof he was ſix years as then poſſeſſed; they went to *Rome*, and to other places, accuſing him every where as guilty of thoſe faults, of which themſelves had lewdly condemned him, pretending that twenty five *African* Biſhops (a thing moſt falſe) had heard and examined his cauſe in a ſolemn Aſſembly, and that they all had given their ſentence againſt him, holding his Election by the Canons of the Church void. The ſame factious and ſeditious perſons coming alſo unto *Florentinus*, who was at that time a man impriſoned for the teſtimony of Jeſus Chriſt, but yet a favourer of the error of *Novatus*, their malicious accuſations he over-willingly hearkned unto, gave them credit, concurred with them, and unto *Cyprian* in fine wrote his Letters againſt *Cyprian*: Which letters he juſtly taketh in marvellous evil part, and therefore ſeverely controulleth his ſo great preſumption, in making himſelf a Judge of a Judge, and as it were, a Biſhops Biſhop, to receive accuſations againſt him, as one that had been his Ordinary. *What height of pride is this,* ſaith *Cyprian*, *what arrogancy of ſpirit, what a puffing up of minde, to call Guides and Prieſts to be examined and ſifted before him? ſo that unleſs we ſhall be cleared in your Court, and abſolved by your ſentence, behold for theſe ſix years ſpace, neither ſhall the Brotherhood have had a Biſhop, nor the people a Guide, nor the Flock a Shepherd, nor the Church a Governor, nor Chriſt a Prelate, nor God a Prieſt.* This is the pride which *Cyprian* condemneth in *Florentinus*, and not the title or name of Archbiſhop, about which matter there was not at that time ſo much as the dream of any controverſie at all between them. A ſilly collection it is, that becauſe *Cyprian* reproveth *Florentinus* for lightneſs of belief, and preſumptuous raſhneſs of judgement, therefore he held the title of Archbiſhop to be a vain and a proud name. Archbiſhops were chief amongſt Biſhops, yet Archbiſhops had not over Biſhops

that

that full Authority which every Bishop had over his own particular Clergy : Bishops were not subject unto their Archbishop as an ordinary, by whom at all times they were to be judged, according to the manner of inferior Pastors, within the compass of each Diocess. A Bishop might suspend, excommunicate, depose such as were of his own Clergy, without any other Bishops Assistants ; not so an Archbishop the Bishops that were in his own Province, above whom divers Prerogatives were given him, howbeit no such Authority and Power, as alone to be judge over them : For as a Bishop could not be ordained, so neither might he be judged by any one onely Bishop, albeit that Bishop were his Metropolitan : Wherefore *Cyprian,* concerning the liberty and freedom which every Bishop had, spake in the Council of *Carthage,* whereat fourscore and seven Bishops were present, saying, *It resteth that every of us declare, what we think* of this matter, neither judging nor severing from the right of communion, any that shall think otherwise: For of us there is not any which maketh himself a Bishop of Bishops, or with Tyrannical fear, constraineth his Colleagues unto the necessity of obedience, inasmuch as every Bishop, according to the reach of his liberty and power, hath his own free judgement, and can no more have another his Judge, then himself be Judge to another.* Whereby it appeareth, that amongst the *African* Bishops, none did use such Authority over any, as the Bishop of *Rome* did afterwards claim over all, forcing upon them opinions by main and absolute power. Wherefore unto the Bishop of *Rome,* the same *Cyprian* also writeth concerning his opinion about Baptism, *These things we present unto your Conscience, most dear brother, as well for common honors sake, as of single and sincere love, trusting that as you are truly your self Religious and faithful, so those things which agree with Religion and Faith, will be acceptable unto you: Howbeit we know, that what some have over-drunk in, they will not let go, neither easily change their minde, but with care of preserving whole amongst their Brethren the bond of peace and concord, retaining still to themselves certain their own opinions wherewith they have been inured: Wherein we neither use force, nor prescribe a Law unto any, knowing that in the Government of the Church, every Ruler hath his own voluntary free judgement, and of that which he doth shall render unto the Lord himself an account.* As for the Council of *Carthage,* doth not the very first Canon thereof establish (a) with most effectual terms, all things which were before agreed on in the Council of *Nice* ? And that the Council of *Nice* did ratifie the pre-eminence of Metropolitan Bishops, who is ignorant ? The name of an Archbishop importeth onely a Bishop, having chiefty of certain Prerogatives above his Brethren of the same Order. Which thing, sith the Council of *Nice* doth allow, it cannot be that the other of *Carthage* should condemn it, inasmuch as this doth yield unto that a Christian unrestrained approbation.

The thing provided for by the *Synod* of *Carthage,* can be no other therefore, then onely that the chiefest Metropolitan, where many Archbishops were within any greater Province, should not be termed by those names, as to import the power of an ordinary Jurisdiction, belonging in such degree and manner unto him, over the rest of the Bishops and Archbishops, as did belong unto every Bishop over other Pastors under him. But much more absurd it is to affirm, that both *Cyprian* and the Council of *Carthage* condemn even such Superiority also of Bishops themselves, over Pastors their inferiors, as the words of *Ignatius* imply, in terming the Bishop, *A Prince of Priests.* Bishops to be termed Archpriests, in regard of their Superiority over Priests, is in the writings of the ancient Fathers a thing so usual and familiar, as almost no one thing more. At the Council of *Nice,* saith (b) *Theodoret,* three hundred and eighteen Archpriests were present. Were it the meaning of the Council of *Carthage,* that the title of Chief-Priest, and such like, ought not in any sort at all to be given unto any Christian Bishop, what excuse should we make for (c) so many ancient, both Fathers, and Synods of Fathers, as have generally applied the title of Archpriest unto every Bishops Office ? High time I think it is, to give over the obstinate defence of this most miserable, forsaken cause, in the favour whereof, neither God, nor, amongst so many wise and vertuous men as Antiquity hath brought forth, any one can be found to have hitherto directly spoken. Irksome confusion must of necessity be the end whereunto all such vain and ungrounded confidence,

Concil. Carthag. de haeret. bapt-zandis.

Lib. 1. ep 1.

a ἀλλὰ τὰ ἐν τῷ Νικαίῳ συνό δῳ ὁρισθέντα ἐμμένῃ πρώτα ἀδιαφυλαχθή σεται.

T. c. l. 1. p. 113.

b *Theod. hist Eccles. lib 1, cap 7,* ἀρχιερεῖς.
c *Hieronymus contra Luciferian. salutem Ecclesiae pendere dicit à summi Sacerdotis dignitate, id est Episcop'. Idem est in Hieronymo summus Sacerdos quod ἀρχιερεύς ἐπισκόπῳ in Carthaginensi concilio.* Vide C. Gratiens 32. dist. item C. Pontifices 12. q. 3. item C. De cis. De consec. dist. 5.

fidence doth bring, as hath nothing to bear it out, but onely an exceſſive meaſure of bold and peremptory words, holpen by the ſtart of a little time, before they came to be examined. In the writings of the ancient Fathers, there is not any thing with more ſerious aſſeveration inculcated, then that it is God which maketh Biſhops, that their Authority hath Divine allowance, that the Biſhop is the Prieſt of God, that he is Judge in Chriſts ſtead, that according to Gods own Law, the whole Chriſtian Fraternity ſtandeth bound to obey him. Of this there was not in the Chriſtian World of old any doubt or controverſie made, it was a thing univerſally every where agreed upon. What ſhould move men to judge that now ſo unlawful and naught, which then was ſo reverendly eſteemed? Surely no other cauſe but this, men were in thoſe times meek, lowly, tractable, willing to live in dutiful aw and ſubjection unto the Paſtors of their ſouls: Now we imagine our ſelves ſo able every man to teach and direct all others, that none of us can brook it to have Superiors; and for a mask to hide our pride, we pretend falſly the Law of Chriſt, as if we did ſeek the execution of his will, when in truth we labour for the meer ſatisfaction of our own againſt his.

XVII. The chiefeſt cauſe of diſdain and murmure againſt Biſhops in the Church of *England*, is, that evil-affected eye wherewith the World looked upon them, ſince the time that irreligious Prophaneneſs, beholding the due and juſt advancements of Gods Clergy, hath under pretence of enmity unto Ambition and Pride, proceeded ſo far, that the contumely of old offered unto *Aaron* in the like quarrel, may ſeem very moderate and quiet dealing, if we compare it with the fury of our own times. The ground and original of both their proceedings, one and the ſame; in Declaration of their greivances they differ not; the complaints as well of the one as the other are, *Wherefore lift ye up your ſelves thus far above the Congregation of the Lord?* it is too much which ye take upon you, too much power, and too much honor. Wherefore as we have ſhewed, that there is not in their power any thing unjuſt or unlawful, ſo it reſteth that in their honor alſo the like be done. The labour we take unto this purpoſe is by ſo much the harder, in that we are forced to wraſtle with the ſtream of obſtinate affection, mightily carried by a wilful prejudice, the dominion whereof ſo is powerful over them in whom it reigneth, that it giveth them no leave, no not as much as patiently to hearken unto any ſpeech which doth not profeſs to feed them in this their bitter humour. Notwithſtanding, foraſmuah as I am perſwaded, that againſt God they will not ſtrive, if they perceive once that in truth it is he againſt whom they open their mouthes, my hope is their own confeſſion will be at the length, *Behold we have done exceeding fooliſhly, it was the Lord, and we knew it not; him in his Miniſters we have deſpiſed, we have in their honor impugned his.* But the alteration of mens hearts muſt be his good and gracious work, whoſe moſt Omnipotent Power framed them. Wherefore to come to our preſent purpoſe, Honor is no where due, ſaving onely unto ſuch as have in them that whereby they are found, or at the leaſt preſumed voluntarily beneficial unto them of whom they are honored. Whereſoever nature ſeeth the countenance of a man, it ſtill preſumeth that there is in him a minde willing to do good, if need require, inaſmuch as by nature ſo it ſhould be; for which cauſe men unto men do honor, even for very humanity ſake. And unto whom we deny all honor, we ſeem plainly to take from them all opinion of humane dignity, to make no account or reckoning of them, to think them ſo utterly without vertue, as if no good thing in the World could be looked for at their hands. Seeing therfore it ſeemeth hard that we ſhould ſo hardly think of any man, the precept of S. *Peter* is, *Honor all men.* Which duty of every man towards all, doth vary according to the ſeveral degrees whereby they are more or leſs beneficial, whom we do honour: *Honor the Phyſician*, ſaith the Wiſeman. The reaſon why, becauſe for neceſſities ſake, God created him. Again, *Thou ſhalt riſe up before the hoary head, and honor the perſon of the aged.* The reaſon why, becauſe the younger ſort have great benefit by their gravity, experience and wiſdom, for which cauſe, theſe things the Wiſeman termeth the Crown or Diadem of the aged. Honor due to Parents: The reaſon why, becauſe we have our beginning from them; *Obey the Father that hath begotten thee, the mother that bare thee deſpiſe thou not.* Honor due unto Kings and Governors: The reaſon

The ſecond main thing wherein the ſtate of Biſhops ſuffereth obloquy, is their honor.

Numb.16,3.

1 Pet.2.17.

Eccleſ 38 1

Levit 19.32.

Eccleſ 25.6.

Prov.23 22.

reafon why, becaufe God hath fet them *for the punifhment of evil doers, and for the* 1 Pet.2,14. *praife of them that do well.* Thus we fee by every of thefe particulars, that there is always fome kinde of vertue beneficial, wherein they excel, who receive honor, and that degrees of honor are diftinguifhed, according to the value of thofe effects which the fame beneficial vertue doth produce.

Nor is honor onely an inward eftimation, whereby they are reverenced, and well thought of in the mindes of men, but honor whereof we now fpeak, is defined to be an External fign, by which we give a fenfible teftification, that we acknowledge the beneficial vertue of others. *Sarah* honored her Husband *Abraham*; this appeareth by the title fhe gave him. The Brethren of *Jofeph* did him honor in the Land of *Egypt*; their lowly and humble gefture fheweth it. Parents will hardly perfwade themfelves that this intentional honor, which reacheth no farther then to the inward conception onely, is the honor which their children owe them.

Touching that Honor which myftically agreeing unto Chrift, was yielded literally and really unto *Solomon*; the words of the Pfalmift concerning it are, *Unto* Pfal.72,15. *him they fhall give of the gold of Sheba, they fhall pray for him continually, and daily blefs him.* Weigh thefe things in themfelves, titles, geftures, prefents, other the like external figns wherein honor doth confift, and they are matters of no great moment. Howbeit, take them away, let them ceafe to be required, and they are not things of fmall importance, which that furceafe were likely to draw after it. Let the Lord Mayor of *London*, or any other unto whofe Office honor belongeth, be deprived but of that title which in it felf is a matter of nothing; and fuppofe we that it would be a fmall maim unto the credit, force, and countenance of his Office? It hath not without the fingular wifdom of God been provided, that the ordinary outward tokens of honor fhould for the moft part be in themfelves things of mean account; for to the end they might eafily follow as faithful teftimonies of that beneficial vertue whereunto they are due, it behoved them to be of fuch nature, that to himfelf no man might over eagerly challenge them, without blufhing; nor any man where they are due withhold them, but with manifeft appearance of too great malice or pride. Now forafmuch, as according to the ancient Orders and Cuftoms of this Land, as of the Kingdom of *Ifrael*, and of all Chriftian Kingdoms through the World, the next in degree of honor unto the chief Soveraign, are the chief Prelates of Gods Church; what the reafon hereof may be, it refteth next to be enquired.

XVIII. Other reafon there is not any, wherefore fuch honor hath been judged What good due, faving onely that publique good which the Prelates of Gods Clergy are Au-doth publiquely grow thors of: For I would know, which of thefe things it is whereof we make any from the Pre-queftion, either that the favour of God is the cheifeft pillar to bear up Kingdoms lacy. and States; or that true Religion publiquely exercifed, is the principal mean to retain the favour of God; or that the Prelates of the Church are they, without whom the exercife of true Religion cannot well and long continue? If thefe three be granted, then cannot the publique benefit of Prelacy be diffembled. And of the firft or fecond of thefe, I look not for any profeft denial: The World at this will blufh not to grant at the leaftwife in word as much as (*a*) Heathens them-a *Quis eft* felves have of old with moft earneft affeveration acknowledged, concerning the *tam vecors qui* force of Divine grace in upholding Kingdoms. Again, though his mercy doth fo *aut cum fu-* far ftrive with mens ingratitude, that all kinde of Publique iniquities deferving *fpexerit in cœ-* his indignation, their fafety is through his gracious Providence, many times *l m Deos effe* neverthelefs continued, to the end that amendment might, if it were poffible, *non fentiat*
& ea que
tanta mente

fiunt, ut vix quifquam arte ulla ordinem rerum ac viciffitudinem perfequi poffit, cafu fieri putet, aut cum Deos effe intellexerit non intelliget eorum numine hoc tantum imperium effe natum, & auctum & retentum? Cic. Orat. de ha-ruf, refpons.

avert their envy : fo that as well Commonweals, as particular perfons, both may
and do endure much longer, when they are careful, as they fhould be, to ufe
the moft effectual means of procuring his favour, on whom their continuance
principally dependeth : Yet this point no man will ftand to argue, no man will
openly arm himfelf to enter into fet Difputation againft the Emperors *Theodofius* and *Valentinian* for making unto their Laws concerning Religion, this Pre-

Tit. \ 13. C de
fumma trinit.

face, *Decere arbitramur noftrum imperium, fubditos noftros de Religione commone-
facere. Ita enim & pleniorem adquiri Dei ac Salvatoris noftri Jefu Chrifti benig-
nitatem poffibile effe exiftimamus, fi quando & nos pro viribus ipfi placere ftudueri-
mus, & noftros fubdetos ad eam rem inftituerimus:* Or againft the Emperor *Jufti-
nian,* for that he alfo maketh the like Profeffion, *Per Sanctiffimas Ecclefias & no-*

L. 3. C de
Epifc. & cler.

*ftrum imperium fuftineri, & communes res clementiffimi Dei gratia muniri credi-
mus.* And in another place, *Certiffime credimus, quia Sacerdotum puritas & de-*

L. 14. C de
Epifc. audiend.

*cus, & ad Dominum Deum ac falvatorem noftrum Jefum Chriftum fervor, & ab ip-
fis miffae perpetuae preces multum favorem noftrae Reipublicae & incrementum prae-
bent.*

Wherefore onely the laft point is, that which men will boldly require us to
prove ; for no man feareth now to make it a queftion, *Whether the Prelacy of
the Church be any thing available or no to effect the good and long continuance of
true Religion?* Amongft the principal bleffings wherewith God enriched *Ifrael,*
the Prophet in the *Pfalm* acknowledgeth efpecially this for one, *Thou didft lead*

Pfal 77. 20.

thy people like fheep by the hands of Mofes and Aaron. That which fheep are, if
Paftors be wanting, the fame are the people of God, if fo be they want Governors : And that which the principal Civil Governors are, in comparifon of
Regents under them, the fame are the Prelates of the Church, being compared
with the reft of Gods Clergy.

Wherefore inafmuch as amongft the Jews, the benefit of Civil Government
grew principally from *Mofes,* he being their principal Civil Governor, even fo
the benefit of fpiritual Regiment grew from *Aaron* principally, he being in the
other kinde their principal Rector, although even herein fubject to the Soveraign
Dominion of *Mofes.* For which caufe, thefe two alone are named as the heads and
Well-fprings of all. As for the good which others did in fervice either of the
Commonwealth, or of the Sanctuary, the chiefeft glory thereof did belong to
the chiefeft Governors of the one fort, and of the other, whofe vigilant care and
overfight kept them in their due order. Bifhops are

Qui vocaniur in veteri teftamento vocabant-
tur hi funt qui nunc Presbyteri op ellantur :
& qui tunc princeps sacerdotum nunc Epifco-
pus vocatur. Raba. Maur. de inftit. cler.
l. 1, c.1.6.

now, as High-Priefts were then, in regard of power
over other Priefts, and in refpect of fubjection unto
High-Priefts : What Priefts were then, the fame now
Presbyters are, by way of their place under Bifhops :
The ones Authority therefore being fo profitable, how
fhould the others be thought unneceffary. Is there any
man profeffing Chriftian Religion, which holdeth it not as a Maxime, That the
Church of Jefus Chrift did reap a fingular benefit by Apoftolical Regiment, not
onely for other refpects, but even in regard of that Prelacy, whereby they had
and exercifed power of jurifdiction over lower Guides of the Church? Prelates are
herein the Apoftles Succeffors, as hath been proved.

Thus we fee, that Prelacy muft needs be acknowledged exceedingly beneficial
in the Church : And yet for more perfpicuities fake, it fhall not be pain fuper-
fluoufly taken, if the manner how be alfo declared at large. For this one thing
not underftood by the vulgar fort, caufeth all contempt to be offered unto higher Powers, not onely Ecclefiaftical, but Civil; whom when proud men have difgraced, and are therefore reproved by fuch as carry fome dutiful affection of
minde : The ufual Apologies which they make for themfelves, are thefe, *What
more vertue in thefe great ones, then in others ? we fee no fuch eminent good which they
do above other men.* We grant indeed, that the good which higher Governors do,
is not fo immediate and neer unto every of us, as many times the meaner labours
of others under them, and this doth make it to be lefs efteemed.

But

But we muſt note, that it is in this caſe, as in a ſhip, he that ſitteth at the ſtern is quiet, he moveth not, he ſeemeth in a manner to do little or Nothing, in compariſon of them that ſweat about other toil, yet that which he doth is in value and force more then all the labours of the reſidue laid together. The influence of the Heavens above, worketh infinitely more to our good, and yet appeareth not half ſo ſenſible as the force doth of things below. We conſider not what it is which we reap by the Authority of our chiefeſt ſpiritual Governors, nor are likely to enter into any conſideration thereof, till we want them, and that is the cauſe why they are at our hands ſo unthankfully rewarded. Authority is a conſtraining power, which power were needleſs, if we were all ſuch as we ſhould be, willing to do the things we ought to do without conſtraint. But becauſe generally we are otherwiſe, therefore we all reap ſingular benefit by that Authority, which permitteth no men, though they would, to ſlack their duty. It doth not ſuffice that the Lord of an houſhold appoint labourers what they ſhall do, unleſs he ſet over them ſome chief workman to ſee they do it. Conſtitutions and Canons made for the ordering of Church affairs, are dead Taskmaſters. The due execution of Laws ſpiritual dependeth moſt upon the vigilant care of the chiefeſt ſpiritual Governors, whoſe charge is to ſee that ſuch Laws be kept by the Clergy and people under them : With thoſe duties which the Law of God, and the Eccleſiaſtical Canons require in the Clergy, lay Governors are neither for the moſt part ſo well acquainted, nor ſo deeply and neerly touched. Requiſite therefore it is, that Eccleſiaſtical perſons have authority in ſuch things. Which kinde of Authority, maketh them that have it Prelates. If then it be a thing confeſt, as by all good men it needs muſt be, to have Prayers read in all Churches, to have the Sacraments of God adminiſtred, to have the myſteries of Salvation painfully taught, to have God every where devoutly worſhipped, and all this perpetually, and with quietneſs, bringeth unto the whole Church, and unto every member thereof, ineſtimable good ; how can that Authority, which hath been proved the Ordinance of God for preſervation of theſe duties in the Church, how can it chooſe but deſerve to be held a thing publiquely moſt beneficial ? It were to be wiſhed, and is to be laboured for, as much as can be, that they who are ſet in ſuch rooms, may be furniſhed with honorable qualities and graces ; every way fit for their calling : But be they otherwiſe, howſoever ſo long as they are in Authoriſy, all men reap ſome good by them, albeit not ſo much good as if they were abler men. There is not any amongſt us all, but is a great deal more apt to exact another mans duty, then the beſt of us is to diſcharge exactly his own ; and therefore Prelates, although neglecting many ways their duty unto God and men, do notwithſtanding by their Authority great good, in that they keep others at the leaſtwiſe in ſome aw under them.

It is our duty therefore in this conſideration, to honor them that rule as Prelates ; which Office if they diſcharge well, the Apoſtles own verdict is, that the honor they ¹ Tim. 5.17. have, they be worthy of, yea, though it were double : And if their Government be otherwiſe, the judgement of ſage men hath ever been this, that albeit the dealings of Governors be culpable, yet honorable they muſt be, in reſpect of that Authority by which they govern. Great caution muſt be uſed, that we neither be emboldned to follow them in evil, whom for Authorities ſake we honor ; nor induced in Authority to diſhonor them, whom as examples we may not follow. In a word, not to diſlike ſin, though it ſhould be in the higheſt, were unrighteous meekneſs, and proud righteouſneſs it is to contemn or diſhonor Highneſs, though it ſhould be in the ſinfulleſt men that live. But ſo hard it is to obtain at our hands, eſpecially as now things ſtand, the yielding of honor, to whom honor in this caſe belongeth, that by a brief Rom. 13.7. Declaration onely, what the Duties of men are towards the principal Guides and Paſtors of their ſouls, we cannot greatly hope to prevail, partly for the malice of their open adverſaries, and partly for the cunning of ſuch as in a ſacrilegious intent work their diſhonor under covert, by more myſtical and ſecret means. Wherefore requiſite, and in a manner neceſſary it is, that by particular inſtances we make it even palpably manifeſt, what ſingular benefit and uſe publique, the nature of Prelates is apt to yield.

First, no man doubteth but that unto the happy condition of Commonweals, it is a principal help and furtherance, when in the eye of Forreign States, their eſtimation and credit is great. In which respect, the Lord himself commending his own Laws unto his people, mentioneth this as a thing not meanly to be accounted of, that their careful obedience yielded thereunto, should purchase them a great good opinion abroad, and make them every where famous for wisdom. Fame and repu-

Deut.4.6.

tation groweth, especially by the vertue, not of common ordinary persons, but of them which are in each estate most eminent, by occasion of their higher place and calling. The mean mans actions, be they good or evil, they reach not far, they are not greatly enquired into, except perhaps by such as dwell at the next door; where-as men of more ample dignity, are as Cities on the tops of Hills, their lives are view-

Mat.5.13.

ed afar off; so that the more there are which observe aloof what they do, the greater glory by their well doing they purchase, both unto God whom they serve, and to the state wherein they live. Wherefore if the Clergy be a beautifying unto the body of this Commonweal in the eyes of Foreign beholders; and if in the Clergy, the Prelacy be most exposed unto the Worlds eye, what publique benefit doth grow from that order, in regard of reputation thereby gotten to the Land from abroad, we may soon conjecture? Amongst the Jews (their Kings excepted) who so renowned throughout the World, as their High-Priest, who so much, or so often spoken of, as their Prelates?

2. Which order is not for the present onely the most in sight, but for that very cause also the most commended unto Posterity: For if we search those Records wherein there hath descended from age to age, whatsoever notice and intelligence we have of those things which were before us, is there any thing almost else, surely not any thing so much kept in memory, as the successions, doings, sufferings, and affairs of Prelates. So that either there is not any publique use of that light which the Church doth receive from Antiquity; or if this be absurd to think, then must we necessarily acknowledge our selves beholden more unto Prelates, then unto others their inferiors, for that good of direction which Ecclesiastical actions recorded do always bring.

3. But to call home our cogitations, and more inwardly to weigh with our selves, what principal commodity that order yieldeth, or at leastwise is of it own disposition and nature apt to yield; Kings and Princes, partly for information of their own consciences, partly for instruction what they have to do in a number of most weighty affairs, intangled with the cause of Religion, having, as all men know, so usual occasion of often consultations and conferences with their Clergy; suppose we, that no publique detriment would follow, upon the want of honorable Personages Ecclesiastical to be used in those cases? It will be haply said, *That the highest might learn to stoop, and not to disdain the advice of some circumspect, wise, and vertuous Minister of God, albeit the Ministery were not by such degrees distinguished.* What Princes in that case might or should do, it is not material. Such difference being presupposed therefore, as we have proved already to have been the Ordinance of God, there is no judicious man will ever make any question or doubt, but that fit and direct it is, for the highest and chiefest order in Gods Clergy, to be employed before others, about so near and necessary Offices as the sacred estate of the greatest on earth doth require. For this cause *Joshua* had *Eliazer*; *David*, *Abiathar*; *Constantine*, *Hosius* Bishop of *Corduba*; other Emperors and Kings their Prelates, by whom in private (for with Princes this is the most effectual way of doing good) to be admonished, counselled, comforted, and if need were, reproved.

Whensoever Sovereign Rulers are willing to admit these so necessary private conferences, for their spiritual and ghostly good, inasmuch as they do for the time while they take advise, grant a kinde of Superiority unto them of whom they receive it, albeit happily they can be contented, even so far to bend to the gravest and chiefest persons in the order of Gods Clergy, yet this of the very best being rarely and hardly obtained, now that there are whose greater and higher callings do somewhat more proportion them unto that ample conceit and spirit, wherewith the minde of so powerable persons are possessed; what should we look for, in case God himself not authorizing any by miraculous means, as of old he did his Prophets, the equal meanness of all did leave, in respect of calling, no more place of decency for one, then for another to be admitted? Let unexperienced wits imagine what pleaseth them, in having to deal with so great Personages, these personal differences are so necessary, that there must be regard had of them.   4.King-

4. Kingdoms being principally (next unto Gods Almightinefs, and the Soveraign-ty of the higheft under God) upheld by wifdom, and by valour, as by the chiefeft humane means to caufe continuance in fafety with honour (for the labours of them who attend the fervice of God, we reckon as means Divine) to procure our pro-tection from Heaven;) from hence it rifeth, that men excelling in either of thefe, or defcending from fuch, as for excellency either way have been enobled, or poffeffing how-foever the rooms of fuch as fhould be in Politique wifdom, or in Martial prowefs eminent, are had in fingular recommendation. Notwithftanding, becaufe they are by the ftate of Nobility great, but not thereby made inclinable to good things; fuch they oftentimes prove even under the beft Princes, as under *David* certain of the Jewifh Nobility were. In Polity and Counfel the World had not *Achitophels* equal, nor Hell his equal in deadly malice. *Joab* the General of the Hoft of *Ifrael*, valiant, in-duftrious, fortunate in War; but withal headftrong, cruel, treacherous, void of piety towards God; in a word, fo conditioned, that eafie it is not to define, whether it were for *David* harder to mifs the benefit of his Warlike hability, or to bear the enormity of his other crimes. As well for the cherifhing of thofe vertues therefore, wherein if Nobility do chance to flourifh, they are both an ornament and a ftay to the Commonwealth wherein they live; as alfo for the bridling of thofe diforders, which if they loofly run into, they are by reafon of their greatnefs dangerous; what help could there ever have been invented more Divine, then the forting of the Clergy into fuch degrees, that the chiefeft of the Prelacy being matched in a kinde of equal yoke, as it were, with the higher, the next with the lower degree of No-bility; the reverend Authority of the one, might be to the other as a courteous bridle, a mean to keep them lovingly in aw that are exorbitant, and to correct fuch exceffes in them, as whereunto their courage, ftate and dignity maketh them over-prone? O that there were for encouragement of Prelates herein, that inclination of all Chriftian Kings and Princes towards them, which fometime a famous King of this Land either had, or pretended to have, for the countenancing of a principal Pre-late under him, in the actions of fpiritual Authority.

Let my Lord Archbifhop know (faith he) *that if a Bifhop, or Earl, or any other great Perfon, yea, if my own chofen Son, fhall prefume to withftand, or to hinder his will and difpofition, whereby he may be withheld from performing the work of the Embaffage com-mitted unto him; fucha one fhall finde, that of his contempt I will fhew my felf no lefs a Perfecutor and Revenger, then if Treafon were committed againft mine own very Crown and Dignity.* Sith therefore by the Fathers and firft Founders of this Commonweal, it hath upon great experience and forecaft, been judged moft for the good of all forts, that as the whole Body Politique wherein we live, fhould be for ftrengths fake a threefold Cable, confifting of the King as a Supreme Head over all, of Peers and Nobles under him, and of the people under them; fo likewife, that in this con-junction of States, the fecond wreath of that Cable fhould, for important refpects, confift as well of Lords Spiritual as Temporal: Nobility and Prelacy being by this mean twined together, how can it poffibly be avoided, but that the tearing away of the one, muft needs exceedingly weaken the other, and by confequent impair greatly the good of all? *(margin: Petr. Blefenf. Ep.5.)*

5. The force of which detriment there is no doubt, but that the common fort of men would feel to their helplefs wo, how goodly a thing foever they now furmife it to be, that themfelves and their godly Teachers did all alone, without controul-ment of their Prelate: For if the manifold jeopardies whereto a people deftitute of Paftors is fubject, be unavoidable without Government; and if the benefit of Go-vernment, whether it be Ecclefiaftical or Civil, do grow principally from them who are principal therein, as hath been proved out of the Prophet, who albeit the people of *Ifrael* had fundry inferior Governors, afcribeth not unto them the pub-lique benefit of Government, but maketh mention of *Mofes* and *Aaron*, onely the chief Prince, and chief Prelate, becaufe they were the well-fpring of all the good which others under them did; may we not boldly conclude, that to take from the people their Prelate, is to leave them in effect without Guides, at leaftwife, with-out thofe Guides which are the ftrongeft hands that God doth direct them by? *Thou didft lead thy people like fheep,* faith the Prophet, *by the hands of Mofes and Aaron.* *(margin: Pfal.77.20.)*

If

If now there arise any matter of grievance between the Paſtor and the people that are under him, they have their Ordinary, a Judge indifferent to determine their cauſes, and to end their ſtrife. But in caſe there were no ſuch appointed to ſit, and to hear both, what would then be the end of their quarrels? They will anſwer perhaps, *That for ſuch purpoſes, their Synods ſhall ſerve.* Which is, as if in the Commonwealth the higher Magiſtrates being removed, every Townſhip ſhould be a State, altogether free and independent; and the Controverſies which they cannot end ſpeedily within themſelves, to the contentment of both parties, ſhould be all determined by ſolemn Parliaments. Merciful God! where is the light of wit and judgement, which this age doth ſo much vaunt of, and glory in, when unto theſe ſuch odd imaginations, ſo great, not onely aſſent, but alſo applauſe is yielded?

6. As for thoſe in the Clergy, whoſe place and calling is lower, were it not that their eyes are blinded, left they ſhould ſee the thing, that of all others, is for their good moſt effectual, ſomewhat they might conſider the benefit which they enjoy by having ſuch in Authority over them, as are of the ſelf ſame Profeſſion, Society and Body with them; ſuch as have trodden the ſame ſteps before; ſuch as know by their own experience, the manifold intolerable contempts and indignities which faithful Paſtors, intermingled with the multitude, are conſtrained every day to ſuffer in the exerciſe of their ſpiritual charge and function, unleſs their Superiors, taking their cauſes even too heart, be by a kinde of ſympathy drawn to relieve and aid them in their vertuous proceedings, no leſs effectually, then loving Parents their dear children.

Iſa.3.5. Thus therefore Prelacy being unto all ſorts ſo beneficial, ought accordingly to receive honor at the hands of all: But we have juſt cauſe exceedingly to fear, that thoſe miſerable times of confuſion are drawing on, wherein *the people ſhall be oppreſſed one of another,* inaſmuch as already that which prepareth the way thereunto is come; to paſs, *children preſume againſt the ancient, and the vile againſt the honorable:* Prelacy, the temperature of exceſſes in all eſtates, the glew and ſoder of the Publique weal, the ligament which tieth and connecteth the limbs of this Body Politique each to other, hath inſtead of deſerved honor, all extremity of diſgrace; the fooliſh every where plead, that unto the wiſe in heart they ow neither ſervice, ſubjection, nor honor.

What kindes of honor be due unto Biſhops. XIX. Now that we have laid open the cauſes for which honor is due unto Prelates, the next thing we are to conſider, is, what kindes of honor be due. The good Government either of the Church, or the Commonwealth, dependeth ſcarcely on any one external thing, ſo much as on the Publique Marks and Tokens, whereby the eſtimation that Governors are in, is made manifeſt to the eyes of men. True it is, that Governors are to be eſteemed according to the excellency of their verties; the more vertuous they are, the more they ought to be honored, if reſpect be had unto that which every man ſhould voluntarily perform unto his Superiors. But the queſtion is now, of that honor which Publique Order doth appoint unto Church Governors, in that they are Governors; the end whereof is, to give open, ſenſible teſtimony, that the place which they hold is judged publiquely in ſuch degree beneficial, as the marks of their excellency, the honors appointed to be done unto them do import. Wherefore this honor we are to do them, without preſuming our ſelves to examine how worthy they are; and withdrawing it, if by us they be thought unworthy. It is a note of that publique judgement which is given of them, and therefore not tolerable that men in private, ſhould by refuſal to do them ſuch honor, reverſe as much as in them lieth the publique judgement. If it deſerve ſo grievous puniſhment, when any particular perſon adventureth to deface thoſe marks whereby is ſignified what value ſome ſmall piece of Coyn is publiquely eſteemed at; is it ſufferable that honors, the characters of that eſtimation which publiquely is had of publique Eſtates and Callings in the Church, or Commonwealth, ſhould at every mans pleaſure be cancelled? Let us not think that without moſt neceſſary cauſe, the ſame have been thought expedient. The firſt Authors thereof were wiſe and judicious men; they knew it a thing altogether impoſſible, for each particular in the multitude to judge what benefit doth grow unto them from their Prelates, and thereupon
                                                                    uniformly

uniformly to yield them convenient honor. Wherefore that all forts might be kept in obedience and aw, doing that unto their Superiors of every degree, not which every mans fpecial fancy fhould think meet, but which being beforehand agreed upon as meet, by publique fentence and decifion, might afterwards ftand as a rule for each in particular to follow; they found that nothing was more neceffary, then to allot unto all degrees their certain honor, as marks of publique judgement, concerning the dignity of their places; which mark, when the multitude fhould behold, they might be thereby given to know, that of fuch or fuch eftimation their Governors are, and in token thereof, do carry thofe notes of excellency. Hence it groweth, that the different notes and figns of Honor, do leave a correfpondent impreffion in the mindes of common beholders. Let the people be asked who are the chiefeft in any kinde of calling? who moft to be liftned unto? who of greateft account and reputation? and fee if the very difcourfe of their mindes, lead them not unto thofe fenfible marks, according to the difference whereof they give their fuitable judgement, efteeming them the worthieft perfons who carry the principal note, and publique mark of worthinefs. If therefore they fee in other eftates a number of tokens fenfible, whereby teftimony is given what account there is publiquely made of them, but no fuch thing in the Clergy; what will they hereby, or what can they elfe conclude, but that where they behold this, furely in that Commonwealth, Religion, and they that are converfant about it, are not efteemed greatly beneficial? Whereupon in time, the open contempt of God and godlinefs, muft needs enfue: *Qui bona fide Deos colit, amat & Sacerdotes,* faith *Papinius.* In vain doth that Kingdom or Commonwealth pretend zeal to the honor of God, *Pref. l. 5. Sisua.* which doth not provide that his Clergy alfo may have honor. Now if all that are imployed in the fervice of God, fhould have one kinde of honor; what more confufed, abfurd, and unfeemly? Wherefore in the honor which hath been allotted unto Gods Clergy, we are to obferve, how not onely the kindes thereof, but alfo in every particular kinde, the degrees do differ. The honor which the Clergy of God hath hitherto enjoyed, confifteth efpecially in pre-eminence of Title, Place, Ornament, Attendance, Priviledge, Endowment. In every of which it hath been evermore judged meet, that there fhould be no fmall odds between Prelates, and the inferior Clergy.

XX. Concerning title, albeit even as under the Law, all they whom God had fevered to offer him facrifice, were generally termed Priefts; fo likewife the name *Honor in ti-* of Paftor or Presbyter, be now common unto all that ferve him in the Miniftery of *tle, place, or-* the Gofpel of Jefus Chrift: Yet both then and now the higher Orders, as well of *tendancy* the one fort, as of the other, have by one and the fame congruity of reafon, their *and privi-* different titles of honor, wherewith we finde them in the phrafe of ordinary fpeech *ledge.* exalted above others. Thus the Heads of the twenty four companies of Priefts, *αρχιερεις.* are in Scripture termed Archpriefts; *Aaron,* and the fucceffors of *Aaron* being above thofe Archpriefts, themfelves are in that refpect further entituled, High and Great. After what fort Antiquity hath ufed to ftile Chriftian Bifhops, and to yield them in that kinde honor more then were meet for inferior Paftors, I may the better omit to declare, both becaufe others have fufficiently done it already, and in fo flight a thing, it were but a lofs of time to beftow further travel. The allegation of Chrifts prerogative to be named an Arch-paftor fimply, in regard of his abfolute excellency over all, is no impediment, but that the like title in an unlike fignification, may be granted unto others befides him, to note a more limited Superiority, whereof men are capable enough, without derogation from his glory, then which nothing is more Soveraign. To quarrel at fyllables, and to take fo poor exceptions at the firft four letters in the name of an Archbifhop, as if they were manifeftly ftollen goods, whereof reftitution ought to be made to the Civil Magiftrate, toucheth no more the Prelates that now are, then it doth the very bleffed Apoftle, who giveth unto himfelf the title of an Archbuilder.

As for our Saviours words, alledged againft the ftile of *Lordfhip* and *Grace,* we have before fufficiently opened how far they are drawn from their natural meaning, to boulfter up a caufe which they nothing at all concern. Bifhop *Theodoret* entituleth

most

Lib 5 cap. 3.
Hiſtor. Eccleſ.
L. 47 C. deſum·
ma Trinit.
L. 33. c. de
Epiſc. & cler.
L. 16. c. de ſa-
croſ. ecleſ.
Mat. 23. 6, 7.
They love to
have the
chief ſeats in
the Aſſem-
blies, and to
be called of
men Rabbi.

Eccluſ 45, 7.

moſt honorable. Emperors writing unto Biſhops, have not diſdained to give them their appellations of honor, *Your Holineſs*, *your Bleſſedneſs*, *your Amplitude*, *your Highneſs*, and the like: Such as purpoſely have done otherwiſe, are noted of inſo-lent ſingularity and pride.

Honor done by giving pre-eminence of place unto one ſort before another, is for decency, order, and quietneſs ſake ſo needful, that both Imperial Laws and Canons Eccleſiaſtical, have made their ſpecial proviſions for it. Our Saviours invective againſt the vain affectation of Superiority, whether in title, or in place, may not hinder theſe ſeemly differences uſual in giving and taking honor, either according to the one, or the other.

Some thing there is even in the Ornaments of honor alſo : Otherwiſe idle it had been for the Wiſeman ſpeaking of *Aaron*, to ſtand ſo much upon the circumſtance of his Prieſtly attire, and to urge it as an argument of ſuch dignity and greatneſs in him : *An everlaſting Covenant God made with Aaron, and gave him the Prieſthood among the people, and made him bleſſed through his comely ornament, and cloathed him with the gar-ment of honor.* The Robes of a Judge do not adde to his vertue ; the chiefeſt Orna-ment of Kings is Juſtice ; holineſs and purity of converſation doth much more adorn a Biſhop , then his peculiar form of cloathing. Notwithſtanding , both Judges, through the garments of judicial Authority, and through the ornaments of Sove-raignty, Princes, yea Biſhops through the very attire of Biſhops, are made bleſſed, that is to ſay, marked and manifeſted they are to be ſuch, as God hath poured his bleſſing upon, by advancing them above others, and placing them where they may do him principal good ſervice. Thus to be called is to be bleſſed, and therefore to be honored with the ſigns of ſuch a calling, muſt needs be in part a bleſſing alſo ; for of good things, even the ſigns are good.

Of honor, another part is Attendancy ; and therefore in the viſions of the glory of God, Angels are ſpoken of as his attendants. In ſetting out the honor of that myſtical Queen, the Prophet mentioneth the Virgin Ladies which waited on her. Amongſt the tokens of *Solomons* honorable condition, his ſervants and waiters, the ſacred Hiſtory omitteth not. This doth prove attendants a part of honor : But this as yet doth not ſhew with what attendancy Prelates are to be honored. Of the High-Prieſts retinue amongſt the Jews, ſomewhat the Goſpel it ſelf doth intimate : And albeit our Saviour came to Miniſter, and not, as the Jews did imagine their Meſſias ſhould, to be miniſtred unto in this World, yet attended on he was by his bleſſed Apoſtles, who followed not onely as ſcholars, but even as ſervants about him. After that he had ſent them, as himſelf was ſent of God, in the midſt of that hatred and extreme contempt which they ſuſtained at the Worlds hands, by Saints and Believers this part of honor was moſt plentifully done unto them. Attendants they had pro-vided in all places where they went ; which cuſtom of the Church was ſtill continued in Biſhops, their ſucceſſors, as by *Ignatius* it is plain to be ſeen. And from hence no doubt, thoſe Acolythes took their beginning, of whom ſo frequent mention is made, the Biſhops attendants, his followers they were, in regard of which ſervice, the name of Acolythes ſeemeth plainly to have been given. The cuſtom for Biſhops to be attended upon by many, is as *Juſtinian* doth ſhew, ancient : The affairs of Regiment, wherein Prelates are employed, make it neceſſary that they always have many about them, whom they may command, although no ſuch thing did by way of honor belong unto them.

Novel. 6.

Some mens judgment is, that if Clerks, Students, and Religious Perſons were moe, common Servingmen and lay Retainers fewer then they are in Biſhops Palaces, the uſe, and the honor thereof would be much more ſuitable then now : But theſe things, concerning the number and quality of perſons fit to attend on Prelates, ei-ther for neceſſity, or for honors ſake, are rather in particular diſcretion to be or-dered, then to be argued of by diſputes. As for the vain imagination of ſome, who teach the original hereof to have been a prepoſterous imagination of *Maximinus* the Emperor, who being addicted unto Idolatry, choſe of the choiſeſt Magiſtrates to be Prieſts ; and to the end they might be in great eſtimation, gave unto each of them a train of followers : And that Chriſtian Emperors thinking the ſame would promote Chriſtianity , which promoted ſuperſtition, endeavoured to make their Biſhops encounter and match with thoſe Idolatrous Prieſts ; ſuch frivolous conceits

T. col. p. 126.
out of uſ. 18.
ca. 15.

having

having no other ground then conceit, we weigh not so much as to frame any answer unto them, our declaration of the true original of ancient attendancy on Bishops being sufficient. Now if that which the light of found reason doth teach to be fit, have upon like inducements reasonable, allowable and good, approved it self in such wise as to be accepted, not onely of us, but of Pagans and Infidels also? doth conformity with them that are evil in that which is good, make that thing which is good evil? We have not herein followed the Heathens, nor the Heathens us, but both we and they one and the self same Divine rule, the light of a true and found understanding, which sheweth what honor is fit for Prelates, and what attendancy convenient to be a part of their honor.

Touching priviledges granted for honors sake, partly in general unto the Clergy, and partly unto Prelates the chiefest persons Ecclesiastical in particular: of such quality and number they are, that to make but rehearsal of them, we scarce think it safe, lest the very entrails of some of our godly Brethren, as they term themselves should thereat haply burst in sunder.

L. 12. C. de sacr. Ecclesf. l. 5 C. de sacr. Ecclef la. C. de Epis. & cler. l. 10 C. de Epif. & cl.t.

XXI. And yet of all these things rehearsed, it may be there never would have grown any question, had Bishops been honored onely thus far forth. But the honouring of the Clergy with wealth, this is in the eyes of them which pretend to seek nothing but meer Reformation of abuses, a sin that can never be remitted.

Honor by endowment with Lands and Livings.

How soon, O how soon might the Church be perfect, even without any spot or wrinkle, if Publique Authority would at the length say Amen, unto the holy and devout requests of those godly Brethren, who as yet with out-stretched necks, groan in the pangs of their zeal to see the Houses of Bishops rifled, and their so long desired Livings gloriously divided amongst the Righteous. But there is an impediment, a let, which somewhat hindreth those good mens prayers from taking effect: They in whose hands the Soveraignty of Power and Dominion over this Church doth rest, are perswaded there is a God; for undoubtedly either the name of Godhead is but a feigned thing, or if in Heaven there be a God, the Sacrilegious intention of Church-Robbers, which lurketh under this plausible name of Reformation, is in his sight a thousand times more hateful then the plain professed malice of those very Miscreants, who threw their vomit in the open face of our blessed Saviour.

They are not words of perswasion by which true men can hold their own, when they are over beset with Theives: And therefore to speak in this cause at all were but labour lost, saving onely in respect of them, who being as yet unjoyned unto this Conspiracy, may be haply somewhat stayed, when they shall know betimes, what it is to see Theives, and to run on with them, as the Prophet in the *Psalm* speaketh, *When thou sawest a Thief, then thou consentedst with him, hast been partakers with Adulters.*

Pfal. 50. 18.

For the better information therefore of men which carry true, honest and indifferent mindes, these things we will endeavour to make most clearly manifest:

First, That in Goods and Livings of the Church, none hath propriety but God himself.

Secondly, That the honour which the Clergy therein hath, is to be, as it were Gods Receivers, the honour of Prelates to be his chief and principal Receivers.

Thirdly, That from him they have right, not onely to receive, but also to use such Goods, the lower sort in smaller, and the higher in larger measure.

Fourthly, That in case they be thought, yea, or found to abuse the same, yet may not such honour be therefore lawfully taken from them, and be given away unto persons of other calling.

*H XXII. Possessions,

XXII. Poſſeſſions, Lands and Livings Spiritual, the wealth of the Clergy, the goods of the Church are in ſuch ſort the Lords own, that man can challenge no propriety in them. His they are, and not ours; all things are his, in that from him they have their being. (a) *My corn, and my wine, and mine oyl,* ſaith the Lord. All things his, in that he hath abſolute power to diſpoſe of them at his pleaſure. *Mine,* ſaith he, *are the ſheep and oxen of a thouſand hills* : All things his, in that when we have them, we may ſay with *Job, God hath given*; and when we are deprived of them, *the Lord,* whoſe they are, hath likewiſe *taken them away* again. But theſe ſacred poſſeſſions are his by another tenure: His, becauſe thoſe men who firſt received them from him, have unto him returned them again, by way of Religious gift, or oblation: And in this reſpect it is, that the Lord doth term thoſe Houſes wherein ſuch gifts and Oblations were laid, *his Treaſuries.*

That of Eccleſiaſtical goods, and conſequently of the Lands and Livings which Biſhops enjoy, the propriety belongeth unto God alone. a Hoſ. 2. 5.

The ground whereupon men have reſigned their own intereſt in things Temporal, and given over the ſame unto God, is that Precept which *Solomon* borroweth from the Law of Nature, *Honor the Lord out of thy ſubſtance, and of the chiefeſt of all thy revenue : ſo ſhall thy barns be filled with plenty, and with new wine, the fate of thy preſs ſhall overflow :* For although it be by one moſt fitly ſpoken againſt thoſe ſuperſtitious perſons that onely are ſcrupulous in external Rites. *Wilt thou win the favour of God? Be vertuous. They beſt worſhip him, that are his followers.* It is not the bowing of your knees, but of your hearts; it is not the number of your oblations, but the integrity of your lives; not your incenſe, but your obedience, which God is delighted to be honored by : Neverthelesse, we muſt beware leſt ſimply underſtanding this, which comparatively is meant, that is to ſay, whereas the meaning is, that God doth chiefly reſpect the inward diſpoſition of the heart, we muſt take heed we do not hereupon ſo worſhip him in Spirit, that outwardly we take all Worſhip, Reverence and honor from him.

Our God will be glorified both of us himſelf, and for us by others : To others, becauſe our hearts are known, and yet our example is required for their good; therefore it is not ſufficient to carry Religion in our hearts, as fire is carried in flint ſtones, but we are outwardly, viſibly, apparently, to ſerve and honor the living God, yea, to employ that way, as not onely our ſouls, but our bodies; ſo not onely our bodies, but our goods, yea, the choice, the flower, the chiefeſt of all thy revenue, ſaith *Solomon* : If thou haſt any thing in all thy poſſeſſions of more value and price then other, to what uſe ſhouldeſt thou convert it, rather then this? *Samuel* was dear unto *Hanna* his Mother : The childe that *Hannah* did ſo much eſteem, ſhe could not but greatly wiſh to advance, and her Religious conceit was, that the honoring of God with it, was the advancing of it unto honor. The chiefeſt of the off-ſpring of men are, the males which be firſt-born, and for this cauſe, in the ancient World, they all were by right of their birth Prieſts to the moſt High. By theſe and the like preſidents, it plainly enough appeareth, that in what heart ſoever doth dwell unfeigned Religion, in the ſame there reſteth alſo a willingneſs to beſtow upon God that ſooneſt, which is moſt dear. Amongſt us the Law is, that ſith Gold is the chiefeſt of mettals, if it be any where found in the bowels of the earth, it belongeth in right of honor, as all men know, to the King : Whence hath this cuſtom grown, but onely from a natural perſwaſion, whereby men judge it decent, for the higheſt perſons always to be honored with the choiceſt things? *If ye offer unto God the blinde,* ſaith the Prophet *Malachi, it is not evil; if the lame and ſick, it is good enough.* *Preſent it unto thy Prince, and ſee if he will content himſelf, or accept thy perſon,* ſaith the Lord of Hoſts. When *Abel* preſented God with an offering, it was the fatteſt of all the Lambs in his whole flock; he honored God not onely out of his ſubſtance, but out of the very chiefeſt therein, whereby we may ſomewhat judge, how religiouſly they ſtand affected towards God, who grudge that any thing worth the having ſhould be his. Long it were to reckon up particularly, what God was owner of under the Law : For of this ſort was all which they ſpent in Legal Sacrifices; of this ſort their uſual oblations and offerings; of this ſort

tythes

Pſal. 50. 10.

Job 1. 21.

Mal. 3. 10.

Prov 3. 9.

Seneca

Mal. 1. 8.

Tithes and First-fruits; of this fort that which by extraordinary occasions they vowed unto God; of this fort all that they gave to the building of the Tabernacle; of
this fort all that which was gathered amongst them for the erecting of the Temple, and the (*a*) adorning of it erected; of this fort
whatsoever their Corban contained, wherein that bles- | (*a*) Because (faith *David*) I have
fed Widows Deodate was laid up. Now either this kinde | delight in the House of my God, there
of honor was prefiguratively altogether ceremonial, and | fore I have given thereunto of mine
then our Saviour accepteth it not, or if we find that | own both Gold and Silver to adorn it
to him also it hath been done, and that with divine ap- | with, 2 *Chron.29.*
probation given for encouragement of the World, to
shew by such kinde of service their dutiful hearts towards Chrift, there will be no
place left for men to make any question at all, whether herein they do well or
no.

Wherefore, to descend from the Synagogue unto the Church of Chrift; al-
beit sacrifices wherewith sometimes God was highly honoured, be not accepted *Pfal.50.13,14*
as heretofore at the hands of men: Yet forasmuch as *Honor God with thy riches*
is an Edict of the unseparable Law of Nature, so far forth as men are therein required by such kind of homage to testifie their thankful minds, this sacrifice God *Phil. 4. 18.*
doth accept still. Wherefore as it was said of Chrift, *That all Kings should worship* *Pfal.72. 11.*
him, and all Nations do him service; so this very kinde of worship or service was
likewise mentioned left we should think that our Lord and Saviour would allow
of no such thing. *The Kings of Tharshish and of the Isles shall bring presents, the Kings*
of Sheba and of Seba shall bring gifts. And as it maketh not a little to the praise of
those sages mentioned in the Gospel, that the first amongst men which did solemn- *Matth.2.11*
ly honour our Saviour on earth were they; so it soundeth no less to the dignity
of this particular kinde that the rest by it were prevented; *They fell down and*
worshipped him, and opened their treasures, and presented unto him gifts, gold, and in-
cense, and mirrh.

Of all those things which were done to the honour of Chrift in his life time
there is not one whereof he spake in such fort, as when *Mary* to testifie the largeness of her affection, seemed to waste away a gift upon him, the price of which *Matth 26.13.*
gift might, as they thought who saw it, much better have been spent in works of
mercy towards the poor, *Verily, I say unto you, wheresoever this Gospel shall be*
preached throughout all the world, there shall also this that she hath done be spoken of
for memorial of her. Of service to God, the best works are they which continue *Joh.15 16.*
longest: And for permanency what like Donation, whereby things are unto him
for ever dedicated? That the ancient Lands and Livings of the Church were
all in such fort given into the hands of God by the just Lords and owners of them,
that unto him they passed over their whole interest and right therein, the form
of sundry the said Donations as yet extant, moft plainly sheweth. And where
time hath left no such evidence as now remaining to be seen; yet the same intention is presumed in all Donors, unless the contrary be apparent. But to the
end it may yet more plainly appear unto all men under what title the several *Aug.cap. 15. de*
kindes of Ecclesiastical possessions are held, *Our Lord himself* (faith Saint *Au-* *menda.*
gustine) *had coffers to keep those things which the faithful OFFERED unto him.*
Then was the form of the Church-treasury first instituted, to the end, that withal we
might understand that in forbidding to be careful for to morrow, his purpose was
not to bar his Saints from keeping money, but to withdraw them from doing God
service for wealths sake, and from forsaking righteousness through fear of losing their
wealth.

The first gifts consecrated unto Chrift after his departure out of the world were
sums of money, in process of time other moveables were added, and at length
goods unmoveable, Churches and Oratories hallowed to the honour of his glorious Name, Houses and Lands for perpetuity conveyed unto him, inheritance
given to remain his as long as the world should endure. (*b*) *The Apostles* (faith *b c.12,9,1. cap.*
Melchiades) *they foresaw that God would have his Church amongst the Gentiles, and* *15.& 16.*
for that cause in Judea they took no lands but price of lands sold. This he conjectu-
reth to have been the cause why the Apostles did that which the History reporteth
of them.

H 2   The

The truth is, that so the state of those times did require as well other where, as in *Judea*: Wherefore when afterwards it did appear much more commodious for the Church to dedicate such inheritances; then the value and price of them being sold, the former custom was changed for this, as for the better. The Devotion of *Constantine* herein all the World even till this very day admireth: They that lived in the prime of the Christian World, thought no Testament Christianly made, nor any thing therein well bequeathed, unless something were thereby added unto Christs Patrimony: Touching which men, what judgement the world doth now give, I know not; perhaps we deem them to have been herein but blind and superstitious persons. Nay, we in these cogitations are blinde; they contrariwise did with *Salomon* plainly know and perswade themselves, that thus to diminish their wealth, was not to diminish, but to augment it, according to that which God doth promise to his own people, by the Prophet *Malachi*, and which they by their own particular experience found true: If *Wickliff* therefore were of that opinion which his adversaries ascribe unto him (whether truly, or of purpose to make him odious, I cannot tell, for in his writings I do not finde it) namely, *That Constantine, and others following his steps did evil, as having no sufficient ground whereby they might gather, that such Donations are acceptable to Jesus Christ*, it was in *Wickliff* a palpable error. I will use but one onely Argument to stand in the stead of many: *Jacob* taking his journey unto *Haram*, made in this sort his solemn vow, *If God will be with me, and will keep me in this journey which I go, and will give me bread to eat, and cloathes to put on, so that I come again to my Fathers house in safety, then shall the Lord be my God, and this stone which I have set up a pillar, shall be the house of God, and of all that thou shalt give me, will I give the tenth unto thee.* May a Christian man desire great things as *Jacob* did at the hands of God? may he desire them in as earnest manner? may he promise as great thankfulness in acknowledging the goodness of God? may he vow any certain kinde of publique acknowledgement before hand; or though he vow it not, perform it after in such sort, that men may see he is perswaded how the Lord hath been his God? Are these particular kinde of testifying thankfulness to the God, the erecting of Oratories, the dedicating of lands and goods to maintain them, forbidden any where? Let any mortal man living shew but one reason wherefore in this point to follow *Jacobs* example, should not be a thing both acceptable unto God, and in the eyes of the World for ever most highly commendable? Concerning goods of this nature, goods whereof when we speak, we term them τὰ τῷ Θεῷ ἀφιερωμένα, the goods that are consecrated unto God; and as *Tertullian* speaketh, *Deposita pietatis*, things which Piety and Devotion hath laid up, as it were, in the bosom of God: Touching such goods, the Law Civil following meer light of Nature, defineth them to be no mans, because no mortal man, or community of men, hath right of propriety in them.

Margin notes:
Prov. 3. 10.
Mal. 3. 10.
2 Chro. 31. 10.
Tb. Had. to 1.
lib. 4 *c.* 39.
Gen. 28. 20.

XXIII. Persons Ecclesiastical are Gods Stewards, not onely for that he hath set them over his Family, as the Ministers of Ghostly food; but even for this very cause also, that they are to receive and dispose his temporal Revenues, the gifts and oblations which men bring him. Of the Jews it is plain, that their tythes they offered unto the Lord, and those (a) offerings the Lord bestowed upon the Levites. When the Levites gave the tenth of their tythes, this their gift, the Law doth term the Lords heave-offering, and (b) appoint that the High-Priest should receive the same. (c) Of spoils taken in War, that part which they were accustomed to separate unto God, they brought it before the Priest of the Lord, by whom it was laid up in the Tabernacle of the Congregation, for a memorial of their thankfulness towards God; and his goodness towards them, in fighting for them against their enemies. As therefore the Apostle magnifieth the honor of *Melchisedec*, in that he being an High-Priest, did receive at the hands of *Abraham* the tythes which *Abraham* did honor God with: so it argueth in the Apostles themselves great honor, that at their feet the price of those possessions was laid, which men thought good to bestow on Christ.

St.

Margin notes:
That Ecclesiastical persons are receivers of Gods rents, and that the honor of Prelates is, to be thereof his chief receivers, not without liberty from him granted, of converting the same unto their own use, even in large manner.
(a, Numb. 18. 24. (b) Numb. 18. 28.
(a) Numb. 31.

Heb. 7. 3.
Acts 4. 34.

S. *Paul* commending the Churches which were in *Macedonia*, for their exceeding liberality this way, faith of them, that he himself would bear record, they had declared their foward mindes, according to their power, yea, beyond their power, and had so much exceeded his expectation of them; *that they seemed, as it were, even to give away themselves first to the Lord,* faith the Apostle, *and then by the will of God unto us*: To him, as the owner of such gifts, to us, as his appointed receivers and dispensers. The gift of the Church of *Antioch*, bestowed unto the use of distressed Brethren which were in *Judea*, *Paul* and *Barnabas* did deliver unto the Presbyters of *Jerusalem*; and the head of those Presbyters was *James*, he therefore the chiefest disposer thereof. ^{2 Cor.8.5. Acts 11.30, Acts 21.19. & 12.17.}

Amongst those Canons which are entituled Apostolical, one is this, *We appoint, that the Bishop have care of those things which belong to the Church*; the meaning is, of Church goods, as the reason following sheweth: *For if the precious souls of men must be committed unto unto him of trust, much more it behoveth the charge of money to be given him, that by his Authority the Presbyters and Deacons may administer all things to them that stand in need.* So that he which hath done them the honor to be, as it were, his Treasurers, hath left them also authority and power to use these his treasures, both otherwise, and for the maintenance even of their own estate; the lower sort of the Clergy, according unto a meaner: the higher after a larger proportion. The use of spirituall goods and possessions, hath been a matter much disputed of; grievous complaints there are usually made against the evil and unlawful usage of them, but with no certain determination hitherto, on what things and persons; with what proportion and measure they being bestowed, do retain their lawful use. Some men condemn it as idle, superfluous, and altogether vain, that any part of the treasure of God should be spent upon costly Ornaments, appertaining unto his service: who being best worshipped, when he is served in Spirit and truth, hath not for want of pomp and magnificence, rejected at any time those who with faithful hearts have adored him. Whereupon the Hereticks, termed *Henriciani* and *Petrobusiani*, threw down Temples and Houses of Prayer, erected with marvelous great charge, as being in that respect not fit for Christ by us to be honored in. We deny not, but that they who sometime wandred as Pilgrims on earth, and had no Temples, but made caves and dens to pray in, did God such honor as was most acceptable in his sight; God did not reject them for their poverty and nakedness sake: Their Sacraments were not abhorred for want of vessels of Gold. ^{Can. 41. Et Concil. Antioch. ca. 25. John 4.24. Heb.11.38.}

Howbeit, let them who thus delight to plead, answer me; when *Moses* first, and afterwards *David*, exhorted the people of *Israel* unto matter of charge about the service of God; suppose we it had been allowable in them to have thus pleaded, *Our Fathers in Egypt served God devoutly, God was with them in all their afflictions, he heard their prayers, pitied their case, and delivered them from the tyrannie of their oppressors; what House, Tabernacle, or Temple had they?* Such Argumentations are childish and fond; God doth not refuse to be honored at all, where there lacketh wealth; but where abundance and store is, he there requireth the flower thereof, being bestowed on him, to be employed even unto the Ornament of his service: In *Egypt* the state of his people was servitude, and therefore his service was accordingly: In the Desart they had no sooner ought of their own, but a Tabernacle is required; and in the Land of *Canaan* a Temple. In the eyes of *David*, it seemed a thing not fit, a thing not decent, that himself should be more richly seated then God.

But concerning the use of Ecclesiastical goods bestowed this way, there is not so much contention amongst us, as what measure of allowance is fit for Ecclesiastical persons to be maintained with. A better rule in this case to judge things by, we cannot possibly have, then the Wisdom of God himself; by considering what he thought meet for each degree of the Clergy to enjoy in time of the Law; what for Levites, what for Priests, and what for High-Priests, somewhat we shall be the more able to discern rightly, what may be fit, convenient, and right for the Christian Clergy likewise. Priests for their maintenance had those first-fruits of (a) Cattel, (b) Corn, Wine, Oyl, and (c) other commodities of the earth, which the ^{a Num 18.15, b Num. 12. c Num. 13.}

the Jews were accustomed yearly to present God with. They had (*d*) the price which was appointed for men to pay in lieu of the first-born of their children, and the price of the first-born also amongst Cattel, which were unclean: They had the vowed (*e*) gifts of the people, or (*f*) the prices, if they were redeemable by the Donors after vow, as some things were: They had the (*g*) free, and unvowed oblations of men: They had the remainder of things (*h*) sacrificed: With (*i*) tythes the Levites were maintained, and with the (*k*) tythe of their tythes, the High-Priest.

In a word, if the quality of that which God did assign to his Clergy be considered, and their manner of receiving it, without labour, expence, or charge, it will appear, that the Tribe of *Levi* being but the twelfth part of *Israel*, had in effect as good as four twelfth parts of all such goods as the holy Land did yield: So that their Worldly estate was four times as good as any other Tribes in *Israel* besides. But the High-Priests condition, how ample? to whom belonged the tenth of all the tythe of this Land, especially the Law providing also, that as the people did bring the best of all things unto the Priests and Levites, so the Levite should deliver the choice and flower of all their commodities to the High-Priest, and so his tenth part by that mean be made the very best part amongst ten: By which proportion, if the Levites were ordinarily in all not above thirty thousand men (whereas when *David* numbred them, he found almost thirty eight thousand above the age of thirty years) the High Priest after this very reckoning, had as much as three or four thousand others of the Clergy to live upon. Over and besides all this, lest the Priests of *Egypt* holding Lands, should seem in that respect better provided for, then the Priests of the true God, it pleased him further to appoint unto them forty and eight whole Cities, with Territories of Land adjoyning, to hold as their own free Inheritance for ever. For to the end they might have all kinde of encouragement, not onely to do what they ought, but to take pleasure in that they did: albeit they were expresly forbidden to have any part of the Land of *Canaan* laid out whole to themselves, by themselves, in such sort as the rest of the Tribes had, forasmuch as the will of God was, rather that they should throughout all Tribes be dispersed, for the easier access of the people unto knowledge: Yet were they not barred altogether to hold a land, nor yet otherwise the worse provided for, in respect of that former restraint; for God by way of special pre-eminence, undertook to feed them at his own table, and out of his own proper treasury to maintain them, that want and penury they might never feel, except God himself did first receive injury. A thing most worthy our consideration, is the wisdom of God herein; for the common sort being prone unto envy and murmure, little considereth of what necessity, use and importance, the sacred duties of the Clergy are, and for that cause hardly yieldeth them any such honor, without repining and grudging thereat; they cannot brook it, that when they have laboured, and come to reap, there should so great a portion go out of the fruit of their labours, and be yielded up unto such as sweat not for it. But when the Lord doth challenge this as his own due, and require it to be done by way of homage unto him, whose meer liberality and goodness had raised them from a poor and servile estate, to place them where they had all those ample and rich possessions, they must be worse then bruit beasts, if they would storm at any thing which he did receive at their hands. And for him to bestow his own on his own servants (which liberty is not denied unto the meanest of men) what man liveth that can think it other then most reasonable? Wherefore no cause there was, why that which the Clergy had, should in any mans eye seem too much, unless God himself were thought to be of an over-having disposition.

This is the mark whereat all those speeches drive, *Levi hath no part nor inheritance with his brethren, the Lord is his inheritance*; again, *To the Tribe of Levi, he gave no inheritance, the Sacrifices of the Lord God of Israel an inheritance of Levi*; again, *The tithes of which they shall offer as an offering unto the Lord, I have given the Levites for an inheritance*; and again, *All the heave-offerings of the holy things which the children of Israel shall offer unto the Lord, I have given thee, and thy sons, and thy daughters with thee, to be a duty for ever, it is a perpetual Covenant of salt before the Lord.* Now that, if such provision be possible to be made, the Christian Clergy ought not herein to be inferior

d Verf. 15.
e Verf. 8.
f Lev. 27. 11.
Verf. 14
Numb. 18. 8.
g Verf. 8.
h Verf. 9.
i Verf. 11.
k Verf. 28.

1 Chron. 2. 3.

Gen. 47. 22.

Numb. 35. 7.
Josh. 14. 4.

Deut. 18. 8.
Lev. 25. 33, 34.

Deut. 10. 9.
Josh. 13. 14.
Numb. 18. 24.

Verf. 19.

ferior unto the Jewish, What founder proof then the Apostles own kinde of Argument? *De ye not know, that they which minister about the holy things, eat of the things* 1 Cor. 9. 13. *of the temple? and they which wait at the Altar are partakers with the Altar? So even SO hath the Lord ordained, that they which preach the Gospel should live of the Gospel.* Upon which words I thus conclude, that if the people of God do abound, and abounding can so far forth finde in their hearts to shew themselves towards Christ their Saviour, thankful as to honour him with their riches (which no Law of God or Nature forbiddeth) no less then the antient Jewish people did honour God; the plain ordinance of Christ, appointeth as large and as ample proportion out of his own treasure unto them that serve him in the Gospel as ever the priests of the law did enjoy? what further proof can we desire? It is the blessed Apostles testimony, That *even so the Lord hath ordained.* Yea, I know not whether it be found to interpret the Apostle otherwise then that whereas he judgeth the Presbyters *which* 1 Tim. 5. 17. *rule well in the Church of Christ to be worthy of double honour,* he means double unto that which the Priests of the Law received; *For if that Ministry which was of the* 2 Cor. 3. 8. *letter were so glorious, how shall not the Ministry of the Spirit be more glorious?* If *Vide 23. 9. 7.* the teachers of the Law of *Moses,* which God delivered written with letters in tables *art. 1.* of stone were thought worthy of so great honour, how shall not the teachers of the Gospel of Christ be in his sight most worthy, the Holy Ghost being sent from heaven to ingrave the Gospel on their hearts who first taught it, and whose successors they that teach it at this day are? So that according to the Ordinance of God himself, their estate for worldly maintenance ought to be no worse then is granted unto other sorts of men, each according to that degree they were placed in. Neither are we so to judge of their worldly condition, as if they were servants of men, and at mens hands did receive those earthly benefits by way of stipend in lieu of pains whereunto they are hired; nay that which is paid unto them is homage and tribute due unto the Lord Christ. His servants they are, and from him they receive such goods by way of stipend. Not so from men? For at the hands of men, he himself being honored with such things, hath appointed his servants therewith according to their several degrees and places to be maintained. And for their greater encouragement who are his labourers he hath to their comfort assured them for ever, that they are in his estimation *worthy the hire* which he allow- 1 Tim. 5. 18. eth them; and therefore if men should withdraw from him the store which those his servants that labour in his work are maintained with, yet he in his Word shall be found everlastingly true, their labour in the Lord shall not be forgoten; the hire he accounteth them worthy of, they shall surely have either one way or other answered.

In the prime of the Christian world, that which was brought and laid down Acts 4. 35. at the Apostles feet, they disposed of by distribution according to the exigence of each mans need. Neither can we think that they who out of Christs treasury made provision for all others, were careless to furnish the Clergy with all things fit and convenient for their estate: And as themselves were cheifest in place of authority, and calling, so no man doubteth but that proportionably they had power to use the same for their own decent maintenance. The Apostles with the rest of the Clergy in *Jerusalem* lived at that time according to the manner of a fellowship or Collegiate Society maintaining themselves and the poor of the Church with a common purse, the rest of the faithful keeping that purse continually stored. And in that sence it is that the sacred History saith, *All which beleeved were in one place, and* Acts 2. 44. *had all things common.* In the Histories of the Church, and in the Writings of the Antient Fathers for some hundreds of years after we finde, no other way for the maintenance of the Clergy but onely this, the treasury of Jesus Christ furnished through mens devotion, bestowing sometimes Goods, sometimes Lands that way, and *Dis. cui P. off.* out of his treasury the charge of the service of God was defrayed, the Bishop and *devita contem p.* the Clergy under him maintained, the poor in their necessity ministred unto. For *l. 2. c. 13. Decon.* which purpose, every Bishop had some one of the Presbyters under him to be *l. 14. c. defer.* * Treasurer of the Church, to receive, keep, and deliver all; which Office in *eccl. & Neul* Churches Cathedral remaineth even till this day, albeit the use thereof be not al- *7. in princip.* together so large now as heretofore. The disposition of these goods was by the *Pros. de vita* appointment of the Bishop. Wherefore (a) *Prosper* speaking of the Bishops care herein *contempl lib. 2.* saith, *cap. 16.*

faith, *It was neceſſary for one to be troubled therewith, to the end that the reſt under him might be the freer to attend quietly their ſpiritual buſineſſes.* And leſt any man ſhould imagine that Biſhops by this means were hindred themſelves from attending the ſervice of God, *Even herein,* faith he, *they do God ſervice; for if thoſe things which are beſtowed on the Church be Gods, he doth the work of God, who not of a covetous mind, but with purpoſe of moſt faithful adminiſtration, taketh care of things conſecrated unto God.* And foraſmuch as the Presbyters of every Church could not all live with the Biſhop, partly for that their number was great, and partly becauſe the people being once divided into Pariſhes, ſuch Presbyters as had ſeverally charge of them were by that mean more conveniently to live in the midſt each of his own particular flock, therefore a competent number being fed at the * ſame table

* Cypr. lib. 4. ep. 5. Presbyterii honorem deſignaſſe nos illis jam ſtatis ut & ſportulis eiſdem cum Presbyteris ononentur, & diviſiones menſurnat aequatis quantitatibus partiantur, jeſſuri nobiſcum provectis & compoſitora is armis ſuis. Which words of *Cyprian* doſhew, that every Presbyter had his ſtanding allowance out of the Church treaſury; that beſides the ſame allowance called *ſportula*, ſome alſo had their portion in that dividend which which was the remainder of every moneths expence; thirdly, that out of the Presbyters under him, the Biſhop as then had certain number of the graveſt, who lived and commoned always with him.

with the Biſhop, the reſt had their whole allowance apart, which ſeveral allowances were called *Sportulæ*, and they who received them, *Sportulantes fratres.* Touching the Biſhop, as his place and eſtate was higher, ſo likewiſe the proportion of his charges about himſelf, being for that cauſe in all equity and reaſon greater, yet foraſmuch as his ſtint herein was no other then it pleaſed himſelf to ſet, the reſt (as the manner of inferiors is to think that they which are over them always have too much) grudged many times at the meaſure of the Biſhops private expence, perhaps not without cauſe: Howſoever, by this occaſion there grew amongſt them great heart-burning, quarrel and ſtrife: where the Biſhops were found culpable, as eating too much beyond their tether, and drawing more to their own private maintenance then the proportion of Chriſts patrimony being not greatly abundant could bear, ſundry conſtitutions hereupon were made to moderate the ſame, according to the Churches condition in thoſe times. Some before they were made Biſhops, having been owners of ample poſſeſ-

Proſp. de vita contemp'. lib. i. c. 9. Pont. Diacon. i. vita Cypr.

ſions, ſold them, and gave them away to the poor: Thus did *Paulinus, Hilary, Cyprian,* and ſundry others. Hereupon, they who entring into the ſame Spiritual and high funĉtion, held their Secular poſſeſſions ſtill, were hardly thought of: And even when the caſe was fully reſolved, that ſo to do was not unlawful, yet it grew a queſtion, *Whether they lawfully might then take any thing out of the Publique Treaſury of Chriſt?* a queſtion, *Whether Biſhops, holding by Civil title, ſufficient to live of their own, were bound in Conſcience to leave the goods of the Church altogether to the uſe of others.* Of contentions about theſe matters there was no end, neither appeared there any poſſible way for quietneſs, otherwiſe then by making partition of Church Revenues, according to the ſeveral ends and uſes for which they did ſerve, that ſo the Biſhops part might be certain. Such partition being made, the Biſhop enjoyed his portion ſeveral to himſelf; the reſt of the Clergy likewiſe theirs; a third part was ſevered to the furniſhing and upholding of the Church; a fourth to the erection and maintenance of Houſes. wherein the poor might have relief. After which ſeparation made, Lands and Livings began every day to be dedicated unto each uſe ſeverally, by means whereof every of them became in ſhort time much greater then they had been for worldly maintenance, the fervent devotion of men being glad that this new opportunity was given, of ſhewing zeal to the Houſe of God in more certain order.

By theſe things it plainly appeareth, what proportion of maintenance hath been ever thought reaſonable for a Biſhop; ſith in that very partition agreed on, to bring him unto his certain ſtint, as much is allowed unto him alone, as unto all the Clergy under him, namely, a fourth part of the whole yearly Rents and Revenues of the Church. Nor is it likely, that before thoſe Temporalities, which now are ſuch eye-ſores, were added unto the honor of Biſhops, their ſtate was ſo mean as ſome imagine: For if we had no other evidence then the covetous and ambitious humour of Hereticks, whoſe impotent deſires of aſpiring thereunto, and extreme diſcontentment as oft as they were defeated, even this doth ſhew that the ſtate of Biſhops was not a few degrees advanced above the reſt. Wherefore of grand Apoſtates which were in the very prime of the Primitive Church, thus *Lactantius.*

above

above thirteen hundred years sithence testified, *Men of a slippery faith they were, who* Lact. de vera *feigning that they knew and worshipped God, but seeking onely that they might grow in* cap lib. 4. c. 30. *WEALTH and Honor, affected the place of the HIGHEST PRIESTHOOD; whereunto when their betters were chosen before them, they thought it better to leave the Church, and to draw their favourers with them, then to endure those men their Governors, whom themselves desired to govern.* Now whereas against the present estate of Bishops, and the greatness of their port, and the largeness of their expences at this day, there is not any thing more commonly objected then those ancient Canons, whereby they are restrained unto a far more sparing life, their houses, their retinue, their diet limited within a far more narrow compass then is now kept; we must know, that those Laws and Orders were made, when Bishops lived of the same purse which served as well for a number of others, as them, and yet all at their disposing: So that convenient it was to provide, that there might be a moderate stint appointed to measure their expences by, lest others should be injured by their wastefulness. Contrariwise there is now no cause wherefore any such Law should be urged, when Bishops live only of that which hath been peculiarly allotted unto them : They having therefore Temporalities and other revenues to bestow for their own private use, according to that which their state requireth, and no other having with them any such common interest therein, their own discretion is to be their Law for this matter; neither are they to be pressed with the rigour of such ancient Canons as were framed for other times, much less so odiously to be upbraided with unconformity unto the pattern of our Lord and Saviours estate, in such circumstances as himself did never minde to require, that the rest of the world should of necessity be like him. Thus against the wealth of the Clergy, they alleage how meanly Christ himself was provided for; against Bishops Palaces, his want of a hole to hide his head in; against the service done unto them, that he came to minister, not to be ministred unto in the world. Which things, as they are not unfit to controul covetous, proud or ambitious desires of the Ministers of Christ, and even of all Christians, whatsoever they be; and to teach men contentment of minde, how mean soever their estate is, considering that they are but servants to him, whose condition was far more abased then theirs is, or can be; so to prove such difference in state between us and him unlawful, they are of no force or strength at all. If one convented before their Consistories, when he standeth to make his answer, should break out into invectives against their Authority, and tell them, that Christ when he was on earth, did not sit to judge, but stand to be judged; would they hereupon think it requisite to dissolve their Eldership, and to permit no Tribunals, no Judges at all, for fear of swarving from our Saviours example ? If those men, who have nothing in their mouthes more usual, then the poverty of Jesus Christ and his Apostles, alleage not this as *Julian* sometime did, *Beati pauperes,* unto Christians, when his meaning was to spoyl them of that they had; our hope is then, that as they seriously and sincerely wish, that our Saviour Christ in this point may be followed, and to that end onely propose his blessed example; so at our hands again they will be content to hear with like willingness, the holy Apostles Exhortation, made unto them of the Laity also, *Be ye* 1 Cor. 11. 1. *followers of us, even as we are of Christ; let us be your example, even as the Lord Jesus* P. il. 3. 16. *Christ is ours, that we may all proceed by one and the same rule.*

XXIV. But beware we of following Christ, as Thieves follow true men, to take their goods by violence from them. Be it that Bishops were all unworthy, not onely of living, but even of life, yet what hath our Lord Jesus Christ deserved, for which men should judge him worthy to have the things that are his given away from him, unto others that have no right unto them; For at this mark it is, that the head lay-Reformers do all aim. That for their unworthiness, to deprive both them and their successors of such goods, and to convey the same unto men of secular calling were extreme sacralegious injustice.

Must these unworthy Prelates give place; what then ? Shall better succeed in their rooms ? Is this desired, to the end that others may enjoy their Honors, which shall do Christ more faithful service then they have done ? Bishops are the worst men living upon earth; therefore let their sanctified Possessions be divided: Amongst whom ? O blessed Reformation ! O happy men, that put to their helping hands for the furtherance of so good and glorious a work ! Wherefore

*I   albeit

albeit the whole World at this day do already perceive, and posterity be likewise hereafter a great deal more plainly to discern; not that the Clergy of God is thus heaved at because they are wicked, but that means are used to put it into the heads of the simple multitude, that they are such indeed; to the end that those who thirst for the spoil of Spiritual Possessions, may till such time as they have their purpose, be thought to covet nothing but onely the just extinguishment of unreformable persons; so that in regard of such mens intentions, practices, and machinations against them, the part that suffereth these things, may most fitly pray with *David, Judge thou me, O Lord, according to my Righteousness, and according unto mine innocency: O let the malice of the wicked come to an end, and be thou the guide of the just.* Notwithstanding, forasmuch as it doth not stand with Christian humility otherwise to think, then that this violent outrage of men, is a rod in the ireful hands of the Lord our God, the smart whereof we deserve to feel: Let it not seem grievous in the eyes of my reverend L L. the Bishops, if to their good consideration, I offer a view of those sores which are in the kinde of their heavenly function, most apt to breed, and which being not in time cured, may procure at the length that which God of his infinite mercy avert. Of Bishops in his time St. *Jerome* complaineth, that they took it in great disdain to have any fault, great or small found with them. *Epiphanius* likewise before *Jerome*, noteth their impatiency this way, to have been the very cause of a Schism in the Church of Christ; at what time one *Audius*, a Man of great integrity of life, full of faith and zeal towards God, beholding those things which were corruptly done in the Church, told the BB. and Presbyters their faults in such sort as those men are wont, who love the truth from their hearts, and walk in the pathes of a most exact life. Whether it were covetousness, or sensuality in their lives; absurdity or error in their teaching; any breach of the Laws and Canons of the Church wherein he espied them faulty, certain and sure they were to be thereof most plainly told. Which thing, they whose dealings were justly culpable, could not bear; but instead of amending their faults, bent their hatred against him who sought their amendment, till at length they drove him by extremity of infestation, through weariness of striving against their injuries, to leave both them, and with them the Church. Amongst the manifold accusations, either generally intended against the Bishops of this our Church, or laid particularly to the charge of any of them, I cannot finde that hitherto their spitefullest adversaries have been able to say justly, that any man for telling them their personal faults in good and Christian sort, hath sustained in that respect much persecution. Wherefore notwithstanding mine own inferior estate and calling in Gods Church, the consideration whereof assureth me, that in this kinde the sweetest Sacrifice which I can offer unto Christ, is meek obedience, reverence and awe unto the Prelates which he hath placed in seats of higher Authority over me, emboldned I am, so far as may conveniently stand with that duty of humble subjection, meekly to crave, my good L L. your favourable pardon, if it shall seem a fault thus far to presume; or if otherwise, your wonted courteous acceptation,
—— *Sinite hæc haud mollia fatu*
Sublatis aperire dolis ——

In government, be it of what kinde soever, but especially if it be such kinde of Government as Prelates have over the Church, there is not one thing publiquely more hurtful then that hard opinion should be conceived of Governors at the first: And a good opinion how should the World ever conceive of them for their after-proceedings in Regiment, whose first access and entrance thereunto, giveth just occasion to think them corrupt men, which fear not that God, in whose name they are to rule? Wherefore a scandalous thing it is to the Church of God, and to the Actors themselves dangerous, to have aspired unto rooms of Prelacy by wicked means. We are not at this day troubled much with that tumultuous kinde of ambition wherewith the elections of (a) *Damasus* in S. *Jeromes* age, and of (b) *Maximus* in *Gregories* time, and of others, were long sithence stained. Our greatest fear is rather the evil which (c) *Leo* and *Anthemius* did by Imperial constitution, endeavour as much as in them lay to prevent. He which granteth, or he which receiveth the office and dig-

Psal. 7. 8.

Epiph. contra hæres. l. 3. to 1. bæ. 70.

a *Ammian. Marcel. li b. 27.*
b *Vide in vita Greg. Naz.*
c *Nemo gradum sacerdotii pretii venalitate mercetur: quantum quisq; mereatur non quantum dare sufficiat æstimetur. Profectò enim quis locus, tutus & quæ causa esse poterit excusata si veneranda Dei templa pecuniis expugnentur?* *Quem murum integritatis aut vallum providebimus si auri sacra fames in penetralia veneranda proserpat? quid demq; cautum esse poterit aut securum si sanctitas incorrupta corrumpatur? Cesset altaribus imminere profanus ardor avaritiæ, & à sacris adytis repellatur piaculare flagitium. Itaq; castus & humilis nostris temporibus eligatur Episcopus, ut quocunq; locorum pervenerit omnia vitæ propriæ integritate purificet. Nec pretio sed precibus ordinetur Antistes, l. 31. C. de Episc. & Cler.*

nity

nity of a Bishop, otherwise then beseemeth a thing Divine and most holy; he which bestoweth, and he which obteineth it after any other sort then were honest and lawful to use, if our Lord Jesus Christ were present himself on earth to bestow it even with his own hands, sinneth a sin by so much more grievous then the sin of *Balshazar*, by how much Offices and Functions heavenly are more precious then the meanest ornaments or implements which thereunto appertain. If it be as the Apostle saith, That the Holy Ghost doth make Bishops, and that the whole action of making them is Gods own deed, men being therein but his Agents; what spark of the fear of God can there possibly remain in their hearts, who representing the person of God in naming worthy men to Ecclesiastical charge, do sell that which in his name they are to bestow, or who standing as it were at the Throne of the Living God do bargain for that which at his hands they are to receive? Wo worth such impious and irreligious prophanations. The Church of Christ hath been hereby made, not a den of theives, but in a manner the very dwelling place of foul spirits; for undoubtedly, such a number of them have been in all ages who thus have climbed into seat of Episcopal Regiment.

2. Men may by orderly means be invested with spiritual Authority, and yet do harm by reason of ignorance how to use it to the good of the Church. It is saith (*bryfostom,* πολλὴ μὲν ἀξιωμάτ☉ δυσκολὸν ἢ ἐπιεικεῖν; *a thing highly to be accompted of, but an hard thing to be that which a Bishop should be.* Yea a hard and a toilsom thing it is, for a Bishop to know the things that belong unto a Bishop. A right good man may be a very unfit Magistrate. And for discharge of a Bishops Office, to be well minded is not enough, no not to be well learned also. Skill to instruct is a thing necessary, skill to govern much more necessary in a Bishop. It is not safe for the Church of Christ, when Bishops learn what belongeth unto Government, as Empericks learn physick by killing of the sick. Bishops were wont to be men of great learning in the Laws both Civil and of the Church; and while they were so, the wisest men in the land for Counsel and Government were Bishops.

3. Know we never so well what belongeth unto a charge of so great moment; yet can we not therein proceed but with hazard of publique detriment if we relye on our selves alone, and use not the benefit of conference with others. A singular mean to unity and concord amongst themselves, a marvellous help unto uniformity in their dealings, no small addition of weight and credit unto that which they do, a strong bridle unto such as watch for occasions to stir against them; finally, a very great stay unto all that are under their Government, it could not chuse but be soon found, if Bishops did often and seriously use the help of mutual consultation. These three rehearsed are things onely preparatory unto the course of Episcopal proceedings. But the hurt is more manifestly seen which doth grow to the Church of God by faults inherent in their several actions, as when they carelesly ordein, when they institute negligently, when corruptly they bestow Church-Livings, Benefices, Prebends, and rooms especially of Jurisdiction, when they visit for gain-sake, rather then with serious intent to do good; when their Courts erected for the maintenance of good Order are disordered; when they regard not the Clergy under them; when neither Clergy nor Laity are kept in that aw for which this authority should serve; when any thing appeareth in them rather then a fatherly affection towards the flock of Christ; when they have no respect to posterity; and finally, when they neglect the true and requisite means whereby their authority should be upheld. Surely the hurt which groweth out of these defects must needs be exceeding great. In a Minister, ignorance and disability to teach is a maim; nor is it held a thing allowable to ordain such, were it not for the avoiding of a greater evil which the Church must needs sustain, if in so great scarcity of able men, and unsufficiency of most Parishes throughout the Land to maintain them, both publick Prayer and the administration of Sacraments should rather want, then any man thereunto be admitted lacking dexterity and skill to perform that which otherwise was most requisite. Wherefore the necessity of ordaining such is no excuse for the rash and careless ordaining of every one that hath but a friend to bestow some two or three words of ordinary commendation in his behalf. By reason whereof the Church groweth burdened with silly creatures more then need, whose noted baseness and insufficiency bringeth their very Order it self into contempt.

It may be that the fear of a *Quare impedit* doth caufe inftitutions to pafs more eafily then otherwife they would. And to fpeak plainly the very truth, it may be that Writs of *Quare non impedit*, were for thefe times moft neceffary in the others place : Yet where Law will not fuffer men to follow their own judgement, to fhew the ir judgement they are not hindred. And I doubt not but that even confciencelefs and wicked Patrons, of which fort, the fwarms are too great in the Church of *England*, are the more imboldened to prefent unto Bifhops any refufe, by finding fo eafie acceptation thereof. Somewhat they might redrefs this fore, notwithftanding fo ftrong impediments, if it did plainly appear that they took it indeed to heart, and we re not in a manner contented with it.

Shall we look for care in admitting whom others prefent, if that which fome of your felves confer, be at any time corruptly beftowed ? A foul and an ugly kinde of deformity it hath, if a man do but think what it is for a Bifhop to draw commodity and gain from thofe things whereof he is left a free beftower, and that in truft, without any other obligation then his facred Order onely, and that religious Integrity which hath been prefumed on in him. Simoniacal corruption I may not for honors fake fufpect to be amongft men of fo great place. So often they do not I truft offend by fale, as by unadvifed gift of fuch preferments, wherein that ancient Canon fhould fpecially be remembred, which forbiddeth a Bifhop to bealed by humane affection, in beftowing the things of God. A fault no where fo hurtful, as in beftowing places of jurifdiction, and in furnifhing Cathedral Churches, the Prebendaries and other Dignities whereof are the very true fucceffors of thofe ancient Presbyters which were at the firft as Counfellors unto Bifhops. A foul abufe it is, that any one man fhould be loaded as fome are with Livings in this kinde, yea fome even of them who condemn utterly the granting of any two Benefices unto the fame man, whereas the other is in truth a matter of far greater fequel, as experience would foon fhew, if Churches Cathedral being furnifhed with the refidence of a competent number of vertuous, grave, wife and learned Divines, the reft of the Prebends of every fuch Church were given within the Diocefs unto men of worthieft defert, for their better encouragement unto induftry and travel; unlefs it feem alfo convenient to extend the benefit of them unto the learned in Univerfities, and men of fpecial imployment otherwife in the affairs of the Church of God. But howfoever, furely with the publick good of the Church it will hardly ftand, that in a ny one perfon fuch favours be more multiplied, then law permitteth, in thofe Livings which are with Cure.

Touching Bifhops Vifitations, the firft inftitution of them was profitable to the end that the ftate and condition of Churches being known, there might befor evils growing convenient remedies provided in due time. The obfervation of Church Laws, the correction of faults in the fervice of God and manners of men, thefe are things that Vifitors fhould feek. When thefe things are inquired of formally, and but for cuftom fake, fees and penfions being the onely thing which is fought, and little elfe done by Vifitations ; we are not to marvail if the bafenefs of the end doth make the action it felf loathfom. The good which Bifhops may do not onely by thefe Vifitations belonging ordinarily to their Office, but alfo in refpect of that power which the Founders of Colledges have given them of fpecial truft, charging even fearfully their confciences therewith : the good I fay which they might do by this their authority, both within their own Diocefe, and in the well-fprings themfelves, the Univerfities, is plainly fuch as cannot chufe but add weight to their heavy accounts in that dreadful day if they do it not.

In their Courts, where nothing but fingular integrity and Juftice fhould prevail, if palpable and grofs corruptions be found, by reafon of Offices fo often granted unto men who feek nothing but their own gain, and make no accompt what difgrace doth grow by their unjuft dealings unto them under whom they deal, the evil hereof fhall work more then they which procure it do perhaps imagine.

At the hands of a Bifhop the firft thing looked for is a care of the Clergy under him, a care that in doing good they may have whatfoever comforts and encouragements his countenance, authority and place may yeild. Otherwife what heart fhall they have to proceed in their painful courfe, all forts of men befides being fo

ready

ready to malign, despise, and every way oppress them? Let them finde nothing but disdain in Bishops; in the enemies of present Government, if that way they list to betake themselves, all kinde of favourable and friendly helps; unto which part think we it likely that men having wit, courage and stomack will incline?

As great a fault is the want of severity when need requireth, as of kindness and courtesie in Bishops. But touching this, what with ill usage of their power · amongst the meaner, and what with disusage amongst the higher sort, they are in the eyes of both sorts as Bees that have lost their sting. It is a long time sithence any great one hath felt, or almost any one much feared the edge of that Ecclesiastical severity, which sometime held Lords and Dukes in a more religious aw then now the meanest are able to be kept.

A Bishop, in whom there did plainly appear the marks and tokens of a fatherly affection towards them that are under his charge, what good might he do ten thousand ways more then any man knows how to set down? But the souls of men are not loved, that which Christ shed his blood for, is not esteemed precious. This is the very root, the fountain of all negligence in Church-Government.

Most wretched are the terms of mens estate when once they are at a point of wrechlesness so extream, that they bend not their wits any further then onely to shift out the present time, never regarding what shall become of their Successors after them. Had our Predecessors so loosely cast off from them all care and respect to posterity, a Church Christian there had not been about the regiment whereof we should need at this day to strive. It was the barbarous affection of *Nero*, that the rnine of his own Imperial Seat he could have been well enough contented to see, in case he might also have seen it accompanied with the fall of the whole World: An affection not more intollerable then theirs, who care not to overthrow all posterity, so they may purchase a few days of Ignominious safety unto themselves, and their present estates, if it may be termed a safety which tendeth so fast unto their very overthrow, that are the Purchasers of it in so vile and base manner.

Men, whom it standeth upon to uphold a reverend estimation of themselves in the minds of others, without which the very best things they do are hardly able to escape disgrace, must before it be over late remember how much easier it is to retain credit once gotten, then to recover it being lost. The Executors of Bishops are sued if their Mansion house be suffered to go to decay: But whom shall their Successors sue for the dilapidations which they make of that credit; the unrepaired diminutions whereof will in time bring to pass, that they which would most do good in that calling, shall not be able, by reason of prejudice generally setled in the mindes of all sorts against them. By what means their estimation hath hitherto decayed, it is no hard thing to discern. *Herod* and *Archelaus* are noted to have sought out purposely the dullest and most ignoble that could be found amongst the people, preferring such to the High-Priests Office, thereby to abate the great opinion which the multitude had of that Order, and to procure a more expedite course for their own wicked Counsels; whereunto they saw the High-Priests were no small impediment, as long as the common sort did much depend upon them. It may be there hath been partly some show and just suspition of like practice in some, in procuring the undeserved preferments of some unworthy persons, the very cause of whose advancement hath been principally their unworthiness to be advanced. But neither could this be done altogether without the inexcusable fault of some preferred before, and so oft we cannot imagine it to have been done, that either onely or chiefly from thence this decay of their estimation may be thought to grow. Somewhat it is that the malice of their cunning Adversaries, but much more which themselves have effected against themselves. A Bishops estimation doth grow from the excellency of vertues suitable unto his place. Unto the place of a Bishop those high Divine Vertues are judged suitable, which vertues being not easily found in other sorts of great men, do make him appear so much the greater in whom they are found.

Devotion, and the feeling sence of Religion are not usual in the noblest, wisest, and chiefest Personages of State, by reason their wits are so much imployed another way, and their mindes so seldom conversant in heavenly things. If therefore wherein themselves are defective, they see that Bishops do blessedly excel, it frameth secretly

Eg.Sup.l.2.c.12.

cretly their hearts to a stooping kinde of disposition, clean opposite to contempt: The very countenance of *Moses* was glorious after that God had conferred with him. And where Bishops are, the powers and faculties of whose souls God hath possest, those very actions, the kind whereof is common unto them with other men, have notwithstanding in them a more high and heavenly form, which draweth correspondent estimation unto it, by vertue of that celestial impression, which deep meditation of holy things, and as it were conversation with God doth leave in their mindes. So that Bishops which will be esteemed of as they ought, must frame themselves to that very pattern from whence those *Asian* Bishops unto whom St. *John* writeth were denominated, even so far forth as this our frailty will permit; shine they must as Angels of God in the midst of perverse men. They are not to look that the world should always carry the affection of *Constantine*, to bury that which might derogate from them, and to cover their imbecillities. More then high time it is, that they bethink themselves of the Apostles admonition; *Attende tibi, Have a vigilant eye to thy self.* They err if they do not perswade themselves that wheresoever they walk or sit, be it in their Churches or in their Consistories, abroad and at home, at their Tables or in their Closets, they are in the midst of snares laid for them: Wherefore as they are with the Prophet every one of them to make it their hourly prayer unto God, *Lead me O Lord in thy righteousness, because of enemies*; so it is not safe for them, no not for a moment to slacken their industry in seeking every way that estimation which may further their labours unto the Churches good. Absurdity, though but in words, must needs be this way a maim, where nothing but wisdom, gravity and judgement is looked for. That which the son of *Syrach* hath concerning the Writings of the old Sages, *Wise sentences are found in them*; should be the proper mark and character of Bishops speeches; whose lips, as doors, are not to be opened, but for egress of instruction and sound knowledge. If base servility and dejection of minde be ever espied in them, how should men esteem them as worthy the rooms of the great Ambassadors of God? A wretched desire to gain by bad and unseemly means, standeth not with a mean mans credit, much less with that reputation which Fathers of the Church should be in. But if besides all this, there be also coldness in works of Piety and Charity, utter contempt even of Learning it self, no care to further it by any such helps as they easily might and ought to afford; no not as much as that due respect unto their very Families about them, which all men that are of account do order as neer as they can in such sort, that no grievous, offensive deformity be therein noted; if there still continue in that most Reverend Order, such as by so many Engines, work day and night to pull down the whole frame of their own estimation amongst men; some of the rest secretly also permitting others their industrious opposites, every day more and more to seduce the multitude, how should the Church of God hope for great good at their hands?

What we have spoken concerning these things, let not malicious Accusers think themselves therewith justified? no more then *Shimei* was by his Soveraigns most humble and meek acknowledgement even of that very crime which so impudent a Caitiffs tongue upbraided him withal; the one in the virulent rancour of a canckred affection, took that delight for the present, which in the end did turn to his own more tormenting wo; the other in the contrite patience even of deserved malediction, had yet this comfort, *It may be the Lord will look on mine affliction, and do me good for his cursing this day.* As for us over whom Christ hath placed them to be the chiefest Guides and Pastors of our souls, our common fault is, that we look for much more in our Governors then a tolerable sufficiency can yield, and bear much less, then Humanity and Reason do require we should. Too much perfection over rigorously exacted in them, cannot but breed in us perpetual discontentment, and on both parts cause all things to be unpleasant. It is exceedingly worth the noting, which *Plato* hath about the means whereby men fall into an utter dislike of all men with whom they converse: *This sowreness of minde which maketh every mans dealings unsavoury in our taste, entereth by an unskilful over-weening, which at the first we have of one, and so of another, in whom we afterwards finde our selves to have been deceived, they declaring themselves in the end to be frail men, whom we judged demigods: When we have oftentimes been thus beguiled, and that far besides expectation, we grow at the length to this plain conclusion, That there is nothing at all found in any man.*

2 Sam. 16. 11.

Plat in Phæd.

man. Which bitter conceit is unseemly, and plain to have risen from lack of mature judgement in humane affairs; which if so be we did handle with art, we would not enter into dealings with men, otherwise then being beforehand grounded in this perswasion, that the number of persons notably good or bad, is but very small; that the most part of good have some evil, and of evil men, some good in them. So true our experience doth finde those Aphorisms of *Mercurius Trismegistus,* Αδυνατον τὸ ἀγαθὸν ἐκκαθαρθῆναι τ κακίας, To purge goodness quite and clean from all mixture of evil here, is a thing impossible. Again, Τὸ μὴ λίαν κακὸν ἐν ἰδία τὸ ἀγαθόν, ἐστι, When in this World we term a thing good, we cannot by exact construction have any other true meaning, then that the said thing so termed, is not noted to be a thing exceedingly evil. And again, Μόνον δ' Ασκληπιέ τὸ ὄνομα τὰ ἀγαθοῦ ἐν ἀνθρώποις, τὸ δὲ ἔργον ἰδαμῦ, Amongst men, O *Esculapius,* the name of that which is good we finde, but no where the very true thing it self. When we censure the deeds and dealings of our Superiors, to bring with us a fore-conceit thus qualified, shall be as well on our part as theirs, a thing available unto quietness: But howsoever the case doth stand with mens either good or bad quality, the verdict which our Lord and Saviour hath given, should continue for ever sure, *Quæ Dei sunt Deo,* let men bear the burthen of their own iniquity, as for those things which are Gods, let not God be deprived of them. For if onely to withhold that which should be given, be no better then to rob God? if to withdraw any mite of that which is but in propose onely bequeathed, though as yet undelivered into the sacred treasure of God, be a sin for which *Ananias* and *Saphyra* felt so heavily the dreadful hand of Divine revenge; quite and clean to take that away which we never gave, and that after God hath for so many ages therewith been possessed, and that without any other shew of cause, saving onely that it seemeth in their eyes who seek it, to be too much for them which have it in their hands, can we term it, or think it less then most impious injustice, most hainous sacriledge? Such was the Religious affection of *Joseph,* that it suffered him not to take that advantage, no not against the very Idolatrous Priests of *Egypt,* which he took for the purchasing of other mens lands to the King; but he considered, that albeit their Idolatry deserved hatred, yet for the honors sake due unto Priesthood, better it was the King himself should yield them relief in publique extremity, then permit that the same necessity should constrain also them to do as the rest of the people did. But it may be men have now found out, that God hath proposed the Christian Clergy, as a prey for all men freely to seize upon; that God hath left them as the fishes of the Sea, which every man that lifteth to gather into his net may; or that there is no God in Heaven to pity them, and to regard the injuries which man doth lay upon them: Yet the publique good of this Church and Commonwealth doth, I hope, weigh somewhat in the hearts of all honestly disposed men. Unto the publique good, no one thing is more directly available, then that such as are in place, whether it be of Civil, or of Ecclesiastical Authority, be so much the more largely furnished even with external helps and ornaments of this life, how much the more highly they are in power and calling advanced above others. For nature is not contented with bare sufficiency unto the sustenance of man, but doth evermore covet a decency proportionable unto the place which man hath in the body, or society of others: For according unto the greatness of mens calling, the measure of all their actions doth grow in every mans secret expectation, so that great men do always know, that great things are at their hands expected. In a Bishop, great liberality, great hospitality, actions in every kinde great are looked for: And for actions which must be great, mean instruments will not serve. Men are but men, what room soever amongst men they hold: If therefore the measure of their Worldly habilities be beneath that proportion which their calling doth make to be looked for at their hands, a stronger inducement it is then perhaps men are aware of, unto evil and corrupt dealings, for supply of that defect. For which cause, we must needs think it a thing necessary unto the common good of the Church, that great Jurisdiction being granted unto Bishops over others, a state of wealth proportionable should likewise be provided for them: where wealth is had in so great admiration, as generally in this golden age it is, that without it Angelical perfections are not able to deliver from extreme contempt, surely to make Bishops poorer then they are, were to make them of less account and estimation then they should be. Wherefore

if

M.Trif in ph. mandro. dial. 6

*Mal 3 8.
Acts 5.2.*

Gen. 47.22.

if detriment and diſhonor do grow to Religion, to God, to his Church, when the publique account which is made of the chief of the Clergy decayeth, how ſhould it be, but in this reſpect, for the good of Religion, of God, of his Church, that the wealth of Biſhops be carefully preſerved from further diminution? The travels and croſſes wherewith Prelacy is never unaccompanied, they which feel them know how heavy, and how great they are. Unleſs ſuch difficulties therefore, annexed unto that eſtate, be tempered by co-annexing thereunto things eſteemed of in this World, how ſhould we hope that the mindes of men, (ſhunning naturally the burthens of each function, will be drawn to undertake the burthen of Epiſcopal care and labour in the Church of Chriſt? Wherefore if long we deſire to enjoy the peace, quietneſs, order and ſtability of Religion, which Prelacy (as hath been declared) cauſeth, then muſt we neceſſarily, even in favour of the publique good, uphold thoſe things, the hope whereof being taken away, it is not the meer goodneſs of the charge, and the Divine acceptation thereof, that will be able to invite many thereunto. What ſhall become of that Commonwealth or Church in the end, which hath not the eye of Learning to beautifie, guide, and direct it? At the length, what ſhall become of that Learning, which hath not wherewith any more to encourage her induſtrious followers? And finally, what ſhall become of that courage to follow learning, which hath already ſo much failed through the onely diminution of her chiefeſt rewards, Biſhopricks? Surely, whereſoever this wicked intendment of overthrowing Cathedral Churches, or of taking away thoſe Livings, Lands and Poſſeſſions which Biſhops hitherto have enjoyed ſhall once prevail, the handmaids attending thereupon will be Paganiſm, and extreme Barbarity. In the Law of *Moſes*, how careful proviſion is made that goods of this kinde might remain to the Church for ever : *Ye ſhall not make common the holy things of the children of Iſrael, leſt ye dye, ſaith the Lord.* Touching the fields annexed unto Levitical Cities, the Law was plain, they might not be ſold; and the reaſon of the Law, this, *for it was their poſſeſſion for ever*; he which was Lord and owner of it, his will and pleaſure was, that from the Levites it ſhould never paſs, to be enjoyed by any other. The Lords own portion, without his own Commiſſion and grant, how ſhould any man juſtly hold? They which hold it by his appointment, had it plainly with this condition, *They ſhall not ſell of it, neither change it, nor alienate the firſt-fruits of the Land; for it is holy unto the Lord.* It falleth ſometimes out, as the Prophet *Habakkuk* noteth, that the very *prey of Savage Beaſts becometh dreadful unto themſelves.* It did ſo in *Judas, Achan, Nebuchadnezzar*, their evil purchaſed goods were their ſnare, and their prey their own terror : A thing no where ſo likely to follow, as in thoſe Goods and Poſſeſſions, which being laid where they ſhould not reſt, have by the Lords own teſtimony, his moſt bitter curſe, their undividable companion. Theſe perſwaſions we uſe for other mens cauſe, not for theirs with whom God and Religion are parts of the abrogated Law of Ceremonies. Wherefore not to continue longer in the cure of a ſore deſperate, there was a time when the Clergy had almoſt as little as theſe good people wiſh. But the Kings of this Realm and others, whom God had bleſt, conſidered devoutly with themſelves, as *David* in like caſe ſometimes had done, *Is it meet that we at the hands of God ſhould enjoy all kindes of abundance, and Gods Clergy ſuffer want?* They conſidered that of *Solomon, Honor God with thy ſubſtance, and the chiefeſt of all thy revenue, ſo ſhall thy barns be filled with corn, and thy veſſels ſhall run over with new wine.* They conſidered how the care which *Jehoſhaphat* had, in providing that the Levites might have encouragement to do the work of the Lord chearfully, was left of God as a fit patern to be followed in the Church for ever. They conſidered what promiſe our Lord and Saviour hath made unto them, at whoſe hands his Prophets ſhould receive but the leaſt part of the meaneſt kinde of friendlineſs, though it were but a draught of water : Which promiſe ſeemeth not to be taken, as if Chriſt had made them of any higher courteſie uncapable, and had promiſed reward not unto ſuch as give them but that, but unto ſuch as leave them but that. They conſidered how earneſt the Apoſtle is, that if the Miniſters of the Law were ſo amply provided for, leſs care then ought not to be had of them, who under the Goſpel of Jeſus Chriſt, poſſeſs correſpondent rooms in the Church. They conſidered how needful it is that they who provoke all others unto works of Mercy and

                                                             Charity,

Marginal notes:

Num. 18. 32.

Levit. 25.

Ezek. 48. 14.

Habak. 2, 17.

Mal. 3. 9.

Prov. 3. 9.

2 Chron. 9.
chap. 19.

Charity, should especially have wherewith to be examples of such things, and by such means to win them, with whom other means without those, do commonly take very small effect.

In these and the like considerations, the Church Revenues were in ancient times augmented, our Lord thereby performing manifestly the promise made to his servants, that they which did *leave either Father, or Mother, or Lands, or goods for his sake, should receive even in this World an hundred fold.* For some hundreds of years together, they which joyned themselves to the Church, were fain to relinquish all worldly emoluments, and to endure the hardness of an afflicted estate. Afterward the Lord gave rest to his Church, Kings and Princes became as Fathers thereunto, the hearts of all men inclined towards it, and by his Providence there grew unto it every day earthly possessions in more and more abundance, till the greatness thereof bred envy, which no diminutions are able to satisfie: For as those ancient Nursing Fathers thought they did never bestow enough, even so in the eye of this present age, as long as any thing remaineth, it seemeth to be too much. Our Fathers we imitate *in perversum*, as *Tertullian* speaketh, like them we are by being in equal degree the contrary unto that which they were. Unto those earthly blessings which God as then did with so great abundance pour down upon the Ecclesiastical state, we may in regard of most neer resemblance, apply the self same words which the Prophet hath, *God blessed them exceedingly, and by this very mean, turned* Psa. 105. 24, 25 *the hearts of their own Brethren to hate them, and to deal politiquely with his servants.* Computations are made, and there are huge sums set down for Princes, to see how much they may amplifie and enlarge their own treasure; how many publique burthens they may ease; what present means they may have to reward their servants about them, if they please but to grant their assent, and to accept of the spoil of Bishops, by wom Church goods are but abused unto pomp and vanity. Thus albeit they deal with one, whose Princely vertue giveth them small hope to prevail in impious and sacrilegious motions, yet shame they not to move her Royal Majestie even with a suit not much unlike unto that wherewith the Jewish High-Priest tried *Judas*, whom they sollicited unto Treason against his Master, and proposed unto him a number of silver pence in lieu of so vertuous and honest a service. But her sacred Majesty disposed to be always like her self, her heart so far estranged from willingness to gain by pillage of that estate, the onely awe whereof under God she hath been unto this present hour, as of all other parts of this noble Common-wealth whereof she hath vowed her self a protector, till the end of her days on earth, which if nature could permit, we wish, as good cause we have, endless: this her gracious inclination is more then a seven times sealed warrant, upon the same assurance whereof touching any and action, so dishonourable as this, we are on her part most secure, not doubting but that unto all posterity, it shall for ever appear, that from the first to the very last of her soveraign proceedings, there hath not been one authorized deed, other then consonant with that *Symachus* saith, *Fiscus bonorum principum, non sacer-* Lib. 10. Ep. 54. *dotum damnis sed hostium spoliis augeatur*; consonant with that imperial law, *ea quæ ad* D D D. *Valent* *beatissimæ ecclesiæ jura pertinent, tanquam ipsam sacrosanctam & religiosam Ecclesiam in-* Theodos & Ar-*tacta convenit venerabiliter custodiri; Ut sicut ipsa religionis & fidei mater perpetua est,* cbad. *ita ejus patrimonium jugiter serveitur illæsum.* As for the case of publique burthens, let L. 14. c. de sa-any politician living, make it appear, that by confiscation of Bishops livings, and crof. Eccles. their utter dissolution, at once the Common-wealth shall ever have half that relief and ease which it receiveth by their continuance as now they are, and it shall give us some cause to think, that albeit we see they are impiously and irreligiously minded, yet, we may esteem them at least to be tolerable Common-wealths-men. But the case is too clear and manifest, the World doth but too plainly see it that no one order of subjects whatsoever within this Land doth bear the seventh part of that proportion which the Clergy beareth in the burthens of the Common-wealth. No revenue of the Crown like unto it, either for certainty or for greatness. Let the good which this way hath grown to the common wealth by the dissolution of religious houses, teach men what ease unto publique burthens there is like to grow, by the overthrow of the Clergy. My meaning is not hereby to make the state of Bishoprick, and of those dissolved companies alike, the one no less unlawful to be removed then the other. For those Religious persons were men which followed onely a

special

special kind of Contemplative life in the Common-wealth, they were properly no portion of Gods Clergy (onely such amongst them excepted, as were also Priests) their goods (that excepted, which they unjustly held through the Popes usurped Power of appropriating Ecclesiastical livings unto them) may in part seem to be of the nature of Civil possessions, held by other kinds of Corporations such as the City of *London* hath divers. Wherefore as their institution was humane, and their end for the most part Superstitious, they had not therein meerly that holy and divine interest which belongeth unto Bishops, who being imployed by Christ in the principal service of his Church, are receivers and disposers of his patrimony, as hath been showed, which whosoever shall with-hold or with-draw at any time from them, he undoubtedly robbeth God himself. If they abuse the goods of the Church unto pomp and vanity, such faults we do not excuse in them. Onely we wish it to be considered whether such faults be verily in them, or else but objected against them by such as gape after spoil, and therefore are no competent judges what is moderate and what excessive in them, whom under this pretence they would spoil. But the accusation may be just, in plenty and fulness it may be we are of God more forgetful then were requisite. Notwithstanding men should remember how not to the Clergy alone it was said by *Moses* in *Deuteronomy*, *Ne cum manducaveris & biberis, & domos optimas edificaveris:* If the remedy prescribed for this disease be good, let it unpartially be applied. *Interest reip. ut re sua* $QUISQUE$ *bene utatur.* Let all states be put to their moderate pensions, let their livings and lands be taken away from them whosoever they be, in whom such ample possessions are found to have been matters of grievous abuse: Were this just? would Noble Families think this reasonable? The Title which Bishops have to their livings is as good as the title of any sort of men unto whatsoever we accompt to be most justly held by them; yea, in this one thing, the claim of *B. B.* hath preeminence above all secular Titles of right, in that Gods own interest is the tenure whereby they hold, even as also it was to the Priests of the Law an assurance of their spiritual goods and possessions, whereupon though they many times abused greatly the goods of the Church, yet was not Gods patrimony therefore taken away from them, and made saleable unto other Tribes. To rob God, to ransack the Church, to overthrow the whole order of Christian Bishops, and to turn them out of Land and Living, out of House and Home, what man of common honesty can think it for any manner of abuse to be a remedy lawful, or just? We must confess that God is righteous in taking away that which men abuse: But doth

Pudet dicere, sacerdotes idolorum, aurigæ; mimi & scorta hæreditates capiunt, so is clericis & monachis id lege prohibetur & prohibetur non à persecutoribus sed principibus Christianis, Nec ea lege conquerer sed dolec qu.d n cautimus bonc legem Ad Nepot. 7.

that excuse the violence of Thieves and Robbers? Complain we will not with * S. *Jerom*, that the hands of men are so straightly tyed, and their liberal minds so much bridled and held back from doing good by augmentation of the Church Patrimony. For we confess that herein mediocrity may be and hath been sometime exceeded. There did want heretofore a *Moses* to temper mens liberality, to say unto them who enriched the Church, *Sufficit*, Stay your hands least fervour of zeal do cause you to empty your selves too far. It may be the largeness of mens hearts being then more moderate, had been after more durable, and one state by too much over-growing the rest, had not given occasion unto the rest to undermine it. That evil is now sufficiently cured, the Church treasury, if then it were over-ful, hath since been reasonable well emptyed. That which *Moses* spake unto givers, we must now inculcate unto takers away from the Church, let there be some stay, some stint in spoiling. If *Grape-gatherers came unto them*, saith the Prophet *would they not leave some remnant behind*? But it hath fared with the wealth of the Church as with a Tower which being built at the first with the highest, overthroweth it self after, by its own greatness, neither doth the ruine thereof cease, with the onely fall of that, which hath exceeded mediocrity, but one part beareth down another, till the whole be laid prostrate; For although the state Ecclesiastical, both others and even Bishops themselves, be now fallen to so low an ebb, as all the World at this day doth see, yet because there remaineth still somewhat which unsatiable minds can thirst for, therefore we seem not to have been hitherto sufficiently wronged. Touching that which hath been taken from the Church in appropriations known to amount to the value of one hundred twenty six thousand pounds yearly, we rest contentedly, and quietly

with-

Obad. vers 5

without it, till it shall please God to touch the hearts of men, of their own voluntary accord to restore it to him again; judging thereof no otherwise then some others did of those goods which were by *Sylla* taken away from the Citizens of *Rome*, that albeit they were in truth *male Capta*, unconscionably taken away from the right owners at the first, nevertheless seeing that such as were after possessed of them, held them not without some title, which law did after a sort make good, *repetitio eorum proculdubio labefactabat compositam civitatem*; What hath been taken away as dedicated unto uses superstitious, and consequently not given unto God, or at the least-wise not so rightly given, we repine not thereat. That which hath gone by means secret and indirect, through corrupt compositions or compacts we cannot help. What the hardness of mens hearts doth make them loath to have exacted, though being due by Law, even thereof the want we do also bear. Out of that which after all these Deductions cometh clearly unto our hands, I hope it will not be said that towards the publique charge, we disburse nothing. And doth the residue seem yet excessive? The ways whereby temporal men provide for themselves and their Families, are foreclosed unto us. All that we have to sustain our miserable life with, is but a remnant of Gods own treasure, so far already diminished and clipt, that if there were any sense of common humanity left in this hard-hearted World, the impoverished estate of the Clergy of God, would at the length even of very commiseration be spared. The mean Gentleman that hath but an hundred pound Land to live on, would not be hasty to change his Worldly estate and condition with many of these so overabounding Prelates; a common Artisan or Tradesman of the City, with ordinary Pastors of the Church. It is our hard and heavy lot that no other sort of men being grudged at, how little benefit soever the publique Weal reap by them, no state complained of for holding that which hath grown unto them by lawful means, onely the governors of our souls, they that study day and night so to guide us, that both in this world we may have comfort and in the world to come endless felicity and joy (for even such is the very scope of all their endeavours, this they wish, for this they labour, how hardly soever we use to construe of their intents; hard that onely they should be thus continually lifted at for possessing but that whereunto they have by law both of God and man most just Title. If there should be no other remedy but that the violence of men in the end must needs bereave them of all succor, further then the inclination of others shall vouchsafe to cast upon them, as it were by way of alms for their relief but from hour to hour; better they are not then their Fathers, which have been contented with as hard a portion at the Worlds hands: let the light of the Sun and Moon, the common benefit of Heaven and Earth be taken from *B. B.* if the Question were whither God should lose his glory, and the safety of his Church be hazarded, or they relinquish the right and interest which they have in the things of this World. But sith the question in truth is whither *Levi* shall be deprived of the portion of God or no, to the end that *Simeon* or *Reuben* may devour it as their spoil, the comfort of the one in sustaining the injuries which the other would offer, must be that prayer powred out by *Moses* the prince of Prophets, in most tender affection to *Levi*, bless *O Lord his substance, accept thou the work of his hands, smite through the loins of them that rise up against him, and of them which hate him, that they rise no more.*

Flor. lib 3. c 13.

Deut. 33. 10, 11.

OF THE
LAWES
OF
Ecclesiastical Polity.

The Eighth Book.

Containing their seventh Assertion;

That, to no Civil Prince or Governour, there may be given such power of Ec-clesiastical Dominion, as by the Laws of this Land belongeth unto the Su-preme Regent thereof.

E come now to the last thing whereof there is Controversie moved, namely, *The Power of Supreme Jurisdiction*, which for distinction sake we call, *The Power of Ecclesiastical dominion*. It was not thought fit in the *Jews Commonwealth*, that the exercise of *Supremacy Ecclesiastical* should be denied unto him, to whom the exercise of *Chiefty Civil* did appertain ; and therefore their Kings were invested with both. This power they gave unto *Simon*, when they consented that he should be their Prince, not onely to set men over their Works, and Countrey, and Weapons, but also to provide for the Holy things ; and that he should be obeyed of every man, and that the Writings of the Countrey should be made in his name ; and that it should not be lawful for any of the people, or Priests to withstand his words, or to call any Congregation in the Countrey without him. And if happily it be surmised, that thus much was given to *Simon*, as being both Prince and High-Priest ; which otherwise (being their *Civil Governor*) he could not lawfully have enjoyned : We must note, that all this is no more then the ancient Kings of that People had, being Kings, and not Priests. By this power, *David*, *Asa*, *Jehoshaphat*, *Josias*, and the rest, made those Laws which sacred History speaketh of, concerning matters of meer Religion, the affairs of the Temple, and service of God. Finally, had it not been by the vertue of this power, how should it possibly have come to pass, that the piety or impiety of the Kings did always accordingly change the publique face of Religion ; which things the Prophets by themselves never did, nor at any time could hinder from being done: Had the Priests alone been possest of all power in Spiritual affairs, how should any thing concerning matter of Religion have been made but onely by them ; in them it had been, and not in the King, to change the face of Religion at any time ; the altering of Religion, the making of Ecclesiastical Laws, with other the like actions belonging unto the Power of Dominion, are still termed *the deeds of the King* ; to shew, that in him was placed the supremacy of power in this kinde over all,

and

Maccab. 14.

and that unto their Priests the same was never committed, (saving only at such times as the Priests were also Kings and Princes over them. According to the pattern of which example, the like power in causes Ecclesiastical is by the Laws of this Realm annexed unto the Crown; and there are which do imagine, that Kings being meere Lay-persons, do by this means exceed the lawful bounds of their callings; which thing to the end that they may perswade, they first make a necessary separation perpetual & personal between *the Church* and *the Common-wealth.* Secondly, they so tie all kind of *power Ecclesiastical* unto the *Church,* as if it were in every degree their only right; who are by proper spiritual functions termed *Church Governours,* and might not unto *Christian Princes* in any wise appertain. To lurk under shifting ambiguities and equivocations of words in matter of principal waight, is childish. A Church and a Common-wealth we grant, are things in nature one distinguished from the other: a Common-wealth is one way, and a Church an other way defined. In their opinions the Church and Common-wealth are corporation, not distinguished only in nature and definition, but in substance perpetually severed: so that they which are of the one, can neither appoint, nor execute, in whole nor in part, the duties which belong to them which are of the other, without open breach of the Law of God which hath divided them; and doth require, that so being divided, they should distinctly or severally work, as depending both upon God, and not hanging one opon the others approbation. For that which either hath to do, we say that the care of Religion being common to all societies Politique, such societies as do embrace the true Religion have the name of the Church given unto every one of them for distinction from the rest: so that every body Politique hath some Religion, but the Church that Religion which is only true. *Truth* of Religion is the proper difference whereby a Church is distinguished from other Politique societies of men; we here mean true Religion in gross, and not according to every particular: for they which in some particular points of Religion do sever from the truth, may nevertheless truly, if we compare them to men of an heathenish Religion)be said to hold and profess that Religion which is true. For which cause there being of old so many Politique societies stablished through the world, only the Common-wealth of Israel which had the truth of Religion, was in that respect the Church of God: and the Church of Jesus Christ is every such Politique society of men, as doth in Religion hold that truth which is proper to Christianity. As a Politique society it doth maintain Religion, as a Church, that Religion which God hath revealed by Jesus Christ: with us, therefore the name of a Church importeth onely a society of men, first united into some publique form of Regiment, and secondly, distinguished from other societies by the exercise of Religion. With them on the other side, the name of the Church in this present question, importeth not onely a multitude of men so united, and so distinguished, but also further, the same divided necessarily and perpetually from the body of the Common-wealth: so that even in such a Politique society as consisteth of none but Christians, yet the Church and Common-wealth are two Corporations, independently subsisting by it self,

We hold, that seeing there is not any man of the Church of *England,* but the same man is also a member of the Common-wealth; nor any member of the Common-wealth, which is not also of the Church of *England.* Therefore, as in a figure Triangle, the base doth differ from the sides thereof, and yet one and the self same line is both a base and also a side; a side simply, a base if it chance to be the bottom and underly the rest. So albeit, properties and actions of one do cause the name of a Common-wealth; qualities and functions of another sort, the name of the Church to be given to a multitude; yet one and the self-same multitude may in such fort be both. Nay, it is so with us, that no person appertaining to the one, can be denied also to be of the other: contrariwise, unless they against us should hold that the Church and the Common-wealth are two, both distinct and separate societies; of which two, one comprehendeth alwayes persons not belonging to the

other,

other, (that which they do) they could not conclude out of the difference betwen the Church and the Common-wealth, namely that the Bishops may not meddle with the affairs of the Common-wealth, because they are Governours of an other Corporation, which is the Church; nor Kings, with making Lawes for the Church, because they have government not of this Corporation, but of another divided from it; the Common-wealth and the walls of separation between these two, must for ever be upheld: they hold the necessity of personal separation which clean excludeth the power of one mans dealing with both; we of natural, but that one and the same person may in both bear principal sway.

The causes of common received errours in this point seem to have been especially two: one, that they who embrace true Religion, living in such Common-wealths as are opposite thereunto; and in other publique affairs, retaining civil communion with such as are constrained for the exercise of their Religion, to have a several communion with those who are of the same Religion with them. This was the state of the Jewish Church both in *Egypt* and *Babylon*, the state of Christian Churches a long time after Christ. And in this case, because the proper affairs and actions of the Church, as it is the Church, hath no dependance on the Laws, or upon the Government of the civil State; an opinion hath thereby grown, that even so it should be alwayes: this was it which deceived *Allen* in the writing of his Apology. *The Apostles* (saith he) *did govern the Church in* Rome *when Nero bare rule, even as at this day in all the Churches dominions: the Church hath a spiritual regiment without dependance, and so ought she to have amongst heathens, or with Christians.* Another occasion of which misconceit is, That things appertaining to Religion are both distinguished from other affairs, and have alwayes had in the Church spiritual persons chosen to be exercised about them. By which distinction of Spiritual affairs, and persons therein employed from Temporal, the errour of personal separation alwayes necessary between the Church and Common-wealth hath strengthened it self. For of every Politique society, that being true which *Aristotle* saith, namely, *That the scope thereof is not simply to live, nor the duty so much to provide for the life, as for means of living well*: And that even as the soul is the worthier part of man, so humane societies are much more to care for that which tendeth properly to the souls estate, then for such temporal things wch the life hath need of. Other proof there needeth none to shew, that as by all men the Kingdom of God is to be sought first, for so in all Common-wealths, things spiritual ought above temporal to be sought for; and of things spiritual, the chiefest is Religion. For this cause, persons and things employed peculiarly about the affairs of Religion, are by an excellency termed spiritual. The Heathens themselves had their spiritual lawes, and causes, and affairs, alwayes severed from their temporal; neither did this make two independent estates among them. God by revealing true Religion doth make them that receive it his Church. Unto the *Jews* he so revealed the truth of Religion, that he gave them in special considerations, Laws, not only for the administration of things spiritual, but also temporal. The Lord himself appointing both the one and the other in that Common-wealth, did not thereby distract it into several independent communities, but institute several functions of one and the self same community: some reasons therfore must there be alledged why it should be otherwise in the Church of Christ.

I shal not need to spend any great store of words in answering that which is brought out of the holy Scripture, to shew that Secular and Ecclesiastical affairs & offices are distinguished; neither that which hath been borrowed from antiquity, using by phrase of speech to oppose the Common-weal to the Church of Christ: neither yet their reasons wch are wont to be brought forth as witnesses, that the Church & Common-weal were always distinct; for whether a Church or Common-weal do differ, is not the question we strive for; but our controversie is concerning the kind of distinction, whereby they are severd the one from the other; whether as under heathen Kings the Church did deal with her own

affairs

affairs within her self, without depending at all upon any in Civil authority; and the Common-weal in hers, altogether without the privity of the Church: so it ought to continue still even in such Common-weals as have now publiquely embraced the truth of Christian Religion; whether they ought evermore to be two societies in such sort, several and distinct. I ask therefore what society was that in *Rome*, whereunto the Apostle did give the name of the Church of *Rome* in his time? If they answer (as needs they must) that the Church of *Rome* in those dayes was that whole society of men, which in *Rome* professed the name of Christ, & not that Religion which the Laws of the Common-weal did then authorize, we say as much, and therefore grant that the Common-weal of *Rome* was one society, and the Church of *Rome* another, in such sort that there was between them no mutual dependence. But when whole *Rome* became Christian where they all embraced the Gospel, and made Laws in defence thereof, if it be held that the Church and Common-weal of *Rome* did then remain as before, there is no way how this could be possible, save only one, and that is, They must restrain the name of a Church in a Christian Common-weal to the Clergy, excluding all the rest of believers both Prince, and people; For if all that believe be contained in the name of the Church, how should the Church remain by personal subsistence divided from the Common-weale, when the whole common-weal doth believe? The Church and the Common-weal are in this case therefore personally one society, which society being termed a Common-weal as it liveth under whatsoever form of secular Law and Regiment, a Church as it liveth under the spiritual Law of Christ; For so much as these two Laws contain so many and different Offices, there must of necessity be appointed in it some to one charge, and some to another, yet without deviding the whole, and making it two several impaled Societies.

The difference therefore either of affairs or offices Ecclesiastical from secular, is no argument that the Church and Common-weal are alwayes separate and independent, the one on the other; which thing even *Allaine* himself considering somewhat better, doth in this point a little correct his former judgement before mentiond, & confesseth in his defence of English Catholicks, that the power political hath her Princes, Laws, Tribunals; the spiritual her Prelates, Canons, Councels, Judgements; and those (when the temporal Princes and Pagans) wholly separate, but in Christian Common-weals joyned; though not confounded. Howbeit afterwards his former sting appeareth again; for in a Common-wealth he holdeth, that the Church ought not to depend at all upon the authority of any civil person whatsoever, as in *England* he saith it doth.

It will be objected that the Fathers do oftentimes mention the Common-weale and the Church of God, by way of opposition. Can the same thing be opposed to it self? If one and the same society, be both Church and Common-wealth, what sence can there be in that speech, *that they suffer and flourish together?* What sence is that which maketh one thing to be adjudged to the Church, and another to the Common wealth? Finally, in that which putteth a difference between the causes of the Province and the Church, doth it not hereby appear, that the Church and the Common-weal, are things evermore personally separate? No, it doth not hereby appear that there is not perpetually any such separation; we speak of them as two, we may sever the rights and the causes of the one well enough from the other, in regard of that difference which we grant is between them, albeit we make no personal difference. For the truth is, that the Church and the Common-wealth, are names which import things really different; but those things are accident, and such accidents as may and alwayes should lovingly dwell together in one subject. Wherefore the real difference between the accidents signified by these names, doth not prove different subjects for them always to reside in. For albeit the subjects wherein they be resident be sometimes different, as when the people of God have their residence among Infidels; yet the nature of them is not such, but that their subject maybe one; and therefore it is but a

A a a 2   changeable

1 Chron. 14. 8. 11.
Heb. 5. 1.
Allain. lib. 31. p. 151.

2. Taken from the speeches of the Fathers opposing the one to the other.

Euseb. de vita constan. lib. 3. *Aug. Epist.* 157

changeable accident in those accidents they are to be divers: There can be
no errour in our conceit concerning this point, if we remember still what
accident is, for which a society hath the name of a Common-wealth, and
what accident that which doth cause it to be termed a Church : a Common-
wealth, we name it simply in regard of some regiment or policy under which
men live ; a Church for the truth of that Religion which they profess.
Now names betokening accidents inabstracted, betoken not only the accidents themselves, but also together with them subjects whereunto they
cleave. As when we name a School-master and a Physitian, those names do
not only betoken two accidents, teaching and curing, but also some person
or persons in whom those accidents are. For there is no impediment but
both may be in one man, as well as they are for the most part divers. The
The Common-weale and the Church therefore being such names, they do
not only betoken these accidents of Civil Government and Christian Religion, which we have mentioned, but also together with them such multitudes
as are the subjects of those accidents. Again, their nature being such as they
may well enough dwell together in one subject, it followeth that their names
though alwayes implying that difference of accidents that hath been set
down, yet do not alwayes imply differet subjects also. When we oppose
therefore the Church and the Common.wealth in Christian Society, we mean
by the Common-wealth that Society with relation to all the publike affairs
thereof, only the matter of true Religion excepted : By the Church the same
Society with only reference unto the matter of true Religion, without any
affairs; besides, when that Society which is both a Church and a Common-
wealth, doth flourish in those things which belong unto it as a Common-
wealth, we then say, the Common-wealth doth flourish ; when in both
them, we then say, the Church and Common-wealth do flourish together.
      The Prophet *Esay* to note corruptions in the Common-wealth, complain-
eth, *That where justice and judgement had lodged , now were murtherers; Princes*
were become Companions of Theeves, every one loved gifts, and rewards ; but the
Esay. 1. 21. *Fatherlesse was not judged, neither did the widdows cause come before them.* To
Mal. 1. 8. shew abuses in the Church, *Malachy* doth make his complaint, *Ye offer unclean*
bread upon mine Altar. If ye offer the blind for sacrifice, it is not evil as ye think ; if
1 *Chron.* 29 3. *the lame and the sick, nothing is amiss.* The Treasure which *David* bestowed upon the Temple, did argue the love which he bore unto the Church : The
Nehem. 2. 27. pains which *Nehemiah* took for building the wals of the City, are tokens of
his care for the Common-wealth. Causes of the Common-wealth, or Pro-
vince, are such as *Gallio* was content to be judge of. *If it were a matter of*
wrong, or an evil deed (O ye Jews) I would according to reason maintain you.
Acts 18. 14. Causes of the Church, are such as *Gallio* there reciteth ; *if it be a question of your*
Law, look ye to it, I will be no Judge thereof : In respect of this difference therefore the Church and the Common-wealth, may in speech be compared or
opposed aptly enough the one to the other ; yet this is no argument, that
they are two independent Societies.

2. Taken
from the ef-
fect of punish-
ment inflict-
ed by the one,
or the other.   Some other reasons there are which seem a little more nearly to make for
the purpose, as long as they are but heard, and not sifted : For what though
a man being severed by Excommunication from the Church, be not thereby
deprived of freedome in the City, or being there discomoned, is not therefore
forthwith Excommunicated and excluded the Church ? What though the
Church be bound to receive them upon repentance, whom the Commonweal
may refuse again to admit ? If it chance the same man to be shut out of both,
division of the Church and Common-weale which they contend for, will very
hardly hereupon follow : For we must note that members of a Christian Common-weale have a triple state, a natural, a civil, and a spiritual : No mans
natural estate is cut off otherwise then by that capital execution. After which,
he that is none of the body of the Common-wealth, doth not I think remain
fit in the body of that visible Church. And concerning mans civil estate, the
same is subject partly to inferiour abatements of liberty, and partly to dimi-
                                                              nution

nution in the highest degree, such as banishment is; sith it casteth out quite and clean from the body of the Common-weale, it must needs also consequently cast the banished party even out of the very Church he was of before; because that Church and the Common-weale he was of, were both one and the same Society; So that whatsoever doth utterly separate a mans person from the one, it separateth from the other also. As for such abatements of civil estate as take away only some priviledge, dignity, or other benefit, which a man enjoyeth in the Common-weale, they reach only to our dealing with publike affairs, from which what may let, but that men may be excluded, and thereunto restored again without diminishing or augmenting the number of persons, in whom either Church or Common wealth consisteth. He that by way of punishment looseth his voyce in a publike election of Magistrates, ceaseth not thereby to be a Citizen; A man dis-franchised may notwithstanding enjoy as a subject the common benefit of protection under Laws and Magistrates; so that these inferiour diminutions which touch men civily, but neither do clean extingish their estates, as they belong to the Commonwealth, or impaire a whit their condition as they are of the Church of God? These I say do clearly prove a difference of the one from the other, but such a difference as maketh nothing for their surmise of distracted Societies.

And concerning Excommunication, it cutteth off indeed from the Church, and yet not from the Common-wealth; howbeit so that the party Excommunicate is not thereby severed from one body which subsisteth in it self, and retained by another in like sort subsisting; but he which before had fellowship with that Society whereof he was a member, as well touching things Spiritual as civil, is now by force of Excommunication, although not severed from the body in Civil affairs, nevertheless for the time cut off from it as touching communion in those things wch belong to the same body, as it is the Church: A man which having been both Excommunicated by the Church, & deprived of Civil dignity in the Common-wealth, is upon his repentance necessarily reunited into the one, but not of necessity into the other. What then? That which he is admitted unto, is a communion in things Divine, whereof both parts are partakers, that from which he is withheld, is the benefit of some humane priviledge, or right, which other Citizens happily enjoy. But are not these Saints and Citizens, one and the same people, are they not one and the same Society? Doth it hereby appear that the Church which received an Excommunicate, can have no dependency on any person which hath chief Authority and power, of these things in the Common-wealth whereunto the same party is not admitted. Wherefore to end this point, I conclude; First, that under the dominions of infidels, the Church of Christ, and their Common-weath, were two Societies independent. Secondly, that in those Common-wealths, where the Bishop of *Rome* beareth sway, one Society is both the Church and the Common-wealth : But the Bishop of *Rome* doth devide the body into two divers bodies, and doth not suffer the Church to depend upon the power of any civil Prince and Potentate. Thirdly, that within this Realm of *England*, the case is neither as in the one, nor as in the other of the former two, but from the state of Pagans we differ; in that with us one Society is both the Church and Common wealth, which with them it was not. As also from the state of those Nations which subjected themselves to the Bishop of *Rome*, in that our Church hath dependance from the chief in our Common-wealth, which it hath not when he is suffered to rule. In a word, our state is according to the pattern of Gods own antient elect people, which people was not part of them the Common-wealth, & part of them the Church of God; but the self-same people whole and entire were both under one chief Governour, on whose *Supream* Authority they did all depend. Now the drift of all that hath been alleadged to prove perpetual separation and independency between the Church and the Commonwealth, is, that this being held necessary, it might consequently be thought fit, that in a Christian Kingdome, he whose power is greatest over the

Common-

Common-wealth, may not lawfully have fupremacy of power alfo over the
the Church, that is to fay, fo far as to order thereby and to difpofe of fpiritual affairs,fo far as the higheft uncommandedCommander in them. Whereupon it is grown a queftion, whether Government Ecclefiafticall, and
power of Dominion in fuch degrees as the Law of this Land do grant unto
the Soveraign Governour thereof, may by the faid fupream Governour lawfully be enjoyd and held : For refolution wherein we are, Firft, to define
what the power of dominion is. Secondly, then to fhew by what right.
Thirdly, after what fort. Fourthly, in what meafure. Fiftly, in
what inconvenieny. According to whofe example Chriftian Kings may
have it. And when thefe generals are opened,to examine afterwards how
lawfull that is which we in regard of Dominion do attribute unto our own :
namely, the title of headfhip over the Church,fo far as the bounds of this
Kingdome do reach. Secondly,the Prerogative of calling and diffolving great
affemblies, about fpiritual affairs publick. Thirdly, the right of affenting
unto all thofe orders concerning Religion, which muft after be in force
as Law. Fourthly, the advancement of Principal Church Governours to
their roomes of Prelacy. Fifthly, judical authority higher then others are capable of. And fixthly, exemption from being punifhable with fuch kind of
Cenfures as the platform of Reformation doth teach, that they ought to be
fubjeſt unto.

What the Power of Dominion is.

Luke 24.
1 Cor.14.

Without order there is no living in publike Society, becaufe the want
thereof is the mother of confufion, whereupon divifion of neceffity
followeth, and out of divifion, deftruſtion. The Apoftle therefore giving
inftruſtion to publike Societies, requireth that all things be orderly done :
Order can have no place in things, except it be fettled amongft the perfons
that fhall by office be converfant about them. And if things and perfons be
ordered, this doth imply that they are diftinguifhed by degrees. For order
is a graduall difpofition : The whole world confifting of parts fo many, fo
different, is by this only thing upheld ; he which framed them hath fet them
in order : The very Deity it felf both keepeth and requireth for ever this to
be kept as a Law, that wherefoever there is a coaugmentation of many, the
loweft be knit unto the higeft, by that which being interjacent, may caufe
each to cleave to the other, and fo all to continue one. This order of things
and perfons in publike Societies,is the work of Policie,and the proper inftrument thereof in every degree in power, power being that hability which
we have of our felves, or receive from others for performance of any aſtion.
If the aſtion which we have to perform be converfant about matters of mear
Religion, the power of performing it is then fpiritual; And if that power be
fuch as hath not any other to over-rule it, we term it Dominion, or Power
Supream;fo far as the bounds thereof extend. When therefore Chriftian Kings
are faid to have Spiritual Dominion or Supream Power in Ecclefiaftical affairs and caufes, the meaning is, that within their own Precinſts and Territories,they have an authority and power to command even in matters of Chriftian Religion, and that there is no higher nor greater that can in thofe cafes
overcommand them,where they are placed to raign as Kings. But withal we
muft likewife note that their power is termed fupremacy, as being the higheft,
not fimply without exception of any thing. For what man is fo brain-fick,
as not to except in fuch fpeeches God himfelf the King of all Dominion ?
who doubteth, but that the King who receiveth it, muft hold it of, and order the Law according to that old axiome, *Attribuat Rex legi, quod lex attribuit
ei poteftatem :* And againe, *Rex non debet effe fub homine, fed fub deo & lege.*
Thirdly, whereas it is altogether without reafon, *That Kings are judged to have
by vertue of their Dominion, although greater power then any,yet not then all the ftate
of thofe Societies conjoyned,wherein fuch Soveraign rule is given them,*there is not any
thing hereunto to the contrary by us affirmed, no not when we grant
fupream

fupream Authority unto Kings;becaufe Supremacy is not otherwife intended or meant to exclude partly forraign powers, and partly the power which belongeth in feveral unto others, contained as parts in that publick body over which thofe Kings have Supremacy ; *Where the King hath power of Dominion, or Supream power, there no forrain State, or Potentate, no State or Potentate Domeftical, whether it confifteth of one or many, can poffibly have in the fame affairs and caufes Authority higher then the King.* Power of Spiritual Dominion, therefore is in caufes Ecclefiaftical that ruling Authority, which neither any forraign State, nor yet any part of that politick body at home, wherein the fame is eftablifhed, can lawfully over-rule. It hath been declared already in general, how *the beft eftablifhed dominion is, where the Law doth moft rule the King;* the true effect whereof particularly is found as well in Ecclefiaftical as civil affairs : In thefe the King, through his Supream Power, may do fundry great things himfelf, both appertaining to Peace and War, both at home, and by command, and by commerce with States abroad, becaufe the Law doth fo much permit. Sometimes on the other fide, *The King alone hath no right to do without confent of his Lords and Commons in Parliament : The King himfelf cannot change the nature of Pleas, nor Courts, no not fo much as reftore blood;* becaufe the Law is a bar unto him ; the pofitive Laws of the Realm have a priviledge therein, and reftrain the Kings Power ; which pofitive Laws, whether by cuftom or otherwife eftablifhed without repugnancy to the Laws of God, and nature, ought not lefs to be in force even in fupernatural affairs of the Church, whether in regard of Ecclefiaftical Laws, we willingly embrace that of *Ambrofe, Imperator bonus intra Ecclefiam, non fupra Ecclefiam eft. Kings have Dominion to exercife in Ecclefiaftical caufes, but according to the Laws of the Church;* whether it be therefore the nature of Courts, or the form of Pleas, or the kind of Governours, or the order of proceeding in whatfoever bufinefs, for the received Laws and Liberty of the Church, *The King hath Supream Authority and power, but againft them never;* What fuch pofitive Laws hath appointed to be done by others then the King, or by others with the King, and in what form they have appointed the doing of it, the fame of neceffity muft be kept ; neither is the Kings fole Authority to alter it ; yet as it were a thing unreafonable, if in civil affairs the King, albeit the whole univerfal body did joyn with him, fhould do any thing by their abfolute power for the ordering of their ftate at home, in prejudice of thofe antient Laws of Nations, which are of force throughout all the World, becaufe the neceffary commerce of Kingdomes dependeth on them : So in principal matters belonging to Chriftian Religion, a thing very fcandalous and offenfive it muft needs be thought, if either Kings or Lawes fhould difpofe of the Law of God, without any refpect had unto that which of old hath been reverently thought of throughout the World, and wherein there is no Law of God which forceth us to fwerve from the wayes wherein fo many and holy Ages have gone : Wherefore not without good confideration, the very Law it felf hath provided, *That Judges Ecclefiaftical appointed under the Kings Commiffion, fhal not adjudge for herefie any thing but that which heretofore hath been adjudged by the Authority of the Canonical Scriptures, or by the firft four general Councels, or by fome other general Council, wherein the fame hath been declared herefie, by the exprefs words of the faid Canonical Scriptures, or fuch as hereafter fhal be determined to be herefie by the high Court of Parliament of this Realm, with the affent of the Clergy in the Convocation, Ann.* 1. *Reg. Eliz.* By which words of the Law, who doth not plainly fee, how that in one branch of proceeding by vertue of the Kings Supream Authority, the credit which thofe four firft general Councels have throughout all Churches, and evermore had, was judged by the making of the forefaid Act a juft caufe wherefore they fhould be mentioned in that cafe, as a requifite part of that rule wherewith Dominion was to be limited. But of this we fhal further confider, when we come unto that which Soverain Power may do in making Ecclefiaftical Laws.

Unto which Supream Power in Kings, two kinds of adverfaries there of adverfaries there are which have oppofed themfelves: one fort defending that *Supream power in caufes Ecclefiaftical throughout the world, appertaineth of Divine Right to the Bifhop of Rome*: Another fort, *That the faid Power belongeth in every National Church unto the Clergy thereof affembled*. We which defend

The Right which men gives, God ratifies.

as well againft the one, as againft the other, *That Kings within their own Precincts may have it*, muft fhew by what right it muft come unto them. Firft, unto me, it feemeth almoft out of doubt & controverfie, that every independent multitude before any certain form of Regiment eftablifhed, hath under God Supream Authority, full Dominion over it felf, even as a man not tyed with the band of fubjection as yet unto any other, hath over himfelf the like power. God creating mankind, did endue it naturally with power to guide it felf, in what kind of Society foever he fhould chufe to live. A man which is born Lord of himfelf, may be anothers fervant. And that power which naturally whole focieties have, may be derived unto many, few, or one; under whom the reft fhall then live in fubjection : Some multitudes are brought into fubjection by force, as they who being fubdued, are fain to fubmit their necks unto what yoak it pleafeth their Conquerors to lay upon them; which Conquerors by juft and lawful Wars do hold their Power over fuch multitudes, as a thing defcending unto them; Divine Providence it felf fo difpofing. For it is God who giveth victory in the day of War, and unto whom Dominion in this fort is derived, the fame they enjoy according to the Law of Nations; which Law authorizeth Conquerours to reign as abfolute Lords over them whom they vanquifh. Sometimes it pleafeth God himfelf by

*Corona eft poteftas delegata a deo.*Bracton

fpecial appointment to chufe out and nominate fuch, as to whom Dominion fhall be given; which thing he did often in the Common-wealth of *Ifrael* : They which in this fort receive power immediately from God, have it by meer Divine Right; they by humane, on whom the fame is beftowed, according to mens difcretion, when they are left freely by God to make choice of their own Governours. By which of thefe means foever it happen, that Kings or Governours be advanced unto their Eftates, we muft acknowledge both their lawful choice to be approved of God, and themfelves to be Gods Lieutenants; and confeffe their Power which they have to be his. As for Supream Power in Ecclefiaftical affairs, the Word of God doth no where appoint that all Kings fhould have it, neither that any fhould not have it; for which caufe, it feemeth to ftand altogether by humane Right, that unto Chriftian Kings there is fuch Dominion given.

Again, on whom the fame is beftowed at mens difcretions, they likewife do hold it by Divine Right: If God in his revealed Word, hath appointed fuch Power to be, although himfelf extraordinarily beftow it not, but leave the appointment of perfons to men; yea, albeit God do neither appoint nor affign the perfon : neverthelefle, when men have affigned and eftablifhed both, who doth doubt but that fundry duties and affairs depending thereupon are prefcribed by the Word of God, and confequently by that very right to be exacted? for example fake, the power which *Romane* Emperours had over foreign Provinces, was not a thing which the Law of God did ever Inftitute: Neither was *Tiberius Cæfar* by efpecial commiffion, from Heaven therewith invefted, and yet paiment of Tribute unto *Cæfar* being now made Emperour, is the plain Law of Jefus Chrift: unto Kings by humane Right, honour by very Divine Right, is due; mans Ordinances, are many times propofed as grounds in the Statutes of God: And therefore of what kind foever the means be, whereby Governours are lawfully advanced to their States, as we by the Laws of God ftand bound meekly to acknowledge them for Gods Lieutenants; and to confeffe their Power his: So by the fame Law they are both authorized, and required to ufe that Power as far as it may be in any State available to his honour. The Law appointeth no man to be a husband; but if a man hath betaken himfelf unto that condition, it giveth him power and authority over his own wife. That the Chriftian world fhould be ordered by the Kingly Regiment, the Law of God doth not any where command : and yet the Law of God doth

give

give them, which once are exalted unto that place of Estate, right to exact at
the hands of their Subjects general obedience in whatsoever affairs their power may serve to command, and God doth ratifie works of that Soveraign Authority, which Kings have received by men. This is therefore the right whereby Kings do hold their power; but yet in what sort the same doth rest & abide
in them, it somewhat behoveth further to search, where that we be not enforced to make overlarge discourses about the different conditions of Soveraign or Supream Power; that which we speak of Kings, shall be in respect of
the State, and according to the nature of this Kingdom, where the people are
in no subjection, but such as willingly themselves have condescended unto
for their own most behoof and security. In Kingdoms therefore of this quality, the highest Governour hath indeed universal Dominion, but with dependency upon that whole entire body, over the several parts whereof he hath
Dominion: so that it standeth for an axiome in this case; The King is *Major
singulis, universis minor.* The Kings dependency, we do not construe as some have
done, who are of opinion that no mans birth can make him a King, but
every particular person advanced to such Authority, hath at his entrance
into his Raign, the same bestowed on him as an estate in condition by the
voluntary deed of the people, in whom it doth lie to put by any one, and to
prefer some other before him, better liked of or judged fitter for the place,
and that the party so rejected hath no injury done unto him; no although
the same be done in a place where the Crown doth go *μία διαδοχή* by succession,
and to a person which is capital and hath apparently if blood be respected the
nearest right. They plainly affirm in all well appointed Kingdoms, the custom
evermore hath been, and is, that children succeed not their Parents, till the
people after a sort have created them anew, neither that they grow to their   *Junius Brutus*
Fathers as natural and proper Heirs, but are then to be reckoned for Kings,   *vindic. pag. 83*
when at the hands of such as represent the Kings Majesty, they have by a Scepter and a Diadem received, as it were, the investure of Kingly power: Their very words are, *That where such power is setled into a family or kindred, the stock it self
is thereby chosen, but not the twig that springeth of it. The next of the stock unto him*   *pag. 85.*
*that raigneth, are not through nearnesse of bloud made Kings, but rather set forth
to stand for the Kingdom; where Regal Dominion is hereditary, it is notwithstanding
(if we look to the persons which have it) altogether elective.* To this purpose
are selected heaps of Scriptures concerning the Solemn Coronation or Inauguration of *Saul,* of *David,* of *Solomon,* and others, by the Nobles, Ancients,
and people of the Common-weal of *Israel;* as if these solemnities were a
kind of deed, whereby the right of Dominion is given, with strange, untrue,
and unnatural conceits, set abroad by seeds-men of Rebellion, onely to animate unquiet spirits, and to feed them with possibility of aspiring to Thrones,
if they can win the hearts of the people, what hereditary title soever any o-
ther before them may have. I say unjust and insolent positions, I would not
mention, were it not thereby to make the countenance of truth more orient;
for unless we will openly proclaim defiance unto all law, equity, and reason,
we must (there is no remedy) acknowledge, that in kingdoms hereditary,
birth giveth right unto Soveraign Dominion; and the death of the predecessour putteth the successor by blood in seisin. Those publique solemnities before
specified, do but serve for an open testification of the inheritours right, or
belong unto the form of inducting him into possession of that thing he
hath right unto: therefore, in case it doth happen, that without right of blood
a man in such wise be possessed, all these new elections and investings are utterly void; they make him no indefeasable estate, the inheritour by blood
may dispossesse him as an usurper. The case thus standing, albeit we judge it a
thing most true, that Kings, even inheritours, do hold their right in the
Power of Dominion, with dependency upon the whole body politique, over
which they have Rule as Kings; yet so it may not be understood as if
such dependency did grow, for that every supream Governour doth personally take from thence his power by way of gift, bestowed of their own

B bb   free

free accord upon him at the time of his entrance into the said place of his soveraign Government. But the cause of dependency is that first Original conveyance, when power was derived from the whole into one ; to passe from *Tuily de Offic.3* him unto them, whom out of him nature by lawful births should produce, and no natural or legal inability make uncapable : *Neither can any man with reason think, but that the first institution of Kings, a sufficient consideration wherefore their power should alwayes depend on that from which it did alwayes flow, by Original influence of power, from the body into the King, is the cause of Kings dependency in Power upon the body.* By dependency we mean subordination and subjection : A manifest token of which dependency may be this; as there is no more certain Argument, that lands are held under any as Lords, then if we see that such lands in defect of heirs fall unto them by escheat : In like manner it doth follow rightly, that seeing Dominion when there is none to inherit it, returneth unto the body; therefore, they which before were inheritours thereof, did hold it with dependency upon the body; so that by comparing the body with the head, as touching power, it seemeth alwayes to reside in both; fundamentally and radically in the one, in the other derivatively ; in the one the habit, in the other the Act of Power. May a body politique then at all times, withdraw in whole or in part the influence of Dominion which passeth from it, if inconveniences do grow thereby? It must be presumed, that supream Governours will not in such case oppose themselves, and be stiff in detaining that, the use whereof is with publique detriment: but surely without their consent I see not how the body by any just means should be able to help it self, saving when Dominion doth escheat; such things therefore must be thought upon before hand, that Power may be limited ere it be granted, which is the next thing we are to consider.

In what Measure.

IN power of Dominion, all Kings have not an equal latitude : Kings by conquest make their own Charter; so, that how large their power, either Civil or Spiritual, is, we cannot with any certainty define further, then onely to set them in the line of the Law of God and Nature for bounds. Kings by Gods own special appointment, have also that largenesse of power which he doth assign or permit with approbation touching Kings which were first instituted by agreement and composition made with them over whom they raign, how far their power may extend ; the Articles of compact between them is to shew not onely the Articles of Compact at the first beginning, which for the most part are either clean worn out of knowledge, or else known to very few; but whatsoever hath been after in free & voluntary manner condiscended unto, whether by expresse consent, (whereof positive laws are witnesses,) or else by silent allowance, famously notified through custome, reaching beyond the me-
Arist. Pol. lib. 3. Cap. 1. mory of man. By which means of after agreement, it cometh many times to passe in Kingdoms, that they whose ancient predecessours were by violence and force made subject, do by little and little grow into that sweet form of Kingly Government, which Philosophers define, *Regency willingly sustained, and indued with Chiefty of power in the greatest things.* Many of the ancients in their writings do speak of Kings with such high and ample tearms, as if universality of Power, even in regard of things and not of persons, did appertain to the very being of a King : The reason is, because their speech concerning Kings, they frame according to the state of those Monarchs, to whom unlimited authority was given ; which some not observing, imagine, that all Kings, even in that they are Kings, ought to have whatsoever power they judge any Soveraigne Ruler lawfully to have enjoyed. But the most judicious Philosopher, whose eye scarce any
Pythagoras : pud Erlant, de Regne. things did escape which was to be found in the bosom of nature, he considering how far the power of one Soveraign Ruler may be different from another regal authory, noteth in *Spartan Kings, that of all others they were most tyed to Law, and so the most restrained power.* A King wch hath not supream power in the greatest things, is rather entituled a King, then invested with real Soveraignty. We
cannot

cannot properly term him a King, of whom it may not be said, at the least wise, as touching certain the chiefest affairs of the State, *ἀἶχεν ἀρχὴς ἴνω ἰσμὸς*, his right in them is to have rule, nor subject to any other predominancy. I am not of opinion that simply in Kings the most, but the best limited power is best, both for them and the people: the most limited is that which may deal in fewest things: the best, that which in dealing is tyed unto the soundest, perfectest, and most indifferent Rule, which Rule is the Law: I mean not onely the Law of Nature, and of God; but the National law consonant thereunto. *Happier that people whose Law is their King in the greatest things, then that whose King is himself their Law : where the King doth guide the State, and the Law the King, that Common-wealth is like an Harp or Mellodious Instrument, the strings whereof are turned and handled all by one hand, following as Laws, the Rules and Canons of Musical Science.* Most Divinely therefore *Archytas* maketh unto publique felicity these four steps and degrees, every of which doth spring from the former as from another cause, *ὁ ᾗ βασιλεὺς ὑμνῶς, ὁ ᾗ ἄρχων ἀκλωθὸς, ὁ ᾗ ἀρχήμενῶς ἀκλωθῶς ὁ ᾗ ἐλα χωρώσα ἰνδαλμων.* *The King ruling by Law, the Magistrate following, the Subject free, and the whole society happy.* Adding on the contrary side, that where this order is not, it cometh by transgression thereof to passe that a King groweth a Tyrant; he that ruleth under him abhoreth to be guided by him or commanded; the people subject unto both, have freedom under neither; and the whole community is wretched. In which respect, I cannot chuse but commend highly their wisdom, by whom the Foundations of the Common-wealth hath been laid; wherein, though no manner of Person, or cause be unsubject unto the Kings Power, yet so is the Power of the King over all, and in all limited, that unto all his proceedings the Law it self is a rule. The Axiomes of our Regal Government are these, *Lex facit Regem* : The Kings grant of any favour made contrary to Law, is void. *Rex nihil potest nisi quod jure potest* : Our Kings therefore, when they are to take possession of the Crown they are called unto, have it pointed out before their eyes, even by the very solemnities and rites of their inauguration, to what affairs by the same Law their Supream Power and Authority reacheth; Crowned we see they are, enthronized and annointed; the Crown a sign of a Military Dominion ; the Throne of Sedentary or Judicial ; the Oyl of Religious and Sacred Power. It is not on any side denyed, that Kings may have Authority in secular affairs. The question then is, *What power they may lawfully have, and exercise in causes of God. A Prince, or Magistrate, or a Community,* (saith Doctor *Stapleton*) *may have power to lay corporal punishment on them which are teachers of perverse things ; power to make Laws for the Peace of the Church : Power to Proclaim, to Defend, and even by revenge to preserve dogmata the very Articles of Religion themselves from violation.* Others in affection no lesse devoted unto the Papacy, do likewise yield, that the Civil Magistrate may by his Edicts and Laws keep all Ecclesiastical Persons within the bounds of their duties, and constrain them to observe the Canons of the Church, to follow the rule of ancient Discipline. That if *Joash* was commended for his care and provision concerning so small a part of Religion, as the Church treasure; it must needs be both unto Christian Kings themselves greater honour, and to Christianity a larger benefit, when the custody of Religion, and the Worship of God in general is their charge. If therefore all these things mentioned be most properly the affairs of Gods Ecclesiastical causes; if the actions specified be works of power ; and if that power be such as Kings may use of themselves, without the fear of any other power superiour in the same thing; it followeth necessarily, that Kings may have Supream power, not only in Civil, but also in Ecclesiastical affairs; & consequently, that they may withstand what Bishop, or Pope soever shall under the pretended claim of higher Spiritual Authority, oppose themselves against their proceedings. But they which have made us the former grant, will never hereunto condescend; what they yield that Princes may do, it is with secret exception always understood, if the Bishop of *Rome* give leave, if he enterpose no prohibition; wherefore, somewhat it is in shew, in truth nothing which they grant. Our own

Stapl. do Do. Princip. lib. 5, 6. 17.

Reor-

T. C. l. 1. p. 192.

mers do the very like, when they make their difcourfe in general, concerning the Authority which Magiftrates may have, a man would think them to be far from withdrawing any jot of that, which with reafon may be thought due. *The Prince and Civil Magiftrate (faith one of them) hath to fee the Laws of God, touching his Worfhip, and touching all Matters, and all Orders of the Church to be executed, and duly obferved; and to fee every Ecclefiaftical Perfon do that office, whereunto he is appointed; and to punifh thofe which fail in their office accordingly.* A-

Farmers def. of the God's Magiftrate.

nother acknowledgeth, *That the Magiftrate may lawfully uphold all truth by his Sword, punifh all perfons, enforce all to their duties towards God and men; Maintain by his Laws, every point of Gods Word, punifh all vice in all men; fee into all caufes, vifit the Ecclefiaftical Eftate, and correct the abufes thereof: Finally to look to his Subjects, that under him they may lead their lives in all godlineffe and honefty.* A

Humble moti-on, page 63.

third more frankly protefteth, *That in cafe their Church Difcipline were eftablifh-ed, fo little it fhortneth the Arms of Soveraign Dominion in caufes Ecclefiaftical, that Her Gracious Majefty for any thing they teach or hold to the contrary, may no leffe then now remain ftill over all perfons, in all things Supream Governeffe; even with that full and Royal Authority, Superiority, and Preheminence, Supremacy, and Prerogative, which the Laws already eftablifhed do give her; and her Majefties Injunctions, and the Articles of the Convocation houfe, and other writings Apologetical of her Royal Au-*

Cicero, lib. 1. de nat. Deor.

thority, and fupream Dignity, do declare and explain. Poffidonius was wont to fay of the Empicure, *That he thought there were no Gods, but that thofe things which he fpake concerning the Gods, were onely given out for fear of growing odious amongft men: and therefore that in words he left Gods remaining, but in very deed overthrew them, in fo much as he gave them no kind of Action.* After the very felf fame manner, when we come unto thofe particular effects, Prerogatives of Dominion which the Laws of this Land do grant unto the Kings thereof, it will appear how thefe men, notwithftanding their large and liberal Speeches, abate fuch parcels out of the afore alleadged grant and flourifhing fhew, that a man comparing the one with the other, may half ftand in a doubt, leaft their Opinion in very truth be againft that Authority, which by their Speeches they feem mightily to uphold, partly for the voiding of pub-like obloquie, envie and hatred, partly to the intent they may both in the end by the eftablifhment of their Difcipline, extinguifh the force of Supream Power, which Princes have, and yet in the mean while, by giving forth thefe fmooth Difcourfes, obtain that their favourers may have fomewhat to alleadge for them by way of Apologie, and that fuch words onely found towards all kind of fulneffe of Power. But for my felf, I had rather con-ftrue fuch their contradictions in the better part, and impute their general acknowledgment of the lawfulneffe of Kingly Power, unto the force of truth, prefenting it felf before them fometimes above their particular con-trarieties, oppofitions, denyals, unto that errour which having fo fully poffeft their minds, cafteth things inconvenient upon them; of which things in their due place. Touching that which is now in hand, we are on all fides fully agreed, Firft, that there is not any reftraint or limitation of matter for regal Authority and Power to be converfant in, but of Religion onely; and of whatfoever caufe thereunto appertaineth Kings may lawfully have charge, they lawfully may therein exercife Dominion, and ufe the temporal Sword.

Kind.

Secondly, that fome kind of actions converfant about fuch affairs are denyed unto Kings: As namely, Actions of Power and Order, and of Spiritual Jurifdiction, which hath with it infeparably joyned Power to Adminifter the Word and Sacraments, power to Ordain, to Judge as an Ordinary, to bind

By what Rule.

and loofe, to Excommunicate, and fuch like. Thirdly, that even in thofe very actions, which are proper unto Dominion, there muft be fome certain rule whereunto Kings in all their proceedings ought to be ftrictly tyed; which rule for proceeding in Ecclefiaftical affairs and caufes by Regal Power, hath not hitherto been agreed upon with fuch uniform confent, and certain-ty as might be wifhed. The different fentences of men herein I will now go about to examine, but it fhall be enough to propofe what Rule doth feem in this cafe moft reafonable. The

The case of deriving Supream Power from a whole intire multitude into some special part thereof; as partly the necessity of expedition in publick affaires, partly the inconvenience of confusion and trouble, where a multitude of equals dealeth; and partly the dissipation which must needs ensue in companies, where every man wholly seeketh his own particular (as we all would do even with other mens hurts) and haply the very overthrow of themselves, in the end also; if for the procurement of the common good of all men, by keeping every several man in order, some were not invested with Authority over all, and encouraged with Prerogative honour to sustain the weighty burthen of that charge. The good which is proper unto each man belongeth to the common good of all, as part to the whole perfection; but these two are things different; for men by that which is proper, are severed; united they are by that which is common; Wherefore, besides that which moveth each man in particular to seek his private, there must be of necessity in all publick Societies also a general mover, directing unto common good, and framing every mans particular unto it. The end whereunto all Government was instituted, was *Bonum publicum, the Universal or Common good.* Our question is of Dominion, for that end and purpose derived into one; such as all in one publick State have agreed, that the Supream charge of all things should be committed unto one: They I say, considering what inconveniency may grow, where States are subject unto sundry Supream Authorities, have for fear of these inconveniencies withdrawn from liking to establish many; *ἐκ ἀγαθῶν πολυκοιρανίη,* the multitude of Supream Commanders is troublesome. *No man* (saith our Saviour) *can serve two Masters*; surely, two supream Masters would make any ones service somewhat uneasie in such cases as might fall out. Suppose that to morrow the Power which hath Dominion in Justice, require thee at the Court; that which in War, at the Field; that which in Religion at the Temple; all have equal Authority over thee; and impossible it is, that then in such case thou shouldst be obedient unto all: By chusing any one whom thou wilt obey, certain thou art for thy disobedience to incur the displeasure of the other two.

Ob utilitatem publicam reip. per unum con-, sult. opereue, prudentissimi docent. I. C. 11. F. de origine juris. Civilis.

But there is nothing for which some comparable reason or other may not be found; are we able to shew any commendable state of Government, which by experience and practice hath felt the benefit of being in all causes subject unto the Supream Authority of one? against the policy of the *Israelites,* I hope there will no man except, where *Moses* deriving so great a part of his burthen in Government unto others, did notwithstanding retain to himself Universal Supremacy; *Jehosaphat* appointing one to be chosen in the affairs of God, and another in the Kings affaires, did this as having Dominion over them in both. If therefore from approbation of Heaven, the Kings of Gods own chosen people had in the affaires of Jewish Religion Supream Power, why not Christian Kings the like, also in Christian Religion? First, unlesse men will answer as some have done, *That the Jews Religion was of far lesse perfection and dignity then ours, ours being that truth whereof theirs was but a shadowish perfigurative resemblance.* Secondly, *That all parts of their Religion, their Laws, their Sacrifices, and their Rights and Ceremonies, being fully set down to their hands, and needing no more, but only to be put in execution; the Kings might well have highest Authority to see that done; whereas with us, there are a number of Mysteries even in belief, which were not so generally for them, as for us necessary to be with sound expresse acknowledgement understood: A number of things belonging to external Government, and our manner of serving God, not set down by particular Ordinances, and delivered to us in writing, for which cause the State of the Church doth now require, that the Spiritual Authority of Ecclesiastical persons be large, absolute and not subordinate to Regal power.* Thirdly, *That whereas God armeth Religion Jewish as Temporal Christian with the sword; But of Spiritual punishment, the one with power to imprison, to scourge, to put to death: The other with bare authority to Censure and Excommunicate: There is no reason that the Church which hath no visible sword, should in Regiment be subject unto any other power, then only unto theirs which have authority to bind and loose.* Fourthly, *that albeit whilst the Church was*

According to what exam- Fl:.

Stapl. de prin: Doct.pag.197. Stapl. ib.

Idem ib.

was

was reſtrained into one people, it ſeemed not incommodious to grant their King the general Chiefty of Power; yet now the Church having ſpread it ſelf over all Nations, great inconveniences muſt thereby grow, if every Chriſtian King in his ſeveral Territory, ſhould have the like power. Of all theſe differences, there is not one which doth prove it a thing repugnant to the Law, either of God, or of nature, that all ſupremacie of external power be in Chriſtian Kingdoms granted unto Kings thereof, for preſervation of quietneſſe, unity, order, and peace, in ſuch manner as hath been ſhewed.

Of the Title of Headſhip.

FOr the Title or State it ſelf, although the Laws of this Land have annexed it to the Crown, yet ſo far we ſhould not ſtrive, if ſo be men were nice and ſcrupulous in this behalf only; becauſe they do wiſh that for reverence to Chriſt Jeſus, the Civil Magiſtrate did rather uſe ſome other form of ſpeech wherewith to expreſſe that Sovereign Authority which he lawfully hath over all, both perſons and cauſes of the Church. But I ſee that hitherto they which condemn utterly the names ſo applyed, do it becauſe they miſlike that ſuch power ſhould be given to Civil Governours. The great exception that Sir *Thomas Moor* took againſt that Title, who ſuffered death for denyal of it, was, *for that it maketh a Lay, a ſecular perſon, the head of the State Spiritual or Eccleſiaſtical*; as though God himſelf did not name *Saul*, the Head of all the Tribes of *Iſrael*; and conſequently of that Tribe alſo among the reſt, whereunto the State Spiritual or Eccleſiaſtical belonged; when the Authors of the Centuries reprove it in Kings and Civil Governours, the reaſon is, *Iſtis non competit iſte primatus*; ſuch kind of power is too high for them, they fit it not: In excuſe of Mr. *Calvin* by whom this Realm is condemned of blaſphemy, for intituling, *H.8. Supream Head of this Church under Chriſt*, a charitable conjecture is made, that he ſpake by miſ-information; howbeit as he profeſſeth utter diſlike of that name, ſo whether the name be uſed or no, the very power it ſelf which we give unto Civil Magiſtrates, he much complaineth of, and proteſteth, *That their Power over all things was it which had ever wounded him deeply: That unadviſed perſons had made them too ſpiritual, that throughout Germany this fault did raign, that in thoſe very parts where* Calvin *himſelf was, it prevailed more then was to be wiſhed, that Rulers by imagining themſelves ſo ſpiritual, have taken away Eccleſiaſtical Government, that they think they cannot raign unleſſe they aboliſh all the Authority of the Church, and be themſelves the chief Judges, as well in Doctrine as in the whole ſpiritual regency.* So that in truth, the queſtion is whether the Magiſtrate by being Head in ſuch ſence as we term him, do uſe or exerciſe any part of that Authority, not which belongeth unto Chriſt, but which other men ought to have.

These things being firſt conſidered thus, it will be eaſier to judge concerning our own eſtate, whether by force of Eccleſiaſtical Government, Kings have any other kind of Prerogative then they may lawfully hold and enjoy. It is as ſome do imagine, too much, that Kings of *England* ſhould be termed Heads in relation to the Church. That which we do underſtand by *Headſhip*, is their only Supream Power in Eccleſiaſtical affairs and cauſes; that which lawful Princes are, what ſhould make it unlawful for men in ſpiritual Stiles or Titles to ſignifie? If the having of Supream Power be allowed, why is the expreſſing thereof by the Title of *Head*, condemned? They ſeem in words, (at leaſtwiſe ſome of them) now at the length to acknowledge, that Kings may have Dominion or Supream Government even over all, both perſons and cauſes. We in terming our Princes *Heads of the Church*, do but teſtifie that we acknowledge them ſuch Governours. Again to this, it will peradventure Replyed, *That whoſoever we interpret our ſelves, it is not fit for a mortal man, and therefore not fit for a Civil Magiſtrate to be intituled the Head of the Church, which was given to our Saviour Chriſt to lift him above all Powers, Rules, Dominions, Titles, in Heaven or in Earth. Where if this Title belong alſo to Civil Magiſtrates, then it is manifeſt that there is a power in Earth whereunto our Saviour Chriſt is not*

Roſſenſis
Epiſt. pag.
5 17.
Pref. cent. 7.
Calvin in
com. 7.
Amos 7. 13.

T. C. lib. 2.
page 411.

in this point superiour. Again, if the Civil Magistrate may have this title, he may be Ephes. 1.21.
termed also the first begotten of all creatures. The first begotten of all the dead, yea Col. 1. 18.
the Redeemer of his people. For these are alike given him as dignities whereby he is
lifted up above all creatures. Besides this, the whole argument of the Apostle in both
places doth lead to shew that this title, Head of the Church, cannot be said of any
creature. And further, the very demonstrative Articles among the Hebrews, espe-
cially whom St. Paul doth follow, serveth to tye that which is verified of one, unto
himself alone: so that when the Apostle doth say that Christ is ὁ κεφαλή, the head, it is
as if he should say, Christ, and none other is the head of the Church. Thus have
we against the entituling of the highest Magistrate, *head,* with relation unto
the Church, four several arguments gathered by strong surmise out of words
marvellous unlikely to have been written to any such purpose, as that whereunto they are now used and urged. To the *Ephesians,* the Apostle writeth, Ephes. 1. 20.
That Christ, God had set on his right hand in the Heavenly places above all Regency 21, 22, 23.
and Authority, and Power, and Dominion, and whatsoever name is named, not in
this world only, but in that which shall be also: and hath under his feet set all things,
and hath given him head above all things unto the Church which is his body, even the
fulnesse of him which accomplisheth all in all. To the Collosians in like manner,
That he is the head of the body of the Church, who is a first born Regency out of the dead, Col. 1, 18.
to the end he might be made amongst them all such an one as both the Chiefty: He mean- Col. 16.
eth amongst all them whom he mentioned before, saying, *By him all things that*
are, were made; the things in the Heavens, and the things in the Earth, the things
that are visible, and the things that are invisible, whether they be Thrones, or Dominions,
or Regencies &c. Unto the fore alleadged arguments therefore we an-
swer: First, that it is not simply the title of *Head,* in such sort understood, as
the Apostle himself meant it; so that the same being imparted in another sence
unto others, doth not any wayes make those others his equals; in as much as
diversity of things is usually to be understood, even when of words there is no
diversity; and it is only the adding of one and the same thing unto divers
persons, which doth argue equality in them. If I term Christ and *Ce'ar*
lords, yet this is no equalizing *Cesar* with Christ, because it is not thereby
intended: *To term the Emperour lord* (saith Tertullian) *I for my own part, will not*
refuse, so that I be not required to call him Lord in the same sence that God is so termed.
Neither doth it follow, which is objected in the second place, that if the Civil Magistrate may be intituled a *Head:* he may as well also be termed *the first*
begotten if all creatures, the first begotten of the dead, and the Redeemer of his people.
For albeit the former dignity doth lift him up no lesse then these, yet these
terms are not appliable and apt to signifie any other inferiour dignity, as the
former term of *head* was. The argument or matter which the Apostle followeth, hath small evidence or proof, that his meaning was to appropriate
unto Christ, that the aforesaid title, otherwise then only in such sence as doth
make it, being so understood, too high to be given to any creature.

As for the force of the Article where our Lord and Saviour is called *the*
Head, it serveth to tie that unto him by way of excellency, which in meaner degrees is common to others; it doth not exclude any other utterly
from being termed *Head,* but from being intituled as Christ is *the Head,*
by way of the very highest degree of excellency; not in the communication of names, but in the confusion of things there is errour. Howbeit,
if *Head* were a name that could not well be, nor never had been used to
signifie that which a Magistrate may be in relation to some Church; but
were by continual use of speech appropriated unto the only thing it signifieth, being applyed unto Jesus Christ, then although we must carry in
our selves a right understanding, yet ought we otherwise rather to speak,
unlesse we interpret our own meaning by some clause of plain speech, because we are else in manifest danger to be understood according to that
construction and sence, wherein such words are personally spoken. But
here the rarest construction and most removed from common sence, is
that which the word doth import being applyed unto Christ; that which
we

which we fignifie by it in giving it to the Magiftrate, is a great deal more familiar in the common conceit of men.

Efay. 7. 9.
Ickah is termed the head of Samaria.
The word is fo fit to fignifie all kinds of Superiority, Preheminence, and Chiefty, that nothing is more ordinary then to ufe it in vulgar fpeech, and in common underftanding fo to take it : If therefore Chriftian Kings may have any preheminence or chiefty above all other, although it be leffe then that which *Theodore Beza* giveth, who placeth Kings amongft the principal members, whereunto publick function, in the Church belongeth; and denieth nor, but that of them which have publick function, the civil Magiftrates power hath all the reft at command, in regard of that part of his office, which is to procure that peace and good order be efpecially kept in things concerning the firft Table; if even hereupon they term him the *Head of the Church*, which is *his Kingdom*, it fhould not feem fo unfit a thing ; which title furely we could not communicate to any other, no not although it fhould at our hands be exacted with torments : but that our meaning herein is made known to the World, fo that no man which will underftand can eafily be ignorant that we do not impart unto Kings when we term them *Heads*, the honour which is properly given to our Lord and Saviour Chrift, when the bleffed Apoftle in Scripture doth term him *the Head of the Church*.

The power which we fignifie in that name, differeth in three things plainly from that which Chrift doth challenge.

Ephef. 1. 21.
Firft, it differeth in order, becaufe God hath given to his Church for the head, ὑπὲρ πᾶσαν, ὑπὲρ ἄνω πᾶσαν ἀρχὴ: *Far above all principalities, and powers, and might, and dominion, and every name that is named, not in this World only, but alfo in that which is to come* : Whereas the power which others have, is fubordinate unto his.

Pfal. 2, 8.
Secondly, again, as he differeth in order, fo in meafure of power alfo ; becaufe God hath given unto him the ends of the Earth for his poffeffion: unto him, dominion from fea to fea, unto him all power both in Heaven and earth, unto him fuch fovereignty, as doth not only reach over all places, perfons, and things, but doth reft in his own only perfon, and is not by any fucceffion continued; he raigneth as Head and King, nor is there any kind of law which tieth him, but his own proper will and wifdom, his power is abfolute, the fame joyntly over all which it is feverally over each : not fo the power of any other Headfhip. How Kings are reftrained, and how their power is limited, we have fhewed before ; fo that unto him is given by the title of *Headfhip over the Church* that largeneffe of power, wherein neither man, nor angel, can be matched nor compared with him.

Thirdly, the laft and greateft difference between him and them, is in the very kind of their power. The Head being of all other parts of the body moft divine, hath dominion over all the reft ; it is the fountain of fence, of motion, the throne where the guide of the foul doth raign; the court from whence direction of all things humane proceedeth. Why Chrift is called *the Head of the Church*, thefe caufes themfelves do yield. As the Head is the chiefeft part of a man, above which there is none, alwayes joyned with the body; fo Chrift the higheft in his Church, is alwayes knit to it. Again as the head giveth fence and motion unto all the body, fo he quickneth us, and together with underftanding of heavenly things, giveth ftrength to walk therein : feeing therefore that they cannot affirm Chrift fenfibly prefent, or alwayes vifibly joyned unto his body the Church which is on earth, in as much as his corporal refidence is in heaven. Again, feeing they do not affirm (it were intolerable if they fhould) that Chrift doth perfonally adminifter the external Regiment of outward actions in the Church, but by the fecret inward influence of his grace, giveth fpiritual life, & the ftrength of ghoftly motions thereunto : Impoffible it is that they fhould fo clofe up their eyes, as not to difcern what odds there is between that kind of operation, which we imply in the *Headfhip* of Princes, and that which agreeth to our Saviours dominion over the Church. The *Headfhip* which we give unto Kings, is altogether vifibly exercifed,

cised, and ordereth only the external frame of the Church affairs here a-
mongst us; so that it plainly differeth from Christs, even in very nature and
kind. To be in such sort united unto the Church as he is, to work as he worketh, either on the whole Church or upon any particular assembly, or in any
one man, doth neither agree, nor hath any possibility of agreeing unto any
one besides him.

Against the first distinction or difference it is to be objected, *That to entitle a*
Magistrate head of the Church, although it be under Christ, is not absurd. For *T.C.l. 2. p.*
Christ hath a two-fold superiority over his, and over Kingdomes : according to the one, 411.
he hath a superiour, which is his Father ; according to the other, none but immediate
authority with his Father ; that is to say, of the Church he is head and governour only
as the sonne of man ; head and governour of Kingdomes onely as the Son of God.
In the Church, as man, he hath officers under him, which officers are Ecclesiastical *T.C.l. 1. p. 418*
persons : As for the Civil Magistrate, his office belongeth unto Kingdomes, and to
Common-wealths, neither is he there an under or subordinate head, considering that
his authority cometh from God, simply and immediately, even as our Saviour Christs
doth. Whereunto the summe of our answer is, First, that as Christ being Lord
or Head over all, doth by virtue of that Soveraignty rule all ; so he hath
no more a superiour in governing his Church, then in exercising soveraign
Dominion upon the rest of the world besides. Secondly, that all authority
as well Civil as Ecclesiastical, is subordinate unto him. And thirdly, the Civil Magistrate being termed head, by reason of that authority in Ecclesiastical affairs which hath been already declared, that themselves do in word acknowledge to be lawful : It followeth that he is a head even subordinated of
Christ, and to Christ. For more plain explication whereof, unto God we acknowledge daily that Kingdome, Power, and Glory are his; that he is the immortal and invisible King of ages, as well the future which shall be, as the present which now is. That which the Father doth work as Lord and King over
all, he worketh not without, but by the Sonne, who through coeternal generation, receiveth of the Father that power, which the Father hath of himself.
And for that cause our Saviours words concerning his own Dominion are;
To me all power both in Heaven and in Earth is given : The Father by the Sonne
did create, and doth guide all ; wherefore Christ hath supream Dominion
over the whole universal world. Christ is God, Christ is λόγος, the consubstantial word of God ; Christ is also that consubstantial word which made man.
As God, he saith of himself ; *I am Alpha and Omega, the beginning and* *Apoc. 1. 8.*
the end ; he which was, and which is, and which is to come ; even the very omnipotent.
As the consubstantial word of God, he hath with God before the beginning
of the world, that glory which as he was man, he requireth to have : *Father,* *John 17. 5.*
glorifie thy Son with that glory which with thee he enjoyed before the world was : Further it is not necessary, that all things spoken of Christ should agree to him,
either as God, or else as man; but some things as he is the consubstantial word
of God, some things as he is that word incarnate. The works of supream Dominion wch have been since the first beginning wrought by the power of the
Son of God, are now most properly and truly the works of the Son of man :
the word made flesh doth sit for ever, and raign as soveraign Lord over all. Dominion belongeth unto the Kingly office of Christ, as Propitiation and Me-dia-
tion unto his Priestly; Instruction, unto his pastoral and prophetical Office His
works of dominion are in sundry degrees and kinds, according to the different
conditions of them which are subject unto it; he presently doth govern ; and
hereafter shal judg the world, intire and wholly; & therefore his Regal power
cannot be with truth restrained unto a proportion of the world only. Notwithstanding, forasmuch as all do not shew and acknowledge with dutiful submission, that obedience which they owe unto him; therefore such as do their
Lord he is termed by way of excellency, no otherwise then the Apostle doth
term God the succour generally of all, but especially of the faithful; these being brought to the obedience of faith, are every where spoken of, as men
translated into that Kingdom, wherein whosoever is comprehended, Christ

is the Author of eternal falvation unto them; they have a high and ghoftly fellowfhip with God and Chrift, and Saints; or as the Apoftle in more ample manner fpeaketh, *Aggregated they are unto Mount Sion, and to the City of* Heb. 12.22. *the living God; the Celeftial Jerufalem, and to the company of innumerable Angels, and to the Congregation of the firft born, which are written in heaven, and to God the Judge of all, and to the Spirits of juft and perfect men, and to Jefus the Mediator of the new Teftament.* In a word, they are of that myftical, body, which we term the Church of Chrift. As for the reft we account them *Aliens from the Commonwealth of Ifrael, and that live in the kingdom of darkneffe, and that are in this prefent world without God.* Our Saviours Dominion is therefore over thefe as over rebels, over them as over dutiful and loving fubjects; which things being in holy Scriptures fo plain, I fomewhat mufe at the ftrange pofitions, that Chrift in the Government of his Church and Superiority over the Officers of it, hath himfelf a Superiour which is the Father: But in governing of Kingdoms and Common-wealths, and in the Superiority which he hath over Kingdoms, no Superiour.

T.C.lib.4.pag. 411. Again, *That the Civil Magiftrates Authority cometh from God immediately, as Chrifts doth, and is fubordinate unto Chrift.* In what Evangelift, Apoftle, or Prophet, is it found, that Chrift (Supream Governour of the Church) fhould be fo unequal to himfelf, as he is Supream Governour of Kingdoms ? The works of his providence for the prefervation of mankind, by upholding Kingdoms not onely obedient unto, but alfo obftinate and rebellious againft him, are fuch as proceed from Divine Power; and are not the works of his providence for fafety of Gods Elect, by gathering, infpiring, comforting, and every way preferving his Church, fuch as proceed from the fame power likewife ? furely if Chrift as God and man have ordained certain means for the gathering and keeping of his Church, feeing this doth belong to the Government of that Church; it muft in reafon follow I think, that as God and man, he worketh in Church Regiment, and confequently, hath no more there any Superiours, then in the Government of the Common-wealth. Again, to be in the midft of his, wherefoever they are affembled in his name, and to be with them to the worlds end, are comforts which Chrift doth perform to his Church as Lord and Governour; yea, fuch as he cannot perform but by that very Power wherein he hath no Superiour. Wherefore unleffe it can be proved that all the works of our Saviours Government in the Church are done by the meer and onely force of his humane nature, there is no remedy but to acknowledge it a manifeft error, that Chrift in the Government of the world is equal to the Father, but not in the government of the Church. Indeed to the honour of this Dominion, it cannot be faid that God did exalt him otherwife then onely according to that humane nature, wherein he was made low. For as the Son of God, there could no advancement or exaltation grow unto him: And yet the Dominion, whereunto he was in his humane nature lifted up, is not without Divine Power exercifed. It is by Divine Power that the Son of man who fitteth in heaven, doth work as King and Lord upon us which are on earth. The exercife of his Dominion over the Church Militant cannot chufe but ceafe, when there is no longer any Militant Church in the World. And therefore as Generals of Armies when they have finifhed their work, are wont to yield up fuch Commiffions as were given for that purpofe, and to remain in the ftate of fubjects and not as Lords, as concerning their former Authority; even fo when the end of all things is come, the Son of man (who till then reigneth) fhall do the like, as touching regiment over the Militant Church on the earth. So that between the Son of man and his brethren, over whom he reigneth now in this their warfare, there fhall be then as touching the exercife of that regiment no fuch difference; they not warfaring any longer under him, but he together with them under God, receiving the joys of everlafting triumph, that fo God may be all in all; all mifery in all the wicked through his Juftice; in all the righteous, through his love all felicity and bliffe. In the mean while he reigneth

over

over the World as King, and doth thofe things wherein none is fuperiour unto him, whether we refpect the works of his providence and Kingdom, or of his regiment over the Church; the caufe of errour in this point,
doth feem to have been a mifconceit that Chrift as Mediator, being inferiour to his Father, doth as Mediator, all works of regiment over the Church,
when in truth, regiment doth belong to his Kingly Office, Mediatorfhip to
his Prieftly; For as the High Prieft both offered Sacrifices, for expiation of
the peoples fins, and entred into the holy place, there to make intercelli- *T.C'.1.p.15.*
on for them: So Chrift having finifhed upon the Croffe that part of his Prieftly Office, which wrought the propitiation for our fins, did afterwards enter *Heb.9,25.*
into very heaven, and doth there as Mediator of the New Teftament, appear
in the fight of God for us. A like fleight of judgement it is, when they hold
that Civil Authority is from God, but not immediately through Chrift, nor
with any fubordination to God, nor doth any thing from God, but by the *Efay 7 25.*
hands of our Lord Jefus Chrift. They deny it not to be faid of Chrift in *Rom.13,1.*
the old Teftament, *By me Princes rule, and the Nobles, and all the Judges of* *Prov.8.15.*
the earth. In the new as much is taught, *That Chrift is the Prince of the Kings* Humble mo-
of the earth. Wherefore to the end it may more plainly appear how all Au- *Rom.1,5.*
thority of man is derived from God through Chrift, and muft by Chriftian
men be acknowledged to be no otherwife held then of, and under him; we are
to note that becaufe whatfoever hath neceffary being, the Son of God doth
caufe it to be, and thofe things without which the world cannot well continue, have neceffary being in the world: a thing of fo great ufe as Government, cannot chufe but be originally from him. Touching that Authority
which civil Magiftrates have in Ecclefiaftical affairs, it being from God by
Chrift, as all other good things are, cannot chufe but be held as a thing received at his hands; and becaufe fuch power is of neceffity for the ordering of Religion, wherein the effence and very being of the Church confifteth, can no
otherwife flow from him, then according to that fpecial care which he hath to
govern and guide his own people: it followeth that the faid Authority is of
and under him after a more fpecial manner, in that *he is Head of the Church,*
and not in refpect of his general Regency over the World. *All things* (faith 1 *Cor.3.11.*
the Apoftle fpeaking unto the Church) *are yours, and ye are Chrifts, and Chrift*
is Gods. Kings are Chrifts as Saints, becaufe they are of the Church, if not
Collectively, yet divifively underftood. It is over each particular perfon
within that Church where they are Kings; furely, Authority reacheth both
unto all mens perfons, and to all kinds of caufes alfo: It is not denyed, but that
they may have and lawfully exercife it; fuch Authority it is, for which and
for no other in the world we term them heads; fuch Authority they have under
Chrift, becaufe he in all things is Lord over all; and even of Chrift it is that
they have received fuch Authority, in as much as of him all lawful Powers
are; therefore the Civil Magiftrate is in regard of this Power, an under and
fubordinate Head of Chrifts people.

It is but idle where they fpeak, *That although for feveral companies of men T.C.l.p.413.*
there may be feverall Heads or Governours, differing in the meafure of their Autho-
rity from the chiefeft who is Head over all, yet feeing it cannot be in the Church,
for that the reafon why Head Magiftrates appoint others for fuch feveral places, is
becaufe they cannot be prefent every where to perform the Office of an Head. But
Chrift is never from his body, nor from any part of it, and therefore needeth not to
fubftitute any, which may be Heads, fome over one Church, and fome over another. Indeed the confideration of mans imbecillity, which maketh many heads neceffary, where the burthen is too great for one, moved *Jethro* to be a perfwader of
Mofes, that the number of Heads or Rulers might be inftituted for difcharge of
that duty by parts, which in whole he faw was troublefom. Now although there
be not in Chrift any fuch defect, or weaknefs, yet other caufes there be divers
more then we are able to fearch into. Wherefore it might feem unto him expedient to divide his Kingdom into many Provinces, and place many Heads
over it, that the power which each of them hath in particular with reftraint,

might

might illustrate the greatnesse of his unlimited Authority. Besides, howsoever Christ be Spiritually alwayes united unto every part of his body, which is the Church: Neverthelesse, we do all know, and they themselves who alledge this, will I doubt confesse also, that from every Church here visible, Christ touching visible and corporal presence, is removed as far as heaven from the earth is distant. Visible government is a thing necessary; for the Church and it doth not appear, how the exercise of visible government over such multitudes every where dispersed throughout the World should consist without sundry visible Governours, whose power being the greatest in that kind so far as it reacheth, they are in consideration thereof termed so far Heads. Wherefore notwithstanding the perpetual conjunction, by vertue whereof our Saviour alwayes remaineth spiritually united unto the parts of his mystical body; Heads indeed with supream power, extending to a certain compasse, are for the exercise of a visible regiment not unnecessary. Some other reasons there are belonging unto this branch, which seem to have been objected, rather for the exercise of mens wits, in dissolving Sophisms, then that the Authors of them could think in likelihood thereby to strengthen their cause. For example, *If the Magistrate be Head of the Church within his own Dominion, then is he none of the Church: For all that are of the Church make the body of Christ, and every one of the Church fulfilleth the place of one member of the body: By making the Magistrate therefore Head, we do exclude him from being a member subject to the Head, and so leave him no place in the Church.* By which reason the name of a body politick, is supposed to be alwayes taken of the inferiour sort alone, excluding the principal Guides and Governours, contrary to all mens customs of speech. The errour ariseth by misconceiving of some Scripture sentences, where Christ as the Head, and the Church as the body, are compared or opposed the one to the other. And because in such comparisons of oppositions, the body is taken for those onely parts which are subject unto the Head, they imagine that whoso is the Head of any Church, he is therefore even excluded from being a part of that Church; That the Magistrate can be none of the Church if so we make him the Head of the Church in his own Dominions : A chief and principal part of the Church therefore next this, is surely a strange conclusion. A Church doth indeed make the body of Christ being wholly taken together; and every one in the same Church fulfilleth the place of a member in the body, but not the place of an inferiour member, the which hath Supream Authority and Power over all the rest. Wherefore by making the Magistrate Head in his own Dominions, we exclude him from being a member subject unto any other person, which may visibly there rule in place of a Superiour or Head over him; but so far are we off from leaving him by this means no place in the Church that we do grant him the chief place. Indeed the Heads of those visible bodies, which are many, can be but parts inferiour in that Spiritual Body which is but one; yea, they may from this be excluded clean, who notwithstanding ought to be honoured, as possessing in order the highest rooms: But for the Magistrate to be termed in his Dominions an Head, doth not bar him from being any way a part or member of the Church of God.

As little to the purpose are those other cavils ; *A Church which hath the Magistrate for head, is perfect man without Christ:* so that the knitting of our Saviour thereunto, should be an addition of that which is too much. Again, *If the Church be the body of Christ, and of the Civil Magistrate, it shall have two heads, which being monsterous, is to the great dishonour of Christ and his Church:* Thirdly, *if the Church be planted in a popular estate, then forasmuch as all govern in common, and all have authority, all shall be heads there, and no body at all, which is another monster.* It might be feared what this birth of so many monsters together might pertend, but that we know how things natural enough in themselves may seem monstrous through misconceit; which errour of mind is indeed a monster : and the skilful in natures mysteries have used to term it the womb of Monsters; if any be, it is that troubled understanding, wherein,

T.C. lib. p. 419.
Vt Hen. 8. 6. 9.

wherein, because things lie confusedly mixt together, what they are it appeareth not. A Church perfect without Christ, I know not how a man shall imagine, unless there may be either Christianity without Christ, or else a Church without Christianity. If Magistrates be heads of the Church, they are of necessity Christians, then is their head Christ. The adding of Christ universal head over all unto Magistrates particular headship, is no more superfluous in any Church then in other societies: each is to be both severally subject unto some head, and to have a head also general for them all to be subject unto. For so in Armies, in civil Corporations, we see it fareth: A body politique in such respects is not like a natural body, in this; more heads then one is superfluous, in that not, it is neither monstrous, nor yet uncomely for a Church to have different heads: for if Christian Churches be in number many, and every of them a perfect body by it self, Christ being Lord & head over all, why should we judge it a thing more monstrous for one body to have two heads, then one head so many bodies? Him that God hath made the supream head of the whole Church, the head not only of that mystical body which the eye of man is not able to discern, but even of every Christian politique society, of every visible Church in the world. And whereas, lastly, it is thought so strange, that in popular states a multitude to it self should be both body and head, all this wonderment doth grow from a little oversight, in deeming that the subject wherein headship ought to reside should be evermore some one person, which thing is not necessary. For in the collective body that hath not derived as yet the principality of power into some one or few, the whole of necessity must be head over each part; otherwise it could not have power possibly to make any one certain person head; in as much as the very power of making a head belongeth unto headship. These supposed *Monsters* we see therefore are no such *Giants*, as that there should need any *Hercules* to tame them.

The last difference which we have between the title of head when we give it unto Christ, and when we give it to other Governours, is, that the kind of Dominion which it importeth is not the same in both: Christ is head as being the fountain of life and ghostly nutriment, the well-spring of spiritual blessings powred into the body of the Church; they heads, as being the principal instruments for the Churches outward government; he head, as founder of the house; they, as his chiefest overseers. Against this is exception especially taken, and our purveyours are herein said to have their provision from the Popish shambles: for by *Pighins* and *Harding*, to prove that Christ alone is not head of the Church, this distinction they say is brought, that according to the inward influence of grace, Christ only is head: but according to the outward government, the being of head is a thing common to him with others. To raise up falshoods of old condemned, and bring it for confirmation of any thing doubtful, which already hath sufficiently been proved an errour, and is worthily so taken, this would justly deserve censuring. But shall manifest truth therefore be reproached, because men convicted in some things of manifest untruth have at any time thought or alledged it? If too much eagerness against their adversaries had not made them forget themselves, they might remember where being charged as maintainers of those very things, for which, others before them have been condemned of heresie, yet left the name of any such heretick holding the same which they do should make them odious, they sticke not frankly to confess, *That they are not afraid to consent in* T.C.l.3.p.63. *some points, with Jews, and Turkes:* which defence, for all that, were a very weak buckler for such as should consent with Jews and Turks, in that which they have been abhorred and hated for in the Church. But as for this distinction of headship, Spiritual and Mystical of Jesus Christ, ministerial and outward in others besides Christ; what cause is there to mislike either *Harding*, or *Pighins*, or any other besides for it? That which they have been reproved for is, not because they did therein utter an untruth, but such a truth as was not sufficient to bear up the cause which they did thereby seek to maintain. By this distinction they have both truly and sufficiently proved
that

that the name of Head importing power and Dominion over the Church, might be given to others besides Christ without prejudice to any part of his honour. That which they should have made manifest, was the name of Head, importing the power of universal dominion over the whole Church of Christ militant, doth, and that by divine right, appertain to the Pope of *Rome*: They did prove it lawful to grant unto others besides Christ the power of Headship in a different kind from his; but they should have proved it lawful to challenge, as they did to the Bishop of *Rome*, a power universal in that different kind. Their fault was therefore in exacting wrongfully so great power as they challenged in that kind, and not in making two kinds of power, unless some reasons can be shewed for which this distinction of power should be thought erroneous and false A little they stir (although in vain) to prove that we cannot with truth make such distinction of power, whereof the one kind should agree unto Christ only, and the other be further communicated.

T C. 2 p.
415.

Thus therefore they argue, *If there be no head but Christ in respect of Spiritual government there is no head but he in respect of the Word, Sacraments, and Discipline administred by those whom he hath appointed, for as much also as it is his Spiritual government:* Their meaning is, that whereas we make two kinds of power, of which two, the one being spiritual, is proper unto Christ, the other men are capable of because it is visible and external. We do amiss altogether in distinguishing, they think, forasmuch as the visible and external power of regiment over the Church is only in relation unto the world, the Sacraments, and Discipline, administred by such as Christ hath appointed thereunto, and the exercise of this power is also his spiritual government : therefore we do but vainly imagine a visible and external power in the Church differing from his Spiritual power. Such disputes as this doth somewhat resemble the practising of well-willers upon their friends in the pangs of death, whose manner is even then to put smoak in their nostrils, and so to fetch them again, although they know it a matter impossible to keep them living. The kind of affection which the favourers of this labouring cause bear towards it, will not suffer them to see it dye, although by what means they should make it live, they do not see; but they may see that these wrestlings will not help . can they be ignorant how little it booteth to overcast so clear a light with some mist of ambiguity in the name of spiritual regiment ? To make things therefore so plain , that henceforward a childs capacity may serve rightly to conceive our meaning, we make the Spiritual regiment of Christ to be generally that whereby his Church is ruled and governed in things Spiritual. Of this general we make two distinct kinds; the one invisible, exercised by Christ himself in his own person , the other outwardly administred by them, whom Christ doth allow to be rulers and guiders of his Church. Touching the former of these two kinds, we teach that Christ in regard thereof is particularly termed *the head of the Church of God*, neither can any other creature in that sence & meaning be termed head besides him, because it importeth the conduct and government of our souls by the hand of that blessed Spirit wherewith we are sealed and marked, as being peculiarly his, him only therefore do we acknowledge to be the Lord, which dwelleth, liveth, and raigneth in our hearts; him only to be that head, which giveth salvation and life unto his body ; him only to be that fountain from whence the influence of heavenly graces distilleth, and is derived into all parts, whether the Word or the Sacraments, or Discipline, or whatsoever be the means whereby it floweth. As for the power of administring these things in the Church of Christ, which power we call the power of order, it is indeed both Spiritual and His ; Spiritual, because such properly concerns the Spirit : His, because by him it was instituted. Howbeit neither Spiritual as that which is inwardly and invisibly exercised ; nor his, as that which he himself in person doth exercise. Again that power of dominion which is indeed the point of this controversie, and doth also belong to the second kind of spiritual government, namely unto that regiment which is external and visible . this likewise being spiritual in regard of the manner about

which

which it dealeth; and being his, in as much as he approveth whatſoever is
done by it muſt notwithſtanding be diſtinguiſhed alſo from that power whereby he himſelf in perſon adminiſtreth the former kind of his own Spiritual regiment, becauſe he himſelf in perſon doth not adminiſter this; we do not
therefore vainly imagine, but truly and rightly diſcern a power external and
viſible in the Church, exerciſed by men, and ſevered in nature from that Spiritual power of Chriſts own regiment, which power is termed Spiritual, becauſe
it worketh ſecretly, inwardly, & inviſibly: His, becauſe none doth, nor can it
perſonally exerciſe, either beſides, or together with him; ſeeing that him only
we may name our Head, in regard of his, and yet in regard of that other power
from this, term others alſo beſides him Heads, without any contradiction at
all; which thing may very well ſerve for anſwer unto that alſo which they
further alledge againſt the aforeſaid diſtinction, namely, *That even the outward
ſocieties and aſſemblies of the Church, where one or two are gathered together in his
Name, either for hearing of the Word, or for Prayer, or any other Church exerciſe, our* T.C.l.2.f.415.
*Saviour Chriſt being in the midſt of them as Mediatour, muſt be their Head: and if he
be not there idle, but doing the office of a head fully, it followeth that even in outward
ſocieties and meetings of the Church, no meer man can be called the head of it, ſeeing
that our Saviour Chriſt doing the whole office of the head himſelf alone, leaveth nothing
to men by doing whereof they may obtain that title.* Which objection I take as
being made for nothing but only to maintain argument: for they are not ſo
far gone as to argue thus in ſooth and right good earneſt. *God ſtandeth (*ſaith
the Pſalmiſt) *in the midſt of gods*; if God be there preſent, he muſt undoubtedly be preſent as God; if he be not there idle, but doing the office of a God
fully, it followeth, that God himſelf alone doing the whole office of a God,
leaveth nothing in ſuch aſſemblies to any other, by doing whereof they may
obtain ſo high a name. The Pſalmiſt therefore hath ſpoken amiſſe, and
doth ill to call Judges Gods. Not ſo; for as God hath his office differing
from theirs, and doth fully diſcharge it even in the midſt of them, ſo they T.C.l.2p.413.
are not hereby excluded from all kind of duty for which that name ſhould
be given unto them alſo; but in that duty for which it was given them, they
are incouraged Religiouſly and carefully to order themſelves after the ſelf
ſame manner. Our Lord and Saviour being in the midſt of his Church as
Head, is our comfort, without the abridgement of any one duty; for performance whereof, others are termed Heads in another kind then he is. If there
be of the ancient Fathers which ſay, *That there is but one head of the Church,
Chriſt; and that the Miniſter that baptizeth cannot be the head of him that is baptized,
becauſe Chriſt is the head of the whole Church: and that Paul could not be head of the
Church which he planted, becauſe Chriſt is the head of the whole body:* They underſtand the name of head in ſuch ſort as we grant that it is not appliable to any
other, no nor in relation to the leaſt part of the whole Church; he which baptizeth, baptizeth into Chriſt; he which converteth, converteth into Chriſt; he
which ruleth, ruleth for Chriſt. The whole Church can have but one to be
head as Lord and owner of all; wherefore if Chriſt be head in that kind, it
followeth, that no other beſides can be ſo either to the whole or to any
part.

To call and diſſolve all ſolemn Aſſemblies about the publick Affairs of the Church.

Amongſt ſundry Prerogatives of *Simons* Dominion over the Jews, there
is reckoned as not the leaſt, *that no man might gather any great aſſembly
in the Land without him.* For ſo the manner of Jewiſh regiment had alwayes
been, that whether the cauſe for which men aſſembled themſelves in peaceable, good, and orderly ſort, were Eccleſiaſtical, or Civil, Supream Authority
ſhould aſſemble them; *David* gathered all *Iſrael* together unto *Jeruſalem*;
when the Arke was to be removed, he aſſembled the ſonnes of *Aaron* and the
Levites. *Solomon* did the like at ſuch time as the Temple was to be dedicated;
when the Church was to be reformed, *Aſa* in his time did the ſame: The
ſame

same upon like occasions was done afterwards by *Ioash*, *Hezekia*, *Iosiah* and others.

The Consuls of *Rome*, *Polybius* affirmeth to have had a kind of Regall Authority, in that they might call together the Senate and People whensoever it pleased him. Seeing therefore the affairs of the Church and Christian Religion, are publick affairs, for the ordering whereof more solemn Assemblies sometimes are of as great importance and use, as they are for secular affairs: It seemeth no less an act of Supream Authority to call the one then the other. Wherefore the Clergy, in such wise gathered together, is an Ecclesiastical Senate, which with us, as in former times the chiefest Prelate at his discretion did use to assemble, so that afterwards in such considerations as have been before specified, it seemeth more meet to annex the said Prerogative to the Crown. The plot of reformed Discipline not liking thereof so well, taketh order that every former Assembly before it breaketh up, should it self appoint both the time and place of their after meeting again. But, because I find not any thing on that side particularly alleadged against us herein, a longer disputation about so plain a cause shall not need. The ancient Imperial Law forbiddeth such assemblies as the Emperours Authority did not cause to be made. Before Emperours became Christians, the Church had never any general Synod, their greatest meeting consisting of Bishops and others, the gravest in each Province. As for the Civil Governours Authority, it suffered them only as things not regarded or not accounted of at such times as it did suffer them. So that what right a Christian King hath as touching Assemblies of that kind we are not able to judge, till we come to latter times, when Religion had won the hearts of the highest Powers. *Constantine* (as *Pighius* doth grant) was not only the first that ever did call any general Council together, but even the first that devised the calling of them for consultation about the businesses of God. After he had once given the example, his Successors a long time followed the same; in so much that S. *Hierom* to disprove the Authority of a Synod which was pretended to be general, useth this as a forcible Argument, *Dic quis Imperator hanc Synodum jusserit convocari?* Their answer hereunto, is no answer, which say, *That Emperours did not this without conference had with the Bishops*: for to our purpose it is enough, if the Clergy alone did it not otherwise then by the leave and appointment of their Soveraign Lords and Kings. Whereas therefore it is on the contrary side alleadged, that *Valentinian* the elder being requested by Catholick Bishops, to grant that there might be a Synod for the ordering of matters called in question by the *Arians*, answered, that he being one of the Laity, might not meddle with such matters, and thereupon willed that the Priests and Bishops, to whom the care of those things belongeth, should meet & consult together by themselves when they thought good. We must with the Emperours speech weigh the occasion & drift thereof. *Valentinian* and *Valens*, the one a Catholick, the other an *Arian*, were Emperours together: *Valens* the Governour of the East; and *Valentinian* of the West Empire. *Valentinian* therefore taking his journey from the East, unto the West parts, and passing for that intent through *Thracia*, there the Bishops which held the soundness of Christian belief, because they knew that *Valens* was their professed Enemy, and therefore if the other was once departed out of those quarters, the Catholick cause was like to find very small favour, moved presently *Valentinian* about a Counsel to be assembled under the countenance of his Authority; who by likelyhood considering what inconvenience might grow thereby, inasmuch as it could not be but a means to incense *Valens* the more against them, refused himself to be Author of, or present at any such Assembly, and of this his denyal gave them a colourable reason, to wit, that he was although an Emperour, yet a secular person, and therefore not able in matters of so great obscurity to fit as a competent judge. But if they wch were Bishops and learned men, did think good to consult thereof together, they might; whereupon when they could not obtain that which they most desired, yet that which he granted unto them they took, and

Polyb.l.6.de milit ac do-mineft. Rom. difcipl.

Lib. 1. de Col. illicit.& de conventiculis. cap. de Epifc. & presbyt.

Hierarch. lib. 6. cap. 1.

Conftant. confil à Theodofio.

Sardicen.confi. à Conflant.

Hieron cont. Ruf finus l.2.

Sozomen.lib. cap.7.

Ambrofe Epift 32.

and forthwith had a Councel. *Valentinian* went on towards *Rome*, they remaining in consultation, till *Valens* which accompanied him returned back; so that now there was no remedy, but either to incure a manifest contempt, or else at the hands of *Valens* himself, to seek approbation of that they had done. To him therefore they became suitors, his answer was short, *Either Arianism, or Exile, which they would* ; whereupon their banishment ensued. Let reasonable men now therefore be judges, how much this example of *Valentinian,* doth make against the Authority, which we say that Soveraign Rulers may lawfully have, as concerning Synods and meetings Ecclesiastical.

Of the Authority of making Laws.

THere are which wonder that we should account any Statute a Law, which the High Court of Parliament in *England* hath established about the matter of *Church Regiment* ; the Prince and Court of Parliament, having (as they suppose) no more lawful means to give order to the Church and Clergy in those things, then they have to make Laws for the Hierarchies of Angels in heaven ; that the Parliament being a meer temporal Court, can neither by the Law of nature, nor of God, have competent power to define of such matters; that Supremacy in this kind cannot belong unto Kings, as Kings, because Pagan Emperours whose princely power was true Soveraignty, never challenged so much over the Church ; that power in this kind cannot be the right of any earthly Crown, Prince, or State, in that they be Christians, forasmuch as if they be Christians, they all owe subjection to the Pastors of their souls ; that the Prince therefore not having it himself, cannot communicate it to the Parliament, and consequently cannot make Laws here, or determine of the Churches Regiment by himself, Parliament or any other Court subjected unto him.

The Parliament of *England* together with the Convocation annexed thereunto, is that whereupon the very essence of all Government within this Kingdom doth depend ; it is even the body of the whole Realm, it consisteth of the King, and of all that within the Land are subject unto him. The Parliament is a Court not so meerly Temporal as if it might meddle with nothing but only leather and wooll: Those dayes of Queen *Mary* are not yet forgotten, wherein the Realm did submit it self unto the Legate of Pope *Julius,* at which time had they been perswaded as this man seemeth now to be, had they thought that there is no more force in Laws made by Parliament concerning Church affairs, then if men should take upon them to make Orders for the Hierarchies of Angels in Heaven, they might have taken all former Statutes of that kind as cancelled, and by reason of nullity abrogated. What need was there that they should bargaine with the Cardinal, and purchase their pardon by promise made before hand, that what Laws they had made, assented unto, or executed, against the Bishop of *Romes* Supremacy, the same they would in that present Parliament, effectually abrogate and repeal ? Had they power to repeal Laws made, and none to make Laws concerning the Regiment of the Church ? Again, when they had by suit obtained his confirmation for such foundations of Bishopricks, Cathedral Churches, Hospitals, Colledges, and Schools ; for such marriages before made, for such Institutions into livings Ecclesiastical, and for all such Judicial Processes, as having been ordered according to the Laws before in force, but contrary unto the Canons and Orders of the Church of *Rome,* were in that respect thought defective, although the Cardinal in his Letters of Dispensation, did give validity unto those Acts, even *Apostolicæ firmitatis robur,* the very strength of Apostolical solidity ; what had all these been without those grave authentical words ? *Be it enacted by the Authority of this present Parliament, that all and singular Articles and Clauses contained in the said dispensation, shall remain and be reputed and taken to all intents and constructions in the Laws of this Realm, lawful, good and effectual to be alleadged and pleaded in all Courts Ecclesiastical and Temporal,*

An 1. & 2.
Phil. & Mar.
cap. 8.

Ddd

poral, for good and sufficient matter either for the Plantiffe or Defendant, without any Allegation or Objection to be made against the validity of them by pretence of any generall Councel, Canon, or Decree to the contrary. Somewhat be like they thought there was in this meer Temporal Court, without which the Popes owne meer Ecclesiastical Legates Dispensations had taken small effect in the Church of *England;* neither did they, or the Cardinal imagine any thing committed against the law of nature, or of God, because they took order for the Churches affairs, and that even in the Court of Parliament. The most natural and Religious course in making laws, is, that the matter of them be taken from the judgement of the wisest in those things which they are to concern; in matters of God to set down a form of prayer, a solemn confession of the Articles of the Christian Faith, and Ceremonies meet for the exercise of Religion. It were unnatural not to think the Pastors and Bishops of our Souls a great deal more fit, then men of Secular Trades, and Callings : Howbeit, when all which the wisdom of all sorts can do, is done for the devising of Laws in the Church, it is the general consent of all that giveth them the form and vigour of Laws, without which they could be no more unto us then the Councels of Physitians to the sick; well might they seem as wholesome admonitions and instructions, but Laws could they never be without consent of the whole Church to be guided by them, whereunto both nature and the practice of the Church of God set down in Scripture, is found every way so fully consonant, that God himself would not impose, no not his own Laws upon his people by the hand of *Moses* without their free and open consent. Wherefore to define and determine even of the Churches affairs by way of assent and approbation, as Laws are defined in that Right of Power, which doth give them the force of Laws: thus to define of our own Churches Regiment, the Parliament of *England* hath competent Authority.

Touching that Supremacy of Power which our Kings have in this case of making Laws, it resteth principally in the strength of a negative voice; which not to give them, were to deny them that without which they were Kings but by meer title and not in exercise of Dominion. Be it in Regiment Popular, Aristocratical, or Regal, Principality resteth in that person, or those persons unto whom is given right of excluding any kind of Law whatsoever it be, before establishment. This doth belong unto Kings, as Kings; Pagan Emperours, even *Nero* himself had no lesse ; but much more then this in the Laws of his own Empire; that he challenged not any interest of giving voice in the Laws of the Church, I hope no man will so construe, as if the cause were conscience, and fear to incroach upon the Apostles right. If then it be demanded by what right from *Constantine* downward, the Christian Emperours did so far intermeddle with the Churches affairs, either we must herein condemn them, as being over presumptuously bold, or else judge that by a Law, which is termed *Regia*, that is to say Regal, the people having derived unto their Emperours their whole Power for making of Laws, and by that means his Edicts being made Laws, what matter soever they did concern, as Imperial Dignity endowed them with competent Authority and Power to make Laws for Religion, so they were thought by Christianity to use their power being Christians unto the benefit of the Church of Christ: Was there any Christian Bishop in the World which did then judge this repugnant unto the dutiful subjection which Christians do owe to the Pastors of their souls, to whom, in respect of their sacred order, it is not by us, neither may be denied, that Kings and Princes are as much, as the very meanest that liveth under them, bound in conscience to shew themselves gladly and willingly obedient, receiving the seals of Salvation, the blessed Sacraments at their hands, as at the hands of our Lord Jesus Christ, with all reverence, not disdaining to be taught and admonished by them, nor with-holding from them as much as the least part of their due and decent honour.? All which, for any thing that hath been alleadged, may stand very well without resignation of supremacy of Power in making Laws, even Laws concerning the most spiritual affairs of the Church ; which

Item quod principi placuit, Legis habet vigorem. Inst. de J. N. G. & C.

Laws being made amongst us, are not by any of us so taken or interpreted, as if they did receive their force from power which the Prince doth communicate unto the Parliament, or unto any other Court under him, but from Power which the whole body of the Realm being naturally possest with, hath by free and deliberate assent derived unto him that ruleth over them, so far forth as hath been declared: so that our Laws made concerning Religion, do take originally their essence from the power of the whole Realm and Church of *England*, then which nothing can be more consonant unto the law of nature and the will of our Lord Jesus Christ.

To let these go, and return to our own Men; *Ecclesiastical Governours*, they say, *may not meddle with making of Civil Laws, and of Laws for the Common-wealth; nor the Civil Magistrate, high or low, with making of Orders for the Church.* It seemeth unto me very strange, that these men which are in no cause more vehement and fierce, then where they plead that Ecclesiastical persons may not *κυριεύειν* be Lords, should hold that the power of making Ecclesiastical laws, which thing of all other is most proper unto Dominion, belongeth to none but Ecclesiastical persons onely: their oversight groweth herein for want of exact observation, what it is to make a Law. *Tully* speaking of the law of nature, saith, *That thereof God himself was inventor, disceptator, lator, the deviser, the discusser, and deliverer;* wherein he plainly alludeth unto the chiefest parts which then did appertain to his publick action. For when Laws were made, the first thing was to have them devised; the second to sift them with as much exactnesse of judgement as any way might be used; the next by solemn voice of *Soveraign* authority to passe them, and give them the force of Laws. It cannot in any reason seem otherwise then most fit, that unto Ecclesiastical persons the care of devising Ecclesiastical Laws be committed, even as the care of Civil unto them which are in those affairs most skilful. This taketh not away from Ecclesiastical persons all right of giving voice with others, when Civil Laws are proposed for regiment of the Common-wealth, whereof themselves, though now the world would have them annihilated; are notwithstanding as yet a part; much lesse doth it cut off that part of the power of Princes, whereby as they claim, so we know no reasonable cause wherefore we may not grant them, without offence to Almighty God, so much authority in making all manner of Laws within their own Dominions, that neither Civil, nor Ecclesiastical do passe without their Royal assent.

In devising and discussing of Laws, wisdom especially is required; but that which establisheth them and maketh them, is power, even power of Dominion, the Chiefty whereof (amongst us) resteth in the person of the King. Is there any Law of Christs which forbiddeth Kings and Rulers of the Earth to have such Soveraign and supream Power in the making of Laws, either Civil or Ecclesiastical? If there be, our controversie hath an end. Christ in his Church hath not appointed any such Law concerning Temporal power, as God did of old unto the Common-wealth of *Israel*; but leaving that to be at the Worlds free choice, his chiefest care is that the spiritual Law of the Gospel might be published far and wide. They that received the Law of Christ, were for a long time people scattered in sundry Kingdoms, Christianity not exempting them from the Laws which they had been subject unto, saving only in such cases as those Laws did injoyn that which the Religion of Christ did forbid: Hereupon grew their manifold persecutions throughout all places where they lived; as oft as it thus came to passe there was no possibility that the Emperours and Kings under whom they lived, should medle any whit at all with making Laws for the Church. From Christ therefore having received power, who doubteth, but as they did, so they might bind them to such orders as seemed fittest for the maintenance of their Religion, without the leave of high or low in the Common-wealth, for as much as in Religion it was divided utterly from them, and they from it. But when the mightiest began to like of the Christian faith, by their means whole free States and Kingdoms became obedient unto Christ. Now the question is, whether

Kings

T. C. l. 1. p. 152.

Kings by embracing Christianity, do thereby receive any such Law as taketh from them the weightiest part of that Soveraignty which they had even when they were Heathens : whether being infidels they might do more in causes of Religion, then now they can by the Laws of God, being true believers. For whereas in Regal States, the King or supream Head of the Common-wealth, had before Christianity a supream stroak in making of Laws for Religion ; he must by embracing Christian Religion utterly deprive himself thereof, and in such causes become subject unto his Subjects, having even within his own Dominions them whose Commandment he must obey ; unlesse his power be placed in the Head of some forraign spiritual Potentate : so that either a forraign or domestical Commander upon Earth he must admit more now then before he had, and that in the chiefest things whereupon Common-wealths do stand. But apparent it is unto all men which are not strangers unto the Doctrine of Jesus Christ, that no State of the world receiving Christianity, is by any law therein contained, bound to resign the power which they lawfully held before : but over what persons, and in what causes soever the same hath been in force, it may so remain and continue still. That which as Kings they might do in matters of Religion, and did in matter of false Religion, being Idolatrous and Superstitious Kings, the same they are now even in every respect fully authorized to do in all affairs pertinent to the state of true Christian Religion. And concerning the supream power of making Laws for all persons, in all causes to be guided by ; it is not to be let passe, that the head enemies of this Headship are constrained to acknowledge the King endued even with this very power, so that he may & ought to exercise the same, taking order for the Church and her affaires, of what nature or kind soever, in case of necessity, as when there is no lawful Ministry, which they interpret then to be (and this surely is a point very remarkable) wheresoever the Ministry is wicked. A wicked Ministry is no lawful Ministry, and in such sort no lawful Ministry, that what doth belong unto them as Ministers by right of their calling, the same to be annihilated in respect of their bad qualities; their wickednesse in it self a deprivation of right to deal in the affaires of the Church, and a warrant for others to deal in them which are held to be of a clean other society, the members whereof have been before so peremptorily for ever excluded from power of dealing for ever with affaires of the Church. They which once have learned throughly this lesson, will quickly be capable perhaps of another equivalent unto it. For the wickednesse of the Ministery transfers their right unto the King; in case the King be as wicked as they, to whom then shall the right descend ? There is no remedy, all must come by devolution at length, even as the family of *Browne* will have it, unto the godly among the people, for confusion unto the wise and the great by the poor and the simple : some *Kimberdoling* with his retinue must take this work of the Lord in hand; and the making of Church Laws and Orders, must prove to be their right in the end. If not for love of the truth, yet for shame of grosse absurdities, let these contentions and stifling fancies be abondoned. The cause which moved them for a time to hold a wicked Ministery no lawful Ministry, and in this defect of a lawful Ministery, authorized Kings to make Laws and Orders for the affaires of the Church, till it were well established, is surely this. First, they see that whereas the continual dealing of the Kings of *Israel* in the affairs of the Church, doth make now very strong against them, the burthen whereof they shall in time well enough shake off, if it may be obtained that it is indeed lawful for Kings to follow these holy examples; howbeit no longer then during the case of necessity, while the wickednesse, and in respect thereof the unlawfulnesse of the Ministery doth continue. Secondly, they perceive right well, that unlesse they should yield authority unto Kings in case of such supposed necessity, the Discipline they urge were clean excluded, as long as the Clergy of *England* doth thereunto remain opposite. To open therefore a door for her entrance, there is no remedy but the tenent must be this ; That now when the Ministery of *England* is universally wicked, and in that respect

hath

T. C. l. 3. 51.

hath loft all authority, and is become no lawful Miniftery, no such Miniftery as hath the right, which otherwife fhould belong unto them if they were vertuous and godly, as their adverfaries are; in this neceffity the King may do fomewhat for the Chnrch: that which we do imply in the name of Head-fhip, he may both have and exercife till they be entered, which will disburthen and eafe him of it: till they come, the King is licenced to hold that power which we call Headfhip. But what afterwards? In a Church ordered, that which the fupream Magiftrate hath, is to fee that the Laws of God touching his Worfhip, and touching all matters and orders of the Church, be executed and duly obferved; to fee that every Ecclefiaftical perfon do that office whereunto he is appointed, to punifh thofe that fail in their office. In a word, that which *Allen* himfelf acknowledgeth unto the earthly power which God hath given him, it doth belong to defend the Laws of the Church; to caufe them to be executed, and to punifh rebels and tranfgreffors of the fame: on all fides therefore it is confeft, that to the King belongeth power of maintaining the Laws made for Church regiment, and of caufing them to be obferved; but principality of Power in making them, which is the thing we attribute unto Kings, this both the one fort, and the other do withftand. *T.C.l.1,p.192* *Apol.fol.40,94*

Touching the Kings fupereminent authority in commanding, and in judging of caufes Ecclefiaftical, Firft, to explain therein our meaning, It hath been taken as if we did hold, that Kings may prefcribe what themfelves think good to be done in the fervice of God: how the Word fhall be taught, how the Sacraments Adminiftred; that Kings may perfonally fit in the Confiftory where the Bifhops do, hearing and determining what caufes foever do appertain unto the Church. That Kings and Queens in their own proper perfons, are by judicial fentence to decide the queftions which do rife about matters of Faith and Chriftian Religion; that Kings may excommunicate; finally, that Kings may do whatfoever is incident unto the office and duty of an Ecclefiaftical Judge; which opinion, becaufe we account as abfurd, as they who have fathered the fame upon us, we do them to wit, that this our meaning is and no otherwife. There is not within this Realm an Eccleliaftical officer, that may by the Authority of his own place command univerfally throughout the Kings Dominions; but they of this people whom one may command, are to an others commandement unfubject; only the Kings Royal Power is of fo large compaffe, that no man commanded by him according to the order of Law, can plead himfelf to be without the bounds and limits of that Authority. I fay according to order of Law, becaufe that with us the higheft have thereunto fo tyed themfelves, that otherwife then fo they take not upon them to command any. And that Kings fhould be in fuch fort fupream Commanders over all men, we hold it as requifite as well for the ordering of Spiritual as Civil affairs; in as much as without univerfal authority in this kind, they fhould not be able when need is, to do as vertuous Kings have done. *Iofiah purpofing to renew the houfe of the Lord, affembled the Priefts and Levites, and when they were together, gave them their charge, faying: Go out unto the Cities of* Judah, *and gather of Ifrael mony to repair the Houfe of God from year to year, and hafte the things: But the Levites haftned not. Therefore the King called* Jehoiada, *the Chief, and faid unto him; why haft thou not required of the Levites to bring in out of* Judah and Jerufalem, *the Tax of* Mofes, *the Servant of the Lord, and of the Congregation of* Ifrael, *for the Tabernacle of the Teftimony? For wicked* Athalia, *and her Children brake up the Houfe of the Lord God, and all the things that were dedicated for the Houfe of the Lord, did they beftow upon* Balaam. *Therefore the King commanded, and they made a Cheft, and fet it at the gate of the Houfe of the Lord without, and they made a Proclamation through* Judah and Jerufalem, *to bring unto the Lord, the Tax of* Mofes *the Servant of the Lord, laid upon* Ifrael *in the Wildernefs.* Could either he have done this, or after him *Ezechias* the like concerning the celebration of the Paffeover, but that all forts of men in all things did owe unto thefe their Soveraign Rulers, the fame obedience, which fometimes *Jofuah* had them by vow and promife bound unto? *Whofoever* *Power to command all perfons, and to be over all Judges in caufes Eccle-fiaftical.* *2 Chron. 24. ver,5,6,7,8,9* *2 Chron,6,30 verf,6.* *Jof,1,v,18,*

ver *shall rebel against thy Commandments, and will not obey thy words in all thou com-*
mandest him, let him be put to death : onely be strong and of a good courage. Furthermore, Judgement Ecclefiaftical we fay is neceffary for decifion of Controverfies rifing between man and man, and for correction of faults committed in
the affairs of God, unto the due execution whereof there are three things neceffary, Laws, Judges, and Supream Governours of Judgements; what Courts
there fhall be, and what caufes fhall belong unto each Court, and what Judges
fhall determine of every caufe, and what order in all judgements fhall be
kept ; of thofe things the Laws have fufficiently difpofed, fo that his duty
who fitteth in any fuch Court, is to judge, not of, but after the fame law.

Juft. de Offic. *Inprimis illud obfervare debet Judex : ne aliter judicet quam legibus, conftitutionibus,*
jus. *ant moribus proditum eft, ut Imperator Juftinianus ;* which Laws (for we mean
the pofitive Laws of our Realm, concerning Ecclefiaftical affairs) if they
otherwife difpofe of any fuch thing, then according to the Law of reafon,
and of God, we muft both acknowledge them to be amiffe, and endeavour
to have them reformed : But touching that point, what may be objected,
fhall after appear. Our Judges in caufes Ecclefiaftical, are either Ordinary
or Commiffionary ; Ordinary, thofe whom we term Ordinaries ; and
fuch by the Laws of this Land are none but Prelates onely, whofe power to
do that which they do, is in themfelves, and belonging to the nature of
their Ecclefiaftical calling. In fpiritual caufes, a Lay Perfon may be no Ordinary ; a Commiffionary Judge there is no let but that he may be ; and that
our Laws do evermore refer the ordinary judgement of fpiritual caufes unto
fpiritual perfons fuch as are termed Ordinaries, no man which knoweth any
of the Practice of this Realm, can eafily be ignorant, Now befides them which
are Authorized to judge in feveral Territories, there is required an univerfal
Power which reacheth over all, imparting Supream Authority of Government, over Courts, all Judges, all Caufes, the operation of which power
is as well to ftrengthen, maintain and uphold particular Jurifdictions, which
haply might elfe be of fmall effect : as alfo to remedy that which they are
not able to help, and to redreffe that wherein they at any time do otherwife
then they ought to do. This power being fometime in the Bifhop of *Rome*,
who by finifter Practifes had drawn it into his hands, was for juft confiderations by publick confent annexed unto the Kings Royal Seat and Crown ;
from thence the Authors of Reformation would tranflate it into their National Affemblies or Synods, which Synods are the onely helps that they
think lawful to ufe againft fuch evils in the Church as particular Jurifdictions
1 Eliz. cap.1. are not fufficient to redrefs. In which caufe, our Laws have provided that
the Kings fupereminent Authority and Power fhall ferve. As namely, when
the whole Ecclefiaftical ftate, or the Principal perfons therein, do need
Vifitation and Reformation ; when in any part of the Church Errours,
Schifms, Herefies, Abufes, Offences, Contempts, Enormities, are grown;
which men in their feveral Jurifdictions, either do not or cannot help. Whatfoever any Spiritual Authority and Power (fuch as Legates from the See of
Rome did fometimes exercife) hath done, or might heretofore have done,
for the remedy of thofe evils in lawful fort (that is to fay, without the violation of the Laws of God, or nature in the deed done) as much in every
degree our Laws have fully granted, that the King for ever may do, not
onely by fetting Ecclefiaftical Synods on work, that the thing may be their
Act, and the King their motion unto it, for fo much perhaps the Mafters of
Reformation will grant : But by Commiffions few or many, who having
the Kings Letters Patents, may in the vertue thereof execute the premifes
as Agents in the right, not of their own peculiar and Ordinary, but of his fupereminent power. When men are wronged by inferiour Judges, or have any
juft caufe to take exception againft them, their way for redrefs, is to make their
appeal ; and appeal is a prefent delivery of him which maketh it, out of the
hands of their power and jurifdictions from whence it is made. Pope *Alexander*
having fometimes the King of *England* at advantage, caufed him amongft o-
ther

other things to agree, that as many of his Subjects as would, might have appeal to the Court of *Rome.* And thus (saith one) *that whereunto a mean person* Machiavil. *at this day would scorn to submit himself, so great a King was content to be subject.* Hist. florent *Notwithstanding even when the Pope* (saith he) *had so great authority amongst Prin-* l. 1 *ces which were far off, the Romans he could not frame to obedience; nor was able to obtain that himself might abide at* Rome *, though promising not to meddle with other then Ecclesiastical Affairs.* So much are things that terrifie, more feared by such as behold them aloof off then at hand. Reformers I doubt not in some causes will admit appeals, but appeals made to their Synods, even as the Church of *Rome* doth allow of them, so they be made to the Bishop of *Rome.* As for that kind of appeal which the *English* Laws do approve from the Judge of any certain particular Court unto the King, as the 15 *Elen. c.* onely Supream Governour on Earth, who by his Delegates may give a final *cap. 13.* definitive Sentence from which no farther appeal can be made : will their platform allow of this ? Surely, for asmuch as in that estate which they all dream of, the whole Church must be divided into Parishes, in which none can have greater or less Authority and power then another : again the King himself must be but as a common member in the body of his own Parish, and the causes of that onely Parish must be by the officers thereof determinable : In case the King had so much favour or preferment as to be made one of those Officers (for otherwise by their positions, he were not to meddle any more then the meanest amongst his Subjects with the judgements of any Ecclesiastical cause) how is it possible they should allow of appeals to be made from any other abroad to the King ? To receive appeals from all other Judges, belongeth unto the highest in power of all, and to be in power over all (as touching judgement in Ecclesiastical causes) this as they think belongeth onely to Synods. Whereas therefore with us, Kings do exercise over all things, persons, and causes Supream Power, both of voluntary and litigious Jurisdiction; so that according to the one they incite, reform and command, according to the other, they judge universally, doing both in far other *T C.l. p. 154.* sort then such as have ordinary spiritual power; oppugned we are herein *2 Chron. 19. 5.* by some colourable shew of Argument, as if to grant thus much to any Secular *Heb 5. 1* Person, it were unreasonable. *For sith it is* (say they) *apparent out of the Chronicles, that judgement in Church matters pertaineth to God, Seeing likewise it is evident out of the Apostles, that the High-Priest is set over those matters in Gods behalf, it must needs follow that the Principality or direction of the judgement of them, is by Gods Ordinance appertaining to the High-Priest, and consequently to the Ministry of the Church, and if it be by Gods Ordinance appertaining unto them, how can it be translated from them to the civil Magistrate ?* Which Argument briefly drawn into form, lyeth thus, That which belongeth unto God, may not be translated unto any other, but whom he hath appointed to have it in his behalf But principality of judgement in Church matters appertaineth unto God, which hath appointed the High-priest, and consequently the Ministry of the Church alone to have it in his behalf, *Ergo* It may not from thence be translated to the Civil Magistrate. The first of which propositions we grant, as also in the second that branch which ascribeth unto God Principality in Church matters But that either he did appoint none but onely the High-Priest to exercise the said Principality for him, or that the Ministry of the Church may in reason from thence be concluded to have alone the same principality by his appointment; these two points we deny utterly. For concerning the High-Priest there is first no such Ordinance of God to be found : *Every High-Priest* (saith the Apostle), *is taken from amongst men, and is ordained for men in things pertaining to God* whereupon it may well be gathered, that the Priest was indeed Ordained of God to have Power in things appertaining unto God. For the Apostle doth there mention the Power of offering gifts and sacrifices for sin, which kinde of Power was not onely given of God unto Priests, but restrained unto Priests onely. The power of jurisdiction and ruling Authority, this also God gave them, but not them alone. For it is held as all men know, that others of the

Laity

Laity, were herein joyned by the law with them. But concerning Principality in Church affairs, (for of this our queſtion is and of no other) the Prieſt neither had it alone, nor at all, but in ſpiritual or Church affairs, (as hath been already ſhewed) it was the Royal Prerogative of Kings onely. Again, though it were ſo that God had appointed the high Prieſt to have the ſaid principality of Government in thoſe matters; yet how can they who alleadge this, enforce thereby, that conſequently the Miniſtry of the Church, and no other ought to have the ſame, when they are ſo far off from allowing ſo much to the Miniſtry of the Goſpel, as the Prieſt-hood of the Law had by Gods appointment : That we but collecting thereout a difference in Authority and Juriſdiction amongſt the Clergy, to be for the Politie of the Church not inconvenient; they forthwith think to cloſe up our mouths by anſwering, *That the Jewiſh High-Prieſt, had authority above the reſt, onely in that they prefigured the Soveraignty of Jeſus Chriſt; as for the Miniſters of the Goſpel, it is altogether unlawful to give them as much as the leaſt title, any ſyllable whereof may ſound to Principality.* And of the Regency which may be granted, they hold others even of the Laity, no leſs capable then the Paſtors themſelves. How ſhall theſe things cleave together ? The truth is, that they have ſome reaſon to think it not at all of the fitteſt for Kings, to ſit as ordinary judges in matters of Faith and Religion. An ordinary Judge moſt be of the quality which in a ſupream Judge is not neceſſary, becauſe the perſon of the one is charged with that which the other Authority diſchargeth, without imploying perſonally himſelf therein. It is an errour to think that the Kings authority can have no force nor power in the doing of that which himſelf may not perſonally do. For firſt, impoſſible it is that at one and the ſame time, the King in perſon ſhould order ſo many, and ſo different affairs, as by his power every where preſent, are wont to be ordered both in peace and war, at home and abroad. Again, the King in regard of his nonage or minority, may be unable to perform that thing wherein years of diſcretion are requiſite for perſonal action; and yet this authority even then be of force. For which cauſe we ſay, that the Kings authority dyeth not but is, and worketh alwayes alike. Sundry conſiderations there may be effectual, to with-hold the Kings perſon from being a doer of that which notwithſtanding his power muſt give force unto, even in civil affairs; where nothing doth more either concern the duty, or better beſeem the Majeſty of Kings, then perſonally to Adminiſter Juſtice to their people (as moſt famous Princes have done;) yet if it be in caſe of Felony or Treaſon, the Learned in the Laws of this Realm do affirm, that well may the King commit his authority to another, to judge between him and the offender, but the King being himſelf there a party, he cannot perſonally ſit to give judgement.

Stamf. Pleas of the Crown, li. cap. 3.

As therefore the perſon of the King may, for juſt conſiderations, even where the cauſe is Civil, be notwithſtanding withdrawn from occupying the ſeat of judgement, and others under his Authority be fit, he unfit himſelf to judge; ſo the conſiderations for which it were haply not convenient for Kings to ſit and give ſentence in Spiritual Courts, where cauſes Eccleſiaſtical are uſually debated, can be no bar to that force and efficacy which their *Soveraign Power* hath over thoſe very *Conſiſtories,* and for which, we hold without any exception that all Courts are the Kings. All men are not for all things ſufficient, and therefore publique affairs being divided, ſuch perſons muſt be authorized Judges in each kinde, as Common reaſon may preſume to be moſt fit. Which cannot of Kings and Princes ordinarily be preſumed in cauſes meerly Eccleſiaſtical; ſo that even common ſenſe doth rather adjudge this burthen unto other men. We ſee it hereby a thing neceſſary, to put a difference, as well between that *ordinary Juriſdiction* which belongeth to the Clergy alone, and that *Commiſſionary* wherein others are for juſt conſiderations appointed to joyn with them, as alſo between both theſe Juriſdictions; and a third, whereby the King hath tranſcendent Authority, and that in all cauſes over both. Why this may not lawfully be granted unto him, there is no reaſon. A time there was when Kings were not capable of any ſuch

power, as namely, when they professed themselves open Enemies unto Christ
and Christianity. A time there followed when they, being capable, took sometimes more, sometimes less to themselves, as seemed best in their own eyes,
because no certainty touching their right was as yet determined. The Bishops who alone were before accustomed to have the ordering of such affairs saw very just cause of grief, when the highest, favouring Heresie, withstood by the strength of Soveraign Authority, Religious proceedings. Whereupon they often times, against this unresistable power, pleaded the use and
custom, which had been to the contrary; namely, that the affairs of the
Church should be dealt in by the Clergy, and by no other; unto which purpose, the sentences that then were uttered in defence of unabolished Orders and Laws, against such as did, of their own heads, contrary thereunto,
are now altogether impertinently brought in opposition against them, who
use but that power which Laws have given them, unless men can shew, that
there is in those Laws some manifest iniquity or injustice. Whereas there- *T.C. l.3. p.153.*
fore against the force Judicial and Imperial, which supream Authority hath, it
is alledged, how *Constantine* termeth *Church-Officers, Overseers of things within the Church,* himself, *of those without the Church* : how *Augustine* witnesseth
that the Emperor not daring to judge of the Bishops cause, committed it to the *Euseb.de vit.*
Bishops; and was to crave pardon of the Bishops, for that by the *Donatists* *Constant l.4.*
importunity, which made no end of appealing unto him, he was, being weary *Ep.162, 166.*
of them, drawn to give sentence in a matter of theirs; how *Hilary* beseecheth
the Emperor *Constance,* to provide that the *Governors* of his Provinces should
not presume to take upon them the judgement of Ecclesiastical causes, *Lib.5. ep.83.*
to whom onely Commonwealth matters onely belonged; How *Ambrose* affirmeth, that *Palaces* belong unto the *Emperor, Churches to the Minister* ; that the
Emperor hath the authority over the Common-walls of the City, and not in
holy things; for which cause he never would yeild to have the causes of the
Church debated in the Princes Consistories, but excused himself to the Emperor *Valentinian,* for that being convented to answer concerning Church matters
in a Civil Court, he came not : We may by these testimonies drawn from antiquity, if we list to consider them, discern how requisite it is that authority
should always follow received Laws in the manner of proceeding. For in as
much as there was at the first no certain Law, determining what force the principal Civil Magistrates authority should be of, how far it should reach,
and what order it should obse. ve; but Christian Emperors from time to time
did what themselves thought most reasonable in those affairs; by this means it
cometh to pass that they in their practice vary, and are not uniform. Vertuous
Emperors, such as *Constantine* the Great was, made conscience to swerve unnecessarily from the custom which had been used in the Church, even when it
lived under Infidels; *Constantine* of reverence to Bishops, and their spiritual
authority, rather abstained from that which himself might lawfully do, then was
willing to claim a power not fit or decent for him to exercise. The order which
hath been before, he ratifieth, exhorting the Bishops to look to the Church,
and promising that he would do the office of a Bishop over the Commonwealth;
which very *Constantine* notwithstanding, did not thereby so renounce all authority in judging of special causes, but that sometime he took, as St. *Augustine* witnesseth, even personall cognition of them; howbeit whether as purposing to give therein judicially any sentence, I stand in doubt; for if the
other of whom St. *Augustine* elsewhere speaketh, did in such fort judge, surely there was cause why he should excuse it as a thing not usually done. Otherwise there is no let, but that any such great person may hear those causes to
and fro debated, and deliver in the end his own opinion of them, declaring on
which side himself doth judge that the truth is. But this kind of sentence
bindeth no side to stand thereunto ; it is a sentence of private perswasion, and
not of solemn jurisdiction, albeit a King or an Emperor pronounce it; again,
on the contrary part, when Governours infected with Heresie were possessed
of the highest power, they thought they might use it as pleased themselves, to
further

further by all means that opinion which they defired fhould prevail, they not respecting at all what was meet, prefumed to command and judge all men in all caufes, without either care of orderly proceeding, or regard to fuch Laws and Cuftomes as the Church had been wont to obferve. So that the one fort feared to do even that which they might, and that which the other ought not they boldly prefumed upon; the one fort of modefty, excufed themfelves where they fcarce needed; the other, though doing that which was inexcufable, bare it out with main power, not enduring to be told by any man how far they roved beyond their bounds. So great odds was between them whom before we mentioned, and fuch as the younger *Valentinian*, by whom Saint *Ambrofe* being commanded to yield up one of the Churches under him unto the *Arians*, whereas they which were fent on his Meffage alledged, That the Emperour did but ufe his own right, for as much as all things were in his power : The Anfwer which the holy Bifhop gave them was, *That the Church is the Houfe of God, and that thofe things that are Gods are not to be yeilded up, and difpofed of at the Emperors will and pleafure; His Palaces he might grant to whomfoever he pleafeth, but Gods own Habitation not fo.* A caufe why many times Emperors do more by their abfolute Authority then could very well ftand with reafon, was the over great importunity of wicked Hereticks, who being enemies to peace and quietnefs, cannnot otherwife then by violent means be fupported,

In this refpect therefore we muft needs think the ftate of our own Church much better fetled then theirs was; becaufe our Laws have with far more certainty prefcribed bounds unto each kinde of Power. All decifion of things doubtful, and corrections of things amifs are proceeded in by order of Law, what perfon foever he be unto whom the adminiftration of Judgement belongeth. It is neither permitted unto Prelates nor Prince to judge and determine at their own difcretion, but Law hath prefcribed what both fhall do. What power the King hath he hath it by Law, the bounds and limits of it are known, the intire community giveth general order by Law how all things publiquely are to be done, and the King as the Head thereof, the higheft in Authority over all, caufeth according to the fame Law every particular to be framed and ordered thereby. The whole Body Politique maketh Laws, which Laws gave power unto the King, and the King having bound himfelf to ufe according unto Law that power, it fo falleth out, that the execution of the one is accomplifhed by the other in moft religious and peaceable fort. There is no caufe given, unto any to make fupplication, as *Hilary* did, that Civil Governors, to whom Commonwealth matters onely belong, may not prefume to take upon them the judgement of Ecclefiaftical caufes. If the caufe be Spiritual, Secular Courts do not meddle with it ; we need not excufe our felves with *Ambrofe*, but boldly and lawfully we may refufe to anfwer before any Civil Judge in a matter which is not Civil, fo that we do not miftake either the nature of the caufe, or of the Court, as we eafily may do both, without fome better direction then can be by the rules of this new-found Difcipline. But of this moft certain we are, that our Laws do neither fuffer a * Spiritual Court to entertain thofe caufes which by the Law are Civil, nor yet if the matter be indeed Spiritual, a meer Civil Court to give judgement of it. Touching Supreme Power therefore to command all men, and in all manner of caufes of judgement to be higheft, let thus much fuffice as well for declaration of our own meaning, as for defence of the truth therein.

The caufe is not like when fuch Affemblies are gathered together by Supreme Authority concerning other affairs of the Church, and when they meet about the making of Ecclefiaftical Laws or Statutes. For in the one they are *rifdictio, ne falcem videatur ponere in Meffem alienam. Again, Non pertinet ad regem injungere pœnitentias, nec ad judicem fecularem, nec etiam ad eos pertinet cognofcere de iis quæ funt fpiritualibus annexa, ficut de decimis & aliis Ecclefiæ proventionibus. Again, Non eft Laicus conveniendus coram judice Ecclefiaftico de aliquo quod in foro feculari terminari poffit & debeat.*

Marginal note:

* *See the ftat. of Edw. 1. and Edw. 2. and Nat. Brev. touching Probibition. See alfo in Bracton thefe fentences, lib. 5. c. 2. Eft Jurifdictio ordinaria quedam delegata, que pertinet ad Sacerdotium, & Forum Ecclefiafticum, ficut in caufis Spiritualibus & Spiritualitati annexis. Eft etiam alia Jurifdictio ordinaria vel delegata que pertinet ad Coronam, & dignitatem Regis & ad Regnum in caufis & placitis rerum temporalium in foro feculari. Again, Cum diverfe fint hinc inde jurifdictiones, & diverfi Judices, & diverfæ caufæ, debet quilibet ipforum inprimis æftimare, an fua fit ju-*

onely to advise, in the other to decree. The persons which are of the one,
the King doth voluntarily assemble, as being in respect of quality fit to consult withal; them which are of the other, he calleth by prescript of Law, as
having right to be thereunto called. Finally, the one are but themselves,
and their sentence hath but the weight of their own judgement; the other
represent the whole Clergy, and their voyces are as much as if all did give
personal verdict. Now the question is, Whether the Clergy alone so assembled, ought to have the whole power of making Ecclesiastical Laws, or else
consent of the Laity may thereunto be made necessary, and the Kings assent so
necessary, that his sole denial may be of force to stay them from being Laws.

If they with whom we dispute were uniform, strong and constant in that
which they say, we should not need to trouble our selves about their persons
to whom the power of making Laws for the Church belongs : for they are
sometimes very vehement in contention, that from the greatest thing unto the
least about the Church, all must needs be immediately from God. And to this
they apply the pattern of the ancient Tabernacle which God delivered unto
Moses, and was therein so exact, that there was not left as much as the least
pin for the wit of man to devise in the framing of it. To this they also apply that streight and severe charge which God so often gave concerning his
own Law, *Whatsoever I command ye, take heed ye do it : Thou shalt put nothing thereto,
thou shalt take nothing from it :* Nothing, whether it be great or small; yet sometimes bethinking themselves better, they speak as acknowledging that it doth suffice to have received in such sort the principal things from God, and that for
other matters the Church hath sufficient Authority to make Laws; whereupon
they now have made it a question, What persons they are whose right it is to take
order for the Churches affairs, when the institution of any new thing therein is requisite. Law may be requisite to be made either concerning things that are onely to be known and believed in, or else touching that which is to be done by
the Church of God. The Law of Nature, and the Law of God, are sufficient
for declaration in both what belongeth unto each man separately as his soul is
the Spouse of Christ, yea so sufficient, that they plainly and fully shew whatsoever God doth require by way of necessary introduction unto the state of everlasting bliss. But as a man liveth joyned with others in common society, and belongeth to the outward politique body of the Church, albeit the same Law of
Nature and Scripture have in this respect also made manifest the things that are
of greatest necessity; neverthelets, by reason of new occasions still arising which
the Church having care of souls must take order for as need requireth, hereby
it cometh to pass, that there is and ever will be so great use even of Humane
Laws and Ordinances, deducted by way of discourse as a conclusion from the former Divine and Natural, serving for principals thereunto. No man doubteth,
but that for matters of action and practice in the affairs of God, for manner in Divine Service, for order in Ecclesiastical proceedings about the regiment of the
Church, there may be oftentimes cause very urgent to have laws made : but the
reason is not so plain, wherefore humane laws should appoint men what to believe. Wherefore in this we must note two things; 1. That in matter of opinion,
the law doth not make to be truth which before was not, as in matter of action
it causeth that to be a duty which was not before, but manifesteth only and giveth
men notice of that to be truth, the contrary whereunto they ought not before to
have believed. 2. That opinions do cleave to the understanding, and are in heart
assented unto, it is not in the power of any humane law to command them, because
to prescribe what men shall think belongeth only unto God; *Corde creditur ore fit
confessio,* saith the Apostle. As opinions are either fit, or inconvenient to be
professed, so mans law hath to determine of them. It may for publique
unities sake require mens professed assent, or prohibite their contradiction
to special articles, wherein as there haply hath been Controversie what
is true, so the same were like to continue still, not without grievous
detriment, unto a number of souls, except Law to remedy that evil, should
set down a certainty, which no man afterwards is to gain-say. Wherefore

(marginal notes)

What Laws
may be made
for the affairs
of the Church
and to whom
the power of
making them
appertain-
eth.

Deut 12.32,
and 4. 2.
Josh 1.7,

Thom. 1.1.quæs.
108.art.2.

Prov. 6. fore as in regard of divine laws, which the Church receiveth from God, we may unto every man apply those words of wisdom in *Salomon* ; *My Son keep thou thy Fathers Precepts. Conserva fili mi precepta patris tui,* even so concerning the statutes and ordinances which the Church it self makes, we may add there-unto the words that followeth, *Et ne dimittas legem matris tue, And forsake thou not thy Mothers Law.*

It is a thing even undoubtedly natural, that all free and *Indepenaent* societies should themselves make their own Laws, and that this power should belong to the whole, not to any certain part of a politique body, though happily some one part may have greater sway in that action then the rest, which thing being generally fit and expedient in the making of all laws, we see no cause why to think otherwise in laws, concerning the Service of God, Which in all well ordered states and Common-wealths, is the * first thing that Law hath care to provide for. When we speak of the right which naturally belongeth to a com-mon-wealth, we speak of that which must needs belong to the Church of God. For if the Common-wealth be Christian, if the people which are of it do pub-liquely imbrace the true Religon, this very thing doth make it the Church, as hath been shewed. So that unless the verity and purity of Religion do take from them which imbrace it, that power where-with otherwise they are possessed, look what Authority as touching Laws for Religion, a Common-wealth hath simply, it must of necessity being Christian Religion.

* Δεῖ ἢ νόμον
τὰ περὶ Θεὸς
ὦ δαίμονας
ὦ γονέας ὦ
ὅλως τὰ καλὰ
ἢ τίμια πρῶτα
τίθεσθαι. Δεύ-
τερο ἢ τὰ συμ-
φέροντα, τὰ
γὰρ μικρὰ τοῖς
μείζοσιν ἀκο-
λουθεῖν προσή-
κει. Aristit.
de leg & Instit.

That is, it behoveth the law, first to establish or settle those things which belong to the Gods, and Divine Powers, and to our Parents, and universally those things which be vertuous and honorable. In the Second place, those things that be convenient and profitable, for it is fit that matters of the less weight should come after the greater.

It will be therefore perhaps alledged that a part of the verity of Christian Re-ligion is to hold the power of making Ecclesiastical Laws a thing appropriated unto the Clergie in their Synods, and that whatsoever is by their onely voices agreed upon, it needeth no further approbation to give unto it the strength of a Law, as may plainly appear by the Canons of that first most venerable assem-bly, where those things the Apostles and *James* had concluded, were after-wards published and imposed upon the Churches of the Gentiles abroad as Laws, Act 15. 7
v 13
v. 23 the records thereof remaining still in the Book of God for a testimony, that the power of making Ecclesiastical Laws, belongeth to the successors of the Apostles, the Bishops and Prelates of the Church of God.

To this we answer, that the Council of *Jerusalem* is no Argument for the power of the Clergy to make Laws ; For first there hath not been sithence any Counsel of like authority to that in *Jerusalem* ; Secondly, the cause why that was of such Authority, came by a special accident ; Thirdly, the reason why other Councels being not like unto that in nature, the Clergie in them should have no power to make Laws by themselves alone, is in truth so forcible, that except some Commandement of God to the contrary can be shewed, it ought notwithstanding the foresaid example to prevail.

The Decrees of the Council of *Jerusalem*, were not as the Canons of other Ecclesiastical assemblies, humane, but very Divine ordinances, for which cause the Churches were far and wide commanded every where to see them kept, no otherwise then if Christ himself had personally on Earth been the Acts 15. 4 Author of them. The Cause why that Councel was of so great Authority and credit above all others which have been sithence, is expressed in those of princi-pal observation, *unto the Holy Ghost, and to us it hath seemed good,* which form of speech though other Councels have likewise used, yet neither could they themselves mean, nor may we so understand them, as if both were in equal sort assisted with the power of the Holy Ghost : but the latter had the favour of that Mat 16.
Mat ult. general assistance and presence which Christ doth promise unto all his, acording to the quality of their several estates and callings, the former the grace of special,

mira-

miraculous, rare, and extraordinary illumination, in relation whereunto the
Apostle comparing the Old Testament and the New together, termeth the
one a Testament of the Letter, for that God delivered it written in stone, the *2 Cor. 3.*
other a Testament of the Spirit, because God imprinted it in the hearts and declared it by the tongues of his chosen Apostles through the power of the Holy
Ghost, feigning both their conceits and speeches in most Divine and incomprehensible manner. Wherefore in as much as the Council of *Jerusalem* did chance
to consist of men so enlightened, it had authority greater then were meet for
any other Council besides to challenge, wherein such kind of persons are, as
now the state of the Church doth stand, Kings being not then, that which now
they are, and the Clergy not now, that which then they were: till it be proved
that some special Law of Christ hath for ever annexed unto the Clergy alone
the power to make Ecclesiastical Laws, we are to hold it a thing most consonant with equity and reason, that no Ecclesiastical Laws be made in a Christian
Common-wealth, without consent as well of the Laity, as of the Clergy, but
least of all without consent of the highest Power.

For of this thing no man doubteth, namely that in all Societies, Compa- *Cap. delicta, de*
nies and Corporations, what severally each sha l be bound unto it must be with *exceſſ. Prælator*
all their assents ratified. Against all equity it were that a man should suffer *L. per fundum*
detriment at the hands of men for not observing that which he never did *Ruſticor.præd.*
either by himself or by others, mediately or immediately agree unto. Much more *& § Religioſum*
then a King should constrain all others unto the strict observation of any *de rerum diviſ.*
such humane ordinance as passeth without his own approbation. In this case
therefore especially that vulgar axiome is of force, *quod omnes tangit ab omnibus*
tractari & approbari debet. Whereupon Pope *Nicholas,* although otherwise not
admitting Lay persons, no not Emperors themselves, to be present at Synods, *Gloſſ. diſt. 9f.*
doth notwithstanding seem to allow of their presence, when matters of faith *c. ubinam.*
are determined, whereunto all men must stand bound. *Ubinam legiſtis Impera-*
tores anteceſſores veſtros, ſynodalibus conventibus interfuiſſe niſi forſitan in quibus
de fide tractatum eſt, quæ non ſolum ad clericos, verum etiam ad laicos & omnes per-
tinet Chriſtianos; A Law, be it *Civil* or *Ecclesiastial*, is a publique obligation,
wherein seeing that the whole standeth charged, no reason it should pass without his privity and will, whom principally the whole doth depend upon. *Sicut*
laici juriſdictionem clericorum perturbare, ita clerici juriſdictionem laicorum non debent
minuere, saith *Innocentius, Extra de judiciis novit. As the Laity ſhould not hin-*
der the Clergie jurisdiction, ſo neither is it reaſon that the Laities right ſhould be
abridged by the Clergy: saith Pope *Innocent.* But were it so that the Clergy alone
might give Laws unto all the rest, for as much as every estate doth desire to inlarge the bounds of their own liberties, is it not easie to see how injurious
this might prove unto men of other conditions. Peace and Justice are maintained by preserving unto every order their rights, and by keeping all estates
as it were in an even ballance, which thing is no way better done, then if the King
their common Parent, whose care is presumed to extend most indifferently over
all, do bear the cheifest sway in the making laws which all must be ordered by.
Wherefore of them which in this point attribute most to the Clergy, I would
demand what evidence there is, whereby it may clearly be shewed, that in
antient Kingdoms Christian, any Canon devised by the Clergy alone in their
Synods, whether Provincical, National, or General, hath by meer force of
their agreement taken place as a law, making all men constrainable to be obedient thereunto, without any other approbation from the King, before or afterwards, required in that behalf. But what speak we of antient Kingdoms,
when at this day, even the papacy it self, the very Tridentine Council, hath
not every where as yet obtained to have in all points the strength of Ecclesiastical Law; did not *Philip* King of *Spain*, publishing that Council in the Low
Countries, add thereunto an express clause of special provision, that the same *Bout Epi. hirto*
should in no wise prejudice, hurt or diminish any kind of priviledge, which *it-queſt. l. 1.*
the King or his vassals a fore time, had enjoyed, touching either possessory *S. 28 ¦.*
judgements of Ecclesiastical livings, or concerning nominations thereunto, or be-

　　　　　　　　　　　　　　　　　　　　　　　　　　　longing

longing to whatſoever rights they had elſe in ſuch affairs. If therefore the Kings exception taken againſt ſome part of the Canons contained in that Councel, were a ſufficient bar to make them of none effect within territories, it followeth that the like exception againſt any other part, had been alſo of like efficacy, and ſo conſequently that no Part thereof had obtained the ſtrength of a Law, if he which excepted againſt a part had ſo done againſt the whole : as what reaſon was there but that the ſame authority which limited might quite and clean have refuſed that Councils who ſo alloweth the ſaid Act of the Catholique Kings for good and lawful, muſt grant that the Canons even of general Councils, have but the face of wiſe mens opinions, concerning that whereof, they treat, till they be publiquely aſſented unto, where they are to take place as Laws, and that in giving ſuch publique aſſent, as maketh a Chriſtian Kingdom ſubject unto thoſe Laws, the Kings Authority is the cheifeſt. That which an Univerſity of men, a Company or Corporation, doth without conſent of their Rector, is as nothing. Except therefore we make the Kings Authority over the Clergy, leſs in the greateſt things, then the power of the meaneſt Governour is in all things over the Colledge, or Society, which is under him, how ſhould we think the matter decent, that the Clergy ſhould impoſe Laws, the Supreme Governours aſſent not asked.

Yea that which is more, the Laws thus made, God himſelf doth in ſuch ſort authorize, that to deſpiſe them, is *to* deſpiſe in them him. It is a looſe and licentious opinion, which the *Anabaptiſts* have embraced, holding that Chriſtian mans liberty is loſt, and the ſoul which Chriſt hath redeemed unto himſelf injuriouſly drawn into ſervitude under the Yoke of humane power, if any Law be now impoſed beſides the Goſpel of Chriſt, in obedience whereunto the Spirit of God, and not the conſtraint of men, is to lead us, according to that of the bleſſed Apoſtle. Such as are led by the Spirit of God, they are the Sons of God, and not ſuch as live in thraldom unto men. Their judgement is therefore that the Church of Chriſt ſhould admit of no Law-makers but the Evangeliſts, no Courts but Presbyteries, no puniſhments but Eccleſiaſtical cenſures : as againſt this ſort, we are to maintain the uſe of humane Laws, and the continuall neceſſity of making them from time to time, as long as this preſent World doth laſt, ſo likewiſe the Authority of Laws, ſo made, doth need much more by us to be ſtrengthened againſt another ſort, who although they do not utterly condemn the making of Laws in the Church, yet make they a great deal leſs account of them then they ſhould do. There are which think ſimply of humane Laws, that they can in no ſort touch the conſcience. That to break and tranſgreſs them, cannot make men in the ſight of God culpable, as ſin doth ; onely when we violate ſuch laws, we do thereby make our ſelves obnoxious unto external puniſhment in this World, ſo that the Magiſtrate may in regard of ſuch offence committed juſtly Coreſt the offender, and cauſe him without injury to indure ſuch pains as law doth appoint, but further it reacheth not. For firſt the conſcience is the proper Court of God, the guiltineſs thereof is ſin, and the puniſhment eternal death, men are not able to make any law that ſhall command the heart, it is not in them to make inward conceit a crime, or to appoint for any crime other puniſhment then corporal ; their laws therefore can have no power over the ſoul, neither can the heart of man be polluted by tranſgreſſing them. St. *Auſtine* rightly defineth ſin to be that which is ſpoken, done or deſired, not againſt any laws, but againſt the Law of the Living God. The Law of God is propoſed unto man, as a glaſs wherein to behold the ſtains and the ſpots of their ſinful ſouls. By it they are to judge themſelves, and when they feel themſelves to have tranſgreſſed againſt it, then to bewail their offences with *David*, Againſt thee onely O Lord, have I ſinned and done wickedly in thy ſight ; that ſo our preſent tears may extinguiſh the flames, which otherwiſe we are to feel, and which God in that day ſhall condemn the Wicked unto, when they ſhall render accompt of the evil which they have done, not by violating ſtatute Laws, and Canons, but by diſobedience unto his law and his word.

For

For our better instruction therefore concerning this point, first we must note, That the Law of God it self doth require at our hands, subjection. Be ye subject, saith S. *Peter*, and S. *Paul*, *Let every soul be subject; subject all unto such powers as are set over us*. For if such as are not set over us, require our subjection, we by denying it are not disobedient to the Law of God, or undutiful unto higher Powers, because though they be such in regard of them over whom they have lawful dominion, yet having not so over us, unto us they are not such. Subjection

Verum ac proprium civis à peregrino discrimen est, quod alter impetio ac potestate e. vult obligatur, alter jussa principis a seni respuere potest illum Princeps ab hostium aquæ ac civium injuria tueri tenetur, hunc non tem nisi rogatus & humanitatis officiis impulsus saith Bodin *de repub.* l 1 c.6. *non multum . fine* p 61.B. Edition Lugdun, in fol 1586.

therefore we ow, and that by the Law of God, we are in conscience bound to yeild it even unto every of them that hold the seats of Authority and Power in relation unto us. Howbeit, not all kinds of subjection, unto every such kind of power: concerning *Scribes* and *Pharisees*, our Saviours precept was, *Whatsoever they shall tell ye, do it*. Was it his meaning, that if they should at any time enjoyn the people to levy an Army or to sell their Lands and Goods, for the furtherance of so great an enterprize; and in a word, that simply whatsoever it were which they did command, they ought without any exception forth-with t be obeyed. No, but whatsoever they shall tell you, must be understood in *pertinentibus ad cathedram*, it must be construed with limitation, and restrained unto things of that kind, which did belong to their place and power. For they had not power general, absolutely given them to command all things. The reason why we are bound in conscience to be subject unto all such power, is because all powers are of God.

They are of God either instituting or permitting them; power is then of Divine institution, when either God himself doth deliver, or men by light of nature find out the kind thereof. So that the power of Parents over Children, and of Husbands over their Wives, the power of all sorts of Superiors, made by consent of Commonwealths within themselves, or grown from agreement amongst Nations, such power is of Gods own institution in respect of the kind thereof; Again, if respect be had unto those particular persons, to whom the same is derived, if they either receive it immediately from God, as *Moses* and *Aaron* did; or from nature, as Parents do; or from men, by a natural and orderly course, as every Governour appointed in any Commonwealth, by the orders thereof doth, then is not the kind of their power, onely of Gods instituting, but the derivation thereof also into their Persons is from him. He hath placed them in their rooms, and doth term them his Ministers; Subjection therefore is due unto all such powers, inasmuch as they are of Gods own institution, even then when they are of mans creation, *Omni humanæ Creaturæ*, which things the Heathens themselves do acknowledge. Ξαντίχ@ Cαεικενα ἀ28 Ζεὺς κυδὸς εδωσι·

As for them that exercise power altogether against order, although the kind of power which they have may be of God, yet is their exercise thereof against God, and therefore not of God, otherwise then by *Permission*, as all Injustice is.

Touching such Acts as are done by that power which is according to his institution, that God in like sort doth authorize them, and account them to be his; though it were not confessed, it might be proved undeniable, for if that be accounted our deed, which others do, whom we have appointed to be our agents, how should God but approve those deeds, even as his own, which are done by vertue of that commission and power which he hath given. *Take heed,* (saith Jehosophat unto his Judges) *be careful and circumspect what ye do, ye do not execute the judgements of man but of the Lord.* 2 Chron. 19.6. The Authority of *Cæsar* over the *Jews*, from whence was it? Had it any other ground then the Law of Nations, which maketh Kingdoms, subdued by just War, to be subject unto their Conquerors? By this power *Cæsar* exacting tribute, our Saviour confesseth it to be his right, a right which could not be withheld without injury, yea disobedience herein unto him, and even rebellion against God. Usurpers of power, whereby we do not mean them that by violence have

A Scepter swaying Kings to whom even Jupiter himself hath given honour, and commandment.

Eff aspired

aspired unto places of highest Authority, but them that use more Authority then they did ever receive in form and manner before mentioned; (for so they may do, whose title unto the rooms of Authority, which they possess, no man can deny to be just and lawful, even as contrariwise some mens proceedings in Government have been very orderly, who notwithstanding did not attain to be made Governors, without great violence and disorder) such usurpers thereof, as in the exercise of their power do more then they have been authorized to do, cannot in Conscience binde any man unto obedience.

That subjection which we owe unto lawful Powers, doth not onely import that we should be under them by order of our state, but that we shew all submission towards them, both by honor and obedience. He that resisteth them, resisteth God: And resisted they be, if either the Authority it self which they exercise be denied, as by Anabaptists all Secular Jurisdiction is; or if resistance be made but onely so far forth, as doth touch their persons which are invested with power; (for they which said, *Nolumus hunc regnare*, did not utterly exclude Regiment; nor did they with all kinde of Government clearly removed, which would not, at the first have *David* to govern) or if that which they do by vertue of their power, namely, their Laws, Edicts, Services, or other acts of Jurisdiction, be not suffered to take effect, contrary to the blessed Apostles most holy rule, *Obey them that have the oversight of you*, Heb. 13. 17. or if they do take effect, yet is not the will of God thereby satisfied neither, as long as that which we do is contemptuously, or repiningly done, because we can do no otherwise. In such sort the Israelites in the Desart obeyed *Moses*, and were notwithstanding deservedly plagued for disobedience. The Apostles Precept therefore is, *Be subject even for Gods cause: Be subject, not for fear, but of meer Conscience, knowing that he which resisteth them, purchaseth to himself condemnation*. Disobedience therefore unto Laws, which are made by men, is not a thing of so small account as some would make it.

Howbeit, too rigorous it were, that the breach of every Humane Law should be held a deadly sin: A mean there is between those extremities, if so be we can find it out.

TO THE
READER.

THe pleasures of thy spacious walks in Mr. Hookers Temple-Garden (not unfitly so called, both for the Temple whereof he was Master, and the Subject, Ecclesiastical Polity) do promise acceptance to these Flowers, planted and watered by the same hand, and for thy sake composed into this Posie. Sufficiently are they commended, by their fragrant smell, in the dogmatical Truth; by their beautiful colours, in the accurate stile; by their medicinable vertue, against some diseases in our neighbour Churches, now proving epidemical, and threatning farther infection; by their strait feature and spreading nature, growing from the root of Faith (which, as here is proved, can never be rooted up) and extending the branches of Charity to the covering of Noahs nakedness; opening the windows of Hope to mens misty conceits of their bemisted forefathers. Thus, and more then thus, do the works commend themselves; the Work-man needs a better Workman to commend him (Alexanders Picture requires Apelles his pencil) nay, he needs it not, His own works commend him in the gates, and, being dead, he yet speaketh; the Syllables of that memorable name Mr. Richard Hooker, proclaiming more, then if I should here stile him a painful Student, a profound Scholar, a judicious Writer, with other due titles of his honour. Receive then this posthume Orphan for his own, yea, for thine own sake; and if the Printer hath with overmuch haste, like Mephibosheths Nurse, lamed the childe with slips and falls, yet be thou of Davids minde, shew kindeness to him for his father Jonathans sake. God grant that the rest of his brethren be not more then lamed, and that as Sauls three sons dyed the same day with him, so those three promised to perfect his Polity, with other issues of that learned brain, be not buried in the grave with their renowned Father. Farewel.

W. S.

The Contents of these Treatises following.

A
SUPPLICATION
Made to the
COUNCEL
BY
Master Walter Travers.

Right Honourable,

THE manifold benefits which all the Subjects within this Dominion do at this present, and have many years enjoyed, under Her Majesties most happy and prosperous reign, by your godly wisdom, and careful watching over this Estate night and day: I truly and unfeignedly acknowledge from the bottom of my heart ought worthily to binde us all, to pray continually to Almighty God for the continuance and encrease of the life and good estate of your Honours, and to be ready with all good duties to satisfie and serve the same to our power. Besides publick benefits common unto all, I must needs, and do willingly confess my self to stand bound by most special obligation to serve and honour you more then any other, for the honourable favour it hath pleased you to vouchsafe both oftentimes heretofore, and also now of late, in a matter more dear unto me then any earthly commodity, that is, the upholding and furthering of my service in the ministring of the Gospel of Jesus Christ. For which cause, as I have been always careful so to carry my self as I might by no means give occasion to be thought unworthy of so great a benefit, so do I still, next unto her Majesties gracious countenance, hold nothing more dear and precious to me, then that I may always remain in your Honours favour, which hath oftentimes been helpful and comfortable unto me in my Ministry, and to all such as reaped any fruit of my simple and faithful labour. In which dutiful regard I humbly beseech your Honours to vouchsafe to do me this grace, to conceive nothing of me otherwise then according to the duty wherein I ought to live, by any information against me, before your Honours have heard my answer, and been throughly informed of the matter. Which although it be a

Eee 2

thing,

thing, that your wisdoms, not in favour but in justice yield to all men, yet the state of the calling into the Ministery, whereunto it hath pleased God of his goodness to call me, though unworthiest of all, is so subject to mif-information, as except we may find this favour with your Honours, we cannot look for any other, but that our unindifferent parties may easily procure us to be hardly esteemed of; and that we shall be made like the poor fisherboats in the Sea, which every swelling wave and billow raketh and runneth over. Wherein my estate is yet harder then any others of my rank and calling, who are indeed to fight against flesh and blood in what part soever of the Lords Host and field they shall stand marshalled to serve, yet many of them deal with it naked and unfurnished of weapons: But my service was in a place where I was to encounter within well appointed and armed with skill and with authority, whereof as I have always thus deserved, and therefore have been careful by all good means to entertain still your Honors favourable respect of me, so have I special cause at this present, wherein mif-information to the Lord Archbishop of *Canterbury*, and other of the High Commission hath been able so far to prevail against me, that by their letter they have inhibited me to preach, or execute any act of Ministry in the Temple or elsewhere, having never once called me before them to understand by mine answer the truth of such things as had been informed against me. We have a story in our books wherein the Pharisees proceeding against our Saviour Christ without having heard him, is reproved by an honorable Counsellor (as the Evangelist doth term him) saying, *Doth our Law judge a man before it hear him, and know what he hath done?* Which I do not mention, to the end that by an indirect and covert speech I might so compare those, who have without ever hearing me, pronounced a heavy sentence against me; for, notwithstanding such proceedings, I purpose by Gods grace to carry my self towards them in all seeming duty agreeable to their places: muchless do I presume to liken my cause to our Saviour Christs, who hold it my chiefest honor and happiness to serve him, though it be but among the hindes and hired Servants, that serve him in the basest corners of his house. But my purpose in mentioning it, is, to shew by the judgement of a Prince and great man in *Israel*, that such proceeding standeth not with the Law of God, and in a princely pattern to shew it to be a noble part of an honorable Counsellor, not to allow of indirect dealings, but to allow and affect such a course in justice, as is agreeable to the Law of God. We have also a plain rule in the Word of God, not to proceed any otherwise against any Elder of the Church; muchless against one that laboureth in the word and in teaching: which rule is delivered with this most earnest charge and obtestation, *I beseech and charge thee in the sight of God, and the Lord Jesus Christ, and the Elect Angels, that thou keep those [rules] without preferring one before another, doing nothing of partiallity or inclining to either part;* which Apostolical and most earnest charge, I refer it to your Honors wisdom how it hath been regarded in so heavy a judgement against me, without ever hearing my cause; and whether, as having God before their eyes, and the Lord Jesu, by whom all former judgements shall be tried again, and as in the presence of the Elect Angels, witnesses and observers of the regiment of the Church, they have proceeded thus to such a sentence. They alleage indeed two reasons in their letters, whereupon they restrain my Ministry, which, if they were as strong against me as they are supposed, yet I refer to your Honors wisdoms, whether the quality of such an offence as they charge me with, which is in effect but an indiscretion, deserve so grievous a punishment both to the Church and me, in taking away my Ministery, and that poor little commodity which it yeeldeth for the necessary maintenance of my life; if so unequal a ballancing of faults and punishments should have place in the Commonwealth, surely we should shortly have no Actions upon the Case, nor of Trespass, but all should be pleas of the Crown, nor any man amerced, or fined, but for every light offence put to his ransom. I have credibly heard, that some of the Ministry have been committed for grievous transgressions of the laws of God and men, being of no ability to do other service in the Church then to read, yet hath it been thought charitable and standing with Christian moderation and temperancy, not to deprive such of Ministry and Beneficency, but to inflict some more tolerable punishment. Which I write not because such, as I think, were to be favoured, but to shew how unlike their dealing is with me, being through the goodness of God not to be touched with any such blame, and one who according to the measure of the gift of God have laboured now some years painfully, in regard of the weak estate of my body, in preaching the Gospel, and as I hope, not altogether un-
pro fitably

1 Tim. 5.19, 21.

profitably in respect of the Church. But I beseech your Honours to give me leave briefly to declare the particular reasons of their Letters, and what answer I have to make unto it.

The first is, that as they say, *I am not lawfully called to the Function of the Ministry, nor allowed to preach according to the Laws of the Church of* England.

For answer to this, I had need to divide the points, and first to make answer to the former, wherein leaving to shew what by the holy Scriptures is required in a lawful calling, and that all this is to be found in mine, that I be not too long for your weighty affairs, I rest.

I thus answer : My calling to the Ministry was such as in the calling of any thereunto, is appointed to be used by the orders agreed upon in the National Synods of the Low Countreys, for the direction and guidance of their Churches, which orders are the same with those whereby the French and Scottish Churches are governed, whereof I have shewed such sufficient testimonial to my Lord the Archbishop of *Canterbury*, as is requisite in such a matter: whereby it must needs fall out, if any man be lawfully called to the Ministry in those Churches, then is my calling, being the same with theirs, also lawful. But I suppose notwithstanding they use this general speech, they mean only my calling is not sufficient, to deal in the Ministry within this land, because I was not made Minister according to that order which in this cause is ordained by our laws. Whereunto I beseech your Honors to consider throughly of mine answer, because exception now again is taken to my Ministery, whereas having been heretofore called in question for it, I so answered the matter, as I continued my ministry, and for any thing I discerned, looked to hear that no more objected unto me. The communion of Saints (which every Christian man professeth to beleive) is such, as that the acts which are done in any true Church of Christ according to his word, are held as lawful, being done in one Church as in another. Which as it holdeth in other acts of ministery, as baptism, mariage and such like, so doth it in the calling to the ministry ; by reason whereof all Churches do acknowledge and receive him for a Minister of the word who hath been lawfully called thereunto in any Church of the same profession. A Doctor created in any University of Christendom, is acknowledged sufficiently qualified to teach in any country. The Church of *Rome* it self, and the Canon law holdeth it, that being ordered in *Spain*, they may execute that belongeth to their order in *Italy*, or in any other place. And the Churches of the Gospel never made any question of it ; which if they shall now begin to make doubt of, and deny such to be lawfully called to the Ministry, as are called by another order then our own, then may it well be looked for that other Churches will do the like : And if a Minister called in the Low-countries be not lawfully called in *England*, then may they say to our preachers which are there, that being made of another order then theirs, they cannot suffer them to execute any act of ministry amongst them ; which in the end must needs breed a schism and dangerous division in the Churches. Further I have heard of those that are learned in the Laws of this land, that by express Statute to that purpose *Anno* 13. upon subscription of the Articles agreed upon *Anno* 62. that they who pretend to have been ordered by another order then that which is now established, are of like capacity to enjoy any place of ministry within the land, as they that have been ordered according to that is now by law in this case established. Which comprehending manifestly all, even such as were made Priests according to the order of the Church of *Rome*, it must needs be, that the law of a Christian land professing the Gospel, should be as favourable for a Minister of the word, as for a Popish Priest, which also was so found in Mr. *Whittinghams* case, who notwithstanding such replies against him, enjoyed still the benefit he had by his Ministry, and might have done until this day if God had spared him life so long ; which if it be understood so and practised in others, why should the change of the person alter the right, which the Law giveth to all other?

The place of Ministry, whereunto I was called, was not presentative : and if it had been so, surely they would never have presented any man whom they never knew ; and the order of this Church is agreable herein to the word of God, and the ancient and best Canons, that no man should be made a Minister *sine titulo*: therefore having none, I could not by the orders of this Church have entred into the Ministry, before I had charge to tend upon. When I was at *Antwerp*, and to take a place of Ministry among the people of that nation, I see no cause why I should have returned again over the seas for

Orders here, nor how I could have done it, without diſallowing the Orders of the Churches provided in the Countrey where I was to live. Whereby I hope it appeareth, that my calling to the Miniſtery is lawful, and maketh me by our Law, of capacity to enjoy any benefit or commodity, that any other by reaſon of his Miniſtery may enjoy. But my cauſe is yet more eaſie, who reaped no benefit of my Miniſtery by Law, receiving onely a benevolence and voluntary contribution; and the Miniſtery I dealt with, being preaching onely, which every Deacon here may do being licenſed, and certain that are neither Miniſters nor Deacons. Thus I anſwer the former of theſe two points, whereof if there be yet any doubt, I humbly deſire for a final end thereof, that ſome competent Judges in Law may determine of it; whereunto I refer and ſubmit my ſelf with all reverence and duty.

The ſecond is, *That I preached without Licenſe.* Whereunto this is my anſwer, I have not preſumed upon the calling I had to the Miniſtery abroad, to preach or deal with any part of the Miniſtery within this Church, without the conſent and allowance of ſuch as were to allow me unto it: my allowance was from the Biſhop of *London,* teſtified by his two ſeveral Letters to the *Inner-Temple,* who without ſuch teſtimony would by no means reſt ſatisfied in it; which Letters being by me produced, I refer it to your Honors wiſdom, whether I have taken upon me to preach, without being allowed (as they charge) according to the Orders of the Realm. Thus having anſwered the ſecond point alſo, I have done with the objection, *Of dealing without calling or licenſe.*

The other Reaſon they alledge, is, concerning a late action, wherein I had to deal with Mr. *Hooker,* Maſter of the *Temple.* In the handling of which cauſe, they charge me with an indiſcretion, and want of duty; *In that I inveighed* (as they ſay) *againſt certain points of Doctrine taught by him as erroneous, not conferring with him, nor complaining of it to them.* My anſwer hereunto ſtandeth, in declaring to your Honors the whole courſe and carriage of that Cauſe, and the degrees of proceeding in it, which I will do as briefly as I can, and according to the truth, God be my witneſs, as near as my beſt memory and notes of remembrance may ſerve me thereunto. After that I have taken away that which ſeemeth to have moved them to think me not charitably minded to Mr. *Hooker;* which is, becauſe he was brought in to Mr. *Alveyes* place, wherein this Church deſired that I might have ſucceeded: which place, if I would have made ſuit to have obtained, or if I had ambitiouſly affected and ſought, I would not have refuſed to have ſatisfied by ſubſcription, ſuch as the matter then ſeemed to depend upon: whereas contrariwiſe, notwithſtanding I would not hinder the Church to do that they thought to be moſt for their edification and comfort, yet did I neither by ſpeech nor letter, make ſuit to any for the obtaining of it; following herein that reſolution, which I judge to be moſt agreeable to the Word and Will of God; that is, that labouring and ſuing for places and charges in the Church is not lawful. Further, whereas at the ſuit of the Church, ſome of your Honors entertained the cauſe, and brought it to a near iſſue, that there ſeemed nothing to remain, but the commendation of my Lord the Archbiſhop of *Canterbury,* when as he could not be ſatisfied, but by my ſubſcribing to his late Articles; and that my anſwer agreeing to ſubſcribe according to any Law, and to the Statute provided in that caſe, but praying to be reſpited for ſubſcribing to any other, which I could not in conſcience do, either for the *Temple* (which otherwiſe he ſaid, he would not commend me to) nor for any other place in the Church, did ſo little pleaſe my Lord Archbiſhop, as he reſolved, that otherwiſe I ſhould not be commended to it. I had utterly here no cauſe of offence againſt Mr. *Hooker,* whom I did in no ſort eſteem to have prevented or undermined me, but that God diſpoſed of me as it pleaſed him, by ſuch means and occaſions as I have declared.

Moreover, as I had taken no cauſe of offence at Mr. *Hooker* for being preferred; ſo there were many witneſſes, that I was glad that the place was given him, hoping to live in all godly peace and comfort with him, both for acquaintance and good will which hath been between us, and for ſome kinde of affinity in the marriage of his neereſt kindred and mine: Since his coming, I have ſo carefully endeavoured to entertain all good correſpondence and agreement with him, as I think he himſelf will bear me witneſs of many earneſt Diſputations and Conferences with him about the matter; the rather, becauſe that contrary to my expectation, he inclined from the

beginning

beginning but fmally thereunto, but joyned rather with fuch as had always oppofed themfelves to any good order in this charge, and made themfelves to be brought in-difpofed to his prefent ftate and proceedings: For both knowing that Gods Com-mandment charged me with fuch duty, and difcerning how much our peace might further the good fervice of God and his Church, and the mutual comfort of us both, I had refolved conftantly to feek for peace; and though it fhould flie from me (as I faw it did by means of fome, who little defired to fee the good of our Church) yet according to the rule of Gods Word, to follow after it: Which being fo (as hereof I take God to witnefs, who fearcheth the heart and reins, and by his Son will judge the World, both the quick and dead) I hope no charitable judgement can fup-pofe me to have ftood evil-affected towards him for his place, or defirous to fall in-to any controverfie with him.

Which my refolution I purfued, that whereas I difcovered fundry unfound mat-ters in his Doctrine (as many of his Sermons tafted of fome four leaven or other) yet thus I carried my felf towards him: matters of fmaller weight, and fo covertly difcovered, that no great offence to the Church was to be feared in them, I wholly paffed by, as one that difcerned nothing of them, or had been unfurnifhed of replies; for others of great moment, and fo openly delivered, as there was juft caufe of fear, left the Truth and Church of God fhould be prejudiced and perilled by it, and fuch as the confcience of my duty and calling would not fuffer me altogether to pafs over, this was my courfe, to dever, when I fhould have juft caufe by my Text, the truth of fuch Doctrine as he had otherwife taught, in general fpeeches, without touch of his perfon in any fort, and further at convenient opportunity to confer with him in fuch points.

According to which determination, whereas he had taught certain things concern-ing Predeftination, otherwife then the Word of God doth, as it is underftood by all Churches profeffing the Gofpel, and not unlike that wherewith *Coranus* fometimes troubled his Church, I both delivered the truth of fuch points in a general doctrine, without any touch of him in particular, and conferred with him alfo privately upon fuch Articles. In which Conference, I remember, when I urged the confent of all Churches and good Writers againft him that I knew; and defired if it were other-wife, what Authors he had feen of fuch Doctrine? He anfwered me, That his beft Au-thor was his own Reafon; which I wifhed him to take heed of as a matter ftanding with Chriftian modefty and wifdom, in a Doctrine not received by the Church, not to truft to his own judgement fo far, as to publifh it before he had conferred with others of his Profeffion, labouring by daily prayer and ftudy, to know the will of God, as he did, to fee how they underftood fuch Doctrine: Notwithftanding, he with wavering replying, That he would fome other time deal more largely in the mat-ter, I wifhed him, and prayed him not fo to do, for the peace of the Church, which by fuch means might be hazarded; feeing he could not but think, that men, who make any confcience of their Miniftery, will judge it a neceffary duty in them, to teach the truth, and to convince the contrary.

Another time, upon like occafion of this Doctrine of his, *That the affurance of that we believe by the Word, is not fo certain, as of that we perceive by fenfe;* I both taught the Doctrine otherwife, namely, the affurance of Faith to be greater, which affured both of things above, and contrary to all fenfe and humane underftanding, and dealt with him alfo privately upon that point: According to which courfe of late, when as he had taught, *That the Church of Rome is a true Church of Chrift, and a fanctified Church by profeffion of that Truth, which God hath revealed unto us by his Son, though not a pure and perfect Church;* and further, *That he doubted not, but that thoufands of the Fathers, which lived and dyed in the Superftitions of that Church, were faved, be-caufe of their ignorance, which excufeth them,* mifalledging to that end a Text of Scri-pture to prove it: The matter being of fet purpofe openly and at large handled by him, and of that moment, that might prejudice the Faith of Chrift, encourage the ill-affected to continue ftill in their damnable ways, and others weak in Faith to fuffer themfelves eafily to be feduced, to the deftruction of their fouls, I thought it my moft bounden duty to God, and to his Church, whileft I might have opportu-nity to fpeak with him, to teach the Truth in a general fpeech in fuch points of Doctrine.

1 Tim. 1. 13.

At

At which time I taught, *That such as dye, or have dyed at any time in the Church of Rome, holding in their ignorance that Faith, which is taught in it, and namely, Justification in part by works, could not be said by the Scriptures to be saved.* In which matter, foreseeing that if I waded not warily in it, I should be in danger to be reported, (as hath fallen out since notwithstanding) to condemn all the Fathers, I said directly and plainly to all mens understanding, *That it was not indeed to be doubted, but many of the Fathers were saved; but the means (I said) was not their ignorance, which excuseth no man with God, but their knowledge and faith of the Truth, which it appeareth God vouchsafed them, by many notable Monuments and Records extant in all Ages.* Which being the last point in all my Sermon, rising so naturally from the Text I then propounded, as would have occasioned me to have delivered such matter, notwithstanding the former Doctrine had been found; and being dealt in by a general speech, without touch of his particular; I looked not that a matter of controversie would have been made of it, no more then had been of my like dealing in former time. But far otherwise then I looked for, Mr. *Hooker* shewing no grief of offence taken at my speech all the week long, the next Sabbath, leaving to proceed upon his ordinary Texts professed to preach again, that he had done the day before, for some question that his Doctrine was drawn into, which he desired might be examined with all severity.

So proceeding, he bestowed his whole time in that discourse, concerning his former Doctrine, and answering the places of Scripture, which I had alledged, to prove that a man dying in the Church of *Rome*, is not to be judged by the Scriptures to be saved. In which long speech, and utterly impertinent to his Text, under colour of answering for himself, he impugned directly and openly to all mens understanding, the true Doctrine which I had delivered; and added to his former points some other like (as willingly one Error followeth another) that is, *That the Galathians joyning with Faith in Christ Circumcision, as necessary to Salvation, might not be saved: And that they of the Church of Rome, may be saved by such a Faith of Christ as they had, with a general Repentance of all their errors, notwithstanding their opinion of Justification, in part, by their works and merits.* I was necessarily, though not willingly, drawn to say something to the points he objected against sound Doctrine; which I did in a short speech in the end of my Sermon, with protestation of so doing, not of any sinister affection to any man, but to bear witness to the Truth, according to my calling; and wished, if the matter should needs further be dealt in, some other more convenient way might be taken for it; wherein I hope, my dealing was manifest to the consciences of all indifferent hearers of me that day, to have been according to peace, and without any uncharitableness, being duly considered.

For that I conferred with him the first day, I have shewed that the cause requiring of me the duty, at the least not to be altogether silent in it, being a matter of such consequence, that the time also being short, wherein I was to preach after him, the hope of the fruit of our communication being small, upon experience of former Conferences, my expectation being, that the Church should be no further troubled with it, upon the motion I made of taking some other course of dealing. I suppose my deferring to speak with him till some fit oportunity, cannot in Charity be judged uncharitable.

The second day, his unlooked for opposition with the former Reasons, made it to be a matter that required of necessity some publique answer; which being so temperate, as I have shewed, if notwithstanding it be censured as uncharitable, and punished so grievously as it is, what should have been my punishment, if (without all such cautions and respects as qualified my speech) I had before all, and in the understanding of all, so reproved him offending openly, that others might have feared to do the like? which yet if I had done, might have been warranted by the rule and charge of the Apostle, *Them that offend openly, rebuke openly, that the rest may also fear;* and by his example, who when *Peter* in this very case which is now between us, had (not in preaching) but in a matter of Conversation, not gone with a right foot, as was fit for the truth of the Gospel, conferred not privately with him, but, as his own rule required, reproved him openly before all, that others might hear, and fear, and not dare to do the like: All which reasons together weighed, I hope, will shew the manner of my dealing to have been charitable, and warrantable in every sort.

Apoc. 18. 4.
Gal. 5. 2, 3, 4.

The

¶. The next Sabbath day after this, Mr. *Hooker* kept the way he had entred into before, and bestowed his whole hour and more onely upon the questions he had moved and maintained; wherein he so set forth the agreement of the Church of *Rome* with us, and their disagreement from us, as if we had consented in the greatest and weightiest points, and differed onely in certain smaller matters: Which agreement noted by him in two chief points, is not such as he would have made men believe. The one, in that he said, *They acknowledged all men sinners, even the blessed Virgin*, though some of them freed her from sin; for the Council of *Trent* holdeth that she was free from sin. Another, in that he said, *They teach Christs Righteousness to be the onely meritorious cause of taking away sin, and differ from us onely in the applying of it*: For *Thomas Aquinas* their chief Schoolman, and Archbishop *Catherinus* teach, *That Christ took away onely Original sin, and that the rest are to be taken away by our selves*; yea, the Council of *Trent* teacheth, *That Righteousness whereby we are righteous in Gods sight, is an inherent Righteousness*: which must needs be of our own works, and cannot be understood of the righteousness inherent onely in Christs person, and accounted unto us. Moreover he taught the same time, *That neither the Galatbians, nor the Church of Rome, did directly overthrow the foundation of Justification by Christ alone, but onely by consequent, and therefore might well be saved; or else neither the Churches of the Lutherans, nor any which hold any manner of Errour could be saved; because* (saith he) *every errour by consequent overthroweth the foundation*. In which discourses, and such like, he bestowed his whole time and more; which, if he had affected either the truth of God, or the peace of the Church, he would truly not have done.

Whose example could not draw me to leave the Scripture I took in hand, but standing about an hour to deliver the Doctrine of it, in the end, upon just occasion of the Text, leaving sundry other his unsound speeches, and keeping me still to the principal, I confirmed the believing the Doctrine of Justification by Christ onely, to be necessary to the Justification of all that should be saved, and that the Church of *Rome* directly denieth, that a man is saved by Christ, or by Faith alone, without the works of the Law. Which my answer, as it was most necessary for the service of God, and the Church, so was it without any immodest or reproachful speech to Mr. *Hooker*: whose unsound and wilful dealings in a cause of so great importance to the Faith of Christ, and salvation of the Church, notwithstanding I knew well what speech it deserved, and what some zealous earnest man of the spirit of *John* and *James*, sirnamed *Boanerges*, sons of Thunder, would have said in such a case; yet I chose rather to content my self in exhorting him to revisit his Doctrine, as *Nathan* the Prophet did the device, which without consulting with God he had of himself given to *David*, concerning the building of the Temple; and with *Peter* the Apostle, to endure to be withstood in such a case, not unlike unto this. This in effect, was that which passed between us concerning this matter, and the invectives I made against him, wherewith I am charged: Which rehearsal, I hope, may clear me (with all that shall indifferently consider it) of the blames laid upon me for want of duty to Mr. *Hooker*, in not conferring with him, whereof I have spoken sufficiently already; and to the High-Commission, in not revealing the matter to them, which yet now I am further to answer. My answer is, That I protest, no contempt nor wilful neglect of any lawful Authority, stayed me from complaining unto them, but these Reasons following:

Mark 3.17.

2 Sam. 7. 2, 3, 4, 5.
Gal. 1, 11. 140.

First, I was in some hope, that Mr. *Hooker*, notwithstanding he had been overcarried with a shew of Charity to prejudice the Truth, yet when it should be sufficiently proved, would have acknowledged it, or at the least induced with peace, that it might be offered without either offence to him, or to such as would receive it; either of which would have taken away any cause of just complaint. When neither of these fell out according to my expectation and desire, but that he replied to the truth, and objected against it, I thought he might have some doubts and scruples in himself, which yet if they were cleared, he would either imbrace sound Doctrine, or at least suffer it to have his course: Which hope of him I nourished so long, as the matter was not bitterly and immodestly handled between us.

Another Reason was the cause it self, which according to the Parable of the Tares (which are said to be sown among the Wheat) sprung up first in his grass: Therefore as the servants in that place are not said to have come to complain to the Lord till,

till the Tares came to shew their fruits in their kinde: so I thinking it yet but a time of discovering of it what it was, desired not their sickle to cut it down.

For further answer, It is to be considered, that the conscience of my duty to God, and to his Church, did binde me at the first to deliver sound Doctrine in such points, as had been otherwise uttered in the place, where I had now some years taught the truth; Otherwise the rebuke of the Prophet had fallen upon me, for not going up to the breach, and standing in it, and the peril for answering the blood of the City, in whose Watch-Tower I sate, if it had been surprized by my default. Moreover, my publique Protestation, in being unwilling, that if any were not yet satisfied, some other more convenient way might be taken for it. And lastly, that I had resolved (which I uttered before to some, dealing with me about the matter) to have protested the next Sabbath day, that I would no more answer in that place, any objections to the Doctrine taught by any means, but some other way satisfie such as should require it.

Ezek 2i.33.
E2.33.6.

These I trust may make it appear, that I failed not in duty to Authority, notwithstanding I did not complain, nor give over so soon dealing in the case: If I did, how is he clear, which can alledge none of all these for himself; who leaving the expounding of the Scriptures, and his ordinary calling, voluntarily discoursed upon School Points and Questions, neither of edification, nor of truth; who after all this, as promising to himself, and to untruth, a victory by my silence, added yet in the next Sabbath day, to the maintenance of his former opinions, these which follow?

That no additament taketh away the foundation, except it be a privative; of which sort, neither the works added to Christ by the Church of Rome, nor Circumcision by the Galatians were: as one denieth him not to be a man, that saith he is a righteous man, but he that saith he is a dead man: Whereby it might seem, that a man might, without hurt, adde works of Christ, and pray also that God and S. Peter would save them.

That the Galatians case is harder then the case of the Church of Rome, because the Galatians joyned Circumcision with Christ, which God hath forbidden and abolished; but that which the Church of Rome joyned with Christ, were good works which God hath commanded. Wherein he committed a double fault, one, in expounding all the questions of the *Galatians,* and consequently of the *Romans,* and other Epistles, of Circumcision onely, and the Ceremonies of the Law (as they do who answer for the Church of *Rome* in their writings) contrary to the clear meaning of the Apostle, as may appear by many strong and sufficient reasons: The other, in that he said, *the addition of the Church of* Rome *was of works commanded of God;* whereas the least part of the works whereby they looked to merit, was of such works, and most were works of supererogation, and of works which God never commanded, but was highly displeased with, as of Masses, Pilgrimages, Pardons, pains of Purgatory, and such like: *That no one sequel urged by the Apostle against the Galatians for joyning Circumcision with Christ, but might be as well enforced against the Lutherans; that is, that for their ubiquity it may be as well said to them, If ye hold the Body of Christ to be in all places, you are fallen from grace, you are under the curse of the Law,* saying, Cursed be he that fulfilleth not all things written in this Book, with such like. He added yet further, *That to a Bishop of the Church of* Rome, *to a Cardinal, yea to the Pope himself, acknowledging Christ to be the Saviour of the world, denying other errours, and being discomforted for want of works whereby he might be justified, he would not doubt, but use this speech, Thou boldest the foundation of Christian Faith, though it be but by a slender thred; thou holdest Christ, though but as by the hem of his garment; why shouldst thou not hope that vertue may pass from Christ to save thee? That which thou boldest of Justification by thy works, overthroweth indeed by consequent the foundation of Christian Faith; but be of good cheer, thou hast not to do with a captious Sophister, but with a merciful God, who will justifie thee for that thou holdest, and not take the advantage of doubtful construction to condemn thee. And if this,* said he, *be an errour, I hold it willingly, for it is the greatest comfort I have in this world, without which I would not wish either to speak or to live.* Thus far, being not to be answered in it any more, he was bold to proceed, the absurdity of which speech I need not to stand upon. I think the like to this, and other such in this Sermon, and the rest of this matter, hath not been heard in publique places within this Land, since Queen *Maries* days. What consequence this Doctrine may be of, if he be not by Authority ordered to revoke it, I beseech your H H. as the truth

of

of God and his Gospel is dear and precious unto you, according to your godly wisdom to consider.

I have been bold to offer to your HH. a long and tedious discourse of these matters; but speech being like to Tapestry, which if it be folded up, sheweth but part of that which is wrought, and being unlapt and laid open, sheweth plainly to the eye all the work that is in it, I thought it necessary to unfold this Tapestry, and to hang up the whole chamber of it in your most Honourable Senate, that so you may the more easily discern of all the pieces, and the sundry works and matters contained in it. Wherein my hope is, your HH. may see I have not deserved so great a punishment, as is laid upon the Church for my sake, and also upon my self, in taking from me the exercise of my Ministery: Which punishment, how heavy it may seem to the Church, or fall out indeed to be, I refer it to them to judge, and spare to write what I fear; but to my self it is exceeding grievous, for that it taketh from me the exercise of my calling. Which I do not say is dear unto me, as the means of that little benefit whereby I live (although this be a lawful consideration, and to be regarded of me in due place, and of the Authority under whose protection I most willingly live, even by Gods Commandment both unto them, and unto me:) but which ought to be more precious to me then my life, for the love which I should bear to the glory and honour of Almighty God, and to the edification and salvation of his Church, for that my life cannot any other way be of like service to God, nor of such use and profit to men by any means: For which cause, as I discern how dear my Ministery ought to be unto me, so it is my hearty desire, and most humble request unto God, to your H.H. and to all the Authority I live under, to whom any dealing herein belongeth, that I may spend my life according to his Example, who in a word of like sound, of fuller sense, comparing by it the bestowing of his life to the Offering poured out upon the Sacrifice of the faith of Gods people, and especially of this Church, whereupon I have already poured out a great part thereof in the same calling, from which I stand now restrained. And if your HH. shall finde it so that I have not deserved so great a punishment, but rather performed the duty, which a good and faithful servant ought in such case to do his Lord, and the people he putteth him in trust withal carefully to keep: I am a most humble Suiter by these presents to your H.H. that by your godly wisdom, some good course may be taken for the restoring of me to my Ministery and place again. Which so great a favour, shall binde me yet in a greater obligation of duty (which is already so great, as it seemed nothing could be added unto it to make it greater) to honour God daily for the continuance and encrease of your good estate, and to be ready with all the poor means God hath given me, to do your HH. that faithful service I may possibly perform: But if notwithstanding my cause be never so good, your HH. can by no means pacifie such as are offended, nor restore me again, then am I to rest in the good pleasure of God, and to commend to your HH. protection, under Her Majesties, my private life, while it shall be led in duty; and the Church to him, who hath redeemed to himself a people with his precious blood, and is making ready to come to judge both the quick and the dead, to give to every one according as he hath done in this life, be it good or evil; to the wicked and unbeliever, justice unto death; but to the faithful, and such as love his truth, mercy and grace to life everlasting.

Your Honours most bounden, and most humble
Suppliant,

WALTER TRAVERS
Minister of the Gospel.

Mr. HOOKERS
ANSWER
TO THE
SUPPLICATION
THAT
Mr. TRAVERS
Made to the
COUNCIL.

To my Lord of Canterbury his Grace.

Y duty in most humble wise remembred: May it please your Grace to understand, That whereas there hath been a late Controversie raised in the *Temple*, and pursued by Mr. *Travers*, upon conceit taken at some words by me uttered, with a most simple and harmless meaning: In the heat of which pursuit, after three publique Invectives, silence being enjoyned him by Authority, he hath hereupon for defence of his proceedings, both presented the Right Honourable Lords and others of Her Majesties Privy Council with a Writing; and also caused or suffered the same to be Copied out, and spred through the hands of so many, that well nigh all sorts of men have it in their bosomes: The matters wherewith I am therein charged being of such quality as they are, and my self being better known to your Grace, then to any other of their Honours besides, I have chosen to offer to your Graces hands a plain declaration of my innocence in all those things wherewith I am so hardly, and so heavily charged, lest if I still remain silent, that which I do for quietness sake, be taken as an Argument, that I lack what to speak truly and justly in mine own defence.

2. First, because Mr. *Travers* thinketh it is expedient to breed an opinion in mens mindes,

mindes, that the root of all inconvenient events which are now sprung out, is, the surly and unpeaceable disposition of the man with whom he hath to do; therefore the first in the rank of accusations laid against me, is, *my inconformity, which have so little inclined to so many, and so earnest Exhortations and Conferences, as my self,* he saith, *can witness, to have been spent upon me, for my better fashioning unto good correspondence and agreement.*

3. Indeed, when at the first, by means of special well-willers, without any suit of mine, as they very well know (although I do not think it had been a mortal sin, in a reasonable sort, to have shewed a moderate desire that way) yet when by their endeavour, without instigation of mine, some reverend and honorable, favourably affecting me, had procured her Majesties grant of the place; At the very point of my entring thereinto the evening before I was first to preach, he came, and two other Gentlemen joyned with him: The effect of his Conference then was, *that he thought it his duty to advise me, not to enter with a strong hand, but to change my purpose of preaching there the next day, and to stay till he had given notice of me to the Congregation, that so their allowance might seal my calling.* The effect of my answer was, *That as in a place where such order is, I would not break; so here where it never was, I might not of mine own head take upon me to begin it:* but liking very well the motion of the opinion which I had of his good meaning who made it, requested him not to mislike my answer, though it were not correspondent to his minde.

4. When this had so displeased some, that whatsoever was afterwards done or spoken by me, it offended their taste, angry informations were daily sent out, intelligence given far and wide, what a dangerous enemy was crept in; the worst that jealousie could imagine, was spoken and written to so many, that at the length some knowing me well, and perceiving how injurious the reports were, which grew daily more and more unto my discredit, wrought means to bring Mr. *Travers* and me to a second Conference. Wherein when a common friend unto us both, had quietly requested him to utter those things wherewith he found himself any way grieved: He first renewed the memory of my entring into this Charge, by vertue onely of an humane creature (for so the want of that formality of popular allowance was thencensured) and unto this was annexed a Catalogue, partly of causless surmizes; as, *That I had conspired against him, and that I sought Superiority over him;* and partly of sauls, which to note, I should have thought it a greater offence then to commit, if I did account them saults, and had heard them so curiously observed in any other then my self, they are such silly things, as, *Praying in the entrance of my Sermon onely, and not in the end; naming Bishops in my prayer, kneeling when I pray, and kneeling when I receive the Communion,* with such like, which I would be as loth to recite, as I was sorry to hear them objected, if the rehearsal thereof were not by him thus wrested from me. These are the Conferences wherewith I have been wooed to entertain peace and good agreement.

A meer formality it had been to me in that place; whereas no man had ever used it before me, so it could neither further me if I did use it, nor hinder me if I did not

5. As for the vehement Exhortations he speaketh of, I would gladly know some reason, wherefore he thought them needful to be used. Was there any thing found in my speeches or dealings that gave them occasion, who are studious of peace, to think that I disposed my self to some unquiet kinde of proceedings? Surely, the special Providence of God I do now see it was, that the first words I spake in this place, should make the first thing whereof I am accused, to appear not onely untrue, but improbable, to as many as then heard me with indifferent ears; and do, I doubt not, in their consciences clear me of this suspicion. Howbeit, I grant this were nothing, if it might be shewed, that my deeds following were not suitable to my words. If I had spoken of peace at the first, and afterwards sought to molest and grieve him, by crossing him in his Function, by storming if my pleasure were not asked, and my will obeyed in the least occurrences, by carping needlesly sometimes at the manner of his teaching, sometimes at this, sometimes at that point of his doctrine: I might then with some likelihood have been blamed, as one disdaining a peaceable hand when it had been offered. But if I be able (as I am) to prove that my self have a now full year together, born the continuance of such dealings, not onely without any manner of resistance, but also without any such complaint, as might let or hinder him in his course, I see no cause in the world, why of this I should be accused, unless it be, lest I should accuse, which I meant not. If therefore I have given him occasion to

F ff use

uſe conferences and exhortations to peace, if when they were beſtowed upon me I have deſpiſed them, it will not be hard to ſhew ſome one word or deed wherewith I have gone about to work diſturbance: one is not much, I require but one. Onely I require if any thing be ſhewed, it may be proved, and not objected orely as this is, *That I have joyned to ſuch as have always oppoſed to any good order in his Church, and made themſelves to be thought indiſpoſed to the preſent eſtate and proceedings.* The words have reference, as it ſeemeth, unto ſome ſuch things as being attempted before my coming to the Temple, went not ſo effectually (perhaps) forward, as he that deviſed them would have wiſhed. An Order, as I learn, there was tendred, that Communicants ſhould neither kneel, as in the moſt places of the Realm; nor ſit, as in this place the cuſtom is; but walk to the one ſide of the table, and there ſtanding till they had received, paſs afterwards away round about by the other. Which being on a ſudden begun to be practiſed in the Church, ſome ſate wondering what it ſhould mean, others deliberating what to do: Till ſuch time as at length by name one of them being called openly thereunto, requeſted that they might do as they had been accuſtomed, which was granted; and as Mr. *Travers* had miniſtred his way to the reſt, ſo a Curate was ſent to miniſter to them after their way. Which unproſperous beginning of a thing (ſaving only for the inconvenience of needleſs alterations, otherwiſe harmleſs) did ſo diſgrace that order in their conceit, who had to allow or diſallow it, that it took no place. For neither could they ever induce themſelves to think it good, and it ſo much offended Mr. *Travers,* who ſuppoſed it to be the beſt, that he ſince that time, although contented to receive it as they do, at the hands of others, yet hath not thought it meet they ſhould ever receive it out of his, which would not admit that order of receiving it, and therefore in my time hath been always preſent not to miniſter, but onely to be miniſtred unto.

6. Another Order there was likewiſe deviſed, but an Order of much more weight and importance. This ſoil in reſpect of certain immunities and other ſpecialties belonging unto it, ſeemed likely to bear that which in other places of the Realm of *England* doth not take. For which cauſe requeſt was made to her Majeſties Privy Councel, that whereas it is provided by a Statute, there ſhould be Collectors and Sidemen in Churches; which thing, or ſomewhat correſpondent unto it, this place did greatly want; it would pleaſe their Honours to motion ſuch a matter to the Ancients of the Temple. And according to their honorable manner of qelpinng forward all motions ſo grounded, they wrote their Letters, as I am informed to that effect. Whereupon, although theſe Houſes never had uſe of ſuch Collectors and Sidemen as are appointed in other places, yet they both erected a Box to receive mens devotion for the poor, appointing the Treaſurer of both Houſes to take care for beſtowing it where need was; and granting further, that if any could be intreated (as in the end ſome were) to undertake the labour of obſerving mens ſlackneſs in divine duties, they ſhould be allowed, their complaints heard at all times, and the faults they complained of, if Mr: *Alveyes* private admonition did not ſerve, then by ſome other means to be redreſſed; but according to the old received Orders of both Houſes. Whereby the ſubſtance of their Honours Letters were indeed fully ſatisfied. Yet becauſe Mr. *Travers* intended not this, but as it ſeemed another thing; therefore notwithſtanding the orders which have been taken, and for any thing I know, do ſtand ſtill in as much force in this Church now, as at any time heretofore; He complaineth much of the good Orders which he doth mean have been withſtood. Now it were hard if as many as did any ways oppoſe unto theſe and the like orders in his perſwaſion good, do thereby make themſelves diſlikers of the preſent ſtate and proceeding. If they whom he aimeth at, have any otherways made themſelves to be thought ſuch; it is likely he doth know wherein, and will I hope diſcloſe wherein it appurtaineth, both the perſons whom he thinketh, and the cauſes why he thinketh them ſo ill affected. But whatſoever the men be, do their faults make me faulty? They do, if I joyn my ſelf with them. I beſeech him therefore to declare wherein I have joyned with them. Other joyning then this with any man here, I cannot imagine: It may be I have talked, or walked, or eaten, or interchangeably uſed the duties of common humanity with ſome ſuch as he is hardly perſwaded of. For I know no Law of God or man, by force whereof they ſhould be as Heathens and Publicans unto me that are not gracious in the eyes of another man, perhaps without cauſe, or if with cauſe,

yet

yet such cause as he is privy unto, and not I. Could he, or any reasonable man think it a charitable course in me, to observe them that shew by external courtesies a favourable inclination towards him, and if I spie out any one amongst them, of whom I think not well, hereupon to draw such an accusation as this against him, and to offer it where he hath given up his against me? which notwithstanding, I will acknowledge to be just and reasonable, if he or any man living shall shew that I use as much as the bare familiar company but of one, who by word or deed hath ever given me cause to suspect or conjecture him, such as here they are termed, with whom complaint is made that I joyn my self. This being spoken therefore, and written without all possibility of proof, doth not Mr. *Travers* give me over-great cause to stand in some fear, lest he make too little conscience how he useth his tongue or pen? These things are not laid against me for nothing, they are to some purpose if they take place. For in a mind perswaded that I am, as he deciphereth me, one which refuses to be at peace with such as imbrace the truth, and side my self with men sinisterly affected thereunto, any thing that shall be spoken concerning the unsoundness of my Doctrine, cannot chuse but be favourably entertained. This presupposed, it will have likelihood enough, which afterwards followeth, that *many of my Sermons have tasted of some sour leaven or other*, that in them he hath *he hath discovered many unsound matters.* A thing much to be lamented, that such a place as this, which might have been so well provided for, hath fallen into the hands of one no better instructed in the truth. But what if in the end it be found that he judgeth my words, as they do colours, which look upon them with green spectacles, and think that which they see is green, when indeed that is green whereby they see.

7. Touching the first point of this discovery, which is about the matter of Predestination, to set down that I spake (for I have it written) to declare and confirm the several branches thereof, would be tedious now in this writing, where I have so many things to touch, that I can but touch them onely. Neither is it herein so needful for me to justifie my speech, when the very place and presence where I spake, doth it self speak sufficiently for my clearing. This matter was not broached in a blinde Alley, or uttered where none was to hear it, that had skill with Authority to control; or covertly insinuated by some gliding sentence.

8. That which I taught was at *Pauls Cross*; it was not hudled in amongst other matters, in such sort that it could pass without noting; it was opened, it was proved, it was some reasonable time stood upon. I see not which way my Lord of *London*, who was present and heard it, can excuse so great a fault, as patiently, without rebuke or controlment afterwards; to hear any man there teach otherwise then *the Word of God doth*; not as it is understood by the private interpretation of some one or two men, or by a special construction received in some few books; but as it is understood by *all Churches professing the Gospel*, by them all, and therefore even by our own also amongst others. A man that did mean to prove that he speaketh, would surely take the measure of his words shorter.

9. The next thing discovered, is an opinion about the assurance of mens perswasion in matters of Faith. I have taught he saith, *That the assurance of things which we believe by the Word, is not so certain as of that we perceive by sense.* And is it as certain? Yea, I taught as he himself, I trust, will not deny, that the things which God doth promise in his Word, are surer unto us, then any thing we touch, handle or see. But are we so sure and certain of them; If we be, why doth God so often prove his promises unto us as he doth, by argument taken from our sensible experience? We must be surer of the proof, then of the thing proved, otherwise it is no proof. How is it, that if ten men do all look upon the Moon, every one of them knoweth it is as certainly to be the Moon as another; but many believing one and the same promises, all have not one and the same fulness of perswasion? How falleth it out, that men being assured of any thing by sense, can be no surer of it then they are; whereas the strongest in faith that liveth upon the earth, hath always need to labour, and strive, and pray that his assurance concerning heavenly and spiritual things, may grow, encrease, and be augmented?

10. The Sermon wherein I have spoken somewhat largely of this point, was long before this late Controversie rose between him and me, upon request of some

of

of my friends, ſeen and read by many, and amongſt many, ſome who are thought
able to diſcern: And I never heard that any one of them hitherto, hath condemned
it as containing unſound matter. My caſe were very hard, if as oft as any thing I
ſpeak diſpleaſing one mans taſte, my Doctrine upon his onely word ſhould be taken
for ſour leaven.

11. The reſt of this diſcovery is all about the matter now in queſtion; wherein he
hath two faults pred minant, would tire out any that ſhould anſwer unto every point
ſeverally: unapt ſpeaking of School-Controverſies, and of my words ſo untoward a
reciting, that he which ſhould promiſe to draw a mans Countenance, and did indeed
expreſs the parts, at leaſtwiſe moſt of them truly, but perverſly place them, could
not repreſent a more offenſive viſage, then unto me my own ſpeech ſeemeth in
ſome places, as he hath ordered it. For anſwer whereunto, that writing is ſufficient, wherein I have ſet down both my words and meaning in ſuch ſort, that where
this Accuſation doth deprave the one, and either miſinterpret, or without juſt cauſe
miſlike the other, it will appear ſo plainly, that I may ſpare very well to take upon
me a new needleſs labour here.

12. Onely at one thing which is there to be found, becauſe Mr. *Travers* doth here
ſeem to take ſuch a ſpecial advantage, as if the matter were unanſwerable, he conſtraineth me either to detect his overſight, or to confeſs mine own in it. In ſetling
the Queſtion between the Church of *Rome* and us, about Grace and Juſtification,
leſt I ſhould give them an occaſion to ſay, as commonly they do, that when we
cannot refute their opinions, we propoſe to our ſelves ſuch inſtead of theirs, as we
can refute; I took it for the beſt and moſt perſpicuous way of teaching, to declare
firſt, how far we do agree, and then to ſhew our diſagreement: not generally (as
Mr. *Travers* his *(a)* words would carry it, for the eaſier faſtning that upon me,
wherewith, ſaving onely by him, I was never in my life touched;) but about the
matter onely of Juſtification: for further I had no cauſe to meddle at this time.
What was then my offence in this caſe? I did, as he ſaith, ſo ſet it out, as if we had
conſented in the greateſt and weightieſt points, and differed onely in ſmaller matters. It will not be found, when it cometh to the ballance, a light difference where
we diſagree, as I did acknowledge that we do, about the very eſſence of the Medicine whereby Chriſt cureth our diſeaſe. Did I go about to make a ſhew of agreement in the weightieſt points, and was I ſo fond as not to conceal our diſagreement about this? I do wiſh that ſome indifferency were uſed by them that have taken
the weighing of my words.

(a) His words be theſe, The next Sabbath day after this Mr. Hooker kept the way he entred in-tred into be-fore, and be-ſtowed his whole hour and more, onely upon the queſtions he had moved and maintained. Wherein he ſo ſet the agreement of the Church f Rome with us, and their diſagreement from us, as if we had conſented in the greateſt and weightieſt points, and differed onely in certain ſmaller matters. Which agreement noted by him in two chief points, is not ſuch as he would have men believe: The one, in that he ſaid they acknow-ledge all men ſinners, even the bleſſed Virgin, though ſome of them freed her from ſin: for the Council of Trent holdeth, that ſhe was free from ſin: Another, in that he ſaid, They teach Chriſt Righteouſaeſs to be the onely meritorious cauſe of taking away ſin, and differ from us onely in the applying of it. For Thomas Aquinas, their chief School-man, and Archbiſhop Catharinus, teach, That Chriſt took away onely Original ſin, and that the reſt are to be taken away by our ſelves: yea, the Council of Trent teacheth, That the Righte-cuſneſs whereby we are righteous in Gods ſight, is inherent righteouſneſs, which muſt needs be our own works, and cannot be underſtood of the righteouſneſs inherent onely in Chriſts perſon, and accounted unto us.

13. Yea, but our agreement is not ſuch in two of the chiefeſt points, as I
would have men believe it is? And what are they? The one is, I ſaid, They acknowledge all men ſinners, even the bleſſed Virgin, though ſome of them free her from
ſin. Put the caſe I had affirmed, That onely ſome of them free her from ſin, and
had delivered it as the moſt currant opinion amongſt them, that ſhe was conceived in
ſin: doth not *Bonaventure* ſay plainly, *Omnes fere,* in a manner all men do hold this? doth
he not bring many reaſons wherefore all men ſhould hold it? Were their voyces ſince
that time ever counted, and their number found ſmaller which hold it, then theirs
that hold the contrary? Let the queſtion then be, Whether I might ſay, The
moſt of them acknowledged all men ſinners, even the bleſſed Virgin her ſelf. To ſhew,
that their general received opinion is the contrary, the *Tridentine* Council is
alledged,

alledged, peradventure not altogether so considerately. For if that Council have by resolute determination freed her, if it hold as Mr. _Travers_ saith it doth, that she was free from sin; then must the Church of _Rome_ needs condemn them that hold the contrary: For what that Council holdeth, the same they all do and must hold. But in the Church of _Rome_, who knoweth not that it is a thing indifferent to think and defend the one or the other? So that by this argument, The Council of _Trent_ holdeth the Virgin free from sin, _ergo_, it is plain that none of them may, and therefore untrue that most of them do acknowledge her a sinner, were forcible to over-throw my supposed Assertion, if it were true that the Council did hold this. But to the end it may clearly appear, how it neither holdeth this nor the contrary, I will open what many do conceive of the Canon that concerneth this matter. The Fathers of _Trent_ perceived, that if they should define of this matter, it would be dangerous howsoever it were determined. If they had freed her from her Original sin, the reasons against them are unanswerable, which _Bonaventure_ and others do alledge, but especially _Thomas_, whose line, as much as may be, they follow. Again, if they did resolve the other way, they should control themselves in another thing, which in no case might be altered. For they profess to keep no day holy in the honour of an unholy thing; and the Virgins Conception they ho-nour with a * Feast, which they could not abrogate without cancelling a Constitution of _Xystus Quartus._ And that which is worse, the world might perhaps suspect, that if the Church of _Rome_ did amiss before in this, it is not impossible for her to fail in other things. In the end, they did wisely quote out their Canon by a middle thred, establishing the Feast of the Virgins Conception, and leaving the other question doubtful as they found it; giving onely a caveat, that no man should take the decree, which pronounceth all mankinde originally sinful, for a definitive sentence concerning the blessed Virgin. This in my sight is plain by their own words, _Declarat hæc ipsa sancta Sy-nodus, &c._ Wherefore our Countreymen at _Rhemes_, mentioning this point, are marvellous wary how they speak; they touch it as though it were a hot coal: _Many godly devout men judge, that our blessed Lady was neither born nor conceived in sin._ Is it their wont to speak nicely of things definitively set down in that Coun-cil?

^{note} This doth much trouble _Thomas_, holding her Conception stained with the natu al blemish inhe-rent in mortal seed. And therefore he putteth it off with two answers; the one, That the Church of _Rome_ doth not allow, but tolerate the Feast, which answer now will not serve: the other, that being sure she was sanctified before birth; but un-sure how long a while after her Conception, there-fore under the name of her Conception-day, they honour the time of her Sanctification. So that besides this, they have now no soder to make the certain allowance of their Feast, and their uncer-tain sentence concerning her sin, to cleave to-gther. _Tom. 3. part. quest. 27. art. 2. ad. 2. & 3._

Annot. in Rom. 5 sect. 9.

In like sort we finde that the rest, which have since the time of the _Tridentine_ Synod written of Original sin, are in this point, for the most part, either silent, or very sparing in speech: and when they speak, either doubtful what to think, or whatsoever they think themselves, fearful to set down any certain determinati-on. If I be thought to take the Canon of that Council otherwise then they them-selves do, let him expound it, whose sentence was neither last asked, nor his pen least occupied in setting it down; I mean _Andradius_, whom _Gregory_ the thirteenth hath allowed plainly to confess, that it is a matter which neither express evidence of Scripture, nor the Tradition of the Fathers, nor the sentence of the Church hath determined; that they are too surly and self-willed, which defending their opinion, are displeased with them by whom the other is maintained: finally, that the Fathers of _Trent_ have not set down any certainty about this question, but left it doubtful and indifferent.

Lib. 5. defens. fidei.

Now whereas my words which I had set down in writing, before I uttered them, were indeed these, _Although they imagine that the Mother of our Lord Jesus Christ, were for his honour, and by his special protection, preserved clean from all sin, yet con-cerning the rest, they teach as we do, that all have sinned._ Against my words they might with more pretence take exception, because so many of them think she had sin: which exception notwithstanding, the Proposition being indefinite, and the matter contingent, they cannot take, because they grant, that many whom they count grave and devout amongst them, think that she was clear from all sin. But whether Mr. _Travers_ did note my words himself, or take them upon the credit of some other mans noting, the Tables were faulty wherein it was noted: _All men sinners, even the_ *blessed Virgin.* When my speech was rather, *All men except the blessed Virgin.* To leave this, another fault he findeth, that I said, *They teach Christ Righteousness to be the onely meritorious cause of taking away sin, and differ from us onely in the applying of it.* I did say, and do, *They teach as we do, that although Christ be the onely meritorious cause of our justice, yet is a medicine which is made for health, doth not heal by being made, but by being applied: So by the merits of Christ there can be no true life no justification, without the application of his merits: But about the manner of applying Christ, about the number and power of means whereby he is applied, we dissent from them.* This of our dissenting from them is acknowledged.

14. Our agreement in the former is denied to be such as I pretend. Let their own words therefore and mine concerning them, be compared. Doth not *Andradius* plainly confess, *our sins do shut, and onely the merits of Christ open the entring unto blessedness?* And *Soto, It is put for a good ground, that all since the fall of Adam, obtained Salvation onely by the Passion of Christ: howbeit, as no cause can be effectual without applying, so neither can any man be saved, to whom the suffering of Christ is not applied.* In a word, who not? When the Council of *Trent* reckoning up the causes of our first Justification, doth name no end, but Gods Glory, and our Felicity; no efficient, but his Mercy; no instrumental, but Baptism; no meritorious, but Christ; whom to have merited the taking away of no sin but Original, is not their opinion: which himself will finde, when he hath well examined his witnesses, *Catharinus* and *Thomas.* Their Jesuits are marvellous angry with the men out of whose gleanings Mr. *Travers* seemeth to have taken this; they openly disclaim it, they say plainly, *Of all the Catholicks there is no one that did ever so teach;* they make solemn protestation, *We believe and profess, That Christ upon the Cross hath altogether satisfied for all sins, as well Original as Actual.* Indeed they teach, that the merit of Christ doth not take away Actual sin, in such sort as it doth Original; wherein if their Doctrine had been understood, I for my speech had never been accused. As for the Council of *Trent,* concerning inherent righteousness, what doth it here? No man doubteth, but they make another formal cause of Justification then we do. In respect whereof, I have shewed you already, that we disagree about the very essence of that which cureth our spiritual Disease. Most true it is which the grand Philosopher hath, *Every man judgeth well of that which he knoweth;* and therefore till we know the things throughly, whereof we judge, it is a point of judgement to stay our judgement.

15. Thus much is our being spent in discovering the unsoundness of my Doctrine, some pains he taketh further to open fault in the manner of my teaching, as that, *I bestowed my whole hour and more, my time, and more then my time, in discourses utterly impertinent to my Text.* Which if I had done, it might have past without complaining of to the Privy Council.

16. But I did worse, as he saith, *I left the expounding of the Scriptures, and my ordinary calling, and discoursed upon School-points and questions, neither of edification, nor of truth.* I read no Lecture in the Law, or in Physick. And except the bounds of ordinary Calling may be drawn like a purse, how are they so much wider unto him then to me, that he which in the limits of his ordinary Calling, should reprove that in me which he understood not; and I labouring that both he and others might understand, could not do this without forsaking my Calling? The matter whereof I spake was such, as being at the first by me but lightly touched, he had in that place openly contradicted, and solemnly taken upon him to disprove. If therefore it were a School-question, and unfit to be discoursed of there, that which was in me but a Proposition onely at the first, wherefore made he a Probleme of it? Why took he first upon him to maintain the negative of that, which I had affirmatively spoken, onely to shew mine own opinion, little thinking that ever it would have a question? Of what nature soever the question were, I could do no less then there explain my self to them, unto whom I was accused of unsound Doctrine; wherein if to shew, what had been through ambiguity mistaken in my words, or misapplied by him in this cause against me, I used the distinctions and helps of Schools, I trust that herein I have committed no unlawful thing. These School-implements are acknowledged by grave and wise men not unprofitable to have been invented. The most approved for learning and judgement do use them without blame; the use of them hath been well liked in some that have taught even in this very place before me:

the

Or bod. lib. 2. In 2 Sent. dist. 3 quest. 4 art. 6.

Bellarm. Judic de lib Concar. Mendac. 18. Nemo Catholicorum qui se docuit, sed credimus & profitemur Christum in Cruce pro omnibus omnino peccatis satisfecisse, tam originalibus qu. m actualibus.

Cat. Just. lib. 1. cap. 5. Sect. 9.

the quality of my hearers is such, that I could not but think them of capacity very sufficient, for the most part, to conceive harder then I used any; the cause I had in hand did in my judgement necessarily require them, which were then used; when my words spoken generally without distinctions had been perverted, what other way was there for me, but by distinctions to lay them open in their right meaning, that it might appear to all men, whether they were so consonant to truth or no? And although Mr. *Travers* be so inured with the City, that he thinketh it unmeet to use any speech which savoureth of the School, yet his opinion is no Canon; though unto him, his minde being troubled, my speech did seem like fetters and manicles, yet there might be some more calmly affected, which thought otherwise; his private judgement will hardly warrant his bold words, that the things which I spake, *were neither of edification nor truth.* They might edifie some other for any thing he knoweth, and be true for any thing he proveth to the contrary. For it is no proof to cry *Absurdities, the like whereunto have not been heard in publique places within this Land since Queen* Maries *days.* If this came in earnest from him, I am sorry to see him so much offended without cause; more sorry, that his sit should be so extreme, to make him speak he knoweth not what. That I neither *affected the truth of God, nor the peace of the Church; Mihi pre minimo est,* it doth not much move me, when Mr. *Travers* doth say that, which I trust a greater then Mr. *Travers* will gainsay.

17. Now let all this which hitherto he hath said be granted him, let it be as he would have it, let my Doctrine and manner of teaching be as much disallowed by all mens judgements as by his, what is all this to his purpose? He alledgeth this to be the cause why he bringeth it in, The High-Commissioners *charge him with an indiscretion and want of duty, in that he inveighed against certain points of Doctrine taught by me as erroneous, not conferring first with me, nor complaining of it to them.* Which faults, a sea of such matter as he hath hitherto waded in, will never be able to scoure from him. For the avoiding Schism and disturbance in the Church, which must needs grow, if all men might think what they list, and speak openly what they think; therefore by a * Decree agreed upon by the Bishops, and confirmed by her Majesties Authority, it was ordered, that erroneous Doctrine, if it were taught publiquely, should not be publiquely refuted, but that notice thereof should be given unto such as are by her Highnes appointed to hear, and to determine such causes. For breach of which Order, when he is charged with lack of duty, all the faults that can be heaped upon me, will make but a weak defence for him: As surely his defence is not much stronger, when he alledges for himself, that *He was in some hope his speech in proving the truth, and clearing those scruples which I had in my self, might cause me either to imbrace sound Doctrine, or suffer it to be imbraced of others; which if I did,*

* In the Advertisements published in the seventh year of her Majesties Reign: *If any Preacher, or Parson, Vicar or Curate so licensed, shall fortune to preach any matter tending to dissention, or to derogation of the Religion and doctrine received, that the bearers denounce the same to the Ordinary, or to the next Bishop of the same place, but not openly to contrary, or to impugn the same speech so disorderly uttered, whereby may grow offence, and disquiet of the people, but shall be convinced and reproved by the Ordinary, after such agreeable order as shall be seen to him according to the gravity of the offence: And that it be presented within one month after the words spoken.*

he should not need to complain: that, It was meet he should discover first what I had sown, and make it manifest to be tares, and then desire their sithe to cut it down: that, Conscience did binde him to do otherwise, then the foresaid Order requireth: that, He was unwilling to deal in that publique manner, and wished a more convenient way were taken for it: that, He had resolved to have protested the next Sabbath day, that he would some other way satisfie such as should require it, and not deal more in that place. Be it imagined, [let me not be taken as if I did compare the offenders, when I do not, but their answers onely] be it imagined that a Libeller did make this Apology for himself, I am not ignorant that if I have just matter against any man, the Law is open, there are Judges to hear it, and Courts where it ought to be complained of; I have taken another course against such or such a man, yet without breach of duty, forasmuch as I am able to yield a reason of my doing, I conceive some hope that a little discredit amongst men would make him ashamed of himself, and that his shame would work his amendment; which if it did, other accusation there should not need; could his answer be thought sufficient, could it in the judgement of discreet men free him from all blame? No more can the hope Mr. *Travers* conceived, to reclaim me by publike speech, justifie his fault against the established Order of the Church.

18. His

18. His thinking it meet *he ſhould firſt openly diſcover to the people the tares that had been ſown amongſt them, and then require the hand of authority to mow them down,* doth only make it a queſtion, whether his opinion that this was meet, may be a priviledge or protection againſt the lawful conſtitution which had before determined of it as of a thing unmeet. Which queſtion I leave for them to diſcuſs whom it moſt concerneth. If the Order be ſuch that it cannot be kept without hazarding a thing ſo precious as a good conſcience, the peril whereof could be no greater to him then it needs muſt be to all others whom it toucheth in like cauſes, then this is evident, it will be an effectual motive, not only for *England,* but alſo for other reformed Churches, even *Geneva* it ſelf [for they have the like] to change or take that away which cannot but with great inconvenience be obſerved. In the mean while the breach of it may in ſuch conſideration be pardoned [which truly I wiſh howſoever it be] yet hardly defended as long as it ſtandeth in force uncancelled.

19. Now whereas he confeſſeth another *way had been more convenient,* and that he found in himſelf ſecret unwillingneſs to do that which he did, doth he not ſay plainly in effect that the light of his own underſtanding, proved the way that he took perverſe and crooked; reaſon was ſo plain and pregnant againſt it, that his mind was alienated, his will averted to another courſe? yet ſomewhat there was that ſo far overruled, that it muſt needs be done even againſt the very ſtream, what doth it bewray? Finally his purpoſed proteſtation, whereby he meant openly to *make it known,* that he did not allow this kind of proceeding, and therefore would ſatisfie men otherwiſe, *and deal no more in this place,* ſheweth his good mind in this, that he meant to ſtay himſelf from further offending; but it ſerveth not his turn. He is blamed becauſe the thing he hath done was amiſs, and his anſwer is, That which I would have done afterwards had been well, if ſo be I had done it.

20. But as in this he ſtandeth perſwaded, that he hath done nothing beſides duty, ſo he taketh it hardly that the High Commiſſioners ſhould charge him with indiſcretion. Wherefore as if he could ſo waſh his hands, he maketh a long and a large declaration concerning the carriage of himſelf: how he waded in *matters of ſmaller weight* and how in things of *greater moment;* how wary he dealt; how *naturally he took his things riſing from the Text;* how cloſely he kept himſelf *to the Scriptures he took in hand;* how much pains *he took to confirm the neceſſity of beleeving Juſtification by Chriſt onely,* and to ſhew how the *Church of Rome denieth that a man is ſaved by faith alone, without works of the Law;* what *the ſons of thunder would have done,* if they had been in his caſe; that his *anſwer was very temperate, without* immodeſt *or reproachful ſpeech,* that when he might *before all have reproved me,* he did not, *but contented himſelf with exhorting me* before all, *to follow Nathans example,* and reviſit *my doctrine;* when he might have followed St. *Pauls* example in *reproving Peter,* he did not, but exhorted me with *Peter, to endure to be withſtood.* This teſtimony of his diſcreet carrying himſelf in the handling of his matter, being more agreeably framed and given him by another then by himſelf, might make ſomewhat for the praiſe of his perſon; but for defence of his action unto them by whom he is thought undiſcreet, for not conferring privately before he ſpake, will it ſerve to anſwer, that when he ſpake, he did it conſiderately? He perceiveth it will not, and therefore addeth reaſons, ſuch as they are. As namely; how he purpoſed at the firſt to take another courſe, and that was this, *Publickly to deliver the truth of ſuch doctrine as I had otherwiſe taught, and at convenient opportunity to confer with me upon ſuch points.* Is this the rule of Chriſt. If thy brother offend openly in his ſpeech, controll it firſt with contrary ſpeech openly, and confer with him afterwards upon it, when convenient opportunity ſerveth? Is there any Law of God or Man, whereupon to ground ſuch a reſolution, any Church extant in the World, where Teachers are allowed thus to do or to be done unto? He cannot but ſee how weak an allegation it is, when he bringeth in his following this courſe, firſt in one matter, and ſo afterwards in another, to approve himſelf, now following it again. For if the purpoſe of doing a thing ſo uncharitable be a fault, the deed is a greater fault; and doth the doing of it twice, make it the third time fit and allowable to be done? The weight of the cauſe, which is his third defence, relieveth him as little. The weightier it was, the more it required conſiderate advice and conſultation, the more it ſtood him upon to take good heed,

that

that nothing were rashly doue or spoken in it. But he meaneth *weighty*, in regard of the wonderful danger, except he had presently withstood me without expecting a time of Conference. *This cause being of such moment that might prejudice the faith of Christ, encourage the ill-affected to continue still in their damnable ways, and other weak in faith, to suffer themselves to be seduced, to the destruction of their souls, he thought it his bounden duty to speak before he talked with me.* A man that should read this, and not know what I had spoken, might imagine that I had at the least denied the Divinity of Christ. But they which were present at my speech, and can testifie, that nothing passed my lips more then is contained in their writings, whom for soundness of Doctrine, Learning and Judgement, Mr. *Travers* himself doth, I dare say, not onely allow, but honor, they which heard, and do know, that the Doctrine here signified in so fearful manner, the Doctrine that was so dangerous to the faith of Christ, that was so likely to encourage ill-affected men to continue still in their damnable ways; that gave so great cause to tremble for fear of the present *destruction of souls*, was onely this, *I doubt not but God was merciful to save thousands of our Fathers, living heretofore in the Popish Superstition, in as much as they sinned ignorantly*; and this spoken in a Sermon, the greatest part whereof was against Popery, they will hardly be able to discerne how C R I S T I A N I T Y should herewith be so grievously shaken.

21. Whereby his fourth excuse is also taken from him. For what doth it boot him to say, *The time was short wherein he was to preach after me*, when his preaching of this matter perhaps ought, surely might have been either very well omitted, or at least more conveniently for a while deferred; even by their judgements that cast the most favourable aspect towards these his hasty proceedings. The poyson which men had taken at my hands, was not so quick and strong in operation, as in eight days to make them past cure; by eight days delay, there was no likelihood that the force and power of his speech could dye; longer meditation might bring better and stronger proofs to minde, then extemporal dexterity could furnish him with: And who doth know whether *Time*, the onely Mother of sound judgement and discreet dealing, might have given that action of his some better ripeness, which by so great festination hath, as a thing born out of time, brought small joy unto him that begat it? Doth he think it had not been better that neither my speech had seemed in his eyes as an arrow sticking in a thigh of flesh; nor his own as a childe whereof he must needs be delivered by an hour? His last way of disburthening himself, is, by casting his load upon my back, as if I had brought him by former conferences out of hope that any fruit should ever come of conferring with me. Loth I am to rip up those Conferences, whereof he maketh but a slippery and loose relation. In one of them the question between us was, Whether the perswasion of faith concerning remission of sins, eternal life, and whatsoever God doth promise unto man, be as free from doubting, as the perswasion which we have by sense concerning things tasted, felt, and seen? For the Negative, I mentioned their example, whose Faith in Scripture is most commended, and the experience which all faithful men have continually had of themselves. For proof of the Affirmative, which he held, I desiring to have some reason, heard nothing but *all good writers* oftentimes inculcated. At the length, upon request to see some one of them, *Peter Martyrs* Common places were brought, where the leaves were turned down, at a place sounding to this effect, *That the Gospel doth make Christians more vertuous, then moral Philosophy doth make Heathens*: which came not near the question by many miles.

22. In the other Conference he questioned about the matter of Reprobation, misliking first, that I had termed God a permissive, and no positive cause of the evil, which the Schoolmen do call *malum culpæ*. Secondly, that to their objection who say, *If I be elected, do what I will, I shall be saved*, I had answered, that the will of God in this thing is not absolute, but conditional, to save his Elect believing, fearing, and obediently serving him. Thirdly, that to stop the mouthes of such as grudge and repine against God for rejecting Cast-aways, I had taught that they are not rejected, no not in the purpose and counsel of God, without a foreseen worthiness of rejection going though not in time, yet in order, before. For if Gods electing do in order (as needs it must) presuppose the foresight of their being that are elected, though they be elected before they be; nor onely the positive foresight of their being, but also the permissive of their being miserable, because election is through mercy, and mercy doth always presuppose

ſuppoſe miſery : it followeth, that the very choſen of God acknowledge to the praiſe of the riches of his exceeding free compaſſion, that when he in his ſecret determination ſet it down, *Thoſe ſhall live and not die,* they lay as ugly ſpectacles before him, as Lepers covered with dung and mire, as ulcers putrified in their Fathers loyns, miſerable, worthy to be had in deteſtation ; and ſhall any forſaken creature be able to ſay unto, God thou did plunge me into the depth, and aſſign me unto endleſſ torments, onely to ſatisfie thine own will, finding nothing in me for which I could ſeem in thy ſight ſo well worthy to feel everlaſting flames ?

23. When I ſaw that Mr. *Travers* carped at theſe things, onely becauſe they lay not open, I promiſed at ſome convenient time to make them clear as light, both to him and all others. Which if they that reprove me will not grant me leave to do, they muſt think that they are for ſome cauſe or other more deſirous to have me reputed an unſound man, then willing that my ſincere meaning ſhould appear and be approved. When I was further asked what my grounds were ? I anſwered, that St. *Pauls* words concerning this cauſe were my grounds. His next demand, what Author I did follow in expounding S. *Paul,* and gathering the Doctrine out of his words, againſt the judgement (he ſaith) *of all Churches and all good Writers.* I was well aſſured that to control this over-reaching ſpeech, the ſentences which I might have cited out of Church Confeſſions, together with the beſt learned monuments of former times, and not the meaneſt of our own, were mo in number then perhaps he would willingly have heard of: but what had this booted me ? For although he himſelf in generality do much uſe thoſe formal ſpeeches, *All Churches* and *all good Writers :* yet as he holdeth it in Pulpit lawful to ſay in general, the *Paynims* think this, or the *Heathens* that, but utterly unlawful to cite any ſentence of theirs that ſay it : ſo he gave me at that time great cauſe to think that my particular alledging of other mens words, to ſhew their agreement with mine, would as much have diſpleaſed his mind, as the thing it ſelf for which it had been alledged, for he knoweth how often he hath in publick place bitten me for this, although I did never in any Sermon uſe many of the ſentences of other Writers, and do make moſt without any, having always thought it meeteſt neither to affect nor contemn the uſe of them.

24. He is not ignorant that in the very entrance to the talk, which we had privately at that time, to prove it unlawful altogether in preaching, either for confirmation, declaration or otherwiſe, to cite any thing but meer Canonical Scripture, he brought in, *The Scripture is given by inſpiration, and is profitable to teach, improve, &c.* urging much the vigour of theſe two clauſes, *The man of God* and *every good work.* If therefore the work were good which he required at my hands, if privately to ſhew why I thought the Doctrine I had delivered to be according to St. *Pauls* meaning, were a good work, can they which take the place before alledged for a Law, condemning every man of God, who in doing the work of preaching any other way uſeth humane authority, like it in me, if in the work of ſtrengthning that which I had preached, I ſhould bring forth the teſtimonies and the ſayings of mortal men? I alledged therefore that which might under no pretence in the world be diſallowed, namely reaſons, not meaning thereby mine own reaſon, as now it is reported, but true, ſound, divine reaſon ; reaſon whereby thoſe Concluſions might be out of S. *Paul* demonſtrated, and not probably diſcourſed of only ; reaſon proper to that ſcience whereby the things of God are known : Theological reaſon without principles in Scripture that are plain, ſoundly deduced more doubtful inferences, in ſuch ſort that being heard they cannot be denied, nor any thing repugnant unto them received, but whatſoever was before otherwiſe by miſcollecting gathered out of dark places, is thereby forced to yield it ſelf, and the true conſonant meaning of ſentences not underſtood, is brought to light. This is the reaſon which I intended. If it were poſſible for me to eſcape the Ferula in any thing I do or ſpeak, I had undoubtedly eſcaped in this. In this I did that which by ſome is enjoyned as the onely allowable, but granted by all as the moſt ſure and ſafe way, whereby to reſolve things doubted of in matters appertaining to Faith and Chriſtian Religion. So that Mr. *Travers* had here ſmall cauſe given him to be weary of conferring, unleſs it was in other reſpects then that poor one which is here pretended, that is to ſay, the little hope he had of doing me any good by conference.

25. Yet behold his firſt reaſon of not complaining to the High Commiſſion,

is,

is, *That sith I offended onely through an over charitable inclination, he conceived good hope, when I should see the truth cleared, and some scruples which were in my minde, removed by his diligence I would yield.* But what experience soever he had of former Conferences, how small soever his hope was that fruit would come of it if he should have conferred, will any man judge this a cause sufficient, why to open his mouth in publique, without any one word privately spoken ? He might have considered that men do sometimes reap where they sow, but with small hope; he might have considered, that although unto me (whereof he was not certain neither) but if to me his labour should be as water spilt, or poured into a torn dish, yet to him it could not be fruitless to do that which Order in Christian Churches, that which Charity amongst Christian men, that which at many mens hands, even common humanity it self, at his, many other things besides did require. What fruit could there come of his open contradicting in so great haste, with so small advice, but such as must needs be unpleasant, and mingled with much acerbity ? surely, he which will take upon him to defend, that in this there was no over-sight, must beware lest by such defences, he leave an opinion dwelling in the mindes of men, that he is more stiff to maintain what he hath done, then careful to do nothing but that which may justly be maintained.

26. Thus have I as near as I could, seriously answered things of weight : with smaller I have dealt as I thought their quality did require. I take no joy in striving, I have not been nuzled or trained up in it. I would to Christ they which have at this present enforced me hereunto, had so ruled their hands in any reasonable time, that I might never have been constrained to strike so much as in mine own defence. Wherefore to prosecute this long and tedious contention no further, I shall wish that your Grace and their Honours (unto whose intelligence the dutiful regard which I have of their judgements, maketh me desirous, that as accusations have been brought against me, so that this my answer thereunto may likewise come) did both with the one and the other, as *Constantine* with Books containing querulous matter. Whether this be convenient to be wished or no, I cannot tell : But sith there cannot come nothing of contention, but the mutual waste of the parties contending, till a common enemy dance in the ashes of them both, I do wish heartily that the grave advice which *Constantine* gave for reuniting of his Clergy so many times, upon some small occasions, in so lamentable sort divided ; or rather the strict commandment of Christ unto his, that they should not be divided at all, may at the length, if it be his blessed will, prevail so far, at least in this corner of the Christian world, to the burying and quite forgetting of strife, together with the causes which have either bred it, or brought it up, that things of small moment never disjoyn them, whom one God, one Lord, one Faith, one Spirit, one Baptism, bands of so great force have linked; that a respective eye towards things wherewith we should not be disquieted, make us not, as through infirmity the very Patriarchs themselves sometimes were, full gorged, unable to speak peaceably to their own brother. Finally, that no strife may ever be heard of again, but this, who shall hate strife most, who shall pursue peace and unity with swiftest paces.

TO THE
Chriſtian Reader.

Hereas *many deſirous of reſolution in ſome points handled in this learned diſcourſe, were earneſt to have it Copied ont; to eaſe ſo many labours, it hath been thought moſt worthy and very neceſſary to be printed: that not onely they might be ſatiſfied, but the whole Church alſo hereby edified. The rather, becauſe it will free the Author from the ſuſpicion of ſome errors, which he hath been thought to have favoured. Who might well* have anſwered *with* Cremutius *in* Tacitus, Verba mea arguuntur, adeo factorum innocens ſum. *Certainly, the event of that time wherein he lived, ſhewed that to be true, which the ſame Author ſpake of a worſe,* Cui deerat inimicus, per amicos oppreſſus; *and that there is not* minus periculum ex magna fama, quam ex mala. *But he hath ſo quit himſelf, that all may ſee, how, as it was ſaid of* Agricola, Simul ſuis virtutibus, ſimul vitiis aliorum in ipſam gloriam preceps agebatur. *Touching whom I will ſay no more, but that which my Author ſaid of the ſame man,* Integritatem, &c. in tanto viro referre, injuria virtutum fuerit. *But as of all other his writings, ſo of this I will adde that which* Velleius *ſpake in commendation of* Piſo, Nemo fuit, qui magis quæ agenda erant curaret, ſine ulla oſtentatione agendi. *So not doubting, good* Chriſtian Reader, *of thy aſſent herein, but wiſhing thy favourable acceptance of this work (which will be an inducement to ſet forth others of his learned Labours) I take my leave, from* Corpus Chriſti Colledge *in* Oxford, *the ſixth of* July, 1612.

Thine in Chriſt Jeſus,

HENRY JACKSON.

A

A
LEARNED DISCOVRSE
OF
Iustification, VVorks, and how the foundation of Faith is overthrown.

HABAK. 1.4.

The wicked doth compass about the righteous : therefore perverse Iudgement doth proceed.

 OR the better manifestation of the Prophets meaning in this place, we are first to confider *the wicked*, of whom he faith, that *They compass about the righteous* : Secondly, *the righteous*, that are compassed about by them : and Thirdly, That which is inferred ; *Therefore perverse judgement proceedeth.* Touching the first, There are two kinds of wicked men, of whom, in the fift of the former to the *Corinthians*, the blessed Apostle speaketh thus : *Do ye not judge them that are within* ; *But God judgeth them that are without.* There are wicked therefore whom the Church may judge, and there are wicked whom God onely judgeth : wicked within, and wicked without the walls of the Church. If within the Church, particular persons are apparently such, as cannot otherwise be reformed ; the rule of the Apostolical judgment, is this, *Separate them from among you* : if whole Assemblies, this : *Separate your selves from among them* : *For what society hath light with darknes ?* But the wicked, whom the Prophet meaneth, were Babylonians, and therefore without. For which cause we have heard at large heretofore in what fort he urgeth God to judge them.

2. Now concerning the righteous, their neither is, nor ever was any meer natural man absolutely righteous in himself, that is to say, void of all unrighteousness of all sin. We dare not except, no not the blessed Virgin her self, of whom although we say with St. *Augustine*, for the honour sake which we ow to our Lord and Saviour Christ, we are not willing in this cause, to move any question of his Mother : yet forasmuch as the Schools of *Rome* have made it a question ; we may answer with (a) *Eusebius Emissenus*, who, speaketh of her and to her in this effect : *Thou didst, by special prerogative nine moneths together entertain within the closet of thy flesh, the hope of all the ends of the Earth, the honour of the world, the common joy of Men* : *He, from whom all things had their beginning, had his beginning from thee* ; *of thy body he took the blood, which was to be shed for the life of the world* ; *of thee he took that which even for thee he payed.* *A peccati enim veteris nexu* (b) *per se non est immunis ipsa genetrix Redemtoris* : the Mother of the Redeemer, her self is not otherwise looked

Ggg from

(marginal notes:)
1,
2,
3.
1 Cor. 5, 12, 13.
2 Cor. 6. 7.
a Or whosoever it be that was the author of those Homiliesthat go under his name.
b Knowing, how the Schoolmen hold this question, some Critical wits may perhaps half suspect that these two words, Per se, are In-mates. But if the place which they have, be their own, their sense can be none other then that which I have given them by a paraphrasti-cal interpreta-tion,

from the bond of ancient sin , then by redemption : if Christ have paid a ransome for all , even for her , it followeth , that all without exception were captives. If one have dyed for all, then all were dead in sin ; all sinful therefore , none absolutely righteous in themselves ; but we are absolutely righteous in Christ. The World then must shew a righteous man , otherwise it is not able to shew a man that is perfectly righteous : *Christ is made to us wisdom , Justice , Sanctification and Redemption : Wisdom*, because he hath revealed his Fathers will : *Justice* because he hath offered up himself a sacrifice for sin : *Sanctification*, because he hath given us his spirit, *Redemption*, because he hath appointed a day to vindicate his Children out of the bands of corruption into liberty, which is glorious. How Christ is made *Wisdom*, and how *Redemption*, it may be declared, when occasion serveth. But how Christ is made the *Righteousness* of men, we are now to declare.

3. There is a glorifying righteousness of men in the World to come : as there is a justifying and sanctifying righteousness here. The righteousness wherewith we shall be clothed in the world to come, is both perfect and inherent. That whereby here we are justified is perfect, but not inherent. That whereby we are sanctified, is inherent, but not perfect. This openeth a way to the understanding of that grand question, which hangeth yet in controversie between us and the Church of *Rome*, about the matter of justifying righteousness.

4. First, although they imagine, that the Mother of our Lord and Saviour Jesus Christ, were for his honour and by his special protection , preserved clean from all sin : yet touching the rest they teach as we do ; that infants that never did actually offend , have their natures defiled, destitute of Justice, averted from God; that in making man righteous , none do efficiently work with God, but God. They teach as we do, that unto Justice no man ever attained , but by the Merits of Jesus Christ. They teach as we do, that although Christ as God , be the efficient ; as Man, the meritorious cause of our Justice : yet in us also there is some thing required. God is the cause of our natural life , in him we live : but he quickneth not the body without the soul in the body. Christ hath merited to make us just : but as a medicine, which is made for health, doth not heal by being made, but by being applied : so by the merits of Christ there can be no Justification , without the application of his Merits. Thus far we joyn hands with the Church of *Rome*.

5. Wherein then do we disagree ? We disagree about the nature and essence of the Medicine , whereby Christ cureth our disease ; about the manner of applying it ; about the number, and the power of means , which God requireth in us for the effectual applying thereof to our souls comfort. When they are required to shew what the righteousness is , whereby a Christian man is justified : they (a) answer, that it is a divine spiritual quality , which quality received into the soul , doth first make it to be one of them , who are born of God : and secondly , indue it with power , to bring forth such works , as they do that are born of him ; even as the soul of man being joyned to his body , doth first make him to be of the number of reasonable creatures; and secondly inable him to perform the natural functions which are proper to his kind : that it maketh the soul amiable and gracious in the sight of God , in regard whereof it is termed grace : that it purgeth, purifieth, and washeth out all the staines , and pollutions of sin, that by it, through the merit of Christ we are delivered as from sin, so from eternal death and condemnation , the reward of sin. This grace they will have to be applyed by infusion : to the end , that as the body is warm by the heat which is in the body , so the soul might be righteous by the inherent grace : which grace they make capable of increase ; as the body may be more and more warm, so the soul more and more justified , according as grace shall be augmented ; the augmentation whereof is merited by good works , as good Works are made meritorious by it. Wherefore, the first receit of grace in their divinity , is the first justification ; the increase thereof the second justification. As grace may be increased by the merit of good works : so it may be diminished by the demerit of sins venial, it may be lost by mortal sin. In as much therefore as it is needful in the one case to repair, in the other to recover

---

Marginal notes:

They teach as we do, that God doth justifie the soul of man alone, without any co-effective cause of justice. *Deus sine medio coeffectivo animam justificat. Casal. de quad. part. 5. q. 6. 1 dim lib. 3. c.*

The difference betwixt the Papists and us about justification.

(a) Tho. Aquin. 1. 2. q. 110. 110. *Gratia gratum faciens, id est justificans, est animæ quiddam reale & positivum qualitas quædam (art. 2. con. c.) supernaturalis, non eadem cum virtute infusa , ut Magister; sed aliquid (art. 3. præter virtutes, ut fidem, spem, charitatem habit. uno que (art. 3. ad 3.) quæ præsupponitur in virtutibus infusis earum principium & radix essentiam animæ tanquam subjectum occupat non potentias ; sed ab ipsa (art 4. ad 1.) effluunt virtutis in potentias : anima, per quas potentiæ moventur ad actus plur. vid. quæst. 113. de justificatione.*

cover the loss which is made: the infusion of grace hath her sundry after-meals, for the which cause, they make many ways to apply the infusion of grace. It is apply-ed to infants through Baptism, without either Faith or Works, and in them really it taketh away original sin; and the punishment due unto it ; It is applyed to Infi-dels and wicked men in the first justification, through Baptism without Works, yet not without Faith ; and it taketh away both sins actual and original together, withal whatsoever punishment, eternal or temporal, thereby deserved. Unto such as have attained the first justification, that is to say, the first receit of grace, it is applyed farther by good works to the increase of former grace, which is the second justifica-tion. If they work more and more, grace doth more increase, and they are more and more justified. To such as diminished it by venial sins, it is applyed by holy water, *Ave Maries*, Crossings, Papal salutations, and such like, which serve for reparations of grace decayed. To such as have lost it through mortal sin, it is apply-ed by the Sacrament (as they terme it) of Penance: which Sacrament hath force to confer grace a new, yet in such sort, that being so conferred, it hath not altogether so much power, as at the first. For it onely clenseth out the stain or guilt of sin committed ; and changeth the punishment eternal into a temporal satisfactory pu-nishment here. if time do serve, if not, hereafter to be indured except it be lightned by Masses, works of Charity, Pilgrimages, Fasts, and such like ; or else shortned by pardon for ter ne, or by plenary pardon quite removed, and taken away. This is the mystery of the man of sin. This maze the Church of *Rome* doth cause her followers to tread ;when they ask her the way to justification. I cannot stand now to unrip this building, and to sift it peece by peece ; onely I will pass by it in few words, that that may befal *Babylon* in the presence of that which God hath builded as hapned unto *Dagon* before the Ark.

6. Doubtless saith the Apostle, *I have counted all things, loss, and judge them to be* Phil. 1. 3;
dung, that I may win Christ ; and to be found in him, not having my own righteousness,
but that which is through the faith of Christ, the righteousness which is of God through
Faith. Whether they speak of the first or second justification, they make it the essence of a divine quality inherent, they make it righteousness which is in us. If it be in us, then is it ours, as our souls are ours though we have them from God, and can hold them no longer than pleaseth him : for if he withdraw the breath of our nostrils, we fall to dust : but the righteousness wherein we must be found, if we will be justified, is not our own; therefore we cannot be justified by any inherent quality. Christ hath merited righteousness for as many as are found in him. In him God find-eth us, if we be faithful, for by faith we are incorporated into Christ. Then al-though in our selves we be altogether sinful and unrighteous yet even the man which is impious in himself, ful of iniquity, full of sin ; him being found in Christ through faith, and having his sin remitted through repentance ; him God upholdeth with a gracious eye, putteth away his sin by not imputing it, taketh quite away the Punish-ment due thereunto by pardoning it, and accepteth him in Jesus Christ, as perfectly righteous, as if he had fulfilled all that was commanded him in the Law : shall I say more perfectly righteous then if himself had fulfilled the whole Law ? I must take heed what I say : but the Apostle saith, *God made him to be sin for us who knew no sin:* : Cor. 5. 21.
that we might be made the righteousness of God in him. Such we are in the sight of God the Father, as is the very Son of God himself. Let it be counted folly or phrensie, or fury, whatsoever ; it is our comfort, and our wisdom ; we care for no know-ledg in the world but this, That Man hath sinned, and God hath suffered ; That God hath made himself the Son of man, and that men are made the righteousness of God. You see therefore that the Church of *Rome*, in teaching justification by inhe-rent grace, doth pervert the truth of Christ, and that by the hands of the Apostles we have received otherwise then she teacheth. Now concerning the righteousness of sanctification, we deny it not to be inherent : we grant, that unless we work, we have it not : onely we distinguish it as a thing different in nature from the righteousness of justification : we are righteous the one way by the faith of *Abraham* ; the other way, except we do the works of *Abraham*, we are not righteous: Of the one St. *Paul* Rom. 4. 8;
To him that worketh not, but believeth, faith is counted for righteousness: Of the other, St. *John*, *Qui facit justitiam justus est;* He is righteous which worketh righteousness: Of the one, St. *Paul* doth prove by *Abrahams* Example; that we have it of faith with-

out works. Of the other, St. *James* by *Abrahams* Example, that by works we have it, and not onely by faith. St. *Paul* doth plainely sever these two parts of Christian righteousnefs one from the other. For in the sixt to the *Rom.* thus he writeth, *Being freed from sin, and made servants to God, ye have your fruit in holinefs, and the end everlasting life. Ye are made free from sin, and made Servants unto God;* this is the righteousnefs of *justification:* ye have your fruit in holinefs; this is the righteousnefs of sanctification. By the one we are interessed in the right of inheriting; by the other we are brought to the actual possession of eternal blifs, and so the end of both is everlasting life.

7. The Prophet *Habak.* doth here term the Jews *righteous* men, not onely becaufe being justified by faith they were free from sin: but alfo becaufe they had their meafure of fruits in holinefs. According to whofe example of charitable judgment, which leaveth it to God to difcern what we are, and fpeaketh of them according to that which they do profefs themfelves to be, although they be not holy men, whom men do think, but whom God doth know indeed to be fuch: yet let every Chriftian man know, that in Chriftian equity, he ftandeth bound for to think and fpeak of his Brethren, as of men that have a meafure in the fruit of holinefs, and a right unto the Titles, wherewith God, in token of fpecial favour and mercy, vouchfafeth to honour his chofen fervants. So we fee the Apoftles of our Saviour Chrift, do ufe every where the name of *Saints*; fo the Prophet, the name of righteous. But let us all be fuch as we defire to be termed. *Reatus impii eft pium nomen,* faith *Salvianus:* Godly names do not juftifie godlefs men. We are but upbraided, when we are honoured with Names and Titles, whereunto our lives and manners are not futable. If indeed we have our fruit in holinefs, notwithftanding we muft note, that the more we abound therein the more need we have to crave that we may be ftrengthned and fupported. Our very vertues may be fnares unto us. The enemy, that waiteth for all occafions to work our ruine, hath found it harder to overthrow an humble Sinner, then a proud Saint. There is no mans cafe fo dangerous, as his whom Sathan hath perfwaded that his own righteoufnefs fhall prefent him pure and blamlefs in the fight of God. If we could fay, we were not guilty of any thing at all in our confciences (we know our felves far from this innocency; we cannot fay we know nothing by our felvs; but if we could) fhould we therefore plead not guilty before the prefence of our Judge, that fees further into our hearts then we our felves can do? if our hands did never offer violence to our brethren, a bloody thought doth prove us Murtherers before him: if we had never opened our mouth to utter any fcandalous, offenfive, or hurtful word, the cry of our fecret cogitations is heard in the ears of God. If we did not commit the fins, which daily and hourly either in deed, word, or thoughts we do commit; yet in the good things which we do, how many defects are there intermingled! God in that which is done, refpecteth the mind and intention of the doer. Cut of then all thofe things wherein we have regarded our own glory, thofe things which men do to pleafe men, and to fatisfie our own liking, thofe things which we do for any by refpect, not fincerely and purely for the love of God: and a fmall fcore will ferve for the number of our righteous deeds. Let the holyeft and beft thing we do be confidered; we are never better affected unto God then when we pray; yet when we pray, how are our affections many times diftracted! How little reverence do we fhew unto the grand Majefty of God, unto whom we fpeak! How little remorfe of our own miferies! How little taft of the fweet influence of his tender mercies do we feel! Are we not as unwilling many times to begin, and as glad to make an end; as if in faying, *Call upon me,* he had fet us a very burthenfome task? It may feem fomewhat extreme, which I will fpeak: therefore let every one judge of it, even as his own heart fhall tell him, and no otherwife; I will but onely make a demand: If God fhould yeild unto us, not as unto *Abraham,* If fifty, forty, thirty, twenty, yea, or if ten good perfons could be found in a City, for their fakes that City fhould not be deftroyed: but, and if he fhould make us an offer thus large; Search all the Generations of men, fithence the Fall of our *Father Adam,* find one man, that hath done one action, which hath paft from him pure, without any ftrain or blemifh at all, and for that one mans onely action, neither man nor Angel fhall feel the torments which are prepared for both. Do you think that this ranfome, to deliver men and Angels, could be found to be among the fons of men? The beft thing which we

do,

do, have somewhat in them to be pardoned. How then can we do any thing meritorious, or worthy to be rewarded? Indeed God doth liberally promise whatsoever appertaineth to a blessed life, to as many as sincerely keep his law, though they be not exactly able to keep it. Wherefore we acknowledge a dutiful necessity of doing well; but the meritorious dignity of doing well, we utterly renounce. We see how far we are from the perfect righteousness of the law; the little fruit which we have in holiness, it is, God knoweth, corrupt and unsound: we put no confidence at all in it, we challenge nothing in the world for it, we dare not call God to reckoning, as if we had him in our debt-books: our continual suit to him, is, and must be, to bear with our infirmities, and pardon our offences.

8. But the people of whom the prophet speaketh, were they all, or were the most part of them such as had care to walk uprightly? Did they thirst after righteousness? Did they wish? Did they long with the righteous Prophet; *Oh that our ways were so direct, that we might keep thy statutes?* Did they lament with the righteous Apostle; *Oh miserable men, the good which we wish and purpose, and strive to do, we cannot?* No, the words of the other Prophet concerning this people, do shew the contrary. How grievously hath *Esay* mourned over them? *Oh sinful nation, laden with iniquity, wicked seed, corrupt Children!* All which notwithstanding, so wide are the bowels of his compassion enlarged, that he denyeth us not, no, not when we were laden with iniquity, leave to commune familiarly with him, liberty to crave and intreat, that what plagues soever we have deserved, we may not be in worse case than unbeleivers, that we may not be hemmed in by Pagans and Infidels. *Jerusalem* is a sinful polluted City: but *Jerusalem* compared with *Babylon*, is righteous. And shall the righteous be overborn? shall they be compas'd about by the wicked? But the Prophet doth not onely complain; Lord how commeth it to pass, that thou handlest us so hardly, of whom thy name is called, and bearest with the Heathen Nations, that despise thee? No, he breaketh out through extremity of grief and inferreth violently: This *proceeding is perverse,* the righteous are thus handled; *therefore perverse judgment doth proceed.*

6. Which illation containeth many things, whereof it were better much both for you to hear, and me to speak, if necessity did not draw me to another task. *Paul* and *Barnabas* being requested to preach the same things again which once they had preached, thought it their duties to satisfie the godly desires of men, sincerely affected to the truth. Nor may it seem burdenous for me nor for you unprofitable, that I follow their example, the like occasion unto theirs being offered me. When we had last the Epistle of St. *Paul* to the *Hebrews* in hand, and of that Epistle these words; *In these last days he hath spoken unto us by his Son:* After we had thence collected the nature of the visible Church of Christ; and had defined it to be a community of men sanctified through the profession of the Truth, which God hath taught the world by his Son; and had declared, that the scope of Christian Doctrine is the comfort of them whose hearts are overcharged with the burden of sin; and had proved that the doctrine professed in the Church of Rome, doth bereave men of comfort both in their lives and in their deaths: the conclusion in the end, whereunto we came, was this; the Church of Rome being in faith so corrupted, as she is, and refusing to be reformed, as she doth, we are to sever our selves from her; the example of our Fathers may not retain us in communion with that Church, under hope that we so continuing, may be saved as well as they. God, I doubt not, was merciful to save thousands of them, though they lived in popish superstitions, inasmuch as they sinned ignorantly: but the truth is now laid before our eys. The former part of this last sentence, namely, these words: *I doubt not, but God was merciful to save thousands of our Fathers living in Popish superstitions, inasmuch as they sinned ignorantly:* this sentence, I beseech you to mark, and to sift it with the severity of austere judgement, that if it be found to be gold, it may be suitable to the precious foundation whereon it was then laid: for I pretest, that if it be hay or stubble, my own hand shall set fire on it. Two questions have risen by reason of this speech before alledged: The one, *Whether our Fathers, infected with Popish errours and superstitions, may be saved?* The other, *Whether their ignorance be a reasonable inducement to make us think, they might?* We are then to examine: first, what possibility: then what probability there is that God might be merciful unto so many of our Fathers.

10. So many of our Fathers living in Popish superstitions, yet by the mercy of

Rom. 7. 19.

Cap. 1. v. 4

Act. 13. 42. 44.

Heb. 1. v. 2

By sanctification, Imaginarie separation from others proceeding as they do. For true holiness consisteth not in professing, but in obeying the truth of Christ

God be saved? No; this could not be: God hath spoken by his Angel from Heaven, unto his people concerning *Babylon* (by *Babylon* we understand the Church of Rome;) *Go out of her my people, that ye be not partakers of her plagues.* For answer whereunto, first, I do not take the words to be meant onely of temporal plagues, of the corpral death, sorrow, famine and fire, whereunto God in his wrath hath condemned *Babylon*; and that to save his chosen people from these plagues, he saith, *Go out,* with like intent, as in the Gospel, (speaking of *Jerusalems* desolations, he saith *Let them that are in* Judea, *flie unto the Mountaines, and them that are in the midst thereof depart out :* or, as in the former times to *Lot,* *Arise, take thy Wife and thy Daughters which are there, lest thou be destroyed in the punishment of the City :* but forasmuch as here it is said, *Go out of Babylon ;* we doubt, their everlasting destruction, which are partakers therein, is either principally ment, or necessarily implyed in this sentence. How then was it possible for so many of your fathers to be saved, sith they were so far from departing out of *Babylon,* that they took her for their Mother, and in her bosome yielded up the Ghost.

11. First, for the plagues being threatned unto them that are partakers in the sins of *Babylon,* we can define nothing concerning our fathers, out of this sentence : unless we shew what the sins of *Babylon* be ; and what they be which are such partakers of them, that their everlasting plagues are inevitable. The sins which may be common both to them of the Church of Rome, and to others departed thence, must be severed from this question. He which saith, *Depart out of Babylon, lest ye be partakers of her sins :* sheweth plainly, that he meaneth such sins, as, except we separate our selves, we have no power in the World to avoyd ; such impieties, as by their Law they have established, and whereunto all that are among them, either do indeed assent, or else are by powerable means forced in shew and appearance, to subject themselves. As for example, in the Church of *Rome* it is maintained, that the same credit and reverence that we give to the Scriptures of God, ought also to be given to unwritten verities ; That the Pope is supreme head ministerial over the universal Church militant ; That the bread in the Eucharist is transubstantiated into Christ ; That it is to be adored, and to be offered up unto God, as a sacrifice propitiatory for quick and dead ; That Images are to be worshipped ; Saints to be called upon, as intercessors, and such like. Now, because some Heresies do concern things, only beleived, as the transubstantiation of the sacramental Elements in the *Eucharist ;* some concern things which are practised and put in ure, as the adoration of the Elements transubstantiated : we must note, that *erroniously,* the practice of that is sometime received, whereof the doctrine, that teacheth it, is not *heretically* maintained. They are all partakers of the maintenance of Heresies, who by word or deed allow them, knowing them, although not knowing them to be heresies ; as also they, and that most dangerously of all others, who knowing Heresie to be, Heresie, do notwithstanding in worldly respects, make semblance of allowing that, which in heart and judgment they condemn : But heresie is heretically maintained, by such as obstinately hold it, after wholesome admonition. Of the last sort, as of the next before, I make no doubt, but that their condemnation without an actual repentance, is inevitable. Lest any man therefore should think, that in speaking of our fathers, I should speak indifferently of them all : let my words I beseech you be wel marked : *I doubt not, but God was merciful to save thousands of our Fathers :* which thing I will now by Gods assistance, set more plainly before your eys.

12. Many are partakers of the errour, which are not of the heresie of the Church of Rome. The people following the conduct of their guides, and observing as they did, exactly, that which was prescribed, thought they did God good service ; when indeed they did dishonour him. This was their error : but the Heresie of the Church of *Rome,* their dogmatical Positions opposite unto Christian truth, what one man amongst ten thousand, did ever understand ? Of them, which understand *Roman* Heresies, and allow them, all are not alike partakers in the action of allowing. Some allow them as the first founders and establishers of them : which crime toucheth none but their Popes and Councels : the people are clear and free from this. Of them which maintain Popish Heresies, not as Authors, but receivers of them from others, all maintain them not as Masters. In this are not the people partakers neither but onely the Predicants and Schoolmen. Of them which have been partakers in this sin of teach-

ing

Apoc. 18. 4.

Mat. 24. 16.

Gen. 19. 15.

ing Popish heresie, there is also a difference; for they have not all been Teachers of all Popish Herefie. *Put a difference*, saith St. *Jude*; *have compassion upon some*. Shall we lap up all in one condition? Shall we cast them all head-long? Shall we plunge them all into that infernal and everlasting flaming lake? Them that have been partakers of the errours of *Babylon*, together with them which are in the herefie? them which have been the Authors of Herefie, with them that by terrour and violence have been forced to receive it? Them who have taught it, with them whose fimplicity hath by flights and conveyances of false Teachers, been seduced to believe it? Them which have been partakers in one, with them which have been partakers in many? Them which in many, with them which in all?

13. Notwithstanding I grant, that although the condemnation of them be more tolerable then of these: yet for the man that laboureth at the plough, to him that fitteth in the Vatican; to all partakers in the sins of *Babylon*; to our Fathers, though they did but erroneously practise that which the guide heretically taught; to all without exception, plagues were due. The pit is ordinarily the end, as well of the guide, as of the guided in blindnefs. But wo worth the hour wherein we were born, except we might promise our selves better things; things which accompany mans salvation, even where we know that worse and such as accompany condemnation are due. Then must we shew some way how possibly they might escape. What way is there that sinners can find to escape the judgement of God, but onely by appealing to the seat of his saving mercy? Which mercy, with *Origen*, we do not extend to Divels and damned spirits. God hath mercy upon thousands, but there be thousands also which he hardeneth. Chrift hath therefore set the bounds, he hath fixed the limits of his saving mercy within the compass of these termes: *God sent not his own Son to condemn the World, but that the world through him might be saved.* In the third of St. *Johns* Gospel mercy is restrained to beleivers: *He that beliveth shall not be condemned; He that beleiveth not, is condemned already, becaufe he beleiveth not in the Son of God.* In the fecond of the Revelation, mercy is restrained to the penitent. For of *Jezabel* and her sectaries, thus he speaketh: *I gave her space to repent, and she repented not. Behold, I will caft her into a bed, and them that commit fornication with her into great affliction, except they repent them of their works, and I will kill her Children with death.* Our hope therefore of the Fathers, is, if they were not altogether faithlef and impenitent, that they are saved.

14. They are not all faithlef that are weak in affenting to the truth, or ftiff in maintaining things opposite to the truth of Christian Doctrine. But as many as hold the foundation which is precious, though they hold it but weakly, and as it were with a flender thred, although they frame many bafe and unfutable things upon it, things that cannot abide the tryal of the fire; yet shall they pass the fiery tryal and be faved, which indeed have builded themselves upon the rock, which is the foundation of the Church. If then our fathers did not hold the foundation of Faith, there is no doubt but they were faithlef. If many of them held it, then is therein no impediment, but many of them might be saved. Then let us see what the foundation of faith is, and whether we may think that thousands of our Fathers being in Popish superstitions, did notwithstanding hold the foundation.

15. If the foundation of Faith do import the general ground, whereupon we reft when we do believe, the writings of the Evangelifts and the Apoftles are the foundation of the Chriftian faith: *Credimus quia legimus*, saith S. *Jerome*: Oh that the Church of *Rome* did as (*a*) foundly interpret these fundamental writings whereupon we build our faith, as she doth willingly hold and imbrace them.

16. But if the name of *Foundation* do note the principal thing which is believed: then is that the foundation of our Faith which S. *Paul* hath to *Timothy*: (*b*) *God manifefted in the flesh, juftified in the Spirit, &c.* that of *Nathaniel*, (*c*) *thou art the Son of the living God: thou art the King of Ifrael*: that of the inhabitants of *Samaria*, (*d*) *This is Chrift the Saviour of the world*: he that directly denyeth this, doth utterly raze the very foundation of our Faith. I have proved heretofore, that although the Church of *Rome* hath plaid the Harlot worfe then ever did *Ifrael*, yet are they not as now the Synagogue of the *Jews*, which plainly deny Chrift Jefus, quite and clean excluded from the new Covenant. But as *Samaria* compared with *Jerufalem* is termed *Aholath*, a Church or Tabernacle of her own; contrar.wife

John 3. 17.

Revel. 2. 22.

a They misinterpret, notonly by making falfe and corrupt gloffes upon the Scripture, but alfo by forcing the old vulgar tranflation as the only authentical; howbeit, they refufe no book which is Canonical, t'ough they admit fundry which are not. *b* 1 Tim. 3. 16. *c* John 1. 49. *d* John 4. 42.

trariwise, *Jerusalim Aholibath*, the resting place of the Lord: so, whatsoever we terme the Church of *Rome*, when we compare her with reformed Churches, still we put a difference, as then between *Babylon* and *Samaria*, so now between *Rome* and the Heathenish assemblies. Which opinion I must and will recal; I must grant and vvill, that the Church of *Rome* together with all her Children, is clean excluded. There is no difference in the World between our Fathers and *Saracens*, *Turks* and *Painims*, if they did directly deny Christ crucified for the Salvation of the World.

17. But how many millions of them were known so to have ended their lives, that the drawing of their breath hath ceased with the uttering of this Faith, *Christ my Saviour, my Redeemer Jesus*? Answer is made, That this they might unfainedly confess, and yet be far enough from Salvation. For behold, saith the Apostle, *I Paul say unto you, that if ye be circumcised, Christ shall profit you nothing.* Christ in the work of mans salvation is alone: the *Galathians* were cast away by joyning *Circumcision* and the other rites of the Law with Christ: the Church of *Rome* doth teach her children to joyn other things likewise with him; therefore their faith, their beleif doth not profit them any thing at all. It is true that they do indeed joyn other things with Christ: but how? Not in the work of redemption it self, which they grant, that Christ alone hath performed sufficiently for the salvation of the whole World; but in the application of this inestimable treasure, that it may be effectual to their salvation: how demurely soever they confess, that they seek remission of sins no otherwise then by the blood of Christ, using humbly the means appointed by him to apply the benefit of his holy blood; they teach indeed, so many things pernicious in Christian Faith, in setting down the means whereof they speak, that the very foundation of Faith which they hold, is thereby (*a*) plainly overthrown, and the force of the blood of Jesus Christ extinguished. We may therefore dispute with them, urge them even with as dangerous sequels, as the Apostle doth the *Galatians*. But I demand, If some of those *Galatians* heartily imbracing the Gospel of Christ, sincere and sound in faith (this one onely errour excepted) had ended their lives before they were ever taught how perilous an opinion they held; shall we think that the danger of this errour did so overwaigh the benefit of their faith, that the mercy of God might not save them? I grant they overthrew the foundation of Faith by consequent: doth not that so likewise which the (*b*) *Lutheran* Churches do at this day so stifly & so firmly maintain? For mine own part I dare not here deny the possibility of their salvation which have bin the chiefest instruments of ours, albeit they carried to their grave a perswasion so greatly repugnant to the truth. Forasmuch therefore as it may be said of the Church of *Rome*, she hath yet a litt'e strength, she doth not directly deny the foundation of Christianity: I may, I trust without offerce, perswade my self, that thousands of our Fathers in former times living and dying within her wals, have found mercy at the hands of God.

a Plainly in all mens sight whose eys God hath enlightned to behold his truth. For they which are in errour, are in darkness, and see not that which in light is plain. In that which the teach concerning the natures of Christ, they hold the same with Nestorius fully, the same with Eutiches about the proprieties of his nature. b The opinion of the Lutherans thoug: it be no direct denyal of the foundation, may notwithstanding be damnable unto some; and I do not think but that in many respects it is less damnable, as at this day some maintain it, than it was in them which held it at first; as Luther and others whom I had an eye unto in this speech. The question is not whether an errour with such and such circumstances: but simply, whether an errour overthrowing the foundation, do exclude all possibility of salvation, if it be not recanted, and expresly repented of.

18. What a'though they repented not of their errours? God forbid that I should open my mouth to gain-say that which Christ himself hath spoken: *Except ye repent, ye shall all perish.* And if they did not repent they perished. But withal note, that we have the benefit of a double repentance: the least sin which we commit in Deed, Thought, or Word, is death, without repentance. Yet how many things do escape us in every of these, which we do not know? How many, which we do not observe to be sins? And without the knowledge, without the observation of sin, there is no actual repentance. It cannot then be chosen, but that for as many as hold the foundation, and have all holden sins and errours in hatred, the blessing of repentance for unknown sins and errours is obtained at the hands of God, through the gracious mediation of Jesus Christ, for such suiters as cry with the Prophet *David*: *Purge me, O Lord, from my secret sins.*

19. But we wash a wall of lome; we labour in vain; all this is nothing; it doth not prove; it cannot justifie that which we go about to maintain. Infidels and Heathen men are not so godless, but that they may no doubt, cry God mercy, and desire in general to have their sins forgiven them. To such as deny the foundation of

faith

faith there can be no salvation (according to the ordinary course which God doth u e in saving men) without a particular repentance of that errour. The Galatians thinking that unlesse they were circumcised, they could not be saved, overthrew the foundation of faith directly: therefore if any of them did die so perswaded, whether before or after they were told of their errours, their end is dreadful; there is no way with them but one, death and condemnation: For the Apostle speaketh nothing of men departed, but saith generally of all, *If you be circumcised, Christ shall profit you nothing. You are abolished from Christ; whosoever are justified by the Law; ye are fallen from grace, Gal.* 5. Of them in the Church of Rome the reason is the same. For whom Antichrist hath seduced, concerning them did not S. *Paul* speak long before, they received not the word of truth; that they might not be saved? therefore God would *send them strong delusions to believe lies, that all they might be damned which believe not the truth, but had pleasure in unrighteousnesse.* And S. *John, All that dwell upon the earth shall worship him, whose names are not written in the book of life, Apoc.* 13. Indeed many in former times as their Books and Writings do yet shew, held the foundation, to wit salvation by Christ alone, and therefore might be saved. God hath always had a Church amongst them, which firmly kept his saving truth. As for such as hold with the Church of Rome, that we cannot be saved by Christ alone without works; they do not onely by a circle of consequence, but directly deny the foundation of faith; they hold it not, no not so much as by a thred.

2 Thess. 2. 11.

Apoc. 13. ver. 8.

20. This to my remembrance, being all that hath been opposed with any countenance or shew of reason, I hope, if this be answered, the cause in question is at an end. Concerning general repentence therefore: what? A Murtherer, a Blasphemer, an unclean person, a Turk, a *Jew*, any sinner to escape the wrath of God by a general repentance; *God forgive me*? Truely it never came within my heart, that a general repentance doth serve for all sins: it serveth onely for the common oversights of our sinful life, and for the faults which either we do not mark, or do not know that they are faults. Our Fathers were actually penitent for sins, wherein they knew they displeased God; or else they fall not within the compass of my first speech. Again, that otherwise they could not be saved, then holding the foundation of Christian Faith, we have not only affirmed, but proved. Why is it not then confessed, that thousands of our Fathers which lived in popish superstitions, might yet by the mercy of God be saved? First, if they had directly denyed the very foundations of Christianity, without repenting them particularly of that sin; he which saith there could be no salvation for them, according to the ordinary course which God doth in saving men, granteth plainly, or at the least closely insinuateth, that an extraordinary priviledge of mercy might deliver their souls from hell, which is more then I required. Secondly, if the foundation be denied, it is denied for fear of some heresie which the Church of *Rome* maintaineth. But how many were there amongst our Fathers, who being seduced by the common error of that Church, never knew the meaning of her Heresies? So that although all popish Hereticks did perish; thousands of them which lived in Popish superstitions, might be saved. Thirdly, seeing all that held Popish Heresies, did not hold all the heresies of the Pope: why might not thousands which were infected with other leaven, live and die unsowred with this; and so be saved? Fourthly, if they all held this Heresie, many there were that held it; no doubt, but onely in a general form of words, which a favourable interpretation might expound in a sense differing far enough from the poysoned conceit of Heresie. As for example; Did they hold, that we cannot be saved by Christ, without good works? We our selves do, I think, all say as much, with this construction, salvation being taken as in that sentence, *Corde creditur ad justitiam, ore fit confessio ad salutem*, except infants and men, cut off upon the point of their conversion: of the rest none shall see God, but such as seek peace and holiness, though not as a cause of their salvation, yet as a way which they must walk, which will be saved. Did they hold, that without works we are not justified? Take justification so as it may also imply sanctification, and St. *James* doth say as much. For except there be an ambiguity in the same terme, St. *Paul* and St. *James* do contradict each the other: which cannot be. Now there is no ambiguity in the name either of faith, or of works, being meant by them both in one and the same sence. Finding therefore, that justification is spoken of by St. *Paul*, without implying sanctification, when

For this is the onely thing alledged to prove the im- possibility of their salvation: The Church of Rome joy- neth works with Christ, which is a de- nyal of the foundati n, and unless we hold the foun- d tion, we ca- not b saved.

he

he proveth, that a man is justified by faith without works; finding likewise that justification doth sometime imply sanctification also with it: I suppose nothing to be more found, then so to interpret St. *James*, speaking not in that sence, but in this.

21. We have already shewed, that there be two kinds of Christian righteousness: the one without us, which we have by imputation; the other in us, which consisteth of faith, hope, and charity, and other Christian vertues: And S. *James* doth prove that *Abraham* had not onely the one, because the thing beleeved was imputed unto him for righteousnesse; but also the other, beause he offered up his son. God giveth us both the one justice and the other: the one by accepting us for righteous in Christ; the other, by working Christian righteousnesse in us. The proper and most immediate efficient cause in us of this latter, is the Spirit of adoption we have received into our hearts. That whereof it consisteth, whereof it is really and formally made, are those infused vertues, proper and peculiar unto Saints, which the spirit in the very moment, when first it is given of God, bringeth with it: the effects whereof are such actions as the Apostle doth call the fruits of works, the operations of the Spirit: The difference of the which operations from the root whereof they spring, maketh it needful to put two kinds likewise of sanctifying righteousnesse, *Habitual*, and *Actual. Habitual*, that holinesse, wherewith our souls are inwardly indued, the same instant, when first we begin to be the Temples of the holy Ghost. *Actual*, that holinesse, which afterwards beautifieth all the parts and actions of our life, the holinesse for which *Enoch*, *Job*, *Zachary*, *Elizabeth*, and other Saints, are in the Scriptures so highly commended. If here it be demanded, which of these we do first receive: I answer, that the Spirit, the vertue, of the spirit, the habitual justice, which is ingrafted, the external justice of *Jesus Christ*, which is imputed: these we receive all at one and the same time; whensoever we have any of these, we have all; they go together. Yet sith no man is justifed except he beleve, and no man beleeveth except he hath faith, and no man except he hath received the spirit of adoption, hath faith: forasmuch as they do necessarily infer justification, and justification doth of necessity presuppose them; we must needs hold that imputed righteousnesse, in dignity being the chiefest, is notwithstanding in order to the last of all these? but *actual righteousnesse*, which is the righteousnesse of good works, succeedeth all, followeth after all, both in order and time. Which being attentively marked, sheweth plainly how the faith of true Beleivers cannot be divorced from hope and love; how faith is a part of sanctification, and yet unto justification necessary; how faith is perfected by good works, and not works of ours without faith: finally, how our Fathers might hold, that we are justified by Faith alone and yet hold truly that without works we are not justified. Did they think that men do merit rewards in heaven, by the works they performe on earth? The ancient use *meriting* for *obtaining*, and in that sence they of *Wittenberg* have it in their confession; *we teach that good Works commanded of God, are necessarily to be done, and by the free kindnesse of God they merit their certain rewards*. Therefore speaking as our Fathers did, and we taking their speech, in a sound meaning, as we may take our Fathers, and might, for as much as their meaning is doubtful, and charity doth always interpret doubtful things favourably: what should induce us to think, that rather the damage of the worst construction did light upon them all, then that the blessing of the better was granted unto thousands? Fiftly, if in the worst construction that may be made, they had generally all imbraced it living, might not many of them dying utterly renounce it? Howsoever men when they sit at ease, do vainly tickle their hearts with the vain conceit of I know not what proportionable correspondence, between their merits and their rewards, which in the trance of their high speculations they dream that God hath measured, weighed, and laid up, as it were in bundles for them: notwithstanding, we see by daily experience, in a number even of them, that when the hour of death approacheth, when they secretly hear themselves summoned forthwith to appear, and stand at the Bar of that Judge, whose brightnesse causeth the eyes of the Angels themselves to dazel, all these idle imaginations do then begin to hide their faces, to name merits then is to lay their souls upon the rack, the memory of their own deeds is lothsome unto them, they forsake all things, wherein they have put any trust or confidence, no staff to lean upon, no ease, no rest, no comfort then, but onely in Jesus Christ.

22. Where-

22. Wherefore if this proposition were true: *To hold in such wise, as the Church of Rome doth, that we cannot be saved by Christ alone without works, is directly to deny the foundation of Faith*; I say, that if this proposition were true: nevertheless so many ways I have shewed, whereby we may hope that thousand of our Fathers which lived in popish superstition, might be saved. But what if it be not true? What if neither that of the *Galathians*, concerning Circumcision; nor this of the Church of Rome by Workes be any direct denial of the foundation as it is affirmed, that both are? I need not wade so far as to discuss this Controversie, the matter which first was brought into question being so clear, as I hope it is. Howbeit, because I desire, that the truth even in that also should receive light, I will do mine indeavour to set down somewhat more plainly; first, the foundation of Faith, what it is: Secondly, what is directly to deny the foundation: Thirdly whether they whom God hath chosen to be heirs of life, may fall so far as directly to deny it: Fourthly, whether the *Galathians* did so by admitting the error about *Circumcision* and the *Law*: last of all, whether the Church of Rome for this one opinion of Works, may be thought to do the like, and thereupon to be no more a Christian Church, then are the Assemblies of Turks and Jews.

23. This word foundation being figuratively used, hath always reference to somewhat which resembleth a material building, as both that Doctrine of *Laws* and the community of Christians do. By the Masters of Civil Policy nothing is so much inculcated, as that *Common-weals are founded upon Laws*; for that a multitude cannot be compacted into one body otherwise then by a common acception of Laws, whereby they are to be kept in order. The ground of all civil Laws is this: *No man ought to be hurt or injured by another*; Take away this perswasion, and ye take away all the Laws: take away Laws, and what shall become of Common-weals? So it is in our spiritual Christian Community: I do not mean that body Mystical, whereof Christ is onely the head, that building undiscernable by mortal eyes, wherein Christ is the chief corner stone: but I speak of the visible Church; the foundation whereof is the doctrine which the Prophets and the Apostles profest. The mark whereunto their Doctrine tendeth, is pointed at in these words of *Peter* unto Christ, *Thou hast the words of eternal life*: in those words of *Paul* to *Timothy*, *The holy Scriptures are able to make thee wise unto salvation*. It is the demand of nature it self, *What shall we do to have eternal life?* The desire of immortality and the knowledge of that, whereby it may be obtained, is so natural unto all men, that even they who are not perswaded, that they shall, do notwithstanding wish, that they might know a way how to see no end of life. And because natural means are not able still to resist the force of Death: there is no people in the earth so savage, which hath not devised some supernatural help or other, to fly for aid and succour in extremities, against the Enemies of the Laws. A longing therefore to be saved, without understanding the true way how, hath been the cause of all the Superstitions in the World. O that the miserable state of others, which wander in darkness, and wot not whither they go, could give us understanding hearts, worthily to esteem the riches of the mercy of God towards us, before whose eys the doors of the Kingdom of Heaven are set wide open! should we offer violence unto it? it offereth violence unto us, and we gather strength to withstand it. But I am besides my purpose, when I fall to bewail the cold affection which we bear towards that whereby we should be saved; my purpose being only to set down, what the ground of salvation is. The Doctrine of the Gospel proposeth salvation as the end: and doth it not teach the way of attayning thereunto? Yet the Damosel possest with a spirit of divination, spake the truth: *These men are the Servants of the most high God, which shew unto us the way of Salvation: A new and living way which Christ hath prepared for us, through the vail, that is, his flesh*; Salvation purchased by the death of Christ. By this foundation the children of God before the written Law, were distinguished from the sons of men; the reverend Patriarks both possest it living, and spake expresly of it at the hour of their death. It comforted *Job* in the midst of grief: as it was afterwards the anker-hold of all the righteous in *Israel*, from the writing of the Law, to the time of grace. Every Prophet maketh mention of it. It was famously spoken of about the time, when the comming of Christ to accomplish the promises, which were made long before it, drew near, that the sound thereof was heard even amongst the

the Gentiles. When he was come, as many as were his, acknowledged that he was their Salvation; he, that long expected hope of *Israel*; he, that *Seed, in whom all the Nations of the earth shall be blessed.* So that now he is a name of ruine, a name of death and condemnation, unto such as dream of a new *Messias*, to as many as look for salvation by any other but by him. *For amongst men there is given no other name under heaven whereby we must be saved.* Thus much S. *Mark* doth intimate by that, which he doth put in the front of this book, making his entrance with these words: *The beginning of the Gospel of Jesus Christ, the Son of God.* His Doctrine he termeth the Gospel, because it teacheth Salvation; the Gospel of Jesus Christ the son of God, because it teacheth salvation by him. This is then the foundation, whereupon the frame of the Gospel is erected; that very Iesus whom the *Virgin* conceived of the holy Ghost, whom *Simeon* imbraced in his armes, whom *Pilat* condemned, whom the *Jews* crucified, whom the *Apostles* preached, he is Christ, the Lord, the onely Saviour of the World: *Other foundation can no man lay.* Thus I have briefly opened that principle in Christianity, which we call the foundation of our faith. It followeth now, that I declare unto you, what is directly to overthrow it. This will be better opened, if we understand, what it is to hold the foundation of Faith.

24. There are which defend, that many of the Gentiles, who never heard the Name of Christ, held the foundation of Cristianity, and why? they acknowledged many of them, the Providence of God, his infinite wisedom, strength, power; his goodnes, and his mercy towards the Children of men; that God hath judgment in store for the wicked, but for the righteous, which serve him, rewards, &c. In this which they confessed, that lyeth covered, which we believe, in the Rudiments of their knowledge concerning God, the foundation of our faith concerning Christ, lyeth secretly wrapt up, and is vertually contained: therefore they held the foundation of Faith, though they never had it. Might we not with as good a colour of Reason defend, that every Plowman hath all the Sciences, wherein Philosophers have excelled? For no man is ignorant of their first Principles, which do vertually contain, whatsoever by natural means is or can be known. Yea, might we not with as great reason affirm, that a man may put three mighty Oaks wheresoever three Akorns may be put? For vertually an Akorn is an Oak. To avoid such Paradoxes, we teach plainly, that to hold the foundation, is in expres terms to acknowledge it.

25. Now, because the foundation is an affirmative Proposition, they all overthrow it, who deny it; they directly overthrow it, who deny it directly; and they overthrow it by consequent, or indirectly, which hold any one assertion whatsoever, whereupon the direct denial thereof may be necessarily concluded. What is the Question between the Gentiles and us, but this, *Whether salvation be by Christ?* What between the *Jews* and us, but this, *Whether by this Jesus, whom we call Christ, yea or no?* This is to be the main point, whereupon Christianity standeth, it is clear by that one sentence of *Festus* concerning *Pauls* accusers: *They brought no crime of such things as I supposed, but had certain questions against him of their superstition, and of one Jesus, which was dead, whom Paul affirmed to be alive.* Where we see that Jesus, dead and raised for the Salvation of the World, is by *Jews* denied, despised by a Gentile, by a Christian Apostle maintained. The Fathers therefore in the Primitve Church when they wrote; *Tertullian,* the book, which he called *Apologeticus; Minutius Fœlix,* the Book which he intitleth *Octavius; Arnobius,* the seven books against the Gentiles; *Chrysostom,* his Orations against the Jewes; *Eusebius,* his ten books of *Evangelical demonstration*: they stand in defence of Christianity against them, by whom the foundation thereof was directly denied. But the writings of the Fathers against *Novations, Pelagians,* and other Hereticks of the like note, refel Positions, whereby the foundation of Christian Faith was overthrown by consequent onely. In the former sort of Writings the foundation is proved; in the later, it is alledged as a proof, which to men that had been known directly to deny, must needs have seemed a very beggerly kind of disputing. All Infidels therefore deny the foundation of Faith directly; by consequent, many a Christian man, yea whole Christian Churches have denied it, and do deny it at this present day. Christian Churches, the foundation of Christianity: not directly, for then they cease to be Christian Churches: but by conse-

Act. 4. 12.

Luke 1. 11.
1 Cor. 3.

confequent, in refpect whereof we condemn them as erroneous, although for holding the foundation we do and muft hold them Chriftians.

26. We fee what it is to hold the foundation; what directly, and what by confequent, to deny it. The next thing which followeth, is, whether they whom God hath chofen to obtain the glory of our Lord Jefus Chrift, may once effectually called, and through faith juftified truly, afterwards fall fo far, as directly to deny the foundation, which their hearts have before imbraced with joy and comfort in the Holy Ghoft; for fuch is the faith, which indeed doth juftifie. Devils know the fame things which we believe, and the mindes of the moft ungodly may be fully perfwaded of the Truth; which knowledge in the one, and in the other, is fometimes termed faith, but equivocally, being indeed no fuch faith as that, whereby a Chriftian man is juftified. It is the Spirit of Adoption, which worketh faith in us, in them not: the things which we believe, are by us apprehended, not onely as true, but alfo as good, and that to us: as good, they are not by them apprehended; as true, they are. Whereupon followeth the third difference; the Chriftian man the more he entreafeth in faith, the more his joy and comfort aboundeth: but they, the more fure they are of the truth, the more they quake and tremble at it. This begetteth another effect, where the hearts of the one fort have a different difpofition from the other. *Non ignoro plerofque confcientia meritorum, nihil fe effe per mortem magis optare quam credere. Malunt enim extingui penitus, quam ad fupplicia reparari.* I am not ignorant, faith *Minutius*, that there be many, who being confcious what they are to look for, do rather wifh that they might, then think that they fhall ceafe, when they ceafe to live, becaufe they hold it better that death fhould confume them unto nothing, then God revive them unto punifhment. So it is in other Articles of Faith, whereof wicked men think, no doubt, many times they are too true: On the contrary fide, to the other, there is no grief or torment greater, then to feel their perfwafion weak in things whereof when they are perfwaded, they reap fuch comfort and joy of fpirit. fuch is the faith whereby we are juftified; fuch, I mean, in refpect of the quality. For touching the principal object of faith, longer then it holdeth the foundation whereof we have fpoken, it neither juftifieth, nor is, but ceafeth to be faith, when it ceafeth to believe, that Jefus Chrift is the onely Saviour of the World. The caufe of life fpiritual in us, is Chrift, not carnally or corporally inhabiting, but dwelling in the foul of man, as a thing which (when the minde apprehendeth it) is faid to inhabite or poffefs the minde. The minde conceiveth Chrift by hearing the Doctrine of Chriftianity, as the light of Nature doth the minde to apprehend thofe truths which are meerly rational, fo that faving truth, which is far above the reach of Humane Reafon, cannot otherwife, then by the Spirit of the Almighty, be conceived. All thefe are implied, wherefoever any of them is mentioned as the caufe of the fpiritual life. Wherefore if we have read, that (a) *the Spirit is our life*; or, (b) *the Word our life*; or, (c) *Chrift our life*: We are in every of thefe to underftand, that our life is Chrift, by the hearing of the Gofpel, apprehended as a Saviour, and affented unto through the power of the Holy Ghoft. The firft intellectual conceit and comprehenfion of Chrift fo imbraced, S. *Peter* calleth, (d) *the feed whereof we be new born:* our firft imbracing of Chrift, is our firft (d) reviving from the ftate of death and condemnation. (e) *He that hath the Son, hath life*, faith S. *John, and he that hath not the Son of God hath not life.* If therefore he which once hath the Son, may ceafe to have the Son, though it be for a moment, he ceafeth for that moment to have life. But the life of them which have the Son of God, (g) is everlafting *in the world to come.* But becaufe as Chrift being raifed from the dead dyed no more, death hath no more power over him: fo juftified man, (h) being allied to God in Jefus Chrift our Lord, doth as neceffarily from that time forward always live, as Chrift (i) by whom he hath life, liveth always. I might, if I had not otherwhere largely done it already, fhew by many and fundry manifeft and clear proofs, how the motions and operations of life are fometime. fo indifcernable, and fo fecret, that they feem ftone-dead, who notwithftanding are ftill alive unto God in Chrift. For as long as that abideth in us, which animateth, quickneth, and giveth life, fo long we live, and we know that the caufe of our faith abideth in us for ever. If Chrift the Fountain of Life, may flit and leave the Habitation, where once he dwelleth, What fhall become of his Promife, *I am with you to the Worlds end?* If the Seed of God, which

a Rom.8.10.
b Phil.1.15.
c Col.3.4.

d 1 Pet.1.
e Ephef.2.5.
f 1 John 5.12.

g 1 John 5. 3. Perp tuity of faith.
b Rom 6.10.
i 1 John 14.19.

a 1 Pet. 1. 1.
b 1 John 3. 9.

* Eph. 1. 1. 14.
John 4. 14.

containeth Christ, may be first conceived, and then cast out: how doth S. *Peter* term it (a) *immortal*? How doth S. *John* affirm, (b) *It abideth*? If the Spirit, which is given to cherish, and preserve the Seed of Life, may be given and taken away, how is it (c) the earnest of our inheritance until Redemption? how doth it continue with us for ever? If therefore the man which is once just by faith, shall live by faith, and live for ever ; it followeth, that he which once doth believe the foundation, must needs believe the foundation for ever. If he believe it for ever, how can he ever directly deny it? Faith holding the direct affirmation; the direct negation, so long as faith continueth, is excluded.

Object. But you will say, *That as he that is to day holy, may to morrow forsake his holiness, and become impure ; as a friend may change his minde, and be made an enemy ; as hope may wither : so faith may dye in the heart of man, the Spirit may be quenched, Grace may be extinguished, they which believe, may be quite turned away from the Truth.*

* Col. 1. 23.

a 1 Tim. 1. 15.
b John 10.

Sol. The case is clear, long experience hath made this manifest, it needs no proof. I grant we are apt, prone, and ready to forsake God ; but is God as ready to forsake us? Our mindes are changeable ; is his so likewise? Whom God hath justified, hath not Christ assured, that it is *his Fathers will to give them a Kingdm*? Notwithstanding, it shall not be otherwise given them, then if they continue * grounded and stablished in the faith, and be not moved away from the hope of the Gospel ; (a) *if they abide in love and holiness.* Our Saviour therefore: when he spake of the sheep effectually called, and truly gathered into his fold, (b) *I give unto them eternal life, and they shall never perish, neither shall any pluck them out of my hands* ; in promising to save them, he promised, no doubt, to preserve them in that, without which there can be no salvation, as also from that whereby it is irrecoverably lost. Every errour in things appertaining unto God, is repugnant unto faith ; every fearful cogitation, unto hope ; unto love, every stragling inordinate desire ; unto holiness, every blemish wherewith either the inward thoughts of our mindes, or the outward actions of our lives are stained. But Heresie, such as that of *Ebion, Cerinthus,* and others, against whom the Apostles were forced to bend themselves, both by word, and also by writing ; that repining discouragement of heart, which tempteth God, whereof we have Israel in the Desart for a pattern ; coldness, such as that in the Angels of *Ephesus* ; foul sins, known to be expresly against the first, or second table of the Law, such as *Noah, Manasses, David, Solomon,* and *Peter* committed : These are each in their kinde so opposite to the former vertues, that they leave no place for salvation without an actual repentance. But Infidelity, extream despair, hatred of God and all goodness, obduration in sin cannot stand where there is but the least spark of faith, hope, love and sanctity ; even as cold in the lowest degree cannot be, where heat in the highest degree is found. Whereupon I conclude, that although in the first kinde, no man liveth, which sinneth not ; and in the second, as perfect as any do live may sin : yet sith the

c 1 John 3. 9.

man which is born of God, hath a promise, that in him *the Seed of God shall abide,* which Seed is a sure preservative against the sins that are of the third suit : Greater and clearer assurance we cannot have of any thing, then of this, that from such sins God shall preserve the righteous, as the apple of his eye for ever. Directly to deny the foundation of faith, is plain infidelity ; where faith is entred, there infidelity is for ever excluded : Therefore by him which hath once sincerely believed in Christ, the foundation of Christian faith can never be directly denied. Did not *Peter* ? Did not *Marcellinus* ? Did not others both directly deny Christ, after that they had believed, and again believe, after they had denied ? No doubt, as they confess in words, whose condemnation is nevertheless their not believing : (for example we have *Judas* :) So likewise, they may believe in heart, whose condemnation, without repentance, is their not confessing. Although therefore, *Peter* and the rest, for whose faith Christ hath prayed, that it might not fail, did not by denial, sin the sin of Infidelity, which is an inward abnegation of Christ (for if they had done this, their faith had clearly failed :) Yet because they sinned notoriously and grievously, committing that which they knew to be expresly forbidden by the Law, which saith, *Thou shalt worship the Lord thy God, and him onely shalt thou serve* ; necessary it was, that he which purposed to save their souls, should, as he did, touch their hearts with true unfeigned repentance, that his mercy might

restore

restore them again to life, whom sin had made the children of death and condemnation. Touching the point therefore, I hope I may safely set down, that if the justified erre, as he may, and never come to understand his errour, God doth save him through general repentance : But if he fall into Heresie, he killeth him at one time or other by actual repentance ; but from infidelity, which is an inward direct denial of the foundation, he preserveth him by special providence for ever. Whereby we may easily know, what to think of those *Galatians*, whose hearts were so possest with the love of the truth, that if it had been possible, they would have pluckt out their eyes to bestow upon their Teachers. It is true, that they were greatly * changed, both in perswasion and affection : so that the *Galatians* when S. *Paul* wrote unto them, were not now the *Galatians* which they had been in former time , for that through errour they wandred, although they were his sheep. I do not deny, but that I should deny, that they were his sheep, if I should grant, that through errour they perished. It was a perilous opinion that they held ; perilous, even in them that held it onely as an errour, because it overthroweth the foundation by consequent. But in them which obstinately maintain it, I cannot think it less then a damnable Heresie. We must therefore put a difference between them which erre of ignorance, retaining nevertheless a minde desirous to be instructed in truth, and them, which after the truth is laid open, persist in the stubborn defence of their blindeness. Heretical defenders, froward and stiff-necked Teachers of Circumcision, the blessed Apostle calls dogs²: Silly men, who were seduced to think they taught the truth, he pitieth, he taketh up in his arms, he lovingly imbraceth, he kisseth, and with more then fatherly tenderness doth so temper, qualifie, and correct the speech he useth toward them, that a man cannot easily discern, whether did most abound, the love which he bare to their godly affection, or the grief which the danger of their opinion bred him. Their opinion was dangerous ; was not theirs also, who thought the Kingdom of Christ should be earthly ? was not theirs, which thought the Gospel onely should be preached to the Jews ? What more opposite to Prophetical Doctrine, concerning the coming of Christ, then the one ? concerning the Catholick Church, then the other ? Yet they which had these fancies, even when they had them, were not the worst men in the world. The Heretie of *Free-will* was a millstone about the *Pelagians* neck ; shall we therefore give sentence of death inevitable against all those Fathers in the Greek Church, which being mis-perswaded, dyed in the errour of *Free-will?* Of these *Galatians* therefore, which first were justified, and then deceived, as I can see no cause, why as many as dyed before admonition, might not by mercy be received, even in errour ; so I make no doubt, but as many as lived till they were admonished, found the mercy of God effectual in converting them from their (*a*) errour, lest any one that is Christs should perish. Of this I take it, there is no controversie, onely against the salvation of them that dyed, though before admonition, yet in errour, it was objected, that at their opinion was a very plain direct denial of the foundation. If *Paul* and *Barnabas* had been so perswaded, they would haply have used the terms otherwise, speaking of the Masters themselves, who did first set that errour abroach (*b*) certain of the Sects of the Pharisees which believed. What difference was there between these Pharisees, and other Pharisees, from whom by a special description they are distinguished, but this ? These which came to *Antioch*, teaching the necessity of Circumcision , were Christians ; the other, enemies of Christianity. Why then should these be termed so distinctly Believers, if they did directly deny the foundation of our belief ; besides which, there was no other thing, that made the rest to be no believers ? We need go no farther then S. *Pauls* very reasoning against them, for proof of this matter ; seeing you know God, or rather are known of God, how turn you again to impotent rudiments ? (*c*) The Law engendreth servants, her children are in bondage : (*d*) They which are gotten by the Gospel, are free. (*e*) Brethren, we are not children of the servant, but of the free-woman, and will ye yet be under the Law ? That they thought it unto salvation necessary, for the Church of Christ, to (*f*) observe days, and moneths, and times, and years, to keep the Ceremonies and Sacraments of the Law, this was their errour. Yet he which condemneth their errour, confesseth, that notwithstanding they knew God, and were known of him ; he taketh not the honour from them to be termed Sons begotten of the immortal Seed of the Gospel. Let the heaviest words they are taught what the truth is, and plainly taught. (*b*) Acts 15.5. (*c*) Galat. 4.8.9. (*d*) Vers. 28. (*e*) Vers. 31. (*f*) Ver. 10.

* Howsoever men be changed, (for changed they may be, even the best amongst men) if they that have received, as it seemeth some of the Galatians which fell into errour, had received the gifts and graces of God which a e called, *apparate Anta*, such as faith, hope and charity are, which God doth never take away from him, to whom they are given, as if it repented him to have given them ; if such might be so far changed by errour, as that the very root of faith should be quite extinguished in them, & so their salvation utterly lost : it would shake the hearts of the strongest and stoutest of us all. See the contrary in *Beza* his observations upon the harmony of confessions. (*a*) Error convicted, and afterwards maintained, is more then errour : for although opinion be the same it was, in which respect I still call it errour, yet they are not now the same they were when

which he useth, be weighed, consider the drift of those dreadful conclusions: *If ye be circumcised, Christ shall profit you nothing: As many as are justified by the Law, are fallen from Grace.* It had been to no purpose in the world so to urge them, had not the Apostle been perswaded, that at the hearing of such sequels, *No benefit by Christ, a defection from Grace,* their hearts would tremble and quake within them: And why? because that they knew, that in Christ, and in Grace, their Salvation lay, which is a plain direct acknowledgement of the foundation. Lest I should herein seem to hold that which no one learned or godly hath done, let these words he considered,

* Bucer. de Venit.Eccles. servanda.

which import as much as I affirm. Surely those brethren, which in S. *Pauls* time, thought that God did lay a necessity upon them to make choice of days and meats, spake as they believed, and could not but in words condemn the liberty, which they supposed to be brought in against the Authority of Divine Scripture. Otherwise it had been needless for S. *Paul* to admonish them, not to condemn such as eat without scrupulosity, whatsoever was set before them. This errour, if you weigh what it is of it self, did at once overthrow all Scriptures, whereby we are taught salvation by faith in Christ, all that ever the Prophets did foretel, all that ever the Apostles did preach of Christ, it drew with it the denial of Christ utterly: Insomuch, that S. *Paul* complaineth, that his labour was lost upon the *Galatians,* unto whom this errour was obtruded, affirming that Christ, if so be they were circumcised, should not profit them any thing at all. Yet so far was S. *Paul* from striking their names out of Christs book, that he commandeth others to entertain them, to accept with singular humanity, to use them like brethren; he knew mans imbecility, he had a feeling of our blindeness which are mortal men, how great it is, and being sure that they are the Sons of God whosoever be endued with his fear, would not have them counted enemies of that whereunto they could not as yet frame themselves to be friends, but did ever upon a very Religious affection to the Truth, willingly reject the truth. They acknowledged Christ to be their onely and perfect Saviour, but saw not how repugnant their believing the necessity of Mosaical Ceremonies was to their faith in Jesus Christ. Hereupon a reply is made, that if they had not directly denied the foundation, they might have been saved; but saved they could not be, therefore their opinion was not onely by consequent, but directly a denial of the foundation. When the question was about the possibility of their salvation, their denying of the foundation was brought to prove, that they could not be saved: now that the question is about their denial of the foundation, the impossibility of their salvation, is alledged to prove, they denied the foundation. Is there nothing which excludeth men from salvation, but onely the foundation of faith denied? I should have thought, that besides this, many other things are death unto as many as understanding that to cleave thereunto, was to fall from Christ, did notwithstanding cleave unto them. But of this enough. Wherefore I come to the last question, *Whether that the Doctrine of the Church of* Rome, *concerning the necessity of works unto salvation, be a direct denial of our faith.*

27. I seek not to obtrude unto you any private opinion of mine own; the best learned in our profession are of this judgement, that all the corruptions of the Church of Rome, do not prove her to deny the foundation directly; if they did, they should grant her simply to be no Christian Church. *But I suppose,* saith one, *that in*

Calv. Ep. 104.

the Papacy some Church remaineth, a Church crazed, or, if you will, broken quite in pieces, forlorn, mishapen, yet some Church: his reason is this, Antichrist must sit in the temple of God. Lest any man should think such sentences as these to be true onely in regard of them whom that Church is supposed to have kept by the special providence of God, as it were, in the secret corners of his bosom, free from infection, and as found in the faith, as we trust, by his mercy, we our selves are; I permit it to your wise considerations, whether it be more likely, that as frenzy, though it take away the use of reason, doth notwithstanding prove them reasonable creatures which have it, because none can be frantick but they: So Antichristianity being the bane and plain overthrow of Christianity, may nevertheless argue, the Church where Antichrist sitteth, to be Christian. Neither have I ever hitherto heard or read any one word alledged of force to warrant, that God doth otherwise, then so as in the two next questions before hath been declared, binde himself to keep his Elect from worshipping the Beast, and from receiving his mark in their foreheads: but

but he hath preserved, and will preserve them from receiving any deadly wound at the hands of the Man of Sin, whose deceit hath prevailed over none unto death, but onely unto such as never loved the truth, such as took pleasure in unrighteousness: They in all ages, whose hearts have delighted in the principal truth, and whose souls have thirsted after righteousness, if they received the mark of Error, the mercy of God, even erring, and dangerously erring, might save them; if they received the mark of Heresie, the same mercy did, I doubt not, convert them. How far Romish Heresies may prevail over Gods Elect, how many God hath kept falling into them, how many have been converted from them, is not the question now in hand: for if Heaven had not received any one of that coat for these thousand years, it may still be true, that the Doctrine which this day they do profess, doth not directly deny the foundation, and so prove them simply to be no Christian Church. One I have alledged, whose words, in my ears, sound that way: shall I adde ✳ another, whose speech is plain? *I deny her not the name of a Church,* saith another, *no more then to a man the name of a man, as long as he liveth, what sickness soever he hath.* His Reason is this, *Salvation in Jesus Christ, which is the mark which joyneth the head with the body, Jesus Christ with the Church is so cut off by many merits, by the merits of Saints, by the Popes Pardons, and such other wickedness, that the life of the Church holdeth by a very thred, yet still the life of the Church holdeth.* ✳ A third hath these words, *I acknowledge the Church of* Rome, *even at this present day, for a Church of Christ, such a Church as* Israel *did* Jeroboam, *yet a Church.* His Reason is this, *Every man seeth, except he willingly hoodwink himself, that as always, so now, the Church of Rome holdeth firmly and stedfastly the Doctrine of truth concerning Christ, and baptizeth in the name of the Father, the Son, and the Holy Ghost; confesseth and avoucheth Christ for the onely Redeemer of the World, and the Judge that shall sit upon quick and dead, receiving true believers into endless joy, faithless and godless men being cast with Satan and his Angels into flames unquenchable.*

✳ *Morn. de Ecclef.*

Zanch. prefat. de Relig.

28. I may, and will, rein the question shorter then they do. Let the Pope take down his top, and captivate no more mens souls by his Papal jurisdiction; let him no longer count himself *Lord Paramount* over the Princes of the World, no longer hold Kings as his servants *paravaile*; let his stately Senate submit their necks to the yoke of Christ, and cease to die their garments like *Edom*, in blood; let them from the highest to the lowest, hate and forsake their Idolatry, abjure all their Errours and Heresies; wherewith they have any way perverted the truth; let them strip their Churches, till they leave no polluted rag, but onely this one about her, *By Christ alone, without works, we cannot be saved:* It is enough for me, if I shew, that the holding of this one thing, doth not prove the foundation of faith directly denied in the Church of Rome.

29. Works are an addition: Be it so, what then? the foundation is not subverted by every kinde of addition: Simply to adde unto those fundamental words, is not to mingle Wine with Water, Heaven and Earth, things polluted with the sanctified blood of Christ: Of which crime indict them, which attribute those operations in whole or in part to any creature, which in the work of our salvation wholly are peculiar unto Christ, and if I open my mouth to speak in their defence, if I hold my peace and plead not against them as long as breath is within my body, let me be guilty of all the dishonor that ever hath been done to the Son of God. But the more dreadful a thing it is to deny salvation by Christ alone; the more slow and fearful I am, except it be too manifest, to lay a thing so grievous to any mans charge. Let us beware, lest if we make too many ways of denying Christ, we scarce leave any way for our selves truly and soundly to confess him. Salvation onely by Christ is the true foundation, whereupon indeed Christianity standeth. But what if I say you cannot be saved onely by Christ, without this addition, Christ believed in heart, confessed with mouth, obeyed in life and conversation? Because I adde, do I therefore deny that which I did directly affirm? There may be an additament of explication, which overthroweth not, but proveth and concludeth the proposition, whereunto it is annexed. He which saith, *Peter* was a chief Apostle, doth prove that *Peter* was an Apostle: He which saith, Our Salvation is of the Lord, ✳ through sanctification of the Spirit, and Faith of the truth, proveth that our salvation is of the Lord. But if that which is added be such a privation as taketh away the very essence of that whereunto it is

2 Thess. 2. 13.

H 3 added,

added, then by the sequel it overthroweth. He which faith *Judas* is a dead man, though in word he granteth *Judas* to be a man, yet in effect he proveth him by that very speech no man, becaufe death depriveth him of being. In like fort, he that should fay, our election is of grace for our works fake, should grant in found of words, but indeed by consequent deny that our election is of Grace; for the Grace which electeth us, is no grace, if it elect us for our works fake.

30. Now whereas the Church of *Rome* addeth works, we muft note further, that the adding of * Works is not like the adding of Circumcifion unto Chrift. Chrift came not to abrogate and put away good works: he did, to change Circumcifion; for we fee that in place thereof, he hath fubftituted holy Baptifm. To fay, ye cannot be faved by Chrift except ye be circumcifed, is to adde a thing excluded, a thing not onely not neceffary to be kept, but neceffary not to be kept by them that will be faved. On the other fide, to fay ye cannot be faved by Chrift without works, is to adde things, not onely not excluded, but commanded, as being in their place, and in their kinde neceffary, and therefore fubordinated unto Chrift, by Chrift himfelf, by whom the web of falvation is fpun: a *Except your righteousness exceed the righteousness of the Scribes and Pharisees, ye shall not enter into the Kingdom of Heaven*. They were *b* rigorous exacters of things not utterly to be neglected, (and left undone, walking and tything, &c. As they were in thefe, fo muft we be in judgement and the love of God. Chrift in works ceremonial, giveth more liberty, in *c* moral much lefs, then they did. Works of righteoufnefs therefore are added in the one propofition; as in the other, Circumcifion is.

Rom. 11. 6.

* I deny not but that the Church of *Rome* requireth fome kinds of works which fhe cught not to require at mens hands. But our queftion is general about the adding of good works, not whether fuch or fuch works be good. In this comparifon it is enough to touch fo much o the matter in queftion between *St. Paul* and the *Galatians*, as inferreth thofe conclufions. *Te ev a fallen from grace, Chrift can profit you nothing* : which conclufions will follow Circumcifion and ufes of the Law Ceremonial, if they be required as things neceffary to falvation. This onely was alledged againft me; and need I touch more then was alledged? a *Mat.* 5. 20. B *Luke* 11. 39. c *Mat.* 5. 11.

31. But we fay, our falvation is by Chrift alone, therefore howfoever, or whatfoever we adde unto Chrift in the matter of falvation, we overthrow Chrift. Our cafe were very hard, if this argument fo univerfally meant as it is propofed, were found and good. We our felves do not teach Chrift alone, excluding our own faith, unto juftification? Chrift alone; excluding our own works, unto fanctification; Chrift alone excluding the one or the other unneceffary unto Salvation. It is a childifh cavil wherewith in the matter of juftification, our Adverfaries do fo greatly pleafe themfelves, exclaiming, that we tread all Chriftian vertues under our feet, and require nothing in Chriftians but faith, becaufe we teach that faith alone juftifieth: whereas by this fpeech we never meant to exclude either Hope or Charity from being always joyned as infeparable Mates with Faith in the man that is juftified; or works, from being added as neceffary duties required at the hands of every juftified man: But to fhew that Faith is the onely hand which putteth on Chrift unto Juftification; and Chrift the onely garment, which being fo put on, covereth the fhame of our defiled natures, hideth the imperfection of our works, preferveth us blamelefs in the fight of God, before whom otherwife, the weaknefs of our faith were caufe fufficient to make us culpable, yea, to fhut us from the Kingdom of Heaven, where nothing that is not abfolute can enter. That our dealing with them be not as childifh as theirs with us: when we hear of Salvation by Chrift alone, confidering that [*alone*] as an exclufive particle, we are to note what it doth exclude, and where. If I fay, *Such a Judge onely ought to determine such a case*, all things incident to the determination thereof, befides the perfon of the Judge, as Laws, Depofitions, Evidences, &c. are not hereby excluded; perfons are not excluded from witneffing herein, or affifting, but only from determining and giving fentence. How then is our falvation wrought by Chrift alone: Is it our meaning, that nothing is requifite to mans falvation but Chrift to fave, and he to be faved quietly without any more ado? No, we acknowledge no fuch foundation. As we have received, fo we teach, that befides the bare and naked work, wherein Chrift without any other Affociate, finifhed all the parts of our Redemption, and purchafed falvation himfelf alone: For conveyance of this eminent bleffing unto us, many things are of neceffity required, as to be known and chofen of God before the foundation of the World; in the World to be called, juftified, fanctified; after we have left the World, to be received unto glory; Chrift in every of thefe hath fomewhat which he worketh alone.

Through

Through him, according to the Eternal purpose of God, before the foundation of the World, Born, Crucified, Buried, Raised, &c. we were in a gracious acceptati- *Eph.16.2.7.* on known unto God, long before we were seen of men: God knew us, loved us, was kinde to us in Jesus Christ, in him we were elected to be heirs of life. Thus far God through Christ hath wrought in such sort alone, that our selves are meer Patients, working no more then dead and senseless Matter, Wood, or Stone, or Iron doth in the Artificers hands; no more then Clay, when the Potter appointeth it to be framed *a Gal. 5.8.* for an honourable use; nay, not so much for the matter whereupon the Craftsman *a 1 Pet. 2.9.* worketh, he chuseth being moved by the fitness which is in it to serve his turn; in *and 5.3.* us no such thing. Touching the rest, which is laid for the foundation of our Faith, *b Ephes. 1.7.* importeth farther, That * by him we are called, that we have a Redemption, b Remissi- *c 1 Es. 3.11.* on of sins through his c blood, Health by his d stripes, Justice by him; that e he doth san- *let.23.6.* ctifie his Church, and make it glorious to himself, that f entrance into joy shall be *d Ephes. 8.26.* given us by him; yea, all things by him alone. Howbeit, not so by him alone, as if f *e Mat.56.230.* in us to our g Vocation, the hearing of the Gospel; to our Justification; Faith, to our *f 1 Thes.2.14.* Sanctification, the fruits of the Spirit; to our entrance into rest, perseverance in *g Cal.1.15. and* Hope, in Faith, in Holiness, were not necessary. *5.23.*
h Thes.1.15.

32. Then what is the fault of the Church of *Rome?* Not that she requireth works at their hands which will be saved: but that she attributeth unto Works a power of satisfying God for sin; yea, a vertue to merit both grace here, and in heaven glory. That this overthroweth the foundation of faith; I grant willingly; that it is a direct deni al thereof, I utterly deny: what it is to hold, and what directly to deny the foun- dation of faith, I have already opened: Apply it particularly to this cause, and there needs no more ado. The thing which is handled, if the form under which it is handled be added thereunto, it sheweth the foundation of any Doctrine whatsoever. Christ is the Matter whereof the Doctrine of the Gospel treateth; and it treateth of Christ as of a Saviour. Salvation therefore by Christ is the foundation of Christiani- ty: as for works, they are a thing subordinate, no otherwise then because our Sancti- cation cannot be accomplished without them: The Doctrine concerning them is a thing builded upon the foundation; therefore the Doctrine which addeth unto them the power of satisfying or of meriting, addeth unto a thing sub-ordinated, builded upon the foundation, not to the very foundation it self; yet is the foundation by this addition consequently overthrown, forasmuch as out of this addition it may be nega- tively concluded, He which maketh any work good and acceptable in the sight of God, to proceed from the natural freedom of our will; he which giveth unto any good works of ours, the force of satisfying the wrath of God for sin, the power of merit- ing either earthly or heavenly rewards; he which holdeth works going before our *Hæc ratio Ec-* Vocation, in congruity to merit our Vocation; works following our first, to merit *clesiastici sacræ* our second Justification, and by condignity our last reward in the Kingdom of Heaven, *menti & Catho-* pulleth up the Doctrine of Faith by the roots; for out of every of these the plain direct *licæ Fidei est, ut* denial thereof may be necessarily concluded. Not this onely, but what other Here- *qui partem di-* fie is there, that doth not raze the very foundation of faith by consequent? Howbeit, *v ni Sacramenti* we make a difference of Heresies, accounting them in the next degree to Infidelity, *negat, partem* which directly deny any one thing to be, which is expresly acknowledged in the Arti- *non valeat con-* cles of our Belief; for out of any one Article so denied, the denial of the very foun- *jt r. Ita enim* dation it self is straightway inferred. As for example, if a man should say, *There is no* *sibi connexa &* *Catholick Church,* it followeth immediately thereupon, that this *Jesus* whom we *contorporata* call the Saviour, is not the Saviour of the World; because all the Prophets bear *funt omnia, ut* witness, that the true *Messias* should *shew light unto the Gentiles;* that is to say, gather *aliud sine alio* such a Church as is Catholick, not restrained any longer unto one circumcised Nation. *flare non possit,* In the second rank we place them, out of whose Positions, the denial of any the fore- *& qui unum ex* said Articles may be with like facility concluded: such as are they which have denied *omnia credidisse* with *Hebion,* or with *Marcion,* his Humanity; an example whereof may be that of *confiteff.lib.6.de In-* *Cassianus,* defending the Incarnation of the Son of God, against *Nestorius* Bishop of *carnat. Dom.* *Antioch,* which held, That the Virgin, when she brought forth Christ, did not bring *si heobstinate-* forth the Son of God, but a sole and meer man: out of which Heresie, the denial of the *ly stand in de-* Articles of the Christian faith he deduceth thus, *If thou dost deny our Lord Jesus Christ,* *nial. pag. 193.* *in denying the Son, thou canst not choose but deny the Father; for according to the voyce of* *Acts 26. 23.* *the Father himself, He that hath not the Son, hath not the Father. Wherefore denying* *Lib. 6. de Incar.* *him* *Dom. cap.16.*

him which is begotten, thou deniest him which doth beget. Again, denying the Son of God to have been born in the flesh, how canst thou believe him to have suffered? believing not his Passion, what remaineth, but that thou deny his Resurrection? For we believe him not raised, except we first believe him dead: Neither can the reason of his rising from the dead stand, without the faith of his death going before. The denial of his death and Passion, inferreth the denial of his Rising from the depth. Whereupon it followeth that thou also deny his Ascension into Heaven. The Apostle affirmeth, That he which ascended, did first descend; so that as much as lieth in thee, our Lord Jesus Christ hath neither risen from the depth, nor is ascended into Heaven, nor sitteth at the right hand of God the Father, neither shall he come at the day of the final account which is looked for, nor shall judge the quick and the dead. And darest thou yet set foot in the Church? Canst thou think thy self a Bishop, when thou hast denied all those things whereby thou dost obtain a Bishoply Calling? Nestorius confessed all the Articles of the Creed, but his opinion did imply the denial of every part of his Confession. Heresies there are of the third sort, such as the Church of *Rome* maintaineth, which be removed by a greater distance from the foundation, although indeed they overthrow it. Yet because of that weaknesse, which the Philosopher noteth in mens capacities, when he saith, *That the common sort cannot see things which follow in reason, when they follow, as it were, afar off by many deductions;* therefore the repugnancy of such Heresie and the foundation, is not so quickly, or so easily found, but that an Heretick of this, sooner then of the former kinde, may directly grant, and consequently neverthelesse deny the foundation of Faith.

33. If reason be suspected, tryal will shew that the Church of *Rome* doth no otherwise, by teaching the Doctrine she doth teach concerning good works. Offer them the very fundamental words, and what man is there that will refuse to subscribe unto them? Can they directly grant, and directly deny one and the very self same thing? Our own proceedings in disputing against their works satisfactory and meritorious, do shew not onely that they hold, but that we acknowledge them to hold the foundation, notwithstanding their opinion. For are not these our Arguments against them? *Christ alone hath satisfied and appeased his Fathers wrath: Christ hath merited salvation alone.* We should do fondly to use such disputes, neither could we think to prevail by them, if that whereupon we ground, were a thing which we know they do not hold, which we are assured they will not grant. Their very answers to all such reasons as are in this Controversie brought against them, will not permit us to doubt, whether they hold the foundation or no. Can any man that hath read their books concerning this matter, be ignorant how they draw all their answers unto these heads? *That the remission of all our sins, the pardon of all whatsoever punishments thereby deserved, the rewards which God hath laid up in Heaven, are by the blood of our Lord Jesus Christ purchased, and obtained sufficiently for all men: but for no man effectually, for his benefit in particular, except the blood of Christ be applied particularly to him, by such means as God hath appointed that to work by. That those means of themselves, being but dead things, onely the blood of Christ is that which putteth life, force, and efficacy in them to work, and to be available, each in his kinde, to our salvation. Finally, that grace being purchased for us by the blood of Christ, and freely without any merit or desert at the first bestowed upon us, the good things which we do, after grace received, be thereby made satisfactory and meritorious.* Some of their sentences to this effect, I must alledge for mine own warrant. If we desire to hear foreign judgements, we finde in one this Confession, *He that could reckon how many the vertues and merits of our Saviour Jesus Christ have been, might likewise understand how many the benefits have been that are to come to us by him, forsomuch as men are made partakers of them all by means of his Passion: by him is given unto us remission of our sins, grace, glory, liberty, praise, salvation, redemption, justification, justice, satisfaction, sacraments, merits, and all other things which we had, and were behoveful for our salvation.* In another we have these oppositions, and answers made unto them. *All grace is given by Christ Jesus:* True, *but not except Christ Jesus be applied. He is the propitiation for our sin; by his stripes we are healed, he hath offered himself up for us: all this is true, but apply it: we put all satisfaction in the blood of Jesus Christ; but we hold that the means which Christ hath appointed for us in the case to apply it, are our penal works.* Our Countreymen in *Rhemes* make the like answer, that they seek salvation no other way then by the blood of Christ; and that humbly they do use Prayers, Fastings, Alms, Faith, Charity, Sacrifice, Sacraments, Priests, onely as

the

Lewis of Granad. Med. cap. l. 1, 3.

Paul. gr. de Just. 11.

Annot. in 1 John 2.

the means appointed by Christ, to apply the benefit of his holy blood unto them; touching our good works, that in their own natures they are not meritorious, nor answerable to the joys of Heaven; it cometh by the grace of Christ, and not of the work it self, that we have by well-doing a right to Heaven, and deserve it worthily. If any man think that I seek to varnish their opinions, to set the better foot of a lame cause formost; let him know, that since I began throughly to understand their meaning, I have found their halting greater then perhaps it seemeth to them which know not the deepness of Satan, as the blessed Divine speaketh. For although this be proof sufficient, that they do not directly deny the foundation of Faith; yet if there were no other leaven in the lump of their Doctrine but this, this were sufficient to prove, that their Doctrine is not agreeable to the foundation of Christian Faith. The *Pelagians* being over-great friends unto Nature, made themselves enemies unto Grace, for all their confessing, that men have their souls, and all the faculties thereof, their wills, and all the ability of their wills from God. And is not the Church of *Rome* still an adversary unto Christs Merits, because of her acknowledging, that we have received the power of meriting by the blood of Christ? Sir *Thomas Moor* setteth down the oddes between us and the Church of *Rome* in the matter of works, In his Book of Consolation. thus, *Like as we grant them, That no good work of man is rewardable in heaven of his own nature, but through the meer goodness of God, that lists to set so high a price upon so poor a thing; and that this price God setteth through Christs Passion, and for that also they be his own works with us; for good works to God-ward worketh no man, without God work in him; and as we grant them also, that no man may be proud of his works, for his imperfect working, and for that in all that man may do, he can do God no good, but is a servant unprofitable, and doth but his bare duty: as we, I say, grant unto them these things: so this one thing or twain do they grant us again, That men are bound to work good works, if they have time and power; and that whoso worketh in true faith most, shall be most rewarded: but then set they thereto, That all his rewards shall be given him for his faith alone, and nothing for his works at all, because his faith is the thing, they say, that forceth him to work well.* I see by this of Sir *Thomas Moor*, how easie it is for men of the greatest capacity, to mistake things written or spoken, as well on the one side as on the other. Their Doctrine, as he thought, maketh the work of man rewardable in the world to come, through the goodness of God, whom it pleased to set so high a price upon so poor a thing: and ours, that a man doth receive that eternal and high reward, not for his works, but for his faiths sake, by which he worketh; whereas in truth our doctrine is no other then that we have learned at the feet of Christ; namely, That God doth justifie the believing man, yet not for the worthiness of his belief, but for the worthiness of him which is believed; God rewardeth abundantly every one which worketh, yet not for any meritorious dignity which is, or can be in the work, but through his meer mercy by whose commandement he worketh. Contrariwise, their Doctrine is, That as pure water of it self hath no savour, but if it pass through a sweet pipe, it taketh a pleasant smell of the pipe through which it passeth: so, although before grace received, our works do neither satisfie nor merit; yet after, they do both the one and the other. Every vertuous action hath then power in such to satisfie; that if we our selves commit no mortal sin, no hainous crime, whereupon to spend this treasure of satisfaction in our own behalf, it turneth to the benefit of other mens release, on whom it shall please the Steward of the house of God to bestow it; so that we may satisfie for our selves and others, but merit onely for our selves. In meriting, our actions do work with two hands; with one they Works of Supererogation. get their morning stipend, the encrease of grace; with the other their evening hire, the Everlasting Crown of glory. Indeed they teach, that our good works do not these things as they come from us, but as they come from grace in us; which grace in us is another thing in their Divinity, then is the meer goodness of Gods mercy towards us in Christ Jesus.

34. If it were not a long deluded Spirit which hath possession of their hearts; were it possible but that they should see how plainly they do herein gain-say the very ground of Apostolick faith? Is this that salvation by grace, whereof so plentiful mention is made in the Scriptures of God? Was this their meaning, which first taught the world to look for salvation onely by Christ? By grace, the Apostle saith, and by grace in such sort as a gift: a thing that cometh not of our selves, nor of our works, lest any man should boast,

boaſt, and ſay, *I have wrought out my own ſalvation.* By grace they confeſs; but by grace in ſuch ſort, that as many as wear the Diadem of bliſs, they were nothing but what they have won. The Apoſtle, as if he had foreſeen how the Church of *Rome* would abuſe the world in time, by ambiguous terms, to declare in what ſenſe the name of *Grace* muſt be taken, when we make it the cauſe of our ſalvation, ſaith, *He ſaved us according to his mercy:* which mercy, although it exclude not the waſhing of our new birth, the renewing of our hearts by the Holy Ghoſt, the means, the vertues, the duties which God requireth of our hands which ſhall be ſaved; yet it is ſo repugnant unto merits, that to ſay, we are ſaved for the worthineſs of any thing which is ours, is to deny we are ſaved by grace. Grace beſtoweth freely; and therefore juſtly requireth the glory of that which is beſtowed. We deny the grace of our Lord Jeſus Chriſt, we abuſe, diſanul and annihilate the benefit of his bitter paſſion, if we reſt in theſe proud imaginations, that life is deſervedly ours, that we merit it, and that we are worthy of it.

35. Howbeit, conſidering how many vertuous and juſt men, how many Saints, how many Martyrs, how many of the ancient Fathers of the Church, have had their ſundry perilous opinions: and amongſt ſundry of their opinions this, that they hoped to make God ſome part of amends for their ſins, by the voluntary puniſhments which they laid upon themſelves, becauſe by a conſequent it may follow hereupon, that they were injurious unto Chriſt: ſhall we therefore make ſuch deadly Epitaphs, and ſet them upon their graves, *They denied the foundation of faith directly, they are damned, there is no ſalvation for them?* S. *Auſtin* ſaith of himſelf, *Errare poſſum, hæreticus eſſe nolo.* And except we put a difference between them that erre, and them that obſtinately perſiſt in error, how is it poſſible that ever any man ſhould hope to be ſaved? Surely in this caſe, I have no reſpect of any perſon alive or dead. Give me a man, of what eſtate or condition ſoever, yea, a *Cardinal* or a *Pope*, whom in the extreme point of his life affliction hath made to know himſelf, whoſe heart God hath touched with true ſorrow for all his ſins, and filled with love towards the Goſpel of Chriſt, whoſe eyes are opened to ſee the Truth, and his mouth to renounce all hereſie and errour, any wiſe oppoſite thereunto: This one opinion of Merits excepted, he thinketh God will require at his hands, and becauſe he wanteth, therefore trembleth, and is diſcouraged; it may be I am forgetful, unskilful, not furniſhed with things new and old, as a wiſe and learned Scribe ſhould be, nor able to alledge that, whereunto if it were alledged, he doth bear a minde moſt willingly to yield, and ſo to be recalled as well from this, as from other errours. And ſhall I think becauſe of this onely errour, that ſuch a man toucheth not ſo much as the hem of Chriſts garment? If he do, wherefore ſhould not I have hope, that vertue may proceed from Chriſt to ſave him? Beecauſe his errour doth by conſequent overthrow his faith, ſhall I therefore caſt him off, as one that hath utterly caſt off Chriſt? one that holdeth not ſo much as by a ſlender thred? No, I will not be afraid to ſay unto a *Pope* or *Cardinal* in this plight, Be of good comfort, we have to do with a merciful God, ready to make the beſt of a little which we hold well, and not with a captious Sophiſter, which gathereth the worſt out of every thing wherein we erre. Is there any Reaſon that I ſhould be ſuſpected, or you offended for this ſpeech? ✳ Is it a dangerous thing to imagine that ſuch men may

† Let all affection be laid aſide; let the matter indifferently be conſidered.

finde mercy? The hour may come, when we ſhall think it a bleſſed thing to hear, that if our ſins were the ſins of the Popes and Cardinals, the bowels of the mercy of God are larger. I do not propoſe unto you a Pope with the neck of an Emperor under his feet; a Cardinal, riding his horſe to the bridle in the blood of Saints: but a Pope or a Cardinal ſorrowful, penitent, diſrobed, ſtript, not onely of uſurped power, but alſo delivered and recalled from errour and Antichriſt, converted and lying proſtrate at the foot of Chriſt: and ſhall I think that Chriſt will ſpurn at him? and ſhall I croſs and gain-ſay the merciful promiſes of God, generally made unto penitent ſinners, by oppoſing the name of a *Pope* or a *Cardinal*? What difference is there in the world between a *Pope* and a *Cardinal*, and *John Stile* in this caſe? If we think it impoſſible for them, after they be once come within that rank, to be afterwards touched with any ſuch remorſe, let that be granted. The Apoſtle ſaith, *If I, or an Angel from heaven preach unto &c.* Let it be as likely, that S. *Paul* or an Angel from heaven ſhould preach Hereſie, as that a *Pope* or *Cardinal* ſhould be brought ſo far forth to acknowledge the truth: yet if a *Pope* or *Cardinal* ſhould, what finde we in their perſons why they might not be ſaved? It is not the perſons you will ſay, but the errour,

✳ wherein

wherein I suppose them to dye, which excluded them from the hope of mercy ; the opinion of merits doth take away all possibility of salvation from them. What if they hold it onely as an errour ? Although they hold the truth truly and sincerely in all other parts of Christian faith ? Although they have in some measure all the vertues and graces of the Spirit, all other tokens of Gods elect children in them ? Although they be far from having any proud presumptuous opinion, that they shall be saved by the worthines of their deeds ? Although the onely thing which troubleth and molesteth them, be but a little too much dejection, somewhat too great a fear, rising from an erroneous conceit that God will require a worthines in them, which they are grieved to finde wanting in themselves ? Although they be not obstinate in this perswasion ? Although they be willing, and would be glad to forsake it, if any one reason were brought sufficient to disprove it ? Although the onely let, why they do not forsake it ere they dye, be the ignorance of the means, by which it might be disproved ? Although the cause why the ignorance in this point is not removed, by the want of knowledge in such as should be able, and are not, to remove it ? Let me dye, if ever it be proved, that simply an errour doth exclude a *Pope* or a *Cardinal* in such a case, utterly from hope of life. Surely, I must confess unto you, if it be an errour that God may be merciful to save men, even when they erre, my greatest comfort is my errour ; were it not for the love I bear unto this errour, I would never wish to speak, nor to live.

36. Wherefore to resume that mother sentence, whereof I little thought that so much trouble would have grown, *I doubt not but that God was merciful to save thousands of our Fathers, living in Popish superstitions, inasmuch as they sinned ignorantly.* Alas! what bloody matter is there contained in this sentence, that it should be an occasion of so many hard censures ? Did I say, that *thousands of our Fathers might be saved ?* I have shewed which way it cannot be denied, Did I say, *I doubt not but they were saved?* I see no impiety in this perswasion, though I had no reason for it. Did I say, *Their ignorance did make me hope they did finde mercy, and so were saved ?* What hindreth salvation but sin ? Sins are not equal; and ignorance, though it doth not make sin to be sin, yet seeing it did make their sin the less, why should it not make our hope concerning their life, the greater ? We pity the most, and doubt not but God hath most compassion over them that sin for want of understanding. As much is confessed by sundry others, almost in the self same words which I have used. It is but onely my evil hap that the same sentences which savour verity in other mens books, should seem to bolster Heresie, when they are once by me recited. If I be deceived in this point, not they, but the blessed Apostle hath deceived me. What I said of others, the same he said of himself, *I obtained mercy, for I did ignorantly.* Construe his words, and you cannot misconstrue mine. I spake no otherwise ; I meant no otherwise then he did.

37. Thus have I brought the question concerning our Fathers, at the length, unto an end. Of whose estate, upon so fit an occasion as was offered me, handling the weighty causes of separation between the Church of *Rome* and us, and weak motives which are commonly brought to retain men in that Society ; amongst which motives, the examples of our Fathers deceased is one ; although I saw it convenient to utter the sentence which I did, to the end that all men might thereby understand, how untruly we are said to condemn as many as have been before us otherwise perswaded then we our selves are ; yet more then that once sentence, I did not think it expedient to utter, judging it a great deal meeter for us to have regard to our own estate, then to sift over-curiously what is become of other men. And fearing, lest that such questions as these, if voluntarily they should be too far waded into, might seem worthy of that rebuke, which our Saviour thought needful in a case not unlike, *What is this unto thee ?* When I was forced, much beside my expectation, to render a reason of my speech, I could not but yield at the call of others, and proceed so far as duty bound me, for the fuller satisfying of mindes. Wherein I have walked, as with reverence, so with fear : with reverence, in regard of our Fathers, which lived in former times ; not without fear, considering them that are alive.

38. I am not ignorant, how ready men are to feed and sooth up themselves in evil. Shall I, will the man say, that loveth the present world more then he loveth Christ, shall I incur the high displeasure of the mightiest upon Earth ? Shall I

hazard my goods, endanger my eftate, put my felf iu jeopardy, rather then to yield to that which fo many of my fathers imbraced , and yet found favour in the fight of God ? *Curfe Meroz,* faith the Lord, *curfe her Inhabitants, becaufe they helped not the Lord, they helped him not againft the mighty.* If I fhould not onely not help the Lord againft the mighty, but help to ftrengthen them that are mighty , againft the Lord; worthily might I fall under the burthen of that Curfe, worthy I were to bear my own judgement. But if the Doctrine which I teach, be a flower gather-ed in the Garden of the Lord; a part of the faving truth of the Gofpel; from whence notwithftanding, poyfoned creatures do fuck venome : I can but wifh it were otherwife, and content my felf with the lot that hath befallen me, the rather, be-caufe it hath not befallen me alone. S. *Paul* taught a truth, and a comfortable truth, when he taught, that the greater our mifery is, in refpect of our iniquities, the readier is the mercy of God for our releafe. If we feek unto him, the more we have finned, the more praife, and glory, aud honor unto him that pardoneth our fin. But mark what lend Collections were made hereupon by fome : *Why then am I condemned for a finner ?* And the Apoftle (as we are blamed, and as fome affirm that we fay, *Why do we not evil that good may come of it ?*) he was accufed to teach that which ill-difpofed men did gather by his teaching , though it were clean, not onely befides, but againft his meaning. The Apoftle addeth, *Their condemna-tion* (which thus do) *is juft.* I am not hafty to apply fentences of Condemnati-on. I wifh from mine heart their converfion , whofoever are thus perverfly af-fected. For I muft needs fay, their cafe is fearful, their eftate dangerous , which harden themfelves , prefuming on the mercy of God towards others. It is true that God is merciful, but let us beware of prefumptuous fins. God delivered *Jo-nah* from the bottom of the Sea, will you therefore caft your felves headlong from the tops of Rocks, and fay in your hearts, God fhall deliver us ? He pitieth the blinde that would gladly fee; but will he pity him that may fee, and hardeneth himfelf in blindenefs ? No, Chrift hath fpoken too much unto you, to claim the priviledge of your Fathers.

39. As for us that have handled this caufe concerning the condition of our Fa-thers, whether it be this thing or any other, which we bring unto you, the counfel is good which the wife man giveth, *Stand thou faft in thy fure underftanding, in the way and knowledge of the Lord, and have but one manner of word, and follow the Word of peace and righteoufnefs.* As a loofe tooth is a grief to him that eateth : fo doth a wavering and unftable word in fpeech, that tendeth to inftruction offend. *Shall a wife man fpeak words of the wind,* faith *Eliphas,* light, unconftant, unftable words ? Surely, the wifeft may fpeak words of the wind, fuch is the untoward conftitution of our nature, that we do neither fo perfectly underftand the way and knowledge of the Lord, nor fo ftedfaftly imbrace it when it is underftood ; nor fo gracioufly utter it, when it is im-braced ; nor fo peaceably maintain it, when it is uttered ; but that the beft of us are overtaken fometime through blindenefs, fometime through haftinefs , fometime through impatience, fometime through other paffions of the minde, whereunto (God doth know) we are too fubject. We muft therefore be contented both to pardon others, and to crave that others may pardon us for fuch things. Let no man, that fpeaketh as a man , think himfelf whiles he liveth, always freed from fcapes and over-fights in his fpeech. The things themfelves which I have fpoken unto you are found, howfoever they have feemed otherwife unto fome: at whofe hands I have, in that refpect, received injury. I willingly forget it: although in-deed, confidering the benefit which I have reaped by this neceffary fpeech of truth, I rather incline to that of the Apoftle, *They have not injured me at all.* I have caufe to wifh them as many bleffings in the Kingdom of Heaven, as they have forced me to ut-ter words and fyllables in this caufe; wherein I could not be more fparing of fpeech then I have been. *It becometh no man,* faith S. *Jerome, to be patient in the crime of Herefie.* Patient, as I take it, we fhould be always, though the crime of Herefie were intended ; but filent in a thing of fo great confequence I could not, beloved, I durft not be : efpecially the love that I bear to the truth of Chrift Jefus being hereby fome-what called in queftion. Whereof I befeech them in the meeknefs of Chrift , that have been the firft original caufe, to confider that a watch-man may cry (*an enemy*) when indeed a friend cometh. In which caufe, as I deem fuch a watch-man more worthy

to be loved for his care, then mif-liked for his Errour: So I have judged it my own part in this, as much as in me lieth, to take away all fuspicion of any unfriendly intent or meaning againft the Truth, from which, God doth know, my heart is free.

40. Now to you, Beloved, which have heard thefe things, I will ufe no other words of admonition, then thofe which are offered me by S. *James, My Brethren, have not the faith of our glorious Lord Jefus in refpect of perfons.* Ye are not now to learn, that as of it felf it is not hurtful, fo neither fhould it be to any fcandalous and offenfive in doubtful cafes, to hear the different judgements of men. Be it that *Cephas* hath one interpretation, and *Apollos* hath another; that *Paul* is of this minde, that *Barnabas* of that; if this offend you, the fault is yours. Carry peaceable mindes, and you may have comfort by this variety.

Now the God of Peace give you peaceable mindes, and turn it to your everlafting comfort.

Iii   A

A Learned
SERMON
OF THE
Nature of Pride.

HABAK. 2. 4.

His Minde swelleth, and is not right in him; But the Just by his faith shall live.

THE nature of man being much more delighted to be led then drawn, doth many times stubbornly resist Authority, when to perswasion it easily yieldeth. Whereupon the wisest law-makers have endeavoured always, that those Laws might seem most reasonable, which they would have most inviolably kept. A Law simply commanding or forbidding, is but dead in comparison of that which expresseth the reason wherefore it doth the one or the other. And surely, even in the Laws of God, although that he hath given Commandment be in it self a reason sufficient to exact all obedience at the hands of men; yet a forcible inducement it is to obey with greater alacrity and cheerfulness of minde, when we see plainly that nothing is imposed more then we must needs yield unto, except we will be unreasonable. In a word, whatsoever be taught, be it Precept, for direction of our Manners; or Article, for instruction of our faith; or Document any way for information of our mindes, it then taketh root and abideth, when we conceive not onely what God doth speak, but why. Neither is it a small thing, which we derogate as well from the honour of his truth, as from the comfort, joy and delight which we our selves should take by it, when we loosly slide over his speech, as though it were as our own is, commonly vulgar and trivial: Whereas he uttereth nothing but it hath besides the substance of Doctrine delivered, a depth of wisdom, in the very choice and frame of words to deliver it in: The reason whereof being not perceived, but by greater intention of brain then our nice mindes for the most part can well away with, fain we would bring the World, if we might, to think it but a needless curiosity, to rip up any thing further then extemporal readiness of wit doth serve to reach unto. Which course, if here we did list to follow, we might tell you, that in the first branch of this sentence, God doth condemn the *Babylonians* pride; and in the second teach, what happiness of state shall grow to the righteous by the constancy of their faith, notwithstanding the troubles which now they suffer; and after certain notes of wholesome instruction hereupon collected, pass over without detaining your mindes in any further removed speculation. But as I take it, there is a difference between the talk that beseemeth Nurses among Children, and that which men of capacity and judgement do or should receive instruction by.

The minde of the Prophet being erected with that which hath been hitherto spoken, receiveth here for full satisfaction a short abridgement of that which is afterwards more particularly unfolded. Wherefore as the question before disputed of doth concern two sorts of men, the wicked flourishing as the Bay, and the righteous like the withered Grass; the one full of pride, the other cast down with utter discouragement: so the answer which God doth make for resolution of doubts hereupon arisen, hath reference unto both sorts, and this present sentence containing a brief Abstract thereof,

thereof, comprehendeth summarily as well the fearful estate of iniquity over-exalted, as the hope laid up for righteousness oppreſt. In the former branch of which sentence, let us first examine what this rectitude or straitneſs importeth, which God denieth to be in the minde of the *Babylonian.* All things which God did create, he made them at the first, true, good and right. True, in respect of correspondence unto that pattern of their being, which was eternally drawn in the counsel of Gods fore-knowledge; Good, in regard of the use and benefit which each thing yieldeth unto other; Right, by an apt conformity of all parts with that end which is outwardly proposed for each thing to tend unto. Other things have ends proposed, but have not the faculty to know, judge, and esteem of them, and therefore as they tend thereunto unwittingly, ſo likewise in the means whereby they acquire their appointed ends, they are by neceſſity ſo held, that they cannot divert from them. The ends why the Heavens do move, the Heavens themselves know not, and their motions they cannot but continue. Onely men in all their actions know what it is which they seek for, neither are they by any ſuch neceſſity tied naturally unto any certain determinate mean to obtain their end by; but that they may, if they will, forsake it. And therefore in the whole World, no creature but onely man, which hath the laſt end of his actions proposed as a recompence and reward, whereunto his minde directly bending it self, is termed right or ſtrait, otherwiſe perverſe.

To make this ſomewhat more plain, we muſt note, that as they which travel from City to City, enquire ever for the ſtraiteſt way, because the ſtraiteſt is that which ſooneſt bringeth them unto their journeys end : *So we having here*, as the Apoſtle ſpeaketh, *no abiding City*, but being always in travel towards that place of Joy, Immortality and Reſt, cannot but in every of our deeds, words and thoughts, think that to be beſt, which with moſt expedition leadeth us thereunto, and is for that very cauſe termed right. That Soveraign good, which is the Eternal fruition of all good, being our laſt and chiefeſt felicity, there is no desperate despiser of God and godlineſs living which doth not wiſh for. The difference between right and crooked mindes, is in the means which the one or the other eschew or follow. Certain it is, that all particular things which are naturally desired in the World, as food, raiment, honor, Wealth, pleaſure, knowledge, they are ſubordinated in ſuch wiſe unto that future good which we look for in the world to come, that even in them there lieth a direct way tending unto this. Otherwiſe we muſt think, that God making promiſes of good things in this life, did seek to pervert men, and to lead them from their right mindes. Where is then the obliquity of the minde of man ? his minde is perverſe, cam, and crooked, not when it bendeth it ſelf unto any of these things, but when it bendeth ſo, that it ſwarveth either to the right hand or to the left, by exceſs or defect, from that exact rule whereby humane actions are measured. The rule to measure and judge them by, is the Law of God. For this cauſe, the Prophet doth make ſo often and ſo earneſt ſuit, *O direct me in the way of thy Commandments : As long as I have reſpect to thy Statutes, I am ſure not to tread amiſs.* Under the name of the *Law*, we muſt comprehend not onely that which God hath written in Tables and leaves, but that which Nature also hath engraven in the hearts of men. Elſe how ſhall thoſe Heathen which never had Books, but Heaven and Earth to look upon, be convicted of perverſneſs ? *But the Gentiles which had not the Law in Books, had,* ſaith the Apoſtle, *the effect of the Law written in their hearts.*

Then ſeeing that the heart of man is not right exactly, unleſs it be found in all parts ſuch, that God examining and calling it unto account with all ſeverity of rigour, be not able once to charge it with declining or ſwarving aſide (which absolute perfection when did God ever finde in the ſons of meer mortal men?) Doth it not follow that all fleſh muſt of neceſſity fall down and confeſs, we are not duſt and aſhes, but worſe, our mindes from the higheſt to the loweſt are not right ? If not right, then undoubtedly not capable of that bleſſedneſs which we naturally ſeek, but ſubject unto that which we moſt abhor, Anguiſh, Tribulation, Death, Wo, endleſs Miſery. For whatſoever miſſeth the way of life, the iſſue thereof cannot be but perdition. By which reaſon, all being wrapped up in ſin, and made thereby the children of death, the mindes of all men being plainly convicted not to be right ; ſhall we think that God hath indued them with ſo many excellencies, more not only then any, but then all the Creatures in the World besides, to leave them in ſuch eſtate, that they had been happier if they had never been ? Here cometh neceſſarily in a new way unto Salvation, ſo that they which

were

were in the other perverfe, may in this be found ftrait and righteous. That the way of Nature, this the way of Grace. The end of that way, Salvation merited, prefuppo-fing the righteoufnefs of mens works; their righteoufnefs, a natural hability to do them; that hability the goodnefs of God which created them in fuch perfection. But the end of this way, Salvation beftowed upon men as a gift, prefuppofing not their righteoufnefs, but the forgivenefs of their unrighteoufnefs, juftification; their juftifi-cation, not their natural ability to do good, but their hearty forrow for their not doing, and unfeigned belief in him, for whofe fake not doers are accepted, which is their vocation; their vocation, the election of God, taking them out from the number of loft children; their election a Mediator in whom to be elect: this medi-ation, inexplicable mercy; his mercy their mifery, for whom he vouchfafed to make himfelf a Mediator. The want of exact diftinguifhing between thefe two ways, and obferving what they have common, what peculiar, hath been the caufe of the great-eft part of that confufion whereof Chriftianity at this day laboureth. The lack of dili-gence in fearching, laying down, and inuring mens mindes with thofe hidden grounds of Reafon, whereupon the leaft particulars in each of thefe are moft firmly and ftrong-ly builded, is the onely reafon of all thofe fcruples and uncertainties wherewith we are in fuch fort intangled, that a number defpair of ever difcerning what is right or wrong in any thing. But we will let this matter reft, whereinto we ftepped to fearch out a way how fome mindes may be, and are right truly even in the fight of God, though they be fimply in themfelves not right.

Howbeit, there is not onely this difference between the juft and impious, that the minde of the one is right in the fight of God, becaufe his obliquity is not imputed; the other perverfe, becaufe his fin is unrepented of: but even as lines that are drawn with a trembling hand, but yet to the point which they fhould, are thought ragged and uneven, neverthelefs direct in comparifon of them which run clean another way; fo there is no incongruity in terming them right-minded men, whom though God may charge with many things amifs, yet they are not as thofe hideous and ugly Monfters, in whom becaufe there is nothing but wilful oppofition of minde againft God, a more then tolerable deformity is noted in them, by faying, that their mindes are not right. The Angel of the Church of *Thyatira*, unto whom the Son of God, fendeth this greet-ing, *I know thy works, and thy love, and fervice, and faith, notwithftanding, I have a few things againft thee*, was not as he unto whom S. *Peter*, *Thou haft no fellowfhip in this bu-finefs, for thy heart is not right in the fight of God.* So that whereas the orderly difpofition of the minde of man fhould be this, perturbations, and fenfual appetites all kept in aw by a moderate and fober will, in all things framed by reafon; reafon, directed by the Law of God and Nature; this *Babylonian* had his minde, as it were, turned upfide down: In him unreafonable cecity and blindenefs trampled all Laws both of God and Nature under feet; Wilfulnefs tyrannized over Reafon; and brutifh Senfuality over Will. An evident token, that his outrage would work his overthrow, and procure his fpeedy ruine. The Mother whereof was that which the Prophet in thefe words fignifi-eth, *His minde doth fwell.*

Immoderate fwelling, a token of very eminent breach, and of inevitable deftruction: Pride, a vice which cleaveth fo faft unto the hearts of men, that if we were to ftrip our felves of all faults one by one, we fhould undoubtedly finde it the very laft and hardeft to put off. But I am not here to touch the fecret itching humour of vanity wherewith men are generally touched. It was a thing more then meanly inordinate, wherewith the *Babylonian* did fwell. Which that we may both the better conceive, and the more eafily reap profit by the nature of this vice, which fetteth the whole World out of courfe, and hath put fo many even of the wifeft befides themfelves, is firft of all to be inquired into. Secondly, the dangers to be difcovered, which it draweth inevita-bly after it, being not cured. And laft of all, the ways to cure it.

Whether we look upon the gifts of Nature, or of Grace, or whatfoever is in the World admired as a part of mans excellency, adorning his body, beautifying his minde, or externally any way commending him in the account and opinion of men, there is in every kinde fomewhat poffible which no man hath, and fomewhat had which few men can attain unto. By occafion whereof, there groweth difparagement neceffarily; and by occafion of difparagement, Pride through mens ignorance. Firft therefore, although men be not proud of any thing which is not at leaft in opinion good, yet every good
thing

thing they are not proud of, but onely of that which neither is common unto many, and being desired of all, causeth them which have it, to be honored above the rest. Now there is no man so void of brain, as to suppose that Pride consisteth in the bare possession of such things ; for then to have Vertue were a Vice, and they should be the happiest men who are most wretched, because they have least of that which they would have. And though in speech we do intimate a kinde of vanity to be in them of whom we say, *They are Wise men, and they know it* ; yet this doth not prove, that every wise man is proud, which doth not think himself to be blockish. What, we may have, and know that we have it, without offence ; do we then make offensive, when we take joy and delight in having it ? What difference between men enriched with all abundance of earthly and heavenly blessings, and Idols gorgeously attired, but this, *the one takes pleasure in that which they have, the other none ?* If we may be possest with beauty, strength, riches, power, knowledge, if we may be privy what we are every way, if glad and joyful for our own welfare, and in all this remain unblameable, neverthelesse some there are who granting thus much, doubt whether it may stand with humility to accept those testimonies of praise and commendation, those titles, rooms, and other honors which the world yieldeth as acknowledgements of some mens excellencies above others. For inasmuch as Christ hath said unto those that are his, *The Kings of the Gentiles reign over them, and they that bear rule over them are called gracious Lords, be ye not so :* The Anabaptist hereupon urgeth equality amongst Christians, as if all exercise of Authority were nothing else but Heathenish Pride. Our Lord and Saviour had no such meaning. But his Disciples feeding themselves with a vain imagination for the time, that the Messias of the world should in *Jerusalem* erect his Throne, and exercise dominion with great pomp and outward statelinesse, advanced in honour and terrene power above al the Princes of the Earth, began to think how with their Lords condition, their own would also rise ; that having left and forsaken all to follow him, their place about him should not be mean : and because they were many, it troubled them much, which of them should be the greatest man : When suit was made for two by name, that of them one might sit at his right hand, and the other at his left ; the rest began to stomack, each taking it grievously, that any should have what all did affect, their Lord and Master to correct this humour, turneth aside their cogitations from these vain and fansiful conceits, giving them plainly to understand that they did but deceive themselves. His coming was not to purchase an earthly, but to bestow an heavenly Kingdom, wherein they (if any) shall be greatest, whom unfeigned Humility maketh in this World lowest, and least amongst others : *Te are they which have continued with me in my temptations, therefore I leave unto you a Kingdom, as my Father hath appointed me, that ye may eat and drink at my Table in my Kingdom, and sit on seats, and judge the twelve Tribes of Israel.* But my Kingdom is no such Kingdom as ye dream of. And therefore these hungry ambitious contentions are seemlier in Heathen in you. Wherefore from Christs intent and purpose nothing further removed, then dislike of distinction in titles and callings annexed for orders sake unto Authority, whether it be Ecclesiastical or Civil. And when we have examined throughly what the nature of this vice is, no man knowing it, can be so simple, as not to see an ugly shape thereof apparent many times in rejecting honors offered, more then in the very exacting of them at the hands of men. For as *Judas* his care for the poor was meer covetousnesse, and that franck-hearted wastefulnesse spoken of in the Gospel, thrift ; so there is no doubt but that going in rags may be Pride, and Thrones be challenged with unfeigned humility.

We must go further therefore, and enter somewhat deeper, before we can come to the Closet wherein this poyson lieth. There is in the heart of every proud man, first, an errour of understanding ; a vain opinion whereby he thinketh his own excellency, and by reason thereof, his worthinesse of estimation, regard, and honor to be greater then in truth it is. This maketh him in all his affections accordingly to raise up himself, and by his inward affections his outward acts are fashioned. Which if you list to have exemplified ; you may either by calling to minde things spoken of them whom God himself hath in Scripture specially noted with this fault, or by presenting to your secret cogitations that which you daily behold in the odious lives and manners of highminded men. It were too long to gather together so plentiful an harvest of examples ï this kinde as the sacred Scripture affordeth. That which we drink in at our ears, doth not so piercingly enter, as that which the minde doth conceive by sight : Is there

there any thing written concerning the Assyrian Monarch in the tenth of *Isaiah*, of his swelling minde, his haughty looks, his great and presumptuous taunts, *By the power of mine own hand I have done all things, and by mine own wisdom I have subdued the World?* Any thing concerning the Dames of *Sion* in the third of the Prophet *Isaiah*, of their stretched out necks, their immodest eyes, their Pageant-like, stately, and pompous gate? Any thing concerning the practices of *Corah*, *Dathan*, and *Abiram*; of their impatience to live in subjection, their mutinies, repining at lawful Authority, their grudging against their Superiors Ecclesiastical and Civil? Any thing concerning Pride in any sort of Sect, which the present face of the world doth not as in the glass, represent to the view of all mens beholding? So that if Books, both prophane and holy, were all lost, as long as the manners of men retain the state they are in: for him that observeth how that when men have once conceived an over-weening of themselves it maketh them in all their affections to swell, how deadly their hatred, how heavy their displeasure, how unappeasable their indignation and wrath is above other mens, in what manner they compose themselves to be as *Heteroclites*, without the compass of all such Rules as common sort are measured by; how the Oathes which Religious hearts do tremble at, they affect as principal graces of speech; what felicity they take to see the enormity of their crimes above the reach of Laws and punishments; how much it delighteth them when they are able to appale with the cloudiness of their look; how far they exceed the terms wherewith mans nature should be limited; how high they bear their heads over others; how they brow-beat all men which do not receive their Sentences as Oracles, with marvellous applause and approbation; how they look upon no man, but with an indirect countenance, nor hear any thing saving their own praise, with patience, nor speak without scornfulness and disdain; how they use their servants as if they were beasts, their inferiours as servants, their equals as inferiours, and as for Superiours acknowledge none; how they admire themselves as venerable, puissant, wise, circumspect, provident, every way great, taking all men besides themselves for cyphers, poor, inglorious silly creatures, needless burthens of the earth, off-scourings, nothing: in a word, for him which marketh how irregular and exorbitant they are in all things, it can be no hard thing hereby to gather, that Pride is nothing but an inordinate elation of the minde, proceeding from a false conceit of mens excellency in things honoured, which accordingly frameth also their deeds and behaviour, unless there be cunning to conceal it. For a foul scar may be covered with a fair cloth. And as proud as *Lucifer*, may be in outward appearance lowly.

No man man expecteth Grapes of Thistles; nor from a thing of so bad a nature, can other then suitable fruits be looked for. What harm soever in private families there groweth by disobedience of children, stubbornness of servants, untractableness in them, who although they otherwise may rule, yet should in consideration of the imparity of their Sex be also subject; whatsoever by strife amongst men combined in the fellowship of greater Societies, by tyranny of Potentates, ambition of Nobles, Rebellion of Subjects in Civil States; by Heresies, Schisms, Divisions in the Church; naming Pride, we name the Mother which brought them forth, and the onely Nurse that feedeth them. Give me the hearts of all men humbled, and what is there that can overthrow or disturb the peace of the world? Wherein many things are the cause of much evil, but Pride of all.

To declaim of the swarms of evils issuing out of Pride, is an easie labour. I rather wish that I could exactly prescribe and persuade effectually the remedies, whereby a sore so grievous might be cured, and the means how the pride of swelling mindes might be taken down. Whereunto so much we have already gained, that the evidence of the cause, which breedeth it, pointeth directly unto the likeliest and fittest helps to take it away: diseases that come of fulness, emptiness must remove. Pride is not cured, but by abating the errour which causeth the minde to swell. Then seeing that they swell by misconceit of their own excellency; for this cause all which tend to the beating down of their pride, whether it be advertisement from men, or from God himself chastisement, it then maketh them cease to be proud, when it causeth them to see their errour in over-seeing the thing they were proud of. At this mark, *Job*, in his Apology unto his eloquent friends, aimeth. For perceiving how much they delighted to hear themselves talk, as if they had given their poor afflicted familiar a schooling of marvellous deep and rare instruction, as if they had taught him more then all

the

the world besides could acquaint him with: His answer was to this effect, Ye swell as though ye had conceived some great matter, but as for that which ye are delivered of, who knoweth it not? Is any man ignorant of these things? At the same mark the blessed Apostle driveth, Ye abound in all things, ye are rich, ye raign, and would to Christ we did reign with you, but boast not. For what have ye, or are ye of your selves? To this mark all those humble confessions are referred, which have been always frequent in the mouthes of Saints, truly wading in the tryal of themselves; as that of the Prophet, *We are nothing but soreness and festered corruption*: our very light is darkness, and our righteousness it self unrighteousness; that of Gregory, *let no man ever put confidence in his own deserts; Sordet in conspectu Judicis, quod fulget in conspectu operantis.* In the sight of that dreadful Judge it is noysome, which in the doers judgement maketh a beautiful shew: That of *Anselm, I adore thee, I bless thee, Lord God of heaven, and Redeemer of the world, with all the power, ability and strength of my heart and soul, for thy goodness so unmeasurably extended, not in regard of my merits, whereunto onely torments were due, but of thy meer unprocured benignity.* If these Fathers should be raised again from the dust, and have the books laid open before them wherein such sentences are found as this, *Works no other then the value, desert price, and worth of the joys, of the Kingdom of Heaven; Heaven, in relation to our works, as the very stipend, which the hired Labourer covenanteth to have of him whose works he doth, as a thing equally and justly answering unto the time and weight of his travels, rather then to a voluntary or bountiful gift.* If, I say, those Reverend fore-rehearsed Fathers, whose books are so full of sentences, witnessing their Christian humility, should be raised from the dead, and behold with their eyes such things written; would they not plainly pronounce of the Authors of such writ, that they were fuller of *Lucifer* then of Christ, that they were proud-hearted men, and carried more swelling mindes then sincerely and feelingly known Christianity can tolerate?

Annot. Rhem. in 1 Cor. 3.

But as unruly children, with whom wholesome admonition prevaileth little, are notwithstanding brought to fear that ever after, which they have once well smarted for: so the minde which falleth not with instruction, yet under the rod of Divine chastisement ceaseth to swell. If therefore the Prophet *David*, instructed by good experience, have acknowledged, Lord, I was even at the point of clean forgetting my self, and so straying from my right minde, but thy rod hath been my reformer; it hath been good for me, even as much as my soul is worth, that I have been with sorrow troubled: If the blessed Apostle did need the corrosive of sharp and bitter strokes, lest his heart should swell with too great abundance of heavenly Revelations, surely, upon us whatsoever God in this world doth, or shall inflict, it cannot seem more then our pride doth exact, not onely by way of revenge, but of remedy. So hard it is to cure a sore of such quality as pride is, inasmuch as that which rooteth out other vices, causeth this, and (which is even above all conceit) if we were clean from all spot and blemish, both of other faults of pride; the fall of Angels doth make it almost a question whether we might not need a preservative still, lest we should haply wax proud that we are not proud. What is vertue, but a medicine; and vice, but a wound? Yet we have so often deeply wounded our selves with medicine, that God hath been fain to make wounds medicinable, to cure by vice where vertue hath stricken, to suffer the just man to fall, that being raised, he may be taught what power it was which upheld him standing. I am not afraid to affirm it boldly with S. *Augustine*, that men puffed up through a proud opinion of their own sanctity and holiness, receive a benefit at the hands of God, and are assisted with his grace, when with his grace they are not assisted, but permitted, and that grievously to transgress, whereby as they were in over-great liking of themselves supplanted, so the dislike of that which did supplant them, may establish them afterwards the surer. Ask the very soul of *Peter*, and it shall undoubtedly make you it self this answer, My eager protestations made in the glory of my ghostly strength, I am ashamed of; but those Chrystal tears wherewith my sin and weakness was bewailed, have procured my endless joy; my strength hath been my ruine, and my fall my stay.

A

A Remedy against Sorrovv and Fear.
Delivered in a Funeral Sermon.

John 14. 27. Let not your hearts be troubled, nor fear.

THE Holy Apostles having gathered themselves together by the special appointment of Christ, and being in expectation to receive from him such instructions as they had been accustomed with, were told that which they least looked for; namely, That the time of his departure out of the world was now come. Whereupon they fell into consideration, first, of the manifold benefits which his absence should bereave them of: and secondly, of the sundry evils which themselves should be subject unto, being once bereaved of so gracious a Master and Patron. The one consideration over-whelmed their souls with heaviness; the other with fear. Their Lord and Saviour, whose words had cast down their hearts, raiseth them presently again with chosen sentences of sweet encouragement. My dear, it is for your own sakes that I leave the world. I know the affections of your hearts are tender, but if your love were directed with that advised and staid judgement which should be in you, my speech of leaving the world, and going unto my Father, would not a little augment your joy. Desolate and comfortless I will not leave you; in Spirit I am with you to the worlds end, whether I be present or absent, nothing shall ever take you out of these hands: My going is to take possession of that, in your names, which is not onely for me, but also for you prepared; where I am, you shall be. In the mean while, *My peace I give, not as the world giveth, give I unto you: let not your hearts be troubled, nor fear.* The former part of which sentence having other where already been spoken of, this unacceptable occasion to open the latter part thereof here, I did not look for. But so God disposeth the ways of men. Him I heartily beseech, that the thing which he hath thus ordered by his providence, may through his gracious goodness turn unto your comfort.

Our nature coveteth preservation from things hurtful. Hurtful things being present, do breed heaviness; being future, do cause fear. Our Saviour to abate the one, speaketh thus unto his Disciples, *Let not your hearts be troubled;* and to moderate the other, addeth, *Fear not.* Grief & heaviness in the presence of sensible evils, cannot but trouble the minds of men. It may therefore seem that Christ required a thing impossible. *Be not troubled:* Why, how could they choose? But we must note, this being natural, and therefore simply not reproveable, is in us good or bad, according to the causes for which we are grieved, or the measure of our grief. It is not my meaning to speak so largely of this affection, as to go over all particulars whereby men do one way or other offend in it, but to teach it so far onely as it may cause the very Apostles equals to swerve. Our grief and heaviness therefore is reproveable, sometime in respect of the cause from whence, sometime in regard of the measure whereunto it groweth.

When Christ the life of the world was led unto cruel death, there followed a number of people and women, which women bewailed much his heavy case. It was a natural compassion which caused them; where they saw undeserved miseries, there to pour forth unrestrained tears. Nor was this reproved. But in such readiness to lament where they less needed, their blindeness in not discerning that for which they ought much rather to have mourned; this our Saviour a little toucheth, putting them in minde that the tears which were wasted for him, might better have been spent upon themselves. *Daughters of Jerusalem, weep not for me, weep for your selves, and for your children* It is not as the Stoicks have imagined, a thing unseemly for a wise man to be touched with grief of minde; but to be sorrowful when we least should; and where we should lament, there to laugh; this argueth our small wisdom. Again, when the Prophet *David* confesseth thus of himself, *I grieved to see the great prosperity of godless men, how they flourish and go untoucht,* Psal. 73. Himself hereby openeth both our common and his peculiar imperfection, whom this cause should not have made so pensive. To grieve at this, is to grieve where we should not, because this grief doth rise from errour. We erre when we grieve at wicked mens impunity and prosperity, because their estate being rightly discerned, they neither

prosper

prosper nor go unpunished. It may seem a Paradox, it is truth, that no wicked mans estate is prosperous, fortunate, or happy. For what though they bless themselves, and think their happiness great? Have not frantick persons many times a great opinion of their own wisdom? It may be that such as they think themselves, others also do account them. But what others? Surely such as themselves are. Truth and Reason discerneth far otherwise of them. Unto whom the Jews wish all prosperity, unto them the phrase of their speech is to wish peace. Seeing then the name of Peace containeth in it all parts of true happiness, when the Prophet saith plainly, that the Wicked have no peace, how can we think them to have any part of other then vainly imagined Felicity? What wise man did ever account fools happy? If Wicked men were wise, they would cease to be wicked. Their iniquity therefore proving their folly, how can we stand in doubt of their misery. They abound in those things which all men desire. A poor happiness to have good things in possession, *A man to whom God hath given riches, and treasures, others also do honour, so that he wanteth nothing for his soul of all that it desireth, but yet God giveth him not the power to eat thereof;* such a felicity Solomon esteemeth but as a vanity, a thing of nothing. If such things adde nothing to mens happiness, where they are not used, surely wicked men that use them ill, the more they have, the more wretched. Of their prosperity therefore, we see what we are to think. Touching their impunity, the same is likewise but supposed. They are oftner plagued then we are aware of. The pangs they feel are not always written in their fore-head. Though wickedness be Sugar in their mouthes, and wantonness as Oyl to make them look with a chearful countenance; neverthelessif their hearts were disclosed, perhaps their glittering state would not greatly be envied. The voyces that have broken out from some of them, *O that God had given me a heart senseless like the flint in the rocks of stone?* which as it can taste no pleasure, so it feeleth no wo; these and the like speeches are surely tokens of the curse which Zophar in the Book of Job poureth upon the head of the impious man, *He shall suck the gall of Asps, and the Vipers tongue shall slay him.* If this seem light, because it is secret, shall we think they go unpunished, because no apparent plague is presently seen upon them? The judgements of God do not always follow crimes, as Thunder doth Lightning, but sometimes the space of many Ages coming between. When the Sun hath shined fair the space of six days upon their Tabernacle, we know not what Clouds the seventh may bring. And when their punishment doth come, let them make their account, in the greatness of their sufferings to pay the interest of that respite which hath been given them. Or if they chance to escape clearly in this World, which they seldom do, in the Day when the heavens shall shrivel as a scrowl, & the mountains move as frighted men out of their places, what Cave shall receive them? what Mountain or Rock shall they get by intreaty to fall upon them? what covert to hide them from that wrath which they shall neither be able to abide nor avoid? No mans misery therefore being greater then theirs whose impiety is most fortunate; much more cause there is for them to bewail their own infelicity, then for others to be troubled with their prosperous and happy estate, as if the hand of the Almighty did not, or would not touch them. For these causes and the like unto these, therefore be not troubled.

Now, though the cause of our heaviness be just, yet may not our affections herein be yeilded unto with too much indulgency and favour. The grief of compassion, whereby we are touched with the feeling of other mens woes, is of all other least dangerous. Yet this is a let unto sundry duties, by this we are to spare somtimes where we ought to strike. The grief which our own sufferings do bring, what temptations have not risen from it? What great advantage Satan hath taken even by the godly grief of hearty contrition for sins committed against God, the near approaching of so many afflicted souls, whom the conscience of sin hath brought unto the very brink of extreme despair, doth but too abundantly shew. These things, wheresoever they fall, cannot but trouble and molest the minde. Whether we be therefore moved vainly with that which seemeth hurtful, and is not; or have just cause of grief, being pressed indeed with those things which are grievous, our Saviours Lesson is, touching the one, Be not troubled, nor over-troubled for the other. For though to have no feeling of that which neerly concerneth us, were stupidity, nevertheless, seeing that as the Authour of our Salvation was himself Consecrated

by

Ecclef. 6.16

by affliction, fo the way which we are to follow him by, is not ftrewed with rufhes, bnt fet with thorns ; be it never fo hard to learn, we muft learn to fuffer with patience, even that which feemeth almoft impoffible to be fuffered, that in the hour when God fhall call us unto our trial, and turn this honey of peace and pleafure wherewith we fwell, into that gall and bitternefs which flefh doth fhrink to tafte of, nothing may caufe us in the troubles of our fouls to ftorm, and grudge, and repine at God, but every heart be enabled with divinely infpired courage, to inculcate unto it felf, *Be not troubled* ; and in thofe laft and greateft conflicts to remember it, that nothing may be fo fharp and bitter to be fuffered, but that ftill we our felves may give our felves this encouragement, *Even learn alfo patience, O my foul.*

Naming Patience, I name that vertue which onely hath power to ftay our fouls from being over-exceffively troubled : A vertue, wherein if ever any, furely that foul had good experience, which extremity, of pains having chafed out of the Tabernacle of this flefh, Angels, I nothing doubt, have carried into the bofom of her Father *Abraham.* The death of the Saints of God is precious in his fight. And fhall it feem unto us fuperfluous at fuch times as thefe are, to hear in what manner they have ended their lives ? The Lord himfelf hath not difdained fo exactly to regifter in the Book of life, after what fort his Servants have clofed up their days on earth, that he defcendeth even to their very meaneft actions , what meat they have longed for in their fieknefs, what they have fpoken unto their Children, Kinsfolks and Friends, where they have willed their dead Carkaffes to be laid, how they have framed their Wills and Teftaments ; yea, the very turning of their faces to this fide or that, the fetting of their eyes, the degrees whereby their natural heat hath departed from them, their crys, their groans, their pantings, breathings, and laft gafpings he hath moft folemnly commended unto the memory of all Generations. The care of the living both to live and to dye well, muft needs be fomewhat encreafed, when they know that their departure fhall not be folded up in filence, but the ears of many be made acquainted with it. Again, when they hear how mercifully God hath dealt with others in the hour of their laft need, befides the praife which they give to God, and the joy which they have, or fhould have, by reafon of their Fellowfhip and Communion of Saints, is not their hope alfo much confirmed againft the day of their own diffolution ? Finally, the found of thefe things doth not fo pafs the ears of them that are moft loofe and diffolute of life, but it caufeth them fometime or other to wifh in their hearts, *Oh, that we might dye the death of the Righteous, and that our end might be like his!* Howbeit, becaufe to fpend herein many words, would be to ftrike even as many wounds into their mindes, whom I rather wifh to comfort : Therefore concerning this vertuous Gentlewoman, onely this little I fpeak, and that of knowledge, *She lived a Dove, and dyed a Lamb.* And if amongft fo many Vertues, hearty Devotion towards God, towards Poverty tender Compaffion, Motherly Affection towards fervants ; towards friends even ferviceable kindenefs, milde behaviour, and harmlefs meaning towards all ; if where fo many vertues were eminent, any be worthy of fpecial mention, I wifh her deareft friends of that fex to be her neareft followers in two things : *Silence,* faving onely where duty did exact fpeech; and *Patience,* even when extremity of pains did enforce grief. *Bleffed are they that dye in the Lord.* And concerning the dead which are bleffed, let not the hearts of any living be over-charged with grief, or over-troubled.

Touching the latter affection of fear; which refpecteth evil to come, as the other which we have fpoken of doth prefent evils ; firft, in the nature thereof it is plain, that we are not of every future evil afraid. Perceive we not how they, whofe tendernefs fhrinketh at the leaft rafe of a Needle's Point, do kifs the fword that pierceth their fouls quite thorow ? If every evil did caufe fear, fin, becaufe it is fin, would be feared; whereas properly fin is not feared as fin, but onely as having fome kinde of harm annexed. To teach men to avoid fin, it had been fufficient for the Apoftle to fay, Flie it. But to make them afraid of committing fin, becaufe the naming of fin fufficed not, therefore he addeth further, that it is as a *Serpent which ftingeth the foul.* Again, be it that fome nocive or hurtful things be towards us, muft fear of neceffity follow hereupon ? Not, except that hurtful things do threaten us either with deftruction or vexation, and that fuch as we,

have

have neither a conceit of ability to refift, nor of utter impoffibility to avoid. That which we know our felves able to withftand, we fear not, and that which we know we are unable to defer or diminifh, or any way avoid, we ceafe to fear, we give our felves over to bear and fuftain it. The evil therefore which is feared, muft be in our perfwafion unable to be refifted when it cometh, yet not utterly impoffible for a time in whole or in part to be fhunned. Nether do we much fear fuch evils, except they be imminent and near at hand; nor if they be near, except we have an opinion that they be fo. When we have once conceived an opinion, or apprehended an imagination of fuch evils-preft, and ready to invade us, becaufe they are hurtful unto our nature, we feel in our felves a kinde of abhorring, becaufe they are thought near, yet not prefent, our nature feeketh forthwith how to fhift and provide for it felf; becaufe they are evils which cannot be refifted, therefore fhe doth not provide to withftand, but to fhun and avoid. Hence it is, that in extreme fear, the Mother of life contracting herfelf, avoiding as much as may be the reach of evil, and drawing the heat together with the fpirits of the body to her, leaveth the outward parts cold, pale, week, feeble, unapt to perform the functions of life; as we fee in the fear of *Balthafar* King of *Babel.* By this it appeareth, that fear is nothing elfe but a perturbation of the minde, through an opinion of fome imminent evil, threatning the deftruction or great annoyance of our nature, which to fhun, it doth contract and dejeсt it felf.

   Now becaufe not in this place onely, but otherwhere often we hear it repeated, *Fear not*; it is by fome made a queftion, *Whether a man may fear deftruction or vexation without finning ?* Firft, the reproof wherewith Chrift checketh his Difciples more then once, *O men of little faith, wherefore are ye afraid ?* Secondly, the punifhment threatned in *Revel.* 21; the Lake, and Fire, and Brimftone, not onely to Murtherers, unclean Perfons, Sorcerers, Idolaters, Lyers, but alfo to the fearful and faint-hearted: This feemeth to argue, that fearfulnefs cannot but be fin. On the contrary fide we fee, that he which never felt motion unto fin, had of this affection more then a flight feeling. How clear is the evidence of the Spirit, that *in the days of his flesh he offered up Prayers and Supplications, with ftrong crys and tears, unto him that was able to fave him from death, and was alfo heard in that which he feared,* Heb.5.7. Whereupon it followeth, that fear in it felf is a thing not finful. For is not fear a thing natural, and for mens prefervation neceffary, implanted in us by the provident and moft gracious giver of all good things, to the end that we might not run headlong upon thofe mifchiefs wherewith we are not able to encounter, but ufe the remedy of fhunning thofe evils which we have not abil ty to withftand ? Let that people therefore which receive a benefit by the length of their Princes days, the Father or Mother that rejoyceth to fee the Off-fpring of their flefh grow like green and pleafant Plants, let thofe children that would have their Parents, thofe men that would gladly have their friends and brethrens days prolonged on earth (as there is no natural-hearted man but gladly would) let them blefs the Father of lights as in other things, fo even in this, that he hath given man a fearful heart, and fettled naturally that affection in him, which is a prefervation againft fo many ways of death. Fear therein it felf being meer nature, cannot in it felf be fin, which fin is not nature, but thereof an acceffary Deprivation.

   But in the matter of fear we may fin, and do, two ways. If any mans danger be great, theirs is greateft that have put the fear of danger fartheft from them. Is there any eftate more fearful then that Babylonian Strumpets, that fitteth upon the tops of feven hills, glorying and vaunting, *I am a Queen,* &c. Rev. 18.7. How much better and happier they, whofe eftate hath been always as his who fpeaketh after this fort of himfelf, *Lord, from my youth have I born thy yoke*: They which fit at continual eafe, and are fetled in the lees of their fecurity, look upon them, view their countenance, their fpeech, their gefture, their deeds, *Put them in fear, O God,* faith the Prophet, *that fo they may know themfelves to be but men*; Worms of earth, duft and afhes, frail, corruptible, feeble things. To fhake off fecurity therefore, and to breed fear in the hearts of mortal men, fo many admonitions are ufed concerning the power of evils which befet them, fo many threatnings of calamities, fo many defcriptions of things threatned, and thofe fo lively, to the end they may leave behind them a deep impreffion of fuch as have force to keep the heart continually waking. All which do fhew; that we are to ftand in fear of nothing more then the extremity of not fearing.

When

When fear hath delivered us from that pit, wherein they are sunk that have put far from them the evil day; that have made a league with death, and have said, *Tush, we shall feel no harm*; it standeth us upon to take heed it cast us not into that, wherein souls destitute of all hope are plunged. For our direction, to avoid, as much as may be, both extremities, that we may know as a Ship-master by his Card, how far we are wide, either on the one side, or on the other; we must note, that in a Christian man there is first, Nature: Secondly, Corruption perverting Nature: Thirdly, Grace, correcting and amending Corruption. In fear, all these have their several operations: Nature teacheth simply, to wish preservation and avoidance of things dreadful; for which cause our Saviour himself prayeth, and that often, *Father, if it be possible.* In which cases, corrupt Natures suggestions are, for the safety of temporal life, not to stick at things excluding from eternal; wherein how far, even the best may be led, the chiefest Apostles frailty teacheth. Were it not therefore for such cogitations, as on the contrary side, Grace and Faith ministreth, such as that of *Job, Though God kill me*; that of *Paul, Scio cui credidi,* I know him on whom I do rely; in all evils would soon be able to overthrow even the best of us. *A wise man,* saith *Solomon, doth see a plague coming, and hideth himself.* It is *Nature* which teacheth a wise man in fear to *hide* himself, but *Grace* and *Faith* doth teach him *where.* Fools care not where they hide their heads: but where shall a wise man hide himself, when he feareth a plague coming? Where should the frighted Childe hide his head, but in the bosom of his loving Father? where a Christian, but under the shadow of the wings of Christ his Saviour? *Come my people,* saith God in the Prophet, *Enter into thy chamber, hide thy self, &c.* Isa. 26. But because we are in danger, like chased Birds, like Doves that seek and cannot see the resting holes, that are right before them; therefore our Saviour giveth his Disciples these encouragements beforehand, that fear might never so amaze them, but that always they might remember, that whatsoever evils at any time did befet them, to him they should still repair for comfort, counsel and succour. For their assurance whereof, his *Peace he gave them, his peace he left unto them, not such a peace as the world offereth,* by whom his name is never so much pretended, as when deepest treachery is meant; but *Peace which passeth all understanding, Peace* that bringeth with it all happiness, *Peace* that continueth for ever and ever with them that have it.

This Peace, God the Father grant, for his Sons sake, unto whom with the Holy Ghost, three Persons, one Eternal and Everliving God, be all honour, and glory, and praise, now and for ever. Amen.

A Learned and comfortable Sermon of the certainty and perpetuity of Faith in the Elect: especially of the Prophet *Habak-kuks* Faith.

HABAK. 1. 4.

VVhether the Prophet Habakkuk, *by admitting this cogitation into his mind,* The Law *doth fail, did thereby shew himself an unbeleiver?*

E E have seen in the opening of this clause, which concerneth the weaknefs of the Prophets faith ; Firft, what things they are whereunto the faith of found beleivers doth affent : Secondly, wherefore all men affent not thereunto : and Thirdly, why they that do, do it many times with fmall affurance. Now becaufe nothing can be fo truely fpoken, but through mif-underftanding it may be depraved ; therefore to prevent if it be poffible, all mifconftruction in this caufe, where a fmall errour cannot rife but with great danger, it is perhaps needful ere we come to the fourth point, that fomething be added to that which hath been already fpoken concerning the third.

That meer natural men do neither know nor acknowledge the things of God, we do not marvel, becaufe they are fpiritually to be difcerned : but they in whofe hearts the light of grace doth fhine, they that are taught of God, why are they fo weak in faith ? Why is their affenting to the Law fo fcrupulous ? fo much mingled with fear and wavering? It feemeth ftrange that ever they fhould imagine the Law to fail. It cannot feem ftrange if we weigh the reafon. If the things which we believe be confidered in themfelves, it may truely be faid, that faith is more certain then any Science: That which we know either by fence, or by infallyble demonftration is not fo certain as the principles, articles and conclufions of Chriftian Faith. Concerning which we muft note, that there is a *certainty of evidence*, and a *certainty of adherence. Certainty of evidence* we call that, when the mind doth affent unto this or that, not becaufe it is true in it felf, but becaufe the truth is clear, becaufe it is manifeft to us. Of things in themfelves moft certain, except they be alfo moft evident, our perfwafion is not fo affured, as it is of things more evident, although in themfelves they be lefs certain. It is as fure if not furer, that there be fpirits as that there be men : but we be more affured of thefe than of them, becaufe thefe are more evident. The truth of fome things is fo evident, that no man which heareth them can doubt of them : as when we hear that *a part of any thing is lef, than the whole*, the mind is conftrained to fay, This is true. If it were fo in matters of Faith, then, as all men have equal certainty of this, fo no beleiver fhould be more fcrupulous and doubtful then another. But we find the contrary. The Angels and Spirits of the righteous in heaven, have certainty moft evident of things fpiritual : but this they have by the light of glory. That which we fee by the light of grace, though it be indeed more certain, yet is it not to us fo evidently certain, as that which fence or the light of nature will not fuffer a

Kkk

man

man to doubt of. Proofs are vain and frivolous , except they be more certain than
is the thing proved : and do we not see how the spirit every where in the Scripture
proveth matters of faith,laboureth to confirme us in the things which we beleive by
things whereof we have sensible knowledge ? I conclude therefore that we have less
certainty of *evidence* concerning things beleived , then concerning sensible or naturally perceived. Of these who doth doubt at any time ? Of them at somtime who
doubteth not ? I will not here alledge the sundry confessions of the perfectest that
have lived upon earth,concerning their great imperfections this way ; which if I did,
I should dwell too long upon a matter sufficiently known by every faithful man that
doth know himself.

The other which we call the *certainty* of *adherence*, is when the heart doth cleave
and stick unto that which it doth beleive. This certainty is greater in us then the other.
The reason is this, The faith of a Christian doth apprehend the words of the Law, the
promises of God , not onely as true, but also as good : and therefore even then when
the evidence which he hath of the truth is so small, that it grieveth him to feel his
weakness in assenting thereto:yet is there in him such a sure adherence unto that which
he doth but faintly and fearfully beleive , that his spirit having once truly tasted the
heavenly sweetness thereof , all the world is not able quite and clean to remove him
from it : but he striveth with himself to hope against all reason of beleiving , being
setled with *Job* upon this unmoveable resolution,*Though God kill me,I will not give over*
thirsting in him. For why ? This lesson remaineth for ever imprinted in him , *It is good*
for me to cleave unto God, *Psal.* 37.

Now the minds of all men being so darkned, as they are with the foggy damp of
original corruption , it cannot be that any mans heart living should be either so inlightned in the knowledge , or so established in the love of that wherein his salvation
standeth,as to be perfect,neither doubting nor shrinking at all. If any such were,what
doth let why that man should not be justified by his own inherent righteousness ? For
righteousness inherent , being perfect, will justifie. And perfect faith is a part of perfect righteousness inherent ; yea a principal part, the root and the Mother of all
the rest : so that if the fruit of every tree be such as the root is , faith being perfect , as it is if it be not at all mingled with distrust and fear, what is there to exclude
other Christian vertues from the like perfections ? And then what need we the righteousness of Christ ? His garment is superfluous ? we may be honourably clothed with
our own robes,if it be thus.But let them beware who challenge to themselvs a strength
which they have not, lest they lose the comfortable support of that weakness which
indeed they have.

Some shew, although no soundness of ground, there is,which may be alledged for
defence of this supposed perfection in certainty touching matters of our faith : as first
that *Abraham* did believe and doubted not : secondly, that the spirit which God hath
given us to no other end, but only to assure us that we are the sons of God ;to embolden us to call upon him as our Father , to open our eyes , and to make the truth of
things beleived evident unto our minds , is much mightier in operation then the common light of nature, whereby we discern sensible things : wherefore we must needs
be more sure of that we beleive , then of that we see ; we must needs be more certain
of the mercies of God in Christ Jesus , then we are of the light of the sun when it
shineth upon our faces. To that of *Abraham* , *he did not doubt* , I answer that this
negation doth not exclude all fear , all doubting ; but onely that which cannot stand
with true faith. It freeth *Abraham* from doubting through *infidelity*, not from doubting through *Infirmity*; from the doubting of *unbeleivers* , not of *weak beleivers* ;
from such a doubting as that whereof the Prince of *Samaria* is attained, who hearing
the promise of sudden plenty in the midst of Extream dearth , answered, *Though the*
Lord would make windowes in heaven, were it possible so to come to pass ? But that *Abraham*
was not void of all doubting,what need we any other proof than the plain evidence of
his own words ? *Gen.* 17. *v.*17. The reason which is taken from the power of the spirit
were effectual, if God did work like a natural Agent , as the fire doth inflame, and the
sun enlighten, according to the uttermost ability which they have to bring forth their
effects. But the incomprehensible wisdom of God doth limit the effects of his power,
to such a measure as seemeth best unto himself. Wherefore he worketh that certainty
in all , which sufficeth abundantly to their salvation in the life to come ; but in none

1 Kings 7.2.

so great as attaineth in this life unto perfection. Even so, O Lord, it hath pleased thee, even so it is best and fittest for us, that feeling still our own infirmities, we may no longer breath, then pray, *Adjuva Domine; Help Lord our incredulity.* Of the third question, this, I hope, will suffice, being added unto that which hath been thereof already spoken. The fourth question resteth, and so an end of this point.

That which cometh last of all in this first branch to be considered concerning the weakness of the Prophets Faith, is, *Whether he did by this very thought, The Law* doth fail, *quench the spirit, fall from faith; and shew himself an unbeleiver or no?* The question is of Moment, therepose and tranquillity of infinite souls doth depend upon it. The Prophets case is the case of many; which way soever we cast for him, the same way it passeth for all others. If in him this cogitation did extinguish grace; why the like thoughts in us should not take the like effect, there is no cause. Forasmuch therefore as the matter is weighty, dear and precious, which we have in hand, it behoveth us with so much the greater charity to wade through it, taking special heed both what we build, and whereon we build, that if our building be pearl, our foundation be not stubble; if the Doctrine we teach be full of comfort and consolation, the ground whereupon we gather it, be sure: otherwise we shall not save, but deceive both our selves and others. In this we know we are not deceived, neither can we deceive you, when we teach that the faith whereby ye are sanctified, cannot fail; it did not in the Prophet, it shall not in you. If it be so, let the difference be shewed between the condition of unbeleivers and his, in this or in the like imbecillity and weakness. There was in *Habakkuk*, that which St. *John* doth call *the seed of God*, meaning thereby, *the first grace* which God poureth into the hearts of them that be incorporated into Christ, which having received, if because it is an adversary to sin, we do therefore think we sin not both otherwise, and also by distrustful and doubtful apprehending of that, which we ought stedfastly to believe, surely, we do but deceive our selves. Yet they which are of God, do not sin either in this, or in any thing any such sin as doth quite extinguish grace, clean cut them off from Christ Jesus: because the *seed of God abideth* in them, and doth shield them from receiving any irremediable wound. Their faith when it is at strongest is but weak; yet even then when it is at the weakest, so strong, that utterly it never faileth, it never perisheth altogether, no not in them who think it extinguished in themselves. There are, for whose sakes I dare not deal slightly in this cause, sparing that labour which must be bestowed to make it plain, Men in like agonies unto this of the Prophet *Habakkuks*, who through the extremity of grief are many times in judgement so confounded, that they find not themselves in themselves. For that which dwelleth in their hearts they seek, they make diligent search and enquiry. It abideth, it worketh in them, yet still they ask where? Still they lament as for a thing which is past finding: they mourn as *Rachel*, and refuse to be comforted, as if that were not, which indeed is; and as if that which is not, were; as if they did not beleive when they do; and as if they did despair when they do not. Which in some, I grant, is but a melancholly passion proceeding only from that dejection of mind, the cause whereof is in the body, and by bodily means can be taken away. But where there is no such bodily cause, the mind is not lightly in this mood, but by some of these three occasions. One, that judging by comparison either with other men or with themselves at some other time more strong, they think imperfection to be plain deprivation, weakness to be utter want of Faith. Another cause is; they often mistake one thing for another. Saint *Paul* wishing well to the Church of Rome, prayeth for them after this sort: *The God of hope fill you with all joy of beleiving.* Hence an errour groweth, when men in heaviness of spirit, suppose they lack faith, because they find not the sugared joy and delight which indeed doth accompany Faith, but so as a separable accident, as a thing that may be removed from it; yea, there is a cause why it should be removed. The light would never be so acceptable, were it not for that usual intercourse of darkness. Too much hony doth turn to gall, and too much joy even spiritually would make us wantons. Happier a great deal is that mans case, whose soul by inward desolation is humbled, then he whose heart is through abundance of spiritual delight lifted up, and exalted above measure. Better it is sometimes to go down into the pit with him, who beholding darkness, and bewailing the loss of inward joy

and

and confolation, cryeth from the bottom of the loweft hell, *My God, my God, why haft thou forfaken me ?* then continually to walk arm in arm with Angels, to fit, as it were, in *Abrahams* bofome, and to have no thought, no cogitation, but, *I thank my God it is not with me as it is with other men.* No ; God will have them that fhall walk in light, to feel now and then what it is to fit in the fhadow of death. A greived fpirit therefore is no argument of a faithlefs mind. A third occafion of mens mif-judging themfelves, as if they were faithlefs when they are not, is ; They faften their cogitations upon the diftruftful fuggeftions of the flefh, whereof finding great abundance in themfelves, they gather thereby, furely, unbelief hath full dominion, it hath taken plenary poffeffion of me: If I were faithful it could not be thus. Not marking the motions of the Spirit and of Faith, becaufe they lye buried and over-whelmed with the contrary : when notwithftanding as the bleffed Apoftle doth acknowledge, that the *Spirit groaneth*, and that God heareth when we do not ; fo there is no doubt, but that our faith may have, and hath her private operations fecret to us, yet known to him by whom they are. Tell this to a man that hath a mind deceived by too hard an opinion of himfelf, and it doth but augment his grief: he hath his anfwer ready ; will you make me think otherwife than I find, then I feel in my felf ? I have throughly confidered and exquifitely fifted all the corners of my heart, and I fee what there is : never feek to perfwade me againft my knowledge, *I do not, I know I do not beleive.* Well to favour them a little in their weaknefs : let that be granted which they do imagine ; be it that they are faithlefs and without beleif. But are they not greived for their unbeleif ? They are. Do they not wifh it might, and alfo ftrive that it may be otherwife ? We know they do. Whence cometh this, but from a fecret love and liking which they have of thofe things that are beleived ? No, man can love things which in his own opinion are not. And if they think thofe things to be, which they fhew that they love when they defire to beleive them ; then muft it needs be, that by defiring to beleive, they prove themfelves true beleivers. For without faith, no man thinketh that things beleived are. Which argument all the fubtilty of infernal powers will never be able to diffolve. The Faith therefore of true Beleivers, though it have many and greivous down-fals, yet doth it ftill continue invincible ; it conquereth, and recovereth it felf in the end. The dangerous conflicts whereunto it is fubject, are not able to prevail againft it. The Prophet *Habakkuk* remained faithful in weaknefs, though weak in faith. It is true, fuch is our weak and wavering nature, we have no fooner received grace, but we are ready to fall from it : we have no fooner given our affent to the law that it cannot fail, but the next conceit which we are ready to imbrace, is, that it may and that it doth fail. Though we find in our felves a moft willing heart to cleave unfeperably unto God, even fo far as to think unfainedly with *Peter*, *Lord, I am ready to go with thee into Prifon and to death* : yet how foon and how eafily, upon how fmall occafions are we changed, if we be but a while let alone and left unto our felves ? the *Galatians* to day, for their fakes which teach them the truth in Chrift, are content if need were to pluck out their own eys, and the next day ready to pluck out theirs which taught them. The love of the Angel to the Church of *Ephefus*, how greatly enflamed, and how quickly flacked ? the higher we flow, the nearer we are unto an ebb, if men be refpected as meer men, according to the wonted courfe of their alterable inclination ; without the heavenly fupport of the Spirit. Again, the defire of our ghoftly enemy is fo incredible, and his means fo forcible to over-throw our faith, that whom the bleffed Apoftle knew betrothed and made hand-faft unto Chrift, to them he could not write but with great trembling : *I am jealous over you with a godly jealoufie, for I have prepared you to one Husband, to prefent you a pure Virgin unto Chrift: but I fear, left as the Serpent beguiled Eve through his fubtilty ; fo your minds fhould be corrupted from the fimplicity which is in Chrift.* The fimplicity of faith which is in Chrift, taketh the naked promife of God, his bare Word, and on that it refteth. This fimplicity the Serpent laboureth continually to pervert, corrupting the mind with many imaginations of repugnancy and contrariety between the promife of God and thofe things which fence or experience, or fome other fore-conceived perfwafion hath imprinted. The word of the promife of God unto his people, is, *I will not leave thee, nor forfake thee* : upon this the fimplicity of faith refteth, and is not afraid of famine. But mark how the fubtilty of Satan did corrupt the minds of that Rebellious

bellious

bellious generation, whose Spirits were not faithful unto God. They beheld the desolate state of the desart in which they were, and by the wisdom of their sence concluded the promise of God to be but folly : *Can God prepare a Table in the Wildernes?* The word of the promise to *Sarah*, was, *Thou shalt bear a Son*. Faith is simple, and doubteth not of it : but Satan, to corrupt this simplicity of Faith, entangleth the mind of the Woman with an argument drawn from common experience to the contrary : *A Woman that is old* ; Sarah, *now to be acquainted again with forgotten passions of youth* ! The word of the promise of God by *Moses* and the prophets, made the Saviour of the World so apparent unto *Philip*, that his simplicity could conceive no other Messias then *Jesus of Nazareth* the son of *Joseph*. But to stay *Nathaniel*, left being invited to come and see, he should also beleive, and so be saved the subtilty of Satan casteth a mist before his eys, putteth in his head against this, the common conceived perswasion of all men concerning *Nazareth* ; *Is it possible that a good thing should come from thence?* this stratagem he doth use with so great dexterity, that the minds of all men are so strangely bewitched with it, that it bereaveth them for the time of all perceivance of that which should releive them and be their comfort ; yea, it taketh all remembrance from them, even of things wherewith they are most familiarly acquainted. The people of *Israel* could not be ignorant, that he which led them through the Sea, was able to feed them in the Desart : but this was obliterated and put out by the sence of their present want. Feeling the hand of God against them in their food, they remember not his hand in the day that he delivered them from the hand of the Oppressour. *Sarah* was not then to learn, that *with God all things were possible*. Had *athaniel never* noted how *God doth chuse the base things of this World to disgrace them that are most honourably esteemed?* The Prophet *Habakkuk* knew that the promises of grace, protection and favour which God in the Law doth make unto his people, do not grant them any such immunity as can free and exempt them from all chastisements; he knew, that as God said, *I will continue my mercy for ever towards them* ; so he likewise said, *Their transgressions I will punish with a rod:* he knew that it cannot stand with any reason, we should set the measure of our own punishments, and prescribe unto God how great or how long our sufferings shall be, he knew that we were blind, a d altogether ignorant what is best for us ; that we sue for many things very unwisely against our selves, thinking we ask Fish, when indeed we crave a Serpent : he knew that when the thing we ask is good, and yet God seemeth slow to grant it, he doth not deny, but deferr our petitions, to the end we might learn to desire great things greatly : all this he knew. But beholding the Land which God had severed for his own people and seeing it abandoned unto Heathen Nations; viewing how reproachfully they did tread it down, and wholy make havock of it at their pleasure; beholding the Lords own Royal Seat made an heap of stones, his temple defiled, the carkases of his servants cast out for the fouls of the air to devour, and the flesh of his m ek ones for the beasts of the field to feed upon; being conscious to himself how long and how earnestly he had cryed, *Succour us, O God of our welfare, for the Glary of thine own Name* ; and feeling that their sore was stil increased : the conceit of repugnancy between this which was object to his eys, and that which faith upon promise of the Law did look for, made so deep an impression and so strong, that he disputeth not the matter, but without any further inquiry or search, inferreth as we see : *The law doth fail.*

Of us who is here, which cannot very soberly advise his brother ? Sir, you must learn to strengthen your faith by that experience which heretofore you have had of Gods great goodnes towards you, *per ea quae agnoscas praestita, discas sperare promissa* ; By those those things which you have known performed, learn to hope for those things which are promised. Do you acknowledge to have received much ? Let that make you certain to receive more. *Habenti dabitur* : *To him that hath, more shall be given.* When you doubt what you shall have, search what you have had at Gods hands. Make this reckoning, that the benefits which he hath bestowed, are Bils obligatory and sufficient Sureties that he will bestow further. His present mercy is stil a warrant of his future love, because *whom he loveth, he loveth to the end.* Is it not thus ? Yet if we could reckon up as many evident, clear, undoubted signes of Gods reconciled love towards us, as there are years ; yea days, yea hours past over our heads ; all these set together have not such force to confirm our faith, as the loss, and

some-

sometimes the only fear of losing a little transitory goods, credit, honour, or favour of men, a small calamity, a matter of nothing to breed a conceit; and such a conceit as is not easily again removed; that we are clean crost out of Gods book, that he regards us not, that he looketh upon others, but passeth by us like a stranger; to whom we are not known. Then we think, looking upon others and comparing them with our selves; their Tables are furnished day by day, earth and ashes are our tread: they sing to the Lute, and they see their children dance before them; our hearts are heavy in our bodys as lead, our sighes beat as thick as a swift Pulse, our tears do wash the beds wherein we lye: The Sun shineth fair upon their fore-heads; we are hanged up like Bottles in the smoke, cast into corners like the sherds of a broken Pot: tell not us of the promises of Gods favour, tell such as do reap the fruit of them, they belong not to us, they are made to others: the Lord be merciful to our weakness, but thus it is. Well, let the frailty of our nature, the Subtilty of Satan, the force of our deceivable imaginations be, as we cannot deny but they are things that threaten every moment the utter subversion of our faith; faith notwithstanding is not hazarded by these things. That which one sometimes told the Senators of Rome, *Ego sic existimabam, P. C. uti patrem saepe meum praedicantem audiveram, qui vestram amicitiam diligenter colerent eos multum laborem suscipere, caeterum ex omnibus maxime tutos esse*: As I have often heard my Father acknowledge, so I my self did ever think, that the friends and favourers of this State charged themselves with great labour, but no mans condition so safe as theirs; the same we may say a great deal more justly in this case: our Fathers and prophets, our Lord and Master hath full often spoken, by long experience we have found it true; as many as have entred their names in the mystical book of life, *eos maximum laborem suscipere*, they have taken upon them a labour-som, a toylesom, a painful profession, *sed omnium maxime tutos esse*, but no mans security like to theirs. *Simon, Simon, Satan hath desired to winnow thee as wheat*; Here is our toyl: *but I have prayed for thee, that thy faith fail not*; this is our safety. No mans condition so sure as ours: the prayer of Christ is more then sufficient both to strengthen us, be we never so weak: and to overthrow all adversary power, be it never so strong and potent. His prayer must not exclude our labour: their thoughts are vain, who think that their watching can preserve the City which God himself is not willing to keep. And are not theirs as vain, who think that God will keep the City, for which they themselves are not careful to watch? the husbandman may not therefore burn his Plough, nor the Merchant forsake his trade, because God hath promised, *I will not forsake thee*. And do the promises of God concerning our stability, think you, make it a matter indifferent for us, to use or not to use the means whereby to attend or not to attend to reading, to pray or not to pray that we fall not into temptation? Surely if we look to stand in the faith of the Sons of God, we must hourly, continually be providing and setting our selves to strive. It was not the meaning of our Lord and Saviour in saying, *Father keep them in thy name*, that we should be careless to keep our selves. To our own safety, our own sedulity is required. And then blessed for ever and ever be that Mothers Child, whose faith hath made him the Child of God. The earth may shake, the pillars of the World may tremble under us: the countenance of the Heaven may be appaled, the Sun may lose his light, the Moon her beauty, the Stars their glory: but concerning the man that trusteth in God, if the fire have proclaimed it self unable as much as to singe a hair of his head; if Lyons, Beasts ravenous by nature, and keen with hunger, being set to devour, have as it were religiously adored the very flesh of the faithful man, what is there in the World that shall change his heart, overthrow his Faith, alter his affection towards God, or the Affection of God to him? If I be of this note, who shall make a separation between me and my God? shall tribulation, or anguish, or persecution, or famine, or nakedness, or peril, or sword? No, I am perswaded that neither tribulation, nor anguish, nor persecution, nor famine, nor nakedness, nor peril nor sword, nor death, nor life, nor Angels, nor principalities, nor powers, nor things present, nor things to come, nor height nor depth, nor any other creature shall ever prevail so far over me. I know in whom I have beleived; I am not ignorant whose precious blood hath been shed for me; I have a shepheard full of kindness, full of care, and full of power: unto him I commit my self; his own finger hath engraven this sentence in the Tables of my heart; *Satan hath desired to winnow thee as wheat, but I have prayed that thy faith fail not*. Therefore the assurance of my hope I will labour to keep as a Jewel unto the end, and by labour, through the gracious mediation of his prayer, I shall keep it.

To

To the VVorshipful Mr. GEORGE SUMMASTER,
Principal of *Broad-Gates Hall* in *Oxford*, *Henry Jackson*
wisheth all Happines.

SIR,

Our kind acceptance of a former testification of that respect I owe you, hath made me venture to shew the World these godly Sermons under your name. In which, as every point is worth observation, so some especially are to be noted, The first, that, as the spirit of Prophecy is from God himself, who doth inwardly heat and enlighten the hearts and minds of his holy Pen-men, (which if some would diligent-
ly consider, they would not puzzle themselves with the contentions of Scot, and Thomas, Whether God only, or his Ministring Spirits, do infuse into mens minds prophetical Revelations, per species intelligibiles) so God framed their words also. Whence the holy Father a St. Augustine religiously observeth, That all those that understand the sacred Writers, will also perceive, that they ought not to use other words then they did, in expressing those heavenly mysteries which their hearts conceived, as the Blessed Virgin did our Saviour, By the Holy Ghost. The greater is Castellio his offence, who had laboured to teach the Prophets to speak otherwise then they have already. Much like to that impious King of Spain, Alphonsus the tenth, who found fault with Gods works, b Si, inquit, creationi affuissem, mundum melius ordinassem, If he had been with God at the Creation of the World, the World had gone better then now it doth. As this man found fault with Gods works, so did the other with Gods words; but because we have a most sure word of the Prophets, to which we must take heed, I will let his words pass with the wind, having a elsewhere spoken to you more largely of his errors, whom notwithstanding for his other excellent parts, I much respect.*

a Lib. 4. cap. 6. de doct. chr.

b Rob. Tolet. lib. 4. cap. 5.

c 2 Pet. 1. d Praf. in Orat. D. Rainold.

You shall moreover from hence understand how Christianity consists not in formal and seeming purity (under which, who knows not notorious villany to mask?) but in the heart root. Whence the Author truly teacheth, that Mockers, which use Religion as a cloak, to put off and on, as the weather serveth, are worse then Pagans and Infidels. Where I cannot omit to shew, how justly this kind of men hath been reproved by that renowned Martyr of Jesus Christ, B. Latimer, both because it will be apposite to this purpose, and also free that Christian Worthy from the slanderous reproaches of him, who was, if ever any, a Mocker of God, Religion, and all good men. But first I must desire you, and in you all Readers, not to think lightly of that excellent man, for using this and the like witty similitudes in his Sermon. For whosoever will call to mind, with what riff-raff Gods people were fed in those days, when their Priests, whose lips should have preserved knowledg, preached nothing else but dreams & false miracles of counterfeit Saints, enrolled in that sottish Legend, coyned and amplified by a drousie head, between sleeping and waking. He that will consider this, and how the people were delighted with such toys (God sending them strong delusions that they should beleive lies) and how hard it would have been for any man, wholly, and upon the sudden, to draw their minds to another bent, will easily perceive, both how necessary it was to use Symbolical Discourse, and how wisely and moderately it was applied by the religious Father, to the end he might lead their understanding so far, till it were so convinced, informed and seiled, that it might forget the means and way by which

e Parsons in 3. convert.

f Mal. 2. 7.

g anus locor. lib. 11. cap. 5. Viva. lib. 2. de corrupt art. Hard lib. 4.

it

it was led, and think only of that I had acquired. For in all such mystical speeches who knows not that the end for which they are used is only to be thought upon? This then being first considered, let us hear the story, as it is related by Mr. Fox:

g Pag. 1973.
edit. 1570.

' Mr. Latimer (saith he) in his Sermon gave the people certain Cards out of the
' fift, sixt & seventh chapter of Matth. For the chief Triumph in the Cards he li-
'mitted the Heart, as the principal thing that they should serve God withal, where-
' by he quite overthrew all hypocritical and external Ceremonies not tending to
' the necessary furtherance of Gods holy Word and Sacraments. By this, he exhor-
' ted all men to serve the Lord with inward heart and true affection, and not
' with outward Ceremonies; adding moreover to the praise of that Triumph, that
' though it were never so small, yet it would take up the best Coat-card beside in
' the Bunch, yea, though it were the King of Clubs, &c. meaning thereby, how the
' Lord would be worshipped and served in simplicity of the heart, and verity,
' wherein consisteth true Christian Religion, &c. Thus Master Fox.

By which it appears, that the holy mans intention was to lift up the peoples hearts to God, and not that he made a Sermon of playing at Cards, and taught them how to play at Triumph, and plaid (himself) at cards in the Pulpit, as that base companion b Parsons reports the matter, in his scurrilous vein of railing, whence he calleth it a Christmass Sermon. Now he that will think ill of such Al-lusions, may out of the abundance of his folly, jest at Demosthenes for his story of the Sheep, Wolves, and Dogs, and Menenius, for his fiction of the Belly. But, hinc illæ lacrymæ, The good Bishop meant that the Romish Religion came not from the heart, but consisted in outward Ceremonies: Which sorely grieved Parsons, who never had the least warmth or spark of honesty. Whether B. Lati-mer compared the Bishops to the Knaves of Clubs, as the fellow interprets him, I know not: I am sure Parsons, of all others, deserved those colours, and so I leave him. We see then, what inward purity is required of all Christians, which if they have, then in prayer, and all other Christian duties, they shall lift up pure hands, as the m Apostle speaks, not as n Baronius would have it, washed from sins with holy water, but pure, this is holy, free from the pollutions of sin, as the Greek word ἁγνὰς doth signifie.

You may also see here refuted those calumnies of the Papists, that we abandon all religious Rites, and godly duties, as also the confirmation of our Doctrine touching certainty of Faith (and so of Salvation) which is so strongly denied by some of that Faction, that they have told the World, o S. Paul himself was un-certain of his own salvation. What then shall we say, but pronounce a woe to the most strict observers of St. Francis rule, and his Canonical Discipline (though they make him even p equal with Christ) and the most meritorious Monk that ever was registred in their Kalender of Saints? But we for our comfort are otherwise taught out of the holy Scripture, and therefore exhorted to build our selves in our most holy faith, that so, when q our earthly house of this Tabernacle shall be destroyed, we may have a building given of God, a house not made with hands, but eternal in the Heavens.

b in the third
part. o 13. con-
versions of
England, in the
Examin. of
Foxes Saints
cap. 14.§ 55.
iS & 55.
k Plut. in De-
mosthen.
l Liv. Dec. 1.
lib. 2. an. V. c. 60

m 1 Tim. 2. 8
n Annal. to. 1.
A. D. 57, n. 109.
110 & to. 2. an.
132. num.
o S. Paulus de
sua salute incer-
tus Kichermus
fuit 1.2 c. 1 s.
Idolat. Haguen.
p. 119. in marg.
dit loc.
Mogunt 113. in-
terpret. Marcel.
Bompar. Iesuita
p Witness the
verses of Hora-
tius a Iesuite,
recited by
Posse. Biblioth.
Select part. 2.

l 11. c. 9 Exue Franciscum tunica laceroq; cucullo, Qui Franciscus erat, jam tibi Christus erit. Francisci exuviis (si qua licet) indue Christum, Iam erat Christus erit, qui modo Christus erat. The like hath sensim another Iesuit.   q 2 Cor. 5. 1.

. This is that, which is most piously and feelingly taught in these few leaves, so that you shall read nothing here, but what I perswade my self, you have long practised in the constant course of your life. It remaineth only, that you accept of these Labours tendred to you by him, who wisheth you the long joys of this world, and the eternal of that which is to come.

Oxon. from Corp. Christi Colledge,
this 13. of January, 1613.

TWO
SERMONS
Upon part of
St. Judes Epistle.

The First Sermon.

Jude, Verse, 17, 18, 19, 20, 21.

But ye, beloved, remember the words which were spoken of before of the Apostles of our Lord Jesus Christ,

How that they told you, that there should be mockers in the last time, which should walk after their own ungodly lusts.

These are makers of Sects, fleshly, having not the Spirit.

But ye, beloved, edifie your selves in your most holy faith, praying in the holy Ghost.

And keep your selves in the love of God, looking for the mercy of our Lord Jesus Christ, unto eternal life.

HE occasions whereupon, together with the end wherefore, this Epistle was written, is opened in the front and entrie of the same. There were then, as there are now, many evil and wickedly disposed persons, not of the mystical body, yet within the visible bounds of the Church, men which were of old ordained to condemnation, ungodly men, which turned the grace of our God into wantonnesse, and denyed the Lord Jesus. For this cause the Spirit of the Lord is in the hand of *Jude*, the servant of *Jesus*, and brother of *James*, to exhort them that are called, and sanctified of God the Father, that they would earnestly contend to maintain the faith, which was once delivered unto the Saints. Which faith because we cannot maintain, except we know perfectly, first, against whom, secondly, in what sort it must be maintained; therefore in the former three verses of that parcel of Scripture which I have read, the enemies of the Crosse of Christ are plainly described; and in the latter two, they that love the Lord Jesus, have a sweet lesson given them, how to strengthen and stablish themselves in the faith. Let us first therefore examine the description of these reprobates, concerning faith; and afterwards come to the words of the exhortation; wherein Christians are taught how to rest their hearts on Gods eternall and everlasting Truth. The description of these godless persons is two-fold, *general* and *special*. The *general* doth point them out, and shew what manner of men they should be. The

parti-

particular pointeth at them, and faith plainly; thefe are they. In the *general* defcription we have to confider of thefe things. *Firft*, when they were defcribed, *they were told of before*. *Secondly*, the men by whom they were defcribed, *They were fpoken of by the Apoftles of our Lord Jefus Chrift*. *Thirdly*, the days, when they fhould be manifefted unto the World, they told you *they fhould be in the laft time. Fourthly*, their difpofition and whole demeanour, *mockers and walkers after their own ungodly lufts*.

2. In the third to the *Philippians*, the Apoftle defcribeth certain. *They are men* (faith he) *of whom I have told you often, and now with tears I tell you of them, their God is their belly, their glory and rejoycing is in their own fhame, they mind earthly things*.

Thefe were enemies of the Crofs of Chrift, enemies whom he faw, and his eys gufht out with tears to behold them. But we are taught in this place how the Apoftles fpake alfo of enemies, whom as yet they had not feen, defcribed a family of men as yet unheard of, a generation referved for the end of the World, and for the laft time, they had not only declared what they heard and faw in the days wherein they lived, but they have prophefied alfo of men in time to come. And *you do well* (faid S. *Peter*) *in that ye take heed to the words of the Prophefie, fo that ye firft know this; that no Prophefie in the Scripture cometh of any mans own refolution.* No Prophefie in Scripture cometh of any mans own refolution. For all prophefie, which is in Scripture, came by the fecret infpiration of God. But there are prophefies which are no Scripture; yea, there are prophefies againft the Scripture: my brethren, beware of fuch Prophefies, and take heed you heed them not. Remember the things that were fpoken of before; but fpoken of before by the Apoftles of our Lord and Saviour Jefus Chrift. Take heed to Prophefies, but to prophefies which are in Scripture: For both the manner and matter of thofe prophefies do fhew plainly, that they are of God.

Of the fpirit of prophefie received from God himfelf.

3. Touching the manner, how men by the fpirit of prophecy in holy Scripture have fpoken and written of things to come, we muft underftand that as the knowledge of that they fpake, fo likewife the utterance of that they knew, came not by thefe ufual and ordinary means, whereby we are brought to underftand the myfteries of our falvation, and are wont to inftruct others in the fame. For whatfoever we know, we have it by the hands and Miniftry of men, which lead us along like children, from a letter to a fyllable, from a fyllable to a word, from a word to a line, from a line to a fentence, from a fentence to a fide, and fo turn over. But God himfelf was their inftructor, he himfelf taught them, partly by Dreams and vifions in the night, partly by Revelations in the day, taking them afide from amongft their brethren, and talking with them, as a man would talk with his neighbour in the way. Thus they became acquainted even with the fecret and hidden counfels of God. They faw things, which themfelves were not able to utter, they beheld that whereat men and Angels were aftonifhed. They underftood in the beginning, what fhould come to pafs in the laft days.

Of the Prophets manner of fpeech.

4. God, which lightned thus the eys of their underftanding, giving them knowledge by unufual and extraordinary means, did alfo miraculoufly himfelf frame and fafhion their words and writings, in fo muchthat a greater difference there feemeth not to be between the maner of their knowledg, then there is between the manner of their fpeech and ours. When we have conceived a thing in our hearts & throughly underftand it, as we think within our felves, ere we can utter in fuch fort that our brethren may receive inftruction or comfort at our mouthes, how great, howlong, how earneft meditation are we forced to ufe? And after much travail, and much pains, when we open our lips to fpeak of the wonderful works of God, our tongues do faulter within our mouthes, yea many times we difgrace the dreadful myfteries of our faith, and grieve the fpirit of our hearers by words unfavory, and unfeemly fpeeches. *Shall a wife man fill his belly with the Eaftern Wind*, faith *Eliphaz*, *fhall a wife man difpute with words not comely? or with talk that is not profitable?* Yet behold, even they that are wifeft amongft us living, compared with the Prophets, feem no otherwife to talk of God, then as if the children which are carried in armes, fhould fpeak of the greateft matters of ftate. They whofe words do moft fhew forth their wife underftanding and whofe lips do utter the pureft knowledge, fo long as they underftand and fpeak as men, are they not

Iob 15, 2, 3.

fain

fain sundry ways to excuse themselves? Sometimes acknowledging with the wise man, *Hardly can we discern the things that are on earth, and with great labour find we out the* Wis'd 9. 1. *things that are before us, who can then seek out the things that are in heaven:* Sometimes confessing with *Job* the righteous, in treating of things too wonderful for us, we have spoken we wist not what. Sometimes ending their talk as doth the History of the *Macchabees*, If we have done well, and as the cause required, it is that we desire, if we have spoken slenderly and barely, we have done what we could. For *God hath made my mouth like a sword*, saith *Esay*. And *we have received*, saith the Esay 49. 2. Apostle, *not the spirit of the World, but the spirit which is of God, that we might know the things which are given to us of God, which things also we speak, not in words, which mans wisdom teacheth, but which the holy Ghost doth teach.* This is that which the Prophets mean by those books written full within, and without; which books were so often delivered them to eat, not because God fed them with Ink and paper, but to teach us, that so oft as he imployed them in this heavenly work, they neither spake nor wrote any word of their own, but uttered syllable by syllable as the Spirit put it into their mouthes, no otherwise then the Harp or the Lute doth give a sound according to the discretion of his hands that holdeth and striketh it with skill. The difference is onely this: An Instrument, whether it be a Pipe or harp, maketh a distinction in the times and sounds, which distinction is well perceived of the hearer, the instrument it self understanding not what is piped or Harped. The Prophets and holy men of God not so. *I opened my mouth*, saith *Ezechiel*, and *God reached me a scroul,* Ezechiel; 3. *saying Son of man, cause thy belly to eat, and fill thy bowels with this I give thee, I eat it and it was sweet in my mouth as hony*, saith the Prophet. Yea sweeter, am perswaded, then either hony or the hony comb. For herein they were not like harps or Lutes, but they felt, they felt the power and strength of their own words. When they spake of our peace, every corner of their hearts, was filled with joy. When they prophecied of mournings, lamentations, and woes to fall upon us, they wept in the bitterness and indignation of spirit, the arm of the Lord being mighty and strong upon them.

5. On this manner were all the Prophesies of holy Scripture. Which Prophecies, although they contain nothing which is not profitable for our instruction, yet as one star differeth from another in glory, so every word of prophecy hath a treasure of matter in it, but all matters are not of like importance, as all treasures, are not of equal price. The chief and principal matter of prophecy is the promise of righteousness, peace, holiness, glory, victory, immortality, unto every soul which beleiveth that Jesus is Christ, of the *Jew* first, and of the *Gentile*. Now because the doctrine of Salvation to be looked for by Faith in him, who was in outward appearance as it had been a man forsaken of God, in him who was numbred judged, and condemned with the wicked; in him whom men did see buffeted on the face, scoft at by Souldiers, scourged by tormentors, hanged on the cross, peirced to the heart, in him whom the eyes of many witnesses did behold, when the anguish of his soul enforced him to roar as if his heart had rent in sunder, *O my God, my God, Why hast thou forsaken me?* I say, because the Doctrine of salvation by him, is a thing improbable to a natural man, that whether we preach it to the Gentile, or to the *Jew*, the one condemneth our faith as madness, the other as blasphemy, therefore to establish, and confirm the certainty of this saving truth in the hearts of men, the Lord together with their preachings, whom he sent immediately from himself to reveal these things unto the world, mingled prophecies of things, both Civil and Ecclesiastical, which were to come in every age from time to time, till the very last of the latter days, that by those things wherein we see dayly their words fulfilled and done, we might have strong consolation in the hope of things which are not seen, because they have revealed as well the one as the other. For when many things are spoken of before in Scripture, whereof we see first one thing accomplished, and then another, and so a third, perceive we not plainly, that God doth nothing else but lead us along by the hand, till he have setled us upon the rock of an assured hope, that no one jot or tittle of his Word shall pass till all be fulfilled? It is not therefore said in vain, that these godless wicked ones *were spoken of before.*

6. But by whom? By them whose words if men or Angels from heaven gainsay they are accursed; by them, whom whosoever despiseth, despiseth not them, but
me,

A natural man
perceiveth not
heavenly
things.

Iam. 2.

Acts 13.

Acts 17.

me, saith Christ. If any man therefore doth love the Lord Jesus (and wo worth him that loveth not the Lord Jesus!) hereby we may know that he loveth him indeed, if he despise not the things that are spoken of by his Apostles ; whom many have despised even for the baseness and simpleness of their persons. For it is the property of fleshly and carnal men to honour, and dishonor, credit, and discredit the words and deeds of every man, according to that he wanteth or hath without. If a man with gorgeous apparel come amongst us , although he be a Thief or a Murtherer (for there are Theeves and Murtherers in gorgeous apparel) be his heart whatsoever , if his Coat be of Purple or Velvet , or Tissue , every one riseth up, and all the reverent Solemnities we can use, are too little. But the man that serveth God, is contemned and despised amongst us for his Poverty. *Herod* speaketh in judgement , and the people cry out, *The voyce of God, and not of man*, *Paul* preacheth Christ, they term him a trifler. Hearken, beloved : hath not God chosen the poor of this World, that they should be rich in faith ? Hath he not chosen the refuse of the World to be heirs of his Kingdom, which he hath promised to them that love him? hath he not chosen the the off-scowrings of men to be Lights of the World, and the Apostles of Jesus Christ ? Men unlearned , yet how fully replenished with understanding ? few in number, yet how great in power ? contemptible in shew , yet in spirit how strong ? how wonderful ? *I would fain learn the mystery of the eternal generation of the Son of God* , saith *Hilary*. Whom shall I seek ? Shall I get me to the Schools of the *Grecians* ? Why ? I have read, *Ubi sapiens ? ubi Scriba ? ubi conquisitor hujus saeculi ?* These wise men in the world must needs be dumb in this , because they have rejected the wisdom of God. Shall I beseech the *Scribes* and interpreters of the Law , to become my teachers ? how can they know this , sith they are offended at the Crosse of Christ ? It is death for me to be ignorant of the unsearchable mystery of the Son of God : of which mystery notwithstanding I should have been ignorant, but that a poor Fisherman, unknown, unlearned, new come from his boat with his clothes wringing wet hath opened his mouth and taught me , *In the beginning was the Word, and the Word was with God, and the Word was God.* These poor silly creatures have made us rich in the knowledge of the mysteries of Christ.

7. Remember therefore that which is spoken of by the Apostles ; Whose words if the Children of this World do not regard, is it any marvaile ? they are the Apostles of our Lord Jesus; not of their Lord, but of ours. It is true which one hath said in a certain place, *Apostolicam fidem saeculi homo non capit* , A man sworn to the World , is not capable of that Faith which the Apostles do teach. What mean the Children of this World then to tread in the courts of our God ? What shall your bodys do at *Bethel* , whose hearts are at *Bethaven* ? the God of this World, whom ye serve, hath provided Apostles and teachers for you , *Chaldeans, Wizards, Soothsayers, Astrologers* , and such like : Hear them. Tell not us that ye will sacrifice to the Lord our God, if we will sacrifice to *Astaroth* or *Melcom* ; that ye will read our Scriptures, if we will listen to your Traditions ; that if ye may have a Mass by permission, we shall have a Communion with good leave and liking ; that ye will admit the things that are spoken of by the Apostles of our Lord Jesus, if your Lord and Master may have his ordinances observed, and his Statutes kept. *Solomon* took it (as he well might) for an evident proof , that she did not bear a motherly affection to her Child, which yeilded to have it cut in divers parts. He cannot love the Lord Jesus with his heart, which lendeth one ear to his Apostles, and another to false Apostles : which can brook to see a mingle-mangle of Religion and Superstition, Ministers and Massing Priests, Light and darkness , Truth and Error , Traditions, and Scriptures. No ; we have no Lord but Jesus ; no Doctrine but the Gospel ; no Teachers but his Apostles. Were it reason to require at the hands of an *English* Subject , obedience to the Laws and Edicts of the *Spaniard* ? I do marvel , that any man bearing the name of a Servant of the Servants of Jesus Christ , will go about to draw us from our Allegiance. We are his sworn Subjects ; it is not lawful for us to hear the things that are not told us by his Apostles. They have told us , that in the last days there shall be Mockers; therefore we beleive it; *Credimus quia legimus*, We are so perswaded, because we read it it must be so. If we did not read it, we would not teach it : *Non que libro legis non continentur, ea nec nosse debemus*, saith *Hilary* : Those things that are not written in the book of the Law, we ought not so much as to be acquainted with them.

We must not
halt between
two opinions.

them. *Remember the words which were spoken of before of the Apostles of our Lord Je-sus Christ.*

8. The third thing to be confidered in the defcription of thefe men of whom we fpeak, is the time, wherein they fhould be manifefted to the World. They to'd *Mockers in the* you, there fhould be mockers in the laft time. *Noah* at the commandement of God, *laft time.* built an Ark, and there were in it Beafts of all forts, clean and unclean. 'A Husbandman planteth a Vineyard, and looketh for Grapes, but when they come to the gathering, behold, together with Grapes there are found alfo wild Grapes. A rich man prepareth a great fupper, and biddeth many, but when he fitteth him down, he findeth amongft his friends here and there a man whom he knoweth not. This hath been the ftate of the Church fithence the beginning. God always hath mingled his Saints with faithlefs and godlefs perfons; as it were the clean with the unclean, Grapes with fowre grapes, his friends and children with aliens and ftrangers Marvel not then, if in the laft days alfo ye fee the men, with whom you live and walk arm in arm, laugh at your Religion, and blafpheme that glorious name, whereof you are called: Thus it was in the days of the Patriarks and Prophets; and are we better then our Fathers? Albeit we fuppofe, that the bleffed Apoftles, in forefhewing what manner of men were fet out for the laft days, meant to note a calamity fpecial and peculiar to the ages and Generations, which were to come: As if he fhould have faid; As God hath appointed a time of Seed for the Sower, and a time of Harveft for him that reapeth, as he hath given unto every herb and every tree his own fruit, and his own feafon, not the feafon nor the fruit of another (for no man looketh to gather figs in the Winter, becaufe the Summer is the feafon for them; nor Grapes of Thiftles, becaufe Grapes are the fruit of the Vine) fo the fame God hath appointed fundry for every Generation of them, other men for other times, and for the laft times the worft men, as may appear by their properties, which is the fourth point to be confidered of in this defcription.

9. They told you, that there fhould be *mockers.* He meaneth men that fhall ufe *Mockers.* Religion as a cloak, to put off, and on, as the weather ferveth; fuch as fhall with *Herod* hear the preaching of *John Baptift* to day, and to morrow condefcend to have him beheaded; or with the other *Herod* fay, they will worfhip Chrift, when they purpofe a maffacre in their hearts; kifs Chrift with *Judas* and betray Chrift with *Judas:* Thefe are Mockers. For *Ifhmael* the fon of *Hagar* laughed at *Ifaac,* which was heir of the promife; fo fhall thefe men laugh at you as the maddeft people under the Sun, if ye be like *Mofes,* choofing rather to fuffer afflifhion with the people of God, than to injoy the pleafures of fin for a feafon. And why? God hath not given them eyes to fee, nor hearts to conceive that exceeding recompence of your reward The promifes of falvation made to you are matters wherein they can take no pleafure, even as *Ifhmael* took no pleafure in that promife, wherein God had faid unto *Abraham, in Ifaac fhall thy feed be called*; becaufe the promife concerned not him, but *Ifaac*. They are termed for their impiety towards God, *mockers,* and for the impurity of their life and converfation, *walkers after their own ungodly lufts.* S. *Peter* in his fecond Epiftle and third Chapter, foundeth the very depth of their impiety: fhewing *firft,* how they fhall not fhame at the length to profefs themfelves prophane, and irreligious, by flat denying the Gofpel of Jefus Chrift, and deriding the fweet and comfortable promifes of his appearing: *fecondly,* that they fhall not be only deriders of all religion, but alfo difputers againft God, ufing Truth to fubvert the truth; yea Scriptures themfelves to difprove Scriptures. Being in this fort *mockers,* they muft needs be alfo followers of *their own ungodly lufts.* Being Atheifts in perfwafion, can they choofe but be beafts in converfation? For why remove they quite from them the fear of God? Why take they fuch paines to abandon and put out from their hearts all fenfe, all tafte, all feeling of Religion? but onely to this end and purpofe, that they may without inward remorfe and grudging of confcience give over themfelves to all uncleannefs. Surely the ftate of thefe men is more lamentable, then is the condition of Pagans and Turks. For at the bare beholding of Heaven and Earth, the Infidels heart by and by doth give *Mockers worfe* him, that there is an eternal, infinite, immortal, and ever-living God; whofe *then Pagans* hands have fafhioned and framed the world; he knoweth that every houfe *and Infidels.* is builded of fome man, though he fee not the man which built the houfe, and he confidereth, that it muft be God, which hath built and created all things;

L l l 　　　　　　　　　　　　　　　　　　　　　although

although becaule the number of his days be few , he could not see when God dif-
poled his works of old , when he caufed the light of his clouds firft to fhine , when
he laid the corner ftone of the earth , and fwadled it with bands of Water ar d darknefs , when he caufed the morning ftar to know his place , and made bars and doors
to fhut up the Sea within his houfe , faying , *Hitherto fhalt thou come , but no farther :*
he hath no eye-witnefs of thefe things. Yet the light of natural reafon hath put
this wifdom in his reins , and hath given his heart thus much underftanding. Bring
a Pagan to the Schools of the Prophets of God ; prophefie to an Infidel , rebuke
him , lay the judgements of God before him , make the fecret fins of his heart manifeft, and he fhall fall down and worfhip God. They that crucified the Lord of Glory,
were not fo far paft recovery , but that the Preaching of the Apoftles was able to
move their hearts and to bring them to this , *Men and brethren , what fhall we do ?*
Agrippa , that fate in judgement againft *Paul* for preaching , yeilded notwithftanding thus far unto him , *Almoft thou perfwadeft me to become a Chriftian.* Although the
Jews for want of knowledge haue not fubmitted themfelves to the righteoufnofs of
God ; yet I bear them record , faith the Apoftle ; *that they have a zeal.* The *Atheni-*

Rom. 10.

ans , a people having neither Zeal, nor knowledge , yet of them alfo the fame Apoftle beareth witnefs , *Ye men of Athens , I perceive ye are δεισιδαιμονεςεροι* , fome way
religious : but Mockers, walking after their own ungodly lufts , they have fmothered every fpark of that heavenly light , they have ftifled even their very natural underftanding. O Lord , thy mercy is over all thy works, thou faveft man and Beaft!
yet a happy cafe it had been for thefe men if they had neuer been born : and fo I leave
them.

10. S. *Jude* having his mind exercifed in the Doctrine of the Apoftles of Jefus
Chrift , concerning things to come in the laft time , became a man of a wife and ftaid
judgement. *Grieved* he was , to fee the departure of many , and their falling away

I udas ver fapi-
ens & criti ju-
dicii. . .

from the Faith , which before they did profefs : grieved , but not *difmayed.* With
the fimpler and weaker fort it was otherwife : Their countenance began by and by to
change , they were half in doubt they had deceived themfelves in giving credit to the
Gofpel of Jefus Chrift. S. *Jude* , to comfort and refrefh thofe filly babes , taketh
them up in his armes , and fheweth them the men at whom they were offended. Look
upon them that forfake this bleffed Profeffion wherein you ftand : they are now
before your eys ; view them , mark them , are they not carnal ? are they not like to
noyfome carrion caft out upon the Earth ? is there that Spirit in them which cryeth
Abba Father in your bofomes ? Why fhould any man be difcomforted ? Have you not
heard that there fhould be mockers in the laft time ? Thefe verily are they , that now
do feparate themfelves.

11. For your better underftanding , what this fevering and feparating of themfelves doth mean , we muft know , that the multitude of them which truely believe
(howfoever they be difperfed far and wide each from other) is all *one body* , whereof
the head is Chrift ; *one building*, whereof he is the corner Stone , in whom they as the
members of the body being knit , and as the ftones of the building , being coupled,
grow up to a man of perfect ftature , and rife to an holy Temple in the Lord. That
which linketh Chrift to us, is his meet mercy and love towards us. That which tyeth
us to him , is our faith in the promifed falvation revealed in the Word of truth. That
which uniteth and joyneth us amongft our felves , in fuch fort that we are now as if
we had but one heart and one foul , is our love. Who be inwardly in heart the lively members of this body, and the polifhed ftones of this building , coupled and joyned to Chrift , as flefh of his flefh , and bones of his bones , by the mutual bond of
his unfpeakable love towards them , and their unfained faith in him, thus linked and
faftned each to other by a fpiritual , fincere , and hearty affection of love , without any manner of fimulation ; who be Jews within , and what their names be; none
can tell , fave he whofe eys do behold the fecret difpofition of all mens hearts. We,
whofe eys are too dim to behold the inward man , muft leave the fecret judgement of
every fervant to his own Lord , accounting and ufing all men as brethren both neer
and dear unto us , fuppofing Chrift to love them tenderly , fo as they keep the profeffion of the Gofpel , and joyn in the outward communion of Saints. Whereof
the one doth warantize unto us their faith , the other their love, till they fall away,
and forfake either the one, or the other, or both; and then it is no injury to term them

as

as they are. When they separate themselves, they are ἀυτακατακειθι, not judged by us, but by their own doings. Men do separate themselves either by Heretie, Schism, or Apostasie. If they loose the bond of faith, which then they are justly supposed to do, when they frowardly oppugn any principal point of Christian Doctrine, this is to separate themselves by *Heresie*. If they break the bond of unity, whereby the body of the Church is coupled and knit in one, as they do which wilfully forsake all external communion with Saints in holy exercises purely and orderly established in the Church, this is to separate themselves by *Schism*. If they willingly cast off, and utterly forsake both profession of Christ, and communion with Christians, taking their leave of all Religion, this is to separate themselves by plain *Apostasie*. And S. *Jude*, to express the maner of their departure, which by *Apostasie* fell away from the faith of Christ, saith, *They separated themselves* ; noting thereby, that it was not constraint of others, which forced them to depart, it was not infirmity and weakness in themselves, it was not fear of persecution to come upon them, whereat their hearts did fail; it was not grief of torment, whereof they had tasted, and were not able any longer to endure them: No, they voluntarily did separate themselves with a fully settled, and altogether determined purpose never to name the Lord Jesus any more, nor to have any fellowship with his Saints, but to bend all their counsel, and all their strength, to raze out their memorial from amongst men.

Threefold Separation:
1. Heresie.
2. Schism,
3 Apostasie.

12. Now because that by such examples, not onely the hearts of Infidels were hardned against the truth, but the mindes of weak Brethren also much troubled, the Holy Ghost hath given sentence of these backsliders, that they were carnal men, and had not the Spirit of Christ Jesus, lest any man having an over-weening of their persons, should be overmuch amazed and offended at their fall. For simple men not able to discern their spirits, were brought by their Apostasie, thus to reason with themselves, If Christ be the Son of the living God, if he have the words of Eternal life, if he be able to bring salvation to all men that come unto him, what meaneth this Apostasie, and unconstrained departure? why do his servants so willingly forsake him? Babes, be not deceived, his servants forsake him not. They that separate themselves were amongst his servants, but if they had been of his servants, they had not separated themselves. They were amongst us, not of us, saith S. *John* ; and S. *Jude* proveth it, because they were carnal, and had not the Spirit. Will you judge of wheat by chaff, which the wind hath scattered from amongst it? Have the children no bread, because the dogs have not tasted it? Are Christians deceived of that salvation they look for, because they were denied the joys of the life to come which were no Christians? What if they seemed to be Pillars and principal Upholders of our Faith? What is that to us, which know that Angels have fallen from Heaven? Although if these men had been of us indeed (O the blessedness of Christian mans estate!) they had stood surer then the Angels that had never departed from their place. Whereas now we marvel not at their departure at all, neither are we prejudiced by their falling away ; because they were not of us, sith they are fleshly, and have not the Spirit. Children abide in the house for ever ; they are Bond-men, and Bond-women, which are cast out.

Infallible evidence in the faithful, that they are Gods Children,

13. It behoveth you therefore greatly every man to examine his own estate, and to try whether you be bond or free, children or no children. I have told you already, that we must beware we presume not to sit as Gods in judgement upon others, and rashly, as our conceit and fancy doth lead us so to determine of this man, he is sincere ; or of that man, he is an hypocrite, except by their falling away they make it manifest and known that they are. For who art thou that takest upon thee to judge another before the time? Judge thy self. God hath left us infallible evidence, whereby we may at any time give true and righteous sentence upon our selves. We cannot examine the hearts of other men, we may our own. That we have passed from death to life we know it, saith S. *John*, because we love our Brethren: *And know ye nat your own selves, how that Jesus Christ is in you, except ye be Reprobates ?* I trust, Beloved, we know that we are not Reprobates, because our spirit doth bear us record, that the faith of our Lord Jesus Christ is in us.

14. It is as easie a matter for the Spirit within you to tell whose ye are, as for the eyes of your body to judge where you sit, or in what place you stand. For what saith the Scripture ? *Ye which were in times past strangers and enemies, because your*

mindes

mindes were let on evil works, Chrift hath now reconciled in the body of his flesh through death, to make you holy, and unblameable, and without fault in his fight: If you continue grounded and eftablifhed in the faith, and be not moved away from the hope of the Gofpel, *Colof.* 1. And in the third to the *Coloffians*, Ye know, that of the Lord ye fhall receive the reward of that inheritance, for ye ferve the Lord Chrift. If we can make this account with our felves, I was in times paft dead in trefpafles and fins, I walked after the Prince that ruleth in the Ayr, and after the Spirit that worketh in the children of difobedience, but God, who is rich in mercy, through his great love, wherewith he loved me, even when I was dead, hath quickned me in Chrift. I was fierce, heady, proud, high-minded; but God hath made me like the childe that is newly weaned: I loved pleafures more then God, I followed greedily the joys of this prefent World; I efteemed him, that erected a Stage or Theatre, more then *Solomon*, which built a Temple to the Lord; the Harp, Viol, Timbrel, and Pipe, Men Singers, and Women fingers were at my feaft; it was my felicity to fee my children dance before me: I faid of every kinde of vanity, O how fweet art thou in my foul! All which things now are crucified to me, and I to them: Now I hate the pride of life, and pomp of this World; now I take as great delight in the way of thy teftimonies, O Lord, as in all riches; now I finde more joy of heart in my Lord and Saviour, then the worldly-minded man, when his Wheat and Oyl do much abound: Now I tafte nothing fweet, but the Bread which came down from Heaven, to give unto the World: Now mine eyes fee nothing, but Jefus rifing from the dead: Now my ear refufeth all kinde of melody, to hear the Song of them that have gotten Victory of the Beaft, and of his Image, and of his mark, and of the number of his Name, that ftand on the Sea of Glafs, having the Harps of God, and finging the Song of *Mofes* the fervant of God, and the Song of the Lamb, faying, Great and marvellous are thy works, Lord God Almighty, juft and true are thy ways, O King of Saints. Surely, if the Spirit have been thus effectual in the fecret work of our Regeneration unto newnefs of life; if we endeavour thus to frame our felves even, then we may fay boldly with the bleffed Apoftle in the tenth to the *Hebrews*, *We are not of them which withdraw our felves to perdition, but which follow faith to the confervation of the foul.* For they that fall away from the grace of God, and feparate themfelves unto perdition, they are fleshly and carnal, they have not Gods holy Spirit. But unto you, becaufe ye are Sons, God hath fent forth the Spirit of his Son into your hearts, to the end ye might know, that Chrift hath built you upon a Rock unmoveable; that he hath regiftred your names in the Book of life; that he hath bound himfelf in a fure and everlafting Covenant, to be your God, and the God of your children after you, that he hath fuffered as much, groaned as oft, prayed as heartily for you, as for *Peter*, *O Father, keep them in thy Name! O Righteous Father, the world hath not known thee, but I have known thee, and thefe have known that thou haft fent me, I have declared thy name unto them, and will declare it, that the love wherewith thou haft loved me, may be in them, and I in them.* The Lord of his infinite mercy give us hearts plentifully fraught with the treafure of this bleffed affurance of faith unto the end.

14. Here I muft advertife all men, that have the teftimony of Gods holy fear within their breafts, to confider how unkindely and injurioufly our own Countreymen and Brethren have dealt with us by the fpace of four and twenty years, from time to time, as if we were the men of whom S. *Jude* here fpeaket 1; never ceafing to charge us, fome with Schifm, fome with Herefie, fome with plain and manifeft Apoftane, as it we had clean feparated our felves from Chrift, utterly forfaken God, quite abjured Heaven, and trampled all Truth and all Religion under our feet. Againft this third fort, God himfelf fhall plead our Caufe in that day, when they fhall anfwer us for thele words, not we them. To others, by whom we are accufed for Schifm and Herefie, we have often made our reafonable, and in the fight of God, I truft, allowable anfwers. For in the way which they call *Herefie*, we worfhip the God of our Fathers, believing all things which are written in the Law and the Prophets. That which they call *Schifm*, we know to be our reafonable fervice unto God, and obedience to his voyce, which cryeth fhrill in our ears, *Go out of Babylon my people, that you be not partakers of her fins, and that ye receive not of her plagues.* And therefore when they rife up againft us, having no quarrel but this, we need not to feek any

The Papifts falfly accufe us of Herefie and Apoftafie.

Acts 15.

Apoc. 18.

any farther for our Apology, then the words of *Abiah* to *Jeroboam* and his Army, **2 Chron. 13.** *O Jeroboam and Israel, hear you me, ought you not to know, that the Lord God of Israel hath given the Kingdom over Israel to David for ever, even to him and to his sons, by a Covenant of Salt?* that is to say, an everlasting Covenant. Jesuits and Papists, hear ye me, ought you not to know, that the Father hath given all power unto the Son, and hath made him the onely Head over his Church, wherein he dwelleth as an Husbandman in the midst of his Vine, manuring it with the sweat of his own brows, not letting it forth to others? For as it is in the *Canticles*, *Solomon* had a Vineyard in *Baalhamon*, he gave the Vineyard unto Keepers, every one bringing for the fruit thereof a thousand pieces of Silver; but my Vineyard, which is mine, is before me, saith Christ. It is true, this is meant of the mystical Head set over the body, which is not seen. But as he hath reserved the mystical Administration of the Church invisible unto himself, so he hath committed the mystical Government of Congregations visible to the sons of *David*, by the same Covenant; whose sons they are, in the governing of the Flock of Christ, whomsoever the Holy Ghost hath set over them, to go before them, and to lead them in several Pastures, one in this Congregation, another in that; as it is written, *Take heed unto your selves, and to all the Flock, whereof the Holy Ghost hath made you Overseers, to feed the Church of God, which he hath purchased with his own blood.* Neither will ever any Pope or Papist, under the Cope of Heaven, be able to prove Romish Bishops usurped Supremacy over all Churches, by any one word of the Covenant of Salt, which is the Scripture. For the children in our streets do now laugh them to scorn, when they force, *Thou art Peter*, to this purpose. The Pope hath no more reason to draw the Charter of his universal Authority from hence, then the Brethren had to gather by the words of Christ, in the last of S. *John*, that the Disciple, whom Jesus loved, should not dye. *If I will that he tarry till I come, what is that to thee?* saith Christ. Straitways a report was raised amongst the Brethren, that this Disciple should not dye. Yet Jesus said not to him, He shall not dye; but, *If I will that he tarry till I come, what is that to thee?* Christ hath said in the sixteenth of S. *Matthews* Gospel, to *Simon* the Son of *Jonas*, I say to thee, thou art *Peter*. Hence an opinion is held in the World, That the Pope is universal Head of all Churches. Yet Jesus said not, The Pope is universal Head of all Churches; but, *Tu es Petrus*, Thou art *Peter*. Howbeit, as *Jeroboam*, the son of *Nebat*, the servant of *Solomon*, rose up and rebelled against his Lord, and there were gathered unto him vain men and wicked, which made themselves strong against *Roboam*, the son of *Solomon*, because *Roboam* was but a childe, and tender-hearted, and could not resist them: So the Son of Perdition, and Man of Sin, being not able to brook the words of our Lord and Saviour Jesus Christ, which forbad his Disciples to be like Princes of Nations, *They bear Rule that are called Gratious, it shall not be so with you*, hath risen up and rebelled against his Lord, and to strengthen his arm, he hath crept into the houses almost of all the Noblest Families round about him, and taken their children from the Cradle, to be his Cardinals: He hath fawned upon the Kings and Princes of the Earth, and by Spiritual Cozenage hath made them sell their lawful Authority and Jurisdiction, for Titles of *Catholicus*, *Christianissimus*, *Defensor fidei*, and such like: He hath proclaimed sale of Pardons, to inveagle the ignorant; built Seminaries to allure young men, desirous of Learning; erected Stews, to gather the dissolute unto him. This is the rock whereupon his Church is built. Hereby the man is grown huge and strong, like the Cedars, which are not shaken with the wind, because Princes have been as children, over-tender hearted, and could not resist.

Hereby it is come to pass, as you see this day, that the Man of Sin doth war against us, not by men of a Language which we cannot understand, but he cometh as *Jeroboam* against *Judah*, and bringeth the fruit of our own bodies to eat us up, that the bowels of the childe may be made the Mothers grave, that hath caused no small number of our Brethren to forsake their Native Countrey, and with all disloyalty to cast off the yoke of their Allegiance to our dread Soveraign, whom God in mercy hath set over them; for whose safegard, if they carried not the hearts of Tygers in the bosomes of men, they would think the dearest blood in their bodies well spent. But now, saith *Abiah* to *Jeroboam*, Ye think ye be able to resist the Kingdom of Lord, which is in the hands of the Sons of *David*. Ye be a great multitude,

the

the golden Calves are with you , which *Jeroboam* made you for gods: Have ye not driven away the Priests of the Lord , the sons of *Aaron* , and the *Levites* , and have made you Priests like the people of Nations ? Whofoever commeth with a young Bullock, and seven Rams, the same may be a Priest of them that are no gods. If I should follow the Comparifon , and here uncover the Cup of thofe deadly and ugly Abominations wherewith this *Jeroboam* , of whom we fpeak, hath made the Earth fo drunk, that it hath reeled under us , I know , your godly hearts would loath to fee them. For my own part , I delight not to rake in fuch filth, I had rather take a garment upon my fhoulders and go with my face from them , to cover them. The Lord open their eys , and caufe them , if it be poffible , at the length to fee, how they are wretched , and miferable, and poor, and blind, and naked ! Put it , O Lord in their hearts, to feek white Rayment , and to cover them felves , that their filthy nakednefs may no longer appear! For, beloved in Chrift , we bow our knees , and lift up our hands to heaven in our Chambers fecretly, and openly in our Churches we pray heartily and hourly , even for them alfo : though the Pope hath given out as a Judge , in a folemn declaratory Sentence of *Excommunication* againft this Land , That our gracious Lady hath quite abolifhed *Prayers* within her Rea'm; and his Scholers, whom he hath taken from the midft of us, have in their publifhed Writings charged us not onely not to have any holy Affemblies unto the Lord for Prayer , but to hold a common School of Sin and flattery ; to hold Sacriledge to be Gods Service ; Unfaithfulnefs, and breach of promife to God , to give it to a ftrumpet, to be a Vertue ; to abandon Fafting ; to abhor confeffion ; to miflike with Penance ; to like well of Ufury ; to charge none with reftitution ; to find no good before God in fingle life ; nor in no well-working; that all men, as they fall to us , are much worfe, and more, than afore, corrupted. I do not add one word, or fyllable, unto that which Mr. *Briftow*, a man both born and fworn amongft us , hath taught his hand to deliver to the view of all. I appeal to the confcience of every foul , that hath been truly converted by us, Whether his heart were never raifed up to God by our Preaching ; whether the words of our exhortation never wrung any tear of a penitent heart from his eys ; whether his foul never reaped any joy, and comfort, any confolation in Chrift Jefus by our Sacraments, and Prayers and Pfalmes, and Thankfgiving ; whether he were never bettered, but always worfed by us.

O merciful God! If Heaven and Earth in this cafe do not witnefs with us, and againft them , let us be razed out from the land of the living ! Let the Earth on which we ftand , fwallow us quick, as it hath done *Corah, Dathan*, and *Abiram*! But if we belong unto the Lord our God, and have not forfaken him : if our Priefts, the fons of *Aaron*, Minifter unto the Lord, and the Levites in their Office : if we offer unto the Lord every morning and every evening the burnt Offerings, and fweet incenfe of Prayers, and thankf-givings; if the Bread be fet in order upon the pure Table, and the Candleftick of Gold, with the Lamps theof, burn every morning; that is to fay , if amongft us Gods blefled Sacraments be duely adminiftred, his holy Word fincerely and daily preached ; if we keep the Watch of the Lord our God, and if ye have forfaken him: then doubt ye not, this God is with us as a Captain, his Priefts with founding Trumpets muft cry alarme againft you ; *O ye children of Ifrael , fight not againft the Lord God of your Fathers, for ye fhall not profper.*

2 Chr. cap. 13.

Verfe 12.

THE

THE SECOND
SERMON.

JUDE, VERSE, 17, 18, 19, 20, 21.

But ye, beloved, remember the words which were spoken of before of the Apostles of our Lord Jesus Christ,

How that they told you, that there should be mockers in the last time, which should walk after their own ungodly lusts.

These are makers of Sects, fleshly, having not the Spirit.

But ye, beloved, edifie your selves in your most holy faith, praying in the holy Ghost.

And keep your selves in the love of God, looking for the mercy of our Lord Jesus Christ, unto eternal life.

Aving otherwhere spoken of the words of Saint *Jude* going next before, concerning *Mockers*, which should come in the last time, and backsliders, which even then should fal away from the faith of our Lord and Saviour Jesus Christ; I am now by the aid of Almighty God, and through the assistance of his good Spirit, to lay before you the words of Exhortation, which I have read.

2. Wherein first of all, whosoever hath an eye to see, let him open it, and he shall well perceive, how careful the Lord is for his children, how desirous to see them profit and grow up to a manly stature in Christ, how loth to have them any way mis-led, either by examples of the wicked, or by inticements of the world, and by provocation of the flesh, or by any other means forcible to deceive them, and likely to estrange their hearts from God. For God is not at that point with us that he careth not whether we sink or swim. No, he hath written our names in the Palme of his hand, in the Signet upon his finger are we graven, in sentences not only of Mercy, but of Judgement also, we are remembred. He never denounceth Judgements against the wicked, but he maketh some *Proviso* for his Children, as it were for some certain priviledged persons, *Touch not mine annointed, do my Prophets no harm, hurt not the Earth, nor the Sea, nor the Trees, till we have sealed the servants of God in their foreheads.* He never speaketh to godless men, but he adjoyneth words of comfort, or admonition, or exhortation, whereby we are moved to rest and settle our hearts on him. In the second to *Timothy*, the third Chapter, *Evil men* (saith the Apostle) *and deceivers shall wax worse, deceiving, and being deceived. But continue thou in the things which thou hast learned.* And in the first to *Timothy* the sixt Chapter, *Some men lusting after money, have erred from the faith, and pierced themselves thorow with many sorrows: But thou, O man of God, flie these things, and follow after righteousness, godliness, faith, love, patience, meekness.* In the second to the *Thessalonians*, the second Chapter, *they have not received the love of the truth, that they might be saved, God shall send them strong delusions, that*

they

they may be'eive lies. But we ought to give thanks alway to God for you, brethren, beloved of the Lord, because God hath from the beginning chosen you to salvation, through sanctification of the Spirit, and faith in the Truth. And in this Epistle of S. Jude; There shall come mockers in the last time, walking after their own ungodly lusts. But, beloved, edifie ye your selves in your most holy faith.

3. These sweet Exhortations, which God putteth every where in the mouthes of the Prophets and Apostles of Jesus Christ, are evident tokens, that God sitteth not in Heaven careless and unmindful of our estate. Can a mother forget her child? Surely, a Mother will hardly forget her child. But if a Mother be haply found unnatural, and do forget the fruit of her own Womb, yet Gods judgements shew plainly, that he cannot forget the man whose heart he hath framed and fashioned a new, in simplicity and truth to serve and fear him. For when the wickedness of man was so great, and the earth so filled with cruelties, that it could not stand with the righteousness of God any longer to forbear, wrathful sentences brake out from him, like Wine from a vessel that hath no vent: *My Spirit* (saith he) *can struggle aud strive no longer,* Gen. 6 3 & 3. *an end of all flesh is come before me.* Yet then did *Noah* find grace in the eys of the Lord, Gen 6 8. & 8. *I will establish my Covenant with thee* (saith God) *thou shalt go into the Ark, thou, and thy sons, and thy wife, and thy sons wives with thee.*

4. Do we not see what shift God doth make for *Lot,* and for his family, in the 19. of *Genesis,* lest the fiery destruction of the wicked should overtake him? Over-night the Angels make enquiry, what sons and daughters, or sons in law, what wealth and Gen. 19. 12. substance he had. They charge him to cary out all, *Whatsoever thou hast in the City, bring it out.* God seemeth to stand in a kind of fear, lest some thing or other would be left behind. And his will was, that nothing of that which he had, not an hoof of any beast, not a thread of any garment, should be singed with that fire. In the morn-Gen. 19 15 ing the Angels fail not to call him up, and to hasten him forward, *Arise, take thy wife and thy daughters which are here, that they be not destroyed in the punishment of the City.* The Angels having spoken again and again, *Lot* for all this lingereth out the time still, till at Verse 16. the length they were forced to take *both him, and his wife and his daughters by the armes,* (*the Lord being merciful unto him*) and to carry them forth, & set them without the City.

5. Was there ever any father thus careful to save his child from the flame? A man would think, that now being spoken unto to escape for his life, and not to look behind him, nor to tarry in the plain, but to hasten to the mountain, and there to save himself, he should do it gladly. Yet behold, now he is so far off from a cheerful and willing heart to do whatsoever is commanded him for his own weal, that he beginneth to reason the matter, as if God had mistaken one place for another, sending him to the Hill, when salvation was in the City. *Not so, my Lord, I beseech thee; Behold, thy servant hath found grace in thy sight, and thou hast magnified thy mercy which thou hast shewed unto me in saving my life. I cannot escape in the Mountain, lest some evil take me and I die. Here is a City hard by, a small thing; O, let me escape thither (is it not a small thing?) and my soul shall live.* Well, God is contented to yeild to any conditions, *Behold, I have received thy request concerning this thing also, I will spare this City for which thou hast spoken; hast thee; save thee there; For I can do nothing till thou come thither.*

6. He could do nothing! Not because of the weakness of his strength (for who is like unto the Lord in power?) but because of the greatness of his mercy, which would not suffer him to lift up his arm against that City, nor to pour out his wrath upon that place where his righteous servant had a fancy to remain, and a desire to dwell. O the depth of the riches of the mercy and love of God! God is afraid to offend us which are not afraid to displease him! God can do nothing ti'l he have saved us, which can find in our hearts rather to do any thing then to serve him. It contenteth him not to exempt us, when the pit is digged for the wicked; to comfort us at every mention which is made of reprobates and godless men; to save us as the apple of his own eye, when fire cometh down from heaven to consume the inhabitants of the earth; except every Prophet; and every Apostle; and every servant whom he sendeth forth, do come loaden with these and the like exhortations, *O beloved, edifie your selves in your most holy faith; Give your selves to prayer in the Spirit, keep your selves in the love of God; Look for the mercy of our Lord Jesus Christ unto eternall life.*

7. *Edifie your selves.* The speech is borrowed from material builders, and must be spiritually understood. It appeareth in the sixt of St. *Johns* Gospel by the

Jews,

Jews, that their mouthes did water too much for bodily food, *Our Fathers*, say they, *did eat Manna in the Defart, as it is written, He gave them bread from Heaven to eat ; Lord, evermore give us of this bread!* Our Saviour, to turn their appetite another way, maketh them this answer, *I am the bread of life ; he, that cometh to me, fhall not hunger , and he that believeth in me, fhall never thirft.*

8. An ufual practice it is of Satan, to caft heaps of worldly baggage in our way, that whilft we defire to heap up gold as duft, we may be brought at length to efteem vilely that fpiritual blifs. Chrift, in *Matth. 6.* to correct this evil affection, putteth us in minde to lay up treafure for our felves in Heaven. The Apoftle, 1 *Tim.* Chap. 3. mifliking the vanity of thofe Women which attired themfelves more coftly then befeemed the Heavenly calling of fuch as profeffed the fear of God, willeth them to cloath themfelves with fhamefaftnefs and modefty, and to put on the apparel of good works. *Taliter pigmentata, Deum habebitis amatorem,* faith *Tertullian.* Put on on Righteoufnefs as a garment , inftead of Civit, have Faith, which may caufe a favour of life to iffue from you, and God fhall be enamoured, he fhall be ravifhed with your beauty. Thefe are the ornaments, and bracelets, and jewels which inflame the love of Chrift, and fet his heart on fire upon his Spoufe. We fee how he breaketh out in the *Canticles* at the beholding of this attire, *How fair art thou, and how pleafant art thou, O my Love, in thefe pleafures!*

9. And perhaps S. *Jude* exhorteth us here not to build our houfes, but our felves ; forefeeing by the Spirit of the Almighty, which was with him, that there fhould be men in the laft days like to thofe in the fift, which fhould encourage and ftir up each other to make Brick, and to burn it in the fire, to build Houfes huge as Cities, and Towers as high as Heaven, thereby to get them a name upon Earth ; men that fhould turn out the poor, and the fatherlefs, and the widow, to build places of reft for Dogs and Swine in their rooms ; men that fhould lay Houfes of Prayer even with the ground, and make them ftables where Gods people have worfhipped before the Lord. Surely this is a vanity of all vanities, and it is much amongft men , a fpecial ficknefs of this age. What it fhould mean, I know not, except God have fet them on work to provide fewel againft that day when the Lord Jefus fhall fhew himfelf from Heaven with his mighty Angels in flaming fire. What good cometh unto the owners of thefe things, faith *Solomon,* but onely the beholding thereof with their eyes ? *Martha, Martha, thou bufieft thy felf about many things, One thing is neceffary.* Ye are too bufie, my Brethren, with Timber and Brick ; they have chofen the better part, they have taken a better courfe that build themfelves. *Ye are the Temples of the living God,* as God hath faid, *I will dwell in them, and will walk in them, and they fhall be my people, and I will be their God.* *Ecclef. 5.*

10. Which of you will gladly remain, or abide in a mifhapen, a ruinous, or a broken houfe ? And fhall we fuffer fin and vanity to drop in at our eyes, and at our ears, and at every corner of our bodies, and of our fouls, knowing that we are the Temples of the Holy Ghoft ? Which of you receiveth a Gueft whom he honoureth, or whom he loveth, and doth not fweep his Chamber againft his coming ? And fhall we fuffer the Chamber of our Hearts and Confciences to lie full of vomiting , full of filth, full of garbige, knowing that Chrift hath faid, *I and my Father will come and dwell with you ?* Is it meet for your Oxen to lie in Parlours, and your felves to lodge in Cribs ? Or is it feemly for your felves to dwell in your feiled Houfes, and the Houfe of the Almighty to lie wafte, whofe Houfe ye are your felves ; Do not our eyes behold, how God every day overtaketh the wicked in their journeys, how fuddenly they pop down into the pit ? how Gods judgements for their crimes come fo fwiftly upon them, that they have not the leifure to cry, Alas ? how their life is cut off like a thred in a moment ? how they pafs like a fhadow ? how they open their mouthes to fpeak, and God taketh them even in the midft of a vain or an idle word ? And dare we for all this lie down, take our reft, eat our meat fecurely and carelefly in the midft of fo great and fo many ruines ? Bleffed and praifed for, ever of the Lords and ever be his Name, who perceiving of how fenflefs and heavy metal we are Supper, made, hath inftituted in his CHURCH a Spiritual Supper, and an Holy Communion, to be Celebrated often, That we might thereby be occafioned often to examine thefe Buildings of ours, in what cafe they ftand. For fith God doth not dwell in Temples which are unclean , fith a Shrine cannot be a Sanctuary *The Sacrament of the Lords Supper.*

M m m unto

unto him; and this Supper is received as a seal unto us, that we are his House and his Sanctuary; that his Christ is as truly united to me, and I to him, as my arm is united and knit unto my shoulder; that he dwelleth in me as verily, as the elements of Bread and Wine abide within me; which perswasion, by receiving these dreadful mysteries, we profess our selves to have a due comfort, if truly; and if in hypocrisie, then wo worth us. Therefore ere we put forth our hands to take this blessed Sacrament, we are charged to examine and to try our hearts, whether God be in us of a truth or no: and if by faith and love unfeigned we be found the Temples of the Holy Ghost, then to judge, whether we have had such regard every one to our building, that the Spirit which dwelleth in us hath no way been vexed, molested and grieved: or if it have, as no doubt sometimes it hath by incredulity, sometimes by breach of charity, sometimes by want of zeal, sometimes by spots of life, even in the best and most perfect amongst us;(for who can say his heart is clean?)O then to fly unto God by unfeigned repentance, to fall down before him in the humility of our souls, begging of him whatsoever is needful to repair our decays, before we fall into that desolation whereof the Prophet speaketh, saying, *Thy breach is great like the Sea, who can heal thee?*

Lam.2.13.

11. Receiving the Sacrament of the Supper of the Lord after this sort (you that are Spiritual, judge what I speak) is not all other Wine like the Water of *Marah*, being compared to the Cup, which we bless? Is not *Manna* like to gall, and our bread like to *Manna?* Is there not a taste, a taste of Christ Jesus, in the heart of him that eateth? Doth not he which drinketh, behold plainly in this cup, that his soul is bathed in the blood of the Lamb? O beloved in our Lord and Saviour Jesus Christ, if ye will taste how sweet the Lord is, if ye will receive the King of glory, *Build your selves*.

12. *Young men,* I speak this to you; for ye are his house, because by faith ye are Conquerers over Satan, and have overcome that evil. *Fathers,* I speak it also to you; ye are his house, because ye have known him, which is from the beginning. Sweet *Babes,* I speak it even to you also; ye are his house, because your sins are forgiven you for his names sake. *Matrons* and *Sisters,* I may not hold it from you; ye are also the Lords building; and as S. *Peter* speaketh, *heirs of the grace of life as well as we.* Though it be forbidden you to open your mouthes in publique Assemblies, yet ye must be inquisitive in things concerning this building, which is of God, with your husbands and friends at home; not as *Dalilah* with *Sampson,* but as *Sara* with *Abraham,* whose daughters ye are, whilst ye do well, and build your selves.

13. Having spoken thus far of the Exhortation, as whereby we are called upon to edifie and build our selves; it remaineth now, that we consider the thing prescribed, namely, wherein we must be built. This prescription standeth also upon two points, the *thing* prescribed, and the *adjuncts* of the *thing.* And that is our most pure and holy *Faith.*

14. The thing prescribed is *Faith.* For as in a chain, which is made of many links, if you pull the first, you draw the rest; and as in a Ladder of many staves, if you take away the lowest, all hope of ascending to the highest will be removed: So, because all the Precepts and Promises in the Law and in the Gospel do hang upon this; Believe; and because the last of the graces of God doth so follow the first, that he glorifieth none, but whom he hath justified, nor justifieth any, but whom he hath called to a true, effectual, and lively faith in Christ Jesus; therefore S. *Jude* exhorting us to *build our selves,* mentioneth here expresly onely faith, as the thing wherein we must be edified, for that faith is the ground and the glory of all the welfare of this building.

15. Ye are not *strangers and forreigners, but Citizens with the Saints, and of the houshold of God* (saith the Apostle) *and are built upon the foundation of the Prophets and Apostles, Jesus Christ himself being the chief corner Stone, in whom all the building being coupled together, groweth unto an holy Temple in the Lord, in whom ye also are built together to be the habitation of God by the Spirit.* And we are the habitation of God by the Spirit, if we believe; for it is written, *Whosoever confesseth that Jesus is the Son of God, in him God dwelleth, and he in God.* The strength of this habitation is great, it prevaileth against Satan, it conquereth sin, it hath Death in derision; neither Principalities nor Powers can throw it down; it leadeth the World captive, and bringeth every enemy, that riseth up against it, to confusion and shame, and all by faith; for this is the victory that overcometh the World, even our faith. Who is it that overcometh the World, but he which believeth that Jesus is the Son of God?

Ephes.4.

1 John 4. & 5.

16. The strength of every Building, which is of God, standeth not in any mans arms

or

or legs; it is onely in our faith, as the valour of *Sampson* lay onely in his hair. This is the reason, why we are so earnestly called upon to *edifie our selves in faith*. Not as if this bare action of our mindes, whereby we believe the Gospel of Christ, were able in it self, as of it self, to make us unconquerable, and invinceable, like stones, which abide in the building for ever, and fall not out. No, it is not the worthiness of our believing, it is the vertue of him in whom we believe, by which we stand sure, as houses that are builded upon a Rock. He is a wise man which hath builded his house upon a Rock; for he hath chosen a good foundation, and no doubt his house will stand; but how shall it stand? Verily, by the strength of the Rock which beareth it, and by nothing else. Our Fathers, whom God delivered out of the Land of *Egypt*, were a people that had no Peers amongst the Nations of the Earth, because they were built by faith upon the Rock, which Rock is Christ. *And the Rock* (saith the Apostle, in the first to the *Corinthians*, the tenth Chapter) *did follow them*. Whereby we learn not onely this, that being built by faith on Christ, as on a Rock, and grafted into him as in an Olive, we receive all our strength and fatness from him; but also, that this strength and fatness of ours ought to be no cause why we should be high-minded, and not work out our salvation with a reverent trembling, and holy fear. For if thou boasteth thy self of thy faith, know this, That Christ chose his Apostles, his Apostles chose not him; that Israel followed not the Rock, but the Rock followed Israel; and that thou bearest not the Root, but the Root thee. So that every heart must thus think, and every tongue must thus speak, *Not unto us, O Lord, not unto us*, nor unto any thing which is within us, but unto thy name onely, onely to thy Name belongeth all the praise of all the Treasures and Riches of every Temple which is of God. This excludeth all boasting and vaunting of our faith.

Mat. 7.

Rom. 11.

17. But this must not make us careless to edifie our selves in Faith. It is the Lord that delivereth mens souls from death, but not except they put their trust in his mercy. It is God that hath given us eternal life, but no otherwise then thus, If we believe in the Name of the Son of God; for he that hath not the Son of God, hath not life. It was the Spirit of the Lord which came upon *Sampson*, and made him strong to tear a Lyon, as a man would rend a Kid; but his strength forsook him, and he became like other men, when the Razor had touched his head. It is the power of God whereby the faithful have subdued Kingdoms, wrought Righteousness, obtained the promises, stopped the mouthes of Lyons, quenched the violence of fire, escaped the edge of the sword: But take away their faith, and doth not their strength forsake them? are they not like unto other men?

1 John 5.

18. If ye desire yet farther to know how necessary and needful it is, that we edifie and build up our selves in faith, mark the words of the blessed Apostles, *Without faith it is impossible to please God*. If I offer unto God all the Sheep and Oxen that are in the World, if all the Temples that were builded since the days of *Adam* till this hour, were of my foundation; if I break my very heart with calling upon God, and wear out my tongue with preaching; if I sacrifice my body and my soul unto him, *and have no faith*, all this availeth nothing. *Without faith it is impossible to please God*. Our Lord and Saviour therefore being asked in the sixth of S. *Johns* Gospel, *What shall we do that we might work the works of God?* maketh answer, *This is the work of God, that ye believe in him whom he hath sent*.

No pleasing of God without faith.

19. That no work of ours, no building of our selves in any thing can be available or profitable unto us, except we be edified and built in faith: What need we to seek about for long proof? Look upon *Israel*, once the very chosen and peculiar of God, to whom the adoption of the faithful, and the glory of Cherubims, and the Covenants of mercy, and the Law of *Moses*, and the service of God, and the promises of Christ were made impropriate, who not onely were the off-spring of *Abraham*, father unto all them which do believe, but Christ their off-spring, which is God to be blessed for evermore.

20. Consider this people, and learn what it is to *build your selves in faith*. They were the Lords Vine: He brought it out of *Egypt*, he threw out the Heathen from their places, that it might be planted; he made room for it, and caused it to take root, till it had filled the earth; the mountains were covered with the shadow of it, and the boughs thereof were as the goodly Cedars; she stretched out her branches unto the Sea, and her boughs unto the River. But when God having sent both his Servants and his Son to visit this Vine, they neither spared the one,

not

nor received the other, but ſtoned the Prophets, and crucified the Lord of glory which came unto them; then began the curſe of God to come upon them, even the curſe whereof the Prophet *David* hath ſpoken, ſaying, *Let their table be made a ſnare, and a net, and a ſtumbling black, even for a recompence unto them: let their eyes be darkned, that they do not ſee, bow down their backs for ever,* keep them down. And ſithence the hour that the meaſure of their infidelity was firſt made up, they have been ſpoiled with wars, eaten up with plagues, ſpent with hunger and famine; they wander from place to place, and are become the moſt baſe and contemptible people that are under the Sun. *Ephraim,* which before was a terrour unto Nations, and they trembled at his voyce, is now by infidelity ſo vile, that he ſeemeth as a thing caſt out to be trampled under mens feet. In the midſt of theſe deſolations they cry, *Return, we beſeech thee, O God of hoſts, look down from heaven, behold and viſit this Vine:* but their very prayers are turned into ſin, and their crys are no better then the lowing of beaſts before him. *Well,* ſaith the Apoſtle, *by their unbelief they are broken off, and thou doſt ſtand by thy Faith: Behold therefore the bountifulneſs, and ſeverity of God; towards them ſeverity, becauſe they have fallen; bountifulneſs towards thee, if thou continue in his bountifulneſs, or elſe thou ſhalt be cut off.* If they forſake their unbelief and be grafted in again, and we at any time for the hardneſs of our hearts be broken off, it will be at ſuch a judgement as will amaze all the powers and principalities which are above. Who hath ſearched the counſel of God concerning this ſecret? And who doth not ſee that *Infidelity* doth threaten *Lo-ammi* unto the Gentiles, as it hath brought *Lo-ruchama* upon the Jews? It may be that theſe words ſeem dark unto you. But the words of the Apoſtle in the eleventh to the *Romans,* are plain enough, *If God have not ſpared the natural branches, take heed,* take heed leſt he ſpare not thee: Build thy ſelf in faith. Thus much of the thing which is preſcribed, and wherein we are exhorted to edifie our ſelves. Now conſider the *Condition* and *Properties* which are in this place annexed unto faith. The former of them (for there are but two) is this, *Edifie your ſelves in your faith.*

21. A ſtrange, and a ſtrong deluſion it is wherewith the *man of ſin* hath bewitched the world; a forcible ſpirit of errour it muſt needs be which hath brought men to ſuch a ſenſleſs and unreaſonable perſwaſion as this is, not onely that men cloathed with mortality and ſin, as we our ſelves are, can do God ſo much ſervice as ſhall be able to make a full and perfect ſatisfaction before the Tribunal ſeat of God for their own ſins; yea, a great deal more then is ſufficient for themſelves: but alſo that a man at the hands of a Biſhop or a Pope, for ſuch or ſuch a price, may buy the *over-plus* of other mens merits, purchaſe the fruits of other mens labours, and build his ſoul by another mans faith. Is not this man drowned in the gall of bitterneſs? Is his heart right in the ſight of God? Can he have any part or fellowſhip with *Peter,* and with the *Succeſſors of Peter,* which thinketh ſo vilely of building the precious Temples of the Holy Ghoſt? Let his money periſh with him, and he with it, becauſe he judgeth that the gift of God may be ſold for money.

22. But, beloved in the Lord, deceive not your ſelves, neither ſuffer ye your ſelves to be deceived: Ye can receive no more eaſe nor comfort for your ſouls by another mans faith, then warmth for your bodies by another mans cloaths; or ſuſtenance by the bread which another doth eat. The juſt ſhall life by his *own faith. Let a Saint,* yea a *Martyr,* content himſelf, *that he hath cleanſed himſelf of his own ſin,* ſaith *Tertullian:* No *Saint* or *Martyr* can cleanſe himſelf of his own ſins. But if ſo be a *Saint* or *Martyr* can cleanſe himſelf of his own ſins, it is ſufficient that he can do it for himſelf. Did ever any man by his death deliver another man from death, except onely the Son of God? He indeed was able to *Safe-conduct* a Thief from the Croſs to Paradiſe: for to this end he came, that being himſelf pure from ſin, he might obey for ſinners. Thou which thinkeſt to do the like, and ſuppoſeſt that thou canſt juſtifie another by thy Righteouſneſs, if thou be without ſin, then lay down thy life for thy brother; dye for me. But if thou be a ſinner, even as I am a ſinner, how can the Oyl of thy Lamp be ſufficient both for thee and for me? *Virgins* that are wiſe, get ye Oyl, while ye have day, into your own lamps: For out of all peradventure, others, though they would, can neither give nor ſell. Edifie your ſelves in your *own* moſt holy faith. And let this be obſerved for the firſt *property* of that wherein we ought to edifie our ſelves.

Pſal.69.
Rom.11.

Pſal.18.14.

Rom.11.20.

Verſe 21.

Hoſea 1.9 not my people.
Ver.6. no: obtaining mercy.

23. Our faith being such, is that indeed which S. *Iude* doth here term *Faith*; namely, a thing most *holy*. The reason is this, We are justified by *Faith* : For *Abraham* believed, and this was imputed unto him for Righteousness. Being justified, all our iniquities are covered; God beholdeth us in the righteousness which is imputed, and not in the sins which we have committed.

24. It is true, we are full of sin, both *original* and *actual*; whosoever denieth it, is a double sinner, for he is both a *sinner* and a *lyar*. To deny sin, is most plainly and clearly to prove it, because he that saith he hath no sin, lyeth, and by lying proveth that he hath sin.

25. But *imputation* of righteousness hath covered the sins of every soul which believeth; God by pardoning our sin, hath taken it away : So that now, although our transgressions be multiplied above the hairs of our heads, yet being justified, we are as free, and as clear, as if there were no one spot or stain of any uncleanness in us. For it is God that justifieth; *And who shall lay any thing to the charge of Gods chosen ?* saith the Apostle in *Rom.* 8.

26. Now sin being taken away, we are made the righteousness of God in Christ : for *David* speaking of this righteousness, saith, *Blessed is the man whose iniquities are forgiven.* No man is blessed, but in the righteousness of God. Every man whose sin is taken away, is blessed. Therefore, every man whose sin is covered, is made the righteousness of God in Christ. This righteousness doth make us to appear most holy, most pure, most unblameable before him.

27. This then is the sum of that which I say, Faith doth justifie, Justification washeth away sin; sin removed, we are cloathed with the righteousness which is of God; the righteousness of God maketh us most holy. Every of these I have proved by the testimony of Gods own mouth. Therefore I conclude, That faith is that which maketh us most holy, in consideration whereof, it is called in this place, *Our most holy faith.*

28. To make a wicked and a sinful man most holy through his believing, is more then to create a World of nothing. Our faith most holy ! Surely, *Solomon* could not shew the Queen of *Sheba* so much treasure in all his Kingdom, as is lapt up in these words. O that our hearts were stretched out like tents, and that the eyes of our understanding were as bright as the Sun, that we might throughly know the riches of the glorious inheritance of the Saints, and what is the exceeding greatness of his power towards us, whom he accepteth for pure, and most holy, through our believing. O that the Spirit of the Lord would give this doctrine entrance into the stony and brazen heart of the Jew, which followeth the Law of righteousness, but cannot attain unto the righteousness of the Law ! Wherefore, saith the Apostle, they seek righteousness, and not by faith; wherefore they stumble at Christ, they are bruised, shivered to pieces as a ship that hath run her self upon a Rock. O that God would cast down the eyes of the proud, and humble the souls of the high-minded ! that they might at the length abhor the garments of their own flesh, which cannot hide their nakedness, and put on the faith of Christ Jesus, as he did put it on which hath said, *Doubtless I think all things but loss, for the excellent knowledge sake of Christ Jesus my Lord, for whom I have counted all things loss, and do judge them to be dung, that I might win Christ, and might be found in him, not having mine own righteousness, which is of the Law; but that which is through the faith of Christ, even the righteousness which is of God through faith.* O that God would open the Ark of Mercy, wherein this Doctrine lieth, and set it wide before the eyes of poor afflicted Consciences, which flie up and down upon the water of their afflictions, and can see nothing but onely the gulf and deluge of their sins, wherein there is no place for them to rest their feet. The God of pity and compassion give you all strength and courage, every day, and every hour, and every moment, to build and edifie your selves in this most pure and holy faith. And thus much both of the thing prescribed in this Exhortation, and also of the properties of the thing, *Build your selves in your most holy faith.* I would come to the next branch, which is of Prayer, but I cannot lay this matter out of my hands, till I have added somewhat for the applying of it, both to others, and to our selves.

29. For your better understanding of matters contained in this Exhortation, *Build your selves,* you must note, that every Church and Congregation doth consist of a multitude of Believers, as every house is built of many stones. And although the

nature

nature of the myſtical body of the Church be ſuch, that it ſuffereth no diſtinction in the inviſible members, but whether it be *Paul* or *Apollos*, Prince or Prophet, he that is taught, or he that teacheth, all are equally Chriſts, and Chriſt is equally theirs: yet in the external adminiſtration of the Church of God, becauſe God is not the Author of Confuſion, but of peace, it is neceſſary that in every Congregation there be a diſtinction, if not of inward dignity, yet of outward degree ; ſo that all are Saints, or ſeem to be Saints, and ſhould be as they ſeem : But are all Apoſtles ? If the whole body were an eye, where were then the hearing ? God therefore hath given ſome to be Apoſtles, and ſome to be Paſtors, &c. for the edification of the body of Chriſt. In which work, we are Gods labourers (ſaith the Apoſtle) and ye are Gods husbandry, and Gods building.

30. The Church, reſpected with reference unto adminiſtration Eccleſiaſtical, doth generally conſiſt but of two ſorts of men ; the *Labourers*, and the *Building* ; they which are miniſtred unto, and they to whom the work of the Miniſtery is committed ; *Paſtors*, and the *Flock* over whom the Holy Ghoſt hath made them Overſeers. If the *Guide* of a Congregation, be his name or his degree whatſoever, be diligent in his vocation, feed the flock of God which dependeth upon him, caring for it, not by conſtraint, but willingly, not for filthy lucre, but of a ready minde ; not as though he would tyrannize over Gods heritage, but as a pattern unto the flock, wiſely guiding them : if the people in their degree do yield themſelves frameable to the truth, not like rough ſtone or flint, refuſing to be ſmoothed and ſquared for the building : if the Magiſtrate do carefully and diligently ſurvey the whole order of the work, providing by ſtatutes and laws, and bodily puniſhments, if need require, that all things may be done according to the rule which cannot deceive ; even as *Moſes* provided that all things might be done according to the patern which he ſaw in the Mount ; there are the words of this Exhortation are truly and effectually heard. Of ſuch a Congregation every man will ſay, *Behold a people that are wiſe, a people that walk in the Statutes and Ordinances of their God, a people full of knowledge and underſtanding, a people that have ſkill in building themſelves*. Where it is otherwiſe, there, *as by ſlothfulneß the roof doth decay* ; and as by *idleneſs of hands the houſe droppeth thorow*, as it is in *Eccleſ.*10. 18. ſo firſt one piece, and then another of their building ſhall fall away, till there be not a ſtone left upon a ſtone.

31. We ſee how fruitleſs this Exhortation hath been to ſuch as bend all their travel onely to build and manage a *Papacy* upon earth, without any care in the World of building themſelves in their moſt holy faith. Gods people have enquired at their mouthes, *What ſhall we do to have Eternal life ?* Wherein ſhall we build and edifie our ſelves ? And they have departed home from their Prophets, and from their Prieſts, laden with Doctrines which are Precepts of men ; they have been taught to tire out themſelves with bodily exerciſe : thoſe things are enjoyned them, which God did never require at their hands, and the things he doth require are kept from them ; their eyes are fed with pictures, and their ears are filled with melody, but their ſouls do wither, and ſtarve, and pine away ; they cry for bread, and behold ſtones are offered them ; they ask for fiſh, ſee they have Scorpions in their hands. Thou ſeeſt, O Lord, that they build themſelves, but not in faith ; they feed their children, but not with food : Their Rulers ſay with ſhame, Bring, and not build, But God is righteous ; their drunkenneſs ſtinketh, their abominations are known, their madneſs is manifeſt, the wind hath bound them up in her wings, and they ſhall be aſhamed of their doings. *Ephraim*, ſaith the Prophet, *is joyned to Idols, let him alone*. I will turn me therefore from the Prieſts which do miniſter unto Idols, and apply this Exhortation to them, whom God hath appointed to feed his choſen in Iſrael.

32. If there be any feeling of Chriſt, any drop of heavenly dew, or any ſpark of Gods good Spirit within you, ſtir it up, be careful to build and edifie, firſt your ſelves, and then your flocks, in this moſt holy faith.

33. I ſay, *firſt your ſelves* ; For, he which will ſet the hearts of other men on fire with the love of Chriſt, muſt himſelf burn with love. It is want of faith in our ſelves, my Brethren, which makes us * wretchleſs in building others. We forſake the Lords inheritance, and feed it not. What is the reaſon of this ? Our own deſires are ſettled where they ſhould not be. We our ſelves are like thoſe women which have a longing to eat coals, and lime, and filth ; we are fed, ſome with honour, ſome with eaſe,

* Careleſs,

ſome

some with wealth; the Gospel waxeth loathsome and unpleasant in our taste; how should we then have a care to feed others with that, which we cannot fancy our selves! If *Faith* wax cold and slender in the *heart* of the *Prophet* it will soon perish from the ears of the people. The Prophet *Amos* speaketh of a famine, saying, *I will send a famine in the Land, not a famine of bread, nor a thirst of water: but of hearing the Word of the Lord.* Amos 8.11. *Men shall wander from sea to sea, and from the North unto the East shall they run to and fro, to seek the Word of the Lord, and shall not finde it. Iudgement must begin at the house of God,* saith Peter. Yea, I say, at the Sanctuary of God, this judgement must begin. 1 Pet. 4.17. This famine must begin at the heart of the Prophet. He must have darkness for a vision, he must stumble at noon days, as at the twi-light; and then truth shall fall in the midst of the streets, then shall the people wander from sea to sea, and from the North unto the East shall they run to and fro, to seek the Word of the Lord.

34. In the second of *Haggai, Speak now,* saith God to his Prophet, *Speak now to Zerubbabel, the son of Shealtiel, Prince of Iudah, and to Iehoshua, the son of Iehozadak the High-Priest, and to the residue of the people, saying, Who is left among you, that saw this house in her first glory, and how do you see it now ? Is not this house in your eyes, in comparison of it, as nothing ?* The Prophet would have all mens eyes turned to the view of themselves, every sort brought to the consideration of their present state. This is no place to shew what duty *Zerubbabel* or *Iehoshuah* doth owe unto God in this respect. They have, I doubt not, such as put them hereof in remembrance. I ask of you, which are a part of the residue of Gods Elect and chosen people, Who is there amongst you that hath taken a survey of the House of God, as it was in the days of the blessed Apostles of Iesus Christ ? Who is there amongst you, that hath seen and considered this Holy Temple in her first glory ? And how do you see it now ? Is it not in comparison of the other, almost as nothing ? when ye look upon them that have undertaken the charge of your souls, and know how far these are, for the most part, grown out of kind, how few there be that tread the steps of their ancient Predecessors, ye are easily filled with indignation, easily drawn unto these complaints, wherein the difference of present, from former times, is bewailed; easily perswaded to think of them that lived to enjoy the days which now are gone, surely they were happy in comparison of us that have succeeded them : Were not their Bishops men unreproveable, wise, righteous, holy, temperate, well reported of, even of those which were without ? Were not their Pastors, Guides and Teachers, able and willing to exhort with wholesome Doctrine, and to reprove those which gain-said the Truth ? had they Priests made of the refuse of the people ? were men, like to the children which were in *Niniveh*, unable to discern between the right hand and the left, presented to the charge of their Congregation ? did their Teachers leave their flocks over which the Holy Ghost had made them overseers? did their Prophets enter upon holy things as spoils, without a reverend calling ? were their leaders so unkindely affected towards them, that they could finde in their hearts to sell them as sheep or oxen, not caring how they made them away?But, Beloved, deceive not your selves. Do the faults of your Guides and Pastors offend you ? it is your fault if they be thus faulty. *Nullus qui malum Rectorem patitur, eum accuset, quia sui fuit meriti perversi Pastoris subjaceri ditioni,* saith S. *Gregory,* whosoever thou art whom the inconvenience of an evil Governor doth press, accuse thy self, and not him : His being such, is thy deserving. O *ye disobedient children, turn again,* saith the Lord, *and then will I* Ier.3.14,15. *give you Pastors according to mine own heart, which shall feed you with knowledge and understanding.* So that the onely way to repair all ruines, breaches, and offensive decays in others, is to begin reformation at your selves. Which that we may sincerely, seriously, and speedily do, God the Father grant for his Son our Saviour Iesus sake, unto whom with the Holy Ghost, three Persons, one Eternal and Everlasting God, be honour, and glory, and praise for ever. Amen.

F I N I S.

AN
Alphabetical Table,
CONTAINING

All the Principal Matters handled in the first, second, third, fourth, fifth, sixth, seventh and eigth Books (being now entire and compleat) of the *Ecclesiasti-cal Polity*, and of other Writings of Mr. *Richard Hooker*.

N n n

F I N I S.

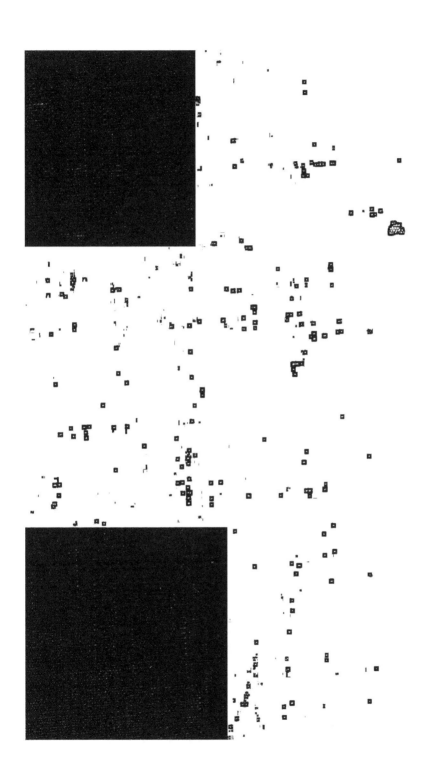

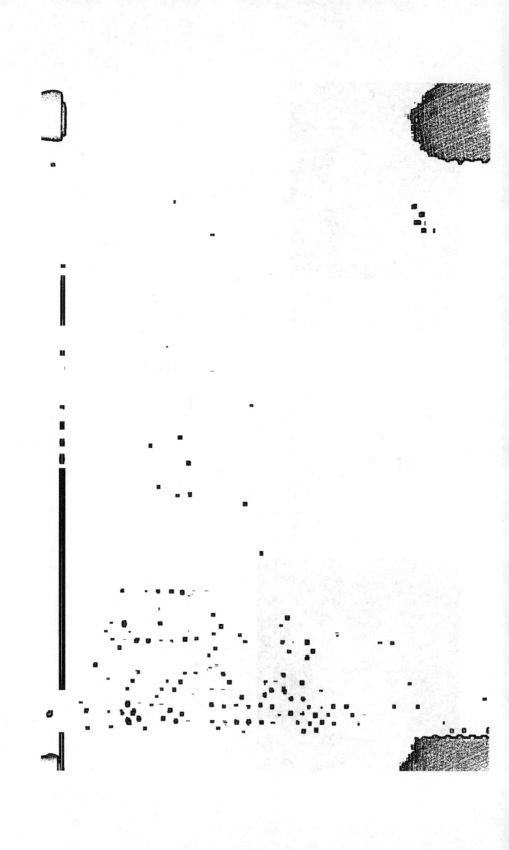

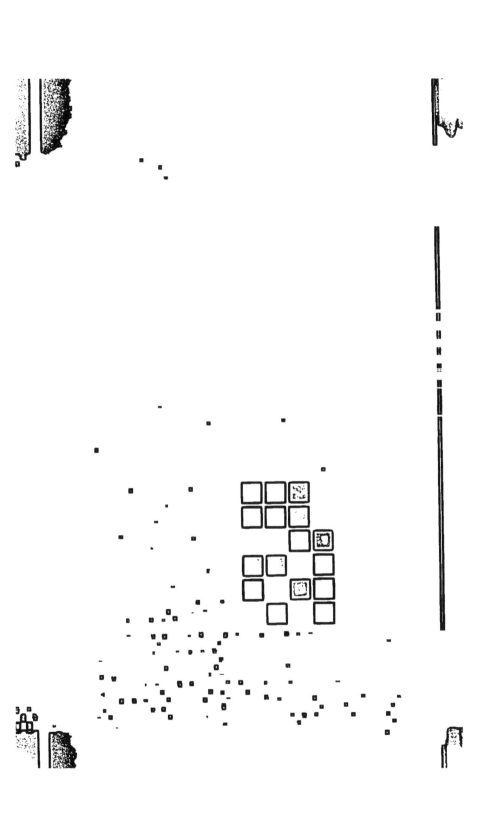

CPSIA information can be obtained
at www.ICGtesting.com
Printed in the USA
LVHW081826271220
675131LV00052B/1834